Handbook of Mental Retardation
(PGPS-121)

Pergamon Titles of Related Interest

Anchin/Kiesler HANDBOOK OF INTERPERSONAL
PSYCHOTHERAPY
Harris FAMILIES OF THE DEVELOPMENTALLY DISABLED:
A Guide to Behavioral Interventions
Hersen/Kazdin/Bellack THE CLINICAL PSYCHOLOGY HANDBOOK
Webster/Konstantareas/Oxman/Mack AUTISM: New Directions in
Research and Education

Related Journals*

ANALYSIS AND INTERVENTION IN DEVELOPMENTAL DISABILITIES
APPLIED RESEARCH IN MENTAL RETARDATION

*Free specimen copies available upon request.

PERGAMON GENERAL PSYCHOLOGY SERIES
EDITORS
Arnold P. Goldstein, *Syracuse University*
Leonard Krasner, *SUNY at Stony Brook*

Handbook of
Mental Retardation

edited by

Johnny L. Matson,
Northern Illinois University

James A. Mulick
*Rhode Island Hospital and
Brown University Program in Medicine*

Pergamon Press

New York   Oxford   Toronto   Sydney   Paris   Frankfurt

Pergamon Press Offices:

U.S.A.	Pergamon Press Inc., Maxwell House, Fairview Park, Elmsford, New York 10523, U.S.A.
U.K.	Pergamon Press Ltd., Headington Hill Hall, Oxford OX3 0BW, England
CANADA	Pergamon Press Canada Ltd., Suite 104, 150 Consumers Road, Willowdale, Ontario M2J 1P9, Canada
AUSTRALIA	Pergamon Press (Aust.) Pty. Ltd., P.O. Box 544, Potts Point, NSW 2011, Australia
FRANCE	Pergamon Press SARL, 24 rue des Ecoles, 75240 Paris, Cedex 05, France
FEDERAL REPUBLIC OF GERMANY	Pergamon Press GmbH, Hammerweg 6, D-6242 Kronberg-Taunus, Federal Republic of Germany

Library of Congress Cataloging in Publication Data

Main entry under title:

Handbook of mental retardation.

(Pergamon general psychology series ; 121)
Includes index.
1. Mental deficiency. 2. Mentally handicapped--
Rehabilitation. I. Matson, Johnny L. II. Mulick,
James A. (James Anton), 1948-   . III. Series.
RC570.H345   1983   616.85'88   82-24520
ISBN 0-08-028060-9

41,762

Printed in the United States of America

CONTENTS

v

PREFACE

The field of mental retardation has seen an amazing growth in information over the last century. This trend in the United States began under the Kennedy administration and has continued with the civil rights movement. The two primary goals that have emerged through these social movements have been the emphasis on the prevention of mental retardation and the emphasis on the rights of the mentally retarded. Through these socially established goals and the remarkable successes that have occurred in medicine and the social sciences, a burgeoning literature on the treatment of this large and highly variable population has occurred. These efforts have been extended further by the fact that parents have become involved with their handicapped children and their rights at an unprecedented level. Thus, another new area of study has grown up around the counseling and training of these parents to deal with their handicapped children.

Over the last 20 years a few books have been written for the professional or advanced graduate student in psychology, medicine, special education, social work, and allied disciplines, but few of them have been comprehensive. This is not to say that they have not been of great importance in the expansion of knowledge in our field. However, the need for such a comprehensive volume continues to increase because of the factors noted above. The present effort is an attempt at producing such a high level professional text that would cover the broad areas of scientific inquiry that have emerged in the field of mental retardation. We, the editors, do not propose a volume that is of extreme depth. That would be impossible, given the vast amount of literature that has accumulated in this field. What we do propose as a goal is the provision of a broad overview of a number of specialized areas with sufficient reference to other materials, so that the reader can explore particular topics in more depth if desired.

While making the book relatively comprehensive in terms of topics, we wished at the same time to present a volume that would be authoritative. It is our belief that we have been exceedingly fortunate in obtaining the cooperation of some of the best scientists in the area of mental retardation to serve as contributors for this book. Thus, we hope to have met our objective of providing a resource that will be valuable to the student or professional in mental retardation.

INTRODUCTION

Johnny L. Matson and James A. Mulick*

The purpose of this handbook is to review the major trends affecting mental retardation. There has been a tremendous growth in knowledge over the past two decades, originating from many areas of study and research. Much of this progress resulted from a commitment in the United States during the Kennedy administration in the early 1960's. This period saw the beginning of a clear mandate to investigate new ways of dealing with mental retardation by raising the number and quality of professional training programs, research and service delivery. Among the most beneficial of trends has been enhanced interdisciplinary collaboration and communication. The result, we would like to think, is increased knowledge.

It is no accident that during this same period an increasing awareness of human rights and a strong political movement occurred to guarantee equal opportunities to many disadvantaged groups. There can be no doubt that mentally retarded people have typically held a disadvantaged position in society. They have been subject to segregation and deprived of both civil and human rights, and efforts to improve their condition have often been withheld. More recently, improvements have begun to appear through efforts of parent groups and advocacy by professional organizations. Recognition of the rights of mentally retarded people and the obligation of society to enhance access and participation to them has occurred.

The most obvious effect of this increased involvement and activity in the field has been an ever increasing number of people eager to gain information about mental retardation—not only students and professionals in areas of biomedical and behavioral sciences, but also educators, parents, legislators, human service professionals, and many individuals involved through work or personal relationships with the mentally retarded. Although no one source can meet all their needs, it is clear that future efforts to collect and disseminate knowledge about mental retardation must result in a wider range of sources and address a much broader audience than in the past.

Contemporary Issues

Selection of topics and contributors in this volume was guided by recognition of several major contemporary issues. These issues are represented by the major subdivisions of the book, but are also represented across subdivisions and within many individual con-

* Supported in part by Maternal and Child Health Grant No. 01-H-000-109-09-0 to the Child Development Center, Rhode Island Hospital to the second author and a Spencer Fellowship from the National Academy of Education to the first author.

tributions. Understanding them is an excellent starting point for the student of mental retardation.

The definition of mental retardation used throughout this book is that provided in the 1977 revision of the *Manual on terminology and classification in mental retardation* of the American Association on Mental Deficiency (Grossman, 1977): "Mental Retardation refers to significantly subaverage general intellectual functioning existing concurrently with deficits in adaptive behavior, and manifested during the developmental period." Thus, the definition is descriptive of a current level of behavioral performance without reference to etiology or prognosis. Social behavior is at the center of this definition, because it assumes a comparison with a larger reference group and in part calls for a judgment concerning an individual's ability to meet sociocultural standards. It is understood that intellectual functioning is determined by assessment with an individually administered general intelligence test, and significantly subaverage performance is defined by a standard score (e.g., IQ) more than two standard deviations below the test mean. Adaptive behavior refers to an individual's personal effectiveness, independence and social responsibility judged on the basis of age and culturally normative expectations. The developmental period is set as the period between birth and the 18th birthday.

Classification of the degree of mental retardation also follows AAMD guidelines. From least to most impaired, these consist of mild, moderate, severe, and profound mental retardation (Grossman, 1977, pp. 16–33). However, other classifications may be used when educational placement (e.g., "educable" or "trainable" mentally retarded classroom placements) or eligibility status under government programs (e.g., disability under the Social Security Act or the Developmental Disabilities Act) are the context of discussion.

Clearly, mental retardation must be viewed within a societal context. Even before a discussion of classification issues can be undertaken, some sense of contemporary philosophical and programmatic standards must be established. Once this is done, the various purposes of classification and the practical effects of classification upon the individual can be recognized for the important issues they do, indeed, represent. Much has been written on these aspects of the disorder and the discussion continues.

Scientific research has been directed toward the two goals of prevention and amelioration of mental retardation. Prevention research aims at understanding the causes of conditions giving rise to retarded intellectual and behavioral development. These conditions are frequently biomedical pathologies associated with genetic and environmentally produced diseases. Other conditions associated with the outcome of mental retardation are related to socioeconomic and experiential factors.

Treatment of mental retardation consists of efforts to improve individual functioning through efficient educational practices and effective support systems. Research in the behavioral and social sciences has created renewed optimism about the ability of many mentally retarded persons to assume contributing roles within their families and communities. Biomedical treatment approaches have also been developed to prevent some of the progressively deleterious consequences of many syndromes associated with mental retardation.

There has been a profound revolution in our understanding of basic processes of human development. Research in medicine, epidemiology, sociology, psychology, education and many related fields of inquiry has yielded a rich data base for constructing new intervention strategies. Without the research efforts of the past decades, the only influences on contemporary practice in the field of mental retardation would have been political and ethical. While these influences are not to be minimized, we are convinced that progress toward a tangible reduction in the human suffering and grief associated with disorders of the developmental process can only be achieved by a strong and actively supported research effort. Selections in this volume reflect this bias and attempt to convey a sense of the fundamental practical value of research. A brief description of these areas covered is next.

Sections one and two of this volume cover a number of practical, legal, and sociological variables that have resulted in many of the present trends in research and habilitation of the mentally retarded. We have selected administration as one area for review. Developments in policies and procedures have rather obvious ramifications in care and prevention. A second area pertains to philosophical, social, and political developments. All these areas are intertwined to a degree, since they affect the type of research and practice that occur. Despite what "pure researchers" would like to think, what government agencies and advocacy groups determine is fundable to a great degree determines the type of research that eventually results.

Another area given considerable emphasis is classification. This reflects the view that such determinations are never done only for their own sake. Classification systems generally reflect the goals of those who devise them as well as the assumed functions that the systems will serve. This point is also related to the discussion in preceding chapters. Therefore, classification always involves systematic biases, including those of the individual classifier, the professional group intending to use the system, and the society in which the system evolves.

Classification systems used in mental retardation reflect the multiple etiologies giving rise to atypical human development and the needs of contemporary sociological and institutional forces such as the family, scientific and professional groups, schools, and government agencies. A major effort has been made over the years to elucidate the biomedical pathologies that give rise to atypical development. This effort has yielded significant advances in our ability to mount successful preventive programs, as well as new ways to ameliorate the developmental impact of many conditions once they have been identified. This section includes three chapters devoted primarily to biomedical factors; namely, those involving injury and disease having adverse effects on the development of the nervous system, inherited diseases, and chromosomal disorders.

The next four chapters focus on broader issues in classification. One chapter is devoted to a critical review of the major classification systems that are in use today. However, we felt strongly that those of us who work in the field of mental retardation need to be more aware of the functional impact of classification both on the mentally retarded individual and on those who share a place in society with them. Even a cursory examination of modern society reveals an astonishing number of important relationships that are in fact determined by formal classification systems. School placement often boils down to a matter of classification, although it should indeed represent a great deal more. Eligibility for specialized services, financial aid, and even for legal recognition of a person's civil rights are all affected by more or less formal use of existing standards for classification. Even such fundamental human relationships as community and social group membership can be determined in part by the effects of the labels a person carries. The impact of classification can truly be immense, and there are clearly a variety of risks as well as benefits involved. Our approach has been to focus on three major areas of impact: legal and administrative issues, educational issues, and sociological issues.

The ensuing major division of the book covers assessment and prevention. In the last two decades this area has been a high priority, given the charge by the President's Commission on Mental Retardation to curtail drastically the incidence of the disorder. Assessment and prevention obviously implies identification of precursors to mental retardation and early identification of children at risk. The latter area is likely to be most difficult but of great importance, since the vast majority of the mentally retarded are in the mild range, with the problem due to many unspecified causes, many of which are likely due at least in part to environmental factors.

Among the areas covered is assessment of different types. The importance of this area in prevention seems fairly straightforward. Subsequently, some common treatment strategies with the mentally retarded are reviewed. These include behavior modification, psychopharmacology, and psychotherapy. Along these same lines, a number of educational approaches are reviewed. Finally, some basic methodological strategies are discussed. These include experimental and descriptive methods. Single-case research methods are not reviewed but are considered of importance. Many approaches cannot be covered as they rightly deserve and this method is one of those areas.

The purpose of this volume as noted is to give an idea of some of the major areas in which research in mental retardation is advancing. This volume is certainly not all inclusive nor the last word on the topic. However, it is hoped that we have been able to demonstrate many of the areas that have value.

Handbook of Mental Retardation
(PGPS-121)

PART I
PHILOSOPHY OF CARE

1 ORGANIZATION AND ADMINISTRATION OF SERVICE DELIVERY SYSTEMS

Matthew P. Janicki,
Paul J. Castellani, and
Robert G. Norris

Much has happened within the past 20 years to overturn an immense pessimism and a pervasive societal rejection of individuals who are different and who demonstrate less than average social and vocational competence. A variety of ideological, political, economic, and clinical factors have contributed to fundamental changes in the structure of services to developmentally disabled persons, as well as in the mode of service delivery and their administrative and fiscal mechanisms. This chapter presents a foundation for planning of developmental services and addresses some of the basic structural, organizational, and administrative consequences of a changing public orientation toward persons with mental retardation and other developmental disabilities.

There has been a pronounced maturing of public perceptions toward disabled persons and the methods through which services to these individuals are organized and delivered. Historically, these perceptions or public attitudes and methods of services provision have run in a cyclical manner (Levine & Levine, 1970; Wolfensberger, 1972, 1974). Unfortunately, cycles of conservatism and pessimism are associated with public beliefs of failure residing within individuals, not society, and these beliefs lead to social ostracism and segregation. Beliefs such as these during the early and middle part of this century led to the institu-

tionalization of the greatest number of "deviant" persons in the history of the United States (Wolfensberger, 1974). Indeed, some 700,000 persons were institutionalized in public institutions for the psychiatrically impaired, mentally retarded, or the otherwise physically different (Bachrach, 1976; Scheerenberger, 1976). In contrast, it is estimated that in the early 1980s, some 140,000 mentally retarded persons still reside within institutional care settings (Scheerenberger, 1981).

Contemporary perceptions and attitudes mirror to some degree the optimism toward competence and relative acceptance of mentally retarded persons that was prevalent in the United States a hundred years ago. The power of parental interest in the welfare of their disabled children, societal reactions to the horrors committed in Nazi Germany, dramatic improvements in medical care, and a swing toward a concern that societal conditions influence behavior and define deviancy all led to enabling legislation on the federal level, and in many instances on the state and provincial level, that in the 1960s set the tone for the development of community systems of care. This trend was also reflected in public policy thinking associated with care for the elderly as well as those persons with acute psychiatric care needs. In general, there was in the late 1960s and 1970s a movement away from reliance on segregation within institutional settings toward community integration and development of alternative care models. Current beliefs support the notion that persons with disabilities are entitled to the same benefits of societal integration as able-bodied persons. Indeed, currently over 60,000 individuals reside in community residential facilities (Bruininks, Hauber, & Kudla, 1980).

The re-emergence of the belief that learning is possible, no matter how intellectually impaired the individual, coupled with the belief that the acquisition of new information and skills would go on throughout a lifetime, has led to the ascendence of the developmental model. These changes were influenced by research and clinical practices that did not support a unitary correspondence between illness or medical care needs and mental retardation. They were also reinforced by research that demonstrated that the effects of environmental and nutritional deprivation could be overcome with the appropriate environmental enrichment and nutritional supplementation. The identification of the scope of mental retardation attributed to intellectual and emotional deprivation, in many cases linked to societal conditions, led to the belief that a medically based care system was not appropriate.

More immediate to substantial shifts in the structure, models, and mechanisms of services to the disabled was the increased public sympathy and awareness of the plight of mentally retarded persons in large custodial institutions. The political pressure for reform and the extension of the civil rights movement to the problems of the disabled resulted in "right to treatment" decisions by federal courts, as well as federal and state legislation that have had an important impact on the structure, mode and administration of developmental services (Rubin, 1978). The community mental health movement and the passage of Medicare and Medicaid legislation in the United States were other powerful factors associated with major changes in services to persons with mental retardation or other developmental disabilities. It would be extremely difficult to measure the relative impact of these forces, but it is nonetheless clear that changes in attitudes, perceptions, and ideology relative to the developmentally disabled have been substantial. These changes are reflected in a structure of services that has become more community than institutionally oriented, models of service delivery that have become more developmental than medical, and a variety of administrative and fiscal mechanisms that have been developed to address these new circumstances.

As a foundation for planning and structuring developmental services, this chapter will explore some of the major issues and developments underlying these changes. The concepts of normalization and communitization are central in this development.

Normalization and Communitization

The concept of normalization owes its current acceptance by most advocates for disabled persons to the American cultural belief in the "equality of opportunity" (Heal, Sigelman, & Switzky, 1980). However, the concept first gained notice in Scandinavia in the 1960s. Bank-Mikkelsen (1969) influenced Danish thought and was instrumental in having the principle nested in the Danish laws governing services for mentally retarded persons. Normalization was subsequently introduced to the English speaking world by Nirje (1969) and extensively elaborated by Wolfensberger (1972; 1980b).

Wolfensberger (1980a) presents three variations of the definition of normalization:

- The use of culturally valued means, in order to enable people to live culturally valued lives.
- Use of culturally normative means to offer persons life conditions at least as good as that of average citizens and, as much as possible, to enhance or support their behavior, appearances, experiences, status, and reputation.
- Use of means that are as culturally normative as possible, in order to establish, enable, or support behaviors, appearances, experiences, and interpretations that are as culturally normative as possible.

This principle is elaborated through a number of corollaries:

- *Cultural normativeness* means that roles, expectations, forms of address, labels, environments, social services, and rhythms of daily, weekly, annual, and lifetime activities should be typical in nature.
- *Developmental expectations* means the stressing of the growth potential of individuals regardless of depth of impairment.
- *Integration of activities and services* means that opportunities, activities and services must be as physically and socially integrated as possible since segregation denies culturally normative opportunities.
- *Integrity of program models* means that the program model used for a service should be internally consistent with the needs of individuals and the most normative means of meeting these needs.

A full discussion of the principle can be found in Wolfensberger (1972) and in the chapter by Jacobson and Schwartz in this volume. An update on the controversy it has aroused in the human services field, along with its various misuses, is presented in Wolfensberger (1980a). The changes occurring in the United States and Canada in the late 1970s and early 1980s make it apparent that the notions inherent in the principle have begun to seep into the organization and administration of services.

Communitization is a concept that is intimately tied to the normalization principle and is linked historically to the deinstitutionalization process in the United States. The term, first used in 1975 and further articulated by Jones (1977) and Hogan (1980), generally refers to the "generation of local capabilities to bear responsibility and provide services at home" (OMRDD, 1978, p. 28). It also provides the "direct redeployment of institutional resources into a developing and integrated continuum of services" (Jones, 1975, p. 3). Communitization thus involves two distinct efforts: the conversion by the state of institutional resources for use in building the evolving community system, and the assumption of responsibility at the local level for developing comprehensive community services.

Planning Foundations

Developmental services encourage a comprehensive approach to planning. Developmental services must be: (1) community-based, with most services provided close to the home of the disabled person; (2) comprehensive, in that all levels of need will be met by a coherent system of services; and (3) founded on the principle of normalization with its implied end, viz., integration of disabled persons within society. An important element in the concept of a system is the existence of strong linkages between all of its components.

Consequently, a system of comprehensive services must encompass all of the resources required to provide assistance to developmentally disabled people. In order to be comprehensive a service system must (1) meet the needs of all age groups, (2) cope with the problems of all degrees of disability, (3) compensate for groups of different socioeconomic backgrounds, and (4) be available when and where needed by an individual or his/her family. "Community-based" means both the access to services by developmentally disabled persons in towns, cities, and regions where people live and a service location that blends in with the surrounding community.

Services, to be fully comprehensive, must also be organized and administered in a manner that will anticipate and meet the needs of a variety of individuals with disabilities with differing levels of impairment. Fundamental to the organization of a service system must be the belief that services can be organized and

delivered effectively at a population specific level that makes sense, a commitment to and internalization of the tenets of normalization and progressive rehabilitative technologies, and a commitment to service comprehensiveness and continuity.

In terms of planning and developing systems of services certain issues have to be addressed. Prominent among those issues is the definition of the scope of the service system in terms of the populations to be served. Defining the boundaries, the scope, and the structure of the service system has become substantially more difficult as a result of the changes in definitions of the population to be served, as well as the shift in the locus of that population. Extension of responsibility beyond mental retardation, to additional and more broadly defined categories of developmental disability—the neurologically impaired, for example—is one dimension of the problem. The movement of thousands of individuals from custodial institutions to the community as well as statutory mandates to provide services to all developmentally disabled persons, including those who have never been institutionalized, is another dimension that makes the scope of the system significantly broader and more indeterminate and often provides the circumstances for variation among the dictates of statute, court decisions, and traditional patterns of service delivery.

An additional issue stems from the fact that in many instances, there is not a statutory guarantee to services or a recognition of rights. A commitment to the rights of persons with disabilities, the goals to be achieved through the rehabilitation process, and the basic organization of service delivery should be encompassed in statute. The Developmentally Disabled Assistance and Bill of Rights Act (PL 95-602) (and, to some degree, the National Health Planning and Resources Development Act—PL 93-641) in part serve this end in the United States at the federal level. In some instances these assurances are found in state statutes. The degree of specificity, clarity, and comprehensiveness of statute and regulation may aid in resolving, but are unlikely to fully address, all of the issues that emerge here.

Another issue that must be addressed is the complexity of the service system. The developmentally disabled and the state agencies primarily responsible for services have been moving from unitary and all-inclusive services provided in institutional settings to complex sets of services provided in the community under many auspices. Questions of continuing the full range of services in the community, relying on existing services, and directly providing, underwriting, or encouraging the development of needed services must be dealt with in the context of greater ambiguity as to what populations are to be served.

The structure of governance is also a crucial issue in defining the service system. Although the fundamental relationships between federal, state or provincial and local governments are defined in statute, responsibility, authority and capacity are often vexing problems in defining the system of service and are further exacerbated by the increasing involvement of private (non-profit and proprietary) providers of services.

As the entire system of services to the developmentally disabled continues to undergo substantial change, there is a continual evolution of each of the sets of issues. Each of the following dimensions of planning must be considered in the context of this changing definition of the service system. These include the (1) integration of disabled individuals within the community, (2) assurance that multi-need individuals are served, (3) provision for quality of services, (4) assurance of economy, and (5) development of consumer independence. To be effective in addressing these dimensions, a service system must offer (or provide for) a wide range of services within a reasonable proximity of the locality, must offer management that effectively coordinates the related services within the region, be administratively set up to encompass an appropriate population size, and must be contained within a reasonable geographic area. This geographic area must have clearly defined boundaries, be of manageable size and distances, contain a manageable configuration of political substructures, and provide for manageable communication and accessibility.

Planning, administration, and service delivery can be organized into subsytems according to the type of service provided. The variety of services can be grouped into the following four major categories: (1) family resources, (2) child development, (3) living alternatives, and (4) habilitation/vocational. These four account for the key elements of any organized, comprehensive service system. Additionally, within this framework, services can be seen as being specialized or generic. However, assurance of access to generic services can be the responsibility of the specialized service system.

In addition, a comprehensive and coordinated system must contain the mechanisms to provide reasonable planning, with open dialogue and exchange of ideas, and must replace a fragmented, piecemeal or territorial system. The process must also have a basic legal framework that enhances cooperation among the various actors in the system, and mechanisms that allow advocacy groups to express their views and make demands.

A developmental service system must also have a reasonable population and resource planning base.

Developmental services in the United States are planned at three levels: state, regional, and local. These are represented by a state's developmental disabilities plan (and in many cases, the state health plan), regional administrative plans (or the health systems plans of the state's health systems agency[ies]) and, if part of the state's structure, plans developed locally.

System planners need to address a number of issues prior to the development of a scheme for the direction or provision of services. These include (1) the definition of the population to be served, (2) the assessment of needs and resources, (3) the definition of the service system, (4) the description of an administrative mechanism to manage the system, (5) the identification of priorities to meet gaps of specific needs in services, and (6) a delineation of fiscal supports. Following is a discussion of each of these steps.

Defining the Population

Population definition includes an agreement on the identification of the population to be served. The use of appropriate terminology permits a more accurate description of the population and a projection of its size and character. Definitional processes can vary from a categorical approach, which relies upon diagnostic classes, to a functional approach, which draws from behavioral descriptions of impairment levels. In some cases the categorical definitions may be restricted to what is characterized as mental subnormality, or expanded to include a range of conditions or impairments termed developmental disabilities. Mental subnormality (a term usually in use in the United Kingdom) can also be used as a generic term defining below average intellectual functioning which originates during early development and is associated with impairments of either learning and social adjustment, or maturation, or both. Mental subnormality is composed of two distinct categories: mental deficiency and mental retardation. Mental deficiency stems from some pathologic condition of the brain which precludes normal development. Mental retardation stems from suboptimum environmental situations causing individuals to function below their potential level of ability (Knoblock & Pasamanick, 1974). Population definitions must account for both categories.

On a broader scale, determining what constitutes a developmental disability is not an easy task (National Task Force, 1977). Legislation predating the current federal developmental disabilities act accounted for conditions including and associated with mental retardation and mental deficiency. Successive renewals of this legislation have expanded the definition to include other similar neurological dysfunctions. Current federal practice is to encourage the use of a functional impairment definition and not to restrict access to developmental disabilities funding simply to retardation associated conditions. This has permitted states to interpret and to apply a definition that includes a variety of impairments which impede normal growth and development.

The prevalent definition of developmental disabilities is embodied in PL 95-602, the "Rehabilitation, Comprehensive Services and Developmental Disabilities Amendments of 1978" to the "Developmentally Disabled Assistance and Bill of Rights Act." These amendments contain a non-categorical, functional definition of developmental disability. Chapter 503, Section 102(b)(7) of this Act stipulates:

The term 'developmental disability' means a severe, chronic disability of a person which:

(A) is attributable to a mental or physical impairment or combination of mental and physical impairments;
(B) is manifested before the person reaches age 22;
(C) is likely to continue indefinitely;
(D) results in substantial limitations in three or more of the following areas of major life activity: (i) self-care, (ii) receptive and expressive language, (iii) learning, (iv) mobility, (v) self-direction, (vi) capacity for independent living, and (vii) economic self-sufficiency; and
(E) reflects the person's need for a combination and sequence of special, interdisciplinary, or generic care, treatment, or other services which are of lifelong or extended duration and are individually planned and coordinated.

In many states, legislation specifically identifies a number of disabling conditions to be included within the focus of services (NASMRPD, 1981). In many instances these include autism, cerebral palsy, epilepsy, mental deficiency or mental retardation, other developmentally linked neurological impairments, or other conditions (Thompson & O'Quinn, 1979). These laws reflect the categorical approach embodied in PL 94-103, the original developmental disabilities legislation.

The difficulty in applying either a categorical or functional approach to defining developmental disability is that neither alone offers guidance to providers on eligibility for services or fiscal reimbursement.

Although difficulties exist in attempting to apply either approach solely, a pragmatic position can be taken. A developmental disability can be defined as a categorical condition with defined functional limitations. In most cases, these categorical conditions will include autism, cerebral palsy, epilepsy, mental retardation, or some other neurological or systemic impairment. The functional limitations can be identical with the life-activity deficits identified in the federal functional definition. In this way, a developmental disability can be seen as a severe, chronic condition, occurring prior to adulthood, which causes a handicap or impairment in life-activity areas. It is essentially "growing up disabled." Practically, categorical disabilities are usually considered developmental disabilities when found in their severest forms.

This pragmatic approach to defining developmental disabilities permits diagnoses of symptomatic and etiologic factors of the conditions that facilitate habilitative planning by focusing upon functional deficits. Experience has shown that, although categorical diagnoses may serve a useful purpose for statistical reporting and planning, they are limiting as a guide for service provision.

Persons with the same categorical disability (e.g., mild mental retardation) may vary markedly in their skills, deficits, and needs. Consequently, functional information is necessary in addition to the determination that a person has a developmental disability. That determination should be based on the skill level and services needed by the individual rather than simply categorical diagnosis. A definition that takes these factors into account represents a better means of assessing needs. Therefore, it is important to view a disability within the context of the degree of impairment present. The identification of a set of life-activity factors and their operational definition in terms of degrees of the impairment are critical contributions to system and program planning. Classification systems such as the *International Classification of Impairments, Disabilities and Handicaps* (WHO, 1980) permit identification of functional impairments within an organized schema. Disease coding systems such as the *International Classification of Diseases-ICD/9* (CPHA, 1978) permit classification of categorical conditions. It is incumbent upon an organization to define the population it intends to serve by couching the definition in operational language. While the federal legislation has received mixed reactions (Lubin, Jacobson, & Kiely, 1982), the use of the functional impairments approach, coupled with the use of diagnostic categories, can assist administrators, staff, and potential consumers to define the boundaries and responsibilities of the system.

Assessment of Needs

Needs assessment determines the number of disabled individuals, the number of persons receiving services, and the unmet service needs within a geographic area. This process also seeks to identify all the existing services within an area. The result is the ability to project the number of people who need specialized services within a geographic area, taking into account severity of disability, age, and residential location. These analyses permit the assessment of the number and characteristics of persons currently receiving services, and the potential capability of service providers to accommodate the unmet need.

The needs-assessment process should determine the nature and scope of the population to be served. As a generic administrative and clinical tool, needs assessment processes have been employed widely in mental health, gerontology and other health systems efforts (Warheit, Bell, & Schwab, 1977). Their uses with mentally retarded and developmentally disabled populations have been more limited (Bradley, 1978; Budde & Edwards, 1978; HCFA, 1979). In most instances, needs assessments conducted in mental retardation have been restricted to limited household surveys (Allen, 1978; Lindberg, 1976) or projections based upon epidemiological statistics (EMC, 1978). The major critiques of needs assessments conducted to date have centered on the design of the techniques. Bradley (1978) notes that many needs analyses are based on abstract national epidemiological statistics that have questionable relevance to particular state circumstances, that some needs-assessment schemes are unfocused and result in the collection of odds and ends of information without cohesion, and that almost all needs assessment projects fail to differentiate between persons whose needs are immediate and those whose needs are merely speculative.

There are a number of data collection techniques that can be employed to avoid these problems. Sallis and Henggeler (1980) have divided these into "hard-data" and "impressionistic" strategies. Hard-data strategies attempt to relate certain social characteristics of a population and/or ecological characteristics of an environment to rates of a condition. Impressionistic strategies rely on subjective evaluations of developmental service needs through the use of a variety of informants. Hard-data approaches include epidemiological research, social and health indicators analysis, and uses of an approach termed "rate-under-treatment."

The use of these strategies produces descriptive information that will have many uses. Whichever procedure is used, however, a needs-assessment process should address the following objectives:

- define the characteristics of the population under study,
- determine which services are most needed or are in most demand,
- determine to what extent the services already available address these needs (i.e., the issue of availability),
- determine the extent to which available services are coordinated and accessible to persons needing them (i.e., the issue of accessibility).

A number of projects that could be characterized as needs assessments have been undertaken to survey target service populations. One such national project in Finland (Kaillo et al., 1980) examined the characteristics of that country's disabled population to determine the extent of various conditions and define specific program needs. Other efforts in the United States, for example, those of California (DDS, 1978), Minnesota (Bock & Roberts, 1979), and New York (Janicki, 1980; Janicki & Jacobson, 1979; Janicki & Jacobson, 1982) examined to various degrees the character of their mentally retarded and/or developmentally disabled population. Massachusetts' efforts were directed toward regional assessments for the purposes of local system development (duPree, 1978; duPree & Hogan, 1979). In most cases the efforts of the needs assessment have addressed the first two objectives; the other two, availability and accessibility issues, were secondary investigations or were undertaken by different mechanisms. A manner of examining the availability issues is offered within a document issued by Alpha Center (1981).

A strategy employed by New York can offer a view of how a rate-under-treatment needs assessment methodology has been used. Beginning in 1978, New York's Office of Mental Retardation and Developmental Disabilities undertook a major statewide survey of all persons with a developmental disability (Janicki & Jacobson, 1982). The survey included all persons who had a combination of a categorical condition and functional deficits that could be termed a developmental disability and who needed specialized interventions of developmental services. It was estimated that of the total 1980 New York population of 17,504,000, some 70,000 persons or 0.40% of the population would be identified through the survey.

The survey process was undertaken in three phases. The first phase included a census of all immediately known persons who were actively receiving services. The second phase included those persons partially served. The third phase included those individuals newly identified through an outreach process. Data

Table 1.1. Characteristics of Developmentally Disabled Persons Residing in Various Living Situations in New York

CHARACTERISTICS	FAMILY LIVING STANDARDS				GROUP LIVING SITUATIONS			CONGREGATE CARE SITUATIONS		
	LIVING WITH FAMILY		FOSTER FAMILY CARE		COMMUNITY RESIDENCES			SKILLED NURSING FACILITIES	STATE DEVELOPMENT CENTERS	
	AGE LT 22	AGE 22+	AGE LT 22	AGE 22+	PRIVATE GROUP HOMES	PUBLIC GROUP HOMES	SUPERVISED APARTMENTS		AGE LT 22	AGE 22+
	(9,505)*	(6,326)	(764)	(2,779)	(2,975)	(567)	(553)	(234)	(2,938)	(11,286)
Age										
Lt 22	100	—	100	—	15	29	7	8	100	—
22–64	—	99	—	82	83	67	91	63	—	91
Gt 64	—	1	—	18	3	5	2	29	—	9
Gender										
Male	60	53	55	45	57	62	52	50	60	55
Female	40	47	45	55	43	38	48	50	40	45
Intellectual level										
Normal	19	12	5	6	10	6	25	20	1	2
Mild MR	18	28	12	21	26	17	39	19	3	6
Moderate MR	17	31	31	29	27	20	17	19	7	12
Severe MR	12	16	30	29	22	28	7	15	18	24
Profound MR	9	7	16	11	10	27	6	17	71	55
Unknown	25	7	7	4	5	2	6	11	1	2
Self-care skills (% Independent or needing minimal assistance with)										
Toileting	65	93	84	98	94	82	98	51	39	64
Eating	70	94	85	98	95	86	98	66	44	66
Dressing	60	88	79	95	91	78	95	48	31	52

Adapted from Janicki, Jacobson, & Schwartz (1980).
* Numbers of individuals indicated in parentheses.

were collected through the completion of a specially designed instrument, the Developmental Disabilities Information Survey (Janicki & Jacobson, 1979). Data collectors, a variety of professional and paraprofessional agency staff, as well as family members, were trained in the use of the instrument prior to its use. The instrument, an eight-page optically scannable computer form, was locally verified and centrally processed. Data were computer analyzed and returned to participating agencies in the form of individual profiles and aggregate reports.

Within a three-year period some 60,000 individuals were identified. Information became available on a variety of variables that included sociodemographics (age, sex, residence, financial status, etc.) disability characteristics (diagnosis, physical, and cognitive and affective limitations), functional capabilities (communication, mobility, activities of daily living, etc.), as well as services received and needed (residential and day program, health and therapy, community generic, etc.).

Through this type of needs assessment comprehensive data became available on a substantial portion of the state's most severely disabled population. The survey results led to a variety of applications. Among these were related epidemiological studies, verification of assumptions for continuum of care models (both in residential and day program services), identification of service system deficiencies by examination of service need trends, various planning applications both at

Table 1.2. Definitions of System Characteristics and Their Criteria

AVAILABILITY: the type and supply of services in an identifiable geographic area.
Criteria

- types of services
- number of services (i.e., beds, program spaces, units of services, etc.)
- utilization rates
- length of stay (LOS)

CONTINUITY: the degree of coordination among similar service providers and relevant generic human service providers.
Criteria

- formal/informal coordinative agreements (i.e., availability of referral mechanisms, staff sharing agreements, mechanisms to transfer client information among providers of services, memoranda of understanding and other signed agreements)
- client tracking/follow-up system (i.e., availability of procedures and policies to ensure that clients are receiving services described in treatment plans; policies and procedures to ensure that clients referred to services receive these services accordingly)
- locus of responsibility (i.e., existence of policies or organizational procedures which ensure that an identifiable service provider has ultimate responsibility for the care of clients or seeing to it that their care is provided)
- client movement policies (i.e., the availability of written criteria for client entry, movement within and exit from the service)
- joint planning activities (i.e., the availability of opportunities which allow similar service providers to plan for the provision of services)

COST: the types and amounts of direct and indirect expenditures incurred in the provision of services.
Criteria

- total operating costs of service by type of service
- total expenditures for services by type of reimbursement (i.e., Medicare, Medicaid, State, local assistance, private insurance, out-of-pocket expenses, etc.)
- per client costs per day or year
- cost per unit of service

ACCEPTABILITY: the level of consumer/client satisfaction with services in relation to all other service system characteristics.
Criteria

- acceptability of the availability, accessibility, quality and cost of services as perceived by the consumer/client (i.e., existence of policies and procedures that allow the consumer/client to evaluate the services provided)
- acceptance of services and goals of the agency/provider by the community (i.e., the extent to which policies and procedures are available to elicit the input of the community when developing new programs, when determining a site for the program, etc.)
- public education and public relations (i.e., the degree to which providers of service inform the community of their mission and goals and gain support from the community for the operation of their programs)
- existence of community boards and advisory councils
- community support (i.e., the extent to which communities support service providers in achieving their goals and objectives and improving their programs via volunteer activities, private financial support, donated space, vehicles, etc.)

Table 1.2 (*continued*)

ACCESSIBILITY: the ability of the population to obtain appropriate services.
Criteria

- proximity of services to target population (i.e., travel time to services, availability of public transportation, etc.)
- architectural barriers (i.e., physical plant characteristics, availability of curbcuts, wheelchair ramps, etc.)
- financial barriers (i.e., reimbursement mechanisms available, existence of sliding fee scales, etc.)
- cultural barriers (i.e., extent to which staff are representative of the target population normally served, availability of bilingual staff etc.)
- organizational barriers (i.e., auspices of services)
- informational barriers (i.e., extent to which services are listed in public telephone directories, information and referral publications, human service directories; extent to which radio spots and public service announcements are utilized to inform public of the services available; extent of advocacy efforts to promote the community's acceptance of developmentally disabled persons.)
- hours of operations (i.e., availability of services during evenings and weekends.)
- response time (i.e., time lag between when services are requested and when received.)

QUALITY: the extent to which services and programs meet established and/or expected professional standards in relation to structural, service delivery and outcome characteristics.
Criteria

- structural aspects (i.e., the extent to which facilities meet federal, state, and local fire and safety standards, living space standards, etc.)
- programmatic aspects (i.e., compliance with licensing/accrediting requirements for service staff and staff/client ratios, existence of admissions criteria to ensure that only clients appropriate for X type of services receive this service, utilization of individual treatment plans which are updated and reviewed regularly, etc.)
- service outcome aspects (i.e., availability of mechanisms to evaluate the effects of service on the health status/behavior of clients, demonstration of expected length of stay and average number of units of service per client, documentation of client movement to less restrictive living environments and service settings, etc.)

Adapted from Malys and Brooks (1981).

local and statewide levels, program research with both individuals and programs, and a variety of operational applications by agency management. Many of these led to shifts in state agency policy due to the availability of more reliable information on populations, programs, and service effects.

New York's experience has shown that the investment in such a needs assessment effort can provide useful results. Not only can this type of process provide data on the characteristics of individuals within various geographic districts or sub-sets of the survey area, but it can also provide data for various inter-program analyses (See Table 1.1). The use of this type of hard-data assessment can overcome Budde and Edwards' (1978) contention that the type of residential alternatives available or the number of persons residing within them are not usually known with any complete accuracy, and that there is usually no standard information or format available that could be used to project how many individuals need various living alternatives.

Needs assessments based on abstract statistics make no distinctions between those individuals receiving and those not receiving services. Additionally, epidemiological statistics based on government or national interest group data are only sporadically updated to reflect new information and, if used without adjust-

ments, will offer questionable outcomes when service projections are made. In most cases, the use of abstract statistics will tend to overinflate need projection figures. A survey approach can overcome these problems and permit the state's administering agency (and/or local program planners) to develop more reliable estimates of persons in service, awaiting services, and to be generally in need. Caution and underestimation seems to be a much better policy when facing legislatures or other potential funders, particularly in times of fiscal conservatism.

Defining the Service System

A service system is a network of specialized and generic services linked for a common purpose. The definition of the service system includes the identification of the full range of specialized mental retardation or developmental services and generic health, social, or educational services needed within a geographic area. While a developmental services organization is not usually responsible for the administration of generic health, social or educational services, it must account for functional relationships with these services. It must also contend with a number of system characteristics that impinge upon its operations. These system characteristics include such aspects as availability, acces-

Table 1.3a. Continuum of Residential Environments

| | | RESTRICTIVENESS | | |
MOST				LEAST
Public and private large congregate care facilities	Public and private small congregate care facilities	Age appropriate group homes or family living	Minimally supervised apartments	Self-maintained apartments or homes

Table 1.3.b. Continuum of Educational/Habilitative Programs for Children

| | | RESTRICTIVENESS | | |
MOST				LEAST
Special education or habilitation in physically and socially segregated settings	Special education or habilitation, socially segregated, but in physically integrated settings	Regular classroom but with special education	Regular classroom education	

Adapted from Hitzing (1980).

Table 1.3.c. Continuum of Vocational Situations for Adults

| | | RESTRICTIVENESS | | |
MOST				LEAST
Work type activities within large public or private congregate settings	Segregated activities center or workshop	Sheltered workshop with other disabled workers	Work station within normative employment location	Competitive employment

sibility, continuity, acceptability, quality, and cost (Table 1.2). For the most part, the system is defined contextually by how well it contends with these system characteristics. It is defined structurally by how it organizes its services to meet these system characteristics.

Individual services can be organized into subsystems or components, according to the type of services provided. This facilitates planning and provides a functional organization for management. Within this approach, similar services can be aggregated within program centers. For example, all programs concerned with living arrangements can be grouped into one subsystem and services dealing with early intervention or early childhood services can be grouped into another subsystem.

Terminology related to identifying these subsystems or components can vary. However, most programs, services, or activities, can be grouped conceptually into the following four major categories addressing needs related to (1) family structures and resources, (2) child developmental activities, (3) living arrangements, and (4) habilitative or vocational activities. These four categories are, for the most part, mutually exclusive and account for the major need areas in any individual's life. These categories are derived from activities that have a common theme. *Family resources services* provide support to the families of individuals,

as well as to individuals with developmental disabilities. The services include information and referral, diagnostic services, case management, respite support, mental health, genetic and parent counseling and parent training, recreation, as well as a range of primary and secondary level prevention services.

All services that directly affect children in their early or school age years can be grouped within *a child development category*. The services within this category should facilitate the maximal growth and development of infants, children and adolescents, as well as providing for related supports for their families. Child development services should include screening and early identification, infant stimulation, early intervention, educational advocacy and assessment, a wide range of both education and habilitative programs, and specialized day and weekend respite services.

Living alternative services should provide for all variations of residential needs of developmentally disabled persons, including structured health or behavioral maintenance care, a range of community living alternatives, assistance with obtaining barrier-free housing, and specialized overnight respite arrangements. The living alternatives include both sheltered housing as well as assistance to persons living independently. This domain also addresses activities that provide for the development of sheltered care housing (site selection, leasing or purchasing, rental assistance),

Table 1.4. Continua of Service Applications

| | INTENSITY | | | |
	MAXIMAL			MINIMAL
Medical orientation	Intense medical	Ameliorative health care	Preventive health care	Ad hoc health care
(Re)habilitation process	Active treatment	Living skills and social interaction	Social interaction	Community living enhancement

and recruitment, training, and supervision of foster care families, as well as personnel to work in group homes and provide oversight on persons in independent housing.

Habilitative and vocational services comprise the last service category. Recognizing that disabled individuals will vary with respect to their day program or employment needs, this category must provide for a variety of both habilitative-level services and a range of vocational and employment support services, including developmental and prevocational activities, worker training, sheltered work, and employment assistance activities.

Owing to the nature of mental retardation and many of the other developmental disabilities, the individuals within a retardation/developmental services system usually represent a finite population with long term care needs. Consequently, services should be organized to provide continua that take into account transitional as well as long term care environments. A good deal has been written about structuring these continua from most to least restrictive (Bradley, 1978; Glenn, 1976; Wolfensberger, 1972). Although the term "least restrictive environment" has at times been controversial, the concept that it represents has remained intact. This notion means that the provision of services that provide for life patterns similar to that of able-bodied persons is tailored to the special needs of each individual, and provides for appropriate opportunities by the disabled individual to participate in activities that draw from the individual's capabilities (Budde & Edwards, 1978). The least restrictive notion can be applied to a variety of environments, each with its particular continuum (Abeson, 1976; Glenn, 1976).

Two primary continua exist that are integral to a service system: residential and activity. The residential continuum encompasses all the places where people live and sleep, and the activity continuum encompasses all the substantive developmental growth activities in which people engage. The activity continuum can be viewed in two subsets, vocational and educational (appropriateness dependent upon the age of the individual). Tables 1.3a-c illustrate the various aspects

of both these continua. The notions inherent in these continua can be applied in all situations, as illustrated in Table 1.4. The use of the notion of a continuum is important for two reasons. It permits service system planners and administrators to develop appropriate variations of services based upon frequency or intensity factors that control for costs of care, and it permits the application of appropriate rehabilitative methods. It also permits the use of an ideological framework that enhances both self- and societal-perceptions of an individual who is disabled as a fully functioning member of the community at large. Economics, rehabilitative technologies, and ideological considerations become prime factors in this process.

Residential Continuum

Although many authors (Glenn, 1976; Lensink, 1974; Madle, 1978; Wolfensberger, 1972) have cited examples of the programs that should be available as options within the residential continuum, most have not framed these options within program models.

Residential settings may vary markedly as to the frequency, variety, and emphasis of on-site formal professional therapeutic or experiential services provided. Every residential program setting, regardless of how unrestricted, possesses some service components, even if such services can be defined as solely advisory or facilitative. Surprisingly, in spite of the focus upon active habilitation services in programs for developmentally disabled persons during the past decade, very little has been written examining distinct services or classes of services and the degree to which they are provided in different residential contexts.

A combination of service need definitions and environments leads to the development of residential models. Bjaanes and Butler (1974) postulated that residential programs could be characterized as custodial, maintaining, or therapeutic. Baker, Seltzer, and Seltzer (1979) offered a taxonomy that characterized residential programs into four categories: group homes, protected environments, training programs, and semi-independent living. Janicki (1981) offered three components for defining residential models: res-

Table 1.5. Comparison of Living Alternative Models

MODEL ELEMENTS	FAMILY LIVING SITUATIONS	GROUP LIVING SITUATIONS	CONGREGATE CARE SITUATIONS
Program environment	• neighborhood house • family residence owned or rented by one or more persons who constitute what is commonly called a family, which incorporates generally no more than six disabled children or adults into the family group. (Bruininks, Hill, & Thorsheim, 1980)	• neighborhood house • a community-based residential facility located within neighborhood housing stock, providing a supervised house for usually more than three but less than 15 disabled adolescents or adults. (O'Conner & Sitkei, 1975)	• purpose built building • an institutional residential environment where specialized services are provided (beyond basic room and board) with varying emphasis on health care or habilitative services provision; for children or adults needing specialized structured institutional care or services. (PILC, 1979)
Rehabilitative intent	• "surrogate family living" • to use the physical environment of a home and the psychological environment of a family to provide for interpersonal and small group living "surrogate kin" group. (Newman & Sherman, 1979–80; Provencal & MacCormack, 1979)	• "cooperative group living" • to use the physical environment of a home and the psychological environment of a peer group to promote development of skills in caring for self, personal space, home common areas, as well as development of interpersonal skills and friendships. (Janicki, 1981)	• "therapeutic care" • to use economy of scale setting to provide health, rehabilitative, educational, or training services in order to enhance the capabilities of disabled individuals to care for themselves or to provide specialized medical services. (PILC, 1979)
Management system	• "parental" • role of "parents" is used to manage home and to use personal style to promote family living.	• "mentoring" • role of "staff" is to manage home, coordinate activities and to carry out rehabilitative goals. Staff integrated as part of system.	• "supervision" • role of "staff" is to provide supervision and specialized health and therapy services; structured administrative systems.
Examples	foster family care	community residence, group homes, shared apartments	state schools, developmental centers, skilled nursing facilities.

Adapted from Janicki, Jacobson, & Schwartz (1980).

idential environment, rehabilitative intent, and management systems, while Janicki, Jacobson, and Schwartz (1980) proposed a matrix that took into account these three components and applied them to program classes identified as family living, group living, or congregate care (see Table 1.5).

A different approach was taken by Budde and Edwards (1978). They integrated abstract notions of service provision within care models. Their model provided a method of classifying services according to setting. According to the dimensions of normalization, size, and service models, four classes of care models could be identified (Table 1.6). Combined, these represent a residential services dimension that stems from both service definitions and care models (Table 1.7).

These models can be reduced to three broad levels of residential care: supervised, structured, and specialized health care (OMRDD, 1982). Supervised care encompasses both family living and group living situations. These settings draw from Budde and Edwards' (1978) "integrated individualized" or "integrated independent" concepts and provide supervision, preventive, and preservation services, and, to a much lesser extent, intensive individual and individual maintenance services. Structured care includes all therapeutic care residential programs, specifically the ICF/MR variants found in the United States. These settings draw from Budde and Edwards' "integrated custodial/habilitative" or "segregated custodial/habilitative" concepts and emphasize comprehensive ha-

Table 1.6. General Service Delivery Models

Segregated Custodial/Habilitative—Intermediate and large units physically and socially segregated from the surrounding community. Most services consolidated for organizational expediency and economy. Typically, more than six clients per sleeping unit, with units grouped like wards or as actual wards.

Integrated Custodial/Habilitative—Intermediate or small units that are physically integrated into but socially segregated from the surrounding community. Most services consolidated for organizational expediency and economy. Sleeping environments often grouped together within one facility.

Integrated Individualized—Small units physically and socially integrated within the surrounding community according to the community's cultural, social, occupational and educational norms. Services are totally individualized and emphasis is foremost on the client. Maximum of 14 clients to a unit with no more than one such unit per 50 in immediate similar environment (e.g., apartment complex).

Integrated Independent—Small units physically and socially integrated within the surrounding community. Services are preventive or preserving and carried out within, or in conjunction with, the client's normal living environment. Services are totally individualized and emphasis is foremost on the clients, their preservation in the normal home and prevention of institutionalization. Services are carried out according to the cultural norm of the community. Maximum of three clients per unit with no more than one such unit per 50 immediate similar environment.

From Budde and Edwards (1978).

bilitation and mass maintenance services. Specialized health care encompasses special medical units, specialty hospitals, skilled nursing facilities, and other congregate care settings where there is a specialized health care motive. These program models are clearly "segregated custodial/habilitative"; the services emphasize subsistence, subsistence and habilitation, and comprehensive habilitative services.

Within the framework of these models, the dimensions presented by Glenn (1976), Lensink (1974), Madle (1978), and others seem reasonable. Table 1.7 represents an amalgam of these types; they should be considered when planning and designing the residential services component of a service system.

Activity Continua

The range and depth of self-determined activity options expand considerably as a person passes from infancy to adulthood. This reflects a normal developmental process through which an individual proceeds beginning with pre-educational preparation, education, and then adoption of a vocational identity. Persons with

mental retardation, and others with severe disabling conditions, find that this process is either delayed or impaired, or that the means to fulfull it are unavailable.

Consequently the developmental activities continua are mechanisms that provide early remedial or enrichment experiences to mitigate cognitive and/or affective deficits. They provide for focused education or habilitation to build upon information retention processes, develop a suitable repertoire of adaptive skills, and develop work behaviors in preparation for sheltered or competitive work. There are two age-dependent subsets of the activity continua.

Education Continuum

Inherent in Public Law 94-142 (Education for All Handicapped Children Act) is the provision for a free and appropriate education. The settings for needed education services can vary greatly (Brown et al., 1980). However, dependent upon the extent of deficits exhibited by an individual, they will normally be provided within either an educational or habilitative environment. The distinction between these two is

Table 1.7. Residential Services Dimensions

Subsistence Services—Mere life subsistence. No or little emphasis on habilitation or social integration.

Subsistence & Habilitation Services—Subsistence treatment and some training to habilitate clients.

Mass Maintenance Services—Maintenance of moderately large groups in the community.

Individual Maintenance Services—Maintenance of small groups in the community.

Intense Individual Services—Provision of a normal environment combined with intensive services that meet specific individual needs.

Suspension Services—Supervision of people in a normal environment. Temporary support services may be included.

Preventive Services—Prevention of client institutionalization; services that meet special needs in a natural or surrogate home setting.

Preservation Services—Preservation of residential status in normal environment, so that client can live a life that is culturally normal. Service is follow-along in nature.

From Budde and Edwards (1978).

important. This distinction is dependent on the model upon which services are based as well as the quirks of the funding mechanisms for special developmental services in the United States. Education services can be characterized by their academically based nature and are predominantly funded through local taxes and federal and state support provided to local educational agencies. Educational services include the provision of specially designed instruction to meet the unique needs of a child according to an Individual Education Plan, and are provided by special educators in a classroom setting. Habilitation services can be characterized by their applied nature and by the fact they they are in part funded through Title XIX of the Social Security Act. Habilitation is the provision of specialized training, assistance and other health maintenance services according to an Individual Program Plan, and directed toward the development of optimal personal competence in intellectual, sensorimotor, and developmental skills. Both types of services can be seen as precursors for a range of adult day services.

Most mental retardation service agencies do not provide direct education services. These are the responsibility of local public education agencies. However, the comprehensiveness tenet of the service system calls for the provision of appropriate habilitative services to severely handicapped preschool and school age children that may fall under the aegis of a retardation/developmental services organization. While this agency may be involved in advocating with local schools to assure appropriate provision of education services within the least restrictive mode of the educational environment continuum (Table 1.3b), it may be also in a position for providing habilitative services under special arrangements with local education authorities. Consequently, provisions have to be made to include habilitative/activity programs for school age youngsters within the overall continuum of activity services. Special efforts must also be made to ensure that a "least restrictive educational environment" is available for each child. As Brown et al. (1980) note, it is critical that educational service delivery models used for severely handicapped students closely approximate the best available educational service delivery models used for non-handicapped students.

The model for habilitative services, structured to provide basic health maintenance, special therapeutic services, and stimulation activities, follows a developmental activities curriculum. Children who are profoundly mentally retarded and/or severely handicapped, and who are not in academically-oriented school programs, must be enrolled in developmental activities programs that provide a combination of di-agnostic, active treatment and habilitative services on a continuous basis. These activities must include the provision of a variety of health and therapy services such as health maintenance care, physical and occupational therapy, and therapeutic recreation, as well as training activities designed to build adaptive behavior skills.

Vocational Continuum

As noted by DuRand and Neufeldt (1980), the primary goal of a vocational services component is to help persons who are handicapped become part of the work community rather than remain in sheltered environments. This component should be organized so that it forms a comprehensive and continuous system. To be comprehensive, it must offer a full range of vocational options, and to be continuous, it must accommodate each individual's growth and needs for a more challenging vocational option.

Vocational service models are similar to those referenced for residential services. The design of vocational services must provide consistency with normal work oriented features that, within the context of a least restrictive environment, encourage challenge and promote greatest transfer of training. Models that operate effectively are those whose designs promote normative work behavior. Design features include training within a building designed for work (and which is perceived by the public as a place of work), tasks that are challenging and related to the development of worker skills and work behavior, and forms of address, methods of supervision, and rates of pay that promote a positive worker identity. Cognitive and experiential deficits will determine the amount of skill capability. However, work training programs are essentially governed by the demands of the marketplace, and what is most needed in terms of building work behavior is exposure to competitive work (Screven, Straka, & LaFond, 1971). Care must be taken to provide tasks, activities, and work assignments that are meaningful and that assure a high degree of challenge as well as self-perception of "real-world" relevance. Bercovici (1981) notes that learning environments that do not heed this notion become counterproductive, that is, "institutional as opposed to normalizing" (p. 143).

The vocational services component has a number of elements. These include mechanisms that evaluate worker potential, provide for worker skill building (by utilizing both appropriate and varied vocational assessment techniques), and provide actual work experience either in a sheltered or competitive work setting. Such services are appropriate for late adolescents or adults who demonstrate prerequisite aptitudes for worker training. However, competitive employment may not be an optimal goal for many developmentally disabled individuals. Nevertheless, a reasonable goal should be to provide each individual with a least restrictive vocational setting capable of maintaining that individual's highest degree of independence and competence (Karan, 1977).

Alternatives to vocational services need also to be available in instances where individuals who, because of cognitive deficits, inexperience, or other reasons, do not yet demonstrate prerequisite worker skills. In this case the continuum must provide for developmental activities, whether called habilitative, day training, prevocational or work activity center programs. These types of activities are usually designed either (1) to prepare individuals for eventual transition to work training programs, or (2) to provide a long-term activities-oriented environment where the emphasis is on maintenance of learned adaptive behaviors as well as continuous development of more complex behaviors. These habilitative programs offer training in basic self-care, toileting, eating, and hygiene skills, in addition to leisure-time experiences, social skill building, and rudimentary academics.

Setting System Priorities

Identification of priorities combines the setting of goals and objectives, and determination of activities of the system within the resources available in order to define a course of action. This course is usually presented through an annual or multi-year plan or other such published documents. Priorities are usually derived by incorporating information from the needs assessment process in combination with the administrative necessities inherent in managing the organization and service system.

Historically, many of the activities related to service priorites of mental retardation/developmental disabilities services have been directed toward institutional management (Scheerenberger, 1975), and the de-institutionalization process (Braddock, 1977; Bradley, 1978; Paul, Stedman, & Neufeld, 1977; Scheerenberger, 1976). As Scheerenberger has noted, the institutionalized population of mentally retarded individuals in the United States peaked at 255,000 in 1969. Since that time more than 100,000 persons have been deinstitutionalized. However, the term "de-institutionalized" does not solely encompass the process of release from institutions. As Scheerenberger (1977) notes, deinstitutionalization encompasses three interrelated processes:

- prevention of admission by finding and developing alternative community methods of care and training;

- return to the community of all residents who have been prepared through programs of habilitation and training to function adequately in appropriate local settings; and
- establishment and maintenance of a responsive residential environment which protects human and civil rights and which contributes to the expeditious return of the individual to normal community living.

This response to federal policy shifts has dramatically changed the structure of most state's services priorities. In most cases, the change has produced a movement toward a community-based services system. This aspect, termed communitization (Jones, 1975), calls for resource and service integration that facilitates normal and full life opportunities for each disabled person. This goal is achieved through the development of comprehensive community services, and the conversion of institutional resources for use in building the evolving community system (Hogan, 1980). As this process has begun to take precedence over the administration of institutional systems, so has the need emerged to re-structure administrative priorities affecting service development and provision.

There are a number of ways to define the priorities of an organization. However, dependent upon the governance mechanisms of that organization, the methods as well as the flexibility in using those methods will vary. State authorities or designated agencies usually are governed by public policies, fiscal economies, and political realities. Regional authorities or local agencies will be more responsive to both their governing body and the voices of participating consumers. Priorities are usually the ranking of objectives; that is, the definition of what the organization wants to achieve and a delineation of methods of attainment. Fiscal resources usually will constrain many agencies in what they want to do. However, these same constraints will also force agencies to set in priority order all the objectives that they want to achieve.

An effective means of organizing priorities can be to trichotomize activities, services, populations, and/or resources according to the primary, secondary, and tertiary prevention levels. In this manner, prevention is viewed within the broadest sense possible so that all activities can be related to this notion. In general, the concept of prevention can be defined as (1) the preempting of the occurrence of certain situations, (2) the early amelioration of situations, and (3) the maintenance of current levels of performance. Within this framework, system priorities can be determined that relate to all three situations. Obviously the care of an existing population often takes precedence because of realistic demands, legislative mandates, strong advocacy, or funding availability.

The institutionalization and deinstitutionalization processes that have occurred in the United States have produced two populations of persons with mental retardation. One population is composed of a state's or locality's institutionalized and deinstitutionalized citizens. They represent a long-term care population that is receiving institutional care or is the obligation of the system for post-release care. Since the number of individuals previously institutionalized and now released is generally known, these individuals represent a finite group. Their needs, both present and future, can be relatively easily assessed and projections can be made as to the shifts in their long term care needs. Since this is an obligatory population, certain dedicated priorities exist that must address this group. These would include residential, vocational, and social rehabilitation services.

The other segment of the population consists of all the individuals within the community who were never institutionalized. This group includes at-risk newborns, preschoolers or school age youngsters, as well as adolescents and adults who may require specialized acute or transitional services as well as long term care. This population poses a more difficult problem in terms of identification, service need projection, and fiscal resource allocations. It also draws upon different levels of services and reflects an organization's priorities in areas of health maintenance and improved pregnancy outcomes, advocacy, public education, appropriate early and remedial intervention services, and a range of services related to families.

The determination of priorities and the structuring of services to meet these needs must take into account these population concepts as well as the trichotomy of prevention strategies. The structuring of priorities should also lead to the agency's publication of a plan detailing its proposed course of action. The priorities setting process should take into account the organization's fiscal resources, legal responsibilities and mandates, advocacy information, needs assessment findings, triage strategies, personnel, and organizational structures. Obviously there will be an interplay between these populations and among the strategies employed to meet their needs. This interplay will be contingent upon how cohesive the organization is and how well the economies of planning affect the determination of management's implementation strategies.

Administrative Mechanisms

The administrative aspects of a service agency define the organization's responsibility for providing and monitoring services. They also detail the processes used for coordinating the units within the service system. These mechanisms outline the legal and organizational relationships among services as well as the responsibility, authority, and accountability for programs and their financing.

The legal aspect stems from the enabling legislation which set up, defined the role and responsibilities, and offered legal authorization for performance of an agency's functions. In most states, the designated state agency is established in law with a clear mandate for its activities. In many localities, the legal authorization comes from either state or provincial statutes, or from the regulatory base of the state or provincial designated agency. Thus, this empowerment permits a course of activity that has legal sanction and permits, within the definition of law or regulations, the workings of the administration of services.

These same legal aspects or regulations also normally define the responsibilities of the service agency in terms of quality assurance. This requires that services be provided in a uniformly acceptable manner and the rights and welfare of clientele are fully protected. This involves the use of qualified and competent employees, approriate therapeutic and habilitative procedures, safe environments, and a regard for the rights of clientele, including due process on admission and discharge decisions, as well as in treatment planning program changes. These monitoring aspects, usually are vested either in a branch of the service agency not directly responsible for operations or in a completely different superior or control agency.

Administrative structures are the framework of the organization and define its ability to deliver the services it has deemed necessary. Consequently, this aspect has two components: structure and process. The structure encompasses the governance mechanisms, as well as the managerial network that oversees the agency's process. The process defines the uses of the prerequisite steps described above, i.e., definition of population, needs assessment, definition of services, determination of priorities, and use of financing mechanisms.

Governance is the power to set policy and make decisions that affect the organization. Developmental service agencies' mandates at the local or regional level will vary as a function of the nature of their form of governance. In some cases, these agencies will be operated by government and consequently governance is vested in public officials designated as managers. In other instances, the agencies will be operated by a public-benefit or not-for-profit corporation. In these instances, the ultimate authority is vested in a board of directors; however some authority in both aspects is delegated to a manager selected and appointed by the board. Boards in these cases are made up of private citizens, not employees, who are vested with certain powers through the corporate charter of the agency. In other cases, governance can be affected through advisory bodies set up specifically to foster dialogue between management and consumer or constituent groups. While advisory bodies may not be vested with real authority or powers, they nevertheless may exercise considerable influence upon the organization and its administrative process. As Thiele, Paul, and Neufeld (1977, p. 33) aptly note, "there must be a decision-making philosophy and the accompanying machinery to effectively involve consumers or their representatives in the decision-making process and keep consumer-revelant decisions made as close to the consumer as possible."

Administrative structure is the managerial network that carries out the agency's policies and oversees service provision. This structure also must encompass the service objectives of the agency. These services must be readily available and accessible, offer continuity, and be comprehensive. To do this, the agency must provide or account for the provision of a range of essential services. These include: evaluation, diagnosis, treatment, day programs, training, education, sheltered employment, recreation, personal care, domiciliary care, special living arrangements, counseling, information and referral, follow-up, protective and other socio-legal services, and transportation.

The organization of these discrete services can be quite difficult unless a domain or clustering approach is taken. An individual's needs should be addressed with a holistic approach; that is, within an assumption that he/she will have differing degrees of need in four primary care domains (social, health, educational, and psychological), and that these domains are interrelated. Consequently, a problem that involves a residential need, i.e., a social domain need, will also most likely affect some other aspect of the individual's life, perhaps health or psychological. Knowing this, this approach can lead to the development of an organizational structure or managerial network that takes into account these personal-need domains by structuring services within the four primary service areas (family resources, residential, vocational, and child development) described elsewhere. These organizational areas then form the framework for an appropriate clustering of a variety of discrete services. The internal consistency of the clusters offers the manager the opportunity to employ staff with appropriate education and experience, as well as meet all aspects of an individual client's needs in a comprehensive manner. It also makes a great deal more sense

when agency territories are set up and interorganizational networks are established. Models of such organizational structures are available in ENCOR (Hitzing, 1980) and COMSERV (Roeher, 1980; NIMR, 1973).

Delineation of Fiscal Support

The fiscal support aspects of a service system structure delineate that system's capabilities to pay for the services it provides. After one has examined planning, structuring, and administering a continuum of care, the next logical step is delineating mechanisms for financing the implementation of the services within the continuum. This step is accomplished primarily through the financial policies of state and local government. As noted by Katzper (1981), "fiscal policy is one of government's main tools for effecting change." Simply stated, the conditions that government imposes on the financing of services determine the character of the service system. Unfortunately, financing policies often do not keep pace with philosophic and program technology changes in serving developmentally disabled persons. It seems rather obvious that, if a continuum of care is being planned with the predetermined goal of its implementation, considerable attention should be given to its financing. The establishment of mutually compatible philosophic, program, and financing principles must receive equal and commensurate attention.

The general requirement of a financing system, beyond compatibility, is that it must be sufficiently flexible so as to accommodate the individualized needs of its clientele. The financing system must be sensitive to the needs of each disabled individual and be able to accommodate the changing needs of the individual for either more or less service, or shifts in types of services. This financing must, just as a program plan, focus on the individual. The financing system must reflect the differences in costs between various program providers where such differences are reasonable. For example, one service provider may be obligated to pay a mortgage on the building housing the program, while another provider is housed in a building donated to the agency. Flat-rate reimbursement methodologies unfairly penalize the provider who did not have the good fortune to receive a donated building. This leaves two possible outcomes. Either providers spend similar amounts of the flat-grant dollars on actual services and the one provider receives a windfall or each provider spends the available dollars on services, with the provider holding a mortgage spending less on its clientele. In the second example, the clientele may receive less service based on happenstance rather than on a rational program or fiscal policy. Obviously, this is inconsistent with the notion of a rational continuum of services based upon individual needs.

An obvious principle of the continuum is that there be equity in the amount of services delivered. Equally important, as the previous example showed, is that there must be equity in the amount of dollars paid to providers. Many states have sought to expand community residential facilities by using contractual processes. In the case of New York, even though guidelines for these processes were developed, subsequent analysis showed that there were inconsistencies in the terms of the contracts. This situation is not too surprising when one considers that New York supervises nearly 800 community residential facilities housing on the average 10 individuals each. Each residence has occupants with different needs as well as different costs for utilities, rent, mortgage, and so forth. Although it is reasonable to think that there would be variations, it is not acceptable.

Providers of service need certainty in their financing in order to focus their attention on managing their services. Certainty in the funding of services would assure continuity of service delivery, allow for good service planning and implementation, and would keep administrative costs to a minimum. Providers must know what funds they will receive, when they will receive them, and what conditions must be met in order to receive the funds. Perhaps no single problem has caused providers of service greater difficulty than trying to assemble myriad sources of payments. As an example, a community residence program might be eligible to receive federal Department of Housing and Urban Development (HUD) rental supplementation funds, Medicaid payments for rendering a variety of services, as well as other federal fiscal support programs authorized under the Social Security Act, such as, Supplemental Security Income (SSI), Aide to Families with Dependent Children (AFDC), Social Security Administration (SSA), and state and local funds.

Typically, major service systems costs are underwritten by federal entitlement programs; for example, AFDC and Medicaid. Problems arise when services for developmentally disabled persons do not fit within the parameters of a given funding stream. For example, AFDC can be used to finance the cost of services to a developmentally disabled child placed in a foster or residential care setting by a family court. However, a facility serving persons with developmental disabilities may well find that not all the children are eligible for AFDC. All too frequently, because AFDC represents a large federal share, the response is to require total eligibility, and exclude those individuals who are not eligible. From a planning and systems administration standpoint this causes havoc for the clinician who finds that access to service is being driven by financial eligibility factors that may be irrelevant to the clinical conditions of the individual. This tyranny of payor systems has been faulted nationally by providers for years (Copeland & Iversen, 1981).

A second and equally troublesome difficulty for providers of service is the blending together of benefits which may be of an intermittent nature such as the rental subsidy program provided through HUD. Typically, funds through this program are made available to housing providers on a year by year contractual basis to cover some number of eligible recipients out of a larger population. This means that a disabled individual, who previously was eligible and has obtained rental subsidy assistance, may find that assistance terminated when entering a different residential program. Conversely, if the individual leaves the residence, the next individual admitted may not be eligible for a rental subsidy contract. This uncertainty, based on varying eligibility and program requirements is not compatible with rational financing of a continuum of services.

The financing of a continuum of services must contain the elements of cost containment. The system must lend itself to quality assurance and fiscal integrity. Within the system, there must also be the ability to link the need for services to the payment for services and, in each case, clearly establish and measure the reasonableness of both against predetermined standards. Various methods such as surveys, utilization reviews and fiscal auditing, are often used as various elements of a quality assurance program. The key element in putting into place the financing system is that it must totally lend itself to quality assurance programs. The principal elements are: client eligibility based on uniform assessment standards, program certification, establishment of reasonable cost, and the assurance that expenditures are consistent with various rules governing the program.

Closing Comments

This chapter provides a general overview of the organization and administration of service delivery systems. Since the political environment of each state or province, as well as areas within states or provinces, will vary widely, no one model can apply equally. However, what is appropriate is the adoption of certain principles and processes that form the framework for planning, developing, and managing a service delivery system addressing the needs of mentally retarded or developmentally disabled persons.

These principles include the notions that organizational systems designed to provide for persons with developmental handicaps should (1) be community-based, so that most, if not all, levels of need can be provided for in a reasonable manner; (2) be comprehensive, so that all levels of need can be met through a coherent system of services; and (3) have an ideological basis, so that the system is founded and maintained on a principle that stresses human dignity and equal access to challenging experiences (i.e., normalization) and is managed in a manner that stresses sound habilitative and rehabilitative practices.

Several steps or processes were proposed that would lead to a system that is organized and administered in a manner that would meet the principles outlined above. These were (1) defining who is to be served, (2) accomplishing a comprehensive assessment of consumer needs and providing resources, (3) adopting an organizationally sound and responsive definition of the service system, (4) developing appropriate administrative structures that would govern and renew the system, (5) determining of needs or gaps in available services that govern the prioritization of service provision strategies, and (6) delineating models and mechanisms for the fiscal support of the system.

References

Abeson, A. Education for handicapped children in the least restrictive environment. In M. Kindred (Ed.), *The mentally retarded citizen and the law*. New York: Free Press, 1976.

Allen, J. R. *Ohio developmental disabilities prevalence and needs survey: Prevalence of developmental disabilities in Ohio*. Columbus, Ohio: Ohio Developmental Disabilities Planning Council, 1978.

Alpha Center for Health Planning. *The relationship between state health planning and mental retardation/developmental disabilities planning*. Bethesda, Md.: Alpha Center for Health Planning, 1981. (Obtainable from 4720 Montgomery Lane, Suite 1102, Bethesda, Md. 20014.)

Bachrach, L. L. *Deinstitutionalization: An analytic review and sociological perspective*. Washington: DHEW, 1976.

Baker, B. L., Seltzer, G. F., & Seltzer, M. M. *As close as possible: Community residences for retarded adults*. Boston: Little, Brown & Co., 1979.

Bank-Mikkelsen, N. E. A metropolitan area in Denmark, Copenhagen. In. R. Kugel and W. Wolfensberger (Eds.), *Changing patterns in residential services for the mentally retarded*. Washington: President's Committee on Mental Retardation, 1969.

Bercovici, S. Qualitative methods and cultural perspectives in the study of deinstitutionalization. In R. H. Bruininks, C. E. Meyers, B. B. Sigford, & K. C. Lakin (Eds.), *Deinstitutionalization and community adjustment of mentally retarded people*. Washington: American Association on Mental Deficiency, 1981.

Bjaanes, A. T., & Butler, E. W. Environmental variation in community care facilities for mentally retarded persons. *American Journal of Mental Deficiency*, 1974, 78, 429–439.

Bock, W., & Roberts, K. The Minnesota experience. In W. Bock (Chair), *Needs assessment as a prelude to community services*. Paper presented at the 103rd Annual Meeting of the American Association on Mental Deficiency, Miami Beach, 1979.

Braddock, D. *Opening closed doors: The deinstitutionalization of disabled individuals*. Reston, Va.: The Council for Exceptional Children, 1977.

Braddock D. Deinstitutionalization of the retarded: Trends in public policy. *Hospital and Community Psychiatry*, 1981, 32, 607–615.

Bradley, V. J. *Deinstitutionalization of developmentally disabled persons: A conceptual analysis and guide*. Baltimore: University Park Press, 1978.

Brown, L., Wilcox, B., Sontag, E., Vincent, B., Dodd, N., & Gruenewald, L. Toward the realization of the least restrictive educational environments for severely handicapped students. In. R. J. Flynn & K. E. Nitsch (Eds.), *Normalization, social integration, and community services*. Baltimore: University Park Press, 1980.

Bruininks, R. H., Hauber, F. A., & Kudla, M. J. National survey of community residential facilities: A profile of facilities and residents in 1977. *American Journal of Mental Deficiency*, 1980, 84, 470–478(a).

Bruininks, R. H., Hill, B. K., & Thorsheim, M. S. A *profile of specially licensed foster homes for mentally retarded people in 1977*. Department of Psychoeducational Studies, University of Minnesota, Minneapolis, 1980.

Budde, J. F., & Edwards, M. E. *Statewide planning: Least-restrictive residential services*. Lawrence, Kans.: University of Kansas, 1978.

Copeland, W. C., & Iverson, I. A. *Refinancing and reorganizing human services: Interagency net budgeting and other fiscal incentives*. (Human Services Monograph Series, No. 20). Rockville, Md.: Project Share, 1981.

CPHA. *International classification of diseases* (9th Revision). Ann Arbor, Mich.: Commission on Professional and Hospital Activities, 1978.

DDS. Analysis of the functioning of residential care rates for regional center clients. Sacramento: California Department of Developmental Services. 1978.

duPree, K. Case management and patient assessment. Paper presented at Tailoring Health Services to Individual States, A Conference held by the Institute for Medicaid Management, Dallas, Texas, September, 1978.

duPree, K. & Hogan, M. The Massachusetts experience. In W. Bock (Chair), *Needs assessment as a prelude to community services*. Paper presented at the 103rd Annual Meeting of the American Association on Mental Deficiency, Miami Beach, 1979.

DuRand, J., & Neufeldt, A. H. Comprehensive vocational services. In. R. J. Flynn & K. E. Nitsch (Eds.), *Normalization, social integration, and community services*. Baltimore: University Park Press, 1980.

EMC Institute. A *compilation of rates of prevalence of the developmental disabilities*. Philadelphia: EMC Institute, 1978.

Glenn, L. The least restrictive alternative in residential care and the principle of normalization. In M. Kindred (Ed.), *The mentally retarded citizen and the law*. New York: Free Press, 1976.

HCFA. *Tailoring health sources to individual needs—conference for States, Washington*: Health Care Finance Administration, 1979.

Heal, L. W., Sigelman, C. K., & Switzky, H. N. Research on community residential alternatives for the mentally retarded. In R. J. Flynn & K. E. Nitsch (Eds.), *Normalization, social integration, and community services*. Baltimore: University Park Press, 1980.

Hitzing, W. ENCOR and beyond. In T. Appolloni, J. Cappuccuilli, & T. P. Cooke (Eds.), *Achievements in residential services for persons with disabilities: Towards excellence*. Baltimore: University Park Press, 1980.

Hogan, M. F. Normalization and communitization. In R. J. Flynn & K. E. Nitsch (Eds.) *Normalization, social integration, and community services*. Baltimore: University Park Press, 1980.

Janicki, M. P. Statewide needs assessment. In J. Mulick (chair), *Computerized recordkeeping systems in developmental disabilities services*. Paper presented at 104th Annual Meeting of the American Association on Mental Deficiency, San Francisco, 1980.

Janicki, M. P. Personal growth and community residence environments. In H. C. Haywood & J. R. Newbrough (Eds.), *Living environments for developmentally retarded persons*. Baltimore: University Park Press, 1981.

Janicki, M. P., & Jacobson, J. W. *New York's needs assessment and developmental disabilities: Preliminary report* (Technical Report 79-10). Albany, N.Y.: New York Office of Mental Retardation and Developmental Disabilities, 1979.

Janicki, M. P., & Jacobson, J. W. The character of developmental disabilities in New York State: Preliminary observations. *International Journal of Rehabilitation Research*, 1982, 5, 191–202.

Janicki, M. P., Jacobson, J. W., & Schwartz, A. S. Community living alternatives: A demographic and model base for community consultation. Paper presented at the 38th Annual Meeting of the American Psychological Association, September, Montreal, 1980.

Jones, W. E. Communitization: The creation of a viable human service delivery system and the institution's role. Paper presented to the New England Regional DHEW Developmental Disabilities Conference, Durham, N.H., 1975.

Jones, W. E. The communitization process. *Western Massachusetts Mental Health Training News*, 1977, 1(5), 1.

Kallio, V., Aromaa, A., Kalimo E., & Maatela, J. Epidemiology of functional limitations in Finland. Paper presented at the 14th World Congress of Rehabilitation International, Winnipeg, Canada, June, 1980.

Karan, O. C. Graduated habilitation programming for the severely developmentally disabled. *Rehabilitation Literature* 1977, 38, 322–327.

Katzper, M. *Modeling of long term care* (Human Services Monograph Services, No. 21). Rockville, Md.: Project Share, 1981.

Knobloch, H., & Pasamanick, B. (Eds.) *Developmental diagnosis: The evaluation and management of normal and abnormal neuropsychologic development in infancy and early childhood*. New York: Harper & Row, 1974.

Lensink, B. One service system at work. In C. Cherington and G. Dybwab (Eds.), *New neighbors: The retarded citizens in quest of a home*. Washington: President's Committee on Mental Retardation, 1974.

Levine, M., & Levine, A. *Social history of helping services: Clinic, court, school and community*. New York: Appleton-Century-Crofts, 1970.

Lindberg, D. *Prevalence of developmental disabilities in West Virginia*. Elkins, W. Va.: Davis and Elkins College, 1976.

Lubin, R. A., Jacobson, J. W., & Kiely, M. Projected impact of the functional definition of developmental disabilities: The categorically disabled population and service eligibility. *American Journal of Mental Deficiency*, 1982, 86, 73–79.

NASMRPD. *Preliminary survey findings on residential rate setting, reimbursement and methods of payment*. Arlington, Va.: National Association of State Mental Retardation Program Directors, November, 1981.

Madle, R. A. Alternative residential placements. In J. T. Neisworth and R. M. Smith (Eds.), *Retardation, issues, assessment and intervention*. New York: McGraw Hill, 1978.

Malys, G. F., & Brooks, W. A. A user's manual for the development of standards and indicators, particularly for developmental disabilities. In Alpha Center for Health Planning (Ed.), *The relationship between state health planning and mental retardation/developmental disabilities planning*. Bethesda, Md.: Alpha Center for Health Planning, 1981.

National Task Force on the Definition of Developmental Disabilities. *Definition of developmental disabilities: Final Report*. Cambridge, Mass.: Abt Associates, Inc., 1977.

Newman, E. S., & Sherman, S. R. Foster-family care for the elderly: Surrogate family or mini-institution? *International Journal of Aging and Human Development*, 1979–80, 10, 165–176.

NIMR. *A plan for comprehensive community services for the developmentally handicapped (COMSERV)*. Toronto: National Institute on Mental Retardation, 1973.

Nirje, B. The normalization principle and its human management implications. In R. Kugel & W. Wolfensberger (Eds.), *Changing patterns in residential services for the mentally retarded*. Washington: U.S. Government Printing Office, 1969.

O'Connor, G., & Sitkei, E. G. Study of a new frontier in community services: Residential facilities for the developmentally disabled. *Mental Retardation*, 1975, 13, 35–39.

OMRDD. *Five-year comprehensive plan for services to mentally retarded and developmentally disabled persons in New York State*. Albany: New York State Office of Mental Retardation and Developmental Disabilities, 1978.

OMRDD. *Comprehensive plan for services to mentally retarded and developmentally disabled persons in New York State: 1981–1984*. Albany: New York State Office of Mental Retardation and Developmental Disabilities, 1980.

OMRDD. *A plan for the availability of specialized living alternatives for the period 1981–1991*. Albany: New York State Office of Mental Retardation and Developmental Disabilities, 1982.

Paul, J. L., Stedman, D. J., & Neufeld, G. R. *Deinstitutionalization: Program and policy development*. Syracuse, N.Y.: Svracuse University Press, 1977.

PILC. Working paper on uses of Title XIX to sustain community residential services for developmentally disabled people. Philadelphia: Public Interest Law Center of Philadelphia, 1979.

Provencal, G., & MacCormack, J. P. Adult foster care: Paradox and possibility. *DD Polestor*, 1979, **1** (7), 4.

Roeher, G. A. Canadian developments: Past, present, and direction. In T. Apolloni, J. Cappuccili, & T. P. Cooke (Eds.), *Achievement in residential services for persons with disabilities: Towards excellence.* Baltimore: University Park Press, 1980.

Rubin, J. *Economics, mental health, and the law.* Lexington, Mass.: D. C. Heath and Co., 1978.

Sallis, J., & Henggeler, S. W. Needs assessment: A critical review. *Administration in Mental Health*, 1980, 7, 200–209.

Scheerenberger, R. C. *Managing residential facilities.* Springfield, Ill.: Charles C. Thomas, 1975.

Scheerenberger, R. C. *Deinstitutionalization and institutional reform.* Springfield, Ill.: Charles C. Thomas, 1976.

Scheerenberger, R. C. Deinstitutionalization in perspective. In J. L. Paul, D. J. Stedman, & G. R. Neufeld (Eds.), *Deinstitutionalization: Program and policy development.* Syracuse, N.Y.: Syracuse University Press, 1977.

Scheerenberger, R. C. Public residential facilities: Status and trends. *Mental Retardation*, 1981, **19**, 59–60.

Screven, C. G., Straka, J. A., & LaFond, R. Applied behavioral technology in a vocational rehabilitation setting. In W. I. Gardner (Ed.), *Behavior modification in mental retardation: The education and rehabilitation of the mentally retarded adolescent and adult.* Chicago: Aldine/Atherton, 1971.

Thiele, R. L., Paul, J. L., & Neufeld, G. R. Institutionalization: A perspective for deinstitutionalization program development. In J. L. Paul, D. J. Stedman, & G. R. Neufeld (Eds.), *Deinstitutionalization: Program and policy development.* Syracuse, N.Y.: Syracuse University Press, 1977.

Thompson, R. J., & O'Quinn, A. N. *Developmental disabilities: Etiologies, manifestations, diagnoses, and treatments.* New York: Oxford University Press, 1979.

Warhert, G. J., Bell, R. A., & Schwab, J. J. *Need assessment approaches; Concepts and methods.* Washington: Alcohol, Drug Abuse and Mental Health Administration, 1977.

Wolfensberger, W. *Normalization: The principle of normalization in human services.* Toronto: National Institute on Mental Retardation, 1972.

Wolfensberger, W. *The origin and nature of our institutional models.* Syracuse, N.Y.: Syracuse University Press, 1974.

Wolfensberger, W. A brief overview of the principle of normalization. In R. J. Flynn & K. E. Nitsch (Eds.), *Normalization, social integration, and community services.* Baltimore: University Park Press, 1980a.

Wolfensberger, W. The definition of normalization. In R. J. Flynn & K. E. Nitsch (Eds.), *Normalization, social integration, and community services.* Baltimore: University Park Press, 1980b.

WHO. *International classification of impairments, disabilities, and handicaps.* Geneva: World Health Organization, 1980.

2 ADVOCATE GROUPS

Philip R. Roos

Contemporary Western societies have little tolerance for deviancy from cherished cultural norms. Mental retardation can be understood as a complex sociocultural condition characterized by difficulty in complying with cultural norms regarding intellectual and social behavior. Mentally retarded persons tend to violate such cherished cultural values as intelligence, emotional independence, economic self-sufficiency and physical attractiveness. As a result, they have traditionally been rejected, isolated, stigmatized, and deprived of society's resources.

Negative reactions to mental retardation contrive to be fostered by enduring negative models of the mentally retarded person, as described in detail by Wolfensberger (1969). These models have generated self-fulfilling prophecies that have contributed to rejection and isolation of mentally retarded people and—to a lesser extent—their families. For example, the model of mental retardation as an illness leads to concerns with contamination and hereditary transmission, inappropriate treatment approaches, and parental shame and helplessness. The model of the mentally retarded person as a subhuman organism has fostered dehumanizing practices and facilities. The model of the mentally retarded person as a menace to society has mitigated against efforts to integrate such persons with society.

Having a mentally retarded child is still often a source of parental shame and self-doubts. Indeed, the possibility of having such a child is so traumatic that most people assume it could not happen to them. Even when new parents are confronted with clear evidence that their child is mentally retarded, denial is a common response.

Furthermore, our culture has no clearly established rituals or practices for dealing with mental retardation. The most common approach has been to abandon these individuals as "hopeless" and to exclude them from society. A report of the International League of Societies for the Mentally Handicapped (1967) aptly summarizes this situation:

To comprehend the handicap, to see what needs doing and to do it, when these three components exist, there is a pulse of communication between the handicapped person and the rest of the community, and everyone, not alone the handicapped, benefits. . . .

In relation to mental handicap, these conditions are difficult to achieve. . . . Because we don't know what to do we feel helpless. In the face of the human distress, which we can do nothing to alleviate, we are embarrassed—so we put the problem out of mind and do nothing [p. 7].

Professional Neglect

Professional services to families of mentally retarded people have traditionally failed to meet their needs (e.g., National Association for Retarded Citizens, 1974; Roos, 1963, 1970, 1975, 1977a, 1977b, in press). Inappropriate handling of parents of mentally retarded children by mental health professionals has been particularly unfortunate. This tragic neglect may reflect the reluctance of many mental health professionals to work with mentally retarded clients.

In general, psychotherapists have selected clients who reflect their own self-concept. Such variables as intelligence, verbal facility, introspective ability, and capacity for highly abstract conceptualizing have typically been identified as favorable prognostic indices for psychotherapy (e.g., Fenichel, 1945; McKinney, 1958). Mentally retarded people, by definition, are lacking in these attributes. Psychotherapy has typically been considered unsuitable with mentally retarded individuals, and those with serious emotional problems have frequently been assigned to institutional "chronic back wards" and provided "custodial care."

These negative attitudes toward mentally retarded people have tended to generalize to their parents as well. Negative stereotypes of these parents are common among professionals, who often inappropriately attribute a variety of "emotional problems" to them (e.g., Roos, 1977a, in press). These include (1) failure to "accept" that their child is mentally retarded, usually interpreted as a form of "denial"; (2) chronic depression, often interpreted as the product of "internalization of unacceptable death wishes" toward the child; (3) overprotectiveness of the child, allegedly stemming from "reaction formation" to latent hostility toward the child; (4) irrational hostility inappropriately displaced from the child to others, particularly health professionals; and (5) chaotic marital relationships, resulting from displaced and/or projected hostility.

In view of these negative stereotypes, it is not surprising that parents of mentally retarded children have traditionally been neglected and, in some cases, mishandled (e.g., Ingalls, 1978; McWilliams, 1976; Menolascino, 1977; Menolascino & Michael, 1978; Murray, 1959; Roos, 1975, 1977a, 1977b, 1978; Turnbull & Turnbull, 1978).

A common misconception of some mental health professionals is the assumption that parents of mentally retarded children are emotionally disturbed and in need of "treatment" (Menolascino, 1977; Menolascino

& Michael, 1978). The psychoanalytic tradition of attributing psychological problems to early parent-child relationships may have fostered this belief (e.g., Fenichel, 1945). Until recently, for example, autism was believed to be the result of parental influences on the affected child (e.g., Bettelheim, 1967; Kanner, 1944).

Surprisingly, many professionals in the medical and behavioral sciences are still grossly misinformed about mental retardation. Misdiagnosis and dispensation of misinformation are common. It is not unusual for parents to be assured that their child will "outgrow" the difficulty, while other parents may be bluntly told that their child is "hopeless" and that immediate institutionalization is the only solution. As recently as 1982, infants suspected of severe mental retardation were denied life-saving surgery and allowed to die (e.g., Barbash & Russell, 1982; Brozek, 1981).

Parental Reactions

Although parents of mentally retarded children generally are not suffering from serious psychological disturbances, having a mentally retarded child is nonetheless usually experienced as highly painful. Western culture places such great value on intelligence that "humanhood" tends to be equated with this attribute (e.g., Fletcher, 1972). Hence, a mentally retarded child may be perceived as "less than fully human" and as a "major disappointment." Research data confirm the assumption that a mentally retarded child produces significant family stress (e.g., Gath, 1977; Holt, 1958; Kramm, 1963).

Typical parental emotional reactions reflect frustration, stress and crisis (McWilliams, 1976; Menolascino, 1977; Menolascino & Michael, 1978; Murray, 1959; Roos, 1963, 1977a, 1978; Schild, 1964). Common reactions include shame, guilt, ambivalence, depression, sorrow, defensiveness, self-sacrifice ("martyr" posture), denial, reaction formation (typically manifested in overprotecting the child), and mourning.

Characteristic patterns of parental reactions to a mentally retarded child have also been identified. Farber (1972), for example, described two kinds of crises: (1) The "tragic crisis" results from frustration of aspirations and dreams for the child and the parents themselves. This response is common in middle class, achievement-oriented parents. (2) The "role organization crisis" is characterized by concern with day-to-day reality problems and is typical of low income parents. Menolascino (1977) identified these common crisis patterns: (1) "novelty shock crisis," in response to the initial diagnosis and the resulting "demolition of expectations;" (2) "crisis of personal values," related to the child's symbolic value and difficulty in fitting the child into the parents' personal value system; and (3) "reality crisis," resulting from practical problems of daily life and associated frustrations.

Roos (1977a, 1977b, 1978) has suggested that having a mentally retarded child tends to exacerbate existential anxieties common to most people. These nonpathological reactions are responses to such existential conditions as disillusionment in self and others, aloneness, vulnerability, inequity, insignificance, and mortality.

Development of Parent Organizations

In view of the serious, chronic frustrations felt by many parents of handicapped children, it is not surprising that some parents inevitably learned to turn toward each other for mutual support and assistance. Yet formal parent organizations are of relatively recent origin. In the United States, small groups of parents of mentally retarded children began to form in a few localities in the 1930s.

The oldest local organization that eventually became a member of what is now the Association for Retarded Citizens (ARC) was founded in 1933 as the Council for the Retarded Child, Cuyahoga County, Ohio. Whereas this early group focused on helping children ineligible for public schools, the Children's Benevolent League was formed in the state of Washington in 1936 to assist children residing in the state's residential institutions. In 1939, parents of residents of New York State's Letchworth Village (a large state institution) formed the Welfare League for Retarded Children. Shortly after World War II, other groups began to appear in such states as Massachusetts, New Jersey, Minnesota, California, Illinois, and Utah.

These local efforts coalesced into a nationwide movement in 1950, when 42 parents representing several local organizations banded together to form what is now the ARC, originally called the National Association of Parents and Friends of Mentally Retarded Children.

Four factors have been identified as responsible for the appearance of the ARC and similar parent organizations in the United States (Mead & Brown, 1966): (1) An acute lack of community services for handicapped children; (2) popular concern with obviously deplorable conditions in many state institutions; (3) stimulation of parent efforts by the opportunity of gaining a platform at the midcentury White House Conference on Children and Youth; and (4) indications of potential federal funding of mental retardation programs. Katz (1961) has identified four general characteristics in American society contributing to the formation of voluntary agencies: (1) The tendency of Americans to form organizations, (2) preference for voluntary rather than governmental programs in the health and welfare field, (3) a highly productive and technological economy, and (4) the strong humanitarian and philanthropic interests of the American people.

Another important stimulant to the emergence of parent associations was the gradual replacement of hopelessness with hope, resulting from progress in the understanding and handling of childhood disabilities. Biomedical advances began to identify preventive approaches, while psychoeducational technologies began to hold out hope for more meaningful lives for many handicapped children. Hence, although the socioeconomic conditions in America may have been particularly propitious for the growth of parent organizations, a combination of parental frustration and hope probably provided a worldwide impetus for parents to seek power and mutual support through unity.

The ARC and similar parent organizations differ significantly from most national voluntary health agencies. Unlike most other organizations, these parent associations did not originate at the initiative of a professional group concerned with a specific disease; rather, they developed as a result of what parents perceived as professional neglect. Whereas many of the other organizations began as centralized national movements, the ARC as a national organization was preceded by local and state units, leading to a strong "grass roots" orientation, which has permeated the association throughout its history. Furthermore, parent organizations have typically been highly democratic and decentralized, encouraging maximum member participation in their governance. Thus, the national board of directors of the ARC has been composed almost exclusively of persons elected by and from its membership. Another difference from most national health organizations is that health per se has not usually been the primary focus of parent organizations. Hence, mental retardation, for example, has not been defined as a medical entity by these groups, but rather as a condition resulting from a wide variety of possible causes, which manifests itself primarily in problems of learning and adaptation. Historically, deficiencies in educational and residential services have been of greater concern to parents than lack of medical or paramedical services.

Parent organizations also differ in important ways from conventionally organized social agencies. Based on a study of four self-organized parent groups, Katz (1961) summarized their differences by concluding that: (1) they were formed for mutual assistance by persons with a common problem, (2) they are "consumer" dominated and emphasize self-help approaches to services and to organizational structure, (3) parent-members share leadership and responsibility with paid professional staff, (4) they encourage "social action" strategies to achieve their objectives, and (5) they often use promotional publicity that does not respect the "confidentiality" of the parent-members.

Composition

The growth of parent organizations has been impressive. For instance, in 1951 the ARC included 125 units with approximately 13,000 active members. By 1955, the membership had grown to 35,000 members in 412 units. A 1961 survey was distributed to 787 local member units with an estimated membership of over 65,000. In 1969, there were 1,370 units and 140,705 members. Membership peaked in 1975 with over 1,800 state and local member units and a membership of approximately 250,000, and it remained relatively static during the rest of the decade.

Most parent organizations have not been restricted to parents. Frequently, the proportion of nonparents has tended to increase. Thus, a survey of the ARC membership in 1952 revealed that three-quarters of all members were parents, that 21% of the units had only parents as members, and that only one unit had an equal number of parent and nonparent members. By 1969, an intensive study of four large units (Segal, 1970) revealed that in some units the parents had become a minority. By 1975, a broad membership survey revealed that 51% of the total membership were parents (NARC, 1975). The latest survey, conducted in 1979, indicated that only 43.9% were parents and that of the members recruited during the previous five years (37% of the membership), only 35% were parents (Neman, 1981).

The socioeconomic level of the ARC membership has been primarily middle and upper middle class, as is common in American voluntary health agencies. The Association has attempted to involve more poor people, and established a Poverty Committee as early as 1968. In spite of continued efforts in this direction, including intensive pilot programs at the local level using indigenous workers, a 1979 survey (Neman, 1981) revealed no significant change had occurred in income levels of the membership. On the other hand, the membership has been getting progressively older. Thus, the percentage of members over 65 increased from 9% in 1974 to 20% in 1979.

The size and composition of local ARC member units has been highly variable. In 1955, a majority of the units (57%) had 10 to 50 members, while 3% reported more than 500 members. A 1962 survey (Boggs, 1963) revealed that 76% of the units had between 10 and 100 members; 16% had between 101 and 250 members; 4% had between 251 and 500 members; 3% had between 501 and 1,500 members, and less than 1% had in excess of 1,501 members. The latest ARC survey (Neman, 1981) revealed that, as of 1976, 72% of the units had less than 101 members, 25% had between 101 and 250 members; 9% had between 251 and 500 members; and 5% had in excess of 501 members, with less than 1% reporting in excess of 2,500 members.

Obviously, the level of sophistication and nature of activities varies widely among these units. For example, many units are operated entirely by volunteer members. The typical sequence in acquiring paid staff is from part-time clerical help, to full-time clerical help, to executive secretary, to professional staff (Katz, 1961). Some local units have developed staff in excess of 100, operating highly sophisticated programs.

In 1952, however, none of ARC's units reported having any staff, other than teachers conducting special classes. By 1955, some 28 units (9%) had an executive director or executive secretary, and 15 units planned to fill such a position shortly. In 1969, approximately 359 of the 1,400 member units had an executive director or its equivalent. This percentage of staffed units has remained relatively constant since, the latest systematic survey (1976) revealing that 31% of the units had executive staff positions (NARC, 1979b).

Functions and Activities

Local parent organizations not only differ markedly in size and level of sophistication, they may also be operating at different evolutionary levels. Katz (1961) has identified characteristic stages through which "self-organized" parent groups evolve. Initially, a small group of parents meet and generate interest in reaching a wider group with similar problems. The next phase ("informal organization") is characterized by increasing group size and informal meetings for information sharing, mutual support, and catharsis. During the third phase, dynamic leadership surfaces which typically molds the organization through personal influence. This informal leadership is replaced by the formal organization typical of the next phase, during which a constitution and bylaws are adopted and leadership roles are formalized and differentiated. Finally, as the organization increases in complexity, paid staff are hired.

The functions of local associations have gradually shifted as they mature. The earliest functions include meeting parents' needs for emotional support, catharsis, and information. Since new parents continue to experience these needs, most local units continue to provide services to meet them. Thus, the local ARC often remains the best source of information about local resources for mentally retarded people.

Early in their development, parent groups often established services to meet the most urgent needs of their members' children. Inadequacy or inaccessibility of suitable services in many areas catalyzed the establishment of direct services by the parent groups themselves.

The early emphasis on providing direct services is evident from surveys of ARC's local units (Roos, 1970). Thus, in 1952, 64% of the units sponsored classes for moderately and severely mentally retarded children, and 36% of the units operated recreational programs. By 1955, units operated 221 classes for "trainable" (i.e., severely and moderately mentally retarded) and 124 classes for "educable" (i.e., mildly retarded) children. Preschool needs were being addressed by 94 nursery classes and 21 day care classes. By 1962, local ARCs operated 80% of the nation's preschool programs for mentally retarded children and 71% of the day care programs.

By 1967, however, parent groups had begun to relinquish operation of direct services as community agencies increasingly assumed these functions. Special education classes were operated by only 31% of the units, while 33% operated preschool programs and 36% provided day care. This shift from providing to obtaining services was consistent with the ARC's enunciated policy as well as with that of the International League of Societies for the Mentally Handicapped (1967). This policy has remained controversial, however, and arguments have been advanced both supporting and opposing the abandonment of direct services (Roos, 1975).

A study conducted in 1976 (Neman, 1979) revealed that at least 34 different services were provided by at least some local ARC's. The most frequently reported services, reported by at least 40% of the units, were information and referral, recreation, parent counseling, parent education, and advocacy. Other frequently reported services were transportation, counseling mentally retarded persons, adult activity centers, and sheltered workshops. This study also revealed that many local ARCs did, indeed, transfer services to other agencies. The most common services transferred included sheltered workshops (18% of ARCs), preschool classes (17%), classes for moderately retarded students (15%), classes for severely and profoundly retarded students (12%), and adult activity centers (12%).

An interesting finding of this study was the tentative conclusion that: "As units provide more and more services, they have (a) significantly larger memberships, (b) staff, (c) budgets, (d) cash reserves, (e) dollars raised through fund raising, and (f) income from grants and United Way" (p. 15). However, financial flexibility of the units, defined as cash reserves and fund raising income relative to total budget, declines with increased service provision.

Clearly, the function of parent groups has gradually shifted away from direct provision of services to handicapped children themselves and increasing emphasis in such areas as public education, governmental affairs, advocacy and litigation. Many local units continue, however, to operate complex and sophisticated direct services.

A relatively recent service provided by some local ARCs is known as citizen advocacy (CA) (NARC, 1974; Wolfensberger & Zauha, 1973). These professionally supervised programs pair selected, interested persons of "normal" intelligence (the "advocates") with mentally retarded "protégés." The resulting one-to-one relationships can focus primarily on meeting the protégé's emotional needs, his needs for coping with practical problems, or a combination of both. Advocates are carefully screened, oriented, and professionally supervised.

The first CA program was established by the Capitol Association for Retarded Children (1971) in Lincoln, Nebraska, in early 1970. In 1972, the ARC initiated a national program to catalyze the development of a nationwide network of CA programs (Copeland, Addison & McCann, 1974). As of 1977, there were 142 local CA programs operating in 32 states and an additional 10 state CA offices providing backup services (Addison, 1977). These programs involved some 5,000 one-to-one advocate-protégé relationships. Approximately 75% of the programs surveyed were administered and operated by local ARCs (Addison, 1976).

Parent organizations have been extremely successful in providing a different type of advocacy through their influence on federal and state governments (Felliceti, 1975; Roos, 1972). The ARC has had a governmental affairs office in Washington, D.C., staffed by professionals skilled in governmental affairs since the late 1960s. Most of the state ARCs have emphasized state level governmental affairs activity. Typically, these efforts have been highly sophisticated and effective in initiating, modifying and supporting new bills, responding to proposed regulations and supporting appropriations. Often volunteers have become very adept at representing positions of the parent groups.

ARCs have increasingly buttressed their legislative efforts by establishing continuing liaison with heads of different state agencies. Frequently, they have participated in drafting and modifying regulations promulgated by these agencies.

Voluntary organizations with common interests have increasingly formed coalitions, often joining forces with professional organizations, such as the Council for Exceptional Children, the American Association on Mental Deficiency, the American Orthopsychiatric Association, and many others.

A related approach by parent organizations to fostering social change has consisted of placing key members on relevant state and national boards, task forces, commissions and advisory committees. For example, the Developmental Disabilities Services and Facilities Construction Act has furnished a fertile arena for ARC's direct participation in planning and evaluating services for the developmentally disabled at the state and national levels. One of the ARC's past national presidents, Dr. Elizabeth Boggs, served as the first chairman of the National Advisory Council on Services and Facilities for the Developmentally Disabled.

ARC has also been instrumental in establishing, in concert with other voluntary and professional organizations, major entities designed as national advocacy and monitoring bodies, including the National Center for Law and the Handicapped, the Accreditation Council for Services for the Mentally Retarded and Other Developmentally Disabled Persons, and National Industries for the Severely Handicapped. ARC representatives have typically served on the governing boards of the organizations, along with administrators and professionals. Through these activities, parent associations have had increasingly potent input into shaping services for handicapped people.

In spite of important advances on behalf of mentally retarded people during the 1960s and 1970s, violations of their legal and human rights continued to frustrate parent organizations and other advocates (e.g., Friedman, 1979; Roos, 1972; *Stanford Law Review*, 1979). Adoption of laudable "bills of rights" and passage of legislation failed in eradicating many discriminating practices. As frustrations mounted, parent groups increasingly turned to the courts to expedite reform.

ARCs have often joined professional and advocacy organizations in class action suits against states to safeguard the rights of mentally retarded citizens and to obtain improved or new types of services for them. This form of litigation spread rapidly among the states during the 1970s (Abeson, 1972; Friedman, 1973; Friedman, 1978; Haggerty, Kane, & Udall, 1972; Ogg, 1973; President's Committee on Mental Retardation, 1973; Roos, 1972, 1973; *Stanford Law Review*, 1979). Cases focused primarily on the issues of "right

to treatment" (e.g., *New York State Association for Retarded Children v. Carey*, 1975; *Wyatt v. Stickney*, 1972) and "right to education" (e.g., *Mills v. Board of Education of District of Columbia*, 1972; *Pennsylvania Association for Retarded Children v. Commonwealth of Pennsylvania*, 1972). Court decisions in the former area were instrumental in eradicating some of the abuses which were all too common in public institutions for mentally retarded people. Suits in the educational area fostered the opening of the doors of the public schools to severely and profoundly mentally retarded children. This "zero reject" approach was eventually codified in the Education for All Handicapped Children Act (P.L. 94-142), enacted by Congress in 1975.

International Aspects

The history of the ARC has been roughly paralleled in many other countries. The first national association for parents of mentally retarded children, the National Society for Mentally Handicapped Children, was established in 1947 in England and Wales. The next national association was the ARC (at the time called the National Association of Parents and Friends of Retarded Children), founded in 1950. By 1955, ARC had contact with mental retardation programs in 22 countries, 11 of which had national or federated associations (Dybwad, 1963). By 1957, 40 countries had some type of parent groups, and by 1959, this number had increased to 60, 20 of which had national associations. In 1963, Boggs reported the existence of national organizations in 26 other countries on six continents. In 1975, the International League of Societies for the Mentally Handicapped (now the International League of Societies for Persons with Mental Handicaps), the international organization composed of national parent organizations, listed 82 national organizations as member societies. By 1981, this number had risen to 84 members in 63 countries.

In general, these associations were founded by parents, and relatively early in their development professionals and other interested persons became involved. In rare instances, an individual professional initiated the movement (Dybwad, 1963).

In 1959, representatives from England, Germany, and Holland met to establish a European league of societies for the mentally handicapped, the precursor of the current League. The League was established in 1960. Its purpose is to secure all quality services needed by mentally retarded people through interchange of experts and information, comparative study of legislation, and fostering of legislation beneficial to mentally retarded persons. The League has regularly held international congresses as well as numerous symposia dealing with a broad range of issues. The latter have resulted in numerous publications, which have been widely disseminated.

New Parental Roles

As already noted, parents of mentally retarded children have played a major role in formal voluntary organizations, such as the ARC. As individuals, they have also adopted new roles reflecting a gradual shift from being passive recipients of services to becoming active participants in the design and delivery of services.

For example, parents have increasingly assumed an important role as members of interdisciplinary teams, participating actively in the evaluation and programming of their own mentally retarded children. This important change in parental roles reflects not only the impact of voluntary organizations, but it can also be related to recent scientific developments, including the following:

- Research has substantiated the importance of mothers' teaching approaches to their children's performance (Brophy, 1970; Hess & Shipman, 1965; Wiegerink, 1969).
- The impact of early intervention on subsequent cognitive and emotional development has been clearly demonstrated (Gray, 1971; Gray & Klaus, 1970; Haywood, 1967; Heber, Garber, Harrington, Hoffman, & Falender, 1972; Hunt, 1961). Long-term effects of a deprived environment during the first five years of life seems particularly destructive and may actually reduce a child's intelligence quotient (Bloom, 1964).
- Curricula, training materials, and audiovisual aids designed to assist parents train their handicapped children have been available for some time (e.g., Bijou, 1968; Ferritor, 1970; Gray & Klaus, 1965; Whaler, 1969; Wildman, 1965).

Pilot demonstration programs have documented the value of parents training their handicapped children. As extensions of professional teams, some parents have become sophisticated trainers. Successful examples of this approach have included preschool programs (Bijou, 1968; Luterman, 1971), programs for severely and profoundly mentally retarded young children (Smith & Murphy, 1969), and programs for brain-injured children (Salzinger, Feldman, & Portnoy, 1970).

Parents have also become more involved in decision making. Whereas, in the past, professionals usually assumed total responsibility for programming for mentally retarded children or avoided any meaningful involvement, parents and professionals are increasingly working cooperatively. The ARC has fostered this rapprochement by developing training programs and materials designed to help parents interact productively with professionals and administrators (e.g., NARC, 1977).

Parents have often been concerned with two types of decisions: they want involvement with decisions regarding their own child, and they want to participate in broader decisions regarding services to mentally retarded persons in general. They have been increasingly successful in both areas. With regard to their own child, parents have gradually been accepted as having a major role to play in developing individual plans for their child's education, habilitation, and programming. Indeed, provisions ensuring direct participation by mentally retarded clients themselves and/or their parents have become embodied in national accreditation standards (e.g., Joint Commission on Accreditation of Hospitals, 1973; Accreditation Council for Services for Mentally Retarded and Other Developmentally Disabled Persons, 1980); federal statutes (e.g., P.L. 94-142); federal court mandates (e.g., *Wyatt v. Stickney*, 1972); and federal guidelines (e.g., Intermediate Care Facilities for the Mentally Retarded [ICF/MR] regulations).

Developments in the past decade have greatly accelerated direct parental participation with decision making and delivery of services. Thus, federal regulations and court decisions have established advisory and monitoring bodies designed to review plans, monitor practices, evaluate programs, and/or approve services. Usually, participation of clients and/or parents is mandated in the composition of these bodies.

Group counseling with parents of mentally retarded children is a relatively new approach enhancing their coping skills, while alleviating negative reactions to having a handicapped child. Such parent groups provide opportunities for mutual support, sharing of information and feelings, and modeling (Ingalls, 1978; McWilliams, 1976; Sternlight & Sullivan, 1974). Some experts contend that providing factual information on mental retardation to parents is the most effective contributor to their acceptance of their retarded child (Ingalls, 1978). Wolfensberger (1967) has proposed a compendium of specific topics suitable for educating such parent groups.

Different types of parent groups have been found successful (McWilliams, 1976). Groups established by parents themselves, using professionals as advisors, have been particularly useful in sharing information. Group counseling by clinicians has also been helpful. Some groups have been successfully led by trained parents with primary emphasis on providing mutual help (Irwin & McWilliams, 1973). Other groups have focused specifically on parenting methods, using such approaches as Parent Effectiveness Training (Gordon, 1972).

Parent-to-parent services have been particularly successful in helping parents recently confronted with the knowledge that they have a mentally retarded child. Several prototypes have demonstrated the value of this approach. For example, the St. Louis Association for Retarded Citizens has developed an outreach program to parents of newly diagnosed retarded children (Bassin & Kreeb, 1978). The "pilot parents" program of the Omaha Association for Retarded Citizens has been another effective approach (Nebraska Association for Retarded Citizens, 1974). The Allegheny County Association for Retarded Citizens (Pennsylvania) has operated a parent-to-parent program emphasizing emotional support to new parents, and the Parent Helper Services of Wisconsin (Wittenmeyer & Nesbitt, 1971) has developed self-help and crisis intervention oriented approaches.

These parent-to-parent services typically include training of "parent helpers" (parents of retarded individuals who have adjusted successfully), establishment of a formal training curriculum, an information referral service, group meetings for support and sharing, and an outreach component. An important element in these approaches is that the "parent helpers" can empathize with the new parents as well as provide them with models of successful coping.

Future Directions

Parents of mentally retarded children have played a major role in putting an end to the decades of rejection, segregation, abandonment, and violation of human rights that have characterized the field of mental retardation. Their efforts were reinforced by the civil rights movement, the advent of consumerism, the growing dissatisfaction with bureaucratic proliferation, the increasing demand for program accountability, and society's growing tolerance for deviation from cultural norms.

Yet forces were at work in the late 1970's that threatened the continued viability of voluntarism in the United States (Manser & Cass, 1976). Shifts in political, legal and economic conditions in the early 1980's appear to be aggravating this trend, and futuristic scenarios (e.g., United Way of America, 1980) suggest that these trends may continue to worsen conditions for voluntary organizations during the next decade.

The ARC is facing additional obstacles that do not bode well for its continued existence as a potent movement on behalf of mentally retarded persons and their families. For instance, the Association's visibility with the public has remained extremely low, owing in part to resistance by state and local member units to adopt a uniform name and identity. Thus, a survey conducted by the Gallup association in 1977 revealed that unaided awareness of the ARC was less than one percent (NARC, 1979a).

A related problem has been the ARC's reluctance to embark on nationwide fund raising campaigns, an approach which has been highly successful with other voluntary organizations. Indeed, many of the ARC's state and local units have refused to actively seek funds from the public. As a result, decreasing government funding of human services has potentially more serious impact on the ARC than on many other similar organizations, which have been more successful in raising funds from the general public. Another obstacle facing the ARC is the increasing internal conflict among its units and fragmentation around potentially divisive issues. Many of the most pressing problems that faced the organization in the 1950s and 1960s have been at least partially resolved, so that much of the urgency and commitment of those decades have been replaced with relative apathy and indifference. The ARC's very success in obtaining services needed by mentally retarded people through legislation, funding, and litigation has reduced its perceived relevance to many parents, whose children's needs were being met in the early 1980s. Concurrently, many of the Association's member units have become increasingly devoted to operating direct services and supporting a national movement has become less relevant to their goals.

The highly decentralized structure of the ARC has impeded coordinated national efforts in increasing visibility and raising funds. As early as 1970, the Association's national executive director predicted organizational demise unless its decentralized structure were significantly modified:

> The highly developed autonomy of the NARC's (now ARC) member units has been a source of strength, in that it has maintained the grassroots flavor of the movement and hence has fostered member involvement and participation. On the other hand, the local and state member units have been jealous of their prerogatives and have seriously curtailed the fund raising potentials of the national body, while insisting on expansion of national services. During recent years, the fiscal situation of the national association has at times been chaotic and, unless rather drastic changes take place in the structure of the organization which would improve national

funding, the continued existence of a viable national association in the United States is questionable [Roos, 1970, p. 216].

This pessimistic forecast was apparently valid. No significant structural changes were implemented, as the organization's power remained with its local units, and its fiscal viability has been gradually declining since the mid-1970s. Writing in the ARC's official newspaper in 1982, its national executive director summarized the current status of the organization as follows:

We must consider the very real possibility of a return to another "dark age" for mentally retarded people and their families.

Unfortunately, the Association's national office has suffered a long series of retrenchments since the mid-1970s. As a result, today's national staff is half as large as it was in 1973. . . . The national office is now operating at such a reduced level that its effectiveness is seriously impaired [Roos, 1982, p. 2].

The parent movement has clearly been immensely effective in ameliorating the lives of millions of mentally retarded individuals. Many of these gains will endure, in spite of shifting political and economical values and priorities. Perhaps it has peaked as a major force in the United States, or conversely, the new challenges and opportunities of the 1980s may revitalize parents and other advocates, so that they will accomplish even more in the future than they have in the past.

References

Abeson, A. *A continuing summary of pending and completed litigation regarding the education of handicapped children.* Arlington, Va.: Council for Exceptional Children, 1972.

Accreditation Council for Services for Mentally Retarded and Other Developmentally Disabled Persons. *Standards for services for developmentally disabled individuals.* Washington, D.C.: Author, 1980.

Addison, M. The theory and application of citizen advocacy. In G. J. Bensberg & C. Rude (Eds.), *Advocacy systems for the developmentally disabled.* Lubbock, Tex.: Texas Tech University Press, 1976.

Addison, M. Some problems regarding citizen advocacy as a component of the protection and advocacy systems. In L. D. Baucom & G. J. Bensberg (Eds.), *Advocacy systems for persons with developmental disabilities: Context components and resources.* Lubbock, Tex.: Texas Tech University Press, 1977.

Barbash, F., & Russell, C. Death of infant "Doe" revives euthanasia debate. *Pittsburgh Press,* 1982, April 18.

Bassin, J., & Kreeb, D. D. *Reaching out to parents of newly diagnosed retarded children.* St. Louis, Mo.: St. Louis Association for Retarded Children, 1978.

Bettelheim, B. *The empty fortress: Infantile autism and the birth of the self.* London: Collier-Macmillan. 1967.

Bijou, S. W. *Research in remedial guidance of young retarded children with behavior problems which interfere with academic learning and adjustment* (ED 024-196). Washington, D.C.: Office of Education, Bureau of Research, June 1968.

Bloom, B. S. *Stability and change in human characteristics.* New York: John Wiley & Sons, 1964.

Boggs, E. M. New hope for the retarded. *The Rotarian Magazine,* 1963, July.

Brophy, J. E. Mothers as teachers of their own preschool children: The influence of socioeconomic status and task structure on teaching capacity. *Child Development,* 1970, **41,** 79–94.

Brozek, D. Defective newborns are dying by design. *Hartford Courant,* 1981, June 14.

Capitol Association for Retarded Children. *History and organization of the citizen advocate program.* Lincoln, Neb.: Author, mimeographed report, 1971.

Copeland, S., Addison, M., & McCann, B. *Avenues to change: Citizen advocacy for mentally retarded children.* Book 1. Arlington, Tex.: National Association for Retarded Citizens, 1974.

Dybwad, R. *The widening role of parent organizations around the world.* Paper presented at the 41st Annual Convention, Council for Exceptional Children, National Education Association, Philadelphia, Pa., April 1963.

Farber, B. Effects of a severely retarded child on the family. In E. P. Trapp & P. Himelstein (Eds.), *Readings on the exceptional child.* (2nd ed.) New York: Appleton-Century-Crofts, 1972.

Felliceti, D. A. *Mental health and mental retardation politics.* New York: Praeger, 1975.

Fenichel, O. *The psychoanalytic theory of neurosis.* New York: W. W. Norton & Co., 1945.

Ferritor, D. E. Modifying interaction patterns: An experimental training program for parents of autistic children. *Dissertation Abstracts,* 1970, **30,** 3114–3115.

Fletcher, J. Indicators of humanhood: A tentative profile of man. *The Hastings Center Report,* 1972, **2**(5), 1–3.

Friedman, P. *Mental retardation and the law: A report on status of current court cases.* Washington, D.C.: Office of Mental Retardation Coordination, U.S. Department of Health, Education and Welfare, 1973.

Friedman, P. *Mental retardation and the law: A report on status of current court cases.* Washington, D.C.: President's Committee on Mental Retardation, U.S. Department of Health, Education and Welfare, 1978.

Friedman, P. R. (Ed.) *Legal rights of mentally disabled persons.* New York: Practising Law Institute, 1979.

Gath, A. The impact of an abnormal child upon the parents. *British Journal of Psychiatry,* 1977, **130,** 405–410.

Gordon, T. *Parent effectiveness training.* New York: Wyden, 1972.

Gray, S. W. Children from three to ten: The early training project. *DARCEE papers and reports.* Vol. 3. Nashville, Tenn.: George Peabody College, 1971.

Gray, S. W., & Klaus, R. A. An experimental preschool program for culturally deprived children. *Child Development,* 1965, **36,** 887–898.

Gray, S. W., & Klaus, R. A. The early training project: The seventh year report. *Child Development,* 1970, **41,** 909–924.

Haggerty, D. E., Kane, L. A., Jr., & Udall, D. K. An essay on the legal rights of the mentally retarded. *Family Law Quarterly,* 1972, **6,** 59–71.

Haywood, H. C. Experimental factors in intellectual development: The concept of dynamic intelligence. In J. Zubin & G. A. Jervis (Eds.), *Psychopathology of mental retardation*. New York: Grune and Stratton, 1967.

Heber, R., Garber, H., Harrington, S., Hoffman, C., & Falender, C. *Rehabilitation of families at risk for mental retardation*. Madison, Wis.: University of Wisconsin, 1972.

Hess, R. D., & Shipman, V. C. Early experience and the socialization of cognitive models in children. *Child Development*, 1965, **36**, 869–886.

Holt, K. S. Home care of severely retarded children. *Pediatrics*, 1958, **22**, 744–755.

Hunt, M. McV. *Intelligence and experience*. New York: Ronald Press, 1961.

Ingalls, R. P. *Mental retardation: The changing outlook*. New York: John Wiley & Sons, 1978.

International League of Societies for the Mentally Handicapped. *The development of national voluntary organizations for the mentally handicapped: Strasbourg Symposium*. Brussels, Belgium: Author, 1967.

Irwin, E. C., & McWilliams, B. J. Parents working with parents: The cleft palate program. *Cleft Palate Journal*, 1973, **10**, 360.

Joint Commission on Accreditation of Hospitals. *Standards for residential facilities for the mentally retarded*. Chicago: Accreditation Council for Facilities for the Mentally Retarded, 1973.

Kanner, L. Early infantile autism. *Journal of Pediatrics*, 1944, **25**, 211–217.

Katz, A. H. *Parents of the handicapped*. Springfield, Ill.: Charles C. Thomas, 1961.

Kramm, E. R. *Families of mongoloid children*. Washington, D.C.: U.S. Government Printing Office, 1963.

Luterman, D. M. A parent-oriented nursery program for preschool deaf children. *Volta Review*, 1971, **73**, 106–112.

Manser, G., & Cass, R. H. *Voluntarism at the crossroads*. New York: Family Service Association of America, 1976.

McKinney, F. *Counseling for personal adjustment*. Cambridge, Ma.: The Riverside Press, 1958.

McWilliams, B. J. Various aspects of parent counseling. In E. J. Webster (Ed.), *Professional approaches with parents of handicapped children*. Springfield, Ill.: Charles C. Thomas, 1976.

Mead, M., & Brown, M. *The wagon and the star*. Chicago: Rand McNally, 1966.

Menolascino, F. J. *Challenges in mental retardation: Progressive ideology and services*. New York: Human Services Press, 1977.

Menolascino, F. J., & Michael, L. E. *Medical dimensions of mental retardation*. Lincoln, Nebr.: University of Nebraska Press, 1978.

Mills v. Board of Education of the District of Columbia, 348 F. Supp. 886 (D.C. 1972).

Murray, M. A. Needs of parents of mentally retarded children. *American Journal of Mental Deficiency*, 1959, **63**, 1084–1099.

National Association for Retarded Citizens. *Avenues to change*. Arlington, Tex.: Author, 1974.

National Association for Retarded Citizens. Survey determines NARC membership profile. *Mental Retardation News*, 1975, **24**(3), 1–4.

National Association for Retarded Citizens. *The partnership: How to make it work*. Arlington, Tex.: Author, 1977.

National Association for Retarded Citizens. *A marketing plan for the National Association for Retarded Citizens*. Unpublished manuscript, author, 1979 (Arlington, Tex.). (a)

National Association for Retarded Citizens. *A survey of local member units*. Arlington, Tex.: Author, 1979. (b)

Nebraska Association for Retarded Citizens. Pilot parents defined. *Focus*, 1974, September.

Neman, R. Service provision by local associations. Unpublished report, Association for Retarded Citizens, 1979 (Arlington, Tex.).

Neman, R. *Time differences in ARC membership samples*. Unpublished report, Association for Retarded Citizens, 1981 (Arlington, Tex.).

New York State Association for Retarded Children v. Carey, 393 F. Supp. 715 (E.D. N.Y. 1975).

Ogg, E. *Securing the legal rights of retarded persons*. New York: Public Affairs Committee, Inc., 1973.

Pennsylvania Association for Retarded Children v. Commonwealth of Pennsylvania, 343 F. Supp. 279 (E.D. Pa. 1972).

The President's Committee on Mental Retardation Legal Rights Work Group. *Compendium of class action law suits related to the legal rights of the mentally retarded*. Washington, D.C.: The President's Committee on Mental Retardation, 1973.

Roos, P. Psychological counseling with parents of retarded children. *Mental Retardation*, 1963, **1**, 345–350.

Roos, P. Parent organizations. In J. Wortis (Ed.), *Mental retardation, an annual review*. Vol. II. New York: Grune & Stratton, 1970.

Roos, P. Mentally retarded citizens: Challenge for the 1970s. *Syracuse Law Review*, 1972, **23**, 1059–1074.

Roos, P. Basic facts about mental retardation. In B. J. Ennis & P. R. Friedman (Eds.), *Legal rights of the mentally retarded*. Vol. 2. New York: Practising Law Institute, 1973.

Roos, P. Parents and families of the mentally retarded. In J. M. Kauffman & J. S. Payne (Eds.), *Mental retardation: Introduction and personal perspectives*. New York: Charles E. Merrill, 1975.

Roos, P. Parents of mentally retarded persons. *International Journal of Mental Health*, 1977, **6**(1), 3–20. (a)

Roos, P. NARC view of parent involvement: A parent's view of what public education should accomplish. *Education and Training of the Mentally Retarded*, 1977, **12**(4) 109–119. (b)

Roos, P. Parents of mentally retarded children: Misunderstood and mistreated. In A. P. Turnbull & H. R. Turnbull (Eds.), *Parents speak out: Views from the other side of the two way mirror*. New York: Charles E. Merrill, 1978.

Roos, P. Avoiding another "dark age." *The arc*, 1982, **31**(2), 2.

Roos, P. The handling and mishandling of parents of mentally retarded persons. In F. J. Menolascino & B. M. McCann (Eds.), *Bridging the gap: Mental health needs of the mentally retarded*. Baltimore, Md.: University Park Press. In press.

Salzinger, K., Feldman, R. S., & Portnoy, S. Training of brain-injured children in the use of operant-conditioning procedures. *Behavior Therapy*, 1970, **1**, 4–32.

Schild, S. Counseling with parents of retarded children living at home. *Social Work*, 1964, January, 86–91.

Segal, R. M. *Mental retardation and social action: A study of the associations for retarded children as a force for social change*. Springfield, Ill.: Charles C. Thomas, 1970.

Smith, D., & Murphy, W. K. A new world for Lori. *Mental Retardation in Illinois*, 1969, **3**, 3–5.

Stanford Law Review, **31**(4), 1979.

Sternlight, M., & Sullivan, I. Group counseling with parents of the MR: Leadership selection and functioning. *Mental Retardation*, 1974, **12**(5), 11–13.

Turnbull, A. P., & Turnbull, H. R. (Eds.) *Parents speak out: Views from the other side of the two way mirror.* New York: Charles E. Merrill, 1978.

United Way of America. *An environmental scan report: What lies ahead.* Washington, D.C.: Author, 1980.

Whaler, R. G. Setting generality: Some specific and general effects of child behavior therapy. *Journal of Applied Behavioral Analysis*, 1969, **4**, 239–246.

Wiegerink, R. A. A comparative study of the teaching behaviors of advantaged and disadvantaged mothers. *Dissertation Abstracts*, 1969, **30**(A), 3808–3809.

Wildman, P. R. A parent education program for parents of mentally retarded children. *Mental Retardation*, 1965, **3**, 17–19.

Wittenmeyer, J. J., & Nesbitt, N. J. *Parent helper service, a self-help program for ARCs.* Paper presented at meeting of the American Association on Mental Deficiency, Houston, Tex., June 1971.

Wolfensberger, W. Counseling the parents of the retarded. In A. A. Baumeister (Ed.), *Mental retardation: Appraisal, education, and rehabilitation.* Chicago, Ill.: Aldine, 1967.

Wolfensberger, W. The origin and nature of our institutional models. In R. B. Kugel & W. Wolfensberger (Eds.), *Changing patterns in residential services for the mentally retarded.* Washington, D.C.: President's Committee on Mental Retardation, 1969.

Wolfensberger, W., & Zauha, H. *Citizen advocacy and protective services for the impaired and handicapped.* Toronto: National Institute on Mental Retardation, 1973.

Wyatt v. Stickney, 344 F. Supp. 373 (M.D. Ala. 1972).

PART II
SOCIAL DEVELOPMENTS

3 THE EVALUATION OF COMMUNITY LIVING ALTERNATIVES FOR DEVELOPMENTALLY DISABLED PERSONS

John W. Jacobson and
Allen A. Schwartz

During the past two decades, increased emphasis has been placed upon the diversification of service alternatives in the area of developmental disabilities, including the decentralization of residential service systems. In this decentralization process, a continuum of community residential settings has evolved, with alternatives as distinct from one another as they are in comparison with larger facilities. One primary type of community residential alternative, which has been developed nationwide, is the community residence (CR), which may be called a hostel, group home, etc. For the purpose of this discussion, the terms *institution* shall apply to a facility housing 30 or more developmentally disabled persons, and *community residence* or CR to a home-like setting for fewer individuals. A community residence may be defined as a "community-based residential facility that operates 24 hours a day to provide services to a small group of disabled people who are presently or potentially capable of functioning in a community setting with some degree of independence" (O'Connor & Sitkei, 1975, p. 35). Although these settings provide residential accommodations for persons around the clock, in general CR residents participate in off-site habilitation, education, or employment activities. The CR is intended to provide a cooperative group living arrangement that is part of the community, not a

small system closed off from that community (Wolfensberger, 1971a). In the author's home state, New York, a CR is a residential setting serving from 4 to 14 persons, staffed either by houseparents or shift staff, and located in a one-family home, apartment, or apartment cluster. The New York community residence system has expanded from a dozen sites in the early 1970s to over 700 sites in 1982, serving over 6,000 persons. It is projected that over 100 new residences will be established annually during the next five years in New York State—an increase that is representative of a similar pattern in many states.

This report will focus on the state-of-the-art research on the effects of CR living upon developmentally disabled individuals, and will suggest directions for the future evaluation of this program type. The review will consider the focus of research to date, instruments applicable to the study of group home settings, and a relevant research design.

The diversity of CR settings is exemplified by a typology developed by Baker, Seltzer and Seltzer (1977). Using four measures of size, presence of protective services, provision of training programs on- or off-site, and extent of permitted resident autonomy, Seltzer and Seltzer (1976) derived a 10-model classification system of community residential alternatives (Baker et al., 1979). Their system includes small group homes, medium group homes, large group homes, mini-institutions, mixed group homes, group homes for older adults, foster family care, the sheltered village, the workshop/dormitory, and the semi-independent unit. Of the programs surveyed by Baker et al. (1977), and the Developmental Disabilities Project on Residential Services and Community Adjustment (1979), small (10 persons or fewer) and medium (11 to 20 persons) group homes bear the closest resemblance to the definition of a CR used in this report and constitute 198 of 381 (52%) and 3,899 of 4,427 (88%) of the settings surveyed, respectively.

From an applied perspective, some writers have warned that CRs are potential mini-institutions (Moen & Aanes, 1979; Roos, 1978), or have implied that the reasons for returning people from institutions to community settings are largely political or economic, rather than humanitarian or habilitative. The relationship between trends in service and demonstrated efficacy of these services through carefully conducted research is complex. Consequently, there is disagreement on whether or not the literature provides a justification for endorsing the establishment of dispersed-site residential settings in the community on the basis of empirical benefit (Balla, 1976; Crawford, Aiello & Thompson, 1979; Throne, 1979; Zigler & Balla, 1979). From an evaluation perspective, several trends underlie current interest in studies of the potential benefits of CRs over institutions. Among these are (1) increasing optimism over the ability of mentally retarded individuals to acquire new skills as the result of behavior technology, intensive services, and enriched environments, (2) increasing interest in the relationship between success or failure in community placement and personal characteristics, (3) increasing availability of community residential settings amenable to analysis, (4) the availability of many behavior measures useful as an alternative to trait/demographic measures, (5) the availability of instruments to describe environmental settings, and (6) an extensive literature concerning the potentially debilitating effects of institutionalization. Building upon this foundation, researchers have shown increasing interest in (1) the effect of community placement upon skill acquisition, (2) the prognosis for successful community placement and adaptation, and (3) the quantification of the manner in which community settings are different from institutional settings. Lastly, political trends as well as technical capability have contributed to research interests. Both federal and state funding now typically require program evaluation activities. Indeed, departures from previous service models may be viewed with skepticism if an evaluation component is not incorporated in program development proposals.

The diversity of opinion about how present knowledge should be interpreted arises in part from procedural incompatibilities among studies; these studies have suffered from methodological problems which restrict their impact upon policy or program development. The status of research on community residential program efficacy stimulated George and Baumeister (1981) to note:

> The question of relative effectiveness is difficult to answer because of the lack of agreed-upon criteria and evaluation strategies. Measurement of quality is further hampered by the great diversity among facilities on basic characteristics, such as size, residents and population, and patterns of organization [p. 639].

Furthermore, Bjaanes and Butler (Note 1) have noted the pitfalls inherent in attributing successful or unsuccessful placement, or changes in level of adaptive growth, to the nature of the residential placement without attending to other program services, or generic settings which individuals encounter and to which they respond.

In spite of these flaws the information base necessary for the implementation of model program evaluation systems for community services exists, and studies can be found which are consistent with movement in this direction (cf. Butler & Bjaanes, 1977; Eyman, Demaine, & Lei, 1979; Hull & Thompson, 1980, 1981). The following review outlines studies that provide a basis for such evaluation activity, and presents a general model for the evaluation of small group homes for mentally retarded and developmentally disabled persons.

The Community Residence: Residents and Setting

The Residents

O'Connor and Sitkei (1975) reported demographic characteristics of 419 community residences serving from one to 20 persons each and 192 residences serving 21 persons or more. Mental retardation was the primary disabling condition for 89% of residents. More recently, in a survey of 4,427 community residential facilities nationwide, Bruininks, Hauber, & Kudla (1980) reported that 97% of the residents were disabled by mental retardation alone, 34% had an additional disability (behavior disorder, epilepsy, cerebral palsy, blindness, deafness, autism), and 19% had two or more additional disabilities. In terms of intellectual functioning, the following breakdown was observed: 8% "borderline," 22% mild retardation, 35% moderate retardation, 22% severe retardation, and 11% profound retardation. These characteristics are elaborated by Hill and Bruininks (1981) in a study of 964 community facility residents. Interestingly, in the latter study, over 50% of the residents were considered capable of performing a variety of self-care and community living tasks with only occasional reminders or assistance.

Disability and intellectual level distributions for the community residence population in New York (which has the largest state CR system of this type) closely resemble those reported by Bruininks et al. (1980). Overall, 25% have a non-neurological physical disability and 25% are considered psychiatricly impaired. Three percent have very limited mobility or ambulation skills, while 1% and 3% are deaf and blind, respectively. The majority have expressive (93%) and receptive (97%) language skills permitting communication of one- or two-word phrases or more complex conversation. The majority are also independent in areas of self-care: toileting (82%), eating (80%), and dressing (60%). Thirty-seven percent are reported to be free of behavior problems requiring intervention. Twenty to 30% of the population are able to use a telephone or a stove, shop in stores, and wash laundry without supervision.

Virtually all (97%) residence program occupants participate in day program activities. Ten percent of this group attend educational programs; 13% attend habilitation, 17% prevocational, and 49% sheltered workshop programs. Four percent are employed. In addition, the majority of program residents receive dental, psychological, recreation therapy, or routine medical services. From 15 to 50% also receive audiology, nursing, nutritional, occupational therapy, physical therapy, professional counseling, specialized medical, or speech therapy services. Ninety-five percent of residents also receive some sort of services from the generic human service system (e.g., public transportation, family planning).

The Setting

Investigators have offered descriptions of the continuum of community residential services intended to meet the needs of developmentally disabled groups with homogeneous or special needs. Reports vary from anecdotal description of several options (Holmes, 1979) to the description of exemplar systems or typologies (Baker, Seltzer & Seltzer, 1977; Seltzer & Seltzer, 1976).

Baker et al. (1977) and Wolfensberger and Glenn (1975b) have offered continua that exemplify the pos-

sible variety of community living alternatives. Options within these continua include childrens' hostels, adolescent hostels, adult training hostels, adult board-and-care homes, apartment clusters, supervised living units, co-resident apartments, independent living, behavior development residential hostels, and developmental maximization units. These programs vary not only in the characteristics of persons served, but also in the type, intensity, and site of day program services provided.

Small size (serving 10 or fewer persons) and medium size (serving 10–20 persons) group home models have been described at length by Baker et al. (1977) and Seltzer and Seltzer (1976). The small group home, typically staffed by houseparents and a relief person, serves predominantly younger, mildly and moderately mentally retarded persons who are accorded greater autonomy than are persons living in other alternatives. Residents tend to come from institutions (57%), and within a year, 19% return to them. Residents usually have extensive contact with the surrounding community, with 21% being competitively employed and 50% attending sheltered workshop or habilitation programs. The average length of stay in this setting is 1.6 years, contrasting sharply with 2.7 years for residents of medium size homes, who tend to be slightly older and slightly less disabled than persons in small size homes. In contrast to findings reported by Butler and Bjaanes (1977), Seltzer and Seltzer (1976) found that residents of medium group homes are generally permitted less autonomy than are persons in small homes, possibly because of more varied staffing patterns and specialized staff. In both types of homes, however, the houseparent model prevails, with such positions usually occupied by young, transient, and minimally-trained persons.

The Effect of Enriched Environments: Institutional vs. Non-Institutional Living

Investigators have presented both anecdotal (cf. King & Raynes, 1967) and quasi-experimental evidence of the harmful effects of institutions (Vogel, Kun, & Meshorer, 1967). Soforenko and Macy (Note 2) found, for example, that, upon follow-up of 265 persons one to eight years after deinstitutionalization, general adaptive functioning had risen for 22% and had fallen for 10%. Zigler and Balla (1979), in a review of articles on institutionalization effects, cited three classes of variables which should be considered: (1) the characteristics of residents, (2) the nature of the institution, and (3) behavioral status and growth. Based upon a series of longitudinal or cross-institutional studies relating measures of interpersonal responsiveness to institutionalization (Balla, Butterfield & Zigler, 1974; Balla & Zigler, 1975; Butterfield & Zigler, 1965; King, Raynes, & Tizard, 1971; McCormick, Balla, & Zigler, 1975; Zigler, 1971; Zigler & Balla, 1972, 1976; Zigler, Balla, & Butterfield, 1968; Zigler, Butterfield, & Capobianco, 1970; Zigler & Williams, 1963), Zigler and Balla reported that institutionalization effects were generally negative, though mediated by family contact and resident-care practices in most instances. Institution-oriented care practices were noted more frequently in large facilities, while resident-oriented care practices occurred more often in group homes (also see King et al., 1971). Balla (1976) and Baroff (1980) have commented extensively upon the studies cited above, noting that the degree of variation in quality of care between different program types has not been demonstrated to occur within programs of the same type (e.g., among CRs).

The widely held premise that habilitation programs should occur in normative settings may be traced to a longitudinal study by Skeels and Dye (1939), who noted that a group of young institutionalized children thought mentally retarded were found to develop more rapidly when placed in a far more stimulating residential setting. Since then, it has become more generally accepted that even profoundly mentally retarded individuals may show improvement in self-help, social, and communications skills with appropriate intervention (Eyman, Silverstein, & McLain, 1975; Webb & Koller, 1979). Vogel, Kun, and Meshorer (1967) have reported that

> the best controlled of the environmental-enrichment studies report widespread individual differences among retarded people in the degree of their cognitive development . . . in response to enrichment conditions; the effect of environmental impoverishment seems to be somewhat more uniform, being generally debilitating to a greater or lesser degree, although individual variation is apparent here also [p. 570].

In a study which compared the effects of institutions with those of a variety of community settings (nursing, foster care, and board-and-care homes), Eyman, Silverstein, McLain, and Miller (1977) concluded that there was little change in residents' adaptive behavior over a three-year interval unless they were provided with specialized day programming. Change was most frequently attributable to environmental factors (e.g., greater participation in activities, greater autonomy, individualization of care), particularly in community

settings, and, to a lesser degree, to the amount of day programming received, preplacement history, and personal characteristics. Residents of foster care and board-and-care homes evinced more positive change than did residents of institutions, although young mildly and moderately disabled institutional residents displayed some adaptive growth.

Aninger and Bolinsky (1977) assessed persons placed in apartments using the A.A.M.D. Adaptive Behavior Scale (ABS) (Nihira, Foster, Shellhaas, & Leland, 1974) and found no measurable increase in adaptive functioning over a six-month period. It should be noted that these clients received no formal habilitative services, a fact that may have attenuated any short-term effect. In a similar report by Aanes and Moen (1976), focusing on 46 residents in group homes receiving day program services, significant gains in adaptive functioning were noted using a one-year test-retest interval for the ABS.

Measures of adaptive behavior have not been the only referents for assessing the impact of enriched environments. Gilbert and Hemming (1979), in a comparison of the psycholinguistic ability of two matched groups (one retained in a traditional institutional unit, the other placed in eight-bed bungalows) reported superior postplacement psycholinguistic performance by bungalow residents, and related this to more resident-oriented care practices in the bungalows.

Successful Community Placement

The extent to which the community adjustment of persons placed from institutions or natural family settings has been successful remains difficult to determine, in part because different authors have different criteria for success (Lakin, Bruininks, & Sigford, 1981). For some, simply remaining in the community is sufficient; others may use additional factors such as employment or day program participation as adjustment indicators.

In a follow-up study of 66 men and 97 women with mental retardation 20 years following their return to the community from institutional living, Wolfson (1970) found that 57.5% of the men were employed and 71% of the women were employed or managing a household. Sixteen percent of the men and 10% of the women had returned to institutional settings where they had thereafter been retained. The remaining individuals were described as leading marginal lives in the community. This pattern is similar to that noted by Eagle (1967) concerning the resettlement of 12,471 developmentally disabled people to community settings; the overall rate of successful adjustment to the community was 60.4%. These studies would

suggest that, while a substantial proportion of institutionalized persons can adjust to community settings,
expectations of successful adjustment have been accurate for only 60% of placements. A more recent
study (Sitkei, 1980) suggests that less than 13% of
developmentally disabled persons placed into group
homes from institutions or other supervised living
situations will return to a more restrictive environment.

If one reviews the factors contributing to the success
or failure of community placement, it becomes apparent that the primary focus has been upon demographic and personal, rather than environmental
or social factors. Variables which favor community
adjustment include longer previous institutionalization
(Soforenko & Macy, Note 2), adequate ambulatory
and self-care abilities (Eyman, Demaine & Lei, 1975),
the willingness of family members to accept the placement (Clark, 1959), and superior work skills (Vogel,
Kun, & Meshorer, 1969). Factors which may limit
adjustment are "special" behavior problems (Clark,
1959; Eagle, 1967; Sutter, Mayeda, Call, Yanagi, &
Yee, 1980; Windle, Stewart & Brown, 1961), psychiatric impairment or poor interpersonal skills (Clark,
1959; Eagle, 1967; Vogel, Kun & Meshorer, 1969;
Windle, Stewart & Brown, 1961), unsatisfactory work
performance (Eagle, 1967; Gordon & Ivy, 1968),
absence of familial support (Gordon & Ivy, 1968),
and adverse environmental supports (Eagle, 1967;
Taylor, 1976). On the other hand, Taylor (1976)
found that psychiatric impairment and "rebellious"
behavior were tolerated in the community and did
not contribute to failure.

The success or failure of community placements
would appear to hinge on a combination of personal
characteristics (good vocational skills and mild behavior
problems) and environmental factors (appropriate social
supports and clinical services). Perhaps an optimal
environment could compensate for poor vocational
preparation or moderately troublesome behavior, but
markedly disturbed behavior might be intolerable in
spite of an adequate environment and result in placement failure. The relative importance of these factors
may pertain to an individual's functional level, with
job-related skills more important for adjustment than
problem behavior for the higher functioning individual,
and appropriate community supports more critical
for the less skilled individual. Understanding of such
relationships becomes more important in light of the
present trend toward deinstitutionalization of increasingly disabled individuals (Braddock, 1981), but our
knowledge of these interactions has not been bolstered
substantially by recent research findings.

In a review of placement practices, Thurlow,
Bruininks, Williams, and Morreau (1978) cite 18
personal characteristics as placement selection criteria
in common use. Questioning the extent to which
individual characteristics may be predictive of community success, they suggest instead that evaluation
of preparatory training, selection of the optimum type
of placement, continuing placement assistance, and
suitable day program activities would provide a more
accurate prognosis for community adaptation. The
question may not be whether certain individuals should
be returned to the community, but when and to
which setting. The importance of sufficient individualization of services, community tolerance of limited
self-care and self-direction abilities, and appropriate
preparatory training to successful placement have been
noted elsewhere as well (Intagliata, Note 3; Mueller
& Porter, 1969; Schalock & Harper, 1981). Further
attention to the interaction between personal characteristics and environmental/social factors is clearly
warranted. This is particularly true for research on
CRs as discussed below.

Interpersonal and Social Behavior
in Community Residences

A number of studies have described the interpersonal
aspects of CRs. Using a life-history reconstruction
approach, Edgarton (1977) has reported preliminary
findings on the experiences of persons with mental
retardation repatriated from institutions. Scheerenberger and Felsenthal (1977) interviewed 75 persons
resettled to foster homes, group homes, and adult
homes (intermediate care facilities and nursing homes).
Respondents in both studies reported they were permitted more autonomy in group homes than they
were in institutions, although the opportunity to exercise choice in many areas of daily activity remained
restricted.

Other investigators have measured interpersonal
aspects of group home settings. Campbell (1968)
compared the extent of community and family contact
enjoyed by selected residents of an institution and
those of a group home. Much more contact with the
community and families was afforded group home
residents, and indeed group home residents lived much
closer to their next of kin. However, the majority of
persons in both settings had no community or family
contact at all. Landesman-Dwyer, Berkson and Romer
(1979) investigated affiliation patterns within several
community residences and found that residents interacted among themselves 28% of the time and with
staff only 12% of the time. Profoundly mentally retarded persons engaged in such social behavior only
slightly less often than did higher functioning individuals. Residents of CRs with a higher average level

of intelligence had more intense social relationships, as did those who shared common preplacement histories. Residents of larger CRs interacted with significantly more peers, but did not appear to have less intense relationships. Interestingly, the data suggest that characteristics of CRs are better predictors of affiliation patterns than are the individual characteristics of residents. These findings should be interpreted cautiously, however, since the CR characteristics noted as associated with affiliation patterns have not as yet been clearly defined or quantified.

Bjaanes, Butler, and Kelly (1981) reported a study of community integration activities undertaken by 142 facilities serving three or more mentally retarded/developmentally disabled persons. Those facilities located in urban areas made greater use of generic resources. Facilities with more than seven residents tended to involve people in more outside activities and to enhance the functioning of the residents. Facilities serving persons aged 45 or older tended to access generic resources less frequently than those serving younger or mixed-aged persons. Schinke and Wong (1977) have shown that training staff in pertinent skills (e.g., behavior modification techniques) may support attitudinal changes in staff which would, in light of the Bjaanes et al. (1981) findings, make it more likely that generic resources would be accessed. The presence of more educated, more experienced, and more therapeutically-oriented staff was associated with greater use of community resources. Again, prediction of community involvement has been more closely related to characteristics of the CR than to those of individual residents.

Landesman-Dwyer, Sackett, and Kleinman (1980) provide a recent study based on observation of resident and staff activity in 20 group homes. Interestingly, while resident activity varied among homes, as found in Landesman-Dwyer, Berkson and Romer (1979), staff activity distributions were relatively homogeneous across programs. To our knowledge, staff activity patterns in community settings have not been otherwise investigated, and there is thus no context in which to interpret this finding at present. The Landesman-Dwyer et al. studies deserve mention aside from their findings, in that they entail behavioral observations as an alternative to paper-and-pencil measures or characterizations of programs through dimensions like size or geographic location. Investigations of this type generally relate frequency distributions of behaviors, classified in taxonomies, to objective characteristics (size, years in operation, etc.) of program sites or to resident characteristics (age, IQ, etc.), but seldom relate activities to secondary measures, such as adherence to normalizing practices. The rationale for developing, conducting, and analyzing studies employing taxonomic descriptions of individual and interpersonal activities in program settings has been addressed by Robinson (1978), Rosenbaum (1978) and Sackett, Ruppenthal, and Gluck (1978).

Normalization, Residence Factors and Residents

Four studies warrant description as models for the analysis of community residential alternatives. The first of these, by Butler and Bjaanes (1977), was a test of the hypothesis that different types of community residential environments result in different patterns of normalization and social competence outcomes for residents. Although these authors compared only two board-and-care and two home-care facilities, they collected extensive data on preplacement characteristics of persons served, the operation of the homes, and caregiver attitudes. Preplacement factors involved individual resident characteristics, including social competence and prior institutional or community placements. The operational intent of each home was categorized as either therapeutic (oriented toward active habilitation), maintaining (oriented toward limited habilitation), or custodial (non-habilitative). Caregiver attitudes were assessed by a Therapeutic Orientation Scale, summarizing staff perceptions of resident capability. Findings indicated that more positive perceptions of resident abilities were associated with increased caregiver interaction with residents and increased access of generic resources. In smaller residences better-educated caregivers tended to interact more frequently with residents, although no such relationship was noted in larger residences. Independent of setting, the longer staff worked in a given setting, the less they interacted with residents. More interaction was apparent in board-and-care homes (which resemble CRs) than in home care facilities (which resemble foster family care settings). The authors concluded that the degree to which generic resources are used by residences was associated with the education and previous experience of caregivers, location of the residence, size of residence, characteristics of the surrounding neighborhood, and extent to which residents participate in normalizing activities. By and large, programs resembling CRs tended to access community resources more frequently and to provide more normalizing activities than other small group living situations.

The second study of note, by Eyman, DeMaine, and Lei (1979), employed a three-year longitudinal design to relate changes in resident adaptive functioning to environmental factors. It involved 245 persons served in 87 family care homes and 11 board-and-care homes (or residential schools). Behavioral measures were obtained through annual administration of the Behavioral Development Survey (BDS) (Individual Data Base, 1978a). Environmental measures were obtained through a single application of the Program Analysis of Service Systems 3 (PASS 3) (Wolfensberger & Glenn, 1975a). Data were analyzed separately for persons over and under 18 years of age. The authors found that, independent of setting factors, older and more mildly mentally retarded persons improved more in functional skills than did their younger or more disabled counterparts. Settings that blended well with the surrounding neighborhood, were located within reach of services, and provided a comfortable and homelike setting were associated with significant changes in some resident self-care skills. The presence of extensive community education programs (and other administrative practices measured by PASS) was negatively associated with changes in personal self-sufficiency scores; apparently time spent by staff in such activities may decrease opportunities for staff-resident interaction which, in turn, may mediate resident adaptive growth. Relationships were noted between PASS scores and resident community living skills, though these varied in association. Higher PASS scores for administrative policies were associated with positive change in older, more retarded residents. Higher PASS scores for location of services were associated with positive change for older, less retarded residents. Higher PASS scores for comfort and appearance of the setting were associated with positive changes for all residents.

The importance of residence operation and environmental considerations has been further underscored by the recent work of Hill and Bruininks (1981), which suggests the presence of environmental constraints to some behaviors in community residential settings. Lack of opportunity to learn or display certain behaviors may affect staff assessments of individual preparedness for movement to a less restrictive living situation. It is possible that, were additional behavioral opportunities afforded residents, they would be judged more capable. The degree to which "opportunity constraints" are present among programs of the same type is not well known, and may be an important variable related both to extent of normalization practices and to changes in client adaptive behavior over time.

The third and fourth studies, reported by Hull and Thompson (1980, 1981) attempted to predict the adaptive functioning level of 369 persons in 144 community facilities based upon resident characteristics, environmental normalization, and facility characteristics (Hull & Thompson, 1980) and to ascertain the

extent to which environmental normalization itself was related to resident, facility and community characteristics and staff/sponsor attitudes (Hull & Thompson, 1981). Their findings are generally consistent with those of Eyman et al. (1979) regarding relationships between adaptive functioning and normalization practices. Specifically, they found that while IQ, resident satisfaction with the setting, and manageability of problem behavior accounted for the greatest proportion of variance in adaptive functioning, six environmental normalization variables also contributed substantially to the explanation of variance (Hull & Thompson, 1980). This finding is explained in part by the fact that the level of environmental normalization was, itself, found to be related to resident characteristics (Hull & Thompson, 1981). These empirical relationships led the authors to note:

> Proponents (of normalization) claim that it is not only an ideology, but a process, a process that promotes the development of individual capabilities and increases the capacity of individuals to function adaptively in a community setting . . . (Findings of) Eyman et al. (1979) . . . as well as those by Butler and Bjaanes (1977) and Zigler and Balla (1977) and the present one, are beginning to provide some empirical basis for the utilization of environmental normalization as a technology as well as an ideology [Hull & Thompson, 1980, pp. 259–260].

While these studies demonstrate the diverse factors which must be assessed in order to analyze and understand the impact of CRs upon their residents, they also have the virtue of elucidating the various research approaches which have evolved to study these complex relationships. But they have obvious limitations. All of these reports include CRs and board-and-care homes (foster family-type settings serving up to thirty persons; Baker, Seltzer, & Seltzer, 1977); but in general, they do not present separate findings for these two, quite different, settings. While Butler and Bjaanes (1977) do compare these settings, their sample size restricts generalization of findings. Eyman et al. (1979) combined data from board-and-care homes with those from residential schools, but still reviewed only 11 board-and-care or residential school facilities altogether, and Hull and Thompson (1980, 1981) present no separate major findings by setting type. Hence, the relevance of these findings to the type of facility characterized as a CR in this report is difficult to assess. To the extent that board-and-care homes in California and Manitoba are similar to the staffed community residences in existence nationally (Hill & Bruininks, 1981), these studies may form a basis for hypotheses guiding the discrete investigation of CR effects.

Residence Program Analysis

While the climate or environmental character of CRs has received a great deal of attention, comparatively little work has been done to relate day or evening habilitation or prevocational training activities to residence or resident functioning. This is surprising, since the day program must be combined with the residential setting in order to consider the total service environment, and the benefits of community day program services are generally acknowledged (cf. Schalock & Harper, 1981).

Residence program activities originating on-site can be defined as (1) those structured activities and tasks in which residents participate on a regular basis (formal program), and (2) less structured recreational or social activities, generally taking place in the community, which provide experiential opportunities to develop and practice skills which require an off-site locale (informal program).

In habilitative program settings it can be expected that services will be provided within a goal-oriented format. Instruments like the Tennessee Goal Domain Dictionary (Tennessee Department of Mental Health & Mental Retardation, 1978), can be employed to record goals targeted and, with modification, to assess the quality of goal statements. Comparisons of goal profiles (goals arrayed in domains) can then be compared with domain or factor scores from adaptive behavior measures. Such evaluations can disclose whether program services remediate deficit behaviors, decelerate excess behaviors, and capitalize on positive behaviors, or fail to address training needs (Jacobson, Janicki, & Unger, Note 4).

An alternative to documentation of goal-related activities and actual utilization of community resources is a review of which and how frequently professional disciplines provide services to an individual, either on-site or off-site. An even more basic approach is to assess whether different types of professional or generic services are provided to each resident on an ongoing basis, regardless of setting.

Although a recent report by Schalock, Harper, and Genung (1981) depicts a negligible relationship between progress in day-program activities and successful residential placement, a number of other reports suggest otherwise. Principal among these are findings by Gollay, Freedman, Wyngaarden and Kurtz (1978), who found that persons who "failed" in CR placements participated in fewer social activities, had more unmet service needs, and had more contact with institutional settings, than did persons remaining in community placement. Further evidence supporting a relationship between day services and community adjustment includes a study by Seltzer (1981), in which resident performance and satisfaction within CR settings were positively associated with participation in formal skills training. The consistency with which service shortfalls in CR settings are reported (cf. Bjaanes, Butler & Kelly, 1981; Gollay, 1981; Savage, Novak, & Heal, 1980) raises some serious issues. While both Schalock et al., and Gollay et al. report that placement failure was often precipitated by behavior problems, the relationship between service shortfall and behavioral problems has not been adequately addressed. It remains unclear whether services are ineffective in dealing with many behaviors (as suggested by Schroeder, Mulick, & Schroeder, 1979), whether the services needed to moderate or modify such behaviors are unavailable, or whether some persons are not provided services because they require too much effort and time (Jacobson & Schwartz, Note 5, Pagel & Whitling, 1978).

Not only have service shortfalls been highlighted in recent studies, but these gaps are most apparent for more disabled individuals (Gollay, 1981). This finding combined with the observation that CRs depend upon previous institutional settings for selected services suggests that (1) local community service networks may be fragmented, ill coordinated, or incomplete (as would be expected in an evolving system); (2) generic service providers may not be prepared to serve a "new," previously institutionalized population, a portion of which has severe multiple handicaps; or (3) that CR managers tend not to refer MRDD individuals to generic service providers.

Existing research generally suggests that formal service provision mediates placement success, although interactions of service, environment, and resident characteristics have not been systematically addressed. In the absence of service provision information, the validity of the results of many investigations of resident "fit" to a setting, and of variables predicting placement success, may be seriously questioned.

Staff Job Satisfaction

The terms "job satisfaction," "job attitudes," and "morale" have been used interchangeably to refer to "affective orientations on the part of individuals toward work roles which they presently occupy" (Vroom, 1964). Several researchers have proposed definitions of job satisfaction, each with a somewhat different emphasis or perspective (Guion, 1958; Likert & Willits, 1940; Locke, 1976; Smith, Kendall, & Hulin, 1969;

Vroom, 1964). Contemporary researchers have rejected any simplistic formulation positing that satisfaction results from good working conditions and leads to increased productivity (see Smith et al., 1969). Similarly, there is general acceptance of the notion that the concept of job satisfaction subsumes a complex set of variables and relationships; individuals may be quite satisfied with certain aspects of their jobs and not with others. Additionally, satisfactions in some areas may be more clearly related to antecedent conditions or resulting work behavior than are satisfactions in other areas.

Several factors have been repeatedly identified in empirical terms which describe the "dimensional space" related to job satisfaction (see Herzberg, Mausner, Peterson, & Capwell, 1957; Smith, Kendall & Hulin, 1969; Vroom, 1964). These factors include aspects of the job related to the work and working conditions, supervision, financial reward, promotional opportunity, coworkers, and company policies. While no universally accepted definition of job satisfaction exists at present, most definitions refer in one way or another to the affective response of the individual toward his or her work situation, considered either globally or as a multifaceted construct of several components.

Job Satisfaction and Attitudes Toward Persons with Mental Retardation

While it makes sense on logical grounds to consider job satisfaction as a relevant dimension in all fields of employment, several sources confirm its relevance as an attitudinal dimension for the developmental disabilities services worker. Bensberg and Barnett (1966) developed a comprehensive attendant opinion assessment in connection with the Attendant Training Project of the Southern Regional Educational Board (SREB). This Attendant Opinion Scale consists of five items in each of 23 attitude categories selected for their relevance to quality of care and worker performance. Respondents indicate their level of agreement or disagreement with each item. Factor analytic studies of the SREB Attendant Opinion Scale by Bensberg and Barnett (1966) and Silverstein, McLain, Brownlee, and Hubbell (1977) have identified job dissatisfaction as the first and largest factor, accounting for approximately 40% of the total variance.

Lounsburg (1976) measured several attendant demographic and attitudinal variables and correlated them with job satisfaction. The attitudinal measure used in this study was derived from Efron and Efron's (1967) Attitude about Mental Retardation Scale (AMS). The AMS has six factors: segregation via institution-alization, cultural deprivation, noncondemnatory etiology, personal exclusion, authoritarianism, and hopelessness. Job satisfaction was assessed through use of the JDI. A minimal but statistically significant relationship ($r = 0.27$; $p = 0.05$) was obtained between job satisfaction and attitudes related to segregation of the mentally retarded. High job satisfaction was associated with opposition to the segregation of mentally retarded individuals from the rest of society. This relationship is consistent with the factor analytic results of the SREB Attendant Opinion Scale. The attitude categories loading on the SREB job dissatisfaction factor included those indicating a desire to avoid giving direct physical care to the mentally retarded, a desire to keep visitors off the wards, and the perception of residents as irritating.

Babow and Johnson (1969) studied attitudes of treatment staff in a newly established MR unit within a state mental hospital. While job satisfaction was not assessed directly, Srole's (1956) Anomia Scale was used to provide a measure of identification with, or alienation from, the hospital's social system and the expected responsiveness of leaders to workers' needs. Hospital employees scoring high on this index of alienation and pessimism toward leadership would likely be job dissatisfied. If this assumption is valid, Babow and Johnson's findings are consistent with those of Lounsburg (1976) and Bensberg and Barnett (1966); highly alienated hospital workers were found to be more authoritarian and to favor a custodial, segregationist approach to the treatment of persons with mental retardation. Alienation was also negatively correlated with orientation toward a humanistic and democratic therapeutic environment. The results of these three studies suggest that mental retardation workers who are dissatisfied with their jobs are more likely to hold pessimistic and segregationist attitudes toward care for their clientele than are workers satisfied with their jobs.

Job Satisfaction in Mental Retardation Programs

Sarata (1974) conducted an extensive study of employee satisfaction ($N = 222$) in three agencies serving persons with mental retardation. The research examined the relationships of job satisfactions of workers through four variable sets: (a) satisfaction with the field of mental retardation, (b) satisfaction with the employing agency, (c) amount of direct client contact, and (d) perceived client progress.

Job satisfaction was measured through use of the Job Descriptive Index (JDI), a rigorously constructed and validated instrument for measuring satisfaction with five job factors: the work itself, supervision, pay, promotions, and coworkers (Smith, Kendall, and Hulin, 1969). Nine job-design variables were included in the questionnaire: variety, autonomy, task identity, feedback, participation, information, learning contact, and informal contact. While satisfaction-with-field and satisfaction-with-agency were highly correlated ($r = 0.55$), these two variables were markedly different in their relationships with other variables. Satisfaction-with-agency correlated 0.59 with the measure of overall satisfaction, and substantially with other component job satisfactions and job design variables, while the measure of satisfaction-with-field was less correlated with most job design variables. It would appear that employees' attitudes toward their specific agency, rather than toward the field of mental retardation, are more likely to impact on overall satisfaction.

Not surprisingly, high-contact employees expressed a significantly lower level of satisfaction-with-agency than did the low-contact group. High-contact employees were more likely to cite client-related matters as sources of satisfaction or dissatisfaction and to mention lack of client progress as a concern (differences in salary and educational level between these two groups did not explain the differences in satisfaction). It is interesting that employees who assumed that limited progress would be made by persons with mental retardation generally displayed a greater degree of satisfaction with the agency. Staff with lower expectations regarding adaptive growth may not be as frustrated or disappointed by actual resident accomplishments. A parallel finding, drawn from Stelmack, Postma, Goldstein, and Shepard (1981), is that attendants working one to one with less physically disabled individuals in home settings were more job satisfied than those working with more seriously physically disabled persons. The authors' measure of satisfaction was a modification of Locke's (1976) Action Tendency Interview Schedule for Job Satisfaction (ATIS). It is possible that either expectations or work effort mediates satisfaction in such settings, since more disabled persons require more hours of care or assistance. Further evidence of this relationship has been provided by George and Baumeister (1981), who found that staff turnover, and job dissatisfaction (as measured by the JDI) were greater in group home settings serving more disabled individuals, particularly those who displayed multiple behavior problems. In general, differences in client characteristics have not been controlled in investigations of job satisfaction. Since client characteristics (such as disability level or problem behaviors) apparently affect job satisfaction, this factor must be controlled in studies which attempt to relate job satisfaction to organizational variables

like decentralization or decision-making power of employees.

A more recent report by Sarata (1977) focused upon job satisfaction and task involvement as correlates of service delivery strategy in three agencies serving persons with mental retardation. Each agency evinced a different service delivery strategy. The first agency was selected as representing those agencies with an operational community-oriented service delivery system; the second agency was in a transitional phase, seeking to develop a fuller community orientation; and the third was chosen because it reflected an institutional service delivery orientation. The measures in this study were identical to those previously employed by the author (Sarata, 1974). Results were consistent with the hypothesis that different service delivery strategies are associated with differences in employee satisfaction, task involvement, and job characteristics. Employees of the first agency showed the highest levels of job satisfaction and overall satisfaction, with less differences observed on these measures between the other two programs. These employees were also more satisfied with most job-design variables (demonstrating more involvement in the tasks that are part of the job) than were employees of the third agency, although results in this area were less compelling.

Organizational Structure, Quality of Care and Job Satisfaction

Several organizational variables—decentralization, participatory decision-making, and quality of care—have been found to be related to job satisfaction among mental retardation workers. Rabinowitz & Hall (1977) have provided an excellent review of the literature relating organizational and personal variables to job involvement. Among their conclusions, they note that "participatory leadership" constitutes one of the best predictors of job involvement (cf. Siegel & Ruh, 1973; White & Ruh, 1973) and, additionally, that job involvement appears clearly to be linked to job satisfaction. Paulson (1974) has reported increased goal attainment in decentralized health care organizations, while Tannenbaum and Masarik (1950) have found higher staff morale to be associated with decentralization. Aiken and Hage (1966) have reported increased worker alienation when authority is centralized.

Within mental retardation agencies, several studies have demonstrated a relationship between decentralized authority and improved quality of care (Holland, 1973; King, Raynes, & Tizard, 1971). Although individualized care appeared to be enhanced by decentralization, neither of these studies actually measured the direct-care staff's feelings of participation in decision-making as it relates to their care-giving responsibilities. The mediating variable of decision-making power was, however, explored by Raynes, Pratt, and Roses (1977), who demonstrated a strong positive association between staff's perceived decision-making power and two measures of quality of care (resident-oriented care practices and use of informative speech with residents). This measurement strategy has been generalized to group homes by Pratt, Luszcz, and Brown (1980), whose findings in group homes are consistent with those obtained in congregate care settings.

To summarize, worker involvement in decision-making was assessed by Raynes et al. (1977), and a general relationship between job involvement and job satisfaction has been noted previously. Taken together, these studies are consistent with research linking decentralization with improved quality of care, and suggest that had job satisfaction been measured, it would have been greater for those working within a decentralized institutional structure.

The relevance of staff attitudes and job satisfaction measures to the overall evaluation of CRs is underscored by reports (Bruininks, Kudla, Wieck, & Hauber, 1980; O'Connor & Sitkei, 1975) which cite the acquisition, training, and retention of qualified staff as prominent problems in development disabilities program operation. Relatively high turnover rates affect continuity of service provision and also divert limited resources from direct service to administrative duties. Evidence that organizational factors affect upon job satisfaction and occupational stability has been provided by Lakin and Bruininks (1981). In a study of staff turnover in 75 public residential and 161 community (private) residential facilities, they found mean turnover rates of 29.5 and 55.4% annually, respectively. It was found that, over a span of five years, only seven percent of staff present at the beginning of that interval were still employed in community residential settings. In community residential facilities serving fewer than 65 persons, greater turnover was associated with lower starting salary, a lower ratio of direct care staff to administrative staff, and a lower ratio of residents to administrative staff. Interestingly, although facility scores on an adaptation of Characteristics of the Treatment Environment were not associated with turnover rate, both intrinsic (nature and rationale of the work itself) and extrinsic (pay, chance for promotion, facility policies, supervision, employer reorganization) job satisfaction scores on the Minnesota Satisfaction Questionnaire (an adaptation of the JDI) discriminated staff who stayed in the programs from those who departed. Relationships between normalization outcomes, resident adaptive growth, employee satisfaction, and turnover, however, remain largely unexplored.

Other Types of Satisfaction Assessment

In addition to studying the satisfaction of staff with their work, the degree of others' (e.g., residents, neighbors, parents) satisfaction with these programs has been investigated. Although studies have addressed questions relative to resident, neighbor, parent, or advocate satisfaction, such measures have not been consistently included in more comprehensive reports. Several methodological problems exist in this area. Principal among these is the difficulty in assessing the satisfaction of nonverbal or marginally verbal residents (as noted by Seltzer, 1981). While satisfaction of parents or advocates with CR placements would logically be considered a possible variable mediating placement success, scant attention has been given to this area.

Finally, there is evidence that shifts in satisfaction may be expected over time among CR residents (Birenbaum & Seiffer, 1976) and among neighbors as well (Lubin, Schwartz, Zigman, & Janicki, 1982). Lubin et al. (1982) found that, although some CRs were opposed by neighbors when they opened, within one to two years neighbors were reported to be indifferent to or supportive of the programs. Furthermore, community acceptance was not related to resident characteristics. Such findings suggest that levels of acceptance determined at one point in time should be qualified as to time of measurement since client placement or program opening.

Analysis of Program Costs

Several authors (Heal & Laidlaw, 1980; Intagliata, Willer, & Cooley, 1979) have investigated the range of program costs related to group homes and other types of community living alternatives, and have compared these to expenses of congregate care settings. Unfortunately, the use of such superficially equivalent measures such as daily cost is often misleading in comparing program cost levels; whereas the analysis of cost levels in congregate care settings remains relatively straightforward (since the setting has definite physical boundaries), community setting cost components must include off-site and generic support services that would be included in the costs of a congregate care setting. Examples of non-comparable allocations to be accounted for in the community include per diem and other formal day-program costs (if these are not included in the CR per diem), trans-

portation costs, case management costs, costs related
to involvement of state agency staff as consultants or
therapists, costs of services purchased from professionals
in the community, and costs engendered through use
of community generic services. Furthermore, variations
in per diems for residential services have not yet been
consistently analyzed to identify labile components
accounting for rate variation. These issues and others
related to cost effectiveness have been discussed in
detail by Heal and Laidlaw (1980).

It is questionable whether the analysis of program
cost, particularly outside of the context of cost effectiveness, is an essential component of community
program evaluation activities, except in those specific
instances where questions are raised about the adequacy
of fiscal supports at selected sites. It is often suggested
that lower cost levels may be useful as a justification
for expanding community service systems in preference
to congregate care settings, and that comparative costs
between community alternatives can be used to guide
program development in the direction of cost containment. Yet the general rationale of cost effectiveness
often fails to take into account needs of the service
population (the lowest cost alternative may not be
the most appropriate for some individuals). Given
the limitations of both research and methodology
related to costs, decisions related to costs are relegated
to policy, rather than evaluation, at present.

Summary

To reiterate areas of consensus, the available evidence
appears to support the view that: (1) persons with
mental retardation, even those who are profoundly
mentally retarded, may benefit from enriched environments and gain skills, if appropriate intervention
strategies are employed; (2) changes in personal competence are often related to the restrictiveness of a
residential setting; (3) the success or failure of persons
placed in CRs, or other community living alternatives,
are related at least as much to the appropriateness of
the particular setting as they are to characteristics of
individuals; (4) persons considered appropriate for CRs
are, as a group, somewhat less disabled than persons
targeted for congregate care programs; (5) living in a
CR is associated with enhanced social or occupational
opportunities for persons with mental retardation
compared to living in an institution; and (6) staff job
satisfaction appears to be enhanced by a decentralized,
community-oriented service delivery strategy, and to
be associated with better care for disabled residents.

Instruments Appropriate for Group Home Research

A primary focus of American psychology has been
the analysis of individual differences among persons,

with the assumption that an understanding of these
differences will enhance the clinician's ability to predict
behavior. However, as Moos (1973) has noted, "no
matter how much information about the individual
one adds to the predictive equation, one cannot bring
the correlation coefficient between individual characteristics and prediction criteria much above .40"
(p. 653). Therefore, the trend toward behavior checklists as a method of assessment has been paralled by
increasing interest in environmental determinants or
correlates of behavior.

Operationalized outcome measures are especially
appealing to social scientists owing to their robustness
and high consensual reliability (Joiner & Krantz, 1979).
In recent years there has been a proliferation of adaptive
behavior scales and checklists and, as will be noted,
consistent application of these in the assessment of
both mentally retarded persons and the quality of
services they receive. For the individual client, behavior
scales may be used (1) to establish a base line, (2) for
the construction of individual habilitation plans, (3)
to evaluate the effectiveness of interventions, and (4)
to describe needed changes in service priorities. On
the administrative level, behavior scales, when used
across persons in service, may permit comparative
evaluation of several different program formats and
thereby provide a description of needed program
planning and development efforts on an agency basis.

Within human services, there is a small but growing
body of literature suggesting relationships between
intervention effectiveness and employee attitudes, organizational structures, and job performance. These
are highly complex variables, and adequate measures
have been developed only recently that permit rigorous
exploration of relationships among them. The following
review will consider the availability of instruments
for assessing adaptive functioning, environmental
factors, and job satisfaction with relevance to the
evaluation of group homes.

Measures of Adaptive Functioning

Bibliographies of behavior scales have been presented
by Esser (1976: 11 scales); Individual Data Base (1978b:
94 scales); Jones (1977: 3 scales); Walls and Werner
(1976: 39 scales); Walls, Werner, and Bacon (1976:
60 scales); and Walls, Werner, Bacon and Zane (1977:
200 scales). Behavioral measures may be classified
along several dimensions: (1) as descriptive or prescriptive, the latter being tied to a curriculum (Walls
et al., 1977); (2) as checklists or scales, the latter
having properties associated with psychometric instruments (Joiner & Krantz, 1978); (3) as setting-specific
or non-specific, the latter measuring behaviors which

might be subject to intervention in a number of settings (Walls et al., 1977); and (4) as limited or global in the assessment of adaptive functioning (Joiner & Krantz, 1978). Criteria for assessing the applicability of behavior instruments have been summarized by Berk (1980).

Walls and Werner (1977) rated each of 39 behavior checklists on a scale of objectivity. Among the scales rated highest for objectivity were the Behavior Characteristics Progression (BCP), Colorado Master Planning Guide for Instructional Objectives, Commonwealth Plan for Education and Training of Mentally Retarded Children (COMPET), Higginsville State School and Hospital Behavioral Scale, Job Seeking Skills Reference Manual, Minnesota Developmental Programming System Behavioral Scales (MDPS), Nebraska Client Progress System, and Washington Assessment and Training Scales. Surprisingly, the A.A.M.D. Adaptive Behavior Scale (ABS), one of the most widely used behavior checklists, was assigned to the lowest range of objectivity. Of the scales noted above, the Colorado Master Planning Guide and COMPET are intended primarily for use with children, while the Job Seeking Manual is recommended for prevocational assessment; these scales generally would be inappropriate for the global assessment of CR residents.

IDB (1978a) has presented information on norm availability, population and setting appropriateness, and reliability for 94 behavior scales. Of those reviewed the ABS (and Behavior Development Survey), Balthazar Scales, Progress Assessment Chart, Rehabilitation Indicators, Personal Skills and Social-Emotional Behavior Checklists, and the MDPS would appear potentially useful for assessing CR residents, given the presence of adequate reliability and evidence of applicability to the population. The ABS, Balthazar Scales, and the Social and Prevocational Information Battery (SPIB) have also been cited by Sundberg, Snowden, and Reynolds (1978) as useful instruments; the Rehabilitation Indicators were found to be of value by Muzzia and Burris (1979).

The Behavior Characteristics Progression (VORT, 1973) is a 59-domain behavior scale, which has been used as a non-standardized, criterion-referenced assessment device in special education, and in management information applications in Texas (Lett, 1979). The Social and Pre-vocational Information Battery and the related Behavior Rating Form have been used in community contexts (Irvin, Halpern & Reynolds, 1976, 1977). Schroeder and Henes (1978) used a two-year interval between applications of the Progress Assessment Chart (Gunzberg, 1969) to compare a group of persons placed in the community with a matched

group remaining in an institution. The Personal Skills, and the Social-emotional Behaviors Checklists, have been used to assess the effects of institutionalization (Vogel, Kun, & Meshorer, 1968), the relationship of EEG abnormality to variability in adaptive behavior (Vogel, Kun, Meshorer, Broverman, & Klaiber, 1969), and relationships between adaptive behavior and probability of repatriation (Vogel, Kun, & Meshorer, 1969). Another recently developed scale is the Behavioral Characteristics Assessment (Hill & Bruininks, 1981), containing 11 domains with a total of 65 items, each rated according to performance quality and/or opportunity. Scores from the BCA domains are summed to provide a total "independence" score reflecting functioning within one of six independence levels. Its brevity—10 minutes to administer—and its provision of a summary score are characteristics of behavior measures developed principally for research purposes; clinical applications are often limited with this type of instrument.

The ABS has been used as a screening measure for special classroom placement (Malone & Christian, 1975; Windmiller, 1977), as a programming tool with a criterion-referenced training program (Berdine, Murphy, & Roller, 1977) and without one (Bogen & Aanes, 1975), for the evaluation of the effects of community placement (Aninger & Bolinsky, 1977; Cohen, Conroy, Frazer, Sneilbecker & Spreat, 1977; Eyman & Call, 1977; Eyman, Silverstein, McLain & Miller, 1977; Intagliata, Note 3), in assessing shifts in adaptive behavior in group homes (Aanes & Moen, 1976; Fletcher, 1979; Taylor, 1976), as a diagnostic tool (Frank & Fiedler, 1969; Gully & Horsch, 1979; Lambert & Nicoll, 1976), in assessing sheltered workshop productivity (Cunningham & Presnall, 1978), and in comparing naturalistic retrospective and controlled observation strategies (Millham, Chilcutt, & Atkinson, 1978).

The Behavior Development Survey (IDB, 1978a: Magni, 1979) is an abbreviated version of the ABS which requires less administration time. The BDS has been employed as the behavioral component of a management information system in California (Mayeda, 1979) and in the investigation of behavioral sequelae to deinstitutionalization (Conroy, 1980). Relationships between changes in BDS scores and characteristics of community settings have been noted (Eyman et al., 1979).

At present there are few reports in the literature addressing the MDPS. Of those available is an article on its use in intermediate care facilities for the mentally retarded (Bock, Roberts, & Bakkenist, 1977), another on its use in service plan development (Bock, 1977), and the MDPS User's Manual (Joiner & Krantz,

1978) in which use of the MDPS with some 2,500 persons is reported. Included in the manual is a study of the congruence between adaptive functioning of persons served in CR settings and admission/discharge criteria for those settings. An investigation of the relationship between group home size and functional progress of clients in developmental programming is also cited (Heiner & Bock, Note 6). In addition to the complete 360 item scales, two other versions of the MDPS have been developed. The first, Form AF, (Janicki, Note 7) is an eight-domain, 80-item extract of the longer form (Heiner, Note 8), used for management information purposes in the Minnesota Individual Information System (MIIS-Bock Associates, Note 9), the New York Developmental Disabilities Information System (DDIS-Janicki & Jacobson, Note 10), the Illinois Client Information System (ICIS-Bock Associates, Note 11), and the Oregon Client Information Survey (OCIS-Bock Associates, Note 12). The second, Form C, is a four-domain, 80-item assessment of very young children and severely multiply handicapped adults.

Measures of Environment and Climate

In the interest of improving clinical prediction, Moos developed several variants of the Community-Oriented Program Environment Scales (COPES, Moos, 1972; Insel & Moos, 1974), to measure the environmental characteristics of halfway houses, rehabilitation centers, day care centers, and community care homes for persons with psychiatric impairments. Moos (1973) stressed six dimensions that should be included in any analysis of environmental influences: (1) geographic situation and architectural/physical plant, (2) the variety of behavior settings, (3) the organizational or administrative structure under which a program operates, (4) the collective behavioral and personal characteristics of the residents, (5) the climate or psychosocial aspects of the setting, and (6) the functional behavior/reinforcement contingencies present in the program. COPES has been used by Pankratz (1975) to evaluate two halfway houses serving developmentally disabled persons. Administration requires responses by both staff and residents, and COPES suitability would be restricted in group homes serving individuals with limited communication skills.

Other investigators have emphasized physical, supportive, attitudinal, or behavioral characteristics of settings as critical in environmental evaluation (Balla, 1976; Bjaanes & Butler, 1974; Butterfield, Barnett, & Bensberg, 1966). Balla (1976), in a review of quality of care studies, cites four factors (resident-oriented care practices, enhanced behavior of residents, ap-

propriate release rates, and greater involvement with the family or community) as correlates of service quality. Balla concludes: "it appears that quality of life . . . is more adequate in smaller community-based institutions, especially in those under a population of 100. However, there seems to be considerable variation in quality of life among small community-based facilities" (p. 123).

The Resident Management Practices Scale (RMPS), first developed by King and Raynes (1968), measures management practices within residential settings. A 30-item version, the "Child Management Scale" was used in a study of institutional care in England (King, Raynes & Tizard, 1971), a 28-item scale termed "Revised RMPS" was employed in an investigation of three large institutions in the United States (Raynes, Pratt, & Roses, 1977), and a 37-item version, the "Group Home Management Schedule (GHMS), was used by Pratt, Luszcz, and Brown (1980) in a study of CR practices. All versions measure the extent to which the management of client activities is institution or resident-oriented. Items in all versions are classifiable into four domains, relating to rigidity of routine, block treatment of residents, depersonalizing practices, and social distance between staff and residents. These domains were originally defined by Goffman (1961) as dimensions of a "total institution." Items from the RMPS and the Characteristics of the Treatment Environment (CTE; Jackson, 1964, 1969) which were descriptive of high-quality facilities have been presented by Magni and Yee (Note 13), based upon a review of 127 Hawaiian care homes. They found that the majority of items in these two measures were endorsed by raters in appropriate directions for high and low quality homes, when quality was described in a global fashion by certifying state agency personnel. Relationships between RMPS scores and quality of care, measured largely by enhanced resident functioning, have been noted consistently in reports (Eyman, Silverstein, McLain, & Miller. 1977; Gilbert & Hemming, 1979; McLain, Silverstein, Hubbell, & Brownlee, 1977; Pratt, Raynes, & Roses, 1977; Raynes, Pratt, & Roses, 1977; Zigler & Balla, 1979).

The Characteristics of the Treatment Environment (CTE) measure (Jackson, 1976, 1969) has been used alone (Silverstein, McLain, Hubbell, & Brownlee, 1977) or in combination with other measures (Eyman et al., 1977; Mayeda, 1979; McLain et al., 1975, 1977) to describe institutional and community residential settings. The CTE consists of 72 items describing staff activities, principally in relation to whether staff perform activities for residents or permit them to exercise choice. Silverstein, McLain, Hubbell, and Brownlee (1977) have derived two CTE factors (autonomy and activity) in an analysis of mental retardation services. The CTE has been used to discriminate among institutional and various community living situations (Eyman et al., 1977; McLain et al., 1977), among community residential settings (Mayeda, 1979; Magni & Yee, Note 13), and among wards within an institution (McLain et al., 1975). Relationships of CTE scores to RMPS scores (Eyman et al., 1977; McLain et al., 1975, 1977), and to both Program Analysis of Service Systems (Wolfensberger & Glenn, 1975a&b) and BDS scores (Mayeda, 1979) have been investigated. In general PASS, CTE, and RMPS scores have been positively correlated, and positively associated with shifts in BDS scores toward greater adaptive functioning.

Program Analysis of Service Systems (PASS), was developed for the evaluation of human service organizations. Several editions of PASS have been published, the most recent being PASS 3 and an abbreviated form entitled PASSING (Flynn, 1980). PASS seeks to describe some 50 major characteristics of service organizations, with characteristics termed "ratings." Ratings may be assigned to three major categories: adherence to normalization principles (73% of ratings), ideology-based services (13% of ratings), and administrative operations (14% of ratings). Twelve other ratings provide an index of facility quality. Overall, about 30% of PASS 3 content is concerned with resident behavior, while 70% reflects administrative processes (Wolfensberger & Glenn, 1975b).

Flynn (1974) analyzed PASS 2 evaluation data from 102 service programs; 68% of these programs served mentally retarded persons, 11% served persons with psychiatric disabilities, and the remainder served mixed populations. Results of an extensive statistical analysis were generally consistent with the hypothesis that PASS ratings constitute a useful index of the degree to which the service program treats the individual as deviant, or engages in nonnormative practices.

PASS 3 evaluation data have been used in a number of studies involving the analysis of community residential settings for developmentally disabled persons (Demaine, 1978; Eyman et al., 1979; Mayeda, 1979; Toedter, 1979). Modifications or abbreviations of the PASS instrument have also been formulated for use with developmental disabilities service providers (Erie County Department of Mental Health, 1975, Erie County Residential Guidelines; Pennsylvania Department of Public Welfare, 1976, Pennsylvania PASS Work Book; Weiss & Flynn, 1980, ANDI—A Normalization and Development Instrument) and psychiatric service providers, (Office of Mental Health, 1978, Community Housing Evaluation Checklist).

Relationships between PASS, BDS and CTE scores have been noted previously in this report, and have also been described by Janicki (1981). In general, variability in PASS scores is associated with quantitative differences in other environmental measures across CRs.

The Rehabilitative Indicators (RI-Diller, Fordyce, Jacobs, & Brown, 1978) presents behavior statements classified as either status indicators or activity indicators. Status indicators are descriptive of a person's present education, employment, income, as well as other aspects of his current situation. Activity indicators are those day-to-day or "special event" activities in which a person has participated during a time interval (e.g., during the past month or year). Activities fall into the three domains of Self-Care/Family, Social/Recreational/Cultural/Political, and Vocational/Educational/Rehabilitation. Since both resident behavior and program features are reviewed in the RI, this instrument can be characterized as a merging of behavioral measures (i.e., ability to participate in various activities) and climate measures (i.e., opportunity to participate), much like Hill and Bruininks' (1981) behavior scale, though with much greater detail.

Measures of Job Satisfaction

Smith, Kendall, and Hulin (1969) have developed a well constructed and validated instrument for measuring job satisfaction, the Job Descriptive Index (JDI). The JDI consists of 72 descriptive terms or phrases associated with five distinct job areas: the work itself, supervision, pay, promotions, and co-workers, with a satisfaction score derived for each area. Extensive normative data are available for each subscale based upon responses from a random sample of nearly 2,600 workers employed in 19 different companies. Adequate discriminant and convergent validity have been demonstrated through the use of several different concurrent measures.

Bensberg and Barnett (1966) developed a comprehensive direct care staff opinion measure, the SREB Attendant Opinion Scale (AOS). It consists of five items in each of 23 attitude categories and has been cited earlier in this report. Respondents indicate their level of agreement of disagreement on a four-point Likert scale. Scores are summed for the five items within each category. The authors performed a factor analysis of this instrument based on a sample of 683 direct care staff. Through rotation, four factors were extracted, accounting for 50% of the total variance. The first and largest factor identified represented job dissatisfaction (accounting for 40% of the total variance). Bensberg and Barnett (1966) state that attendants with high scores on this factor are apparently job dissatisfied; they find their work unrewarding, too demanding, and are job insecure; they perceive residents as irritating and therefore avoid providing direct physical care. Silverstein, McLain, Brownlee, and Hubbell (1976) have replicated the factor structure obtained by Bensberg and Barnett (1966) on this measure with 105 attendants from an institution for mentally retarded persons. Recently, an abridged form of the SREB/AOS has been developed (Community Residence Employee Opinion Scale, Living Alternatives Research Project, Note 14) for use in the evaluation of direct care staff attitudes toward employment in a CR.

Organizational Measures

A number of measures are available that describe the organization/management contexts within which employees function on the job. Hackman and Oldham (1974a,b) developed a self-report scale, the Job Diagnostic Survey (JDS), for the purpose of assessing five core dimensions of jobs: (1) skill variety—the degree to which a job requires the performance of different activities as part of work, (2) task identity—the degree to which a job requires completion of identifiable pieces of work (e.g., projects, permanent products), (3) task significance—the degree to which a job affects the lives of other people, (4) autonomy—the degree to which a job provides freedom, independence, and discretion in scheduling and carrying out work activities, and (5) feedback—the degree to which workers are informed about their performance effectiveness. These constructs are posited to bear upon motivation for work. Utilization of the JDS in CRs is suggested by its demonstrated applicability in a public retardation institution (MacEachron & Driscoll, 1981) and consistency between self-reported data and independent behavioral observations of work behavior (Hackman & Oldham, 1974b).

Although organizational factors and employee turnover have been investigated in CRs, little attention has been given to the roles of decision-making practices or leadership in behavior in these settings. Decision-making has been assessed in mental retardation institutions (MacEachron & Driscoll, 1981) and psychiatric institutions (Buffum & Holland, 1980) using another self-report scale, the Employee Influence Scale (EIS-Tannenbaum, 1968, 1974). EIS scores reflect dimensions of participation and centralization in decision-making practices, dimensions which are proposed by Likert (1966), Argyris (1973) and Pennings (1976) to mediate staff effectiveness. Participation reflects the involvement of the individual employee in

decision-making within the program itself while centralization represents the distribution of decision-making prerogatives throughout an organization. Srole's (1956) Anomia Scale, a measure of alienation from a facility's social system, may also be useful as an index of organizational involvement.

Leadership behavior has been assessed through both questionnaire (Halpin & Winer, 1957) and observational (Mintzberg, 1973) strategies. The Leadership Behavior Description Questionnaire (LBDQ, Halpin & Winer, 1957) considers two dimensions, (consideration, and initiation of structure) which are posited by Stodgill (1974) to be related to job productivity and satisfaction. Consideration relates to perceived positive aspects of supervisor/surpervisee relationships, and initiations of structure encompasses perceptions of the supervisor's actions in defining and clarifying roles, goals, and communication patterns. The observational strategy involves the recording of leader behaviors in a taxonomic fashion similar to that employed in observational studies of resident and staff interaction.

Since the amount of time a CR manager actually spends supervising staff may vary, and since manager turnover in residences is relatively high, another construct which may bear on CR organizational structure is that of leadership substitutes (Kerr, 1977). Such substitutes are design characteristics of programs which compensate for intermittent supervision. Substitutes for leadership may be documented through application of a questionnaire entitled the Measurement of Substitutes for Leadership (MSL, Kerr & Jermier, 1978).

Measures of motivation, decision-making practices, and leadership behavior provide a context within which job satisfaction, general environmental climate, and resident growth need to be considered. Relationships among organizational framework, management practices and job satisfaction have been demonstrated. Given the inferred relationships of job satisfaction to staff turnover, care practices, and aspects of organization, one could anticipate that management practices would influence resident functioning. At present, the character of CRs as small work places remains virtually unnoted as an issue in the mental retardation literature (Janicki, 1981).

Development of an Evaluation Framework for Community Living Alternatives

The absence of consistent, generalizable effects of settings independent of size or program category, coupled with the projected growth of CRs, underscores the need for further research and the refinement of suitable evaluation strategies. Frequent methodological barriers to the integration of diverse CR research studies are founded in several design considerations. Designs often do not discriminate among different types of community programs when comparisons are made to large residential facilities. Designs focusing upon specific programs often do not identify these programs within a typology of residential alternatives derived from evaluation measures. Designs often concentrate on one measurement modality without assessing other factors which are known situational predictors (for example, research employing extensive measures of behavior change may not include detailed environmental measures). Designs often relate client characteristics to setting characteristics at only one point in time, rendering data descriptive rather than longitudinal. Studies which include test-retest of behavior often do not provide the same information for environmental factors. Designs using a large number of sites often employ brief or superficial measures. Studies that focus on fewer settings tend to involve the types of measures necessary to draw inferences, but sampling considerations may seriously restrict the generalization of findings. Random selection of target programs or clients within programs is seldom achieved.

More extensive evaluation of CRs should permit the clinician and policymaker alike to determine more accurately who should be considered appropriate for CR placement and what elements of CR environment and operation should be modified. The basis for such decision has not yet been documented sufficiently in the literature.

There are a number of elements which increase the likelihood that an evaluation of habilitation settings will be used to improve services in those settings. Care should be taken to insure that data collected as part of the evaluation process will be useful by the program itself as part of its clinical or management activities. Ideally, it should be possible to employ measures which yield information suitable to decision-making processes at every organizational level, from direct-care to top administration. From the evaluator's standpoint, the use of more than one instrument to measure a variable (e.g., resident adaptive behavior change) can contribute to the credibility of results by permitting construct validation. A secondary motive for using redundant measures is the opportunity to validate or assess the reliability of less widely used instruments when a less frequently used tool is more appropriate to the sample or easier to administer. However, in order to obtain optimal cooperation by service providers, the evaluation strategy should collect data in the manner that intrudes least upon the daily operations of programs, and for practical reasons it may be necessary to forego the use of redundant measures.

These approaches are closely related to evaluation elements cited as necessary by persons currently operating evaluation systems which review CRs. Doucette (1979), in identifying criteria for the selection of measurement tools, has listed as primary considerations (1) an immediate relationship to the phenomenon of concern, (2) reasonable administration time, (3) readily interpretable data, (4) practical applicability, (5) sufficient history of use, and (6) adequate validity and reliability. More technical issues have been addressed by Finarelli (1979), including (1) the preliminary selection of outcomes to be measured, (2) the establishment of standards as to how much change in client activity shall be judged to constitute "progress," (3) the definition of the evaluation focus, and (4) the importance of being able to relate progress to specific aspects of a program setting. Irvin, Crowell, and Bellamy (1979) have stressed that data must be of sufficient quality to engender the credibility of findings. Other researchers have criticized the predominance of outcome measures in program evaluation, noting that outcomes are interpretable only if one has an adequate assessment of content and process factors mediating these outcomes (Kiresuk, 1979; Rowitz, 1979; Yaron, 1979). Finally, instruments should be applicable to residential, day program, and generic service settings that the individuals under study encounter.

A Model Evaluation System for Community Residences

It would be reasonable to derive an empirical taxonomy of CRs upon which a more exhaustive analysis and evaluation of an entire CR system may be based. The elucidation of such taxonomies has, by and large, been achieved through either the preselection of parsing variables (e.g, number of residents) which are expected to discriminate among programs, or, far less frequently, by the administration of one or two measures of either personal functioning or environmental quality, with the taxonomy based upon combinations of measurement factor loadings.

In adopting the second strategy, one would incorporate general and specific measures of adaptive functioning, demographic and historical information, measures of environmental quality (physical plant, therapeutic orientation, and service provision) and measures of staff attitude as a reference base for the taxonomy. The taxonomy would ideally be extracted from data gathered from a sizable, geographically stratified, random sample of residences. An exhaustive analysis of the residence system itself would incorporate the same measures as those employed for the taxonomy.

Program/system evaluation should include repeated measures of the following domains: (1) resident characteristics, (2) physical plant factors, (3) residence climate, (4) administration, (5) residence program, (6) staff training and attitudes, and, if possible, (7) program costs. On the basis of previous research, resident characteristics should include consideration of demographics, preplacement history, functional status, and specific measures of adaptive skills and deficits. Physical plant factors would include compliance with regulatory standards and adherence to principles of normalization, specifically community integration and resemblance to a home-like setting. Residence climate should include consideration of the program's service orientation, and compliance with normalization principles. Administration encompasses management style and the degree to which practices are management- or facility-oriented vs. resident-oriented. Resident program measures should include documentation of the opportunities provided for growth, and should encompass specific habilitation goals and services, in-service education activities, and staffing patterns. Staff training and attitude measures should focus upon staff education and experience, attitudes toward one's work role, and attitudes toward those persons receiving services. Program costs refer to per-diem operating costs of a residence for both in-house and off-site programs and services including transportation, recreation, routine medical and summer camp costs.

An idealized evaluation design for CRs would first address issues that are of concern in the current literature and secondly, attempt to provide a basis for linkage and rapprochment with previous research. More specifically, the evaluation should be based in a model which takes into account the dynamics of the CR context. A model of this type is presented in Fig. 3.1. In Fig. 3.1, three classes of variables (occupants, organization, and environment) are expected

to impact (scanning the figure from left to right) singly, in two-way interactions, and in a three-way interaction, upon the developmental progress of residents, the quality of life afforded them, and the degree to which a CR can be described as homelike. These issues are of present concern in the literature. Futhermore, a feedback process, wherein changes in inputs to the setting (or outcomes reflected back as inputs) must be continuously taken into account in CR assessment.

In developing an evaluation design, barriers to generalization of findings would be addressed by incorporating design characteristics which enhance the integration of findings. Specifically, this would entail:

- Careful discrimination among programs in terms of type, and, preferably, the inclusion of only one type of program in the study sample (e.g., group homes, residential schools, intermediate care facilities for the mentally retarded serving 15 persons or fewer).
- Careful delineation of the position of the program type within a continuum of care settings, in terms of as many as possible of the constructs addressed by measurement tools.
- Inclusion of at least one, but preferably more than one, measurement tool in the design, which addresses occupant, environment, and organization factors.
- Longitudinal application of measures representing occupant, environment, and organization factors.
- Use of measures which are detailed and reliable enough that there can be a reasonable expectation that changes which do occur will be detected.
- Use of a random sample of program sites, stratified so as to be representative of a larger system of such settings.
- Incorporation of both "paper-and-pencil" measures and behavioral observation procedures.
- Derivation of residence models through explicit combinations of measures (sample size permitting), or alternatively, interpretation of general factors, processes, or effects.

Overall, the literature suggests that the evaluation of CRs requires a recognition that the factors which contribute to the effects of such settings are complex. Consequently, the evaluation design must address the relative contribution of a number of variables, singly and in combination, to resident/residence status and change. Sources of effect for CR settings are delineated in Fig. 3.2. Analyses must address the relationships of these factors to observable changes in resident/residence measures. Proposed areas of analysis and related measurement tools which address occupant, environment, and organization factors are presented in Table 3.1.

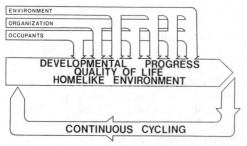

FIG. 3.1. Community residence/group home process model.

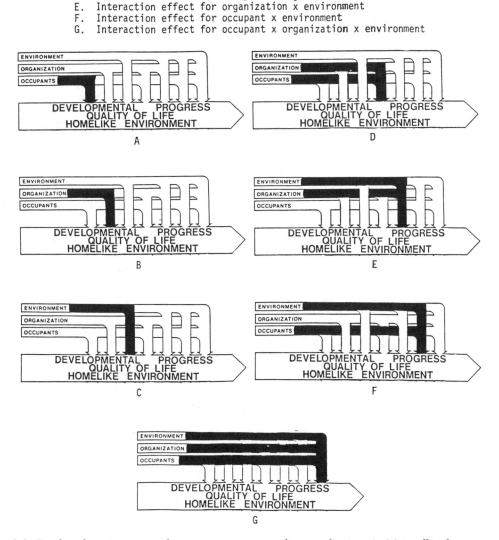

A. Main effect for occupant factors
B. Main effect for organizational factors
C. Main effect for environmental factors
D. Interaction effect for occupant x organization
E. Interaction effect for organization x environment
F. Interaction effect for occupant x environment
G. Interaction effect for occupant x organization x environment

FIG. 3.2. Focal analyses in a comprehensive community residence evaluation. A. Main effect for occupant factors. B. Main effect for organizational factors. C. Main effect for environmental factors. D. Interaction effect for occupant × organization. E. Interaction effect for organization × environment. F. Interaction effect for occupant × environment. G. Interaction effect for occupant × organization × environment.

As in most multi-dimensional designs, there may be severe restrictions upon statistical analyses. For example, within the context of the proposed design, the types and number of analyses to be performed will be limited by the number of program sites included in the sample. Given that an adequate sample of sites has been selected, statistical tests will have sufficient power to discriminate effects, and Type I error will be minimized. However, it may be valuable to treat some scores as independent variables in some analyses and as dependent variables in others; therefore, the sequence and variety of analyses must be carefully selected to control for Type II errors. Furthermore, the sheer number of independent variables in the proposed design, even if represented by factor scores rather than the item scores, is such that the possible combinations of high and low factor scores may greatly exceed the number of sites. For this reason, it may

Table 3.1. Relationship of Assessment Areas, Domains, Characteristics and Instruments

AREA	DOMAINS INCLUDED	CHARACTERISTICS SET	MEASURES
Occupant	Resident characteristics	physical	standardized demographic and functional attributes data set*
		functional	Minnesota Developmental Programming System Behavior Scales Behavior Development Survey
	Residence program	experiential	Rehabilitation Indicators
		habilitative service	standardized service receipt data set* Tennessee Goal Domain Dictionary
		movement	standardized record of admissions/ discharges*
Organization	Administration	occupational commitment	Job Diagnostic Survey
		management style	Employee Influence Survey Leadership Behavior Description Questionnaire
		staff	Adapted SREB Attendent Opinion Scale Job Descriptive Index standardized record of turnover** standardized record of in-service training activities**
	Program costs	per capita expenditures	standardized fiscal allocation protocol**
Environment	Physical plant	site	standardized data set on physical structure and resources***
	Residence climate	normalization	Program Analysis of Service Systems (PASS) or PASS-SF
		relation to community	standardized data set on community relations and residence neighborhood***
		responsiveness to resident needs	Group Home Management Schedule Characteristics of the Treatment Environment

   * Could be consolidated in single protocol.
  ** Could be consolidated in single protocol.
 *** Could be consolidated in single protocol.

be valuable to combine separate measures and derive factors based on an area of measurement (e.g., environment) before proceeding to further analyses. An example of this approach is found in Eyman and Arndt (1982), who combined RMPS and CTE scores before assessing their relationship to adaptive growth of persons with mental retardation living in institutions. However, since each of the variable classes of interest are probably of themselves multi-factored, this procedure will only diminish analytic complexity moderately. The evaluation strategy outlined here would provide a perspective on the relative contribution of independent variables to variance in dependent variables, rather than on direct cause and effect relationships.

The proposed model evaluation system would encompass groups of instruments which would be administered several times in a longitudinal design. Each instrument would be completed at each assessment interval to assure the measurement of change, if any, over time in each domain. Measures completed during the initial (baseline) stage could be analyzed through multivariate techniques and form the basis for a description of program types (e.g., CRs). When longitudinal data are available for each domain, and resident functional skills and service outcomes (retention in CR, transition to a less restrictive setting) are treated as dependent variables, optimum resident/ program/site matching would become possible. In addition, information from a range of instruments on the same individuals and sites would permit extraction and consolidation of separate scales into new instruments which might be less extensive but sufficiently comprehensive and sensitive as indicators of individual/site change.

Among the requirements for such an investigation are a sufficient number of sites, adequate instrumentation, and the necessary funding supports. However, many states now operate or support enough CRs to permit this type of research, and a variety of instruments is available with demonstrated efficiency and applicability in community contexts.

Extending the Logic of Research to Evaluation

Scientific research attempts to discover and understand the lawful relationships among forces and factors, people and their surroundings, often through the elucidation of cause and effect. The scientist endeavors to discover or verify effects which may not be readily apparent. The tradition of psychological research has involved the isolation of variables and the precise description of the manner in which these (either singly or in combination) result in alterations in personal functioning. In the context of applied research, this historical tendency has been reflected in attention being given to selected aspects of community living alternatives. Quite clearly, an approach entailing the isolation of variables is most appropriate when investigating issues about which little is known. However, the time has come for further investigation to be shifted from the disclosure of isolated effects to a delineation of the influence of combinations of variables that mediate the direction and degree of effects.

The presence of relationships among setting and occupant variables forms a necessary condition for evaluation activities. Employment of previously used measures, which therefore have known properties (e.g., reliability, expectation that meaningful changes will be reflected), is central to the design of credible evaluation studies. Such instrumentation, when used in combination with multivariate analyses, forms a primary model for program evaluation.

As noted by Butler and Bjaanes (1978), "it has often been assumed, without carefully assessing the internal programs available and the extent of utilization of external community resources, that placing a developmentally disabled person in a community facility (such as a CR) is equivalent to providing a normalizing (and otherwise beneficial) environment" (p. 398). They point out that their findings suggest otherwise. We still lack an understanding of the typical benefits of community residences for mentally retarded and developmentally disabled persons. In spite of extensive previous and ongoing research many pressing questions remain unanswered. Among the many critical issues to be addressed more fully are: Which facility characteristics affect quality of care? What are the best methods for encouraging normal life patterns? Which CR models are best suited for which individuals? Until the focus of research can be narrowed to studies

of unitary program types, and results generalized to most community residential alternatives, the continued national expansion of CRs remains a venture of faith, based more on good intentions than good results. It must be remembered that those same institutions now criticized were lauded by their proponents in earlier years. If, as Wolfensberger (1969) has predicted, CRs will become a primary supervised living environment for persons with mental retardation, it behooves us to understand how and why and what these programs accomplish, so that we can promote a higher quality of life for people, and not just a different life situation.

Reference Notes

1. Bjaanes, A. T., & Butler, E. W. Environmental demand, client competencies, and support services: Implications for placement outcome. Paper presented in M. P. Janicki (chair), *Community Services for Developmentally Disabled Persons: Individual and Program Differences*, 89th Annual Convention of the American Psychological Association, Los Angeles, August, 1981.
2. Soforenko, A. Z., & Macy, T. W. A study of the characteristics and life status of persons discharged from a large state institution for the mentally retarded during the years 1969–1977, 1978 (manuscript).
3. Intagliata, J. Factors related to the quality of community adjustment in family care homes. Paper presented at the Conference on Community Adjustment, Minneapolis, 1979.
4. Jacobson, J. W., Janicki, M. P., & Unger, L. Determining behavior intervention priorities for marginally disabled persons: A pilot study. Paper presented at the 104th Annual Meeting of the American Association on Mental Deficiency, San Francisco, 1980.
5. Jacobson, J. W., & Schwartz, A. A. Trends in deinstitutionalization: Impact of problem behavior upon community services. Paper presented in M. P. Janicki (chair), *Community services for Developmentally Disabled Persons: Individual and Program Differences*, 89th Annual Convention of the American Psychological Association, Los Angeles, August, 1981.
6. Heiner, K. & Bock, W. H. *Preliminary Report on the Relationship of Client Capacity to Client Development and Costs in Small Community Residential Facilities (ICF/MR) for the Mentally Retarded: A Working Paper*, 1978.
7. Janicki, M. P. *Report of the Committee on Instrument Selection*. Albany: New York Office of Mental Retardation and Developmental Disabilities, 1979.
8. Heiner, K. Item selection and the development of a management information data base. In M. P. Janicki (chair), *Rehabilitation Planning with Disabled Persons Using the Minnesota Developmental Programming System Behavior Scales*. Paper presented at the 86th Annual Convention of the American Psychological Association, Toronto, 1978.
9. Bock Associates, *Minnesota Individual Information System*, St. Paul, Minn.: Bock Associates, 1978.
10. Janicki, M. P. & Jacobson, J. W. *New York Developmental Disabilities Information System: Preliminary Report*. Albany, New York State Office of Mental Retardation and Developmental Disabilities, 1979.

11. Bock Associates, *Illinois Client Information System*, St. Paul, Minn.: Bock Associates, 1979.
12. Bock Associates, *Oregon Client Information Survey*, St. Paul, Minn.: Bock Associates, 1981.
13. Magni, T., & Yee, S. CTE & RMS ratings of Hawaii care homes, Individual Data Base, April, 1979 (report).
14. Living Alternatives Research Project. *Community residence employee opinion scale*. Staten Island, NY: New York State Institute for Basic Research in Developmental Disabilities, 1981.

References

Aanes, D. & Moen, M. Adaptive behavior changes of group home residents. *Mental Retardation*, 1976, **14**, 36–40.

Adams, J. Adaptive behavior and measured intelligence in the classification of mental retardation. *American Journal of Mental Deficiency*, 1973, **78**, 77–81.

Aiken, M., & Hage, J. Organizational alienation: A comparative analysis. *American Sociological Review*, 1966, **31**, 497–507.

Aninger, M., & Bolinsky, K. Levels of independent functioning of retarded adults in apartments. *Mental Retardation*, 1977, **15**, 12–16.

Argyris, C. Personality and organization theory revisited. *Administrative Science Quarterly*, 1973, **18**, 141–167.

Babad, E. Y., & Budoff, M. Sensitivity and validity of learning potential measurement in three levels of ability. *Journal of Educational Psychology*, 1974, **66**, 439.

Babow, I., & Johnson, A. Staff attitudes in a mental hospital which established a mental retardation unit. *American Journal of Mental Deficiency*, 1969, **74**, 116–124.

Baker, B. L., Seltzer, G. B., & Seltzer, M. M. *As close as possible: Community residences for retarded adults*. Boston, Mass.: Little, Brown & Co., 1977.

Balla, D., Relationship of institution size to quality of care. *American Journal of Mental Deficiency*, 1976, **81**, 117–124.

Balla, D., Butterfield, E. C., & Zigler, E. Effects of institutionalization on retarded children: A longitudinal cross-institutional investigation. *American Journal of Mental Deficiency*, 1974, **78**, 530–549.

Balla, D., Kossan, N., & Zigler, E. Effects of preinstitutional history and institutionalization on the behavior of the retarded. Unpublished manuscript, Yale University, 1976.

Balla, D., & Zigler, E. Preinstitutional social deprivation and responsiveness to social reinforcement in institutionalized retarded individuals: A six-year follow-up study. *American Journal of Mental Deficiency*, 1975, **80**, 228–230.

Baroff, G. S. On "size" and the quality of resident care: A second look. *Mental Retardation*, 1980, **18**, 113–118.

Bensberg, G. J., & Barnett, C. D. *Attendant training in Southern residential facilities for the mentally retarded, Report of the SREB Attendant Training Project*. Atlanta, Ga.: Southern Regional Educational Board, 1966.

Berdine, W. H., Murphy, M., & Roller, J. D. A criterion-referenced training program based on the ABS: The Oakwood resident scale for training and evaluating programs. *Mental Retardation*, 1977, **15**, 19–22.

Berk, R. A. Psychometric properties of adaptive behavior scales: Guidelines for producers and consumers. *Mental Retardation*, 1980, **18**, 47–49.

Birenbaum, A., & Seiffer, S. *Resettling retarded adults in a managed community*. New York: Praeger, 1976.

Bjaanes, A. T., & Butler, E. W. Environmental variation in community care facilities for mentally retarded persons. *American Journal of Mental Deficiency*, 1974, **78**, 429–439.

Bjaanes, A. T., Butler, E. W., & Kelly, B. R. Placement type and client functional level as factors in provision of services aimed at increasing adjustment. In R. H. Bruininks, C. E. Meyers, B. B. Sigford, & K. C. Lakin (Eds.), *Deinstitutionalization and community adjustment of mentally retarded people*. Washington, D.C.: American Association on Mental Deficiency, 1981.

Bock, W. How to design and evaluate a developmental plan of care. In Institute for Medicaid Management (Ed.). *Assessment of resident care in intermediate care facilities for mentally retarded*. Washington, D.C.: DHEW (HFCA), 1977.

Bock, W. Minnesota developmental programming system. In P. Sanofsky (Ed.), *Evaluating program effectiveness: The administrator's dilemma*. Watertown, Mass.: Social Planning Services, 1979.

Bock, W. H., Roberts, K., & Bakkenist, K. The Minnesota developmental programming system: Its history and application in ICF/MRs and SNFs. *Journal of Medicaid Management*, 1977, **1**, 17–26.

Bogen, D., & Aanes, D. The ABS as a tool in comprehensive mental retardation programming. *Mental Retardation*, 1975, **13**, 38–40.

Braddock, D. Deinstitutionalization of the retarded: Trends in public policy. *Hospital and Community Psychiatry*, 1981, **32**, 607–615.

Bruininks, R. H. Hauber, F. A., & Kudla, M. J. National survey of community residential facilities: A profile of facilities and residents in 1977. *American Journal of Mental Deficiency*, 1980, **84**, 470–478.

Bruininks, R. H., Kudla, M. J., Wieck, C. A., & Hauber, F. A. Management problems in community residential facilities. *Mental Retardation*, 1980, **18**, 125–130.

Buffum, W. E., & Holland, T. P. *Measuring employee influence in residential institutions* (SASS Working Paper), Cleveland, Ohio: Case Western Reserve University, 1980.

Butler, E. W., & Bjaanes, A. T. A typology of community care facilities and differential normalization outcomes. In P. Mittler & J. deJong (Eds.), *Research to practice in mental retardation: Care and intervention*. Baltimore, Md.: University Park Press, 1977.

Butler, E. W., & Bjaanes, A. T. Activities and use of time by retarded persons in community care facilities. In G. P. Sackett (Ed.), *Observing behavior, Volume 1: Theory and applications in mental retardation*. Baltimore, Md.: University Park Press, 1978.

Butler, E. W., Lei, T., & McAllister, R. J. Childhood impairments and subsequent social adjustment. *American Journal of Mental Deficiency*, 1978, **83**, 223–232.

Butterfield, E. C., Barnett, C. D., & Bensberg, G. J. Some objective characteristics of institutions for the mentally retarded: Implications for attendant turnover rate. *American Journal of Mental Deficiency*, 1966, **70**, 786–794.

Butterfield, E., Barnett, C., & Bensberg, G. A. A measure of attitudes which differentiates attendants from different institutions. *American Journal of Mental Deficiency*, 1968, **72**, 890–899.

Butterfield, E. C., & Zigler, E. The influence of differing institutional social climates on the effectiveness of social reinforcement in the mentally retarded. *American Journal of Mental Deficiency*, 1965, **70**, 48–56.

Campbell, A. Comparison of family and community contacts of mentally subnormal adults in hospital and in local authority hostels. *British Journal of Preventive and Social Medicine*, 1968, **22**, 165–169.

Clark, M. J. I. A community placement program for the mentally retarded. *American Journal of Mental Deficiency*, 1959, **64**, 548–555.

Cohen, J., Conroy, J., Frazer, D., Sneilbecker, G., & Spreat, S. Behavioral effects of institutional relocation of mentally retarded residents. *American Journal of Mental Deficiency*, 1977, **82**, 12–18.

Conroy, J. *Longitudinal study of the court-ordered deinstitutionalization of Pennhurst: Report on assessment of adaptive functioning changes*. Philadelphia, Pa.: Temple University Developmental Disabilities Center, 1980.

Crawford, J. L., Aiello, J. R., & Thompson, D. E. Deinstitutionalization and community placement: Clinical and environmental factors. *Mental Retardation*, 1979, **17**, 59–64.

Cunningham, T., & Presnall, D. Relationship between dimensions of adaptive behavior and sheltered workshop productivity. *American Journal of Mental Deficiency*, 1978, **82**, 386–394.

Demaine, G. *Empirical validation of Pass 3: A first step in service evaluation through environmental assessment*. Pomona, Calif.: Individualized Data Base, 1978.

Developmental Disabilities Project on Residential Services and Community Adjustment, *Brief #3*, Minneapolis, Minn.: University of Minnesota, March, 1979.

Diller, L., Fordyce, W., Jacobs, D., & Brown, M. *Postinstitutional placement project evaluation report*. New York: Rehabilitation Indicators Projects, NYU Medical Center, 1978.

Doucette, J. Identifying appropriate instruments for use in evaluating programs for the developmentally disabled. In P. Sanofsky (Ed.), *Evaluating program effectiveness: The administrator's dilemma*. Watertown, Mass.: Social Planning Services, 1979.

Duckett, J. Adaptive and maladaptive behavior of idiot savants. *American Journal of Mental Deficiency*, 1977, **82**, 308–310.

Eagle, E. Prognosis and outcome of community placement of institutionalized retardates. *American Journal of Mental Deficiency*, 1967, **72**, 232–243.

Edgarton, R. B. The study of community adaptation: Toward an understanding of lives in process. In P. Mittler & J. deJong (Eds.), *Research to practice in mental retardation: Care and intervention*, Baltimore, Md.: University Park Press, 1977.

Efron, R. E., & Efron, H. Y. Measurement of attitudes toward the retarded and an application with educators. *American Journal of Mental Deficiency*, 1967, **72**, 100–107.

Erie County Department of Mental Health, *Erie county residential guidelines*. Buffalo, N.Y.: ECDMH, 1975.

Esser, T. *Client rating instruments for use in vocational rehabilitational agencies*. Stout, Wis.: University of Wisconsin, 1976.

Eyman, R. K., & Arndt, S. Life-span development of institutionalized and community-based mentally retarded residents. *American Journal of Mental Deficiency*, 1982, **86**, 342–350.

Eyman, R., & Call, T. Maladaptive behavior and community placement of mentally retarded persons. *American Journal of Mental Deficiency*, 1977, **82**, 137–144.

Eyman, R. K., Demaine, G. C., & Lei, T. Relationship between community environments and resident changes in adaptive behavior: A path model. *American Journal of Mental Deficiency*, 1975, **83**, 330–338.

Eyman, R. K., Silverstein, A. B., & McLain, R. Effects of treatment programs on the acquisition of basic skills. *American Journal of Mental Deficiency*, 1975, **79**, 573–582.

Eyman, R. K., Silverstein, A. B., McLain, R., & Miller, C. Effects of residential settings on development. In P. Mittler & J. deJong (Eds.), *Research to practice in mental retardation: Care and intervention*, Baltimore, Md.: University Park Press, 1977.

Finarelli, H. The design for a model statewide evaluation system. In P. Sanofsky (Ed.), *Evaluating program effectiveness: The administrator's dilemma*. Watertown, Mass.: Social Planning Services, 1979.

Fletcher, D. N. The relationship of visitation to adaptive behavior of institutionalized mentally retarded persons. *Mental Retardation*, 1979, **17**, 152–153.

Flynn, R. J. Assessing human service quality with Pass II: An empirical analysis of 102 service program evaluations, 1974. Unpublished manuscript.

Flynn, R. J. Normalization, PASS, and service quality assessment: How normalizing are current human services? In R. J. Flynn & K. E. Nitsch (Eds.), *Normalization, social integration, and community services*. Baltimore, Md.: University Park Press, 1980.

Foster, R. W. *Camelot behavioral checklist manual*. Lawrence, Kans.: Camelot Behavior Systems, 1974.

Frank, H., & Fiedler, E. R. A multifactor behavioral approach to the genetic-etiological diagnosis of mental retardation. *Multivariate Behavioral Research*, 1969, **4**, 131–145.

Gardner, J. Community residential alternatives for the developmentally disabled. *Mental Retardation*, 1977, **15**, 3–8.

George, M. J., & Baumeister, A. A. Employee withdrawal and job satisfaction in community residential facilities for mentally retarded persons. *American Journal of Mental Deficiency*, 1981, **85**, 639–647.

Gilbert, K. A., & Hemming, H. Environmental change and psycholinguistic ability of mentally retarded adults. *American Journal of Mental Deficiency*, 1979, **83**, 455–459.

Goffman, E. *Asylums: Essays on the social situation of mental patients and other inmates*. Garden City, N.Y.: Doubleday & Co., 1961.

Gollay, E. Some conceptual and methodological issues in studying the community adjustment of deinstitutionalized mentally retarded people. In R. H. Bruininks, C. E. Meyers, B. B. Sigford, & K. C. Lakin (Eds.), *Deinstitutionalization and community adjustment of mentally retarded people*. Washington, D.C.: American Association on Mental Deficiency, 1981.

Gollay, E., Freedman, R., Wyngaarden, M., & Kurtz, N. R. *Coming back: The community experiences of deinstitutionalized mentally retarded people*. Cambridge, Mass.: Abt Books, 1978.

Gordon, L. R., & Ivey, A. E., Reintegrating institutionalized mental retardates in the community: A descriptive survey. *Community Mental Health Journal*, 1968, **4**, 395–401.

Guarnaccia, V. J. Factor structure and correlates of adaptive behavior in non-institutionalized retarded adults. *American Journal of Mental Deficiency*, 1976, **80**, 543–547.

Guion, R. M. Industrial morale (A symposium) 1. The problem of terminology. *Personnel Psychology*, 1958, **11**, 59–64.

Gully, K. J., & Horsch, H. M. Adaptive behavior scale: Development as a diagnostic tool via discriminant analysis. *American Journal of Mental Deficiency*, 1979, **83**, 518–523.

Gunzberg, H. C. *P-A-C manual.* (3rd ed.) Birmingham, England: SEFA Publications, Ltd., 1969.

Hackman, J. R., & Oldham, G. R. *Motivation through the design of work: Test of a theory* (Tech. Rept. No. 6). New Haven, Conn.: Yale University, Department of Administrative Studies, 1974.(a)

Hackman, J. R. & Oldham, G. R. *The job diagnostic survey: An instrument for the diagnosis of jobs and the evaluation of job redesign projects* (Tech. Rept. No. 4). New Haven, CT: Yale University, Department of Administrative Studies, 1974.(b)

Halpin, A. W., & Winer, B. J. A factorial study of the leader behavior descriptions. In R. M. Stodgill & A. E. Coons (Eds.), *Leader behavior: Its description and measurement.* Columbus, Ohio: Bureau of Business Research, Ohio State University, 1957.

Hamilton, J. L., & Budoff, M. Learning potential among the moderately and severely retarded. *Mental Retardation*, 1974, **12**, 33–36.

Heal, L. W., & Laidlaw, T. J. Evaluation of residential alternatives. In A. R. Novak & L. W. Heal (Eds.), *Integration of developmentally disabled individuals into the community.* Baltimore, Md.: Paul H. Brooks, 1980.

Herzberg, F., Mausner, B., Peterson, R. O., & Capwell, D. F. *Job attitudes: Review of research and opinion.* Pittsburgh, Pa.: Psychological Service of Pittsburgh, 1957.

Hill, B. K., & Bruininks, R. H. *Physical and behavioral characteristics and maladaptive behavior of mentally retarded people in residential facilities* (Project Report No. 12), Minneapolis, Minn.: Department of Psycho-educational Studies, University of Minnesota, 1981.

Hill, B. K., Sather, L. B., Kudla, M. J., & Bruininks, R. H. *A survey of the types of residential programs for mentally retarded people in the United States in 1978.* Unpublished report, Minneapolis, Minn.: Department of Psychoeducational Studies, University of Minnesota, 1978.

Holland, T. Organizational structure and institutional care. *Journal of Health and Social Behavior*, 1973, **14**, 241–251.

Holmes, R. F. Characteristics of five community living arrangements serving mentally retarded adults in southwest urban Pennsylvania. *Mental Retardation*, 1979, **17**, 181–183.

Hull, J. T., & Thompson, J. C. Predicting adaptive functioning of mentally retarded persons in community settings. *American Journal of Mental Deficiency*, 1980, **85**, 253–261.

Hull, J. T., & Thompson, J. C. Factors contributing to normalization in residential facilities for mentally retarded persons. *Mental Retardation*, 1981, **19**, 69–73.

Individual Data Base, *Behavior development survey.* Pomona, Calif.: Pacific State Neuropsychiatric Institute, 1978.(a)

Individual Data Base, *Review of behavioral instruments.* Pomona, Calif.: Pacific State Neuropsychiatric Institute, 1978.(b)

Insel, P. M., & Moos, R. H. Psychological environments: Expanding the scope of human ecology. *American Psychologist*, 1974, **29**, 179–188.

Intagliata, J. C., Willer, B. S., & Cooley, F. B. Cost comparison of institutional and community based alternatives for mentally retarded persons. *Mental Retardation*, 1979, **17**, 154–156.

Irvin, L. K., Crowell, F. A., & Bellamy, G. T. Multiple assessment evaluation of programs for severely retarded adults. *Mental Retardation*, 1979, **17**, 123–128.

Irvin, L. K., Halpern, A. S., & Reynolds, W. M. *Measuring client gain in group homes*, Eugene, Oreg.: University of Oregon Rehabilitation Research and Training Center in Mental Retardation, 1976.

Irvin, L. K., Halpern, A. S., & Reynolds, W. M. Assessing social and prevocational awareness in mildly and moderately retarded individuals. *American Journal of Mental Deficiency*, 1977, **82**, 266–272.

Isett, R. D., & Spreat, S. Test-retest and interrater reliability of the AAMD adaptive behavior scale. *American Journal of Mental Deficiency*, 1979, **84**, 93–95.

Jackson, J. Toward the comparative study of mental hospitals: Characteristics of the treatment environment. In A. F. Wessen (Ed.), *The psychiatric hospital as a social system.* Springfield, Ill.: Thomas, 1964.

Jackson, J. Factors of the treatment environment. *Archives of General Psychiatry*, 1969, **21**, 39–45.

Janicki, M. P. Personal growth and community residence environments: A review. In C. Haywood & J. R. Newborough (Eds.), *Living environments for developmentally retarded persons.* Baltimore, Md.: University Park Press, 1981.

Joiner, L. M., & Krantz, G. C. (Eds.) *Assessment of behavioral competence of developmentally disabled individuals: The MDPS*, Minneapolis, Minn.: University of Minnesota, 1978.

Jones, W. E. The communitization process. *Western Massachusetts Mental Health Training News*, 1977, **1**, 1.

Kerr, S. Substitutes for leadership: Some implications for organizational design. *Organization and Administrative Services*, 1977, **8**, 135–153.

Kerr, S., & Jermier, J. Substitutes for leadership: Their meaning and measurement. *Organizational Behavior and Human Performance*, 1978, **22**, 375–403.

King, R. D., & Raynes, N. V. An operational measure of inmate management in residential institutions. *Social Science and Medicine*, 1968, **2**, 41–53.

King, R. D., & Raynes, N. V. Patterns of institutional care for the severely subnormal. *American Journal of Mental Deficiency*, 1967, **72**, 700–709.

King, R. D., Raynes, S. V., & Tizard, J. *Patterns of residential care: Sociological studies in institutions for handicapped children.* London: Routledge & Kegan Paul, 1971.

Kiresuk, T. The role of evaluation in managing human service systems. In P. Sanofsky (Ed.), *Evaluating program effectiveness: The administrator's dilemma*, Watertown, Mass.: Social Planning Services, 1979.

Lakin, K. C., Bruininks, R. H. *Occupational stability of direct care staff of residential facilities for mentally retarded people* (Project Report No. 14) Minneapolis, Minn.: Department of Psycho-educational Studies, University of Minnesota, 1981.

Lakin, K. C., Bruininks, R. H., & Sigford, B. B. Deinstitutionalization and community adjustment: A summary of research and issues. In R. H. Bruininks, C. E. Meyers, B. B. Sigford, & K. C. Lakin (Eds.), *Deinstitutionalization and community adjustment of mentally retarded people.* Washington, D.C.: American Association on Mental Deficiency, 1981.

Lambert, N. M., & Nicoll, R. C. Dimensions of adaptive behavior of retarded and nonretarded public-school children. *American Journal of Mental Deficiency*, 1976, **81**, 135–146.

Landesman-Dwyer, S., Berkson, G., & Romer, D. Affiliation and friendship of mentally retarded residents in group homes. *American Journal of Mental Deficiency*, 1979, **83**, 571–580.

Landesman-Dwyer, S., Sackett, G. P., & Kleinman, J. S. Relationship of size to resident and staff behavior in small community residences. *American Journal of Mental Deficiency*, 1980, **85**, 6–17.

Landesman-Dwyer, S., Schuckit, J. J., Keller, L. S., & Brown, T. R. A prospective study of client needs relative to community placement. In P. Mittler & J. deJong (Eds.), *Research to practice in mental retardation: Care and intervention*, Baltimore, Md.: University Park Press, 1977.

Lett, M. Use of the behavior characteristics progression scale in Texas. In P. Sanofsky (Ed.), *Evaluating program effectiveness: The administrator's dilemma.* Watertown, Mass.: Social Planning Services, 1979.

Leva, R. A. Relationship among the self-direction, responsibility, and socialization domains of the adaptive behavior scale. *American Journal of Mental Deficiency*, 1976, **81**, 297–299.

Likert, R. *The human organization.* New York: McGraw-Hill, 1966.

Likert, R., & Willets, J. M. *Morale and agency management.* Volume 1. Morale: the mainspring of management. Hartford, Conn.: Life Insurance Sales Research Bureau, 1940.

Locke, E. The nature and causes of job satisfaction. In M. Dunnette (Ed.), *Handbook of industrial and organizational psychology.* Chicago, Ill.: Rand McNally, 1976.

Lounsburg, K. R. Exploratory investigation of the ability of attendants to plan their own training program. *American Journal of Mental Deficiency*, 1976, **80**, 446–453.

Lubin, R. A., Schwartz, A. A., Zigman, W. B., & Janicki, M. P. Community acceptance of residential programs for developmentally disabled persons. *Applied Research in Mental Retardation*, 1982, **3**, 191–200.

MacEachron, A. E., & Driscoll, J. W. *Organizational redesign of physical structure, quality of work life, and performance: A field experiment in the human services.* Hiller School Working Paper, Waltham, Mass.: Brandeis University, 1981.

Magni, T. *Behavior development survey user's manual*, Pomona, Calif.: Individualized Data Base, 1979 (draft version).

Malone, D. R., & Christian, W. P. Adaptive behavior scale as a screening measure for special-education placement. *American Journal of Mental Deficiency*, 1975, **79**, 367–371.

Mayeda, T. The use of client data in program planning and analysis. In P. Sanofsky (Ed.), *Evaluating program effectiveness: The administrator's dilemma.* Watertown, Mass.: Social Planning Services, 1979.

McCormick, M., Balla, D., & Zigler, E. Resident-care practices in institutions for retarded persons: A cross-institutional, cross-cultural study. *American Journal of Mental Deficiency*, 1975, **80**, 1–17.

McDevitt, S. C., & Rosen, M. Adaptive behavior scale. Part II: A cautionary note and suggestions for revisions. *American Journal of Mental Deficiency*, 1977, **82**, 210–211.

McLain, R. E., Silverstein, A. B., Hubbell, M., & Brownlee, L. The characterization of residential environments within a hospital for the mentally retarded. *Mental Retardation*, 1975, **13**, 24–27.

McLain, R. E., Silverstein, A. B., Hubbell, M., & Brownlee, L. Comparison of the residential environment of a state hospital for retarded clients with those of various types of community facilities. *Journal of Community Psychology*, 1977, **5**, 282–289.

Millham, J., Chilcutt, J., & Atkinson, B. Comparability of naturalistic and controlled assessment of adaptive behavior. *Mental Retardation*, 1978, **83**, 52–59.

Mintzberg, H. *The nature of managerial work.* New York: Harper & Row, 1973.

Moen, M. G., & Aanes, D. Eclipse of the family group home concept. *Mental Retardation*, 1979, **17**, 17–19.

Moos, R. Assessment of the psychosocial environments of community-oriented psychiatric treatment programs. *Journal of Abnormal Psychology*, 1972, **79**, 9–18.

Moos, R. H. Conceptualizations of human environments. *American Psychologist*, 1973, **28**, 652–655.

Mueller, B. J., & Porter, R. Placement of adult retardates from state institutions in community care facilities. *Community Mental Health Journal*, 1969, **5**, 289–294.

Muzzia, T. C., & Burris, C. T. *Functional limitations: A state of the art review.* Falls Church, Va.: Indices, Inc., 1979.

National Association of Private Facilities for the Mentally Retarded. Study evaluates community integration of residents, *Links*, July, 1979.

Nihira, K. Factorial dimensions of adaptive behavior in adult retardates. *American Journal of Mental Deficiency*, 1969, **73**, 868–878.

Nihira, K., Foster, R., Shellhaas, M., & Leland, H. *AAMD adaptive behavior scale, 1974 revision.* Washington, D.C.: American Association on Mental Deficiency, 1974.

Nihira, K. Dimensions of adaptive behavior in institutionalized mentally retarded children and adults: Developmental perspective. *American Journal of Mental Deficiency*, 1976, **81**, 215–216.

O'Connor, G., & Sitkei, E. G. Study of a new frontier in community services. *Mental Retardation*, 1975, **13**, 35–38.

Office of Mental Health, *Community housing evaluation checklist (CHEC).* Albany, N.Y.: NYSOMH, 1978.

Pagel, S., & Whitling, C. Readmissions to a state hospital for mentally retarded persons: Reasons for community placement failure. *Mental Retardation*, 1978, **16**, 164–166.

Pankratz, L. Assessing the psychosocial environment of halfway houses for the retarded. *Community Mental Health Journal*, 1975, **11**, 341–345.

Paulson, S. R. Causal analysis of inter-organizational relations: An axiomatic theory revisited. *Administrative Science Quarterly*, 1974, **19**, 319–337.

Pennings, J. M. Dimensions of organizational influence and their effectiveness correlates. *Administrative Science Quarterly*, 1976, **21**, 688–699.

Pennsylvania Department of Public Welfare, *Pennsylvania PASS work book.* Philadelphia, Pa.: PDPW, 1976.

Polivka, C. H., Marvin, W. E., Brown, J. L., & Polivka, L. J. Selected characteristics, services and movement of group home residents. *Mental Retardation*, 1979, **17**, 227–230.

Pratt, M., Bumstead, D., & Raynes, N. Attendant staff speech to the mentally retarded: Language use as a measure of the quality of care. *Journal of Child Psychology and Psychiatry*, 1976, **17**, 133–143.

Pratt, M. W., Luszcz, M. A., & Brown, M. E. Measuring dimensions of quality of care in small community residences. *American Journal of Mental Deficiency*, 1980, **85**, 188–194.

Pratt, M. W., Raynes, N. V., & Roses, S. Organizational characteristics and their relationship to the quality of care. In P. Mittler & J. deJong (Eds.), *Research to practice in mental retardation: Care and intervention*. Baltimore, Md.: University Park Press, 1977.

Rabinowitz, S., & Hall, D. T. Organizational research on job involvement. *Psychological Bulletin*, 1977, **84**, 265–288.

Raynes, N. V., Pratt, M. W., & Roses, S. Aides' involvement in decision-making and the quality of care in institutional settings. *American Journal of Mental Deficiency*, 1977, **81**, 570–577.

Robinson, N. M. Introduction: Observational studies of behavior in community settings. In G. P. Sackett (Ed.), *Observing behavior, Volume I: Theory and applications in mental retardation*. Baltimore, Md.: University Park Press, 1978.

Roos, S. The future of residential services for the mentally retarded in the United States: A delphi study. *Mental Retardation*, 1978, **16**, 355–356.

Rosen, M., Floor, L., & Baxter, D. Prediction of community adjustment: A failure at cross-validation. *American Journal of Mental Deficiency*, 1972, **77**, 111–112.

Rosenbaum, L. A. The creation of a behavioral taxonomy. In G. P. Sackett (Ed.), *Observing behavior, Volume II: Data collection and analysis methods*. Baltimore, Md.: University Park Press, 1978.

Rowitz, L. The importance of client/program impact measures in evaluation design. In P. Sanofsky (Ed.), *Evaluating program effectiveness: The administrator's dilemma*. Watertown, Mass.: Social Planning Services, 1979.

Sackett, G. P., Ruppenthal, G. C., & Gluck, J. An overview of methodological and statistical problems in observational research. In G. P. Sackett (Ed.), *Observing behavior, Volume II: Data collection and analysis methods*. Baltimore, Md.: University Park Press, 1978.

Sarata, B. P. V. Employee satisfactions in agencies serving retarded persons. *American Journal of Mental Deficiency*, 1974, **79**, 434–442.

Sarata, B. P. V. Job characteristics, work satisfactions, and task involvement as correlates of service delivery strategies. *American Journal of Community Psychology*, 1977, **5**, 99–109.

Savage, V. T., Novak, A. R., & Heal, L. W. Generic services for developmentally disabled citizens. In A. R. Novak and L. W. Heal (Eds.), *Integration of developmentally disabled individuals into the community*. Baltimore, Md.: Paul H. Brooks, 1980.

Schalock, R. L., & Harper, R. S. A systems approach to community living skills training. In R. H. Bruininks, C. E. Meyers, B. B. Sigford, & K. C. Lakin (Eds.), *Deinstitutionalization and community adjustment of mentally retarded people*. Washington, D.C.: American Association on Mental Deficiency, 1981.

Schalock, R. L., Harper, R. S., & Genung, T. Community integration of mentally retarded adults: Community placement and program success. *American Journal of Mental Deficiency*, 1981, **85**, 478–488.

Scheerenberger, R. C. *Public residential services for the mentally retarded*, Madison, Wis.: National Association of Superintendents of Public Residential Facilities for the Mentally Retarded, Central Wisconsin Center for the Developmentally Disabled, 1978.

Scheerenberger, R. C., & Felsenthal, D. Community settings for mentally retarded persons. *Mental Retardation*, 1977, **15**, 3–7.

Schinke, S., & Wong, S. Evaluation of staff training in group homes for retarded persons. *American Journal of Mental Deficiency*, 1977, **82**, 130–136.

Schroeder, S. R., & Henes, C. Assessment of progress of institutionalized and deinstitutionalized retarded adults: A matched-control comparison. *Mental Retardation*, 1978, **16**, 147–148.

Schroeder, S. R., Mulick, J. A., & Schroeder, C. S. Management of severe behavior problems of the retarded. In N. R. Ellis (Ed.), *Handbook of mental deficiency, psychological theory and research*. (2nd edition) Hillsdale, N.J.: Lawrence Erlbaum, 1979, pp. 341–366.

Seltzer, G. B. Community residential adjustment: The relationship among environment, performance, and satisfaction. *American Journal of Mental Deficiency*, 1981, **85**, 624–630.

Seltzer, G. B., & Seltzer, M. M. *The community adjustment scale*. Cambridge, Mass.: Educational Projects, 1976.

Seltzer, M. M., & Seltzer, G. B. Community living: Accommodations and vocations. In P. Mittler (Ed.), *Research to practice in mental retardation: Care and intervention*. Baltimore, Md.: University Park Press, 1977.

Siegel, A. L., & Ruh, R. A. Job involvement, participation in decision-making, personal background and job behavior. *Organizational Behavior and Human Performance*, 1973, **9**, 318–327.

Silverstein, A. B., McLain, R. E., Hubbell, M., & Brownlee, L. Characteristics of the treatment environment: A factor analytic study. *Educational and Psychological Measurement*, 1977, **37**, 367–371.

Sitkei, E. G. After group home living—what alternatives? Results of a two-year mobility follow up study. *Mental Retardation*, 1980, **18**, 9–14.

Skeels, H. M., & Dye, H. B. A study of the effects of differential stimulation on mentally retarded children. *Proceedings of the American Association on Mental Deficiency*, 1939, **44**, 114–136.

Smith, P. C., Kendall, L. M., & Hulin, C. L. *The measurement of satisfaction in work and retirement*. Chicago, Ill.: Rand McNally and Co., 1969.

Srole, L. Social integration and certain corollaries: An exploratory study. *American Sociological Review*, 1956, **21**, 709–716.

Stelmach, J., Postma, J., Goldstein, S., & Shepard, K. F. Selected factors influencing job satisfaction of attendants of physically disabled adults. *Rehabilitation Literature*, **42**, 1981, 130–137.

Stodgill, R. M. *Handbook of leadership: A survey of theory and research*. New York: The Free Press, 1974.

Sundberg, N. D., Snowden, L. R., & Reynolds, W. M. Toward assessment of personal competence and incompetence in life situations. *Annual Review of Psychology*, **29**, 1978, 179–221.

Sutter, P., Mayeda, T., Call, T., Yanagi, G., & Yee, S. Comparison of successful and unsuccessful community-placed mentally retarded persons. *American Journal of Mental Deficiency*, 1980, **85**, 262–267.

Tannenbaum, A. S. *Control in organizations.* New York: McGraw-Hill, 1968.

Tannenbaum, A. S., Kavcic, B., Rosner, M., Vianellow, M., & Wieser, G. *Hierarchy in organizations.* San Francisco, Calif.: Jossey-Bass Publishers, 1974.

Tannenbaum, R., & Masarik, F. Participation by subordinates in the managerial decision-making process. *Canadian Journal of Economics and Political Science*, 1950, **16**, 408–418.

Taylor, J. R. A comparison of the adaptive behavior of retarded individuals successfully and unsuccessfully placed in group living homes. *Education and Training of the Mentally Retarded*, February, 1976, 56–64.

Taylor, R. L., Warren, S. A., & Slocumb, P. R. Categorizing behavior in terms of severity: Considerations for Part II of the adaptive behavior scale. *American Journal of Mental Deficiency*, 1979, **83**, 411–413.

Tennessee Department of Mental Health and Mental Retardation, *Tennessee goal domain dictionary*, Nashville, Tenn.: TDMHMR, 1978.

Throne, J. M. Deinstitutionalization: Two wide a swath. *Mental Retardation*, 1979, **17**, 171–176.

Thurlow, M. L., Bruininks, R. H., Williams, S. M., & Morreau, L. E. *Deinstitutionalization and residential services: A literature survey.* Minneapolis, Minn.: University of Minnesota Information and Technical Assistance Project on Deinstitutionalization, 1978.

Toedter, A. Operation pinpoint in California. In P. Sanofsky (Ed.), *Evaluating program effectiveness: The administrator's dilemma.* Watertown, Mass.: Social Planning Services, 1979.

Vogel, W., Kun, K. J., & Meshorer, E. Effects of environmental enrichment and environmental deprivation on cognitive functioning in institutionalized retardates. *Journal of Consulting and Clinical Psychology*, 1967, **31**, 570.

Vogel, W., Kun, K. J., & Meshorer, E. Changes in adaptive behavior in institutionalized retardates in response to environmental enrichment or deprivation. *Journal of Consulting and Clinical Psychology*, 1968, **32**, 76–82.

Vogel, W., Kun, K. J., & Meshorer, E. Determinants of institutional release and prognosis in mental retardates. *Journal of Abnormal Psychology*, 1969, **74**, 685–692.

Vogel, W., Kun, K. J., Meshorer, E., Broverman, D. M., & Klaiber, E. L. The behavioral significance of EEG abnormality in mental defectives. *American Journal of Mental Deficiency*, 1969, **74**, 62–68.

VORT, *Behavior characteristics progression.* Palo Alto, Calif.: VORT Corporation, 1973.

Vroom, V. H. *Work and motivation.* New York: John Wiley & Sons, 1964.

Walls, R. T., & Werner, T. J. Vocational behavior checklists. *Mental Retardation*, 1977, **15**, 30–35.

Walls, R. T., Werner, T. J., & Bacon, A. *Behavior checklists.* Morgantown, W. Va.: Research and Training Center, West Virginia University, 1976.

Walls, R. T., Werner, T. J., Bacon, A., & Zane, T. Behavior checklists. In J. D. Cone & R. P. Hawkins (Eds.), *Behavioral assessment: New directions in clinical psychology.* New York: Brunner-Mazel, 1977.

Webb, R. C., & Koller, J. R. Effects of sensorimotor training on intellectual and adaptive skills of profoundly retarded adults. *American Journal of Mental Deficiency*, 1979, **83**, 490–496.

Weiss, C., & Flynn, R. J. *A normalization and development instrument.* Sacramento, Calif.: Department of Developmental Services, 1980.

White, J. K., & Ruh, R. A. Effects of personal values on the relationship between participation and job attitudes. *Administrative Science Quarterly*, 1973, **18**, 506–514.

Whorton, J. E., & Algozzine, R. F. A comparison of intellectual, achievement, and adaptive behavior levels for students who are mildly retarded. *Mental Retardation*, 1978, **16**, 320.

Windle, C. D., Stewart, E., & Brown, S. Reasons for community failure of released patients. *American Journal of Mental Deficiency*, 1961, **66**, 213–217.

Windmiller, M. An effective use of the public school version of the AAMD ABS. *Mental Retardation*, 1977, **15**, 42–45.

Wolfensberger, W. Twenty predictions about the future of residential services in mental retardation. *Mental Retardation*, 1969, **7**, 51–54.

Wolfensberger, W. Will there always be an institution? I: The impact of epidemiological trends. *Mental Retardation*, 1971, **9**, 14–20.(a)

Wolfensberger, W. Will there always be an institution? II: The impact of new service models. *Mental Retardation*, 1971, **9**, 31–38.(b)

Wolfensberger, W., & Glenn, L. *Pass 3. A method for the quantitative evaluation of human services.* Toronto: National Institute on Mental Retardation, 1975.(a)

Wolfensberger, W., & Glenn, L. *Pass 3: A method for the quantitative evaluation of human services,* (handbook, 3rd ed.). Toronto: National Institute on Mental Retardation, 1975.(b)

Wolfson, I. N. Adjustment of institutionalized mildly retarded patients twenty years after return to the community. *Mental Retardation*, 1970, **8**, 20–23.

Wyngaarden, M., Freedman, R., & Gollay, E. *Descriptive data on the community experience of deinstitutionalized mentally retarded persons.* Vol. IV of a study of the community adjustment of deinstitutionalized mentally retarded persons. Contract No. 0EC-0-74–9183, U.S. Office of Education. Cambridge, Mass.: Abt Associates, Inc., 1976.

Yaron, A. Program evaluation: The Colorado model. In P. Sanofsky (Ed.), *Evaluating program effectiveness: The administrator's dilemma.* Watertown, Mass.: Social Planning Services, 1979.

Zigler, E. The retarded child as a whole person. In H. E. Adams & W. K. Boardman (Eds.), *Advances in experimental clinical psychology.* (Vol. I) New York: Pergamon Press, 1971.

Zigler, E., & Balla, D. A. Developmental course of responsiveness to social reinforcement in normal children and institutionalized retarded children. *Developmental Psychology*, 1972, **6**, 66–73.

Zigler, E., & Balla, D. A. Motivational factors in the performance of the retarded. In R. Koch & J. C. Dobson (Eds.), *The mentally retarded child and his family: A multidisciplinary handbook.* (2nd ed.) New York: Brunner-Mazel, 1976.

Zigler, E., & Balla, D. A. Impact of institutional experience in the behavior and development of retarded persons. *American Journal of Mental Deficiency*, 1979, **82**, 1–11.

Zigler, E., Balla, D., & Butterfield, E. C. A longitudinal

investigation of the relationship between preinstitutional social deprivation and social motivation in institutionalized retardates. *Journal of Personality and Social Psychology,* 1968, **10,** 437–445.

Zigler, E., Butterfield, E. C., & Capobianco, F. Institutionalization and the effectiveness of social reinforcement: A five- and eight-year follow-up study. *Developmental Psychology,* 1970, **3,** 255–263.

Zigler, E., & Williams, J. Institutionalization and the effectiveness of social reinforcement: A three-year follow-up study. *Journal of Abnormal and Social Psychology,* 1963, **66,** 197–205.

4 MAINSTREAMING MENTALLY RETARDED CHILDREN

Jay Gottlieb,
Mark Alter, and
Barbara W. Gottlieb

There is little doubt that one of the major elements of contemporary special education involves mainstreaming handicapped learners. Ever since Dunn (1968) questioned the justifiability of self-contained classes for educable mentally retarded (EMR) pupils, there has been an accelerating movement to avoid placing handicapped learners in self-contained classes. At this time, however, we have few reliable data on the effectiveness of mainstreamed programs. There are a number of reasons for this state of affairs, some of which we hope to elaborate in this chapter. The general outline followed involves an introductory section in which we present some of the problems in defining mainstreaming, especially as they relate to the distinction between least restrictive environment and mainstreaming. Then, we examine the impact of changing definitions of educable mental retardation as it affects the extent to which EMR children are being mainstreamed. Next, we review some representative data on the effects of mainstreaming EMR children. Finally, we discuss several issues pertinent to the mainstreaming of severely mentally retarded children.

Definitional Issues in Mainstreaming

As with many aspects of educational programming, mainstreaming may be viewed from different perspectives: a practical perspective—how it is actually implemented by the schools, or an idealized perspective—how it should or could be done. From a practical orientation, school personnel define mainstreaming as placement of handicapped children in regular classrooms for a portion of the school day. Although the exact percentage of time that EMR children must spend in regular classes varies, an accepted figure is at least 50% (Semmel, Gottlieb, & Robinson, 1979). It does not matter whether the mainstreamed time occurs for academic or nonacademic activities, whether the mainstreamed children have specific educational objectives established for the time they attend regular-education programs, or whether there are clearly established criteria against which their academic growth may be judged. The mere placement of EMR children in a regular-education program in contact with nonhandicapped peers for an arbitrary fixed minimum amount of time is defined by the schools as mainstreaming. The intensive emphasis on the placement of handicapped children in contact with nonhandicapped peers is the primary indication that, from a practical perspective, mainstreaming has focused almost exclusively on administrative and process issues. The content of the educational program to which EMR children should be exposed while they are in the mainstream and the specialized methods that may be required to deliver the content have seldom been a major consideration either in the professional literature or in legal decrees (e.g., *Jose P. v. Ambach*, 1979).

The idealized version of mainstreaming departs dramatically from the practical definition. The most idealized definition of mainstreaming that appears was offered by Kaufman, Gottlieb, Agard, and Kukic (1975), who defined it as "the temporal, instructional, and social integration of eligible exceptional children with normal peers, based on an ongoing, individually determined, educational planning and programming process . . . [that] requires clarification of responsibility among regular and special education administrative, instructional, and supportive personnel" (p. 4).

The intent of this definition was to indicate that mainstreaming involves more than the simple placement of handicapped children in regular-education programs; it also involves the development of an instructional plan that serves not only to identify handicapped children's academic needs, but also indicates the curriculum and teaching methods that are necessary for them to achieve stated objectives. Kaufman et al. (1975) were concerned with the need to provide mainstreamed handicapped children, especially EMR children, with appropriate educational content that could be provided in regular classrooms and that would not be completely dissonant with the educational content engaged in by the nonretarded classmates. The definition deliberately pointed out the necessity of collaboration between regular- and special-education personnel in order to stress the importance of identifying and tracking the education that EMR children receive during the time they spend in regular-education settings.

It is well recognized that the term mainstreaming does not appear in Public Law 94-142; the term that is used is "least restrictive environment" (LRE). Section 612(5)(B) of this law requires assurances that to the maximum extent appropriate handicapped children will be educated with their nonhandicapped peers. Does mainstreaming differ from LRE? The intent of the law is that the educational provisions offered to handicapped children should be appropriate and that they should be provided in the least restrictive environment insofar as they maximize opportunities for contact with nonhandicapped children. Thus, two concerns must be addressed when planning a least restrictive environment: The placement must be appropriate *and* contact with nonhandicapped peers must be available. Presumably, if it can be demonstrated that contact with nonhandicapped peers is not appropriate, alternative placements would be desirable.

A major obstacle preventing schools from providing handicapped children with the least restrictive environment has been in establishing criteria by which the appropriateness of the environment may be determined. What do we mean when we speak of an appropriate placement? Do we mean appropriate insofar as it offers the mentally retarded child opportunities to interact with nonhandicapped peers? Do we mean that it is appropriate insofar as it maximizes opportunities for academic achievement? For improved social behavior? Do we mean that it maximizes opportunities for the child to function normally only during his school career, or are we also concerned with enabling the child to lead an independent life as an adult? Ideally, we would like to achieve all of these objectives. However, as we shall indicate in a later section, evidence to date fails to demonstrate that mainstreamed environments will accomplish all of these objectives.

What, if any, are the distinctions between the terms *mainstreaming* and *least restrictive environment*? The answer depends upon which definition of mainstreaming we select. If the practical definition is chosen with mainstreaming equated with contact with nonhandicapped peers, mainstreaming and LRE differ appreciably. The practical version of mainstreaming fails to consider the appropriateness of the placement, as is attested to by available evidence, which indicates that the sheer placement of handicapped children with nonhandicapped peers has little impact on the handicapped child's social acceptance (Gottlieb, Semmel, & Veldman, 1978), other aspects of social adjustment (Gottlieb & Baker, 1975) or on academic achievement (Gottlieb et al., 1978). On the other hand, if we select the idealized version of the definition presented earlier, then mainstreaming is more nearly equivalent to a least restrictive environment. When MacMillan and Semmel (1977) questioned whether any existing mainstreaming program fulfills the criteria in the idealized definition, they were questioning at the same time our ability to develop least restrictive environments.

Obviously, the appropriateness of an environment is largely dependent upon the children who are educated in that environment. In many respects, it is impossible to speak of a least restrictive environment or a mainstreamed environment without knowing the characteristics of children who comprise the mainstreamed population. As we shall indicate, the population of mentally retarded children who are being mainstreamed has undergone substantial changes during the past few years; a factor further complicating our efforts to develop appropriate environments.

Who Is Mainstreamed?

When we speak of the fact that federal and state legislation mandates that all handicapped children should be given opportunities to interact with non-handicapped peers, it is of interest to examine the characteristics of children who are given these opportunities. As a general rule, we might expect that the more mildly mentally retarded a child is, the more likely (s)he is to be mainstreamed. Although we are not aware of any research that has examined this issue, we are well aware that within the range of mild mental retardation, decisions as to who is best mainstreamed are extremely complex (MacMillan, Meyers, & Morrison, 1980).

It is well known that the definition of mild mental retardation has changed over the past several years (Grossman, 1977). Whereas some years earlier a defining feature of mental retardation was an IQ score of one standard deviation below the mean, an IQ score of two standard deviations is now required. The role of IQ becomes more problematic when we consider that classification and placement issues within special education are governed primarily by state laws that may or may not have changed through the years.

It is equally well known that a major reason for the definitional changes in mental retardation was the fact that minority group members were disproportionately represented in classes for EMR children. The resulting litigation has resulted in a diminished role for the IQ test within the jurisdiction where the case was tried (*Larry P. v. Riles*, 1979). As a result of the continued disfavor with IQ tests, especially for minority group children, there has been a discernable trend to classify many minority group children as learning disabled rather than the more disfavored classification of mentally retarded (Tucker, 1980). Consequently, many children who previously would have been classified as mentally retarded are now being classified as learning disabled, a fact stated somewhat differently by Ysseldyke et al. (1979), who reported that as many as 40% of learning disabled children are being misclassified.

There is conceptual confusion between the categories of educable mental retardation and learning disabilities (LD). Therefore, the recent literature in school psychology chronicling a host of errors in the entire diagnostic and placement process casts an even greater pall over the appropriateness of decisions to mainstream or not to mainstream. To illustrate, Bennett (1980) questioned the competence of diagnosticians to classify children correctly. Bennett (1980) found that school psychologists were deficient in their knowledge of basic principles of psychological and educational measurement. The errors inherent in the identification of children as handicapped are perhaps nowhere better illustrated than a study by Miller and Chansky (1974).

Miller and Chansky (1974) scored 64 psychologists' ratings of a bogus WISC protocol. All subjects were experienced psychologists who were members of the American Psychological Association. Analysis of the ratings revealed a range of 78 to 95 in psychologists' scorings of the same protocol. Furthermore, the standard deviation of the psychologists' responses exceeded the standard error of the test. The range in scores observed must be considered in light of the fact that additional sources of error that occur during actual test administrations were absent from the scores. That is, because the authors asked their raters to score already completed protocols, errors that occur during testing, such as children's variations in responses from time to time, did not enter into the score. Furthermore, because the psychologists who participated in this study were all volunteers, it is likely that those who did not volunteer (68%) may not have been as proficient as those who did, i.e., psychologists who are uncertain of their ability may not be likely to volunteer and expose their deficiencies.

In another investigation concerning psychologists' ability to score WISC protocols accurately, Oakland, Lee, and Axelrad (1975) asked psychologists to score three real protocols taken from the files of one of the investigators. Each protocol represented a child of different ability—low, medium, and high. A total of 94 psychologists who were members of the divisions of educational and/or school psychology of the American Psychological Association returned the protocols scores (out of a total of 400 who were asked to score them). As was the case with the investigation by Miller and Chansky (1974), Oakland et al. (1975) found that the standard deviation of the scores exceeded the standard error of the test, at least on the verbal IQ score. Mechanical errors, such as mistakes in arithmetic, and judgmental errors, such as not giving proper credit for a response, were the two most often made mistakes in both investigations.

The data reported by Miller and Chansky (1974) and Oakland et al. (1975) must be interpreted in light of the fact that the respondents were not under any time pressures to score the test protocols. It is of interest to speculate how much of an increase in errors could occur when severe time pressures, which result from heavy work loads, require psychologists to complete a maximum number of protocols in a minimum amount of time.

The difficulties inherent in the identification of educable mentally retarded children may also be illustrated somewhat differently. In recent years, the adaptive behavior component of the definition of mental retardation has been stressed more heavily than in the past. That is, in order for a child to be classified as mentally retarded not only must he/she obtain a low IQ score, but in addition the child must possess deficits in adaptive behavior. Although adaptive behavior difficiencies have been included in the definition of mental retardation for a considerable period of time, it was seldom used in school related contexts, primarily because few reliable or valid instruments were available. Now that new adaptive behavior scales are available, school systems contend, with a certain legitimacy, that classification of children as mentally retarded is not made solely on the basis of IQ scores; they claim that a wide variety of inputs are used including IQ, adaptive behavior, social and developmental histories, and so forth. However, evidence exists suggesting that despite the compilation of a wide assortment of academic, social, and behavioral indices of children's performance, school systems continue to emphasize the IQ score as the overriding determinant of a child's eventual classification and placement (Berk, Bridges, & Shih, 1981). That is, despite the "advances" made in developing a wider array of indices on which to base a classification decision of mental retardation, practitioners still rely most heavily on the IQ test score.

The definitional problems with mental retardation and its substitution on many occasions by the diagnosis of learning disabilities, could explain why relatively few children diagnosed by the schools as mentally retarded are actually mainstreamed for activities other than lunch or assembly. A survey conducted in 1978 in northern Illinois indicated that only about three percent of EMR children were mainstreamed into regular classrooms. The same survey indicated that approximately 50% of learning disabled children were mainstreamed, with the remaining half attending self-contained classrooms. It is interesting to speculate as to the characteristics of learning disabled children who remain in self-contained classrooms. Are they the same children who might have been labeled as educable mentally retarded several years ago?

The importance of the impact of changing definitions of educable mental retardation was raised recently by MacMillan and Borthwick (1980), who also reported that few educable mentally retarded pupils are being mainstreamed, according to teacher reports. The relatively low functioning nature of children who are presently identified as EMR may preclude their being mainstreamed into regular education programs. In their investigation, MacMillan and Borthwick (1980)

reported that 7.3% of their EMR sample was mainstreamed for academic activities.

We are raising the issue of the characteristics of children who attend the mainstream, because it is a critical element in our understanding of mainstreaming effects. The history of "efficacy" research in mental retardation is one of poor design, in large part because of a subject selection bias in which children who attended regular class programs were different from those who were educated in self-contained special classes. To the extent that studies of mainstreaming employ subjects who systematically differ across treatment conditions, it is impossible to offer any meaningful statements about treatment effects. Indeed, one of the major cautions in the literature on mainstreaming is that we must scrutinize carefully the description of subjects before we draw any conclusions.

In summary, the mainstreaming of mentally retarded children is fraught with difficulties. Not only is there confusion as to how a child is to be defined by the schools as mentally retarded there is the further problem of how to decide how much time a child should spend in the mainstream. In Project PRIME, a large-scale study of mainstreaming in Texas, analyses of that very substantial data base failed to detect any significant correlations between characteristics of the mainstreamed child and the amount of time for which s/he was mainstreamed (Kaufman, Agard, & Semmel, in press). In fact, the only consistent correlate of amount of time mainstreamed was a school district policy, a policy that appeared to be totally unrelated to children's measured abilities.

We now turn to the core issue of this paper, the review of mainstreaming effects. As has been done before, the review is organized around two major effects: (1) academic achievement and (2) psychological and social adjustment.

Research on Mainstreaming Effects

Academic Achievement

Without doubt, the majority of studies that have compared the performance of handicapped children in special and regular classes have focused on EMR children. To illustrate, prior to the mainstreaming movement in the early 1970's, 10 studies appeared in the professional literature in which the academic achievement and social adjustment of EMR children in self-contained classes was compared with that of EMR children who attended regular classes on a full-time basis. Beginning with Bennett's investigation in 1932 and ending with the most methodologically sophisticated study by Goldstein, Moss, and Jordan (1965), this series of investigations failed to demonstrate that EMR children who were enrolled in self-contained classes achieved at higher levels than EMR children who remained in regular classes. Five studies in the series found no significant achievement differences (Ainsworth, 1959; Blatt, 1958; Goldstein et al., 1965; Thurstone, 1959; Wrightstone et al., 1959), and five reported achievement differences favoring the regular class program (Bennett, 1932; Cassidy & Stanton, 1959; Elenbogen, 1957; Mullen & Itkin, 1961; Pertsch, 1936). With respect to these studies' findings on social adjustment, Kirk's review (1964) concluded that special classes promoted better social adjustment than regular classes.

The 10 studies cited, collectively referred to as the "efficacy" studies, were largely responsible for the disenchantment with special classes by special educators. The fact that special classes did not promote better achievement gains than regular classes despite smaller class sizes, specially trained teachers, and a higher per-capita cost, was most distressing to those who believed that special education was indeed "special" (Blackman, 1963). The reader is reminded, however, of the criticisms of this research voiced earlier, i.e., that the "deck was stacked" against children in special classes. That five of the 10 studies reported no significant achievement differences could conceivably indicate that differences might have emerged had the subjects been equal prior to the study and/ or had the instrumentation been appropriate to evaluate achievement growth in special classes.

It should be mentioned that of the 10 "efficacy" studies, only the one conducted by Goldstein et al. (1965) randomly assigned pupils to special and regular education settings, thus avoiding the subject selection bias. Results of this investigation revealed that, at the conclusion of the first year, there were significant achievement differences between the two groups that favored the regular class, but that these differences disappeared by the end of the third year, when the two groups exhibited equal achievement scores.

The earlier research on the efficacy of special class placement, when viewed within the constraints of the subject selection biases that existed in every study except the investigation conducted by Goldstein et al. (1965), failed to reveal that special classes fostered improved academic achievement. Attendance in regular classes without any special education assistance whatever was found to result in equal levels of academic achievement by EMR children as full-time attendance in special classes. For this reason, among others, special classes lost favor as a philosophy for special education.

A number of alternative arrangements were advanced in the literature. The major distinction between the alternatives was whether children should attend regular classes and be pulled out of the class to receive their special education support, or whether that support should be provided within the regular classroom. From an empirical viewpoint, the bulk of the research has been conducted on the "pull-out" variety of support, usually in the form of resource room instruction, and we will confine our review to this body of research.

Four studies serve to illustrate the findings with respect to the academic achievement of EMR children. Budoff and Gottlieb (1976) compared the academic achievement of 31 EMR children randomly assigned to special classes and regular classes with resource room support. No differences in academic achievement were reported either two months after the study began or at the end of a full year. Walker (1974) also compared the academic achievement of EMR children who attended either resource room programs or special classes, although she did not randomly assign children to the respective placements. Results of this investigation indicated that the resource room group scored significantly higher in word reading and vocabulary than the special class group, but that there were no significant differences in arithmetic achievement.

A third study in which the special class/resource room comparison was made was conducted by Carrol (1967) on 39 EMR children who were studied in their naturally existing groups, i.e., random assignment was not made. After one year, the investigator reported that the special class group made greater gains on a reading subtest than the resource room children. Finally, Smith and Kennedy (1967) in a random assignment procedure compared a resource room group (45 minutes daily) with a comparable group of EMR children who attended only regular class programming. No significant achievement differences occurred between the two groups.

It is noteworthy that two of the four studies of the effectiveness of resource room programming that were reviewed randomly assigned children to their respective placements. Both studies failed to obtain significant achievement differences, corroborating the results of the Goldstein et al. (1965) efficacy study. Results of the more recent studies could have been anticipated; if placement in regular classes without any special education support yielded the same achievement data as placement in special classes without regular education support, then a mixture of special and regular education should not have differed significantly from either total regular education or total special education.

Why are there no significant achievement differences between EMR children in the different placements? Results of one large-scale study provide one answer to this question.

Kaufman et al. (in press) conducted in-depth observations of 150 special and 400 mainstreamed regular classes for an average of 10 hours each. The data were intriguing in their demonstration of instructional similarities and differences between special and regular classes. For example, the regular class teachers taught in large groups (to the class as a whole) 75.7% of the time. Special class teachers used large group instruction only 44.8% of the time. Conversely, special education teachers provided individual instruction 26.7% of the time, whereas regular class teachers did so only 12.0% of the time. Substantial differences were also observed in the percentage of time that special and regular class teachers allocated to reading instruction. Regular class teachers reported that they spent an average of 16% of the school day on reading instruction. Special class teachers, on the other hand, reported that they spent an average of 27% of the time on reading instruction.

Despite these rather dramatic differences, the kinds of teaching behavior that occurred in special and regular classes were remarkably consistent. Questioning was done by regular and special class teachers 10.7% and 12.2% of the time, respectively. Directing was done 19.3% and 22.6% of the time by regular and special class teachers. Likewise, pupils in regular classes interacted with the teacher for 27.8% of the observations, whereas self-contained class children interacted for 26.5% of the observations. Children in regular and special classes interacted with other pupils 5.3% and 5.2% of the time respectively.

The Kaufman et al. (in press) data indicate strongly that, with the exception of the grouping arrangements that are used for instruction, there are few differences between the types of education offered in regular and special classes. It is not surprising, therefore, that research has uniformly failed to indicate achievement differences between EMR pupils in special and regular classes (Semmel et al., 1979); there are few, if any, meaningful instructional differences.

Social Adjustment

Although the vast majority of resource rooms are designed to provide supplemental academic assistance to handicapped learners, more research has been conducted on their effectiveness in improving social adjustment than in improving academic achievement. Of the studies of handicapped children's social adjustment, the majority focus on sociometric status or the extent to which handicapped children are liked or rejected by their peer group. A smaller number of adjustment studies focus on the children's classroom behavior. Still other studies are concerned with hand-

icapped children's self-concept in different class placement.

SOCIOMETRIC STATUS OF MENTALLY RETARDED CHILDREN

Historically, one of the main criteria that have been used to assess the adjustment of mentally retarded youngsters has been their sociometric status. The assumption underlying the use of sociometric analysis is that all children, including mentally retarded children, have a strong need to be liked and accepted by others. To the extent that the individuals are not accepted, or perceive that they are not accepted, adjustment problems could be anticipated.

The literature on the sociometric acceptance of mainstreamed EMR children was built upon previous sociometric research on EMR children who attended regular classes on a full-time basis. The first such investigation was conducted by Johnson (1950), who found that EMR children (more precisely, children whose IQ scores were below 70) were rejected significantly more often and accepted significantly less often than their nonretarded classmates. Similar results were found by others as well (Baldwin, 1958; Heber, 1956; Johnson & Kirk, 1950). Despite the consistency of early data indicating that EMR children were socially rejected far more often in regular classes than nonretarded children were rejected, and the availability of still other data that indicated that EMR children in regular classes were rejected more than EMR children in special classes (Thurstone, 1959), proponents of mainstreaming stated either explicitly (Christoplos & Renz, 1969) or implicitly (Dunn, 1968) that mentally retarded children would be known more and liked better if they were placed in regular classrooms in contact with nonhandicapped peers. The early sociometric research provided clues that perhaps EMR children would be known more in regular classes, but the data were not encouraging that EMR children would also be liked more.

One of the earliest sociometric studies directed toward mainstreamed handicapped pupils was conducted by Goodman, Gottlieb, and Harrison (1972), who compared the sociometric status of elementary-school-age EMR children in regular classes with those who remained in self-contained classes. Results indicated that the mainstreamed children were rejected significantly more often than the segregated children despite the efforts of the principal to mainstream only the most promising children. The findings of Goodman et al. (1972), which were obtained on an upper-middle class sample, were replicated in a subsequent investigation on primarily lower middle-class children

(Gottlieb & Budoff, 1972). The results were replicated once again on an upper-middle class sample, this time with an attitudinal instrument rather than a sociometric scale. Finally, a social choice experiment in which a nonhandicapped child was asked to choose between a mentally retarded or a nonretarded partner as a teammate revealed that the retarded child was almost never chosen regardless of whether s/he was mainstreamed or segregated (Gottlieb & Davis, 1973). The fact that the series of studies mentioned above consistently indicated that mainstreamed placement did nothing to improve EMR children's social acceptance, a finding also reported by Iano (1972), but rather tended to suggest that such children were more rejected socially casts serious doubt on one of the major assumptions underlying the mainstreaming movement: that mainstreaming would promote better acceptance of EMR children (Christoplos & Renz, 1969).

In perhaps the most direct investigation of the relationship between amount of mainstreaming, i.e., amount of contact with nonhandicapped peers, Gottlieb, Semmel, and Veldman (1978) correlated the number of hours weekly for which EMRs were mainstreamed with their social acceptance and social rejection scores. Results indicated that amount of time failed to correlate significantly with either social acceptance or social rejection. Interestingly, other analyses conducted as part of this investigation did not detect any significant correlations between characteristics of EMR children and the amount of time for which they were mainstreamed.

DIRECT OBSERVATION OF HANDICAPPED LEARNERS IN THE MAINSTREAM

Studies that employ direct observation procedures usually concentrate on describing behavior that occurs naturally (i.e., with experimental intervention) in classroom settings. Behaviors that the researcher or the classroom teachers consider to be important are selected for observation. Consequently, this line of research is valid in that selected variables actually measure what they were intended to measure.

The complexity of the findings of mainstreaming effects is typified by direct observational research. To illustrate, it was mentioned earlier that the data consistently indicated that EMR children were sociometrically rejected more than their nonmainstreamed peers. Yet, studies of the classroom behavior of mainstreamed EMR children found them to behave more like that of nonhandicapped children than EMR children in segregated classrooms (Gampel, Gottlieb, &

Harrison, 1974), and that these differences persisted over an entire school year, even when controlling for behavioral differences that occurred prior to the experimental program (Gottlieb, Gampel, & Budoff, 1975). The observational data indicate some of the complexities about conclusions that can be drawn about mainstreaming effects. Despite the fact that the observational data suggest that EMR children in the mainstream behave as their nonretarded peers, previous data reviewed earlier indicate clearly that mainstreamed EMR children are less well accepted than their nonretarded classmates.

Self-concept. Research on mainstreaming has compared the self-concept of mildly handicapped children in resource rooms and special or regular classes. As with a good deal of other research on the effects of mainstreaming, conclusions with respect to self-concept are inconclusive. That is, some research reported no significant differences in EMR children's self-concept as a function of class placement (Budoff & Gottlieb, 1976; Knight, 1967; Walker, 1972), while other studies reported differences favoring self-contained placements (Hoeltke, 1967; Schurr & Brookover, 1967). Still other studies, including one conducted with learning disabled children, reported the most favorable self-concept scores for children who were partially enrolled in self-contained classes and partially enrolled in resource room programs. Regardless of what the outcomes of these studies indicate, however, it should be born in mind that the measures themselves are questionable indices, especially for handicapped children whose lack of verbal skills may at least partially invalidate the measures.

Other areas of adjustment. In a study of 456 EMR children who were integrated into first through sixth grade regular classes, Gottlieb and Baker (1975) examined the relationship between amount of academic integration, children's race, and a variety of socioemotional measures of adjustment. Included among these measures were the child's feelings of social and academic effectiveness, school enthusiasm, attitudes toward selected academic areas, and attitudes towards friends. Results indicated that, overall, the predictive power of the variable percentage of academic integration was very weak. More specifically, with respect to social effectiveness, the more time white children were mainstreamed for academics, the more socially ineffective they felt, as measured by self-report instruments. Chicano and black children, on the other hand, felt more socially effective as they were mainstreamed more for academics. With respect to academic effectiveness, all children perceived themselves to be less effective the more time they spent in regular classes. Yet, as was the case in research cited earlier, the more time children spent mainstreamed for academics, the more they expressed enthusiasm for school.

Mainstreaming Severely and Profoundly Retarded Children

The severely/profoundly handicapped (S/PH) are serving as catalysts for major changes in public education. First, because recognition of their rights to education makes people realize that effective education for all students is and must be a science, not an art, and second, current thinking regarding the definition of the S/PH proposes a restructuring of society's ideas on the whole of service delivery in special education (McDowell & Sontag, 1977). The inclusion of the W/PH within the educational system has redefined education broadly as any endeavor involving the attainment of cognitive, affective, and behavioral improvement. The usual specifics of academic and socio-occupational objectives, while not excluded from the new definition, are no longer delimiting criteria. Any intervention that leads to new and/or improved skills in any aspect of human growth and development is seen as education. Consequently, the traditional narrow conceptualization of the function of the school, of school staffing patterns, and of the school as a structure in the community are broadened. The onus is on the educational system to find handicapped children, to test and classify them educationally, to provide the least restrictive educational setting, to describe, recruit, train, and deploy staff, to designate curriculum and methods of instruction, and to assess all the resultant cognitive, affective, and/or behavioral changes in the students. In other words, regardless of the degree of handicap, the end product of education, and implicitly the objective of education, is to equip all children with the behavioral repertoire that will enable them to participate, if they choose to, in the mainstream of society.

The questions, what is the most appropriate education for a child, and how and what are the "best" ways to manage the child's learning, are not mainstreaming questions. A mainstreaming question is what are the competencies that are *required* by the society to be a functional member of that society. Consequently, with the delineation of societal competencies comes the goals of education. The difference then among children is not what competencies they need to master, but the degree to which they master the competencies. The task of education, more appropriately educators, is to identify the pedagogic factors

that will enable and facilitate a child's acquisition of societal competencies.

There is no doubt whatsoever that the framers of Public Law 94-142 intended that all mentally retarded children, even those who are severely or profoundly retarded, should participate in the "least restrictive environment" appropriate to their needs. It was Senator Hubert Humphrey, one of the major proponents of the law, who indicated that the time had come when we could no longer tolerate the invisibility of the handicapped in America. There is also very little doubt that attitudes toward severely mentally retarded people are essentially negative (e.g., Gottlieb & Siperstein, 1976) and that the inclusion of severely retarded people into the mainstream of the schools is likely to meet with resistance, at least initially.

One of the major needs at the present time is for empirical evidence that the inclusion of severely or profoundly mentally retarded (SPMR) children benefit as well as their nonhandicapped classmates. This was suggested by Brown et al. (1977). Unfortunately, to date there are few published data on the effects of mainstreaming SPMR children, either on themselves or on others.

McCauley, Morris, and Cooper (1978) assessed the attitudes and knowledge of Canadian school personnel toward mainstreaming of handicapped populations. Teachers, administrators and guidance counselors were asked to place 30 children in a seven-step continuum of educational placement on the basis of brief behavioral descriptions. Results indicated that regular elementary education teachers and administrators were the most positive toward integrated placement with support services, whereas special education teachers relied more often on special class placements.

Miller, Miller, and Repp (1978), interviewed representatives of three mental health facilities in Illinois about procedures for determining least restrictive environment, parental involvement in decision making, public school placement, effect of community attitude, public school response and funding considerations, and available programs in schools. The respondents indicated that least restrictive environment is often not implemented because of a lack of cooperation and enthusiasm on the part of public schools. The respondents all indicated that efforts to place students in schools were based primarily on expected community acceptance and not on educational considerations.

Concern about the lack of research on the population of SPMR is a persistent theme of the literature. The paucity of the research base for developing mainstreaming programs was decried by Meyen and Altman (1976), who urged researchers to process available research into usable forms and to focus attention on priority problems of a practical nature in the areas of general curriculum development and of educational programming. They also urged emphasis be removed from classification, organization, and teaching methodology and placed on the development of appropriate skill and concept curricula.

Conclusions

The literature on mainstreaming presents a fairly consistent portrait—that it neither benefits mentally retarded children academically nor socially in comparison with self-contained classes. Whatever results and conclusions emerge from the literature, however, must be interpreted cautiously. Much of the corpus of the research in mental retardation suffers from the systematic bias that results when children are not randomly assigned to their respective treatments. In the absence of random assignment, there is the definite likelihood that children who attend regular classes will be superior to the students who remain in self-contained classes.

At the present time, there is a critical lack of information on the characteristics of regular classrooms into which mentally retarded children should be mainstreamed. Should these classes be homogeneous or heterogeneously grouped with respect to the ability levels of the nonhandicapped classmates? How many EMR children can most profitably be mainstreamed into a single classroom? What role do classroom teachers' attitudes play in the academic and social growth of mainstreamed mentally retarded children? Many statements appear in the literature regarding the importance of teachers' expectations and attitudes; few data are available with respect to the extent to which findings from nonhandicapped children generalize to handicapped pupils who often function at substantially lower levels than their classmates. The safest conclusion of all with respect to the mainstreaming is that at the present we know very little about how to decide which children are to be mainstreamed and into which classes they should be mainstreamed. Until these two questions—at the very least—can be answered, discussions of the virtues or evils of mainstreaming cannot progress beyond the realm of speculation.

References

Ainsworth, S. H. An exploratory study of social and emotional factors in the education of educable mentally retarded children in Georgia public schools. *U.S. Office of Education Cooperative Research Program, Project Number 171.* Athens, Georgia: University of Georgia, 1959.

Baldwin, W. K. The educable mentally retarded child in the regular grades. *Exceptional Children*, 1958, **25**, 106–108, 112.

Bennett, A. *A comparative study of subnormal children in the elementary grades.* New York: Teachers College, Columbia University, Bureau of Publications, 1932.

Bennett, R. Methods for evaluating the performance of school psychologists. *School Psychology Monograph*, 1980, **4**(1), 45–59.

Berk, R. A., Bridges, W. P., & Shih, A. Does IQ really matter? A study of the use of IQ scores for the tracking of the mentally retarded. *American Sociological Review*, 1981, **46**, 58–71.

Blackman, L. S. What is special about special education revisited: The mentally retarded. *Exceptional Children*, 1965, **31**, 242–247.

Blatt, B. The physical, personality, and academic status of children who are mentally retarded attending special classes as compared with children who are mentally retarded attending regular classes. *American Journal of Mental Deficiency*, 1958, **62**, 810–818.

Brown, L., Branston, M. B., Hamre-Niepupski, S., Johnson, S., Wilcox, B., Sontag, E., & Gruenewald, L. *A rationale for comprehensive longitudinal interactions between severely handicapped students and nonhandicapped students and other citizens.* Paper prepared by Grant number G007501004, Grant number G007801740, and Contract number 300784345, Washington, D.C., 1978.

Budoff, M., & Gottlieb, J. Special class EMR students mainstreamed: A study of an aptitude (Learning Potential) X treatment interaction. *American Journal of Mental Deficiency*, 1976, **81**, 1–11.

Carroll, A. W. The effects of segregated and partially integrated school programs on self-concepts and academic achievement of educable mental retardates. *Exceptional Children*, 1967, **34**, 93–96.

Cassidy, V., & Stanton, J. An investigation of factors involved in the educational placement of mentally retarded children. *U.S. Office of Education Cooperative Research Program, Project No. 43.* Columbus, Ohio: Ohio State University, 1959.

Christoplos, F., & Renz, P. A critical evaluation of special education programs. *Journal of Special Education*, 1969, **3**, 371–379.

Dunn, L. M. Special education for the mildly retarded: Is much of it justifiable? *Exceptional Children*, 1968, **35**, 5–22.

Elenbogen, M. L. A comparative study of some aspects of academic and social adjustment of two groups of mentally retarded children in special classes and regular classes. *Dissertation Abstracts*, 1957, **17**, 2496.

Gampel, D. H., Gottlieb, J., & Harrison, R. H. A comparison of the classroom behaviors of special class EMR, integrated EMR, low IQ, and nonretarded children. *American Journal of Mental Deficiency*, 1974, **79**, 16–21.

Goldstein, H., Moss, J. W., & Jordan, L. J. The efficacy of special class training on the development of mentally retarded children. *U.S. Office of Education Cooperative Project No. 619.* Urbana, Ill.: University of Illinois, 1965.

Goodman, H., Gottlieb, J., & Harrison, R. H. Social acceptance of EMR's integrated into a nongraded elementary school. *American Journal of Mental Deficiency*, 1972, 76, 412–417.

Gottlieb, J., & Baker, J. L. Socio-emotional characteristics of mainstreamed children. *Paper presented at National Conference of the Council for Exceptional Children*, 1975.

Gottlieb, J., & Budoff, M. Attitudes toward school by segregated and integrated retarded children. *Proceedings of the American Psychological Association*, 1972, 713–714.

Gottlieb, J., & Davis, J. E. Social acceptance of EMRs during overt behavioral interaction. *American Journal of Mental Deficiency*, 1973, 78, 141–143.

Gottlieb, J., Gampel, D. H., & Budoff, M. Classroom behaviors of retarded children before and after reintegration into regular classes. *Journal of Special Education*, 1975, 9, 307–315.

Gottlieb, J., Semmel, M. I., & Veldman, D. J. Correlates of social status among mainstreamed mentally retarded children. *Journal of Educational Psychology*, 1978, 70, 396–305.

Gottlieb, J., & Siperstein, G. N. Attitudes toward mentally retarded persons: Effects of attitude referent specificity. *American Journal of Mental Deficiency*, 1976, 80, 376–381.

Grossman, J. H. Manual on terminology and classification in mental retardation. *American Association on Mental Deficiency Special Publication Series No. 2*, 1977.

Heber, R. J. The relation of intelligence and physical maturity to social status of children. *Journal of Educational Psychology*, 1956, 47, 158–162.

Hoeltke, G. Effectiveness of special class placement. *Dissertation Abstracts*, 1967, 27, 3311.

Iano, R. P. Shall we disband special classes. *Journal of Special Education*. 1972, 6, 167–178.

Johnson, G. O. A study of social position of mentally handicapped children in the regular grades. *American Journal of Mental Deficiency*, 1950, 55, 60–89.

Johnson, G. O., & Kirk, S. A. Are mentally handicapped children segregated in the regular grades? *Exceptional Children*, 1950, 17, 65–68, 87–88.

Jose P. v. Ambach. 79 C 270, United States Eastern District Court of New York, 1979.

Kaufman, M. J., Agard, J. A., & Semmel, M. I. *Mainstreaming: Learners and their Environments*. Baltimore, Md.: University Park Press. In press.

Kaufman, M., Gottlieb, J., Agard, J., & Kukic, M. Mainstreaming: Toward an explication of the construct. In E. L. Meyen, G. A. Vergason, & R. J. Whelan (Eds.), *Alternatives for teaching exceptional children*. Denver: Love Publishing Co., 1975.

Kirk, S. A. Research in education. In H. A. Stevens & R. Heber (Eds.), *Mental retardation*. Chicago: University of Chicago Press, 1964.

Knight, O. The self-concept of educable mentally retarded children in special and regular classes. *Dissertation Abstracts*, 1967, 27, 4483.

Larry P. v. Riles, Civil Action No. C-71-2270 343 F. Supp. 1306 (N.D. Cal., 1979).

MacMillan, D. L., & Borthwick, S. The new educable mentally retarded population: Can they be mainstreamed? *Mental Retardation*, 1980, 18(4), 155–158.

MacMillan, D. L., Meyers, C. E., & Morrison, G. M. System-identification of mildly mentally retarded children: Implications for interpreting and conducting research.

American Journal of Mental Deficiency, 1980, 85, 108–115.

MacMillan, D. L., & Semmel, M. I. Evaluation of mainstreaming programs. *Focus on Exceptional Children*, 1977, 9(4).

McCauley, R. W., Morris, P. S., & Cooper, J. K. The placement of handicapped children by Canadian public school personnel. *Education and Training of the Mentally Retarded*, 1978, 13, 367–379.

McDowell, F., & Sontag, E. The severely and profoundly handicapped as catalysts for change. In E. Sontag, J. Smith, and N. Certo. *Educational programming for the severely and profoundly retarded*. Reston, Va.: Council for Exceptional Children, 1977.

Meyen, E., & Altman, R. Public school programming for the SPH: Some researchable problems. *Training and Education of the Mentally Retarded*, 1976, 11(1), 40–45.

Miller, C., & Chansky, N. Psychologists' scoring of WISC protocols. *Psychology in the Schools*, 1974, 11, 422–424.

Miller, S., Miller, T., & Repp, A. Are profoundly and severely retarded people given access to the least restrictive environment? An analysis of one state's compliance. *Mental Retardation*, 1978, 16, 123–126.

Mullen, F., & Itkin, W. The value of special classes for the mentally handicapped. *Chicago Schools Journal*, 1961, 42, 353–363.

Oakland, T., Lee, S., & Axelrad, K. Examiner differences on actual WISC protocols. *Journal of School Psychology*, 1975, 13, 227–233.

Pertsch, C. F. *A comparative study of the progress of subnormal pupils in the grades and in special classes*. New York: Teachers College, Columbia University, 1936.

Schurr, K. T., & Brookover, W. B. *The effect of special class placement on the self-concept-of-ability of the educable mentally retarded child*. East Lansing, Mich.: Michigan State University, 1967.

Semmel, M. I., Gottlieb, J., & Robinson, N. Mainstreaming: Perspectives on educating handicapped children in the public schools. In D. Berliner (Ed.), *Review of Research in Education*. Vol. 7. Washington, D.C.: American Educational Research Association, 1979.

Smith, H. W., & Kennedy, W. A. Effects of three educational programs on mentally retarded children. *Perceptual and Motor Skills*, 1967, 24, 174.

Thurstone, T. G. An evaluation of educating mentally handicapped children in special classes and in regular grades. *U.S. Office of Education Cooperative Research Program*, Project Number OE-SAE 6452. Chapel Hill: University of North Carolina, 1959.

Tucker, J. A. Ethnic proportions in classes for the learning disabled: Issues in nonbiased assessment. *Journal of Special Education*, 1980, 14, 93–105.

Walker, V. The resource room model for educating educable mentally retarded children. Unpublished doctoral dissertation. Temple University, 1972.

Walker, V. The efficacy of the resource room for educating retarded children. *Exceptional Children*, 1974, 40, 288–289.

Wrightstone, J. W., Forlano, G., Lepkowski, J. R., Sontag, M., & Edelstein, J. D. A comparison of educational outcomes under single-track and two-track plans for educable mentally retarded children. *U.S. Office of Education, Cooperative Research Program*, Project Number 144. New York: New York City Board of Education, 1959.

Ysseldyke, J. E., Algozzine, B., Shinn, M. R., & McGue, M. *Similarities and differences between underachievers and students labelled learning disabled: Identical twins with different mothers.* University of Minnesota: Institute for Research on Learning Disabilities: Research Report Number 13, 1979.

5 LITIGATION WITH THE MENTALLY RETARDED*

Henry A. Beyer

Prior to the 1970s, personal legal rights for individuals with mental retardation were practically nonexistent but during the 1970s the growth of such rights was remarkable; and, as the 1980s begin, many questions are being raised concerning their continuing viability. In this chapter, the recent recognition and development of these rights through litigation will be described, an assessment will be given of their current status, and some speculation will be made as to their future.

"Rights" is a word used to which a wide range of meanings is ascribed. Individuals and organizations sometimes use the term in referring to a privilege or benefit that they believe some person or group of persons "ought" to possess. Although such rights may be moral or human rights, they are not legal rights unless and until they are enforceable in a court of law. When a sufficient societal consensus exists concerning what "ought" to be (i.e., a moral right), and when it is the type of right which is susceptible of enforcement by the legal system, then sometimes a court, or a state legislature, or the U.S. Congress will transform that moral right into a legal right—a right enforceable in a court of law.

An early indication of changing societal perceptions regarding what rights mentally retarded persons ought to possess appeared in a working paper prepared by Professor Gunnar Dybwad for the 1960 White House Conference on Children and Youth. In discussing trends and issues, he observed that "[i]nsufficient attention has been given in the past to the legal status of the mentally retarded child and adult. . . . Our great valuation of a person's rights and liberty is apt to come in conflict . . . with a temptation to apply too forcefully the state's inherent guardian function and to deal summarily with the retarded by divesting them of personal rights" (Dybwad, 1964, pp. 210–211). A 1963 Report of the Task Force on Law of the President's Panel on Mental Retardation provided further evidence of such change: "In the past the law has seemed to place more emphasis on the protection of property rights of the retarded than on protection of their personal rights. Both are important and we would seek to redress the balance" (President's Panel on Mental Retardation, 1963, pp. 24–25).

Attitudinal changes were not confined to the United States. In 1967, member organizations of the International League of Societies for the Mentally Handicapped, representing 14 nations, met in Stockholm, Sweden. They concluded that "no examination of the legislative aspects of the problem of mental re-

* I gratefully acknowledge the research assistance of law students Kim M. Cooke and Lily C. Towers.

tardation would be complete without general consideration being given to the basic rights of the mentally retarded, not only from the standpoint of their collective rights and those of their families, but also from that of the individual rights of the retarded person as a human being" (ILSMH, 1967, p. 15). One year later the International League issued a "Declaration of General and Special Rights of the Mentally Retarded" (ILSMH, 1968). And, in December 1971, the General Assembly of the United Nations proclaimed a "Declaration on the Rights of Mentally Retarded Persons" and called for "national and international action to ensure that it will be used as a common basis and frame of reference for the protection of these rights" (UN, 1971).

These developments demonstrated burgeoning worldwide acknowledgement of what rights mentally retarded individuals ought to have. During the past decade, courts, state legislatures, and the U.S. Congress transformed a sizable number of these human rights into legal rights. Since most of the new legal rights gained their first recognition in a federal or state court, this chapter will focus primarily on the litigation out of which these rights arose. We will examine the rights under the headings of education, institutions, deinstitutionalization, problems of implementation, community living, sterilization, parenthood, and medical treatment. This will not be an exhaustive treatment of all relevant litigation. Moreover, since law is a "seamless web," any division of rights into specific categories is rather arbitrary. We have nevertheless limited discussion to the above divisions in order to hold the chapter to a reasonable length and to help structure an otherwise amorphous subject.

Education

More than a quarter of a century ago, in the *Brown v. Board of Education*[1] school integration suit, the U.S. Supreme Court held that public education is "a right which must be made available to all on equal terms."[2] Yet, 17 years later, an enormous number of children were still being denied such education. In 1971 in the District of Columbia, for example, there lived an estimated 22,000 children who had disabilities which interfered with learning. Twelve to 18 thousand of these children were receiving no specialized education, and a large percentage of this group was receiving no education whatsoever.[3] A similar situation existed in Pennsylvania and, to a greater or lesser degree, in every other state.

Early in the 1970's, some parent advocacy groups and a few public interest lawyers, encouraged by the gains which civil rights groups had been making

through litigation, instituted lawsuits in the federal district courts of Eastern Pennsylvania and the District of Columbia. These two suits, the *Pennsylvania Association of Retarded Children* [PARC] v. *Commonwealth of Pennsylvania*[4] and *Mills v. Board of Education*,[5] were "class actions," that is, suits brought on behalf of a few named children who were being denied an appropriate public education and all others within the jurisdiction who were "similarly situated." In 1971 and 1972, consent agreements and court orders, the *PARC* and *Mills* decisions established the following legal principles and rights which have since served as a basis of education rights in every state in the nation:

(1) All children are capable of benefiting from education and training.
(2) All children are entitled to free public education and training appropriate to their learning capacities.
(3) All children are entitled to an opportunity to develop to their full potential as human beings.
(4) All children are entitled to as normalized an educational placement as possible. That is, placement in a regular public school class is preferable to placement in a special public school class; placement in a special class in the public school is preferable to the placement in a special school or program.[6]

In *Mills*, the federal court rejected the District of Columbia's argument that the District lacked the funding to educate all of its handicapped children.

If sufficient funds are not available to finance all of the services and programs that are needed and desirable in the system, then the available funds must be expended equitably in such a manner that no child is entirely excluded from a publicly supported education consistent with his needs and ability to benefit therefrom. The inadequacies of the District of Columbia Public School system, whether occasioned by insufficient funding or administrative inefficiency, certainly cannot be permitted to bear more heavily on the "exceptional" or handicapped child than on the normal child.[7]

Following the *PARC* and *Mills* decisions, a number of state legislatures enacted special education statutes embodying the principles laid down in those cases.[8] And, in 1975, the U.S. Congress followed suit by enacting Public Law 94-142, the Education for All

Handicapped Children Act.[9] The goal of the Act is to make available a "free, appropriate, public education" to all handicapped persons three to 21 years of age. A great portion of the judiciary's subsequent efforts has been devoted to interpreting the word "appropriate." Several of these court interpretations have challenged the traditional 180-day school year. In a leading case, *Battle v. Commonwealth of Pennsylvania*,[10] the U.S. Court of Appeals for the 3rd Circuit recognized that some children who are severely and profoundly impaired "tend to learn much more slowly than nonhandicapped children and tend much more quickly to forget what they have learned."[11] The court concluded that, for such children, a state rule limiting the school year to 180 days precludes the proper determination of the content of a free appropriate public education and, accordingly, that it violates the Act.[12]

In other cases, courts have been struggling to define precisely what "related services" a public school is required to provide under the Act. The regulations promulgated by the U.S. Department of Education (formerly the Department of Health, Education, and Welfare) have identified these as "transportation and such developmental, corrective, and other supportive services as are required to assist a handicapped child to benefit from special education."[13] The U.S. Court of Appeals for both the 3rd and 5th Circuits have agreed that "clean, intermittent catheterization" is such a related service which must be provided by the school to enable certain handicapped children to attend.[14]

A number of courts have held that an appropriate education should include services needed to bring a handicapped child's educational opportunity up to the level offered to that child's nonhandicapped peers. In perhaps the foremost of these cases, *Rowley v. Board of Education of the Hendrick Hudson School District*,[15] both the U.S. District Court and the Court of Appeals held the school district responsible for providing a deaf child, Amy Rowley, with the services of a sign language interpreter in her public, grammar school classroom. The U.S. Supreme Court, however, did not agree.[16] Although three justices dissented,[17] the Court decided that a "requirement that States provide 'equal' educational opportunities would . . . seem to present an entirely unworkable standard requiring impossible measurements and comparisons."[18]

The high Court held that a state satisfies P.L. 94-142's requirement of a free, appropriate education when it provides

> personalized instruction with sufficient support services to permit the child to benefit

educationally from that instruction. Such instruction and services must be provided at public expense, must meet the State's educational standards, must approximate the grade levels used in the State's regular education, and must comport with the child's IEP [individualized education program]. In addition, the IEP, and therefore the personalized instruction, should be formulated in accordance with the requirements of the Act and, if the child is being educated in the regular classrooms of the public education system, should be reasonably calculated to enable the child to achieve passing marks and advance from grade to grade.[19]

Noting that Amy Rowley was already receiving many specialized services (e.g., a school-supplied FM hearing aid, five hours of tutoring, and three hours of speech therapy per week), and was performing well academically, the Court concluded that Amy's educational program already complied with the requirements of the Act—she was not entitled to the services of a sign language interpreter in her classroom.[20]

In considering the future of education rights, most legal advocates for handicapped children are greatly concerned about recent federal and state emphasis on reducing public expenditures. Courts have frequently stated that a lack of funds is no justification for denial of legal rights, particularly constitutional rights. Defining and interpreting those rights in specific situations, however, necessitates the making of difficult judgments by fallible human beings. It should be recognized that judges are not immune from the influences which affect the rest of society. The political humorist, Mr. Dooley, once remarked that the Supreme Court follows the election returns (Dunne, 1901, pp. 22, 26). It is likely that the justices also read the financial pages. A major challenge now confronting legal advocates for individuals with mental retardation is to ensure the survival of the principle established in *PARC* and *Mills*—that any inadequacies in educational services "certainly cannot be permitted to bear more heavily on the 'exceptional' or handicapped child than on the normal child."[21]

Institutions

While the courts in Pennsylvania and the District of Columbia were establishing the educational rights discussed above, a U.S. District Court in Alabama was hearing evidence in a class action brought on behalf of Ricky Wyatt and the other involuntary patients at Alabama's Bryce Hospital, a public mental institution. In March of 1971, the court held that those patients "unquestionably have a constitutional right to receive such individual treatment as will give each of them a realistic opportunity to be cured or to improve his or her mental condition."[22] Shortly thereafter, the plaintiff class was enlarged to include involuntarily confined residents of Alabama's Partlow State School and Hospital for mentally retarded people. And, in April 1972, the court held that, because the only constitutional justification for civilly committing a mentally retarded person to an institution is habilitation, "it follows ineluctably that once committed such a person is possessed of an inviolable constitutional right to habilitation."[23]

This Order by Judge Frank M. Johnson in the *Wyatt v. Stickney* case was a major milestone in establishing legal rights for persons with mental retardation. The preceding year, the General Assembly of the United Nations, in its "Declaration on the Rights of Mentally Retarded Persons," had proclaimed that "[t]he mentally retarded person has a right to proper medical care and physical therapy and to such education, training, rehabilitation and guidance as will enable him to develop his ability and maximum potential" (UN, 1971, sec. 2). The court, in its April 1972 Order, converted this moral right into a legal right for Partlow's involuntary residents.

In *Wyatt*, the district court noted that the evidence had "vividly and undisputedly portrayed Partlow as a warehousing institution which, because of its atmosphere of psychological and physical deprivation, is wholly incapable of furnishing [habilitation] to the mentally retarded and is conducive only to the deterioration and the debilitation of the residents."[24] The court observed that "atrocities occur daily" at Partlow. Incidents cited at the court hearing included: "a resident was scalded to death by hydrant water; . . . a resident was restrained in a straightjacket for nine years in order to prevent hand and finger sucking . . . a resident was inappropriately confined in seclusion for a period of years . . . [and] a resident died from the insertion by another resident of a running water hose into his rectum."[25]

To address these conditions and give substance to the residents' newly recognized right to habilitation, the court ordered the implementation of "Minimum Constitutional Standards for Adequate Habilitation of the Mentally Retarded."[26] In an appendix to his Order, Judge Johnson set forth 49 such minimum standards covering almost 13 printed pages. Like the rights established in the *PARC* and *Mills* education cases, the *Wyatt* standards incorporated developmental and normalization principles.

Although most of the standards related to rights and conditions within the institution—services, staffing, and the physical and psychological environment—they also recognized a right to live in the least restrictive setting. "No persons shall be admitted to the institution unless a prior determination shall have been made that residence in the institution is the least restrictive habilitation setting feasible for that person. . . . [T]he institution shall make every attempt to move residents from (1) more to less structured living; (2) larger to smaller facilities; (3) larger to smaller units; (4) group to individual residences; (5) segregated from the community to integrated into the community living; (6) dependent to independent living."[27]

A major innovation of the *Wyatt* Order was its establishment of a standing "Human Rights Committee" for Partlow. The seven-member committee, composed of parents and other individuals with an interest but not professional experience in mental retardation, was to "review . . . all research proposals and all habilitation programs to ensure that the dignity and human rights of residents are preserved. The committee also shall advise and assist residents who allege that their legal rights have been infringed."[28] In the Order's appended standards, the committee was assigned specific responsibility for all experimental research, unusual or hazardous treatment procedures," and behavior modification programs involving the use of noxious or aversive stimuli, and for reviewing reports of alleged mistreatment, abuse, or neglect of residents.[29]

After *Wyatt*, similar institutional class actions were brought in a number of states. One of the more noteworthy suits was that on behalf of the residents of New York's Willowbrook State School, a case entitled *New York State Association for Retarded Children v. Rockefeller*.[30] Testimony showed that conditions at Willowbrook were generally as abhorrent as those at Partlow. In addition, the Willowbrook case presented the issues of institutionalized residents serving as research subjects. Physicians at Willowbrook had been attempting to develop a vaccine for fecally borne infectious hepatitis. In this effort, they deliberately infected a number of mentally retarded children newly admitted to the school. Some of the children became quite ill; all risked serious illness (Annas et al., 1977, pp. 179–180). In defense of their methods, the researchers argued that, because the disease was epidemic at the facility, most of the children would have contracted it even without deliberate exposure. And the research did succeed in development of a vaccine. Although the children's parents had given at least nominal consent to the experiment, there was evidence that many had done so only to avoid having the children placed at the bottom of a long list of those waiting for admission to the school (Annas et al., 1977, p. 181). The case thus challenged the efficacy of consent obtained under such coercion and the propriety of using incompetent subjects for experimentation, as well as the generally terrible conditions of the institution.

In a 1973 opinion, the federal court considering the Willowbrook issues rejected the *Wyatt* conclusion that the U.S. Constitution guaranteed mentally retarded residents of a state institution a right to habilitation. The court did recognize, however, that they have a constitutional "right to protection from harm."[31] According to the court, this right encompasses not only protection from assaults by other residents or staff,[32] but also a right to a "tolerable living environment" satisfying "civilized standards of human decency" and an absence of "conditions which 'shock the conscience' of the court."[33]

In 1975, after two more years of listening to testimony about Willowbrook, the court demonstrated its growing understanding of the nature of institutional life by observing that "harm can result not only from neglect but from conditions which cause regression or which prevent development of an individual's capabilities. . . . Somewhat different legal rubrics have been employed in these cases—'protection from harm' in this case and 'right to treatment' and 'need for care' in others. It appears that there is no bright line separating these standards."[34] The court then approved a 29-page Consent Judgment. The Judgment's "steps, standards, and procedures . . . are based on the recognition that retarded persons, regardless of the degree of handicapping conditions, are capable of physical, intellectual, emotional and social growth, and . . . that a certain level of affirmative intervention and programming is necessary if that capacity for growth and development is to be preserved, and regression prevented."[35]

The standards are, in many respects, similar to those decreed in *Wyatt*. There are differences, however, responding to specific Willowbrook problems and conditions. The experience with hepatitis research, for example, resulted in a provision mandating that "no physically intrusive, chemical, or bio-medical research or experimentation shall be performed at Willowbrook or upon members of the plaintiff class. This standard, however, recognizes the possibility that such research or experimentation, under proper safeguards, may be appropriate for persons who are not members of the class, in other facilities or programs."[36]

To monitor compliance with the Willowbrook standards, the Consent Judgment ordered the creation of a seven-person Review Panel. In an attempt to avoid problems which had arisen with the *Wyatt* Human Rights Committee, the panel was granted greater authority, staff, and support services than that committee.[37] Establishment of the Review Panel, however, like *Wyatt's* establishment of a Human Rights Committee, represented a continuing judicial belief that a group of persons with a special interest in mental retardation, but enjoying independence of the institution and state service-providing agency, is a useful mechanism for dealing (at least at the initial level) with the myriad issues encountered in implementing such decrees. Elsewhere in the nation, other federal courts were adapting the *Wyatt* committee model to address other institutional issues. In 1974, for instance, a U.S. District Court in Tennessee ordered the creation of an Admissions Review Board for the state's Clover Bottom Developmental Center.[38] That three-member board, consisting of a mental retardation professional, a member of the Tennessee Association for Retarded Children and Adults, and a representative of the State Developmental Disabilities Council, was to approve or deny every proposed admission to the Center. Variations on the independent committee model have also been adopted in federal and state regulations and by accreditation agencies concerned with assuring compliance with institutional standards and procedures.[39]

Deinstitutionalization—the Least Restrictive Alternative

As discussed above, the *Wyatt* and similar institutional decisions recognized the right of mentally retarded clients to receive services in the least restrictive setting, and required the discharge of residents to community placements whenever and wherever feasible. Several years' experience made clear, however, that the orders were bringing about only a modest expansion in community services. The bulk of increased state spending resulting from the early decrees was going toward renovations and greater staffing for the large institutions. In 1974 and 1975, therefore, the advocates bringing a federal class action on behalf of the residents of Pennsylvania's Pennhurst State School and Hospital[40] adopted a somewhat different approach. They argued, not for the improvement of the institution, but for the rapid development of adequate residential and other services in the community, so that all of Pennhurst's residents could be discharged and the institution closed. To ensure that the requested court order could accomplish this result, the plaintiffs sued not only the facility, its administrators, and the Pennsylvania Department of Public Welfare, but also various state and county officials with responsibility for the state's and counties' community mental retardation programs.[41]

On December 23, 1977, Judge Broderick of the U.S. District Court for Eastern Pennsylvania delivered an opinion which some have called his Christmas present to Pennhurst's residents. In it, the court held "that when a state involuntarily commits retarded persons, it must provide them with such habilitation as will afford them a reasonable opportunity to acquire and maintain those life skills necessary to cope as effectively as their capacities permit." Then, breaking new judicial ground, the court found "that minimally adequate habilitation cannot be provided in an institution such as Pennhurst; . . . [and that] Pennhurst does not provide an atmosphere conducive to normalization which is so vital to the retarded." It also found "that the confinement and isolation of the retarded in the institution called Pennhurst is segregation in a facility that clearly is separate and *not* equal; . . . [and] that the retarded at Pennhurst have been and presently are being denied their Equal Protection Rights as guaranteed by the Fourteenth Amendment to the Constitution."[42]

The court ordered the defendants "to provide suitable community living arrangements for the retarded residents of Pennhurst . . . together with such community services as are necessary to provide them with minimally adequate habilitation until such time as the retarded individual is no longer in need of such living arrangement and/or community service."[43]

To assure the appropriateness of community services, the court ordered the defendants to develop written, individualized program plans for each resident, and prescribed procedures for the development and periodic review of those plans. Finally, instead of a Human Rights Committee or Review Panel, this court appointed a Special Master, "with the power and duty to plan, organize, direct, supervise, and monitor the implementation of this and any further Orders of the Court."[44]

The Pennsylvania defendants, although generally agreeing that community residences and services should be provided for Pennhurst residents, maintained that this should be done in a manner and at a pace determined by the state rather than by a federal court. They turned to the 3rd Circuit Court of Appeals. In 1979, that court affirmed almost all of the district court's order, but it based its decision upon statutory, rather than constitutional, grounds.[45] The principal statute relied upon by the Court of Appeals was the federal Developmentally Disabled Assistance and Bill of Rights Act (the DD Act).[46] According to the court, that Act

provides to mentally retarded persons the right to the least restrictive environment. . . . The clear preference of the Act . . . is deinstitutionalization, and . . . we have no doubt about Congressional power to impose the least restrictive alternative requirement upon the states for patients who do not require institutionalization for adequate habilitation.[47]

On the other hand, the appeals court said it could not agree with the trial court that Pennhurst must be entirely closed. It believed that

there may be some individual patients who, because of advanced age, profound degree of retardation, special needs or for some other reason, will not be able to adjust to life outside of an institution and thus will be harmed by such change. The case must therefore be remanded [to the district court] for individual determinations by the court, or by the Special Master, as to the appropriateness of an improved Pennhurst for each such patient.[48]

On the whole, however, the court of appeals gave strong affirmation of the district court's decision: "Of course, deinstitutionalization is the favored approach to habilitation. The federal statutory material makes clear and we acknowledge that constitutional law developments incline in that direction as well."[49] The court cited 14 federal decisions as authority for this assertion.[50] Most of these, including *Wyatt* (which had been affirmed in relevant part by the 5th Circuit Court of Appeals),[51] did indeed support a right to habilitation or treatment in the least restrictive environment. Three of the citations, however, were to decisions of the U.S. Supreme Court, and that Court's view of such rights was far less clear. The high Court had never decided whether institutionalized mentally retarded individuals enjoy a right to habilitation, much less whether they have a right to habilitation in the least restrictive setting. The Court's 1975 opinion in *O'Connor v. Donaldson*[52] marked its closest approach to dealing with the question. Mr. Donaldson had been involuntarily confined for almost 15 years to a Florida state mental hospital. In reviewing the lower court holdings that Donaldson enjoyed a constitutional right to treatment, the Supreme Court had held only that "a State cannot constitutionally confine *without more* a nondangerous individual who is capable of surviving safely in freedom by himself or with the help of willing and responsible family members or friends[53] (emphasis added). The phrase "without more" has been widely interpreted to mean "without treatment."[54] The court, however, had explicitly noted in *Donaldson* that "there is no reason now to decide whether mentally ill persons dangerous to themselves or to others have a right to treatment upon compulsory confinement by the State, or whether the State may compulsorily confine a nondangerous, mentally ill individual for the purpose of treatment."[55]

Thus, when the Commonwealth of Pennsylvania appealed the *Pennhurst* opinion to the Supreme Court, there was considerable doubt that the Court would rule in favor of Pennhurst's residents.

When, in April 1981, the Supreme Court handed down its opinion in *Pennhurst*,[56] it again sidestepped the question of whether there exists a constitutional right to habilitation and, if so, whether habilitation services must be provided in the least restrictive setting. The Court focused instead on the much narrower question of whether such rights are guaranteed by the federal DD Act. It ruled that they are not. According to the high Court, the major provision of the Act relied upon by the court of appeals "does no more than express a congressional preference for certain kinds of treatment. It is simply a general statement of 'findings' and, as such, is too thin a reed to support the rights and obligations imposed on it by the Court below. . . . Congress intended to encourage, rather than mandate, the provision of better services."[57]

Because it limited itself to the narrow question of the meaning of the DD Act, the Supreme Court did not ultimately dispose of the substantive questions concerning the right to treatment. It remanded the case to the court of appeals for reconsideration of those issues in light of its opinion. The appeals court was to determine, in particular, whether the U.S. Constitution, a different federal statute, or Pennsylvania's state law mandates that the state provide treatment or habilitation in the least restrictive environment.[58]

As directed, the Third Circuit Court of Appeals again considered the questions raised by *Pennhurst* and, in February 1982, issued another opinion.[59] On the major question of whether the state is required to provide habilitation services in the least restrictive setting, the court reaffirmed its 1979 holding that the state is indeed under such a legal obligation.[60] This time, however, instead of relying on federal law, the court based its decision squarely upon Pennsylvania's Mental Health and Mental Retardation statute,[61] as interpreted by the Pennsylvania Supreme Court in a 1981 case.[62] Thus, as matters now stand, residents of Pennsylvania's public institutions for the mentally retarded have a legal right to receive habilitative services in the least restrictive environment. Each resident has a right to receive an individual determination of his or her particular needs and, if those needs so dictate, a right to a suitable community living arrangement. Because these rights are based on Pennsylvania state law, they are not automatically possessed by residents of other states. It is certain, however, that this most recent *Pennhurst* decision is prompting legal advocates throughout the nation to examine their own states' laws for provisions similar to Pennsylvania's.

The Supreme Court's *Pennhurst* opinion did not lay to rest the question of whether there exists a constitutional right to at least minimal, least restrictive, habilitative services. In a December 1980 decision, the same court of appeals that decided the *Pennhurst* class action upheld the treatment rights of a single Pennhurst resident, Nicholas Romeo.[63] Mr. Romeo, a profoundly mentally retarded 30-year-old man, involuntarily committed to the facility since 1974, filed suit for being "improperly shackled," and for being denied adequate protection and appropriate treatment. In remanding the case for a new trial, the court of appeals directed that the jury be instructed that, under the Fourteenth Amendment's due process clause, "shackling may be justified only by a compelling necessity, i.e., that the shackling was essential to protect the patient or to treat him. . . . [E]xcept in emergency situations, inadequate resources or administrative rationales offer an insufficient basis for intrusions of this kind on a fundamental liberty interest."[64] With respect to Romeo's claim regarding adequacy of treatment, the court ruled that "for the plaintiff to prevail it is necessary to find that an individual involuntarily confined in a facility for the mentally retarded did not receive a form of treatment that is regarded as acceptable for him in light of present medical or other scientific knowledge."[65]

Pennsylvania appealed the *Romeo* decision to the U.S. Supreme Court and, in June 1982, that tribunal handed down its most positive ruling ever concerning the rights of persons with mental retardation.[66] The Court held that mentally retarded persons in state institutions have a constitutional right under the Fourteenth Amendment to safe conditions, freedom from unreasonable restraint, and at least "minimally adequate" training in caring for themselves.[67] The Court's reasoning regarding safety and freedom from unreasonable restraint was that, since convicted criminals have these rights, it is evident that mentally retarded people, involuntarily institutionalized in state facilities, "who may not be punished at all," are entitled to as much legal protection.[68]

The Court found the claim of a right to treatment or training more troubling. It agreed unanimously that Mr. Romeo was entitled to enough training to enable him to control his aggressive behavior better, so that he could be allowed more freedom of movement. But it explicitly declined to decide the more general question of whether an institutionalized mentally retarded person "has some general constitutional right to training per se."[69]

Associate Justices Blackmun, Brennan, and O'Connor stated, in a concurring opinion, that they would have gone beyond the Court's narrow holding to rule that a mentally retarded individual is entitled to enough training to "prevent a person's pre-existing self-care skills from deteriorating because of his commitment."[70] Chief Justice Burger, however, in a separate concurring opinion, said he "would hold flatly that respondent has no constitutional right to training, or 'habilitation,' per se."[71]

The *Romeo* case has thus firmly established institutionalized mentally retarded individual's constitutional rights to safe conditions, freedom from unreasonable restraint, and at least minimal training. It remains for future litigation or legislation to establish definitively and nationally their legal right to *adequate* training and habilitation services.

Problems in the Implementation of Rights

As farsighted observers recognized early on (Lottman, 1976, pp. 72–73; Diver 1979; Note, "Enforcement," 1970; Note, "Implementation," 1977), the gaining of judicial recognition of the rights of mentally retarded persons has proven considerably less difficult than effective enforcement of those rights. In 1979, for example, the *Wyatt* district court found "defendants are in substantial and serious noncompliance with the orders entered . . . over seven years ago, in several critical areas. Among these are: (1) Failure to provide adequate habilitation programming; (2) Insufficiently trained staff; (3) Failure to move residents from the large institutions to less restrictive settings; (4) Failure to provide privacy for residents"; etc. The court concluded that "over seven years of failure to comply . . . mandates the appointment of a receiver."[72]

Similarly, in 1980, the District of Columbia court, which had handed down the landmark *Mills* decision eight years previously, found the defendants to be in contempt of court for ignoring orders of the court and, through "willful and deliberate actions," proceeding on their own initiative.[73]

The U.S. District Court for Eastern Pennsylvania has likewise held that state's Department of Public Welfare and its Secretary in civil contempt for failing to make a good faith effort to obtain continuing funding for the court-appointed Special Masters.[74] That contempt holding was affirmed on appeal,[75] and fines totalling $1.2 million have been paid by the state.[76] On the other hand, the Second Circuit Court of Appeals has ruled that New York's governor and other state officials cannot be held in contempt for failing to provide continuing funding for the Willowbrook Review Panel. The court found that the governor, acting in good faith, had taken "all steps within his lawful authority to secure funding for the Panel."[77] He was not required to act in violation of New York law by transferring funds from another section of the state's budget.

The question of what are the limits on a federal court's power to enforce its orders or consent decrees against a "sovereign" state is as old as our federal system. The problem is most acute when enforcement requires the expenditure of state funds. No reputable body of legal opinion holds that a court can compel a legislature to levy taxes or appropriate funds. Many believe, however, that a court can order that state funds which have been allocated for one purpose be spent for a different purpose, particularly where failure to fund the latter activity would result in a violation of constitutional rights.[78] For example, early in the *Wyatt* case, the district court hinted that it might "order the sale of a portion of defendant Mental Health Board's land holdings and other assets" to fund implementation of its minimum constitutional standards.[79] The court has not, however, actually attempted to do so.

A different approach has been taken by several other courts. In 1977, the Eighth Circuit Court of Appeals held that "[i]f Minnesota chooses to operate hospitals for the mentally retarded, the operation must meet minimum constitutional standards, and that obligation may not be permitted to yield to financial considerations."[80] The court said that, if the means were not available to eliminate unconstitutional conditions in state facilities, "[a]n extreme alternative would be the closing of the hospitals and the abandonment by the State of any program of institutional care and treatment for mental retardees."[81] Courts have understandably been extremely reluctant to order the closing of constitutionally substandard institutions, believing that such an outcome would be a Pyrrhic victory for the residents.

Another type of implementation problem has arisen during the last few years from a difference of opinion among mental retardation professionals over the efficacy and appropriateness of various court-ordered standards. This problem has been most clearly manifested in the *Wyatt* case. In late 1978, the *Wyatt* defendants filed a motion with the district court requesting modification in a number of the 1972 "minimum constitutional standards."[82] The motion was accompanied by a memorandum[83] from 10 professionals in the field who, at the request of the defendants, had formed a Partlow Review Committee. The memorandum reported the Committee's consensus that:

(a) Only a small number of the present Partlow residents can reasonably be expected to adjust to community living.

(b) The potential for behavioral improvement in a substantial number of Partlow residents is very low and *training* programs seem inappropriate for them.

(c) The 1972 court standards set unrealistic goals and are so restrictive that professional judgment is often precluded in the treatment of individual residents.[84]

On the basis of this consensus, the Committee recommended that the standards be modified to state that

[r]esidents who fail to improve with extensive education and training efforts will not be subjected to further training or education per se. Residents who are not continued in training or education will received [sic] a full program of enriching activities including recreational and leisure time activities, work activities, sheltered employment, physical exercise and therapies, and other such programs that tend to give meaning and dignity to their lives. . . . [Habilitation] programs that do not result in significant improvement and do not hold promise of altering the functional independence of the resident should not be continued. . . . Caution should be exercised to insure that residents are not expected to live in environments to which they cannot reasonably adapt nor in those which tax their adaptive capacity to the extent that marginal adaption may be stressful and unpleasant.[85]

These and additional proposed modifications were intended to implement the Committee's views that to harbor "unrealistic expectations" for severely handicapped persons "is to do them and their families a serious disservice"; that certain of the original standards were "pejorative and demeaning"; and that "[t]o require a human being to participate involuntarily in a futile daily training regimen extending over months, even years, may constitute cruel and inhuman treatment."[86]

In October, 1979, after considering opposing briefs and additional testimony, the district court responded

to these recommendations.[87] The court strongly rebuffed the defendants and some of their expert witnesses on a number of points. For instance, it said that their interpretation

that the 1972 order requires that each resident receive a structured program for six hours per day has no basis. This issue is a straw man which defendants have painstakingly raised and then elaborately struck down. The minimum constitutional standards explicitly state that 'residents shall have a right to habilitation . . . *suited to their needs*. . . .' Further the Court notes, and the parties and amici have recognized, that there is no requirement in the orders of this Court that *every* resident receive six hours of habilitation programming per day.[88]

The court denied defendants' request that the standards be modified to allow defendants to provide an "enriched environment" rather than habilitation programming. "The constitutional rights of each resident to a habilitation program which will maximize his human abilities and enhance his ability to cope with his environment would be threatened by this [proposed] modification."[89]

The court did, however, agree to modify one standard to create "a very *narrow*" exception. "While the evidence has not persuaded the Court that in general borderline or mildly mentally retarded individuals should be institutionalized, the evidence does indicate that in a very limited number of circumstances such individuals cannot be satisfactorily placed in the community."[90] Therefore, "[i]n unusual cases in which borderline or mildly mentally retarded persons have severe additional handicaps which preclude their living in the community, they may reside in Partlow."[91]

Despite ubiquitous shortcomings in actual implementation of court orders, it would be grossly unfair to characterize the institutional litigation movement as a failure. Although conditions and services in both the institutions and the community continue to fall far short of the standards of court orders and consent decrees, they are vastly improved over the conditions and services which existed before commencement of these suits. In some actions, the improvements have been dramatic. In Maine, for example, a class action brought on behalf of the residents of the state's Pineland Center was settled in July 1978 with a lengthy consent decree in which the plaintiffs and defendants agreed upon the improvements to be made. The decree specified detailed standards to be achieved in both the institution and in less restrictive community placements.[92] By January 1981, the Pineland plaintiffs and defendants were able to report, in a joint Stipulation Agreement filed with the court, that "Pineland Center is in substantial compliance with the provisions of the decree." The parties agreed that the Center is providing programming and care necessary to develop their abilities as identified in their individual prescriptive program plans, that residents are provided "a safe, healthy environment," and that the staffing ratios called for in the decree "are met throughout the institution."[93] They acknowledged that "programming in the community does not fully meet Decree standards" and that there remain "gaps in providing a continuum of residential and program services."[94] But the defendants agreed to undertake corrective actions to hasten the achievement of full compliance with that portion of the decree.[95]

Even in suits where events have moved less amicably, the progress has been significant. In 1979, although it found the Alabama defendants in serious noncompliance in several areas with its seven-year-old order, the *Wyatt* court acknowledged that Partlow's "hazardous and deplorable conditions" of 1972 "have to some degree been ameliorated, . . . [that] severe overcrowding has been eliminated . . . that the size of the staff has increased . . . [and that] the physical conditions have improved."[96]

Community Living

One right most Americans would probably support, at least in the abstract, is that of a citizen to live in the neighborhood of his or her choice, economic considerations permitting. A significant amount of litigation of the past decade has been devoted to converting that moral right into a legal right for mentally retarded citizens, in particular for individuals attempting to move from large institutions into the community.

The major legal obstacle confronting mentally retarded persons in obtaining an appropriate community living arrangement has been exclusionary zoning. Zoning ordinances, enacted by towns, cities, and counties, are the primary means by which these local governments regulate the use and development of land. Some ordinances prohibit the establishment of any but "single-family" residences in certain areas. These are frequently the same areas in which a consumer group, a state agency, or others have attempted to establish a group home for citizens with mental retardation or other disabilities. On many occasions, local residents, fearing an adverse impact on the neighborhood's property values, safety, or lifestyle, or merely fearing the unknown, have gone to court to block such plans.[97]

The resulting zoning cases have addressed such questions as whether a number of adults living together, unrelated by blood or marriage, but sharing kitchen and dining facilities as a single housekeeping unit, constitute a "family" for purposes of zoning; whether a group home constitutes a "public educational use," thereby exempting it from the provisions of certain ordinances; and whether a state statute or policy providing for the establishment of group homes as part of a statewide deinstitutionalization plan may override a local exclusionary ordinance (Boyd, 1979–80; Note, "A Review of the Conflict," 1980; Mental Health Law Project, Reference Note 1; National Center for Law and the Handicapped, Reference Note 2).

Although the legal rationales and bases for decisions have differed considerably from state to state, the results have been overwhelmingly and increasingly in one direction—against exclusion of the homes. In 1981, for example, "[a]lmost every court decision which addressed the issue found legal grounds for allowing small group homes to be established in residential neighborhoods."[98] Some of the legal restrictions on group residents which *have* generally been upheld arise from state statutes and relate principally to the maximum number of occupants (six residents and two houseparents is a typical limit) and to the density of group houses in a geographic area (regulated, e.g., by a specific minimum distance between residences).[99]

In most states, the most difficult remaining "legal" hurdle to the establishment of sufficient community living arrangements arises not from "the law," but from "the legal process." It comes from the ability of neighborhood groups to file suit opposing the establishment of a residence, claiming that it would violate a zoning ordinance, restrictive covenant, or state statute. Even though the state's law may be settled, and such a suit would fail if pursued to a final decision, the proponents of a residence in many cases lack the resources for protracted litigation. They may therefore shift the proposed home to another, frequently less desirable, location. This is a "legal" problem for which the solution appears to lie in a non-legal area—the need for heightened public awareness and education concerning the needs, capabilities, and both legal *and* moral rights of mentally retarded citizens.

Sterilization

The sexual sterilization of mentally retarded persons and others deemed "unfit" had its roots in the eugenics movement of the late nineteenth and early twentieth centuries.[100] By 1930, 28 states had enacted legislation authorizing the compulsory sterilization of people in various categories—certain criminals, persons with mental and physical impairments, and others institutionalized as "unfit." Although a number of these statutes were ruled unconstitutional by state courts,[101] the U.S. Supreme Court took an approving stand when, in 1927, it considered the Virginia sterilization law. In the infamous *Buck v. Bell*[102] decision, Justice Oliver Wendell Holmes, speaking for the court, held that "[i]t is better for all the world, if instead of waiting to execute degenerate offspring for crime, or to let them starve for their imbecility, society can prevent those who are manifestly unfit from continuing their kind. The principle that sustains compulsory vaccination is broad enough to cover cutting the fallopian tubes. . . . Three generations of imbeciles are enough."[103]

In the 1930's, as it was discovered that the scientific bases of the eugenics theories were more questionable than had been assumed, the movement waned, and with it, the emphasis on compulsory sterilization. Although the *Buck* holding has never been explicitly overruled, there is some doubt that it could still survive Supreme Court scrutiny.

Sterilization of mentally retarded citizens has not disappeared, however. Rather, the eugenics basis has generally been superseded by a different rationale—that mentally retarded individuals are incapable of adequate parenting (Vitello, 1978). And "compulsory" sterilization has been largely replaced by so-called "voluntary" sterilization. From one viewpoint, it seems only fair that mentally retarded persons have as much right to be voluntarily sterilized as do nonretarded persons. From another perspective, however, serious questions are apparent. In cases where individuals with mental retardation have "chosen" to be sterilized, how fully informed were they regarding that choice; how intellectually and emotionally competent were they to make it; and how free from coercion or undue influence? Even more questionable is the very common situation in which it is assumed that a mentally retarded person is incapable of personally deciding whether or not to be sterilized, and the choice is made for him or her by a parent, guardian, or other representative. In most states, sterilization in such cases of substituted consent is legally characterized as "voluntary."

Recent litigation in a number of states has resulted in considerable progress toward the establishment of legal standards and procedural safeguards for "voluntary" sterilization of individuals with mental disabilities.[104] Although differing somewhat from state to state, the legal principles emerging would, in general, require that before a mentally retarded person is sterilized, there must be a hearing before an impartial fact finder (a court), at which the mentally retarded individual is assisted by counsel. At the hearing, it must be shown by clear and convincing evidence that: (1) the mentally retarded person's consent is truly informed and voluntary, *or* (2) if substituted consent is to be accepted, that (a) the person is capable of procreation; (b) there is an actual or potential opportunity and likelihood of sexual activity; (c) there is good reason to believe that the person, if capable of deciding, would not wish to procreate; (d) no alternative means (e.g., birth control methods, sex education, counseling), reversible and less drastic than sterilization, would be sufficient to prevent undesired procreation; (e) the person will not develop sufficiently in the foreseeable future to be able to make the decision personally; (f) there is no likelihood that a reversible sterilization procedure or other less drastic contraceptive method will soon be available; *and* (g) the decision to sterilize is based on the best interests of the mentally retarded person him- or herself, rather than the interests of a family member, the state, or other caretaker. Some advocates would go further, prohibiting substitute consent unless there is a medical necessity for the sterilization, and banning all sterilizations of persons who have not reached the age of majority. Although few, if any, states currently require that all of these provisions be satisfied, the current trend by both courts and legislatures across the nation is decidedly toward their greater recognition.[105]

Parenthood and Medical Treatment

A great many other rights of mentally retarded citizens have gained legal recognition during the past decade, either through litigation or legislation. Most, still inchoate, have yet to be uniformly defined and clearly delineated. A brief mention of some of the issues being addressed, however, may serve to indicate some directions in which the law seems to be moving.

It is clear that the power of parents over their children may be subject to limitation or termination, if it appears that parental decisions, actions, or incapacities will jeopardize the health or safety of the children.[106] There is growing judicial recognition, however, that mental retardation of parents is, by itself, not sufficient reason to assume such jeopardy will occur. The Utah Supreme Court, for example, ruled in 1978 that a mere showing of mental retardation and mental illness is insufficient to terminate parental rights on the grounds of unfitness or incompetency.[107] A New York Family Court expressed this new awareness in 1980 by overturning a state law that forced the termination of parental rights of mentally retarded parents and the adoption of their children. As the court stated, "the idea that adoption of such children invariably promotes their welfare and best interests is simply not true."[108] On the other hand, where a mentally retarded mother could not understand or cope with the special needs of her developmentally delayed child who had a low frustration level, was self-injurious, and required almost constant attention, an Idaho court found it to be in the best interests of both mother and child to terminate their relationship.[109] Even in this case, however, the court permitted the mother to retain custody of a younger child for whom special parenting requirements were not evident.

A different aspect of the parental rights issue is presented in cases where the nonretarded parents of a mentally retarded child with a correctable physical defect refuse permission for surgical correction of the child's problem. There is considerable evidence that many such cases, particularly when they involve a newborn infant, never reach a court of law, and the child is permitted to die (Affleck, 1980; Bridge & Bridge, 1981; Canadian Psychiatric Association, 1979; Duff & Campbell, 1973; Fletcher, 1975; Hardman & Drew, 1980; Sargeant, 1978; Smith, 1974). When such a situation is brought to a court's attention, however, the traditional judicial reaction has been to intervene in the parent-child relationship, and to provide at least temporary custody of the child to an agency or other adult who may then consent to the required operations.[110]

Two recent, publicized cases have appeared to run counter to this general rule. One is that of Phillip B., a California boy with Down's syndrome. Phillip's parents have, since his birth, refused permission for heart surgery, which doctors say is required to prevent his premature, slow, and painful death. When the California courts originally upheld the parents' right to make such a decision and, in 1980, the U.S. Supreme Court refused to review the case,[111] Phillip's chances for an operation appeared to be at an end. It now appears, however, that this case may yet be brought into the mainstream of judicial law. In 1981, A California Superior Court awarded custody of Phillip, by then 14 years old, to another family, the H.'s, who through their attention, care, and love had assumed the role of "psychological parents."[112] As Phillip's biological parents are appealing this decision, it remains to be seen whether the surgery will actually be performed, if, indeed, the critical time for its performance has not already passed.

The other recent case in which courts appear not to have followed their traditional approach of intervening to sustain life occurred in April 1982 in Bloomington, Indiana. "Infant Doe" was the name used to refer to a child born with Down's syndrome and a deformity in the esophagus that prevented food taken by mouth from reaching the child's stomach. The parents refused to consent to corrective surgery and the state courts refused to order it. Infant Doe died before an appeal could be made to the U.S. Supreme Court (Petroskey, 1982).

It is not at all clear that the high Court would have acted to save the child's life, as this would have been viewed by some as intruding on both parental and states' rights. The U.S. Department of Health and Human Services, however, has responded by notifying all 6,800 hospitals which receive federal financial assistance that it is unlawful for them to withhold from an infant medically indicated treatment required to correct a life-threatening condition if the withholding is based on the fact that the infant is handicapped.[113] Such withholding, the Department said, constitutes discrimination on the basis of handicap in violation of Section 504 of the Rehabilitation Act of 1973,[114] and may result in the termination of federal funding.

Although the judicial actions (and inactions) in the *Phillip B.* and *Infant Doe* cases are deeply troubling, it is hoped that they are anomalies in the law, and that future cases will reaffirm the basic legal principle that a child's (or adult's) right to needed medical services is not diminished by the fact that he or she happens to be mentally retarded. As the Supreme Court of Massachusetts proclaimed in the 1977 case of Joseph Saikewicz, an institutionalized man with profound mental retardation who was dying of leukemia, "the chance of a longer life carries the same weight for Saikewicz as for any other person, the value of life under the law having no relation to intelligence or social position.[115] (See chapter 20 in this volume, "Ethical Decision Making in Medical Intervention," for a more detailed discussion of this issue.)

As is evident from even this general survey, a great many legal questions are still to be answered. But they are subsidiary to the major principle established during the past decade—that the rights of persons who are mentally retarded are not just moral rights, but are legal rights, enforceable in a court of law. The affirmation, extension, and enforcement of this principle are law's primary tasks for the future.

Notes

1. 347 U.S. 483 (1954).
2. *Id.*, at 493.
3. Mills v. Board of Education, 348 F. Supp. 866, 868 (D.D.C. 1972).
4. 334 F. Supp. 1257 (E.D. Pa. 1971).
5. 348 F. Supp. 866.
6. 348 F. Supp. 866; 334 F. Supp. 1257.
7. 348 F. Supp. at 876.

8. See, e.g., 1972 Mass. Acts 766, "An Act Further Regulating Programs For Children Requiring Special Education and Providing Reimbursement Therefore."
9. 20 U.S.C. §§1401 et seq. (1976).
10. 629 F.2d 269, (3d Cir. 1980).
11. *Id.*, at 274.
12. *Id.*, at 280–81.
13. 34 C.F.R. §222.70(c) (7) (1981).
14. Tatro v. Texas, 625 F.2d 557 (5th Cir. 1980); Tokarcik v. Forest Hills School District (mem.) 49 U.S.L.W. 2336 (Oct. 18, 1980), *aff'd*, 665 F.2d 443 (3d Cir. 1981).
15. 483 F. Supp. 528 (S.D.N.Y. 1980); 632 F. 2d 945 (2d Cir. 1980); 73 L. Ed 2d 690 (1982).
16. 73 L. Ed. 2d 690 (1982).
17. *Id.*, at 715.
18. *Id.*, at 707.
19. *Id.*, at 710.
20. *Id.*, at 714.
21. 348 F. Supp. at 876.
22. Wyatt v. Stickney, 325 F. Supp. 781, 784 (M.D. Ala. 1971).
23. Wyatt v. Stickney, 344 F. Supp. 387, 390 (M.D. Ala. 1972).
24. *Id.*, at 391.
25. *Id.*, at 393–94, n. 13.
26. *Id.*, at 396, App. A §2.
27. *Id.*, at 396. App. A §3.
28. *Id.*, at 392.
29. *Id.*, at 400–02. App. A §§24, 28, 30.
30. 357 F. Supp. 752 (E.D.N.Y. 1973).
31. *Id.*, at 758.
32. *Id.*
33. *Id.*, at 765.
34. N.Y. State ARC v. Carey, 393 F. Supp. 715, 718–19 (E.D.N.Y. 1975).
35. N.Y. State ARC v. Carey, No. 72-C-356/357 (E.D.N.Y. April 30, 1975), *approved*, 393 F. Supp. 715 (E.D.N.Y. 1975), *reprinted at* 1 Mental Disability Law Reporter 58 (1976).
36. N.Y. State ARC v. Carey, 1 Mental Disability Law Reporter at 65 (1976).
37. *Id.*, at 66.
38. Saville v. Treadway, No. 6969 (M.D. Tenn. April 18, 1974).
39. See, e.g., 45 CFR ¶249.13(a)(1)(x) and 249.13(b)(1)(xiii); "Standards for Services for Developmentally Disabled Individuals," Accreditation Council for Services for Mentally Retarded and Other Developmentally Disabled Persons (March 1980), §3.17 et al.; and Mass. DMR Regs., 104 CMR ¶20.14.
40. Halderman v. Pennhurst, 446 F. Supp. 1295. (E.D. Pa. 1977).
41. *Id.*, at 1301–02.
42. *Id.*, at 1319–22.
43. *Id.*, at 1326.
44. *Id.*, at 1366.
45. Halderman v. Pennhurst, 612 F.2d 84 (3d Cir. 1979).
46. Pub. L. No. 94–103, 89 Stat. 486 (1975), *codified at* 42 U.S.C. §§6001–6081 (1976).
47. 612 F.2d at 107.
48. *Id.*, at 114.
49. *Id.*, at 115.
50. *Id.*, at 115, n. 38.
51. Wyatt v. Aderholt, 503 F.2d 1305 (5th Cir. 1974).
52. 422 U.S. 563 (1975).
53. *Id.*, at 576.
54. See, e.g., R. Spece, "Preserving the Right to Treatment: A Critical Assessment and Constructive Development of Constitutional Right to Treatment Theories," 20 Ariz. L. Rev. 1 (1978), at p. 13, n. 46.
55. 422 U.S. at 573.
56. Halderman v. Pennhurst, 451 U.S. 1 (1981).
57. *Id.*, at 19.
58. *Id.*, at 31.
59. Halderman v. Pennhurst, 673 F.2d 647 (3d Cir. 1982).
60. *Id.*, at 654.
61. Pa. Stat. Ann. tit. 50, ¶4101–4704 (Purdon 1969).
62. In re Schmidt, 429 A.2d 631 (Pa. 1981).
63. Romeo v. Youngberg, 644 F.2d 147 (3d Cir. 1980); 102 5. Ct. 2452 (1982).
64. 644 F.2d at 160–61.
65. *Id.*, at 169.
66. Romeo v. Youngberg, 102 5. Ct. 2452 (1982).
67. *Id.*, at 2460.
68. *Id.*, at 2458.
69. *Id.*, at 2459.
70. *Id.*, at 2464.
71. *Id.*, at 2465.
72. Wyatt v. Ireland, No. 3195 (N.D. Ala. October 25, 1979).
73. Mills v. Board of Education, 348 F. Supp. 866 (D.D.C. 1980).
74. Halderman v. Pennhurst, 533 F. Supp. 649 (E.D. Pa. 1982).
75. Halderman v. Pennhurst, 673 F.2d 628 (3d Cir. 1982).
76. 533 F. Supp. at 651.
77. N.Y. State ARC v. Carey, 631 F.2d 162 (2d Cir. 1980).
78. See Jackson v. Bishop, 404 F.2d 571, 580 (8th Cir. 1968); Martarella v. Kelley, 359 F. Supp. 478, 481 (S.D.N.Y. 1973); cf. Edelman v. Jordan, 415 U.S. 651, 665 (1974).
79. 344 F. Supp. at 389–90, n. 3 and 394.
80. Welsch v. Likins, 550 F.2d 1122, 1132 (8th Cir. 1977).
81. *Id.*, at 1132, n. 8.
82. Wyatt v. Hardin, No. 3195–N (M.D. Ala. October 20, 1978), Motion for Modification. The history of the *Wyatt* case, with special attention to the proposal for modification of the 1972 standards, is addressed in four articles at 19 Mental Retardation 209–229 (1981).
83. Wyatt v. Hardin, No. 3195–N (M.D. Ala. October 20, 1978), Motion for Modification, Exhibit "A".
84. *Id.*
85. *Id.*
86. *Id.*
87. Wyatt v. Ireland, No. 3195–N (M.D. Ala. Oct. 25, 1979).
88. *Id.*, slip op. at 5–6.
89. *Id.*, at 10.
90. *Id.*, App. at 3.
91. *Id.*
92. Wuori v. Zitnay, No. 75–80–50 (D. Me. July 14, 1978).
93. Wuori v. Zitnay, No. 75–80–P (D. Me. Jan. 14, 1981) (stipulation agreement).
94. *Id.*
95. *Id.*
96. Wyatt v. Ireland, No. 3195–N (M.D. Ala. Oct. 25, 1979), slip op. at 5.
97. A number of studies have failed to discover a valid basis for such fears. See, e.g., "Community Acceptance:

A Realistic Approach," Board of Mental Retardation and Developmental Disabilities, Montgomery County, Ohio; S. Breslow, "The Effects of Siting Group Homes on the Surrounding Environs," Princeton University (1976).

98. "Summary and Analysis: Group Homes Overcome Exclusionary Zoning," 6 Mental Disability Law Rptr. 3 (1982). The major exceptions to this national trend have occurred in Ohio (Garcia v. Siffrin Residential Association, 63 Ohio St. 2d 259, 407 N.E. 2d 1369 (Ohio Sup. Ct. 1980) and Brownfield v. Ohio, 63 Ohio St. 2d 282, 407 N.E. 2d 1365 (Ohio Sup. Ct. 1980)) and Maine (Penobscot Area Housing Development Corp. v. City of Brewer, 434 A. 2d 14 (Me. Sup. Ct. 1981)).

99. See, e.g., City of Schenectady v. Caughlin, 74 A.D. 2d 985, 426 N.Y.S. 2d 328 (1980).

100. Ferster, E. Z., "Eliminating the Unfit—Is Sterilization the Answer?" 27 Ohio St. L. J. 591 (1966); Burgdorf, R. L. and Burgdorf, M. P., "The Wicked Witch is Almost Dead: _Buck v. Bell_ and the Sterilization of Handicapped Persons," 50 Temp. L.Q. 955 (1977). See also the _amicus curiae_ brief filed by Adams, et al., of Advocacy, Inc., in In re Guardianship of Gonzalez. (Probate Session, Bexar County Court, Texas, Feb. 22, 1980), _reprinted in_ "Mental Retardation and the Law", President's Committee on Mental Retardation (June 1980). It provides an excellent discussion of the history of sterilization in the United States and its current legal status, and concludes by recommending specific standards and procedures.

101. See _Adams_, at 3.

102. Buck v. Bell, 274 U.S. 200 (1927).

103. _Id._, at 207.

104. In re Mary Moe, 385 Mass. 555 (1982); In re Grady, 85 N.J. 235 (1981); In re A.W., 637 P. 2d 366 (Colo. Sup. Ct. 1981); In re Marcia R., 136 Vt. 47 (1978); In re Hayes, No. 45612, 93 Wash. 2d 228, (Wash. Sup. Ct. 1979); N.C. ARC v. North Carolina, 420 F. Supp. 451 (M.D. N.C. 1976); Wyatt v. Aderholt, 368 F. Supp. 1383 (M.D. Ala. 1974).

105. _Id._

106. Wisconsin v. Yoder, 406 U.S. 205, 233–34 (1971).

107. In re E., 578 P. 2d 831 (Utah 1978). See also, In re Anna Maria R., 98 Misc. 2d 910, 414 N.Y.S. 2d 982 (1979); Helvey v. Rednour, 86 Ill. App. 3d 154, 408 N.E. 2d 17 (1980).

108. In re Gross, 102 Misc. 2d 1073, 425 N.Y.S. 2d 220 (1980).

109. In re Waggoner, No. L-33123 (Idaho Nov. 27, 1979). See also, In re P.L.L., 597 P. 2d 886 (Utah 1979); In re David B., 5 Fam. L. Rptr. 2531 (Cal. App. 1979).

110. Houle v. Maine Medical Center, No. 74–145 (Me. Feb. 14, 1974); In re Custody of a Minor, 379 N.E. 2d 1053 (Mass. 1978).

111. In re Philip B., 92 Cal. App. 3d 796, 156 Cal. Rptr. 48 (1979), _cert. denied sub nom_ Bothman v. Warren B., 445 U.S. 949 (1980).

112. Guardianship of Philip Becker, No. 101981 (Cal. Aug. 7, 1981).

113. 47 Fed. Reg. 26,027 (June 16, 1982).

114. Rehabilitation Act of 1973, 29 U.S.C. §794 (1976).

115. Superintendent of Belchertown v. Saikewicz, 370 N.E. 2d 417, 431 (Mass. 1977).

Reference Notes

1. Mental Health Law Project. _Combatting exclusionary zoning: The right of the handicapped people to live in the community._ Washington, D.C., 1979.

2. National Center for Law and the Handicapped. _Community living: Zoning obstacles and legal remedies._ South Bend, Indiana, 1977.

References

Affleck, G. G. Physicians' attitudes toward discretionary medical treatment of Down's syndrome infants. _Mental Retardation_, 1980, **18**, 79–81.

Annas, G., Glantz, L., & Katz, B. _Informed consent to human experimentation: The subject's dilemma._ Cambridge, Mass.: Ballinger Publishing, 1977.

Boyd, P. Strategies in zoning and community living arrangements for retarded citizens: _Parens patriae_ meets police power. _Villanova Law Review_, 1979–1980, **25**, 273.

Bridge, P., & Bridge, M. The brief life and death of Christopher Bridge. _The Hastings Center Report_, December 1981.

Canadian Psychiatric Association. Withholding treatment. _Mental Retardation_, 1979, **17**, 18–23.

Diver, C. S. The judge as political powerbroker: Superintending structural change in public institutions. _Virginia Law Review_, 1979, **65**, 43.

Duff, R. S., & Campbell, A. G. M. Moral and ethical dilemmas in the special-care nursery. _New England Journal of Medicine_, 1973, **289**, 890.

Dunne, P. _Mr. Dooley's opinions._ New York: R. H. Russell, 1901.

Dybwad, G. Trends and issues in mental retardation. _Challenges in mental retardation._ New York: Columbia University, 1964.

Fletcher, J. Abortion, euthanasia, and care of defective newborns. _New England Journal of Medicine_, 1975, **292**, 75–77.

Hardman, M. L., & Drew, C. J. Parent consent and the practice of withholding treatment from the severely defective newborn. _Mental Retardation_, 1980, **18**, 165–169.

International League of Societies for the Mentally Handicapped. _Legislative aspects of mental retardation._ Stockholm: 1967.

International League of Societies for the Mentally Handicapped. Declaration of general and special rights of the mentally retarded. Oct. 24, 1968.

Lottman, M. Enforcement of judicial decrees: Now comes the hard part. _Mental Disability Law Reporter_, 1976, **1**, 69.

Note, Enforcement of judicial financing orders: Constitutional rights in search of a remedy. _Georgetown Law Journal_, 1970, **59**, 393.

Note, Implementation problems in institutional reform litigation, _Harvard Law Review_, 1977, **91**, 428.

Petroskey D., Court's involvement makes infant's death noteworthy. _Indianapolis Star_, April 27, 1982.

President's Panel on Mental Retardation. _Report of the Task Force on Law_, 1963.

Sargeant, K. J. P. Withholding treatment from defective newborns: Substituted judgment, informed consent, and the *Quinlan* decision. *Gonzaga Law Review*, 1978, **13,** 781.

Smith, D. H. On letting some babies die. *Hastings Center Studies*, 1974, **2,** 36–45.

United Nations. Resolution of United Nations General As-sembly, 26th Session, 2027th plenary meeting, December 20, 1971.

Vitello, S. J. Involuntary Sterilization: Recent developments. *Mental Retardation*, 1978, **16,** 405–408.

PART III
CLASSIFICATION

6 PERINATAL FACTORS IN MENTAL RETARDATION*

Ira T. Lott

With the advent of sophisticated monitoring techniques in the labor room and improved intervention at delivery, the mortality rate among critically ill neonates has decreased. Yet, optimism over the salvage rate for sick neonates has not always been reflected in the quality of life for survivors. Perinatal factors continue to be highly represented in the etiology of mental retardation. This chapter will review the current status of hypoxic-ischemic brain damage, intracranial hemorrhage, intrauterine infections, and trauma in terms of neurological pathogenesis and outcome. A comprehensive monograph on neonatal neurology reviews many aspects of this subject (Volpe, 1981).

Hypoxic-Ischemic Disease of the Newborn

Basic Concepts

A brief review of some basic concepts in the pathophysiology of neonatal hypoxic-ischemic insults will help to place the clinical manifestations into perspective. Subnormal oxygen concentration in arterial

blood (hypoxemia) and pathologically decreased blood perfusion (ischemia) can be separated in animal models, but generally occur together in the sick neonate (asphyxia). The pathophysiological and biochemical findings in asphyxic disorders have been studied in animals and humans, as reviewed by Volpe (1981). The biochemical changes include an increased glucose flux into the brain, increased breakdown of glycogen and glucose, an increased production of lactate, and a diminution in adenosine triphosphate (ATP) (Vannucci and Plum, 1975; Holowach-Thurston et al., 1974; Kobayashi et al., 1977). The reduction in brain glucose is associated with a change over to anaerobic metabolism, but this is an ineffective way of generating ATP. After an asphyxic insult, the infant may not be able to reestablish normal cerebral perfusion, a phenomenon referred to as "no-reflow" (Ames et al., 1968). As this concept has been further studied, it appears to involve an aggregation of red blood cells, vasoconstriction, and swelling of endothelial and perivascular elements.

Some protection is afforded against these insults in the newborn brain. It has been shown in newborn animals that ATP levels decline less than in adults (Holowach-Thurston & McDougall, 1969). In addition, the myocardium appears to have increased resistance to the effects of ischemia in many newborn

* Supported in part by National Institutes of Health grants HD 05515 and HD 04147.

species. The role of glucose in the production of brain damage in the newborn is more controversial. Vannucci and Vannucci (1978) conclude from animal experiments that the best neurological outcome is related to endogenous brain glucose reserves at the time of the insult. Myers (1976), on the other hand, finds that pretreatment of Rhesus monkeys aggravates brain edema and worsens lactate accumulation during an asphyxic challenge.

Physiological monitoring of cerebral blood flow in human newborns has suggested that autoregulation of the intracranial circulation is impaired by perinatal asphyxia (Lou et al., 1979a). Cerebral vessel autoregulation, which is only marginally operative in normal newborns, is an important means by which intracerebral perfusion may continue during a drop in systolic blood pressure. Cerebral atrophy and abnormal neurological signs have been shown to occur in human newborns whose cerebral blood flow rate has fallen below 20 ml/100 g tissue/min.

Success in preventing the biochemical and physiological changes described above has been partially achieved through intrauterine assessment of infants at risk for perinatal asphyxia. One major advance has been electronic fetal monitoring (Hobbins et al., 1979), a technique that allows a precise measurement of fetal heartbeat in relation to uterine contractions. A late deceleration in heart rate (peaking well after the peak of uterine contraction) has been correlated with placental insufficiency and perinatal asphyxia (Cibilis, 1978). Fetal acid-base measurements (through capillary blood testing) are directly related to abnormal neurological signs within the first hour of life (Low et al., 1977).

The earliest systematic recording of newborn well-being was the Apgar score, a scale in which equal weight on a 3-point scale is given to five different neonatal parameters (heart rate, cry, muscle tone, color, and reflexes). The predictive value of the 1-minute Apgar score has been questioned (Hobbins et al., 1980), but the extended score (after five minutes) has been shown to correlate with the likelihood of cerebral palsy in survivors (Nelson & Ellenberg, 1979).

Neuropathological Findings in Perinatal Asphyxia

In term fetal monkeys in whom partial asphyxia had been induced by sustained maternal hypotension, a consistent band of cortical necrosis (destruction) was found that was particularly marked in the posterior parasagittal regions (Brann & Myers, 1975). This pattern of necrosis is also seen in term human infants as a manifestation of hypoxic-ischemic encephalop-

athy. Partial asphyxia in the newborn infant is further characterized by selective neuronal necrosis with regional vulnerability noted in the following areas: cerebral cortex (border zones between major cerebral arteries), diencephalon (thalamus, hypothalamus, geniculate body), basal ganglia, brain stem (inferior colliculus, fifth and seventh nerves of pons, vagus nucleus in medulla) and cerebellum (Purkinje cells). The reasons for this striking selective vulnerability are unknown. Since the injuries do not follow a vascular distribution, the vulnerability may be determined by high metabolic rates and disproportionate susceptibilities in the areas effected (Norman, 1978).

Status marmoratus is a common manifestation of asphyxic disease in the term newborn characterized by neuronal loss, gliosis, and hypermyelination (Malamud, 1950). The hypermyelination provides a marbled appearance of the caudate nucleus and putamen. Coexistent with this lesion is "ulegyria" of the cerebral cortex, in which a smooth firm scar involves one or more gyri. The abnormal myelin staining appears to involve the aberrant deposition of myelin upon astrocytic fibers (Borit and Herndon, 1970).

In premature infants who have experienced partial asphyxia due to cardiorespiratory disturbances, a characteristic white matter scar is noted at the angles of the lateral ventricles. This lesion, termed periventricular leukomalacia by Banker and Larroche (1962), occurs predominantly in the border zones between penetrating branches of the middle and posterior cerebral arteries. An early form of this lesion has been termed perinatal telencephalic leukoencephalopathy and may involve leakage of material from injured blood vessels (Gilles & Murphy, 1969).

Another type of neuropathological lesion in perinatal asphyxia tends to be asymmetrically focal or multifocal and involves tissue necrosis and subsequent cavity formation within brain tissue. The destructive brain lesions designated porencephaly, hydranencephaly, or multiple cystic encephalomalacia are generally thought to be the result of circulatory accidents within the distribution of the major cerebral arteries. The middle cerebral artery was involved in approximately 50% of 592 infants examined pathologically (Bormada et al., 1979). It is not known why generalized hypotension should produce focal cavitation of the neonatal brain. Explanations have included variations in the development of cerebral vessels or regional metabolic vulnerabilities to ischemia.

Intracranial Hemorrhage

With the advances in obstetrical care of the past two decades, traumatic hemorrhage has declined as a cause of neonatal birth injury. Conversely, the support systems which have permitted premature infants to survive have been associated with an increase in periventricular-intraventricular hemorrhage. Computerized cranial tomography (CT-scan) has facilitated visualization of some hemorrhagic conditions not otherwise appreciated on the basis of the clinical examination. Trauma, of course, often coexists with hypoxic-ischemic insults, and both factors might thus be responsible for intracranial hemorrhage in the perinatal period. As a general rule, subarachnoid and intraventricular hemorrhages are associated with hypoxia-ischemia, whereas subdural and intracerebellar hemorrhage involve trauma as the precipitating factor (Page & Wigglesworth, 1979).

Subdural hemorrhage is related to tearing of the bridging cerebral veins or venous sinuses. Traumatic insults of this type are particularly likely when a large infant is delivered through a small birth canal, when labor is precipitous or prolonged, or when delivery follows a difficult extraction. Most of the infants with infratentorial hemorrhage are greater than 4,500 grams body weight (Cooke et al., 1979). The clinical signs of hemorrhage include a hyperalert state or irritability, full fontanelle, deviation of the eyes, followed by seizures and stupor (Lou et al., 1979a; Ross & Dimette, 1965). The diagnosis of this type of hemorrhage is achieved through CT-scan and needle tapping (or paracentesis) of the subdural space.

In subarachnoid hemorrhage, blood is largely localized over the cerebral convexities. The origin is probably venous. Seizures may occur frequently in the early stages of primary subarachnoid hemorrhage because of irritability of the cortex underlying the pial laptomeninges (Volpe, 1977). Unless complicated by other intracranial hemorrhages, primary subarachnoid hemorrhage has a good prognosis and would not be expected to be a cause of severe mental retardation.

Intracerebellar hemorrhage is a relatively rare but increasingly reported phenomenon in premature infants (Moylan et al., 1978). It is possible that many cerebellar hemorrhages arise from the dissection of blood from an intraventricular source into the substance of the cerebellar tissue. Pathogenetic explanations include the presence of a tenuous cerebellar vascular integrity in premature infants; the compliant skull in this population may predispose toward hemorrhage from traumatic changes in intravascular pressure.

The most common and serious hemorrhage in the perinatal period for mental retardation is that arising in periventricular and intraventricular locations. This lesion occurs most commonly in infants at 32 weeks of gestation or less, and is thus a phenomenon increasing in proportion to the salvage rate for sick premature infants.

The basic lesion is bleeding into the subependymal germinal matrix. This highly cellular area is active metabolically and is extremely well vascularized. Approximately 80–90% of these hemorrhages have originated in the germinal matrix at the head of the caudate nucleus (Yakovlev & Rosales, 1970). In these infants coming to autopsy, over 80% of these hemorrhages have ruptured into the ventricle (Leech & Kohnen, 1974). The blood then spreads throughout the ventricular system and is likely to lead to an obliterative fibrosing arachnoiditis. In these circumstances, hydrocephalus may result from acute obstruction of cerebrospinal fluid flow at the level of the acqueduct or obliteration of the subarachnoid space. This hemorrhage appears to arise from capillaries but not from larger vessels (Hambleton & Wigglesworth, 1976).

The role of hypoxia-ischemia appears to be central to the pathogenesis of periventricular-intraventricular hemorrhage. Asphyxia may increase cerebral perfusion and overload the tenuous vascular complex in the germinal matrix (Lou et al., 1979b). Hypercapnia (increased CO_2 content) may have the same effect (Kenney et al., 1978). When the hypotension of perinatal asphyxia is treated by plasma expanders, the increase in arterial pressure may be transmitted directly to the capillary bed with resultant intraventricular hemorrhage (Simmons et al., 1974). As studied by microangiographic techniques, the capillary endothelial cells of the neonatal brain may be particularly susceptible to asphyxic injury with subsequent rupture and loss of vasoautoregulation (Takashima & Tanaka, 1978).

The clinical manifestations of periventricular-intraventricular hemorrhage have been divided into a catastrophic syndrome (sudden deterioration with stupor, apnea, seizures, and paralysis) and a saltatory syndrome (gradual evolution with abnormal eye movements, hypotonia, and respiratory disturbances). The diagnosis is substantiated by the CT-scan (Scott et al., 1974), which has facilitated the use of a clinical grading system corresponding to the evolution of the intracranial hemorrhage (Krishnamoorthy et al., 1977). Ultrasonography of the infantile skull has been made possible by the thinness of the cranium and has permitted a bedside confirmation of intracranial hemorrhage (Babcock et al., 1980).

Intrauterine Infections

Non-bacterial intracranial infections account for a significant etiologic category in mental retardation.

The offending organisms may exert their pathologic effect on the brain in either the prenatal or perinatal period. Although most intrauterine infections exert a destructive effect on nervous tissue that has already formed, recent observations suggest that developmental aberrations of brain may be associated with fetal viral exposure before an antibody or inflammatory response may be mounted (Thompson & Glasgow, 1980).

Cytomegalovirus (CMV)

CMV infection is said to be the most frequent and serious form of intrauterine infection. Those offspring with serious neurologic injury and mental retardation almost always have sustained the infection before birth rather than during a passage through an affected birth canal (Ballard et al., 1979). CMV excretion is seen in the urine of 3 to 6% of pregnant women (Hanshaw & Dudgeon, 1973). Infection of the fetal nervous system appears to take place during the first and second trimester (Monif et al., 1972), and several weeks may be required for the virus to exert a destructive effect. CMV causes an inflammation of brain tissue and its meningeal coverings (meningoencephalitis). In addition to an inflammatory reaction, the CMV may cause actual necrosis of brain tissue, particularly in the germinal matrix of the periventricular region. Intranuclear inclusions have been noted in neurons (Griffith, 1977). As the result of inflammatory cell loss, periventricular cerebral calcification occurs and forms the distinguishing radiologic hallmark of this disorder. Microcephaly is very common in CMV infection and various developmental malformations of brain have been reported (Crome & France, 1959). CMV infection often has sytemic manifestations in the newborn period, including enlarged liver and spleen, generalized skin rash, and low platelet count. Neonatal seizures are a common association with the meningoencephalitis. The outcome will be discussed in the section on prognostic studies.

Toxoplasmosis

The intrauterine infection is caused by the protozoan parasite *Toxoplasma gondii*, as the result of transplacental passage from the mother. As with all the congenital infections, the maternal illness may be quite mild, with nonspecific features suggestive of influenza or infectious mononucleosis. The major sequelae for the fetus appear to follow a maternal infection in the first trimester, although the frequency of milder infection rises in the third trimester (Desmonts and Couvreur, 1974).

The primary neuropathologic manifestations result from tissue destruction as opposed to developmental malformation (Frenkel, 1974). The meningoencephalitis may lead to multiple destructive areas where the encysted organism is surrounded by an inflammatory reaction (granuloma). Hydrocephalus is a common complication in toxoplasmosis due both to a blockage of spinal fluid flow from viscous inflammatory breakdown products and to necrosis around the cerebral aqueduct. The hallmark clinical manifestation is chorioretinitis in which the mature lesions appear as punched out pigmented areas in the retina (Remington & Desmonts, 1976). As in CMV, a systemic infection may ensue with skin rash, liver dysfunction, and anemia. The spinal fluid protein concentration may be astronomically high in toxoplasmosis. Toxoplasmosis-like CMV infection is generally limited to a single pregnancy, but we have recently seen a case in which a subsequent sibling was affected, probably secondary to conception acquired shortly after delivery of an affected infant. In contrast to CMV infection, the radiographic features of congenital toxoplasmosis include diffuse multifocal calcification throughout the cerebral cortex.

Rubella

Congenital rubella is a transplacental infection in which timing of the insult bears a characteristic relationship to the outcome (Cooper et al., 1969). Neurological manifestations occur after maternal rubella infection in the first four months of gestation (particularly the first two months) as to the ocular and cardiac defects. The sensorineural deafness in rubella may still occur when the fetal infection is experienced in the fourth month or shortly thereafter. The rubella virus appears to interfere with cellular proliferation in the developing brain and, in addition, causes an inflammation and tissue necrosis (Singer et al., 1967). This infection also causes a distinctive inflammation of the walls of blood vessels, a lesion which contributes to brain necrosis. The full rubella syndrome consists of a large spectrum of anomalies including intrauterine growth retardation, meningoencephalitis, cataracts, hearing loss, narrowing of the pulmonary artery, dysfunction of the reticuloendothelial system, and bony abnormalities. Preventative intervention for congenital rubella has been approached through active immunization of children (to prevent the circulation of virus in the general population) and passive immunization of a susceptible pregnant woman exposed to rubella.

Other Congenital Infections

Neonatal herpes simplex meningoencephalitis is a true perinatal infection acquired during the passage of an infant through an infected birth canal or, more commonly, by ascending spread of the virus after ruptured fetal-maternal membranes. The infection may take a highly fatal disseminated form or may be localized to the central nervous system, eyes, skin, or mouth. When severe, herpes simplex type 2 virus causes massive hemorrhage necrosis and brain swelling (Nahmias & Visintine, 1976).

Congenital syphilis declined to vanishing low levels with the advent of penicillin treatment, but owing to a change in social trends the incidence appears to be rising again (Ingall & Norins, 1976). The spirochete *Treponema pallidum* infects the fetus by a transplacental mechanism. The mother may be entirely asymptomatic and often shows evidence of the infection only by serological testing. The fetus may be protected in the early stages of gestation and has been shown to acquire the infection after 24 weeks (Dippel, 1944). When it affects the nervous system, congenital syphilis causes an acute and subacute meningitis. If this process becomes chronic, fibrosis of the meninges with subsequent hydrocephalus is possible. The mucocutaneous eruption and teeth abnormalities are highly characteristic of congenital syphilis, but the rest of the clinical manifestations are nonspecific. Serologic testing is thus mandatory for any newborn in whom the suspicion is raised since treatment with penicillin is efficacious after a diagnosis has been promptly established.

Bacterial Intracranial Infection

Bacterial meningitis of the newborn may have its origins in utero and requires prompt diagnosis and therapy if neurologic sequelae are to be prevented. The early onset perinatal form of this infection is generally caused by bacterial contamination in an affected birth canal. The offending organisms are those that tend to frequent the birth canal, including Group B streptococcus, staphylococci, *Escherichia coli*, and *Listeria monocytogenes*. Obviously, factors that complicate delivery and those that may lower the immunity of the infant predispose towards bacterial meningitis. The inflammatory phase of bacterial meningitis includes an arachnoiditis, vasculitis, and cerebral edema.

Prognostic Studies

All of the insults to the perinatal brain which have been described in this chapter form a continuum of reproductive casualty in survivors. At one end is severe psychomotor retardation and at the other mild disturbances of learning and behavior. Prognostic features of these illnesses are determined as much by variables in recognition and neonatal management as they are by the severity of the individual insult. Finer et al. (1981) have recently examined 95 infants at 37 weeks' gestation or greater and graded the perinatal encephalopathy according to a neonatal staging system (Sarnat & Sarnat, 1976). Thirty-five percent of these term infants had a moderate to severe neurologic handicap, somewhat less than the 48% reported by Brown et al. (1974). The presence of early seizures as the result of perinatal asphyxia was correlated with poor outcome, as was prolonged voltage suppression on the electroencephalogram (Amiel-Tison, 1973; Brann & Dykes, 1977; Rose & Lombroso, 1970). Poor progress for mental retardation has also been correlated with a low five-minute Apgar score (Drage & Berendes, 1966; Nelson & Ellenberg, 1979). Prognostic studies in perinatal asphyxia are increasingly reflective of improvement in neonatal management. Thus, within Finer's recent study, there appeared to be an improved outcome in the last two years (1977–78) compared with the first two years (1975–76). The CT-scan has also been useful in predicting neurologic outcome in neonatal brain hypoxia and injury (Schrumpf et al., 1980). Radiographic evidence of severe periventricular leukomalacia and cortical low density zones were seen to correlate with abnormal motor and mental development.

In CMV infections, the presence of the full-blown neurologic state of microcephaly, intracranial calcifications, and chorioretinitis is correlated with mental retardation, seizures, deafness, and motor deficits in 95% of survivors (MacDonald & Towbin, 1978). The prognosis appears to improve in infants whose neonatal neurological manifestations are less severe. The same paradigm holds for congenital toxoplasmosis. Of those with prominent neonatal neurological features, only 9% are normal on follow-up examination. In those with asymptomatic toxoplasmosis, none had hearing loss, but 25 to 60% developed chorioretinitis after the neonatal period. The mean IQ of this group was 93 (Stagno et al., 1977). In rubella, the outcome is less clearly related to neonatal manifestations. Even infants who appear to be less severely affected often show significant neuromotor and auditory sequelae (Desmond et al., 1978). In part, the uncertainty of predicting prognosis may be related to the chronicity of congenital rubella. For the remaining infectious diseases, the prognosis appears to be correlated with the severity of the initial manifestations.

References

Ames, A., III, Wright, R. L., Kowada, M. D., Thurston, J. M., & Majno, G. Cerebral ischemia. II. No reflow phenomenon. *The American Journal of Pathology*, 1968, **52**, 437–453.

Amiel-Tison, C. Neurologic disorders in neonates associated with abnormalities of pregnancy and birth. *Current Problems in Pediatrics*, 1973, **3**, 3–37.

Babcock, D. S., Han, B. K., & LeQuesne, G. W. B-mode gray scale ultrasound of the head in the newborn and young infant. *American Journal of Roentgeneology*, 1980, **134**, 457–468.

Ballard, R. A., Drew, W. L., Hufnagle, K. G., & Riedel, P. A. Acquired cytomegalovirus infection in preterm infants. *American Journal of Diseases in Children*, 1979, **133**, 482–485.

Banker, B. Q., & Larroche, J-C. Periventricular leukomalacia of infancy. *Archives of Neurology*, 1962, **7**, 386–410.

Bormada, M. A., Moossy, J., & Shuman, R. M. Cerebral infarcts with arterial occlusion in neonates. *Annals of Neurology*, 1979, **6**, 495–502.

Borit, A., & Herndon, R. M. The fine structure of plaques fibromyeliniques in ulegyria and in status marmoratus. *Acta Neuropathologica*, 1970, **14**, 304–311.

Brann, A. W., Jr., & Dykes, F. D. The effects of intrauterine asphyxia in the term neonate. *Clinics in Perinatology*, 1977, **4**, 149–161.

Brann, A. W., & Myers, R. E. Central nervous system findings in the newborn monkey following severe in utero partial asphyxia. *Neurology*, 1975, **25**, 327–338.

Brown, J. K., Purvis, R. J., Forfar, J. O., & Cockburn, F. Neurological aspects of perinatal asphyxia. *Developmental Medicine and Child Neurology*, 1974, **16**, 567–580.

Cibilis, L. A. Clinical significance of fetal heart rate patterns during labor. V. Variable decelerations. *American Journal of Obstetrics and Gynecology*, 1978, **132**, 791–805.

Cooke, R. W. I., Rolfe, P., & Howat, P. Apparent cerebral blood-flow in newborns with respiratory disease. *Developmental Medicine and Child Neurology*, 1979, **21**, 154–160.

Cooper, L. Z., Ziring, P. R., Ockerse, A. B., Fedon, B. A., Kiely, B., & Krugman, S. Rubella. *American Journal of Disease in Children*, 1969, **118**, 18–29.

Crome, L., & France, N. E. Microgyria and cytomegalic inclusion disease in infancy. *Journal of Clinical Pathology*, 1959, **12**, 427–434.

Desmond, M. M., Fisher, E. S., Vorderman, A. L., Schaffer, H. G., Andrew, L. P., Zion, T. E., & Catlin, F. I. The longitudinal course of congenital rubella encephalitis in nonretarded children. *Journal of Pediatrics*, 1978, **93**, 584–591.

Desmonts, G., & Couvreur, J. Toxoplasmosis in pregnancy and its transmission to the fetus. *Bulletin of the New York Academy of Medicine*, 1974, **50**, 146–159.

Dippel, A. L. The relationship of congenital syphilis to abortion and miscarriage and the mechanism of intrauterine protection. *American Journal of Obstetrics and Gynecology*, 1944, **47**, 369–379.

Drage, J. S., & Berendes, H. W. Apgar scores and outcome of newborn. *Pediatric Clinics of North America*, 1966, **13**, 637–643.

Finer, N. N., Robertson, C. M., Richards, R. T., Pinnell, L. E., & Peters, K. L. Hypoxic-ischemic encephalopathy in term neonates: Perinatal factors and outcome. *Journal of Pediatrics*, 1981, **98**, 112–117.

Frenkel, J. K. Pathology and pathogenesis of congenital toxoplasmosis. *Bulletin of the New York Academy of Medicine*, 1974, **50**, 182–191.

Gilles, F. H., & Murphy, S. F. Perinatal telencephalic leukoencephalopathy. *Journal of Neurology, Neurosurgery, and Psychiatry*, 1969, **32**, 404–413.

Griffith, J. F. Neurobacterial infections of the fetus and newborn. *Clinics in Perinatology*, 1977, **4**, 117–130.

Hambleton, G., & Wigglesworth, J. S. Origin of intraventricular hemorrhage in the preterm infant. *Archives of Disease in Childhood*, 1976, **51**, 651–659.

Hanshaw, J. B., & Dudgeon, J. A. *Viral disease of the fetus and newborn*. Philadelphia: W. B. Saunders, 1973.

Hobbins, J. C., Freeman, R., & Queenan, J. T. The fetal monitoring debate. *Pediatrics*, 1979, **63**, 942–951.

Hobbins, J. C., Freeman, R., & Queenan, J. T. Reply (Letter). *Pediatrics*, 1980, **65**, 367.

Holowach-Thurston, J., Hauhart, R. E., & Jones, E. M. Anoxia in mice: Reduced glucose in brain with normal or elevated glucose in plasma and increased survival after glucose treatment. *Pediatric Research*, 1974, **8**, 238–243.

Holowach-Thurston, J., & McDougal, D. B., Jr. Effects of ischemia on metabolism of the brain of the newborn mouse. *American Journal of Physiology*, 1969, **216**, 348–352.

Ingall, D., & Norins, L. Syphilis. In J. S. Remington & J. O. Klein (Eds.), *Infectious Diseases of the Fetus and Newborn Infant*. Philadelphia: W. B. Saunders, 1976, 414–463.

Kenny, J. D., Garcia-Prats, J. A., Hilliard, J. L., Corbet, A. J. S., & Rudolph, A. J. Hypercarbia at birth: A possible role in the pathogenesis of intraventricular hemorrhage. *Pediatrics*, 1978, **62**, 465–467.

Kobayashi, M., Lust, W. D., & Passonneau, J. V. Concentrations of energy metabolites and cyclic nucleotides during and after bilateral ischemia in the gerbil cerebral cortex. *Journal of Neurochemistry*, 1977, **29**, 53–59.

Krishnamoorthy, K. S., Fernandez, R. A., Momose, K. J., DeLong, G. R., Moyian, M. B., Todres, I. D., & Shannon, D. C. Evolution of neonatal intracranial hemorrhage by computerized tomography. *Pediatrics*, 1977, **59**, 165–172.

Leech, R. W., & Kohnen, P. Subependymal and intraventricular hemorrhages in the newborn. *The American Journal of Pathology*, 1974, 77, 465–475.

Lou, H. C., Lassen, N. A., & Friis-Hansen, B. Impaired autoregulation of cerebral blood flow in the distressed newborn infant. *Journal of Pediatrics*, 1979, **94**, 118–121. (a)

Lou, H. C., Lassen, N. A., Tweed, W. A., Johnson, G., Jones, M., & Palahniuk, R. J. Pressure passive cerebral blood flow and breakdown of the blood-brain barrier in experimental fetal asphyxia. *Acta Paediatrica Scandinavica*, 1979, **68**, 57–63. (b)

Low, J. A., Pancham, S. R., Piercy, W. N., Worthington, D., & Karchmar, J. Intrapartum fetal asphyxia. Clinical characteristics, diagnosis, and significance in relation to pattern of development. *American Journal of Obstetrics and Gynecology*, 1977, **129**, 857–872.

MacDonald, H., & Tobin, J. O'H. Congenital cytomegalovirus infection: A collaborative study on epidemiological, clinical, and laboratory findings. *Developmental Medicine in Child Neurology*, 1978, **20**, 471–482.

Malamud, N. Status marmoratus: A form of cerebral palsy following either birth injury or inflammation of the central nervous system. *Journal of Pediatrics*, 1950, **37**, 610–619.

Monif, G. R. G., Egan, E. A., Held, B., & Eitzman, D. V. The correlation of maternal cytomegalovirus infection during varying stages in gestation with neonatal involvement. *Journal of Pediatrics*, 1972, **80**, 17–20.

Moylan, F. M. B., Herrin, J. T., Krishnamoorthy, K., Todres, I. D., & Shannon, D. C. Inappropriate antidiuretic hormone secretion in premature infants with cerebral injury. *American Journal of Diseases in Children*, 1978, **132**, 339–402.

Myers, R. E. Anoxic brain pathology and blood glucose. *Neurology*, 1976, **26**, 345.

Nahmias, A. J., & Visintine, A. M. Herpes simplex. In J. S. Remington & J. O. Klein (Eds.), *Infectious Diseases of the Fetus and Newborn Infant*. Philadelphia: W. B. Saunders, 1976, 156–190.

Nelson, K. B., & Ellenberg, J. H. Neonatal signs as predictors of cerebral palsy. *Pediatrics*, 1979, **64**, 225–232.

Norman, M. G. Perinatal brain damage. *Perspectives in Pediatric Pathology*, 1978, **4**, 41–92.

Page, K. E., & Wigglesworth, J. S. *Haemorrhage, Ischemia, and the Perinatal Brain*. Philadelphia: Lippincott, 1979.

Remington, J. S., & Desmonts, G. Toxoplasmosis. In J. S. Remington & J. O. Klein (Eds.), *Infectious Diseases of the Fetus and Newborn Infant*. Philadelphia: W. B. Saunders, 1976, 191–332.

Rorke, L. B., & Spiro, A. J. Cerebral lesions in congenital rubella syndrome. *Journal of Pediatrics*, 1967, **70**, 243–255.

Rose, A. L., & Lombroso, C. T. Neonatal seizure states. A study of clinical, pathological, and electroencephalographic features in 137 full-term babies with a long-term follow-up. *Pediatrics*, 1970, **45**, 404–425.

Ross, J. J., & Dimette, R. M. Subependymal cerebral hemorrhage in infancy. *American Journal of Diseases in Children*, 1965, **110**, 531–542.

Sarnat, H. B., & Sarnat, M. S. Neonatal encephalopathy following fetal distress. A clinical and electroencephalographic study. *Archives of Neurology*, 1976, **33**, 696–705.

Schrumpf, J. D., Sehring, S., Killpack, S., Brady, J. P., Hirata, T., & Mednick, J. P. Correlation of early neurologic outcome and CT findings in neonatal brain hy-

poxia and injury. *Journal of Computer Associated Tomography*, 1980, **4**, 445–450.

Scott, W. R., New, P. F. J., Davis, K. R., & Schnur, J. A. Computerized axial tomography of intracerebral and intraventricular hemorrhage. *Radiology*, 1974, **112**, 73–80.

Simmons, M. A., Adcock, E. W., Bard, H., & Battaglia, F. C. Hypernatremia and intracranial hemorrhage in neonates. *New England Journal of Medicine*, 1974, **291**, 6–10.

Singer, D. B., Rudolph, A. J., Rosenberg, H. S., Rawls, W. E., & Boniuk, M. Pathology of the congenital rubella syndrome. *Journal of Pediatrics*, 1967, **71**, 665–675.

Stagno, S., Reynolds, D. W., Amos, C. S., Dahle, A. J., McCollister, F. P., Mohindra, I., Ermocilla, R., & Alford, C. A. Auditory and visual defects resulting from symptomatic and subclinical congenital cytomegaloviral toxoplasma infections. *Pediatrics*, 1977, **59**, 669–678.

Takashima, S., & Tanaka, K. Microangiography and vascular permeability of the subependymal matrix in the premature infant. *Canadian Journal of Neurological Sciences*, 1978, **5**, 45–50.

Thompson, J. A., & Glasgow, L. A. Intrauterine viral infection and the cell-mediated immune response. *Neurology*, 1980, **30**, 212–215.

Vannucci, R. C., & Plum, F. Pathophysiology of perinatal hypoxic-ischemic brain damage. In G. E. Gaull (Ed.), *Biology of Brain Dysfunction*. Vol. 3. New York: Plenum Press, 1975, 1–45.

Vannucci, R. C., & Vannucci, S. J. Cerebral carbohydrate metabolism during hypoglycemia and anoxia in newborn rats. *Annals of Neurology*, 1978, **4**, 73–75.

Volpe, J. J. Neonatal intracranial hemorrhage: Pathophysiology, neuropathology, and clinical features. *Clinics in Perinatology*, 1977, **4**, 77–102.

Volpe, J. J. *Neurology of the Newborn*. Philadelphia: W. B. Saunders, 1981.

Yakovlev, P. I., & Rosales, R. K. Distribution of the terminal hemorrhages in the brain wall in stillborn premature and nonviable neonates. In C. R. Angle & E. A. Bering, Jr., (Eds.), *Physical Trauma as an Etiologic Agent in Mental Retardation*. Washington, D.C.: U.S. Government Printing Office, 1970, 67–78.

7 GENETIC DISORDERS*

Dianne N. Abuelo

It has been estimated that approximately half of the individuals with IQ's below 50 have a genetically related condition (Kaveggia, Durkin, & Pendleton, 1973). The true figure is probably higher since these data are derived from studies of institutionalized populations and do not include some of the most severe inherited disorders, for example, inborn metabolic errors, which can cause death in infancy or early childhood. It is therefore important that professionals dealing with mentally retarded individuals and their families be aware of the origins and mechanisms of transmission of these genetic disorders. This awareness is of particular importance during the initial clinical evaluation process and often can determine whether a genetic condition is diagnosed or goes undiscovered.

This chapter will describe the types of inherited conditions that may cause mental retardation, either as an isolated problem or associated with other abnormalities. Its major aim is to provide the reader with a general insight into the manner in which genetic factors influence intellectual function. In addition, a practical step-by-step approach for evaluating the individual affected with mental retardation will be recommended, which may lead to a diagnosis or provide clues as to whether or not the mental retardation is related to an inherited disorder. Frequently, if one is able to establish a diagnosis of a specific inherited disorder, it is then possible to provide information as to the natural history and prognosis of the condition. This may in turn aid in formulating a treatment plan, as well as in anticipating and guarding against known potential complications. Moreover, since other relatives are frequently concerned about their own reproductive risks, this information helps the genetic counselor determine whether other family members are at risk for problems in themselves or in their future offspring.

Types of Genetic Disorders

There are three major classes of genetic disorders (Table 7.1). The first consists of single-gene disorders, which may be transmitted by dominant, recessive, or X chromosome-linked genes. Phenylketonuria is an example of a recessive genetic disease. The number of individuals with this type of disorder is small; approximately 1% of newborns are affected with a single-gene disorder. A complete catalogue of all known and suspected single-gene disorders has been compiled and is updated periodically by McKusick (1978). Each entry in the catalogue consists of a brief descriptive summary of the condition and a list of pertinent references.

* The author would like to thank Miss Jocelyn Blanchet for typing the manuscript.

Table 7.1. Classes of Genetic Disorders

1. Single gene
   A. Dominant
   B. Recessive
   C. X-linked
2. Multifactorial
3. Chromosomal

The second major class of genetic disorders to be considered consists of the multifactorial problems, an example of which is spina bifida, an open defect of the spine. These malformations are thought to be transmitted by a multifactorial combination of several genes interacting with environmental factors. This type of gene-environment interaction also accounts for a large proportion of persons with mild familial mental retardation.

The third class comprises the chromosomal disorders, such as Down syndrome, in which the abnormalities usually result from meiotic errors that occur during formation of either the sperm or the egg, and are usually not hereditary. The major chromosomal disorders are covered elsewhere.

Basic Mechanisms of Inheritance

In the human cell, the genetic material or DNA in the nucleus has subunits known as chromosomes. A human karyotype (Fig. 7.1) normally has 23 pairs of chromosomes; one chromosome from each pair is maternally derived, the other is paternal in origin. A female normally has two X chromosomes; a male has an X and a Y. With present-day laboratory techniques, the chromosomes are easily seen, but the genes, which are arranged linearly along the chromosomes, are not yet microscopically visible. Since the chromosomes are present in pairs, each gene contributed by one parent has a counterpart derived from the other parent. This is true for all of the genes with the exception of the X-linked genes in the male, which do not have counterparts on the Y chromosome.

A gene may "mutate" or become abnormal as a result of some change in its DNA structure. If the mutated gene is able to produce a clinical abnormality in the presence of its normal counterpart, it is known as a dominant gene. Abnormal dominant genes frequently cause structural defects which can involve single organ systems, for example, the connective tissue or skeletal system, but the disorders can also be multisystemic and affect, for example, both the skin and the central nervous system. Recessive genes, on the other hand, usually produce a clinical abnormality only when *both* genes of the pair are abnormal. The genes for X-linked recessive disorders are located on the X chromosome and, therefore, since men do not have a second X, these genes generally cause severe clinical disease only in males. Several examples of genetic disorders from each of these categories will be described.

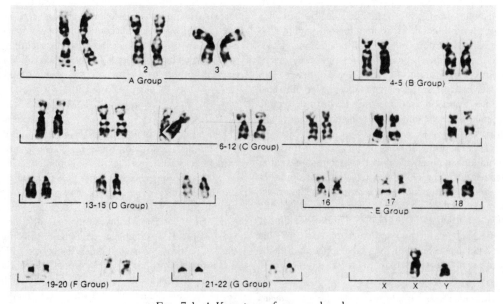

FIG. 7.1. A Karyotype of a normal male.

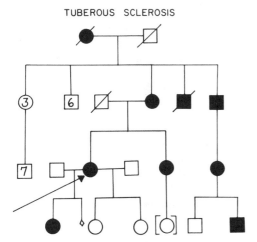

TUBEROUS SCLEROSIS

FIG. 7.2. Pedigree showing dominant transmission; circles are females, squares are males. Solid circles and squares are affected individuals.

Transmission and Characteristics of Dominant Genetic Disorders

In general, during formation of the gametes, one chromosome of each pair is incorporated into the egg or sperm. Thus, the chance for an individual with a dominant gene to pass it on to his or her future offspring, is one in two, or 50%, for each pregnancy. If the dominant disorder is compatible with normal reproductive fitness, one may see a pedigree, or family tree, with transmission from one generation to another (see Fig. 7.2) in a vertical direction.

For certain dominantly inherited disorders, the clinical findings can vary considerably in severity from one individual to another (Table 7.2). This is termed *variable expressivity* of the gene. From time to time, the gene's expression is so mild in a particular individual that its presence cannot be detected at all, in which case, it is stated that the gene is *nonpenetrant* in that individual. For other types of dominant disorders, e.g., achondroplasia, the effects of the gene are quite similar in all affected persons.

With regard to mental retardation, it is clear that if significant mental handicap were invariably associated with a particular dominant disorder, reproductive fitness would be considerably diminished, and little genetic transmission would occur. This situation is not always the case, however, as one of the characteristics of dominant genetic disorders associated with mental retardation is a variable and sometimes late onset as may be seen in myotonic dystrophy. Individuals with this condition may reproduce before they develop any symptoms or before they are diagnosed. Other disorders, e.g., neurocutaneous diseases, show variable expressivity which can allow reproduction and transmission of the gene by the mildly affected individuals.

Neurofibromatosis

The most comon of these disorders is neurofibromatosis, also known as Von Recklinghausens Disease, which has an incidence of 1 in 3,000. The characteristic skin lesion is the café-au-lait spot, which usually appears as an irregular oval-shaped patch of light brown pigmentation. These spots are frequently present at birth and may also multiply during the first two decades (see Fig. 7.3). The presence of six or more spots of at least 1.5 cm in diameter is considered reliable diagnostic evidence of the disease in adults (Crowe, Schull & Neel, 1956). For children, it has been suggested that criteria be five or more spots of 0.5 cm in diameter (Whitehouse, 1966). Physical problems include the development of scoliosis, in-

Table 7.2. Characteristics of Some Dominantly Inherited Disorders

1. Variable expressivity
2. Variable penetrance
3. Variable age of onset

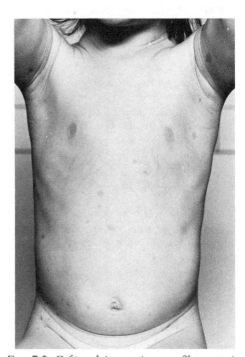

FIG. 7.3. Café-au-lait spots in neurofibromatosis.

Table 7.3. Findings in Neurofibromatosis

	%
Café-au-lait spots	94
Mental deficiency	10
Seizures	12
Macrocranium	24
Scoliosis	40

From Smith (1976).

creased head circumference, and multiple cutaneous and subcutaneous nodules, which may become quite disfiguring. Approximately 12% of affected persons have seizures, and about 10% are mentally retarded. The exact cause of mental retardation is not entirely clear, but probably has to do with an abnormality in brain structure. Neuropathologic studies (Rosman & Pearce, 1967) have shown disorders of the architecture of the cerebral cortex and malposition of neurons that appear to be more severe in mentally retarded than nonretarded persons with neurofibromatosis. Table 7.3 lists the major clinical features.

Persons with neurofibromatosis can differ considerably in the type and severity of clinical manifestations. Because of this, whenever a child is suspected of having this disease, the other family members, especially the parents, should be examined thoroughly for any evidence of the condition. If a parent also is affected, dominant inheritance is documented and the recurrence risk for another affected child to these parents is 50%. If both parents and all sibs are apparently free of the disorder, one usually assumes that it probably resulted from a new gene mutation that occurred in either the sperm or egg that formed the affected individual. The spontaneous mutation rate of neurofibromatosis is relatively high, with approximately 50% of cases thought to result from new mutations. A new mutation would imply a very low recurrence risk for the parents' future offspring, since they themselves do not have the gene. Of course, as far as the affected individual himself, there still exists a 50% risk for each pregnancy that the gene will be passed to the offspring.

Another neurocutaneous disorder, tuberous sclerosis, has a much lower incidence than neurofibromatosis, and is estimated to be approximately 1 in 30,000. Although the incidence is lower, a higher percentage have mental retardation and, in fact, tuberous sclerosis accounts for approximately 0.5% of the institutionalized mentally retarded. Fig. 7.2 illustrates the pedigree of a family with multiple affected members. The typical skin lesions are oval-shaped depigmented areas or "white spots," present on the trunk and extremities from an early age.

The "classic triad" of findings is mental deficiency, epilepsy, and adenoma sebaceum, but many persons with tuberous sclerosis do not have all of these. Also characteristic is the appearance during childhood or adolescence of a nodular eruption in a butterfly distribution on the cheeks that looks somewhat similar to acne. Other manifestations, with their frequencies, are listed in Table 7.4. The basic defect is not yet known. The incidence of mental retardation in tuberous sclerosis is approximately 60% (Vinken & Bruyn, 1972). Seizures are very common, of many types, and may be quite difficult to control. The seizures and mental defect are related to structural abnormalities of the brain including nodules of glial tissue present in the cerebrum, cerebellum, midbrain, and spinal cord, many of which are calcified and can be seen on skull X-ray. Fig. 7.4 is the pedigree of a family with achondroplasia, a fairly common type of skeletal dysplasia causing short stature, a characteristic physical appearance, and a disproportionately large head. It should be pointed out that achondroplasia is not a cause of true mental retardation. A great many patients with achondroplasia have, unfortunately, been misdiagnosed as being mentally retarded, generally on the basis of delayed motor milestones. They usually demonstrate some delay in independent sitting and walking. However, this is probably due to a combination of hypotonia (which slowly improves), ligamentous laxity, and altered body proportions, rather than to true mental deficiency. Parents of children with achondroplasia should be made aware of this and should be told that eventual intellect is usually normal. Fortunately, a timetable for milestones in achondroplasia has recently been published (Todorov, Scott, Warren, & Leeper, 1981), and developmental progress can now be assessed more rationally. Head circumference may be disproportionately large, and mild hydrocephalus usually not requiring treatment may be present. Special graphs for following head growth in achondroplasia are available (Horton, Rotter, Rimoin, Scott, & Hall, 1978).

In addition to achondroplasia, there are many other rarer skeletal dysplasias that can cause dwarfism,

Table 7.4. Findings in Tuberous Sclerosis

	%
Mental retardation	62
Seizures	93
Adenoma sebaceum	83
White skin lesions	82
Retinal phakoma	53
Angiomyolipoma of kidney	45–81
Intracranial mineralization	51

From Smith (1976).

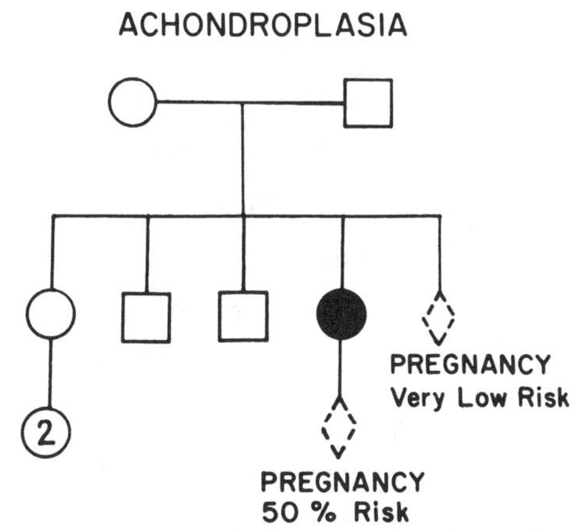

ACHONDROPLASIA

FIG. 7.4. Pedigree of a dominant disorder resulting from a new mutation.

a few of which may be associated with mental retardation. It is, therefore, imperative that an exact clinical and X-ray diagnosis be made for each case so that appropriate treatment and follow-up can be planned. This would best be undertaken in a multidisciplinary setting, such as a genetics clinic which has personnel with expertise in dysmorphology and radiology.

Myotonic Dystrophy

This disorder is also due to a dominant gene with variable expressivity, i.e., manifestations that can vary considerably in character and severity from patient to patient. Myotonic dystrophy is one of the most common types of muscular dystrophy present in adult life. Onset may be at any time from infancy to old age, although the average is the late 20's. Expressivity can be quite variable, and, therefore, at-risk family members should be examined quite thoroughly for suggestive signs of the condition. It is not unusual to discover several previously undiagnosed relatives upon careful family study.

Affected persons have myotonia (difficulty in relaxing a contracted muscle), particularly of the hand and jaw muscles. Weakness of the extremities tends to progress from the proximal to distal musculature. The characteristic facial appearance is described as "expressionless" and includes a drooping mouth, wasting of the temporal areas, and ptosis (drooping of the eyelids) (see Fig. 7.5). The gene that causes myotonic dystrophy can affect many organs in addition to the neuromuscular system. Males may have evidence of gonadal insufficiency, such as testicular atrophy and early frontal baldness. Patients may also have cataracts, cardiac conduction defects, as well as skeletal and endocrine abnormalities. Mental retardation of variable degree is often a feature of this condition,

but the precise cause is not clear. The course is slowly progressive. Patients tend to develop increasing debility and susceptibility to respiratory infections, and their average life span is shortened.

Pregnancy represents a high risk situation for these individuals as they are especially susceptible to complications of labor and delivery, including accentuation of muscle weakness, inadequate ventilation secondary to the interaction of anesthetic drugs with their muscle weakness, and postpartum hemorrhage due to poor uterine contractions. Another potential complication for these women is the occurrence of the severe neonatal form of myotonic dystrophy in their offspring. The disorder appears to be particularly severe in the neonate, and prognosis can be quite poor. Severe muscle weakness, present from early life in utero, can cause club foot and other joint deformities. Facial diplegia is striking, and weakness of the respiratory muscles can lead to ventilatory insufficiency. This severe form of myotonic dystrophy appears to occur exclusively in infants who have inherited the gene from their mothers. It would seem that in pregnant women with myotonic dystrophy, the intrauterine milieu has some unfavorable effect on the expression of the gene in the fetus. It may be that a humoral factor is passed transplacentally from the mother to the fetus, but such a factor has not yet been discovered. In any event, if these infants survive, mental retardation and orthopedic deformities are continuing problems. Of 14 patients with respiratory symptoms in the neonatal period, the average IQ was 56 (Dyken & Harper, 1973). Genetic counseling should be offered to these women, to make them aware of the nature and variability of the disorder, the risks of transmission, and the potential problems associated with childbearing. Many persons with myotonic dystrophy, even if mildly or moderately retarded, can be provided with a basic understanding of the problems and risks involved.

Craniosynostosis Syndromes

Another type of genetic disorder often associated with mental retardation which frequently shows dominant inheritance patterns is the group of craniosynostosis syndromes. Craniosynostosis, which is due to premature closure of one or more sutures, may occur as an isolated finding or may be associated with other physical malformations. The cause is an abnormality in development of the bones of the skull. During fetal life, the skill is formed from several membranous cranial bones which are separated by areas of fibrous tissue called sutures. Growth of the skull bones occurs with and depends on the growth of the underlying brain. After termination of brain growth, the cranial

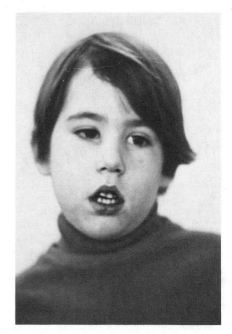

FIG. 7.5. Myotonic dystrophy, mother and son.

bones fuse at the sutures. Premature fusion of a suture causes inability of the cranial bones to grow in that direction, which results in deformity of the skull and a subsequent decreased ability of the brain to grow outward in that area.

Children with premature closure of only one suture usually have normal intelligence (Shillito & Matson, 1968), whereas those with several closed sutures may be mentally retarded, probably due to in-utero damage to the developing brain. In patients with multiple suture involvement, early corrective surgery is recommended for both cosmetic reasons and to hopefully prevent further brain damage.

Table 7.5 lists the more common of the dominantly inherited syndromes, which include both craniosynostosis and frequent mental retardation. The reader is referred to Holmes Atlas (1972) for a thorough consideration of these conditions.

Table 7.5. Craniosynostosis Syndromes

SYNDROME	SUTURES INVOLVED	OTHER FINDINGS
Apert syndrome (acrocephalo-syndactyly)	coronal, lamb-doid, others	total syndactyly fingers and toes
Carpenter	coronal	large thumbs and great toes, variable syndactyly
Crouzon	coronal, others	normal extremities

Apert Syndrome is the most common of the craniosynostosis syndromes. These patients have a striking appearance, including a tower-like skull with a decreased anterior-posterior diameter due to premature closure of the coronal sutures. The eyes are protuberant and have a downward slant. The nasal bridge is underdeveloped, and the nose appears beak-like. There is total syndactyly (fusion) of all the digits resulting in "mitten-like" hands and "sock-like" feet. Early surgical treatment of these abnormalities is recommended. Most of these patients are moderately to severely mentally retarded, but there have been occasional affected persons (see Fig. 7.6) with normal intelligence.

Autosomal Recessive Disorders

A recessive disease is one that is caused by the presence of two abnormal genes for the condition, one having been inherited from the father and one from the mother. In general, one abnormal recessive gene does not cause an abnormality in a person if its counterpart is normal. We are all "carriers" of several abnormal recessive genes, which cause no ill effects if they are present in only one "dose." However, if two parents both carry the same abnormal gene, there is a 1 in 4, or 25% risk for each pregnancy that the offspring will inherit two doses of this gene, and thereby inherit the disorder. Some of these recessive genes are present in higher incidence in certain ethnic groups. For

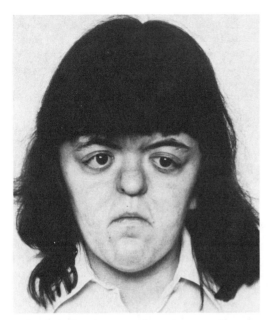

FIG. 7.6. Facial appearance in Apert syndrome.

example, 1 in 30 Ashkenazic Jews is a carrier of Tay-Sachs disease, although the carrier frequency in the general population is approximately one in 300. Autosomal recessive inheritance is characterized by a horizontal pedigree, i.e., affected individuals are usually present only in one generation (see Fig. 7.7). In small families, it may be difficult to establish recessive inheritance from the pedigree pattern, since a child with a recessive disorder may be the only affected family member. Most recessively inherited disorders associated with mental retardation are either metabolic in origin, isolated CNS malformations, or multiple congenital anomaly—mental retardation (MCA/MR) syndromes, as seen in Table 7.6.

A couple who are consanguinous (related to each other), is at an increased risk to have a child affected with a recessive disease, and this risk increases with the closeness of the relationship. The reason is that consanguinity increases the chance that both members of the couple may have inherited the same deleterious recessive gene from a common ancestor. Fig. 7.7 illustrates the pedigree of a family with an extremely rare mental retardation syndrome. In general, the rarer a particular recessive gene, the more likely consanguinity might be present in the parents of an affected individual. Because first cousins have one-eighth of their genes in common, offspring of first cousin marriages theoretically have a substantially increased risk for having birth defects or mental retardation of a recessive nature. However, the increase that is actually

seen in this situation is lower than expected. The risk for any couple in the general population to have a child with a malformation or mental retardation is approximately 3–4%, whereas the risk for first cousins is approximately 6–8%. However, it should be noted that for incestuous matings (father-daughter, brother-sister), the risk for abnormalities in the offspring rises to approximately 30%. It has been suggested (Hall, 1978) that children of consanguinous unions be examined thoroughly with a battery of physical, developmental, and laboratory tests in order to screen them for possible genetic disorders. Moreover, whenever, conversely, a rare recessive disorder is discovered in an offspring of a young teenage mother, especially if there is a negative family history for the condition, one should consider incest as a possibility.

Inborn Errors of Metabolism

Metabolism refers to a stepwise series of biochemical reactions, each of which is catalyzed by a particular enzyme. An inborn error of metabolism is defined as a genetically determined biochemical disorder in which a defect in an enzyme produces a metabolic block which may have pathologic consequences. The metabolic block may involve pathways of metabolism of amino acids, carbohydrates, mucopolysaccharides, etc. The most common of these are the amino acid disorders.

The importance of early detection of inborn errors of amino acid metabolism is that mental retardation is often preventable when the diagnosis is made early and appropriate treatment initiated. For example,

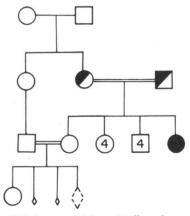

FIG. 7.7. Laurence-Moon-Biedl syndrome. Pedigree of a recessively inherited disorder; double lines indicate consanguinity. Partially shaded squares are normal carriers.

Table 7.6. Recessively Inherited Causes of Mental Retardation

I. Inborn errors of metabolism
    A. Amnioacidurias; e.g., phenylketonuria
    B. Disorders of carbohydrate metabolism; e.g., galactosemia
    C. Lysosomal storage diseases:
        1. Mucopolysaccharidoses: e.g., Hurler syndrome
        2. Sphingolipidoses; e.g., Tay-Sachs disease
        3. Mucolipidoses, e.g., I-cell disease
II. Unclassified Mental Retardation
III. Multiple congenital anomaly—mental retardation (MCA/MR) syndromes; e.g., Laurence-Moon-Biedl syndrome
IV. Isolated CNS malformations; e.g., microcephaly

phenylketonuria (PKU), with an incidence of approximately 1 per 14,000 newborns, used to be associated almost invariably with marked mental retardation, seizures, and behavioral abnormalities. With the advent of neonatal screening programs, since approximately the mid-1960's, affected newborns have been detected at birth and dietary treatment initiated in the neonatal period, with excellent results (Dobson, Williamson, Azen, & Koch, 1977).

The biochemical defect in phenylketonuria is an abnormality of the liver enzyme phenylalanine hydroxylase which is either decreased in amount or defective in activity. The normal function of this enzyme is to convert phenylalanine, a constituent of protein in the normal diet, to tyrosine. The absence of this enzyme produces a "metabolic block," causing a decreased production of tyrosine and a build-up of high levels of phenylalanine (see Fig. 7.8). The high levels of phenylalanine and its metabolites are toxic to the developing brain, although the exact mechanism is not yet clear. In addition to neurologic abnormalities, the untreated child develops an unusual or musty odor which is characteristic of phenylketonuria. Dietary treatment was first reported in 1953 (Bickel, Gerrard, & Hickmans). It is based on the principle that since one cannot supply patients with the missing liver enzyme, one can still aim at lowering the high concentrations of the toxic amino acids into the normal range by prescribing a special diet restricting phe-

nylalanine intake. This is now the standard treatment for PKU and is carried out in special PKU clinics. Close attention is paid to periodic monitoring of phenylalanine blood levels, which assures proper dietary prescription and patient compliance. A recent report from the Collaborative study of children treated for phenylketonuria (Williamson, Koch, Azen, & Chang, 1981) indicates that the children treated from an early age (average 21 days) whose dietary control is satisfactory, attain normal IQ's at age 6. In some clinics, the restricted diet has been liberalized or discontinued at school age, often without major ill effects, in spite of the fact that the children's blood phenylalanine levels may rise to levels known to adversely affect brain development in early infancy. Whether it is truly safe over the long term to discontinue the diet is presently a point of controversy and requires further study. Whatever the result, an even more pressing problem has emerged. There now are an increasing number of successfully treated patients whose diets have been discontinued and who are beginning to reach childbearing age. It has long been known that maternal phenylketonuria can cause intrauterine growth retardation, microcephaly, mental retardation, and congenital heart disease in the developing fetus (Lenke & Levy, 1980). Ironically, if successfully treated females with PKU begin to bear offspring without proper medical management during and almost certainly even before pregnancy, the rate of mental retardation due to PKU may well begin to rise toward levels of the pretreatment era. It is not yet known whether reinitiation of dietary therapy during pregnancy would be effective at preventing these birth defects, but it is clear that a well planned prospective clinical evaluation of preconceptional dietary treatment is sorely needed. Obtaining these data will be the most important clinical and epidemiological challenge to workers in the field of PKU during the next decade.

Galactosemia

Galactosemia is an inborn error of carbohydrate metabolism with an incidence of approximately 1 in 40,000 births. The defective enzyme is galactose-L-

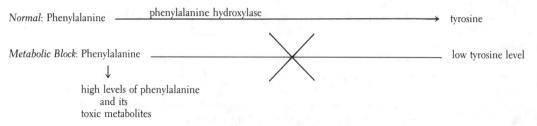

FIG. 7.8. Metabolic block in PKU.

phosphate uridyl transferase which functions in the conversion of galactose to glucose. A defect or absence in this enzyme causes a metabolic block that produces an abnormal accumulation of galactose and its metabolites in the body.

The symptoms of galactosemia begin quite early in infancy and can include failure to thrive, jaundice, enlarged liver, and an unusual susceptibility to fatal neonatal infection. If the patient survives infancy, he eventually develops cataracts, mental retardation, and cirrhosis of the liver.

Since it is not yet possible to supply the missing enzyme, management is directed toward exclusion of galactose from the diet. Since galactose is a component of lactose, which is milk sugar, the dietary prescription consists of excluding milk and its products from the diet. In general, the earlier the diagnosis is made and treatment initiated, the better the results. In one study (Fishler, Koch, Donnell, & Wenz, 1980), children whose treatment was initiated before one month of age had a mean IQ of 95. However, it was noted that half of the children were found to have some difficulties in visual-perceptual functions, so that it should be recognized that treated galactosemic patients with normal IQ levels may nevertheless require some remedial educational intervention. Of particular interest in this respect is that some infants identified and treated from the time of birth do not escape this visual-perceptual handicap. It may be that some damage has occurred prenatally, or that even what is felt to be optimal dietary therapy cannot completely prevent this complication.

Most important with regard to galactosemia, however, is the fact that results from metabolic screening studies in newborn infants usually become available within 2–3 weeks after birth, but these infants are at risk for developing severe clinical illness prior to that time, along with a high risk of death from infection. For those galactosemic infants who become infected and die before they can be screened, the diagnosis may never be made. In order to save as many of these infants as possible, performing and reporting of results of general newborn screening must be done rapidly. In terms of specific cases, if one has a sick newborn who has a family history of a previous sibling with mental retardation or who died in the newborn period either of infection or unknown causes, galactosemia, as well as other metabolic disorders, should be considered and tested for immediately.

There are a number of large regional screening programs in the United States. The New England program presently screens for PKU, galactosemia, homocystinuria, and maple syrup urine disease, as well as hypothyroidism. This latter condition is usually not genetic but has a higher incidence than the above mentioned genetic conditions, is amenable to screening, and can be successfully treated (The New England Congenital Hypothyroidism Collaborative, 1981).

The Lysosomal Storage Diseases

This group of disorders includes the mucopolysaccharidoses, sphingolipidoses, and mucolipidoses. Mental retardation and other abnormalities usually result from lack of a particular enzyme which normally functions in processing certain chemical waste products for excretion. These degradative enzymes are usually present in intracellular organelles called lysosomes. If a particular enzyme is defective, the resulting abnormal material accumulates and is "stored" within the lysosomes. These disorders are not detected in newborn screening programs and most are presently untreatable.

In the mucopolysaccharidoses (e.g., the Hurler syndrome), there is a defect in the degradation of acid mucopolysaccharides, also known as glycoseaminoglycans. These materials are stored in the lysosomes of the brain, heart, viscera, bone, and connective tissue. Affected children, at a few months of age, begin to develop coarse facial features, enlarged heads, enlargement of liver and spleen, and mental retardation. The mucolipidoses are a similar group of conditions in which abnormal physical signs may be present at birth. Here again, treatment is unavailable and prognosis is generally poor.

The most well known of the sphingolipidoses is Tay-Sachs disease, which is due to a defect in the enzyme hexoseaminidase A. Affected infants are usually normal at birth and for the first few months of life, but then development slows, and they lose previously attained skills. The infants develop blindness and spasticity, with death occurring at approximately four years of age. Since carriers have about half of normal enzyme levels, they can be identified. Screening the at-risk adult population on a voluntary basis to detect carriers has been done in many large cities and has resulted in prevention of a considerable number of cases (Kaback, Nathan & Greenwald, 1977). A recent estimate (Kaback, 1980) indicates that this screening program has resulted in a 65–85% reduction of Tay-Sachs disease in North America within the past decade.

There are other lysosomal disorders in addition to many other inherited neurological disorders, some of which are associated with mental retardation, and the interested reader is referred to a recent review of the biochemical genetics of neurologic disease (Rosenberg, 1981).

Unclassified Mental Retardation

It has been noted that some cases of unclassified mental retardation may be caused by recessive factors. Studies done in institutions (Priest, Thaline, & Laveck, 1961; Wright, Tarjan, & Eyer, 1959) have shown that mental retardation occurs in multiple siblings in a considerable number of cases.

Multiple Congenital Anomaly—Mental Retardation (MCA/MR) Syndromes

In addition to these cases in which no specific diagnosis can be made, there are a number of other recessively inherited malformation and malformation-retardation syndromes that are identifiable. Diagnosis of these syndromes is usually based on a certain constellation of clinical findings that is typical for the condition. It should be noted that karyotype analysis is unrevealing in recessively inherited syndromes, but may have to be done in individual cases to rule out a possible chromosomal cause.

The Laurence-Moon-Biedl syndrome is one example of a MCA/MR syndrome that is recessively inherited. Fig. 7.7 illustrates the pedigree of a patient with this condition, whose parents were consanguinous. The patient's sister, who is clinically normal does have an elevated risk of having a similarly affected offspring on the basis of her own marriage to her first cousin.

The characteristic features of the condition include obesity, polydactyly, renal disease, and progressive visual handicap, as well as mental retardation. Multidisciplinary evaluation is necessary for these individuals, who should then be followed by developmental pediatricians, nutritionists, and ophthalmologists, and often by nephrologists as well.

Microcephaly

Microcephaly is defined as a head circumference that measures less than two standard deviations below the mean for a child's age and sex. In general, severe microcephaly is usually associated with mental retardation, but medical professionals should be aware that not every microcephalic child is necessarily mentally retarded (Avery, Meneses, & Lodge, 1972; Sassaman & Zartler, in press). Parents of a newborn infant with a small head size should therefore not be told that mental retardation will definitely occur based on the small head measurement alone. Rather, these infants should be considered to be at risk, evaluated carefully, and followed closely.

The onset of microcephaly is variable; it may be present at birth or may become apparent during infancy. It may be the only malformation present or it can also be associated with other abnormalities.

Microcephaly is considered in this section along with the recessively inherited disorders, but it should be pointed out that there are many different causes of microcephaly, both genetic and nongenetic (see Table 7.7). It is important to make every possible effort to identify the cause of a child's microcephaly, both for prognostic purposes, and also to allow proper genetic counseling to the parents with regard to the recurrence risk for future offspring.

A nongenetic cause may occasionally be identified by a careful pregnancy history which may identify infectious diseases, drugs such as anticonvulsants, alcohol ingestion, etc. Perinatal brain damage can cause mental retardation with or without the later development of microcephaly and spasticity. Again, the birth history should be taken very carefully and documented with delivery records whenever possible in cases where brain damage is presumed to have been caused by perinatal asphyxia.

Malformations intrinsic to the brain itself can also be associated with small head size. Rarely, microcephaly occurs secondary to a congenital malformation such as premature suture synostosis, which, as mentioned previously, should be corrected promptly.

Other genetic causes of microcephaly include the common chromosomal disorders, e.g., Down syndrome. Many of the rare chromosomal disorders are also associated with microcephaly. Even when the head measurement is normal, as a general rule, nearly all persons with abnormal karyotypes (except those involving the sex chromosomes) have some degree of mental retardation.

Isolated microcephaly, when inherited, is usually recessive in origin although it has been X-linked in some families (Holmes, 1972). Recently, a dominant

Table 7.7. Causes of Microcephaly

I. Nongenetic
  1. Teratogens; e.g., alcohol, hydantoin
  2. Intrauterine infections; e.g., due to "TORCH" agents
  3. Perinatal brain damage; e.g., due to asphyxia, infections
  4. Congenital malformations; e.g., premature suture synostosis
II. Genetic
  1. Chromosomal disorders; e.g., Down syndrome
  2. Familial microcephaly (recessive, X-linked, dominant)
  3. Multiple anomaly syndromes with microcephaly

NOTE: "TORCH" agents include the agents which cause toxoplasmosis, rubella, cytomegalic inclusion disease, herpes infection, and syphilis.

form of microcephaly has been suggested (Haslam & Smith, 1979). In addition, there are a large number of syndromes in which microcephaly is associated with other congenital anomalies.

X-Linked Disorders

In X-linked recessive disorders, the abnormal recessive gene is located on the X chromosome. As previously mentioned, only males are affected by X-linked disorders, since they have only one X chromosome. Transmission is by carrier females who have the abnormal gene but also have its normal counterpart on their second X. Table 7.8 lists some X-linked disorders associated with mental retardation.

The Lesch-Nyhan Syndrome

A well-known example of an X-linked mental retardation syndrome is the Lesch-Nyhan syndrome, a metabolic disorder characterized by mental retardation, spasticity, and self-mutilation.

The Lesch-Nyhan syndrome is an inherited type of cerebral palsy. The abnormal gene on the X chromosome causes an inborn error of purine metabolism. These patients have a deficiency of the enzyme hypoxanthine - guanine - phosphoribosyltransferase (HPRT). Clinical signs of the condition include mental retardation, abnormal neurological signs and behavioral abnormalities. Lesch-Nyhan is the first condition identified in which a biochemical defect has been associated with a specific type of aberrant behavior (Seegmiller, 1972).

Affected infants, always male, appear normal at birth and for the first few months of life. The first sign of the condition is often the parents' discovery of some orange sand in the diapers, which are crystals of uric acid (Nyhan, 1978). The infants lose the ability to sit independently and develop signs of cerebral palsy, including marked hypertonia, athetoid posturing, dysarthria, and choreic movements. Compared to other types of cerebral palsy, the motor deficit is said to appear worse than the degree of mental retardation. Most affected patients do develop some speech, but the IQ is usually less than 50.

Medical complications that may develop include urinary tract stones, renal failure, and gout. Untreated,

these problems could lead to death before the time of puberty. Treatment with the drug allopurinol has been successful in medical management, but has not been effective in modifying the neurological or behavioral problems in these children (Nyhan, Johnson, Kaufman & Jones, 1980).

The behavioral manifestations consist of self-mutilation; patients bite their lips and fingers so severely that permanent tissue damage and loss results. These children are often aggressive against others. Until a treatment becomes available for this condition, or one that at least can ameliorate the behavioral manifestations, day-to-day management of most patients with the Lesch-Nyhan syndrome consists of physical restraint in order to protect them from themselves. Behavior modification techniques have been employed; some of the results have been encouraging while others have not (Nyhan, 1978). The Lesch-Nyhan syndrome should be considered a possibility whenever cerebral palsy in males "runs in the family" or in any spastic child with aggressive or self-injurious behavior. Prevention by use of amniocentesis in future pregnancies of carrier women is possible since affected fetuses can be identified (Seegmiller, 1972).

X-Linked Mental Retardation

It has long been known that there are more males than females in institutions for the mentally retarded (Penrose, 1938). A survey from Australia (Turner & Turner, 1974) of all mentally retarded persons born during a 10-year period showed that this increased population of males was present in both the institutionalized and non-institutionalized groups. It was also noted that mentally retarded males were more likely to have affected male relatives than mentally retarded females to have affected female relatives. These findings suggested that X-linked disorders could account for many cases of nonspecific mental retardation in males, that is, retardation of unknown cause unaccompanied by physical abnormalities.

Many families have now been described, including that studied by Renpenning (1962), with mental retardation without abnormal physical findings and pedigrees consistent with X-linked inheritance. This finding has been termed the "Renpenning Syndrome."

Fragile X-Associated Mental Retardation

In 1969, a family was described (Lubs, 1969), with nonspecific X-linked mental retardation in which the affected males had a chromosomal abnormality consisting of a constriction or narrowing near the end of the long arm of the X chromosome. In some of the

Table 7.8. X-linked Causes of Mental Retardation

I. Metabolic; e.g. Lesch-Nyhan syndrome
II. Nonchromosomal; e.g., Renpenning
III. Possibly chromosomal; e.g., Fragile X-associated retardation
IV. Malformation syndrome; e.g., X-linked aqueductal stenosis

chromosomes studied, the piece below this constriction was found to actually break off, leading to the designation "fragile X chromosome" for the unusual chromosome and "fragile X syndrome" for the mental retardation syndrome associated with it (see Fig. 7.9).

After this initial observation, no further families with this abnormality were detected for several years. Recently, however, the syndrome has been rediscovered (Harvey, Judge, & Wiener, 1977) and, in fact, has been found to affect a considerable proportion of mentally retarded males. The reason it had gone undetected after the initial observation was found to be due to the composition of the culture medium used for growing white blood cells for karyotype preparation. In the late 1960s, Medium 199 was in general use and allowed expression and detection of the fragile site on the X chromosome due to its relative deficiency of folic acid. In the early 1970s, Medium 199 was replaced in most laboratories by an enriched culture medium, which in retrospect, appears to have suppressed this fragile site. Since 1977, studies using the original culture technique have led to the rediscovery of the fragile X. A large number of reports have now appeared that have further defined the syndrome. Physical signs associated with the condition are not striking, except for enlargement of the testicles. The incidence is not yet known, but it appears to be relatively high, and may well be second to Down syndrome as a diagnosable cause of mental retardation (Gerald, 1980). Interestingly, some female carriers have been

found to be mildly affected (Turner, Brookwell, Daniel, Selikowitz, & Zilibowitz, 1980). It is not yet known whether the fragile site relates to the mental retardation in any causative manner. It should be noted that all males with X-linked mental retardation do not necessarily exhibit this fragile site. The exact proportion who do is not yet known. In fact, when studied for the fragile X, Renpenning's original family was found not to have it (Fox, Fox, & Gerrard, 1980).

In summary, the fragile X syndrome should be specifically looked for in non-malformed mentally retarded males, particularly if there is a history of other affected family members. Since carrier mothers and sisters often exhibit this fragile site on one of their X chromosomes, prenatal diagnosis will doubtless become available in the near future.

Malformation Syndrome

There are other X-linked disorders associated with mental retardation, including a type of familial sex-linked mental retardation often associated with hydrocephalus due to aqueductal stenosis. These male infants with hydrocephalus may appear similar to those without the genetic form, but may be distinguished by the presence of a flexed or adducted thumb (which is present in about half of these patients), or a positive family history. Other brain malformations may be present in these patients, and their overall outlook is poor.

Multifactorially Inherited Disorders

As was mentioned earlier, the single gene disorders account for only a small percentage of mentally retarded individuals. The larger proportion comprises those individuals affected with mild, familial mental retardation, which is caused by multifactorial transmission. Multifactorially inherited disorders are caused by the additive effects of both genetic and environmental factors. The mechanism of multifactorial inheritance is not completely understood at present, especially with regard to which environmental factors play a role and how they exert their effects. Recurrence risk is much lower than for the single gene defects, usually on the order of 3–5%.

Neural Tube Defects

Neural tube defects, which are open defects of the brain and spinal cord, are also considered to be multifactorially inherited. This group of birth defects includes anencephaly, a severe and fatal defect in brain development, encephalocele (a protrusion of brain tissue through a defect in the cranium), and spina

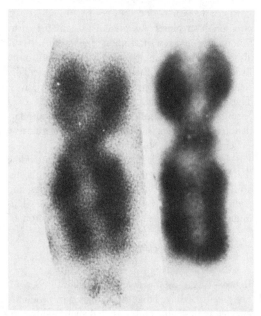

FIG. 7.9. "Fragile" site on X chromosome of a related male.

bifida, which includes meningoceles and meningo-myloceles. The incidence of neural tube defects in the United States is about 1 per 500 births. The prognosis in the 1950's for these children was fairly bleak and most were left to die. In the 1960's, vigorous treatment was implemented, but some of the survivors were left with rather severe deficits. Currently, with early and comprehensive treatment, prognosis is much improved. Survival is now 80–95% (Leonard & Free-man, 1981), and there have been many advances in the treatment of the secondary problems of bladder and bowel incontinence. Hydrocephalus develops in 70–90% of these children. The complications of hy-drocephalus used to account for the frequent intel-lectual impairment seen in these individuals in the past. Again, recent improvements in shunt technology and medical and surgical management have improved the prognosis for intellectual function in persons with spina bifida and a much smaller percentage are mod-erately or severely mentally retarded. Most of the children can attend regular schools, but it should be noted that even those with normal IQ scores are at risk for visual or perceptual problems, which should be specifically looked for and remediated if present. Parents of children with neural tube defects should be referred for genetic counseling, since prenatal di-agnosis is available for future pregnancies. The in-cidence of neural tube defects appears to be decreasing somewhat during recent years for reasons that are not clear. In addition, the availability of prenatal diagnosis and the increasing utilization of maternal serum alpha-fetoprotein screening during pregnancy should decrease the incidence still further in the future.

Familial Mental Retardation

The types of genetically transmitted mental retardation that have been discussed so far, usually involve some type of brain pathology, and are associated with either an intrinsic brain malformation, or a metabolic ab-normality that causes brain damage. However, there are a large number of mentally retarded individuals without demonstrable brain pathology. They are usu-ally borderline or mildly mentally retarded, and other family members are frequently mentally retarded as well. The explanation for this relates to the fact that like many other population traits, human intelligence is distributed along a continuous, bell-shaped curve. It is thought that mild, familial mental retardation is due to the combined effects of being on the low end of the population curve for intelligence along with the sociocultural problems that frequently are associated with it, such as poverty, environmental deprivation, etc. (Moser & Wolf, 1971). Whenever multiple sibs

in one family have mental retardation without striking physical abnormalities, and the parents are similarly affected, multifactorial inheritance should be con-sidered. In this situation, it may be useful to consider and test for other causes, such as maternal PKU, and one should also try to rule out teratogenic causes. Maternal anticonvulsant ingestion and alcohol abuse are two examples of teratogens that can mimic ge-netically caused mental retardation by affecting several sibs in one family with mental and growth retardation and mildly dysmorphic features.

Genetic Evaluation of the Mentally Retarded Child

As mentioned previously, an accurate diagnosis of the etiology of mental deficiency is essential for many reasons: for determining prognosis, for planning and evaluating treatment, and for counseling the family accurately with regard to the cause (whether genetic or not), recurrence risk, and potential means for pre-vention in future offspring in the family. The results of one study (Hunter, Evans, Thompson, & Ramsey, 1980) indicated that between 31 and 44% of moderately to profoundly mentally retarded institutionalized pa-tients were mentally retarded owing to causes that might be prevented.

It should be stressed that there is no laboratory test or tests that should be obtained routinely for diagnostic reasons on all mentally retarded individuals. The most important exercise in the evaluation of a mentally retarded person is the performance of an appropriate history and physical examination as out-lined by Smith and Simons (1975), and in the diagrams in Figs. 7.10 and 7.11.

First, the pregnancy and neonatal history is con-sidered in detail, including duration of gestation, ill-ness, drugs (including alcohol), onset and quality of fetal movements and maternal weight gain. Birth rec-ords should be obtained for descriptions of the pre-sentation, length of labor, Apgar scores, condition at delivery, the infant's weight, length, and head cir-cumference, and any perinatal problems, including jaundice and hypoglycemia. For early infancy, a careful developmental history is noted as well as any significant illnesses or hospitalizations.

The family history can provide important clues, both for diagnosis and counseling. A pedigree diagram is fairly simple to draw and can be helpful for deter-mining patterns of inheritance. The result of each pregnancy, including miscarriages, premature births, and stillbirths, should be included on the pedigree, and notations should be made as to whether there

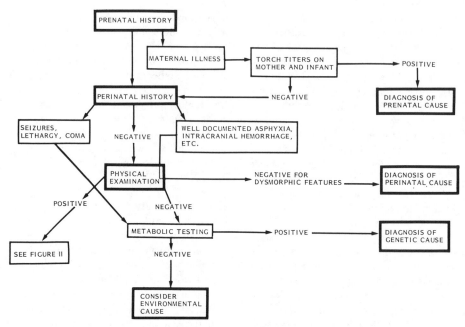

FIG. 7.10. Algorithm for evaluation of patient with mental retardation.

are other similarly affected individuals, persons with congenital malformations, mental retardation, etc., and whether consanguinity is present. Parents' ages should be included, as there is a correlation between advanced maternal age and chromosome abnormalities (e.g., Down syndrome) and also between advanced paternal age and some new dominant mutations (e.g., Apert syndrome).

The physical examination should include the percentiles for the child's height, weight, and head circumference, and a careful examination for major and minor congenital anomalies. The distinctions between major and minor anomalies and definitions of normal variant findings are described in Smith (1976).

The combined results of the history and physical examinations may indicate or point toward a specific diagnosis. If at this point, however, a definite diagnosis has not become evident, it may be helpful to go through the exercise of postulating the possible timing of the damage to the central nervous system, i.e., whether the insult may have been prenatal, perinatal, or postnatal in origin. This may suggest a direction for further testing.

A prenatal abnormality in development of the brain, often manifest as abnormal size of the head, may account for as many as 53% of the more severely affected (Smith & Simons, 1975). This includes microcephaly and macrocephaly, conditions with both genetic and nongenetic etiologies. In cases of macrocephaly, the first test that should be done is the simplest and cheapest—transillumination of the

cranium with a flashlight. Abnormal transillumination can suggest hydrocephalus, hydroencephaly, porencephalic cyst, subdural effusion, etc. Recently, C-T scans or ultrasound examinations have become routine in investigation of macrocephaly. One recent study (Donat, 1981) indicates that 75% of these children have hydrocephalus, while many of the others had primary megalencephaly (increased brain size). Although some authors feel that megalencephaly is usually associated with abnormal neurologic development (Donat, 1981), others (Lorber & Priestley, 1981) feel that the vast majority are normal.

The workup for microcephaly includes skull X-rays to rule out premature suture synostosis and to look for intracranial calcifications as well as TORCH titers (see note to Table 7.7). If these are negative, chromosomal analysis should be performed. It should be noted that TORCH studies involve comparisons of antibody levels to the putative infecting organism, and can be truly diagnostic only if done shortly after birth and only if any high antibody levels that are found are shown to be nonmaternal in origin. Results from studies undertaken several months after birth can only be suggestive, since postnatal infection and antibody formation is possible.

Those patients with both CNS and other congenital malformations and those with MCA/MR syndromes should usually be karyotyped.

Perinatal causes of mental retardation accounted for three percent in Smith, Estelle, and Simons' study (1975) and can include prematurity with its many

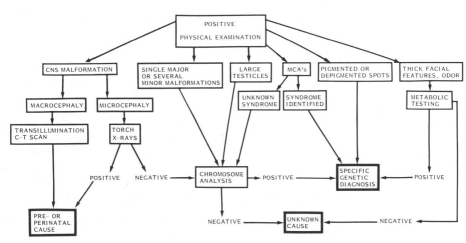

FIG. 7.11. Algorithm for evaluation of patient with mental retardation.

complications, birth asphyxia, sepsis, etc. However, in evaluating individual patients, one should use caution before invoking any of these as the cause of the mental retardation until appropriate efforts have been made to consider and rule out all possible prenatal causes. The author has seen several cases in which a genetic problem has been overlooked and mental retardation attributed mistakenly to the umbilical cord around the infant's neck at delivery. It is also important to note that preexisting central nervous system anomalies, neuromuscular disorders, or hypotonia of any cause, appear to predispose to abnormal presentations, difficult deliveries, and breathing difficulties at birth, which could result in birth asphyxia superimposed on an underlying genetic disorder. Mental retardation then could be due to a combination of both causes, which unfortunately sometimes act synergistically. For this reason, every infant who has been depressed at birth should be carefully examined for an underlying cause for the depression before attributing subsequent retardation to birth injury alone.

Another group of infants may have a benign prenatal history and appear normal at birth, but mental retardation is suspected postnatally, when their developmental landmarks are found to be delayed. Some may reach a plateau in their accomplishments and then begin to regress. This is a frequent presentation for mentally retarded patients with inborn errors of metabolism, which accounted for 4.2% in Kaveggia's study (Kaveggia, Durken, & Pendelton, 1973). Specific testing for metabolic errors and hypothyroidism is therefore appropriate for patients in this category. Environmental causes should certainly be considered as well, such as sociocultural deprivation, lead poisoning, etc. Appropriate investigations may include social service evaluation of the family circumstances, blood lead levels, etc.

The utility of this type of evaluation is that all relevant diagnostic laboratory determinations can be performed, and those which would not be contributory are omitted. Certainly, not all patients can be easily categorized, and some may have evidence of not only prenatal but perinatal and postnatal complications as well. In conclusion, the direction and extent of the evaluation must be individualized, and consideration for further laboratory testing should be based upon a thoughtful interpretation of the history and physical examination as outlined above. If no firm diagnosis can be made, the family should be so informed. Even in these cases, referral for genetic counseling is appropriate since empiric recurrence risk figures are available (Lubs & Maes, 1977).

References

Avery, G. B., Meneses, L., & Lodge, A. The clinical significance of "measurement microcephaly." *American Journal of Diseases of Children*, 1972, **123**, 214–217.

Bickel, H., Gerrard, J., & Hickmans, E. M. Influence of phenylalanine intake on phenylketonuria. *Lancet*, 1953, **2**, 812.

Crowe, F. W., & Schull, W. J. Diagnostic importance of cafe-au-lait spot in neurofibromatosis. *Archives of Internal Medicine*, 1953, **91**, 758–766.

Crowe, F. W., Schull, W. J., & Neel, J. V. *A clinical, pathological, and genetic study of multiple neurofibromatosis*. Springfield, Illinois: Charles C. Thomas, 1956.

Dobson, J. C., Williamson, M. L., Azen, C., & Koch, R. Intellectual assessment of III four-year-old children with phenylketonuria. *Pediatrics*, 1977, **60**, 822–827.

Donat, J. F. G. Evaluation of macrocrania using computed tomography. *American Journal of Diseases of Children*, December, 1981, **135**, 1118–1121.

Dykin, P. R., & Harper, P. S. Congenital dystrophia myotonica. *Neurology*, 1973, **23**, 465–473.

Fishler, K., Koch, R., Donnell, G. N., & Wenz, E. Developmental aspects of Galactosemia from infancy to childhood. *Metabolism*, 1980, **19**, 38–44.

Fox, P., Fox, D., & Gerrard, J. W. X-linked mental retardation: Renpenning revisited. *American Journal of Medical Genetics*, 1980, 7, 491–495.

Gerald, P. S. X-Linked mental retardation and an X-Chromosome Marker. *The New England Journal of Medicine*, 1980, 303, 696–697.

Gorlin, R. J., Pindborg, J. J., & Cohen, M. M. *Syndromes of the head and neck*. New York: McGraw-Hill, 1976.

Hall, J. G. Children of incest: When to suspect and how to evaluate. *American Journal of Diseases of Children*, 1978, 132, 1045.

Harper, P. S., Tyler, A., Walker, D. A., Newcombe, R. G., & Davies, K. Huntington's chorea: The basis for long-term prevention. *Lancet*, 1979, 1, 346–349.

Harvey, J., Judge, C., & Wiener, S. Familial X-linked mental retardation with an X chromosome abnormality. *Journal of Medical Genetics*, 1977, 14, 45–50.

Haslam, R. H. A., & Smith, D. W. Autosomal dominant microcephaly. *Journal of Pediatrics*, 1979, 95, 701–705.

Holmes, L. B., Moser, H. W., Halldorsson, S., Mack, C., Pant, S. S., & Matzilevich, B. *Mental retardation. An atlas of disease with associated physical abnormalities*. New York: Macmillan, 1972.

Horton, W. A., Rotter, J. I., Rimoin, D. L., Scott, C. I., & Hall, J. G. Standard growth curves for achondroplasia. *The Journal of Pediatrics*, 1978, 93, 435–438.

Hunter, A. G. W., Evans, J. A., Thompson, D. R., & Ramsay, S. A study of institutionalized mentally retarded patients in Manitoba, I: Classification and preventability. *Developmental Medicine and Child Neurology*, 1980, 22, 145–162.

Kaback, M. M. Unpublished data. Los Angeles: University of California, 1980.

Kaback, M. M., Nathan, T. J., & Greenwald, S. Tay-Sachs disease: Heterozygote screening and prenatal diagnosis: U.S. experience and world perspective. *Prognostic Clinical Biological Research*, 1977, 18, 33–36.

Kaveggia, E. G., Durkin, M. V., & Pendleton, E. Diagnostic genetic studies on 1,224 patients with severe mental retardation. Paper read before the Third Congress of the International Association for Scientific Study of Mental Deficiency. The Hague, September 4–12, 1973.

Lenke, R. R., & Levy, H. Maternal phenylketonuria and hyperphenylalanemia: An international survey of the outcome of untreated and treated pregnancies. *New England Journal of Medicine*, 1980, 303, 1202–1208.

Leonard, C. O., & Freeman, J. M. Spina Bifida: A New Disease. *Pediatrics*, 1981, 68, 136–137.

Lorber, J., & Priestley, B. L. Children with large heads: A practical approach to diagnosis in 557 children, with special reference to 109 children with megalencephaly. *Developmental Medicine and Child Neurology*, 1981, 23, 494–504.

Lubs, H. A. A marker X chromosome. *American Journal of Human Genetics*, 1969, 21, 231–244.

Lubs, M. L. E., & Maes, J. A. Recurrence risk in mental retardation. *Biomedical Aspects*, 1977.

McKusick, V. *Mendelian inheritance in man: Catalogs of autosomal dominant, autosomal recessive, and X-linked phenotypes.* 5th Ed. Baltimore: The Johns Hopkins University Press, 1978.

Monaghan, H. P., Krafchik, B. R., MacGregor, D. L., & Fitz, C. R. Tuberous sclerosis complex in children. *American Journal of Diseases of Children*, 1981, 135, 912–917.

Moser, H. W., & Wolf, P. A. The nosology of mental retardation: Including the report of a survey of 1,378 mentally retarded individuals of the Walter E. Fernald State School. *Birth Defects: Original Article Series*, 1971, 7, 117–134.

The New England Congenital Hypothyroidism Collaborative. Effects of neonatal screening for hypothyroidism: Prevention of mental retardation by treatment before clinical manifestations. *Lancet*, 1981, 1, 1095–1098.

Nyhan, W. L. The Lesch-Nyhan syndrome. *Developmental Medicine and Child Neurology*, 1978, 20, 376–387.

Nyhan, W. L., Johnson, H. G., Kaufman, I. A., & Jones, K. L. Serotonergic approach to the modification of behavior in the Lesch-Nyhan syndrome. *Applied Research in Mental Retardation*, 1980, 1, 25–40.

Penrose, L. S. A clinical and genetic study of 1,280 cases of mental defect (Special Report Series No. 299). London: Medical Research Council, 1938.

Priest, J. H., Thaline, H. C., & Laveck, G. D. An approach to genetic factors in mental retardation: Studies of families containing at least two siblings admitted to a state institution for the retarded. *American Journal of Mental Deficiency*, 1961, 66, 42–50.

Renpenning, H., Gerrard, J. W., Zaleski, W. A., & Tabata, T. Familial sex-linked mental retardation. *Canadian Medical Association Journal*, 1962, 87, 954–956.

Rosenberg, R. N. Biochemical Genetics of Neurologic Disease. *New England Journal of Medicine*, 1981, 305, 1181–1193.

Rosman, N. P., & Pearce, J. The brain in multiple neurofibromatosis (Von Recklinghausen's disease): A suggested neuropathological basis for the associated mental defect. *Brain*, 1967, 90, 829–838.

Sassaman, E. A., & Zartler, A. S. Mental retardation and head growth abnormalities. *Journal of Pediatric Psychology*. In press.

Seegmiller, J. E. Lesch-Nyhan syndrome and X-linked uric acidurias. *Hospital Practice*, 1972, 79–90.

Shillito, J., Jr., & Matson, D. D. Craniosynostosis: A review of 519 surgical patients. *Pediatrics*, 1968, 41, 829–853.

Smith, D. W., Estelle, F., & Simons, R. Rationale diagnostic evaluation of the child with mental deficiency. *American Journal of Diseases of Children*, 1975, 129, 1285–1290.

Todorov, A. B., Scott, C. I., Warren, A. E., & Leeper, J. D. Developmental screening tests in achondroplastic children. *American Journal of Medical Genetics*, 1981, 9, 19–23.

Turner, G., & Turner, B. X-linked mental retardation. *Journal of Medical Genetics*, 1977, 14, 46–50.

Turner, G., Brookwell, R., Daniel, A., Selikowitz, M., & Zilibowitz, M. Heterozygous expression of X-linked mental retardation and X-chromosome marker fra(X) (q27). *The New England Journal of Medicine*, 1980, 303, 662–664.

Vinken, P. J., & Bruyn, G. W. Phakomatosis. In P. J. Vinken & G. W. Bruyn (Eds.), *Handbook of Clinical Neurology*. Vol. 9. New York: Elsevier Publishing Co., Inc., 1972.

Whitehouse, D. Diagnostic value of the cafe-au-lait spot in children. *Archives of Diseases in Childhood*, 1966, 41, 316–319.

Williamson, M. L., Koch, R., Azen, C., & Chang, C. Correlates of intelligence test results in treated phenylketonuria children. *Pediatrics*, 1981, 68, 161–167.

Wright, S. W., Tarjan, G., & Eyer, L. Investigation of families with two or more mentally defective siblings: Clinical observations. *American Journal of Diseases of Children*, 1959, 97, 445–456.

8 CHROMOSOME DISORDERS

Siegfried M. Pueschel and Horace C. Thuline

Historical Considerations

There has been extraordinary progress in the field of cytogenetics during the past century. This has been primarily the result of technical advances and innovative methods that allowed identification of chromosome structural elements. Early investigators such as Naegeli (1842) observed thread-like bodies in cell nuclei; later, Virchow (1858) studied cell division, and in 1882 Fleming described mitosis in human corneal epithelial cells. In 1888, Waldeyer introduced the term "chromosomes" and united theories about cell nuclei and chromosomes into the concept that chromosomes maintain genetic continuity from generation to generation. Later, Sutton (1903) demonstrated that chromosomes were the segregating and recombination units of reproduction.

Hansemann (1891) made an early attempt to determine the number of human chromosomes; he reported counts of 18, 24, and over 40 chromosomes in three respective cells from human tissue. In 1912, von Winiwarter found 47 chromosomes in a spermatogonial metaphase plate and 23 pairs of chromosomes plus one unpaired chromosome in primary spermatocytes. He concluded that the human male had 47 chromosomes and that the female had 48 chromosomes. Painter (1921) reported that the number of chromosomes in cells from spermatogonial material

was either 46 or 48. In a later paper, Painter (1923) concluded that the correct diploid number of chromosomes for both human sexes was 48.

During the mid-1930s, Heitz (1936) developed the squash technique which allowed examining chromosomes in a thin spread. This squash technique was refined during the following years by the use of non-hardening fixatives such as acetic acid, lactic acid, and alcohol. In 1937, Gavaudan, Gavaudan, and Pomriaskinsky-Kobozieff observed colchicine to be a potent spindle poison and this prompted scientists to use colchicine to prevent the formation of the metaphase plate.

Although the effects of anisotonic solutions on cells had already been noted during the 1930s, this technique was not utilized until the early 1950s when Hughes (1952) and Hsu (1952) independently reported the results of the hypotonic treatment in producing improved separation of chromosomes in metaphase spreads. Moreover, tissue culture methods developed for the production of polio vaccine in the 1950s made it possible to study large numbers of easily accessible dividing mammalian cells.

Thanks to these technical advances, Tjio and Levan (1956) were able to demonstrate the correct number of chromosomes in human cells. They found 46 chromosomes in cultured cells of fetal lung tissue.

Ford and Hamerton (1956) confirmed Tjio and Levan's findings, using testicular tissue. They identified 46 chromosomes in spermatogonial metaphases and 23 bivalents in primary spermatocytes at metaphase. The subsequent introduction of short term tissue culture procedures for peripheral blood, using phytohemagglutin to stimulate cell division in small lymphocytes, brought human cytogenetics within the reach of non-research laboratories. Medical cytogenetics became a reality when Lejeune, Gauthier, and Turpin (1959) found an additional small chromosome in patients with Down syndrome. Shortly thereafter, Jacobs, Baikie, Court-Brown, and Strong (1959) also observed a supernumerary small acrocentric chromosome in cells from bone marrow preparation of a patient with Down syndrome. During subsequent years, many other chromosomal aberrations have been reported in the literature.

Tissue Cultures

The introduction of peripheral blood leukocyte culture methods (Arakaki & Sparkes, 1963; Edwards, 1962; Froland, 1962; Hungerford, Donnelly, Nowell, & Beck, 1959; Moorhead, Nowell, Mellman, Battips, & Hungerford, 1960) made cytogenetics a fairly routine procedure. Among the various cells in the circulating blood, only the small lymphocyte is routinely used for chromosome studies.

The other most common cell type studied for cytogenetic diagnosis is the fibroblast grown from a tissue biopsy, most often taken from skin. Since fibroblasts do not respond to mitogens, as lymphocytes do, the procedure is more prolonged. The biopsy tissue which is minced and seeded into culture medium requires incubation from two to four weeks (small lymphocytes can be harvested after three days) before there is assurance of adequate fibroblast growth. Rigid aseptic techniques have to be followed from collection of tissue through every step of the procedure to prevent contamination by bacteria or mycoplasma.

The quickest method for cytogenetic diagnosis is by bone marrow aspiration and processing of cells already in mitosis. The usual procedure is to suspend the bone marrow in tissue culture media containing colchicine, then treat it with hypotonic solution and harvest. With this methodology for newborns, when it is necessary to establish a diagnosis quickly for management decisions, the chromosome status can usually be determined within a few hours (Francke, Brown, & Jones, 1979).

The tissue culture methods used for amniotic fluid cells obtained by amniocentesis for prenatal diagnosis of fetal chromosome status are critical. There is great pressure on a laboratory to complete the study in less than three weeks, to have no laboratory failures or false or equivocal results. Consequently, procedures must be meticulous, control of all elements of the procedure must be maintained, and the cytogeneticist must be experienced in the interpretation of the findings.

Staining and Banding

The three types of stains most commonly used prior to the advent of banding techniques in 1969, were the Feulgen reaction for DNA, orcein, and the azure-based dyes including Giemsa, Leishman's, and Wright's stains. The previously preferred Giemsa stain is still most commonly used.

During the 1960s, cytogeneticists would occasionally find a Giemsa-stained metaphase spread in which the chromosomes had faint bands transverse to the axis of the chromatids. However, this finding was inconsistent and infrequent enough that it was not recognized as a potentially important phenomenon. Only when Caspersson, Zech, Wagh, Modest, and Simonsson (1969) and Zech (1969) began working with fluorescent dyes was banding observed reproducibly and recognized as a demonstrable characteristic of chromosome structure. The fluorescent banding obtained with quinacrine dihydrochloride and quinacrine mustard, was discovered in plant chromosomes. Within two years, Caspersson, Zech, Johansson and Modest (1970) had described the consistent banding pattern for each human chromosome pair and had shown that every pair of chromosomes could be conclusively identified, including the three 21 chromosomes in Down syndrome (Caspersson, Hulten, Linsten, & Zech, 1970).

The banding pattern produced by the quinacrine derivatives is called Q-banding. Q-banding is useful in rapid analysis of chromosomes for sequential staining (Magenis, Palmer, Wang, Brown, Chamberlain, Parks, Merritt, Rivas, & Yu, 1977). Fig. 8.1 illustrates unbanded and Q-banded chromosomes of the G group and the Y chromosome. Disadvantages of Q-banding and other fluorescent methods are the lack of permanence, the need for fluorescence microscopy, and great technical photomicroscopic skills.

Once it was realized that chromosome banding could be produced, reports of various techniques appeared. Arrighi and Hsu (1971) and Yunis, Roldan, Yasmineh, and Lee (1971) published procedures for selective staining of constitutive heterochromatin in the centromeres and secondary constrictions of human chromosomes based on the method of Pardue and Gall (1970) for mouse chromosomes. The denatur-

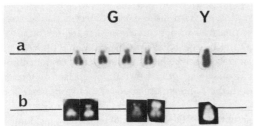

FIG. 8.1. Standard staining and Q-banding of the G & Y group. (a) Pairs 21 and 22 stained with orcein or Giemsa without pre-treatment cannot be distinguished. The Y-chromosome usually can be identified by morphology. (b) Q-banding allows distinction of pairs 21 from 22 and gives the Y-specific bright fluorescence in the long arm of the Y. The chromosomes of pairs 21 and 22 illustrate the Q-band polymorphisms which are used in identifying the parental origin of given chromosomes.

ation/renaturation technique (C-banding) was modified by Sumner, Evans, and Buckland (1971) and by Drets and Shaw (1971) to produce banding patterns along the chromatids of all the chromosomes. The same type and pattern of banding was obtained by enzyme pretreatment, rather than by the denaturation technique, followed by Giemsa staining. Pronase was used by Dutrillaux, de Grouchy, Finaz, and Lejeune (1971) and trypsin by Seabright (1971). Because of the common pattern obtained by employing Giemsa for the

stain in these methods, the bands are called G-bands (Fig. 8.2). G-banding has become a widely used banding method for describing normal and abnormal chromosomes (Seabright, 1971).

A fourth banding method, the so-called reverse or R-banding, was introduced by Dutrillaux and Lejeune (1971). "Reverse" refers to pale Q- or G-bands that are darkly stained by R-banding. The usual R-banding technique involves denaturation of chromosomal DNA, followed by partial reannealing and differential staining with Giemsa. Fluorescent procedures using acridine orange instead of Giemsa were reported by Bobrow, Collacott, and Madan (1972) and by Wyandt, Vlietinck, Magenis, and Hecht (1974).

Another staining method developed by Bloom and Goodpasture (1976) identifies the nucleolus-organizer regions on the short arms of the acrocentric chromosomes (Fig. 8.3).

Other procedures have been published that produce staining or banding of specific parts or regions of some or all chromosomes; these are generally limited to research use. The Paris Nomenclature diagrammatic banded karyotype is illustrated in Fig. 8.4.

Chromosome Counts

The first procedure during routine chromosome analysis is to count the number of chromosomes. In general,

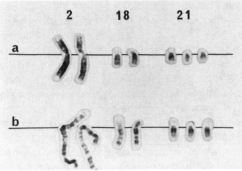

FIG. 8.2. Effect of relative chromosome condensation on G-banding detail. (a) Chromosome pairs 2, 18 and 21 from a G-banded metaphase spread of the common degree of condensation. Note lack of detail distal to the dark band in the long arm of #21 chromosomes. (b) Chromosomes from a spread on the same slide but in late prophase. The increased number of bands for pairs 2 and 18 is obvious. In the long arm of #21 chromosomes the bands 21q22.1, 21q22.2 and 21q22.3 can be distinguished. The common intra-pair variation in condensation and staining is also illustrated.

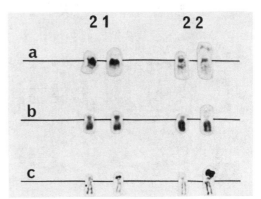

FIG. 8.3. Distinction of nucleolar-organizing-region (NOR) from small translocation by silver-staining. (a) G-banded chromosomes of pairs 21 and 22 with minor polymorphism of a #21 and a major polymorphism of a #22. (b) R-banding on the same pairs from this patient. The polymorphism in pair 21 is more marked than with G-banding and the variant #22 is marked. (c) Silver-staining identifies the NORs and shows the polymorphisms observed by G- and R-banding to be variations in the NOR. A small translocation to the #22 is considered ruled-out by this result.

there are two main questions: what is the modal number, and is there evidence for mosaicism? When no mosaicism is present, the modal number can be determined from any cell that is intact and not altered by laboratory or processing artifacts. This is the reason why some laboratories offer a two-cell count as a cytogenetic study. Although such a limited approach may be adequate for confirming a clinical diagnosis in the majority of cases, it does not take into consideration two important factors: first, a chromosome count without karyotyping will not detect translocations that do not change the normal number of chromosomes, and second, counting two cells only is inadequate to find mosaicism. Consequently, it is essential to obtain a complete karyotype routinely in all chromosomal analyses and to count an adequate number of cells to assess mosaicism when indicated.

The question of mosaicism is approached through the chromosome count followed by karyotyping of cells to establish that more than one modal number characterizes the cells in the patient. A common practice is to count the chromosomes of 16 to 20 metaphase spreads. If one cell shows an increase or a decrease from the normal number of 46, the cell is analyzed to determine whether the abnormality would be consistent with the syndrome under consideration or whether it resulted from a random chromosome loss or gain. If two or more metaphase spreads with the same abnormal count and carrier type are found in the initial 16 to 20 cells, mosaicism is strongly suspected and the count should be extended for another 10 to 15 spreads.

Chromosome Disorders

The human karyotype consists of arrangement of chromosome pairs according to a standard format, as seen in Fig. 8.5 for a G-banded prometaphase spread from a girl with Down syndrome. A karyotype is considered to be abnormal if there is extra or missing chromosome material or if structural rearrangements of chromosomes are identified.

Numerical chromosome abnormalities involve either whole sets of chromosomes or only one of a chromosome pair. Changes in the former result in karyotypes with multiples of the 23 elements (triploidy and tetraploidy). Although most conceptuses with triploidy or tetraploidy are aborted early in pregnancy, some fetuses with triploidy have been live born but only survived for a short time.

Numerical changes which involve only one chromosome of a given pair may result in karyotypes with a modal chromosomal number of 45 or between 47 and 51 chromosomes, depending on the number of missing or extra elements. The mechanisms resulting in abnormal chromosome numbers are nondisjunction and anaphase lag. In nondisjunction, the separation of chromatids occurs, but without normal segregation into the two daughter cells. Monosomic conceptuses involving autosomes are practically always miscarried. The only relatively common condition with a missing chromosome is monosomy for the X (Turner syndrome). Nondisjunction may take place during the first or second meiotic division in either sperm or ovum or during early mitosis after formation of the zygote. In anaphase lag, the migration of the chromosomes on the spindle is affected by the nuclear membrane, which forms before all the chromosomes have migrated to the poles and usually leads to a monosomic condition.

Both nondisjunction and anaphase lag may result in mosaicism. This is when two or more stemlines of cells coexist within a single individual. Usually mosaicism results from a postfertilization event taking place during one of the earliest cleavage divisions.

Structural rearrangements require the occurrence of breaks in chromosomes. Balanced rearrangements or translocations show no apparent loss or gain of

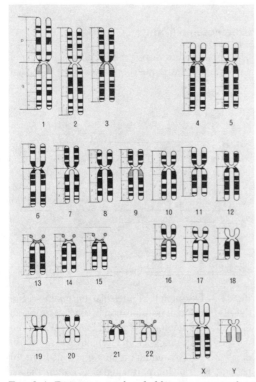

FIG. 8.4. Diagrammatic banded karyotype according to the Paris nomenclature. The banding patterns given were derived from Q-, G-, and R-banding methods as a composite. Reproduced through the courtesy of The National Foundation and is from the 1972 Paris Conference.

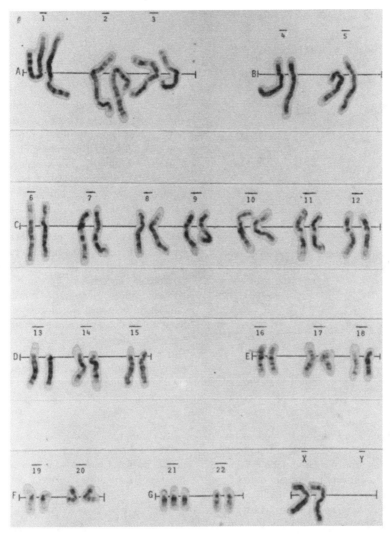

FIG. 8.5. Karyotype of G-banded chromosomes. This formalized arrangement of the chromosomes (karyotype) was prepared from a prometaphase spread from a girl with Down syndrome. It shows trisomy-21.

chromosome material. One form of these is the reciprocal translocation which involves the exchange of material between two chromosomes as the result of single breaks in each. In Fig. 8.6, four reciprocal translocations are depicted. Apparently nonreciprocal translocations occur, but there is always the question of whether a very small part of one may be present, but not detected. Two such translocations are illustrated in Fig. 8.7.

Another type of single-break rearrangement is the Robertsonian translocation, in which there may or may not be the loss of a centromere from one of the acrocentric chromosomes. Loss of a centromere in a Robertsonian translocation results from a break in the short arm of one and the long arm of the other

involved chromosomes to give a monocentromeric translocation chromosome. If the break occurs in the short arms of both, the result is a dicentric translocation. In the "balanced" Robertsonian translocation of two acrocentric chromosomes, there does not seem to be any detectable phenotypic consequence due to the loss of the short arms from both acrocentric chromosomes. Four Robertsonian translocations are shown in Fig. 8.8. Three of these involve a chromosome 21 and three of the four were found to be dicentric by C-banding.

The least common of the balanced single-break translocations is the tandem translocation in which material from another chromosome of the same pair or from a different pair may be attached to the end

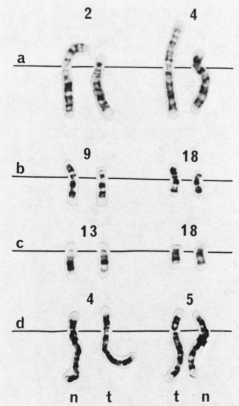

FIG. 8.6. Reciprocal Translocations. Chromosomes in the columns "n" are normal, those in "t" are derivatives. (a) A translocation in which all the short arm of a #2 is found attached to the short arm of a #4. The break point in the #4 is in 4p15, with the short arm of 4 distal to this point attached to the centromere of the #2. This translocation would be obvious in an unbanded karyotype. (b) This translocation is between the short arms of a #9 and a #18. Most of the short arm of the 9 is attached to the short arm of the 18, with the distal band of the 18 short arm on the 9. This translocation should be detected in unbanded karyotypes because of the lack of a normal pair 18. (c) Long arm portions have been translocated between a #13 and a #18. Because the derivative chromosomes in this translocation are the same length as normal homologues, this translocation could not be detected without banding. (d) There is exchange of the short arms between a #4 and a #5. This translocation would be missed unless the banding and chromosome length are adequate to distinguish the double band in short arm of #4 from the single band in short arm of #5.

of a chromosome. The principle of tandem translocation is illustrated in Fig. 8.9 by a translocation of part of the long arm of a chromosome 4 to the end of the long arm of another chromosome 4.

A deletion-insertion translocation results from two breaks in one chromosome and insertion of the segment from between the breaks into a single-break location of another chromosome. This type of translocation may be very difficult to find if the inserted segment is small. In Fig. 8.10, a small segment from the middle of the long arm of a chromosome 3 was inserted into the long arm of a chromosome 11 in the balanced carrier state. The unbalanced state associated with translocation may be from trisomy or from monosomy for varying amounts of chromosome material.

Deletion of a portion of a chromosome more commonly involves a terminal chromosome segment as illustrated in Fig. 8.11. In one situation, the deletion is a two-break event of short and long arms with ring formation while the other four examples are considered single break deletions of distal segments from short or long arms. They illustrate the karyotypes of 4p- (Wolf-Hirschhorn syndrome), 5p- (cri-du-chat syndrome), 18p- and 18q- syndromes. The ring -18 is from a child with clinical 18p- syndrome.

Isochromosomes are formed during cell division when the centromere of a chromosome mistakenly divides so that it separates the two arms rather than the two chromatids. The most common isochro-

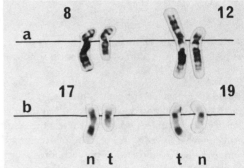

FIG. 8.7. Apparent non-reciprocal translocations. (a) Translocation of about one-half the long arm of a #8 to the end of the short arm of a #12. Theoretically the telomere from the short arm of 12 is on the break in the long arm of the 8 but it is undetectable. (b) The long arm segment from a #17 is attached to the long arm of a #19. As in the 8;12 translocation above, there is no apparant translocation of 19 to 17.

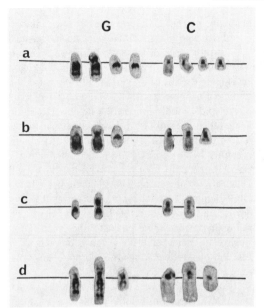

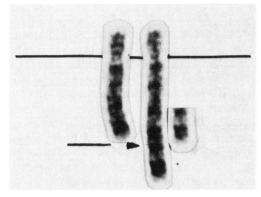

FIG. 8.9. Tandem translocation of 4q. The left member of this pair is a normal #4 by G-banding. The right member is the homologue showing an additional segment which, from the arrow to the end, duplicates the distal segment of the normal long arm. This segment has been cut from the translocation chromosome and aligned with the segment duplicated.

FIG. 8.8. Robertsonian translocations. (a) Both G- and C-banding of pairs 14 and 21 for a person with translocation Down syndrome is shown. The G-banding identifies the translocation and the trisomy with the extra #21 long arm replacing the short arm of a #14. The C-banding shows a single centromeric band indicating this to be a true Robertsonian translocation. (b) A 13;21 translocation carrier. The C-banding shows two centromeric bands in the translocation chromosome indicating it to be dicentric and formed from breaks in the short arms of both the #13 and #21. (c) An apparent 21;21 translocation or an iso-long arm-21 chromosome in Down syndrome. It is not possible to distinguish between these alternatives without C-banding. In this case C-banding shows a dicentric chromosome indicating a translocation. (d) A 14;22 translocation carrier. The G-banding does not show two centromeric constrictions but the C-banding confirms the translocation chromosome to be dicentric with one centromere (that of the #22) "repressed."

mosomes are those of the X-chromosome long arms and are observed in approximately 15 to 20% of women with Turner syndrome.

Not all variations in the chromosomes of a karyotype are abnormal or associated with clinical symptoms. Inspection of any series of karyotypes from different individuals shows marked variability in the short arm-stalk-satellite regions of all the acrocentric chromosomes, variation in the secondary constrictions of chromosomes 1, 9, and 16, and differences in the length of the long arms of the Y chromosome. Per-

icentric inversions with familial transmission are also seen and included in the category of familial polymorphisms. Both secondary constrictions, heterochromatin polymorphism and inversions are depicted in Fig. 8.12. The Q-banding variants for acrocentric short arms, stalks, and satellites have been the most useful in ascertaining the parent of nondisjunction. The meiotic division of error has been identified by

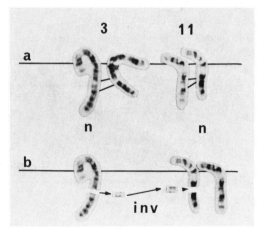

FIG. 8.10. Deletion insertion translocation. (a) Normal #3 and #11 are indicated by "n". The marker bands in the 3 and the 11 which indicate that a deletion and an insertion have occurred are connected by lines between the homologues. (b) The deletion and insertion are represented. The segment deleted from the long arm of #3, as the result of two breaks, is inserted into the single break site in the long arm of the #11.

this method in studies to assess the relative proportion of children with trisomy 13 and trisomy 21 that result from paternal or maternal gametodysgenesis. Fig. 8.1 illustrates the polymorphism of chromosome 21.

Of the many known chromosome syndromes, only a select number of autosomal and sex chromosome disorders will be described here. Since Down syndrome is the most common autosomal disorder and since it has been studied extensively, it will be discussed as a "prototype" in more detail while other chromosome abnormalities can be presented only in an abbreviated way within the framework of this chapter.

Trisomy 21

Although Dr. Langdon Down is credited with first describing as a group the features of persons who today bear his name (Down, 1866), Down syndrome had already been recognized earlier by Esquirol (1838) and Sequin (1866). Down syndrome is the most common autosomal abnormality in man with an incidence of 1/800 to 1/1,200 live births. Trisomy 21 is found

in approximately 1/200 conceptuses; thus, 75 to 85% of embryos with trisomy 21 are spontaneously aborted.

The phenotype of persons with Down syndrome is well known to professionals working in the field of developmental disabilities. It should be noted that some children with Down syndrome have many phenotypic features consistent with this syndrome, while others present only a few such characteristics. Moreover, some of the phenotypic features change over time. Some physical findings such as the abundant tissue in the posterior neck area in the infant with Down syndrome are less evident later in life, whereas other stigmata become more apparent as the child grows, such as fissuring of the tongue, dental abnormalities, etc. Some characteristics such as the single palmar crease and the wide separation between first and second toes, of course, do not change over time.

Children with Down syndrome are usually of small stature. The head of the child with Down syndrome is reduced in size and in infancy the fontanels are wide open. The sagittal suture is often separated and

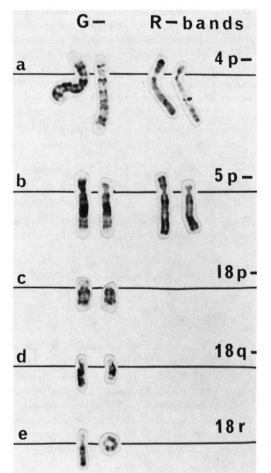

FIG. 8.11. Chromosome deletions. (a) The 4p- deletion associated with the Wolf-Hirschhorn syndrome. G-banding of pair 4 shows the normal chromosome on the left with the deleted short arm chromosome on the right. The same order is shown for the R-banded pairs. This is considered a single break terminal deletion. (b) This 5p- deletion is associated with the "cri-du-chat" syndrome. More of the short arm has been deleted in this chromosome than in the 4p- and would be more easily detected in unbanded preparations. (c) The 18p- illustrated with G-banding only is associated with a characteristic clinical syndrome. Essentially the whole short arm has been deleted. (d) The 18q- deletion is associated with a specific clinical syndrome quite different from the 18p- syndrome. (e) An 18 ring formed by two terminal deletions. The amount of chromosomal material lost by deletion appears minimal but is associated in this case with microcephaly, mental retardation and the phenotype of 18p- syndrome.

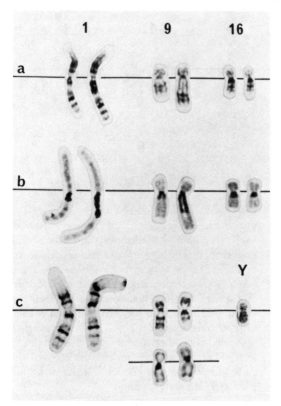

Fig. 8.12. Familial chromosomal polymorphisms. (a) G-banding of pair 1, 9 and 16 homologues. The polymorphisms for the secondary constriction regions in one member of each pair are shown in extreme form for pairs 1 and 9. The distinction between members of pair 16 is in the more common range. (b) C-banding of pairs 1, 9 and 16 from the same individuals as above. The polymorphisms are emphasized by this banding method. (c) G-banded pericentric inversions in members of pairs 1, 9 and in a Y. The 9 inversion is also shown by C-banding. The effect of pericentric inversions is to alter the arm ratio for the affected chromosome.

frequently a third fontanel, which is a widening of the sagittal suture at the parietal area, is noted between the anterior and posterior fontanels. The ears are often small with overlapping helices. The ear canals are narrow. Epicanthal folds, slanting of palpebral fissures, and Brushfield spots are noted in many children with this syndrome. Sometimes congenital nystagmus is observed, and many persons with Down syndrome have refractive errors. The midfacies is hypoplastic with a small nose and a depressed nasal bridge giving the impression of a flat facies. Intraoral structures show broadening of the alveolar ridges with narrowing of the palatal vault. In the older child

and adult with Down syndrome, fissuring of the tongue has been described. Reports of enlargement of the tongue have not been substantiated by accurate measurements. Delayed dentition, abnormally shaped teeth, and absence of teeth have occasionally been noted. The neck is usually short and broad. In infants, commonly, there is abundant loose skin in the posterior neck area. Thirty to 40% of children with Down syndrome have congenital heart disease and 2 to 5% have duodenal obstruction. Umbilical hernias are seen at a high frequency. The distal extremities are short, with stubby hands and feet. Brachyclinodactyly of the fifth finger is noted in approximately 50% of children and a single flexion crease of the fifth finger in about 20%. A unilateral or bilateral single palmar crease is found in half of the children with Down syndrome. Wide separation between first and second toes with an interdigital plantar crease is often observed. Infants with Down syndrome are usually hypotonic and their joints are hyperextensible. As the children grow, their muscle strength increases markedly and their muscle tone becomes normal. The dermatoglyphics show a high frequency of ulnar loops on most fingers with a radial loop on the fourth finger, distal axial triradii, and tibial arch in the hallucal area.

The physical and psychomotor development of children with Down syndrome is frequently delayed. During the first few months of life, they are more like other infants and follow a similar sequence of development. Their intellectual limitations and the marked delay in language acquisition becomes more apparent during the subsequent years. It should be noted that there is a wide variation in mental abilities, behaviors, and developmental progress among children with Down syndrome. Previously, it was thought that most children with Down syndrome were severely mentally retarded and many were institutionalized. Today, with supportive counseling of parents, appropriate home care, early intervention, and environmental enrichment during the first few years of life, followed by stimulating preschool experiences and later special education, most children with Down syndrome will be functioning in the mild to moderate range of mental retardation. A few children's intellectual functioning will be in the borderline to low average range and on the other end of the spectrum severe mental retardation will be infrequently observed. Contrary to previous reports, individuals with Down syndrome who have appropriate education and who later engage in vocational training usually can become productive citizens.

Three main chromosome abnormalities have been described in Down syndrome. Most children with this syndrome (90 to 95%) have a supernumerary 21 chromosome (trisomy 21). A karyotype of a child with trisomy 21 is depicted in Fig. 8.5. Four to six percent of children with clinical features of Down syndrome have a translocation. Most of the translocations involve the attachment of the long arms of chromosome 21 in place of the short arms of a D group or another of the G group chromosomes, most frequently onto chromosomes 14 or 21, but occasionally to chromosomes 13, 15, or 22 as shown in Fig. 8.8. For a child with Down syndrome found to have a translocation, it is important to determine whether the translocation is derived from one of the parents; thus, parental chromosomes need to be studied. If one of the parents is found to be a carrier, family studies need to be pursued because of the increased risk persons with balanced carrier status have for giving birth to a child with Down syndrome. It has been estimated that in 30 to 45% of children with 14/21 translocation Down syndrome, the translocation is derived from a carrier parent, whereas most 21/21 translocation cases are de novo in origin and only in 3 to 4% is this translocation familial (Thuline & Pueschel, 1982). Empiric data suggest that the risk of recurrence for women who are 14/21 translocation carriers is about 15%, if men carry such a translocation, the recurrence risk is about 5% (Miller, 1979). In 21/22 translocation carriers, the risk for giving birth to a child with Down syndrome in future pregnancies is 2 to 3%. If a child has a 21/21 translocation and if there are normal siblings in this family, karyotyping is not usually indicated, since neither father nor mother can be a translocation carrier (with the rare exception of a mosaic situation). Ordinarily, a 21/21 carrier parent can only have one of two outcomes in a pregnancy: a spontaneous abortion with a monosomy or trisomy 21 embryo or a live born child with a 21/21 translocation Down syndrome.

In addition to the Robertsonian translocations where the long arms of chromosome 21 replace the short arms of the D or G group chromosome, there are also tandem translocations where the long arms of chromosome 21 are attached at the distal end of another chromosome. Other rare chromosome translocations in Down syndrome have been described in the literature (Pueschel, Mendoza, & Ellenbogen, 1980). Two are illustrated in Fig. 8.13.

The third form of chromosome aberration found in persons with Down syndrome is mosaicism in which both normal and trisomic cells are observed in blood and other tissues. Mosaicism occurs at a frequency of 1 to 2% in persons with Down syndrome. It has been noted that children with the mosaic form of

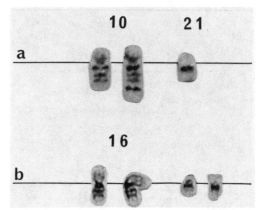

FIG. 8.13. Unusual translocations associated with Down syndrome (G-banded). (a) Carrier for a 10;21 translocation. The long arm of a #21 is translocated to the end of the long arm of a #10 as a balanced translocation with no phenotypic effect for the carrier. (b) Carrier for a 16;21 translocation. The long arm of one #21, nearest to the #16, is deleted at band 21q22.2 and the segment 21q22.2→21qtr is attached to the end of the short arm of a #16 where it can be seen. The child of this carrier, who received the derivative 16 and two normal 21's shows the full phenotype of Down syndrome.

Down syndrome have, as a group, a more advanced psychomotor development and higher intelligence test scores than children with trisomy 21 (Fishler, 1975). A more complex mosaic situation is seen in double aneuploidy as reviewed by Thuline and Pueschel (1982).

It is well known that the risk of having a child with Down syndrome increases significantly with advancing age of the mother. There are also data available concerning the correlation of paternal age and increased risk of having a child with Down syndrome. Although some investigators feel that such a relationship exists, others did not find evidence for a significant correlation between paternal age and increased risk of having a child with Down syndrome (Hook, 1982).

During the past decade, new staining methods (as described above) allowed identification of the parental origin of trisomy 21 in about 75% of cases with Down syndrome. While in 20 to 30% the extra chromosomes derived from the father, in 70 to 80% the nondisjunctional event had occurred in the mother, most often during the first meiotic division (Thuline & Pueschel, 1982).

Trisomy 18

Trisomy 18 was first recognized as a specific entity by Edwards, Harnden, Cameron, Crosse, and Wolff

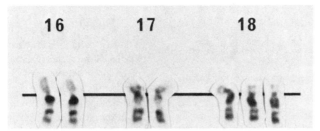

FIG. 8.14. Trisomy 18. The E-group, pairs 16, 17 and 18 in G-banded preparations from an infant with Trisomy-18 syndrome, confirms the clinical diagnosis.

(1960). Trisomy 18 is the second most common autosomal disorder with an incidence of 1/3,000 to 1/5,000 live births. Females are more often affected than males; the female:male ratio being 3:1. Trisomy 18 is clinically a more severe chromosome aberration than trisomy 21. Only 10% of affected infants survive the first year of life. Survival appears related to sex. The average age at time of death for males is 2 to 3 months and for females 10 months (Weber, 1967). The cause of death usually is from congenital heart disease. Infants with trisomy 18 are born at an average of 42 weeks of gestation. They have low Apgar scores and often need to be resuscitated. They are small for gestational age and have low birth weight. Later, if they survive, they exhibit failure to thrive. They often display feeding difficulties, poor sucking ability and occasionally apneic episodes. Children with trisomy 18 change from early hypotonia to increased muscle tone (de Grouchy & Turleau, 1977).

The major phenotypic features are prominent occiput, dolichocephaly, low-set pointed ears with hypoplastic helix and aplastic antihelix, epicanthal folds, narrow palpebral fissures and ptosis of eyelids, retromicrognathia, short sternum with widely spaced nipples, congenital heart disease, narrow pelvis with limited abduction of hips, fingers short and held in overlapping position, distally placed retroflexible thumbs with ulnar deviation of the hands, and protruding calcaneus (rocker-bottom feet).

Other less often observed features include corneal opacities, narrow arched palate, cleft lip and/or palate, abundant skin on the back of the neck, eventration of the diaphragm, umbilical and inguinal hernias, diastasis recti, Meckel's diverticulum, malrotation of the large bowel, renal anomalies, cryptorchidism, hypoplastic nails, club foot, and partial syndactylies.

There is much variation in the clinical expression with over 130 abnormal features described in children with this chromosome disorder (Summitt, 1973). For 80% of the children, the cytogenetic finding is free trisomy 18 (Fig. 8.14). In 10%, mosaicism is observed

and for 10% there is either translocation or double aneuploidy involved. Adequate studies to estimate a recurrence risk are not available.

Trisomy 13

In 1960, Patau et al. reported on a new chromosome syndrome, trisomy 13, associated with multiple anomalies (Patau, Smith, Therman, Inhorn, & Wagner, 1960). The frequency of trisomy 13 has been estimated to be 1/8,000 to 1/15,000 live births. There is a high mortality for this syndrome. The mean life expectancy is 130 days without regard to sex, 50% die in the first month, nearly 70% are dead by six months, and only 18% survive the first year of life. Children with trisomy 13 are usually profoundly mentally retarded, thrive poorly, and often have seizures with hypsarrhythmic electroencephalographic pattern. In infancy, these children often have apneic episodes, show persistence of Hemoglobin Gower-2,

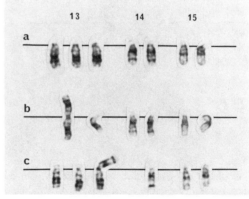

FIG. 8.15. Trisomy 13. The phenotype of trisomy-13 required only the presence of trisomy for the long arm of 13 in the karyotype. This results from (a) free trisomy in pair 13, (b) translocation between two 13s or an isochromosome of the long arm of 13 plus a normal 13, (c) a 13q;14q translocation in addition to a normal pair of 13s.

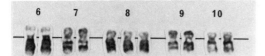

FIG. 8.16. Trisomy 8. A G-banded partial karyotype for pairs 6 through 10 shows trisomy in pair 8.

and have increased frequency of nuclear projections in neutrophils.

The cardinal features at birth are cleft lip and/or palate, microphthalmia, and hexadactyly. Other reported characteristics include microcephaly with receding forehead and holoprosencephaly, broad fontanels and suture lines, defect in scalp at vertex, broad flat nose, occasionally cebocephaly, low set ears with abnormal poorly defined flat helix, hemangiomas on face or nape of neck, loose skin at nape of neck, fingers flexed, rocker-bottom feet, cryptorchidism, scrotal anomalies, clitoral hypertrophy, double vagina and bicornuate uterus, hypoplastic or absent 11th rib and vertebral anomalies, hypoplastic pelvis, cardiac and urinary tract malformations, defects in the organ of Corti, agenesis of corpus callosum, hydrocephalus, cerebellar hypoplasia, and meningomyelocele.

Karyotyping shows free trisomy 13 in 80% of cases, and mosaicism, double aneuploidy or translocation for 20%. The karyotype for free trisomy, and for two translocation trisomies are illustrated in Fig. 8.15.

Trisomy 8

The first patients with trisomy 8 were described by Stadler, Buhler, and Weber (1963). The natural history of children with trisomy 8 is largely dependent on the severity of the intellectual deficit. Patients with this syndrome are mildly to severely retarded. There is an excess of males, giving a female to male ratio of 1:3. Two thirds of individuals reported have had mosaicism for trisomy 8 (de Grouchy and Turleau, 1977). Lifespan appears to be normal.

The most characteristic clinical features are deepset eyes with strabismus, full everted lower lip, deep palmar and plantar flexion creases, and osteoarticular anomalies, including absent or hypoplastic patellae, long slender trunk, and narrow pelvis. Other features reported include macrocephaly, slight hypertelorism, large low-set ears with thick helices, plump broadbased and upturned nose, microretrognathia, occasional cleft palate, short wide neck, kyphoscoliosis, abnormal or supernumerary vertebrae and ribs, spina bifida, hollow chest, supernumerary nipples, urinary tract abnormalities, brachydactyly or arachnodactyly, clinodactyly, restricted function of joints, hypoplastic convex nails, cryptorchidism, and delayed puberty. A karyotype for trisomy 8 is shown in Fig. 8.16.

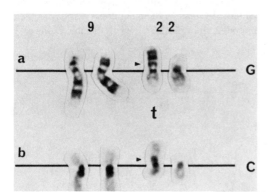

FIG. 8.17. Trisomy 9p. In this 9p;22p translocation loss of the 22p is not clinically significant with the result that there is pure 9p trisomy. (a) G-banding of pairs 9 and 22, with what appears as an extra G-positive band in the 9p segment of the translocation chromosome. (b) C-banding for centromeric heterochromatin shows the centromere in the translocation to be that of the 22 and the extra G-band in 9p to actually be the centromere of the 9 in a "repressed" state. Use of both G- and C-banding shows the translocation to be structurally dicentric.

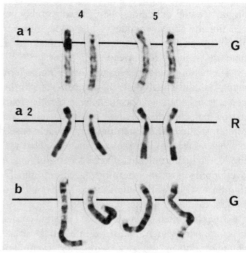

FIG. 8.18. Deletion of Short-arm 4 (4p−). Pairs 4 and 5 from two patients with the Wolf-Hirschhorn syndrome. (a1) G-banded preparation showing deletion of the distal-half of the short arm from p14, (a2) R-banded preparation for the same patient showing apparently a larger deletion than would have been estimated by G-banding but with the same break point, (b) G-banding of pairs 4 and 5, from another patient, showing deletion of about the distal third of 4p from p15.2.

9p+ Syndrome

On the basis of four observations, Rethore et al. (1970) delineated the 9p + syndrome. It is a relatively frequent syndrome with about 60 cases reported by 1978. Females predominate with a 2:1 female to male ratio. Mental retardation is constant with variability about a mean IQ of 55. Delayed language development, agitation, instability and disorders of coordination are common. Life expectancy is normal.

The most characteristic features are brachycephaly, prominent bulbous nose with inverted nostrils, short upper lip, cup mouth and asymmetric grin, and a worried look in the older child. Other reported features are microcephaly, prominent forehead, hypertelorism, deep-set small eyes with excentric pupils and strabismus, prominent nose with fullness at tip, thin and protruding nasal septum, round chin with horizontal dimple, large protruberant but normally set ears, short neck, widely spaced nipples, pectus excavatum, subacromial and coccygeal dimples, diastasis recti and umbilical hernia, hands with palms too long for the fingers, single palmar crease, brachymesophalangy, proximal implantation of thumb, dysplastic nails, and malformed feet.

Trisomy for 9p may be pure, arising from breakage, as a derivative chromosome in translocation of 9p to an acrocentric, or associated with partial monosomy of some other chromosome involved in reciprocal translocation. The karyotype of 9p + is illustrated in Fig. 8.17.

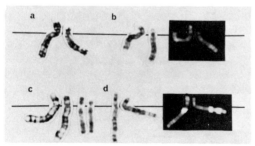

FIG. 8.19. Deletion of Short-arm 5 (5p−). Pair 5s from four patients with the Cri-du-chat syndrome illustrating differing degrees of deletion and the use of varied stains in evaluating the anomaly. (a) deletion of nearly all 5p with the break point at p13.3 (G-banding), (b) left hand set is G-banded and right hand set is stained with chromomycin A₃-methyl green (Chr A₃), to produce fluorescent R-banding, with localization of the break point to 5p13.3, (c) G-banded, left set, and R-banded, right set, showing a terminal deletion from 5p15.1, (d) G- and Chr A₃ banding showing an interstitial deletion of 5p15.1→p15.32 with retention of p15.33.

4p− Syndrome

The 4p− syndrome was first described in Europe by Wolf, Porsch, Baitsch, and Reinwein (1965) and in the United States by Hirschhorn, Cooper, and Firschein (1965). Children with the 4p− syndrome are usually profoundly mentally retarded. They often have grand mal seizures which are difficult to control. Growth retardation is evident at birth. Life expectancy is not well documented but several individuals in their 20's are known.

Features that are most characteristic are microcephaly, "Greek warrior helmet" facies, broad bridge of the nose, wide prominent glabella, deep narrow nasal philtrum with marked pillars, hypertelorism with shallow orbital sockets. Other features reported are hypotonia, cranial asymmetries, high forehead, downward slanting palpebral fissures, epicanthus, ptosis of upper eyelid, strabismus, nystagmus, atresia of lacrimal ducts, severe ocular malformation such as coloboma of the iris, short and occasionally cleft upper lip, cleft palate, down-turned corners of mouth, small receding chin, pre-auricular dimple or tag, long slender neck, long trunk, frequent skeletal anomalies, long big toe, hypospadias in males, cardiac malformations, and renal anomalies. For the syndrome to be manifest the distal portion of 4p, and band 4p16 in particular, must be deleted. Illustrative partial karyotypes are given in Fig. 8.18.

5p− Syndrome

The cri-du-chat syndrome (5p−) was first reported by Lejeune et al. (1963). They described an infant who had significant mental retardation, microcephaly, and other minor phenotypic aberrations. Most remarkable was the infant's high pitched cat-like cry which led to the term "cri-du-chat" syndrome. Since then many individuals with this syndrome have been described. A rough frequency estimate among newborns of 1/50,000 has been made by de Grouchy and Turleau (1977). Birth weight is low and weight gain slow. Neither sex predominates in the sex ratio. Survival to adulthood is to be expected. About 30% of children have congenital heart disease and mental retardation is severe.

The most common features of the syndrome in infants are shrill cry resembling a mewing kitten, microcephaly, rounded moonlike facial appearance, micrognathia, hypertelorism, and hypotonia. In the older child and adult the characteristic features are: long face, small mandible with effacement in the jaw angle, lack of speech, and loss of characteristic cry. Other common features reported are downward slanting palpebral fissures, epicanthal folds, strabismus, wide

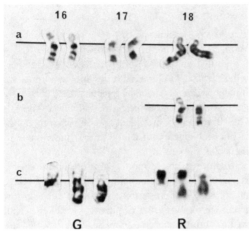

FIG. 8.20. Deletion of Short arm 18 (18p −). Partial karyotypes from three patients with the 18p − syndrome. (a) partial 18p − with apparent terminal deletion from p11.23. (b) deletion of the whole short arm from 18p11. (c) deletion of 18p from translocation of the long arm of a 22 to the long arm of an 18. The G-banded left set consists of a normal 22, (placed in inverted position to show identity with the 22q part of the 18q;22q translocation) the translocation chromosome (the centromere is from the 22) and the normal 18. The R-banded right hand set confirms the G-banding interpretation of break points in 22p11 and 18q11 with loss of all the 18p and 18 centromere.

flat nasal bridge, preauricular tag, narrow auditory canals, facial asymmetry, occasionally cleft lip and palate, congenital heart disease, and narrow arched palate.

The chromosomal lesion, deletion of 5p involving 5p 14→15 (Fig. 8.19) is *de novo* in a majority with about 20% of reported cases having a parental translocation as etiology (de Grouchy & Turleau, 1977).

18p− Syndrome

The deletion of the short arm of chromosome 18 was first described by de Grouchy, Lamy, Thieffry, Arthuis, and Salmon (1963) as the first known deletion syndrome for humans. Since then, nearly 100 children with this chromosomal disorder have been reported in the literature. Occurrence in females is more common, with a 3:2 female to male ratio. Mental retardation varies from profound with severe malformation of the cranium and face (such as cebocephaly or arhinencephaly) to mild in those with fewer anomalies. IQ is said to range from 15 to 75, with most individuals around 50 and with a discrepancy between verbal and performance scores. Except for those individuals with

severe malformation, life expectancy does not appear altered.

The features most characteristic of the syndrome, for individuals without severe craniofacial malformations, are growth retardation, epicanthal folds, ptosis of upper eyelids, and large soft ears with aplastic antihelix. Also reported have been dental anomalies, micrognathia, round face, short neck with low hairline and suggestion of webbing, wide thin thorax with widely spaced nipples, small hands and feet, apparent susceptibility to connective tissue disease (Schinzel et al., 1974), and decrease or absence of serum IgA in 50% of patients.

The deletion of 18p arises *de novo* in two-thirds of instances. The remainder have shown loss of 18p in a *de novo* translocation, malsegregation of a parental translocation and occasionally ring formation with loss of 18p. Uchida, McRae, Wang, and Ray (1965) have reported pregnancy with an 18p − offspring to a mother with 18p−. The range of deletions seen is illustrated in Fig. 8.20.

18q− Syndrome

The deletion of a segment of the long arm of chromosome 18 was first reported by Summitt and Patau (1964) and by de Grouchy, Royer, Salmon, and Lamy (1964). The phenotype of patients with 18q − syndrome is significantly different from that of children with 18p − syndrome and was delineated by Lejeune, Berges, Lafourcade, and Pethore (1966). The syndrome

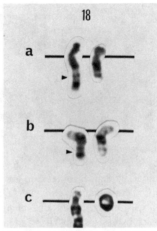

FIG. 8.21. Deletion of Long-arm 18 (18q −). Pair 18 from three patients with clinical 18q − syndrome. (a) terminal deletion from 18q21.31. (b) terminal deletion from 18q21.33. (c) ring-18 formed by a break at pter and in the long arm at a point not defined but with loss of enough of 18q to produce typical clinical 18q − syndrome.

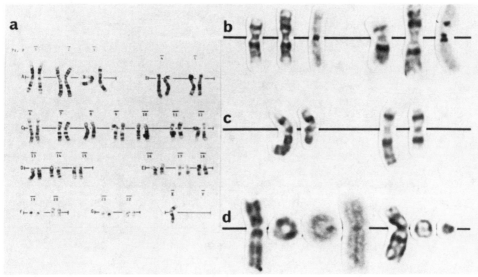

FIG. 8.22. X-chromosome Findings Associated with the Turner Phenotype. (a) A full karyotype for a patient with 45,X status. (b) X-chromosomes from two patients with 45,X,isoXq karyotypes. The normal X is to the left in each G-banded pair and the isoXq to the right. Beside each pair, on the right, is C-banding of the isoXq. For the first patient only one C-banded centromere is seen and the isoXq is judged to be a true isochromosome. For the second patient two C-banded centromeres are seen and this is probably not an isochromosome but an Xq;Xq translocation. (c) Two examples of deletion of Xq with break points in the region of the long arm critical for normal fertility. (d) Two examples of ring-X. The first two are the R-banded normal X and the ring, with the next two C-banding of the same pair, done to locate the centromeres. The last three are the normal G-banded X and the ring-X followed by the C-banded ring-X. Ring formation involves loss from both short and long arms.

had been reported for over 50 cases by 1977 and does not appear to be rare. Among reported cases the sex ratio is 3:2, female to male, mental retardation is severe with IQ below 30 in about one fourth of cases, another one fourth are from 30 to 50, one fourth from 50 to 70 and one fourth over 70. Behavior problems and language difficulties are common. Although about 10% of affected infants die in infancy, the life expectancy for the rest appears normal.

Features most characteristic of the syndrome are depressed mid-face with deeply set eyes, round head with moderate microcephaly, cup-shaped mouth, strongly folded ears, genital anomalies—small penis, hypospadias, hypoplastic scrotum, and undescended testes in the male; atrophy of the labia minora and clitoris in the female—hypotonia, and low birth weight. Other reported features include growth retardation, prominent jaw, eye anomalies such as hypertelorism, epicanthal folds, nystagmus, strabismus, and ptosis, anteverted nostrils, atretic external auditory canals, cleft lip and palate, wide-spread nipples, subacromial dimples, proximally placed thumbs, long thin fingers with "hanging water-drop" fingertips, abnormal

placement of the toes, club feet, coloboma, supernumerary ribs, costal synostosis, cardiac and renal malformations and serum IgA deficiency in one third of cases. Pregnancy in a female with 18q− syndrome has been reported by Subrt and Pokorny (1970).

The deletion occurs *de novo* for 80% of cases, is mosaic in 10% and results from parental 18 inversion or translocation in 10%. Two terminal deletions and a ring-18 are illustrated in Fig. 8.21.

XO Syndrome

In 1938, Turner described a syndrome of sexual infantilism, short stature, webbing of the neck, and cubitus valgus. The physical features of a child with Turner syndrome include epicanthal folds, narrow maxilla, micrognathia, narrow arched palate, low hairline at the nape of the neck, which usually is short and webbed. Children have a shieldlike chest with widely spaced nipples, which may be hypoplastic or inverted. Cardiovascular abnormalities are present in more than one fifth of the patients, the majority of whom have coarctation of the aorta, whereas aortic

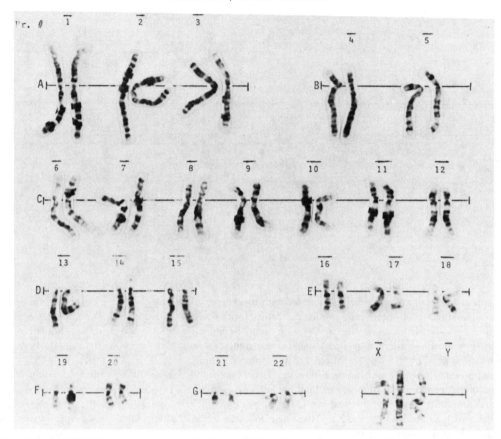

FIG. 8.23. 47,XXX. The most common poly-X syndrome in females is 47,XXX as illustrated in this karyotype.

stenosis, ventricular septal defects and atrial septal defects are less often observed. Infants with Turner syndrome present at times with edema of the dorsum of hands and feet. The external genitalia are juvenile. There are also urinary tract anomalies such as horseshoe kidneys and cleft renal pelvix. Other characteristics of Turner syndrome include cubitus valgus, narrow hyperconvex fingernails, short metacarpals and metatarsals, unusual dermatoglyphics with a high total ridge count, distal palmar triradii, and excessive pigmented nevi. Sensorineural hearing loss is common (50%) and defective vision is observed in 22% of individuals with Turner syndrome. Mental retardation is not usually seen in children with Turner syndrome, although 18% of patients have been reported to have intellectual limitations (Palmer & Reichmann, 1976).

The chromosomal abnormality, 45,XO in Turner syndrome was first reported by Ford, Jones, Polani, deAlmeida, and Briggs, 1959 (Fig. 8.22a). Whereas about 57% of children with Turner syndrome have 45,XO, true monosomy, 15–20% have a 46,X,i(Xq) karyotype, which represents an isochromosome of the long arm of the X as illustrated in figure 8.22b. Mo-

saicism, including 45,X/46,XX; 45,X/47,XXX; 45,X/46,XY accounts for approximately 15% of individuals with Turner syndrome. The remaining 10% of patients have various forms of deletion of the long arm of one of the X chromosomes or formation of a ring X chromosome (Hamerton, 1971; Ferraro et al., 1980) (see Fig. 8.22c&d). The phenotype in patients with mosaicism Turner syndrome varies depending on the time of the postzygotic accident and the proportion of abnormal cell lines in different tissues. Deletions of the long arm of the X at a critical point regularly produces gonadal dysgenesis while deletion of the short arm is responsible for the physical characteristics in Turner syndrome (Forabosco, Giorgi, Formica, Tarantino, & Dallapiccola, 1979).

The buccal smear in patients with Turner syndrome resulting from a deletion of part of the X chromosome may be either X-chromatin positive or X-chromatin negative, depending on whether the abnormal X is large enough to form a discernible X chromatin mass. Cells of children with true monosomy 45,XO, of course, will be chromatin negative. However, because of the difficulties in obtaining suitable preparations

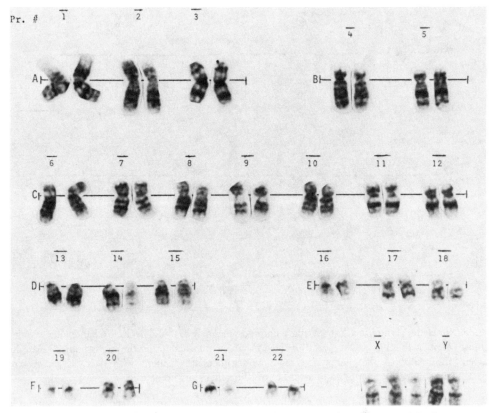

FIG. 8.24. 49,XXXXX. This is a karyotype of a patient with pentasomy of the X.

and problems in correct interpretation of buccal smears, they are no longer recommended for definitive diagnosis of X chromosome disorders.

XXX, XXXX, and XXXXX Syndromes

Trisomy (Fig. 8.23), tetrasomy and pentasomy of the X (Fig. 8.24) have been reported in the literature. Usually XXX females are not phenotypically abnormal and the majority of these women are not mentally retarded. Many of the XXX females probably remain undiagnosed. Several XXX women have borne children, most of whom apparently have normal karyotypes.

The phenotype of poly-X females is variable. Women with the XXXX syndrome usually have midfacial hypoplasia, epicanthal folds, hypertelorism, micrognathia, clinodactyly of fifth finger and narrow shoulder girdle. Some patients with the XXXXX syndrome have a resemblance to a child with Down syndrome. XXXX and XXXXX females often have significant mental retardation. The approximate frequency of the poly-X female syndrome is 1/1,000 live born females (Tennes et al., 1975).

XXY Syndrome

In 1942, Klinefelter and coworkers described a syndrome characterized by gynecomastia, aspermatogenesis, and increased secretion of follicle-stimulating hormone (Klinefelter, Reifenstein, & Albright, 1942). The most constant phenotypic features of Klinefelter syndrome are small genitalia, infertility, and scant facial and pubic hair. Affected men are usually taller than the general population, have a eunuchoid habitus with long limbs and a decreased upper to lower body segment ratio. Some individuals with Klinefelter syndrome have brachycephaly, minor ear abnormalities, clinodactyly of fifth finger, single palmar crease, unusual dermatoglyphic patterns, such as distal placement of the axial triradii and decreased finger ridge counts. Rare congenital anomalies in Klinefelter syndrome include cryptorchidism, hypospadias, scoliosis during adolescent years, and diabetes mellitus during adulthood. Some individuals with Klinefelter syndrome are phenotypically normal. Behavior problems may become evident during the school years. Mental retardation is observed in about 20% of children with Klinefelter syndrome.

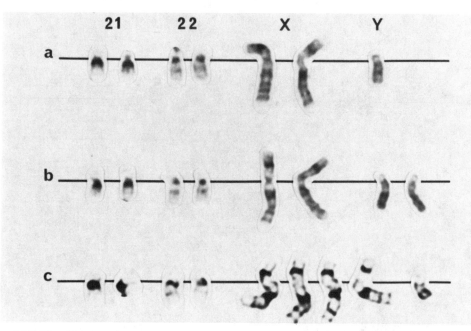

FIG. 8.25. Klinefelter's syndrome. Extra X and Y chromosomes may be found in clinical Klinefelter's syndrome. The most common finding, 47,XXY, is illustrated in (a). A not uncommon finding is both an extra X and Y as seen in (b). Although the phenotype is far more detrimental for patients with 49,XXXXY karyotype, as in (c), it is still commonly referred to as a variant of Klinefelter's syndrome.

The karyotype of patients with Klinefelter syndrome (Fig. 8.25) is 47,XXY in 82%. Others with more severe phenotypic involvement may have 48,XXXY, 48,XXYY and 49,XXXXY karyotypes (Fig. 8.25). A few patients have been reported to have various forms of mosaicism such as 46,XY/47,XXY; 46,XX/47,XXY; 46,XY/47,XXY/48,XXYY; 47,XXY/48XXYY (Becker et al., 1966; Opitz, 1973).

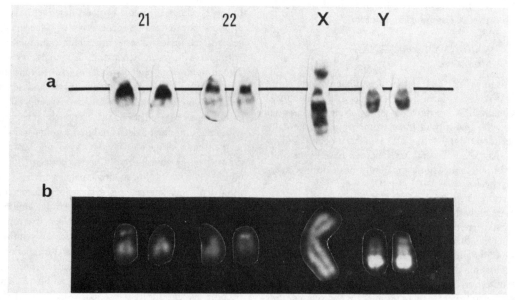

FIG. 8.26. XYY Karyotype. (a) G-banding of a partial karyotype from a male with XYY. (b) Q-banding confirming the identity of both Y- chromosomes.

XYY Syndrome

In 1961, Sandberg and coworkers reported a man with a 47,XYY karyotype (Sandberg, Koepf, Ishihara, & Hauschka, 1961). Since then, many publications on this subject have appeared in the literature. In newborn chromosomal surveys, the incidence of 47,XYY syndrome has been found to be approximately 1/1,000. About 3% of males in prisons and mental hospitals have the chromosomal constitution of 47,XYY. Among the same population with selection for those over six feet tall, the proportion is over 20%.

The majority of individuals with 47,XYY syndrome are phenotypically unremarkable except for their tall stature. Some males with this syndrome have abnormalities of the external genitalia, such as cryptorchidism and small penis and testes. Other features may include a prominent glabella, mild pectus excavatum, and increased nodular cystic acne during adolescence. Poor fine motor coordination and a fine intention tremor have been noted in some individuals with this syndrome. Behavior disturbances such as temper tantrums, explosiveness, and aggressiveness have been observed in many individuals. It is of note, however, that not all persons with the 47,XYY karyotype manifest aggressive behavior or are over six feet in height. Some men with this syndrome have psychosexual problems and many of them function intellectually in the low-average to borderline range.

The extra Y chromosome in persons with the 47,XYY syndrome (see Fig. 8.26) usually does not affect gonadal function and most offspring of 47,XYY males have normal karyotypes. The origin of the 47,XYY karyotype is paternal nondisjunction at the second meiotic division producing the YY sperm. The less common syndromes of 48,XXYY and 49,XXXYY, which share features of Klinefelter syndrome, probably also originate in the father (Voorhees, Wilkins, Hayes, & Harrell, 1972).

Other Chromosomal Abnormalities

Autosomal abnormalities associated with a recognized syndrome were reviewed by Summitt (1978), Lubs and Walknowska (1977), de Grouchy and Turleau (1977), and Borgoanbar (1980). Added to that number are the various X and Y number and structural anomaly syndromes. Of particular interest are the recent reports of association of 13q− with retinoblastoma, 11p− with an aniridia, neuroblastoma and mental retardation syndrome, 15q− with Prader-Willi syndrome, and expression of a fragile site on the X-chromosome with X-linked mental retardation. It is apparent that the place of cytogenetics in relation to diagnosis in mental retardation is assured.

In summary, it can be said that enormous progress has been made during the past 20 years in the identification of numerous chromosomal disorders, only few of which could be discussed within the framework of this chapter. The importance of the recognition of specific chromosomal aberrations in patients with mental retardation is twofold: knowledge of well defined chromosomal disorders allows better prognostic estimations (although it is realized that there is much variability) and second, the identification of a specific karyotype in a patient (in particular, those with translocation chromosome disorders) makes genetic counseling for families with an affected individual more complete and accurate.

References

Arakaki, D. T., & Sparkes, R. S. Microtechnique for culturing leukocytes from whole blood. *Cytogenetics*, 1963, **2**, 57–60.

Arrighi, F. E., & Hsu, T. C. Localization of heterochromatin in human chromosomes. *Cytogenetics*, 1971, **10**, 81–86.

Becker, K. L., Hoffman, D. L., Albert, A., Underdahl, L. O., & Mason, H. L. Klinefelter's syndrome. Clinical and laboratory findings in 50 patients. *Archives of Internal Medicine*, 1966, **118**, 314.

Bloom, S. E., & Goodpasture, C. An improved technique for selective silver staining of nucleolar organizer regions in human chromosomes. *Human Genetics*, 1976, **34**, 199–206.

Bobrow, M., Collacott, H. E. A., & Madan, K. Chromosome banding with acridine orange. *Lancet*, 1972, **2**, 1311.

Borgaonkar, D. F. *Chromosomal variation in man: A catalogue of chromosomal variants and anomalies*. (3rd ed.) Appendix II, pp. 645–710. New York: Liff, 1980.

Caspersson, T., Hulten, M., Linsten, J., & Zech, L. Distinction between extra G-like chromosomes by quinacrine mustard fluorescence analysis. *Experimental Cell Research*, 1970, **63**, 240–243.

Caspersson, T., Zech, L., Johansson, C., & Modest, E. J. Identification of human chromosomes by DNA-binding fluorescent agent. *Chromosoma*, 1970, **30**, 215–227.

Caspersson, T, Zech, L., Wagh, U., Modest, E. J., & Simonsson, E. DNA-binding fluorochromes for the study of the organization of the metaphase nucleus. *Experimental Cell Research*, 1969, **58**, 141–152.

Down, J. L. H. Observations on an ethnic classification of idiots. *Clinical Lecture Reports*, London Hospital, 1866, **3**, 259–262.

Drets, M. E., & Shaw, M. W. Specific banding patterns of human chromosomes. *Proceedings of the National Academy of Sciences of United States of America*, 1971, **68**, 2073–2077.

Dutrillaux, B., de Grouchy, J., Finaz, C., & Lejeune, J. Mise en évidence de la structure fine des chromosomes humains per digestion enzymatique (pronase en particulier). *Comptes Rendus Hebdomadaires Des Séances de l Académie des Sciences. D: Sciences Naturelles* (Paris) 1971, **273**, 587–588.

Dutrillaux, B., & Lejeune, J. Sur une nouvelle technique d'analyse du caryotype humain. *Comptes Rendus Heb-*

domadaires Des Séances de l Académie des Sciences. D: Sciences Naturelles (Paris), 1971, **272**, 2638–2640.

Edwards, J. H. Chromosome analysis from capillary blood. *Cytogenetics*, 1962, **1**, 90–96.

Edwards, J. H., Harnden, D. G., Cameron, A. H., Crosse, V. M., & Wolff, O. H. A new trisomic syndrome. *Lancet*, 1960, **1**, 787–793.

Esquirol, J. E. D. Des maladies mentales considerées sous les rapports médical, hygiénique et médico-légal. 2 vols. Paris: Ballière, 1838.

Ferraro, M., Capoa, A. de, Mostacci, C., Pelliccia, F., Zulli, P., Baldini, M. A., & DiNisio, Q. Cytogenetic and clinical studies in gonadal dysgenesis with 46,X,Xt(qtr→p221::p223→qtr) karyotype: Review and phenotype/karyotype correlations. *Journal of Medical Genetics*, 1980, **17**, 457–463.

Fishler, K. Mental development in mosaic Down's syndrome as compared with trisomy 21. In R. Koch & F. F. de la Cruz (Eds.), *Down's syndrome (mongolism), research, prevention and management.* New York: Brunner/Mazel, 1975.

Fleming, W. Beiträge zur Kenntniss der Zelle und ihrer Lebenserscheinungen. III. *Archiv fur mikroskopische Anatomie*, 1882, **20**, 1–86.

Forabosco, A., Giorgi, L., Formica, A., Tarantino, E., & Dallapiccola, B. Ovarian dysfunction in balanced X-autosome translocations: Report of two cases involving band Xq21. *Annals of Genetics*, 1979, **22**, 11–16.

Ford, C. E., & Hamerton, J. L. The chromosomes of man. *Nature*, 1956, **178**, 1020–1023.

Ford, C. E., Jones, K. W., Polani, P. E., Almeida, J. C. de, & Briggs, J. H. A sex chromosomal anomaly in a case of gonadal dysgenesis (Turner's syndrome). *Lancet*, 1969, **1**, 711–713.

Francke, U., Brown, M. G., & Jones, K. L. Immediate chromosome diagnosis on bone marrow cells: An aid to management of the malformed newborn infant. *Journal of Pediatrics*, 1979, **94**, 289–292.

Froland, A. A micromethod for chromosome analysis on peripheral blood cultures. *Lancet*, 1962, **2**, 1281–1282.

Gavaudan, P., Gavaudan, N., & Pomriaskinsky-Kobozieff, N. Sur l'influence de la colchicine sur la caryocinese dans les meristemes de l'Allium cepa. (Effect of colchicine on karyokinesis in the meristems of Allium cepa). *Comptes Rendus Des Séances De La Société De Biologie Et De Ses Filiales* (Paris), 1937, **125**, 705–707.

Grouchy, J. de, Lamy, M., Thieffry, S., Arthuis, M., & Salmon, C. Dysmorphie complexe avec oligophrenie: Deletion des bras courts d'un chromosome 17-18. *Comptes Rendus Hebdomadaires Des Séances de l Académie des Sciences. D: Sciences Naturelles* (Paris), 1963, **256**, 1028.

Grouchy, J. de, Royer, P., Salmon, C., & Lamy, M. Deletion partielle du bras long du chromosome 18. *Pathologie Biologie* (Paris), 1964, **12**, 579.

Grouchy, J. de, & Turleau, C. *Clinical atlas of human chromosomes.* New York: John Wiley & Sons, 1977.

Hamerton, J. L. Human cytogenetics. Volume II. *Clinical cytogenetics.* New York: Academic Press, 1971.

Hansemann, D. Über pathologische Mitosen. *Archiv fur Pathologische Anatomie*, 1891, **123**, 356–370.

Heitz, E. Die Nucleal-Quetschmethode. *Berichte der Deutschen Botanischen Gesellschaft*, 1936, **53**, 870–878.

Hirschhorn, K., Cooper, H. D., & Firschein, I. L. Deletion of short arms of chromosome 4-5 in a child with defects of midline fusion. *Humangenetik*, 1965, **1**, 479.

Hook, E. B. Epidemiology of Down syndrome. In S. M. Pueschel & J. E. Rynders, (Eds.), *Down Syndrome: Advances in biomedicine and the behavioral sciences.* Cambridge: The Ware Press, 1982.

Hsu, T. C. Mammalian chromosomes in vitro. The karyotype of man. *Journal of Heredity*, 1952, **43**, 167–172.

Hughes, A. *The mitotic cycle.* New York: Academic Press, 1952.

Hungerford, D. A., Donnelly, A. J., Nowell, P. C., & Beck, S. The chromosomes constitution of a human phenotypic intersex. *American Journal of Human Genetics*, 1959, **11**, 215–236.

Jacobs, P. A., Baikie, A. G., Court Brown, W. M., & Strong, J. A. The somatic chromosome in mongolism. *Lancet*, 1959, **1**, 710.

Johnson, V. P., Mulder, R. D., & Husen, R. The Wolf-Hirschhorn (4p−) syndrome. *Clinical Genetics*, 1976, **10**, 104–112.

Klinefelter, H. F., Jr., Reifenstein, E. C., Jr., & Albright, F. Syndrome characterized by gynecomastia, aspermatogenesis without A-Leydigism, and increased secretion of follicle-stimulating hormone. *Journal of Clinical Endocrinology and Metabolism*, 1942, **2**, 615–627.

Lejeune, J., Berges, R., Lafourcade, J., & Pethore, M. O. La deletion du bras long du chromosome 18. Individualisation d'un nouvel état morbide. *Annales De Génétique*, 1966, **9**, 32–28.

Lejeune, J., Gauthier, M., & Turpin, R. Étude des chromosomes somatiques de neuf enfants mongoliens. *Comptes Rendus Hebdomadaires Des Séances de l'Académie des Sciences. D: Sciences Naturelles* (Paris), 1959, **248**, 1721–1722.

Lejeune, J., Lafourcade, J., Berger, R., Vialatte, J., Boeswillwald, M., Seringe, P., & Turpin, R. Trois cas da déletion partielle du bras court du un chromosome 5. *Comptes Rendus Hebdomadaires Des Séances de l Académie des Sciences. D: Sciences Naturelles* (Paris), 1963, **257**, 3098–3102.

Lubs, H. A., & Walknowska, J. New chromosomal syndromes and mental retardation. In P. Mitter & J. M. de Jong (Eds.), *Research to practice in mental retardation. Volume III. Biomedical aspects.* Baltimore: University Park Press, 1977.

Magenis, E., Palmer, C. G., Wang, L., Brown, M., Chamberlain, J., Parks, M., Merritt, A. D., Rivas, M., & Yu, P. L. Heritability of chromosome banding variants. In E. B. Hook, *Population cytogenetics: studies in humans.* New York: Academic Press, 1977.

Miller, O. J. Chromosome twenty-one trisomy syndrome. In D. Bergsma (Ed.), *Birth Defects Compendium.* (2nd edition) New York: Alan R. Liss, Inc., 1979.

Moorhead, P. S., Nowell, P. C., Mellman, W. J., Battips, D. M., & Hungerford, D. A. Chromosome preparations of leukocytes cultured from human peripheral blood. *Experimental Cell Research*, 1960, **20**, 613–616.

Naegeli, C. Von Zur Entwicklungsgeschichte des Pollens bei den Phanerogamen. Zurich: Orell-Fussli, 1842.

Opitz, J. M. Klinefelter syndrome. In E. Bergsma (Ed.), *Birth Defects Atlas and Compendium.* Baltimore: Williams & Wilkins, 1973.

Painter, T. S. The Y chromosome in mammals. *Science*, 1921, **53**, 503.

Painter, T. S. The spermatogenesis of man. *Journal of Experimental Zoology*, 1923, **37**, 291–334.

Palmer, C. G., & Reichmann, A. Chromosomal and clinical findings in 110 females with Turner syndrome. *Human*

Genetics, 1976, **35**, 35.

Pardue, M. L., & Gall, J. G. Chromosomal localizations of mouse satellite DNA. *Science*, 1970, **168**, 1356–1358.

Patau, K., Smith, D. W., Therman, E., Inhorn, S. L., & Wagner, H. P. Multiple congenital anomaly caused by an extra autosome. *Lancet*, 1960, **1**, 790–793.

Pueschel, S. M., Mendoza, T., & Ellenbogen, R. Partial trisomy 21. *Clinical Genetics*, 1980, **18**, 392–395.

Pueschel, S. M., Scola, F. H., Perry, C. D., & Pezzullo, J. C. Atlanto-axial instability in children with Down syndrome. *Pediatric Radiology*, 1981, **10**, 129–132.

Rethore, M. O., Larget-Piet, L., Abonyi, D., Boeswillwald, M., Berger, R., Carpentier, S., Cruveiller, J., Dutrillaux, B., Lafourcade, J., Penneau, M., & Lejeune, J. Sur quatre cas de trisomie pour le bras court du chromosome 9. Individualisation d'une nouvelle entité morbide. *Annales De Génétique*, 1970, **13**, 217–232.

Sandberg, A. A., Koepf, G. F., Ishihara, T., & Hauschka, T. S. XYY human male. *Lancet*, 1961, **2**, 488.

Santana, J. A. M., Gardner, L. I., & Neu, R. L. The X isochromosome-X syndrome 46,X,i(Xq): Report of three cases with review of the phenotype. *Clinical Pediatrics*, 1977, **16**, 1021–1026.

Schinzel, A., Schmid, U., Luscher, U., Nater, M., Brook, C., & Steinmann, B. Structural aberrations of chromosome 18. I. The 18p- syndrome. *Archiv fur Genetik*, 1974, **47**, 1–15.

Seabright, M. A rapid banding technique for human chromosomes. *Lancet*, 1971, **2**, 971–972.

Sequin, E. *Idiocy and the treatment by the physiological method*. New York: W. Wood and Company, 1866.

Stadler, G. R., Buhler, E. M., & Weber, J. R. Possible trisomy in chromosome group 6-12. *Lancet*, 1963, **1**, 1379.

Subrt, I., & Pokorny, J. Familial occurrence of 18q-. *Humangenetik*, 1970, **10**, 181–187.

Summitt, R. L. Abnormalities of the autosomes and their resultant syndromes. *Pediatric Annals*, 1973, **2**, 40–70.

Summitt, R. L. Autosomal syndromes. *Pediatric Annals*, 1978, **7**, 94–122.

Summitt, R. L., & Patau, K. A. Cytogenetics in mental defectives with anomalies. *Journal of Pediatrics*, 1964, **65**, 1097.

Sumner, A. T., Evans, H. J., & Buckland, R. A. New technique for distinguishing between human chromosomes. *Nature/New Biology* (London), 1971, **232**, 31–32.

Sutton, W. S. The chromosomes in heredity. *Biological Bulletin*, 1903, **4**, 231–251.

Tennes, K., Puck, M., Bryant, K., Frankenburg, W., & Robinson, A. A development study of girls with trisomy X. *American Journal of Human Genetics*, 1975, **27**, 71–80.

Thuline, H. C., & Pueschel, S. M. Cytogenetics in Down's syndrome: In *Down syndrome: Advances in biomedicine and the behavioral sciences*. Cambridge: The Ware Press, 1982.

Tjio, J. H., & Levan, A. The chromosome number of man. *Hereditas*, 1956, **42**, 1–6.

Turner, H. D. A syndrome of infantilism, congenital webbed neck, and cubitus valgus. *Endocrinology*, 1938, **23**, 566–574.

Uchida, I. A., McRae, K. N., Wang, H. C., & Ray, M. Familial short arm deletion of chromosome 18 concomitant with arhinencephaly and alopecia congenita. *American Journal of Human Genetics*, 1965, **17**, 410–419.

Virchow, R. *Cellular biology as based upon physiological and pathological histology*, 1858. (English translation by F. Chance, London: Churchill, 1860).

Voorhees, J. J., Wilkins, J. W., Jr., Hayes, E., & Harrell, R. F. Nodulocystic acnes as a phenotypic feature of the XYY genotype. Report of five cases, review of all known XYY subjects with severe acne, and discussion of XYY cytodiagnosis. *Archives of Dermatology*, 1972, **105**, 913–919.

Waldeyer, W. Über Karyokinese und ihre Beziehungen zu den Befruchtungsvorgängen. *Archiv für mikroskopische Anatomie*, 1888, **30**, 159–181.

Weber, W. W. Survival and the sex ratio in trisomy 17–18. *American Journal of Human Genetics*, 1967, **19**, 369–377.

Winiwarter, H. de von. Études sur la spermatogenèse humaine. (Studies on human spermatogenesis.) *Archives of Biology*, 1912, **27**, 91–189.

Wolf, U., Porsh, R., Baitsch, H., Reinwein, H. Deletion on short arms of a B-chromosome without "cri-du-chat" syndrome. *Lancet*, 1965, **1**, 769.

Wyandt, H. E., Vlietinck, R. F., Magenis, R. E., & Hecht, R. Colored reverse-banding of human chromosomes with acridine orange following alkaline-formalin treatment: Densitometric validation and applications. *Humangenetik*, 1974, **23**, 119–130.

Yunis, J. J., Roldan, L., Yasmineh, W. G., & Lee, J. C. Staining of satellite DNA in metaphase chromosomes. *Nature* (London), 1971, **231**, 532–533.

Zech, L. Investigation of metaphase chromosomes with DNA binding fluorochromes. *Experimental Cell Research*, 1969, **58**, 463.

9   SYSTEMS OF CLASSIFICATION

Gary B. Seltzer

The problem which we have to solve presents many difficulties both theoretical and practical. It is a hackneyed remark that the definitions, thus far proposed, for the different states of subnormal intelligence lack precision [Binet & Simon, 1976, pp. 331–332].

This quote is from a paper published in 1905, one year before the first Binet-Simon Scales of Intelligence became available. Many professionals in the field of mental retardation would argue that even some 75 years after the introduction of the intelligence test—or perhaps partially because of it—agreement about the diagnostic classification of mental retardation remains elusive (Baumeister & Muma, 1975; Leland, 1972; Mercer, 1973). Kuhlmann, as early as 1913, suggested that changes in methods of classification occur "with changing standards of the normal progress of time and under different social and other circumstances of the person examined" (p. 380). He noted the importance of examining the diverse criteria of functioning as they relate to different age levels.

Conceptual and operational definitions guiding the classification of mental retardation have been controversial throughout this century, with the debate focusing on the importance that should be placed on such variables as IQ score, age, functional disabilities, and social and cultural circumstances. In order to understand both the debate that has occurred histor-

ically and the debate that is currently being engaged in by professionals in the field of mental retardation, it is necessary to examine the purposes and functions of classification. At least three perspectives on the purposes and functions of classification have been advanced by professionals. Each of these is briefly discussed below.

A somewhat cynical perspective on this issue, which was articulated by Mercer (1973), among others, is that at least one of the functions of classification is to sustain the activity of professionals. As Mercer has noted regarding the professionalization of diagnostic function,

The more formal the norms and the more elaborate the measuring devices, the stronger the tendency to professionalize the diagnostic function and to adopt a clinical prospective. . . . Only those who have received special training are regarded as having the requisite skills for administering intelligence tests and/or making medical diagnosis [p. 15].

Another understanding about the functioning of the classification process builds on a sociopolitical perspective and asserts that by classifying or labeling certain members of society, professionals are stigmatizing and regulating deviant individuals. This argument has been advanced by a number of professionals including Mercer (1973) and Turnbull and Wheat (in this book). Turnbull and Wheat point out that the classification process has the effect of assigning classified individuals to "lower echelons of life, to second-class citizenship."

The traditional view of the purposes and functions of classification is that classification aids in the identification of the characteristics and problems of an individual, the enumeration of client needs, the specification of treatments and intervention strategies, and the determination of eligibility for services. As Filler et al. (1975) note,

> Classification systems in mental retardation provide an objectively specifiable way of delimiting populations of individuals who for various reasons are likely to encounter difficulty in acquiring the skills necessary for successful community living. The provision of ways to identify and categorize people is, perhaps, absolutely necessary for distributing funds for special programs. In addition, scientific efforts to provide explanations of human development assume, as a prerequisite, adequate systems of description [p. 202].

To some extent, all three of the diverse perspectives about the purpose of classification are valid. Classification does have the purpose of regulating those who are classified and of providing professionals with a special function. In addition, classification enables professionals in the field of mental retardation to understand the incidence and prevalence of the phenomenon, to organize services in a somewhat orderly fashion, and to determine eligibility for services.

Classification actually has somewhat different functions for different types of professionals who are involved in either classifying or utilizing the classification outcomes. For example, clinicians and educators primarily use classification to determine eligibility for treatments and services; researchers use classification to define the population under study, to facilitate replication of findings, and generally to promote the development of empirical models and the theory building process; and policy makers use classification in the regulation, certification, and funding of services that are directed to specific subsegments of the population.

It is important to recognize that a conceptual distinction exists between the *purposes* of classification and its *effects*. Many who have articulated the negative features of classification have in fact been referring to the unintended effects of classification, not to its purposes or objectives. This chapter focuses almost exclusively on the intended purposes and uses of classification, not on the unintended effects of this process. Specifically, this chapter has three overall objectives:

1. to provide a conceptual overview for use in critically evaluating the various classification systems;
2. to describe four of the major classification systems that are used by professionals in the field of mental retardation and to identify published sources that can be used in the further exploration of each system; and
3. to discuss the relative advantages and disadvantages of the various systems for use in different situations.

This chapter begins with an overview of the conceptual issues involved in classification, followed by discussion of four systems currently used in classification. These four systems are the AAMD system (which is largely statistical in its foundations), the DSM-III system (which is largely psychiatric in its foundations), the ICD-9 system (which is largely medical in its foundations), and the Developmental Disabilities definition (which is largely functional in its foundations). Following these sections, the relative advantages and disadvantages of the four systems will be discussed.

Classification: Overview and Conceptual Issues

Any system by which a person is diagnosed as mentally retarded and is classified into one of several subgroups of mental retardation consists of a series of formalized rules. These rules specify the characteristics that a person must possess or must fail to possess in order that diagnostic and classification decisions can be made. However, there is no single "correct" system or valid set of rules for classification, because mental retardation and its levels (mild, moderate, severe, profound) are hypothetical constructs that must be inferred from other phenomena (e.g., behavior, test performance, physical signs) rather than from direct observation.

Because mental retardation is a hypothetical construct, there is room for much debate regarding the best method of defining this phenomenon. The various systems that have been developed therefore reflect different ideological perspectives regarding the conceptualization of mental retardation. No single approach is inherently superior to the others, because each is reflective of a different ideological perspective. However, there are advantages and disadvantages of each approach, as will be discussed throughout this chapter. The three ideological approaches to classification that will be presented in this discussion are the categorical approach, the functional approach, and the social systems approach.

· By far the most commonly accepted approach to the classification of mental retardation is the *categorical approach*. Systems that are based on this approach accomplish classification by determining the presence or absence of a phenomenon, or the degree to which a phenomenon is present or absent. Often the etiology of the problem forms the basis of the categorization. Regarding mental retardation, the phenomenon most often used as the basis of categorization is intelligence, as measured by the IQ test. Persons with IQ scores within certain ranges are categorized as mentally retarded and are differentiated from persons who have higher IQ scores but who may exhibit similar performance deficits. In this schema, it is possible that two persons who have been placed in different categories actually behave very similarly. It is their category, not their behavior that is salient.

An alternative to the categorical approach is the *functional approach*. In this approach to classification, the salient phenomenon is the behavior of the person being classified. The etiology of the person's problem is less important. Thus, in the functional approach to classification, two persons whose problems are caused by different etiological conditions but whose behavior patterns are similar would be classified similarly.

A third approach to the classification of mental retardation is *the social systems* approach. A social system is an environment within which a person functions, such as a school, a job, or a family. According to the social systems perspective, mental retardation is neither the presence or absence of a characteristic of the individual, as postulated by the categorical approach, nor simply the manifest behavior of the individual, as postulated by the functional approach, but rather a *role* played by an individual in a particular social system. A social role is defined as the part one plays as the occupant of a particular social status (Mercer, 1973). For example, the psychologist's role is to administer psychometric tests, provide psychotherapy, write clinical reports, etc. A person plays a role in part because of his/her characteristics and in part because of the label assigned to him or her by others. According to Mercer (1979) "Behavioral norms are politically, not biologically determined; values of the dominant group are enforced. . . . Multiple definitions of 'normal behaviors' are role and system specific" (p. 40). Being mentally retarded is to be labeled retarded. From this perspective, then, mental retardation is defined as a role played by a person in some social systems, but not necessarily in all social systems. For example, some children are given the label "mentally retarded" only for the six

hours during which they attend special education classes, but not while playing with their friends after school. Other children, who have fewer skills, tend to be labeled mentally retarded in most of the environments or social systems in which they play a role. Thus, although the social systems approach examines the behavior of a person as in the functional approach, it differs from the latter and from the categorical approach in that it argues against the underlying clinical assumption accepted by these two approaches—namely that a person either is or is not mentally retarded.

In the next section of this chapter, four of the most commonly used systems for classifying mental retardation are presented. Three of these (the AAMD, the DSM-III, and the ICD-9) utilize a combination of the categorical and functional approaches, while the fourth (the Developmental Disabilities definition) relies exclusively on the functional orientation. None of the most commonly used classification systems utilizes the social systems approach.

Regardless of the ideological perspective that forms the basis of a classification schema or its specific operational features, all classification systems ideally should share five characteristics. To the extent to which any system fails to meet all five of these criteria, the system is deficient and needs improvement. These criteria will be useful to consider when evaluating the advantages and disadvantages of the four classifications systems presented below. The five criteria are: clarity, coverage, reliability, clinical utility, and acceptability. Each is defined briefly as follows:

Clarity refers to the extent to which the decision rules for making the diagnoses are stated clearly, precisely and explicitly.

Coverage refers to the extent to which the classification system results in the inclusion of all individuals who should be included and the exclusion of all individuals who are not part of the relevant population.

Reliability refers to the extent to which the classification system is guided by procedures that result in the same decision being applied to identical patients by different clinicians. The more that the system relies on observable phenomena, the less inter-clinician variability will result.

Clinical utility refers to the extent to which the classification system facilitates continuity between initial diagnosis and subsequent treatments or interventions.

Acceptability refers to the extent to which professionals who use the classification system and the individuals who are classified (the consumers) find the system to contain few or no pejorative features. A feature believed by a professional to be nonpejorative may be found by a consumer to be pejorative and vice versa. Both perspectives are important.

Classification systems vary not only by ideological perspectives and on the extent to which they meet the five criteria presented above, but also on the element or elements they stress. For example, some definitions emphasize the incurability of mental retardation (e.g., Doll, 1941; Ewalt, 1972), while others emphasize the manifestation of social incompetence (e.g., Tredgold, 1952). Other elements that are stressed to varying degrees in different classification systems include age of onset, severity, prognosis, etiology, and degree of impairment. With regard to some of these elements (e.g., age of onset), there is widespread consensus among professionals and consumers. Thus, nearly all definitions and classification systems stress that mental retardation must be manifested prior to adulthood. Regarding other elements (such as social incompetence), there is much disagreement regarding their importance (Clark, 1965).

The great deal of variability among classification systems in all of the respects discussed in this section is not necessarily reflective of a lack of sophistication in the field of mental retardation. Rather, it may reflect the phenomenon of mental retardation itself. As noted earlier, this must be inferred and not directly observed. Thus, each classification system currently in use is flawed in various important respects, but each also has unique advantages. These will be explored in the discussion that follows.

Systems Used in Classifying Mental Retardation

AAMD Classification System

The American Association on Mental Deficiency (AAMD) has pioneered in the development of classification schema in the field of mental retardation. A landmark year in the history of AAMD's classification activities was 1959 when the Association published a *Manual on Terminology and Classification* (Heber, 1959). According to Heber, mental retardation was defined as

subaverage general intellectual functioning which originates during the developmental

period and is associated with impairment in one or more of the following; (1) maturation, (2) learning, and (3) social adjustment [p. 3].

This definition relied on the statistical model in which the IQ score was used to separate mentally retarded from nonretarded persons and to further subdivide those defined as mentally retarded into various levels of retardation. When the IQ scores of the population in general are plotted on a graph, a bell-shaped curve results as shown in Fig. 9.1.

Because of the statistical properties of the normal curve, a known proportion of the population falls between any two IQ scores. Fifty percent of the population have IQ scores below the average score of 100. Obviously, not all these persons are mentally retarded. A valid statistically-based classification schema is one which identifies the IQ score below which a person can appropriately be classified as mentally retarded.

At different points in history, various demarcation points have been used by the AAMD. For example, prior to 1959, the AAMD used an IQ cutoff of 70, below which individuals were diagnosed as mentally retarded. With this cutoff point, approximately 2½% of the population was classified as mentally retarded. In the 1959 revision of the AAMD classification schema, a change was made in the cutoff point; instead of 70, an IQ of 85 was used to demarcate mental retardation from nonretardation. This change had dramatic consequences; rather than 2½% of the population being classified as mentally retarded, as many as 17% of the population was thus labeled. The large segment of the population who had IQ scores above 70 but below 85 were considered "borderline intelligence" by the AAMD after 1959. However in the AAMD's 1973 revision of the classification schema (Grossman, 1977), the cutoff point was again set at an IQ of 70 and the category of "borderline intelligence" was no longer officially accepted. According to the 1973 revision, the four levels of mental retardation and their associated IQ ranges were roughly as follows

Level	IQ score
mild	56–70
moderate	41–55
severe	26–40
profound	25 and below

This brief overview of the changes in the IQ cutoff point used by the AAMD to define mental retardation highlights the central difficulty in using the IQ score

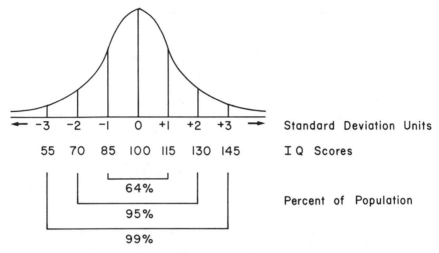

FIG. 9.1. Distribution of IQ scores.

in classification, namely the arbitrariness of the selection of any numerical cutoff point.

Dissatisfaction with this arbitrariness existed prior to 1959 and was largely responsible for the decision made by the AAMD in 1959 to add a second dimension (in addition to IQ) to the classification of mental retardation, namely, adaptive behavior. The dimension of adaptive behavior was added to the classification schema in order to include the functional abilities of the mentally retarded person as well as his or her IQ score in the process of defining mental retardation. This was considered to be important because it is very possible that two individuals who have the same IQ score may be very different in their functional abilities.

In keeping with this perspective, since 1959 the AAMD classification requires that a person have *both* a low IQ score and deficits in adaptive behavior in order to be classified as mentally retarded. Adaptive behavior is defined as

> the effectiveness or degree to which the individual meets the standards of personal independence and social responsibility expected of his age and cultural group [p. 11].

This definition states that the individual's behavior must be assessed in relation to the behavior of other persons—agemates and members of the person's cultural group. Grossman (1977) delineates the types of adaptive behaviors by age as follows:

During infancy and early childhood in:
1. sensory motor skills development,
2. communication skills (including speech and language),

3. self help skills,
4. socialization (development of ability to interact with others).

During childhood and early adolescence in:
5. application of basic academic skills in daily activities,
6. application of appropriate reasoning and judgement in mastery of the environment,
7. social skills (participation in group activities and interpersonal relationships).

During late adolescence and adult life in:
8. vocational and social responsibilities and performances [p. 13].

It is important to note that although the two dimensions of IQ and adaptive behavior are conceptually distinct, they are not empirically independent of one another. Many researchers have reported a high, although not a perfect correlation between IQ and adaptive behavior (Gollay, Freedman, Wyngaarden, & Kurtz, 1978; Jones & Jones, 1976; Seltzer & Seltzer, 1978). Among severely mentally retarded persons, classification by means of the IQ score and by means of adaptive behavior level are usually in agreement. Among mildly and moderately mentally retarded persons, discrepancies in the two classification outcomes are more likely to occur but agreement is still more common than disagreement (Roszokowski & Spreat, 1981).

Although there is widespread philosophical acceptance of the inclusion of adaptive behavior along with the IQ score in classification, some criticisms have been levelled. For example, as Baumeister and Muma (1975) note, it is a deficit in adaptive behavior that first identifies a child as potentially having a problem, leaving only the IQ score to define him/her officially mentally retarded. Baumeister and Muma argue that the AAMD definition in fact uses the IQ score as the single criterion.

There is even less agreement among professionals about how adaptive behavior is best assessed. The most commonly used measure of adaptive behavior at the present time is the AAMD Adaptive Behavior Scale (Nihira, Foster, Shellhaas, & Leland, 1975) a scale in which the mentally retarded person's performance of selected skills is evaluated by an informant. The informant might be a parent, residential staff member, or social worker who knows the client well.

The Adaptive Behavior Scale has been criticized on two points: conceptually and methodologically. Conceptually, it has been criticized because it purportedly focuses exclusively on the individual being assessed and neither compares his/her behavior to others in the cultural group nor considers the person's physical and social environment (Seltzer, 1981). Baumeister and Muma (1975) argue:

It is assumed that the determinants of adaptive capacity are exclusively within the providence of the individual's faculties. The logical extension is that mental retardation should be determined only in terms of individual capacities. This position simply attributes retardation to a person without due regard to the functional context in which he lives. . . . Adaptation is not simply a matter of one's capacities measured in neutral gear, so to speak, but also of environmental opportunities [p. 298].

In addition to this conceptual criticism, the inter-rater reliability of the ABS and the validity of the responses of the informant have been criticized (Isett & Spreat, 1979; Millham, Chilcutt, & Atkinson, 1978). Many alternative scales have been developed to assess adaptive behavior including the Minnesota Developmental Programming System (Bock & Weatherman, 1975) the Personal Competency Scale (Reynolds, 1981), and the Progress Adjustment Chart (Gunzberg, 1969). No single scale, however, has achieved the widespread use of the Adaptive Behavior Scales.

The Diagnostic and Statistical Manual of Mental Disorders

The third edition of this work (DSM-III), published by the American Psychiatric Association in 1980, is a second diagnostic system that can be used to define mental retardation and to classify mentally retarded

persons into various levels of retardation. The DSM-III is a multidimensional (or multi-axial) system, which means that the diagnosis given to an individual reflects not only his/her "major mental disorder," but also any physical disorder that the person might have, as well as a rating of the severity of psychosocial stresses operating in the person's life, and a rating of the highest level of adaptive functioning achieved by the person during the past year. As a classification system, the DMS-III thus provides more detailed descriptive information about the individual being classified than does the AAMD system. However, in spite of this greater degree of elaboration, the criteria used by the DSM-III to classify a person as mentally retarded are almost identical to the AAMD criteria. In fact, a footnote appearing at the beginning of the section on mental retardation in the DSM-III states that "the definitions of mental retardation were written in accordance with the terminology and classification of the American Association on Mental Deficiency" (p. 36).

The DSM-III differs from its predecessors (DSM-I published in 1952, and DSM-II published in 1968) in a number of ways. The DSM-I represented a particular theoretical framework for understanding mental disorders, namely a psychobiological perspective. In contrast, the DSM-II was designed to be more general and to minimize the use of terminology specific to any particular theoretical perspective. The DSM-III also attempts to be atheoretical. A difference between the DSM-II and the DSM-I is that the DSM-II based its classification of mental disorders on the International Classification of Diseases (the ICD-8) and the DSM-I did not. This linking of two major classification systems (DSM and ICD) was seen as an important advantage of the DSM-II. The DSM-III continues to be linked to the ICD system, now in its 9th revision, but differs from the DSM-I and DSM-II in that it is multi-axial (i.e. multidimensional).

Any understanding of the DSM-III classification system is dependent upon familiarity with the five axes of which the DSM-III is composed. Each axis is intended to represent a distinct dimension.

Axis I and *Axis II* include all of the categories of mental disorders. All categories of mental disorders except specific developmental disorders and personality disorders are included in Axis I. Specific developmental disorders and personality disorders are included in Axis II. The separation of mental disorders into two axes represents a departure from the basic definition of an axes as a distinct dimension. However, the rationale for the separation of mental disorders onto two axes, according to the DSM-III manual, is that those disorders that are frequently overlooked will be less often ignored if they are placed on a separate axis. These frequently overlooked categories are found in Axis II. It may be useful to note that in diagnosing a person with multiple problems, there is no restriction in the number of diagnoses that can be given in Axis I and Axis II. Mental retardation is included in Axis I and specific developmental disorders (e.g., learning disabilities) are included in Axis II.

Axis III involves the identification of the physical disorders or conditions that a person might have. The particular codes used for Axis III are taken from the ICD-9. Again, there is no restriction in the number of physical conditions that can be included on Axis III. Thus, if a person has Down's syndrome and a seizure disorder, both are coded under Axis III.

Axis IV involves the rating of the severity of psychosocial stresses operative in a person's life. The rating represents a judgment of the *total* amount of stress to which the person is exposed. Stressors are rated as to how the "average" person would react if exposed to them. Thus, even if a person has an extreme reaction to a mild stressor, the stressor is coded as mild. The Axis IV scale of stressors includes the following points:

1. none
2. minimal
3. mild
4. moderate
5. severe
6. extreme
7. catastrophic
0. unspecified

Types of psychosocial stressors rated in Axis IV include marital problems, parenting problems, and other interpersonal problems, occupational problems, problems in living circumstances, financial problems, legal problems, life cycle problems (e.g., puberty), physical illness or injuries not related to the development or management of an Axis I or Axis II disorder, other psychosocial stresses (e.g., rape), and family problems.

Axis V involves a rating of the highest level of adaptive functioning exhibited by the person during the past year. This rating is not intended to reflect fleeting levels of adaptive functioning but rather the level achieved by the person for at least a few months. Axis V consists of three key areas: social relations, occupational functioning, and use of leisure time. Unlike Axis IV, which involves the ratings of the stressors in a person's life, Axis V involves the rating of the person's behavior. The Axis V scale of adaptive functioning includes the following points:

1. superior
2. very good
3. good
4. fair
5. poor
6. very poor
7. grossly impaired
0. unspecified

This scale is not synonymous with adaptive behavior and therefore mentally retarded persons are not uniformly considered to have low Axis V ratings.

As noted previously, the classification of mental retardation in Axis I is based on the AAMD criteria. The AAMD system relies heavily on the results of adaptive behavior scales that have been developed. In the DSM-III, however, the clinician's judgment tends to be given more weight. Specifically, the DSM-III manual states that although "there are scales defined to quantify adaptive behavior . . . , none is considered sufficiently reliable and valid to be used alone to evaluate this aspect of functioning. Therefore clinical judgment is necessary for the assessment of general adaptation" (p. 37). Thus, users of DSM-III system might be more likely than users of the AAMD system to use the IQ score alone in the classification of mental retardation.

The following codes are used in the DSM-III to classify mental retardation:

317.0 (x) mild mental retardation (IQ 50 through 70)
318.0 (x) moderate mental retardation (IQ 35 through 49)
318.1 (x) severe mental retardation (IQ 20 through 34)
318.2 (x) profound mental retardation (IQ 19 or less)
319.0 (x) unspecified mental retardation (for untestable persons)

The x is replaced by a 0 when no behavior problems are present or by a 1 when the client has associated behavior problems. The use of the DSM-III in diagnosing mental retardation requires not only familiarity with the DSM-III itself but also the AAMD criteria and with the ICD-9 medical codes for use in Axis III.

International Classification of Diseases (ICD)

The ICD system of classification provides the international health community with a means for classifying comparable data about morbidity and mortality. Specifically, the principal objective of the ICD is to classify "morbidity and mortality information for statistical purposes, and for the indexing of hospital records by disease and operations, for data storage and retrieval" (ICD-9-CM p. XXI). The ICD has been adapted for use in medical records in order to encourage a standardized means of organizing medical information and for the purpose of creating a world-wide data bank of information.

The ICD is presently in its ninth revision, having been revised at approximately 10-year intervals since 1893. The ICD system was first published as the International Classification of Causes of Death, having been adopted by the International Statistical Institute in Paris in 1893. The first revision conference of the International List of Causes of Death was held in Paris in 1900. As evident in its original title, the classification system was intended to code only causes of death and did not include morbidity data. The 6th revision was the first to include data about morbidity as well as mortality (Kramer, 1980).

The fifth revision of the ICD in 1938 included a subsection for mental disorders for the first time. Four subcategories were contained within the section on disease of the nervous system and sense organs: (a) mental deficiency; (b) schizophrenia; (c) manic-depression psychosis; and (d) all other mental disorders (Kramer, 1980). The ICD-6 contained the first separate section on mental disorders.

Following the publication of ICD-8, the WHO organized a series of seminars, the intent of which was to thoroughly evaluate the classification system for the major psychiatric disorders and to offer recommendations for reformulating this section. A fascinating series of papers on the classification of mental retardation was published as a result of this effort (American Psychiatric Association, 1972). Prominent professionals such as George Tarjan, Jack Tizard, Jack Ewalt, Joseph Wortis and others contributed individual papers and as a group agreed that

> The current classification of mental retardation is inadequate and that a multiaxial scheme should be adopted. This scheme would consist of three axes: (1) intellectual level, (2) associated or etiological factors, and (3) clinical psychiatric system, and would require that each axis be recorded. Information that should be considered in classifying mental retardation includes: degree, organic aspects, psychiatric and behavioral aspects, and psychosocial aspects [p. 3].

Some noteworthy changes were made from ICD-8 to ICD-9, although not particularly reflective of the above recommendations. The ICD-9 is not a multiaxial classification system as is the DSM-III nor does it combine etiological factors together with the presence and degree of mental retardation as was done in the ICD-8. That is, in ICD-8, after a three-digit code for mental retardation (ranging from 310, borderline mental retardation to 315 unspecified mental retardation), 10 additional etiological and/or associated physical condition codes were included. The use of "combination categories" was cross-referenced in the 1977 AAMD (Grossman, 1977) with the following listing of associated physical conditions:

.0 following infection and intoxication
.1 following trauma or physical agent
.2 with disorders of metabolism and nutrition
.3 associated with gross brain disease (post)
.4 associated with diseased conditions due to unknown prenatal influence
.5 with chromosomal abnormality
.6 gestational disorders
.7 following psychiatric disorders
.8 environmental influences
.9 other conditions

ICD-9 requires that the above conditions be coded separately by using two code numbers: one for mental retardation and another for the associated physical and/or psychiatric disorders.

Code 8, "environmental influences" was eliminated in the ICD-9 classification schema. This was noteworthy because of the conflicting array of interpretations associated with this etiological category (Tarjan & Eisenberg, 1972). Environmental influences as a cause of mental retardation was inferred only in certain circumstances. That is, etiological terms such as sociocultural retardation, cultural familial retardation, and psychogenic mental retardation were used when an organic cause for mental retardation was not found and when the person was often from a minority or ethnic background and/or from a low socioeconomic background. In the ICD-9 a supplementary classification of external causes of injury and poisoning (E codes) is included to permit classification of tangible environmental events that cause mental retardation. The need for coding environmental influences was further reduced by the elimination in the ICD-9 of the borderline mental retardation code (as in the AAMD 1973 revision and DSM-III).

The definition of mental retardation found in the ICD-9 CM* Glossary of Mental Disorders is as follows:

> A condition of arrested or incomplete development of mind which is especially

---

* "CM" stands for Clinical Modification, as adopted for use in the United States revision of ICD-9.

characterized by subnormality of intelligence. The coding should be made on the individual's *current* level of functioning *without regard to its nature* or causation, such as psychosis, cultural deprivation, Down's syndrome, etc. Where there is a specific cognitive handicap—such as in speech—the diagnosis of mental retardation should be based on assessments of cognition *outside the area of specific handicap*. The assessment of intellectual level should be based on whatever information is available, including clinical evidence, adaptive behavior, and psychometric findings. The IQ levels given are based on a test with a mean of 100 and a standard deviation of 15, such as the Wechsler Scales. They are provided only as a guide and should not be applied rigidly. Mental retardation often involves psychiatric disturbances and may often develop as a result of some physical disease or injury. In these cases, an additional diagnosis should be recorded to identify any associated condition, psychiatric or physical [p. 1098].

The ICD-9 definition stresses the use of the current level of functioning as opposed to some definitions (e.g., the British definition, Ewalt, 1972) that emphasize the use of etiology and a lifetime progress of mental subnormality. Moreover, the assessment of intellectual level in the ICD-9 definition can be based upon a broader array of *combined* sources (i.e., clinical evidence, adaptive behavior and psychometric findings) than is true of the DSM III and AAMD definition. That is, the architects of this definition seem not to have categorized adaptive behavior and IQ as separate criteria for diagnosing mental retardation. Instead, it seems that users of this definition are given more license to employ their clinical judgment in diagnosing mental retardation than is true with the DSM-III and AAMD definitions.

The Developmental Disabilities (DD) Definition

In recent years, there has been a move toward using a functional perspective to classify persons with developmental problems. In this approach, the focus is on an analysis of the skills—or adaptive behaviors—performed by a person in his/her daily life. In addition, some proponents of this approach advocate that an examination of the environmental conditions that promote, maintain, or impede the performance of adaptive behaviors should be included in any assessment of the individual (e.g., Nagi, 1976; Seltzer & Seltzer, in press; Wood, 1978). A variety of professionals in different disciplines have contributed to the general conceptual development of the functional approach (although not specifically to the development of the DD definition), including behavioral psychologists (Bijou, 1961; Skinner, 1953), sociologists (Lemert, 1967; Mercer, 1973), and rehabilitation physicians (Granger, in press; Wood, 1980). In this section, a discussion of the functional approach as applied to the definition of developmental disabilities is presented.

The functional perspective classifies a mentally retarded person according to observable behaviors. As Bijou (1963) noted, "a retarded individual is one who has a limited repertory of behavior evolving from interactions of the individual with his environmental contacts which constitute his history" (p. 101). The functional perspective has rejected the use of the IQ score (or any other single characteristic) for classification purposes. According to Skinner (1953), it is inappropriate to equate an IQ score with intelligence, because the numerical IQ score gives *excess meaning* to the limited sample of behavior assessed by IQ tests. To illustrate, Skinner notes that "we begin with intelligent behavior, pass to behavior which shows intelligence, and then to behavior which is the effect of intelligence" (p. 202). Thus, the functional perspective rejects the basic foundations of the AAMD, DSM-III, and ICD-9 classification systems, which all utilize the IQ score in defining and classifying mental retardation.

One operationalization of the functional approach is the definition adopted in 1978 by Congress and incorporated in Section 102 (7) of Public Law 95-602, the Developmental Disabilities Assistance and Bill of Rights Act (often referred to as the "DD Act"). The definition of "developmental disability" in the DD Act qualifies persons to receive services and benefits and is used by state Developmental Disabilities Councils in the planning of services, the development of policy regarding services, advocacy for services, and at times the funding of services.

Developmental Disabilities Councils often provide state legislatures with projections regarding the service needs of persons with developmental disabilities. Therefore, Council members need a definition from which they can determine criteria of eligibility and population estimates. The operational definition first introduced into P.L. 91-517, the Developmental Disabilities Act of 1970 (section 401) defined persons as developmentally disabled by means of *impairment status*, not by means of a functional approach.

> The term developmental disability means a disability attributable to mental retardation, cerebral palsy, epilepsy or another neurological condition of an individual found by the

Secretary to be closely related to mental retardation or to require treatment similar to that required for mentally retarded individuals, which disability originates before such individual attains age 18, which has continued or can be expected to continue indefinitely, and which constitutes a substantial handicap to such individual.

In 1975, autism was added to the qualifying conditions of mental retardation, cerebral palsy, and epilepsy, when the Developmental Disabilities Act was amended by P.L. 94-103.

Over time, the definition presented in P.L. 91-517 and amended by Public Law 94-103 was found by many professionals to be unsatisfactory because the definition excluded from eligibility many individuals whose disabilities are functionally similar to those with mental retardation, cerebral palsy, epilepsy, or autism, but which were due to some other etiology. By specifying only three (and later four) categorical disabilities, the definition was believed to alter the broader philosophy intended within the original legislation (Boggs & Henney, 1979). An alternative definition, which was noncategorical and based on a functional perspective, was therefore adopted within P.L. 95-602 in 1978. This act defined a developmental disability as follows:

The term developmental disability means a severe, chronic disability of a person which
(A) is attributable to a mental or physical impairment or combination of mental and physical impairments;
(B) is manifested before the person attains age 22;
(C) is likely to continue indefinitely;
(D) results in substantial functional limitations in three or more of the following areas of major life activity, (i) self care, (ii) receptive and expressive language, (iii) learning, (iv) mobility, (v) self direction, (vi) capacity for independent living, and (vii) economic sufficiency; and
(E) reflects the person's need for a combination and sequence of special, interdisciplinary, or generic care, treatment, or other services which are of lifelong or extended duration and individually planned and coordinated.

The emphasis in this functionally oriented definition is on chronicity, age-specific onset, multiple areas of functional limitations, and need for an extended array of long-term services from a multiplicity of service providers, not on specific category of disability (e.g., mental retardation, cerebral palsy, etc., as in P.L. 91-517 and P.L. 94-103). The concepts of severity and substantiality are crucial in the application of this definition. Boggs and Henney (1979) note that the determination of a substantial functional limitation for a particular individual is a *clinical* determination; it does not depend simply on a person's label. It was hoped that the clinical measurement of functional limitations and abilities would broaden the target group defined as developmentally disabled. Whereas under the P.L. 91-517 definition, a mentally retarded person would *always* have been labeled as developmentally disabled, under the P.L. 95-602 definition, many functionally competent mentally retarded persons living on their own and not in need of services would not be considered developmentally disabled. This definitional approach attempts to link planning, service provision, and eligibility determination to the level of competence a person displays in performing life sustaining and enhancing activities, not to a categorical label.

Because the functional definition of developmental disabilities is new, there has been limited experience in applying it to definitional and classification problems. It should be noted that the operational clarity of this definition is somewhat weak, especially regarding Sections D and E. Its reliance on clinical judgment, as noted above, is said to be a strength of the definition. This is also a weakness because of the reliability and validity problems that are encountered when clinicians are expected to make judgments in the absence of clear guidelines.

To summarize, the advantage of the DD definition is its function orientation and the disadvantage is its lack of operational clarity. With use over several years and with the development of operational guidelines, it is hoped that this disadvantage will diminish.

Comparisons Among Classification Systems

An important issue to address when comparing the four classification systems is the extent to which the same person would be classified comparably if each of the four systems was used. Are the definitional and classification criteria among the systems very highly correlated, or, alternatively, are the criteria discrete enough to result in some definitional and classification variability among the systems? This question is explored in the discussion that follows through an examination of the unique and common features of each classification system.

As noted earlier, the DSM-III and the AAMD systems use the same criteria for diagnosing and classifying mental retardation. The two systems differ in the emphasis each places on adaptive behavior. The AAMD system provides much greater specificity and much clearer guidelines than the DSM-III in defining adaptive behavior and in using adaptive behavior in defining and classifying mental retardation. However, as Taylor (1980) noted, there has been very little actual use of adaptive behavior in defining mental retardation and in classification as evidenced in published articles, and perhaps also in clinical practice. In light of the limited use of the criterion of adaptive behavior in the AAMD system, it is probable that the AAMD and DSM-III systems are likely to result in similar diagnosis and classification outcomes if used with the same person despite their formal differences in the adaptive behavior domain. However, the DSM-III will provide additional psychological detail, especially through Axes IV and V, that would not be provided by the AAMD system.

The ICD-9 system is quite similar to the DSM-III and AAMD systems in the definitional and classification criteria employed. It too emphasizes the use of both adaptive behavior and IQ in defining and classifying mental retardation. However, to a greater extent than in either the AAMD or DSM-III systems, the ICD-9 suggests the use of "clinical evidence" in diagnoses and classification. Reliance on clinical evidence, in the absence of clear guidelines regarding the nature of such evidence or its interpretation, is likely to result in operational ambiguity. Different ICD-9 users might use different types of clinical evidence when diagnosing a person as mentally retarded and might interpret similar evidence in different ways. However, in spite of this problem of unreliability, since the ICD-9 uses definitional and classification criteria comparable to the DSM-III and AAMD, the three systems would be likely to produce similar outcomes if used by the same diagnostician to classify one mentally retarded person.

The greatest contrast among the systems is most likely to occur between the Developmental Disabilities (DD) functional definition and each of the other three systems. In fact a recent study (Lubin, Jacobson, & Kiely, 1982) reported that only 78.8% of the persons classified as mentally retarded and receiving developmental disabilities services in New York State would be classified as developmentally disabled if the DD definition were to be used. Not surprising, this study did find a significant relationship between IQ score and the manifestation of substantial impairment. Substantial impairment was defined by functional limitations in three of the following areas: mobility,

language, independent living, economic self sufficiency, self direction, self care, and learning. The authors reported that the proportions of individuals with substantial impairment increased as the degree of retardation became more severe, with 41.5% of mildly mentally retarded persons substantially impaired in three or more areas, 86.7% of the moderately mentally retarded, 96.7% of the severely mentally retarded, and 99.7% of the profoundly mentally retarded.*

In regard to the comparability of the AAMD and DD systems, it is important to note that the operational criteria for measuring substantial impairments in the DD systems and in the Lubin et al. (1982) study are obviously similar to the criteria for assessing adaptive behavior by means of the Adaptive Behavior Scale (Nihira et al., 1975). However the finding reported by Lubin et al. (1982) that only 41.5% of those persons labelled mildly mentally retarded actually function as substantially handicapped is consistent with other reports (Baumeister & Muma, 1975; Smith & Polloway, 1979; Taylor, 1980) that adaptive behavior is often ignored by researchers and clinicians who use the AAMD system in diagnosing and classifying a person as mentally retarded. It seems that the IQ score remains the dominant criterion in diagnoses and classification of mental retardation.

Another basis on which to compare the four classification systems is to examine the extent to which each of them meets the five criteria delineated above: clarity, coverage, reliability, clinical utility, and acceptability. Of course, the extent to which any of the classification systems meets each of these criteria is a matter of judgment; there is no objective manner of determining the relative strength and weakness of each system in the absence of an empirical research project. Nevertheless, it may be useful to rate the relative strength and weaknesses of each of the four classification systems on each of the five criteria. Table 9.1 contains the author's ratings, each made on a 5-point scale in which 5 represents the most favorable ruling and 1 represents the least favorable rating.

Regarding *clarity*, the highest ratings were given to the AAMD and DMS-III systems. Both of these

---

* It is important to note that the Lubin et al. study selected as their criterion of substantial impairment within the life activity area of learning "intellectual functioning within the *moderately*, severely or profoundly retarded ranges" [p. 74, emphasis added]. The decision to select moderate rather than mild or *three* rather than *two* standard deviations below the mean IQ score deviates from the criterion used by the other three classification systems and obviously skews their findings. Furthermore, the authors do not justify their selection of moderate retardation or below as the criterion of substantial impairment for the life activity area of learning.

Table 9.1. Ratings of the Classifications System

CRITERIA	AAMD	DSM-III	ICD-9	DD
Clarity	4	4	3	2
Coverage	4	4	4	2
Reliability	4	3	3	2
Clinical utility	4	5	3	4
Acceptability	4	4	3	4

systems have been extensively pilot tested and revised in order to maximize the clarity of the definition and classification decision rules which they contained. The 1977 revision of the AAMD system specifically focused on improving clarity. Lower ratings were given to the ICD-9 and DD systems. The ICD-9 is lacking the detailed specificity of the AAMD and the DSM-III and the DD definition includes a minimum of operational definitions and guidelines. A number of task forces (e.g., Abt Associates, 1977; Gollay, 1980) have attempted to address the problem with the clarity of the DD definition. If the recommendations of any of the task forces are adopted officially, it is likely that the clarity of the DD definition will improve.

Regarding *coverage*, the AAMD, DSM-III, and ICD-9 systems were given comparable ratings. Coverage refers to the extent to which the classification system would correctly classify all mentally retarded persons as mentally retarded. The DD definition was given a lower rating because the requirement of "substantial impairment" may exclude many mildly mentally retarded persons as found in the Lubin et al. (1982) study. Additional incidence and prevalence studies using the DD definition are needed; thus the rating given to the DD definition for the criterions of clarity should be seen as preliminary.

Regarding *reliability*, the highest rating was given to the AAMD system. The guidelines for making judgment about levels of adaptive behavior are clearer in the AAMD system than in either the DSM-III or ICD-9 systems. It should be noted that the reliability of the other criterion used in defining mental retardation by these three systems—the IQ score—is very high. In contrast, the DD system received the lowest rating for reliability because of the lack of clear guidelines and operational definitions, which are prerequisites for high levels of reliability.

Regarding *clinical utility*, the highest rating was given to the DSM-III system. The inclusion of multiple axes provides information to the clinician about the client that is rich in detail and broad in scope, much more so than in any of the other classification systems. The AAMD and DD systems received the next highest ratings. The AAMD system focuses on adaptive behavior as well as IQ score alone. Similarly, the DD

definition focus on the functional abilities of the clients is helpful in service planning for clients as well as program planning for groups of clients. For example, an examination of the life activities in which significant impairment is present can guide the development of the behavioral objectives of an Individual Service Plan. The ICD-9 system received a lower rating for clinical utility because of its focus on facilitating the systematic collection of data rather than information targeted for clinical interventions.

Finally, regarding *acceptability* of the classification system to both professionals and consumers, equally high ratings were given to the AAMD, DSM-III, and DD systems. The AAMD system is the most widely accepted system among professionals in the field of mental retardation. Similarly, the DSM-III system has received recent widespread support from the mental health community. The DD system probably has the highest level of acceptability to consumers, because it exclusively focuses on the present functioning of clients and is not dominated by the use of IQ score. However, the DD system also poses problems to policy makers. The noncategorical approach (i.e., not accepting clinical labels such as mental retardation, autism, etc.) for determining service eligibility necessitates more complex estimates of the number of persons in need (Boggs & Henney 1979). The ICD-9 system is used by hospitals for reimbursement of costs and as such is important for both consumers and professionals, but its limited clinical utility makes the system less acceptable to both consumers and professionals. However, as an instrument to collect uniform morbidity and mortality data, the ICD-9 system is quite valuable to researchers and health planners.

To summarize, the classification system that received the most consistently high ratings across the five criteria is the AAMD system, with the DSM-III system a close second. The ICD-9 system and the DD system both received lower and more variable ratings. However, the system with the greatest potential for improvement appears to be the DD system which, with some additional operational definition and guidelines, could receive significantly higher ratings in the areas of clarity and reliability. While the ratings presented in Table 9.1 represent judgments, not objective assessments, these ratings hopefully will be useful in guiding decisions made by clinicians, policy makers, program planners, researchers and consumers about which classification system is most useful under varying circumstances and for varying objectives.

References

Abt Associates. *Final report on the definitions developmental disabilities*. Cambridge, Mass.: Abt Assoc., 1977.

Baumeister, A. A., & Muma, J. R. On defining mental retardation. *The Journal of Special Education*, 1975, **9**, 293–306.

Bijou, S. W. Theory and research in mental (developmental) retardation. *Psychological Record*, 1963, **13**, 95–110.

Binet, A., & Simon, J. Upon the necessity of establishing a scientific diagnosis of inferior states of intelligence. In M. Rosen, G. R. Clark, & M. Kivitz (Eds.), *The history of mental retardation*. Vol. 1. Baltimore: University Park Press, 1976.

Bock, W., & Weatherman, R. *Minnesota Developmental Programming System*. St. Paul: University of Minnesota, 1975.

Boggs, E. M., & Henney, R. L. *A numerical and functional description of the developmentally disabled population in the United States by major life activities as defined in the Developmental Disabilities Assistance and Bill of Rights Act as amended in P.L. 95-602*. Washington, D.C.: EMC Institute, 1979.

Clarke, A. M. Criteria and classification of mental deficiency. In A. M. Clarke & A. D. B. Clarke (Eds.), *Mental deficiency; the changing outlook*. (Rev. ed.) New York: The Free Press, 1965.

Diagnostic and statistical manual of mental disorders. (3rd ed.) Washington, D.C.: American Psychiatric Association, 1980.

Doll, E. A. The essentials of an inclusive concept of mental deficiency. *American Journal of Mental Deficiency*, 1941, **46**, 214–219.

Ewalt, J. R. Differing concepts of diagnoses as a problem in classification. *American Journal of Psychiatry*, 1972, **128** (Suppl.), 18–20.

Filler, J. W., Robinson, C., Smith, R. A., Vincent-Smith, L. J., Bricker, D. D., & Bricker, W. A. Mental retardation, In N. Hobbs (Ed.), *Issues in the classification of children*. Vol. 1. San Francisco: Jossey-Bass, 1975.

Gollay, E., Freedman, R., Wyngaarden, M., & Kurtz, N. *Coming back: The community experiences of deinstitutionalized mentally retarded persons*. Cambridge, Mass.: Abt Books, 1978.

Gollay, E. *Operational definition of developmental disabilities (Preliminary report)*, Columbia, Md.: Morgan Management Systems, 1980.

Granger, C. V. A conceptual model for functional assessment. In C. V. Granger & G. E. Gresham (Eds.), *Functional Assessment in Rehabilitation Medicine*. In press.

Grossman, H. (Ed.) *Manual on terminology and classification in mental retardation*. Washington, D.C.: American Association on Mental Deficiency, 1977.

Gunzberg, H. C. *The P-A-C Manual*. London: National Association for Mental Health, 1969.

Heber, R. *Manual on terminology and classification in mental retardation*. Washington, D.C.: American Association on Mental Deficiency, 1959.

International classification of diseases, 9th revision; clinical modification. Ann Arbor: Commission on Professional and Hospital Activities, 1978.

Isett, R. D., & Spreat, S. Test-retest and interrater reliability of the AAMD Adaptive Behavior Scale. *American Journal of Mental Deficiency*, 1979, **84**, 93–95.

Jones, K. J., & Jones, P. P. *The measurement of community placement success and its associated costs*. Waltham, Mass.: Brandeis University, 1976.

Kramer, M. Historical review and mental disorders sections of ICD-9 and ICD-9CM. In *Diagnostic and statistical manual of mental disorders*. (3rd ed.) Washington, D.C.: American Psychiatric Association, 1980.

Kuhlmann, F. Degree of mental deficiency in children as expressed by the relation of age to mental age. *Journal of Psycho-Asthenics*, 1913, **17**, 132–144.

Leland, H. Mental retardation and adpative behavior. *Journal of Special Education*, 1972, **6**, 71–80.

Lemert, E. M. *Human deviance, social problems, and social control*. Englewood Cliffs, N.J.: Prentice-Hall, 1967.

Lubin, R., Jacobson, J. W., & Kiely, M. Projected impact of the functional definition of developmental disabilities: the categorically disabled population and service eligibility. *American Journal of Mental Deficiency*, 1982, **87**, 73–79.

Mercer, J. R. *Labelling the mentally retarded: Clinical and social system perspectives on mental retardation*. Berkeley: University of California Press, 1973.

Mercer, J. *Sompa technical manual*. New York: The Psychological Corporation, 1979.

Millham, J., Chilcutt, J., & Atkinson, B. L. Comparability of naturalistic and controlled observation assessment of adaptive behavior. *American Journal of Mental Deficiency*, 1978, **83**, 52–59.

Nagi, S. Z. An epidemiology of disability among adults in the United States. In *Health and society*. *Milbank Memorial Fund Quarterly*, 1976, **54**, 439–467.

Nihira, K., Foster, R., Shellhass, M., & Leland, H. *AAMD-Adaptive Behavior Scale*, Washington, D.C.: American Association on Mental Deficiency, 1975.

Reynolds, W. M. Measurement of personal competence of mentally retarded individuals. *American Journal of Mental Deficiency*, 1981, **85**, 368–376.

Roszkowski, M. J., & Spreat, S. A comparison of the psychometric and clinical methods of determining level of mental retardation. *Applied Research in Mental Retardation*, 1981, **2**, 359–366.

Seltzer, G. B. Community residential adjustment: the relationship among environment, performance, and satisfaction. *American Journal of Mental Deficiency*, 1981, **85**, 624–630.

Seltzer, M. M., & Seltzer, G. B. *Context for competence: A study of retarded adults living and working in the community*. Cambridge, Mass.: Educational Projects, Inc., 1978.

Seltzer, M. M., & Seltzer, G. B. Functional assessment of persons with mental retardation. In C. V. Granger & C. E. Gresham (Eds.), *Functional assessment in rehabilitation medicine*. Baltimore: William and Wilkens. In press.

Skinner, B. F. *Science and human behavior*. New York: The Free Press, 1953.

Smith, J. D. & Polloway, E. A. The dimension of adaptive behavior in mental retardation research: An analysis of recent practices. *American Journal of Mental Deficiency*, 1979, **84**, 203–206.

Stengel, E. Classification of mental disorders. *Bulletin of the World Health Organization*, 1960, **21**, 601–663.

Tarjan, G., & Eisenberg, L. Some thoughts on the classification of mental retardation in the United States of America. *American Journal of Psychiatry*, 1972, **128** (Suppl.), 14–18.

Taylor, R. L. Use of the AAMD Classification System: A review of recent research. *American Journal of Mental Deficiency*, 1980, **85**, 116–119.

Tizard, J. A note on the international statistical classification of mental retardation. *American Journal of Psychiatry*, 1972, **128** (Suppl.), 25–29.

Tredgold, A. F. *A textbook of mental deficiency.* (8th ed.) London: Bailliere, Tindall & Cox, 1952.

Wood, P. H. N. Setting disablement in perspective. *International Rehabilitation Medicine,* 1978, **1,** 32–37.

Wood, P. H. N. Appreciating the consequences of disease: the International Classification of Impairments, Disabilities and Handicaps. *WHO Chronicle,* 1980, **34,** 376–380.

World Health Organization: Fifth WHO seminar on the standardization of psychiatric diagnosis, classification, and statistics. *American Journal of Psychiatry,* 1972, **128** (Suppl.), 3–14.

Wortis, J. Comments on the ICD classification of mental retardation. *American Journal of Psychiatry,* 1972, **128** (Suppl.), 21–24.

10 LEGAL RESPONSES TO CLASSIFICATION

H. Rutherford Turnbull, III and Mary J. Wheat

John Merrick to Dr. Frederick Treves:
"If your mercy is so cruel, what do you have for justice?"

Treves to Merrick:
"I am sorry. It is just the way things are."

—B. Pomerance, *The Elephant Man*

Dual System

Classification of a person as mentally retarded can have horrendous consequences for the person, his family, and society. In a nutshell, classification as mentally retarded subjects a person to a dual system of law, relegating him or her to second-class citizenship in a wide variety of important areas of life. The dual system affects the person's family because, as a rule, the family is ultimately responsible for its handicapped member. The dual system affects society because its existence enables all of us to treat each other as though some of us were less worthy than others because of disability.

This chapter will show how a dual system occurs by discussing the classification "system" and its consequences at law. We begin with a description of society's perceptions of mentally retarded people, because those perceptions too often are reflected in law, and show how and why society's agents classify. We then discuss the legal effects of classification. Throughout, we show how the law has responded to classification issues.

In a society that values competence and sometimes institutionalizes Social Darwinism in its educational and economic systems, it is no wonder that disabled people are little valued and ill served. Sadly, mental retardation is but one of the hallmarks of disability, others being mental illness, physical disability, and old age. Unlike these conditions, however, mental retardation is always chronic, usually diagnosed at birth or soon thereafter and generally lasting throughout a person's lifetime.

A consequence of chronicity is that a mentally retarded person frequently has been regarded as wholly incompetent for all time, despite easily proved contrary conclusions (AAMD, 1979). Thus, the "permanent child" has been presumed unable to execute wills, enter into contracts, make valid gifts, consent to treatment or services, be held liable for civil or criminal wrongs, survive without assistance from guardianship or involuntary commitment or voluntary admission procedures, reside safely (in safety to self and others) in "the community", establish residence in the community without having to leap elaborate legal and attitudinal hurdles, have unsupervised enjoyment of the family and sexual liberties that the constitution guarantees nonretarded people (Wald, 1976), be treated in a decent and humane way by the state when in its custody, or even benefit from medical treatment that nonretarded ("unclassified") people receive as a matter of course. The most telling attribute of autonomy (of "liberty"), the power to give or withhold consent, has been routinely unavailable to the mentally retarded person either because of *de jure* or *de facto* declarations of incompetence. Today, no other person is so disadvantaged at law as the mentally retarded citizen (Burgdorf, 1980; Kindred, 1976; Practicing Law Institute, 1979). As recent legal history involving discrimination on account of race and sex demonstrates, dual systems of law are not unknown but the dual system that is still the most intact is the one involving the mentally retarded citizen. How can this be?

Perceptions and the Basis for Classification

Consider the mentally retarded person. The moving characteristic—the one on which action usually is predicated—is "mentally retarded," not "person." Mentally retarded people are seen to be qualitatively different from nonretarded people in this important and debilitating sense: they are "deviant." The mentally retarded newborn is commonly called a "defective child." Because the defect is considered to inhere in the child itself, rather than in the society into which the child is born (Sarason & Doris, 1979), it must be "treated" in the sense of being subjected to diagnosis, prescription, regimen, and "cure." The treatment is rendered by many "helping" professionals, not just physicians. But this kind of treatment frequently strips the mentally retarded person of social being and reduces him to mere biology (Gliedman & Roth, 1980).

The mentally retarded person is regarded as a "perpetual patient," as one for whom a cure can never be found, as a person defined by what he is not, not by what he is or may become. Regarded as "sick" and not responsible for his own condition, he is treated in a way that has disastrous consequences for him and his family. Since he is deemed sick, he is obliged to "fulfill permanently the role obligations of the good patient." In this role, people learn to be helpless and inferior; they are expected to accept, and then in fact do come to accept, the medical professions' control over their lives (Gliedman & Roth, 1980). Infrequent rebellion against medical dominance is itself treated as a symptom of sickness; parents or family also become "patients" (Turnbull & Turnbull, 1978). Inculcated passivity of the patient and family reinforces the original perception that the person is continuously and permanently incapable and indeed incurable; there is, after all, no present cure for extant mental retardation, only relief from its effects. "Treatment" of this sort essentially reflects the prevailing social mores (Sarason & Doris, 1979). Classifying a person as mentally re-

tarded enables "us" to use a convenient concept, one ostensibly rooted in science, to do unto others what we would abhor being done to us, all in the name of altruism. Incorrectly seeing the mentally retarded person as sick and not responsible for his condition (Gliedman & Roth, 1980; Sarason & Doris, 1979), "we" can easily conclude, as "the law" traditionally did, that he is not responsible ("competent") and must be dealt with in unusual ways (Morse, 1978).

The able-bodied and mentally competent come to regard the mentally retarded person's chronic incapacity as a kind of failure of the person. Given that the person is a failure, there is a reduced duty, if any, of the professions and of society as a whole to act on the person's behalf. "We" are off the hook for any responsibility to "them" (Gliedman & Roth, 1980). We have, ultimately, no responsibility for their exclusion from normality and, with relatively clean conscience and legal impunity, we can assign them to lower echelons of life, to second-class citizenship at law.

Who Classifies

Every society needs its "operatives," those professionals who will do the bidding of society by bringing their purported expertise to bear on difficult situations, resolving the difficulties by the use of special training, talents, and status.

Physicians

It is ironic in the extreme that physicians and educators are society's principal agents for dealing with mentally retarded people—ironic because, while they have great ability to help them, they also have great ability to injure. Thus, the physician's curative abilities—to prevent mental retardation, intervene early so that its effects are minimized, and be a sustaining force throughout mentally retarded people's lives—render him a primary resource for saying who is mentally retarded. He does this through developmental testing of newborns and infants. The developmentally delayed child is the one in need of treatment; the physical disability is the province of the physician. Given the need of society and its lawgivers for professional operatives, it is little wonder that physicians also have become the law's agents for deciding what to do about mental retardation. Exactly how the law has allowed them to discharge their agentry will be discussed later.

Educators

Educators are another of society's classifiers. Schools label more children as mentally retarded than any other governmental or social entity (Sorgen, 1976). Their classification of children as mentally retarded has massive consequences, both positive and negative, for a child, especially one whose mental retardation is questionable or mild. Educational classification as mentally retarded can, among other things, determine the nature or effectiveness of the child's curriculum (Sorgen, 1976), the characteristics of his peers and thereby his tendency to learn from peer interactions (Sorgen, 1976; Gliedman & Roth, 1980), the extent of teacher demands on him and the type of teacher expectations surrounding him (*Hobson v. Hanson*, 1969; Kirp, 1973, 1974), his self-image, the nature of educational resources made available to him, his mobility within or even out of special education, the nature of discriminary proceedings, and his potential for higher educational opportunities, especially those that are vocational in nature.

Some disabled children are spotted and classified well before they enter the public school system; their disabilities are such that they are unmistakably handicapped. Others, however, become "known to us" only when schools tell us they are different, "special," "exceptional," or otherwise euphemistically labeled as atypical (Hobbs, 1975), as not being easily subjected to the mass education of the masses. The reasons for and techniques of educational classification, and the procedures for challenging them, are not relevant here. The fact that schools classify people as handicapped who frequently "become" unhandicapped when they have exited from public education's jurisdiction should, however, give us pause.

Other Professionals and Agencies

Educators and physicians are not the only professional sorters, though they are the principal ones (Gliedman & Roth, 1980; Sarason & Doris, 1979). Any profession having contact, however tangential, with different people classifies, notwithstanding its limited competence to do so. Social workers, psychologists, and rehabilitation specialists classify for the purpose of providing or withholding services or for other reasons. Institutions of higher education, particularly vocational, technical, and community colleges, do their own classification. Law enforcement and criminal justice agencies classify. Courts accept classification arguments in order to assess whether, and, if so, to what extent, a person is criminally or civilly liable for his actions or failures to act. The armed forces classify. Nearly every agency of government classifies; none comes to mind that does not.

Professional Organizations

Professional organizations classify. The American Association on Mental Deficiency classifies by changing its definition of mental deficiency (the lower the cutoff point of mentally subaverage, the more people are "cured" and classified by exclusion from being mentally retarded) and creating and altering its adaptive behavior scales. The American Psychiatric Association classifies when it changes the standards and definitions in its Diagnostic Standards Manual. The learning disabilities societies (ACLD, CEC-DCLD) classify by defining a specific learning disability to exclude some types of children.

Families

Finally, families classify. It is not so much that families say that their child, brother or sister, or relative is mentally retarded; others do that for them. It is more that they classify by determining how they will react to what others say. The decision to risk placement of a mentally retarded child in one's own home or in an institution or to try a mainstream education instead of a more specialized one is in the first (and sometimes in the last) place a family decision. Among other things, it reflects a decision to classify a person more or less into or out of mentally retarded status. The option is less likely to be available if the person is severely or profoundly mentally retarded than mildly retarded. For that reason, it is all the more important that it be made carefully.

Everyone classifies. We all make choices to associate or not with certain other people. Human beings are discriminating in the neutral sense of the word: we make discriminations about ourselves and others. We also are discriminating in a different sense: we discriminate for invidious as well as altruistic purposes. We let defective newborns die because their existence horrifies us, but we say we do it because we are concerned about the quality of their and others' lives. Classification is not inherently wrong, merely natural.

How We Classify

By Resort to Science

There is some magical quality in the concept of "science." Call something scientific and it becomes less assailable; there is a presumption that science and its products are researched, reliable, validated, evaluated, and unbiased. But what we do—our policies—are not always based on good science, on defensible science. It is little wonder, then, that our policies are not always good. The medical model's fallibility is pervasive (Gliedman & Roth, 1980, Sarason & Doris, 1979; Blatt, 1966). After all, science taught that mentally retarded people were a menace; so the eugenics movement spawned legalized compulsory institutionalization and sterilization (Wald, 1976). Science teaches that intelligence can be measured; so classification as mentally retarded and categorization into special education receive the blessings of the law. It is no great matter that the basis for either of these "scientific facts" is open to doubt, so long as it is not clearly erroneous. The fallibility of many "scientific" tests of intelligence, of the potential for school success, or of both, is well known, especially at law (Kirp, 1973, 1974; *Larry P. v. Riles*, 1972; *Parents v. Hannon*, 1980; Sorgen, 1976). There is far less debate about the fallibility of medical assessment for developmental delay (whether physical or mental), yet decisions by physicians, other service providers, and families, made on the basis of relatively acceptable assessment techniques, can still be highly debatable. The recent case of Phillip Becker proves the point. There was no doubt about the fact that he was a young boy with Down's syndrome and a heart defect that could be corrected surgically, with little risk to his life, as a means of substantially prolonging his life. Yet his family decided to refuse to authorize the surgery and, up to a point, so did the courts of California, because of debatable medical decision making (*In re Phillip B.*, 1979). Thus, we classify by using relatively fallible or infallible science or by acting in someone's interests on the basis of what that science tells us.

By Social Vulnerability

Classification is effected by other "scientific" means and by nonscientific ones as well. Educators, for example, identify students as handicapped who make life difficult for them. Boys are more subject to special education classification than girls; aggressive students more than acquiescent ones; racial and ethic minority students more than white students (Hobbs, 1975; *Hobson v. Hansen*, 1969; Kirp, 1973, 1974; *Larry P. v. Riles*, 1972; Mercer, 1973). The "science" of these classifications is highly doubtful; instead, student's differential vulnerability to special education classification appears to be a factor of cultural, social, or economic differentness.

By Legal Proceedings

Likewise, classification as mentally disabled occurs in a host of legal proceedings, often without a "scientific" basis. For example, if a person is aggressive, unable to care for himself, or, because of mental disability, "in need of treatment," society's caretakers—family, mental health, public health, or social services agencies—may choose to intervene by having the person involuntarily committed, adjudicating him to be incompetent so that third-party consent to treatment

or placement can be obtained, securing temporary social services custody for neglected or abused people, or obtaining criminal prosecution for alleged violation of a crime. Any one of these four responses is legally sanctioned and may be effective as a way of intervening appropriately. So, too, is doing nothing; inaction is a form of action. Whatever the choice—whether or not to intervene and, if so, how—a classification results. In Alan Stone's (1976) typology, the "classified" person becomes mad, sad, or bad—mad if committed involuntarily, sad if referred to social services or mental retardation agencies, or bad if convicted of a crime. The classifier, of course, is "good."

By Reason of Serendipity

There is, moreover, no clear reason why a particular intervention prevails. So much depends on serendipity. Is the state psychiatric hospital full; are there enough beds in an MR Center; does the prosecutor have a good case; what agency does the family or the person have the most contact with; are private or third-party funds available to pay for services; is the presiding judge likely to be amenable to the desired disposition of the case; do the jailers, who influence the prosecutor, want to avoid the responsibility of caring for the person; is it summer, when people can survive without shelter, or winter, when they cannot; is the person an "interesting case" for the staff at a psychiatric hospital or mental retardation center; what are the desires of the party initiating the legal proceedings; how effectively does a lawyer represent the parties; have political or social influences been brought to bear on the agencies or courts; have community resources been tried unsuccessfully? These are some of the factors—all of them far removed from the allegedly precise scientific basis for classification that is supposed to be obtained in special education or mental health intervention, for example—that affect whether a person is classified and, if so, how, why, and with what effect.

Legal Responses to How We Classify

Fair, Individualized Assessment

Legal efforts to rescue mentally retarded citizens from second-class citizenship through classification have addressed both the techniques for classification and action founded on the classification. As an illustration of the techniques issue, the Education for All Handicapped Children Act (1975) requires a multidisciplinary, multifaceted, nonbiased evaluation of a child before he is classified as mentally retarded or not and before he is furnished special education. It prohibits sole reliance on "scientific" assessment measures, such as IQ tests, and provides instead that "soft" data, such as teacher observations, may be used to evaluate and then classify someone as mentally retarded. By the same token, in some states a person may not be declared mentally incompetent unless it can be proven by an interdisciplinary evaluation consisting of medical, psychological, and social work assessments that the incompetence is a result of mental retardation (among other causes).

It should be obvious that the requirement of a fair evaluation as a prerequisite to classification is a requirement of individualization. Due process mandates nothing less (AAMD, 1981). If a person is not assessed individually when the result of the assessment could be that a benefit (e.g., special education, if needed) is made available to him or a special burden (e.g., assignment to special education when he is not handicapped) is placed upon him, his constitutional rights to due process—to enjoyment of life, liberty, and property—may be violated. Thus, legal requirements for fair assessment reflect not only constitutional concerns but also an attempt to prevent people from being relegated to a second-class citizenship. In addition, they reflect sound professional practice, assuring that service providers will deal appropriately with people whom they are trained to serve. This result benefits the person and the provider alike.

Restraints on Consequences of Classification

It is not legally sufficient, however, that the techniques of classification be regulated. The use that one makes of the techniques is an important concern as well. The techniques may be entirely acceptable but invidious classification and treatment of mentally retarded citizens could still obtain unless their uses were scrutinized. Thus, as interpreted by the courts, the federal constitution prohibits a person found not guilty of a crime because of mental disability from simply being institutionalized in a mental health facility for an undefined time period (*Jackson v. Indiana*, 1972). Self-injurious behavior in a mentally retarded person may be effectively curtailed by aversive therapy, but usually only if other "less drastic" intervention has been found unsuccessful (AAMD, 1981). If a newborn child is mentally retarded, it must be patently clear that he or she is very seriously "damaged" or "injured" before courts will allow life-saving or life-prolonging medical treatment to be denied. The fact that a man is severely or profoundly mentally retarded can affect whether he will be treated for cancer and, if so, how and why (*Superintendent v. Saikewicz*, 1977). Thus law reins in the scientific basis for classification by a

rigorous insistence that the techniques and effects of classification be mutually compatible.

Just as the law seeks to minimize the potential for bias or error in educational or other "scientific" classifications, so it seeks to eliminate the "whimsy factors" in other classifying actions. It does so by four principal techniques. First, it insists on knowable and measurable standards; second, it requires procedural safeguards; third, it sometimes provides affected parties access to professionals' records; and, finally, it enables the affected person or his representative to participate in decisions ordinarily made by professionals.

Standards

For example, to find that a person may be involuntarily committed, it is necessary in most states to show by clear, cogent, and convincing evidence that the person is mentally disabled and imminently dangerous to himself or others (ABA, in press). To adjudicate a person incompetent, the same burden of proof usually must be met and the person must be proven to be unable to make and communicate important decisions concerning himself, his family, or his property (ABA, 1979). To convict someone, there must be proof beyond a reasonable doubt that the person committed the crime with which s/he was charged and has no valid defenses. Thus, the standards and the burden of proof have been tightened up so that erroneous classification—through commitment, adjudication, or conviction—is less apt to occur incorrectly.

Procedures

Procedural safeguards also tend to minimize the risk of error. As a general rule, the disabled person is entitled to notice of action that the state proposes to take, an attorney or guardian *ad litem* to represent him, a hearing before an impartial trier of fact and law, an opportunity to present and rebut evidence, and the right to appeal from the initial decision. These safeguards obtain in nearly all states in almost every proceeding at which personal or property rights—i.e., at which classification as disabled—are at stake, such as involuntary commitment, adjudication as incompetent, conviction of crime, or, under federal law, placement in special education.

Access to Records

A third technique is to grant the affected person or his representatives access to the professionals' records concerning him or service systems that may be brought to bear on him. For example, federal education law allows a student's parents to see his school records or records of the school system special education programs (Education for all Handicapped Children Act, 1976). Some states have enacted statutes that allow mentally retarded people or their representatives access to social work, health, or mental health records (Schwitzgebel & Schwitzgebel, 1980). Court and quasi-judicial proceedings or records (such as the "impartial hearing" guaranteed under Education for All Handicapped Children Act) normally can be accessed by disabled people or their representatives. And some courts have taken the innovative step of requiring service professionals to divulge their records or make known certain information to the affected person or interested others (Schwitzgebel & Schwitzgebel, 1980).

Participatory Decision Making

Finally, federal laws governing special education (Education for All Handicapped Children Act), vocational rehabilitation (DD Act, 1975), and institutional care of developmentally disabled people (DD Act, 1975), provide that the disabled person or his representative may participate with professionals in planning the goals and methods of professional services.

Why We Classify

It may be impossible to avoid classification. We are, after all, discriminating, choosy, selective, and exclusive in almost every aspect of our lives, whether the issue be so trivial as the choice of food at a carry-out restaurant or so momentous as the choice of a mate. In addition to our natural restrictions (age, sex, race, and ability), we restrict ourselves voluntarily (AAMD, 1981), such as by the jobs we choose. And in most cases, the law recognizes our rights to be selective in the important matters of speech, religion, and personhood as well as in less significant matters such as the types of clothes we wear (so-called "symbolic speech").

Yet our natural instincts and legal rights to be selective, to classify ourselves and others, are not unbridled. Our rights of free speech do not extend to publishing pornography. Consensual sexual conduct is regulated and, of course, so is nonconsensual conduct (crimes against person or property). One reason for regulation is that the effects of absolute liberty for anyone are unacceptable to someone. Thus, the possession of pornography may be protected but its sale and distribution are not. Another reason is that the reasons for governmental classification must be examined; the due process and equal protection clauses of the federal constitution forbid invidious, irrational, indefensible classifications (such as those made on

the basis of race). It is legally relevant, therefore, to inquire into why people classify others as mentally retarded.

Altruism

Sometimes classification is done for the most altruistic of purposes. When someone is classified as mentally retarded, it enables him or her to be the recipient of services that the classifier and, sometimes the classified, thinks will be helpful, such as special education, vocational rehabilitation, or institutional care. Classification also may prevent the person from being subjected to disadvantaging conditions; segregation of prisoners by mental disability has been thought by some to protect mentally retarded prisoners from non-retarded inmates and the ordinary conditions of imprisonment.

There are, however, negative results of classification motivated by social beneficence. Lionel Trilling (1980) has made the point that people who are the objects of our pity become the objects of our coercion, and Kai Erickson (1966) has highlighted the paradox that deviancy—difference on account of mental retardation—is nourished by the agencies that were designed to inhibit it, in proportion to society's ability to control it. Blatt (1966) has documented the horrible conditions to which mentally retarded people have been subjected in institutions originally predicated on a medical model. Sarason and Doris (1979) have cast doubt on the motives and efficacy of special education systems. And Gliedman and Roth (1980) have produced strong evidence of the shortcomings of the medical model in a host of "helping" professions.

Negative Reactions

We also classify for reasons having to do with our instinctive negative reaction to mental retardation. After all, the grossly macrocephalous child may not be easily or immediately lovable; fecal smearers can be unpleasant to live or work with. Many aspects of mental retardation, such as severe self-injurious behavior, are not only especially intractable, but deeply disturbing to families and caretakers alike. Thus, when the decision to institutionalize a child or, more seriously, to withhold medical treatment of a defective newborn is made, it seems inevitable that our instincts for being with pleasant, attractive, able, "promising" people are at work. By the same token, our ability to "succeed" with a mentally retarded person—if we are a physician, to "cure," or an educator, to "teach"—is threatened by some handicapped people. Surely the emotional reactions of parents are not the only ones operating in a classification decision. Physicians report the terribly difficult task of telling a parent that the child is mentally retarded (Sarason & Doris, 1979). To "place" the child in an institution—to put it out of sight and out of mind in America's Siberias—is partly a human condition. And the human condition is an imperfect one.

Riddance Motive

We also classify because we sometimes actively and admittedly wish to rid ourselves of the mentally retarded person. The decision to abort a defective fetus, while constitutionally protected, may reflect the mother's wish to avoid life with a handicapped child. Decisions to withhold life sustaining medical treatment (*In re Phillip B.*, 1979) or to institutionalize a child may reflect similar reactions of parents to not be handicapped by reason of having a mentally retarded child (Ziskin, 1978). Nor are parents alone in their reaction to mental retardation. The educator who refers a child to a special education program, the community agency social worker who counsels for institutionalization, and the institutional psychologist who recommends deinstitutionalization all may be motivated by a desire to rid themselves of a "problem" person (Hobbs, 1975; Milofsky, 1974).

Agency Self-Interest

Another motive explains classification, and it is more related to agency interests than to personal interests. Educators test and thereby engage in classification decisions to absolve themselves of moral responsibility for decisions about what happens to mentally retarded people, taking refuge in "science." By resorting to science, they also gain credibility with parents of children. Finally, they serve school interests in categorization and program efficiency; a well organized school system needs to have categories of children so that programs can be planned, financed, operated, and perpetuated (Kirp, 1973, 1974; Sorgen, 1976). By the same token, social services, health, and mental health agencies sometimes classify a person as mentally retarded or as having a certain degree of mental retardation (mild to profound) for self-serving purposes. They want to include or exclude a person from a service category because it will increase their headcount (numbers of people served) and thereby their budget or constituency base, or decrease it and thereby enable them to serve someone else. Resource allocation is a powerful motivation.

Dual Diagnosis

One familiar but subtle issue in classification, not yet addressed, is that of "double diagnosis." Some mentally retarded people display symptoms of emotional disturbance. And some mentally ill people (or people whose behavior can be characterized as mental illness) may be mentally retarded. How should the person be classified, as mentally retarded or as mentally ill? Or can he be classified as both mentally retarded and mentally ill? The choice of diagnosis is important. It may determine whether the person receives a label as "MR" or "ED," whether he receives one type of special education service or another, whether confinement in a mental retardation center or psychiatric hospital could occur, whether the person will be placed in one type of community-based residential or service system or another, and so on.

Many times, service agencies are required by their regulations or operating procedures to classify a person as having a single disability. As a result, they report a single diagnosis, even though a double diagnosis would be professionally defensible. The regulations or agency procedures may be valid in the sense that they seek to channel into the agency's service streams only those people who can benefit by the services provided or who can be served effectively by agency personnel. But they also may have untoward consequences. They may prevent a person from obtaining services for a coexisting disability and, in the long run, make intervention less than maximally useful. They also may have the consequence of locking the person into the primary system and preventing him from transferring out of it and into another (or into none) when the system has outlived its usefulness to him or has become dysfunctional and harmful to him. The choice of diagnosis therefore is a critical one when there may be a possibility to make a double diagnosis. Special attention to the motivation of the classifier and the effects of classification are warranted in these difficult cases. Since professionals cannot help but take into account parental or family wishes (e.g., the "learning disabilities" classification seems to be far less stigmatizing to families and client than "mental retardation"), the motives of parents and family also are of concern (*Parham v. J. R.*, 1979).

Desire to Dominate

Finally, classification occurs because the classifier seeks to subject the person to a position of powerlessness. An intelligence test given in English to a Spanish-speaking student may, but is not likely to, test accurately the student's potential to be successful in school or his or her inherent or acquired skills. Persuasive arguments have been made that classification, especially by public schools, is a means for subjecting ethnic or racial minorities to a second-class status, thereby perpetuating the political, economic, or social dominance of nonminority people (Hobbs, 1975; *Larry P. v. Riles*, 1972; Mercer, 1973).

Legal Responses to Why We Classify

As already noted, the law's response to the reasons we classify a person as mentally retarded or as having a certain degree of mental retardation is to insist on knowable and precise standards (e.g., subaverage intelligence and inability in adaptive behavior), procedural safeguards (notice, hearing, counsel, and appeal), access to records, and patient/client participation in decision making.

Eligibility

More than that, however, the law has created eligibility standards (e.g., if a person is mentally retarded, he becomes entitled to special education) and accompanying funding streams (federal special education funds may be spent only on handicapped students or for administrative costs associated with their education). Sometimes the law selects certain kinds of mentally retarded people for special benefits (and thereby denies others those same benefits). For example, federal special education (Education for All Handicapped Children Act, 1975) and vocational rehabilitation (DD Act, 1975) funds are earmarked for the more disabled person, not the mildly handicapped person. This type of "bottom up" legislation—it attacks the social problems of disability at their most severe level and works upward to benefit the least mentally retarded person—contrasts with the "creaming" legislation or executive-administrative action that furnishes services to the mildly mentally retarded person in preference to the severely mentally retarded one (e.g., deinstitutionalization by transfer to group homes affects mildly mentally retarded people more often than severely mentally retarded ones).

Prohibiting Discrimination

Another legal response is to prohibit governmental agencies or recipients of governmental aid from discriminating against otherwise qualified people solely because of their handicaps (Sec. 504, Rehabilitation Act, 1973). For example, it is a violation of federal law for a state corrections system that receives federal aid to exclude a mentally retarded prisoner from prison-operated vocational rehabilitation programs solely because he is retarded (*Sites v. McKenzie*, 1976) or for a school system to exclude handicapped children soley because they are handicapped (*Hairston v. Drosick*, 1976).

Effect and Motive

The law entitles an advocate to inquire into both the effects of classification as well as the intent of the classifier. If a discriminatory (invidious) effect can be found (e.g., the child may not attend school because he is mentally retarded and disruptive, *S-1 v. Turlington*, 1980), the intent of the classifier may be irrelevant. But if the classifier also has an invidious intent and seeks to discriminate against the person solely because he is mentally retarded, the law will provide a remedy (*N. Mexico ARC v. N. Mexico*, 1980).

Advocacy

To challenge the discriminatory effect or intent of classification, a mentally retarded person must have an advocate. Recent federal law has established a "protection and advocacy" system (DD Act, 1975) to enable mentally retarded and other disabled people to challenge unwarranted classification. Under this law, states that receive federal funds for use in serving disabled people must create a system to advocate for them against state and local governmental agencies. Federally financed P & A offices have been extensively involved in special education law suits involving mentally retarded children's classification and education. Another federal effort to provide advocates for disabled people has been by way of funding the Legal Services Corporation, which in turn allocates its money for local legal services for handicapped and other disadvantaged citizens. Some states also have enacted laws that, independent of federal requirements, create advocacy systems for mentally retarded people.

Personal Liability and Attorney Fees

A similar legal response has been the courts' use of a provision of the Civil Rights Act (1871) that holds a state or local official liable for depriving someone of his rights under the federal constitution or federal statutes. If, for example, a public school superintendent expels a mentally retarded child from school without cause and thereby violates the child's right to a free appropriate education or if a school psychologist deliberately classifies someone as mentally retarded who is not, violating the Education for All Handicapped Children Act, a court may require the official to pay damages to the child (*Maine v. Thiboutot*, 1980; *Maher v. Gagne*, 1980). Likewise, if the superintendent of a state institution for mentally retarded people deprives them of their constitutional rights to proper care and treatment, a court may hold the person liable (*Romeo v. Youngberg*, 1980). An extra measure of protection for a mentally retarded person exists under

Section 1988 of the Civil Rights Act (1871), which allows a court to charge the defendant the legal fees the mentally retarded person incurred if he wins his law suit (*Maher*, 1980; *Maine*, 1980).

Least Restrictive Alternative

In its many responses to classification, the law recently has taken the posture that the government itself is the victimizer and the mentally retarded person is the victim (Burt, 1979). The issue is how to govern the government, recognizing that government becomes involved in classification because it offers services (education, social, mental health, and rehabilitation) and responds in a variety of ways (by excluding an otherwise qualified person from services, by subjecting a person to improper or unconstitutional treatment in a service system, or by treating a person as mentally retarded who is not retarded) to a complex set of explanations for classification.

A major principle of constitutional law—the doctrine of "the least restrictive (drastic) alternative"—has become a useful device for curbing governments that harm mentally retarded citizens (AAMD, 1981). The doctrine forbids a government from acting in a way that restricts a person's liberty any more than necessary to accomplish its legitimate purposes. If a government has a defensible reason for restricting someone and may accomplish that restriction in either of two ways—one that infringes individual liberty to a greater extent and another to a lesser extent—it must chose the lesser of the two ways. For example, sometimes it is legitimate to confine a person against his will because he is dangerous to others. But the nature of confinement may not be excessive. Thus, under the doctrine of least restriction, courts have been able to reform the conditions in institutions in which mentally retarded people have been placed and prevent institutional placement when community-based placement would be as effective to serve the state's purposes.

Substitute Consent

Courts have even been able to address one of the most debilitating aspects of classification as mentally retarded, which is the loss of legal autonomy. It is a general rule of law that a person may not legally consent or withhold consent to health or mental health services if he is not mentally competent; mental capacity is an indispensible element of consent (AAMD, 1979). Since some mentally retarded people do not have legally sufficient capacity to consent to governmental services that may be furnished only if they do consent, it has been necessary for legislatures and courts to

provide for the appointment of a legal guardian for them and to authorize the guardian to consent to those services on their behalf. Thus, courts have allowed a mentally retarded person's parents to consent to sterilization (*In re Grady*, 1978) or to refuse treatment for cancer (*Superintendent v. Saikewicz*, 1977). When courts allow guardians to consent to or refuse such important medical procedures as are involved in sterilization or cancer treatment, they are using the "substitute consent" doctrine to help the mentally retarded person vindicate rights (to consent or not) that he can not exercise because he is mentally retarded and that he could exercise, under law, if he were not.

The courts thus place mentally retarded and non-retarded people on the same footing, legally. If the courts were to hold that a mentally incompetent person may not have his legal rights exercised, they would deny that the person has the right in the first place. That result would have a doubly disabling effect. First, it would deny the mentally retarded person any of the substantive legal rights that nonretarded people have. Second, it would deny the mentally retarded person any procedural due process rights, such as a judicial hearing on whether he is incompetent and the nature of his substantive rights, if any. Were the courts to reject the "substitute consent" doctrine, they would leave the mentally retarded person in a legal limbo: the person has no right to consent or not, and the person also has no right to have someone else consent or not on his behalf. This result would be tantamount to an admission that the mentally retarded person has no standing at law, that he is indeed subject to a dual standard—legal rights for competent people, but not for incompetent ones. Of course, one may disagree about the results of the substitute consent doctrine in a particular case or series of cases; indeed, as in the circumstance of sterilization under a substitute consent, the results are indeed the subject of great debate.

Nature of Decision and Decision-Making Process

As useful as the substitute consent doctrine is for establishing the proposition that mentally retarded citizens have rights under law and are not subject to the full effect of a dual system of law, there are great problems concerning how much legal process should be brought to bear in deciding whether a government may deal with a mentally retarded person in one way or another. Simply stated, the issue is: how much due process—how many legal safeguards—must come into play. The answer seems to be that the greater the nature of the decision, the more the law requires procedural safeguards to assure that the government deals fairly with the person. For example, in the case in which substitute consent was used to decide that a mentally retarded person with cancer should not be given chemotherapy, the court itself decided whether treatment should be authorized. In this case, it was a matter of life and death, and the decision was made by a court (*Saikewicz*, 1979). In the case involving heart surgery for the Down's syndrome boy, the court eventually made a decision to allow surgery (*Becker*, 1981). In a case where the issue was whether parents may place their mentally retarded children in a state institution, the decision was that, given the nature of the action (institutionalization), the process for making the decision need not be a judicial one but can be medical (*Parham*, 1979). Thus, the nature of the decision shapes the process for making a decision.

Principles and Professionals

Characterizing the Decision

There is one major problem with the approach that ties the substance of a decision to the process for making it. It is that a court is relatively free to characterize the nature of the decision as extremely important or not, thereby affecting the decision-making process. This is exactly what the constitution allows (*Matthews v. Eldridge*, 1976). The nature of the decision is critical. A court can characterize it as a matter of life, as in the case of cancer therapy or heart surgery (*Saikewicz*, 1977; *Becker*, 1979), or as a matter that simply involves a risk of medical judgments being erroneous (*Parham*, 1979).

Value-laden Decision Making

The nature of the decision as the crux of the matter creates a real problem for mentally retarded people. This is so because the nature of the decision is nothing more or less than what a court says it is. In the absence of unavoidable precedent, value-laden decision making is given an open invitation; the door is shut in the face of principled decision making.

It is precisely this kind of flexibility that allows a court to impose its predetermined results in a case. If a court wants a certain result, it need only downgrade the nature of the decision in order to reduce the amount of safeguards that a retarded person may receive, or elevate it to increase the safeguards.

Parham and Pennhurst

It is perfectly clear that the U.S. Supreme Court is inclined to downgrade the substance of the issues presented to it in cases involving mentally retarded people. By doing so, it of course depreciates the procedural safeguards available to them. For example, it refused to characterize the institutionalization case as one involving the children's interests to liberty (*Parham*, 1979). Instead, it said the real issue was whether physicians might make a mistake; by describing the case as raising a risk-benefit issue (Ellis, 1980), it could avoid the "liberty" aspect and refuse to follow its long line of cases requiring judicial proceedings when the liberty of a mentally diasabled person is at stake (*Addington v. Texas*, 1974; *Jackson v. Indiana*, 1972; *O'Connor v. Donaldson*, 1975).

By the same token, the Court refused to deal with the right of mentally retarded people to treatment and an unharmful life in an institution (*Pennhurst*, 1981). Instead, it held that Congress did not intend to require states that receive federal money for developmentally disabled people to deal with institutionalized mentally retarded people in certain ways. The Court refused to consider the right to treatment issue; it thereby refused to create a powerful right for mentally retarded people. By regarding the case as one in which the only issue was the effect and meaning of a federal statute as drafted, the Court kept in abeyance the implementation of an important right for mentally retarded people.

The Medical Model

But more than a nature-process issue was at stake in *Parham* and *Pennhurst*. Both cases dramatically show the power of the "medical model," the very approach to mental retardation that, as briefly described earlier in this chapter, has caused so many problems for mentally retarded people. The medical model describes mental retardation as a deviance from a biological norm and posits that the deviancy is best handled by medical intervention. Medical intervention requires a physician (or, in the extended conceit of the model, some other professional) to deal with a "patient" (or "student" or "client"). The model ascribes the problem to the person and holds that the "cure" can best be found—or alleviation of the "condition" can best be furnished—by physicians ("professionals"). The major criticism of the model is that it fails to recognize that mental retardation is as much a "condition" determined by social mores as by a physical anomaly (Gliedman & Roth, 1980; Morse, 1978; Sarason & Doris, 1979; Szasz, 1963, 1973). Another criticism is that is has spawned social policy, reflected in law, that reduces the personhood of mentally retarded people. Because, under the medical-model view, mentally retarded people are significantly different from the "rest of us" in significant ways, they may be treated significantly different than the rest of us.

The Dual System and the Supreme Court

That is precisely the view that *Parham* and *Pennhurst* reflect. If the Supreme Court had seen mentally retarded children to be "children" first and "retarded" second, if it had not made so much of the fact of mental retardation, it would have been able to see *Parham* as a case involving the liberty of children, not the medical treatment of "retardates." It then would have imposed higher standards of due process; it would have given mentally retarded children more due process, consistent with its precedents (*In re Gault,* 1967).

The consequence of the belief that different people require different treatment is to deny mentally retarded children the rights of children. It is to focus on their retardation in a way that denigrates them because it highlights a "condition," not a personhood.

Pennhurst had a similar flaw, only not as obvious. The Justices who ducked the right-to-treatment issue and took refuge in the "problem" of Congressional intent managed thereby to perpetuate an institution in which mentally retarded people were subjected to conditions that would have been unacceptable if they had not been mentally retarded but, instead, simply "people" (*In re Gault,* 1967).

Both *Parham* and *Pennhurst* have disastrous consequences for mentally retarded people and public policy. They sanction the deprivation of normal legal rights; they deprive children who happen to be mentally retarded of liberty, autonomy, and dignity by allowing them to be confined on a basis that would not justify the confinement of nonretarded people. The cases thereby perpetuate a dual system of law, one that treats mentally retarded people more harshly solely because they are mentally retarded.

Who Should Make Policy?

These cases rely mightily on the perceived expertise of professionals (physicians and mental retardation "experts" who decide who will be admitted to institutions and, to a large extent, what will happen to them there), although their expertise is certainly unexceptional in informing anyone what to do about social policy and "different" people. These cases advance and nearly canonize the medical model, although the model is highly suspect.

By turning to medicine or other professions, the Court avoids coming to grips directly with the social, political, and moral dilemmas posed by mental re-

tardation (Morse, 1978). Thus, decisions about institutionalization, institutions, and families with mentally retarded members are glibly characterized as "medical" (just as other types of decisions are called "educational" or otherwise dignified by being seen as "professional"). The consequence is that the true nature of the decisions—what shall be done about mental retardation and retarded people—is obscured and a convenient solution is found: let the doctors (professionals) decide!

Classification, Professionals, and Policy

By the fiction that different people really are different and should be treated differently, largely by "professionals," the "law"—or, at least, the Supreme Court—has avoided the ultimate questions: Who should decide who should care for mentally retarded people, where, how, at whose expense, and why? Even more fundamentally, who is different enough to be treated differently? And, who has the sagacity to tell us the answer? These are the issues of classification. The answers to these questions have been, "the professionals." Once "we" know that "they" can tell us the answers, we tend to seek answers to other questions from them: Is this psychological examination valid for the purpose it is used? Is aversive therapy effective? Thus it is that our responsibility (or lack of it) for "other" people, for mentally retarded people, is made manifest to us: do as the professionals say.

John Merrick and Dr. Treves

But John Merrick, the Elephant Man, asked a question of his physician, friend, and savior, Dr. Treves, that we cannot escape and that the law does not let us escape: "If your mercy is so cruel, what do you have for justice?" Merrick knew, as we must now admit, that our altruism, our willingness to justify professional decision making and to cloak it in the excusing garment of *parens patriae* requires restraint. Trilling (1980), Erickson (1966), Gliedman and Roth (1980), Morse (1978), Sarason and Doris (1979), and Szasz (1963, 1973) are contemporaries who recognize, as Merrick did, that even the most beneficent professional, even a Dr. Treves, must be held accountable lest he reflect and act upon society's devaluation of mentally retarded people.

By allowing them to be devalued, by reflecting social mores, the law does an injustice not only to them but to itself. It condones a double standard, a dual system. The Supreme Court's shame, as revealed in *Parham* and *Pennhurst,* is that it has blessed the double standard. To its credit, however, "the law" is more than the *Parham* and *Pennhurst* decisions. It is the courts and legislatures that advance mentally retarded people's rights in the ways described earlier in this chapter. By insisting on substantive and procedural changes in how "we" deal with mentally retarded people, a body of reformist law is not only reshaping our culturally responsive law but, it is hoped, our culture itself. Dr. Treves' answer, "I am sorry. It is just the way things are," need not be and in large part is not the law's answer.

References

Addington v. Texas, 441 U.S. 418 (1979).

American Association on Mental Deficiency. *The consent handbook*, (H. Turnbull et al., Eds.). Washington, D.C., 1979.

American Association on Mental Deficiency. *The least restrictive alternative: Principle and practice*, (H. Turnbull et al., Eds.), Washington, D.C., 1981.

American Bar Association, Commission on the Mentally Disabled, *Involuntary commitment*. Washington, D.C.: A.B.A., in press.

American Bar Association, Commission on the Mentally Disabled, *Guardianship and conservatorship*. Washington, D.C.: A.B.A., 1979.

Blatt, B. & Kaplan, F. *Christmas in purgatory*. Boston, Mass.: Allyn and Bacon, 1966.

Burgdorf, R. *The legal rights of handicapped persons*. Baltimore, Md., Brookes Publishing Co., 1980.

Burt, B. *Souls in extremis*. Boston, Mass.: Allyn and Bacon, 1973.

Burt, R. Children as victims. In P. Vardin and I. Brody (Eds.), *Children's rights: Contemporary perspectives*. New York: Columbia University Teachers College Press, 1978.

Burt, B., McNally, J., & Ozolins, A. *The family papers*. Boston, Mass.: Longman Press, 1979.

Ellis, J. Commitment proceedings for mentally ill and mentally retarded children. *Child Psychiatry and the Law*, 1980.

Erickson, K. T. *Wayward puritans: A study in the sociology of deviance*. New York: John Wiley & Sons, 1966.

Gliedman, J. & Roth, W. *The unexpected minority: Handicapped children in America*. New York: Harcourt Brace Jovanovich, 1980.

Hairston v. Drosick, 423 F. Supp. 180 (S.D.W. Va. 1976).

Halderman v. Pennhurst, 446 F. Supp. 1295, 612 F. 2d 84, ___ U.S. ___, 67 L. Ed. 2d 694 (1981).

Hobbs, N. (Ed.), *The futures of children*. San Francisco: Jossey-Bass, 1975.

Hobson v. Hanson, 269 F. Supp. 401, *aff'd. sub nom. Smuck v. Hobson*, 408 F. 2d 175 (D.C. Cir. 1969).

In re Gault, 387 U.S. 1 (1967).

In re Grady, 426 A. 2d 467 (N.J. Super. Ct., 1978).

In re Phillip B., 92 Cal. App. 3d 796, 156 Cal. Reptr. 48 (1979), *cert. den.* 100 S. Ct. 1597 (1980), Civ. Action No. 101981, (Super. Ct. Santa Clara Co., Cal., Aug. 7, 1981).

Jackson v. Indiana, 406 U.S. 715 (1972).

Kindred, M., et al. (Eds.) *The mentally retarded citizen and the law*. New York: The Free Press, 1976.

Kirp, D. Schools as sorters. *Pennsylvania Law Review*, 1973, **121**, 705.

Kirp, D., et al. Reform of special education: Empirical studies and procedural proposals. *California Law Review*, 1974, **62**, 40.

Larry P. v. Riles, 343 F. Supp. 1306, *aff'd*. 502 F. 2d 963 (9th Cir. 1974), 495 F. Supp. 926 (N.D. Cal. 1979).

Maher v. Gagne, 448 U.S. 122 (1980).

Maine v. Thiboutot, 448 U.S. 1 (1980).

Matthews v. Eldridge, 424 U.S. 319 (1976).

Mercer, J. Implications of current assessment procedures for Mexican American children. *Journal of the Association of Mexican American Educators*, 1973, **1**, 25–33.

Mercer, J., and Ysseldyke, J. Designing diagnostic intervention programs. In T. Oakland (Ed.), *Non-biased assessment of minority grown children, with bias toward none*. Lexington, Ky.: University of Kentucky, CORRC, undated.

Milofsky, C. Why special education isn't special. 1974 *Harv. Educ. Review*, **44**, 437.

Morse, S. Crazy behavior. *Southern California Law Review*, 1978, **51**, 528.

New Mexico ARC v. New Mexico, 495 F. Supp. 391 (D. N. Mex. 1980).

O'Connor v. Donaldson, 422 U.S. 563 (1975).

Parents in Action on Special Education v. Hannon, F. Supp., (N.D. Ill. 1980).

Parham v. J.R., 442 U.S. 584 (1979).

Practicing Law Institute. *Legal rights of mentally disabled persons* (P. Friedman, Ed.). New York: Practicing Law Institute, 1979.

Romeo v. Youngberg, Civ. Act. No. 76-3429 (E.D. Pa. 1976), 644 F. 2d 147 (3d Cir. 1980), remanded, ___U.S. ___ 50 V.S.L.W. 4681 (June, 1982).

Sarason, S. & Doris, J. *Educational handicap, public policy, and social history: A broadened perspective on mental retardation*. New York: The Free Press, 1979.

Schwitzgebel, R. & Schwitzgebel, R. *Law and psychological practice*. New York: John Wiley & Sons, 1980.

Sites v. McKenzie, 423 F. Supp. 1190 (N.D.W. Va. 1976).

S-1 v. Turlington, N. 78-8020-C1V-CA-WPB (S.D. Fla. 1980), *aff'd.* 49 U.S. L.W. 2504 (Feb. 10, 1981).

Sorgen, M. The classification process and its consequences. In M. Kindred et al. (Eds.), *The mentally retarded citizen and the law*. New York: The Free Press, 1976.

Stone, A. *Mental health and law: A system in transition*. Washington, D.C.: National Institute of Mental Health, 1976.

Superintendent v. Saikewicz, 370 N. E. 2d 417 (Mass. Sup. Jud. Ct., 1977).

Szasz, T. *Law, Liberty, and Psychiatry*. New York: MacMillan, 1963.

Szasz, T. *Psychiatric Slavery*. New York: MacMillan, 1973.

Trilling, L. Quoted in D. Rothman, *Convenience and conscience: The asylum and its alternatives in progressive America*. Boston: Little, Brown and Company, 1980.

Turnbull, A. & Turnbull, H. *Parents speak out: Views from the other side of the two-way mirror*. Columbus, Ohio: Charles E. Merrill Co., 1978.

Wald, P. Basic personal and civil rights. In M. Kindred et al. (Eds.), *The mentally retarded citizen and the law*. New York: The Free Press, 1976.

Ziskin, L. Jenny's story. In A. Turnbull and H. Turnbull (Eds.), *Parents speak out: Views from the other side of the two-way mirror.* Columbus, Ohio: Charles E. Merrill Co., 1978.

Statutory References

Civil Rights Act of 1871, 42 U.S.C. Secs. 1983 and 1988.
Developmentally Disabled Assistance and Bill of Rights Act, 42 U.S.C. Secs. 6001–6081.
Education for All Handicapped Children Act, PL 94-142, 89 Stat. 773, 20 U.S.C. Sec. 1401 et seq.
Rehabilitation Act Amendments of 1973 (enacting Section 504), 29 U.S.C. Sec. 794.

11 CLASSIFICATION: EDUCATIONAL ISSUES

Esther Sinclair and Steven Forness

Historical Perspectives

The genesis of current practices in educating the mentally retarded goes back to the late eighteenth century in Europe. The early history of the United States records no formal programs for the education of handicapped children. A historical perspective is nonetheless worthwhile, because trends and issues in the field today regarding classification of mentally retarded school children continue to reflect these early concerns (Hewett & Forness, in press).

Jean Marc Itard is acknowledged to be the first person to use systematic techniques in teaching a mentally retarded boy. In 1800, at age 12, a boy was found in Aveyron forest in southern France. Itard, a physician, examined the boy Victor and found him to be mentally retarded. It was posited that this mentally retarded child was abandoned by his parents in the forest and that his animal-like behavior was due to isolation and lack of human stimulation. Itard taught Victor self-help skills, language, and attempted to socialize him with the ultimate goal of being normal. Self-help skills, language, and socialization are recognized today as major objectives in special classes for the moderately mentally retarded (Dunn, 1973).

Edward O. Sequin established the first public residential facility in France for moderately mentally retarded children. He was a student of Itard and believed that motor and sensory training could be used to remedy nervous system inadequacies of the mentally retarded child. He advocated training of gross motor functions that would ultimately lead to finer perceptual-motor exercises (Sequin, 1907).

Samuel Gridley Howe introduced Sequin's teaching methods into the first state residential facility for the mentally retarded in the United States. In 1848, Howe requested funds from the Massachusetts legislature to create a residential school for 10 mentally retarded children. Prior to the creation of the Massachusetts State School, mentally retarded children either stayed at home or were sequestered in charity and alms houses. In 1850, 60% of the residents of poor houses were mentally retarded.

In the latter half of the nineteenth century, many residential schools were established in the United States. These years also saw the parallel establishment of large residential asylums for the mentally ill. Mental illness and mental retardation were viewed similarly, and like provisions and services were provided at both types of facilities.

Asylums were often located in rural areas, as opposed to more heavily populated urban areas, where agricultural work was available. Two divergent needs of American society were met, in that treatment was being offered to those citizens who needed it and the intellectually normal citizen was sheltered from the mentally retarded community by their isolation in asylums.

Public school programs for the mentally retarded did not receive much attention until the end of the nineteenth century. Parents of mentally retarded children joined together to establish parent-sponsored day schools. They furthermore demanded that local public school systems assume responsibility for operating these schools. The first such special class for the mentally retarded was opened in Providence, Rhode Island, in 1896.

Public school subsidy and sponsorship increased between 1920 and 1970. In 1950, the National Association for Retarded Children (NARC) was established with the chief goal of developing public school programs for the mentally retarded. In 1961, President Kennedy's First Panel on Mental Retardation established the courts and subsequent federal legislation to identify and enforce the rights of the mentally retarded to appropriate education and services. Increased state subsidies and federal aid, as well as the opening of the Bureau for the Handicapped under the Department of Health, Education, and Welfare in 1966 were responsible for the increased provision of services to the mentally retarded. The U.S. Office of Education has estimated the prevalence of all school-age mentally retarded children at 2.3%, but statistics gathered during the 1978–79 school year indicate that only 1.6% of school-age children were actually identified at all levels of mental retardation (Hewett & Forness, in press).

Since 1970, there has been a strong movement to place mentally retarded citizens in a more normal community setting and to provide services for all handicapped children, no matter how severely handicapped. Three major factors seemed to play an important role in the trend away from segregation of the handicapped from typical life settings and normal peers: (1) An accumulation of research evidence that shows little improvement for the educable mentally retarded child in special classes over what could be accomplished in the regular grades (Carlberg & Kavale, 1980; Forness, 1981); (2) strong legal pressures from organized minority groups who are concerned that minority-group children are being mislabeled and segregated in special education programs inappropriately (Guskin, Bartel, & MacMillan, 1975); (3) a growing emphasis on, and legal attention to, the rights of the individual citizen, particularly the poor and those with special problems (Gilhool, 1973). This recommitment to the principle that all should share equally in the opportunities available in the society raised questions as to whether being placed in an institution is to be deprived of individual freedom and whether being placed in a special class limits the child's educational opportunities.

In 1975, a landmark piece of legislation was passed primarily as a response to the above issues. Public Law 94-142 was designed to guarantee that all handicapped individuals from ages 3 to 21 in the United States receive a free and appropriate education. The law directly addresses issues of neglect as well as other grievances involving handicapped persons. Public Law 94-142 specifies that all testing and assessment procedures employed by the school be nondiscriminatory and not penalize anyone because of background or nature or mode of communication. The law also states that the education must be individualized and appropriate for the child. Unless the educational opportunity is meaningful and significant to the child, it is tantamount to no education at all (Turnbull & Turnbull, 1978). In this regard the law requires that an Individualized Education Program (IEP) be written for each child (Forness, 1979b).

Another provision of Public Law 94-142 is that handicapped individuals be integrated or mainstreamed into regular education programs "to the maximum extent possible." The law further specifies that should the handicapped individual's parents or the handicapped individual himself or herself be dissatisfied with the educational program provided by the school, they have the right to challenge the school in a fair hearing. As we shall see, this law has led to a deemphasis on traditional classification systems for the mentally retarded. However, a discussion of these systems is in order since the field is in a decided state of transition from old systems to new.

Educational Classification

It is difficult to describe the abilities, disabilities, and behavioral characteristics of mentally retarded children, because of the heterogeneous nature of the group. To organize an educational program for groups, however, it has been necessary for researchers to study the distinctive characteristics of different levels of mentally retarded children. Important points to keep in mind are that the observed characteristics of a mentally retarded child may be a result of how the child has been treated, as well as part of the essential condition.

For example, if children are given less opportunity to participate in physical activities and sports, they may appear physically awkward and uncoordinated. In other words, the retardation may be as much a function of the learning environments, as a function of the organism. Secondly, descriptions reflect group tendencies. Individual children may well reveal characteristics counter to the group norm.

For over two decades the field of mental retardation has been dominated by the broad, socioeducational definition prepared by Heber (1961) for the American Association on Mental Deficiency. The definition includes the three dimensions of (1) subaverage intellectual functioning, (2) association with impairments in adaptive behavior, and (3) origination during the developmental period.

An important aspect of this definition is its emphasis on both intelligence and behavior. The school-age child who performs below average on a test of intelligence but still manages to succeed in the regular classroom, if only on a marginal level, cannot strictly be considered mentally retarded according to this definition. The assumption is that the child's adaptive behavior reflects a higher level of intellect than is reflected by the test. The child who is not able to adapt to the regular classroom but whose measured intelligence is in the normal range would not be considered mentally retarded either. Impaired adaptive behavior in his case might be a result of some factor other than low intellectual ability, such as emotional disturbance. A system of checks and balances is thereby established to avoid such practices as labeling children as mentally retarded on the basis of a single criterion.

For educational placement, children with low intelligence are classified for the most part on grounds of the level of intellectual subnormality. Three groups are singled out for educational attention: (1) the educable mentally retarded (IQ of 50 to 70 or 75), (2) the trainable mentally retarded (IQ of 30 to 50), and (3) the totally dependent or severely mentally retarded (IQ below 30). Other factors besides IQ are considered for special services, especially in those gray areas between subgroups and in relation to the child's capabilities and needs (Smith & Knoff, 1981). The category of borderline or the slow learner (IQ of 70 to 85) is no longer considered as a valid subclassification, though it should be kept in mind that a great deal of research on education of "mentally retarded" children prior to the 1970s and even later was conducted on children in this IQ range (MacMillan, Meyers, & Morrison, 1980).

Educable Mentally Retarded (EMR)

An EMR child (this designation corresponds approximately to the mildly retarded child in the AAMD classification) is one who, because of subnormal mental development, is not always able to profit sufficiently from the normal program of the regular elementary school, but who is considered to have potential for development in three areas: (1) educability in academic subjects at the primary or advanced elementary grade level, (2) educability and social adjustment to a point at which he can get along independently in the community, and (3) occupational adequacy to such a degree that he can later be self-supporting partially or totally at the adult level.

In many instances, during infancy and early childhood, the EMR child may not be known to be mentally retarded. Retardation and growth in mental and social activities can sometimes be noted, however, if the child is observed closely during the preschool years and in a structured environment. Most of the time, retardation is not evident because expectations for the child are not heavily weighted with intellectual content during the preschool years. The child may be slightly delayed in talking, language development, and sometimes walking. The retardation may not be so great as to cause alarm on the part of the parents. Many of the children are not identified as mentally retarded until they enter school and begin to fail to learn the required subject matter. The EMR child is usually first identified by the school when such learning ability becomes an important part of social expectations. In most instances, there are no obvious pathological biomedical conditions to account for the mental retardation (MacMillan, 1977).

Public Law 94-142 mandates that 3–5-year-old children be served in special education programs. There is a federal incentive for earlier identification of exceptional children. Many states have child find or "search and serve" teams to evaluate and identify EMR 3–5-year olds. Without such a vigorous screening program in the early grades, the potential EMR child might remain in the regular class program competing with normal peers until such time as the severity of his language problems or cognitive limitations lead the teacher to seek special assistance. In many cases, a potential EMR child may not be referred for assistance until he has spent two or more years in regular grades (Forness, 1972). The classroom teacher is often the person who initiates the referral to the school psychologist for evaluation (Meyers, MacMillan, & Yoshida, 1978). Results are generally discussed by a school evaluation team designated to consider admissions to special programs. If the team's determination is that the child's inability is due primarily to low intelligence and not other factors, and if he cannot be expected to make satisfactory progress unassisted in the regular grades, the child is then referred for some form of special education. Special education goals at the primary level tend toward development of oral language, sensory and motor development, self-awareness, group membership, and social adjustment. Academic tasks may not be greatly emphasized, except for beginning work habits, direction-following, and readiness training in reading and mathematics. At the elementary level EMR children are usually ready to begin learning the subjects of reading, writing, spelling, and arithmetic. The secondary program (adolescence) provides further consolidation in the use of academic subjects, but with increasing emphasis on preparation for work and independent home living.

The EMR curriculum varies widely because of the heterogeneity of the EMR population. This population differs in all dimensions except IQ. Even in IQ, there may be different variations among subgroups that reflect different strengths and weaknesses in areas such as social judgment, verbal-conceptual skills and the like (Jensen, 1970). The commonality among EMR children is their inability to learn efficiently in the regular classroom. The educational program must therefore address as its major goal, the skills and abilities that are necessary for successful living and working in society, thus certain vocational, personal and social objectives are seen as necessary requisites for any successful EMR program (Goldstein, 1974; Payne, Polloway, Smith, & Payne, 1977; Smith, 1974).

The EMR curriculum typically is designed to develop competency in several areas. Kolstoe (1976) mentioned a variety of outcomes contained in various programs, including arithmetic competencies, social competencies, communicative skills, safety, health, vocational competencies, motor and recreation skills and avoidance of drug and alcohol abuse. These can probably be subsumed under the three major rubrics suggested by Kirk and Johnson (1951): Occupational adequacy, social competence, and personal adequacy. Occupational success is important in order for the individual to be self-supporting. Since the EMR student may, in many cases, live in the community as a parent, neighbor, and citizen, it is also important that the EMR program develop the knowledge, skills, and attitudes that will enable him to be an active member of the adult community. The third objective, a sense of personal adequacy, is very difficult for the mentally retarded child to develop if he meets with constant frustration and failure. Thus, the emotional well-being of the child should be considered as he is educated to help him develop a sense of belonging to the class and friendships with peers (Lawrence & Winschel, 1973).

For purposes of instruction, regular classrooms are generally organized according to specific grade levels. In EMR programs, especially in special classes, this organization usually consists instead of (1) primary classes, (2) elementary or intermediate classes, (3) secondary classes (sometimes separated into prevocational and vocational programs), and (4) postschool programs. Although it is becoming more common to have preschool programs for EMR children, this assumes that EMR children can be identified during the preschool years, which is often difficult unless a vigorous early identification program exists (Hayden, 1979).

Trainable Mentally Retarded (TMR)

The TMR child (this designation corresponds to the moderately retarded child in the AAMD classification, although the upper levels of severe retardation are also included) is one who was not considered educable in the sense of minimal (first grade) academic achievement, independent social adjustment in the community, and total occupational adjustment at the adult level. These differences between the TMR child and the EMR child are sometimes matters of degree and frequently depend on environmental and educational opportunities.

The problems of the TMR children emerge quite early in the preschool years, and many are likely to have multiple handicapping conditions that complicate their education. The TMR child, however, has a potential for learning self-help skills, social adjustment in the family and in the neighborhood, and economic usefulness in the home, in a residential school, or in a sheltered workshop. The mental retardation is generally noted at an early age because of known clinical or physical stigmata or deviations, or because the children are markedly delayed in talking and walking.

These children can profit from systematic training in dressing, feeding, and toileting. Special day schools are now being established, albeit in limited numbers (Hayden, 1979), to provide habit training and language development programs for TMR children below school age. With the aid of other professionals, such as public health nurses who visit the home and provide guidance in child care and management, parents can usually maintain the child at home through the school years.

As TMR children reach school age, public educational facilities are available, as early as age three, usually in the form of special day school. Educational emphasis is on oral language development, self-help skills, socialization, and, ultimately, preparation for living and working in a sheltered environment. Language activities include practice in listening, following directions, communicating with others, reading and recognizing commonly encountered signs and labels, counting, and telling time. Self-help activities include lessons in dressing, grooming, eating, care of personal belongings, toileting, and safety. Trainable mentally retarded children also engage in arts and crafts, recreational activities, and, as they reach adolescence, vocational experiences and practice in home-living skills. There is, in fact, increasing emphasis on teaching TMR children within the context of simulated home or vocational settings (Smith, 1974).

Severely Mentally Retarded (SMR)

Until recently, special education was concerned exclusively with EMR and TMR children. Children usually had to be toilet trained and able to communicate, in order to be admitted even to a TMR class. Children functioning at lower levels were often left to be served by mental health facilities. However, recent court cases have resulted in broadening the responsibility of departments of education, requiring them to provide programs for all handicapped children. As a result, educational classification systems have been forced to go beyond two groups to include the severely and profoundly mentally retarded children.

It has been suggested that their educational goals emphasize skills that will maximize their happiness within the environment rather than unrealistic expectations for a future role in everyday society (Cleland, 1979; Rago & Cleland, 1978). Subgroupings of such children according to their need for supervision has been attempted as a means for more effective programming since this is often a critical factor in retention of institutionalized mentally retarded children in school programs (Peterson, 1977; Storm & Willis, 1978).

Severely and profoundly mentally retarded children can learn. However, the types of learning of which SMR children are capable, are more restricted than those of TMR children, and usually consist of toileting, self-dressing, and self-feeding. Even these tasks may be beyond some SMR children. The beginnings of methods to increase basic socialization and communication among even SMR individuals are evident in research on these groups (Meyers, 1978). The prognosis for SMR children is that they will be unable to achieve any marked degree of independence as adults. They will generally be dependent on others economically and will require rather constant supervision.

Severely and profoundly mentally retarded (SMR) people have long been thought to be the responsibility of the medical profession. But within the past decade, behavior modification techniques have been used in attempts to establish more appropriate behaviors in SMR patients. Early applications of behavioral techniques have been in the areas of toileting (Azrin & Foxx, 1971), feeding (Azrin & Armstrong, 1973),

self-dressing (Karen & Maxwell, 1976), and grooming (Hunt, Fitzhugh, & Fitzhugh, 1968).

Practical Distinctions Among EMR, TMR, and SMR

EMR and TMR programs are based on predictions about the different capabilities of each group. EMR children are those who are thought to be capable of learning fundamental academic skills, and who, as adults, will be able to be self-sufficient and live independently in society. On the other hand, most TMR children are considered capable of mastering only the most basic word and number concepts. As adults they will seldom be self-sufficient or capable of living independently in the community. SMR children, however, will need almost total care and supervision on a continued basis from the earliest years. Table 11.1 depicts these differences in terms of school expectations and adult outcomes.

In many states, EMR and TMR are defined by legislation in terms of IQ ranges. Such definitions run counter to the educational principle of placing the child into the program that is individually appropriate. IQ should be treated as one, and only one, of the many kinds of information needed to make an appropriate placement. Special educators have become increasingly concerned in the past 10 years about their use of diagnostic or categorical labels. What brings the field into such a ferment is that special education itself has often been shown to have precipitated and added to many of the problems of exceptional children, not only because of the labels which it uses, but also because of programs which result from assumptions behind these labels (Forness, 1974; Guskin, Bartel, & MacMillan, 1975; MacMillan, Jones, & Aloia, 1974). Educators have borrowed categorical designations and diagnostic terms emanating from other professions, such as medicine and psychology. Yet it is not altogether clear that these terms are at all useful or helpful when directed toward special education practices, in which tasks, settings, and procedures are markedly dissimilar.

Learning can be defined as a relatively permanent change in behavior due to experience, as distinguished from maturation, growth, or aging. Researchers have identified areas of relative difficulty of learning in the mentally retarded (Baumeister, 1967; Denny, 1964; Mercer & Snell, 1977). Mentally retarded children require a great deal of structure from teachers as well as awareness of their own learning strategies if they are to be successful in learning situations. Instructional opportunities may often be far more important than IQ in determining ultimate educational outcome.

Table 11.1. Levels of Mental Retardation*

	EDUCABLE (EMR)	TRAINABLE (TMR)	SEVERE (SMR)
Prevalence**	About 15 to 20 per 1,000 school children.	About 3 to 5 per 1,000 school children.	About 1 to 3 per 1,000 school children.
Preschool expectations	Marginal delays in language and motor development but able to profit from early instruction in readiness skills.	Moderate delays in motor and language; preschool emphasis on communication skills and early stimulation experiences.	Severe delays in walking and motor development with little if any meaningful language; preschool emphasis on motor development and some basic communication.
School expectations	Capable of 2nd- to 7th-grade learning such as reading stories, communicating in handwriting, and handling simple financial transactions.	Capable of 1st- or 2nd-grade learning, such as reading simple sentences and basic addition and subtraction. Emphasis on survival vocabulary and self-care skills.	Capable of some communication and socialization, with very little potential for academic learning.
Adult expectations	Capable of achieving social and vocational skills adequate for minimum self-support; may live independently and marry but may need guidance and support.	Capable of skilled and unskilled work in a sheltered situation; may contribute partially to self-maintenance; usually not capable of independent living.	Capable of self-help and simple chores, but will need nursing care or continued supervision.

* Note that children at each of these levels encompass a wide range of abilities and that considerable variability is likely. This table should by no means be construed as an absolute "table of limitations" but as an indication of the mean or modal levels of expected behavior for each group.
** Source: Hewett & Forness (1982).

EMR, TMR and SMR designations should therefore be considered as program needs rather than crystalized as invariable categories into which children fall on an all-or-none basis. Some educators (e.g., Dunn, 1973) use the terms "general learning disorders" and "specific learning disorders" in lieu of TMR and EMR to soften the distinction between these groups. The problems with the present categorical models center primarily on the debilitating effects that labels regarding degrees of mental retardation may have on a child's eventual school progress.

In addition to academic or classroom considerations, increased attention is being given to both physical and vocational development as well, since physical and vocational education are increasingly regarded as important parts of the school day for mentally retarded children. Studies by Cratty (1974) and Rarrick (1976) show mentally retarded children to be less proficient in physical or motor behavior than normal children of the same chronological age. However, in many cases, differences are not as marked in gross motor areas or when tasks are relatively simple, and there is speculation that delays in motor development may begin with the mentally retarded infant's inability

to use feedback effectively to regulate his or her posture (Molnar, 1978).

Mildly mentally retarded children frequently demonstrate a propensity toward greater visual, auditory, and neurological problems. The more severely mentally retarded the child is, the more likely it is that there will be accompanying physical handicaps, since the possibility is greater than the same disease or organic factor that has affected physical functioning will be associated with retarded overall development. Therefore, poorer physical and motor abilities might generally be expected. The same distinction is generally true of vocational abilities, with expectations for EMR children having some difficulty but still capable of success in unskilled and semi-skilled occupations and more severely mentally retarded needing sheltered workshop situations (Forness, 1982). This means that considerable adaptation may be needed in most school vocational classes. However, one must be continually cognizant of the heterogeneity and range of ability levels within the mentally retarded population and, therefore, not be surprised by wide variance in physical and vocational skills in individual children in addition to their variability in academic or instructional situations.

Placement Alternatives

Since the mentally retarded population is extremely heterogeneous with respect to virtually every attribute, various educational options are needed to provide a reasonably good fit with differing individual needs. No placement for a mentally retarded child should therefore be considered appropriate for a prolonged time period. Rather, periodic evaluation of each mentally retarded child is needed to determine if educational placement needs are still current. The following educational settings describe the current options for school placement and their advantages and disadvantages.

Regular Class

In the classic study on effectiveness of special classrooms, there were some EMR children who manifested particular learning problems that required special programs and others who seemed to be able to profit relatively unassisted from regular class instructional programs (Goldstein, Moss, & Jordan, 1965). Research evidence on EMR children in the regular class further suggests that EMR children are often rejected by their nonretarded peers not necessarily because of their lowered intellect, but because of their behavior (Gottlieb & Leyser, 1981). It is frequently the case that mentally retarded children will be unable to compete favorably with their more able classmates and will therefore experience undue failure and suffer a loss of self-esteem. Likewise, teachers and parents of nonhandicapped children may be concerned lest the presence of mentally retarded children hamper the learning of the nonretarded children in the regular classroom, though available evidence does not support this contention (A. F. Johnson, 1980).

In the case of mildly mentally retarded children, the current trend in placement seems to be to retain them in the regular classroom whenever possible. In contrast to the state of affairs when special classes were being promoted for most EMR children, there is now considerable reluctance to remove them from the regular classroom. Before Public Law 94-142 some children in special EMR programs were returned to regular classes by court mandates (Collins, 1973). The burden of proof now falls on those who would label and place a child in a special program. Unless it can be shown that special placement is going to benefit the child, he should not be classified as mentally retarded and placed in a special program. Today, the clear assumption is that the regular class is a placement preferable to the special class. Even when a child is in need of special help, he may be kept in the regular

educational program as much as possible, depending on his abilities. The contemporary issue is not so much whether to place a child in a regular or special class but rather what placement can ensure delivery of needed services with the minimum degree of segregation.

The concept of least restrictive environment was one of the more controversial aspects of Public Law 94-142. In a general sense, the concept has come to mean that handicapped children be provided services in as normal and integrated a fashion as possible (Thurman & Fiorelli, 1979). In a particular sense, the concept has become equated with mainstreaming children into regular classrooms. Although mainstreaming means different things to various professions, there is some agreement that it is defined by the following four features (MacMillan, Jones, & Meyers, 1976):

1. The mainstreamed child must spend more than half the time in the regular classroom.
2. The regular classroom teacher must have primary responsibility for the child's progress.
3. No categorical labels (e.g., mentally retarded, emotionally disturbed) must be applied to the child.
4. The child's learning handicaps must not be so severe as to preclude his effective remediation in a regular classroom setting.

One way to retain the advantage of regular class placement without sacrificing the presumed benefits of special education is to leave the mentally retarded child in the regular class for the greater part of the school day but to provide special assistance the rest of the time through an itinerant special teacher or a resource room teacher. As with regular class placement, this option is generally applicable only to EMR children, not to TMR or SMR children. Hammill (1972; cf. Wiederholt, Hammill, & Brown, 1978) lists some advantages of the resource room over the special classroom situation.

1. A label is not needed in order to receive special assistance.
2. Resource rooms are not as costly as special classrooms.
3. Students can continue to be with their classmates for part of the school day.
4. More children can be served for limited hours than in the all day special classroom.
5. Children who do not qualify for special class placement can still get needed special attention.

Thus, the regular classroom becomes the child's primary assignment but special assistance can be provided to the regular teacher through resource specialists who either teach the mentally retarded child directly in a separate classroom for one or two hours daily or provide consultation to his or her regular teacher (Sargent, 1981).

Special Class

Special classes were developed because they were thought to protect the EMR child from undue failure, peer rejection, and loss of self-esteem. Placing a mentally retarded child in a classroom with a smaller enrollment supposedly afforded him more individualized instruction and a curriculum that would prepare him for kinds of occupations he was likely to enter upon leaving school. Generally, such classrooms contain only 10 to 15 pupils.

Despite the humane reasons for the creation of special classes, this administrative arrangement ran into criticism from parents on the grounds that they were discriminatory. Dunn (1968), J. L. Johnson (1969), and Mercer (1973) pointed to the disproportionate numbers of minority children in EMR classes and argues that special class placement represented a form of institutional racism. Legal action has mandated modification in the identification process, particularly the use of intelligence tests.

To contend that any one administrative arrangement is the best for all EMR children, or conversely, to argue that one is bad for all EMR children, is naïve and ignores variation in individuals within the population of EMR. Hewett and Forness (in press) state that the debate over special class versus regular class placement may have little relevance for two reasons. First, litigation has forced the field from the unitary special class model, regardless of the research or logic that can be generated in defense of the special class alternative. Second, even under the present system, special class placement does not mean complete segregation from regular class children. For example, EMR children have commonly been integrated for nonacademic subjects such as art, physical education and music as a matter of traditional practice in special class placement. This discussion is also applicable to TMR children as well. Being in a special class within the regular school offers TMR children the advantages of contact with nonretarded peers with whom the mentally retarded child can interact as abilities allow (Thomason & Arkell, 1980).

Much of the research into the direct effects of such placement was, furthermore, based on studies that compare EMR children in special class to children who score in a similar IQ range (usually 60 to 85) but who, for a variety of reasons, were never placed in an EMR program. Comparisons of children in these two settings are referred to as "efficacy studies" (Carlberg & Kavale, 1980) in that they evaluated the effectiveness of the two administrative arrangements for educating mildly mentally retarded children. Usually, the children left in regular programs and not identified as EMR had evinced either better academic achievement or better adjustment; this is why they were not classified. Comparisons of the adjustment or achievement of the two groups were frequently specious because the outcome was already determined by the way the groups were created.

Despite the selective bias inherent in the formation of the groups, a number of studies published in the early 1960s indicated that mildly mentally retarded children left in regular classrooms achieved academically at a higher level than comparable mentally retarded children assigned to special classes (Guskin & Spicker, 1968; MacMillan, 1977). The evidence was not necessarily conclusive. Even in the classic research by Goldstein, Moss, and Jordan (1965), mentally retarded children in the lowest IQ groups who were assigned to special classes at the beginning of the first grade, and whose teachers employed a specifically designed curriculum for four years, were achieving at a higher level than mentally retarded children with equally low IQ's in regular classrooms. This situation was the case in certain academic areas but not all. Recent metaanalysis of some 50 studies in this area suggests that, on the average, mentally retarded children in regular classes may have an academic advantage of only one or two months of achievement gain over their special class counterparts (Carlberg & Kavale, 1980). Nor was the evidence clear on effects of placement on self-concept and social adjustment of mentally retarded children. While early research indicated that mentally retarded children seemed to be better adjusted and to have better self-concepts after special class placement, other data have appeared showing that special class placement may in some cases have had a harmful effect on the self-concept of the mentally retarded child and on his or her readiness to interact with peers (Jones, 1972; Lawrence & Winschel, 1973).

A related area of study is follow-up of mentally retarded children returned to regular classes after placement in special class settings. These were generally children in California (Keogh & Levitt, 1976) whose return to regular classes was determined by court action. The studies demonstrated that mentally retarded children did not perform very well on social and academic measures when compared to nonretarded peers in the same classrooms. It is important to note that these children were mainstreamed *after* special class placement and were returned en masse to regular classes, often without full individual consideration of the particular benefits or disadvantages of each child.

It is clear that a fair test of either special classes or mainstreaming has not yet been made (MacMillan & Semmel, 1977). The least restrictive environment may not be synonymous with the most effective environment. Criteria for deciding whether or not to place or to mainstream a particular child relate to such factors as the child's age, the pervasiveness and degree of handicap, the curriculum modification which might be needed, the child's peer relationships and social skills, the number of children in the regular classroom, attitude or competency of the regular class teacher, and the type of family support system the child has (Forness, 1979a; Guralnick, 1981).

Special Schools

Special schools are frequently used with TMR children because a particular school district or geographic area may not have enough TMR children to warrant the establishment of a special class for TMR children under their own aegis. In such a case, a larger unit of organization (such as the office of the county superintendent of schools) may establish a school for TMR children. It may thus serve children from several school districts that cannot offer their own TMR program. Under these circumstances, the consideration is largely an economic one. The cost required to provide the varied services—medical, speech, psychological, vocational, social welfare, and physical therapy—is considerable, making a centralized facility the most economically feasible alternative.

There is a great deal of variety among special schools. Some schools serve only the mentally retarded, while others serve different types of exceptional children (e.g., mentally retarded, physically handicapped, deaf, and blind) in one school. In this case, children are usually grouped by disabilities, with classes for the mentally retarded containing only mentally retarded children. In the past, all classes for the TMR child, regardless of whether in a regular elementary school or in a community sponsored special school, required that the child be toilet trained and able to communicate basic needs prior to admission. Children who had not mastered these self-care criteria and who were unacceptable for TMR programs were frequently excluded from public education.

Public education facilities are now increasingly available for severely and profoundly mentally retarded children of school age. Impressive progress has been made in recent years much of it through the courts, in mandating public school programs for all such children (Collins, 1973; Gilhool, 1973).

Residential Schools and Institutions

Residential facilities range from medically oriented hospitals sesrving severely mentally retarded children in which the treatment is primarily medical in nature, to residential schools, in which the treatment consists of an educational program for children who do not need constant medical attention. Retarded children who receive instruction on a residential basis are usually in the TMR range or below. The major advantage claimed for residential programs is that services of a multidisciplinary nature such as medical, psychological, social welfare, and education can be concentrated on relatively few sites and benefit many children.

The disadvantages are widely cited. First, the child is removed from his home and is thereby denied the benefit of his or her parents and siblings; at the same time he is denied an opportunity to have informal and spontaneous contact with nonretarded children of similar ages or with similar interests. A second criticism is that there is often a stigma attached to such a school. Despite these disadvantages, institutional placement for mentally retarded children is often done following public school placement in which the child's needs have not been met. Many of these mentally retarded children are institutionalized for secondary problems of emotional disturbance, home instability, or multiple handicaps.

School Placement and Classification Issues

In the past two decades, a large body of research has emerged that questions basic concepts of learning and instruction in mentally retarded students and, by implication, their placement in programs separate from other types of handicapped children. Although it is not possible to give adequate coverage to all relevant findings, some major areas may at least be mentioned.

Zeaman (Zeaman & House, 1963; Fisher & Zeaman, 1973), who has documented the marked deficit which mentally retarded persons demonstrate in discrimination learning, has shown that such deficits can be greatly attenuated in a number of ways, i.e., enhancing the novelty of the learning stimuli, training the mentally retarded person beforehand in verbal mediation, and proper sequencing of stimuli. Campione and Brown (1977) and Ellis (1970) have shown that the mentally retarded youngster's supposed deficit in memory is actually a deficit in use of memory strategies in which the child could be trained to improve his performance. Jensen (1970) has suggested that there are actually two subgroups of mild or borderline mentally retarded persons who differ markedly from one another in their performance on certain associative learning tasks, although their school performance may appear, at first glance, as quite similar. Feuerstein and his colleagues (Feuerstein, Miller, Hoffman, Rand, Mintzker, & Jensen, 1981) have demonstrated how learning can be mediated in mentally retarded populations by a variety of strategies to enhance the learner's interpretation of incoming stimuli. Zigler (1966; Zigler, Abelson & Seitz, 1975) has shown that certain motivational differences exist among mentally retarded persons as a function of past experience, so that some mentally retarded persons would be more likely to respond to the social aspects of a learning situation at the expense of adequate performance on the learning task itself.

Implicit in these formulations is that teaching strategies can make a difference in the outcome of mental retardation. Classification schemes based on intelligence levels alone therefore have both benefits and detriments. Undoubtedly the legislation caused by the efforts of advocacy groups, such as the National Association for Retarded Citizens, has improved services for the mentally retarded. Various categories or classifications have provided focal points around which these groups have worked. There is a need, however, to make categories more precise and discriminating in order to develop more detailed educational and instructional goals.

The negative aspects of categorical designations are most cogently evident in the relationship between diagnosis and treatment. The disease model in medicine indicates a direct relationship between diagnosis and treatment. In medicine, treatment is dictated by diagnosis. This situation is not the case in education where diagnosis frequently tells little of the appropriate treatment to follow. As implied above, much of the psychological data used to diagnose mild mental retardation implies very little concerning effective educational treatment.

In the past, special education pupils have been separated into categories on the assumption that their educational needs were different. It was accepted that the thought processes, educational content, needs, and optimal instructional methods of handicapped children were different based on their handicapping condition. Blind, deaf, emotionally disturbed, learning disabled, language disordered, and mentally retarded children were generally not grouped together in school. These categorical distinctions have been questioned and there is a new trend toward noncategorical special programs that do not distinguish between disturbed, learning disabled, and mentally retarded children for placement and instructional purposes (Forness, 1974; MacMillan, 1973). Conversely, MacMillan (1977)

concludes that available evidence on labeling, teacher expectancy and self-concept fails to support the argument that devastating effects result from labeling a child and providing him or her with special help in the form of special programs. However, the label of mental retardation is harmful when it triggers off automatic expectations of dependency, helplessness, or hopelessness.

The State of California, among others, has adopted a "master plan" for special education which is essentially noncategorical. The plan states that all handicapped children are henceforth given a single designation as "individuals with exceptional needs" and this term "should have four subclassifications, which should be used only for data collection and reporting purposes" (California Master Plan for Special Education, 1974, p. 23). One of these subclassifications, Learning Handicapped (LH), includes all behavior disordered, learning disabled, and EMR children. It was the implicit hope that LH classrooms might contain all three types of students, grouped according to their educational needs and that for the EMR children, the label of mental retardation would be avoided. The other three subclassifications are: Communicatively Handicapped which includes deaf, aphasic, and speech disordered children; Physically Handicapped which includes blind, orthopedically handicapped and other health impaired children; and Severely Handicapped which includes TMR, SMR, autistic, and seriously emotionally disturbed children.

Public Law 94-142 provides for an individualized educational program for each child. Therefore, each child's particular strengths and weaknesses are given individual consideration in planning school programming needs. The individual educational program (IEP) has been considered one of the most significant developments in the education of handicapped children (Forness, 1979b). For most parents, teachers, and administrators, it has been a relatively new experience to meet together to design a year-long school plan for a single child, but the IEP does serve to disabuse educators from the notion of specific educational classifications because of its very nature as an *individualized* plan.

The issues thus involved in considering new classification systems are: (1) Should children who are classified as exceptional on the basis of a handicapping condition, whether it be mental retardation, emotional disturbance, or learning disability, be segregated from normal school children, and (2) should these children be labeled in ways that distinguish them from each other, i.e., should separate programs be maintained for each type of exceptional child?

There is in fact a widely used special education placement model which does address both issues. The Madison School Plan (Hewett & Forness, in press) is a learning center located in the regular elementary school. Mildly mentally retarded, emotionally disturbed, learning disabled, hearing impaired, and speech handicapped children are indeed grouped together. Placement in the learning center is based on the child's readiness for regular classroom functioning. Each child is assigned a place in one of the regular classrooms and spends as much time in that classroom's daily routine as possible. The learning center itself is composed of four classroom levels, based on the child's preacademic and academic skills, his ability to learn in traditional classroom settings, and on his responses to incentives normally available in the classroom. Another important feature of the learning center is that it is virtually disbanded at the beginning of each school year, and children are given a chance to succeed in the regular classroom. It is of interest to note that the Madison School Plan itself developed out of a special classroom model which was based on the use of behavior modification. Since behavior modification tends to minimize the use of labels and concentrates instead on performance, the widespread use of behavioristic approaches to educational problems has generally led to a deemphasis on traditional diagnostic labels.

An opposite approach to the minimal use of labels would be to divide children with special needs into smaller categories than are now used and to generate more categories of exceptional needs. The following subgroups were identified by MacMillan (1971) within the EMR category. (1) Bilingual children who need accommodation in the area of language, but who are not necessarily biomedically handicapped. (2) Children from environments that are described as impoverished because they are lacking in materials or experience considered beneficial to a child in adjusting to school; again, these children may not be biomedically handicapped. (3) Children who have developed failure; that is, who have poor self-concept and expect to fail before they even attempt a task. (4) Children of low-normal measured intelligence with so much emotional overlay that their performance in school and on the intelligence test itself is temporarily depressed below accepted IQ cut-off points. (5) Children who inherit genetic abnormalities or suffer prenatal, or postnatal damage resulting in lowered cognitive development, whose progress may sometimes be less likely to be amenable to instructional modifications.

Additional subtypes could be specified. The point is that no single program would maximally benefit all these children. They are alike only in their failure to achieve academic success in regular classrooms, but they differ greatly in their needs for special education and in their social characteristics. According to critics of ethnic minority group testing, some may not even be mentally retarded; their placement in the category may be based on tests and judgments that are biased and invalid (Mercer, 1973). But faced with the fact of the academic failure they have in common, we could handle the considerable differences between EMR children in two possible ways: (1) develop specific programs for the various subgroups, or (2) go to a broad category and attempt to accommodate the differences by individualizing instruction to meet individual needs. The field of special education will no doubt continue classifying mentally retarded children for educational purposes by using traditional EMR, TMR, SMR designations, while at the same time searching for individually more relevant means of describing each child's educational needs.

References

Azrin, N. H., & Armstrong, P. M. The "mini-meal": A method for teaching eating skills to the profoundly retarded. *Mental Retardation*, 1973, **11**, 9–13.

Azrin, N. H., & Foxx, R. M. A rapid method of toilet training the institutionalized retarded. *Journal of Applied Behavior Analysis*, 1971, **4**, 89–99.

Baumeister, A. A. Learning abilities of the mentally retarded. In A. A. Baumeister (Ed.), *Mental retardation: Appraisal, education, & rehabilitation*. Chicago: Aldine, 1967. Pp. 181–211.

California Master Plan for Special Education. Sacramento: Bureau of Publications, California State Department of Education, 1974.

Campione, J. C., & Brown, A. L. Memory and metamemory development in educable retarded children. In R. V. Kail and J. W. Hagen (Eds.), *Perspectives on the development of memory and cognition*. Hillsdale, N.J.: Erlbaum, 1977.

Carlberg, C., & Kavale, K. The efficacy of special versus regular class placement for exceptional children: A meta-analysis. *Journal of Special Education*, 1980, **14**, 296–309.

Cleland, C. C. *The profoundly mentally retarded.* Englewood Cliffs, N.J.: Prentice-Hall, 1979.

Collins, G. D. Case review: Rights of the retarded. *Journal of Special Education*, 1973, **7**, 27–37.

Cratty, B. J. *Motor activity and the education of retardates.* (2nd edition) Philadelphia: Lea & Fobiger, 1974.

Denny, M. R. Research in learning and performance. In H. A. Stevens & R. Heber (Eds.), *Mental retardation: A review of research*. Chicago: University of Chicago Press, 1964. Pp. 100–142.

Dunn, L. M. Special education for the mildly retarded: Is much of it justifiable? *Exceptional Children*, 1968, **35**, 5–22.

Dunn, L. M. (Ed.) *Exceptional children in the schools: Special education in transition.* (2nd edition) New York: Holt, Rinehart, & Winston, 1973.

Ellis, N. R. Memory processes in retardates and normals. In N. R. Ellis (Ed.), *International review of research in mental retardation*. Vol. 4. New York: Academic Press, 1970. Pp. 1–32.

Feuerstein, R., Miller, R., Hoffman, M., Rand, Y. Mintzker, Y., & Jensen, M. Cognitive modifiability in adolescence: Cognitive structure and the effects of interaction. *Journal of Special Education*, 1981, **15**, 269–287.

Fisher, M. A., & Zeaman, D. Growth and decline of retardate intelligence. In N. R. Ellis (Ed.), *International review of research in mental retardation*. Vol. 4. New York: Academic Press, 1973. Pp. 151–191.

Forness, S. R. The mildly retarded as casualties of the educational system. *Journal of School Psychology*, 1972, **10**, 117–125.

Forness, S. R. Implications of recent trends in educational labeling. *Journal of Learning Disabilities*, 1974, 7, 445–449.

Forness, S. R. Clinical criteria for mainstreaming mildly handicapped children. *Psychology in the Schools*, 1979, **16**, 508–514.(a)

Forness, S. R. Developing the individual educational plan: Process and perspectives. *Education and Treatment of Children*, 1979, **2**, 43–54.(b)

Forness, S. R. Concepts of learning and behavior disorders: Implications for research and practice. *Exceptional Children*, 1981, **48**, 56–64.

Forness, S. R. Prevocational academic assessment of children and youth with learning and behavior problems: The bridge between the school classroom and vocational training. In K. Lynch, W. Kiernan, & J. Stark (Eds.), *The hard to train*. Baltimore: Paul Brookes, 1982.

Gilhool, T. K. The uses of litigation: The right of retarded children to a free public education. *Peabody Journal of Education*, 1973, **50**, 120–127.

Goldstein, H. *The social learning curriculum*. New York: Charles Merrill, 1974.

Goldstein, H., Moss, J., & Jordan, L. The efficacy of special class training on the development of mentally retarded children. USOE Project No. 619. Washington, D.C.: U.S. Office of Education, 1965.

Gottlieb, J., & Leyser, Y. Facilitating the social mainstreaming of retarded children. *Exceptional Education Quarterly*, 1981, **1**, 57–69.

Guralnick, M. J. Programmatic factors affecting child-child social interactions in mainstreamed preschool programs. *Exceptional Education Quarterly*, 1981, **1**, 71–91.

Guskin, S. L., Bartel, N. R., & MacMillan, D. L. Perspective of the labeled child. In N. Hobbs (Ed.), *Issues in the classification of children*. Vol. 2. San Fancisco: Jossey-Bass, 1975. Pp. 189–212.

Guskin, S. L., & Spicker, H. H. Educational research in mental retardation. In N. R. Ellis (Ed.), *International review of research in mental retardation*. Vol. 3. New York: Academic Press, 1968. Pp. 217–278.

Hammill, D. The resource-room model in special education. *Journal of Special Education*, 1972, **6**, 349–354.

Hayden, A. H. Handicapped children, birth to age 3. *Exceptional Children*, 1979, **45**, 510–516.

Heber, R. A manual on terminology and classification in mental retardation. *Monograph Supplement of the American Journal of Mental Deficiency*. (2nd ed.) 1961.

Hewett, F. M., and Forness, S. R. *Education of exceptional learners*. (3rd ed.) Boston: Allyn and Bacon. In press.

Hunt, J. G., Fitzhugh, L. C., & Fitzhugh, K. B. Teaching "exit-ward" patients appropriate appearance behaviors by using reinforcement techniques. *American Journal of Mental Deficiency*, 1968, **73**, 41–45.

Jensen, A. R. A theory of primary and secondary familial mental retardation. In N. R. Ellis (Ed.), *International review of research in mental retardation*. Vol. 4. New York: Academic Press, 1970. Pp. 33–105.

Johnson, A. F. Retrospective study of the relationship between regular class integration of learning handicapped students and academic achievement of their nonhandicapped classmates. Los Angeles: UCLA Doctoral Dissertation, 1980.

Johnson, J. L. Special education and the inner city: A challenge for the future or another means for cooling the mark out? *Journal of Special Education*, 1969, **3**, 241–251.

Jones, R. L. Labels and stigma in special education. *Exceptional Children*, 1972, **38**, 553–564.

Karen, R. L., & Maxwell, S. J. Strengthening self-help behavior in the retardate. *American Journal of Mental Deficiency*, 1976, **71**, 546–550.

Keogh, B. K., & Levitt, M. L. Special education in the mainstream: A confrontation of limitations? *Focus on Exceptional Children*, 1976, **8**, 1–11.

Kirk, S. A., & Johnson, G. O. *Educating the retarded child*. Cambridge, Mass.: Riverside Press, 1951.

Kolstoe, O. P. *Teaching educable mentally retarded children*. (2nd edition) New York: Holt, Rinehart, and Winston, 1976.

Lawrence, E. A., & Winschel, J. F. Self-concept and the retarded: Research and issues. *Exceptional Children*, 1973, **39**, 310–319.

MacMillan, D. L. Special education for the mildly retarded: Servant or savant? *Focus on Exceptional Children*, 1971, **2**, 1–11.

MacMillan, D. L. Issues and trends in special education. *Mental Retardation*, 1973, **11**, 3–8.

MacMillan, D. L. *Mental retardation in school and society*. Boston: Little, Brown and Co., 1977.

MacMillan, D. L., Jones, R. L. & Aloia, G. R. The mentally retarded label: A theoretical analysis and review of research. *American Journal of Mental Deficiency*, 1974, **79**, 241–261.

MacMillan, D. L., Jones, R. L., & Meyers, C. E. Mainstreaming the mentally retarded: Questions, cautions, and guidelines. *Mental Retardation*, 1976, **14**, 3–10.

MacMillan, D. L., Meyers, C. E., & Morrison, G. M. System-identification of mildly mentally retarded children: Implications for interpreting and conducting research. *American Journal of Mental Deficiency*, 1980, **85**, 108–115.

MacMillan, D. L., & Semmell, M. I. Evaluation of mainstreaming programs. *Focus on Exceptional Children*, 1977, **9**, 1–14.

Mercer, C. D., & Snell, M. E. *Learning theory research in mental retardation. Implications for teaching*. Columbus, Ohio: Charles E. Merrill, 1977.

Mercer, J. R. *Labeling the mentally retarded*. Berkeley: University of California Press, 1973.

Meyers, C. E. (Ed.) *Quality of life in severely and profoundly mentally retarded people*. Washington, D.C.: AAMD Monograph Series, 1978.

Meyers, C. E., MacMillan, D. L., & Yoshida, R. K. Validity of psychologists' identification of EMR students in the perspective of the California decertification experience. *Journal of School Psychology*, 1978, **16**, 3–15.

Molnar, G. E. Analysis of motor disorder in retarded infants and young children. *American Journal of Mental Deficiency*, 1978, **83**, 213–222.

Payne, J. S., Polloway, E., Smith, J. E., & Payne, R. *Strategies for teaching the mentally retarded*. Columbus, Ohio: Charles E. Merrill, 1977.

Peterson, C. P. Retention of MR children in a community school program: Behaviors and teacher ratings as predictors. *Mental Retardation*, 1977, **15**, 46–49.

Rago, W. V. Jr., & Cleland, C. C. Future directions in the education of the profoundly retarded. *Education and Training of the Mentally Retarded*, 1978, **13**, 184–186.

Rarrrick, G. L. (Ed.) *Physical activities: Human growth and development*. New York: Academic Press, 1976.

Sargent, L. R. Resource teacher time utilization: An observational study. *Exceptional Children*, 1981, **47**, 420–425.

Sequin, E. *Idiocy and its treatment by the physiological method*. New York: Columbia University Press, 1907.

Smith, C. R., & Knoff, H. M. School psychology and special education student's placement decisions: IQ still tips the scale. *Journal of Special Education*, 1981, **15**, 55–64.

Smith, R. M. *Clinical teaching: Methods of instruction for the retarded*. New York: McGraw-Hill, 1974.

Storm, R. H., & Willis, J. H. Small group training as an alternative to individual programs for profoundly retarded persons. *American Journal of Mental Deficiency*, 1978, **83**, 283–288.

Thomason, J., & Arkell, C. Educating the severely/profoundly handicapped in the public schools: A side by side approach. *Exceptional Children*, 1980, **47**, 114–122.

Thurman, S. K., & Fiorelli, J. S. Prescriptives on normalization. *Journal of Special Education*, 1979, **13**, 339–346.

Turnbull, H. R., & Turnbull, A. P. *Free appropriate public education: Law and implementation*. Denver: Love Publishing Co., 1978.

Wallin, J. E. Training of severely retarded, viewed in historical perspective. Journal of General Psychology, 1966, **74**, 107–127.

Wiederholt, J. L., Hammill, D. D. & Brown, V. *The resource teacher*. Boston: Allyn & Bacon, 1978.

Wolfensberger, W. *The principle of normalization in human services*. Downsview, Ontario, Canada: National Institute on Mental Retardation, 1972.

Zeaman, D., & House, B. J. The role of attention in retardate discrimination learning. In N. R. Ellis (Ed.), *Handbook of mental deficiency*. New York: McGraw-Hill, 1963. Pp. 159–223.

Zigler, E. Research on personality structure in the retardate. In N. R. Ellis (Ed.), *International review of research in mental retardation*. Vol. 1. New York: Academic Press, 1966.

Zigler, E., Abelson, W., & Seitz, V. Motivational factors in the performance of economically disadvantaged children on the Peabody Picture Vocabulary Test. *Child Development*, 1973, **44**, 294–303.

12 CLASSIFICATION AND SOCIAL STATUS

Marsha Mailick Seltzer and Gary B. Seltzer

The process of diagnosing a person as mentally retarded usually involves two stages. First, the person is *defined* as mentally retarded and second, the person is *classified* into one of four levels of retardation: mild, moderate, severe, or profound. The consequences of the first stage of this diagnostic process (definition) are obviously highly significant—for the person, the family, and for society at large. For example, when a child is diagnosed as mentally retarded, it is often the case that family aspirations change, plans are modified, and opportunities narrow. With regard to the second stage of the diagnostic process—classification into a particular level of retardation—there often are equally significant consequences. For example, in the educational arena, classification has an effect on the type of classroom in which a child is placed.

The purpose of this chapter is to examine the implications of the second stage of the diagnostic process—the classification stage—with regard to the social status ascribed to or achieved by a mentally retarded person. An exploration will be made of the relationship between classified level of retardation and social status in three areas: residential status, vocational status, and receipt of services. The following overall question is examined: What is the relationship between classified level of retardation and where a mentally retarded person lives, where a mentally retarded person works, and the services he or she receives? This is not a question about the effect of diagnosis or labeling *per se*, but rather of the effect of the intellectual characteristics possessed by a person on his/her social status.

In the sociological literature, theorists have defined two types of processes by which an individual is assigned to a particular social status (Linton, 1936). An *ascribed* status is one to which an individual is assigned on the basis of his or her fixed characteristics, such as race or caste. An ascribed status cannot be changed because the characteristics used in assigning the status are fixed. An *achieved* status is one which an individual can occupy because of efforts that he or she extends or actions that he or she takes. Examples of achieved statuses are occupation and marital status. An achieved status can be changed because the actions which brought about the assignment of the status were voluntary, and can thus be changed. In this chapter an attempt will be made to determine whether the process by which a mentally retarded person is assigned to various social statuses is ascribed on the basis of classified level of retardation and thus fixed, or alternatively achieved on the basis of a combination of functional abilities and the environmental conditions encountered, and thus is not fixed solely by classified level of retardation.

This chapter thus examines the impact of classification and addresses the following question: Does classified level of retardation cause (or largely determine) residential status, vocational status, and the services received by a mentally retarded person? If so, classified levels are largely ascribed statuses. If not, then what other factors contribute to the probability that a mentally retarded person will achieve various social statuses? Three such factors in addition to classified level of retardation that will be examined in this discussion are: (1) broad social trends, such as deinstitutionalization, (2) environmental opportunities, such as a low unemployment rate, and (3) societal expectations about what mentally retarded people are capable of achieving.

The question examined in this chapter is important because of the implications of its answer for the planning and delivery of services to mentally retarded persons. If classified level of retardation is found to largely determine social status, it follows that prescriptive statements such as "profoundly retarded persons are not able to benefit from a community residence" can be made without much risk of contradiction. If, alternatively, it is found that the social status of a mentally retarded person is a function of his/her classified level of retardation along with social trends, environmental opportunities, and societal expectations, it follows that the optimal match between the client and the service is not totally a function of the characteristics of the client, but also of the broader social context.

The extent to which there is a relationship between classified level of retardation and social status is largely an empirical issue, and for this reason this chapter relies heavily on published research. As noted earlier, classified level of retardation will be related to three social statuses: residential status, vocational status, and receipt of services. The section on residential status is by far the longest, because there is much more published literature on this issue than the other two areas.

Additionally, it should be noted that the discussion that follows includes past research that relates both classified level of retardation and IQ score to social status. Although level of retardation and IQ score are not synonymous, they have been found to be highly correlated. Therefore, although classified level of retardation is more closely tied to the central issue of this chapter, when IQ score alone is reported in a relevant article it will be discussed.

Finally, this chapter takes a longitudinal/historical perspective in examining the relationship between classification and social status. Although at any single point in time social status may appear to be very strongly related to classification, a longitudinal perspective allows for identification of shifts in the strength and nature of this relationship over time.

Classification and Residential Status

Classification and Institutionalization/ Deinstitutionalization

Since public institutions were first developed in the middle-to-late 19th century, there has been a considerable degree of movement of mentally retarded persons into and out of these facilities. Nevertheless, from the turn of the century through the 1950's, there was a great deal of stability in the characteristics of residents of institutions, with approximately 50% of the residents classified as "morons," 35% as "imbeciles," and 15% as "idiots" during this period of time (Lakin, undated). Since the 1950s, however, there has been a change in the population of institution residents. There has been a gradual increase in the proportion of more severely retarded residents, until by 1976 nearly three-quarters of institution residents were labelled severely or profoundly retarded, as shown in Table 12.1.

Other recent studies of the population of state institutions have found comparable distributions. For example, Landesman-Dwyer and Sulzbacher (1981) studied the residents of institutions in the state of Washington in 1975 and 1976 and found that 79% were classified as either severely or profoundly retarded. Similarly, Hill and Bruininks (1981) reported that 75.7% of institutionalized residents in their study were either severely or profoundly retarded. Thus, the classified level of retardation of institution residents has changed over time from approximately 50% mildly retarded in 1950 to predominantly severely and profoundly retarded presently.

Interestingly, there is some evidence to suggest that persons admitted for the first time during the past 10 years to state institutions were somewhat *less*

Table 12.1. Level of Retardation of Residents in U.S. Institutions, 1976

	n	%
"Borderline"	3,384	2.22
Mild	12,040	7.92
Moderate	24,370	16.03
Severe	45,424	29.87
Profound	66,833	43.96
	152,051	100.00

From Scheerenberger, 1976.

severely retarded than the residents already living in these facilities. For example, whereas approximately 75% of the long-term residents of institutions were severely and profoundly retarded, only 58.7% of the new admissions to state institutions in the Hill and Bruininks (1981) study and only 61.2% of the new admissions to U.S. public institutions in 1976 (Lakin, undated) were labeled severely or profoundly retarded.

Hill and Bruininks (1981) provide additional data comparing new admissions with long-term residents of institutions. These data indicate that although the new admissions functioned at a higher level and had fewer chronic health problems and handicaps than the long-term residents, they were more likely to display behavior problems. Similar findings were reported by Campbell, Smith, and Wool (1982), who compared persons living in community residential settings who had been referred for placement to an institution with those living in community residential settings who had never been referred. Pairs were matched on age, sex, race, and IQ. No differences between the groups were found in self-help skills and cognitive abilities, but significant differences were found in maladaptive behavior, with the clients who were referred to institutions having many more reported behavior problems. Thus, while the long-term population of state institutions has over time become increasingly severely retarded, new admissions are somewhat less mentally retarded but display more serious behavior problems.

An additional trend is that over time the clients who are moved from institutional settings to community residences are increasingly severely retarded. Whereas in the early 1970s the institution residents who moved to community residences were largely mildly and moderately retarded, by the end of this decade those leaving institutions were more likely to be classified as moderately and severely retarded. Schalock, Harper, and Genung (1981) provided data about this trend. They reported that, whereas in 1970 the mean IQ score of clients deinstitutionalized in Nebraska was 64, by 1978 the mean IQ score of newly deinstitutionalized clients was 39. In a related vein, Mayeda and Sutter (1981) compared deinstitutionalized clients who lived in the community with those who still lived in the institution but who were considered "placeable" in the community. The two groups were found to differ significantly in level of retardation, as shown in Table 12.2. These data suggest that residents currently living in institutions but who are considered to be "placeable" are classified at a lower level of retardation than those who were placed in the community in the past.

A number of other studies have compared the

Table 12.2. Level of Retardation, Community Clients, and "Placeable" Institution Clients

	"PLACEABLE" INSTITUTION CLIENTS	COMMUNITY CLIENTS
"Borderline"	0.0	4.5
Mild	4.9	26.7
Moderate	14.8	34.8
Severe	29.6	26.0
Profound	50.6	7.8

From Mayeda & Sutter, 1981.

level of retardation or mean IQ score of institution and community residence clients, and in every instance a substantially greater proportion of the clients who lived in institutions than those who lived in community residences were classified as severely and profoundly retarded. For example, Hill and Bruininks (1981) reported that 47% of their institution sample members were profoundly retarded, as compared with 12% of their community residence sample members, whereas only 8% of their institution sample members were classified as mildly retarded, as compared with 24% of their community residence sample members. Bjaanes, Butler, and Kelly (1981) and Eyman and Call (1977) reported that approximately 50% of their institution clients were severely retarded, whereas 50% of their community residence clients were classified as mildly retarded. Borthwick, Meyers, and Eyman (1981) and Eyman and Arndt (1982) reported the mean IQ score of institution residents to be in the middle 20's and the mean IQ score of community residence clients to be in the middle 40's. Thus, the level of retardation (or mean IQ score) of institution residents was consistently lower than that of those in community residences. However, as noted earlier both populations are shifting over time as the more severely retarded institution group filters into the community residence group.

When groups of institution and community residence clients who are classified at the *same level of retardation* are compared, those who live in institutions were found in several studies to be functioning at a lower level than those who live in the community. For example, Landesman-Dwyer and Sulzbacher (1981) compared severely/profoundly retarded persons who lived in the institution with those who lived in the community on the basis of 20 measures of skills and behavior problems, and found that the community residence clients functioned at a superior level on all but two of these measures. Similarly, Eyman and Arndt (1982) reported the mean Adaptive Behavior Scale (ABS) score of institution and community residents at comparable levels of retardation and found that in each level (mild, moderate, severe, profound), the community residence clients had higher ABS scores than the institution clients. Thus, the correlation between level of retardation and level of functioning, although high, is not perfect, and this relationship appears to be mediated by the residential environment.

However, it might be that the differences in functioning between institutional and community residence clients classified at the same level of retardation could in part be a function of the environmental constraints placed by institutions on residents' performance of mastered skills. Hill & Bruininks (1981) examined this issue and found that on the average, institution residents were significantly less likely to perform skills that they had previously mastered than were community residence clients. This difference in performance was attributed to the higher degree of environmental constraints in institutions than in community residences. A similar point was raised by G. B. Seltzer (1981) regarding the relationship between environmental opportunity and performance of mastered skills. Recidivists (i.e., those who returned to the institution) were less likely to perform the skills they had mastered than those who remained in the community. Thus, the functional level of residents of institutions is likely to be underestimated, because of the environmental constraints of the institutions. This has the effect of magnifying differences in performance between institution and community residence clients of comparable levels of retardation.

To summarize, the population of clients in state institutions has over time become largely severely and profoundly retarded. This census change is largely accounted for by the release of the majority of mildly and moderately retarded institution residents to the community during the 1970s. Presently, the newly admitted residents tend to be somewhat less severely retarded and to have more behavior problems than those who had lived in the institution over time.

The relationship between classified level of retardation and institutionalization/deinstitutionalization is not a simple one, and is apparently affected in large part by evolving trends in the residential service system. Conceptions about the type of person most appropriate for deinstitutionalization have evolved over time. Whereas in the early 1970s only mildly retarded persons were seen by many professionals to be appropriate for deinstitutionalization, by the end of this decade professional opinion had shifted, and many severely retarded persons were released to the community. Only a longitudinal perspective can detect such an evolving relationship between classified level of retardation and placement into and out of institutions.

Classification and Community Residential Placement

LEVEL OF RETARDATION AND TYPE OF COMMUNITY RESIDENCE

Table 12.3 presents data about the level of retardation or IQ score of clients placed in different types of community residential facilities. These data were drawn from 19 published studies. As shown in Table 12.3 (Section A), approximately equal numbers of mildly and moderately mentally retarded clients are found in community residences (approximately 30% each), with fewer severely retarded clients included in these settings (approximately 20%). Clients classified as profoundly retarded were relatively infrequently found in community residences (approximately 10%).

When the various types of community residences are compared, some differences emerge with respect to the level of retardation of clients. For example, the clients in group homes tend to be less severely mentally retarded than those in foster homes. Specifically, across studies, about 35% of group home clients and 25% of foster home clients were classified as moderately retarded, whereas approximately 17% of group home clients and 27% of foster home clients were classified as severely retarded. Moreover, the residents of semi-independent/independent living arrangements were found to have higher IQs or to be classified as less severely retarded than either group home or foster home clients.

Several possible explanations can be forwarded for such differences in resident level of retardation in different types of community residences. For one, differential *admissions criteria* used by group homes, foster homes, and semi-independent units could account for the observed differences in level of retardation in their respective clients. Another possibility is that the differences in level of retardation are due to the differential *effects* of the different types of settings on the individual clients subsequent to placement. A third explanation is that the differences in client level of retardation could be due to differential *perception* of the residents by the staff of differing facility types. This latter hypothesis suggests the possibility that foster parents may perceive their residents to be more severely retarded than they actually are, while staff of semi-independent apartments may intentionally or unintentionally inflate the functional level of their residents in order to make the resident level of retardation more consistent with the higher level of demands placed on residents by these settings. Seltzer and Seltzer (1978) analyzed the relationship between IQ and type of setting using IQ scores obtained prior to the time

Table 12.3 Types of Community Residences by Level of Retardation

	LEVEL OF RETARDATION					
	"BORDERLINE"	MILD	MODERATE	SEVERE	PROFOUND	MEAN IQ SCORE
A. Community residences in general						
Baker, Seltzer, & Seltzer (1977)	14.0	32.0	42.0	12.0		
Bruininks, Hauber, & Kudla (1979)	8.0	22.4	35.3	21.8		
Eyman & Call (1977)			← 63.0 →	24.0	13.0	
Gollay, Freedman, Wyngaarden, & Kurtz (1978)		41.3	33.1	25.6		
Hill & Bruininks (1981)	10.1	23.8	28.7	25.8	11.7	
Mayeda & Sutter (1981)	4.5	26.7	34.8	26.0	7.8	
O'Connor (1976)	22.6	30.2	27.7	17.1	2.4	
Seltzer & Seltzer (1978)	17.0	30.0	31.0	14.1	8.0	
B. Group homes						
Baker, Seltzer, & Seltzer (1977)	4.0	35.0	48.0	13.0		
Bjaanes, Butler, & Kelly (1981)		50.1	32.8	17.1		
Eyman, Demaine, & Lei (1979)			← 41.0 →	26.0	33.0	
Landesman-Dwyer, Berkson, & Romer (1979)	11.0	28.0	39.0	18.0	3.0	
Landesman-Dwyer, Stein, & Sackett (1978)		← 65.0 →		35.0		
Landesman-Dwyer & Sulzbacher (1981)					← 20.0 →	
Willer, Intagliata, & Wicks (1981)		42.2	26.7	29.6	1.5	
C. Foster homes						
Bruininks, Hill, & Thorsheim (1980)	8.1	21.0	38.0	27.0	6.0	
Eyman, Demaine, & Lei (1979)		← 46.0 →		35.0	19.0	
Landesman-Dwyer & Sulzbacher (1981)					← 22.0 →	
Lei, Nihira, Sheeny, & Meyers (1981)		← 65.4 →			← 34.6 →	
Willer, Intagliata, & Wicks (1981)		24.4	20.5	44.9	10.3	
Borthwick, Meyers, & Eyman (1981)						39.8
Eyman & Arndt (1982)						36.4
Seltzer & Seltzer (1978)						43.0
D. Relatives						
Bjaanes, Butler, & Kelly (1981)		55.8	27.2	17.0		
Eyman & Call (1977)			← 78.0 →	19.0	3.0	
Landesman-Dwyer & Sulzbacher (1981)					← 14.0 →	
Willer, Intagliata & Wicks (1981)			30.8	61.5	7.7	
Borthwick, Meyers, & Eyman (1981)						51.7
Eyman & Arndt (1982)						44.2
E. Semi-independent and independent apartments						
Baker, Seltzer, & Seltzer (1977)		56.0	43.0	1.0		
Schalock & Harper (1981)						59.5-83.6*
Seltzer & Seltzer (1978)						64.0

* Range of mean annual IQs of clients placed in independent settings over a seven-year period.

that residents were deinstitutionalized, thereby eliminating the possibility that it was the differential perception of staff of different types of community residences that accounted for the differences in IQ score. Seltzer and Seltzer (1978, Table 4) found substantial differences when comparing the average IQ scores of residents in foster homes (mean IQ = 43), group homes (mean IQ = 53), and semi-independent apartments (mean IQ = 64). These findings provide support for the first hypothesis put forward above, namely that differences among residents' IQ scores in different types of community residences were at least in part a function of differential admissions criteria (selection) used by the different types of facilities.

It is not surprising that community residences select clients on the basis of the characteristics possessed by these clients at the time of placement. It is probable that referral agencies refer the clients whom they believe to have the most potential to the residences which they perceive to have the best environments. Since the early 1970's, conceptions about the types of residences that are most desirable have been shaped by the normalization principle. In general, the more independent the residence the more normalized it is believed to be. Thus, semi-independent living arrangements are generally viewed as more normalized than either group homes or foster homes, and group homes are likewise perceived to be more normalized than foster homes. It is also likely that beliefs held by community residence staff regarding the types of clients with whom they believe they will have the most success have an influence on client selection. Generally the more intelligent the client, the more likely staff are to perceive the client having a high potential for community success. According to this argument, the settings considered most normalized have the "right of first refusal" of the less desirable clients (or the less desirable clients are not referred to them in the first place) and these types of clients eventually "filter down", or are referred, to the environments perceived to be less normalized.

Thus, one possible explanation for the observed relationship between type of residence and classified level of retardation of clients is that the preplacement characteristics of the clients influence placement decision *differentially* in the various types of community residences. Furthermore, if the various types of community residences have a differential impact on clients, by placing the more severely retarded clients in what are believed to be less desirable residences, the service system may in fact be making valuable opportunities for growth and development less available to severely retarded persons than to mildly and moderately retarded persons. However, conclusive evidence about the differential effects of different types of residences on clients is not yet available in the mental retardation literature, and therefore it cannot be unequivocally argued that the observed relationship between type of residence and classified level of retardation implies any negative or positive *effects* of the residences on the clients.

TRENDS IN COMMUNITY RESIDENTIAL PLACEMENT

Earlier in this chapter, trends in the placement and release of institution clients of different levels of retardation were discussed. The data indicate that over time the population served in and released from institutions is becoming increasingly more cognitively impaired. These trends obviously have had an effect as well on the population of mentally retarded persons in community residences, since a large proportion of community residence clients lived in institutions prior to their placement in the community. In this section, similar trends will be discussed, only the focus will be on data pertaining to shifts over time in the composition of the population of community residence clients.

Examination of Table 12.3 supports the existence of the trend toward more severe retardation in community residence clients. Two early nationwide studies of community residences (Baker et al., 1977; O'Connor, 1976), both of which were conducted in the early 1970's, found that approximately 30% of the clients were classified as mildly retarded and 12–14% as severely retarded. The most recent nationwide study of community residences (Bruininks et al., 1979) reported approximately 20% of the clients to be mildly retarded and 20% to be severely retarded, representing a shift of about 10% of the population from the mild to severe category.

A similar trend was noted by Schalock and Harper (1981) who studied clients placed in independent living arrangements between the years 1972 and 1978. As shown in Table 12.4, there has been a decrease in the IQ scores of these clients during this period of time, particularly among males.

As lower functioning clients have increasingly been placed in community residences, concomitant changes in the support services provided in the residences have also occurred. Staff-to-client ratios have often been increased and the expectations held by staff regarding the extent to which residents can function independently have often been tempered. Thus, although over time the classified level of retardation of clients entering a given type of residence has decreased, the services provided in many residences have evolved

Table 12.4. Mean IQ Scores of Clients Placed in Independent Living, 1972–1978

YEAR	MALES	FEMALES
	mean IQ	
1972	71.39	64.75
1973	83.60	69.30
1974	71.25	68.50
1975	70.91	69.33
1976	60.07	69.80
1977	62.00	67.89
1978	59.50	61.55

From Schalock & Harper, 1981.

along with clients' abilities. Thus, conceptions about the type of client best suited to a particular type of community residence must not be too rigidly held by professionals, because community residences appear to be rather flexible in accommodating a wide variety of client types.

Classification and Recidivism

A related issue of considerable importance that has received attention in the literature is the problem of recidivism, i.e., the return of mentally retarded persons from community residences to institutions. As can be seen from an examination of Table 12.5, the reported rates of recidivism vary considerably from study to study. However, it is possible to detect patterns regarding differential rates of recidivism from different types of community residential facilities. Perhaps even more important, Table 12.5 reveals that in no study and for no type of facility was recidivism unimportant.

In general, higher recidivism rates were reported for foster homes than for group homes. An exception was the Willer and Intagliata (1980) study, in which fewer than 10% of the foster-home residents of their New York State sample returned to institutions. In contrast, the average reinstitutionalization rate from foster homes was found by the other studies to be nearly 30%, while the average recidivism rate from

group homes across studies was approximately 15%. Eagle's (1967) early literature review generally concurs with this finding, with nearly a 40% reinstitutionalization rate from foster family care reported.

It may be useful to speculate about the reasons for the difference in recidivism in group homes and foster homes. As was noted earlier in this chapter, residents of foster homes tended to be more severely retarded than residents of other types of community residences, which might make recidivism more probable. Moreover, foster families might be subject to considerably more strain simply by having mentally retarded persons live with them in their own homes than group home staff, who often have other homes. Furthermore, foster parents may have very limited professional back-up support services available to them to ease the strain. This lack of back-up services might also make it more likely for foster families than group home staff to return residents to the institution as a crisis management strategy.

There is reason for concern with the relatively high rates of recidivism from both foster homes and group homes. Undoubtedly, some of this recidivism is a function of poor placement decisions. Until better knowledge is available regarding the type of client likely to do best in each type of setting, a certain rate of recidivism can be expected simply because there will continue to be inappropriate placements. In addition, recidivism is probably also a function of limited, uneven, or poor quality back-up services for clients, especially for those with behavior problems or medical problems. A final point to note regarding Table 12.5 is that additional research is needed with regard to recidivism from semi-independent settings, in that the two studies reporting data (Baker et al., 1977; Gollay et al., 1978) found widely discrepant results.

The reasons for recidivism among community residence clients were explored in a number of studies. Hill and Bruininks (1981) compared recidivists with those who remained in the community and found a number of differences between the two groups. For

Table 12.5. Recidivism Rates of Mentally Retarded Persons from Different Types of Community Residences

	GROUP HOMES	FOSTER HOMES	SEMI-INDEPENDENT APARTMENTS	ALL TYPES
Aanes & Moen (1976)	15.0			
Baker, Seltzer, & Seltzer (1977)	15.4	34.0	23.0	22.0
Bruininks, Hauber, & Kudla (1979)	15.9			
Bruininks, Hill, & Thorsheim (1980)		20.0		
Gollay et al. (1978)	10.1	32.1	9.0	
Moen, Bogen, & Aanes (1975)	15.0			
Seltzer & Seltzer (1978)				22.0
Willer & Intagliata (1980)	26.4	9.2		14.9

example, although the two groups contained nearly identical proportions of mildly, moderately, and severely mentally retarded persons, the recidivist group contained half as many clients labelled "borderline" and twice as many profoundly retarded persons. In contrast, no difference in IQ score among recidivists and non-recidivists was reported by Thiel (1981), while Sutter, Mayeda, Call, Yanagi, and Yee (1980) found the recidivists to be less severely retarded than the non-recidivists. Thus, the available evidence on the relationship between level of retardation and recidivism is mixed.

More agreement among studies was found regarding the relationship between recidivism and maladaptive behavior. For example, Pagel and Whitling (1978) conducted a study of all former residents of Pacific State Hospital who had previously been released to the community but who had returned to the institution during a two-year period of time (1974 to 1976). Ninety-two percent of the sample members were returned to the state school either because of health problems, maladaptive behavior, or a combination. Gollay et al. (1978) compared the recidivists in their sample of deinstitutionalized mentally retarded persons with those who remained in the community and found that the recidivists were more likely to have psychological problems (55% of the recidivists vs. 17% of the nonrecidivists). Jones and Jones (1976) reported a similar finding. In their study, Part II of the Adaptive Behavior Scale, which measures maladaptive behavior, was useful in distinguishing those who returned to the institution from those who did not, with the recidivists tending to have more behavior problems. Similarly, Sutter et al. (1980) compared successful and unsuccessful clients placed in group homes in Hawaii and found that the recidivists tended to display more behavior problems than those who were more successful. Maladaptive behavior was also more common among the recidivists than among the nonrecidivists in the Hill and Bruininks (1981) and Thiel (1981) studies.

All of these studies agree that recidivists are more likely to have psychological problems and to manifest maladaptive behaviors than non-recidivists. It is possible that those who are returned to the institution manifested their psychological problems prior to their placement in the community residence. It is also possible that at least some of these individuals were mismatched with the settings in which they were placed. To the extent to which a community residence does not meet the needs of a mentally retarded person, maladaptive behavior may occur even in the absence of prior maladaptive behavior. Thus in an effort to reduce recidivism, there is a need to effect optimal placements

and to design highly specialized community settings for clients who manifest severe behavior problems.

To summarize, recidivism from community residential facilities back to state institutions appears serious. Apparently, recidivism is related less to classified level of retardation than to the manifestation of maladaptive behavior by the deinstitutionalized clients. The probability of recidivism is affected not only by the characteristics of mentally retarded individuals but also by the conditions encountered in the community. In part, the community success of deinstitutionalized persons is dependent upon the availability of community support services; however, these services do not remain constant over time. Supporting data are provided by McCarver and Craig (1974) who reviewed 44 studies in which the criterion of success was "remaining in the community vs. returning to the institution." They presented the following data reflecting the percentage of released clients who remained in the community during four time periods:

1918–1935	72%
1936–1953	89%
1954–1959	65%
1960–1970	53%

The declining success rates of the 1950s and 1960s are perhaps an indication of shrinkage in the labor market following World War II, and more significantly, a relatively dormant period in the development of community residential programs. However, as shown earlier in Table 12.5, by the mid-1970s the trend had been reversed, with success rates of 75% or more reported by most studies. Thus, it appears that the general economic trends and the resiliency of the service system in the community may be equally as important in determining recidivism as are characteristics of the individual client.

Summary

To summarize, the literature reviewed leads to a number of conclusions regarding the relationship between classified level of retardation and residential status. First, although at any given time the residents of state institutions are generally more severely retarded than residents of community-based facilities, both populations have over time shifted substantially toward more severe retardation. Persons once considered too severely retarded to succeed in the community are now routinely released to community programs. Thus, the impact of classification on the residential status of a mentally retarded person will be different at different points in time. The identified trends in the level of retardation of clients in institutions and in community residences are parallel to other trends ongoing in the field of mental retardation. For example, court-mandated deinstitutionalization, the normalization principle, and the emerging community residence movement all have had an impact on the relationship between level of retardation and residential status. As was pointed out earlier, because of these trends in predicting a client's residential status, the current status of the residential service system at any particular point in time must be taken into account along with the client's level of retardation.

Additionally, when institution and community residence clients of the same level of retardation are compared, the institution clients are found to function on a lower level. One group of investigators (Hill & Bruininks, 1981) presented data suggesting that this difference was due to the more limited opportunity for performance available in institutions. Thus, it appears that the relationship between classified level of retardation and residential status is mediated not only by trends in the mental retardation service system, but also by the particular type of residential facility in which an individual is placed.

Classified level of retardation is not strongly related to recidivism. Instead, recidivism appears to be in part a function of the extent to which an individual displays maladaptive behavior while in the community. Recidivism rates were found to fluctuate widely from decade to decade, and thus broad economic and social policy trends as well as individual maladaptive behavior appear to have an effect on recidivism rates.

Classification and Vocational Status

Many studies have examined the relationship between vocational success and IQ scores or classified level of retardation, in order to determine whether mentally retarded adults with better cognitive skills are more likely to succeed at work than those individuals who are more limited. The utility of the IQ score as a predictor of vocational success has been the subject of considerable controversy, with most studies finding IQ to be a significant predictor of success, although other studies have found no significant relationship. *

* Studies reporting *no relationship* between IQ and vocational success include: Appell et al., 1965; Barrett, Relos, & Eisele, 1965; Collman & Newlyn, 1956; Cowan & Goldman, 1959; Ferguson & Kerr, 1960; Gellman & Glaser, 1959; Kraus, 1972; McIntosh, 1949; O'Connor & Tizard, 1956; Schalock & Harper, 1981; and Voelker, 1962. Studies reporting a *positive relationship* between IQ and vocational success include: Abel, 1940; Albizu-Miranda et al., 1966; Baller, 1936; Bell, 1974; Daniels, 1974; Elkin, 1974; Fry, 1956; Jackson, 1968; Jackson & Butler, 1963; Kaufman, 1970; Lambert, 1972; Larson, 1964; Phelps, 1965; Pearson, 1975; Pinkard, 1963; Seltzer & Seltzer, 1978; Song & Song, 1969; Stephens & Peck, 1968; Tobias & Gorelick, 1974.

The definition of successful vocational adjustment varies widely in these studies, but there seems to be some evidence to suggest that those with higher IQ scores are more likely to be successful at work in both sheltered and competitive settings.

A recent in-depth study of the vocational adjustment of a sample of deinstitutionalized mentally retarded adults provides some additional insight into the relationship between IQ and various vocational outcomes (M. M. Seltzer, 1981). This study reported that there was a significant difference in IQ scores between sample members who had held a competitive job at some point since their release from the institution (mean IQ = 66), those who had worked exclusively in sheltered settings (mean IQ = 54), and those who had never been employed in either competitive jobs or sheltered workshops (mean IQ = 35). Thus, level of retardation was positively related to the probability that a deinstitutionalized mentally retarded person would find a competitve job.

However, no such relationship was found between level of retardation and job mobility. Persons who had been fired, laid off from, or quit competitive jobs were comparable in IQ score to those who retained their competitive jobs. Similarly, unemployed persons who in the past attended sheltered workshops but who no longer did so were comparable in IQ score to those who continued to attend the workshop. Although comparable in IQ score, the downwardly mobile sample members were more likely to have behavior problems than the stable status group. These findings are similar to those reported earlier in this chapter regarding the relationships among level of retardation, residential status, and return to the institution (recidivism).

An additional finding reported in the G. B. Seltzer (1981) study was that there was a positive relationship between IQ score and job performance among workers in both competitive and sheltered settings. Thus, IQ was found to be a predictor of job attainment and performance, but not job mobility.

Although the overall relationship between vocational status and classified level of retardation appears generally positive, the probability that any given mentally retarded person will find a job at any particular time is also a function of the labor market, of societal receptivity to hiring mentally retarded adults, and of the extent to which support services are available in the community. Illustrative of the influence of labor market factors is the experience of mentally retarded persons during World War II. A number of reports in the literature noted that during World War II, many mentally retarded individuals who previously were considered so handicapped as to warrant institutionalization were re-evaluated and released to the community in order to fill jobs left vacant by draftees.

For example, Hegge (1944) studied 177 exresidents from the Wayne County Training School who were living in the community but who "in other times would not have been considered ready for parole" (p. 91). He found that over 80% of the men and women were successfully participating in community life, in the armed forces, in war industries, civilian jobs, or homemaking. Several other studies reported similar findings (Coakley, 1945; Haskell & Strauss, 1943; McKeon, 1946; Weaver, 1946).

These studies of the employment success of mentally retarded adults during World War II suggest that, as economic opportunities and societal expectations increased, so did the demonstrated functional competence of mentally retarded individuals. They often moved from institutional to community living; they obtained positions either in the armed forces or in industry that were more sophisticated and complex than had been available before; and they earned substantially higher wages. At least half of the sample members in each of the studies were successful in their work endeavors, and often the percentage was much higher. Thus, it appears that when society widens the opportunities, it is more likely for mentally retarded persons to be successful.

Two societal trends which have had an impact on the vocational success of mentally retarded persons during the second half of this century are the increase of automation in industry and the increase in urbanization and societal complexity. A number of influential professionals in the field of mental retardation have argued that both of these trends have had and will continue to have a negative impact on the vocational success of mentally retarded persons (e.g., Heber & Dever, 1970; Wolfensberger, 1967). Evidence about the effect of increased urbanization and societal complexity was provided by a study conducted in Puerto Rico (Albizu-Miranda, Matlin, & Stanton, 1966) in which the authors categorized the island into six types of communities, ranging from peasant (least urban and complex) through urban middle and upper class (most urban and complex). As predicted, the more complex the community, the less likely it was for mentally retarded persons to succeed vocationally. Thus, vocational success was more likely for a person who lived in a peasant community than for a person of the same level of retardation who lived in an urban middle class community. Mercer's (1973) social system perspective on mental retardation provides a theoretical framework within which to interpret the findings of the Albizu-Miranda et al. (1966) study:

> Mental retardation is not viewed as individual pathology but as a status which a person holds

in a particular social system and a role which he plays as an occupant of that status [p. 76].

As was discussed earlier in this chapter regarding residential status, although classified level of retardation is a valuable predictor of vocational status, this outcome is a function of general societal trends as well as individual intellectual capacity.

Classification and the Receipt of Services

Thus far, the relationship between classified level of retardation and both residential status and vocational status were discussed, and on the basis of reviews of extensive amounts of literature it was shown that both societal and individual variables were related to the residential and vocational status of a mentally retarded person. In contrast, surprisingly little information is available concerning the relationship between classified level of retardation and the receipt of nonresidential and nonvocational services. Although it would seem reasonable to assume that persons who have a demonstrated need for particular types of services are more likely to receive such services, in fact, the relationship between need for services and receipt of services is much less clear. Bjaanes, Butler, and Kelly (1981) examined the need for and distribution of services to clients in four types of residential settings in California: institutions, large care facilities, small care facilities, and clients' own homes. The services that were studied in these four types of settings were: supportive counseling, behavior therapy, independent living skills training, and social interaction training. It was found that residents who were more severely retarded and who thus had more pronounced needs for habilitation tended to receive *fewer* services than the less severely retarded residents. As the authors note:

> this [finding] raises the philosophical and moral dilemma: to whom should services be provided? Should services be provided to those for whom the greatest gain can be expected or to those with the greatest need for services? Without consciously addressing this issue, it appears that the service system has opted for the former course [p. 346].

Another major finding of this study pertained to the issue of the differential rates of provision of different types of needed services. In the two types of community residential facilities (large care facilities and small care facilities), nearly all clients who were judged to need supportive counseling and independent living skills training received these services, whereas the percentage of clients who received needed services in the areas of social interaction training and behavior therapy was considerably lower. The latter two service areas (social interaction and behavior therapy) require a greater degree of technical expertise on the part of service providers than do the former two areas (supportive counseling and independent living skills training), which may in part account for their lower frequency of delivery in community residential facilities.

The results of the Bjaanes et al. (1981) study raise important issues and areas of concern, but because of the geographic restriction of their sample of facilities (California only), the generalizability of results may be limited. A more nationwide perspective was taken by Gollay et al. (1978) who examined the *unmet* needs of exresidents of state institutions, and compared those who eventually returned to the institution (recidivists) with those who did not. Recidivists tended to have higher rates of unmet needs than nonrecidivists in each of the following five areas:

1. social/recreational services
2. behavior management
3. education/employment
4. community use training
5. domestic living training

It is interesting to note that the first two of these areas of unmet needs were the same as those identified by the Bjaanes et al. (1981) study as being provided *less* frequently to those judged to be in need of such services in community residences. These findings, coupled with those discussed above that recidivists tended to have more behavior problems than nonrecidivists, together suggest that a key area in which community residences are deficient is the extent to which they can meet the needs of residents who have emotional problems and maladaptive behavior. In addition, questions can be raised about the appropriateness of the distribution of services in general to residents of all types of facilities in light of the Bjaanes et al. (1981) finding that those most in need of services are least likely to receive them.

Summary and Conclusions

The available evidence appears to suggest that at any one point in time there is a strong relationship between level of retardation and residential status, with the more severely mentally retarded clients more likely to live in institutional settings and the less severely retarded clients more likely to live in community residential settings. Among the clients who live in community residential settings, the most severely re-

tarded lived in foster homes, the least severely retarded lived in semi-independent apartments, and those in the middle lived in group homes. Similarly, it was found that, at any particular time, level of retardation was related to vocational status, with the less severely retarded clients more likely to hold competitive jobs and the more severely retarded clients more likely to attend sheltered workshops or have no day placement at all.

However, a longitudinal perspective reveals that the relationships among level of retardation and residential and vocational statuses have fluctuated considerably across time periods. For example, during the 1970s the population of state institutions shifted toward more severe retardation as the less severely retarded residents were released to community-based facilities. Similarly, clients once considered to be much too severely retarded to live in community residential facilities are now routinely accepted into such programs. Thus, the service delivery system and professional opinion have shifted considerably during the 1970s. Level of retardation appears not to dictate residential status in any absolute manner. Rather, the relationship between level of retardation and residential status is reflective of the contemporary situation regarding availability of services and professional beliefs about the types of clients most appropriate for different types of services, which in turn have been influenced by broad trends such as normalization and deinstitutionalization.

Similarly, an examination of trends over time reveals that although vocational status is related to level of retardation, broad social trends and conditions also have exerted a powerful influence on this outcome. For example, the number of mentally retarded persons holding competitive jobs was much higher during World War II than either before or after, owing to labor market factors. Moreover, even at one point in time, it appears that vocational success is more probable among mentally retarded persons of all levels of retardation who live in less complex communities than in more complex communities. Thus, the relationship between vocational status and level of retardation appears to be mediated by social trends and social conditions.

It was interesting to find that although residential and vocational status were in part related to level of retardation, no such relationship was found between level of retardation and either downward vocational mobility or downward residential mobility (recidivism). Both types of downward mobility appeared to be related to the presence of maladaptive behavior, not to level of retardation. Societal trends also were found to be related to downward mobility. For example, whereas in the 1950s approximately half of the institution residents who were released to the community were returned to the institution, by the 1970s the recidivism rate dropped to 25%, as the availability of community residential alternatives increased dramatically.

Much less is known about the relationship between level of retardation and receipt of services. However, one study did suggest that an inverse relationship exists, with those most severely retarded and most in need of services least likely to receive such services.

Earlier in this chapter, a question was raised regarding the nature of the relationship between classified level of retardation and social status. Is the process by which a mentally retarded person is assigned to a particular social status *ascribed* on the basis of the fixed characteristics of the individual (particularly level of retardation) or *achieved* on the basis of the voluntary actions taken by the individual? The available evidence suggests that the process of assigning a mentally retarded person to a social status contains elements characteristic of both ascribed and achieved statuses. To illustrate, level of retardation was found to be related to residential and vocational statuses, but not to completely determine these outcomes. Thus, in the strictest sense of the concept, residential and vocational statuses are not ascribed statuses because they are not wholly determined by the fixed characteristics of the individual. On the other hand, residential and vocational statuses are not wholly determined by the voluntary actions of the individual and are therefore not true achieved statuses. Although voluntary activity does have a role in determining vocational and residential statuses, mentally retarded persons are far from free to independently select places in which to live and work. Professionals are in greater control, and they in turn are limited by the limits of the service delivery system and are influenced by broad social and economic trends.

To summarize, the social status of a mentally retarded person appears to be determined by at least four categories of factors:

1. the characteristics of the individual, particularly classified level of retardation and maladaptive behavior;
2. the voluntary actions taken by the individual—his/her preferences, level of motivation, etc.;
3. the beliefs held by professionals in the field of mental retardation; and
4. broad social trends and conditions.

The level of mental retardation does not wholly determine social status. Instead, this level interacts with the broad social context in determining where a mentally retarded person will live and work, and what services he or she will receive.

References

Aanes, D., & Moen, M. Adaptive behavior changes of group home residents. *Mental Retardation*, 1976, **14**, 36–40.

Abel, T. M. A study of a group of subnormal girls successfully adjusted in industry in the community. *American Journal of Mental Deficiency*, 1940, **45**, 66–72.

Albizu-Miranda, C., Matlin, N., & Stanton, H. *The Successful Retardate*. Hato Rey, Puerto Rico: Commonwealth of Puerto Rico, mimeo, 1966.

Appell, M. J., Williams, C. M., & Fishell, K. N. Factors in the job holding ability of the mentally retarded. *Vocational Guidance Quarterly*, Winter 1964–65, 127.

Baker, B. L., Seltzer, G. B., & Seltzer, M. M. *As close as possible: Community residences for retarded adults*. Boston: Little, Brown and Company, 1977.

Baller, W. R. A study of the present social status of a group of adults who, when they were in elementary schools, were classified as mentally deficient. *Psychological Monographs*, 1936, **18**, 165–244.

Barrett, A. M., Relos, R., & Eisele, J. Vocational success and attitudes of mentally retarded toward work and money. *American Journal of Mental Deficiency*, 1965, **70**, 102–107.

Bell, N. *IQ as a factor in a community lifestyle of previously institutionalized retardates*. Research and Training Center in Mental Retardation, Lubbock, Texas. Paper presented at Region V AAMD Meeting, New Orleans, October 1974.

Bjaanes, A. T., Butler, E. W., & Kelly, B. R. Placement type and client functional level as factors in provision of services aimed at increasing adjustment. In R. H. Bruininks, C. E. Meyers, B. B. Sigford, & K. C. Lakin (Eds.), *Deinstitutionalization and community adjustment of mentally retarded people*. Washington, D.C.: American Association on Mental Deficiency, 1981.

Borthwick, S., Meyers, C. E., & Eyman, R. K. Comparative adaptive and maladaptive behavior of mentally retarded clients of five residential settings in three Western states. In R. H. Bruininks, C. E. Meyers, B. B. Sigford, & K. C. Lakin (Eds.), *Deinstitutionalization and community adjustment of mentally retarded people*. Washington, D.C.: American Association on Mental Deficiency, 1981.

Bruininks, R. H., Hauber, F. A., & Kudla, M. J. *National survey of community residential facilities: A profile of facilities and residents in 1977*. Project Report No. 5. Minneapolis: University of Minnesota, 1979.

Bruininks, R. H., Hill, B., & Thorsheim, M. J. *A profile of specially licensed foster homes for mentally retarded people in 1977*. Project Report No. 6. Minneapolis: University of Minnesota, 1980.

Campbell, V., Smith, R., & Wool, R. Adaptive behavior scale differences in scores of mentally retarded individuals referred for institutionalization and those never referred. *American Journal of Mental Deficiency*, 1982, **86**, 4, 425–428.

Coakley, F. Study of feebleminded wards employed in war industries. *American Journal of Mental Deficiency*, 1945, **50**, 301–306.

Collman, R. D., & Newlyn, D. Employment success of educationally subnormal ex-pupils in England. *American Journal of Mental Deficiency*, 1956, **60**, 733–743.

Cowan, L., & Goldman, M. The selection of the mentally deficient for vocational training and the effect of this training on vocational success. *Journal of Consulting Psychiatry*, 1959, **23**, 78–84.

Daniels, L. K. Intelligence and vocational adjustment. In L. K. Daniels (Ed.), *Vocational rehabilitation of the mentally retarded*. Springfield, Ill.: Charles C. Thomas, 1974.

Eagle, E. Prognosis and outcome of community placement in institutionalized retardates. *American Journal of Mental Deficiency*, 1967, **72**, 232–243.

Elkin, L. Predicting productivity of trainable retardates on experimental workshop tasks. In L. K. Daniels (Ed.), *Vocational rehabilitation of the mentally retarded*, Springfield, Ill.: Charles C. Thomas, 1974.

Eyman, R. K., & Arndt, S. Life-span development of institutionalized and community-based mentally retarded residents. *American Journal of Mental Deficiency*, 1982, **86**, 342–350.

Eyman, R. K., & Call, T. Maladaptive behavior and community placement of mentally retarded persons. *American Journal of Mental Deficiency*, 1977, **82**, 137–144.

Eyman, R. K., Demaine, G. C., & Lei, T. Relationship between community environments and resident changes in adaptive behavior: A path model. *American Journal of Mental Deficiency*, 1979, **83**, 330–338.

Ferguson, T., & Kerr, A. W. Handicapped youth: A report on the employment problems of handicapped young people in Glasgow. London: Oxford University Press, 1960.

Fry, L. M. A predictive measure of work success for high grade mental defectives. *American Journal of Mental Deficiencies*, 1956, **61**, 402–408.

Gellman, W., & Glaser, N. M. *A scale for evaluating and predicting the employability of vocationally handicapped persons*. Chicago: Jewish Vocational Service, mimeo, Bulletin 7, 1959.

Gollay, E., Freedman, R., Wyngaarden, M., & Kurtz, N. R. *Coming back: The community experiences of deinstitutionalized mentally retarded people*. Cambridge, Mass.: Abt Associates Inc., 1978.

Haskell, R. H., & Strauss, A. A. One hundred institutionalized mental defectives in the armed forces. *American Journal of Mental Deficiency*, 1943, **48**, 67–71.

Heber, R. F., & Dever, R. B. Research on the habilitation of the mentally retarded. In H. C. Haywood (Ed.), *Socio-cultural aspects of mental retardation*. New York: Appleton-Century-Crofts, 1970.

Hegge, T. G. The occupational status of higher-grade mental defectives in the present emergency: A study of parolees from Wayne County Training School at Northville, Michigan. *American Journal of Mental Deficiency*, 1944, **49**, 86–98.

Hill, B. K., & Bruininks, R. H. *Physical and behavioral characteristics & maladaptive behavior of mentally retarded people in residential facilities*. Project Report No. 12. Minneapolis: University of Minnesota, 1981.

Jackson, R. N. Employment adjustment of educable mentally handicapped ex-pupils in Scotland. *American Journal on Mental Deficiency*, 1968, **72**, 924–930.

Jackson, R. N., & Butler, A. J. Prediction of successful community placement of institutionalized retardates. *American Journal of Mental Deficiency*, 1963, **68**, 211–217.

Jones, P. P., & Jones, K. J. *The measurement of community placement success and its associated costs*. HEW Contract No. 05-74-278. Waltham: Brandeis University, 1976.

Kaufman, H. I. Diagnostic indices of employment with the mentally retarded. *American Journal of Mental Deficiency*, 1970, **74**, 777.

Kraus, J. Supervised living in the community and residential and employment stability of retarded male juveniles. *American Journal of Mental Deficiency*, 1972, **77**, 283–290.

Lakin, K. C. *Demographic studies of residential facilities for the mentally retarded*. Project Report No. 3. Minneapolis: University of Minnesota, undated.

Lambert, C. Examining career opportunities for the trainable retarded. *Canada's Mental Health*, 1972, **20**, 2.

Landesman-Dwyer, S., Berkson, G., & Romer, D. Affiliation and friendship of mentally retarded residents in group homes. *American Journal of Mental Deficiency*, 1979, **83**, 571-580.

Landesman-Dwyer, S., Stein, J. G., & Sackett, G. P. A behavioral and ecological study of group homes. In G. P. Sackett (Ed.), *Observing behavior*. Vol. 1. Baltimore: University Park Press, 1978.

Landesman-Dwyer, S., & Sulzbacher, F. M. Residential placement and adaptation of severely and profoundly retarded individuals. In R. H. Bruininks, C. E. Meyers, B. B. Sigford, & K. C. Lakin (Eds.), *Deinstitutionalization and community adjustment of mentally retarded people*. Washington, D.C.: American Association on Mental Deficiency, 1981.

Larson, K. H. *The characteristics of vocationally successful mentally retarded youth as described by two types of intelligence tests*. Unpublished doctoral dissertation, University of Oregon, 1964.

Lei, T., Nihira, L., Sheehy, N., Meyers, C. E. A study of small family care homes for mentally retarded people. In R. H. Bruininks, C. E. Meyers, B. B. Sigford, & K. C. Lakin (Eds.), *Deinstitutionalization and community adjustment of mentally retarded people*. Washington, D.C.: American Association on Mental Deficiency, 1981.

Linton, R. *The study of man*. New York: Appleton-Century-Crofts, 1936.

Mayeda, T., & Sutter, P. Deinstitutionalization phase II. In R. H. Bruininks, C. E. Meyers, B. B. Sigford, & K. C. Lakin (Eds.), *Deinstitutionalization and community adjustment of mentally retarded people*. Washington, D.C.: American Association on Mental Deficiency, 1981.

McCarver, R., & Craig, E. Placement of the retarded in the community: Prognosis and outcome. *International Review of Research in Mental Retardation*, 1974, **7**, 145–207.

McIntosh, W. J. Follow-up study of 1000 non-academic boys. *Exceptional Children*, 1949, **15**, 167–169.

McKeon, R. M. Mentally retarded boys in war time. *Mental Hygiene*, 1946, **30**, 47–55.

Mercer, J. R. *Labelling the mentally retarded: clinical and social system perspectives on mental retardation*. Berkeley: University of California Press, 1973.

Moen, M., Bogen, D., & Aanes, D. Follow-up of mentally retarded adults successfully and unsuccessfully placed in community. *Hospital and Community Psychiatry*, 1975, **26**, 752–754.

Nihira, L., & Nihira, K. Normalized behavior in community placement. *Mental Retardation*, 1975, **13**, 9–13.

O'Connor, G. *Home is a good place: A national perspective of community residential facilities for developmentally disabled persons*. Washington, D.C.: American Association on Mental Deficiency, 1976.

O'Connor, N., & Tizard, J. *The social problem of mental deficiency*. London: Pergamon Press, 1956.

Pagel, S. E., & Whitling, C. A. Readmissions to a state hospital for mentally retarded persons: Reasons for community placement failure. *Mental Retardation*, 1978, **16**, 164–166.

Pearson, D. M. Social class and vocational outcomes of adult mentally retarded males. *Social Service Review*, 1975, **49**, 2.

Phelps, W. R. Attitudes related to the employment of the mentally retarded. *American Journal of Mental Deficiency*, 1965, **69**, 575–585.

Pinkard, C. *Predicting the vocational capacity of retarded young adults*. MacDonald Training Center Foundation, Research Division, Tampa, Florida, 1963.

Schalock, R. L., & Harper, R. S. A systems approach to community living skills training. In R. H. Bruininks, C. E. Meyers, B. B. Sigford, & K. C. Lakin (Eds.), *Deinstitutionalization and community adjustment of mentally retarded people*. Washington, D.C.: American Association on Mental Deficiency, 1981.

Schalock, R. L., Harper, R. S., & Genung, T. Community integration of mentally retarded adults: Community placement and program success. *American Journal of Mental Deficiency*, 1981, **85**, 478–488.

Scheerenberger, R. C. A study of public residential facilities. *Mental Retardation*, 1976, **14**, 32–35.

Seltzer, G. B. Community residential adjustment: The relationship among environment, performance, and satisfaction. *American Journal of Mental Deficiency*, 1981, **85**, 624–630.

Seltzer, M. M. Deinstitutionalization and vocational adjustment. In P. Mittler (Ed.), *Frontiers of knowledge in mental retardation*. Vol. 1. Baltimore: University Park Press, 1981.

Seltzer, M. M., & Seltzer, G. B. *Context for competence: A study of retarded adults living and working in the community*. Cambridge, Mass.: Educational Projects Inc., 1978.

Song, A. Y., & Song, R. H. Prediction of job efficiency of institutionalized retardates in the community. *American Journal of Mental Deficiency*, 1969, **73**, 567–571.

Stephens, W. B., & Peck, J. R. *Success of young adult male retardates*. Washington, D.C.: The Council for Exceptional Children, 1968.

Sutter, P., Mayeda, T., Call, T., Yanagi, G., & Yee, S. Comparison of successful and unsuccessful community-placed mentally retarded persons. *American Journal of Mental Deficiency*, 1980, **85**, 262–267.

Thiel, G. W., Relationship of IQ, adaptive behavior, age and environmental demand to community placement success of mentally retarded adults. *American Journal of Mental Deficiency*, 1981, **86**, 208–211.

Tobias, J., & Gorelick, J. Work characteristics of retarded adults at trainable levels. In L. K. Daniels (Ed.), *Vocational rehabilitation of the mentally retarded*. Springfield, Ill.: Charles C. Thomas, 1974.

Voelker, P. H. The value of certain selected factors in predicting early post-school employment for educable mentally retarded males. *Dissertation Abstracts*, 1962, **23**, 3243.

Weaver, T. R. The incident of maladjustment among mental defectives in the military environment. *American Journal of Mental Deficiency*, 1946, **51**, 238–246.

Willer, B., & Intagliata, J. *Deinstitutionalization of mentally retarded persons in New York State*. Final Report submitted to DHEW Region II, Office of Human Development, Developmental Disabilities Office, 1980.

Willer, B., Intagliata, J., & Wicks, N. Return of retarded adults to natural families: Issues and results. In R. H. Bruininks, C. E. Meyers, B. B. Sigford, & K. C. Lakin (Eds.), *Deinstitutionalization and community adjustment of mentally retarded people*. Washington, D.C.: American Association on Mental Deficiency, 1981.

Wolfensberger, W. Vocational preparation and occupation, in A. A. Baumeister (Ed.), *Mental retardation: Appraisal, education, and rehabilitation*. Chicago: Aldine Publishing Co., 1967.

PART IV
ASSESSMENT

13 STANDARD INTELLIGENCE TESTS AND RELATED ASSESSMENT TECHNIQUES

Murry Morgenstern

Historical Trends

After almost a century of conflict over the uses and abuses of standard tests, the critics of the tests are now in the ascendant—in professional and lay literature and in the courts.

The controversy within the framework of mental retardation has historically centered upon the use of a psychometric definition of intelligence as sole criterion for determining school placement, institutional commitment and legal incompetence. Although experts in the field such as Doll, Penrose, and Tredgold objected to this use, reliance on IQ as sole determinant became standard practice.

While IQ-yielding tests measure a behavioral performance on tasks assumed to be characteristic of an individual's intellectual development at successive ages, the momentum of the tests, rapidly accelerating to national influence, generated a set of assumptions about the meaning of IQ. These assumptions became, in effect, an act of faith that: (1) IQ reflected a global intelligence, culture-transcendent and unmodifiable; (2) IQ constituted a set of intellectual attributes that were not simply those most socially valued, but represented inherent or constitutional capacity of an individual for competent participation in society (Anastasi, 1968).

However, concurrently with the traditional reliance on IQ in mental retardation, a series of ongoing advances by investigators in the general field of intelligence emerged; in effect, pluralistic considerations were challenging the simplistic view of a test-measured global intelligence. Multifactored analyses of intelligence were introduced by Spearman (1927), elaborated by B. B. Cattell (1963), Guilford (1967), Thorndike (1927), Thurstone (1938), Vernon (1950). A gradual trend developed which led to a definition of intelligence in terms of functions and processes. Factor analysis indicated that intelligence is not a single trait or attribute but a composite of dynamic components that can be respectively identified and related to aspects of behavioral performance. The earlier emphasis on structural definitions and on etiology, and the related emphasis on a dual perspective (endogenous or exogenous, hereditary or familial, and so on) were yielding to a holistic view of individual behavior in which the psychometric measurement of intelligence played a less dominant role.

Consideration of the social aspects of that performance also became significant. Longitudinal studies of children released from institutional care and adopted at early ages showed high rates of social adaptation as well as empirical evidence of significant improvement in IQ. (Skodak & Skeels, 1949; Wellman, 1945).

Nevertheless, despite such advances and the successive recommendations by the American Association on Mental Deficiency that measures of adaptive behavior be used in conjunction with IQ for the determination of mental retardation, very few states adopted this recommendation as mandatory. In the schools particularly, administrative policy continued to place reliance on the IQ alone for placement in special classes, despite the continued support of the significance of social-adaptive behavior in studies in mental retardation (Geloff, 1963; Robinson and Robinson, 1978). Of the many definitions in this regard, Heber's (1961) was the most influential. Mental retardation, according to Heber, refers to subaverage general intellectual functioning which originates during the developmental period and is associated with impairment in adaptive behavior. Heber's definition, as analyzed by Sattler (1974), has many implications which shape current clinical views: (1) the diagnosis of mental states must be only a description of present behavior; prediction of later intelligence is a separate process; (2) the contribution of individually administered intelligence tests is specifically recognized; (3) diagnosis is tied to the developmental process, rather than to etiology, with behavioral description related to the individual; (4) the emphasis is given to mild forms of retardation. Mental retardation is seen as no more or less than a behavioral symptom, not necessarily stable from one time of life to another, and accompanied by any of several genetic, physiological, emotional, and experiential factors.

Another aspect of IQ significance underwent investigation, namely the relation of test scores to environmental influences. Findings in this regard posed the first powerful challenge to the dominance of IQ in a national forum of controversy during the decade of 1965 to 1975.

It is now well known that children of minorities and of the lower socioeconomic classes of society in general are overly represented in mental retardation populations, particularly among those in classes for the mildly retarded (EMR). Whether this overrepresentation results primarily from intelligence test results is not fully clear. As MacMillan (1977) pointed out, testing is not the first step in the decision to place a child in a special class. School adjustment, academic achievement, as well as teacher referral may have equal importance in overrepresentation. In fact, Anhurst and Meyers (1973) suggest that test results may protect minority children from erroneous classification decisions.

Recent studies by Mercer (1973, 1974) and others have shown the extent to which cultural bias on the tests may account for the frequency with which minority children are considered mentally retarded. Black, Mexican-American, Puerto Rican, Indian, and children of impoverished families in general are identified as mentally retarded in numbers disproportionate to their respective distributions in the national population. Assessment of these children shows that a high proportion are not significantly impaired when their adaptation to nonschool environments is evaluated. Mercer (1973) refers to the term "situationally retarded" as a description of these children, in distinction to the "comprehensively retarded." Critics of the labeling process attribute the classification of many of these children as mentally retarded in any form to the selective cultural orientation of the IQ tests, which by virtue of the measures of statistical regression from the mean, place them automatically within the framework of mental retardation without supportive evidence.

Looking at these issues in historical perspective, a broad range of studies were taken, starting in the 1940s, on the differences in group-mean IQ relative to environmental criteria. These earlier classic studies on large population samples provided massive data that higher mean IQ correlates with higher social, economic, racial, and occupational status; the lower mean IQ correlates all too well with disadvantaged segments of the population, white or black, ethnically differentiated or not (Anastasi, 1968; McNemar, 1942; Shuey, 1966; Tyler, 1966). Children also differ in group mean IQ by regional environment, relative to metropolitan, suburban, and rural circumstance (Coleman, 1966).

These data clearly indicate that limitations implicit in disadvantaged settings will tend to limit the developmental experience associated with certain aspects of intelligence as measured by IQ, in comparison with the expansion of that developmental experience offered by the more advantaged settings: in short, that differences in preparative experience for the tests are reflected in the differences in group mean IQ. If so, the findings provide a basis for the many well articulated changes in the literature that the tests are culturally biased. That is, tests, in their emphasis, content, structure, administration, and possibly intent (Jencks, 1972; Kamin, 1974), favor the children of the white, middle class majority and are thus discriminatory against the children of disadvantaged populations.

The findings also challenge another traditional assumption regarding standardization practices in intelligence testing, namely the assumption that the sample populations used for standardization properly represent demographic and cultural variance in the composition of national population and that the tests are therefore valid for use with children of differing social, economic, cultural, ethnic, and racial strata.

The environmentalist issue thus posed a challenge to the cultural neutrality of IQ, both in terms of the test orientation and in terms of the test technology. Several studies provided evidence that: (1) environmental variance affects variance in group mean IQ, (2) environmental intervention can produce an increase in IQ, (3) IQ does not measure a genetically based limitation in intelligence unless other evidence in addition to IQ is presented, and (4) an IQ score represents significant developmental experience and that all children do not share equally in the quality of that experience. These postulations represent, in essence, the position of the environmentalists (Cronbach, 1975; Hilliard, 1980; Kamin, 1974; Lewontin, 1970).

The hereditarians take the opposite position that: (1) underlying genetic processes significantly affect racial intelligence, (2) environment plays a much smaller role in shaping intelligence, and (3) intervention, in view of racially based genetics, cannot achieve significant improvement in IQ (Eyesenck, 1971; Herrnstein, 1971; Jensen, 1969). The controversy thus flared into open public debate when Jensen (1969) published a long paper in the Harvard Educational Review, presenting his findings derived from studies of resemblance between identical twins raised apart, identical versus fraternal twins reared together, families having their own children versus adopted children. These findings formed the basis of Jensen's conclusions: (1) 80% of the variation in intelligence among group mean IQ is determined by heredity; (2) only 20% can be attributed to environmental factors; (3) the lower mean IQ of black Americans, compared with whites, represents genetically based inferiority among blacks; and (4) owing to the limitations in genetic potential, interventions with disadvantaged groups have little chance of success. Herrnstein (1971) took a more moderate position, observing that "the IQ test is merely a measurable sample of an individual's performance, lasting about a half-hour, and useful for predicting behavior of the sort that is thought of as "intellectual." He also observes that significant heritability, in practical terms, translates into significant individual differences in learning from a given educational curriculum.

In a major work on mental retardation, Jensen (1970) gave a more cogent explanation of his thinking, summarized as follows: (1) although the intelligence tests emphasize those attributes of intelligence most socially valued, they nevertheless provide an unbiased measure of general intelligence, owing to the following factors: (a) two types of mental ability exist, "associative abilities" and "cognitive abilities"; (b) these two types of ability have underlying genetic processes that are essentially different; (c) socioeconomic considerations in intelligence are largely independent of associative abilities, but are correlated with cognitive abilities. Jensen then goes on to say that in severe grades of mental retardation both associative and cognitive abilities are markedly deficient. In mild forms of mental retardation, the deficiency occurs primarily in cognitive abilities. He then proposes that primary retardation should be the term used to refer to deficits in both sets of abilities and secondary retardation be employed to refer to deficit in cognitive abilities. Individuals who achieve IQs in the range between -1 and -2 standard deviations below the mean (IQ 70 to 85) are largely from groups referred to as culturally disadvantaged. Those who are average in associative abilities but deficient in cognitive abilities should not be designated as retarded.

Despite the merits of this 1970 work, the controversy incited by his paper of 1969 continued to erupt, with cultural bias of the standard intelligence tests as the central issue. As Cronbach (1975) remarked, "It is the struggle for the minds of men and not the specifics of mental tests which generate such controversies." Both sides of the hereditary-environment controversy have supported their positions with a collection of evidence that has important implications in regard to test interpretation. Regardless of one's position, Anastasi (1967) makes the point that the most usable knowledge about psychological characteristics is not the relative contributions of an individual's heredity and environment, but how amenable and under what conditions these characteristics are subject to change. Furthermore, at this time, there is no feasible way of separating these influences when interpreting test results for an individual.

Social issues, however, which represent a "struggle for the minds of men," do not wait for science to resolve them; the California litigation on discriminatory uses of the standard intelligence tests went on for eight years, from 1971 to 1979. In this case (*Larry P. v. Wilson Rileys, Superintendent of Public Instruction for the State of California et al.*) a landmark decision was handed down in 1979. It found unconstitutional the use of intelligence tests to place black children in classes for the educable mentally retarded. In the middle of this lengthy trial, the Education For All Handicapped Children Act of 1975 was passed. Thus, before the decision was handed down, the state of California banned the use of the tests for EMR placement of all children, white or black.

This controversy, the culmination of six decades of debate, has been instructive. In spite of the California case, intelligence tests are not irremediably damaged, since administrative abuses of IQ for placement were well known before the litigation ensued. The case simply emphasizes that such practices must be stopped. The various accusations against the cultural bias of the tests were needed in order to emphasize among clinicians that adjustments and accountability for cultural deficiency must be undertaken both in the analysis of the test scores and in unbiased assessment (Bersoff, 1981).

Most importantly, the controversy served to improve the current state of the art in the evaluation of low IQ children. The opposing arguments, the court decisions and the Education For All Handicapped Children Act of 1975 succeeded, to a greater degree than any previous effort to put national emphasis on an assessment approach to the determination of mental retardation, and to reduce the use of IQ to its proper role as an alert to the need for assessment and as a guide to interventional action (Reschly, 1979).

Looking retrospectively at the trends and events occurring in the period from Goddard's first applications of the Binet-Simon Scale to a psychometric definition of mental retardation up to the present implementation policies of PL 94-142, work in mental retardation has come a long way. Implementation of the 1975 Act now supports the movement toward pluralistic and multifactored unbiased assessment of individuals. In this current philosophy, mental retardation is viewed in behavioral terms, involving these components: (1) intellectual behavior, in terms of the analyses of individual functions in the mental process which have a relationship to learning and academic performance; (2) adaptive behaviors relative to the ability to learn and to perform, which includes aspects of motivation, cooperation, emotional stability, and related characteristics of personality as expressed in behavior; and (3) evaluation of interventions available and applicable to the individual which appear feasible for altering negative aspects or limitations of behavior.

The causes of an individual's retardation are not directly relevant to this process, whether organic, genetic, or environmental. The relevance of work in assessment is that, at a particular point in an individual's life, that person is unable, for whatever reason, to conform to the expectations which society sets for an individual in relation to his peers. Mental retardation is not a state unto itself nor a behavior that exists in a vacuum. It is a reflection of the social perceptions of others in regard to the intellectual and social behavior of a given individual. What we do, conceptually, is

bring clinical techniques combined with responsive perception and experience to the problem.

Current Trends

The Assessment Process

Although it is beyond the scope of this chapter to discuss at length the concepts, elements, and use of assessment, a brief description is presented since intelligence testing is a major aspect of this process.

A multidimensional model of behavior in which each dimension, intellectual, adaptive, developmental, physiological, and psychosocial, interacts with all other dimensions to produce one continuum of individual behavior underpins current assessment philosophy. This model is viewed in the context of the individual's age and his environmental milieu.

The pivotal functions in this assessment strategy are observation, measurement, interpretation, structural development of inferences and hypotheses, and synthesis of findings from both empirical and inferential sources (Kaplan, 1970). Based on data from antecedent events in an individual's life in relation to current characteristics, specific interventions are monitored.

In addition to test instruments and evidence of physical, neurological or psychological impairments, there are cognitive, perceptual, discriminative, adaptive, and emotional functions not directly accessible from the instruments, observations, or client history which call for inferential conceptualization by the psychologist. Clinical understanding and technology must be malleable and applicable to diverse types of clients, each of whom presents variable behaviors. Mental retardation has usually been defined in negative terms; a behavior deviation from the standards and expectations of society (Throne, 1970). This deficit has historically been the focus of social judgment and research procedures. While assessment necessarily considers such deficits, it also explores observable and potential assets on which possibilities for positive change rest.

In work with individuals considered severely retarded, the clinician deals with impairment of such severity that standardized instruments may have little applicability so that innovative efforts are required to secure enough information about remaining functions upon which to base a useful evaluation. In regard to clients who are mildly mentally retarded, assessment especially requires depth analysis of the role of environmental influences or disorders in the family setting, and, in some instances, the determination whether mental retardation is an appropriate designation for presenting problems (Karp, Michal-Smith, & Morgenstern, 1978).

The task of the clinician is to identify and differentiate variations in behavior through sensitive observations, test findings, and analysis and to ascertain that all these findings corroborate any evaluatory hypothesis (Pruyser, 1979). In effect, much depends on the individual psychologist, which is both a strength and weakness. The weakness, in this form of clinical assessment, is its dependence on the quality of the clinician. A strength, given the theoretical and implementary integrity of the psychologist, lies in the flexibility of observation he brings to efforts that extend beyond the obvious. In so doing, the psychologist must call upon his resources of experience in the inferential process since the analysis of test scores, although considered as empirical data, is fundamentally inferential. The inferential quality of assessment is safeguarded to the degree that it does not rely on any one measurement instrument or technique; it correlates data from a variety of sources and from a multidimensional view of behavior; it constitutes an intensive effort to perceive the client in the round, so to speak, as a composite of interactive modalities of behavior, and yet as more than the sum of his parts. It is, in effect, a holistic approach to behavior at the philosophical level; an analytic and inferential process at the scientific level (Hirt & Kaplan, 1967). In essence, assessment is neither defined by nor limited to the administration of tests; it cannot be an evaluation solely in terms of psychometric validity. It also requires conceptual validity or the extent to which hypotheses about a person are confirmed and consistent with observations that follow from the model of that individual constructed in the assessment process (Rapaport, Gill, & Schafer, 1968).

Concepts of Intelligence and IQ

The development of tests to measure intelligence precisely has intensified efforts to describe and understand it. However, definitions of intelligence continue to plague the philosopher, scientist and educator. Intelligence is generally considered easier to measure than define (Jensen, 1969). It is an ambiguous term, referring both to processes of intellection and their accumulated outcome as evinced in a body of knowledge, store of insights, acquired cognitive skills, and their ever-ready generalization and application to new situations (Pruyser, 1979). Textbook definitions of intelligence vary widely because of such factors as heredity, cultural influence, early learning, and how much general ability is complemented by specific talents. In regard to processes of intelligence, the information-processing approach has attempted to add to the understanding of the factors of intelligence (Sternberg, 1981). Examples of processes include encoding stimulus information, inferring relations between stimuli, and applying these relations to new contexts.

A wide variety of competencies including personality or behavioral factors are subsumed in prominent theories and definitions. Among them are Wechsler's global definition (1958) and Guilford's three dimensional model (1956) which suggest that intelligence is a multifaceted rather than a unitary characteristic and that IQ tests do not measure all aspects of intelligence. Several general subjects appear across many definitions; learning capacity, acquired knowledge and adaptability (Cronbach, 1975; Guilford, 1972). A motivational component also appears frequently in many definitions. For example, Thurstone in an early symposium (1921) defined the intelligent organism as one with the volitional capacity to translate the products of the mind into actions that benefit the organism in its social milieu.

It seems inconceivable to define and understand mental retardation without including intelligence as a fundamental concept. Various studies to understand the nature of intelligence have investigated what it is that mentally retarded persons lack. Borkowski and Cavanaugh (1979) and Zeaman (1978) have attempted to understand retardation in terms of ineffective functioning of the operations of acquisition, retention, and transfer components in their interaction with control processes. Some of their research results has shown marked improvement in the learning and recall of mentally retarded individuals. Budoff (1968) and Feuerstein (1979) utilized performance components (reasoning) for the solution of items such as analogies, series completions, and classifications at the time the test is actually taken with consequent improvement in IQ scores.

In all tests, intelligence is considered a biopsychological variable that follows the normal distribution curve in large populations. In large samples, which include those with handicapping conditions, the distribution of IQs is skewed to the left which represents an increment over the expected biological variation. This increment, above the statistically expected distribution of intelligence, represents individuals who could be considered deviant in some special way (i.e., culturally deprived, having psychotic disturbances, or neurological disorders).

Intelligence quotients are compound measures derived from number values assigned to successes on a range of diverse tasks graded for difficulty. The IQ is determined by the particular intelligence test used and is based on the intellectual behavior sampled by the test, the statistical treatment of the scores, the ratio of mental age to chronological age, and the standard deviation from the mean. Essentially, the IQ summarizes in numerical language, a pattern of intellectual functioning. "No major, reputable test today uses an actual IQ score; that is a score based on the ratio of mental age to chronological age, multiplied by 100. Yet, test descriptions in basic texts continue to report the ratio IQ concept" (Reschly, 1981).

Nature of Intelligence Tests

Standard intelligence tests provide a predetermined set of conditions and demands, both of which call for a diversity of cognitive, perceptual, and organizational skills. Competence in these skills is based on social and educational expectancies of "normal behavior" in life situations. Whether an individual will or will not need to face equal demands and need to utilize all of these skills remains an assumption. The tests create conditions of variable levels of stress and other emotional components in the testing situation. In their content, they also create conditions of direction, communication, ambiguity, interpretation and discrimination that require the client to engage in some very complex processes to understand the task and to perform it. Organization and integration of these processes produce an appropriate response that is communicated appropriately to the examiner. These responses are considered to be the finished or end products of a complex processing system, from which the integrity or impairment of these various processes are inferred. Inferences drawn from the nature and patterns of responses are considered to indicate the variability of strengths and weaknesses respective to the different processes mobilized by the client to meet performance criteria. In the mobilization of these behaviors and in the stress situation of testing, other behaviors emerge, which provide observational data to form a basis for the examiner's understanding of personality organization, its stability or vulnerability, control of attention and concentration, comprehension of social reality, control and range of energy deployment, interpersonal reactions, and tolerance for anxiety and stress. Consequently, the results of the tests must be submitted to an analysis of functions underlying the test tasks and demands and of the behaviors exhibited by the client which relate to disturbance in these underlying functions.

Some Assumptions Underlying Tests

(a) The examiner is skilled in administering tests; knowledgeable about normal and abnormal development; familiar with the interests and needs of various age groups and acquainted with the wide variety of available tests. Such a wide body of knowledge and competencies go hand in hand with discriminating observations of behavior patterns and the qualitative features of test performance and proficiency in interpreting test results.

(b) In order to assure the quality of data, tests must be reliable and valid. The obtained information should be internally consistent and similar over time. Information must be stable for it to be accurate. By using norm-referenced measures, estimates of reliability can be made by the Standard Error of Measurement, which establishes a range around the obtained score (Newland, 1974).

(c) Measures are valid when they provide accurate descriptions of behaviors they are designed to assess. A particular test cannot have validity for every purpose. Thus, the information it provides for a specific purpose determines its selection. The validity is all the more useful if it enhances the prediction of nontest behavior (Allen & Jefferson, 1962).

In a review of research, Cronbach (1956) concludes that statistical procedures are more useful in predicting human behavior than clinical judgment, particularly when complex, meaningful data are involved. However, considering the present state of knowledge, it does not seem wise to replace clinical test data with the computer hopper. It is sounder to make good use of both validation and reliability and statistical procedures, as well as clinical clues and insights.

(d) Another assumption is that the individual is performing at his best effort (Anastasi, 1976). Factors such as anxiety, difficulty in concentration, and poor motivation reduce the validity of test performance and must be accounted for. Zigler and Butterfield (1968), for example, obtained improved function of mentally retarded children on cognitive tasks by effecting quantitative and qualitative changes in their motivational levels.

Tests in Current Usage

Tests used today are based on those initially developed by Binet (1905), which were designed to identify slow children enrolled in regular classes rather than to resolve theoretical problems about the meaning of intelligence. His scales provided quantifiable and consistent observations, which heretofore were done informally by different observers, using different criteria from which different conclusions were drawn about the same person. Standardized procedures that involved specific administration criteria and norms as constructed in intelligence tests helped to protect individuals from uninformed and personal observations.

Currently, clinical practice further protects the individual against the vagaries of IQ test results by including adaptive behavior as a determining factor in mental retardation (Grossman, 1977).

The Stanford-Binet and the Wechsler Scales continue to be the main instruments to evaluate intellectual behavior in the field of mental retardation. The reliability of these tests for the normal population is well known, as are their limitations in regard to cultural neutrality, reviewed earlier. The Stanford-Binet originally designed for children can be divided into five broad categories of cognition: language, discrimination, manipulation, memory, reasoning, and problem solving (Lutey, 1967, Sattler, 1974, Valett, 1964). Considered as an indication of overall rate of mental growth, translated as mental age, the Binet reflects a conceptualization of intelligence as a general factor.

It taps a variety of mental tasks mainly manipulative and visual at the younger age levels (C.A. 5−) becoming increasingly weighted with verbal requirements, generally abstract, at the older levels (C.A. 6+) (McNemar, 1942). This task pattern of the Binet is both helpful and a disadvantage when evaluating slow developing individuals or those with special disabilities. It can be used with individuals whose general functioning is as low as the two-year level. Similarly within this range, the nonverbal child or adult can be tested on a wider array of abilities, thus reducing the limited response range imposed by the absence of speech. However, the Binet reduces the response repertoire of the motorically limited client at these same age levels, since few abilities can be tapped. At the higher age levels, the situation is reversed: a wider array of abilities to be tapped for the verbal but motor involved subject. Since many mentally retarded subjects do not reach the upper levels, which emphasize abstract and symbolic aspects of thought processes, its use is limited to pointing out an individual's deficits and not sufficiently helpful in determining the ability of many of these individuals to think or to perform on a practical and concrete level. Concreteness in problem presentation and in response processes is a frequent characteristic among mentally retarded persons. Thus, intelligence tests that favor certain kinds of mental activity over other kinds (e.g., the abstract and symbolic aspects of thinking) do not provide an exclusive foundation for the study of intellectual behavior, since it is clear that there are many functions within that behavior which are not represented or are underrepresented in the tests (Jones, 1949).

As is generally known, the Wechsler Scales are given as part of the test battery since they provide the most structure clarifying the characteristics of the person's response in relatively routine, sometimes over-learned, habituated, detached situations. The tests ask for facts, conventionally held judgments, and specified manipulations of materials. Meanings and definitions are requested, not associations, not what could be, but what is. In respect to age, flexibility of orientation, the capacity to adapt to diverse situations, and the ability to shift and alter intentions to meet different requirements may reflect an important value of our society (Boyer, 1964). The WISC-R, WPPSI, and WAIS are all clinically valuable, in that the structure of these tests and their respective subtests are easily accessible to identification of functions measured.

Research in mental retardation on comparative data obtained from both the Verbal and Performance Scales is conflicting; some of the studies indicate that mentally retarded subjects obtain significantly higher Performance Scale IQ than Verbal Scale IQ; other research indicates insignificant differences between the two scales (Baumeister & Bartlett, 1962). It is necessary then, in spite of the structural convenience of the Wechsler tests, to analyze the function and performance on each of the subtests on each scale to arrive at data upon which to base individual patterns of performance.

Stability of IQ

In clinical practice, pressures are often felt to make predictions about future intellectual functioning for planning purposes. Data from several studies (Walker & Gross, 1970) indicate that IQ test results are fairly stable for groups of mentally retarded individuals above age six. As is true for the general population, similarity of IQ depends on the age when the test was first given, the time interval between tests and retests, the reliability of the test, and the consistency of its content from one level to another (Robinson & Robinson, 1978). In some individual cases, there have been reports of dramatic changes of 15 points or more in IQ, which usually are associated with significant changes in the individual's environment and/or personal-social adjustment rather than representing random fluctuations.

Test Procedures Used

Prior to the implementation of test procedures, there are several sources of information used as guides to test planning and selection. These include an analysis of the client's history, initial observations of behavior, and consideration of the purpose of assessment. These considerations are used in test interpretation as well.

CLIENT HISTORY

Among other forms of data, there may be a record of a previous evaluation. It is well understood that many factors in a client's history contribute to the various successes and failures in the composite represented by previous IQ; cultural, situational, psychological, physical health, and other elements present at the time previous tests were taken. These factors are particularly relevant during childhood. It is this vulnerability of the IQ to other factors (Pruyser, 1979) that makes intelligence tests clinically significant. This aspect of the history provides a frame of reference in which to initiate informal and tentative hypotheses about the nature and pattern of developmental experience in a child's life which has relevance to IQ. What may emerge is a picture of stability or instability; chronic or acute difficulties; progressive deterioration or improvement, turning points either way that may be accessible to identification; and areas of specific behavioral assets or deficits that may have been environmentally observed.

By using the person as his own standard, present intellectual functioning is compared to previous findings. The study of client history is useful in providing inferential clues.

INITIAL CLIENT OBSERVATION

Initial observation of the client in the clinical setting prepares the examiner for the forthcoming evaluation. Behavior in interaction with the accompanying adult(s), with other staff members, and with objects and situations in the environment set the stage. Body behaviors, emotional behaviors, energy levels, distractibility, mannerisms in speech, language, tone and quality of voice, gait, posture, movements are also noteworthy. Physical appearance in itself is a factor to be reckoned with, not only as it may suggest physically based syndromes in mental retardation, but as it relates to the social and emotional attitudes of others toward the examinee in terms of social acceptance or repulsion (Ross, 1971). Developmental lags can also be observed by informal comparison with the norms for the pertinent age level: delayed motor development, delayed speech, delayed psychomotor skills, delayed judgment, delayed attention.

Recognition of overt physiological barriers to performance on certain testing tasks avoids raising the levels of client frustration by not introducing tests or test tasks that are inappropriate for his physical capabilities. For example, there are physical abilities necessary in order for the individual to respond to certain subtests on the WISC or WPPSI. Vision and/or hearing are necessary for most of the Verbal Scale subtests, while vision and hand use are necessary for the Performance Scale subtests. Allan and Jefferson

(1962) provide a table that outlines the physical abilities needed for performance on the Wechsler scales.

Culturally related problems can also be informally observed; i.e., linguistic styles and usage, comprehension of verbal communications, defensive or stressful behaviors, unfamiliarity with commonly known events. All of these observations are useful for informal evaluation of some of the presenting problems and for the planning of tactics in testing (Olmedo, 1981).

Bilingualism is directly related to the measurement of intelligence, since bilingual persons differ widely in terms of receptive and expressive dominance. It is the examiner's responsibility to determine in which language the client feels most comfortable or is most sophisticated. The goal is to use a language which maximizes the client's opportunity to understand requirements and to be able to respond by using his best language abilities. Testing repertoires have been increased by translating tests into other languages and by developing parallel forms. However, translation alone may not remove language biases unless the language used in the translation is characteristic of the client. Formal Spanish, for example, is not characteristic of the Spanish dialect spoken by Puerto Ricans or Mexican-Americans. This is compounded by the different dialects spoken by the various Spanish speaking subgroups. In addition, direct translations are still culture bound and do not yield technically equivalent forms. Until such time as the technical problems to minimize language differences of minority groups are resolved it will be necessary to use a wider variety of tests with emphasis on nonverbal measures. Examiner variables also affect test outcomes of minority clients. Some of the factors to be considered include the examiner's ethnic background, sex, level of acculturation of the client, and whether an interpreter is used when bilingualism is involved. The reader is directed to Mercer's research (1973), on the relevance of acculturation, socioeconomic status and family constellation to testing. Her work has resulted in the development of the SOMPA (System of Multicultural Pluralistic Assessment) (1974), in which estimated learning potentials are measured in relationship to sociocultural characteristics.

PURPOSE OF ASSESSMENT

Referrals for assessment come from a variety of different sources: schools, parents, clinics, hospitals, sheltered workshops, courts and other social and rehabilitative agencies. The reasons for requesting the assessment are equally varied: the school may be concerned about difficulties in academic learning, parental concern may be confined to unmanageable or immature behavior at home, a hospital may request determination of mental disability underlying physical symptoms, or the court may request findings for a determination of legal competence. The reasons, then, provided in the request for testing serve as guideposts to the overall direction and emphasis of the forthcoming assessment process and also serve as a frame of reference for the answers to be supplied later in the formal evaluation and report.

The Interpretive Process

The process of interpretation of test results beyond the obvious data of test and subtest scores is inferential, since in the previously presented theoretical framework, the responses are considered overt manifestations of a complex chain of cognitive, perceptual, and psychological processes. For example, in a task of manipulation, the skill also implicitly involves comprehension of the task, direction of attention, control of movement and other voluntary actions, form perception and discrimination, spatial relations and visual memory. Moreover, all these functions and processes are subject to the influence of other behavioral factors. In addition, a developmental view is required, since test results relative to an age group and other evidence of impairment are being examined. Thus, test results represent the interplay of maturation, cognitive and perceptual functions, sociocultural influences, emotional factors, and psychological/physiological processes. Each client, drawing upon these resources in terms of his or her respective integrity, produces a pattern of responses which reflect his or her successes and failures in these resources. Establishing the pattern from test and subtest scores is a relatively simple procedure; interpreting the pattern in a way that recognizes areas of dysfunction and function and then applying this recognition to objective intervention is, obviously, far more difficult.

Analysis of Test Results

Both the Binet and Wechsler Scales are structured to provide a high degree of goal and stimulus clarity. The goal or expected behavior is relatively clear and explicitly stated within a certain range. A particular task may have a built-in control error, in that the response itself provides the fit. For example, solutions to the Block Design test on the Wechsler Scales or Block Building on the Binet can be immediately checked against the model. The Information test on the Wechsler also has a degree of clarity, in that an item tells the subject what kind of an answer is required (e.g., "how *many* legs does a dog have?").

Although both tests are highly structured in goal and stimulus clarity, there are degrees of variation in these dimensions. Thus, comparisons of the subject's ability to deal with the varying demands of the subtests or tasks can be made. Some subtests are relatively clear in what they require. In the information subtest, instructions are explicit. The area of functioning tested is a narrow segment involving past learning and memory with a minimum of judgment and organization required. Comprehension, however, has less clarity. Though the questions require logical responses, there is less intrinsic directiveness as to the nature of the answers. Responses depend on an element of judgment relevant to what the questions implicitly rather than explicitly demand.

Therefore, intelligence test results can be analyzed in terms of both kinds of response: the response to a narrowly defined goal and the involved mental functions compared to the response to ambiguously defined tasks and other involved mental functions which call for a more sophisticated organizational process on the part of the subject. One can also consider that high-clarity goals draw to a larger degree upon the knowledge and the cultural and educational background of the subject, as in Information, Vocabulary, and Arithmetic; the high-ambiguity tasks call for decision making, comprehension of alternatives, and reasoning.

Consequently, it is extremely important that analysis of test results reflect the professional awareness of which test items measure what functions, in order to build structural inferences as to the respective functions and their capabilities in the individual client's response behavior.

THE STANFORD-BINET

The Binet, as discussed, measures general intelligence in a general way. It does not offer, in its construct, differentiated or identified sets of mental functions. Consequently, methodologies have been developed to provide this differentiation of cognitive functions considered to underlie the test structure. These include factor analysis, classification systems, and determination of spread of successes, the standard deviation method.

The results of factor analysis have been incorporated into the various classification systems; scatter analysis has been found to be limited in its applications to this test (Jones, 1949, Silverstein, 1968). In practice, then, one of the classification systems is used, combined with spread of successes and information derived from the standard deviation tables as a methodology for the analysis of results. The most well known classification systems were mentioned previously. All three are based on the factor-analytic studies of Jones (1949) and McNemar (1942).

Technically, respective tests scores are applied to the respective test classifications, using Sattler (1974) as an example: language, memory, conceptual thinking, reasoning, visual motor, and social intelligence. An individual analysis, rather than a deviation analysis of the spread of successes is undertaken, interpreting variability in relation to the client's own mental age (MA). For example, a child who is functioning in the mentally retarded range, but who has specific successes that are above the norms in relation to his MA, may be described as being better developed in those success areas than those at his average level of functioning, but overall at a level that is below average for children of his age. Thus, in this brief recapitulation of the essentials of the analytic process, we arrive at a pattern of strengths and weaknesses that in turn can be used to reflect larger patterns of behavior upon which to base an initial hypothesis. These larger patterns would reflect (1) the general level of intelligence as shown by MA or IQ, (2) the ability to profit from school experience, (3) the ability to synthesize or integrate perceptions in a comprehension of reality, and (4) the ability to comprehend relationships, verbal or spatial. These areas are, in essence, the intellectual function measurements provided by the Stanford-Binet. They also represent factors external to the Stanford-Binet, i.e., the behavioral characteristics of the client during the test situation as cross validated with observation data on that situation, cultural advantages or cultural deficits as confirmed by other data, neurological dysfunctions as confirmed by other evidence, and so on. In effect, by placing the pattern of test results in the context of all relative confirming or negating data, we form a hypothesis regarding the intellectual behavior of the client that reflects the IQ data, other forms of clinical evidence, and the inferential perceptions of the examiner derived from the pattern analysis.

THE WECHSLER SCALES

As mentioned, the various subtests are relatively rich in associative content in terms of such behavior as planning, judgment, attention, concentration, persistence, discrimination, and so on. Many of the subtests, however, preclude their interpretation as a strict measure of general intelligence. For example, the Digit Span test is a measure of attention, as well as short-term memory. The Picture Arrangement test requires nonverbal reasoning but also requires interpretation by the subject of social situations and planning ability in those social situations.

Other tasks represent a variety of functions that relate closely to the individual's cultural environment and previous education experience, such as specific information concept formations, and language development. The Arithmetic subtest requires many operations that are easier for subjects who have automized simple arithmetical tasks and require functions of reflection and mental operations for those who have not.

The tendency to use subtest scores or score clusters (factorial analysis) can be useful in serving as cues concerning an individual's habitual approach to various problem solving situations, his inclination to guess, persist or give up quickly. Qualitative interpretations of such behavior and the test scores provide tentative hypotheses until verified by other sources of data. Such analysis requires careful and thorough recording of responses and events which can become laborious but a critical endeavor.

Scatter analysis, while not appropriate with the Stanford-Binet, may be helpful with the Wechsler Scales in determining differentials affecting the respective functions, provided that (1) cultural and educational experience are accounted for and ruled out, and (2) the differentials observed are statistically significant. Also, performance on the Wechsler can be substantially affected by the examiner's behavior, in terms of the rephrasing (testing of limits) procedures used, and the degree to which the examiner provides clarification of tasks or cues to methods in problem solving. With these caveats in mind, scatter analysis is helpful for generating tentative hypotheses as to factors underlying the successes and weaknesses revealed by the pattern of "profiles" (Sattler, 1974). Marked variability then can be further assessed by placing the hypotheses derived from such analysis in the context of clinical observations and other forms of evidence. A comprehensive analysis and interpretation of the WISC-R has been done by Kaufman (1979).

In regard to mental retardation and levels of intelligence, Kaufman and Doppelt (1976) found no relationship to test scatter in the standardization of the WISC-R. Apparently, mentally retarded children are no more likely than normal children to have flat test profiles.

Alternate Measures

The IQ range of the Wechsler Scales (IQ 44-160) obviously does not meet the range requirements when there is a question of retardation in the severe or profound level. On these same levels, the actual number of items on the Binet may be quite narrow, so that an adequate representation of the many functions reflected in both tests may not be possible. In these instances, the Cattell (1950) may be used, the Bayley (1969), or the Gesell (1949), which investigate the chronological course of growth and development in four major areas: social, adaptive, language, and motor.

Tests such as the Peabody Picture Vocabulary Test (1965), the Slosson Intelligence Test (1963), and the Columbia Mental Maturity Scale (1959) are often used as substitute or alternate measures for the more conventional instruments. These brief devices can save time and provide individuals with physical handicaps or severe language problems with a response format to intelligence test items. Such tests must be used with caution even when the subject does not have the verbal or motor resources or abilities to respond to the other major tests as they sample only a limited range of abilities and do not permit qualitative analysis of responses. Comparability of scores to the Wechsler Scales or Stanford-Binet is particularly important when a decision about intellectual classification is to be made. Although very high correlations may be reported, it does not necessarily mean that the scores are comparable or interchangeable, but rather that the tests are measuring similar attributes. The scores may not be comparable because of differences in normative samples and/or differences in score scales (Reschly, 1979). It is therefore recommended that these measures should not be used as the only or primary source for classification decisions on intelligence functioning.

From the clinical or qualitative viewpoint, determination of a broad range of cognitive skills for programmatic purposes is as important as classification decisions. Accordingly, other well known tests such as the Merrill-Palmer Scale (1948) and the Leiter International Performance Scale (1980), which do not meet desired reliability or standardization criteria, can provide useful information when the Binet or Wechsler has limited applicability. The age range of the Merrill-Palmer is from 2 to 5+ years, focusing on nonverbal developmental tasks, and it does not penalize for lack of speech. It is also useful with the older severely or profoundly retarded individual, since the test items describe functioning in basic discrimination and eye-hand coordination skills applicable to training programs at these levels. The recent instruction manual for the Leiter (1980) now provides more explicit guides to test administration and scoring. In addition, a profile of the test constructs have been devised by Levine, Allen, Alker, and Fitzgibbon (1975), although the authors do not indicate whether it is based on clinical judgment or statistical analysis.

Deviations from Standardized Testing Procedures

Of major concern in testing retarded or developmentally disabled individuals is adherence to standardized procedures. Some clinicians (Allison, 1978) believe that the usual tendency to cover over ambiguities, normalize them, and fail to take note of their idiosyncrasies must be vigorously resisted. On the other hand, the limited applicability of available tests to the heterogeneous retarded population using standardized procedures can result in incomplete or invalid conclusions. Current approaches to assessment consider the analysis of strengths and weaknesses more significant than a specific score. Deviations from the prescribed manner may be unnecessary for subjects without physical or sensory-motor difficulties and at higher functioning levels. However, in situations of severely retarded mental functioning and/or multiple handicaps, sufficient information may not be available to develop educational or treatment plans and to make appropriate placement decisions.

On the practical level, the issue is expressed in whether discretionary changes in the phrasing of certain types of questions should be made by the examiner, based on his clinical judgment, in the direction of concreteness and simplicity in order to facilitate comprehension of the item. Recommended changes in phrasing have been developed for three of the WISC subtests (Information, Comprehension and Arithmetic) by Volle (1957).

In reality, the control of the test situation is in the examiner's hands. How he exercises this control may be a significant factor in testing individuals with low IQs. He may choose to go "by the book" to get a rigorously standardized test score or he may consider introducing some types of changes that are relevant to the special needs of low functioning children. The question arises as to how important the standardization aspect is to the clinical picture, a particularly difficult problem when using nonstandardized procedures for the next examiner who, if he uses standardized techniques, may be troubled by discrepancies between the two test results.

Various test adaptations have been made. Responses which are fundamentally correct in comprehension but expressed linguistically in an unconventional manner may be accepted. The examiner may, on ambiguous questions or tasks, provide a series of cues to the client. He may show him the first step or additional steps toward solving a problem; he may tell the examinee that his method in problem solving is wrong and ask him to try again; he may encourage participation and motivation by little rewards; he may accept a "don't know" answer only after questioning again; he may ask the subject to clarify his answer when the response borders on a correct response, but is incomplete. Giving extra trials which lead to a correct response suggests how the environment can be adapted to individual needs so that the individual achieves success. Thus, information of individual learning styles and conditions under which learning occurs is provided. Altering the environment may be helpful in eliciting representative behaviors; permitting parents in the testing room; providing a warm, encouraging atmosphere; providing for the individual's physical needs. However, Field reports (1981) the effects of manipulating test situations with young handicapped children. Her data indicates that intelligence test scores of these children may be artificially inflated or deflated by variables such as examiner's recent experience with testing normal children, examination sequences, and familiarity with the child's record and condition.

Since a standardized score obtained under all these cited conditions would be invalid, modifications in test administration must be related to the purposes for which the examination was given. If the purpose is to measure mental retardation in terms of statistical regression from the mean, then the standardized procedure is in order. However, if the purpose is to understand mental processes underlying actual test items and to obtain as comprehensive a picture as is possible of an individual's intellectual behavior, then variations are in order. The basic issue then is the value of a "standardized IQ" for assessment purposes compared to the value of obtaining a more accurate picture of the individual's intellectual behavior and the clinical need of compensating for possibly discriminatory aspects of the test. Considering the question of validity and the need to adapt existing tests to provide information on the mentally retarded individual, it is recommended that evaluation is initiated and carried out using standardized procedures. When expected task behaviors are not elicited, possibly because of specific disabilities or other attitudinal-behavioral factors, alterations or adaptations may be in order. In the latter event, test performance should be reported in both situations. Modifications should be reported and test results qualified explaining why and how deviations were made and under what conditions an individual is able to respond effectively.

Summary and Future Trends

In this chapter, the history of intelligence testing, concepts of intelligence and rationales for tests, and test procedures as these relate to mentally retarded individuals have been briefly reviewed. The issues of bias in testing minority as well as economically disadvantaged groups persist. Considering test results as a current indication of intellectual functioning and as one element in a multifaceted assessment for developing effective programs may be a positive approach to reduce bias and unfairness. How tests are administered and how test results are reported and used in decision making require careful and expert attention by the examiner.

Testing by its nature discriminates the strengths and weaknesses of the individual for developing learning or remedial strategies and behavioral goals. It is likely to continue but in a positive discriminatory manner taking into account the total milieu of the individual, keeping in mind the limitations of test instruments. An important criticism of tests and test results is that they have relatively little value in helping to predict future behavior of an individual other than in a narrow sense. If we have nothing but a statistical interpretation of a test score and can evaluate nothing but those personal characteristics that can be represented by a numerical index, the criticism is justified. If test results are interpreted clinically as well as statistically and qualitative as well as quantitative values are considered, accuracy of prediction is increased. Although the individual is now what he has become and will tend to continue in the same direction of development, changes in circumstances can alter his characteristic modes of behavior. Nowhere is this more salient than in regard to children who are arbitrarily designated mildly retarded or at the borderline on the basis of a particular quotient; an artificial dichotomy between "retarded" and "normal."

Finally, in view of the various limitations of the tests, it is quite legitimate to question their continued use. There are several answers: (1) in terms of predictability for the academic skills related to school achievement, the tests are the most proven instruments; as such, they provide information on a vital aspect of behavior; (2) the massive normative data acquired by the tests provide a strong guide to the degree in which an individual meets the expectations of society in general mental behavior; (3) the tests provide clues, through analysis of the processes underlying test results, to the determination and identification of impairment in specific functions; and (4) the tests provide an important part of the criteria for the determination of legal competence. In short, the standard intelligence tests do not exist in a vacuum; they are still despite the controversy institutionalized in national educational and legal practices which affect mentally retarded individuals and they reflect the intellectual standards of the nation in general.

It is perhaps the emphasis on certain forms of thinking, namely its abstract and symbolic functions, which is reflected in the tests, that discriminates against mentally retarded persons. But that value system, derived from the complexities of an advanced and industrialized country, is very real, whether just or not. So the issue, in this line of thought, is the value conceptualizations of a society, which is more difficult (to say the least) to alter than it is to conduct test analyses, to be aware of test limitations, and to include other assessment strategies to compensate for the basic unfairness. It is indeed one of the major rationales for psychological evaluation that it seeks to equalize whatever prejudice, cultural or functional, that exists in the tests through the multidimensions of its techniques.

References

Allen, R. M., & Jefferson, T. W. *Psychological evaluation of the cerebral palsied person.* Baltimore: C. C. Thomas, 1962.

Allison, J. Clinical contributions of the Wechsler Adult Intelligence Scale. In B. B. Wolman (Ed.), *Clinical diagnosis of mental disorders. A handbook.* New York: Plenum Press, 1978.

Alper, A. E. An analysis of the Wechsler Intelligence Scale for children with institutionalized mental retardates. *American Journal of Mental Deficiency,* 1967, **71**, 624–630.

Anastasi, A. Psychology, psychologists, and psychological testing. *American Psychologist,* 1967, **22**, 297–306.

Anastasi, A. *Differential psychology,* New York: MacMillan, 1968.

Anastasi, A. *Psychological testing.* (4th Ed.) New York: MacMillan, 1976.

Anhurst, D., & Meyers, E. Social system and clinical model in school identification of the educable retarded. In R. Eyman, E. Meyers, & G. Tarjan (Eds.), *Social-behavioral studies in mental retardation.* Washington, D.C.: American Association on Mental Deficiency, 1973.

Baumeister, A. A., & Bartlett, C. J. A comparison of the factor structure of normals and retardates on the WISC. *American Journal of Mental Deficiency,* 1962.

Bayley, N. *Bayley Scales of Infant Development,* New York: Psychological Corporation, 1969.

Bersoff, D. N. The judicial report card. *New York University Education Quarterly,* 1981, **13**, 2–8.

Borkowski, J. G., & Cavanaugh, T. C. Maintenance and generalization of skill and strategies by the retarded. In N. R. Ellis (Ed.), *Handbook of Mental Deficiency,* Hillsdale, N.J.: Erlbaum, 1979.

Boyer, L. B. Comparisons of the Shamans and pseudo-Shamans of the Apaches of the Mescalero Indian Reservation. *Journal of Projective Techniques,* 1964, **28**, 173–180.

Budoff, M. A. A learning potential assessment procedure, rationale and supporting data. In B. W. Richards (Ed.), Proceedings of the First Congress of the International Association for the Scientific Study of Mental Deficiency. Relgate, England: Jackson, 1968.

Burgemeister, B., Blum, L. H., & Lorge, I. *Columbus Mental Maturity Scale.* New York: Harcourt, Brace and World, 1959.

Cattell, B. B. Theory of fluid and crystalized intelligence. A critical experiment. *Journal of Educational Psychology,* 1963, **54**, 1–22.

Cattell, P. *The measurement of intelligence of infants and young children.* New York: Psychological Corporation, 1950.

Coleman, J. S., Campbell, E., Hobson, C., McPortland, J., Mood, A., & York, R. *Equality of educational effort unity.* Washington, D.C.: United States Government Printing Office, 1966.

Cromwell, R., Blashfield, R., & Strauss, J. Criteria for classification systems. In N. Hobbs (Ed.), *Issues in the classification of children.* San Francisco: Jossey-Bass, 1975.

Cronbach, L. J. Assessment of individual difficulties. In P. Farnsworth and A. McNamar (Eds.), *Annual Review of Psychology,* 1956, **3**, 173–196.

Cronbach, L. Five decades of public controversy over mental testing, *American Psychologist,* 1975, **30**, 1–15.

Dunn, L. M. *Expanded manual for the Peabody Picture Vocabulary Test,* Minneapolis: American Guidance Service, 1965.

Education for all handicapped children, PL 94-142, United States, November, 1975.

Environment, heredity and intelligence. Compiled from Harvard Educational Review, reprint series 2, Cambridge, Mass.

Eyesenck, H. J. *The I.Q. argument: Race, intelligence and education.* New York: Library Press, 1971.

Feuerstein, R. *Redevelopment of cognitive functions of retarded performers.* Baltimore, Md.: University Park Press, 1979.

Field, T. Ecological variables and examiner biases in assessing handicapped preschool children. *Journal of Pediatric Psychology,* 1981, **6**, 155–163.

Geloff, M. Comparisons of systems of classification relating degree of retardation to measured intelligence. *American Journal in Mental Deficiency,* 1963, 297–317.

Gesell, A. *Gesell Developmental Schedules.* New York: Psychological Corporation, 1949.

Grossman, H. (Ed.) *Manual terminology and classification in mental retardation.* Washington, D.C.: American Association on Mental Deficiency, 1977.

Guilford, J. P. The structure of intellect. *Psychological Bulletin,* 1956, **53**, 267–293.

Guilford, J. P. *The nature of human intelligence.* New York: McGraw-Hill, 1967.

Heber, R. Modifications in the manual on terminology and classification in mental retardation. *American Journal on Mental Deficiency,* 1961, 499–500.

Hermnstein, R. In defence of intelligence tests. *Atlantic Monthly,* September, 1971, 43–64.

Hilliard, A. Cultural diversity and special education. *Exceptional Children,* 1980, **46**, 584–588.

Hirt, M. L., & Kaplan, M. L. Psychological testing II, current practice. *Comprehensive Psychiatry,* 1967, **8**, 310–20.

Jackson, G. On the report of the ad hoc committee on educational uses of tests with disadvantaged students. *American Psychologist,* 1975, **30**, 88–92.

Jencks, C. *Inequality: a reassessment of family and schooling in America.* New York: Basic Books, 1972.

Jensen, A. How much can we boost IQ and scholastic achievement? *Harvard Educational Review*, 1969, **39**, 1–123.

Jensen, A. A theory of primary and secondary familial mental retardation. In N. R. Ellis (Ed.), *International Review of Research in Mental Retardation*. Vol. 4. New York: Academic Press, 1970.

Jensen, A. Another look at culture-fair testing. In J. Hellmuth (Ed.), *Disadvantaged Child*. Vol. III. New York: Brunner/Mazel, 1976.

Jones, L. A factor analysis of the Stanford-Binet at four age levels. *Psychometrika*, 1949, 299–331.

Kamin, L. *The science and politics of IQ*. New Jersey: Laurence Erlbaum Associates, 1974.

Kaplan, M. Collavelli, N., Gross, R., Leventhal, S. D., & Siegel, S. *The structural approach in psychological testing*. New York: Pergamon Press, 1970.

Karp, E., Michal-Smith, H., & Morgenstern, M. Diagnosing mental deficiency. In B. J. Wolman (Ed.), *Clinical diagnosis of mental deficiency: A handbook*. New York: Plenum Press, 1978.

Kaufman, A., & Doppelt, J. Analysis of WISC-R standardization data in terms of stratification variables. *Child Development*, 1976, **47**, 165–171.

Kaufman, A. *Intelligent testing with the WISC-R*. New York: John Wiley & Sons, 1979.

Larry P. et al. vs. Wilson Riles et al. United States District Court, Northern District of California, Case #C-71-2270, RFP, 1974.

Leiter, R. G. *Leiter International Performance Scale Instruction Manual*. Chicago: Stoelting Co., 1980.

Levine, M. N., Alker, L. N., Allen, R. N., & Fitzgibbon, W. *Leiter International Performance Scale Clinical Profile*. Chicago: Stoelting Co., 1975.

Lewontin, R. C. Race and Intelligence. *Bulletin of the Atomic Scientists*, March, 1970, 2–8.

Lutey, C. L. *Individual intelligence testing, a manual*. Creeley, Colo.: 1967.

MacMillan, D. L. *Mental retardation in school and society*. Boston: Little Brown and Co., 1977.

McNemar, Q. *The revision of the Stanford-Binet Scale*. Boston: Houghton Mifflin, 1942.

Mercer, J. R. *Labeling the mentally retarded*. Berkeley: University of California Press, 1973.

Mercer, J. Psychological assessment and the rights of children. *Harvard Educational Review*, February, 1974.

Mercer, J. R., & Leurs, J. P. *System of multicultural pluralistic assessment: Technical manual*. New York: Psychological Corporation, 1979.

Merrill-Palmer Scale of Mental Tests. New York: Harcourt, Brace and World, 1948.

Newland, T. E. Assumptions underlying psychological testing. In T. Oakland and B. N. Phillips (Eds.), *Assessing minority group children*. New York: Human Sciences Press, 1974.

Olmedo, E. L. Testing linguistic minorities. *American Psychologist*, 1981, **36**, 1078–1085.

Palmer, J. O. *Psychological assessment of children*. New York: John Wiley & Sons, Inc., 1970.

Pruyser, P. W. *The psychological examination: A guide for clinicians*. New York: International University Press, Inc., 1979.

Rapaport, D., Gill, M. M., & Schafer, R. *Diagnostic psychological testing*. New York: International Universities Press, 1968.

Reschly, D. Nonbiased Assessment. In G. Phye and D. Reschly (Eds.), *School Psychology: perspectives and issues*. New York: Academic Press, 1979.

Reschly, D. J. Psychological testing on educational classification and placement. *American Psychologist*, 1981, **36**, 1094–1102.

Robinson, H. B., & Robinson, N. M. *The mentally retarded child, a psychological approach*. New York: McGraw-Hill, 1978.

Ross, A. O. A clinical psychologist examines retarded children. Paper presented at the Workshop on Research for the Educable Mentally Retarded. Harrisburg, Pa.: *Journal of Clinical Child Psychology*, 1971, 67–80.

Sattler, J. M. *Assessment of children's intelligence*. Philadelphia: A. B. Saunders Co., 1974.

Shuey, A. *The testing of negro intelligence*. (2nd ed.) New York: Social Science Press, 1966.

Silverstein, A. B. Variants components in five psychological tests. *Psychological Reports*, 1968, **28**, 141–142.

Skodak, M., & Skeels, H. M. A final follow-up study of 100 adopted children. *Journal of Genetic Psychology*, 1949, **75**, 85–125.

Slosson, R. L. *Slosson Intelligence Test*. New York: Slosson Educational Publications, 1963.

Spearman, C. E. *The measurement of intelligence*. New York: Bureau of Publications, Teachers' College, Columbia University, 1927.

Sternberg, R. The nature of intelligence. *New York University Education Quarterly*, 1981, **3**, 10–17.

Terman, L. M., & Merrill, M. A. *Stanford-Binet Intelligence Scale*. Boston: Houghton Mifflin, 1960.

Throne, J. M. *The assessment of intelligence: Towards what end?* Reprint of paper presented to joint meeting of the American Academy on Mental Retardation and the American Association on Mental Deficiency. Washington, D.C., 1970.

Thurstone, L. L. Intelligence and its measurement: a symposium. *Journal of Education Psychology*, 1921, **12**, 195–216.

Thurstone, L. L. Primary mental abilities. *Psychometric monographs*, 1938.

Tyler, L. E. *The psychology of human differences*. (3rd Ed.) New York: Appleton Century Crofts, 1966.

Vallet, R. E. A clinical profile for the Stanford-Binet. *Journal of School Psychology*, 1964, 49–54.

Vernon, P. E. *The structure of human abilities*. New York: Wiley, 1950.

Volle, F. O. A proposal for testing the limits with mental defectives for purposes of subtest analysis of the WISC Verbal Scales. *Journal of Clinical Psychology*, 1967, 64–67.

Walker, K. P., & Gross, F. L. IQ stability among educable mentally retarded children. *Training School Bulletin*, 1970, **66**, 181–187.

Wechsler, D. *The measurement and appraisal of adult intelligence*. (4th ed.) Baltimore: Williams and Wilkins, 1958.

Wellman, B. L. IQ changes of preschool and nonpreschool years: A summary of the literature. *Journal of Psychology*, 1945, **20**, 34–71.

Zeaman, D. Some relatives of general intelligence and selective attention. *Intelligence*, 1978, **2**, 55–73.

Zigler, E., & Butterfield, E. Motivational aspects of changes in IQ test performance of culturally deprived nursery school children. *Child Development*, 1968, **39**, 1–14.

14 ADAPTIVE BEHAVIOR SCALES

Henry Leland

The ethics of testing require that if the tester does not know how to use the derived information or has little understanding of the purpose of deriving it, (s)he should not be asking the questions. If there is a valid reason for the questions, if the examiner understands the reason, and can use the information for the benefit of the client—then the questions should be asked. This principle has been the underlying ethical basis for the development of a measurement approach to handicapped persons based on "the manner in which they cope with the natural and social demands of their environment" (Heber 1961). The concept of adaptive behavior measurement has been derived from this definition.

What is adaptive behavior? It is obviously many and varied things. Historically the term emerged in psychology with the work of people such as Helson (1964), who were attempting to deal with the relationship between psychological and biological phenomena. That particular approach goes back into reflexology and classical conditioning literature around the work of Pavlov, Anokhin, and others (Anokhin, 1974). The organism has ways of dealing with noxious stimuli to make them less noxious and permit the organism to benefit. A standard example is the eye blink. If one does not blink, the surface of the eye becomes dry, which is both very painful and impairs vision. If one closes the eye it will prevent drying but

also impedes vision. Therefore, we have an "adaptive response which permits us to close the eye ("blink") without actually cutting off vision. This aspect of adaptive behavior study is valuable; it has been extremely fruitful and can be considered the basis for looking at human behavior. That is, how can an individual utilize available resources to meet social stimuli in a manner both protective and valuable. This concept of adaptive behavior is very broad and challenges many of the typical approaches to the measurement of behavior, because it says, in effect, that all factors present at the time a behavior is performed are significant to the production of that behavior, and that any reductionist effort to isolate the behavior only results in the loss of necessary information.

This topic is broad and far reaching. Since we are dealing with mental retardation we restrict our approach to those elements of adaptive behavior measurement that relate primarily to the mentally retarded, developmentally disabled, or similarly handicapped persons. This is not to say that adaptive behavior is only relevant to that group, but that the measurement processes, the effort at scaling which we will discuss, and the theoretical constructs surrounding these approaches have been narrowed to this population.

What is unique about this population? Most standard measurement is based on the assumption that the elements being measured will progress in an orderly

215

fashion and that one looks at the developmental dimensions, rates of learning, mental age, etc. that reflect systematic progression.

This basic assumption has to be challenged when dealing with handicapped persons. First, we have a group of atypically developing individuals who do not follow an orderly progression. They do not follow the same developmental phases, or if they seem to, the phases do not emerge within the same time period. These differences in time periods reflect differences in physical growth, differences in personal experiences and other aspects of psychological growth, and differences in basic physical make-up. The human endowment is an individual with two arms, two legs, two eyes facing forward, two ears, etc., with all parts, both external and internal, within an acceptable level of appropriate working order. This basic endowment is not always available in the mentally retarded or handicapped population. While the external physiognomy may be consistent with the pattern, according to the social definition of mental retardation, there is certainly an underlying presumption that the brain, the rest of the nervous system, and the related chemical apparatus that creates the human as a cognitive organism are not in appropriate working order; otherwise, the individuals would not be described as mentally retarded.

We are not only dealing with individuals who are psychologically and biologically described as representing atypical patterns of growth and development but who, because of this very fact, also present a number of very unique measurement problems in terms of how, with their handicap, they are able to develop appropriate coping skills or strategies to deal with external stimuli.

We are thus faced with two questions. (1) "What do we want to know from these people (remembering that what we want to know has to be directly related to why we want to know it)?" (2) "How do we measure these individuals to insure the highest practical level of valid information?"

What We Need to Know and Why

What kind of information are we seeking from measurement of this population? The decision as to what to measure has to follow an earlier decision of what kinds of living patterns are we trying to establish or modify. The ongoing behavior of an individual changes regularly dependent on the types of social situations to which the individual must respond. Many behaviors are appropriate in one setting and totally inappropriate in another, e.g., screaming at a football game vs. in a classroom, and we recognize that handicapped persons often lose track of the "appropriateness of a setting." Furthermore, just because a person is mentally retarded does not mean that he has to be open to constant intrusion and exploitation from the more knowing members of the community. They should enjoy the same kinds of personal rights as other people, to the extent of their ability to utilize those rights. Part of our reason for developing measurements around them is to determine how they might be aided to utilize their rights and function within the realm of the normative aspects of the community.

This does not mean that the purpose of measurement is to establish normalcy, but rather to determine what areas need special help, special training, special intrusion, possibly leading even to the denial of certain specific rights for a prescribed period of time (with the understanding that those rights will be restored, whether or not the habilitation program has been a success); and to determine what things the individual is currently able to do, what particular areas are currently within a "normative" range, what specific behaviors can go forward without intrusion and without the denial of personal rights to the individual (Nihira, 1973). Thus, measurement must reflect the strengths of the individual as well as the weaknesses if we are to properly establish a pattern of overall improvement in the quality of life of a person. The primary reason for measurement has to be an effort to answer the question of how we can help these individuals learn to improve themselves and to function within socially acceptable lines, recognizing that we are not eliminating the handicaps. This, in a sense, is saying that the basis for measurement is for us to gain the information we need to help particular individuals prevent their handicap from turning into a major disability.

The second reason for measurement obviously derives from the first. We have to have indications as to what kinds of behaviors tend most to interfere with the achievement of major goals. What are the specific things that this particular individual is doing that makes it difficult for the broader goal of preventing the handicap from becoming a disability to be achieved? It is important to underlie that with atypically developing individuals the reason for failure to achieve goals differs from person to person and one cannot begin establishing generalized causes or even generalized errors, but rather must look at each situation in terms of its own points of reference. Since it is obviously impossible to evolve a different measurement scale for each handicapped person, a general concept must be utilized. We have found that the most useful centers around the question of *visibility* (Leland, 1964). In other words, what is it that the handicapped person is doing that makes him especially visible in the eyes of society? This question is a highly personal one, and some behaviors are more visible in some cultural groups than they are in others. Thus, for example, specific patterns of childrearing relating to the use of a pacifier vary widely so that the same mother will be reinforced for such usage and criticized for doing exactly the same thing, in different parts of the same city. This problem of visibility as it relates to the mentally retarded centers around many aspects of so called "creative" behaviors which are not consistent with usual social expectations. Those of us who emerge in public, who write books, profess in universities, carry out various and sundry business activities, etc., consider visibility part of our stock-in-trade. We expect to be visible and we are reinforced for it by jobs, salary increases, and a wide variety of other tangible and intangible rewards. Handicapped people tends to be highly "creative," but what they create is often completely contrary to what society wants or expects, and as a result this high level of unusual unpredictable behavior sets up within society a fear or annoyance which puts the handicapped person into jeopardy. They cannot afford this visibility because they have not become sufficiently aware of society's level of tolerance to enter into that kind of activity without some jeopardy. One of the major goals of persons working with the handicapped must be to help them develop sufficient understanding of a situation or sufficient levels of social competency (Edmonson et al., 1969; 1970) that they will be able to appear in most matters to be behaving like everyone else, dressing the same, entering the same doorways, walking at about the same pace on the street, talking in about the same tone of voice, etc., so that they do not emerge as obnoxiously visible and are thus able to maintain a place in society. One needs to determine the specific behaviors which seem to produce excessive levels of visibility and at the same time identify behaviors which might be supported or trained to help produce necessary levels of "invisibility."

The third aspect of measurement must center around knowledge of how the child is actually performing within the structure of the community system. If individuals, as we indicated above, are not to be considered disabled and if they are to be able to function within a sufficient level of social invisibility they must be able to perform certain tasks. However, because of their atypical level of development and the nature of their handicap it is often impossible for them to perform in exactly the way that society defines the activity. This social phenomenon is not unusual. Most of the activities people perform are performed somewhere within what we call a "tolerance range." That is, there is no exact way to walk or sit or eat,

etc. Society at times enters into a rigid construct for some of these behaviors, e.g. official protocol at the White House, but generally there are a great variety of options, as long as certain specific types of results emerge, for example, with sitting, as long as the individual can bend in the middle and has sufficient knowledge to utilize the appropriate furniture or make an appropriate adaptation if the usual furniture is not present, the exact pose or exact manner in which the individual sits is usually not brought into question. If for some reason, either physical or psychological, the individual is unable to meet those requirements, another aspect of visibility emerges, and society observes how the individual deals with the situation. If it seems predictable and adequate, society leaves it alone. Thus, if a person cannot bend in the middle because of a physical disability society does not get upset as long as that individual can find a mode of leaning comfortably so that the other members of an audience do not become uncomfortable. People in a crowd become very conscious and uneasy if someone comes through on crutches, but if they seem to be managing them properly and seem to be getting along without any obvious need for additional help, the crowd makes way for them and no further attention is paid. But if the crutches are not being managed properly, if for example, they are hitting people as they pass, if the individual looks constantly as though they were going to fall, etc., the normal persons around them become very concerned, and while they may not intervene, they try to see to it that somebody intervenes so that this situation can be brought under a different kind of control. With this overall pattern in mind and recognizing that our mentally retarded and handicapped clients cannot always cope with situations in the manner in which society has prescribed, this problem of "what the individual is doing instead of what society had anticipated" becomes an extremely important question (Leland 1977; 1978). These "instead" behaviors become extremely important psychological questions all the way down the line.

This is a major problem with usual standard measurement. The individual fails to do the test item in the manner in which it was administered and is marked as having failed. No notice is taken of what was done instead and yet the "instead" activity may be extremely important in learning about the client's ability. Thus, we may have a child who completely fails all gross and fine motor tasks which have been administered, who cannot properly classify different objects, who cannot distinguish between colors or shapes, who cannot stay on task, etc., etc., and who fails all test items and is thus marked as "untestable." This same individual may have a history of throwing rocks at windows. Here we find a graphic example of "instead" behaviors. Typically such an individual does not pick up a leaf to throw at the window so there is an obvious ability to distinguish between substances. He picks up the stone to throw it and seems to have throwing ability, indicating something about his gross and fine motor behavior. If the stone reaches the window, there is a certain amount of goal direction, this was obviously not a random toss, and there is some judgement of force. Obviously, we are not interested in reinforcing window breaking behavior, but this is a very graphic example of an individual who though designated as "untestable" and having no visible skills, nonetheless has a number of usable skills. This "instead" behavior tells us more about the child than any of the formal testing did. This understanding of the relationship between social requirements and the manner in which the individual has chosen to deal with them becomes as much a part of the measurement problem as any other aspect and the better we are able to ascertain the "instead" behaviors the more accurate and valid will be the measurement. Furthermore since our object is to know how individuals, when left to their own devices, cope with a social stimulus, this becomes the most revealing type of information that we can get.

Thus, to review, we assess the handicapped person to determine (1) how we can help prevent the handicap from becoming a disability, (2) what behaviors are present that interfere with the individual functioning within the normative range, and (3) what behaviors are present that represent the individual's efforts to cope with the situation on an "instead" basis. There may be many more reasons for testing within a wide variety of other kinds of questions, but when dealing with the adaptive behavior of the individual these are the three primary bases which emerge, all relating to eventual efforts to set up curricula and procedures for either modifying on-going behaviors or developing a program of habilitation or educational progress with the individual. Adaptive behavior measurement is that aspect of measurement which indicates the potentially reversible areas of mentally retarded and handicapped behavior in the individual (Leland et al., 1967; Leland, 1977). This is vastly different from those aspects of measurement which merely try to determine what is wrong or the level of how wrong it is.

Having determined why we want the information, the next question in adaptive behavior measurement relates to what we want to know and the best way to learn it. Considering once again our interest in preventing the handicap from becoming a disability, we need to know the areas where the handicap emerges.

Again, adaptive behavior assessment, which is based on the direct reporting of observable behavior, gives us specific information concerning what it is that the individual is doing or not doing. Since we are dealing with coping strategies and skills the behavior that goes into what the individual *is* doing is qualitatively different than the behavior relating to things which the individual *is not* doing. The things which the individual is not doing may fall into four possible categories. One, the individual may never have had experience or opportunity to carry out those particular behaviors. Second, the individual may have certain physical limitations which prevent the performance of those behaviors. Third, the behaviors themselves may be inappropriate for this particular individual, e.g., the child is too young. Four, the individual may be totally undermotivated for those particular behaviors because of certain cultural patterns or experiences, e.g., expecting Oriental children trained with chopsticks to use a spoon and fork. To look only at what the individual is not doing gives us an unclear picture of coping skill because, as indicated above, the reasons for the absence of the behavior are not clear. Conversely, what the individual does is based on having had to cope with certain kinds of environmental demands in order to reach success in these areas. Thus, we have some evidence of ability to cope successfully in those domains. It is thus necessary to develop indications of where these coping successes have occurred and of what the "hills" in the individual's performance are, and to chart these success areas as part of the priorities for evolving a program designed to prevent the development of a disability. If the emphasis is put on the "valleys" or the failure areas, since we have no immediate knowledge as to the cause of the failures, the programming becomes guesswork, the outcomes become problematical, and the whole exercise becomes futile. We have to have measurement that will provide us with an indication of the "hills," in order to continue with our overall objective (Nihira, Foster, Shellhaas, & Leland, 1974).

In trying to determine the behaviors that interfere most or provide the greatest degree of "visibility," we have another situation. Generally speaking, adaptive behaviors can be divided into necessary behaviors and desirable behaviors (Leland, 1977). There is a group of behaviors that would probably be considered essential across most cultures and, within normal physical limitations, based on growth throughout most age groups. These behaviors include such things as elimination of waste, consummation of nutriment, protection against cold or heat, mobility, etc. These necessary behaviors are the core of adaptive behavior measurement concerning questions relating either to functional independence or the development of adaptive cognitive processes. They demand both awareness of societal needs and understanding of what the satisfaction of those needs requires. There is, however, a major contradiction in the relationship between these necessary behaviors and those behaviors we have described as desirable. The desirable behavior often has a higher priority than some of the necessary behaviors. The extreme is the situation around elimination where an individual cannot just eliminate wastes, even though this is an absolute necessity, but is expected to do it in a certain place under certain prescribed circumstances and is open to punishment if it is done in the wrong place under the wrong circumstances. Thus, the priority clearly goes to the desirable behavior—"toilet training"—over the necessary behavior, waste elimination. There are many other examples of this same phenomenon on a less extreme basis. The taking in of nutriment is very highly structured within our culture in terms of time, place, and quantity. Protection against the elements is also very highly structured in terms of the quantity of clothing to be worn, the nature of the clothing (particularly in terms of gender identification), and other elements of this sort. All point to the fact that the desirable behavior is often more important than the necessary behavior. This creates additional difficulty, because the desirable behavior is not as structured across cultures and what is desirable in one culture may not be desirable in another culture. Since one of the aspects of mental retardation is the inability to make these kinds of transfers easily, a person may meet the demands of desirable behavior at home and find that because the school represents a different approach they do not meet those demands as readily. Thus, the whole pattern of learning experience, working experience, school experience, etc., is constantly fraught with confusion because different behaviors are given priority. One of our functions in testing is to try to establish some way of recognizing how it is the individual must cope in order to survive in his/her particular environment or his/her particular social group while at the same time having sufficiently broad understanding to cope with the community at large. The function of the adaptive behavior information is to give us an indication of which priority item the individual may be having difficulty with so that the programming and planning can be developed around those issues.

In the third area, the question of "instead" behaviors, we have an entirely different phenomenon with which to deal. It is often the case with handicapped persons that they develop an idiosyncratic way of coping with social and cultural demands. This idiosyncratic pattern may be counterproductive in terms of the needs of the situation, in which case it would be considered unsuccessful coping; but there are occasions in which it is productive and will bring the individual to the desired end. Thus, in the area of eating, cerebral palsied individuals have a great deal of trouble controlling their feeding procedures and coordinating their chewing and swallowing. One feels a high degree of success has been achieved if the cerebral palsied individual can successfully feed himself even though some of the procedures may be far afield from the usual way of accomplishing this objective. If society is going to take the stand that there is only one way that one can drink out of a cup or only one way that certain foods can be taken, the only alternative would be to have someone else feed him. This would not only represent an extreme loss of independence and increase in total social dependency but also would limit his freedom and damage his self concept affecting growth and development in other areas. Coping processes outside of the realm of social expectations must also be measured to help to determine if the idiosyncratic pattern developed by the individual can fall within the realm of social acceptability. Sometimes, the coping style adopted is unsightly or creates additional annoyance. This can occur when idiosyncratic behaviors, compared with expected behaviors, give an additional pattern of information concerning expectations surrounding the individual, and additional indications of strengths in unexpected areas.

This overall measurement process relates to reversible aspects of mental retardation, and is important for the reasons suggested above, plus the provision of additional very important information concerning whether the basic needs of the individual fall into a training area or a treatment area, and further what kinds of training or treatment curricula would be most appropriate. *Training* is essentially described as the introduction of new information, and includes educational as well as specific training efforts such as prevocational and vocational instruction. It also relates to activities of daily living and other activities where the handicapped person needs new and specific information in order to accomplish a degree of functional independence. *Treatment* on the other hand, implies that much of the knowledge base has already been acquired—that the individual has had and benefited from various types of instruction, that there is demonstrated understanding or ability to perform the task, and that the behavior is not being performed because of either failure in motivation or failure in social adaptation involving either extrapunitive or intrapunitive affect and emotional structures. It is necessary to know what the area of interference is, if the behaviors break down for these reasons. Beyond that, we think in terms of a treatment program which might include psychotherapy, behavior modification, medical therapy, occupational therapy, or other types of work which involve the reordering and the reorganization of information which the individual already possesses. Obviously for most individuals the question is a mixture of treatment and training, and adaptive behavior measurement is designed to help set the areas of emphasis, so that given an individual's 16 waking hours a day, the interventions which occur in either the area of training or treatment can be the most productive for the development of this individual. Extreme treatment needs will interfere with the success of training programs and extreme training needs will slow down progress in the treatment realm. These are not to be considered completely independent concepts, but rather a basis for determining where the major emphasis needs to be placed with any specific individual. This is not to claim all important testing to adaptive behavior but rather to point out that since we are dealing with the reversible aspects of mentally retarded behavior, if we can get valid indication of individual needs in this area, the possibility of success in other areas becomes greatly enhanced.

Adaptive Behavior Scales

When we are faced with the question of how to measure the kinds of behaviors we have described, we find that there are a number of interlocking areas which have to be brought together in a pattern or profile to enable us to use the material. These adaptive behaviors come under a broad heading of functional independent skills, personal and social responsibility, motivation, cognitive development, etc. There are also a number of other elements to be measured, such as physical development, social maladaptation, and the presence or absence of a condition requiring regular medication, which, while not described as adaptive, are nonetheless closely tied into the coping skill of the individual. These diverse elements can then be combined like the threads in a Persian carpet to form an organized "picture" of the individual.

Since different social and cultural groups make different demands on the individual, and since there are a variety of ways to approach many necessary behaviors, we could look at adaptive behavior measurement in terms of a large number of scales representing different population groups from different areas of the country in different settings. There would be scales based on age, sex, rural areas, urban areas, representing different racial or national groups, etc. However, a measurement process is not really appropriate if it is not practical or useful to the people

who must of necessity do the measurement so that they can plan the modification programs. It becomes totally impractical to conceptualize having a completely individualized scale for each of the populations described. Plus the additional fact that once one begins to break these groups down in this manner, every individual area of the population—every individual group—certainly has some things which are different and which would demand particular attention. It becomes more functional to develop a basic measurement instrument which will center on broad patterns of necessary and desirable behaviors in a variety of realms and allow the professionals within each of the settings (training programs, community residences, etc.) to make their own modifications concerning the specific needs within their specific setting. Rather than try to set up an all-inclusive series of scales with thousands of items, it was felt that it was both more efficient and effective to develop a prototypic set of scales which would have a more limited number of items, but which could be easily administered and would produce enough information to permit the development of individual educational, or individual habilitation plans.

The first question to be answered is how much personal, functional independence does this individual have? It should be noted that historically this has been consistently the area that adaptive behavior measurement has most generally assessed (Doll, 1947; Leland, Shellhaas, Nihira & Foster, 1967; Voisin, 1843). Functional independence has to be viewed in terms of some age differences and at least one sex difference (menstruation). One needs to look at both specific kinds of behaviors relating to daily living and also more socialized types of activities relating to domestic and work activities (Leland, Shoaee, & Vayda, 1975), all of which will give the examiner some indication of the level of personal independence that the client has been able to achieve at the time of the assessment.

The second question relates to the level of the cognitive growth and development (described as species specific behavior for the human organism; Lenneberg, 1967). The elements included under the heading of cognitive growth relate to functional independence and are considered behavior elements. These include *language development*, which occurs through the individual's relationship with a social group, and is a primary coping procedure oriented toward communication. Communication can be thought of as a very unique, human strategy in adaptation. Cognitive development also includes the response to efforts at teaching. These can be based on socially oriented areas of *number and time concepts* and can teach the individual and determine how much of the intellectual demands of the surrounding world the individual is able to handle, based on incidental or untaught learning. Since one of the major problems that one has with the mentally retarded individual is the inability to utilize social cues as a guide to behavior, measuring this aspect of adaptation becomes a very strong indicator of the potential for training programs. This domain is an important combined measure of independent functioning and cognitive ability. All of these "cognitive" elements would require too many items to give a complete picture. To keep the measurement basis efficient, it was necessary to subsume an amount of information by reduction, i.e., if behavior C is being perfomed we can assume that some sort of an A or B preceded it. We say "some sort of an A or B," because individuals with atypical growth and development do not necessarily use the same paths toward achievement, but nonetheless, we can assume that the existing observable behavior had antecedents within the same behavioral realm and that the ability to achieve certain, ongoing behaviors can indicate a potential for developing the next expected level. There is no effort to predict that this will be achieved. This combination of measurement of functional independence and cognitive development can give us some measure of a "level of adaptive behavior" to be used for "bookkeeping" purposes. These data are the most usually reported types of information (Leland et al., 1967).

When some type of "bookkeeping" result is required (usually because of an interest in placing the individual in a program with a homogeneous group or putting the individual in a residence or working situation based on certain levels of ability), the adaptive behavior level, derived from the combination of functional independence and cognitive development, can be one of the best ways of meeting those bookkeeping needs. We must underline that this is not moving in the direction of an "ABQ," but rather on an individual criterion basis, taking the performance of a specific individual and comparing that performance with other individuals in order to derive some degree of commonality for the purpose of grouping, placing, or recording. This is not leading to a quotient or some other mathematical single score, because it cannot be assumed that individuals functioning at the same level are functioning there for the same reasons, or with the same mental processes at work. All that can be said is that these individuals have been seen to perform certain discrete behaviors similarly.

Alongside of *functional independence*, we must also look at elements such as personal and social motivation, conformity and cooperation. These adaptive behaviors are part of a more general pattern described as *personal responsibility*. How much personal involvement the individual feels with the outcome of the behavior, how much knowledge of potential consequences the individual possesses, are some of the main determining factors in whether individuals will do what they can do. Now, with a slight detour back to normal adaptation, it is certainly not unexpected, for example, that adolescents will leave a bed unmade or teeth unbrushed in the normal proceedings of their daily activities. The assumption is generally that they have learned to make their beds, they have learned to brush their teeth, and that they will do it under certain types of pressure, but left to their own devices it is not a predictable activity. Unfortunately, the same kind of conclusion cannot be drawn around the mentally retarded. It cannot be said that because they have once done something they can still do it.

The problem here is that, besides the general possibility of neurological or medical deterioration which may be occurring, there is also the possibility of emotional disturbance or other factors, which may in fact have inhibited the performance of learned behaviors. We are dealing with brain damaged, emotionally disturbed, mentally retarded, neurologically handicapped, etc. individuals and these symptoms take on different impact as the individual grows older. One cannot automatically assume that age is a guarantee of development progress. Therefore, we have to be aware of how much social responsibility or how much personal responsibility the individual is willing to take in terms of his daily activities as part of our judgement between whether or not the individual can do certain things and just doesn't do them or actually cannot do them. The measurement of motivation becomes a very important part of our understanding of the ongoing adaptive skills of the individual. This involves elements relating to personal responsibility when dealing with other people on a day-to-day basis, cooperating, standing in line, etc.; it also involves seeking and holding employment. It further involves some degree of self-direction in both the sense of how one uses one's leisure or unplanned time and how one proceeds to use planned time in terms of the effective use of that time.

Beyond these dimensions of functional independence and personal responsibility is the area of social responsibility and social adaptation. This is the most difficult area to measure because society typically does not look at social adaptation but, rather at social maladaptation. This is very much the same as defining health as the absence of illness. Society expects persons to behave in a generally responsible manner. They expect that people will walk down the street without breaking windows or without hitting other people. They expect that they will stop at red lights and obey other such regulations. And they have set up various punitive processes to deal with those individuals who consistently do not do this. Society does not differentiate in their punitive processes between people who do not do these things because they are angry or disturbed or brain damaged or psychotic or mentally retarded. Society just says that maladaptive behaviors have occurred and they must be dealt with. If the behavior that has occurred has not been that bad, society tends to ignore it. The assumption is that adaptive behaviors are occurring but these are never defined. With this in mind, a measurement procedure in this area must be based on the behaviors which society will not tolerate. This of necessity has to be set up on a negative basis because their positive counterparts are not always discernable; e.g., it is easy to determine when a person is hitting another person, it is impossible to determine whether nonhitting behavior is specific rather than nonspitting or nonyelling or non- some other behavior. So that in order to be sure of what it is that is being recorded in the areas of social adaptation this becomes the measurement of the presence of social maladaptation.

Finally, there are domains included which are not specifically measures of adaptive behavior. An individual who has no legs cannot run, nor can he do a number of other things that require that type of mobility, so that physical development including both sensory development and motoric development has to be recorded if we are to be able to fully judge what is happening in relationship to specific behaviors. This information is thus extremely important and has to be included even though it sets a level of inconsistency with the other kinds of items being measured. Of equal importance is the knowledge whether the individual is on a regular prescription of medication. Presuming the medication is doing anything, it is certainly affecting the individual's behavior in a variety of realms. It may also effect his motivation and his skill level and has to be considered a factor in determining the final adaptive element being measured.

All of these pieces should be brought together into a single scale which cannot be too long, must be easily administered and must contain the items written in such a way that both professionals and nonprofessionals, particularly parents, can respond to them with some degree of reliable consistency. This does not mean that teachers and parents for example, should of necessity respond to the same items in the same way (Crawford, 1974; Estreicher, 1978). It is recognized that children behave differently at home and in school. But, presuming that both observe the same behavior,

they should be able to report it reliably and the item must be based on easily recognizable observable behaviors which can be recorded in such a manner that another person observing the same thing at the same time would record it in the same way. This latter requirement comes about through another aspect of adaptive behavior measurement which requires direct observation by a party other than the person administering the material (Leland et al., 1975).

Since it is impossible to get an accurate, naturalistic view of an individual's behavior through the direct administration of testing tasks, it was found that the most effective way of getting information was from a reporter who had made direct observations of the behaviors. This reporter should be well enough acquainted with the individual being assessed to be able to report those observations over a sufficient period of activities incorporating most of the 16 waking hours. In this way we are able to deal with the problem that staged or laboratory type tasks are artificial and do not directly indicate how the individual copes with those stimuli in a field demand situation. Since it is this latter type of demand situation which provides the "survival" information, one has to depend on reports of individuals who know the client as thoroughly as possible (Nihira et al., 1974).

A wide range of attempts has been made to develop adaptive behavior instruments to accomplish some of those objectives. A review in 1967 revealed over a dozen instruments designed to measure some of the same elements (Leland et al., 1967). A more recent review done by Coulter and Morrow (1978) revealed 19 measures which specifically called themselves "adaptive behavior" and which did not necessarily include the measures reviewed in 1967. Currently, state departments, agencies and programs have begun to develop their own checklists, inventories, and other types of scales. Blackman (1980) has identified literally hundreds of these "in-house" checklists and inventories which contain some adaptive behavior type items. Most have not been developed in a sufficiently systematic manner to permit the clinical judgements or assessment information required of the broader based nationally oriented measures. Of these latter, the following are the scales currently receiving the most attention. Only the AAMD Scales cover all of the areas in the described manner, but many of the others serve very important specialized roles and have a high level of utility. It will take a great deal of additional research to determine which approach will be the most productive in the long run:

The *AAMD adaptive behavior scale* (Nihira et al., 1974)

AAMD adaptive behavior scale: - Public school version (Lambert, N.; Windmiller, M.; Cole, L.; and Figuerra, R., 1981)

Adaptive behavior inventory for children. In *System of multicultural pluralistic assessment* (Mercer, J. and Lewis, J. F., 1977).

Adaptive behavior scale for infants and early childhood (Leland, H.; Shoaee, M.; McElwain, D.; & Christie, R., 1980)

Balthazar's scales of adaptive behavior (Balthazar, E. E., 1973)

Callier-Azusa scale (Stillman, R. (Ed.), 1975)

Family behavioral profile (Kennett, K. F., 1973)

Progressive assessment chart (Gunzburg, H. C., 1974).

Looking Ahead

All of the concepts that have been presented need greater and more careful investigation. This is, in a way, a measurement revolution. It is becoming clear from the experiences we have had with norm-referenced methods, and clinic-based testing, that both of those approaches have to be reviewed and new ways of assessing field experiences based on individual criteria have to be enhanced.

We have spoken about the importance of developing programming around "invisibility training." This is directly related to the modification in the definition of mental retardation which now refers to: "significantly subaverage general intellectual functioning existing concurrently with *deficits in adaptive behavior* (our emphasis) and manifested during the developmental period" (Grossman, 1973). Since both dimensions are treated as equally important, we must begin examining further aspects of this question. The *Larry P.* case (1974) has raised many important questions concerning the types of assessment that should be used with mentally retarded and handicapped persons in order to determine the most appropriate kind of program intervention and these questions need to be examined in much greater detail.

We have indicated that the most appropriate pattern for selection of priority training areas is the "hill and valley" approach. A mentally retarded individual's capacity for immediate benefit from training and treatment processes is often limited to one element at a time. Major priorities are absolutely necessary to determine which domains to approach first, and which items within the domain should receive emphasis. There is increasing evidence that this is the way handicapped children learn (and there is some possibility it may also be the way normal children learn). Fur-thermore, this "hill and valley" approach is clearly indicated for the development of individual education plans (IEP's) and individual habilitation plans (IHP's). Adaptive behavior measurement which indicates ongoing behaviors, the antecedents to those behaviors and proposed next steps in that same behavioral category, become the primary basis for the establishment of long range goals and objectives within the structuring of individual programs. The "hill and valley" concept gives priorities for these programs, allowing the adaptive behavior approach to emerge as one of the more essential guidelines in the development of individual program plans for both children and adults. As programs of early intervention develop, increased investigation is required concerning these same types of concepts in relationship to the infant population, who, while not yet designated as mentally retarded, nonetheless may evidence delay or potential handicap.

We need further to look at questions relating to quality of life of the handicapped individual. Adaptive behavior measurements can also make a major contribution in this area by indicating where the strengths of the individual lie, what are in effect the things that the individual can do which are consistent with society's overall demands. The indication of these strengths as compared with areas of deficiency gives a clear picture of what is for this individual a truly "least restrictive environment." The needs of training, treatment and other types of modification programs can be introduced alongside the expressed elements which are required for the individual to survive in a particular social community and still maintain a pattern of life consistent with his personal needs as modified by his handicap. This becomes a process of not allowing the handicap to become a disability but rather utilizing his strengths ("hills") to develop a pattern of living which permits the highest level of personal freedom that he is able to enjoy. This is a matter of our insuring that we do as much for these individuals as they need but that we make very sure that we do no more for them than they absolutely need, so that they have the best possible opportunity to function as self-sufficient persons.

Furthermore, it should be remembered that, while the major emphasis is based on functional independence, no person should always have to be alone. The social support system of the individual is as important a part of his adaptive behavior as any other specific aspect. In many respects it is a more important part than much of their skill behavior. Individuals working together can achieve many things that persons alone cannot and so specific skills are not always that important, but the ability to draw on a social chain of support in terms of both crisis situations and normal average activities of daily living as vital, if the individual is really to be able to maintain a life quality consistent with the highest levels of humanity.

Obviously, adaptive behavior assessment does not help in developing a support system, but it does help in bringing together individuals who are functioning at similar adaptive levels so that there is a basis for communication between them. It also helps indicate what specific types of maladaptive behaviors may be present which are driving people away and corrective programs of treatment can be introduced to help these individuals function at a more "lovable" level. Furthermore, through understanding of the adaptive behavior of the individual, the adaptive behavior of their family and of the people around them, it is possible to develop family-related groups (defining family "as groups of individuals who are living together with shared responsibility"). These groups can become the basis for assuring that not only will the handicap not become a disability, but that as the individuals develop additional problems related to aging, we do not get intensive deterioration.

In this short overview, an attempt has been made to outline the concept of adaptive behavior and measurement from essentially two philosophical approaches. First, I have presented the meaning of the idea itself; and, second, I have tried to present the functional, sociocultural considerations related to adaptive behavior assessments. I have also tried to raise some of the practical applied questions relative to the utilization of the obtained information. An attempt has been made to tie this material into some of the general problems of handicapped individuals as they live in our world. Through this approach, I have tried to indicate that while adaptive behavior measurement has some very distinct and precise objectives, the overall question of an "adaptive behavior approach" is far reaching. As research develops, this method should become a more important way of looking at handicaps than through the historical precedence of IQ or single categories leading to a labeling process which gives no guidance concerning the growth or development of the person.

References

Anokhin, P. K. (Ed.) *Biology and neurophysiology of the conditioned reflex and its role in adaptive behavior.* Oxford: Pergamon Press, 1974.

Balthazar, E. E. *Balthazar scales of adaptive behavior,* Palo Alto; Consulting Psychologists Press, 1973.

Blackman, D. H. Personal communication, 1980.

Coulter, W. A., & Morrow, H. W. (Eds.) *Adaptive behavior.* New York: Grune & Stratton, 1978.

Crawford, C. A. *Comparisons of parents' and teachers' perceptions of adaptive behavior and psycholinguistic functioning with young school age children of low socioeconomic status.* Unpublished Master's Thesis, The Ohio State University, 1974.

Doll, E. A. *Vineland social maturity scale: Manual of directions.* Minneapolis, Minn.: Educational Test Bureau, 1947.

Edmonson, B., Leach, E. M., & Leland, H. *Social perceptual training for community living.* Freeport, N.Y.: Educational Activities, 1969.

Edmonson, B., Leland, H., & Leach, E. M. Social inference training of retarded adolescents. *Education and Training of the Mentally Retarded,* 1970, **5**, 169–176.

Estreicher, D. G. *An investigation of the relationship between adaptive behavior and self-esteem of educable mentally retarded children as perceived by parents and teachers.* Unpublished Master's Thesis, The Ohio State University, 1978.

Grossman, H. J. (Ed.) *Manual on terminology and classification in mental retardation.* Washington, D.C.: American Association on Mental Deficiency, 1977.

Gunzburg, H. *Progress assessment chart of social and personal development,* Bristol, Ind.: Aux Chandelles, 1974.

Heber, R. (Ed.) A manual on terminology and classification in mental retardation. *American Journal of Mental Deficiency.* Monograph Supplement, 2nd ed., 1961.

Helson, H. *Adaptation-level theory.* New York: Harper and Row, 1964.

Kennett, K. F. *The family behavior profile.* Sydney, Australia: Saint Francis Xavier Univ., 1973.

Lambert, N., Windmiller, M., Cole, L., & Figuerra, R. *AAMD adaptive behavior scale: Public school version.* Monterey, Calif.: Publishers Test Service, 1981.

Larry P. v. Riles, 502 F. 2d 963 (9th Cir.), N.D. Cal. 1974.

Leland, H., What is a mentally retarded child? *Journal of Psychiatric Nursing,* 1964, **2**, 21–37.

Leland, H. Adaptation, coping behavior, and retarded performance. In P. Mittler (Ed.), *Research to practice in mental retardation: Education and training.* Vol. 2. London: University Park Press, 1977.

Leland, H. Theoretical considerations of adaptive behavior. In W. A. Coulter and H. W. Morrow (Eds.), *Adaptive behavior.* New York: Grune & Stratton, 1978. Chap. 2.

Leland, H., Schellhaas, M., Nihira, K., & Foster, R. Adaptive behavior: A new dimension in the classification of the mentally retarded. *Mental Retardation Abstracts,* 1967, **4**, 359–387.

Leland, H., Shoaee, M., McElwain, D., & Christie, R. *Adaptive behavior scale for infants and early childhood.* Columbus, Ohio: Nisonger Center, Ohio State University, 1980.

Leland, H., Shoaee, M., & Vayda, S. *Guidelines for the clinical use of the AAMD adaptive behavior scale.* Columbus, Ohio: Nisonger Center, Ohio State University, 1975.

Lenneberg, E. H. *Biological foundations of language.* New York: John Wiley & Sons, 1967.

Mercer, J. R., & Lewis, J. F. *System of multicultural pluralistic assessment: Parent interview manual and student assessment manual.* New York: The Psychological Corporation, 1977.

Nihira, K., Importance of environmental demands in the measurement of adaptive behavior. In G. Tarjan, R. J. Eyman, & C. E. Meyers (Eds.), *Sociobehavioral studies in mental retardation.* Monograph No. 1. Washington, D.C.: American Association on Mental Deficiency, 1973. Pp. 101–106.

Nihira, K., Foster, R., Shellhaas, N., & Leland, H. *AAMD adaptive behavior scale, Manual.* Washington, D.C.: American Association on Mental Deficiency, 1974.

Stillman, R. (Ed.) *Callier-Azusa scale.* Dallas, Tex.: University of Texas/Dallas, 1975.

Voisin, F. *De l'idiotie chez les enfants.* Paris: J. B. Bailliere, 1843.

15 BEHAVIORAL ASSESSMENT*

Johannes Rojahn and
Stephen R. Schroeder

B ehavioral assessment is quantification of behavioral phenomena through the systematic
recording of response parameters; its major
purpose is monitoring and evaluating behavior changes
in relation to manipulations of independent variables.
In recent years, behavioral assessment has been one
of the most rapidly developing areas within the field
of applied behavior analysis, behavior modification,
and behavior therapy. This increased interest is reflected
in a number of books (Barlow, 1981; Ciminero, Calhoun, & Adams, 1977; Cone & Hawkins, 1977;
Haynes, 1978; Hersen & Bellack, 1976; Keefe, Kopel,
& Gordon, 1978; Mash & Terdal, 1976, 1981a,b;
Sackett, 1978a,b; Schulte, 1974), in special issues of
leading journals (*Journal of Applied Behavior Analysis*,
1979, **12**[4]), and in the appearance of two new journals
(*Journal of Behavioral Assessment* and *Behavioral Assessment*) that are exclusively devoted to this topic.
It is the purpose of this chapter to discuss technological
and conceptual issues of behavioral assessment, with

a focus on applied research with severely and profoundly retarded persons in particular. Behavioral assessment as it is presented here also applies to other
groups of clients (Kazdin & Straw, 1976). The emphasis
on the lower functioning mentally retarded people
in this chapter, however, allows for a selection of
those techniques and methods that are more typical
for research in mental retardation than for any other
clinical population.

Behavioral assessment constitutes an important type
of evaluation for mentally retarded people. It differs
greatly and in various aspects from other types of
assessment such as IQ testing, the measurement of
adaptive functioning relative to sociocultural standards,
or the assessment of educational achievement. In
specifying the main characteristics of behavioral assessment, we will point out some of these differences.

First and foremost, behavioral assessment is change
oriented. Its major purpose is to provide the basis for
the development, performance, and evaluation of behavior change programs. Behavior is assessed to enhance the chances for its improvement.

Secondly, behavioral technology and behavioral
assessment are based on a specific set of assumptions
with respect to the level of inference from the data.
Observed and measured behavior under natural conditions is regarded as a sample of an individual's be-

* We wish to acknowledge NICHD grant HD-10570, "The
Neuropharmacology of Developmental Disorders," George
Breese, Ph.D. and C. T. Gualtieri, M.D., Principal In-
vestigators; USPHS grant HD-03110, and MCH project 916
to the Division for Disorders of Development and Learning.
We are especially grateful for the careful reading and the
critical comments of an earlier version of this chapter to
Dr. Jan Wallander and Dr. G. Summer.

havior repertoire, rather than as a symptomatic phe-nomenon that reflects some underlying cause (as is assumed in the medical model), or psychological trait (psychometric theory). Observable behavior is accepted as the true object of interest in its own right. Ac-cordingly, the behavioral approach to mental retar-dation recognizes the main issue as retarded *behavior*, rather than as retarded *mentality* (Bijou, 1966).

Thirdly, mental retardation from an experimental point of view refers to the total behavior of an individual who is classified as being retarded as the dependent variable. Retarded behavior is a function of independent variables and can—at least theoretically—be changed by the manipulation of those independent variables. In other words, the behavior is of primary interest for treatment, and not for diagnosis of some biological condition that is believed to exist among all those who display a similar set of behaviors. Of course, we do not have the ability yet to recognize and manipulate *all* of the causal factors of retarded behavior, but some of them have been found to be manipulable. This heuristic point of view seems to be justified, because organic abnormalities cannot be detected in the ma-jority of cases of mental retardation (Kazdin & Straw, 1976) and because sociocultural and environmental factors obviously are important variables in the de-velopment of human behavior. Furthermore, the biomedical model seems to have a disadvantageous effect on mentally retarded people through labeling and a causal attribution for failure. This view em-phasizes uncontrollable causes, such as brain damage, while it deemphasizes controllable factors, such as educational opportunities (cf. Weisz, 1981).

However, behavioral scientists generally do not discard the notion of behavior as being partly dependent upon organismic variables. Behavior can be assumed to be determined by the environment *and* by orga-nismic variables. Yet, since a behaviorist is an em-piricist, he/she has to prove his/her hypotheses about behavior change mechanisms through the systematic variation of the independent variables. Since the exact manipulation of aberrant biological conditions, such as structural defects of the brain, for example, is often beyond our control, behavior management programs have mostly focused on variables of nurture rather than nature. Therefore, behavioral assessment has been geared towards monitoring behavior changes as a function of environmental events such as ecologi-cal conditions (individual space, noise level, furnish-ing, etc.) or of behavioral-antecedent and behavior-contingent stimuli.

Studies investigating the direct impact of biological processes on behavior have been carried out and will have a major influence in the future with the growing sophistication of pharmacology and medical tech-nology. Nyhan, Johnson, Kaufman, and Jones (1980), for example, were able to reduce self-injurious behavior in seven of nine patients with Lesch-Nyhan syndrome through the alteration of the balance of biogenic amines in the central nervous system. This alteration was achieved through pharmacological agents (5-hydroxy-tryptophan in combination with carbidopa and im-ipramine). Although the subjects had become tolerant to the medication within one to three months, the type of question asked fits into a behavioral-experimental framework: Is there a functional de-pendency between certain biochemical variations (independent variables) and self-injurious behavior (dependent variable)? Behavior assessment techniques have become useful in this type of research.

Fourthly, behavioral assessment has abandoned the standards of age norms for interindividual com-parisons. In the development of behavior management programs that are individually designed or adapted for the unique conditions of a single person, norm-oriented assessment has proven to be of little value. For behavior change programs, the assessment of levels of responding and of intraindividual change was needed. Therefore, behavior assessment follows a *criterion*-oriented approach. Criterion-oriented as-sessment sets individual, task-oriented criteria for the estimation of specified response classes that are selected on the basis of a thorough problem analysis and the treatment goal (Linehan, 1980). For example, if one were to work with a mentally retarded client on a self-help dressing program, it would be of minor interest to know his/her percentile in a theoretical distribution of the respective age group for buttoning a shirt (norm-oriented assessment). What is of interest, however, is information on how close a particular person actually is to buttoning a shirt independently, whether the prerequisite fine motor skills are already developed to start training at a certain level, how many more training sessions this person would need to reach a certain criterion, whether the individual is improving with training, and whether training achievements are maintained and generalized to buttoning other gar-ments as well.

Fifthly, applied research asks for the analysis of behavior *in vivo*, and under conditions that are relevant for an individual's environment. Therefore, behavioral assessment is supposed to yield data that pertain directly to the behaviors as they appear in the actual situation. Observation of behavior under laboratory conditions can also be useful. This applies particularly to cases in which a behavior management program needs to be performed in a special therapy setting, rather than in the person's natural surrounding. Nevertheless, it is a priority of behavior assessment to train, as well as to observe, a person's behavior in his or her own environment.

Three interrelated response domains have traditionally been addressed with behavioral assessment, each of which requires a different approach and a special technology: observable *motor* responses are mostly assessed by direct observation; other possibilities are automatic recording, which is often found in basic experimental research, but also in applied studies. For instance, Schroeder (1972a,b) used electromechanical programming and recording equipment for the use of tools of retarded workers in an assembly line. Another possibility is indirect measurement, such as permanent product evaluation. An example of permanent product would be the production rate of a mentally retarded person on a sheltered workshop task. *Cognitive* behavior is usually inferred from responses to items on rating scales, checklists, questionnaires, semantic differentials, or questions during an interview. *Physiological* aspects of behavior are measured by special mechanical and electronic equipment. With severely and profoundly retarded people, direct observation techniques have been the almost exclusive choice. This is based on certain population-specific features, such as a generally limited communication repertoire. It is quite evident that the application of rating scales for cognitive attribution preferences or depressive thoughts would hardly be useful with a person apparently lacking expressive and receptive language. Direct observation does not require any skills from the client whatsoever. Since it is the most frequently used tool for behavioral assessment with the mentally retarded, direct observation will be the subject of this chapter. A more detailed account on recording equipment for various behavior topographies in applied research with the mentally retarded for response detection and for data storage can be found in Mulick, Scott, Gaines, and Campbell (1983).

Other observation techniques, such as rating scales for adaptive behavior, which have had an increased relevance for mentally retarded people in recent years (Grossman, 1977), are discussed in chapter 14 of this volume.

Observational Assessment Strategies and Units of Measurement

Behavior observation includes monitoring selected response parameters from an ongoing behavioral sequence within predetermined time periods. These response parameters together with the observation periods determine the units of measurement or the assessment strategy. Three basic parameters exist in behavioral observation data: the onset-time of a response, its frequency of occurrence, and its duration. These parameters are the essential ingredients of quantified response characteristics that are frequently used as dependent variables in applied research. Among them are rate, simple and cumulative frequency, probability, interresponse time, latency, sequential pattern, topography, precision, etc.

Within observation time periods, behavior can be observed continuously or only during certain intervals. A direct, real time behavior record is evidently more accurate than an arbitrary time sample, yet it is not always feasible. For instance, continuous recording is usually more expensive and time consuming, tends to amass a large amount of information that is often difficult to analyze, and is strenuous for the observers. So the selection of a dependent variable (unit of measurement) and the time characteristics of observation (observation periods) are among the first of a number of important decisions that have to be made prior to the collection, analysis, and interpretation of data. They have direct impact on the quality and meaningfulness of an assessment procedure.

For the recording procedure a large variety of materials and technical aids can be employed. They include the simple paper-pencil-stopwatch outfit, oven timers, manual punching of computer cards with a stylus, checklists, mechanical counters, multitrack mechanical event recorders with keys on a control board connected to pens that mark on a strip chart, data entry and storage on a computer-readable medium such as paper tape, magnetic tape, or solid-state memory (Sackett, Stephenson, & Ruppenthal, 1973), which are commercially available by Electro/General's "Datamyte" and IBM's Data Acquisition Computer. A detailed description and discussion of recording techniques and instrumentation for observational data has been given by Holm (1978).

The choice of a particular assessment strategy depends on numerous factors, some of which will be of a pragmatic/economical nature, such as the availability of certain technological devices or manpower. Other factors will be related to more theoretical considerations. For instance, certain analysis techniques require specific characteristics of the data, or the choice of a response parameter, which is the most valid to describe a specific behavior. The following observational assessment strategies that will be discussed are the ones most widely used in applied research.

Their major characteristics as well as advantages and disadvantages will be highlighted.

Frequency Recording

Frequency recording refers to counting the number of responses (and/or stimulus events) within a given observation period. Frequency recording yields the *rate* of responding. The actual time of response onset within each observation frame (temporal pattern) is not recorded.

It is usually assumed that response rates are readily comparable, even between sessions with variable observation periods. Yet, this assumption might not always be valid; for instance, when dealing with a highly variable pattern of responding. For example, a bout of 15 rapid head hits in a self-injurious child at one point in a 30-minute observation period might have a different "clinical meaning" than 15 randomly distributed hits during the same amount of time, or 30 hits during one hour. This term, "clinical meaning," can be easily operationalized here: it is conceivable that a bout of 15 hits is a different type of responding, because it is likely that these 15 hits are controlled by entirely different stimuli and consequences from the other two cases. This certainly would have consequences for the behavior analysis. Furthermore, 15 hits are much more likely to result in visible, short-term consequences such as tissue reddening or even swelling than the spread-out hits. It is also more dramatic to watch and could therefore easily affect the caretaker's behavior in a different way.

Frequency data can be useful for discrete and brief behavioral events, when only the rate of responding is of interest. Yet frequency measures do not permit a detailed within-session analysis of observer agreement. This means that only rough estimates of the data quality based on session-total scores can be achieved.

Duration Data

Duration data reflect the amount of time that a particular behavior was emitted by an individual during a set period of time. Duration data provide a percentage score of actual time engaged in a certain activity.

Duration data neglect a great deal of other information on the behavioral process; duration, however, is an important measure in time allocation studies, such as attention research, or studies of behavioral preferences. Observer agreement evaluation is similarly limited as with frequency recording, because moment-to-moment comparisons of observer records are not possible in either case. Only a rough comparison of the total duration score per session can be used.

Continuous Recording or Continuous Real Time Measurement

Continuous recording means the behavior-synchronized, real time recording of each onset and each end (and therefore also of each duration and frequency) of responding during an observation period. It represents the most complete strategy available in observational assessment and, most importantly, contains precise information of temporal structures of a response, such as pattern of occurrence, sequence, torque, bouts, inter-response times, and cyclic variations.

The natural trade-off is the work-intensity during all stages of data work. The completeness, however, leaves a large variety of options for data analysis.

Interval Recording or Modified Frequency Time Sampling

Interval recording is an interrupted time observation, in which the observer scans for present and usually fixed time intervals that alternate with nonobservation intervals. The nonobservation intervals can be used for recording. Behavioral events are scored in a dichotomous fashion as having occurred or having not occurred during the last observe interval. This means, for example, that three occurrences of one response during one observe interval lead to the same record as one or five occurrences. Observe intervals usually range between five and 30 seconds. Record intervals are either as long, or shorter.

Apparently, with interval recording, one loses important information, particularly on temporal response characteristics. It does not yield an accurate record of the frequency, the duration, or the onset. For this reason, interval recording has also been labelled "modified frequency time sampling" (Sackett, 1978b). Interval recording is also relatively insensitive to the analysis of functional stimulus-response relationships, because it does not account for small sequential order effects. On the other hand, because of the interruptions that give the observer time to record, interval recording may allow for a greater number of behavior codes to be monitored simultaneously than other strategies.

Actually, there are two subtypes of interval-recording that differ in their specification of temporal characteristics of a scorable response. The one strategy described above would then be called *partial interval time sampling*, whereas in the *whole interval time sampling* a response has to be present and ongoing throughout the whole observe interval. Powell, Martindale, and Kulp (1975) demonstrated in an empirical study that the partial interval method had overestimated the actual response occurrence, whereas the whole interval method had underestimated it. Generally, it is true that the accuracy improves with the increase of the number of observe intervals.

Momentary Time Sampling or Discontinuous Probe-time Sampling

With momentary time sampling, the observer scans the subject after certain, equally long intervals for a "moment," checking whether a specified response was occurring at that moment or not. The interobserve intervals are usually fixed and the length of the observe "moment" is often specified more precisely, such as "two seconds." Probe-time sampling will be more appropriate for behavior which is ongoing rather than momentary in its appearance.

In the study by Powell et al. (1975), it was also demonstrated that momentary time sampling both under- as well as overestimated actual response rate at random. They found that the larger the interobserve interval, the larger were the intersession differences. However, since momentary time sampling equally over- and underestimated response rates in single observe sessions, the mean over several sessions was reported as being a reasonably accurate account of the true response rate. Yet, it needs to be remembered that the Powell et al. (1975) results were achieved with only one specific subject (a secretary) and one specific response-type (in-seat behavior); generalizations to other populations and response types might not always be warranted.

Interaction Recording

Interaction recording is designed to monitor behavior of one person in the context of the behavior of another person in a dyad. The recording of dyadic social interaction has been mostly used in families of developmentally delayed children and children with behavior problems (Forehand & King, 1977; Johnson & Lobitz, 1974). The basic idea of interaction recording is to uncover contingency patterns in the sequence of two people's behaviors. For instance, a purpose could be to reveal "unintentional" reinforcement of a mother for inappropriate child behavior, to demonstrate ongoing countercontrol of the child, and to pinpoint antecedent events that set off undesirable behavior. In such a case, the child's behavior would be viewed as the target-response, whereas the mother's behavior would be seen as either antecedent or consequent events.

The recording usually proceeds in a behavior/event pace, rather than being controlled by arbitrary time intervals. In setting up an interaction recording system, critical classes of behaviors from each of the two persons involved in the dyad are summarized, defined, and categorized. The observer scores the ongoing interaction by recording interaction chains (contiguous, alternate behaviors from both members), and behaviors that are not followed by a response of the partner. The resulting record can be analyzed as to which functional relationship existed between the behavior of two people in a dyadic interaction.

Interfacing Data from Different Observation Systems

Most clinical assessment protocols involve large data acquisition packages, partly to control for inherent problems and weaknesses of single observation strategies, partly because of the need for different types of information that cannot be accomplished by one single data system.

As a result, a multitude of information gathering media are employed, reaching from systematic observation techniques, rating scales, clinical impressions, and interviews. To integrate all this information in a scientifically appropriate fashion is obviously a highly complex task that requires a strict rationale. But even within one type of data gathering medium, such as direct observation, the interfacing of results from multiple systems, which are used in different settings, or by different observers, and that focus on different response units, can be a problem.

For example, Schroeder, Rojahn, and Mulick (1978) developed a multiple data package of direct observation systems for a developmental day-care program for chronically self-injurious mentally retarded people. The data package consisted of two interval recording systems, one momentary time-sample system, and frequency recording. The purpose of this observation system was to serve day-to-day clinical decision making, as well as more sophisticated analyses of complex stimulus-response interactions. Each system consisted of multiple categories, including self-injurious behavior, but employed different response units. The data indicate that variability can be expected from the application of different response units and the differential control during various time periods. Observation system A was *frequency recording*; the data in the graph show response-rate per minute. Observation system B was interval recording or *partial interval time sampling* with 10-second observe intervals and 10-second record intervals. Both were used simultaneously for the same period of time by the same observer for 16 minutes daily between 9:00 a.m. and 12:30 p.m. Observation system C was the second *partial time sampling system*, that had longer observe intervals (10 minutes) and 10-second record intervals. *Momentary time sampling* was employed with system

D, where the observers had to scan the clients every 10 minutes for 2 seconds. Systems C and D were applied by trained staff personnel, who were also involved in behavior management programs during the same time. These two systems covered the whole period between 9:00 a.m. and 12:30 p.m. Pearson correlations for the time-matched systems were $r_{A+B} = 0.90$, and $r_{C+D} = 0.69$. The other pairwise correlations were $r_{A+C} = 0.59$, $r_{A+D} = 0.66$, $r_{B+C} = 0.62$, and $r_{B+D} = 0.68$. As a matter of fact, these results are unusually high, given the various differences between the systems. The reason for the high correlations between these for different response parameters can be attributed to the high rate of responding and the fairly equally distributed incidences during the 2½-hour observation sessions. A skewed distribution, or burst responding would lower the correlations between response parameters. Nevertheless, this example shows the difference between data systems even under favorable conditions. The similarity of the observation parameters will yield higher similarity in the results.

The usage of data packages permits "multidimensional" and "trans-situational" evaluation of outcomes, but what if the different measures disagree? In fact, disagreement among multiple outcome measures is more the rule than the exception. Which measures should be used as criteria, and which should be used as covariants? For instance, parents' impression of therapy outcomes with their children often agrees poorly with other observational data. Which is the more valid measure? There are many reasons why the measures may disagree. For instance, the variances contained in the several measures may not be comparable statistically; or each measure may be selectively sensitive to a different set of covariates, e.g., sex, race, age, maternal IQ, the care-taking environment, time, etc.; or each measure may reflect idiosyncratic aspects of the clinical phenomenon under study. All of these hypotheses are plausible explanations for lack of correlation among multiple measures. Yet, they would be more convincing if stated *a priori* rather than *a posteriori*. In other words, when multiple types of data in data packages are used, a commitment should be made prior to the analysis as to what role each data set is expected to play in determining what the total behavior outcome will be.

Coding Systems

The description of observational assessment strategies involves discussion of the unit of measurement and some implications of the most frequently employed strategies. Another aspect of describing and differentiating observational assessment tools is the complexity of a coding system. Complexity here refers to the number of events that are simultaneously monitored by one system.

Simple Behavioral Events

The simplest form of behavioral assessment is the observation of *one* target behavior or the recording of *one* dependent variable. Behavioral analysis started out in animal laboratories. A high degree of experimental control over the independent variable can be achieved in the laboratory at the expense of immediate applied significance of the results. A great amount of operant research in the laboratory uses strictly operationalized response measures such as lever presses and button pushing. Equally precisely controlled are environmental variables like visual and acoustic stimuli, reinforcers, and punishers. Under such conditions, it is often sufficient to record a single behavior as the dependent variable, since behavioral options are usually very restricted; unpredictable effects almost by definition hardly ever occur and if they do, they are considered the result of inadequate experimental planning.

In the beginnings of applied behavior analysis, the condition of one-dimensional observation was preserved, along with the behavioral technology from laboratory research, and as a matter of fact, the majority of publications in behavior analysis journals are still based on single response measures. However, the effects of an intervention procedure in applied settings through the medium of a single response record might not be representative enough. Measures of a single response, usually the "target response," most likely give an incomplete picture of the resulting changes. In the natural environment, we do not exert the same rigorous control over the variables. For example, target behaviors are part of the whole behavior repertoire of a person. It cannot be assumed that the clinically significant behavioral events in such a repertoire are unrelated or isolated. It seems evident, therefore, that our understanding of certain responses is enhanced when we look at them as parts of a dynamic system.

Additionally, behavioral interventions are found to cause changes that are not limited to one target behavior. They often result in changes of collateral behavior. This can either appear in a positive fashion in terms of response generalization or in a negative way, such as "side effects." For instance, Rollings, Baumeister, and Baumeister (1977) demonstrated that suppression of body rocking through overcorrection was associated with increased collateral stereotypic behavior. During treatment, previously unobserved behaviors like self-pinching, self-scratching, complex finger manipulations, and screaming were exhibited by one subject. In the second subject, head nodding increased while stereotyped body rocking was being treated. Similar effects on the increase of collateral stereotypes during suppression of a target response with overcorrection were reported by Rollings and Baumeister (1981).

This example shows that the evaluation of an intervention procedure that is based on a single-target-response measure is likely to lack important information. In Rollings et al.'s example, the major dependent variable was clearly reduced, but this certainly was not the only effect. Had they only observed body rocking, the results would have given a favorable, yet incomplete, picture of what had actually happened. Particularly with response elimination procedures, a multiple-event observation system is clearly warranted.

Multiple Events

The fact that behavioral intervention procedures can be expected to occasion a whole variety of changes in the client's behavior repertoire, not only in the target behavior, suggests that the appropriate evaluations of treatment outcomes must take this complexity into account. The assessment of a decrease of an inappropriate target behavior by itself proves the "effectiveness" of treatment; yet this does not guarantee its clinical relevance and usefulness. One possible adaptation of assessment instruments for the investigation of more complex intervention effects would be the extension of the number of behavioral events that are included in the observation (Willems, 1974).

MULTIPLE BEHAVIOR SYSTEMS

These contain more than one response category of an individual that are observed simultaneously. The purpose of multiple behavior systems is the analysis of intervention procedures on a variety of behaviors and their interactions that are likely to be affected by treatment. The selection of response categories will depend on various factors and is based on the treatment goal or on the expected changes, respectively. Informed observations prior to setting up the category system will help to identify the repertoire of relevant behaviors.

Fig. 15.1 shows an example of the type of data that can be expected from such a multiple behavior system, which applied a *partial interval time sampling* strategy (5-minute interobserver interval, 2-second observation). The client, M. M., was a severely mentally retarded male adult of 26 years, who was abruptly withdrawn from 200 mg of Mellaril (thioridazine) per day in a double blind, placebo-controlled fashion for 8 weeks. After that, he was put back on 50 mg of

Mellaril per day. During withdrawal, nurses and caretakers reported noncompliance, hyperactivity, agitation, and weight loss. The client had also developed severe withdrawal symptoms (tardive dyskinesia) in the third week of the study. Observational data presented in Fig. 15.1 shows an increase in "out of seat" and "vocalization" as well as a decrease of "work and play" after drug withdrawal. This tendency in the data, which is reversed after Mellaril is reintroduced, might reflect those behaviors that were reported by the nurses as hyperactivity, agitation, and noncompliance.

Owing to the strategy of momentary time sampling, these data do not lend themselves to sophisticated interresponse interaction analysis. Nevertheless, the system has proven to be sensitive as a clinical assessment tool for drug effects. More detailed analysis would require an interval or continuous recording strategy.

MULTIPLE STIMULUS-RESPONSE SYSTEMS

Multiple response systems are designed to reflect changes and interrelationships in a set of responses. They therefore will be able to reveal interresponse relationships such as indirect treatment effects on collateral behaviors or other behavioral phenomena. Multiple response systems, however, will be insensitive to the detection of "unexpected" functional dependencies between a person and some uncontrolled variables in his/her natural environment. Behavior management techniques that are used on applied problems in natural environments need to be evaluated within this context. There, a certain behavior is evidently

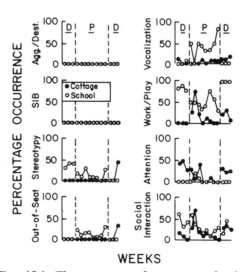

FIG. 15.1. The percentage of occurrence of eight different response types emitted by M.M. during drug-placebo-drug conditions.

not exclusively dependent on the programmed contingencies. Behavior does not occur independently from other behaviors, but is part of a dynamic response system, which is mutually dependent with the environment. The whole system can be called an ecology.

This ecology consists of the physical and social environment as well as the behavior of the individuals. These three components mutually influence one another, e.g., the behaviors of one person are interrelated with one another. However, the change of one particular response will not only affect other behaviors of that same person, but possibly some aspects of the physical and social context (Rogers-Warren & Warren, 1977). Ecological research in the sense of the investigation of the influences of environmental characteristics on behavior had been pursued mainly by experimental psychologists, who have carried out studies about complex nonverbal social behavior such as territoriality, dominance, food sharing, social behavior with peers, and communication (Berkson & Landesman-Dwyer, 1977). Ecological psychology itself has not given much attention to research with the developmentally disabled (Schoggen, 1978), but its basic assumptions have been recognized and integrated into applied behavior analysis. Owing to an increased interest in "clinical usefulness" within the reality of applied work, behavior analysts have been looking for strategies that help to identify conditions that are favorable for a given treatment procedure and others that are not. Applied behavior analysis has developed to the point where it requires different criteria for intervention techniques from the mere demonstration of a functional relationship between the dependent and the independent variable. Issues such as generalization, maintenance, and possible side effects of treatment procedures have become important. This is reflected in discussions of ecological and social validity or consumer satisfaction. These interests in more complex intervention effects in natural experiments put new demands on behavioral assessment.

Ecobehavioral analysis, a term coined by Rogers-Warren and Warren (1977), is the attempt to investigate how the environment and the behavior of its inhabitants affect one another and how to operate with them as a behavior change agent for the purpose of long-term behavioral management. Ecobehavioral analysis is clearly change oriented and not only descriptive of complex behavior-environment systems. This ecobehavioral approach has had a strong impact on assessment. As Willems (1977) suggested, new kinds of data, in addition to those of traditional behavior analysis, are required. Basically, he called for an expansion of data collection. Willems (1977) offered some specific suggestions as to how to alter data collection, although

"it is impossible to offer *a priori* specification of the degree of expansion for each and every study" (p. 53). Data systems should be expanded by (*a*) increasing the number of behavior categories, (*b*) increasing the number of persons observed, (*c*) observing other dimensions of behavior in addition to its type, (*d*) lengthening the time period of observation, and (*e*) increasing the number of settings in which the observations are made.

Ecobehavioral studies have already yielded important results with the emotionally disturbed (Wahler, House, & Stambaugh, 1976), with autistic children (Lichstein & Wahler, 1976), and with the analysis and treatment of self-injurious behavior in the mentally retarded (Schroeder, Rojahn, & Mulick, 1978; Schroeder, Kanoy, Mulick, Rojahn, Thios, Stephens, & Hawk, in press).

Many other multiple stimulus-response observation systems have been applied with mentally retarded persons on a more descriptive nonintervention-oriented approach. For example, Berkson and Romer (1980) used a 41-category system with a momentary time sampling strategy in combination with staff ratings and client reports to study various aspects of the social ecology of mentally retarded adults in a supervised communal facility. They carried out research on prediction of affiliation (Romer & Berkson, 1980a), and social choice (Romer & Berkson, 1980b), on characteristics of social behavior (Romer & Berkson, 1981), on social and work adjustment (Berkson, 1981), and initial social adaptation (Heller, Berkson, & Romer, 1981).

Another example of multiple stimulus-response observations was reported by Lewis, McLean, Johnson and Baumeister (1981), in a descriptive study of the rhythm of stereotyped behaviors in five mentally retarded people. Using a multiple category system, including the target behaviors, social interactions, settings, and activities, they investigated the environmental influence on the patterning of stereotyped behavior.

A multiple-category data system can have certain properties in terms of coding regulations that play a role for the selection of data analysis techniques. Sackett (1978b) argues that behavior categories should be mutually exclusive (only one activity can be recorded at any time) and exhaustive (there must be no point in time without a scorable category), in order to permit the calculation of behavioral probabilities relative to time and the total alternative behavioral output.

Data Analysis

Behavioral assessment, and direct observation in particular, have developed as the information gathering procedure of applied behavior analysis. It has been based on repeated measures on single subjects rather than on single measures on subject groups within the operant baseline logic of experimentation. Applied behavior analysis, as it is today, is mainly a result of the work by Skinner (1953) and some of his followers (e.g., Sidman, 1960), who strongly opposed the scientific tradition of the hypotheticodeductive method, group experiments and inferential statistics (cf. Parsonson & Baer, 1978).

The main method of data presentation has been the use of graphs. The data plotted in these graphs are usually direct behavioral scores of the basic measurement units, e.g., frequencies of occurrence or response duration. Simple transformations of the raw data, such as rate of responding or percentage of responses, are also used in these graphs. The construction and different types of graphical presentation of behavioral data are closely described in Parsonson and Baer (1978).

The most important purpose of behavioral assessment is the demonstration of behavioral control. This demonstration is usually based on the comparison of different behavioral data from different experimental phases (time series data). The simplest case would be the comparison of baseline responding (nontreatment phase) with responding during treatment. For a detailed discussion of single subject experimental design see Hersen and Barlow (1976).

Visual Analysis of Graphic Data

Visual analysis of graphic data is the most widely used and straightforward procedure in behavioral assessment. Yet, visual inference is a highly complex process, and there are many possibilities for distortions in the interpretation of graphs (e.g., Wampold & Furlong, 1981; Gottman & Glass, 1978; Jones, Weinrott, & Vaught, 1978). Parsonson and Baer (1978) discussed the literature on statistical properties of data that are critical to visual analysis. These involve the stability of baseline, the variability within experimental phases, the variability between phases, overlap between scores of adjacent phases, number of data points in each phase, changes in trend within phases, changes in trend between adjacent phases, changes in level between phases, analysis of data across similar phases, and the evaluation of the overall pattern of the data. Another factor, serial dependency of the data could be added (see Jones et al., 1978). Other attempts at a rationale for visual inference from graphs were given by Hersen and Barlow (1976) and Kazdin (1976).

Although visual inference of graphically displayed data has great practical advantages (see, e.g., Parson-

son & Baer, 1978), it lacks a strong conceptual and methodological basis. One approach to systematize the process of visual analysis is the description of factors, as presented above. Another way would be its empirical investigation. Wampold and Furlong (1981) presented a theoretical framework (schema theory) to study visual inference.

Discussion about visual inference has mainly dealt with single behavior scores. With an increase of observational sophistication and the quantity of observed events, the data become more and more complex. A reliable analysis of phenomena, such as side effects of behavioral interventions and collateral behaviors is difficult to achieve from the inspection of graphs alone without the help of statistical analysis.

There are several different statistical approaches to the analysis of single subject data. Some of them shall be discussed here on a descriptive, nontechnical level. Kazdin (1976) has given an excellent introduction to the basics of these techniques for the applied behavior analyst. An updated version of this topic is Hartmann, Gottman, Jones, Gardner, Kazdin, and Vaught (1980).

Time Series Analysis

Time series analysis evaluates differences of two or more sequences of serial data in terms of their level and slope, while taking the serial dependency of the data into account. Serial dependency means that the series of data is autocorrelated, or that correlations exist among successive data points. Correlations can appear between data separated by different time intervals (lags) in the series. These autocorrelations are used as part of the analysis to describe the specific structure and dependency of the data. This is accomplished by fitting the model to the data series that describes its structure best. A variety of different model types exists (Anderson, 1976; Box & Jenkins, 1970; Glass, Willson, & Gottman, 1975).

The model chosen then transforms the data so that they match the requirements of traditional statistical analysis by removing the serial dependency. After the transformation, *t*-tests are applied for hypothesis testing. A testable null hypothesis could be: baseline data do not differ in a statistically significant degree from the ones collected during the intervention phase, either in level or in slope.

Time series analysis is a fairly complicated and expensive data analysis technique for serially dependent data. It is useful for experimental rather than for clinical behavior analysis, where even subtle but statistically significant changes are important to recognize. As an additional means to visual inspection for data analysis, as Kazdin (1976) recommends, time series analysis seems to be as yet rather uneconomical.

Other statistical methods for the analysis of time-sequential data are various types of *Markov chain analyses* (Gottman & Notarius, 1978). Sackett (1978) suggested an alternative method, called *lag-sequential analysis* (cf. Gottman & Notarius, 1978). It is based on principles of auto- and cross-lag correlation. The analysis focuses on the temporal dependencies between behavioral events.

As an alternative to time series analysis, one may wish to consider a relatively new procedure called MATPAR, i.e., *matched-pair partial correlation procedure* (Johnson & Quade, 1980). MATPAR will calculate a correlation between any two variables while matching (or partialing out or controlling for) any other specific variables. For example, suppose one wishes to correlate time with a target behavior in order to see if the behavior decreases over time and that this decrease in behavior is independent of environmental changes, e.g., a change in room decorations (old and new) occurring during this period. To remove or partial out any effects on the behavior due to the change in room decorations, it would be necessary to correlate only data points within a condition which in effect matches on the environmental change of room decorations.

Foster and Cone (1980) used the term *ecological validity* of direct observation coding systems to call attention to the fact that important aspects related to coding systems have received relatively little attention by behavioral assessors. While it has been a critical issue, for example, as to how behavioral categories are defined, not much attention has been paid to the selection of the "right" behaviors, the units of measurement or the times and places for observation. A coding system is considered ecologically valid when all of these factors have been appropriately considered. Similar neglect can often be found in the area of data management: the type of data presentation in graphs, the transformation of data (e.g., the presentation of the means over several sessions to reduce variability within experimental phases), or the methods of statistical analysis.

The Practice of Quality Estimation of Observational Data

The calculation of observer agreement is the most frequently used method in behavioral assessment to evaluate and control the quality of observational data. Some of the more prominent measures will be discussed here. As will be shown, the choice of such a formula depends on a number of factors. The decision of

which of these formulae to choose is certainly an important one. How critical this choice can be is partly reflected in Table 15.1, which demonstrates the strikingly different results that are yielded by different formulae on the same data. This table can also be consulted to investigate the "face-validity" of each formula as far as their results with selected cases of data configurations are concerned.

The presented formulae can be applied to categorical data. Categorical data are yielded by *interval*, *time-sampling*, and *continuous** recording. These formulae are developed for a detailed analysis of agreement on an interval-by-interval basis within observation sessions rather than just on the comparison of observation session totals.

Frequency and duration recording usually do not provide within-session time intervals, so that only session totals can be considered. For the comparison of session total measures, which are continuous rather than categorical, Pearson correlations or similar statistics can be recommended. For *interaction recording*, the calculation of observer agreement depends on how the data are being transformed into either categorical or continuous data. If they are transformed into categorical data through superimposing time intervals and dichotomous scoring decisions within intervals, the following part also applies for interaction recording strategies.

Observer Agreement Formulae Based on Percent Agreement

Percentage agreement formulae will be briefly discussed by using the nomenclature in Table 15.2. The estimated values lie between 0 (no agreement) and 1 (total agreement).

Percentage agreement on occurrence (PO) =

$$\frac{A}{A + B + C} \times 100 \qquad (1)$$

Percentage agreement on nonoccurrence (PNO) =

$$\frac{D}{D + B + C} \times 100 \qquad (2)$$

Overall percentage agreement on occurrence and nonoccurrence (OPA) =

---

* Continuous recording may also be evaluated on an interval-by-interval basis if the records contain time intervals that divide them into recording trials with dichotomous data within intervals.

Table 15.1. Comparison of Different Results of Observer Agreement Yielded by Nine Different Formulae for 16 Illustrative Cases.

	2 × 2 Table $\frac{A|B}{C|D}$	PO	CO	PNO	CNO	OPA	OCA	WA	κ	φ
1.	$\frac{50|0}{0|0}$	100	100	0	0	100	100	0	0	0
2.	$\frac{45|0}{0|5}$	100	81	100	1	100	82	100	100	100
3.	$\frac{49|1}{0|0}$	98	98	0	0	98	98	98	0	0
4.	$\frac{48|1}{0|1}$	98	94	50	8	96	84	51	66	70
5.	$\frac{0|1}{0|49}$	0	0	98	98	98	98	98	0	0
6.	$\frac{1|0}{1|48}$	50	8	98	94	96	94	51	66	70
7.	$\frac{25|0}{0|25}$	100	25	100	25	100	50	100	100	1
8.	$\frac{35|0}{0|15}$	100	49	100	9	100	58	100	1	1
9.	$\frac{24|1}{0|25}$	96	24	96	26	98	50	96	96	96
10.	$\frac{20|10}{0|20}$	67	24	67	24	80	48	67	62	66
11.	$\frac{9|16}{9|16}$	26	18	39	32	50	50	38	0	0
12.	$\frac{1|24}{24|1}$	2	25	2	25	4	50	2	−92	−92
13.	$\frac{14|12}{13|11}$	36	28	31	22	50	50	41	−3	−3
14.	$\frac{11|12}{13|14}$	31	22	36	28	50	50	41	−3	−3
15.	$\frac{13|12}{13|12}$	34	26	32	24	50	50	29	0	0
16.	$\frac{12|12}{13|13}$	32	24	34	26	50	50	29	0	0

The results were multiplied by 100. The 16 cases have been placed into three groups: (1) Cases 1–6 illustrative of extremely skewed distributions of observations toward one cell in the 2 × 2 table. (2) Cases 7–12 illustrate more even distributions of observations across diagonally opposite cells. (3) Cases 13–16 illustrate even distributions across all four cells. See text for definition of abbreviations.

$$\frac{A + D}{A + B + C + D} \times 100 \qquad (3)$$

These three formulae have been the most basic, straightforward, and the most used measures of agreement in observational research (Berk, 1979). No the-

oretical assumption precludes their application for behavioral data and they do not account for agreement by chance.

The most serious drawback of percent agreement formulae is that they are positively related to the base rate of occurrence of the behavior of interest. This

Table 15.2. Two × Two Contingency Table of Possible Agreements and Disagreements of Two Observers on the Occurrence (O) or Nonoccurrence (NO) of an Event

		Observer 2	
		O	NO
Observer 1	O	A	B
	NO	C	D

would mean an inflation of some results by chance agreement (e.g., Hopkins & Hermann, 1977). E.g., high occurrence of an event would inflate PO, low occurrence would automatically increase PNO (see also Table 15.1).

A recently developed modification of OAP, called weighted agreement (WA), attempts to correct for chance by weighting every measure according to the observed rate of behavior (Harris & Lahey, 1978).

Weighted agreement (WA) =

$$\frac{A\left(\dfrac{B + C + 2D}{A + B + C + D}\right)}{2(A + B + C)}$$

$$+ \frac{D\left(\dfrac{2A + B + C}{A + B + C + D}\right)}{2(B + C + D)} \times 100 \qquad (4)$$

As will be discussed below, correction for chance agreement might be a problem by itself, at least on a more theoretical level.

Computational Formulae for Chance Agreement

Hopkins and Hermann (1977) presented three computation formulae to estimate change agreement, which were deduced from the basic theorems of probability theory for independent events.

Chance agreement on occurrence (CO) =

$$\frac{(A + B)(A + C)}{(A + B + C + D)^2} \times 100 \qquad (5)$$

Chance agreement on nonoccurrence (CNO) =

$$\frac{(D + B)(D + C)}{(A + B + C + D)^2} \times 100 \qquad (6)$$

Overall chance agreement (OCA) =

$$\frac{(A + B)(A + C) + (D + B)(D + C)}{(A + B + C + D)^2} \times 100$$

$$(7)$$

The formulae on chance agreement are mainly dependent on the frequency of observed events and to a lesser degree on the ratio of B/C (if $B < C$), given that A and D are constant. The smaller the ratio, the smaller the chance agreement.

Correlation and Correlation-like Statistics

Kappa (κ) is an agreement measure for both occurrence and nonoccurrence for categorial data (Cohen, 1960; Fleiss, 1971). Its main characteristic is the ability to estimate agreement after clearing the data from chance agreement.

$$\kappa = \frac{2\left[A - \dfrac{(A + B)(A + C)}{A + B + C + D}\right]}{B + C + 2\left[A - \dfrac{(A + B)(A + C)}{A + B + C + D}\right]}$$

$$(8)$$

Kappa's upper limit is 1.00, its lower limit is zero, and an inverse relationship between observers' records is expressed by values between zero and −1.00. Kappa has also been generalized for multiple raters (Conger, 1980; Fleiss, 1971; Light, 1971).

Phi (ϕ) is the product-moment correlation for dichotomous data (from Kent & Foster, 1977):

$$\phi = \frac{(A \times D) - (B \times C)}{[(A + B)(C + D)(A + C)(B + D)]^{1/2}} \qquad (9)$$

In case the rate of occurrence of the target event is approximately equal for the two observers $[(A+B/A+B+C+D) \cong (A+C/A+B+C+D)]$, κ and ϕ are almost identical in value (Hartmann, 1977). Phi, like kappa, was developed for independent data.

The primary assumption underlying the use of correction for chance in the kappa and percentage agreement formulae is that the emitted behavioral responses are independent. However, in the typical behavioral analysis study, one is dealing with response-series of a single person. As noted by Jones (1977), "single subject scores replicated over occasions (i.e., trials) are likely to be non independent" (p. 338). Unless empirically demonstrated to the contrary, serial dependency has generally been accepted as the usual case with regard to the analysis of between-occasion or between-session scores of a single subject. As a result, correction for chance (WA, κ, φ, chance agreement formulae) as well as probability-based formulae (κ, φ) are not entirely appropriate for most of single subject response series data from a statistical point of view (Wasik, Rojahn, & Schroeder, 1978).

What can be assumed to be an acceptable level of observer agreement? As a rule of thumb, the level of observer disagreement must not override the experimental effects. Usually, values of 0.75 to 0.80 indicate acceptable agreement.

A very different approach was offered by Birkimer and Brown (1979) in an attempt to circumvent statistical problems of percentage formulae and issues of chance agreement. The idea was to present graphically the disagreement range as a bandwidth around reported rates of the behavioral event. The graphic presentation of disagreements conveys and summarizes all information obtained from percentage agreement formulae (PO, PNO, OPA), as well as from chance agreement percentage (CO, CNO, OCA). It permits the easy determination of whether sound observer agreement relative to the amount of corresponding chance agreement has been demonstrated. It is also a simple and rather direct method of comparing observer disagreement with changes in behavior rates due to experimental manipulations. Nevertheless, it needs to be pointed out that the method by Birkimer and Brown (1979) is based on percentage statistics. This means that the earlier comments on the difficulties with these formulae also apply here. For further discussions of this procedure see Hartmann and Gardner (1979), Hawkins and Fabry (1979), Hopkins (1979), Kratochwill (1979), and Yelton (1979).

In yet another conceptually different approach to observer agreement, Gottman (1980) argues for the comparison of sequential structures in the data streams generated by two observers. His suggestions are of particular interest for continuous recording strategies when sequential behavior patterns and behavioral covariations are of primary interest. In his opinion, interval-by-interval comparisons of categorical data are sufficient, and in fact, even too stringent for that purpose. Gottman's concept of comparing two observers' records does not consider whether a response was unanimously recognized by both observers at one given point in time. It rather compares the temporal structure of behavior onsets and duration. He, therefore, developed a z-statistic which is appropriate for testing the hypothesis that two independent observers had detected the same structure of response occurrence in their records. The limitation of this procedure is that it is useful with only a few behavior categories and a large number of data for each (Gottman, 1980).

Inter- Versus Intraobserver Agreement

In the literature on behavioral assessment, observer agreement is commonly understood as the agreement between two independent observers, who have both observed and recorded the same events: *interobserver agreement*. This index has been frequently mislabeled as observer reliability. Berk (1979) distinguished reliability from agreement, because the latter does not assume underlying observed-score and true-score variance components as does the former. In behavioral assessment, it is well recognized that there can be distortions of the data due to various sources of bias and error (Kazdin, 1977; Kent & Foster, 1977), but the true score concept of psychometric theory does not immediately apply to observational data (Rojahn, 1978). Furthermore, observer agreement is not a measure of consistency or stability of data as is reliability.

Another measure of data quality is the *intraobserver agreement*, or *observer drift index* (Rojahn, 1978). Observer drift refers to a gradual change in the way an observer uses behavior definitions. Procedurally, this index is established by the comparison of two records from one observer who has viewed the same events twice.

Every therapy session should be video-taped (if only a few of them can be taped, the observer must be naïve as to the selection of scenarios). The time lapse between the first observation and the second observation ought to be controlled by a variable schedule. The systematically varied time lapses will identify unsystematic short-term drifts as well as systematic long-term drifts. Therefore, some of the sessions should be reobserved shortly after the first observation (between three and five hours later), and others after a longer period of time (days and weeks later).

Thus, the consistency of control that a definition has over the observing/recording behavior can be evaluated. For a procedural description see Rojahn (1978).

Intra- and interobserver agreement correlate highly with each other, suggesting that an observer who agrees with himself also would agree well with other observers. A recent paper by Rojahn and Wool (1979) raises several of the theoretical issues concerning validation of multicategory systems. This experiment examined the effect of different types of behavior definitions on observer agreement. Six behaviors were chosen for simultaneous observation with the interval-recording method. The very same subject behaviors were defined either "operationally," i.e., objective, clear and complete (Hawkins & Dobes, 1977) or more subjectively and vaguely. Two independent groups of observers with nine subject-observers each were trained to use one of these systems of behavior categories. Each observer worked independently. They viewed a series of four videotapes twice in balanced order, so that time lapses between first and second observation were different for each tape. The tapes showed an autistic child with a psychologist engaging in table-top tasks. Intraobserver agreement reached higher levels than the agreement between observers. There was also a high correlation between the two reliability measures ($r = 0.913$). This result suggests that intraobserver agreement can be a substitute for interobserver agreement, which can be of considerable importance in applied settings. The problem of an intraobserver index is ceiling effects. In the Rojahn and Wool study (1979), intraobserver scores were 33% higher on the average than the respective interobserver agreement. This indicates an insensitivity to small but perhaps significant observer errors. More stringent levels of acceptance than 80% are required for intraobserver agreement.

Another important result was that the type of behavior definition did not affect observer agreement. Both definition types achieved the same level of inter- and intraobserver agreement. Large differences between groups, however, were found for single behaviors in the levels of observer agreements, as well as in the total frequency of recorded behavioral events. Their results were similar to those found by Wahler and Leske (1973), i.e., subjective impressions resulted in higher observer agreement than "objective" ones based on frequency counts. Operational definitions do not guarantee *a priori* better results in terms of observer agreement than vague definitions.

A different method to measure observer drift is to check the accuracy of observers (Kazdin, 1977). Accuracy refers to the extent to which an observer agrees with a predetermined standard score. Repeated reobservation of training materials and the comparison to the standard score would indicate the degree of observer drift over time.

The Experimental Development of an Observational System

The process of an experimental validation and development of an observation system starts after the gross selection of behavior classes. These categories will be "operationally" defined, i.e., objective, clear, and complete (Hawkins & Dobes, 1977). Before a category can be included into a complex recording system, it has to reach a certain level of interobserver agreement. Therefore, the first draft of a definition is given to a group of independent observers. These observers apply the definition to the corresponding behavior of a subject in a recording session. The quality of that definition will then be characterized by the level of interobserver agreement. The index will be calculated on the basis of the two most extreme scores. If this index does not meet pre-established standards (e.g., a level of 80% agreement), the category has to be either dropped or redefined. In another recording session, this new definition is tried out to check whether it reaches a better agreement. This process continues until each of the categories of the entire observation category system is unambiguous and enables the observers to agree with one another. The validity of the integrated system can be evaluated in the same fashion and by the same group of observers. The category index shows how much of observational variability lies in the system itself. If the internal validity of the categories is high, it will reduce observer errors.

In other words, each category and category system should be evaluated prior to its use and the level should be reported in all published experiments that use observational data.

Conclusion

Behavioral assessment in the field of mental retardation has developed rapidly over the last ten years. This development was partly triggered by the growing sophistication of questions asked. The nature of those questions again was influenced by changes in the philosophy of care for the mentally retarded people in the United States and other Western countries. This development of behavior observation is reflected in the technology as well as in conceptual changes. Technologically, behavior observation instruments have become more complex which in turn demanded a new approach to data collection, storage, and analysis. Conceptually, issues such as ecological and social validity were raised. Problems of data quality control have been confronted with an array of assessment methods.

This chapter highlights important current issues of direct, naturalistic observation as the most important technology of behavioral assessment for applied research in mental retardation.

References

Anderson, O. D. *Time series analysis and forecasting: The Box-Jenkins approach.* London: Butterworth, 1976.

Barlow, D. H. (Ed.) *Behavioral assessment of adult disorders.* New York: Guilford Press, 1981.

Berk, R. Generalizability of behavior observations: A clarification of inter-observer agreement and interobserver reliability. *American Journal of Mental Deficiency,* 1979, **83,** 460–472.

Berkson, G. Social ecology of supervised communal facilities for mentally disabled adults. V. Residence as a predictor of social and work adjustment. *American Journal of Mental Deficiency,* 1981, **86,** 39–42.

Berkson, G., & Landesman-Dwyer, S. Behavioral research on severe and profound retardation (1955–1974). *American Journal of Mental Deficiency,* 1977, **81,** 418–454.

Berkson, G., & Romer, D. Social ecology of supervised communal facilities for mentally disabled adults. I. Introduction. *American Journal of Mental Deficiency,* 1980, **85,** 219–228.

Bijou, S. W. A functional analysis of retarded development. In N. R. Ellis (Ed.), *International review in mental retardation.* New York: Academic Press, 1966.

Birkimer, J. C., & Brown, J. H. A graphical judgmental aid which summarizes obtained and chance reliability data and helps assess the believability of experimental effects. *Journal of Applied Behavior Analysis,* 1979, **12,** 523–534.

Box, G. E. P., & Jenkins, G. M. *Time-series analysis: Forecasting and control.* San Francisco: Holden-Day, 1970.

Ciminero, A. R., Calhoun, K. S., & Adams, H. E. (Eds.) *Handbook of behavioral assessment.* New York: Wiley, 1977.

Cohen, J. A coefficient of agreement for nominal scales. *Educational and Psychological Measurement,* 1960, **20,** 37–46.

Cone, J. D., & Hawkins, R. P. (Eds.) *Behavioral assessment.* New York: Brunner/Mazel, 1977.

Conger, A. J. Integration and generalization of kappas for multiple raters. *Psychological Bulletin,* 1980, **88,** 322–328.

Fleiss, J. L. Measuring nominal scale agreement among many raters. *Psychological Bulletin,* 1971, **76,** 378–382.

Forehand, R., & King, H. E. Noncompliant children: Effects of parent training on behavior and attitude change. *Behavior Modification,* 1977, **1,** 93–108.

Foster, S. L., & Cone, J. D. Current issues in direct observation. *Behavioral Assessment,* 1980, **2,** 313–338.

Glass, G. V., Willson, V. L., & Gottman, J. M. *Design and analysis of time-series experiments.* Boulder: Colorado Associated University Press, 1975.

Gottman, J. M. Analyzing for sequential connection and assessing interobserver reliability for the sequential analysis of observational data. *Behavioral Assessment,* 1980, **2,** 361–368.

Gottman, J. M., & Glass, G. V. Analysis of interrupted time-series experiments. In T. R. Kratochwill (Ed.), *Single subject research: Strategies for evaluating change.* New York: Academic Press, 1978.

Gottman, J. M., & Notarius, C. Sequential analysis of observational data using Markov chains. In T. Kratochwill (Ed.), *Single subject research.* New York: Academic Press, 1978. Pp. 237–286.

Grossman, H. J. *Manual on terminology and classification in mental retardation.* Washington: American Association on Mental Deficiency, 1977.

Harris, F., & Lahey, B. B. A method for combining occurrence and non-occurrence interobserver agreement scores. *Journal of Applied Behavior Analysis,* 1978, **11,** 523–527.

Hartmann, D. P. Considerations in the choice of interobserver reliability estimates. *Journal of Applied Behavior Analysis,* 1977, **10,** 103–116.

Hartmann, D. P., & Gardner, W. On the not so recent invention of interobserver reliability: A commentary on two articles by Birkimer and Brown. *Journal of Applied Behavior Analysis,* 1979, **12,** 559–560.

Hartmann, D. P., Gottman, J. M., Jones, R. R., Gardner, W., Kazdin, A. E., & Vaught, R. S. Interrupted time-series analysis and its application to behavioral data. *Journal of Applied Behavior Analysis,* 1980, ·**13,** 543–559.

Hawkins, R. P., & Dobes, R. W. Behavioral definitions in applied behavior analysis: Explicit or implicit? In B. C. Etzel, J. M. LeBlanc, & D. M. Baer (Eds.), *New developments in behavioral research: Theory, method, and application. In honor of Sidney W. Bijou.* Hillsdale, N.J.: L. Erlbaum Associates, 1977.

Hawkins, R. P., & Fabry, B. D. Applied behavior analysis and interobserver reliability: A commentary on two articles by Birkimer and Brown. *Journal of Applied Behavior Analysis,* 1979, **12,** 545–552.

Haynes, S. N. *Principles in behavioral assessment.* New York: Gardner Press, 1978.

Heller, T., Berkson, G., & Rowen, D. Social ecology of supervised communal facilities for mentally disabled adults. VI. Initial social adaptation. *American Journal of Mental Deficiency,* 1981, **86,** 43–49.

Hersen, M., & Barlow, D. H. (Eds.) *Single case experimental designs: Strategies for studying behavior change.* Oxford: Pergamon Press, 1976.

Hersen, M., & Bellack, A. S. (Eds.) *Behavioral assessment.* Oxford: Pergamon Press, 1976.

Holm, R. A. Techniques of recording observational data. In G. P. Sackett (Ed.), *Observing behavior.* Vol. II. Baltimore: University Park Press, 1978.

Hopkins, B. L. Proposed conventions for evaluating observer reliability: A commentary on two articles by Birkimer and Brown. *Journal of Applied Behavior Analysis,* 1979, **12,** 561–569.

Hopkins, B., & Hermann, J. Evaluating interobserver reliability of interval data. *Journal of Applied Behavior Analysis,* 1977, **10,** 121–126.

Johnson, R. E., & Quade, D. Proc MATPAR: A SAS procedure for calculating matched-pair partial correlations. *Proceedings of the Fifth Annual SAS User's Group International Conference,* 1980, 188–93.

Johnson, S. M., & Lobitz, G. K. Parents manipulation of child behavior in home observations. *Journal of Applied Behavior Analysis,* 1974, **7,** 23–31.

Jones, R. R., Weinrott, M. R., & Vaught, R. S. Effects of serial dependency on the agreement between visual and statistical inference. *Journal of Applied Behavior Analysis,* 1978, **11,** 277–289.

Kazdin, A. E. Statistical analyses for single-case experimental designs. In M. Hersen & D. H. Barlow (Eds.), *Single case experimental designs: Strategies for studying behavior change.* Oxford: Pergamon Press, 1976.

Kazdin, A. E. Artifact, bias, and complexity of assessment: The ABCs of reliability. *Journal of Applied Behavior Analysis*, 1977, **10**, 141–150.

Kazdin, A. E. Assessing the clinical or applied significance of behavior change through social validation. *Behavior Modification*, 1977, **1**, 427–452.

Kazdin, A. E., & Straw, M. K. Assessment of behavior of the mentally retarded. In M. Hersen & A. S. Bellack (Eds.), *Behavioral assessment*. Oxford: Pergamon Press, 1976.

Keefe, F. J., Kopel, S. A., & Gordon, S. B. *A practical guide to behavioral assessment*. New York: Springer, 1978.

Kent, R. N., & Foster, S. L. Direct observational procedures: Methodological issues in naturalistic sessions. In A. R. Ciminero, K. S. Calhoun, & M. E. Adams (Eds.), *Handbook of behavioral assessment*. New York: John Wiley & Sons, 1977.

Kratochwill, T. R. Just because it's reliable doesn't mean it's believable: A commentary on two articles by Birkimer and Brown. *Journal of Applied Behavior Analysis*, 1979, **12**, 553–558.

Lewis, M. H., MacLean, W. E., Johnson, W., & Baumeister, A. A. Ultradian rhythms in stereotyped and self-injurious behavior. *American Journal of Mental Deficiency*, 1981, **85**, 601–610.

Lichstein, K. L., & Wahler, R. G. The ecological assessment of an autistic child. *Journal of Abnormal Psychology*, 1976, **4**, 31–54.

Light, R. J. Measures of response agreement for qualitative data: Some generalizations and alternatives. *Psychological Bulletin*, 1971, **76**, 365–377.

Linehan, M. M. Content validity: Its relevance to behavioral assessment. *Behavioral Assessment*, 1980, **2**, 147–160.

Mash, E. J., & Terdal, L. G. (Eds.) *Behavior therapy assessment*. New York: Springer, 1976.

Mash, E. J., & Terdal, L. G. (Eds.) *Behavioral assessment of childhood disorders*. New York: Guilford Press, 1981. (a)

Mash, E. J., & Terdal, L. G. (Eds.) *Behavioral assessment of adulthood disorders*. New York: Guilford Press, 1981. (b)

Mulick, J. A., Scott, F. D., Gaines, R. F., & Campbell, B. M. Devices and instrumentation for skill development and behavior change. In J. L. Matson & F. Andrasik (Eds.), *Treatment issues and innovations in mental retardation*. New York: Plenum Press, 1983. In press.

Nyhan, W. L., Johnson, H. G., Kaufman, I. A., & Jones, K. L. Serotonergic approaches to the modification of behavior in the Lesch-Nyhan syndrome. *Applied Research in Mental Retardation*, 1980, **1**, 25–40.

Parsonson, B. S., & Baer, D. M. The analysis and presentation of graphic data. In T. R. Kratochwill (Ed.), *Single subject research*. New York: Academic Press, 1978.

Powell, J., Martindale, A., & Kulp, S. An evaluation of time-sample measures of behavior. *Journal of Applied Behavior Analysis*, 1975, **8**, 463, 470.

Rogers-Warren, A., & Warren, J. *Ecological perspectives in behavior analysis*. Baltimore: University Park Press, 1977.

Rojahn, J. Validity and reliability of data from naturalistic observational studies: A new approach. *Behavior Analysis and Modification*, 1978, **2**, 296–305.

Rojahn, J., & Wool, R. Inter- and intra-observer agreement as a function of explicit behavior definitions in direct observation. *Behavioural Analysis and Modification*, 1979, **3**, 211–228.

Rollings, J. P., & Baumeister, A. A. Stimulus control of stereotypic responding: Effects on target and collateral behavior. *American Journal of Mental Deficiency*, 1981, **86**, 67–77.

Rollings, J. P., Baumeister, A. A., & Baumeister, A. A. The use of overcorrection procedures to eliminate the stereotyped behaviors of retarded individuals: An analysis of collateral behaviors and generalization of suppressive effects. *Behavior Modification*, 1977, **1**, 29–46.

Romer, D., & Berkson, G. Social ecology of supervised communal facilities for mentally disabled adults. II. Predictors of affiliation. *American Journal of Mental Deficiency*, 1980, **85**, 229–242. (a)

Romer, D., & Berkson, G. Social ecology of supervised communal facilities for mentally disabled adults. III. Predictors of social choice. *American Journal of Mental Deficiency*, 1980, **85**, 243–252. (b)

Romer, D., & Berkson, G. Social ecology of supervised communal facilities for mentally disabled adults. IV. Characteristics of social behavior. *American Journal of Mental Deficiency*, 1981, **86**, 28–38.

Sackett, G. P. (Ed.) *Observing behavior*. Vol. I & II. Baltimore: University Park Press, 1978. (a)

Sackett, G. P. Measurement in observational research. In G. P. Sackett (Ed.), *Observing behavior*. Vol. II. Baltimore: University Park Press, 1978. (b)

Sackett, G. P., Stephenson, E., & Ruppenthal, G. C. Digital data acquisition systems for observing behavior in laboratory and field settings. *Behavior Research Methods and Instrumentation*, 1973, **5**, 344–348.

Schoggen, P. Ecological psychology and mental retardation. In G. Sackett (Ed.), *Observing behavior*. Vol. I. Baltimore: University Park Press, 1978.

Schroeder, S. R. Automated transduction of sheltered workshop behaviors. *Journal of Applied Behavior Analysis*, 1972, **5**, 523–525. (a)

Schroeder, S. R. Parametric effects of reinforcement frequency, amount of reinforcement, and required response force on sheltered workshop behavior. *Journal of Applied Behavior Analysis*, 1972, **5**, 431–441. (b)

Schroeder, S. R., Kanoy, J. R., Mulick, J. A., Rojahn, J., Thios, S. J., Stephens, M., & Hawk, B. The effect of the environment on programs for self-injurious behavior. In C. E. Meyers (Ed.), *AAMD Monograph No. 5*. Washington: American Association on Mental Deficiency. In press.

Schroeder, S. R., Rojahn, J., & Mulick, J. A. Ecobehavioral organization of developmental day care for the chronically self-injurious. *Journal of Pediatric Psychology*, 1978, **3**, 81–88.

Schulte, D. *Verhaltensanalyse*. Munich: Urban & Schwartzenberg, 1974.

Sidman, M. *Tactics of scientific research*. New York: Basic Books, 1960.

Skinner, B. F. *Science and human behavior*. New York: MacMillan, 1953.

Wahler, R. G., House, A. E., & Stambaugh, E. E. *Ecological assessment of child problem behavior*. New York: Pergamon Press, 1976.

Wahler, R. G., & Leske, G. Accurate and inaccurate observer summary reports: Reinforcement theory interpretation and investigation. *Journal of Nervous and Mental Disease*, 1973, **156**, 386–389.

Wampold, B. E., & Furlong, M. J. The heuristic of visual inference. *Behavioral Assessment*, 1981, **3**, 79–92.

Wasik, J. L., Rojahn, J., & Schroeder, S. R. A note on the use of correction for change responding in estimating interobserver agreement. Unpublished manuscript, 1978. (Available from the second author.)

Weisz, J. R. Effects of the "mentally retarded" label on adult judgements about child failure. *Journal of Abnormal Psychology*, 1981, **90**, 371–374.

Willems, E. P. Behavioral technology and behavioral ecology. *Journal of Applied Behavior Analysis*, 1974, **7**, 151–165.

Willems, E. P. Steps towards an ecobehavioral technology. In A. Rogers-Warren, & S. F. Warren (Eds.), *Ecological perspective in behavior analysis*. Baltimore: University Park Press, 1977.

Yelton, A. R. Reliability in the context of the experiment: A commentary on two articles by Birkimer and Brown. *Journal of Applied Behavior Analysis*, 1979, **12**, 565–570.

16 EDUCATIONAL ASSESSMENT

Esther Sinclair

I n this chapter, we will examine the content and process involved in the assessment of mental retardation in the schools. Traditional methods, as well as procedures instituted to meet the criteria for assessment set forth in Public Law 94-142 (the Education for All Handicapped Children Act), will be described. Educational assessment of mental retardation is performed by various professionals within the school system. The specific functions and roles of members of this interdisciplinary team will be discussed. The types of educational assessment tools will be explained, along with discussion of the utility and implementation of educational placement and programming recommendations made in diagnostic reports of individual, mentally retarded children. The educational assessment of mentally retarded children includes dimensions of cognitive functioning, measures of adaptive behavior, language, academic achievement, and perceptual integrity. Cognitive testing, measures of adaptive behavior, and language testing will be discussed in detail in other chapters. Finally, the impact of Public Law 94-142 on assessment will be discussed. The law provides for nondiscriminatory testing, parent involvement in the interdisciplinary assessment team, and due process safeguards in diagnostic and classification procedures.

Assessment in special education is broadly defined as the process of collecting data for the purpose of helping professionals make educational decisions about children. The assessment techniques themselves are characterized by diversity and multiformity, rather than by invariability and uniformity. There is often little agreement in the choice of specific tests and the integration of specific data (Sinclair & Kheifets, 1982). Sinclair (1980) and McDermott (1981) point to the rather unimpressive relationship between diagnostic categories and specific educational placement recommendations as well as sources of error in the psychoeducational diagnostic process itself. However, the overall process by which children are referred for evaluation and, ultimately, placed in special education programs is uniform and faithful to legislative requirements of Public Law 94-142. Assessment is not synonymous with testing (Feuerstein et al., 1981); testing is simply one part of assessment. Assessment may include direct observation of individuals in natural environments (Bagnato, 1981), obtaining data from others by means of interviews (Wall & Paradise, 1981), and obtaining historical and current information by reviewing records (Sinclair, 1980). Clearly, many different kinds of data may be collected in the process of decision making. In its broadest sense, this data collection procedure is assessment.

To add to the numerous definitions of what constitutes educational assessment, Cromwell, Blashfield, and Strauss (1975) propose that the diagnostic intervention process consist of historical-etiological information of currently assessable characteristics, specific treatments or interventions, and a particular prognosis; all elements required in one form or other by Public Law 94-142. To attain such comprehensiveness, a combination of assessment techniques or models must be used.

Assessment is a *continuous process*. Since conditions surrounding a child are always changing, decisions regarding a child's placement should always be considered tentative and subject to review, as well as to periodic, comprehensive assessment and possible revision. Prior to Public Law 94-142, a child could have been placed in a class for the educable mentally retarded (EMR) on the basis of a single intelligence test. If the IQ was low, the child could be placed in such a class for the remainder of his school attendance. This practice was based on the erroneous assumption that the administration of a particular IQ test, at a given time, could predict the continuous development of a child (Cleary et al., 1975). Fortunately, current pedagogy views the mentally retarded child as being capable of benefitting from school, if the school environment is appropriately oriented and stimulating. Therefore, regular periodic educational assessment, which includes teacher observation, testing with standardized instruments, and review of, and assimilation of, data by an interdisciplinary team is needed. It is only with this kind of continued reassessment that the most effective educational programs can be developed.

What are the *objectives of educational assessment* of the mentally retarded child? The educational assessment should furnish information about the extent of the learning deficit. The educational assessment should yield information about the qualitative aspects of the learning deficit. And finally, the educational assessment should determine which educational placement option is the most appropriate and the most potentially beneficial to the child.

Evaluation of academic abilities and disabilities is part of the total assessment program. For example, in relation to the EMR child, it would be important to know the child's level of reading recognition, reading comprehension, spelling, handwriting skills, and arithmetic computation. It is of particular importance to determine whether the child's academic achievement levels are at a level commensurate with mental-age expectancy as measured by intellectual functioning level. The assessment should include a description of the skill areas where the child may have a relatively high degree of proficiency. Retarded children frequently develop skill in specific areas such as mechanical ability, ability to perform various industrial

tasks, and, less frequently, skill in some academic area (Gajar, 1980). It is important that these proficiency areas be labeled and assessed, so that effective guidance counseling, in relation to the child's vocational aptitudes and vocational interests, can be provided.

It is significant to note that the process whereby children come to be classified as mentally retarded is different for educable mentally retarded (EMR) from that for trainable mentally retarded (TMR), or for severely mentally retarded (SMR) children. Although mention will be made of educational assessment techniques that are appropriate for TMR and SMR populations, the majority of educational assessment techniques relate to the assessment and placement of EMR children. The explanation for this phenomenon is self-evident to educators. Diagnosis of EMR denotes school failure, is school-oriented, and usually made by educational personnel. These children are unlikely to continue in the status of mentally retarded after leaving school; for in many other settings their behavior is likely to be primarily adaptive (MacMillan, 1977). To summarize the differences between diagnosis of EMR versus TMR or SMR children, one can make the generalization that the earlier in the child's life that a diagnosis of mental retardation is made, the more likely it is that the degree of retardation will be severe (Hutt & Gibby, 1976). The severely retarded tend to be identified before the end of the first year of life. Identification may be made at birth as well, or soon thereafter by physicians. On the other hand, the mildly mentally retarded tend to be diagnosed as such only after they have entered school and have experienced failure in a school setting. These children are usually energetic youngsters, who during the preschool years walk and talk at about the same age as other children. They tend to get along well with neighborhood children and may not be regarded by their parents as significantly different from other children (Meyers, Sundstrom, & Yoshida, 1974).

While professionals often estimate that 1 to 3% of the population is mentally retarded (depending on how retardation is defined), such prevalence estimates cannot be used as a guide by school districts in setting policy. School professionals cannot decide that a certain percentage of their enrollment will be classified as mentally retarded on an a priori basis, and then attempt to find the specified percentage of mentally retarded students. Similarly, schools do not establish an IQ cutoff and then survey their enrollment population to determine which children fall below that cutoff point (Ashurst & Meyers, 1973). Furthermore, EMR classification is not a categorization by means of intelligence test scores alone. Those who contend that children are placed in EMR programs on the basis of IQ alone are either unaware of the diagnostic process or so intent on condemning the process that they overstate their case (MacMillan, 1971; MacMillan et al., 1974).

Criteria for Identification in the Schools

Identification of mild mental retardation in the schools is made primarily for educational reasons, in order to remove the child from the regular program where he is constantly frustrated by repeated failure, and to place the child in an EMR program (or some other type of special program) where he/she can be provided with extra help and where his/her special educational needs can be attended to. Historically, programs for the EMR were created as a means to provide an academic education for certain children who were normal in every sense except that they were slow learners. The impetus for classifying these children as mentally retarded came from legislation for mandatory special education. The formulation of clinical guidelines, in terms of academic deficits and IQ cutoffs, provided a way to justify the excess costs over the monies given every district per pupil for each child so classified.

Much *ability differentiation* takes place within the regular classroom. Students are frequently placed in homogeneous ability groups for reading and mathematics instruction. In addition, further group differentiation takes place when children are placed outside of the classroom for remedial or accelerated instruction in a particular subject area. For example, a second grade student, who reads at the fourth grade level, may be too advanced for reading programs in the second-grade classroom. The child may participate in the reading program in the fourth-grade classroom instead. The same second-grade classroom may contain several students who have not yet mastered basic phonics instruction and who require remedial reading instruction not available in the regular classroom. These children may receive small-group or individual instruction with a remedial reading teacher. These examples illustrate the range of individual differences and abilities that is expected in the regular classroom. It is only when students deviate significantly from what would be expected by a normal distribution of abilities within the classroom that some other form of educational intervention is considered.

Grade retention is frequently the first educational intervention for a child who deviates sufficiently from classroom norms (Mercer, 1973). The philosophy behind retention is that the child who, for whatever reason, is below average in intellectual ability, learning disability, or emotional disturbance would benefit from repeated exposure to the same academic material for another academic year. Retention, as a form of educational intervention, is more frequently recommended in the primary elementary grades as there may be numerous social and emotional difficulties that appear when an older child is placed with a younger peer group. In addition, older children are more aware of their failure to perform in school, which is implied in grade retention. Many educational professionals may not wish to jump over retention as an educational intervention because they see it as a logical step in general intervention for a child who is failing the regular program.

If the child continues to remain significantly behind academically after being retained one year, he/she is at a critical point. Since schools prefer to keep children with their chronological age-group peers, it is unlikely that a child will be retained for a second year. Furthermore, when a particular educational intervention proves ineffective with a child, the frequent tactic is to try another form of intervention rather than to repeat the same educational intervention that did not work the previous year. The options to the teacher can be simplified to indicate social promotion (despite failure in the retained grade), or referral to the school psychologist or school assessment team to initiate special education placement.

Once the assessment team has determined that a child meets the criteria for placement in an EMR program, the child's specific learning strengths and weaknesses must be assessed. The mildly mentally retarded child, perhaps contrary to public opinion, does not usually present with a characteristic profile of learning abilities that represent all mildly retarded children. There is as much heterogeneity within the EMR classroom as there is within the regular classroom. For example, some mildly retarded children will easily grasp the content material that the teacher presents, some children will demonstrate learning disabilities as well as mild mental retardation and have difficulty comprehending and mastering certain learning tasks. Still others may be emotionally disturbed and a fourth group may meet the general population's stereotype of a mildly mentally retarded child with learning problems in all areas.

Types of Assessment Information

There are many different models of educational assessment. Two basic models will be presented to illustrate the diversity of theoretical background supporting each model. The *psychoeducational model*, sometimes called the diagnostic-prescriptive model, has traditionally been used to evaluate mentally retarded students in school (Howell, Kaplan, & O'Connell, 1979). The basic tenet of this model is that the disorder, disability or reason for school failure resides within the child and, therefore, the evaluation consists of measuring the child's cognitive and perceptual ability levels.

The *diagnostic psychoeducational report* is the format used by the school psychologist to translate diagnostic results of observation and testing into appropriate goals for developmental intervention. Through the clear synthesis, integration, and practical communication of diagnostic information from multiple sources, the psychoeducational report should comprehensively describe current levels of functioning upon which individualized goals and educational interventions can be constructed. Critical content areas in the psychoeducational report typically include background educational information and current classroom observation, as well as standardized testing in the areas of cognitive functioning, language, achievement, perception, and social-emotional development. As previously stated, several of these areas are explored in detail in other chapters. The emphasis in this chapter on educational assessment is with educational issues and academic achievement tests.

Norm-referenced tests are the assessment tools that are primarily used in the psychoeducational model. Testing information in academic achievement is expressed as "below grade level," "at grade level," or "above grade level." Norm-referenced testing allows for a comparison between the individual child's score and some standardization sample. The major purpose of norm-referenced testing is to aid educators in comparing a particular child with other children of the same age. Furthermore, the child's skills can be evaluated in relation to what is believed to be his capacity or potential. The Peabody Individual Achievement Test (Dunn & Markwardt, 1970) with subtests in mathematics, reading recognition, reading comprehension, spelling, and general information is an example of a norm-referenced achievement test which relates one child's performance in these five areas to the performance of other children of the same chronological age or chronological grade placement.

An alternate model of educational assessment is the task-analytic model, which is a model of *behavioral analysis*. In this model, it is not the child but the child's behavior, that is measured and evaluated. The reason for failure in school does not reside within the child, but within the child's environment. Therefore, behavioral analysis attempts to identify the environmental contingencies that support or reinforce desired behavior and which contingencies do not. Obtaining

reinforcement preference information is useful in determining how to motivate a particular child to learn. Not all children are motivated to work for the same reinforcers. For example, the intrinsic reward of being successful may be reinforcing for one child. Another child may require the presentation of a secondary reinforcer such as teacher approval or a grade of A. A third child may only demonstrate the desired behavior for food, tokens, or other external rewards. Bateman (1967) identifies the following three issues as important questions behind curriculum planning with the behavioral approach: (1) What specific educational tasks are important for the child to learn? (2) What are the sequential steps in learning this task? And (3) what specific behaviors does the child need to perform this task? The task-analytic model primarily utilizes *criterion-referenced tests* as assessment tools to measure the child's behavior.

These two models exemplify two different philosophical viewpoints in educational assessment practices. They are based on opposite premises regarding the supposed source of failure in school. Frequently, psychologists and teachers borrow assessment tools from each model, as both models seem to have strengths in different areas of assessment. The psychoeducational model appears more appropriate for general identification or classification of mental retardation, whereas the task-analytic model appears more appropriate for specific diagnostic identification. The identification of specific target behaviors is a necessary requisite for effective curriculum planning. Therefore, both models have their place in usefulness and effectiveness.

Bloom, Hastings, and Madaus (1971) identify two general types of evaluation procedures that parallel the psychoeducational and task-analytic models. Standardized, norm-referenced achievement tests are designed to measure how much learning has taken place and are, therefore, called *summative evaluation* procedures. Summative evaluation would indicate the grade-level equivalent performance of a child in a given academic area. Even standardized diagnostic tests are summative evaluation procedures as the diagnostic tests measure the grade level of prior achievement in order to determine the appropriate grade level of current instruction.

In contrast to summative evaluation procedures, *formative evaluation* procedures measure learning as the skills are being taught and are used to measure the child's progress toward specific instructional goals. This necessitates ongoing behavioral analysis and observation of cognitive, motivational, and learning subskills and, therefore, more closely resembles the task-analytic model of evaluation. Formative evaluation is a means of measuring learning or growth as it occurs naturalistically. The evaluation is direct, continuous and allows for the constant exchange of feedback between teacher and student. Since the evaluation takes place as learning is occurring, changes in programming or instruction are feasible. Examples of formative evaluation procedures include *diagnostic-prescriptive teaching* (Peter, 1965), *diagnostic teaching* (Kirk, 1972), *clinical teaching* (Lerner, 1971), *narrative log* (Stephens, 1970), *management by objectives* (Mali, 1977), and *criterion-referenced testing*.

These evaluation systems all allow for constant, continuous data collection in order to make instructional decisions. Diagnostic-prescriptive teaching and diagnostic teaching differ from one another in that diagnostic teaching does not utilize case history information but relies on standardized test results to plan educational interventions. Clinical teaching combines case history and standardized test results in an alternating test-teach-test-teach approach. Narrative logs provide a written record of teacher observations of child behavior. Accurate behavioral observation is a preliminary step toward structuring the learning environment to meet the child's needs. Management by objectives, as an evaluation procedure, consists of writing individual short-term objectives and long-term goals for a student based on all the assessment information that is available. The *Individual Educational Program*, mandated by Public Law 94-142, is an example of the management by objectives evaluation system.

Criterion-referenced testing compares an individual child's behavior on a given task to an objective performance standard or criterion. Intraindividual differences, rather than comparison with standardized groups, are at the core of criterion-referenced testing. The major purpose of testing is to provide specific measurement of a child's skills, so that instructional goals can be established and so that instructional techniques can be implemented. A criterion-referenced test is either passed or not passed. All items are at approximately the same level of difficulty. Since criterion-referenced tests do not lose reliability if frequently administered, it is possible to chart a child's performance in one particular area of the curriculum. If the speed of skill attainment is too slow, the teacher may change the method of teaching or alter the instructional content in order to achieve better results. *Task analysis* is the process by which criterion-referenced tests are analyzed in terms of the elements and subelements that constitute the criterion. Task analysis includes determining the specific educational tasks that are significant for the child to learn; the sequential steps involved in learning the task and the specific behaviors that the child needs in order to perform the task

(Lerner, 1971). According to Wallace and Kauffman (1973), task analysis is "a sequence of evaluative activities which pinpoint the child's learning problem and guides the teacher in planning an effective remedial sequence of instructional tasks" (p. 105).

Formal testing, as a source of diagnostic information, primarily consists of standardized test instruments with accompanying statistical data such as validity indices and reliability coefficients. Formal tests are generally categorized under two broad headings; *prognostic tests* and *diagnostic tests*. Prognostic tests are usually administered by a testing specialist such as a school psychologist. They are often called tests of general ability (i.e. Stanford-Binet Intelligence Scale) and yield global scores of mental ability (Terman & Merrill, 1972). Another type of prognostic test is a test of general academic achievement (i.e. Wide Range Achievement Test), which identifies grade-equivalent scores in achievement areas of reading, spelling, and arithmetic (Jastak & Jastak, 1978).

Diagnostic tests are frequently teacher-administered and identify specific levels of skill attainment in specific subject areas. Since teachers teach children and not grade levels, the assessment information ideally needs to provide a profile of what skills the child has mastered in specific subject areas, so that the teacher will know where to begin instruction. For example, the Gray Oral Reading Test (Gray, 1967) allows for the identification of various sources of error in reading, such as gross mispronunciation, partial mispronunciation, word omission, word substitution, repetition, and inversion of word order. This type of diagnostic test indicates specific information about the child's strengths and weaknesses in subskills of reading recognition. The Woodcock Reading Mastery Tests (Woodcock, 1973) is a diagnostic test which divides reading into five areas of letter identification, word identification, word attack, word comprehension, and passage comprehension. The KeyMath Diagnostic Arithmetic Test (Connolly, Nachtman, & Pritchett, 1976) divides mathematics into 13 skill areas of numeration, fractions, geometry and symbols, addition, subtraction, multiplication, division, mental computation, numerical reasoning, word problems, missing elements, money, measurement, and time. Sequential skills are identified in each area to provide a comprehensive diagnostic profile in four general performance areas.

In summary, both prognostic and diagnostic tests are useful, in that they provide different kinds of assessment information. General prognostic tests complement the legal and administrative requirements for identification and placement of mentally retarded children according to Public Law 94-142. Specific diagnostic tests encourage the development of curriculum specifically geared to the child's level of skill development.

Informal assessment, as a source of diagnostic information, may include *teacher observation* of the child in the classroom, informal *teacher-made tests* to pinpoint development in certain cognitive, academic achievement or perceptual areas, and *behavior rating scales* and *check lists*. *Precision teaching* (Lindsley, 1971) is perhaps the best known of the informal assessment, formative evaluation techniques. Precision teaching differs from all the other formative techniques in that, in addition to charting current learning and growth accurately, it allows future learning and growth to be predicted. Mathematical principles are used to evaluate the developmental sequence of a particular skill, such as addition regrouping in arithmetic computation. A particular instruction program is applied toward achieving each level of skill development involved in mastery of this computational skill. Following the application of the instructional program, the child's skill level is again evaluated to determine whether the instructional program was effective.

Teacher observation and assessment of classroom behavior is best accomplished when the target behaviors are specific, observable, and quantitative. Teachers of the retarded often deal with hyperactive, aggressive, and withdrawn children (Payne et al., 1977). An aggressive child may hit or bite other children, push others while standing in line, or destroy or otherwise mar other children's work. Identifying the specific behaviors, rather than stating that the child is aggressive, assists the teacher in behavioral intervention. Behavior rating scales and check lists aid the teacher in pinpointing behavior that may inhibit learning. The Devereux Child Behavior Rating Scale (Spivack & Spotts, 1966) identifies behaviors such as distractibility, social isolation, incontinence, messiness, sloppiness, and need for adult contact. The Pupil Rating Scale (Myklebust, 1971) focuses on behavioral characteristics of auditory comprehension, spoken language, orientation, motor coordination and personal-social behavior. The public school version of the AAMD Adaptive Behavior Scale (Lambert et al., 1974) is widely used by the public schools. Part I evaluates skills and habits in 10 behavioral domains considered important to the development of personal independence in daily living. Part II quantifies maladaptive behavior related to personality and behavior disorders. Diagnosis of specific behaviors is indispensable in facilitating behavioral change and facilitating behavioral change is the primary purpose of collecting diagnostic data.

A Word on Curriculum Planning

Educational assessment techniques in mental retardation should provide prescriptions for educational planning and curriculum. To reiterate, general, prognostic tests are useful in determining the child's overall developmental level. Specific, diagnostic tests help the educator identify which skills need to be taught and how the instructional approach may best be implemented. Curriculum, regardless of the level of mental retardation, should not be based on the classification label, but on the interests, capabilities, and needs of those children who will be receiving instruction.

Curriculum for the mild-to-moderately mentally retarded individual has been well documented throughout the years (Bender, Valletutti, & Bender, 1976; Morganstern & Michel-Smith, 1973). Most educational programs contain specific objectives in arithmetic competencies, social competencies, communicative skills, safety, health, vocational competencies, motor and recreational skills, and avoidance of drug and alcohol abuse (Kolstoe, 1976). In general, mild-to-moderately mentally retarded students will benefit from instruction in functional reading and writing at the second to sixth grades in terms of comprehension (Brown et al., 1970). Since the mildly mentally retarded student will, in most cases, live in the community as a parent, neighbor, and citizen, it is also important that the educational program develop the knowledge, skills, and attitudes that will enable him to be an active member of the adult community.

The curriculum objectives for the moderate-to-severely retarded individual have undergone close scrutiny since the formation of the Bureau of Education for the Handicapped in 1967 (see chapter 11 in this volume, by Sinclair & Forness). Curricular goals and objectives are usually expressed from a developmental point of view and developmental sequences are stated in hierarchical terms. The necessary range of skills that needs to be taught to moderately and severely mentally retarded students is far greater than the range of skills required by nonhandicapped and mildly mentally retarded students. The curriculum needs to include functional skills in self-help areas, gross and fine motor development, nonverbal and verbal communication, and social adjustment in society, home, and neighborhood (Bellamy, Greiner, & Laffin, 1972; Domnie & Bellamy, 1972; Molloy, 1972; Schmidt, 1979). The philosophy underlying all educational programs for mentally retarded individuals, regardless of the level of retardation, is to enable the student to develop his full potential, regardless of how limited this potential may be in comparison to others.

Individualized Educational Program

Public Law 94-142, passed by the 94th Congress in November 1975, is the culmination of legislative and judicial efforts on behalf of the mentally retarded. The law requires that states wishing financial assistance from the federal government, develop policies which will (1) assure a *free*, *"appropriate public education* to all handicapped children between the ages of 3 and 21"; (2) provide "procedural safeguards to assure, to the maximum extent possible, that handicapped children are educated with children who are not handicapped"; (3) assure that handicapped children and their parents are guaranteed procedural safeguards of *due process* which shall include an opportunity to examine all relevant records, receive written prior notice in the parent's native language of proposed changes in educational programs, and have an impartial due process hearing with the findings subject to appeal; and (4) "insure that *testing* and evaluation materials for classification and placement are selected and administered so as *not to be racially or culturally discriminatory.*"

Evaluation and placement decisions must be made by an interdisciplinary team. An *individualized educational program* (IEP) is adopted by the team in consideration of each individual child's strengths and weaknesses in meeting his or her school needs (Hawkins-Shepard, 1978). This interdisciplinary team represents a change from traditional practices in the educational assessment of not only mentally retarded children, but all special education children. The rationale for employing a team approach is the belief that a group decision provides safeguards against individual errors in judgment, while ensuring greater accuracy in evaluation, classification, and placement decisions. In addition, the interprofessional team ensures greater adherence to due process requirements (Pfeiffer, 1980). A number of researchers have advocated applying the team approach to the schools (Buktenica, 1970; Falik, Grimm, Preston, & Konno, 1971; Hogenson, 1973). Yet an equally articulate group has criticized the interdisciplinary team concept; pointing out that it increases role confusion, is duplicative in effort, unnecessarily costly, raises issues of territoriality, and leads to ambiguous decisions (Hefferin & Katz, 1971; Pluckum, 1972; Taylor, 1978; Wallace, 1976). There is a great deal of prima facie validity in the notion that an interdisciplinary team has the potential to facilitate greater accuracy in decision making. In support of this notion, Thurlow and Ysseldyke (1979) found that a group makes more accurate decisions than do individuals acting alone.

The IEP participants typically include an administrative designee such as the school principal, the school psychologist, the special education teacher, the resource program teacher, the regular education teacher, the school physician, and the school nurse. Educational roles of these professionals are self-evident with the possible exception of the resource program teacher. The resource program teacher works with the regular education teacher by providing individualized, usually remedial instruction to children who are deficient in specific subject areas. A child may attend this program daily or weekly from one to three hours at a time, depending on his disabilities. IEP teams dealing with mentally retarded children may include a speech and language specialist as well as an adaptive physical education teacher.

The IEP requires parental involvement. The parent is encouraged to attend the IEP meeting, as the IEP cannot be implemented until the parent signs the IEP document indicating agreement with the assessment, eligibility for special educational classification, needed educational services, and the instructional setting. Singer, Bossard, and Watkins (1977) discovered that when parents were present at team meetings, more staff members attended and more recommendations were generated. In spite of the fact that parents, teachers, and administrators are partners on the interdisciplinary committee, recent studies indicate that the members of the partnership may not be perceived as having equal status in terms of committee input and ultimate decision-making influence. Hyman et al. (1972, 1973) found that school psychologists were particularly influential members of the IEP team. They often functioned as chairpersons of teams and, perhaps as Goldstein, Arkell, Ashcroft, Hurley and Lilly (1975) suggest, were in such a dominant position because of their experience and knowledge of various placement options. Gilliam (1979) asked IEP team members to rank the importance of each other team member. Prior to the IEP, parents and school administrators (school principals) were perceived as high status participants. After the IEP, they were ranked much lower in terms of their contribution. Special education teachers and school psychologists maintained their very high ranking both before and after the IEP committee hearing. Parents were seen as relatively uninvolved during the planning process. Regular education teachers were seen as the least involved professional discipline in the team decision-making process (Yoshida, Fenton, Maxwell, & Kaufman, 1978). They tended to contribute in a very limited way to the generation of recommendations (Semmel, Yoshida, Fenton, & Kaufman, 1978), and perceived the majority of team activities as inappropriate to their particular discipline (Fenton, Yoshida, Maxwell, & Kaufman, 1978).

The studies that suggest minimal involvement of parents and regular education teachers in decision making and program implementation are disconcerting. Comprehensive, nondiscriminatory assessment should include evaluation of the child's performance in the classroom, school, home, and community (Wall & Paradise, 1981). Who could better assist in such ecological evaluation than the teacher and the parent? Furthermore, the success of any intervention plan is enhanced by the involvement of the parent and classroom teacher, as these individuals have the most contact with the individual child on a regular basis.

The IEP must include a functional description of the child's exceptionality with descriptive statements in the areas of academic achievement, cognitive functioning, communication status, motor abilities, and health and social/emotional status. Although teams vary in the type of evaluative information that they collect and analyze and the specific reason for referral to the team dictates the type of assessment information needed, the psychoeducational report, completed by the school psychologist, is typically included in the educational assessment (Goldbaum & Rucker, 1977). To date, no one has explored the incremental validity of the various diagnostic information sources that teams typically use, or the validity of the data based on the interaction of type of information with type of presenting problems (Morrow, Powell, & Ely, 1976; Ysseldyke, Algozzine, Regan, & McGue, 1981). In relation to the inclusion of psychoeducational data, Goldbaum and Rucker found that cases written in norm-referenced terminology were preferred by educators and that cases written in criterion-referenced terminology were preferred by clinicians. Additionally, it was found that criterion-referenced data led to "less restrictive" educational placement.

The child's educational functioning level is determined by assessment in various areas of development. For example, assessment of a mildly mentally retarded child might include assessment in the following areas: Assessment of the child's health history and medical background including evaluation of the health record kept by the school nurse as well as the results of recent medical examination. Screening tests for vision and hearing would be included as well. The school nurse or physician might review developmental history records and interview the parent, if possible, in order to obtain a current developmental history of the child. As previously mentioned, cognitive functioning, academic achievement, sensorimotor/perceptual functioning and social/emotional func-

tioning would be assessed by the teacher and the school psychologist. Adaptive behavior measures may be provided by the parent along with other descriptions of the child's social role functioning at home and in the community. Teacher rating scales, direct classroom observational data, teacher-made tests and anecdotal records which describe classroom behavior are usually the responsibility of the child's classroom teacher as he/she works with the child on a daily basis. Assessment of motor abilities is usually made by the adaptive physical education teacher or the psychomotor specialist on the team. Communication status is determined by the speech and language specialist.

Assessment information representative of the above-mentioned areas is consolidated into individually-determined educational goals and objectives. In addition, the IEP indicates who will be responsible for the acquisition of these goals and objectives. According to Holland (1980) and Morgan (1981), putting goals into writing for each individual child is still a relatively new exercise. The team members must agree on whether the child's deficits are capable of being remedied and which goals and objectives are feasible for the child to achieve (Page, 1980). For example, the classroom teacher may be accountable for academic achievement goals, while the speech therapist is accountable for the attainment of communication skills.

The IEP indicates which educational and related services are required in order to achieve the goals and objectives outlined by the committee. The frequency with which services will be delivered to the child needs to be specified in terms of the initiation date and duration of services. In the case of speech therapy and adaptive physical education, the time framework of delivery of services must be delineated, so that it is clear whether these services will be provided once, twice, or three times per week. The duration of each session must be indicated and, if possible, the name of the therapist responsible for the delivery of the service.

Lastly, the IEP must contain an *accountability model* for determining whether annual goals and objectives were attained. Evaluation criteria are needed to provide information to facilitate decision-making on the IEP team in general. Although the Education for All Handicapped Children Act has required public school districts to become more accountable for their special education programs (Gotts, 1976; Maher, 1978), little attention has been given to special education program evaluation itself (Maher, 1981). Ultimately, the adequacy of any educational assessment technique must be measured not only in relation to adequacy and efficiency of educational diagnosis or classification but in relation to adequacy of the recommended educational setting. Selection of an effective program depends on continual evaluation of the child's progress. Many approaches and techniques are utilized in program evaluation (Dunst, 1979; Maher & Barbrack, 1980). It is necessary for the entire IEP team to understand and agree upon measures of progress. Furthermore, it is important to begin to develop assessment instruments that measure application of skills learned in educational settings, since long-term goals for mentally retarded children are ultimately concerned with career and vocational outcomes (Lynch, Kiernan, & Stark, 1982).

Conclusion

The goal of educational intervention in mental retardation is to enhance development, i.e., to bring about a level of development that a particular individual has never experienced before. Educational assessment techniques are needed that lead directly to such development-enhancing educational interventions. In recent years, legislative action has had a profound impact on the educational assessment of the mentally retarded. Prior to 1970, it was not uncommon for teacher referral and IQ testing to be the sole considerations for special education placement of a mentally retarded child. A variety of assessment techniques including psychoeducational diagnosis, behavioral analysis, summative evaluation, formative evaluation, norm-referenced testing, and criterion-referenced testing have been presented. A plethora of assessment instruments and observational techniques are now a *sine qua non* and are only a part of the total individual educational planning procedure for each child needing special education. While these procedures are still in the process of ongoing scrutiny and refinement, it is clear that the public schools have embarked on a new era of assessing the educational needs of mentally retarded children at all levels.

References

Ashurst, D. E., & Meyers, C. E. Social system and clinical model in school identification of the educable retarded. In R. K. Eymans, C. E. Meyers, & G. Tarjan (Eds.), Sociobehavioral studies in mental retardation, *Monographs of the American Association on Mental Deficiency*, 1973, **1**, 150–163.

Bagnato, S. J. Developmental diagnostic reports: Reliable and effective alternatives to guide individualized intervention. *Journal of Special Education*, 1981, **15**, 65–76.

Bateman, B. Three approaches to diagnosis and educational planning for children with learning disabilities. *Academic Therapy Quarterly*, 1967, **2**, 215–222.

Bellamy, T., Greiner, C., & Laffin, K. Arithmetic computation for trainable retarded students: Continuing sequential instructional program. In L. Brown and E. Sontag (Eds.), *Toward the development and implementation of an empirically based public school program for trainable mentally retarded and severely emotionally disturbed students*. Part II. Madison, Wisconsin: Madison Public Schools, 1972.

Bender, M., Valletutti, P. J., & Bender, R. *Teaching the moderately and severely handicapped: Curriculum objectives, strategies, and activities*. Vol. III. *Functional academics for the mildly and moderately handicapped*. Baltimore: University Park Press, 1976.

Bloom, B. S., Hastings, J. T., & Madaus, G. F. *Handbook of formative and summative evaluation of student learning*. New York: McGraw-Hill, 1971.

Brown, L., Hermanson, J., Klemme, H., Haubrion, P., & Ora, J. Using behavior modification principles to teach sight vocabulary. *Teaching Exceptional Children*, 1970, **2**, 120–128.

Buktenica, M. A multidisciplinary training team in the public schools. *Journal of School Psychology*, 1970, **8**, 220–225.

Cleary, T. A., Humphreys, L. G., Kendrick, S. A., & Wesman, A. Educational uses of tests with disadvantaged students. *American Psychologist*, 1975, **30**, 15–41.

Connolly, A. J., Nachtman, W., & Pritchett, E. M. *KeyMath diagnostic arithmetic test*. Circle Pines, Minnesota: American Guidance Service, Inc., 1976.

Cromwell, R., Blashfield, R. K., & Strauss, J. S. Criteria for classification. In N. Hobbs (Ed.), *Issues in Classification*. Vol. 1. San Francisco: Jossey-Bass, 1975.

Domnie, M., & Bellamy, T. A sequential procedure for teaching reading skills to trainable retarded students. In L. Brown and E. Sontag (Eds.), *Toward the development and implementation of an empirically based public school program for trainable mentally retarded and severely emotionally disturbed students*. Part II. Madison, Wisconsin: Madison Public Schools, 1972.

Dunn, L. M., & Markwardt, F. C. *Peabody Individual Achievement Test*. Circle Pines, Minnesota: American Guidance Service, Inc., 1970.

Dunst, C. J. Program evaluation and the Education for All Handicapped Children Act. *Exceptional Children*, 1979, **46**, 24–31.

Falik, L., Grimm, M., Preston, F., & Konno, T. Evaluating the impact of the counseling-learning team on the elementary school. *School Counselor*, 1971, **19**, 25–37.

Fenton, K. S., Yoshida, R. K., Maxwell, J. P., & Kaufman, M. J. *Recognition of team goals: An essential step toward rational decision making*. Washington, D.C.: U.S. Office of Education, Bureau of Education for the Handicapped, Division of Innovation and Development, State Programs Studies Branch, 1978.

Feuerstein, R., Miller, R., Hoffman, M., Rand, Y., Mintzker, Y., & Jensen, M. Cognitive modifiability in adolescence: Cognitive structure and the effects of interaction. *Journal of Special Education*, 1981, **15**, 269–287.

Gajar, A. H. Characteristics across exceptional categories: EMR, LD, and ED. *Journal of Special Education*, 1980, **14**, 166–173.

Gilliam, J. E. Contributions and status rankings of educational planning committee participants. *Exceptional Children*, 1979, **45**, 466–468.

Goldbaum, J., & Rucker, C. Assessment data and the child study team. In J. A. C. Vatour & C. M. Rucker (Eds.), *Child study team training program: Book of Readings*. Austin, Texas: Special Education Associates, 1977.

Goldstein, H., Arkell, C., Ashcroft, S. C., Hurley, D. L., Lilly, M. S. Schools. In N. Hobbs (Ed.), *Issues in the classification of children.* Vol. II. San Francisco: Jossey-Bass, 1975.

Gotts, E. Individual Education Program: Potential change agent for special education. *In conference Summary of Public Law 94-142.* Washington, D.C.: Roy Littlejohn Associates, 1976, 61–73.

Gray, W. S. *Gray oral reading tests.* Indianapolis: Bobbs-Merrill Company, Inc., 1967.

Hawkins-Shepard, C. Working with the IEP: Some early reports. *Teaching Exceptional Children*, 1978, **10**, 95–97.

Hefferin, E. A., & Katz, A. H. Issues and orientations in the evaluation of rehabilitation programs. *Rehabilitation Literature*, 1971, **32**, 66–73.

Hogenson, D. A multidisciplinary approach to the school management of acutely anxious and depressed students in a large urban senior high school setting. *Pupil Personnel Services Journal*, 1973, **3**, 29–31.

Holland, R. P. An analysis of the decision making processes in special education. *Exceptional Children*, 1980, **46**, 551–554.

Howell, K. W., Kaplan, J. S., & O'Connell, C. V. *Evaluating exceptional children.* Columbus: Charles E. Merrill Publishing Company, 1979.

Hutt, M. L., & Gibby, R. G. *The mentally retarded child: Development, education and treatment.* Boston: Allyn and Bacon, Inc., 1976.

Hyman, I., Caroll, R., Duffey, J., Manni, J., & Winikur, D. Conflict resolution by school child study teams. Monograph. *School Psychology in New Jersey*, 1972.

Hyman, I., Caroll, R., Duffey, J., Manni, J., & Winikur, D. Patterns of interprofessional conflict resolution on school child study teams. *Journal of School Psychology*, 1973, **11**, 187–195.

Jastak, J. F., & Jastak, S. *Wide range achievement test.* Wilmington, Del.: Jastak Associates Inc., 1978.

Kirk, S. *Educating exceptional children.* Boston: Houghton-Mifflin Company, 1972.

Kolstoe, O. P. *Teaching educable mentally retarded children.* (2nd ed.) New York: Holt, Rinehart, and Winston, 1976.

Lambert, N., Windmiller, M., Cole, L., & Figueroa, R. *AAMD Adaptive Behavior Scale Public School Version 1974 Revision.* Washington, D.C.: American Association on Mental Deficiency, 1975.

Lerner, J. N. *Children with learning disabilities: Theories, diagrams, and teaching strategies.* Boston: Houghton Mifflin, 1971.

Lindsley, O. R. Precision teaching in perspective: An interview with Ogden R. Lindsley. *Teaching Exceptional Children*, 1971, **3**, 114–119.

Lynch, K. P., Kiernan, W. E., & Stark, J. A. (Eds.) *Prevocational and vocational education for special needs youth: A blueprint for the 1980's.* Baltimore: Paul Brookes, 1982.

MacMillan, D. L. Special education for the mildly retarded: Servant or savant? *Focus on Exceptional Children*, 1971, **2**, 1–11.

MacMillan, D. L. *Mental retardation in school and society.* Boston: Little, Brown and Co., 1977.

MacMillan, D. L., Jones, R. L., & Aloia, G. R. The mentally retarded label: A theoretical analysis and review of research. *American Journal of Mental Deficiency*, 1974, **79**, 241–261.

Maher, C. A. A synoptic framework for school program evaluation. *Journal of School Psychology*, 1978, **16**, 322–333.

Maher, C. A. School psychologists and special education program evaluation: Contributions and considerations. *Contemporary School Psychology*, 1981, 114–119.

Maher, C. A., & Barbrack, C. R. A framework for comprehensive evaluation of the Individualized Education Program (IEP). *Learning Disability Quarterly*, 1980, **3**, 49–55.

Mali, P. *Managing by objective.* New York: John Wiley & Sons, 1977.

McDermott, P. A. Sources of error in the psychoeducational diagnosis of children. *Journal of School Psychology*, 1981, **19**, 31–44.

Mercer, J. R. *Labeling the mentally retarded.* Berkeley: University of California Press, 1973.

Meyers, C. E., Sundstrom, P. E., & Yoshida, R. K. The school psychologist and assessment in special education. *School Psychology Monographs*, 1974, **2**, 3–57.

Molloy, J. S. *Trainable children: Curriculum and procedures.* New York: John Day, 1972.

Morgan, D. P. *A primer on individualized education programs for exceptional children: Preferred strategies and practices.* (2nd ed.) Reston, Virginia: Foundation for Exceptional Children, 1981.

Morganstern, M., & Michel-Smith, H. *Psychology in the vocational rehabilitation of the mentally retarded.* Springfield, Illinois: Thomas, 1973.

Morrow, H. W., Powell, G. O., & Ely, D. D. Placement or placebo: Does additional information change special education placement decisions. *Journal of School Psychology*, 1976, **14**, 186–191.

Myklebust, H. R. *The Pupil Rating Scale.* New York: Grune & Stratton, Inc., 1971.

Page, E. B. Tests and decisions for the handicapped: A guide to evaluation under the new laws. *Journal of Special Education*, 1980, **14**, 423–483.

Payne, J. S., Polloway, E. A., Smith, J. W., & Payne, R. A. *Strategies for teaching the mentally retarded.* Columbus: Charles E. Merrill Publishing Company, 1977.

Peter, L. *Prescriptive teaching.* New York: McGraw-Hill, 1965.

Pfeiffer, S. I. The School-based interprofessional team: Recurring problems and some possible solutions. *Journal of School Psychology*, 1980, **18**, (4), 388–394.

Pluckum, M. Professional territoriality. *Nursing Forum*, 1972, **11**, 300–310.

Schmidt, R. A. *Motor skills.* New York: Harper & Row, 1975.

Semmel, D. S., Yoshida, R. K., Fenton, K. S., & Kaufman, M. J. *The contribution of professional role to group decision-making in a simulated pupil-planning team setting.* Washington, D.C.: U.S. Office of Education for the Handicapped, Division of Innovation and Development, State Program Studies Branch, 1978.

Sinclair, E. Relationship of Psychoeducational Diagnosis to Educational Placement. *Journal of School Psychology*, 1980, **18**, 349–353.

Sinclair, E., & Kheifets, L. Use of clustering techniques in deriving psychoeducational profiles. *Contemporary Educational Psychology*, 1982, **7**, 81–89.

Singer, J., Bossard, M., & Watkins, M. Effects of parental presence on attendance and input of interdisciplinary teams in an institutional setting. *Psychological Reports*, 1977, **41**, 1031–1034.

Spivack, G., & Spotts, J. *Devereux child behavior rating scale*. Pennsylvania: Devereux Foundation, 1966.

Stephens, T. *Directive teaching of children with learning and behavioral handicaps*. Columbus: Charles E. Merrill, 1970.

Taylor, A. Assessment myths and current fads: A rejoinder to a position paper on nonbiased assessment. *Psychology in the Schools*, 1978, **15**, 205–209.

Terman, L. M., & Merrill, M. A. *Stanford-Binet intelligence scale*. Boston: Houghton Mifflin Company, 1972.

Thurlow, M. L., & Ysseldyke, J. E. Current assessment and decision-making practices in model programs for learning disabled students. *Learning Disability Quarterly*, 1979, **2**, 15–24.

Wall, S. M., & Paradise, L. V. A comparison of parent and teacher reports of selected adaptive behaviors of children. *Journal of School Psychology*, 1981, **19**, 73–77.

Wallace, G. Interdisciplinary efforts in learning disabilities: Issues and recommendations. *Journal of Learning Disabilities*, 1976, **9**, 511–526.

Wallace, G., & Kauffman, J. M. *Teaching children with learning problems*. Columbus, Ohio: Charles E. Merrill, 1973.

Woodcock, R. W. *Woodcock Reading Mastery Tests*. Circle Pines, Minnesota: American Guidance Service, Inc., 1973.

Yoshida, R. K., Fenton, K. S., Maxwell, J. P., and Kaufman, M. J. Group decision making in the planning team process: Communication of planning team decisions to program implementers. *Journal of School Psychology*, 1978, **16**, 178–183.

Ysseldyke, J. E., Algozzine, B., Regan, R., & McGue, M. The influence of test scores and naturally-occurring pupil characteristics on psychoeducational decision-making with children. *Journal of School Psychology*, 1981, **19**, 167–177.

PART V
PREVENTION ISSUES

17 GENETIC COUNSELING

Siegfried M. Pueschel and Amy Goldstein

enetic counseling is a communication process which deals with the human problems associated with the occurrence or risk of occurrence of a genetic disorder in a family (American Society of Human Genetics Committee on Genetic Counseling, 1975). If a counseling experience is to be successful, the genetic counselor should make the counselee aware of the nature of the genetic disorder, its medical facts and clinical expectations, the inheritance pattern and risk of recurrence, reproductive options, and the availability of prenatal diagnosis. Along with this basic information, there is also a need for the counselor to help the counselee and his family cope with emotional responses and deal with adjustment to caring for and accepting an affected child as a family member. The scope of the genetic counseling experience is, therefore, aimed at allowing the family to make educated, rational decisions about themselves and the affected child.

Genetic counseling is often requested by families who have a mentally retarded child or other family member who is retarded. Since mental retardation can have many different causes, before genetic counseling is possible one should attempt to determine the cause of the retardation. Of particular concern to the genetic counselor are those mental retardation syndromes which are associated with genetic defects;

these may include chromosomal abnormalities, specific neurological diseases, and biochemical disorders. However, the existence of a genetic cause for mental retardation is often difficult to prove. Unless a clearly nongenetic reason is found for the retardation, such as neonatal anoxia or congenital infection, genetic counseling may depend on empiric risks assessment (see below). The more documentation of family history and medical records that can be obtained, the more accurate and helpful will be the genetic counseling process. The gathered information, in addition to phenotype evaluation and specific laboratory investigations, will allow differentiation between genetically caused mental retardation including chromosome, single gene and multifactorial disorders and idiopathic mental retardation.

Chromosome Disorders

An increased risk of having a child with a chromosome abnormality is observed in women who are 35 years of age and older, in families who have had a previous child with a chromosomal disorder, and in persons who carry a balanced translocation. Several epidemiological studies have demonstrated an increase in occurrence of nondisjunction in offspring of older mothers (Hook & Chambers, 1977; Hook & Fabia, 1978; Hook & Lindsjo, 1978). While the relationship between increased incidence and advanced maternal age has been well documented for Down syndrome (Table 17.1), it also has been observed for trisomy 13, trisomy 18, Klinefelter syndrome, XXX syndrome, and some other chromosome disorders.

The reason for the increase of chromosome disorders in offspring as a woman gets older remains unknown. Because a woman's ova are in a state of "suspended animation" throughout most of her premenopausal life, it is possible that those eggs remaining to be ovulated during the later reproductive years have had more exposure to environmental agents or endogenous processes that may interfere with normal meiosis. Warburton (1981) has found evidence which may suggest a failure in older women of some recognition rejection mechanism which would thereby increase the number of chromosomally abnormal fetuses that would normally have been spontaneously aborted. An alternative explanation of the increased prevalence of chromosomally abnormal offspring at advanced maternal ages may relate to hormonal

changes noted at that time in a woman's life. Other hypotheses elaborating on this phenomenon are discussed in detail by Crowley, Hayden, and Gulati (1982).

Counseling of a couple concerning future pregnancies when the woman is over 35 usually includes a discussion of the type of abnormalities for which there is an increased risk, as well as of the availability, technical aspects, and risks of amniocentesis. Although one can never guarantee that an infant will be born free of any birth defects, the prospective parents should be made aware that amniocentesis can eliminate the added risk of a chromosomally abnormal child.

A discrepancy has been noted in the risk of finding a chromosomally abnormal fetus at 16 weeks of gestation when amniocentesis is performed, compared with the risk of delivering a liveborn child with a chromosome anomaly as noted in Table 17.2 (Hook, 1978). Reasons for this discrepancy may include spontaneous abortion of fetuses with Down syndrome during the second trimester and incomplete recording

Table 17.1. Rates of Down Syndrome per 1,000 Live Births by Single-year Maternal Age Intervals

MATERNAL AGE, YEARS	HOOK & FABIA (1978)	HOOK & CHAMBERS (1977)	HOOK & LINDSJO (1978)
20	0.57	0.52	0.65
21	0.60	0.59	0.67
22	0.64	0.65	0.71
23	0.67	0.71	0.75
24	0.70	0.77	0.79
25	0.74	0.83	0.83
26	0.77	0.89	0.87
27	0.80	0.95	0.92
28	0.84	1.01	0.97
29	0.87	1.07	1.02
30	0.90	1.13	1.08
31	0.93	1.21	1.14
32	1.15	1.38	1.25
33	1.55	1.69	1.47
34	1.98	2.15	1.92
35	2.53	2.74	2.51
36	3.22	3.49	3.28
37	4.11	4.45	4.28
38	5.24	5.66	5.60
39	6.68	7.21	7.32
40	8.52	9.19	9.57
41	10.86	11.71	12.51
42	13.85	14.91	16.36
43	17.66	19.00	21.39
44	22.51	24.20	27.96
45	28.71	30.84	36.55
46	36.61	39.28	47.79
47	46.68	50.04	62.47
48	59.52	63.75	81.67
49	75.89	81.21	106.76

Adapted from Hook (1982).

Table 17.2. Risk of Down Syndrome in Fetuses at Amniocentesis and in Live Births

MATERNAL AGE	FREQUENCY OF DOWN SYNDROME	
	FETUSES	LIVE BIRTHS
35	1/350	1/350
36	1/260	1/300
37	1/200	1/225
38	1/160	1/175
39	1/125	1/150
40	1/70	1/100
41	1/35	1/85
42	1/30	1/65
43	1/20	1/50
44	1/13	1/40
45	1/25	1/25

Adapted from Hook and Chambers (1977).

of Down syndrome births. In addition, some chromosome disorders such as XXX and XXY syndromes cannot be diagnosed in a newborn unless a chromosome analysis is done (Hook, 1978).

When there is already one child with a chromosome abnormality such as Down syndrome in a family, there is approximately a 1% chance that there will be another child born with either Down syndrome or another of the trisomy syndromes resulting from a nondisjunctional event (Carter, 1961; Hamerton et al., 1980). This risk appears to remain nearly the same regardless of the age of the mother until about the age of 40 years, at which time the risk increases.

Genetic counseling of a family who has given birth to a child with a chromosome abnormality should take place in several stages. If possible, initial contact immediately following the birth of the child can establish a source of information and support. At this stage, the counselor should start to help the family cope with the emotional concerns subsequent to the birth of a child who is not the perfect infant they expected. If a child has multiple congenital anomalies due to a chromosome anomaly such as trisomy 18 or 13, counseling of the parents during the neonatal period will often require discussion of the poor prognosis observed in these disorders. Confirmation of the diagnosis of such chromosome abnormalities by bone marrow aspiration is a technique that provides an opportunity to study the child's chromosomes immediately.

Infants with Down syndrome usually survive the neonatal period, and have a much better prognosis than infants with trisomy 13 or 18. Counseling following the initial shock of the diagnosis of a baby with Down syndrome is most helpful if the counselor will provide support to the parents and show understanding of their grief, anger, disappointment, and denial reactions. Parents should be allowed to see their baby as a human being and as an individual with the potential for a meaningful life.

At one or more follow-up visits, the facts about the chromosome abnormality should be explained. Illustrations of various karyotypes (trisomy and translocations) and diagrams of the nondisjunctional event will give parents a better understanding of the subject matter (see Figs. 17.1–4). Discussion of prenatal diagnosis and future pregnancies can be deferred until parents can be expected to be more able to make rational decisions and ask appropriate questions.

Individuals carrying a balanced translocation (normal amount of genetic material is present) are often discovered because of the birth of a child with an unbalanced translocation. Therefore, when a child is found with a translocation, both parents' chromosomes should be examined. If one of the parents carries the translocation in a balanced form, that individual may also have relatives with the same balanced translocation who also would be at risk for having a child with the unbalanced translocation. Each translocation has its own risk of occurring in a conceptus and live birth, therefore one cannot usually predict any specific risk based on past experiences with other types of translocations. If conception should occur, the embryo/fetus may be spontaneously aborted either before or after pregnancy is recognized. Translocations which are unlikely to allow complete development of a fetus if they are unbalanced, would, therefore, have a low risk for causing the live birth of a child with multiple malformations. Most children born to such a couple would either have no translocation or have the balanced arrangement.

Robertsonian translocations involving D and G group chromosomes have more predictable risks. In such families, an empiric risk can be given which may range from as low as 2% to as high as 100%, depending on the rearrangement involved and whether the translocation is carried by the father or mother (see Table 17.3).

If a translocation is found to occur spontaneously, or *de novo*, in a phenotypically abnormal child, the likelihood of another child being born to a couple with normal chromosomes is low, probably less than 1%. In most mosaic chromosomal conditions, the risk of recurrence is not known; it is probably also less than 1%.

In all cases of translocation and other types of chromosome anomalies such as ring formations and deletions, amniocentesis is an option available to allow

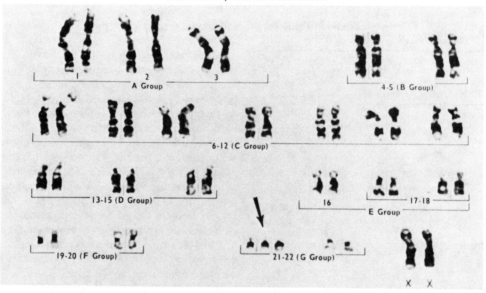

FIG. 17.1. Chromosomes (karyotype) of a girl with Down syndrome. Note the extra #21 chromosome as shown by the arrow.

prenatal diagnosis of unbalanced fetal chromosome disorders.

Single Gene Disorders

Genetic diseases caused by mutation of a single gene can be inherited in one of four ways: autosomal recessive, autosomal dominant, X-linked recessive, and X-linked dominant. If the inheritance of a mental retardation syndrome is known, counseling of the family includes education and guidance about the genetic facts of the condition, recurrence risk information, and discussion of possible prenatal diagnosis if available.

Almost all of the inborn errors of metabolism such as phenylketonuria, galactosemia, and Hurler syndrome are *autosomal recessive* disorders. Parents at risk for having a child with an autosomal recessive disease are for the most part phenotypically normal. They each carry one copy of the mutated gene and one normal gene which compose the pair of genes at this particular gene locus. With each pregnancy,

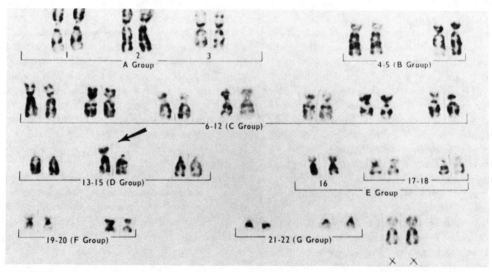

FIG. 17.2. Karyotype of a girl with translocation Down syndrome. The arrow indicates the extra #21 chromosome which is "translocated" or attached to a #14 chromosome.

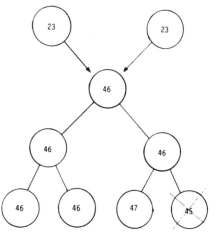

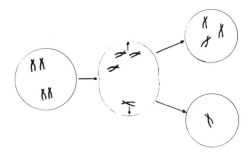

Table 17.3. Recurrence Risk of Balanced Carriers

TRANSLOCATION	FATHER	MOTHER
14/21	5	10–15
21/21	100	100
21/22	2–3	10–15

derstandable grief reaction. The counselor should point out that nearly all people have several mutated genes and that we all are carriers for several genetic diseases. The carrier state is most often discovered when a couple has a child with an autosomal recessive disorder or if the heterozygote state is identified by screening such as for Tay-Sachs disease. Unless this occurs, an individual's genetic makeup remains an unknown factor.

Autosomal dominant conditions are expressed when only one member of a pair of genes is affected. For autosomal dominant conditions there is a 50% chance that a child will inherit the disease from an affected mother or father (Fig. 17.6). Autosomal dominant conditions often show variable expression, so that one person with the disease can be more or less severely affected than another. When an autosomal dominant disease is phenotypically not apparent (nonpenetrance), the gene may appear to skip a generation; i.e., even though the affected gene is present in an individual, its effect is so mild that it cannot be detected clinically.

Autosomal dominant conditions frequently occur as new mutations in families where there is no family history. Achondroplasia, Apert syndrome, and neurofibromatosis are autosomal dominant disorders that

FIG. 17.3. In mosaicism the "accident of nature" (nondisjunction) is thought to occur during one of the early cell divisions. When this infant is born, one will find some cells with 46 chromosomes and others with 47 chromosomes. Cells with 45 or less chromosomes usually do not survive.

there is a 25% chance that the child will inherit the mutated gene from both parents and, thereby, will have the genetic disease (see Fig. 17.5). When counseling such a family, it is important to stress that chance has no memory and therefore, there is an equal risk (again one chance in four) that each pregnancy may produce an affected child, one chance in four that the child will have normal genes at this particular gene locus, and one chance in two that the child will be a carrier.

Parents often express feelings of unworth because of their guilt at having "bad" genes. This is an un-

FIG. 17.4. During the process of cell division two #21 chromosomes "stick together" (nondisjunction). In the following cell generation, one cell will have one chromosome less (this is not a viable cell) and the other cell will have one additional chromosome. For demonstration purposes only two pairs of chromosomes are shown here.

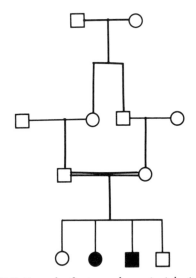

FIG. 17.5. Example of autosomal recessive inheritance. The parents who are first-degree cousins are heterozygotes; they have two affected children.

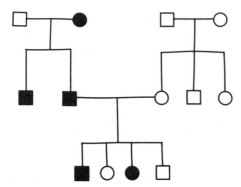

FIG. 17.6. In autosomal dominantly inherited disorders, affected individuals are often observed in each generation as noted in this pedigree.

commonly occur as a new mutation in a family with no history of the disease.

All these factors must be taken into account when a family is counseled for autosomal dominant inheritance. Parents must realize the high risk of recurrence (50%) if one of them is affected. Because there are usually other affected relatives who may not be aware of the risk to their future children, it is important to pursue extended family counseling. It is in the family's interest to diagnose other people at risk and to make sure that the rest of the family understands the risks involved for future generations.

Genes located on the X chromosomes are called X-linked or sex-linked genes. Because a female has two X chromosomes, a recessive mutation on one of the X-chromosomes usually has no effect. However, since all males have only one X in addition to the Y chromosome, any mutation on their X chromosome would be expressed. Because of this, X-linked recessive disorders are almost always found only in males who either inherit the mutated gene from their carrier mother (Fig. 17.7) or who have a new mutation.

X-linked recessive mental retardation has been suggested as the cause for the preponderance of moderately mentally retarded males (Turner & Turner, 1974). X-linked mental retardation is sometimes associated with the "fragile" or "marker" X chromosome, a recently delineated syndrome (Sutherland & Ashforth, 1979). Macroorchidism is a frequent finding in these patients. Carrier females of the fragile X syndrome do not always have the marker chromosomes in their cells, making carrier detection difficult. Turner, Brookwell, Daniel, Selkiowitz, and Zilbowitz (1980) examined a population of 128 mildly mentally retarded girls and found that about 7% of those who were physically normal had the marker X chromosome in some of their cells.

When counseling a family in which mental retardation appears to be inherited in an X-linked pattern, carrier risks and recurrence risks must be calculated, taking the entire pedigree into account. For example, a woman whose mother is an obligate carrier because of several affected sons, has a 50% chance of also being a carrier. However, if this daughter already has three normal sons, her actual risk is much lower. Calculation of this risk figure requires Bayesian analysis (Murphy & Chase, 1975).

If an X-linked recessive condition is a new mutation in the affected male there will be a very low risk of recurrence and other female relatives would not be at risk. Unfortunately, accurate carrier detection is not available for many X-linked conditions and it is, therefore, very difficult to assure any mother or other female relative of a son with X-linked mental retardation that she is not a carrier.

X-linked dominantly inherited conditions are quite rare. When a female is heterozygous for a dominant mutation on her X chromosome, she will express the disorder. Males are usually more severely affected than females. At times the condition may be lethal, resulting in spontaneous abortions of affected male conceptuses. In X-linked dominant diseases, an affected female has a 50% chance of passing the condition to either her sons or daughters. An affected male will pass the gene to 100% of his daughters and to none of his sons (Fig. 17.8).

Multifactorial Inheritance

In some genetic conditions, there is a familial tendency for recurrence of the disorder. The risk of recurrence

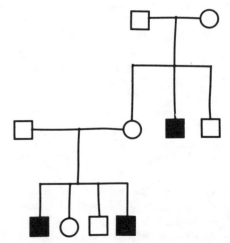

FIG. 17.7. Example of X-linked recessive inheritance where the mutant gene is carried by the female but only males are affected.

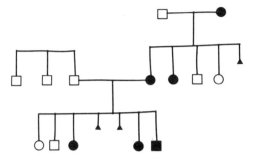

FIG. 17.8. In X-linked dominantly inherited disorders, both males and females can be affected.

is, however, significantly less than that for single gene diseases. These conditions are called multifactorially inherited disorders. They are believed to result from the additive effect of many genes that are influenced by environmental factors. Multifactorial diseases include the majority of the more common birth defects such as spina bifida, congenital hip dislocation, club foot, pyloric stenosis, cleft lip and/or cleft palate, and most congenital heart diseases.

The main characteristics of multifactorial inheritance are:

- after one affected child the recurrence risk averages between 2 and 5%;
- if more than one child is affected the risk of recurrence is increased;
- the more severe the malformations in the affected individual, the higher the recurrence risk will be;
- the incidence of multifactorial conditions sometimes varies with different ethnic groups and socioeconomic classes;
- the risk to relatives declines sharply with decreasing degrees of relationship;
- some multifactorial disorders are often found at a higher frequency in one sex than the other. The recurrence risk is higher for relatives if the patient is of the less susceptible sex.

The genetic and environmental components of multifactorial inheritance can be best observed in twin births. The likelihood that both of a set of identical or monozygotic twins will be affected with the same malformation is less than 100%, but this likelihood is much greater than the chance that both of a set of nonidentical twins will be affected. The concordance rate for monozygotic twins ranges from 20 to 40%, depending on the type of malformation. If only genetic factors were involved as in single gene Mendelian disorders, monozygotic concordance would be 100%.

Idiopathic Mental Retardation

Counseling with regard to the recurrence risk of a condition is relatively simple if the mode of inheritance of the disorder is known. Empiric risk estimates can thus be discussed and used as a basis for decision making. However, there are a large number of mentally retarded patients for whom no recognized etiology is known for their condition. The actual recurrence risk for this group can range from less than 2% up to 45% (see below). However, it is usually impossible to know where within this spectrum an individual actually belongs.

Several studies have been done in an attempt to derive more specific recurrence risk estimates. When one or both parents are mentally retarded, pooled data from three studies (Brandon, 1957; Scally, 1968; Shaw and Wright, 1960) revealed the overall risk to be about 11% for mentally retarded offspring. When one parent is mentally retarded and there is already one mentally retarded child in the family, the recurrence risk rises to almost 20%. Two mentally retarded parents who have already had one mentally retarded child have a 40 to 45% risk for a child with an IQ of less than 70. The recurrence risk for parents of normal intelligence after having one child who is moderately to severely mentally retarded was found to be about 6%. Similarly, Penrose (1938) had noted that the risk to intellectually normal parents after they had one mentally retarded child was about 5%, but their risk of having a child of borderline intelligence was 10%.

It has been observed that males have a lower threshold to express polygenic mental retardation. In the mild to moderate range of mental retardation Turner, Collins, and Turner (1971) found that the recurrence risk for future siblings was 9% if the proband was male and 4% if the proband was female. The male-to-female sex ratio in this group was 1.5:1.0. In the severe to profound range of mental retardation the sex ratio was appropriately equal 1.1:1.0 and the recurrence rate was 4% regardless of the sex of the proband.

Since chromosome banding techniques became available during the past decade it is possible now to look for minute chromosome anomalies. Some patients, who in the past had been said to have idiopathic mental retardation, may presently be diagnosed if the chromosome analysis is repeated. Lubs and Lubs (1973), who studied 191 pediatric patients with mental retardation, do not recommend that all patients with mental retardation have a chromosomal analysis, since they found no chromosome abnormalities in the group with no physical anomalies or seizures. However,

14% of the group with major anomalies did have an abnormal karyotype.

The Counseling Experience

Providing facts about the inheritance of a genetic disease and suggesting tests and appropriate medical management are essential aspects of genetic counseling. In addition, the genetic counselor should help families to cope and adjust, since the information given to a family during the genetic counseling session is often emotionally burdensome. The birth of an abnormal child or being told of a serious diagnosis can elicit guilt, denial, anger, and unforeseen anxieties. A sensitive counselor will be attuned to these reactions and understand the symbolism of behaviors in stress and the applications of defense mechanisms.

The timing of genetic counseling sessions is important to allow optimal absorption of the provided information. At the time of diagnosis, the resulting shock and grief may prevent counselees from "hearing" any recurrence risk information or understanding the explanation of the condition. Follow-up counseling after a diagnostic informing session is not only beneficial, but in many situations a necessity as counselees need time to adjust to each piece of information.

By encouraging comments and questions from the counselees, the genetic counselor can elicit information to help guide the counseling efforts. In order to communicate effectively, the counseling has to be a give-and-take process. The initial counseling contact may only include an introduction, some basic reassurances, and answers to questions. By the second meeting, after the initial shock has subsided, more detailed information can be communicated.

After the counselees are able to assimilate the genetic information, the educational process can begin in earnest. Most patients have learned from past experience that physicians, for the most part, tell them what tests or actions are best for them. The approach to genetic counseling may, therefore, come as a surprise to these individuals because of the nondirective manner which is commonly used. The counselor usually provides information, various options and guidance to the family, but, for example, does not tell a couple whether to become pregnant, or what to do if they are already pregnant. Counselees are asked to make independent decisions based upon the knowledge they have gained through genetic counseling. The way information and choices are discussed by the counselor may influence these decisions, however. Sorenson et al. (1980) found that 54% of all counselors leave all decisions to the parents, but that 64% did feel that

it was always appropriate to inform counselees in a way that would guide them toward rational decision.

As part of the genetic counseling process, parents should be introduced to the sources of help they will be using throughout the life of their child. Referrals to early intervention programs, support groups, parent organizations, and social service agencies are appropriate contacts for the parents to make as a result of the genetic counseling experience. The genetic counselor also may be the family's unifying point in the care of their child. Often a coordinator is needed to make sure that medical evaluations and tests are carried out and this coordinating task may at times fall upon the genetic counselor.

Options

The outcome of genetic counseling usually involves some decision making about future reproduction. If the genetic counseling process is to be successful, the couple who has been counseled is prepared to make rational, educated decisions about whether more children are to be planned. Depending on the type of genetic disorder and its risks of recurrence, the couple will be faced with varying options which should be considered in light of these risks as well as the emotional, financial, and physical burden placed on the family and any future handicapped child. The way these burdens are experienced can cause one family to view a 1% risk as extremely great, while another family might consider a 25% risk as one with relatively good odds. Possible options may include prenatal diagnosis with abortion of an abnormal fetus, birth control, adoption, artificial insemination, sterilization, or taking the risk and playing the odds.

For certain types of genetic defects, such as biochemical abnormalities, chromosomal anomalies and neural tube defects, prenatal diagnosis by amniocentesis can be performed. Amniocentesis which is usually done at about the 16th week of pregnancy requires the withdrawal of a small amount of amniotic fluid transabdominally with a syringe. This option allows a couple to attempt a pregnancy and choose to give birth only to babies unaffected with the disorder in question.

Depending on the specific disorder, various tests can be performed on the fluid. The fetal cells in the fluid can be cultured for either biochemical or chromosomal analysis. The fluid itself can also be assayed biochemically, for such substances as abnormal amounts of α-fetoprotein which escapes into the fluid through open neural tube defects. The results of amniocentesis are most often reassuring to couples who have had children with a chromosome abnormality or a neural tube defect, because the recurrence risk for these conditions is usually no more than 1 to 3%. To couples at risk for a child with an autosomal recessive biochemical disease, a risk of 25% may be much too great to plan another pregnancy unless the condition can be diagnosed prenatally. For X-linked mental retardation couples may choose to give birth only to females and to thereby use amniocentesis for sex selection. For any of these reasons, a couple should be prepared for the possibility of having to make a decision regarding termination of a pregnancy. This decision may be especially difficult in the case of X-linked disorders, when 50% of males if aborted would have been normal.

Whenever amniocentesis is an option for a counselee, the risks of the procedure must be discussed and compared with the likelihood that the test will diagnose an abnormal fetus. If this likelihood is less than the risk of complication from the amniocentesis, such as miscarriage or fetal injury, then parents may decide against having an amniocentesis performed. As an example, a young couple who has a child with mental retardation for which no cause can be found becomes pregnant again. They may request amniocentesis because they want "to make sure that their baby is normal." However, the counselor must inform them that although their risk for having another child with mental retardation may be about 6%, a completely normal amniocentesis result could not rule out mental retardation, but would only serve to rule out chromosome disorders and neural tube defects. The possible 0.5% risk of miscarriage from the amniocentesis is much greater than the 0.1% chance that their child might have Down syndrome, a condition for which they do not have an increased risk. Hence, amniocentesis would not be beneficial to this couple.

For conditions caused by autosomal recessive inheritance, or a dominant gene in the father, artificial insemination by donor is a possibility that the counselor can discuss with a couple. It makes recurrence highly unlikely and it allows a pregnancy which a couple can experience together. This option, however, may be distasteful for many individuals. Counseling can be particularly difficult when one member of a couple agrees to such a procedure and the spouse is repulsed by it.

Techniques involving in vitro fertilization of donor eggs with the husband's sperm may be developed in the future. This technique would be applicable in cases of X-linked and dominant conditions present in the mother.

Extended Counseling Responsibilities

Genetic counseling often reaches out to patients rather than having the patient seek counseling. Situations calling for this outreach responsibility may be encountered in families where a translocation has been found as discussed previously. Relatives of the individual with the translocation may also be at risk for children with multiple anomalies and an attempt should be made to contact them for testing and counseling.

Maternal aunts, sisters, and female cousins of boys with X-linked genetic disorders may be at risk for affected children. If carrier testing is available, the women at risk could be identified. However, for most cases of X-linked mental retardation, no carrier test can be done and risks are mathematically derived. It is tragic when a relative who is at risk has an affected child before knowing the risk she was taking.

Newborn screening projects also serve to reach out and contact families for genetic services immediately following the birth of a child with a biochemical condition such as phenylketonuria.

During the early 1960s, mass screening for metabolic disorders was introduced in many states when simple methods (the Guthrie test) became available. These innovative techniques allow collection of blood specimens by heel puncture of newborns and subsequent absorption on filter paper. Without special handling the air-dried specimens can be sent to a competent laboratory for further processing. During the sixties and early seventies, these blood specimens were primarily tested for the presence of increased phenylalanine to identify those children who had phenylketonuria. Today, in addition to phenylketonuria and its variants, other metabolic diseases such as homocystinuria, maple syrup urine disease, galactosemia, and most recently hypothyroidism have been added to the newborn testing program (Levy, 1973). Many states have organized regional programs with central laboratories, where the blood specimens are processed. While it is possible today to detect a variety of other rare inborn errors of metabolism, most screening programs usually focus on those metabolic disorders that are associated with preventable clinical disease and mental retardation, and those that have a relatively high frequency for which early instituted therapy will be beneficial.

In addition to homozygote screening for rare inborn errors of metabolism in newborns, there has been a great deal of interest in heterozygote screening over the past two decades. This interest is understandable since identification of carriers for certain "abnormal" genes could provide information which might assist in making decisions regarding family planning and childbearing. The present techniques of detecting the carrier state for most inborn errors of metabolism are not developed to the point that they could be applied to general population screening. A reliable method for heterozygote screening is readily available for Tay-Sachs disease. This screening test can accurately determine the presence of the activity of the enzyme hexosaminidase A. Screening for this disease has had particular success because of the single ethnic group (Ashkenazi Jews) who have a high proportion of carriers, about 1 in 30. It is of note that beyond the medical aspect of screening there are ethical, financial and legislative aspects that need to be taken into account.

Once a diagnosis has been established that either a newborn child has a certain metabolic disease or that a person has been identified as a heterozygote, this information, of course, has to be shared with those immediately involved. In the former situation, the parents will need to be notified that their child has a metabolic genetic disease such as phenylketonuria. They should be provided with a detailed explanation in simple understandable terms of the specific metabolic error and its genetic basis. The respective approach to treatment will also need to be communicated to the parents. Appropriate follow-up counseling should not only review the medical and genetic aspects, but also should deal with the parents' guilt feelings, their disappointment, frustration, and other possible causes of emotional stress.

Summary

As detailed in this paper, genetic counseling involves much more than explaining risks and recommending tests. The counselor remains involved in the functioning of the family from the time initial contact is made. This contact can be because of the birth of a child with a genetic problem, the prenatal diagnosis of an abnormality, or the discovery of a genetic condition in a relative. For parents of a mentally handicapped child, the genetic counselor can become an important source of information and referral.

References

Brandon, M. W. G. The intellectual and social status of children of mental defectives. *Journal of Mental Science.* 1957, **103**, 710–725.

Carter, C. A., & Evans, K. A. Risk of parents who have one child with Down syndrome having another child similarly affected. *Lancet.* 1961, **2**, 785–787.

Committee on Genetic Counseling. Genetic counseling. *American Journal of Human Genetics.* 1975, **27**, 240–242.

Crowley, P. H., Hayden, T. L., & Gulati, D. K. Etiology of Down syndrome. In S. M. Pueschel & J. E. Rynders, (Eds.). *Down syndrome: Advances in biomedicine and the behavioral sciences.* Cambridge, Mass.: The Ware Press, 1982.

Evers-Kieboome, G., & Van Den Berghe, H. Impact of genetic counseling: A review of published follow-up studies. *Clinical Genetics.* 1979, **15**, 465–474.

Golbus, M. S., Loughman, W. D., Epstein, C. J., Halbasch, G., Stephens, J. D., & Hall, B. D. Prenatal genetic diagnosis in 3000 amniocenteses. *New England Journal of Medicine.* 1979, **300**, 157–163.

Guthrie, R., & Susi, A. A simple phenylalanine method for detecting phenylketonuria in large populations of newborn infants. *Pediatrics.* 1963, **32**, 338–343.

Hamerton, J. L., Boue, A., Cohen, M. M., De La Chapelle, A., Hsu, L. Y., Lindsten, J., Mikkelsen, M., Robinson, D., Stengel-Rutkowski, D., Webb, T., Willey, A., & Worton, R. Chromosome disease. *Prenatal Diagnosis* (Special Issue). December, 1980, 4–21.

Hook, E. B. Differences between rates of trisomy 21 Down syndrome (DS) and other chromosome abnormality diagnosis in livebirths and in cell culture 2nd trimester amniocentesis. Suggested explanations for genetic counseling and program planning. *Birth Defects.* 1978, **14**, 249.

Hook, E. B., & Chambers, G. M. Estimated rates of Down's syndrome in livebirths by one year maternal age intervals for mothers aged 20 to 49 in a New York State study: Implications of the "risk" figures for genetic counseling and cost benefit analysis of prenatal diagnosis programs. In D. Bergsma, R. B. Lowry, B. K. Trimble & M. Feingold (Eds.), *Numerical taxonomy on birth defects and polygenic disorders.* (Birth Defects Original Article Series Vol 13, No. 3A) New York: Alan R. Liss, Inc., 1977. Pp. 123–141.

Hook, E. B., & Fabia, J. J. Frequency of Down syndrome by single-year maternal age interval: Results of a Massachusetts study. *Teratology.* 1978, **17**, 223–228.

Hook, E. B., & Lindsjo, A. Down syndrome in live births by single year maternal age interval in a Swedish study: Comparison with results from a New York study. *American Journal of Human Genetics.* 1978, **30**, 19–27.

Hook, E. B. Epidemiology of Down syndrome. In S. M. Pueschel & J. E. Rynders (Ed.) *Down syndrome: Advances in biomedicine and the behavioral sciences.* Cambridge: The Ware Press, 1982.

Ives, E. J., Petersen, E. M., & Cardwell, S. E. Evaluation of a genetic counseling service. *Pediatric Research.* 1973, **7**, 345. (Abstr.)

Levy, H. L. Genetic screening for inborn errors of metabolism. In H. Harris, & K. Hirschhorn (Eds.), *Advances in human genetics.* Vol. 4. New York: Plenum Press, 1973.

Lubs, M. L. E., & Lubs, H. A. New cytogenetic technic applied to a series of children with mental retardation. Nobel Symposia XXIII. Medicine and natural sciences, chromosome identification technique and application. In T. Caspersson & L. Zech (Eds.), *Biology and medicine.* New York: Academic Press, 1973. P. 241.

Lubs, M. L. E., & Maes, J. A. Recurrence risk in mental retardation. In P. Mittler (Ed.). *Research to Practice in Mental Retardation.* Vol. III. *Biomedical Aspects.* Baltimore, Maryland: University Park Press, 1973.

Murphy, E. A., & Chase, G. A. *Principles of genetic counseling.* Chicago: Yearbook, 1975.

Penrose, L. S. A clinical and genetic study of 1280 cases of mental deficit. MRC Spec. Rep. Ser. No. 229, 1938, London, HMSU.

Scally, B. G. The offspring of mental defectives. Proc. 1st. Cong. Assoc. Ment. Defic. 1968. P. 246.

Schreinemachers, D. M., Cross, P. K., & Hook, E. B. Rates of 47, + 21, 47, + 18, 47, + 13, XXY and XXX detected in 21,864 prenatal cytogenetic diagnoses by one year maternal age intervals. *American Journal of Human Genetics.* 1981, **33**, 120a. (Abstr.)

Shaw, C. H., & Wright, C. H. The married mental defective. *Lancet.* 1960, **1**, 273.

Sorenson, J. R., Swazey, J., Scotch, N. A. Summary and recommendations: A two year study of genetic counseling at clinics receiving support from the March of Dimes–Birth Defects Foundation. Jan., 1980.

Sutherland, G. R., & Ashforth, P. X-linked mental retardation with macroorchidism and the fragile site at Xq 27 or 28. *Human Genetics.* 1979, **48**, 117–120.

Turner, G., & Turner, B. X-linked mental retardation. *Journal of Medical Genetics.* 1974, **11**, 109.

Turner, G., Brookwell, R., Daniel, A., Selkiowitz, M. & Zilbowitz, M. Heterozygous expression of X-linked mental retardation and X-chromosome marker fra(x) (q27). *New England Journal of Medicine.* 1980, **303**, 662–664.

Turner, G., Collins, E., & Turner, B. Recurrence risk of mental retardation in sibs. *Medical Journal of Australia.* 1971, **1**, 1165.

Warburton, D. Environmental cytogenetic interaction in the origin of spontaneous abortion. American Society of Human Genetics, 32nd Annual Meeting, October 30, 1981.

18 NUTRITION AND MENTAL RETARDATION

Agnes M. Huber

The relevancy of nutrition to mental retardation was first convincingly demonstrated in the fifties when diet intervention in phenylketonurics proved effective in preventing the associated brain damage and mental retardation (Bickel, Gerrard, & Hickmans, 1953). Of the large number of monogenic disorders described (McKusick, 1968) since the publication of the Croonian lecture by Sir Archibald Garrod in 1908, some respond to dietary treatment. The aim of diet intervention is to minimize the biochemical changes brought about by the genetic defect, thus normalizing the metabolic events. For dietary intervention to be successful, the basic biochemical lesion of the genetic disorder must be known, early diagnosis must be made before permanent brain damage occurs, and the appropriate diet modification should be available and acceptable to the patient.

Dietary intervention for inborn errors of metabolism is essentially of two types: (1) exclusion diets, in which one or several dietary constituents are greatly reduced and adjusted to such dietary intakes to produce normal blood and tissue levels, and (2) diets to which greater than normal amounts of a specific nutrient are added. Exclusion diets usually are much more difficult to prepare and adhere to because each nutrient is found in many different foods, thus requiring extensive dietary changes. Addition of a vitamin or a mineral element, on the other hand, poses no difficulties since most nutrients are available in purified form and can be obtained at reasonable cost.

Although the benefit of nutrition in the treatment of certain inborn errors is well known, the relevancy of nutrition to the wider field of mental retardation is less well accepted. Studies indicate that, even when conservative estimates are made, the incidence of nutritional problems in the mentally retarded is high (Palmer & Ekvall, 1978). Problems may relate to food ingestion, nutrient needs that are higher than average, or behavioral problems that affect eating.

The following chapter will give an overview of work done in the area of nutrition as it relates to mental retardation and will discuss its current status and point out further trends. Since nutrition approaches to mental retardation are comparatively recent, much of our knowledge is fragmentary and requires updating as new data become available.

Nutrition and Brain Development

Calorie and nutrient needs must be met all through life. During periods of rapid growth, such as occur prenatally, postnatally, and during the adolescent growth spurt, nutritional requirements are greatest. Nutrient deficiencies during growth may result in stunting (Cravioto, DeLicardie, & Birch, 1966; György, 1960; Mitchell, 1962). Although temporary deficiency states leading to growth depression may be overcome by refeeding, catch-up growth is limited and may not occur if the nutritional deficiency had occurred during a critical period of development.

The growth spurt of the human brain occurs early in life. There is controversy as to what extent nutritional insults may affect brain development. Controlled animal studies indicate that malnutrition during the hyperplastic phase of brain growth affects cell numbers, cell size, protein, and lipid content of the brain (Dobbing, 1971; Winnick & Noble, 1966).

The study of human brain growth related to nutrition is hampered by the fact that nutritional factors are difficult to separate from social and genetic factors. The use of the term "malnutrition" may cover a multitude of nutritional conditions. Malnutrition can be due to chronic or acute deficiency; it can be related to low intakes of all nutrients, a group of nutrients, or single nutrients, thus producing different manifestations. In general, the nutritional assessment tools are still too crude to define type and severity of malnutrition. Depending upon timing during development, nutritional insults may have vastly different effects.

In spite of these difficulties, many studies suggest that malnutrition in early life may affect brain growth (Rosovski, Novoa, Aberzua, & Mönkeberg, 1971; Winnick & Rosso, 1966; Winnick, Rosso, & Waterlow, 1970).

Many studies carried out during the last 25 years have related early malnutrition to mental development, learning, and behavior. Although some conflicting results have been recorded, related to timing, severity, and type of malnutrition, in general, developmental problems are associated with early malnutrition. Stoch and Smyth (1963) for instance, have reported lower than average IQ's in children from Africa who were malnourished in early life. A follow-up study of children in Chile who were malnourished in infancy also showed significantly reduced IQ's (Mönkeberg, Tisler, Toro, Gattas, & Vegal, 1972). Deficits from kwashiorkor have been described in motor behavior during rehabilitation (Cravioto & Robles, 1965), cognition (Freeman, Klein, Kagan, & Yarborough, 1977), behavior development (Chavez, Martinez, & Yaschine, 1975; Richardson, Birch, & Hertzig, 1973), and school performance (Cravioto & DeLicardie, 1970).

As knowledge has been accumulating on the effects of undernutrition on mental development, it has become increasingly clear that effects of malnutrition are extremely difficult to separate from those of other environmental factors. In a recent review, Ricciuti (1981) summarizes present knowledge of the unfavorable consequences of adverse nutritional and environmental influences on children's mental development. He makes a strong point that cause and effect relationships between malnutrition and suboptimal mental development cannot be viewed without consideration of other socioenvironmental influences.

Several studies on the effects of refeeding after malnutrition have taken socioeconomic factors into consideration (Hepner & Maiden, 1971; Herrera et al., 1980). In the Atwater Memorial Lecture given at the XII International Congress of Nutrition in San Diego in August of 1981, Joaquin Cravioto reviewed the various approaches to the study of malnutrition and development. In his own longitudinal studies using the ecological approach, Cravioto has elucidated the nature of effective variables and their interrelationships in a given population. The results of these studies indicate the importance of the social environment in the etiology of malnutrition, as well as in the rehabilitation from malnutrition. Infants rehabilitated from malnutrition by refeeding improved markedly in motor, adaptive, language and social-personal development when refeeding was coupled with systematic environmental stimulation.

Congenital Defects Linked to Nutrients

Effects of single-nutrient deficiencies or excesses have been well studied in many laboratory experiments. In recent years, these studies have been extended to prenatal development, in particular, to organogenesis. Although there are some earlier publications, such as those of Daniels and Everson (1935), the recent studies of Lucille Hurley and coworkers from the University of California at Davis have been leading. Her book entitled "Developmental Nutrition" (Hurley, 1980), summarizes much of the present knowledge in the field.

The mineral element that has been known for many years to affect development is iodine. Too little iodine (Pharaoh, Butterfield, & Hetzel, 1971), as well as excess iodine intake (Carswell, Kerr, & Hutchinson, 1970) result in goiter. Infants with neonatal goiter, if not treated, become mentally retarded, have stunted growth and abnormal bone growth, may be deaf, and have characteristic faces with thick, coarse skin. Goiter due to iodine deficits has been endemic in many areas of the globe before iodization of salt was introduced as a public health measure to prevent goiter. Recent concern has arisen over excessive dietary iodine intake. The U.S. Food and Drug Administration has published data indicating markedly increasing amounts of iodine in the food supply and reports of increased incidence of goiter in school children (Review, Division of Foods, FDA, 1976).

Another mineral deficiency, which has been shown to lead to congenital abnormalities in experimental animals, is zinc deficiency. This has resulted in congenital defects such as cleft lip and palate, brain abnormalities, clubbed legs, syndactyly, lung malformations and herniations (Hurley, Gowan, & Swenerton, 1971). Copper deficiency also has resulted in morphological changes in the developing brain (Everson, Shrader, & Wang, 1968; Hurley & Keen, 1979). A deficiency of manganese during gestation led to defective skeletal development and otolith formation with resulting deafness (Erway, Hurley, & Fraser, 1970).

Very little is known at present as to the extent of congenital defects related to nutrient status occurring in man. The fact that nutrient deficiencies may result in similar defects in humans was demonstrated in the case of acrodermatitis enteropathica, a hereditary zinc deficiency, where women delivered infants with a variety of brain anomalies, including an anencephalic infant (Moynahan, 1974). While copper and manganese deficiencies have not been described in pregnant women, low zinc states during pregnancy have been described in alcoholics (Flynn et al., 1981), and could occur temporarily during virus infections.

Of the vitamins linked to birth defects, vitamin A deficiency (Wilson & Wakany, 1950), as well as excess vitamin A intake, can result in congenital defects (Stange, Carlstrom & Erikson, 1978). Although adults may be able to tolerate megadoses of vitamin A to some degree, the fetus may receive lasting damage during such exposure. The coumadin syndrome, related to the excessive use of a vitamin K inhibitor (Kerber, Warr, & Richardson, 1968) and neural tube defects related to folic acid deficiency (Gross, Newberne, & Reid, 1974; Smithells, Sheppard, & Schorah, 1976) are other examples where birth defects have been linked to nutrient deficiencies.

There is at present scant data on the prevalence of congenital defects related to nutrient abnormalities in man. From the few data we have, it has become clear that deficiencies as well as excesses of nutrients can cause congenital anomalies. Nutrient deficiencies can be primary (inadequate dietary intake) or secondary (deficiency produced by nondietary causes, such as a drug-nutrient interaction). Although much more research is necessary to delineate the role of nutrition in teratology, good dietary practices before and during pregnancy cannot be advocated strongly enough. Fad diets, as well as megadose intakes of vitamins and minerals, may pose a comparatively low risk in the adult, but may be devastating in the fetus.

From the sampling of references cited, it has become clear that optimum nutrition is a prerequisite for normal fetal and later development. Currently, there are no data to link chromosomal disorders in man to any nutritional deficiency. In view of the unexplained etiologies of chromosomal disorders, it is interesting to note the provocative animal studies of Bell, Branstrator, Roux, and Hurley, (1975), which

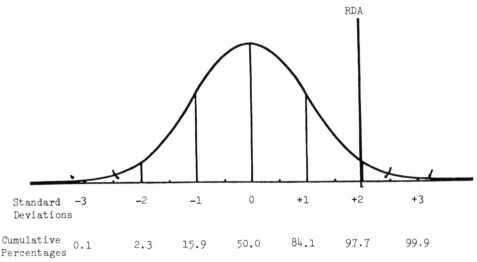

FIG. 18.1. Definition of the RDA. The RDA covers the nutrient requirements of 98% of all healthy people (2 SD above mean).

Table 18.1. Metabolic Disorders among or Directly Relating to Newborns in Massachusetts

DISORDER	TOTAL SCREENED	TOTAL DETECTED	ESTIMATED FREQUENCY
* Hypothyroidism**	414,733	103	1:3,800
* Phenylketonuria	1,406,221	95	1:15,000
Phenylketonuria (atypical)	1,406,221	86	1:16,000
* Phenylketonuria (DHPR)	1,406,221	1	< 1:1,000,000
* Maternal PKU and PMH	532,506	16	1:33,000
* Galactosemia	973,244	15	1:65,000
* Maple syrup urine disease	1,266,864	3	1:400,000
* MSUD (intermediate variant)	1,266,864	2	1:600,000
* MSUD (intermittent variant)	1,266,864	1***	< 1:1,000,000
* Homocystinuria	974,475	3	1:300,000
Histidinemia	666,736	37***	1:18,000
Histidinemia (atypical)	666,736	2	1:300,000
Maternal Histidinemia	207,699	4	1:50,000
* Cystinuria	666,736	53	1:13,000
Hartnup Disorder	666,736	36	1:18,000
Iminoglycinuria	666,736	55	1:12,000
* Argininosuccinic acidemia	666,736	9***	1:75,000
Cystathioninemia	666,736	11	1:60,000
* Hyperglycinemia (non-ketotic)	666,736	4***	1:150,000
* Methylmalonic acidemia	666,736	7***	1:95,000
* Propionic Acidemia	666,736	2***	1:300,000
Hyperprolinemia (type I)	666,736	2	1:300,000
Hyperprolinemia (type II)	666,736	2	1:300,000
Hyperlysinemia	666,736	2	1:300,000
Sarcosinemia	666,736	3	1:300,000
Hyperornithinemia	666,736	1	< 1:600,000
Carnosinemia	666,736	1	< 1:600,000
Urocanic Aciduria	666,736	1	< 1:600,000
Hyperglutamic aciduria	666,736	1	< 1:600,000
α-Aminoadipic aciduria	666,736	1	< 1:600,000
* Fanconi syndrome	666,736	1	< 1:600,000
* Rickets (Vit D Dep)	666,736	1	< 1:600,000
* Hereditary Tyrosinemia	666,736	1***	< 1:600,000
* Hereditary Fructosemia	666,736	1***	< 1:600,000

Compiled by Harvey L. Levy, M.D. (Through 2/28/79.)
* Disorders with definite clinical significance; the others are either not yet established as clinically important or are known to be benign.
** Includes screening throughout New England.
*** Includes infants who were born in Massachusetts but "missed" by newborn screening as follows:

MSUD (intermittent variant)	1
Histidinemia	1
Argininosuccinic acidemia	1
Hyperglycinemia	1
Methylamalonic acidemia	3
Propionic acidemia	1
Hereditary tyrosinemia	1
Hereditary fructosemia	1

have shown that zinc and magnesium deficiency cause chromosomal aberrations such as deletions, fragments, and gaps.

Euphenic Nutrition

Euphenic Nutrition describes the interaction of nutrition and genes (Scriver, 1977). Nutritional requirements are influenced by environmental factors and the genetic make-up of an individual. The environmental factors which influence nutrient needs relate to the composition of diet consumed, as well as stress and disease states. Genes determine each individual's chemical make-up, such as enzyme and hormone patterns, which, in turn, affect nutrient needs. The sum of all these variables results in individual nutrient requirements which, for a normal healthy population, is represented by a Gaussian distribution (Fig. 18.1). The recommended dietary allowances (RDA) for nutrients are set two standard deviations above the mean. The RDA for each nutrient, therefore, will cover the requirement of 97% of all normal healthy people.

Any genetic disorder, whether chromosomal or gene related, has the potential of affecting nutrient requirements. In comparison with norms, nutrient needs may be either much lower or considerably higher. Examples of interactions of nutritional and genetic factors in controlled research studies have been discussed in a symposium chaired by Hurley (1976).

Lower than normal requirements of one or several nutrients have been identified in a variety of monogenic disorders, especially those involving inborn errors of amino acid metabolism. If diet modification to address the lower requirement is not instituted early in life, permanent brain damage with mental retardation results. The prototype of diet intervention for inborn errors of metabolism is that of phenylketonuria (Williamson, Koch, Azen, & Chang, 1981). Neonatal screening for phenylketonuria is mandated by law in the United States, so that early intervention can be started (Levy, 1973). For each infant with phenylketonuria, the optimum level of dietary phenylalanine must be determined by trial, during which blood phenylalanine levels are monitored, since an extreme exclusion of phenylalanine from the diet results in growth depression. There is still controversy as to whether dietary restriction should continue beyond 5 years of age (Giffin, Clarke, & d'Entremont, 1980). Dietary phenylalanine restriction is again necessary should a female phenylketonuric become pregnant. In untreated maternal PKU, the fetus is exposed to very high levels of phenylalanine in utero and, although the fetus is heterozygous and would not have phenylketonuria, brain damage can occur because of high maternal phenylalanine levels (Bazel, 1980).

Inborn errors of metabolism can occur at any stage of metabolism. They may relate to protein, carbohydrate, and fat metabolism. They may be benign or may result in devastating effects to the individual. Table 18.1, provided by Dr. Harvey Levy, summarizes inborn errors screened in Massachusetts through February, 1979. Once an infant is identified, comprehensive intervention is started to prevent lasting damage.

For the dietary management of inborn errors, a variety of dietary products are commercially available. In Table 18.2, the nutrient modification of a number of commonly available products is listed which is used in the treatment of inborn errors of metabolism of amino acids. Such foods for special dietary uses must be carefully labeled for content and specific use. Products designed for one metabolic disorder must not be used for any other purpose than that specified. They must be given only when appropriate, under surveillance and careful monitoring (Food and Drug Administration. Rules and Regulations, 1971).

The question whether genetic disorders may in some cases result in much higher than normal nutrient needs can at present be answered only partially. Examples of elevated nutrient requirement relate to vitamin B_6 dependency (Scriver & Whelan, 1969), elevated zinc requirement in acrodermatitis enterohepathica (Nelder & Hambidge, 1975), and to elevated vitamin B_{12} requirement in methylmalonic aciduria (Hsia, Lilljequist, & Rosenberg, 1970). In these disorders, specific biochemical abnormalities have been identified leading to greater than normal needs of these nutrients.

Table 18.2. Dietary Products Used in Certain Inborn Errors

PRODUCT	AMINO ACID MODIFICATION	USED IN
Lofenalac†	Low phenylalanine	PKU
PKU-Aid*	Low phenylalanine	PKU
Phenylfree†	No phenylalanine	PKU
MSUD-Aid*	Free of valine, leucine, isoleucine	Maple syrup urine disease
MSUD Diet†	Free of valine, leucine, isoleucine	Maple syrup urine disease
Histinaid*	Free of histidine	Histidinemia
Low methionine isomil#	Low in methionine	Homocystinuria
Methionaid†	Low in methionine cystine supplemented	Homocystinuria

† Mead Johnson.
* Milner Scientific.
# Ross Laboratories.

Table 18.3. Estimated Safe and Adequate Daily Dietary Intakes of Selected Vitamins and Minerals*

VITAMINS

	AGE (YEARS)	VITAMIN K (μg)	BIOTIN (μg)	PANTOTHENIC ACID (mg)
Infants	0–0.5	12	35	2
	0.5–1	10–20	50	3
Children and adolescents	1–3	15–30	65	3
	4–6	20–40	85	3–4
	7–10	30–60	120	4–5
	11+	50–100	100–200	4–7
Adults		70–140	100–200	4–7

TRACE ELEMENTS**

	AGE (YEARS)	COPPER (mg)	MANGANESE (mg)	FLUORIDE (mg)	CHROMIUM (mg)	SELENIUM (mg)	MOLYBDENUM (mg)
Infants	0–0.5	0.5–0.7	0.5–0.7	0.1–0.5	0.01–0.04	0.01–0.04	0.03–0.06
	0.5–1	0.7–1.0	0.7–1.0	0.2–1.0	0.02–0.06	0.02–0.06	0.04–0.08
Children and adolescents	1–3	1.0–1.5	1.0–1.5	0.5–1.5	0.02–0.08	0.02–0.08	0.05–0.1
	4–6	1.5–2.0	1.5–2.0	1.0–2.5	0.03–0.12	0.03–0.12	0.06–0.15
	7–10	2.0–2.5	2.0–3.0	1.5–2.5	0.05–0.2	0.05–0.2	0.10–0.3
	11+	2.0–3.0	2.5–5.0	1.5–2.5	0.05–0.2	0.05–0.2	0.15–0.5
Adults		2.0–3.0	2.5–5.0	1.5–4.0	0.05–0.2	0.05–0.2	0.15–0.5

ELECTROLYTES

	AGE (YEARS)	SODIUM (mg)	POTASSIUM (mg)	CHLORIDE (mg)
Infants	0–0.5	115–350	350–925	275–700
	0.5–1	250–750	425–1275	400–1200
Children and adolescents	1–3	325–975	550–1650	500–1500
	4–6	450–1350	775–2325	700–2100
	7–10	600–1800	1000–3000	925–2775
	11+	900–2700	1525–4575	1400–4200
Adults		1100–3300	1875–5625	1700–5100

Research Dietary Allowances (1980), p. 178.
* Because there is less information on which to base allowances, these figures are not given in the main table of RDA and are provided here in the form of ranges of recommended intakes.
** Since the toxic levels for many trace elements may be only several times usual intakes, the upper levels for the trace elements given in this table should not be habitually exceeded.

The use of megadoses of nutrient supplements to improve intelligence (as measured by IQ) in mentally retarded children, including Down syndrome children, has been tried and is under discussion (Harrell, Capp, & Davis et. al., 1981). Such treatments have no well defined rationale and must be considered experimental until more data become available. The quantities of micronutrients administered over considerable periods of time are considered excessive and not without risk in normal children. There are at present no data supporting the appropriateness of such supplements, and their experimental use must be monitored for side effects. If beneficial effects of one or several nutrients can be shown, a careful analysis of dose effect relationships must be made. Many nutrient interrelationships have been documented in the nutrition literature; excess of certain nutrients may produce deficiency of another, excessive intake of nutrients can also produce dependency, and toxic reactions have been described with excess intakes of fat soluble vitamins (RDA, 1980).

In view of the popularity of megadose supplements of vitamins and minerals, the 1980 RDA has specified

Table 18.4. Eating from the Four Food Groups for Variety

| | NUMBER OF SERVINGS | | |
FOOD GROUP	CHILD	ADO-LESCENT	ADULT
Milk			
1 cup milk 1 cup yogurt 1½ oz cheddar cheese 1¾ cup ice cream	3	4	2
Meat			
2 oz cooked lean meat 2 oz fish 2 oz poultry 2 eggs 4 tablesp. peanut butter	2	2	2
Grain-cereals			
1 slice bread 1 cup ready to eat cereal ½ cup cooked cereal ½ cup pasta	4	4	4
Vegetables-fruits			
½ cup vegetables 1 cup fruit juices 1 fresh fruit, apple, banana	4	4	4

for a number of nutrients adequate and safe levels of intakes (Table 18.3). According to the definition of the Food and Drug Administration, nutrient supplements providing more than 150% of the RDA per day are considered drugs.

Nutritional Factors in the Prevention of Lead Toxicity

Children between one and six years of age are the main victims of lead toxicity (Lin-Fu, 1975). This is due to various factors. Children absorb a greater percentage of an ingested lead dose than adults (50% in children versus 5 to 10% in adults) (Alexander, Delves, & Clayton, 1973). During the mouthing stage, when children explore their environment, they may inadvertently ingest and swallow flaking paint or house dust containing lead (Vosteal, Taves, Sayre, & Charney, 1974). Because of their high metabolic rate, they also may inhale a proportionately higher amount of airborn lead from gasoline exhaust in addition to the lead present in various concentrations in foods and beverages (Mahaffey, 1977).

The clinical effects of lead poisoning are well documented. They include deleterious effects on the hemotopoietic system, the kidney, and the central nervous system. Whereas the anemia and effects on the kidney are reversible, those on the central nervous system are not, and children with lead toxicity may have lasting brain damage which requires total care (Moore, Meredith, & Goldberg, 1977).

The average lead intake in children from all sources, such as airborn lead, food, and water is estimated to be in the order of 100 to 200 μg of lead per day (Mahaffey, 1977). It is thought that safe levels of ingestion are less than 500 μg per day. There is evidence that subclinical levels of lead toxicity may be related to learning difficulty (Needleman et al., 1979).

Although it is impossible to eliminate all lead from the environment of children, much can be done to minimize exposure by appropriate public health measures. Thus, apartments must be stripped of lead before being occupied by families with infants and children, commercially prepared infant foods must not be sold in lead soldered containers, and drinking water supplies must be monitored for lead.

In the prevention of lead toxicity, good nutrition also plays a crucial role, since children with suboptimal nutrient status are more prone to deleterious effects of lead (Mahaffey, 1981). The interactions of lead with nutrients are complex. When dietary intake of iron is low, and borderline iron deficiency anemia is present, the absorption of lead from the gastrointestinal tract is greatly elevated. The increased body lead bur-

Table 18.5. Recommended Daily Dietary Allowances[a]

	AGE (YEARS)	WEIGHT		HEIGHT		PROTEIN (g)	FAT-SOLUBLE VITAMINS		
		(kg)	(lb)	(cm)	(in)		VITA-MIN A (µg RE)[b]	VITA-MIN D (µg)[c]	VITA-MIN E (mg α-TE)[d]
Infants	0.0–0.5	6	13	60	24	kg × 2.2	420	10	3
	0.5–1.0	9	20	71	28	kg × 2.0	400	10	4
Children	1–3	13	29	90	35	23	400	10	5
	4–6	20	44	112	44	30	500	10	6
	7–10	28	62	132	52	34	700	10	7
Males	11–14	45	99	157	62	45	1000	10	8
	15–18	66	145	176	69	56	1000	10	10
	19–22	70	154	177	70	56	1000	7.5	10
	23–50	70	154	178	70	56	1000	5	10
	51+	70	154	178	70	56	1000	5	10
Females	11–14	46	101	157	62	46	800	10	8
	15–18	55	120	163	64	46	800	10	8
	19–22	55	120	163	64	44	800	7.5	8
	23–50	55	120	163	64	44	800	5	8
	51+	55	120	163	64	44	800	5	8
Pregnant						+30	+200	+5	+2
Lactating						+20	+400	+5	+3

From Food and Nutrition Board, National Academy of Sciences-National Research Council. Revised 1980.

[a] The allowances are intended to provide for individual variations among most normal persons as they live in the United States under usual environmental stresses. Diets should be based on a variety of common foods in order to provide other nutrients for which human requirements have been less well defined.

[b] Retinol equivalents. 1 retinol equivalent = 1 µg retinol or 6 µg β carotene.

[c] As cholecalciferol. 10 µg cholecalciferol = 400 IU of vitamin D.

[d] α-tocopherol equivalents. 1 mg d-α tocopherol = 1 α-TE.

den, which in turn aggravates the anemia, thus results in a vicious cycle eventually leading to frank lead toxicity. Similar effects occur when calcium intake in children is low, thus also enhancing lead absorption. Infants and children with lactose intolerance whose milk intake is comparatively low are especially at risk, especially since many of them also live in the inner city where lead pollution may be greatest. Other nutrients besides iron and calcium may interact with lead, but their roles in the prevention of lead intoxication are less well understood.

Nutritional Assessment of Mentally Retarded Individuals

In mentally retarded children and adults, a high prevalence of nutrition problems have been reported (Coffey & Crawford, 1971; Danford & Huber, 1981; Palmer & Ekvall, 1978). If such problems are not addressed, they may cause further handicapping conditions. Periodic assessment of nutrient status should be part of the comprehensive care of all developmentally delayed persons. There is no question that the prevention of nutritional problems is more effective than treatment of nutrition problems of long standing. Unfortunately, preventive aspects are often completely ignored.

The nutrition problems described relate to inadequate nutrient intake (Gouge & Ekvall, 1975), prob-lems with digestion and assimilation of food, and factors which modify nutrient requirement. Some nutritional problems reflect those observed in the general population such as obesity or poor food habits, whereas others are unique and very specific for the mentally retarded.

There are no simple criteria to assess nutrient status, and the question whether a person is well nourished cannot be answered with certainty. However, by evaluating a variety of assessment parameters it is possible to assess the risk of nutritional problems and to formulate preventive or therapeutic intervention. The following parameters are part of a nutritional assessment:

1. Food intake
2. Growth and other anthropometric data
3. Blood and tissue laboratory parameters
4. Feeding skills and problems
5. Factors which alter nutrient needs
6. Medical and family history

Food Intake

Whether a child or adult is consuming an acceptable diet can be evaluated by a number of parameters:

Variety of Food Consumed

No one food provides all nutrients, and diets that include only a few foods cannot provide adequate

Table 18.5. (continued)

	WATER-SOLUBLE VITAMINS						MINERALS					
VITA-MIN C (mg)	THIA-MIN (mg)	RIBO-FLAV-IN (mg)	NIACIN (mg NE)[e]	VITA-MIN B-6 (mg)	FOLA-CIN[f] (µg)	VITA-MIN B-12 (µg)	CAL-CIUM (mg)	PHOS-PHO-RUS (mg)	MAG-NE-SIUM (mg)	IRON (mg)	ZINC (mg)	IO-DINE (µg)
35	0.3	0.4	6	0.3	30	0.5[g]	360	240	50	10	3	40
35	0.5	0.6	8	0.6	45	1.5	540	360	70	15	5	50
45	0.7	0.8	9	0.9	100	2.0	800	800	150	15	10	70
45	0.9	1.0	11	1.3	200	2.5	800	800	200	10	10	90
45	1.2	1.4	16	1.6	300	3.0	800	800	250	10	10	120
50	1.4	1.6	18	1.8	400	3.0	1200	1200	350	18	15	150
60	1.4	1.7	18	2.0	400	3.0	1200	1200	400	18	15	150
60	1.5	1.7	19	2.2	400	3.0	800	800	350	10	15	150
60	1.4	1.6	18	2.2	400	3.0	800	800	350	10	15	150
60	1.2	1.4	16	2.2	400	3.0	800	800	350	10	15	150
50	1.1	1.3	15	1.8	400	3.0	1200	1200	300	18	15	150
60	1.1	1.3	14	2.0	400	3.0	1200	1200	300	18	15	150
60	1.1	1.3	14	2.0	400	3.0	800	800	300	18	15	150
60	1.0	1.2	13	2.0	400	3.0	800	800	300	18	15	150
60	1.0	1.2	13	2.0	400	3.0	800	800	300	10	15	150
+20	+0.4	+0.3	+2	+0.6	+400	+1.0	+400	+400	+150	h	+5	+25
+40	+0.5	+0.5	+5	+0.5	+100	+1.0	+400	+400	+150	h	+10	+50

[e] 1 NE (niacin equivalent) is equal to 1 mg of niacin or 60 mg of dietary tryptophan.
[f] The folacin allowances refer to dietary sources as determined by *Lactobacillus casei* assay after treatment with enzymes (conjugases) to make polyglutamyl forms of the vitamin available to the test organism.
[g] The recommended dietary allowance for vitamin B-12 in infants is based on average concentration of the vitamin in human milk. The allowances after weaning are based on energy intake (as recommended by the American Academy of Pediatrics) and consideration of other factors, such as intestinal absorption.
[h] The increased requirement during pregnancy cannot be met by the iron content of habitual American diets nor by the existing iron stores of many women; therefore the use of 30–60 mg of supplemental iron is recommended. Iron needs during lactation are not substantially different from those of nonpregnant women, but continued supplementation of the mother for 2–3 months after parturition is advisable in order to replenish stores depleted by pregnancy.

nutrients. Children and adults are at risk for nutrient deficiencies if they do not consume a variety of foods. For instance, children with feeding problems living on milk diets or mushy foods or pasta cereals will eventually lack a variety of nutrients provided by vegetables, fruits and meats.

Eating from the Four Food Groups

Since foods provide different nutrient densities, one can class them in groups which have strengths in some nutrients and weaknesses in others. Grouping foods in four food groups is a convenient way to plan diets and to evaluate whether a person consumes a balanced diet. The cereal group should include some whole grain products. It provides energy, B vitamins, and fiber. The meat group, which is high in protein, niacin and iron, includes all meats, fish, and fowl, as well as meat substitutes such as peanut butter, dried beans, lentils, and soybean products. The dairy group, with milk, cheese, and also eggs, provides high quality protein, riboflavin, and calcium, and if milk is fortified, also vitamin D. The vegetable and fruit group provides vitamins, trace minerals, and fiber.

The four food groups are useful for menu planning and portion size can be adjusted to individual needs.

In Table 18.4, the servings from the four food groups are outlined for different age groups. Using this food system, dieticians can plan menus that provide adequate nutrients. Evaluation of a diet by the four food groups is a rapid way to evaluate the likelihood of an adequate diet and to identify glaring omissions, monotony, and bizarre food habits.

Calculation of Nutrient Intakes

From 24-hour food intakes or food records obtained over three to seven days, the nutrients consumed are calculated from food composition tables. This method is time consuming. Computerized food analysis programs have simplified the methodology considerably. Once the nutrient intakes for each day have been calculated, they are compared to the recommended allowances for the appropriate age and sex.

Recommended Dietary Allowances (RDA)

The RDA has been established as recommendations for normal healthy people (RDA, 1980; Munro, 1977). They are updated every four or five years as new data

Table 18.6. Drug–Nutrient Effects

DRUG	NUTRIENTS AFFECTED	DEFICIENCY INDUCED	RECOMMENDED SUPPLEMENTS/DAY
Anticonvulsants	Folic acid	Anemia	400–1,000 µg folate
Dilantin	Vitamin D	Rickets	400–800 IU Vit. D
Phenobarbital	Vitamin B_{12}	Anemia	2–4 µg Vit. B_{12}
Primidone			60 mg ascorbic acid
Mineral oil	Vitamins A, E, D, K; essential fatty acids	Fat soluble vitamins	Fat soluble vitamins; discontinue mineral oil
Oral contraceptive	Folic acid	Anemia	400–1,000 µg folacin
Agents	Vitamin B_6	Low B_6 states	10 mg Vitamin B_6; possibly others
Dextroamphetamines	All nutrients, appetite suppressant	Growth retardation	Vigorous refeeding when off medication
Antidepressant MAO inhibitors	Breakdown of amino acid metabolites		Avoid tyramine containing foods: banana, aged cheese etc.
Antacids	Phosphate	Osteomalacia	Calcium and iron
	Calcium	Anemia	Supplements not effective
	Iron		
Lithium	Sodium		
Aspirin (chronic use)	Iron	Anemia	Iron and zinc
	Zinc		

become available (Table 18.5). In view of the possibility that some trace minerals may be consumed in excess, and the fact that salt intakes in U.S. diets are generally excessive, adequate and safe intakes are recommended for a number of nutrients (Table 18.3).

Since the RDA addresses the nutrient recommendations for normal healthy people, the question arises whether these recommendations are appropriate for mentally retarded people. In a court case, *Wyatt vs. Hardin*, Alabama (1972), the adequacy of nutritional care of the mentally retarded living in institutions was discussed and resulted in court ordered dietary standards. As part of a more extensive care plan, the dietary guidelines address the nutrient intakes of mentally retarded patients in institutions and the staffing practices of dietary personnel working with them. The court ordered that each retarded patient must receive daily amounts of nutrients stipulated by the RDAs and also ordered periodic surveillance to ensure that these recommendations are put into effect (Ponder & Bergman, 1980).

The appropriateness of using the RDAs as guidelines for mentally retarded persons has been questioned by nutritionists since the RDA was set up as guidelines for normal healthy people and may not meet the specific needs of the mentally retarded. Since we do

Table 18.7. Anthropometry

PUBLICATION	USE	REFERENCE
Weighing and measuring children	Training manual for professionals	Weighing and measuring children (1980)
Nutritional screening of children	Manual for screening and follow-up of children	Nutrition screening (1981)
NCHS growth curves	For children to 18 years of age	Natl. Center for Health Statistics (1977)
Growth of Down syndrome children	Birth to 3 years of age	Cronk (1978)
Body ratios: upper/lower height	Handicapped children	Wilkens, Blizzard, & Migion (1965)
Arm anthropometry	Adipose tissue muscle mass in children	Gurney & Jelliffe (1973)
Obesity standards	Children 5–17 years of age	Committee on Nutrition (1968)
Height-weight standards	Adults 18–74 years of age	National Center for Health Statistics (1976)
Minimum triceps fat fold	Identifying obesity	Seltzer & Mayer (1965)
Percentage body fat	Obesity-underweight in adults	Durnin & Womersley (1974)

not have better guidelines for mentally retarded children and adults, the RDA should be used as baseline recommendations that must be modified, taking into account the specific problems of each individual. Nutrition intervention and diet planning, therefore, must be based on such individual approaches which take into account the specific needs of the mentally retarded. For a variety of conditions, group recommendations are possible. One such example is the recommendation for vitamin D and folic acid supplements over and above the RDA for persons on long-term seizure medication (Table 18.6).

Anthropometric Parameters

Measurements include height, body weight, head circumference, skinfold thickness and mid-arm circumference. During childhood these parameters evaluate growth patterns and, in the adult, stability of weight as well as obesity and underweight (Table 18.7).

One measurement in time usually is not very useful, since only comparisons with norms can be made, which may not be appropriate. Growth standards have been obtained for Down syndrome children (Cronk, 1978). Growth patterns of children with mental retardation of unknown etiology are charted on NCHS growth charts (National Center for Health Statistics, 1976) to insure that stable growth patterns are obtained. A child whose growth is parallel to the third percentile may grow according to his or her own growth potential. If unstable growth patterns occur, careful analysis of the changes which lead to this altered growth must be made. Examples of stable and nonstable growth patterns are given in Fig. 18.2.

Growth patterns in children, as well as height and weight in adults, are often difficult to measure in the physically handicapped, who may have a scoliosis or

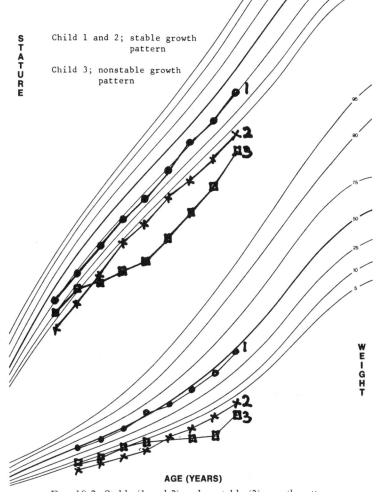

FIG. 18.2. Stable (1 and 2) and unstable (3) growth patterns.

Table 18.8. Minimum Triceps Skinfold Thickness
Indicating Obesity

AGE	MALES	FEMALES
Years		No.
5	12	14
6	12	15
7	13	16
8	14	17
9	15	18
10	16	20
11	17	21
12	18	22
13	18	23
14	17	23
15	16	24
16	15	25
17	14	26
18	15	27
19	15	27
20	16	28
21	17	28
22	18	28
23	18	28
24	19	28
25	20	29
26	20	29
27	21	29
28	22	29
29	22	29
30–50	23	30

From Seltzer, C. C. and Mayer, J. *Postgrad. Med.* 1965, **38**, A 101.

contractures or may not be able to stand. In such cases, body parts may be measured, for instance sitting height. Comparison of these measurements with standards from normal populations again is a problem since such standards may not be appropriate.

The amount of adipose tissue indicating obesity or underweight is evaluated by measuring skinfold thickness with skinfold calipers (Lange calipers). Triceps skinfold measurements are the most commonly used. Minimum triceps skinfold thickness indicating obesity is given in Table 18.8. The method is not useful in persons whose major adipose tissue is distributed on the body rather than the upper arm. In such cases, skinfold measurements can be on four body sites (triceps, biceps, subscapular, and suprailiac). The sum of all four readings is compared to standards published by Durnin and Womersley (1974). Obesity and underweight are common in the mentally retarded. Nutrition intervention is more effective in the prevention of these extremes than in the treatment of long-term obesity or underweight. Regular measurements of selected anthropometric parameters aid in the identification of detrimental changes early, before they have developed into chronic conditions.

Biochemical Parameters

Biochemical parameters are the most objective assessment parameters, because blood and tissue levels of nutrients or nutrient metabolites are measured directly, indicating nutrient status. However, since such measurements require blood or tissue samples and may be very expensive assays, one must have good reasons for their inclusion into a comprehensive nutritional assessment. The coordination of the nutritional assessment with medical evaluation is desirable since blood samples collected for medical purposes may, at the same time, be utilized to assess nutritional parameters.

Blood parameters estimated are related to red blood cell and white blood cell indices, to plasma proteins, electrolytes, and nutrient levels in blood. Care must be taken that blood and tissue samples are collected and handled under specified conditions. The interpretation of biochemical data requires evaluation of confounding factors, and almost always a differential diagnosis is necessary. An example is low hematocrit and hemoglobin, indicating anemia, which as Table 18.9 shows, may be due to different nutritional causes as well as to non-nutritional ones. For proper treatment, the type of anemia must be ascertained.

In Table 18.10, biochemical parameters frequently utilized are summarized. For more extensive information, consult other texts (Thiele, 1980; Wallach, 1978).

Evaluation of Feeding Problems

Inability or refusal to eat may relate to neuromotor dysfunction, psychological factors, pain during food ingestion, or obstruction. Palmer and Ekvall (1978), classifying feeding problems, have observed 73.5% as neuromotor dysfunction, 21.3% as behavior mismanagement, and 5.2% with mechanical obstruction.

Feeding problems are best assessed by a feeding team consisting of professionals from various disciplines. The nutritionist will evaluate the appropriateness of nutrient intake, the occupational therapist oral structure and motor development, the physical therapist positioning, the dentist will check whether faulty dentition may interfere with the feeding process, and the psychologist will evaluate behavior and devise strategies for changing behavior. Based on joint evaluation, priorities and intervention strategies are set. Excellent reviews on feeding assessment and therapy, as well as the use of special eating utensils and adaptive equipment, are found in occupational therapy texts.

Factors Which Alter Nutrient Needs

The mentally retarded are a heavily medicated population that receives single or multiple drug regimen

Table 18.9. Nutrition Anemias*

NUTRIENT DEFICIENCY	TYPE OF ANEMIA	DIAGNOSTIC PARAMETERS	TREATMENTS/SUPPLEMENTS
Iron	Microcytic hypochromic	Ferritin, MCV Transferrin saturation	Iron sulfate Organic iron
Copper	Microcytic hypochromic	Serum copper ceruloplasmin	0.2 mg/kg body wt of $CuSO_4 \cdot 5H_2O$
Pyridoxine	Hypochromic	Responds to vitamin B_6	Vitamin B_6
Folic acid	Megaloblastic	MCV, folate in serum & RBC	0.1 mg/d therapeutic, 0.04 mg maintenance
Vitamin B_{12}	Megaloblastic	Serum B_{12}, MCV	B_{12} either by mouth or I.M.
Vitamin E	Hemolytic	Serum tocopherol < 0.5 mg/dl	Tocopherol-polyethylene glycol
Protein-calorie malnutrition	Normocytic normo-chromic	Diagnostic tools for PCM	Protein, iron folate
Excess intake			
Zinc	Microcytic hypochromic	Low iron and copper, high serum zinc	Omit zinc supplement, add iron and copper
Lead	Microcytic hypochromic	Blood lead and ALA	Chelation treatment and subsequent refeeding

* Abnormally low Hematocrit and Hemoglobin Values

for extended periods of time (Springer & Fricke, 1975). Such long-term drug use has the potential of affecting nutrient status (Rowe 1976). Drugs can affect absorption of nutrients from the gastrointestinal tract, or may interfere with the metabolism of nutrients. Drug-nutrient interactions are complex, and much more research is necessary to understand them.

Medications most commonly prescribed are anticonvulsants, psychotropic drugs, laxatives, antibiotics, and oral contraceptives, as well as a variety of over-the-counter drugs such as aspirin, antacids, and cold medicines.

In Table 18.6, drugs commonly administered to the mentally retarded are summarized with their effects

Table 18.10. Selected Laboratory Parameters Useful in Nutritional Assessment

PARAMETER	NORMAL RANGE	LEVELS INCREASED	DECREASED
Hematocrit, %	42–50 male 40–48 female	Dehydration	Anemia
Hemoglobin, g/dl	13–16 male 12–15 female	Dehydration	Anemia
Erythrocyte count	4.2–5.9/mm³	Dehydration	Anemia
MCV	80–92 µm³	Macrocytic anemia	Microcytic anemia
Ferritin	20–200 mg/ml	Iron overload	Iron deficient
Lymphocyte	1500/mm³		PCM
Albumin	3.5–5 g/dl		PCM
Transferrin	150–250 mg/dl		PCM
Alkaline Phosphatase	age dependent	Rickets	
Calcium	8.5–10.5 mg/dl	Hypervit. D	Hypovit. D
Magnesium	1.5–2.5 mEqu/L		In starvation
Sodium	134–145 mEqu/L	Dehydration	Rumination diarrhea
Chloride	100–106 mEqu/L	Dehydration	
Zinc	80–120 µg/dl	Zn Excess	Zn deficiency
Copper	70–140 µg/dl	Cu Excess	Cu deficiency
Vitamin A	30–65 µg/dl	Hypervit. A	Vit. A deficient
Carotene	80–200 µg/dl		
Tocopherol	0.6 mg/dl		Vit. E deficient
Ascorbic acid	0.5–1.5 mg/dl		Vit. C deficient
Folic acid	5–6 ng/ml		Megaloblastic anemia
Vitamin B_{12}	200–1,000 pg/ml		Megaloblastic anemia
Transketolase	Positive TPP effect		Vitamin B_1 deficient

Each Blood and Plasma Parameter cited may be affected also by non-nutritional factors. Differential Diagnoses are required to rule out such confounding factors.

on nutrients. Suggestions for the prevention of these effects are given in the last column of the same table.

A drug history should be part of any nutritional assessment. Information should be obtained on the types of medications used, dosage, and duration of use. At present, not all drug effects on nutrient status are known. As new drugs are introduced, their nutritional side affects must be evaluated. There is evidence accumulating that nutrient status affects drug metabolism, and the effectiveness of drugs may be influenced by dietary considerations.

Pica

Pica can be defined as the eating of nonfood items and/or the excessive ingestion of food items. Danford and Huber (1981), surveying an institutionalized, predominantly adult mentally retarded population, found an incidence of 26%. Pica was lowest in individuals with borderline and mild retardation (10%) and was greatest in the profoundly retarded (34%). Although the diets consumed by the surveyed population appeared adequate in terms of nutrients, those individuals who practiced geophagia (eating of clay and dirt) had lower serum iron and zinc levels, which indicates deficiencies of these nutrients (Danford, Smith, & Huber, 1982). Studies of nonretarded clay eaters have shown that clay interferes with the gastrointestinal absorption of zinc and iron (Arcasoy, Cavdar, & Babcan, 1978). Marginal zinc deficiency may lead to decreased wound healing and decreased growth. Iron deficiency is associated with increased irritability. The practice of Pica in growing children may also increase the lead burden of the body if lead-containing nonfood items are consumed (Kalisz, Ekvall, & Palmer, 1978), and may expose children to parasitic infestations of the gastrointestinal tract which interfere with nutrient absorption.

Gastrointestinal Problems

Problems such as vomiting, diarrhea, and rumination have serious effects on nutrient status if they are of a chronic nature. Before dietary requirements can be addressed, the underlying medical causes must be identified. Chronic diarrhea can be due to partial or complete lactose intolerance (Barr, Levine, & Watkins, 1979). If lactose in milk products cannot be broken down into galactose and glucose (because lactase is low in the small intestine), the milksugar is fermented in the large intestine by bacteria. The resulting lactic acid produces cramps, gas, and rashes around the anus. Many individuals have partial lactose intolerance. They are able to consume some milk products without

ill affects. Yogurt prepared by fermentation is free of lactose and can be substituted for milk.

The etiology of chronic vomiting and rumination is at present not well understood. Chronic ruminators may be extremely emaciated and malnourished, even to the point of death. Behavior intervention by satiation procedures has benefitted some cases (Borreson & Anderson, 1982; Jackson, Johnson, Ackron, & Crowley, 1975). Reflux therapy may also include nutritional considerations such as composition of meals, timing of food intake, and positioning during and after feeding (Ingelfinger, 1974). Rumination should be identified before growth stunting has occurred and before frank malnutrition further interferes with the digestion and absorption of nutrients.

Summary

Nutrition is relevant in the prevention of mental retardation and the care of mentally retarded children and adults. In both areas, much more research is necessary to delineate specific relationships. Nutrition problems related to prevention and/or treatment are closely interwoven with medical, behavioral, educational and economic issues. They must be addressed within the context of multidisciplinary approaches. The American Dietetic Association has published a position statement on the consensus regarding the developmentally disabled, which succinctly summerizes further approaches (Statement by the American Dietetic Association, 1981).

References

Alexander, F. W., Delves, H. T., & Clayton, B. E. The uptake and excretion by children of lead and other contaminants. In D. Barth, A. Berlin, & R. Engel (Eds.), *Environmental health aspects of lead.* Commission of the European Communities Center for Information, Luxembourg, 1973. Pp. 319–330.

Arcasoy, A., Cavdar, A. O., & Babcan, E. Decreased iron and zinc absorption in Turkish children with iron deficiency and geophagia. *Acta Hematologica,* 1978, **60,** 76–84.

Barr, R. G., Levine, M. D., & Watkins, J. B. Recurrent abdominal pain of childhood due to lactose intolerance. *New England Journal of Medicine,* 1979, **300,** 1449–1452.

Bazel, P. Maternal phenylketonuria: Nutritional management. In E. A. Wilson (Ed.), *Nutrition in Pregnancy.* Lexington: University of Kentucky, 1980.

Bell, L. T., Branstrator, M., Roux, C., & Hurley, L. S. Chromosomal abnormalities in maternal and fetal tissue of magnesium or zinc deficient rats. *Teratology,* 1975 **12,** 221–226.

Bickel, H., Gerrard, J., & Hickmans, E. M. Influence of phenylalanine intake on phenylketonuria. *Lancet* 1953, **2,** 812–813.

Borreson, P. M., & Anderson, J. L. The elimination of chronic rumination through a combination of procedures. *Mental Retardation* 1982, **20**, 34–38.

Carswell, F., Kerr, M. M., & Hutchinson, J. H. Congenital goiter and hypothyroidism produced by maternal ingestion of iodides. *Lancet* 1970, **1**, 1241–1243.

Chavez, A., Martinez, C., & Yaschine, T. Nutrition, behavioral development and mother child interaction in young rural children. *Federation Proceedings*, 1975, **34**, 1574–1582.

Coffey, K. R., & Crawford, J. *Nutritional problems commonly encountered in the developmentally handicapped*. In M. A. Smith (Ed.), *Feeding the handicapped child*. Memphis: University of Tenn. Child Development Center. 1971. Pp. 63–77.

Committee on Nutrition. Measurement of skinfold thickness in childhood. *Pediatrics*, 1968, **42**, 538–542.

Cravioto, J. Nutrition, Stimulation, mental development and learning. *Nutrition Today*, 1981, **16**, 4–15.

Cravioto, J., & DeLicardie, E. R. Mental performance in school-age children. *American Journal Diseases of Children* 1970, **120**, 404–410.

Cravioto, J., DeLicardie, E. R., & Birch, H. G. Nutrition growth and neuro integrative development. An experimental and ecological study. *Pediatrics*, 1966, **38**(Suppl. 2), 319–372.

Cravioto, J., & Robles, B. Evolution of adaptive and motor behavior during rehabilitation from kwashiorkor. *American Journal of Orthopsychiatry*, 1965, **35**, 449–464.

Cronk, C. E. Growth of children with Down's syndrome: birth to age 3 years. *Pediatrics*, 1978, **61**, 564–568.

Danford, D. E., & Huber, A. M. Eating dysfunction in an institutionalized mentally retarded population. *Appetite: Journal for Intake Research*, 1981, **2**, 281–292.

Danford, D. E., Smith, J. C., & Huber, A. M. Pica and mineral status in the mentally retarded. *American Journal of Clinical Nutrition*, 1982, 141–146.

Daniels, A. L., & Everson, G. J. The relation of manganese to congenital debility. *Journal of Nutrition*, 1935, **9**, 191–203.

Dobbing, J. Undernutrition and the developing brain. The use of animal models to elucidate the human problem. *Psychiatria, Neurologia, Neurochirurgia*, 1971, **74**, 433–442.

Durnin, J. V. G. A., & Womersley, J. Body fat assessment from total body density and its estimation from skinfold thickness 16 to 72 years. *British Journal of Nutrition*, 1974, **32**, 77–97.

Erway, L., Hurley, L. S., & Fraser, A. Congenital ataxia and otolith defects due to manganese deficiency in mice. *Journal of Nutrition*, 1970, **100**, 643–654.

Everson, G. J., Shrader, R. E., & Wang, T. Chemical and morphological changes in the brains of copper-deficient guinea pigs. *Journal of Nutrition*, 1968, **96**, 115–125.

Flynn, A., Martier, S. S., Sobol, R. J., Miller, S. I. Gorden, N. L., & Villano, B. C. Zinc status of pregnant alcoholic women. A determination of fetal outcome. *The Lancet*, **1**, 1981, 572–574.

Food and Drug Administration Rules and Regulations: *Label statement concerning dietary properties of food purporting to be or represented for special dietary use*. Part 125. Federal Reg. 36. 23553. December 10, 1971.

Freeman, H. E., Klein, R. E., Kagan, J., & Yarborough, C. Relations between nutrition and cognition in rural Guatemala. *American Journal of Public Health*, 1977, **67**, 233–243.

Garrod, A. E. Inborn errors of metabolism. (Croonian Lectures) *Lancet*, 1908, **2**, 1–7.

Giffin, F. D., Clarke, J. T. R., & d'Entremont, D. M. Effect of dietary phenylalanine restriction on visual attention span in mentally retarded subjects with phenylketonuria. *Journal Canadien des Sciences Neurologique*, 1980, **7**, 127–131.

Gouge, A. L., & Ekvall, S. Diets of handicapped children: Physical psychological and socio-economic correlations. *American Journal on Mental Deficiency*, 1975, **80**, 149–157.

Gross, R. L., Newberne, P. M., & Reid, J. V. O. Adverse effects on infant development associated with maternal folic acid deficiency. *Nutrition Reports International*, 1974, **10**, 241–248.

Gurney, J. M., & Jelliffe, D. B. Arm anthropometry in nutritional assessment. Nomogram for rapid calculation of muscle circumference and cross-sectional muscle and fat areas. *American Journal of Clinical Nutrition*, 1973, **26**, 912.

György, P. The late effects of early malnutrition. *American Journal of Clinical Nutrition*, 1960, **8**, 344–915.

Harrell, R. F., Capp, R. H., Davis, D. R., Peerless, J., & Ravitz, L. R. Can nutritional supplements help mentally retarded children? An exploratory study. *Proceedings of the National Academy of Sciences, U.S.A.*, 1981, **78**, 574–578.

Hepner, R., & Maiden, N. C. Growth rate, nutrient intake and "mothering" as determinants of malnutrition in disadvantaged children. *Nutrition Reviews*, 1971, **29**, 219–223.

Herrera, M. G., Mora, J. O., Christensen, N., Ortiz, N., Clement, J., Vuori, L., Waber, D., DeParedes, B., & Wagner, M. Effects of nutritional supplementation and early education on physical and cognitive development. In R. R. Turner, & H. W. Reese (Eds.), *Life Span Developmental Psychology: Intervention*. New York: Academic Press, 1980.

Hsia, Y., Lilljequist, A., & Rosenberg, L. Vitamin B_{12} dependent methyl-malonic aciduria. Amino acid toxicity, long chain ketonuria and protective effect of vitamin B_{12}. *Pediatrics*, 1970, **46**, 497–507.

Hurley, L. S. Symposium, Interactions of nutrition and genetic factors. *Federation Proceedings*, 1976, **35**, 2270–2299.

Hurley, L. S. *Developmental Nutrition*. Englewood Cliffs, New Jersey: Prentice Hall, 1980.

Hurley, L. S., Gowan, J., & Swenerton, H. Teratogenic effects of short-term and transitory zinc deficiency in rats. *Teratology*, 1971, **4**, 199–204.

Hurley, L. S., & Keen, C. L. Teratogenic effects of copper. In J. D. Nriagu (Ed.), *Copper in the environment*. New York: John Wiley & Sons, 1979.

Ingelfinger, F. J. How to swallow and belch and cope with heart burn. *Nutrition Today*, 1973, **8**, 4–13.

Jackson, G. M., Johnson, C. R., Ackron, G. S., & Crowley, R. Food satiation as a procedure to decelerate vomiting. *American Journal of Mental Deficiency*, 1975, **80**, 223–227.

Kalisz, K., Ekvall, S., & Palmer, S. Pica and lead intoxication. In S. Palmer & S. Ekvall (Eds.), *Pediatric Nutrition in Developmental Disorders*. Springfield, Ill.: Charles C. Thomas, 1978. Pp. 150–155.

Kerber, I. J., Warr, III, O. S., & Richardson, C. Pregnancy in a patient with a prosthetic mitral valve. *Journal of the American Medical Association*, 1968, **203**, 223–225.

Levy, H. L. *Genetic screening for inborn errors of metabolism.* U.S. Department of Health, Education, and Welfare. Public Health Services Administration. Bureau of Community Health Services. Rockville, Maryland: DHEW Publication No (HSA) 75-5708. 1973.

Lin-Fu, J. S. *Lead poisoning in children.* U.S. Department of Health, Education, and Welfare. Washington, D.C.: 1975. Pp. 1–25.

Mahaffey, K. R. Quantities of lead producing health effects in humans. Sources and bioavailability. *Environmental Health Perspectives*, 1977, **19**, 285–295.

Mahaffey, K. R. Nutritional factors in lead poisoning. *Nutrition Reviews*, 1981, **39**, 353–362.

McKusick, V. A. *Mendelian inheritance in man: Catalogs of autosomal, dominant, recessive and X-linked phenotypes.* (2nd ed) Baltimore: Johns Hopkins, 1968.

Mitchell, H. S. Nutrition in relation to stature. *Journal American Dietetic Association*, 1962, **40**, 521–524.

Mönkeberg, F., Tisler, S., Toro, S., Gattas, V., & Vegal, L. Malnutrition and mental development. *American Journal of Clinical Nutrition*, 1972, **25**, 766–772.

Moore, M. R., Meredith, P. A. & Goldberg, A. A retrospective analysis of blood-lead in mentally retarded children. *Lancet*, 1977, **1**, 717–719.

Moynahan, E. J. Acrodermatitis enteropathica: A lethal inherited human zinc disorder. *Lancet*, 1974, **2**, 399–400.

Munro, H. N. How well recommended are the recommended dietary allowances? *Journal of the American Dietetic Association*, 1977, **71**, 490–494.

National Center for Health Statistics. *Height and weight of adults, 18–74 years of age in the United States.* Advance data from vital and health statistics, No 3. Washington, D.C.: Nov. 19, 1976.

National Center for Health Statistics: *NCHS Growth curves for children. Birth to 18 years of age in the United States.* Vital and health statistics, Public Health Service. Publication 78-1650 Series II, No 165, Washington, D.C.: Government Printing Office, 1977.

Needleman, H. L., Gunnoe, C., Leviton, A., Reed, R., Peresie, Maher, C., & Barrett, P. Deficits in psychologic & classroom performance of children with elevated dentine lead levels. *New England Journal of Medicine*, 1979, **300**, 689–695.

Nelder, K. H., & Hambidge, K. M. Zinc therapy of acrodermatitis enterohepatica. *New England Journal of Medicine*, 1975, **292**, 879–882.

Nutritional screening of children: *A manual for screening and follow-up.* U.S. Department of Health and Human Services. Public Health Service. Health Service Administration. Bureau of Community Health Services. Office for Maternal & Child Health. Rockville, Md.: DHHS Publication No (HSA) 91-5114, 1981. Pp. 1–15.

Palmer, S., & Ekvall, S. Nutritional Developmental Disorders: An overview. In *Pediatric nutrition in developmental disorders.* Springfield: Charles C. Thomas, 1978. Pp. 21–24.

Pharaoh, P. O. D., Butterfield, I. H., & Hetzel, B. S. Neurological damage to the fetus resulting from severe iodine deficiency during pregnancy. *Lancet*, 1971, **1**, 308–310.

Ponder, K. B., & Bergman, J. S. Court ordered dietary standards: RDAs and mental retardation. *Journal of the American Dietetic Association*, 1980, 77, 428–433.

Recommended Dietary Allowances, 1980. (9th ed.) *The National Research Council*, Washington, D.C.

Review of the effects of dietary iodine on certain thyroid disorders. Prepared by the Division of Foods FDA. July 1976.

Ricciuti, H. N. Adverse environmental and nutritional influences on mental development. A perspective. *Journal American Dietetic Association*, 1981, **79**, 115–120.

Richardson, S. A., Birch, H. G., & Hertzig, M. E. School performance of children who were severely malnourished in infancy. *American Journal of Mental Deficiency*, 1973, 77, 623–632.

Rosovski, J., Novoa, F., Aberzua, J., & Mönkeberg, F. Craneal transillumination in early and severe malnutrition. *British Journal of Nutrition*, 1971, **25**, 107–111.

Rowe, D. A. *Drug-induced nutritional deficiencies*, Westport, Conn.: The Avi Publishing Company, 1976.

Scriver, C. R. Diets and genes: Euphenic nutrition. *New England Journal of Medicine*, 1977, **297**, 202–203.

Scriver, C. R., & Whelan, D. T. Glutamic acid decarboxylase in mammalian tissue outside the central nervous system and its possible relevance to hereditary vitamin B_6 dependency with seizures. *Annals New York Academy of Sciences*, 1969, **166**, 83–96.

Seltzer, C. C., & Mayer, J. A simple criterion of obesity. *Postgraduate Medicine*, 1965, **38**, A101 - A 107.

Smithells, R. W., Sheppard, S., & Schorah, C. J. Vitamin deficiencies and neural tube defects. *Archives of Disease in Childhood*, 1976, **51**, 944–950.

Springer, N. F., & Fricke, N. L. Nutrition and drug therapy for persons with developmental disabilities. *American Journal on Mental Deficiency*, 1975, **80**, 317–322.

Stange, L. K., Carlstrom, K., & Erikson, M. Hypervitaminosis A in early pregnancy and malformations of the central nervous system. *Acta Obstetrica Gynecologica Scand.* 1978, **57**, 289–291.

Statement by the American Dietetic Association on infant and child nutrition. Concerns regarding the developmentally disabled. *Journal of the American Dietetic Association*, 1981, 78, 443–452.

Stoch, M. B., & Smyth, P. M. Does undernutrition during infancy inhibit brain growth and subsequent intellectual development? *Archives Disease Childhood*, 1963, **38**, 546–552.

Thiele, V. F. *Clinical nutrition.* St. Louis: C. V. Mosby Co, 1980. Pp. 23–39.

Vosteal, J. J., Taves, E., Sayre, J. W., & Charney, E., Lead analysis of house dust: a method of detection of another source of lead exposure in inner city children. *Environmental Health Perspective*, 1974, **11**, 87–91.

Wallach, J. *Interpretation of diagnostic tests. A handbook synopsis of laboratory medicine.* (3rd ed.) Boston: Little-Brown, 1978.

Weighing and measuring children: *A training manual for supervisory personnel.* U.S. Department of Health and Human Services, Public Health Service, Center for Disease Control, Nutrition Division, Atlanta, Georgia: 1980. Pp. 1–10.

Wilkens, L., Blizzard, R., & Migion, C. *The diagnosis and treatment of endocrine disorders in childhood and adolescence.* (3rd ed.) Springfield: Charles C. Thomas, 1965.

Williamson, M. L., Koch, R., Azen, C., & Chang, C. Correlates of intelligence test results in treated phenylketonuric children, *Pediatrics*, 1981, **68**, 161–167.

Wilson, J. G., & Wakany, J. Cardiac and aortic arch anomalies in the offspring of vitamin A deficient rats correlated with similar human anomalies. *Pediatrics*, 1950, **5**, 708–725.

Winnick, M., & Noble, A. Cellular response in the rat during malnutrition at various ages. *Journal of Nutrition*, 1966, **89**, 300–306.

Winnick, M., & Rosso, P. Effects of severe malnutrition on cellular growth of human brain. *Petriatric Research*, 1966, **3**, 181–184.

Winnick, M., Rosso, P., & Waterlow, J. Cellular growth of cerebrum, cerebellum and brain stem in normal and marasmic children. *Experimental Neurology*, 1970, **26**, 393–400.

Wyatt vs. Hardin (formerly Wyatt and Stickney) 344 F Supp. 387 (M D Alabama, 1972).

19 COMMUNITY HEALTH ISSUES

Sterling D. Garrard

The widespread implementation of policies of deinstitutionalization during the seventies resulted in the relocation of mentally retarded people on a large scale in a variety of community-based residential settings. In fiscal year 1978–1979, Scheerenberger (1981; Note 1) reported that more than 8,700 people were resettled from 172 public residential facilities (PRF). In a nationwide survey in 1977, Bruininks, Hauber, and Kudla (1980; Note 2) found that there were more than 16,000 first admissions to community residential facilities (CRF). In that same year, more than 60,000 mentally retarded people were living in CRFs. In effect, a new community-based residential system was established for mentally retarded people during the seventies.

From a health perspective, the relocation movement of the seventies had one distinctive feature. It was anticipated that the generic system of health services would provide care for the occupants of community residences (Savage, Novack, & Heal, 1980). There was, however, no *a priori* evidence that the services delivered would meet the requirements of the population or that access to the system could be readily achieved. To date, the problems associated with the delivery of health services have not been sufficiently examined. Similarly, the health consequences of the relocation of people from their own homes and public institutions to CRFs have not been adequately analyzed. Although relevant empirical data are scanty, this chapter will address some of the issues.

Health Services and CRFs

From the standpoint of health services, community-based residential facilities can be divided into two groups. In the first group, mentally retarded people obtain all or most of their health services in generic settings *outside* the facility, although in some instances a nurse may periodically visit the facility. These facilities often house 10 people or fewer. In 1977, Bruininks et al., (1980; Note 2) reported that 73% of the 4,400 CRFs included in a nationwide survey had one to 10 occupants; another 15% had 11–20 occupants.

In the second group of CRFs, mentally retarded people receive all or most of their health services *within* the facility. Health professionals from the generic system, under an agreement or contract, bring services into these facilities. The people themselves enter generic settings only when their diagnostic or therapeutic requirements are exceptional. In some instances, the intramural health services of these facilities are designed to meet federal regulations for intermediate care facilities (ICF) under the medical assistance program of Title XIX of the Social Security

Act (Intermediate Care Facility Services, 1974). Facilities with intramural health services usually house more than 15–20 people, although size alone does not indicate the pattern of health services. In the study of Bruininks et al. (1980; Note 2), 10% of CRFs nationwide had 21–100 occupants; another 2% had 101 or more.

The two groups of CRFs differ in the frequencies with which their occupants enter the generic system of health services. The two groups also differ in the initiative that is assigned to the mentally retarded person for obtaining health services. In the first group, the mentally retarded person, usually with an advocate, is expected to seek services actively in generic settings along with the general population. In the second group, the mentally retarded person is a passive recipient of services in the residential setting apart from the general population. Finally, the two groups differ in the ease with which the health problems of their occupants, individually and collectively, can be monitored. In facilities which have an extramural pattern of health services, monitoring is difficult because of the dissemination of care among multiple providers in the community. In facilities that have an intramural pattern of health services, monitoring is easily accomplished, because of the concentration of care and records in a single place.

Distribution of the Population by Type of Health Services

The proportionate distribution of the population between CRFs with extramural and intramural health services is unknown. Estimates are possible, however, if it is assumed that the size of CRFs and the pattern of health services are related. The costs of providing intramural services would almost certainly be prohibitive in small facilities. At the time of the national survey of CRFs by Bruininks et al. (1980; Note 2) in 1977, 28% of the population lived in CRFs with one to 10 people, 16% in facilities with 11–20 people, 32% in facilities with 21–100 people, and 24% in facilities with 101 or more people. It is hypothesized that most people in CRFs with 10 or less occupants and many in CRFs with 11–20 occupants would obtain extramural health services for purposes of normalization as well as cost control. Most of the remainder would receive intramural health services. If these assumptions are correct, the demographic data (Bruininks et al., 1980; Note 2) suggest that approximately 40% of the total population in CRFs would obtain health care in generic settings and 60% in residential facilities. As a corollary, the health care of 40% of the population in CRFs would be disseminated in the generic system and would be difficult to monitor.

Distribution of Physical and Behavioral Characteristics

The physical and behavioral characteristics of the populations in CRFs with extramural and intramural patterns of health services have not been separately analyzed. Accurate profiles of the two populations would clarify the differences in the requirements of each for day to day residential care, health and medical services, and monitoring.

Two nationwide surveys have included data concerning the characteristics of the overall population in CRFs (O'Connor, 1976; Hill & Bruininks, Note 3). Unfortunately, these surveys utilized a single, operational definition of CRFs, which precluded the identification of gradients of severity between the populations in CRFs with extramural and intramural health services. In the more recent study of the two (Hill & Bruininks, Note 3), the data indicated that the rates of physical and behavioral disabilities were high in the population as a whole in CRFs. Severe and profound levels of mental retardation were present in 38%. Forty-seven percent exhibited maladaptive behaviors, which included aggression toward others, property damage, and self-injury. Forty percent had one or more associated impairments, including cerebral palsy and severe visual and auditory disorders. Ten percent were not ambulatory. Seizures had been observed within the preceding year in 13%. Other chronic medical disorders were attributed to 17%. Sixteen percent were totally dependent or required direct assistance with most daily activities. Twenty percent were unable to communicate in a verbal mode. A reversed reading of these percentages would indicate that a relatively large proportion of the population was unaffected by each of these groups of disabilities and, hence, that the population was heterogeneous.

It is hypothesized that the most disabled people, physically and behaviorally, are placed in CRFs which house more than 21 people, have a staff sufficient to meet the requirements for daily care, and have intramural health services. It is further hypothesized that the least disabled people are placed in small facilities, which rely chiefly upon extramural health services. It would be expected that the people in the latter facilities would be relatively free of antisocial behaviors, would be ambulatory, would have few chronic medical problems that would be difficult to manage, and would have at least some capacity for verbal communication. Heterogeneity would be expected in both populations, however, as a result of the lack of precision in placement, the unavailability of appropriate places, and other variables.

Several of the behavioral characteristics just cited would have important implications for the provision of health care: (1) the absence of speech would preclude reliance upon articulated complaints for the recognition of health problems, (2) limited modes of communication would interfere with most transactions between mentally retarded people and health professionals, and (3) severe maladaptive behaviors would restrict access to generic health settings.

Age of the Population

Community residential facilities are occupied primarily by adults and late teenage children. In a national sample of the population in CRFs in 1978–1979, Hill and Bruininks (Note 3) found that 65% were 21 years of age or older and 18% were 16–20 years of age. The population is physically mature, therefore, and requires health care which is appropriate for *chronological age* and *sex*.

To date, relatively few health professionals have had experience in the provision of services for fully grown, mentally retarded people. Prior to the seventies, the contacts of health professionals with mentally retarded people were often limited to young children in the context of the natural family. The development of the community residential system, however, increased the probability of encounters with adult, mentally retarded people in the generic health system. As a result, health professionals, agencies, and facilities in many communities are now gaining experience in the provision of care for mentally retarded adults. These experiences have not yet been systematically analyzed or reported.

Issues in Health Care in CRFs

Seven important questions related to the health care of mentally retarded people in CRFs are addressed in the remainder of this chapter: (1) Can generic health services be obtained by mentally retarded people in CRFs? (2) What are the deterrents to care? (3) Will the health problems of institutional populations be replicated in the community? (4) Will health care be monitored? (5) What are the health consequences of placement in the community residential system? (6) How will accountability in health care be achieved? (7) Does the concept of normalization require compromises with respect to the quality of health care?

Can Generic Health Services Be Obtained?

For CRFs with intramural health services, it is important to know, first, that health professionals from the generic system are available and accessible to the people *within* the facilities and, secondly, that access to the extramural health system can be obtained when required. For CRFs with extramural health services, it is important to establish that generic health services are available and accessible to the occupants *outside* the facilities. Availability refers to the existence of resources in a defined geographical area. Accessibility refers to differential rates of entry of individuals with particular characteristics into available services due to obstacles to utilization.

Three studies have included data concerning the availability and utilization of generic health services (Gollay, Freedman, Wyngaarden, & Kurtz, 1978; O'Connor, 1976; Scheerenberger, 1981, Note 1). These studies employed the methodology of opinion polls and were not rigorous analyses of health care. In the reports of Gollay et al. (1978) and O'Connor (1976), the results were confounded by the fact that institutions continued to provide some health services for the populations in the community. These reports all provided favorable interpretations, however, concerning the availability and accessibility of health services for mentally retarded people in CRFs and other community settings. The studies did not differentiate between the populations in facilities with extramural and intramural patterns of health services.

Scheerenberger (1981, Note 1) obtained data from 176 PRFs in fiscal year 1978–1979 regarding institutional perceptions of the availability, accessibility, and quality of medical services in the community. Availability and accessibility were considered to be only occasional barriers to placement in the community of mildly and moderately mentally retarded people from PRFs. A threshold emerged, however, in relation to the placement of severely and profoundly mentally retarded people. At the latter levels of mental retardation, the accessibility of services was considered to be a frequent obstacle to placement. Overall, problems with medical services were judged to be the least frequent among nine causes of failure of placement in the community from PRFs.

These relatively favorable reports do not provide a sufficient basis for generalization about the availability and accessibility of generic health services to the population in CRFs. Since placement involves a process in which requirements of the individual and the availability of services are weighed, whether systematically or not, the favorable assessment of the availability of services in these reports is a self-fulfilling prophecy. Scheerenberger's data (1981, Note 1) suggest that medical services in the community are less accessible to severely and profoundly mentally retarded people than to mildly and moderately mentally retarded people. The same report also indicates that chronic medical disorders are the third most important obstacle to community placement. These findings imply that barriers to services exist in the community. At this time, it is concluded that very little is known concerning the accessibility of generic health services to mentally retarded people with differing physical and behavioral characteristics in CRFs of different types.

What Are the Deterrents to Care?

A number of subtle obstacles may limit access to generic health services for mentally retarded people in CRFs, although quantitative data are lacking to assess the relative importance of each. Identifiable barriers include (1) negative attitudes, (2) lack of training, (3) procedural uncertainties, (4) consent issues, (5) double standards in decision making, (6) insufficient financial reimbursement, (7) turnover of direct-care staff, (8) characteristics of the person, (9) behavioral requirements of health facilities, (10) intramural health services, and (11) mismatched placement.

Negative Attitudes

It is hypothesized that groups of health professionals will have prejudicial or stereotypic attitudes toward mentally retarded people with the same frequency as comparable socioeconomic and cultural groups in the general population (Gottlieb, 1975). Deprecatory attitudes may or may not be linked with rejecting behaviors which restrict the access of mentally retarded people to health services. Evidence for rejection is suggested by the fact that mentally retarded people in CRFs with extramural health services are not randomly distributed among the health professionals of a community. Instead, health professionals seem to be selected for their willingness to accept mentally retarded people.

To date, the modifiability of negative attitudes and rejecting behaviors of health professionals through educational methods has not been convincingly demonstrated. Experience suggests, however, that a group of practitioners with positive attitudes toward the provision of services for mentally retarded people can be identified within all health professions. Predictably, a network of responsive providers for mentally retarded people can be developed within the generic health system of many communities.

Lack of Training

Health professionals may lack clinical experience with mentally retarded adults. In these instances, resistance to the provision of services may reflect the uncertainty of professionals concerning the adequacy of their skills for examining and communicating with mentally retarded people. For some professionals, discomfort may

be the chief determinant of resistance to the provision of services rather than prejudicial attitudes.

Procedural Uncertainties

Health professionals may occasionally be frustrated by the resistance of mentally retarded people to preventive, diagnostic, or therapeutic procedures. The dilemma is especially acute, if the mentally retarded person is an adult whose right to refuse must be respected. The distinctions between resistance and refusal are often ambiguous. Even when informed consent has been given by a legal guardian, there are no guidelines to indicate how forcibly diagnostic measures should be pursued in the face of strong resistance. Similarly, guidelines are not available to indicate when compromise is acceptable in the implementation of therapeutic regimens which the person resists or unwittingly defeats. Whenever coercive measures, such as anesthesia, psychoactive medications, or physical restraints, are required to achieve the objectives of health care, the health professional is confronted with moral and ethical quandaries. The right to be treated and the right not to be treated may also be in conflict in a legal framework. Some health professionals may opt to avoid accepting mentally retarded adults entirely rather than confront these dilemmas.

Consent Issues

Questions concerning appropriate mechanisms for obtaining informed consent may be a source of considerable uncertainty for professionals in caring for a mentally retarded adult who is not an adjudicated incompetent and who has no legally appointed guardian (Christie & Hoffmaster, 1979). Judicial orders may be required in relation to major clinical decisions in some states (Curran, 1981; Ramsey, 1978). The confusion of health professionals, especially physicians, regarding the legal requirements for consent and the wish to avoid unnecessary risks of liability may create barriers to care for some mentally retarded adults.

Double Standards in Clinical Decision Making

If diagnostic or therapeutic decisions are influenced by value judgments concerning the social worth of a mentally retarded person rather than medical criteria alone, the mentally retarded individual may be denied access to services which would be provided for nonretarded people under identical medical circumstances. A double standard of medical indications may develop in which barriers are created for some mentally retarded people, especially those who are severely or profoundly mentally retarded. Clinical decisions that incorporate judgments concerning "a meaningful life" or the "quality of life" of a mentally retarded person may result in the exclusion of the person from therapies which would be life saving (Brown, 1982; Fletcher, 1972; McCormick, 1974).

Insufficient Reimbursement

Many mentally retarded adults are eligible for third party payment for health services through Medicaid. The scale of reimbursement for a physician under Medicaid may be low enough to create a disincentive for the provision of care to mentally retarded people from CRFs (Schor, Smalky, & Neff, 1981). A physician may spend unusual amounts of time, which are not reimbursable in evaluating the health problems of a mentally retarded person, in communicating findings and recommendations to responsible agencies and interested parties, and in educating the staff of a CRF in order to obtain compliance with a preventive or therapeutic regimen. *Mental retardation and Medicaid may act synergistically, therefore, in creating barriers to care in the generic health system.*

A rigorous analysis of the costs of dental services for mentally retarded adults from CRFs has been reported (Gotowka & Johnson, in press). When compared with the revenues available for program maintenance, a net hourly deficit of $18.82 per dentist hour and $9.89 per dental hygienist hour resulted. Insufficient funding may deter health professionals in the community from accepting patients from CRFs.

Finally, health maintenance organizations (HMO) may resist the enrollment of groups of mentally retarded people for prepaid care, because actuarial data are not available to indicate the level of financial risk. In the absence of data, it is assumed *a priori* that the mentally retarded population presents a high risk with respect to the utilization of health services.

Turnover of Direct-care Staff

Direct-care personnel are the first line of defense for health problems in many CRFs. The identification of the presumptive signs of a health problem by direct-care personnel may be a prerequisite for obtaining medical care for individuals who reside in CRFs with extramural health services. If a mentally retarded person cannot articulate complaints effectively, the ability of the direct-care staff to interpret nonverbal signs or behavioral changes is crucial. Failure of the staff to make a correct inference from the cues can be a temporary barrier to services. Training, experience, and familiarity with the mentally retarded person are helpful in making these interpretations.

In 1977, Lakin and Bruininks (Note 4) found that the mean annual turnover rate for direct-care personnel in a national sample of CRFs was approximately 55%. One-fourth of direct-care employees left their jobs in less than three months. Rapid turnover rates translate operationally into untrained and inexperienced personnel who may inadvertently impede access to health services.

Characteristics of the Mentally Retarded Person

In some instances, mentally retarded individuals with physical disabilities may be unable to gain access to offices or facilities that present architectural barriers. The cognitive and verbal limitations of a person may interfere with the ability of the staff to tap subjective complaints for the early recognition of health problems. If the complaint-response loop is inoperative under these circumstances, the person's own disabilities may create the principal barriers to care. Finally, adaptive behavioral deficiencies or maladaptive behaviors of a person may elicit barriers to care in generic health settings as noted below.

Behavioral Requirements of Health Settings

Because health care occurs in a social context, the social behavior of the mentally retarded person may be an issue in many generic health facilities. Severe, adaptive behavioral deficiencies can present difficulties in facilities that are not prepared to cope with low functioning adults. Maladaptive behaviors that impinge upon the well-being of other patients are a predictable source of difficulty in most generic facilities. Even behaviors that represent "appropriate" responses of the person to aversive experiences in health care may be considered to be disturbing and appropriate targets for further treatment.

The generic system of health services is seldom prepared to respond supportively to adults with frequent or severe maladaptive behaviors, especially if interpersonal aggression, property damage, self-injury, hyperactivity, impulsiveness, and explosive tantrums are the manifestations. The tolerance for these behaviors is low in all community settings (Eyman & Call, 1977; Scheerenberger, 1981, Note 1).

In general, generic health facilities emphasize tight schedules, the efficient utilization of time, cost effectiveness, rigorous adherence to procedures, and the compliance of patients. Noncompliant or disruptive people are not readily integrated into generic health settings and may elicit responses which present serious obstacles to care.

CRFs with Intramural Health Services

Community residential facilities which have intramural health services may present intrinsic barriers to the utilization of the generic health system. Although many of the individuals who reside in facilities of this type have disabilities that make access to the generic system difficult, the range of disabilities of the occupants is often broad. In some instances, therefore, individuals may be locked into segregated care in these facilities who, if housed elsewhere, would obtain care in the generic health system.

Mismatching

The frequency with which individuals are placed in CRFs in medically underserved areas is unknown. In 1977, approximately 25% of CRFs were located in rural areas or in towns with less than 2,500 population (Bruininks *et al.*, 1980; Note 2). The probability that generic health services would be unavailable in areas with a low population density might be high. This failure to achieve an appropriate match between the requirements of the person for health services and the resources available in a particular locale could pose serious obstacles to health care.

Will Health Problems of Populations in PRFs Be Replicated in CRFs?

There is a risk that health problems with excessive prevalences in institutional populations will carry over into the new community residential system. Several problems of this type are identified for discussion here as follows: (1) high rates of utilization of psychopharmacologic medications, (2) infections with the hepatitis B virus, (3) intestinal parasitism, (4) tuberculosis, (5) unsatisfactory control of seizure disorders, and (6) high rates of injuries.

Psychopharmacologic Medications

The excessive utilization of antipsychotic medications to control the behavior of mentally retarded people in institutions has been repeatedly documented in published studies and reviews (Lipman, 1970; Lipman, DiMascio, Reatig, & Kirson, 1978; Pulman, Pook, & Singh, 1979; Sewall & Werry, 1976; Sprague, 1977; Tu, 1979; Lipman, Note 5). Thioridazine, chlorpromazine, and haloperidol are the most widely used agents (Lipman, Note 5). Every class of psychoactive medication has been utilized, however, including lithium, antianxiety agents, stimulants, sedatives and hypnotics, tricyclic antidepressants, and anticonvulsants.

In the studies cited, 40–70% of institutional populations were receiving antipsychotic medications. In addition to excessive utilization rates, high or excessive doses were frequently prescribed. All studies reported that the administration of two or more psychoactive medications concurrently was a common practice. This practice has been labeled "polypharmacy." Finally, antipsychotic drugs were often continued for months, years, or indefinite periods (Lipman, 1970; Sprague, 1977; Tu, 1979).

Several of the class action suits in federal courts during the seventies addressed the question of the excessive and inappropriate utilization of antipsychotic medications in institutions (Kenefick, 1981; Sprague & Baxley, 1978; Breuning & Sprague, Note 6; Fielding & Reagan, Note 7). As a result, court orders often specified the conditions that were to be met or the procedures that were to be followed when antipsychotic medications were prescribed. Court orders, federal regulations pertaining to intermediate care facilities for the mentally retarded (Intermediate Care Facility Services, 1974), strong advocacy programs, utilization reviews, and professional education undoubtedly have curbed the institutional use of antipsychotic medications in the past decade (Fielding, Murphy, Reagan, & Peterson, 1980; Inoue, 1982; LaMendola, Zaharia, & Carver, 1980).

The replication of institutional patterns of antipsychotic drug utilization in the new community residential system was documented for the first time on a large scale by Davis, Cullari, and Breuning (1981). A sample of 3,496 people from a population of 15,000 in community foster homes and group homes in Illinois, Indiana, Michigan, and Ohio was obtained. Fifty-eight percent (2,014 people) of the individuals in the sample were receiving an antipsychotic medication alone or in combination with another antipsychotic agent. Operational definitions of the target behaviors were available for only 5.4% of the 2,014 individuals who were receiving antipsychotic medications. In 21%, the reasons for the administration of medication were not documented. Thirty-nine percent were not examined by a nurse or a physician when the medication was prescribed or renewed. Drug free periods were scheduled for only 4% of individuals. Monitoring for adverse reactions was systematic in only 12%. The authors concluded that the prevalence of drug utilization, classes of drugs prescribed, dosages administered, duration of treatment, and frequency of polypharmacy in the community residential system resembled those previously reported in institutions.

Scheerenberger (1981; Note 1) reported that the unavailability and insufficient quality of services for behavioral management of mentally retarded people in the community were consistent problems. He also found that problems with services for behavioral management were the leading cause of placement failures. Under these circumstances, it could be anticipated that physicians would be subjected to strong pressures to prescribe antipsychotic medications in the community. It could also be anticipated that the geographical separation of physicians from residential settings and programs would complicate the problem of obtaining reliable behavioral observations and of monitoring for adverse drug effects. For these reasons, attempts to control the use of antipsychotic medications may be even more difficult in the community than in institutions.

If systematic monitoring of the utilization of antipsychotic agents is not undertaken in the community residential system, irrational utilization may easily escape recognition. Institutional gains in reducing utilization in the recent past can readily be dissipated in the new community system. The realistic difficulties of monitoring the utilization of these drugs in a disseminated population with multiple prescribing physicians are considerable. The alternative, however, may be the replication of institutional abuses. Court orders in the *Wuori v. Zitnay* (1978) case are unique, in that they extended controls over the utilization of antipsychotic medications to mentally retarded people in the community residential system.

Hepatitis B Virus

Immunological markers for hepatitis B virus (HBV) infections have been reported in 60–80% of institutional populations (Gust, Dimitrakakis, & Sharma, 1978; Kingham, McGuire, Paine, & Wright, 1978; Madden et al., 1976; Szmuness, Prince, Etling, & Pick, 1972). Placement of carriers of HBV from institutions with susceptibles from the community introduces a risk that exceptionally high institutional rates of infection will be replicated in the new community residential system. Approximately one-third of first admissions to CRFs come directly from natural or adoptive homes and the remainder from PRFs or other community residential situations (Baker, Seltzer, & Seltzer, 1974; O'Connor, 1976; Bruininks et al., 1980, Note 2). The public health dilemmas and legal issues which can arise when carriers and susceptibles are juxtaposed in a community classroom have been described (Bakal, Marr, Novick, Millner, Goldman, & Pitkin, 1980; Bakal, Novick, Marr, Millner, Goldman, & Pitkin, 1980).

For purposes of community placement, individuals can be divided into three groups with respect to HBV infections. The first group is presumed to be susceptible

and is negative for HBV markers on immunological tests. The second group is presumed to be immune and reveals antibody to the surface antigen of the virus (anti-HBs) on immunological tests. The third group includes carriers of HBV and reveals positive results for hepatitis B surface antigen (HBsAg) on immunological tests. Carriers are potential transmitters of the viral agent. Carriers differ, however, in the relative infectiveness of their blood, serum, and secretions. Carriers of HBsAg who are, in addition, positive for the hepatitis "e" antigen (HBeAg) may be relatively more infective than carriers who are positive for antibody to the "e" antigen (anti-HBe). The probability that a carrier will transmit the virus is further influenced by the individual's level of social skills and interactional behaviors with contacts, e.g., biting, indiscriminate kissing, and mouth-to-mouth sharing of food. Finally, the probability of transmission is influenced by the immunological status, social skills, and hygienic behaviors of contacts.

People with the Down syndrome (DS) pose a special problem with respect to the carrier state. Numerous studies have demonstrated that the DS population is predisposed to chronic antigenemia following infection with HBV (Aldershvile, Skinhoj, Frosner, Black, Deinhardt, Hardt, & Nielsen, 1980; Boughton, Hawkes, Schroeter, & Harlor, 1976; Chaudhary, Perry, & Cleary, 1977; Gust et al., 1978; Hawkes, Boughton, Schroeter, Decker, & Overly, 1980; Madden et al., 1976; Szmuness, Neurath, Stevens, Strick & Harley, 1981). These studies suggest that, once infected, 30–40% of the DS population will become carriers for indefinite periods by comparison with 8 to 14% of the non-DS, mentally retarded population. In addition, 30–80% of DS carriers will be positive for HBeAg by comparison with 10–20% of non-DS, mentally retarded carriers. When infected, therefore, DS individuals will become chronic carriers three to four times as frequently as non-DS, mentally retarded individuals. DS individuals who become chronic carriers will also be potentially effective transmitters three to four times as frequently as non-DS, chronic carriers. The potential for the transmission of HBV is related to the random mixing of carriers and susceptibles in CRFs and is not specific to the placement of the DS population. It is hypothesized, however, that the probability of replicating institutional rates of HBV in the community residential system will be appreciably increased by the indiscriminate placement of individuals with DS.

Hypothetically, the transmission of the virus in CRFs could be prevented by systematic efforts to house susceptibles only with other susceptibles or immunes, and carriers only with other carriers or immunes. Carriers with a positive test for anti-HBe and adequate social skills might also be appropriate for placement with susceptibles, although no prospective epidemiological data are available to evaluate the risks. There is no evidence to suggest that placement practices in any section of the country have been guided by immunological criteria. In most areas, the availability of places and the behavioral characteristics of individuals have been the overriding practical considerations in placement.

Empirical data are not available to indicate the rates of transmission of HBV infections to susceptible mentally retarded people and staff in CRFs. Few, if any, programs for monitoring attack rates for HBV infections in CRFs have been established. Accordingly, the extent to which institutional prevalences of immunological markers have been replicated in the community residential system is unknown. The importance of HBV infections as a public health problem in PRFs, however, underscores the seriousness of the failure to monitor the population in CRFs. The dissemination of people in the community residential system complicates the process of monitoring, decreases the probability that monitoring will occur, and reduces the general level of awareness of a health problem to which the group as a whole is highly vulnerable.

In the future, the chief hope for preventing the spread of the virus to susceptible occupants and staff in the community residential system will be the hepatitis B vaccine that was approved by the U.S. Food and Drug Administration in late 1981. The vaccine's efficacy has been demonstrated in rigorously controlled trials with high-risk, nonretarded populations (Szmuness, Stevens, Zang, Harley, & Kellner, 1982). Studies have not yet been reported in mentally retarded populations. In particular, the efficacy of the vaccine for people with DS is an unanswered question in view of the failure of many in this group to develop anti-HBs for prolonged periods following natural infections. The availability of the vaccine, however, should reduce the occupational hazard of HBV infection for direct-care staff and the residential hazard of infection for susceptible mentally retarded people. For the moment, the relatively high cost of the vaccine may limit its use.

Intestinal Parasitism

Intestinal parasites may be found in 20–60% of populations in PRFs (Krogstad, Spencer, Healy, Gleason, Sexton, & Herron, 1978; Thacker, Simpson, Gordon, Wolfe, & Kimball, 1979; Yoeli, Most, Hammond, & Scheinesson, 1972; Yoeli & Scheinesson, 1976). Parasites commonly found in institutional populations include *E. histolytica*, *G. lamblia*, *S. stercoralis*, *T. trichiura*, and *H. nana*. Infestation with two or more parasites may occur. Infected individuals may be symptomatic or asymptomatic but, in either instance, may transmit disease. Asymptomatic individuals who are infected with *E. histolytica*, for example, may transmit severe forms of intestinal amebiasis to contacts (Thacker et al., 1979) and may be a potential health hazard for a residential group. Since the transmission of intestinal parasites occurs via the fecal-oral route, high prevalence rates are indicative of low levels of social skills in the population or inadequate public health measures, or both (Garrard, 1979).

The replication of high institutional prevalence rates for intestinal parasites should be preventable in the community residential system by identifying and successfully treating infected individuals prior to placement in CRFs, obtaining follow-up stool examinations after placement, conducting epidemiological investigations if cases are subsequently identified, and monitoring the prevalence of infections. In the absence of a program for control, the population in CRFs may be predisposed to replicate the problem of intestinal parasitism that has plagued many PRFs. To date, no attempt has been made to determine the magnitude of the carry-over health problem, if any, due to intestinal parasitism in the community residential system.

Tuberculosis

The risk of transmission of tuberculosis in some PRFs is greater than in the general population (Screening for Pulmonary Tuberculosis in Institutions, 1977; Toward Eradication—A Contemporary Tuberculosis Control Strategy, 1978; Tuberculosis in a Nursing Home, 1980). If individuals are placed in CRFs from institutions with a high incidence or prevalence of tuberculous infection or disease, a control program should be implemented for the population as a whole in the community residential system.

An appropriate protocol for the control of tuberculosis in a community residential system should be developed in consultation with a local or state department of public health, if the risks are judged to be increased for the occupants and staff in the community system. The program might include two-step tuberculin skin testing of direct-care employees when hired, with appropriate follow-up and treatment of positives (Thompson, Glassroth, Snider, & Farer, 1979). Preadmission screening of residents under 35 years of age might include tuberculin skin testing followed by chest roentgenograms of those who were skin test positive. Decisions concerning isoniazid preventive therapy, unless contraindicated, or further investigation for current disease due to *M. tuberculosis* would be determined by the normality or abnormality of findings on the chest roentgenogram. Preadmission screening of residents over 35 years of age might include two-step tuberculin skin testing *and* a chest roentgenogram. Investigation for current disease due to *M. tuberculosis* would be dictated by the normality or abnormality of the chest roentgenogram (Screening for Pulmonary Tuberculosis in Institutions, 1977; Tuberculosis in a Nursing Home, 1980).

The dissemination of the mentally retarded population throughout the community residential system complicates the problem of implementing a uniform protocol for the control of tuberculosis. The dissemination also complicates the problem of collecting and aggregating data in order to determine rates of infection and disease and, hence, the necessity for a control program. Without a control program, some community residential systems are undoubtedly at risk of replicating the problems of tuberculosis which have characterized some PRFs.

Unsatisfactory Control of Seizures

The prevalence of convulsive disorders in samples of the mentally retarded population in CRFs exceeds by many fold the frequency of 0.34% in the general population (Prevalence of Chronic Conditions, 1977). Hill and Bruininks (Note 3) found that 13% of a nationwide sample of the population in CRFs had had an observed seizure during the preceding year; 21% of the sample were receiving anticonvulsant medications. Gollay et al. (1978) reported a seizure frequency of 12% in a sample of 414 people in community placement. Schor et al. (1981) found a frequency of 31% in a group of 48 children in a CRF.

Systematic studies of institutional populations have demonstrated unsatisfactory levels of seizure control. Unacceptable frequencies were identified for unrecognized seizures, unnecessary administration of anticonvulsants, overmedication and drug toxicity, undermedication and inadequate control, and episodes of status epilepticus and seizure related deaths (Freeman, Holden, & Schoenfeld, 1980; O'Neill, Ladon, Harris, Riley, & Dreifuss, 1977). These studies also demonstrated that unsatisfactory control was an important cause of disability and interference with habilitative programs in institutional populations. When intensive programs were developed, which included staff training, the judicious use of blood levels to guide anticonvulsant treatment, and rational therapeutic regimens, marked improvement was effected in the level of control (Freeman et al., 1980; O'Neill et al., 1977).

These institutional studies suggest that the magnitude of the problem of unsatisfactory seizure control may be unrecognized, even in a circumscribed population, in the absence of a system for the collection and analysis of group data. Furthermore, improved care for such a population may require a coordinated approach to the management of the group as a whole. Community placement of mentally retarded people with seizure disorders presents the problems of dissemination, multiple providers of care, and loss of the ability to monitor the overall level of control. Problems of staff turnover, insufficient staff training, difficulties in obtaining observer reliability, and lack of a centralized programmatic thrust would seem to cloud the prospect for achieving effective control in the community residential system. Although it is possible that some individuals may experience improved control in community placement, the institutional problem of unsatisfactory control for the population as a whole could easily be replicated without recognition.

Injuries

Accidents and injuries are frequent occurrences in PRFs. In a facility with 639 residents, Pierce (1977) found that one in 40 referrals to health services was due to an injury. In addition, one in 38 bed days in the infirmary was utilized for a person with an injury. Hill and Bruininks (Note 3) reported that 17.7% of a nationwide sample of mentally retarded people in PRFs saw a physician for an accident or injury during a one-year period in 1978–1979. Injuries, especially fractures and lacerations, are a public health problem for populations of mentally retarded people in PRFs. Hill and Bruininks (Note 3) reported that 5.6% of a nationwide sample of mentally retarded people in CRFs saw a physician for an accident or an injury during 1978–1979. Schor et al., (1981) found that 12% of all visits for primary medical care by 48 children, ages six to 17 years, in a CRF were due to trauma. At this time, however, the data are insufficient to establish the incidence of injuries in the community residential system.

Without a mechanism for collecting and aggregating data, the relative importance of injuries for the health of the population in CRFs cannot be estimated. If excessive rates are obscured by a lack of data, opportunities will be missed for the development of preventive programs. In the absence of a system for monitoring, the replication of the institutional health problem would not be recognized in the community residential system.

Conclusions

Several health problems which have high prevalences in the populations of PRFs may carry over into the community residential system. The replication of these health problems and, perhaps, others could be prevented if appropriate surveillance and control measures were implemented for the population as a whole in CRFs. At this time, data are insufficient to determine the extent to which replication has already occurred.

Will Health Care Be Monitored?

Monitoring of health problems may be undertaken for the population as a whole and for individuals in CRFs.

Group Monitoring

Monitoring of group health problems is more difficult in the community residential system than in PRFs where records are centralized. The concept of a single population with common health problems is lost when people are disseminated among multiple, small CRFs with separate administrations. Although the obstacles to monitoring may be lessened in CRFs with intramural health services and on-site health records, the difficulties are compounded in CRFs with extramural health services. In the latter situations, care is disseminated among multiple providers who are oriented to individuals rather than groups. Even if the issue of confidentiality of individual records could be easily resolved, the collection and aggregation of data from numerous sites in the generic system would be costly, time-consuming, and difficult. For these reasons, the monitoring of group health problems is often abandoned in the community residential system.

In the absence of preventive programs, the risks are high that health problems which have been excessively frequent in institutional populations will be reestablished in the new community residential system. Systematic monitoring at the time of entry into CRFs would define the extent of the carry-over from PRFs and other community settings. Continued monitoring would establish the direction of change in the frequencies of these problems and would allow preventive programs to be assessed. If the data did not substantiate the replication of serious institutional problems in the community residential system, the monitoring program could be modified or discontinued. The feasibility, costs, and benefits of a monitoring program would require careful analysis in order to justify continuation. Central direction of the monitoring program by a state department of public health or other superordinate agency would be required in order to ensure participation of the CRFs in the community residential system.

The suggestion that the population in CRFs should be monitored as if it were a single population may appear to be a perpetuation of the concept of an institution or a subversion of the principle of normalization. Until data are available that establish that the population is not at risk for serious institutional health problems, however, monitoring of the entire population will be medically defensible. The downside risk of not monitoring will be the unrecognized duplication of institutional health problems in the new community residential system.

Individual Monitoring

Monitoring at the level of the individual serves the purposes of "case" management and accountability. Individual monitoring is readily accomplished in CRFs which have intramural health services and on-site health records. Individual monitoring may be difficult, however, in facilities that have extramural health services, multiple providers of health care, and scattered health records. In addition, the generic health system may not be responsive to external monitoring by personnel from CRFs.

In general, quantitative monitoring can be accomplished more readily than qualitative monitoring; that is, services can be counted more easily than they can be evaluated for quality. Three types of data are required for individual monitoring: (1) data related to preventive health care, (2) data related to encounters with the generic health system, and (3) data related to the management of chronic diseases. The difficulties of monitoring increase from the first through the last.

Individual monitoring of *preventive health care* may be limited to the verification of the fact that an annual health examination has been performed. As performed, however, the content of a routine, annual health examination may vary widely among physicians. In the absence of a specific protocol, the probability is low that a uniform content of preventive care will be provided for the people in CRFs. Monitoring for item content, as well as for the performance of the examination, would be required to detect major omissions.

For the general population, the American College of Physicians now recommends individually planned, *periodic* health examinations in lieu of a traditional *annual* physical examination (Periodic Health Examination, 1981) for the asymptomatic person. The recommended items and schedules could be used as a guide for monitoring the content of periodic health examinations for the population in CRFs.

Individual monitoring of the frequency of *encounters* with the generic health system would identify high consumers of health services. If the causes of these contacts were also determined, the individuals who were identified could become the objects of intensified health maintenance and preventive programs. If data of this type were collected and aggregated for the population as a whole in CRFs, the ensuing recognition of excessive morbidity would offer the possibility of developing targeted preventive programs for the entire population. At this time, the extent to which the prevalence of diseases in the mentally retarded population may deviate from prevalences in the population at large is unknown.

Individual monitoring of *chronic diseases* would identify people with satisfactory and unsatisfactory progress. Individuals whose course was marked by frequent episodes of instability would be candidates for intensified health care. Monitoring of chronic diseases would require a detailed transfer of information from the generic service system to personnel in CRFs. Problems in obtaining information from the generic system would be accentuated in this context. Ideally, individualized protocols for surveillance, management, and periodic evaluations of the person with a chronic disease would be prepared in the generic service system. Portions of these protocols would then be incorporated in the individual service plan (ISP) and would provide the blueprint for individual monitoring.

Conclusions

Accountability in the community residential system requires individual monitoring. In many CRFs, the implementation of the ISP must be verified. Individual monitoring can be utilized to achieve uniformity in the content of preventive health care, to identify individuals with increased morbidity rates who might benefit from intensified health care, and to assess the progress of chronic diseases. In addition, the collection and analysis of data for the population as a whole in CRFs could provide information concerning the replication of institutional health problems, the indications for targeted preventive programs for the entire population, and the overall utilization rates of health services. At this time, group monitoring is uncommon. Its benefits and costs are unknown as are the risks of not monitoring. In the absence of data from group monitoring, no definitive conclusions can be reached concerning the merits of care for mentally retarded people in the generic health system as opposed to care in the institutional health system. Although the inadequacy of health care in PRFs was publicized in numerous class action suits in federal courts during the seventies (Kenefick, 1981), the superiority of health care in the community residential system has yet to be demonstrated.

What Are the Health Consequences of Placement in CRFs?

The relocation of people from PRFs or their own homes to CRFs is associated with two important changes which could have health consequences: (1) a change in environmental variables and (2) a change in the source of health services. Changes in mortality and morbidity of the population could provide indications of the health consequences of placement in the community residential system.

Mortality

If monitored, comparative mortality rates in CRFs and PRFs could provide a gross measure of the impact of placement in the community residential system upon the health of people. In a nationwide survey of the population in CRFs during the year 1976–1977, Bruininks et al. (1980, Note 2) reported a crude mortality rate of 1.0%, or 10/1,000 population. In a nationwide survey of the population in PRFs during 1979–1980, the crude mortality rate was 1.5%, or 15/1,000 population (Krantz, Bruininks, & Clumpner, Note 8). Since these rates were not obtained in the same calendar year, they cannot be compared. In addition, death rates for a single year are not necessarily representative of all years. Finally, unless crude rates are adjusted for significant differences between the populations in the distribution of age and level of retardation, no meaningful comparisons can be made.

Severe and profound levels of retardation are associated with much of the excess mortality in the mentally retarded population (Eyman & Miller, 1978; Miller & Eyman, 1978). Death rates are approximately 50% higher at profound than at severe levels. Hill and Bruininks (Note 3) provided data for the differences in levels of retardation in the populations of CRFs and PRFs in 1978–1979. In CRFs, 26% were severely and 12% profoundly retarded, a combined total of 38%. In PRFs, 29% were severely and 47% profoundly retarded, a combined total of 76%. In view of these differences in the proportionate distribution of severe and profound retardation, lower crude death rates would be expected in CRFs than PRFs.

Miller and Eyman (1978) reported comparative death rates in community settings and institutions in southern California for the years 1973–1975, inclusive. Data were analyzed by placement, age, level of retardation, previous institutionalization, and ambulation. Within the profoundly and severely retarded groups, death rates were significantly higher for the nonambulatory subgroup than for the ambulatory. It was concluded that death rates in the community were generally lower than those for comparable institutional residents. Additional studies would be required in other sections of the country, however, before these findings could be generalized. At this time, no sophisticated program for monitoring specific or adjusted death rates exists. As a result, the capacity of the new forms of residential facilities to maintain life relative to home and institution is unknown (Miller & Eyman, 1978).

Rago (1976) reported that mortality rates for profoundly mentally retarded people who were transferred to community facilities from a PRF were nearly double the rates of those who remained in the institution. It was not clear that these populations were comparable, however, with respect to relevant variables such as age, nonambulatory status, epilepsy, and associated disabilities. A relocation syndrome has also been postulated which may include depression and increased mortality (Cochran, Sran, & Varano, 1977; Coffman & Harris, 1980). At present, the available data are insufficient to evaluate this syndrome or its associated mortality.

Morbidity

Changes in morbidity rates might also provide a measure of the health consequences of placement in the community residential system. In this instance, it would be necessary to compare the morbidity rates of matched groups in CRFs, PRFs, and family homes. In addition, it would be important to analyze morbidity experiences longitudinally for groups of mentally retarded people before and after placement in CRFs. At this time, however, no adequate system is in operation for the collection and analysis of data related to morbidity rates in the community residential system.

Conclusions

To date, the impact of placement in the community residential system upon mortality and morbidity has not been clarified. From a research perspective, the null hypothesis is still untested with respect to the health status of the populations in CRFs and PRFs.

How Will Accountability For Health Care Be Achieved?

The locus of accountability for health care is less clear in CRFs with extramural health services than in CRFs with intramural services. *Professional accountability* for the occupants of CRFs with extramural services is disseminated among multiple providers in the generic health system. *Administrative accountability* remains with the agency which operates the CRF and is met by efforts to monitor the delivery of services. For the reasons previously stated, monitoring of the care provided in the generic health system is difficult for the staff of a CRF, especially when the responsible staff member is not a health professional. Because of the difficulties in monitoring, administrative accountability may be attenuated in facilities with extramural health services. The monitoring function of the CRF, however, is essentially for mentally retarded people who are incapable of monitoring their own health services. Under the circumstances, the quality and content of health care may not be scrutinized. The quality of care is often entrusted blindly to providers in the generic health system, since the assessment of quality is beyond the capabilities of most CRFs.

Does Normalization Require Compromises in the Quality of Health Care?

Normalization is achieved in the area of health care when mentally retarded people and the general population are afforded equal access and receive identical services in the community. It should be recognized, however, that situations may arise in which the generic health services of a community are inadequate even for the general population. Under these circumstances, a dilemma exists. On the one hand, an effort to provide services of acceptable quality for the mentally retarded population that are not also available to the general population would violate the principle of normalization. On the other hand, acceptance of the available services in order to uphold the principle of normalization would compromise the quality of care for the mentally retarded population. Under these circumstances, the appropriateness of the placement would usually be questioned. Since the mentally retarded person seldom has an option regarding placement, the accountable agency is considered to be obligated to obtain an acceptable level of health care by all means necessary.

Medical Mainstreaming

Mainstreaming in the generic system of health services justifies strategies which are analogous to those which are applied in the educational system. Four strategies can be proposed for the health system: (1) full integration without special supports, (2) full integration with special support by the staff and procedural adaptations, (3) partial integration with special support by the staff, procedural adaptations, and environmental modifications, and (4) separation with partial integration under unusual diagnostic and therapeutic circumstances.

Strategies

The *first strategy* for health care in a generic setting would be the full integration of mentally retarded people with nonretarded people. In this situation, the mentally retarded person would ordinarily be free of socially disruptive, maladaptive behaviors. The intellectual level, communicative ability, and social skills would be high enough to permit integration without the necessity for a specially trained staff, procedural alterations, or environmental modifications. At most, the person would benefit from the assistance of an advocate. If this strategy were appropriate, no aversive consequences or experiences would follow for the mentally retarded person or for nonretarded people in the same setting. This strategy would be applicable to many individuals in CRFs with extramural health services.

The *second strategy* for health care in a generic setting would involve the full integration of mentally retarded people combined with special support by the staff and changes in routines or procedures as indicated. In these situations, the mentally retarded person generally would be free of maladaptive behaviors that would have a negative impact upon other people in the same setting. As a result, the staff could focus primarily upon the support of the mentally retarded person without diverting attention to the protection of other people. The issue of separation of the mentally retarded person should not arise.

In this situation, the ability of the mentally retarded person to conceptualize health problems, to understand the experiences of health care, and to communicate verbally with staff would be limited to varying degrees. These limitations would underscore the importance of having personnel in the facility who were skilled in relating interpersonally, reducing apprehension, providing reassurance, and generally supporting mentally retarded people at verbal and nonverbal levels. Appointments could be scheduled to allow added time for realizing the objectives of a visit. Procedures could be altered to allow familiarizing trial runs in order to diminish the likelihood of interfering responses. Programs could be devised that would enable the person to learn in advance the cooperative behaviors which would be required during specific diagnostic or therapeutic procedures. The availability of a behavioral analyst for consultation could assist the staff in several of these areas. Again, an advocate would be useful who could act as a bridge between familiar and unfamiliar situations, who could assist in the interpretation of events to the person, and who could interpret the person to health professionals. This strategy should permit the utilization of generic health facilities for the majority of mentally retarded people in CRFs.

The *third strategy* for health care in a generic setting would involve partial integration with special support by the staff, procedural changes, and environmental modifications. In this situation, the mentally retarded person would exhibit maladaptive behaviors at a frequency and level of intensity that would have an adverse impact upon other people in the same setting. Attention would be directed, in part, therefore, to the well-being of other people. In these instances, the staff would require special training in order to respond supportively to the behaviors of the mentally retarded individual. Again, the availability of a behavioral analyst for consultation with the staff could be important. Visits might be scheduled at times when few, if any, nonretarded people were present. Environmental modifications might be improvised that would permit the partial separation of mentally retarded people in waiting and service areas, although the risk of categorical separation would be introduced thereby. Generic facilities could be utilized for individuals with difficult behaviors, if routines and space could be adapted sufficiently to avoid imposing an excessive burden on others in the setting. Mentally retarded people who would present antisocial, maladaptive behaviors and who would require a strategy of partial integration would be proportionately few in numbers.

The *fourth strategy* would involve partially segregated care in a CRF with an intramural health system. If diagnostic or therapeutic services were required that exceeded the intramural capacity or if hospitalization were indicated, however, the mentally retarded person would be referred to generic facilities. One of the preceding strategies would then be activated. Totally segregated and self-contained systems of health, medical, and surgical care were discontinued in most PRFs in the seventies. It is doubtful that current CRFs are operating systems of this type, although no data are available to settle the question. In general, the indications for intramural health care are limited to individuals with multiple or severe physical and maladaptive behavioral disabilities, precarious physical states that require daily surveillance by health professionals, and situations in which intensive or complex maintenance or therapeutic regimens are necessary.

Accommodation by Generic Services

The low volume of mentally retarded adults in most generic settings does not provide a sufficient incentive to prepare specifically for this group, especially in the absence of funds to defray the costs. If the volume of mentally retarded adults increases in generic settings with the growth of the community residential system, however, facilities and health professionals will undoubtedly conclude that suitable preparations could reduce the frequency of traumatic encounters between mentally retarded individuals, other patients, and staff. Even now, hospitals and clinics in some communities are increasing their capacity for supportive care in the face of increased utilization by mentally retarded people from CRFs.

State of the Art

Currently, no studies of medical mainstreaming are available. The types and frequencies of difficulties encountered by mentally retarded people in health facilities, the effects of integrated care upon mentally retarded and nonretarded people, and the behaviors of professional and nonprofessional personnel in response to mentally retarded people in generic settings have not been analyzed. The effectiveness of the strategies and techniques which have been noted here have not been empirically studied. Similarly, the quality of care obtained in generic health settings by mentally retarded people has not been compared with the quality of care which is obtained in segregated, intramural health systems.

Utilization of Health Services

The data concerning the physical characteristics of the population in CRFs (Hill & Bruininks, Note 3) support the hypothesis that the population as a whole would have an increased utilization of health services. The heterogeneity of the population, however, suggests that three groups would be present. The *first* would be a low consuming group, probably a sizable minority of the population in CRFs, whose requirements for health services would be similar to those of people of the same age and sex and of equivalent economic status in the general population. The major service requirements would be for primary care with an emphasis upon health maintenance and periodic preventive health examinations. The *second* would be an intermediate consuming group, probably also a sizable minority of the population in CRFs, whose increased morbidity rates would necessitate frequent medical encounters and intensified care for the maintenance of health. The major service requirements would be for primary care with occasional specialized consultations. The *third* would be a high consuming group, probably the smallest minority of the population in CRFs, whose increased utilization of health services would be attributable to chronic medical disorders. The major service requirements would be for primary care often supplemented by specialized consultations. Systematic monitoring, therapeutic compliance, and periodic evaluations would be essential for the main-

tenance of biomedical homeostasis in this group. The level of consumption of health services at any given time in the community residential system would be determined by the proportionate mix of these three groups.

Schor et al. (1981) described the provision of primary medical care for 48 ambulatory, previously institutionalized children, ages six to 17 years, in a community-based residential facility. Sixty-nine percent of the children were teenagers. Fifty-two percent were severely or profoundly retarded, and 42% were moderately retarded. No similar documentation of care in a CRF has been reported. The group had five times as many medical encounters as an age matched general population. Medical encounters occurred at an average rate of 12 per person per year during the first year of the program but were reduced to 7.4 by the third year. Chronic problems were much more frequent than in the general population. Convulsive disorders were present in 31%. Specialized consultations were required for approximately half of the children per year. A health associate provided primary health care, reviewed seizure control, and monitored dietary regimens in the CRF. The health associate also conferred with caretakers and school personnel in relation to behavioral and school problems. The commitment of time of the health associate to these activities totalled eight hours per week.

Summary

The impact of placement in the community residential system for the health of the mentally retarded population has been discussed. To date, the health status and health care of the population in CRFs have received much less attention than behavioral considerations. From a health perspective, community residential facilities can be divided into two groups: (1) those which have an extramural pattern of care and (2) those which have an intramural pattern of care. The following issues were considered in relation to the health of the population in the community residential system: (1) the availability and accessibility of generic health services, (2) deterrents to health care in the generic system, (3) the replication of institutional health problems in the community residential system, (4) monitoring of health care in the generic system, (5) the health consequences of placement in the community residential system, (6) accountability for health care in the generic system, (7) potential conflicts between the principle of normalization and inadequate health care in a community, (8) mainstreaming in the generic health system, and (9) the utilization of health services by the mentally retarded population in CRFs. At this time, the data are insufficient to conclude that health care in the generic health system is superior to intramural health care in an institution. Similarly, the data are insufficient to conclude that placement in the community residential system from an institution will have beneficial consequences for health.

Reference Notes

1. Scheerenberger, R. C. *Public residential services for the mentally retarded, 1979.* Madison, Wis.: National Association of Superintendents of Public Residential Facilities for the Mentally Retarded, 1979.
2. Bruininks, R. H., Hauber, F. A., & Kudla, M. J. *National Survey of community residential facilities: A profile of facilities and residents in 1977.* (Project Report No. 5) Minneapolis: University of Minnesota, Department of Psychoeducational Studies, 1979.
3. Hill, B. K., & Bruininks, R. H. *Physical and behavioral characteristics and maladaptive behavior of mentally retarded people in residential facilities.* (Project Report No. 12) Minneapolis: University of Minnesota, Department of Psychoeducational Studies, 1981.
4. Lakin, K. C., & Bruininks, R. H. *Occupational stability of direct-care staff of residential facilities for mentally retarded people.* (Project Report No. 14) Minneapolis: Department of Psychoeducational Studies, University of Minnesota, 1981.
5. Lipman, R. S. Psychotropic drugs and the mentally retarded: What we know and what we need to know. In R. Young & J. Kroll (Eds.), *The use of medications in controlling the behavior of the mentally retarded: Proceedings.* Minneapolis: University of Minnesota, Department of Conferences, 1981.
6. Breuning, S. E., & Sprague, R. L. Assessing medication effects with institutionalized mentally retarded individuals: A legal and empirical analysis. In R. Young & J. Kroll (Eds.), *The use of medications in controlling the behavior of the mentally retarded: Proceedings.* Minneapolis: University of Minnesota, Department of Conferences, 1981.
7. Fielding, L. T., & Reagan, M. W. Behavioral analysis techniques in assessing drug efficacy and dosage in mentally retarded persons. In R. Young & J. Kroll (Eds.), *The use of medications in controlling the behavior of the mentally retarded: Proceedings.* Minneapolis: University of Minnesota, Department of Conferences, 1981.
8. Krantz, G. C., Bruininks, R. H., & Clumpner, J. L. *Mentally retarded people in state-operated residential facilities: Year ending June 30, 1980.* Minneapolis: University of Minnesota, Department of Psychoeducational Studies, 1980.

References

Aldershvile, J., Skinhoj, P., Frosner, G. G., Black, F., Deinhardt, F., Hardt, F., & Nielsen, J. O. The expression pattern of hepatitis B e antigen and antibody in different ethnic and clinical groups of hepatitis B surface antigen carriers. *The Journal of Infectious Diseases,* 1980, **142,** 18–22.

Bakal, C. W., Marr, J. S., Novick, L. F., Millner, E. S., Goldman, W. D., & Pitkin, O. E. Deinstitutionalized mentally retarded hepatitis-B surface antigen carriers in public school classes: A descriptive study. *American Journal of Public Health,* 1980, **70,** 709–711.

Bakal, C. W., Novick, L. F., Marr, J. S., Millner, E. S., Goldman, W. D., & Pitkin, O. Mentally retarded hepatitis-B surface antigen carriers in NYC public school classes: A public health dilemma. *American Journal of Public Health,* 1980, **70,** 712–716.

Baker, B. L., Seltzer, G. B., & Seltzer, M. M. *As close as possible: Community residences for retarded adults.* Boston: Little, Brown and Company, 1977.

Boughton, C. R., Hawkes, R. A., Schroeter, D. R., & Harlor, J. A. The epidemiology of hepatitis B in a residential institution for the mentally retarded. *Australian and New Zealand Journal of Medicine,* 1976, **6,** 521, 529.

Brown, J. K. Ethical dilemmas in paediatrics. *Developmental Medicine and Child Neurology,* 1982, **24,** 1–2.

Bruininks, R. H., Hauber, F. A., & Kudla, M. J. National Survey of community residential facilities: A profile of facilities and residents in 1977. *American Journal of Mental Deficiency,* 1980, **84,** 470–478.

Chaudhary, B. K., Perry, E., & Cleary, T. E. Prevalence of hepatitis B infection among residents of an institution for the mentally retarded. *American Journal of Epidemiology,* 1977, **105,** 123–126.

Christie, R. J., & Hoffmaster, C. B. Ethical considerations in caring for retarded patients. *Canadian Family Physician,* 1979, **25,** 1369–1372.

Cochran, W. E., Sran, P. K., & Varano, G. A. The relocation syndrome in mentally retarded individuals. *Mental Retardation,* 1977, **15,** 10–12.

Coffman, T. L., & Harris, M. C. Transition shock and adjustments of mentally retarded persons. *Mental Retardation,* 1980, **18,** 3–7.

Curran, W. J. Court involvement in right-to-die cases: Judicial inquiry in New York. *New England Journal of Medicine,* 1981, **305,** 75–76.

Davis, J. J., Cullari, S., & Breuning, S. E. Drug use in community foster-group homes. In S. E. Breuning & A. D. Poling (Eds.), *Drugs and mental retardation.* Springfield, Ill.: Charles C. Thomas, 1981.

Eyman, R. K., & Call, T. Maladaptive behavior and community placement of mentally retarded persons. *American Journal of Mental Deficiency,* 1977, **82,** 137–144.

Eyman, R. K., & Miller, C. Introduction: A demographic overview of severe and profound mental retardation. In C. E. Meyers (Ed.), *Quality of life in severely and profoundly mentally retarded people: Research foundations for improvement.* (Monograph No. 3) Washington, D.C.: American Association on Mental Deficiency, 1978.

Fielding, L. T., Murphy, R. T., Reagan, M. W., & Peterson, T. L. Individualized drug and behavioral assessment for preventing excessive utilization of major tranquilizers in intermediate care facilities for the mentally retarded. *Hospital and Community Psychiatry,* 1980, **31,** 771–773.

Fletcher, J. Indicators of humanhood: A tentative profile of man. *The Hastings Center Report,* 1972, **2,** 1–4.

Freeman, J. M., Holden, K. R., Schoenfield, E. Comprehensive care of institutionalized persons with epilepsy. In J. A. Wada & J. K. Penry (Eds.), *Advances in epileptology: Xth Epilepsy International Symposium.* New York: Raven Press, 1980. (Abstr.)

Garrard, S. D. Intestinal parasitism and public health practices in institutions for mentally retarded people. *American Journal of Public Health,* 1979, **69,** 1211–1213.

Gollay, E., Freedman, R., Wyngaarden, M., & Kurtz, N. R. *Coming Back: The community experiences of deinstitutionalized mentally retarded people.* Cambridge, Mass.: Abt Books, 1978.

Gotowka, T. D., & Johnson, E. S. Costs of providing dental services to adult mentally retarded: A preliminary report. *American Journal of Public Health.* In press.

Gottlieb, J. Public, peer, and professional attitudes toward mentally retarded persons. In M. J. Begab & S. A. Richardson (Eds.), *The mentally retarded and society: A social science perspective.* Baltimore: University Park Press, 1975.

Gust, I. D., & Dimitrakakis, M., & Sharma, D. L. B. The prevalence of HBeAg and anti-HBe in an institution for the mentally retarded. *Australian and New Zealand Journal of Medicine,* 1978, **8**, 471–473.

Hawkes, R. A., Boughton, C. R., Schroeter, D. R., Decker, R. H., & Overby, L. R. Hepatitis B infection in institutionalized Down's syndrome inmates: A longitudinal study with five hepatitis B virus markers. *Clinical Experimental Immunology,* 1980, **40**, 478–486.

Inoue, F. A clinical pharmacy service to reduce psychotropic medication use in an institution for mentally handicapped persons. *Mental Retardation,* 1982, **20**, 70–74.

Intermediate care facility services. *Federal Register,* January 17, 1974. Pp. 2220–2235.

Kenefick, B. Court decisions: The impact of litigation. In J. Wortis (Ed.), *Mental retardation and development disabilities.* Vol. XII. New York: Brunner/Mazel, 1981.

Kingham, J. G. C., McGuire, M., Paine, D. H. D., & Wright, R. Hepatitis B in a hospital for the mentally subnormal in Southern England. *British Medical Journal,* 1978, **2**, 594–596.

Krogstad, D. J., Spencer, H. C., Healy, G. R., Gleason, N. N., Sexton, D. J., & Herron, C. A. Amebiasis: Epidemiologic studies in the United States, 1971–1974. *Annals of Internal Medicine,* 1978, **88**, 89–97.

LaMendola, W., Zaharia, E. E., & Carver, M. Reducing psychotropic drug use in an institution for the retarded. *Hospital and Community Psychiatry,* 1980, **31**, 271–272.

Landesman-Dwyer, S. Living in the community. *American Journal of Mental Deficiency,* 1981, **86**, 223, 234.

Lipman, R. S. The use of psychopharmacological agents in residential facilities for the retarded. In F. J. Menolascino (Ed.), *Psychiatric approaches to mental retardation.* New York: Basic Books, 1970.

Lipman, R. S., DiMascio, A., Reatig, N., & Kirson, T. Psychotropic drugs and mentally retarded children. In M. A. Lipton, A. DiMascio, & K. F. Killam (Eds.), *Psychopharmacology: A generation of progress.* New York: Raven Press, 1978.

Madden, D. L., Dietzman, D. E., Matthew, E. B., Sever, J. L., Lander, J. J., Purcell, R. H., Rostafinski, M., & Mata, A. Epidemiology of hepatitis B in an institution for mentally retarded persons. *American Journal of Mental Deficiency,* 1976, **80**, 369–375.

McCormick, R. A. To save or let die: The dilemma of modern medicine. *Journal of the American Medical Association,* 1974, **229**, 172–176.

Miller, C., & Eyman, R. Hospital and community mortality rates among the retarded. *Journal of Mental Deficiency Research,* 1978, **22**, 137–145.

O'Connor, G. *Home is a good place: A national perspective of community residential facilities for developmentally disabled persons.* (Monograph No. 2) Washington, D.C.: American Association on Mental Deficiency, 1976.

O'Neill, B. P., Ladon, B., Harris, L. M., Riley, H. L., & Dreifuss, F. E. Comprehensive interdisciplinary approach to care of the institutionalized person with epilepsy. In J. K. Penry (Ed.), *Advances in Epileptology: Eighth International Symposium.* New York: Raven Press, 1977.

Periodic health examination: A guide for designing individualized preventive health care in the asymptomatic patient. *Annals of Internal Medicine,* 1981, **95**, 729–732.

Pierce, C. H. The costs of accidents and injuries at an institution for retarded adults. *Mental Retardation,* 1977, **15**, 23–24.

Prevalence of chronic conditions of the genitourinary, nervous, endocrine, metabolic, and blood and blood forming systems. National Health Survey, Vital and Health Statistics, Series 10, No. 109. Washington, D.C.: Department of Health, Education, and Welfare, Public Health Service, 1977.

Pulman, R. M., Pook, R. B., & Singh, N. N. Prevalence of drug therapy for institutionalized mentally retarded children. *Australia Journal of Mental Retardation,* 1979, **5**, 212–214.

Rago, W. V., Jr. On the transfer of the PMR. *Mental Retardation,* 1976, **14**, 27.

Ramsey, P. The Saikewicz precedent: What's good for an incompetent patient? *The Hastings Center Report,* 1978, **8**, 36–42.

Savage, V. T., Novak, A. R., & Heal, L. W. Generic services for developmentally disabled citizens. In A. R. Novak & L. W. Heal (Eds.), *Integration of Developmentally Disabled Individuals into the Community.* Baltimore: Paul H. Brookes, 1980.

Scheerenberger, S. M. Deinstitutionalization: trends and difficulties. In R. H. Bruininks, C. E. Meyers, B. B. Sigford, & K. C. Lakin (Eds.), *Deinstitutionalization and community adjustment of mentally retarded people.* (Monograph No. 4) Washington, D.C.: American Association on Mental Deficiency, 1981.

Schor, E. L., Smalky, K. A., & Neff, J. M. Primary care of previously institutionalized retarded children. *Pediatrics,* 1981, **67**, 536–540.

Screening for pulmonary tuberculosis in institutions. *American Review of Respiratory Disease,* 1977, **115**, 901–906.

Sewall, J., & Werry, J. S. Some studies in an institution for the mentally retarded. *New Zealand Medical Journal,* 1976, **84**, 317–319.

Sprague, R. L. Overview of psychopharmacology for the retarded in the United States. In P. Mittler (Ed.), *Research to practice in mental retardation.* Vol. III. *Biomedical aspects.* Baltimore: University Park Press, 1977.

Sprague, R. L., & Baxley, G. B. Drugs for behavior management with comment on some legal aspects. In J. Wortis (Ed.), *Mental retardation and developmental disabilities: An annual review.* Vol. X. New York: Brunner/Mazel, 1978.

Szmuness, W., Neurath, A. R., Stevens, C. E., Strick, N., & Harley, E. J. Prevalence of hepatitis B "e" antigen and its antibody in various HBsAg carrier populations. *American Journal of Epidemiology,* 1981, **113**, 113–121.

Szmuness, W., Prince, A. M., Etling, G. F., & Pick, R. Development and distribution of hemagglutinating antibody against hepatitis B antigen in institutionalized populations. *The Journal of Infectious Disease,* 1972, **126**, 498–506.

Szmuness, W., Stevens, C. E., Zang, E. A., Harley, E. J., & Kellner, A. A controlled clinical trial of the efficacy of the hepatitis B vaccine (Heptavax B): A final report. *Hepatology*, 1982, **1**, 377–385.

Thacker, S. B., Simpson, S., Gordon, T. J., Wolfe, M., & Kimball, A. M. Parasitic disease control in residential facility for the mentally retarded. *American Journal of Public Health*, 1979, **69**, 1279–1281.

Thompson, N. J., Glassroth, J. L., Snider, D. E., & Farer, L. S. The booster phenomenon in serial tuberculin testing. *American Review of Respiratory Disease*, 1979, **119**, 587–597.

Toward eradication—A contemporary tuberculosis control strategy. *American Review of Respiratory Disease*, 1978, **118**, 641–644.

Tu, J. B. A survey of psychotropic medication in mental retardation facilities. *Journal of Clinical Psychiatry*, 1979, **40**, 125–128.

Tuberculosis in a nursing home—Oklahoma. *Morbidity and Mortality Weekly Report*, 1980, **29**, 465–467.

Welsch v. Dirkswager, 373, F. Supp. 487 (D. Minn. 1974), 550 F. Supp. 2d 1122 (8th Cir. 1977).

Wuori v. Zitnay, No. 75–80–5D (D. Maine, July 14, 1978), 4 MDLR35.

Yoeli, M., Most, H., Hammond, J., & Scheinesson, G. P. Parasitic infections in a closed society. *Transactions of Royal Society of Tropical Medicine and Hygiene*, 1972, **66**, 764–776.

Yoeli, M., & Scheinesson, G. P. Infections in residential institutions. In J. Wortis (Ed.), *Mental retardation and developmental disabilities: An annual review*. Vol. VIII. New York: Brunner/Mazel, 1976.

20 ETHICAL CONSIDERATIONS IN MEDICAL TREATMENT

Edward A. Sassaman

Over the past decade, there has been an explosion of ethical and legal decisions relating to mentally retarded citizens. Well meaning professionals have explored many of the personal aspects of the mentally retarded citizen's life in an attempt to better define and protect the rights of the incompetent. Although it would be historically interesting to review these statements as they relate to the growth of personal freedom for the mentally retarded, it is perhaps more appropriate to review two individual cases histories and analyze them as to how they affect larger populations. Those issues to be covered, the right of the mentally retarded adult to receive or refuse medical care and the right of the birth-deformed neonate to be treated, are among the most crucial relating to medical care. Other issues such as sterilization, equal access to medical care, and the quality of medical care, which are just as important, are not mentioned, since each would require a lengthy separate analysis. Rather, by closely examining only these two issues, the reader will be provided a more thorough understanding of some of the most fundamental ethical concepts relating to medical care for the mentally retarded.

Ethical Problems of the Terminally Ill

Case Study I

On April 19, 1976, Joseph Saikewicz, a 67-year-old profoundly mentally retarded man who had resided at Belchertown State School in Massachusetts for 48 years was diagnosed as having acute myeloblastic monocytic leukemia. One week later, William E. Jones, superintendent of Belchertown State School, and Paul R. Rogers, a staff attorney at the school, petitioned the Probate Court for Hampshire County for the appointment of both a legal guardian and a guardian ad litem for Mr. Saikewicz. A guardian ad litem was appointed by the judge on May 5th. The next day the guardian ad litem filed a report with the court stating that Mr. Saikewicz had an incurable illness. The report continued that although chemotherapy was the indicated medical treatment for this form of leukemia, the side effects from this treatment would be significant. Furthermore, if remission does occur with chemotherapy, it usually lasts less than one year. It was the recommendation of the guardian ad litem not to treat Mr. Saikewicz.

On May 13, 1976, a hearing was held in Probate Court for Hampshire County. The judge agreed with the guardian ad litem that the side effects of the recommended treatment for Mr. Saikewicz outweighed the small chance that he might benefit from such treatment. The judge based that decision on the fact that the negative considerations in treating Mr. Saikewicz (his age, his inability to cooperate with the treatment, the side effects of the treatment, the low chance of producing a remission, the suffering associated with the treatment, and the quality of Mr. Saikewicz's life) outweighed the positive considerations (the chance of lengthening his life, and the fact that most people choose treatment). The judge ordered that Mr. Saikewicz not be treated for his acute myeloblastic leukemia. The judge then referred the decision to the Massachusetts Appeals Court.

That Court issued its review on November 28, 1977. The Court (the decision was written by Justice Liacos) reaffirmed the basic doctrines of informed consent and the right of a patient to refuse medical treatment in certain cases. For an incompetent person, these rights may be asserted by a guardian.

The Court then maintained that the State has claimed interest in four areas: the preservation of life, the protection of innocent third parties, the prevention of suicide, and preserving the ethical integrity of physicians. Relating to these four areas, the Court continued that an individual has the right to decline medical treatment in a situation of incurable illness, and it is only by failing to allow that competent individual the right of such choice that the value of life is lessened. The Court felt that suicide and protection of innocent third parties were not relevant to this case. The Court concluded this part of the decision by maintaining that the doctrines of informed consent and the right to privacy are superior to any considerations preserving existing medical mores.

The next section of the Court opinion dealt with the joint issues of choice and decision making for an incompetent person. The Court recognized the right of all persons, competent and incompetent, to refuse medical treatment. Indeed, although, many courts in the past have argued that the medical treatment of an incompetent person facing a life-threatening danger is the proper course, to do so deprives the incompetent person of the rights enjoyed by others. Thus, the choice to accept or decline medical treatment is one to be enjoyed by all citizens. The problem of decision making, however, is the more difficult one. In reference to the Karen Ann Quinlan decision (In re Quinlan, 70 N.J. 10, 1976) written by Chief Justice Hughes of the New Jersey Supreme Court, Justice Liacos agreed that the principle of substituted judgment

in which one acts on behalf of the incompetent person is correct. In Karen Ann Quinlan's case, her father could perform that responsibility. Mr. Saikewicz was entitled to that same representation.

Thus, the Court determined that Mr. Saikewicz had the same right to choose between treatment and nontreatment as anyone else, but that since he could not exercise that right the probate court was within its jurisdiction in appointing a guardian ad litem to represent him.

Regarding the decision to withhold chemotherapy, the Court felt that the negative considerations outlined by the probate court did indeed outweigh the positive factors and that the guardian ad litem and the probate court judge were correct in their decision.

The final section of the judgement related to the procedures appropriate in deciding whether to provide care for an incompetent. The Court felt that it is well within the legal responsibility of the probate court to appoint a guardian and a guardian ad litem to protect the interests of an incompetent person. Moreover, it is the responsibility of the guardian ad litem to present to the judge all arguments in favor of and against the proposed treatment before the court could issue the appropriate decision. The Court differed with the New Jersey Supreme Court in deciding that rendering such decisions would be an "encroachment upon the medical profession's field of competence" and that it would be burdensome to the court system. Justice Liacos concluded by stating that life and death questions "require the process of detached but passionate investigation and decision that forms the ideal on which the judicial branch of government was created".

Mr. Saikewicz died of pneumonia on September 4, 1976, at Belchertown State School three months after diagnosis. He did not receive chemotherapy and he died 15 months before a final decision in his case was handed down.

Case Study II

On May 5, 1978, a case was argued in Probate Court of Massachusetts relating to a three-year-old child with acute lymphocytic leukemia (ALL). This form of leukemia, in contrast to the form that had afflicted Mr. Saikewicz, is highly treatable, with a better than 50% long-term survival rate. After the child was initially diagnosed as having ALL, he was started on chemotherapy. He quickly went into remission and seemed to be doing well. Soon thereafter, as part of routine blood studies, it was noted that the child was not responding as expected and that the leukemic cells had begun to appear again in the child's blood. The physicians, on questioning the child's parents, learned that they had stopped giving their son his medications and had begun using alternative treatments which they felt were less noxious to their son. They stated that they loved their son and felt that the treatment they were using was a more natural one. A compromise was reached between the parents and their child's doctors, in which both treatments were to be used. The parents were informed that the chances for a complete remission in their son, although lessened by the relapse, were still good if they adhered to the chemotherapeutic regimen. The child did well for a few months and then relapsed again. The parents admitted that they were not giving their son his chemotherapy. The case was referred to Probate Court by child welfare agencies, representatives of the physicians and their hospital, and legal counsel for the parents.

A decision was handed down on July 10, 1978, by the Superior Court of Massachusetts. Early in that decision the court stated that family autonomy is not absolute and can be limited where it appears that parental decisions might jeopardize the health or safety of their child. Furthermore, it is well within the power of the Superior Court to hear issues concerning medical care for children when such issues affect the child's very chances for survival. The Court continued that it has the power and responsibility to care for all persons who, by virtue of some legal disability, are unable to protect themselves. The Court did state that parents are the natural guardians of their children with the moral obligation to care for them. Parents must be protected from unwarranted state interference. This principle does not, however, grant parents life and death authority over their children. Rather, the Court felt that parental rights represented a trust to care for and protect their children. That trust was felt to be terminable upon any failure by the parents to discharge their responsibility to their children. The Court also reaffirmed the principle of substituted judgment and extended its applicability to children. Thus, the Court decided to remove the child from his parent's legal custody. The boy's parents, however, fled with their son to Mexico. He continued receiving nontraditional treatment for his leukemia for several months. At times, according to statements made by his parents, he also received more accepted methods of therapy. The boy died from complications of his disease while still in Mexico.

Thus, in these extremely important decisions the Massachusetts Superior Court ruled that an incompetent person is entitled to the same legal rights as a competent individual, that the quality of life has no bearing in determining what should be decided in a specific case, that the priniciple of substituted judgment

is a valid one in the broader context of using a guardian ad litem to represent incompetent people, and that all of these rights apply to those patients incompetent by reason of age as well as by reason of cognitive status.

Professional Response to Judicial Decisions

Within a few months of the Saikewicz decision, articles began appearing in the medical literature analyzing its effects. Among the first were two commentaries and a letter to the editor in *The New England Journal of Medicine*, perhaps the most prestigious medical journal in the country. The first article was written by William Curran (Curran, 1978a) a lawyer who writes the medical legal column for *The New England Journal of Medicine* and who is on the faculty of the Harvard Medical School. Curran pointed out that he agreed with the majority of the decision written by Justice Liacos. He continued that the Saikewicz decision is in the tradition of recent "enlightened jurisprudence." It is the requirement for use of a guardian ad litem with which Curran strongly disagreed. Curran stated that in his own opinion the Court did not realize how many cases would be affected by the Saikewicz decision and how the Probate Court could literally be flooded with requests for emergency hearings. Curran felt that the approach used in New Jersey in relationship to the Karen Ann Quinlan decision where a hospital "prognosis committee" composed of hospital and lay personnel who might advise the family and physician quickly about individual cases was a more appropriate method for dealing with these situations. In that same issue Arnold Relman (Relman, 1978a), senior editor of *The New England Journal of Medicine*, and Professor of Medicine at the Harvard Medical School, went even further in attacking the Saikewicz decision. Relman stated that traditionally physicians and families have made medical decisions in behalf of the incompetent. Relman conceded that this system may have led to some abuses, but, in his opinion, this system of joint decision is far better than any alternative. He believed that the Massachusetts Supreme Court had interfered in the patient-physician-family trust in taking care of dying patients. He continued that the decision had already disrupted medical care in Massachusetts and that physicians of terminally ill patients as of March, 1978, were unclear as to what treatment they should provide for their patients.

Two months later six letters to the editor were published in *The New England Journal of Medicine* about the Saikewicz decision. One article strongly supported the Supreme Court's decision, the others, including a reply from Mr. Curran, strongly opposed. Moreover, one of the letters opposing the Court decision was written by the most respected and senior pediatricians of the Department of Pediatrics of the Harvard Medical School (Avery, Janeway, Berenberg & Medearis; 1978). These doctors questioned whether physicians any longer were free to make decisions for their seriously ill patients. Mr. Curran (1978b) in his letter stated, "I suggest instead that Saikewicz is part of a broader contemporary phenomenon: an attempt by government and by many other elements in society to diminish the privileged status of medicine as a profession, to make it more open, more responsive to public need and, of course, less costly."

George Annas, Director of the Center for Law and Health Sciences at Boston University, answered most of these charges in two articles. In the first (Annas, 1978a), he reviewed the Saikewicz decision. He stated that (according to the court) the incompetent person has the same right to decline medical services as does the competent person. He continued that the Court stressed it is the responsibility of the state to prove that it should override an individual's decision to refuse treatment. In Annas' opinion, however, the most important parts of the Saikewicz decision related to the issue of substituted judgment. The Saikewicz decision, unlike the Quinlan decision, maintained that it would be unfair to determine what the majority of people would do in a certain situation and then force the incompetent to abide by that judgment. If that were the case then Saikewicz would have had to be treated for his leukemia since most adults elect to be treated. Rather, the Saikewicz Court rejected the objective reasonable person standard upheld by the Quinlan Court. Instead, Justice Liacos, writing for the majority, felt that Joseph Saikewicz should be treated as an individual with the goal being to try to determine what Saikewicz himself would have decided if he were competent. That is the doctrine of *substituted judgment*. The entire issue of quality of life according to Justice Liacos, as interpreted by Annas, never had any place in this decision. In Annas' opinion, the thorniest issue of the entire Saikewicz decision was implementation of the principle of substituted judgment. Here, too, Justice Liacos disagreed with the Quinlan decision. The New Jersey Supreme Court maintained that applying to a court to decide these issues would represent not only an infringement on the medical profession but also would be too time-consuming. Justice Liacos, however, felt that questions as important as life-prolonging treatment for the incompetent could best be decided by the judiciary. He stated that "achieving this ideal is the responsibility of the lower court, and is not to be entrusted to any group purporting to represent the 'morality and conscience of our society,' no matter how highly motivated or impressively constituted."

Annas anticipated the furor this might cause in the medical community. He stated, however, that it was the Court's opinion that only judges could decide cases such as Saikewicz with legal immunity and that, furthermore, ethics committees were to be used as advisors, not decision makers. Annas concluded this article by maintaining that the judiciary was the best means to ensure the rights of the incompetent.

Within four months, parts of the medical community in Massachusetts were arguing that their ability to care for their patients had been interfered with by the Saikewicz decision. Annas, in a follow-up article (Annas, 1978b), reviewed the six cases that had been referred to the probate court. He found that of the six only one was of the type that the Supreme Judicial Court had previously defined as appropriate. It was obvious that no flood of cases had occurred. In fact, according to Annas, much of the anger of the medical community derived from their fear of litigation for not obtaining court approval prior to terminating life support on a terminally ill incompetent patient. In Annas' opinion, this is a nonexistent risk, since there has never been a criminal indictment in Massachusetts for discontinuing treatment of a terminally ill adult. To argue immunity from prosecution and civil suit for physicians in Saikewicz-type cases (as the Massachusetts Medical Society and Massachusetts Hospital Association did) is to grant physicians "unreviewable life-and-death decision-making authority to a group of individuals who are afraid to take responsibility for their decisions."

Charles Baron (1978), Professor of Law at Boston College Law School, felt that the Saikewicz decision did not go far enough. It was his feeling that in the Saikewicz case the guardian ad litem did not forcefully defend Saikewicz's right to treatment. Baron advocated that it is the responsibility of the guardian ad litem to oppose whatever petition is presented to the Court. Thus, Baron maintained that the guardian ad litem in the Saikewicz case did not protect the legal and moral rights of his charge.

Relman (1978b) was the next to write a major article on the Saikewicz decision. This article again went over the same basic arguments in favor of the Quinlan decision and against the Saikewicz decision. Relman did concede that the statements in the Saikewicz case granting the incompetent the same rights as the competent, and favorably formalizing the traditional medical view not to use extraordinary means to prolong life where there was unquestionably no hope for recovery were both welcome. Relman then went on to discuss the case of Shirley Dinnerstein (Dinnerstein, 1978). Dinnerstein was a woman dying of Alzheimer's Disease, an incurable progressively deteriorating neurologic condition. In this decision, the Massachusetts Appeals Court ruled that in the case of a dying woman with no hope of cure, prior judicial approval was not required to withhold life-saving support systems. Relman viewed this as a useful clarification of the Saikewicz decision, but only a partial clarification. He went on to say that in the newborn nursery life-and-death decisions about keeping alive defective infants are made by physicians every day with the help of parents. Indeed, Relman maintained that most physicians would advise against providing life support to severely defective newborns, but that physicians should always defer to parents' wishes. It was Relman's feeling that in cases where family and physicians agree as to what should be done and where that decision is in conformity with high professional standards involvement of the judiciary would actually interfere with medical care. Relman concluded that a peer review system of objective professional colleagues would certainly be preferable to any judicial format.

In another follow-up article, Annas (1979) tried to reconcile his and Relman's positions. Annas stated that there were many similarities between the two decisions. Both the Quinlan Court and the Saikewicz Court held that the incompetent had the same right to refuse treatment and the same right to avoid bodily invasion as the competent. Both Courts used the principle of substituted judgment to help make a decision. The Quinlan Court gave this power to Karen Ann's family. The Saikewicz Court reserved this decision for itself. There were, however, a few basic differences as pointed out by Annas. The medical community in Karen Ann Quinlan's case was agreed that withholding treatment was the proper approach. Physicians, however, feared civil and criminal liability and therefore desired a mechanism by which they might be granted immunity. Thus, the Quinlan Court resorted to prognosis committees. The Saikewicz Court, however, did not have a question of medical prognosis, but rather whether an accepted medical treatment should be used on an incompetent individual. The Court felt that this was a legal decision and such a decision could be delegated to a nonjudicial body. Therefore, in Annas' opinion, the two decisions were not irreconcilable but rather complementary since each pertained to a different legal principle.

Thus, by looking at both Quinlan and Saikewicz cases, one is left with some basic truths and some disturbing questions relating to the rights of the incompetent to medical care. Both the New Jersey Supreme Court and the Massachusetts Superior Court agree that the incompetent is entitled to the same medical care as everyone else. Both Courts also agree that the quality of life concept should never enter into any decisions relating to medical care for the incompetent. The Courts differ, however, as to how those decisions can be made. The Massachusetts Court uses the principle of substituted judgment through a guardian ad litem procedure as decided by the judiciary. The New Jersey Court relies heavily on the use of recommendations made by ethics (prognosis) committees composed of professional and lay people.

Discussion

To understand better how each decision works, it would perhaps be appropriate now to see how each would view the same hypothetical case. Let us suppose that a six-year-old mildly mentally retarded boy with Down syndrome living in a state-run residential facility has severe congenital heart disease and is in need of cardiac surgery. With surgery (which has about a 20% mortality risk), the boy has the chance for a longer life. Without surgery, the child would die within a few years. Both Courts would say that the issue of mental retardation should not enter into the decision (although both Courts were influenced by this very issue since the Massachusetts Court said Saikewicz could not cooperate with treatment since he was retarded, and the New Jersey Court said Quinlan would never have wanted to live as a profoundly retarded woman). The New Jersey Court would rely heavily on medical evidence that the child would die without surgery and probably would survive the operation. The Massachusetts Court would say that the child would die without treatment and, therefore, would have to have surgery since the associated risks were low. Thus, both Courts would probably reach a common decision. Now let us change just one thing. Let us say that even with surgery the child's chances for survival for more than two or three years were minimal. The Massachusetts Court would probably say that the child would not survive anyway and therefore should be allowed to die with dignity (a similar case and decision were in fact just reached by the Massachusetts Superior Court). The New Jersey Court might reach a similar decision. Again it would be based primarily on medical recommendations and there could be no way of saying beforehand what those recommendations would be. Some physicians might say that no matter what happens, the child should be treated, whereas others might argue that to subject the child to heroic treatment would be unfair. There does exist some question as to how a court might apply the Quinlan decision in an individual case.

It is, however, irresponsible of physicians to say that the Saikewicz decision has provided guidelines by which to work in difficult moral situations.

Ethical Problems in the Newborn Nursery

Having analyzed some of the issues involved in treating the terminally ill developmentally disabled adult, it is now appropriate to focus on another morally perplexing area, the neonatal nursery.

In a fascinating review of English and American law, Catherine Damme (1978) reviewed the attitudes of English and American Courts toward infanticide. Although infanticide was a prevalent practice in medieval England, it was not until 1237 A.D. that it was elevated from a minor to major sin with punishment to be determined solely by the Church. Furthermore, the murder of a malformed infant was not even considered by the Church as a sin. During the second half of the sixteenth century, however, English courts began prosecuting those few found guilty of infanticide. In 1623, the English Parliament passed an act preventing the murder of illegitimate children. The act also reversed previous common law practice that a dead newborn was considered stillborn until proven otherwise. The Act remained in force until 1803, when the previous common-law practice of presuming a dead infant stillborn was re-instituted. In 1864, the Crown Prosecutor began refusing to ask for the death penalty for proven infanticide. The last execution for infanticide in England was in 1849. With the passage of the Infanticide Act of 1938, prison sentences became mandated. Even so, by 1965, according to Damme, of those women found guilty of infanticide only 1.3% were in prison. The rest were on probation or institutionalized in psychiatric units. American legal practices concerning infanticide derive partly from English law and partly from the American Constitution reserving for the states all rights not delegated to the federal government. The landmark Roe v. Wade decision in 1973 established the wishes and the health of the mother as pre-eminent to those of the fetus. Furthermore, although no state differentiates between homicide and infanticide, the dearth of trials in American legal history for deaths of infants brings into question, according to Damme, the issue of equality under the law.

In 1977, a report was presented to the Anglican Church in Canada dealing with death and dying. Part of that report (Walmsley, 1978) stated that infants "with severe neurological defects may not be 'human'

as defined earlier in this paper and it is a fundamental error to treat it as human." The Church did not accept this report. Walmsley in his review of the events surrounding this episode stated that many were "stunned" that such a report and recommendations could even have been written. Walmsley concluded that in his opinion society could never objectively measure humanness. Every child by definition is human even if we do not like its appearance or lack of cognitive skills. He continued, "we must stop the meaningless and pointless play on words, the excusing of ourselves because we feel guilt, inadequacy, embarrassment or that advantage may be taken of us. A creature is a human being who is the product of the union of a man and woman, is conceived by woman and born of woman."

Three groups of physicians detailed in a series of articles how their institutions dealt with this problem of the birth deformed newborn (Duff & Campbell, 1979; McLaughlin & Shurtleff, 1979; Stahlman, 1979).

Duff and Campbell using the newborn infant with spina bifida as an example, showed how the philosophy in treating these children had changed from that of a nonintervention in the 1950s to aggressive medical care in the 1960s and then to a more selective approach in the 1970s. It was their recommendation that since parents must live with any decisions made, it is the parents who ultimately must make all decisions. It is the role of health professionals to provide parents with the information necessary to make an intelligent decision. Duff and Campbell admit, however, that physicians can influence decisions "by limiting or controlling the information made available to patients or families."

Stahlman stated that in her hospital all live-born infants are resuscitated. "The severely malformed infant at birth creates a special dilemma, since the possibility of intact salvage may not easily be decided on the spot. If the deformity is not immediately life threatening, which means if the infant will survive despite benign neglect and he is likely to suffer further damage, I have no alternative but to resuscitate for a reasonable length of time." Stahlman continued, "I believe that most decisions must be made by the physician, with discussion, consultation, and understanding of all personnel involved in the patient's care, especially the nurse to whom the details of daily care are entrusted and with whom we share our medical responsibility. The parents should be fully informed as to the alternatives open, with the best alternative, in our opinion, presented as a plan of action for their approval. The burden of decision making and of personal guilt in the death of their child can, therefore, be relieved."

Finally, McLaughlin and Shurtleff described how they care for newborns with spina bifida. They state how they "defer to the desires of parents for aggressive treatment," despite even a poor prognosis. Indeed, the authors admit that they have learned a great deal from those particular cases since it helps to prove that each child and family is unique despite what might appear to be very similar circumstances. The authors show that almost 50% of infants with spina bifida who are untreated still survive despite nonaggressive care.

In an attempt to define a rational approach to this ethical dilemma, MacMillan (1978) proposed a standard for caring with deformed infants. The current standard for decision making, according to MacMillan, is the "best interests of the child." Although such a policy can be influenced by those defining it, it does conform to the practice that all men are equal and that parental or societal wishes are not superior to those of the infant. Such a standard could in some instances where further medical treatments were hopeless (as in a widely disseminated tumor with no hope of cure or even amelioration) lead to a decision to protect an infant's right to not receive therapy. The same right is granted to competent adults. Furthermore, according to MacMillan, when professionals disagree as to the right therapy, parents should be absolved of any responsibility for a nontreatment decision. Moreover, if parents could not afford the care needed for their child or if the available medical care could not benefit the child, then that care would be described "as an impossible duty." And if that care would be more than society could expect or would be of doubtful benefit, then a nontreatment decision would not be inappropriate. Thus, in a legal situation unless the prosecution could prove that treatment was going to succeed, a parental decision for nontreatment should not be culpable. Other standards used to justify nontreatment decisions, according to MacMillan, are based on the quality of life left to a severely deformed newborn. MacMillan rightly pointed out, however, that a quality-of-life standard implies that some lives are worth more than others. This principle is contrary to the whole legal system. What MacMillan proposed instead is the medical feasibility standard: if it is futile, then it can be withheld. The process for this medical feasibility decision would be simple. The infant's physician would have the responsibility to diagnose the defect and determine whether medical care was feasible. If the physician decided that treatment was not feasible, the parents would become the primary decision makers. If the parents determined that they wanted their child treated, that decision would be final. If the parents concurred with the physician's recommendation for nontreatment, a judicial hearing where the court could review the nontreatment decision would be in order. The court would determine whether treatment of the infant's condition were feasible and whether the proper decisional roles have been followed. In such a manner the rights of infant, the parents and society would be guarded.

Conclusion

It appears evident that the medical community on the whole is opposed to much of the new legislation protecting the rights of the incompetent. It is not so much that physicians are opposed to equal care for and rights of the diabled or even to equal access to medical care. It is more that physicians resent having to share the decision making roles with the courts. In both extremes of life as shown in this report (the right to die as analyzed by the Saikewicz and Quinlan cases, and the rights of the newborn as shown in the articles reviewed), most physicians feel that any form of judicial review is an infringement upon their right to practice medicine in the best possible manner. Some lawyers and judges, on the other hand, feel that physicians for too long have made arbitrary decisions for the patients, avoiding some of the ethical issues implicit in that decision making process. Both sides share in the truth. Medical decisions frequently cannot be deferred. They must be made within a matter of hours. Unless the judiciary can respond rapidly to requests from families and doctors its helpfulness is questionable at best. But in those cases where decisions can be deferred, physicians have the responsibility to address the ethical considerations involved in their decisions. Hospital prognosis committees can be helpful investigating alternative treatments or pointing out moral correlates of proposed approaches. They are not there to share responsibility or blame. Medicine is not treatment by committee. Yet, can morality be legislated? The Saikewicz Court said that the quality of Saikewicz's life did not enter into their decision. But in part they based their decision on Saikewicz's inability to understand or cooperate with the needed therapy.

Ultimately, there is only the hope that professionals, medical and legal, will be able to work out some solution protecting the rights of those unable to decide for themselves, while preserving the dignity of all citizens.

References

Annas, G. J. The incompetent's right to die: The case of Joseph Saikewicz. *The Hastings Center Report*, 1978, 8, 21–23.(a)

Annas, G. J. After Saikewicz: No-fault death. *The Hastings Center Report*, 1978, **8**, 10–18.(b)

Annas, G. J. Reconciling Quinlan and Saikewicz: Decision making for the terminally ill incompetent. *American Journal of Law and Medicine*, 1979, **4**, 367–396.

Avery, M. E., Janeway, C. A., Berenberg, W., & Medearis, D. N. The Saikewicz decision. *New England Journal of Medicine*, 1978, **298**, 1208–1209.

Baron, C. H. Assuring "detached but passionate investigation and decision": The role of guardians ad litem in Saikewicz-type cases. *American Journal of Law and Medicine*, 1978, **4**, 112–130.

Curran, W. J. Law-medicine notes. The Saikewicz decision, *New England Journal of Medicine*. 1978, **289**, 499–500.(a)

Curran, W. J. The Saikewicz decision. *New England Journal of Medicine*. 1978, **289**, 1209.(b)

Custody of a Minor. *Northeast Reporter*, 1978, **379** (2nd series), 1053–67.

Damme, C. Infanticide: The worth of an infant under law. *Medical History*, 1978, **22**, 1–25.

In the Matter of Shirley Dinnerstein, 1978, *Mass. App. Adv. Sh.*, 736.

Duff, R. S., & Campbell, A. G. M. Moral and ethical dilemmas in the special-care nursery. *New England Journal of Medicine*, 1979, **289**, 890–894.

MacMillan, E. S. Birth-defective infants: A standard for nontreatment decisions. *Stanford Law Review*, 1978, **30**, 599–633.

McLaughlin, J. F. and Shurtleff, D. B. Management of the newborn with myelodysplasia. *Clinical Pediatrics*, 1979, **18**, 463–476.

Relman, A. S. The Saikewicz decision: Judges as physicians. *New England Journal of Medicine*, 1978, **298**, 508–529.(a)

Relman, A. S. The Saikewicz decision: A medical viewpoint. *American Journal of Law and Medicine*, 1978, **4**, 233–242.(b)

Stahlman, M. J. Ethical dilemmas in perinatal medicine. *Journal of Pediatrics*, 1979, **94**, 516–520.

Superintendent of Belchertown State School et al v. Joseph Saikewicz. *1977 Mass. Adv. S1*. 2401, 1977, 370 N.E., 2d 417.

Walmsley, S. A. A life and death issue. *Mental Retardation*, 1978, **16**, 387–389.

PART VI
TREATMENT APPROACHES

21 PHARMACOLOGICAL INTERVENTION*

Michael G. Aman and Nirbhay N. Singh

R ecent years have witnessed a great deal of interest regarding the use of psychoactive drugs in mental retardation. For reasons that will become clear later in this chapter, both medical and nonmedical professionals in the field have taken an active role in evaluating the degree of drug usage as well as the effects of these agents. Unfortunately, there were few published surveys of drug prescription in retarded persons before the 1970's, so that the patterns of utilization before that time are to some extent a matter of conjecture.

In large part, drug prescription patterns in mental retardation appear to have paralleled those in adult psychiatry. There have been notable exceptions, such as in the 1940's and 1950's when a number of researchers were exploring the possible utility of glutamic acid for enhancing intellectual performance. However, psychotropic drug prescription in mentally retarded people received a great impetus in the late 1950's, following the introduction of chlorpromazine (Largactil, Thorazine), which was synthetically produced and found to have value in treating psychotic behavior

in nonretarded persons. Since that time, it has been common to see drugs employed in this field shortly after their introduction for treating various types of psychiatric disorders.

This chapter will first assess the patterns of usage of psychoactive drugs in mentally retarded persons. Because these drugs are used in large part to suppress maladaptive behaviors, the most common types of behavior problems in mentally retarded people will then be surveyed. This will be followed by a discussion of the major drug categories, with particular emphasis on behavioral and cognitive effects. Following the drug survey, major issues in need of further study will be explored.

For the purposes of this chapter, *psychotropic drug* will refer to any substance that is prescribed for the purpose of causing cognitive, behavioral, or emotional changes. *Psychoactive drug* will be used in a broader sense to refer to any agent that causes such changes, irrespective of the intention for prescribing such a drug.

Prevalence of Psychoactive Drug Use

Recently, there have been several surveys of psychoactive drug prescription in institutions for retarded persons (see Table 21.1). The prevalence of psychotropic medication has been found to range from a

* This work was supported in part by a grant from the Medical Research Council of New Zealand. The authors wish to thank Denise Reynolds for her meticulous typing and practical assistance. We also thank Marsha Aman and Judy Singh for their support above and beyond the call of duty.

Table 21.1. Prevalence of Drug Treatment in the Mentally Retarded

AUTHORS	NUMBER OF PATIENTS SURVEYED	PERCENTAGE RECEIVING PSYCHOTROPIC MEDICATION	PERCENTAGE RECEIVING ANTICONVULSANT DRUGS	TOTAL PERCENTAGE	MOST COMMON DRUGS PRESCRIBED
Lipman, 1970	Residents of 109 institutions	51*	?	?	Thioridazine, chlorpromazine, trifluoperazine, diazepam, chlordiazepoxide
Spencer, 1974	585	22+ (only antipsychotics surveyed)	24	51+	Phenobarbitone, haloperidol, chlorpromazine, phenytoin, thioridazine
Bullmore (in Kirman, 1975)	617	?	27	60	NR
Sewell & Werry, 1976	254	40	NR	NR	Thioridazine, chlorpromazine, methotrimeprazine, nitrazepam
Cohen & Sprague, 1977	1,924	51	36	66	Thioridazine, phenytoin, phenobarbital, diazepam, primadone, mesoridazine
Hughes, 1977	219	NR	NR	68	Phenobarbital, phenytoin, diazepam (usually as an anticonvulsant), chlorpromazine, thioridazine, haloperidol
Pulman, Pook, & Singh, 1979	435	47	34	60	Phenytoin, diazepam, carbamazepine, trimeprazine, haloperidol, phenobarbitone, promethazine
Silva, 1979	260	?	24	66	Phenytoin, phenobarbital, thioridazine, hydroxyzine, primadone
Tu, 1979	2,238	42	27	58	Thioridazine, chlorpromazine, mesoridazine, diazepam, thioxanthene
Jonas, 1980	596	?	?	70	Chloral hydrate, carbamazepine, thioridazine, diazepam, haloperidol, phenytoin, sodium valproate
Gadow & Kalachnik, 1981	3,306 TMR pupils	7	12	18	Phenytoin, phenobarbital, methylphenidate, primadone, thioridazine, diazepam
Davis, Cullari & Breuning, in press	3,496 residents of community group homes	58 (antipsychotics only)	46	74	Thioridazine, phenytoin, phenobarbital, chlorpromazine, diazepam, haloperidol

NR, not reported. Since there is overlap (some patients received both psychotropic and anticonvulsant drugs), the two component percentages will not necessarily equal the total percentage.

* This figure may represent an overestimate of drug incidence, since the survey asked how many patients had been, or were currently being, treated with psychotropic medication.

low of 22% (which included only antipsychotic drugs) (Spencer, 1974) to a high of 51% (Cohen & Sprague, 1977; Lipman, 1970). As a group, these surveys suggest that between 40 and 50% of institutional residents can be expected to be receiving psychotropic medication at any given time. The most commonly used psychotropic drugs appear to be thioridazine (Mellaril), chlorpromazine (Largactil, Thorazine), diazepam (Valium), and haloperidol (Haldol, Serenace). Anticonvulsant drug usage has also been summarized in Table 21.1, because there is increasing recognition in this and related fields that these drugs may have important effects on behavior and cognition. The prevalence of antiepileptic drugs in institutions was found to range from 24 to 36%. The most frequently reported anticonvulsant drugs were phenytoin (Dilantin), phenobarbital (Luminal), and primadone (Mysoline). When the total prevalence of psychoactive drugs is examined, it is seen to range from 51% to a high of 68%. These figures are remarkably high and they indicate that psychoactive drugs comprise a prevalent form of treatment in mental retardation, although, as we shall see later, there is substantial controversy as to whether certain drugs have much in the way of therapeutic value.

The writers know of only two surveys of drug prescription practices in noninstitutionalized retarded people. Gadow and Kalachnik (1981) carried out a study of 3,306 trainable mentally retarded children and adolescents attending special classes in public schools. They found that 12% were receiving anticonvulsant medication and a further 7% were receiving psychotropic drugs to render a total prevalence rate of 18%. Unlike the surveys mentioned above, the pattern for psychotropic drugs differed in this study, the stimulants being reported as the most commonly used behavior modifying drug. Davis, Cullari, and Breuning (in press) surveyed prescription practices in 3,496 mentally retarded persons residing in community foster homes and group homes. They found that 58% of this group were receiving antipsychotic drug treatment, whereas 46% were administered anticonvulsant drugs. This resulted in a combined total of 74% of these residents receiving psychoactive medication. The disparities between the surveys by Gadow and Kalachnik (1981) and by Davis et al. (in press) can probably be accounted for by differences in age, degree of mental retardation, and the likelihood that more behaviorally disordered people may be found outside the nuclear home.

All of these surveys indicate that consistently large percentages of mentally retarded people receive psychoactive medication and, in fact, the mentally retarded are probably among the most medicated people in society. Given that these drugs may have pervasive effects on behavioral adjustment, learning performance, and physical health, it behooves all workers in this field to have at least a passing familiarity with the effects of psychoactive drugs as they are used in mental retardation.

Psychopathology of Mentally Retarded Persons

Because psychotropic drugs are usually prescribed to suppress maladaptive and nonconforming behavior, it would be instructive to take a brief look at the most commonly occurring types of psychopathology in mental retardation. Unfortunately, there is a paucity of systematic information on both the prevalence and specific etiology of behavior problems in this population. What little is known has been derived mainly from studies of persons from institutions or psychiatric clinics, where the proportion of disturbed persons is relatively high. As such, these findings are not directly applicable to the field as a whole.

In a large-scale study, Payne, Johnson, and Abelson (1969, in Gadow, 1979) found hyperactivity, aggression, running, and self-destruction to be the most common problem behaviors in a sample of over 24,000 institutionalized residents. Some form of antisocial behavior (e.g., fighting, destructive and disruptive behavior, stealing, lying, screaming) was reported as occurring at least once a month among 27% of all institutionalized mentally retarded persons in California (Ross, 1972). In a study of 100 consecutive referrals of mentally retarded children to a child psychiatric clinic, Phillips and Williams (1975) found 38 to have psychotic symptoms and 49 to have nonpsychotic disorders. Aggression, inappropriate social relations, and "neurotic" traits were found to be the most commonly occurring behavior problems.

Behavior problems are often a crucial factor leading to institutionalization, with the result that institutions are heavily attended by behaviorally disordered residents. The more severely and profoundly retarded residents often show little interest in their environment and most can be seen exhibiting some form of self-stimulatory or self-injurious behavior. Two out of every three residents in large institutions engage in self-stimulatory behavior (Berkson & Davenport, 1962), from 5 to 23% in self-injurious behavior (Singh, 1982), and about 6% in ruminative vomiting (Singh, 1981). Furthermore, a large number of these residents display aggressive and destructive behaviors (e.g., fighting, window breaking, clothes tearing, food throwing) serious enough to require some form of therapy.

The behavior problems of those living in the community are generally not as severe or debilitating as of those who have been institutionalized. In general, the mild and moderately retarded are thought to suffer from such problems as low frustration tolerance, hyperactivity, aggression, and general problems of motivation (Baroff, 1974). However, antisocial behaviors are quite common in these populations and, as noted by Mulick and Schroeder (1980), inadequate management of such behavior in the community may result in eventual institutionalization.

The psychiatric aspects of mental retardation have been adequately presented by Menolascino (1970, 1976) and Matson & Barrett (1982). The incidence of depressive illness is fairly low, with at least four studies estimating it to be below 1.5% (Gardner, 1967). Problems in assessing depression increase in direct proportion to the degree of mental retardation of the client. It has been suggested that children with mild-to-moderate degrees of mental retardation often get depressed because of their feelings of inadequacy and hopelessness when faced with rejection by their normal peers and elders (Glaser, 1967).

Survey of Psychoactive Drug Effects

Other Reviews

Owing to limitations of space, the review of drug effects in this chapter will be very brief. The interested reader is strongly urged to consult other surveys of psychoactive drug effects in mental retardation. Recent years have witnessed a number of excellent papers. Freeman (1970) conducted a thorough and detailed summary, and Sprague and Werry (1971) carried out a review from a rigorous methodological stance that was to prove very influential in this field. More up-to-date analyses have appeared by Aman (in press, a), Breuning, Davis, and Poling (in press), and Lipman, DiMascio, Reatig, and Kirson (1978). Sprague and Baxley (1978) and Ferguson and Breuning (in press) have recently completed chapters highlighting social issues. Schain's (1979) review is one of the few which is devoted exclusively to anticonvulsant drug effects in the mentally retarded. Finally, there are two papers dealing with drugs and learning in mentally retarded persons. That by Wolfensberger and Menolascino (1968) discusses important theoretical issues whereas that by Aman (in press, b) presents a comprehensive summary of empirical data.

Methodological Considerations

In order to arrive at scientifically interpretable results, drug studies must meet a number of design criteria, some of which are unique to drug research. Sprague and Werry (1971) have enumerated several principles that they regard as minimal standards for assessing the effects of psychoactive drugs. These include the use of suitable control groups, random assignment of subjects to treatments, the provision of placebo and blind evaluations to minimize bias, standardized measures of drug effect, adequate statistical analysis, and use of standardized doses. With the possible exception of the last standard, these are widely acknowledged today as necessary components of a controlled study of behavior modifying drugs. Aman and Singh (1980) added the further recommendation that other contemporaneous drug treatments be discontinued, so that the effects of the drug under study are not confounded. This has been a common problem, particularly in older investigations where patients under study often received several medications. It has also been suggested that drug treatment should regularly be compared with some alternative therapy (Sprague & Baxley, 1978) and that assessments of neuroleptic drug effects, when this follows drug discontinuation, should be maintained for at least 12 to 16 weeks (Breuning, Davis, Matson, & Ferguson, 1982; Breuning, O'Neill, & Ferguson, 1980). All of the above design caveats have been violated regularly in earlier work in the field of mental retardation. However, there are signs that the field is entering a new phase now and that obvious blunders, such as the complete absence of drug controls, are encountered far less often.

Antipsychotics (Neuroleptics, Major Tranquilizers)

INTRODUCTION

Antipsychotics are the most frequently prescribed medication in mental retardation, with recent surveys indicating that about 40 to 50% of institutionalized mentally retarded are receiving them at any given time (see Table 21.1). As already discussed, antipsychotic drug prevalence in community foster and group homes is somewhat similar, with one study reporting a figure of 58% (Davis, Cullari, & Breuning, in press). However their use among students attending special classes is substantially less (Gadow & Kalachnik, 1981). The antipsychotics include four major classes of compounds: phenothiazines (e.g., thioridazine, chlorpromazine), butyrophenones (e.g., haloperidol), thioxanthenes, and rauwolfia alkaloids, with the first two being the most widely used. The pharmacology of the antipsychotics has been adequately dealt with in several recent reviews (Breuning, Davis, & Poling, in press; Werry, in press; Winsberg & Yepes, 1978).

EFFECTS ON BEHAVIOR

The antipsychotics, mainly chlorpromazine, thioridazine, and haloperidol, are most frequently prescribed for aggressive, destructive, hyperactive, and antisocial behaviors in mentally retarded persons. Although a great deal of research has focused on the efficacy of antipsychotics in controlling such behaviors, there is still a dearth of well controlled studies from which firm conclusions can be drawn (see Aman, in press, a; Aman & Singh, 1980; Breuning, Davis & Poling, in press; Ferguson & Breuning, in press; Sprague & Werry, 1971).

Chlorpromazine (Largactil, Thorazine). Uncontrolled studies of chlorpromazine, reviewed by Sprague and Werry (1971), Freeman (1970), and Lipman, DeMascio, Reatig, and Kirson (1978), suggest that chlorpromazine produces a reduction in problem behaviors in mentally retarded children. However, the data from more recent and well-controlled studies (see Aman, in press, a; Breuning, Davis, & Poling, in press) challenge the earlier findings and suggest that chlorpromazine may actually worsen some appropriate behaviors (e.g., Marholin, Touchette, & Stewart, 1979; Moore, 1960) in some subjects. No general conclusions can be reached on the efficacy of chlorpromazine in controlling maladaptive behaviors in mentally retarded persons. Further research utilizing some degree of methodological sophistication is urgently needed.

Thioridazine (Mellaril). Aman and Singh (1980) conducted a comprehensive review of the effects of thioridazine in childhood disorders. Of 24 studies located, only six fulfilled the methodological criteria necessary for scientifically valid studies. In general, these studies tended to rely upon global impressions of change; surprisingly little was reported about the specific nature of drug induced changes. However, where specific changes were noted, they tended to appear as improvements in hyperactivity, aggression, eating behavior, and stereotypy.

Two recent studies suggest that this drug is useful, although in circumscribed ways, in mentally retarded subjects. Singh and Aman (1981) reported the reduction of self-stimulatory behavior, hyperactivity, and bizarre behavior in severely and profoundly retarded persons with a low (2.5 mg/kg) dose of thioridazine. Furthermore, they found that this dose was as effective in controlling stereotypy as were substantially higher doses individually determined by titration. In an extension of the Singh and Aman (1981) study, Breuning (in press) found that different doses were optimal for controlling different behaviors in patients who were known responders. It was found that while

a dose of 5.9 mg/kg was optimal in reducing aggressive behaviors, a dose of only 2.5 mg/kg was sufficient to reduce self-stimulatory behaviors. Higher doses led to more inappropriate behaviors, but had no additional effects on either aggression or stereotypy. The frequency of inappropriate behaviors increased in non-responders as the dose of thioridazine was increased. This study suggests that different classes of behavior may well respond to different doses of thioridazine and, further, that thioridazine only worsens the behaviors of non-responders.

On current evidence, it appears that thioridazine is more useful than chlorpromazine in altering some of the behaviors of mentally retarded persons. However, as discussed later, there are some potential costs with this medication (as in the case of all antipsychotics), even when the patients involved show drug induced improvements.

Haloperidol (Haldol, Serenace). Haloperidol has been used to control hyperactive, aggressive, hostile, and impulsive behaviors in mentally retarded persons (Sprague & Baxley, 1978). However, only a handful of studies have attempted to establish its efficacy in this regard. Unfortunately, most of these studies are methodologically unsophisticated and are from an earlier era of drug research when enthusiasm outweighed scientific rigor. In general, these studies suggest that haloperidol may be superior to the phenothiazines (Claghorn, 1972; Le Vann, 1971; Ucer & Kreger, 1969) and may be useful in reducing hyperactive, aggressive, and stereotyped behavior. However, such a conclusion is based on rather tenuous grounds and definitive conclusions must await further, more scientific, study.

Other Antipsychotics. Experimental evidence for the usefulness of other phenothiazines (e.g., mesoridazine, fluphenazine, peracetazine, and pericyazine), butyrophenones (e.g., pipaperone), and rauwolfia alkaloids is rather sparse and the literature has been reviewed by Aman (in press, a). Sprague and Baxley (1978) briefly review the use of thioxanthenes in the management of behavior problems in mentally retarded persons.

Antipsychotic Drugs and Stereotypic Behavior. Thus, much of the evidence attesting to the clinical value of antipsychotic drugs is rather weak. This may be partly because of the clinical variables that have been emphasized in the past. Researchers have generally looked at certain maladaptive behaviors such as hyperactivity, aggressiveness, destructiveness, and other acting-out behaviors to assess drug effects. However, recent well controlled studies indicating beneficial effects due to antipsychotics have reported a reduction in stereotypic behavior as *the major therapeutic effect* of antipsychotic drugs (e.g., Davis, Sprague, & Werry, 1969; Hollis, 1968; Singh & Aman, 1981; Zimmerman & Heistad, 1982). On the other hand, studies showing adverse or no drug effects (e.g., Breuning, Ferguson, Davidson, & Poling, in press; Breuning, O'Neill, & Ferguson, 1980; Marholin, Touchette, & Stewart, 1979; McConahey, Thompson, & Zimmerman, 1977) have tended to emphasize clinical measures other than stereotypy.

This suggests that the antipsychotics may have a more-or-less specific effect on this behavioral dimension and, furthermore, that other positive effects (when they occur) may be a byproduct of the individual engaging in less stereotypy. The finding that self-stimulatory behaviors are affected at much lower doses of thioridazine than are other classes of behavior (Breuning, in press) also supports this notion of a specific behavioral effect. This would suggest further that the patients most likely to respond beneficially to such medication would be those characterized by high levels of stereotypic behavior rather than by aggressiveness and other acting out behavior, as has traditionally been believed to be the case. However, this must be regarded as speculative and it is clear that further research, which examines subject characteristics as well as stereotypy and other measures of drug effect, is badly needed.

Effects on Behavior: Summary. It appears that antipsychotic drugs do suppress stereotypic behavior in some patients, and as a secondary consequence of this adaptive behaviors *may* be indirectly promoted. However, their effects on acting out behaviors such as aggressiveness, destructiveness, and hyperactivity are still the subject of debate.

EFFECTS ON COGNITIVE PERFORMANCE

Aman (in press, b) has reviewed the evidence pertaining to antipsychotic drug effects on intellectual level and achievement variables. It was found that as a group these studies lacked methodological rigor. Only three of the studies showed significant changes on learning indices, with two (Alexandris & Lundell, 1968; Bair & Herold, 1955) indicating improvement and one (Moore, 1960), worsening. It is noteworthy that the two studies suggesting improvement used very low doses of either chlorpromazine or thioridazine.

Some studies have suggested that antipsychotic drugs may be inimical to learning in children with normal IQ (Aman, 1978, in press, b). A recent study by Wysocki, Fuqua, Davis, and Breuning (1981) provides some evidence that this may also be the case in the mentally retarded. Wysocki et al. used a matching-to-sample task with a group of four mild/moderately retarded adults who were phased off their current medication (thioridazine) in a multiple baseline design. Their results showed that the limit of delay over which accurate performance could be maintained systematically increased with reduction in dosage. The conclusion drawn from these data is that thioridazine impeded learning in these subjects, possibly by interfering with attention or memory.

In a series of innovative studies, Breuning and his colleagues have investigated the interactive effects of antipsychotic drugs and the consequences of reinforcement. Breuning et al. (1980) evaluated the effects of antipsychotic drugs and a token economy program, used independently and in combination. Little or no difference between the drug and placebo conditions were noted in terms of altering inappropriate behavior. Of more interest, however, was the finding that the token economy program produced socially significant improvements but only in the absence of concomitant drug therapy. This prompted Breuning at al. to conclude that the antipsychotic drugs were interfering with the rehabilitative programs of these patients.

One way of increasing an individual's IQ score is by providing reinforcement contingent on the correct performance on each test item (Clingman & Fowler, 1976). Recent studies have shown, however, that no such increases are to be found when the subject is on some form of antipsychotic medication (Breuning & Davidson, 1981; Breuning et al., in press) and that such an effect may be noticed even at very low doses (Breuning, in press). Breuning et al. have suggested that medication impairs the subject's responding to external reinforcement. That is, antipsychotic drugs are said to interfere actively with the conditioning process and consequently reinforcement is believed to have a negligible impact on the test performance of these subjects.

Aman (in press, b) has raised two issues regarding these studies which need to be mentioned. First, the doses used were high and the impairments which were noted may not occur at moderate or low doses. Second, some subjects included in these studies were chosen because they were nonresponders (i.e., they showed a poor clinical response to medication). Further research is needed with lower doses and drug responders before we can unequivocally conclude that the antipsychotics render the effects of reinforcement negligible. Nevertheless, on current evidence, it does appear that higher doses of antipsychotics may impair learning performance in mentally retarded persons.

Antipsychotic agents may produce side effects that are wide ranging and often severe (see Charalampous & Keepers, 1978). These include the following: (1) Anticholinergic effects—dry mouth, constipation, urinary retention, blurred vision, meiosis, reduced gastric motility, mental confusion, and tachycardia. (2) Alpha adrenergic blockade—postural hypotension, mydriasis, and flushing of the skin. (3) Dopaminergic—acute dystonia, akathisia, and tardive dyskinesia (a drug-induced movement disorder). Other side effects include weight gain, photosensitivity (especially from chlorpromazine) and agranulocytosis during the first two months of treatment. Furthermore, alertness may decrease because of the nonspecific sedative nature of most antipsychotics. Further discussion of these side effects can be found in Breuning, Davis, and Poling (in press), Ferguson and Breuning (in press), and Werry (in press).

Anticonvulsant Drugs (Antiepileptics)

INTRODUCTION

Some readers may be surprised to see the anticonvulsant drugs featured in this chapter, regarding them instead as strictly "medical" agents, bereft of behavioral effects. However, there is growing recognition that anticonvulsants may be important to the behavioral adjustment of retarded persons for several reasons beyond the fact that they help to control seizures. First, they are regarded by some workers as having useful psychotropic properties in their own right and are sometimes prescribed specifically for this purpose. Second, a number of the antiepileptic drugs appear to have psychoactive effects, even when prescribed exclusively for seizure control. Third, some of these agents can cause toxic reactions which mimic symptoms of neurological disease and can be particularly difficult to identify in severely retarded persons. In addition, anticonvulsant drugs are prescribed to approximately 30% of institutionalized retarded persons (see Table 21.1), which parallels the estimated prevalence of epilepsy in this group (Jasper, Ward, & Pope, 1969; in Gadow, 1979). Furthermore, antiepileptic drugs are often administered for many years or even life-long (Reynolds, 1975). Consequently, even subtle effects on behavior must be regarded as important over such periods.

ANTICONVULSANT DRUGS AS PSYCHOTROPIC AGENTS

Anticonvulsant medication is, of course, most commonly prescribed for the suppression of seizures in epileptic patients. However, there are some workers who advocate the use of certain antiepileptic drugs for the control of behavior problems. In their survey, Davis et al. (in press) found that 19% of patients receiving anticonvulsant drugs had no documentation of either an EEG abnormality or a clinical seizure. Kaufman and Katz-Garris (1979) assessed the prescription of anticonvulsants on one ward of a state institution for the mentally retarded. Of 41 patients receiving such medication, 24 (59%) had no clinical evidence of a seizure disorder.

This prescription of antiepileptic medication in patients who apparently are not epileptic suggests that these drugs are being administered for their purported psychotropic effects. Much of the earliest work claiming a psychotropic action for the various anticonvulsant drugs was based on the belief that behavior disturbances in certain children were a manifestation of an underlying "subconvulsive" epileptic-like disorder. Many of the earlier studies evaluated phenytoin (Dilantin) and made exorbitant claims of psychotropic effectiveness, but these were usually uncontrolled studies or anecdotal reports (see Aman, in press, a; Conners & Werry, 1979; Stores, 1978). However, subsequent well controlled investigations (e.g., Conners, Kramer, Rothschild, Schwartz, & Stone, 1971; Looker & Conners, 1970) were unable to establish any benefit due to phenytoin.

More recently, carbamazepine (Tegretol) has been discussed as an anticonvulsant with useful psychotropic effects. Remschmidt (1976) has summarized 28 studies of the drug in nonepileptic children with behavior disorders. There was sufficient information to assess only 17 of 21 uncontrolled studies. Symptoms of hyperkinesis and aggressiveness were found to be improved in nine and five of the studies, respectively. However, of the seven well controlled studies, only three found evidence of significant improvement, usually expressed in terms of social adaptation, enhanced "drive," and promotion of purposeful activity. In his review of this drug, Stores (1978) noted that "Most favourable reports are based on uncontrolled studies of heterogeneous clinical groups with little effort made to measure particular aspects of behavior" (p. 296). Nevertheless, he tentatively concluded that carbamazepine may have beneficial effects on overactivity and aggression, although this requires confirmation.

There have been very few trials of antiepileptic drugs in mentally retarded patients to determine whether these drugs exert psychotropic effects. Goldberg and Kurland (1970) compared phenytoin to placebo in a group of mildly retarded boys. The results were equivocal with only one of numerous measures showing significant drug-related improvement, this being expressed as reduced distractibility. Reid, Naylor, and Kay (1981) evaluated carbamazepine in severely and profoundly retarded institutional residents. As determined by global impressions of each patient's most salient problem behaviors, carbamazepine failed to produce significant changes for the overall group.

In summary, there is very little evidence that phenytoin has useful psychotropic properties in its own right. There is more widespread enthusiasm for the use of carbamazepine in this respect, but where "psychotropic" effects have been observed this may have been due to improved suppression of seizures or concomitant withdrawal of other, sedative-type antiepileptic drugs (Dalby, 1975). Most other anticonvulsants have been studied far less in this regard and are equally unproven as psychotropic agents. Therefore, as argued elsewhere (Aman, in press, a, b; Conners & Werry, 1979; Stores, 1978) *these drugs should be administered only for a bona fide seizure disorder and should not be prescribed for behavior control.* We believe that their use for behavior control should be regarded as strictly experimental and unproven at this time.

UNINTENDED BEHAVIORAL EFFECTS (PSYCHOACTIVE EFFECTS)

Recent years have witnessed a growing concern that anticonvulsant drugs may cause untoward behavioral, cognitive, or motoric effects in patients receiving chronic pharmacotherapy for seizure disorders. Space does not allow for detailed examination of this evidence and the interested reader is referred to reviews by Aman (in press, a, b), Schain (1979), Stores (1975, 1978), Trimble (1979), and Trimble and Reynolds (1976).

In brief, the evidence suggests that phenobarbital, phenytoin, and primadone, when administered singly, may be associated with psychomotor deterioration, especially at higher drug concentrations. This has been assessed in a variety of ways, including IQ tests, specialized tests of learning and cognitive style, neuropsychological tests, retrospective clinical judgements, and rating-scale techniques. The evidence is mixed and some studies actually indicate improvement, especially at low doses. Studies of these drugs given in various combinations tend to be more damning and indicate a more consistent pattern of worsening. However, in these latter studies, it is difficult to disentangle drug effects from the possibility that the patients were suffering from a progressive neurological condition.

With respect to phenobarbital, one other point is relevant. It has long been noted that this drug (as well as primadone) may cause some children to become hyperactive (Ounsted, 1955; Schain, 1979). Wolf and Forsythe (1978) found that 42% of children treated with phenobarbital developed a behavior disturbance, as compared with 18% who received no treatment. Another study (Camfield, Chaplin, Doyle, Shapiro, Cummings, & Camfield, 1979) failed to observe hyperactivity as a result of phenobarbital treatment, but the criteria for detection of hyperactivity may have been so stringent as to preclude its occurrence. The tendency of phenobarbital to elicit hyperactive and aggressive behavior has been widely reported and workers should be vigilant for this reaction in mentally retarded patients so treated.

The research on carbamazepine (Tegretol) is more optimistic, with little or no evidence of drug-related deterioration in psychomotor functions. In fact, cognitive enhancement has been observed when patients have begun treatment with this drug. However, this may well reflect cessation of treatment with previous sedative types of medication (such as phenobarbital or primadone) rather than a direct psychoactive effect.

Most of the studies that have evaluated ethosuzimide (Zarontin) have been suggestive of cognitive improvement. This was probably due to control of absence (petit mal) seizures in some cases. If so, this would reflect the anticonvulsant properties of the drug rather than a true psychoactive effect. Most of the remaining anticonvulsant drugs have been poorly studied for their behavioral effects and little can be said with confidence about possible cognitive, behavioral, or motoric effects.

It is significant that phenobarbital, primadone, and phenytoin are thought to have adverse effects on behavior, as these are among the most commonly prescribed drugs in mentally retarded persons (Davis et al., in press; see Table 21.1). It is also important that the subjects in the above reports generally received moderate doses, which were regarded as within the therapeutic range. This area of investigation is still in its infancy and many of these studies were methodologically flawed. Nevertheless, they do suggest caution in the use of these drugs and indicate that the lowest clinically effective doses should be employed. Schain (1979) has suggested that, where possible, the sedative types of antiepileptic drugs should be avoided in favor of carbamazepine, which is often used for similar types of clinical conditions.

TOXIC EFFECTS

All drugs are capable of producing untoward effects, but the toxic effects of antiepileptic drugs may be particularly troublesome in the case of mentally retarded people. This is because the symptoms of intoxication (mental confusion, nystagmus, ataxia, lethargy, slurred speech) may be readily confused with the developmental disability of the person concerned.

There are a number of case reports that demonstrate that anticonvulsant drugs can have serious effects on both behavior and cognition. Cordes (1973) reported the case of a young girl who was placed on phenobarbital and assorted other drugs at the age of one year. Phenobarbital caused an apparent arrest of development with virtually no improvements in speech until all antiepileptic drugs were subsequently withdrawn at the age of 3½ years. From this period onward, there were regular increments in IQ, ranging from a low of 69 to a high of 108 at the age of 7 years. Vallarta, Bell, and Reichert (1974) described 10 patients in an institution for the mentally retarded who presented progressive neurological deterioration. Deterioration included neurological symptoms, an apparent reduction in IQ, and behavioral abnormalities. When phenytoin treatment was terminated, deterioration was arrested in all except one patient. Neurological symptomatology was actually reversed in six instances and intellectual decline was abated. Logan and Freeman (1969) reported four children with phenytoin toxicity. In each case, intoxication had previously gone undetected for one of the following reasons: (*a*) occurrence with relatively low doses, (*b*) confusion of toxic symptoms with coexisting neurological disease, and (*c*) absence of classical symptoms or difficulty in detecting them in small children.

These reports indicate the necessity for keeping doses to the absolute minimum required for clinical seizure control. There are at least two reports from institutions suggesting that toxic drug levels may be commonplace in institutionalized mentally retarded persons. Iivanainen, Viukari, Seppäläinen, and Helle (1978) carried out a survey of phenytoin toxicity in 127 mentally retarded epileptic residents. On the basis of clinical signs of toxicity or serum levels exceeding 25 µg/ml, they diagnosed phenytoin intoxication in 70 (55%) of the patients treated with this drug! Weiss, Heffelfinger, and Buchanan (1969) found that blood-level determinations exceeded the upper limit of the "therapeutic range" in four of nine residents surveyed. Probably owing to the degree of disability in these children, none of the usual side effects was detectable. Together, these two reports suggest that untoward effects due to antiepileptic drugs are easily missed in severely retarded people. Without determined and explicit probing for intoxication, it is probable that instances of excessive medication will go undetected.

Stimulant Drugs

HISTORY

In 1937, Charles Bradley first reported the value of stimulants in treating behavior problems in a diagnostically mixed group of children. Stimulant drugs were subsequently found to have a marked beneficial effect in many hyperactive children whose behavior is characterized by inattention, distractibility, excessive activity, conduct problems, and (frequently) specific learning problems. The most commonly used stimulant drugs are methylphenidate (Ritalin), dextroamphetamine (Dexedrine), and magnesium pemoline (Cylert), but other agents such as caffeine and deanol (Deaner) are sometimes claimed to have similar clinical effects (see Cantwell & Carlson, 1978). The most apparent clinical changes resulting from stimulant drugs in hyperactive children are reduced physical activity, improved attentiveness, and lessened distractibility, especially in structured situations such as the classroom.

Unlike many other psychotropic drugs which appear to cause CNS depression, the stimulants have been shown to enhance performance on a variety of cognitive functions in the short term. Stimulant related improvements have most consistently been demonstrated on tests of attention span, but enhancement in short-term memory, verbal learning, cognitive style, and visual and auditory discrimination have also frequently been reported (see reviews by Aman, 1978, 1980; Cantwell & Carlson, 1978; Douglas, 1974; Sroufe, 1975). However, studies of hyperactive children receiving long term stimulant medication have generally been unable to document any academic gains due to pharmacotherapy (Aman, 1978, 1980, 1982; Barkley & Cunningham, 1978; Rie, Rie, Stewart, & Ambuel, 1976a,b).

It has been maintained by some workers that the beneficial effects of cerebral stimulants are largely confined to children with symptoms of hyperactivity. However, investigators have recently evaluated dextroamphetamine and methylphenidate in psychiatrically normal children and adults (Rapoport, Buchsbaum, Zahn, Weingartner, Ludlow, & Mikkelson, 1978; Werry & Aman, in press). Both studies found reduced physical activity and improved learning performance similar to, although less dramatic than, changes found in hyperactive children. This suggests that stimulant drugs frequently have beneficial effects irrespective of diagnostic group.

STIMULANT DRUGS AND MENTAL RETARDATION

Stimulant medication is not commonly prescribed in

institutions for the mentally retarded. Surveys show that between 2 and 3% of residents are so treated (Cohen & Sprague, 1977; Lipman, 1970). This is perhaps surprising, because the behavior of many residents can be characterized as grossly overactive with inattention as a prominent feature and one might expect a therapeutic action similar to that found in hyperactive children. In fact, there have been a substantial number of studies of stimulant drugs in institutionalized mentally retarded persons (see reviews by Aman, in press, a,c; Lipman, DiMascio, Reatig, & Kirson, 1978; Sprague & Werry, 1971; Walker, in press). Behavioral indices have most frequently emphasized measures of overactivity, aggressiveness, and conformity toward activities (e.g., Alexandris & Lundell, 1968; McConell, Cromwell, Bialer, & Son, 1964), although some studies have also looked at self-stimulatory behaviors (e.g., Davis, Sprague, & Werry, 1969). These studies have produced results that are nearly uniformly negative, although there have been some isolated variables showing drug-related benefits.

Similarly, the stimulants do not appear appreciably to influence the learning performance of the mentally retarded, especially in severely retarded people (Aman, in press, b). In contrast to the research in hyperactivity, most of these studies failed to find any drug effects on learning variables, although a few investigators did document scattered areas of improvement. Two studies (Bell & Zubek, 1961; Lobb, 1968) actually demonstrated drug related worsening on learning tests. Lobb's (1968) study deserves special mention because it is probably the only one in which a classical conditioning task has been used to assess drug effects in the mentally retarded. It was found that amphetamine resulted in less successful conditioning and that a conditioned response persisted less in the subjects who had been conditioned under amphetamine.

In summary, the stimulants do not appear to produce beneficial behavioral or cognitive changes. This appears to be particularly the case in more severely retarded persons (Aman, in press, c). Elsewhere, it has been suggested that this generally poor response may be due to a characteristically narrow focus of attention in severely retarded persons which is confined further still by stimulant drugs (Aman, in press, c).

SIDE EFFECTS

The most frequent side effects of stimulant drugs are insomnia, decreased appetite, weight loss, abdominal pain, and headaches (see Cantwell & Carlson, 1978). Less common reactions include drowsiness, sadness, increased talkativeness, and dizziness. Dyskinetic episodes and toxic psychoses have been reported, but these are relatively rare. It has also been reported that chronic administration of methylphenidate and the amphetamines can cause depression of growth rate (Safer, Allen, & Barr, 1972) but more recent work has challenged this finding (Roche, Lipman, Overall, & Hung, 1979).

Antidepressant and Antimanic Drugs

The monoamine oxidase inhibitors (MAOI) and the tricyclic and quadricyclic antidepressants form the major subgroups of the antidepressant drugs. The pharmacology of the antidepressants has been dealt with by Breuning, Davis, and Poling (in press), Rapoport and Mikkelsen (1978) and Werry (in press). Antidepressants are infrequently used with the mentally retarded, with Lipman's (1970) survey showing the tricyclics as representing only 4% of psychotropic drug use in institutions.

According to Werry (in press), the MAO inhibitors are seldom, if ever used in pediatric psychopharmacology, mainly because of their dangerous side effects (also see Breuning, Davis, & Poling, in press). Only a few studies, all completed before the mid-1960's (Carter, 1960; Davies, 1961; Heaton-Ward, 1962), have examined their efficacy with mentally retarded persons. The methodologically sound studies report negative results.

While the tricyclic group of antidepressants (imipramine, desipramine, amitriptyline, and nortriptyline) has replaced the MAO inhibitors, the research with tricyclics is also rather limited and dated. Imipramine has been used the most (Bender & Fareta, 1961; Drew, 1967; Fisher, Murray, Walley, & Kiloh, 1963; Pilkington, 1962), but no new studies have been published since 1967. As with children of normal IQs, imipramine is most commonly prescribed for enuresis in mentally retarded persons. While any curative effect of the tricyclics is extremely doubtful, their symptomatic effect appears to be well established (Blackwell & Currah, 1973). Amitriptyline and nortriptyline have been investigated in four studies (Carter, 1966; Drew, 1967; Kraft, Ardali, Duffy, Hart, & Pearce, 1966; Smith & Gonzalez, 1967), but no general conclusions can be drawn from such a limited sample of methodologically weak investigations. The same is generally true of the entire class of antidepressant drugs in the pharmacotherapy of the mentally retarded.

Lithium carbonate is the only important antimanic drug that has received some attention in the treatment of behavioral disorders in mentally retarded persons. The pharmacology of lithium carbonate has been documented in several excellent reviews (e.g., Gerbino, Oleshansky, & Gershon, 1978; Johnson, 1979; Rapoport, Mikkelsen, & Werry, 1978). The prevalence of its use with the mentally retarded is unknown at this stage, although several drug prevalence surveys do not mention its use with either institutionalized (e.g., Lipman, 1970) or noninstitutionalized (e.g., Davis et al., in press) populations.

One group of studies has dealt with the treatment of affective disorders in mentally retarded persons. The two best controlled studies (Naylor, Donald, Le Poidevin, & Reid, 1974; Rivinus & Harmatz, 1979), in which the subjects clearly exhibited affective symptoms, showed modest but clinically significant improvements. However, any general conclusions are unwarranted on the basis of only two studies.

Another group of studies has dealt with the treatment of chronic hyperactivity, aggressiveness, and self-injurious behavior. A group of five case studies (Cooper & Fowlie, 1972; Lion, Hill, & Madden, 1975; Goetzl, Grunberg, & Berkowitz, 1977; Sovner & Hurley, 1981) provide some evidence for the efficacy of lithium carbonate in controlling these behaviors. A small group of clinical trials, mostly uncontrolled studies with various methodological weaknesses (Dale, 1980; Dostal & Zvolsky, 1970; Micev & Lynch, 1974; Mullerova, Novtua, Rehan, & Skula, 1974; Worrall, Moody, & Naylor, 1975) have also reported drug-induced improvements, including increased "adaptability" and reduced aggressiveness, motor activity, restlessness, excitability, and self-injury. However, these are mostly uncontrolled studies, and while their data are suggestive of its efficacy, only well controlled studies will provide more definitive evidence. Indeed, more studies are needed, since lithium carbonate appears to control those behaviors that are resistant, in their more chronic forms, to other types of therapy (e.g., behavior modification).

The effects of antidepressant and antimanic drugs on learning, cognition, and adaptive behaviors are yet to be investigated with the mentally retarded. Recently, a study with hospitalized aggressive school-age children, who had no evidence of psychosis and/or mental retardation, has indicated that lithium carbonate may cause a very mild depression of cognition on circumscribed tests (Platt, Campbell, Green, Perry, & Cohen, 1981). Squire, Judd, Janowsky, and Huey (1980) studied lithium carbonate in adult psychiatric patients and found that the drug caused slowing of performance but without measureable impairment of learning and memory. Studies examining the cognitive effects of antidepressant and antimanic drugs in mentally retarded persons are certainly long over-due.

SIDE EFFECTS

The antidepressants have anticholinergic side effects similar to those found with antipsychotics. Tricyclics may also precipitate postural hypotension, tachycardia, and heart conduction defects (Jefferson, 1975). The most important side effect of lithium carbonate is the CNS confusional state, which occurs at serum levels around and above 1.5 mEq/l. This may include sluggishness, tremor, ataxia, and coma, and electrolyte changes leading to seizures and death may occur (Brown, 1976). Milder side effects may be present even at therapeutic levels, the most common being gastrointestinal irritability (e.g., nausea, anorexia, epigastric cramping, or diarrhea). Finally, lithium carbonate is noted for its disputed renal and nephron toxicity (Schou, 1979). Further discussion of these side effects can be found in Breuning, Davis, and Poling (in press), Rapoport, Mikkelsen, and Werry (1978), and Werry (in press).

Anxiolytic Drugs

BENZODIAZEPINES

The use of chlordiazepoxide (Librium) appears to be quite extensive in institutionalized populations, with surveys reporting prevalences between 8% (Lipman, 1970) and 13% (Tu, 1979) of residents receiving these drugs. However, it is often difficult to determine whether these drugs are being used only sporadically as hypnotics, alternatively as anticonvulsants (in the case of diazepam), or on a daily basis for behavioral control.

There is a dearth of behavioral research on these drugs in mentally retarded persons. Most of the relevant studies have employed the benzodiazepines in the hopes of suppressing aggressive and destructive behavior and to reduce hyperactivity. In one study of a diagnostically mixed group which included mentally retarded children, diazepam was found to produce less improvement than placebo (Zrull, Westman, Arthur, & Rice, 1964). Walters, Singh, and Beale (1977) compared lorazepam (Ativan) with placebo in moderately and severely retarded hyperactive residents. Inactive and appropriate behaviors were unaffected by this drug, but the degree of hyperactivity actually increased because of lorazepam. LaVeck and Buckley (1961) treated nonretarded, behavior problem children with chlordiazepoxide (Librium). Contrary to expectation, the active drug condition produced nonsignificant increases in undesirable behavior and less constructive play. There are other, uncontrolled, studies of the benzodiazepine group, which have often suggested that these drugs produce more salutary effects. However, overall it must be concluded that there is little evidence that the benzodiazepines improve noncompliant and hyperactive behavior in the mentally retarded, and indeed there is a possibility that these agents exacerbate such behaviors. This is obviously a class of drugs in serious need of further study.

The cognitive effects of these drugs are unstudied in mentally retarded persons, although research with other groups has frequently suggested depression of learning performance (McNair, 1973).

ANTIHISTAMINES

These drugs have received remarkably little investigation in mentally retarded persons. No studies of diphenhydramine (Benadryl) could be located. Hydroxyzine (Atarax), the other antihistamine occasionally used in mentally retarded persons, was assessed in at least three studies. Of the better controlled studies one evaluated hydroxyzine in maladjusted children (Segal & Tansley, 1957) and one in aggressive and destructive residents (Craft, 1957). Both trials were essentially negative. The antihistamines are unstudied with respect to their effects on learning or other adaptive skills in this population.

ANXIOLYTIC DRUGS: CONCLUSIONS

There is a paucity of research on this group of drugs in the mentally retarded. The well controlled studies have consistently failed to reveal any role for these agents in treating destructive, aggressive, impulsive, or hyperactive behavior. Apparently little effort has been made to locate subgroups whose behavior problems are a manifestation of high levels of anxiety. This is perhaps surprising, given the use of these drugs, especially the benzodiazepines, in treating anxiety related symptoms in nonretarded people.

Other Drugs

5-HYDROXYTRYPTOPHAN

5-Hydroxytryptophan is a biochemical that is the metabolic precursor of serotonin. Serotonin, in turn, is a neurotransmitter that has been implicated in a wide range of psychological processes and disorders (Cohen & Young, 1977). Of note for the current discussion is the fact that serotonin levels have been found to be depressed in Down syndrome persons (Rosner, Ong, Paine, & Mahanand, 1965; Tu & Zellweger, 1965). In an attempt to normalize their serotonin levels and hence overall developmental functioning, Bazelon, Paine, Cowie, Hunt, Houck, and Mahanand (1967) administered 5-hydroxytryptophan to a group of Down syndrome infants. Bazelon et al. reported that the drug caused a prompt and substantial improvement in muscle tone, which is often otherwise depressed in these children. However, subsequent investigators who conducted trials of 5-hydroxytryptophan in Down syndrome children have been unable to document neurological, developmental,

or behavioral changes (Partington, MacDonald, & Tu, 1971; Weise, Koch, Shaw, & Rosenfeld, 1974).

Others have employed 5-hydroxytryptophan in Lesch-Nyhan syndrome patients. Mizuno and Yugari (1975) reported that the drug relieved self-mutilation, but did not alleviate choreoathetoid movements in four cases. Nyhan, Johnson, Kaufman, and Jones (1980) employed 5-hydroxytryptophan to treat nine male patients with Lesch-Nyhan syndrome. They found a striking reduction in self-mutilative behavior due to the drug, but this reduction diminished over time, owing to the development of tolerance. However, Nyhan et al. cited other investigators (Anderson, Herrman, & Dancis, 1976; Ciaranello, Anders, Barchas, Berger, & Cann, 1976), who were unable to demonstrate such an effect due to 5-hydroxytryptophan.

The foregoing evidence suggests that 5-hydroxytryptophan is of dubious value in Down syndrome patients. If it is effective in suppressing self-mutilation in Lesch-Nyhan syndrome, its action appears to be transitory. For this reason the drug should be regarded as unproven and strictly experimental. However, the real significance of these trials is that this agent was adopted because of plausible neurochemical relationships which pointed to a possible therapeutic intervention. Such attention to patient characteristics has been unusual in this field and these studies may well provide a model for future work.

GLUTAMIC ACID

This drug is mentioned primarily because of its historical place in the pharmacotherapy of the mentally retarded. A body of research in the 1930's and the 1940's suggested that glutamic acid was the only amino acid that caused increased oxygen uptake by the brain. In addition, it was shown that glutamic acid increased brain respiration and that it was a catalyst for the formation of acetylcholine, one of the first neurotransmitters to be discovered (see Gadson, 1951; Waelsch, 1948). An early report (Price, Waelsch, & Putnam, 1943) also claimed that glutamic acid reduced petit mal seizures and improved mental and physical alertness in epileptic patients.

Following these reports, there was a virtual explosion of research into the effects of glutamic acid in mentally retarded persons. Indeed, interest was so great that the number of these investigations exceeded 50 (Vogel, Broverman, Draguns, & Klaiber, 1966). The earliest of these reports were very optimistic, frequently claiming a direct effect of glutamic acid on cognitive functioning as well as on behavioral adjustment. However, many of these studies, especially those reporting positive effects, were characterized by inadequate controls and were methodologically weak. The *Zeitgeist* of investigations on glutamic acid was largely over by the early 1950's, a time that coincided with the introduction of chlorpromazine and the other antipsychotics. Astin and Ross (1960) later reviewed the evidence and found that positive findings tended to be associated with a lack of experimental controls. They concluded that there was no compelling evidence that glutamic acid has a specific effect on human intelligence. However, in a subsequent review, Vogel et al. (1966) challenged several of Astin and Ross's interpretations and they argued that glutamic acid has not been disproved as a therapeutic agent.

Methodological Critique

As noted by previous reviewers, the caliber of drug studies with mentally retarded persons has been abysmally poor, with the vast majority of them defying a scientifically valid interpretation. Most studies, particularly those of the pre-1970 era, have lacked a number of the basic methodological controls outlined by Sprague and Werry (1971). More recent studies have been far more cognizant of the methodological niceties of drug research and a small number of well controlled studies are now available. As such, virtually the whole area of psychopharmacology in the mentally retarded still remains to be investigated.

In the past, the great bulk of drug studies employed group designs. A recent but important development has been the use of single-subject methodology in psychopharmacological research (Campbell, Cohen, & Anderson, 1981; Campbell, Geller, & Cohen, 1977; Liberman & Davis, 1975). These workers are advocating a move away from the large group-design research to within-subject evaluations of given drugs. They argue that generalizing from averaged group data to individual subjects is often questionable. The reversal and multiple baseline designs are thought to be the most appropriate designs to use when employing single-subject methodology. Although the reversal design has been used infrequently for some time now (see Hersen & Barlow, 1976), the multiple baseline design has not been used until very recently (e.g., Breuning, et al., 1980; Davis, Poling, Wysocki, & Breuning, in press; Wysocki et al., 1981).

Our position is that both, group and single-subject designs, are needed in this area of research and that they are useful in answering different questions. We are fortunate that such a diversity of experimental designs has been developed and refined in recent years. These should be employed to maximum effect to resolve the many outstanding issues in this complex field. The methodology of psychopharmacological

studies has been discussed in depth in several reviews, including those by Aman (in press a,b), Breuning, Davis, and Poling (in press), Conners (1977), Hersen and Barlow (1976), Liberman and Davis (1975), Marholin and Phillips (1976), Sprague and Baxley (1978), Sprague and Werry (1971), and Wysocki and Fuqua (in press).

Major Issues Requiring Attention

There are a number of issues that appear to be in particular need of attention in the pharmacotherapy of mentally retarded persons. In the sections below, we attempt to identify some of these issues and to suggest profitable directions for future research.

Dosage Effects

The vast majority of drug investigations in the field of mental retardation have established dose levels by titration. Most frequently, dosage has been individualized for each patient in the study against the end point of behavioral improvement. However, the use of titration in drug research poses several difficulties. First, it is a subjective procedure of unknown reliability and it is plausible that different clinicians would disagree on appropriate doses for a given group of patients. Second, when dosage is titrated against some criterion, such as behavioral improvement, it is difficult to know what behaviors are emphasized in the adjustment process. As we have argued elsewhere (Aman, in press, a), the use of titration in the drug research appears tautological and suggests that the investigator can identify optimal drug effects before having access to his own data.

We believe that there is a serious need in this field for research that explores the effects of various doses standardized on the basis of body weight, surface area, blood level, or other compelling indicators. Research with hyperactive children has shown that drugs often have complex effects, influencing different classes of behavior at different doses (e.g., Sprague & Sleator, 1975, 1977; Werry & Aman, 1975). In the case of the mentally retarded, Singh and Aman (1981, discussed earlier) carried out one of the few existing dosage studies. They compared a low standardized dose of thioridazine with the previous individualized doses that had been determined by titration. It was found that the standardized dose, which was less than half the mean titrated level, resulted in an equivalent therapeutic response. This, of course, suggests that there may be a tendency in institutions to administer doses which are unnecessarily high. Breuning's (in press) study of thioridazine has also been discussed.

He demonstrated that various types of maladaptive behavior appear to be controlled at different dosage levels. In addition, adaptive behavior (workshop performance) was impeded at still higher dosage levels. This study is very useful, because it provides specific guidelines on what doses can be administered without producing drug-related impairment.

Such dosage research is rare in this field and thus far has been largely confined to the antipsychotic drug thioridazine. Obviously, if psychotropic drugs are to be prescribed rationally, it is imperative that much more information be available regarding the types of adaptive and maladaptive behavior likely to be affected at various drug levels.

Lack of Studies Examining Learning

In their oft-quoted review of this area, Sprague and Werry (1971) noted that, although mental retardation is primarily a disorder of learning, few studies have used learning, cognitive, or educational performance variables as indices of drug effect. Yet with only a few notable exceptions from the very recent literature, the latest review on this topic has concluded in a similar vein (see Aman, in press, b).

In the past, the most common measure of learning has been the IQ score, even though (when obtained in the standard manner) it has repeatedly been found to be insensitive to drug manipulations in the mentally retarded (Breuning & Davidson, 1981; Werry & Sprague, 1972). Other indices, which may provide more specific and sensitive measures, have virtually been ignored. Remarkably, only one study has evaluated drug effects on the acquisition of a conditioned response, that being Lobb's (1968) study of amphetamine, mentioned earlier. Only four studies have used operant paradigms to assess the behavioral effects of drugs (Davis, 1971; Hollis, 1968; Hollis & St. Omer, 1972; Wysocki et al., 1981). This is surprising, since operant techniques have consistently demonstrated their value and flexibility in elucidating learning mechanisms.

Another notable omission has been in the general area of discrimination learning of the type espoused by Zeaman and House (1963). Only one group of researchers seems to have used this paradigm to assess drug effects, albeit with a rather obscure drug (Sandman, George, Walker, & Nolan, 1976; Walker & Sandman, 1979). Few studies have used attentional variables as a measure of drug effects. Useful methodologies for measuring breadth of attention (Ullman, 1974) and attentional changes during discrimination learning (Singh & Beale, 1978) have already been developed but have yet to be utilized in drug studies.

Other research strategies involving short-term memory (Scott, 1971) and incidental learning (Singh & Ahrens, 1978) are potentially useful for measuring the drug effects on learning, but have not yet been employed in the mentally retarded.

Hence, we presently have very little information about the nature and extent of drug effects on learning in the mentally retarded. There are signs that researchers are beginning to apply far more sophisticated techniques to the study of drug effects in this area (e.g., Wysocki et al., 1981; Breuning & Davidson, 1981). However, most drugs are still poorly studied, if at all. We are only likely to make substantial gains in this respect if investigators take cognizance of the large body of research, already available, relating to cognitive correlates of mental retardation. Unfortunately, such intra- and interdisciplinary awareness has not been a hallmark of psychopharmacology in the past.

Predictors of Drug Response

Historically, there has been remarkably little attention in this field to subject characteristics that may forecast outcome to pharmacological intervention. Even salient cognitive/behavioral measures, such as IQ level and behavioral profile, have seldom been systematically explored as predictors of drug response. Similarly, extent and nature of brain damage and neurological dysfunction have only rarely been utilized for their possible predictive value.

Recently there has been a great deal of interest in neurotransmitter systems and the possibility that drug response may be determined by a limited number of such systems (see Cohen & Young, 1977; Smith & Copolov, 1979). There have been isolated attempts to formulate treatment on the basis of biochemical imbalances, as in the case where Down syndrome children were treated with 5-hydroxytryptophan, already mentioned (Bazelon et al., 1967). Following a preliminary investigation, Greenberg and Coleman (1976) reported that drugs which elevated serotonin levels (in patients with previously depressed levels) also caused marked improvements in behavior. However, systematic research into such relationships between biochemical status and therapeutic response is still a rarity in mental retardation, despite the fact that this is becoming a lively area of investigation in other fields.

It is clear that attention to basic subject characteristics is required if we are to understand the nature of the drug response in mentally retarded persons. Only in this way can pharmacotherapy of the mentally retarded become a true scientific discipline, matching therapeutic mode to organismic factors, as opposed to the crude hit-and-miss approach as is frequently the case now.

Absence of Research in Noninstitutionalized Retarded People

The vast majority of drug studies in the mentally retarded have been carried out with institutionalized populations. The survey of drug use in community foster-group homes (Davis et al., in press) indicated that the prevalence of drug prescription is often very high outside of institutions. Furthermore, Gadow and Kalachnick's (1981) survey of mentally retarded children attending special classes indicated a substantially different pattern of drug prescription, with the stimulants being the most commonly prescribed psychotropic drugs. In addition, Lipman (1982) has pointed out that the numerical preponderance of mentally retarded people do not reside in institutions. All of these points indicate a serious need for more research with noninstitutionalized mentally retarded persons. It can then be determined whether the prevalence and pattern of pharmacotherapy are appropriate in this group or whether prescription practices have merely been inappropriately extrapolated from other clinical populations.

Paucity of Follow-up Studies

There has been a near absence of long-term studies of psychoactive drugs in the mentally retarded, despite the fact that such drugs are frequently prescribed for a number of years. Although long term effects may parallel those observed in the short term, there is no justification for blithely assuming that this will necessarily be the case.

Moore (1960) monitored the learning performance of a group of female residents who had received long-term treatment with chlorpromazine. Subjects discontinuing treatment showed significantly improved performance on the Stanford Achievement Tests, whereas those continuing treatment failed to show similar changes. McAndrew, Case, and Treffert (1972) found that when thioridazine treatment was discontinued in children on long-term therapy, three patients showed dramatic increases in achievement upon discontinuation of the drug.

Breuning and his associates have occasionally used the strategy of withdrawing existing pharmacological treatment from residents who had received pharmacotherapy for substantial periods (Breuning, Ferguson, & Cullari, 1980; Breuning, Davis, Matson, & Ferguson, 1982). These studies have frequently shown high levels of withdrawal emergent symptoms,

as well as a disappointing lack of therapeutic effect. However, these studies are only suggestive in terms of long-term effects, because it is unknown whether these patients ever benefited from pharmacotherapy in the first place.

We are unaware of any long term, prospective follow-up studies in this field. However, there are indications that workers are attempting to develop less formal techniques for monitoring the clinical behavioral effects of pharmacotherapy after treatment has begun (e.g., Fielding, Murphy, Reagan, & Peterson, 1980). The investigations cited above would certainly justify more long-term prospective studies with particular reference to drug effects on learning, physiology, and behavioral effects.

Physiological Risk

In the treatment of mentally retarded persons, the beneficial effects of drugs must always be weighed against their possible untoward effects. While serious immediate side effects due to most antipsychotics are rare in children (Engelhardt & Polizos, 1978), there are several long-term side effects which are cause for some concern. These include those factors which influence cognition, growth, and the endocrine system.

Another risk factor was discussed when the anticonvulsant drugs were reviewed. Various of the anticonvulsants have the potential of causing progressive and irreversible cognitive impairment when given in excessive doses (Vallarta et al., 1974; Logan & Freeman, 1969). In the case of antipsychotic drugs, it has been found that some of these are capable of causing retinal stippling (McAndrew, Case, & Treffert, 1972) as well as triggering epileptic seizures upon withdrawal of medication (Heistad & Zimmerman, 1979).

Another side effect which has recently gained considerable attention is tardive dyskinesia. This is a drug-induced movement disorder characterized by involuntary, rhythmic, and repetitive movements of the face, mouth, and extremities (Gualtieri & Hawk, 1980). It is rarely noticed in its early stages, since it appears to be masked by the very agents that cause it, namely neuroleptic medication. Although the incidence of tardive dyskinesia in mentally retarded populations is difficult to ascertain, current data suggest that it could be relatively high. Paulson, Rizvi, and Crane (1975) reported an incidence of 20% in a sample of 103 mentally retarded youngsters who had been on long-term phenothiazine therapy. Other studies indicate its prevalence to be about 17% following gradual drug reduction and 23% following abrupt termination (Breuning, 1981; Gualtieri, Breuning, Schroeder, & Quade, in press). Tardive dyskinesia is a particularly serious side effect, because no effective treatment is currently available (Baldessarini & Tarsy, 1978), because of its permanence and because it actively interferes with adaptive functioning.

It is clear that a decision to employ pharmacotherapy does involve genuine risks to the persons so treated. There has been a recent increase in work carried out in this area, especially in relation to tardive dyskinesia (e.g., Breuning, Davis et al., in press; Gualtieri et al., in press). However, further work is needed to identify persons most at risk, to locate the safest dosage ranges and drug types, and to develop appropriate forms of treatment.

Conclusions

We have now witnessed three decades of research and several hundred studies since the synthetic antipsychotic drugs were introduced to treat behavior problems in retarded persons. Despite this fact, there is a remarkable lack of information regarding any of the drug groups commonly used in mental retardation. Standards and expectations regarding drug research have risen dramatically in the last five or so years. It is hoped that we can now look forward to an era of discovery and consolidation, so that the true value of these agents is known. Only in this way can pharmacotherapy genuinely contribute to the well-being of those receiving such treatment.

References

Alexandris, A., & Lundell, F. W. Effect of thioridazine, amphetamine, and placebo on the hyperkinetic syndrome and cognitive area in mentally deficient children. *Canadian Medical Association Journal*, 1968, 98, 92–96.

Aman, M. G. Drugs, learning, and the psychotherapies. In J. S. Werry (Ed.), *Pediatric psychopharmacology: The use of behavior modifying drugs in children*. New York: Brunner/Mazel, 1978.

Aman, M. G. Psychotropic drugs and learning problems: A selective review. *Journal of Learning Disabilities*, 1980, 13, 87–96.

Aman, M. G. Psychotropic drugs in the treatment of reading disorders. In R. N. Malatesha & P. G. Aaron (Eds.), *Neuropsychological and neurolinguistic aspects of reading disorders*. New York: Academic Press, 1982.

Aman, M. G. Psychoactive drugs in mental retardation. In. J. L. Matson & F. Andrasik (Eds.), *Treatment issues and innovations in mental retardation*. New York: Plenum Press, in press.(a)

Aman, M. G. Drugs and learning in mentally retarded persons. In G. D. Burrows & J. S. Werry (Eds.), *Advances in human psychopharmacology*. Vol. III. Greenwich, Conn.: JAI Press, in press.(b)

Aman, M. G. Stimulant drug effects in developmental disorders and hyperactivity: Toward a resolution of disparate findings. *Journal of Autism and Developmental Disorders*, in press.(c)

Aman, M. G., & Singh, N. N. The usefulness of thioridazine

for treating childhood disorders: Fact or folklore? *American Journal of Mental Deficiency*, 1980, 84, 331–338.

Anderson, L. T., Hermann, L., & Dancis, J. The effect of L-5 hydroxtryptophan on self-mutilation in Lesch-Nyhan disease: A negative report. *Neuropaediatrie*, 1976, 7, 439–442.

Astin, A. W., & Ross, S. Glutamic acid and human intelligence. *Psychological Bulletin*, 1960, 57, 429–434.

Bair, H. V., & Herold, W. Efficacy of chlorpromazine in hyperactive mentally retarded children. *Archives of Neurology and Psychiatry*, 1955, 74, 363–364.

Baldessarini, R. A., & Tarsy, D. Tardive dyskinesia. In M. A. Lipton, A. DiMascio, & K. Killiam (Eds.), *Psychopharmacology: A generation of progress*. New York: Raven Press, 1978.

Barkley, R. A., & Cunningham, C. E. Do stimulant drugs improve the academic performance of hyperkinetic children? A review of outcome research. *Clinical Pediatrics*, 1978, 17, 85–92.

Baroff, G. S. *Mental retardation: Nature, cause and management*. New York: Halsted Press, 1974.

Bazelon, M., Paine, R. S., Cowie, V. A., Hunt, P., Houck, J. C., & Mahanand, D. Reversal of hypotonia in infants with Down's syndrome by administration of 5-hydroxytryptophan. *Lancet*, 1967, 1, 1130–1133.

Bell, A., & Zubek, J. P. Effects of deanol on the intellectual performance of mental defectives. *Canadian Journal of Psychology*, 1961, 15, 172–175.

Bender, L., & Fareta, G. Organic therapy in pediatric psychiatry. *Diseases of the Nervous System*, 1961, 22, 110–111.

Berkson, G., & Davenport, R. K. Stereotyped movements of mental defectives: Initial survey. *American Journal of Mental Deficiency*, 1962, 66, 849–852.

Blackwell, B., & Currah, J. The psychopharmacology of nocturnal enuresis. In I. Kolvin, R. McKeith, & S. Meadow (Eds.), *Bladder control and enuresis*. London: Heineman, 1973.

Bradley, C. The behavior of children receiving benzedrine. *American Journal of Psychiatry*, 1937, 94, 577–585.

Breuning, S. E. Drug use with the mentally retarded: Efficacy, behavioral effects, side effects, and alternative treatments. Paper presented at the American Association on Mental Deficiency Conference, Detroit, 1981.

Breuning, S. E. An applied dose-response curve of thioridazine with the mentally retarded: Aggressive, self-stimulatory, intellectual, and workshop behaviors. A preliminary report. *Psychopharmacology Bulletin*. In press.

Breuning, S. E., & Davidson, N. A. Effects of psychotropic drugs on the intelligence test performance of mentally retarded adults. *American Journal of Mental Deficiency*, 1981, 85, 575–579.

Breuning, S. E., Davis, V. T., Matson, J. L., & Ferguson, D. G. Effects of thioridazine and withdrawal dyskinesias on workshop performance of mentally retarded young adults. *American Journal of Psychiatry*. 1982, 139, 1447–1454.

Breuning, S. E., Davis, J. J., & Poling, A. D. Pharmacotherapy with the mentally retarded: Implications for clinical psychologists. *Clinical Psychology Review*. In press.

Breuning, S. E., Ferguson, D. G., & Cullari, S. Analysis of single-double blind procedures, maintenance of placebo effects, and drug induced dyskinesia with mentally retarded persons. *Applied Research in Mental Retardation*, 1980, 1, 175–192.

Breuning, S. E., Ferguson, D. G., Davidson, N. A., & Poling, A. D. Effects of thioridazine on the intelligence of mentally retarded drug responders and non-responders. *Archives of General Psychiatry*. In press.

Breuning, S. E., O'Neill, J., & Ferguson, D. G. Comparison of psychotropic drug, response cost, and psychotropic drug plus response cost procedures for controlling institutionalized retarded persons. *Applied Research in Mental Retardation*, 1980, **1**, 253–268.

Brown, W. T. Side effects of lithium therapy and their treatment. *Canadian Psychiatric Association Journal*, 1976, **21**, 13–21.

Camfield, C. S., Chaplin, S., Doyle, A., Shapiro, S. H., Cummings, C., & Camfield, P. R. Side effects of phenobarbital in toddlers: Behavioral and cognitive aspects. *Journal of Pediatrics*, 1979, **95**, 361–365.

Campbell, M., Cohen, I. L., & Anderson, L. T. Pharmacotherapy for autistic children: A summary of research. *Canadian Journal of Psychiatry*, 1981, **26**, 265–273.

Campbell, M., Geller, B., & Cohen, I. L. Current status of drug research and treatment with autistic children. *Journal of Pediatric Psychology*, 1977, **2**, 153–161.

Cantwell, D. P., & Carlson, G. A. Stimulants. In J. S. Werry (Ed.), *Pediatric psychopharmacology: The use of behavior modifying drugs in children*. New York: Brunner/Mazel, 1978.

Carter, C. H. Isocarboxazid in the institutionalized mentally retarded. *Diseases of the Nervous System*, 1960, **21**, 568–570.

Carter, C. H. Nortriptyline HCL as a tranquilizer for disturbed mentally retarded patients: A controlled study. *American Journal of Medical Science*, 1966, **251**, 465–467.

Charalampous, K. D., & Keepers, G. A. Major side effects of antipsychotic drugs. *Journal of Family Practice*, 1978, **6**, 993–1002.

Ciaranello, R. D., Anders, T. F., Barchas, J. D., Berger, P. A., & Cann, H. M. The use of 5-hydroxytryptophan in a child with Lesch-Nyhan syndrome. *Child Psychiatry and Human Development*, 1976, **7**, 127–133.

Claghorn, J. L. A double-blind comparison of haloperidol (Haldol) and thioridazine (Mellaril) in outpatient children. *Current Therapeutic Research*, 1972, **14**, 758–789.

Clingman, J., & Fowler, R. The effects of primary reward on the IQ performance of grade school children as a function of initial IQ level. *Journal of Applied Behavior Analysis*, 1976, **9**, 19–23.

Cohen, D. J., & Young, J. G. Neurochemistry and child psychiatry. *Journal of the American Academy of Child Psychiatry*, 1977, **16**, 353–411.

Cohen, M. N., & Sprague, R. L. Survey of drug usage in two midwestern institutions for the retarded. Paper presented at the Gatlinburg Conference on Research in Mental Retardation, Gatlinburg, Tennessee, March 1977.

Conners, C. K. Methodological considerations in drug research with children. In J. M. Wiener (Ed.), *Psychopharmacology in childhood and adolescence*. New York: Basic Books, 1977.

Conners, C. K., Kramer, R., Rothschild, G. H., Schwartz, L., & Stone, A. Treatment of young delinquent boys with diphenylhydantoin sodium and methylphenidate. *Archives of General Psychiatry*, 1971, **24**, 156–160.

Conners, C. K., & Werry, J. S. Pharmacotherapy of psychopathology in children. In H. C. Quay & J. S. Werry (Eds.), *Psychopathological disorders of childhood*. New York: John Wiley & Sons, 1979.

Cooper, A. F., & Fowlie, H. C. Control of gross self-mutilation with lithium carbonate. *British Journal of Psychiatry*, 1972, **122**, 370–371.

Cordes, C. K. Chronic drug intoxication causing pseudoretardation in a young child. *Journal of the American Academy of Child Psychiatry*, 1973, **12**, 215–222.

Craft, M. Tranquilizers in mental deficiency: Hydroxyzine. *Journal of Mental Science*, 1957, **103**, 855–857.

Dalby, M. A. Behavioral effects of carbamazepine. In J. K. Penry & D. D. Daly (Eds.), *Advances in neurology*. Vol. II. New York: Raven Press, 1975.

Dale, P. G. Lithium therapy in aggressive mentally subnormal patients. *British Journal of Psychiatry*, 1980, **137**, 469–474.

Davies, T. S. A monoamine oxidase inhibitor (Niamid) in the treatment of the mentally subnormal. *Journal of Mental Science*, 1961, **107**, 115–118.

Davis, K. V. The effect of drugs on stereotyped and non-stereotyped operant behaviors in retardates. *Psychopharmacologia*, 1971, **22**, 195–213.

Davis, V. J., Cullari, S., & Breuning, S. E. Drug use in community foster-group homes. In S. E. Breuning & A. D. Poling (Eds.), *Drugs and mental retardation*. Springfield, Illinois: Charles C. Thomas. In press.

Davis, V. J., Poling, A. D., Wysocki, T., & Breuning, S. E. Effects of phenytoin withdrawal on matching to sample and workshop performance of mentally retarded persons. *Journal of Nervous and Mental Disease*. In press.

Davis, K. V., Sprague, R. L., & Werry, J. S. Stereotyped behavior and activity level in severe retardates: The effect of drugs. *American Journal of Mental Deficiency*, 1969, **73**, 721–727.

Dostal, T., & Zvolsky, P. Antiaggressive effect of lithium salts in severe mentally retarded adolescents. *International Pharmacopsychiatry*, 1970, **5**, 203–207.

Douglas, V. I. Differences between normal and hyperkinetic children. In C. K. Conners (Ed.), *Clinical use of stimulant drugs in children*. Amsterdam: American Elsevier Publishing Co., 1974.

Drew, R. L. H. Drug control of incontinence in adult mental defectives. *Medical Journal of Australia*, 1967, **2**, 202–207.

Engelhardt, D. M., & Polizos, P. Adverse effects of pharmacotherapy in childhood psychosis. In M. A. Lipton, A. DiMascio, & K. Killam (Eds.), *Psychopharmacology: A generation of progress*. New York: Raven Press, 1978.

Ferguson, D. G., & Breuning, S. E. Antipsychotic and antianxiety drugs. In S. E. Breuning & A. D. Poling (Eds.), *Drugs and mental retardation*. Springfield, Ill: Charles C. Thomas. In press.

Fielding, L. T., Murphy, R. J., Reagan, M. W., & Peterson, T. L. An assessment program to reduce drug use with the mentally retarded. *Hospital and Community Psychiatry*, 1980, **31**, 771–773.

Fisher, G. W., Murray, F., Walley, M. R., & Kiloh, L. G. A controlled trial of imipramine in the treatment of nocturnal enuresis in mentally subnormal patients. *American Journal of Psychiatry*, 1963, **67**, 536–538.

Freeman, R. D. Psychopharmacology and the retarded child. In F. J. Menolascino (Ed.), *Psychiatric approaches to mental retardation*. New York: Basic Books, Inc., 1970.

Gadow, K. D. *Children on medication: A primer for school personnel*. Virginia: The Council for Exceptional Children, 1979.

Gadow, K. D., & Kalachnik, J. Prevalence and pattern of drug treatment for behavior and seizure disorders of TMR students. *American Journal of Mental Deficiency*,

1981, **85**, 588–595.

Gadson, E. P. Glutamic acid and mental deficiency: A review. *American Journal of Mental Deficiency*, 1951, **55**, 521–529.

Gardner, W. I. Occurrence of severe depressive reactions in the mentally retarded. *American Journal of Psychiatry*, 1967, **124**, 142–144.

Gerbino, L., Oleshansky, M., & Gershon, S. Clinical use and mode of action of lithium. In M. A. Lipton, A. DiMascio, & K. F. Killam (Eds.), *Psychopharmacology: A generation of progress*. New York: Raven Press, 1978.

Glaser, K. Masked depression in children and adolescents. *American Journal of Psychotherapy*, 1967, **26**, 565–574.

Goetzl, J., Grunberg, F., & Berkowitz, B. Lithium carbonate in the management of hyperactive aggressive behavior of the mentally retarded. *Comprehensive Psychiatry*, 1977, **18**, 599–606.

Goldberg, J. B., & Kurland, A. A. Dilantin treatment of hospitalized cultural-familial retardation. *Journal of Nervous and Mental Disease*, 1970, **150**, 133–137.

Greenberg, A. S., & Coleman, M. Depressed 5-hydroxyindole levels associated with hyperactive and aggressive behavior. Relationship to drug response. *Archives of General Psychiatry*, 1976, **33**, 331–336.

Gualtieri, C. T., Breuning, S. E., Schroeder, S. R., & Quade, D. Tardive dyskinesia in mentally retarded children, adolescents, and young adults. *Psychopharmacology Bulletin*. In press.

Gualtieri, C. T., & Hawk, B. Tardive dyskinesia and other drug-induced movement disorders among handicapped children and youth. *Applied Research in Mental Retardation*, 1980, **1**, 55–69.

Heaton-Ward, W. A. Inference and suggestion in a clinical trial (Niamind in Mongolism). *Journal of Mental Science*, 1962, **108**, 865–870.

Heistad, G. T., & Zimmerman, R. L. Double-blind assessment of Mellaril in a mentally retarded population using detailed evaluations. *Psychopharmacology Bulletin*, 1979, **15**, 86–88.

Hersen, M., & Barlow, D. H. *Single-case experimental designs: Strategies for studying behavior change*. New York: Pergamon Press, 1976.

Hollis, J. H. Chlorpromazine: Direct measurement of differential behavioral effect. *Science*, 1968, **159**, 1487–1489.

Hollis, J. H., & St. Omer, V. V. Direct measurement of psychopharmacologic response: Effects of chlorpromazine on motor behavior of retarded children. *American Journal of Mental Deficiency*, 1972, **76**, 397–407.

Hughes, P. S. Survey of medication in a subnormality hospital. *British Journal of Mental Subnormality*, 1977, **23**, 88–94.

Iivanainen, M., Viukari, M., Seppäläinen, A., & Helle, E. Electroencelphalography and phenytoin toxicity in mentally retarded epileptic patients. *Journal of Neurology, Neurosurgery, and Psychiatry*, 1978, **41**, 272–277.

Jasper, H. H., Ward, A. A., & Pope, A. (Eds.), *Basic mechanisms of the epilepsies*. Boston: Little, Brown & Co., 1969.

Jefferson, J. W. A review of the cardiovascular effects and toxicity of tricyclic antidepressants. *Psychosomatic Medicine*, 1975, **37**, 160–179.

Johnson, F. M. The psychopharmacology of lithium. *Neuroscience and Biobehavioral Reviews*, 1979, **3**, 15–30.

Jonas, O. Pattern of drug prescribing in a residential centre for the intellectually handicapped. *Australian Journal of Developmental Disabilities*, 1980, **6**, 25–30.

Kaufman, K. R., & Katz-Garris, L. Epilepsy, mental retardation, and anticonvulsant therapy. *American Journal of Mental Deficiency*, 1979, **84**, 256–259.

Kirman, B. Drug therapy in mental handicap. *British Journal of Psychiatry*, 1975, **127**, 545–549.

Kraft, I. A., Ardali, C., Duffy, J., Hart, J., & Pearce, P. R. Use of amitriptyline in childhood behavioral disturbances. *International Journal of Neuropsychiatry*, 1966, **2**, 611–614.

LaVeck, G. D., & Buckley, P. The use of psychopharmacologic agents in retarded children with behavior disorders. *Journal of Chronic Diseases*, 1961, **13**, 174–183.

Le Vann, L. Clinical comparison of haloperidol with chlorpromazine in mentally retarded children. *American Journal of Mental Deficiency*, 1971, **75**, 719–723.

Liberman, R. P., & Davis, J. Drugs and behavior analysis. In M. Hersen, R. M. Eisler, & P. M. Miller (Eds.), *Progress in behavior modification* Vol. I. New York: Academic Press, 1975.

Lion, J. R., Hill, J., & Madden, D. J. Lithium carbonate and aggression: A case report. *Diseases of the Nervous System*, 1975, **36**, 97–98.

Lipman, R. S. The use of psychopharmacological agents in residential facilities for the retarded. In F. J. Menolascino (Ed.), *Psychiatric approaches to mental retardation*. New York: Basic Books, 1970.

Lipman, R. Psychotropic drugs in mental retardation: The known and the unknown. In K. D. Gadow & I. Bialer (Eds.), *Advances in learning and behavioral disabilities*. Vol. I. Greenwich, Conn.: JAI Press, 1982.

Lipman, R. S., DiMascio, A., Reatig, N., & Kirson, T. Psychotropic drugs and mentally retarded children. In M. A. Lipton, A. DiMascio & K. F. Killam (Eds.), *Psychopharmacology: A generation of progress*. New York: Raven Press, 1978.

Lobb, H. Trace GSR conditioning with benzedrine in mentally defective and normal adults. *American Journal of Mental Deficiency*, 1968, **73**, 239–246.

Logan, W. J., & Freeman, J. M. Pseudodegenerative disease due to diphenylhydantoin intoxication. *Archives of Neurology*, 1969, **21**, 631–637.

Looker, A., & Conners, C. K. Diphenylhydantoin in children with severe temper tantrums. *Archives of General Psychiatry*, 1970, **23**, 80–89.

Marholin, D., & Phillips, D. Methodological issues of psychopharmacological research: Chlorpromazine—A case in point. *American Journal of Orthopsychiatry*, 1976, **46**, 477–495.

Marholin, D., Touchette, P. E., & Stewart, R. M. Withdrawal of chronic chlorpromazine medication: An experimental analysis. *Journal of Applied Behavior Analysis*, 1979, **12**, 159–171.

Matson, J. L. & Barrett, R. P. *Psychopathology in the mentally retarded*. New York: Grune & Stratton, 1982.

McAndrew, J. B., Case, Q., & Treffert, D. A. Effects of prolonged phenothiazine intake on psychotic and other hospitalized children. *Journal of Autism and Childhood Schizophrenia*, 1972, **2**, 75–91.

McConahey, O. L., Thompson, T., & Zimmerman, R. A token system for retarded women: Behavior therapy, drug administration, and their combination. In T. Thompson & J. Grabowski (Eds.), *Behavior modification of the mentally retarded*. (2nd ed.) New York: Oxford University Press, 1977.

McConnell, T. R., Cromwell, R. L., Bialer, I., & Son, C. D. Studies in activity level: VII. Effects of amphetamine drug administration on the activity level of retarded children. *American Journal of Mental Deficiency*, 1964, **68**, 647–651.

McNair, D. M. Antianxiety drugs and human performance. *Archives of General Psychiatry*, 1973, **29**, 611–617.

Menolascino, F. J. (Ed.) *Psychiatric approaches to mental retardation*. New York: Basic Books, 1970.

Menolascino, F. J. Psychiatric aspects of retardation in young children. In R. Koch & J. C. Dobson (Eds.), *The mentally retarded child and his family*. New York: Brunner/Mazel, 1976.

Micev, V., & Lynch, D. M. Effect of lithium in disturbed severely mentally retarded patients. *British Journal of Psychiatry*, 1974, **125**, 110.

Mizuno, T., & Yugaris, Y. Prophylactic effect of L-5-hydroxytryptophan on self-mutilation in the Lesch-Nyhan syndrome. *Neuropaediatrie*, 1975, **6**, 13–23.

Moore, J. W. The effects of a tranquilizer (Thoraxine) on the intelligence and achievement of educable mentally retarded women. *Dissertation Abstracts*, 1960, **20**, 3200.

Mulick, J. A., & Schroeder, S. R. Research relating to management of antisocial behavior in mentally retarded persons. *Psychological Record*, 1980, **30**, 397–417.

Mullerova, S., Novtua, J., Rehan, V., & Skula, E. Lithium treatment of behavioral disturbances in patients with defective intellect. *Activitas Nervosa Superior*, 1974, **16**, 196.

Naylor, G. J., Donald, J. M., Le Poidevin, & Reid, A. H. A double-blind trial of long-term lithium therapy in mental defectives. *British Journal of Psychiatry*, 1974, **124**, 52–57.

Nyhan, W. L., Johnson, H. G., Kaufman, I. A., & Jones, K. L. Serotonergic approaches to the modification of behavior in the Lesch-Nyhan syndrome. *Applied Research in Mental Retardation*, 1980, **2**, 25–40.

Ounsted, C. The hyperkinetic syndrome in epileptic children. *Lancet*, 1955, **2**, 303–311.

Partington, M. W., MacDonald, M. R. A., & Tu, J. B. 5-Hydroxytryptophan (5-HTP) in Down's syndrome. *Developmental Medicine and Child Neurology*, 1971, **13**, 362–372.

Paulson, G. W., Rizvi, C. A., & Crane, G. E. Tardive dyskinesia as a possible sequel of long-term therapy with phenothiazines. *Clinical Pediatrics*, 1975, **14**, 953–955.

Payne, D., Johnson, R. G., & Abelson, R. B. *Comprehensive description of institutionalized retardates in Western United States*. Boulder, Colo.: Western Interstate Commission for Higher Education, 1969.

Phillips, I., & Williams, N. Psychopathology and mental retardation: A study of 100 mentally retarded children: I. Psychopathology. *American Journal of Psychiatry*, 1975, **132**, 1265–1271.

Pilkington, T. L. A report on "Tofranil" in mental deficiency. *American Journal of Mental Deficiency*, 1962, **66**, 729–732.

Platt, J. E., Campbell, M., Green, W. H., Perry, R., & Cohen, I. L. Effects of lithium carbonate and haloperidol on cognition in aggressive hospitalized school-age children. *Journal of Clinical Psychopharmacology*, 1981, **1**, 8–13.

Price, J. C., Waelsch, H., & Putnam, T. J. d-1-Glutamic acid hydrochloride in treatment of petit mal and psychomotor seizures. *Journal of the American Medical Association*, 1943, **122**, 1153.

Pulman, R. M., Pook, R. B., & Singh, N. N. Prevalence of drug therapy for institutionalised mentally retarded children. *Australian Journal of Mental Retardation*, 1979, **5**, 212–214.

Rapoport, J. L., Buchsbaum, M. S., Zahn, T. P., Weingartner, H., Ludlow, C., & Mikkelsen, E. J. Dextroamphetamine: Cognitive and behavioral effects in normal prepubertal boys. *Science*, 1978, **199**, 560–563.

Rapoport, J. L., & Mikkelsen, E. J. Antidepressants. In J. Werry (Ed.), *Pediatric psychopharmacology: The use of behavior modifying drugs in children*. New York: Brunner/Mazel, 1978.

Rapoport, J. L., Mikkelsen, E. J., & Werry, J. S. Antimanic, antianxiety, hallucinogenic and miscellaneous drugs. In J. S. Werry (Ed.), *Pediatric psychopharmacology: The use of behavior modifying drugs in children*. New York: Brunner/Mazel, 1978.

Reid, A. H., Naylor, G. J., & Kay, D. S. G. A double-blind, placebo controlled, crossover trial of carbamazepine in overactive, severely mentally handicapped patients. *Psychological Medicine*, 1981, **11**, 109–113.

Remschmidt, H. The psychotropic effect of carbamazepine in non-epileptic patients, with particular reference to problems posed by clinical studies in children with behavioural disorders. In W. Birkmayer (Ed.), *Epileptic seizures, behaviour, pain*. Bern, Switzerland: Hans Huber Publishers, 1976.

Reynolds, E. H. Chronic antiepileptic toxicity: A review. *Epilepsia*, 1975, **16**, 319–352.

Rie, H. E., Rie, E. D., Stewart, S., & Ambuel, J. P. Effects of methylphenidate on underachieving children. *Journal of Consulting and Clinical Psychology*, 1976, **44**, 250–260.(a)

Rie, H., Rie, E., Stewart, S., & Ambuel, J. Effects of Ritalin on underachieving children: A replication. *American Journal of Orthopsychiatry*, 1976, **46**, 313–322.(b)

Rivinus, T. M., & Harmatz, J. S. Diagnosis and lithium treatment of affective disorder in the retarded: Five case studies. *American Journal of Psychiatry*, 1979, **136**, 551–554.

Roche, A. F., Lipman, R. S., Overall, J. E., & Hung, W. The effects of stimulant medication on the growth of hyperkinetic children. *Pediatrics*, 1979, **63**, 847–850.

Rosner, F., Ong, B. H., Paine, R. S., & Mahanand, D. Blood-serotonin activity in trisomic and translocation Down's syndrome. *Lancet*, 1965, **1**, 1191.

Ross, R. T. Behavioral correlates of levels of intelligence. *American Journal of Mental Deficiency*, 1972, **76**, 545–549.

Safer, D., Allen, R., & Barr, E. Depression of growth in hyperactive children on stimulant drugs. *New England Journal of Medicine*, 1972, **287**, 217–220.

Sandman, C. A., George, J., Walker, B. N., & Nolan, J. D. Neuropeptide MSH/ACTH 4-10 enhances attention in the mentally retarded. *Pharmacology, Biochemistry and Behavior*, 1976, **5**, 23–28.

Schain, R. J. Problems with the use of conventional anticonvulsant drugs in mentally retarded individuals. *Brain and Development*, 1979, **1**, 77–82.

Schou, M. Lithium prophylaxis: Is the honeymoon over? *Australian & New Zealand Journal of Psychiatry*, 1979, **13**, 109–114.

Scott, K. G. Recognition memory: A research strategy and a summary of initial findings. In N. R. Ellis (Ed.), *International review of research in mental retardation*. Vol. 5. New York: Academic Press, 1971.

Segal, L. J., & Tansley, A. E. A clinical trial with hydroxyzine (Atarax) on a group of maladjusted educationally subnormal children. *Journal of Mental Retardation*, 1957, **103**, 677–681.

Sewell, J., & Werry, J. S. Some studies in an institution for the mentally retarded. *New Zealand Medical Journal,* 1976, **84,** 317–319.

Silva, D. A. The use of medication in a residential institution for mentally retarded persons. *Mental Retardation,* 1979, **17,** 285–288.

Singh, N. N. Rumination. In N. R. Ellis (Ed.), *International review of research in mental retardation.* Vol. 10. New York: Academic Press, 1981.

Singh, N. N. Current trends in the treatment of self-injurious behavior. In L. A. Barnes (Ed.), *Advances in pediatrics.* Vol. 28. Chicago: Year Book Medical Publishers, 1982.

Singh, N. N., & Ahrens, M. G. Incidental learning in the mentally retarded. *Exceptional Child,* 1978, **35,** 53–63.

Singh, N. N., & Aman, M. G. Effects of thioridazine dosage on the behavior of severely mentally retarded persons. *American Journal of Mental Deficiency,* 1981, **85,** 580–587.

Singh, N. N., & Beale, I. L. Attentional changes during discrimination learning by retarded children. *Journal of the Experimental Analysis of Behavior,* 1978, **29,** 527–533.

Smith, E. H., & Gonzalez, R. Nortriptyline hydrochloride in the treatment of enuresis in mentally retarded boys. *American Journal of Mental Deficiency,* 1967, **71,** 825–827.

Smith, G. C., & Copolov, D. Brain amines and peptides: Their relevance to psychiatry. *Australian and New Zealand Journal of Psychiatry,* 1979, **13,** 283–291.

Sovner, R., & Hurley, A. The management of chronic behavior disorders in mentally retarded adults with lithium carbonate. *Journal of Nervous and Mental Disease,* 1981, **169,** 191–195.

Spencer, D. A. A survey of the medication in a hospital for the mentally handicapped. *British Journal of Psychiatry,* 1974, **124,** 507–508.

Sprague, R. L., & Baxley, G. B. Drugs for behavior management, with comment on some legal aspects. *Mental Retardation and Developmental Disabilities,* 1978, **10,** 92–129.

Sprague, R. L., & Sleator, E. K. What is the proper dose of stimulant drugs in children? *International Journal of Mental Health,* 1975, **4,** 75–118.

Sprague, R. L., & Sleator, E. K. Methylphenidate in hyperkinetic children: Differences in dose effects on learning and social behavior. *Science,* 1977, **198,** 1274–1276.

Sprague, R. L., & Werry, J. S. Methodology of psychopharmacological studies with the retarded. In N. R. Ellis (Ed.), *International review of research in mental retardation.* Vol. 5. New York: Academic Press, 1971.

Squire, L. R., Judd, L. L., Janowsky, D. S., & Huey, L. Y. Effects of lithium carbonate on memory and other cognitive functions. *American Journal of Psychiatry,* 1980, **137,** 1042–1046.

Sroufe, L. Drug treatment of children with behavior problems. In F. Horowitz (Ed.), *Review of child development research.* Vol. 4. Chicago: University of Chicago Press, 1975.

Stores, G. Behavioural effects of anti-epileptic drugs. *Developmental Medicine and Child Neurology,* 1975, **17,** 647–658.

Stores, G. Antiepileptics (anticonvulsants). In J. S. Werry (Ed.), *Pediatric psychopharmacology: The use of behavior modifying drugs in children.* New York: Brunner/Mazel, 1978.

Trimble, M. The effects of anticonvulsant drugs on cognitive abilities. *Pharmacology and Therapeutics,* 1979, **4,** 677–685.

Trimble, M., & Reynolds, E. Anticonvulsant drugs and mental symptoms. *Psychological Medicine,* 1976, **6,** 169–178.

Tu, J. A survey of psychotropic medication in mental retardation facilities. *Journal of Clinical Psychiatry,* 1979, **40,** 125–128.

Tu, J. B., & Zellweger, H. Blood serotonin deficiency in Down's syndrome. *Lancet,* 1965, **2,** 715.

Ucer, E., & Kreger, C. A double-blind study comparing haloperidol with thioridazine in emotionally disturbed mentally retarded children. *Current Therapeutic Research,* 1969, **11,** 278–283.

Ullman, D. G. Breadth of attention and retention in mentally retarded and intellectually average children. *American Journal of Mental Deficiency,* 1974, **78,** 640–648.

Vallarta, J. M., Bell, D. B., & Reichert, A. Progressive encephalopathy due to chronic hydantoin intoxication. *American Journal of Diseases of Children,* 1974, **128,** 27–34.

Vogel, W., Broverman, D. M., Draguns, J. G., & Klaiber, E. L. The role of glutamic acid in cognitive behaviors. *Psychological Bulletin,* 1966, **65,** 367–382.

Waelsch, H. A biochemical consideration of mental deficiency. The role of glutamic acid. *American Journal of Mental Deficiency,* 1948, **52,** 305–313.

Walker, B. B., & Sandman, C. A. Influences of an anolog of the neuropeptide ACTH 4-9 on mentally retarded adults. *American Journal of Mental Deficiency,* 1979, **83,** 346–352.

Walker, M. K. Stimulant drugs. In S. E. Breuning & A. D. Poling (Eds.), *Drugs and mental retardation.* Springfield Ill.: Charles C. Thomas. In press.

Walters, A., Singh, N., & Beale, I. L. Effects of lorazepam on hyperactivity in retarded children. *New Zealand Medical Journal,* 1977, **86,** 473–475.

Weise, P., Koch, R., Shaw, K. N., & Rosenfeld, M. J. The use of 5-HTP in the treatment of Down's syndrome. *Pediatrics,* 1974, **54,** 165–168.

Weiss, C. F., Heffelfinger, J. C., & Buchanan, R. A. Serial Dilantin levels in mentally retarded children. *American Journal of Mental Deficiency,* 1969, **73,** 826–830.

Werry, J. S. Pharmacotherapy. In B. B. Lahey & A. E. Kazdin (Eds.), *Advances in clinical child psychology.* Vol. 5. New York: Plenum Press. In press.

Werry, J. S., & Aman, M. G. Methylphenidate and haloperidol in children. Effects on attention, memory, and activity. *Archives of General Psychiatry,* 1975, **32,** 790–795.

Werry, J. S., & Aman, M. G. Methylphenidate in hyperactive and enuretic children. In B. Shopsin & L. Greenhill (Eds.), *The psychobiology of childhood: Profile of current issues.* Jamaica, N.Y.: Spectrum Publications. In press.

Werry, J. S., & Sprague, R. L. Psychopharmacology. In J. Wortis (Ed.), *Mental retardation.* Vol. 4. New York: Grune and Stratton, 1972.

Winsberg, B. G., & Yepes, L. E. Antipsychotics (major tranquilizers, neuroleptics). In J. Werry (Ed.), *Pediatric psychopharmacology: The uses of behavior modifying drugs in children.* New York: Brunner/Mazel, 1978.

Wolf, S. M., & Forsythe, A. Behavior disturbance, phenobarbital, and febrile seizures. *Pediatrics,* 1978, **61,** 728–731.

Wolfensberger, W., & Menolascino, F. Basic considerations in evaluating ability of drugs to stimulate cognitive development in retardates. *American Journal of Mental Deficiency*, 1968, **73**, 414–423.

Worrall, E. P., Moody, J. P., & Naylor, G. J. Lithium in non-manic depressives: Antiaggressive effect and red blood cell lithium values. *British Journal of Psychiatry*, 1975, **126**, 464–468.

Wysocki, T., & Fuqua, R. W. Methodological issues in the evaluation of drug effects. In S. E. Breuning & A. D. Poling (Eds.), *Drugs in mental retardation.* Springfield, Ill.: Charles C. Thomas, in press.

Wysocki, T., Fuqua, R. W., Davis, W. J., & Breuning, S. E. Effects of thioridazine (Mellaril) on titrating delayed matching-to-sample performance of mentally retarded adults. *American Journal of Mental Deficiency*, 1981, **85**, 539–547.

Zeaman, D., & House, B. J. The role of attention in retardate discrimination learning. In N. R. Ellis (Ed.), *Handbook of mental deficiency.* New York: McGraw-Hill, 1963.

Zrull, J. P., Westman, J. C., Arthur, B., & Rice, D. L. A comparison of diazepam, d-amphetamine and placebo in the treatment of the hyperkinetic syndrome in children. *American Journal of Psychiatry*, 1964, **121**, 388–389.

22 BEHAVIORAL TREATMENT

John W. Scibak

The history of treatment approaches for dealing with the mentally retarded could be compared to the swinging of a pendulum. Public sentiment ranged from the humanitarianism exemplified by Itard in his work with the "Wild Boy of Aveyron" in the early 1800's to the emergence of the Eugenics movement which called for sterilization and segregation a century later. As MacMillan (1977) pointed out, the welfare of the mentally retarded has in large part depended on the sway of public opinion and philosophy.

In the last 20 years, a technology has emerged that focused on a behavioral approach to treatment with the mentally retarded. Through the monitoring and systematic manipulation of antecedents and consequences, it has been possible to develop rudimentary self-help skills and complex vocational assembly tasks while controlling inappropriate responses such as aggression and self-injurious behavior (Whitman & Scibak, 1979; Matson & McCartney, 1981). Over 400 studies have appeared in the literature demonstrating the efficacy of this technology in modifying the behavior of mentally retarded individuals. In all of these investigations, emphasis has been placed upon the systematic observation and measurement of human behavior, rather than on the postulation of some hypothetical construct, personality trait, or other intervening variable.

The application of behavioral treatment procedures with the mentally retarded in recent years parallels the evolution of how society has defined the phenomenon of retardation. While early conceptualizations emphasized biological factors (Jervis, 1952; Penrose, 1949) and psychometric scores (Clausen, 1967; Wechsler, 1958), the contemporary view characterizes retardation in terms of behavioral deficiencies and excesses (Bijou, 1963, 1966; Lindsley, 1964). In fact, the most widely accepted contemporary definition, published by the American Association on Mental Deficiency, included a criterion of adaptive behavior or social competence. According to Grossman (1973), this definition "denotes a level of behavioral performance without reference to etiology. . . . [It] is descriptive of current behavior and does not imply prognosis" (p. 11). Attention centers around the behaviors which an individual does or does not exhibit, with the emphasis placed on the development of active habilitation programs directed toward overt behavioral performance.

This chapter will examine the impact of behavioral treatment approaches with the mentally retarded. A brief review of learning theory and the techniques which emerged from this perspective will be presented together with illustrations of how these specific procedures have been applied to various problem areas. Practical considerations influencing the selection of a particular intervention strategy will also be discussed. Some researchers have referred to these approaches under the label "behavior modification" (e.g., Kazdin, 1978), while others prefer to classify them as "behavior therapy" (e.g., Yates, 1971). Since there has been no clear distinction between these two labels in the literature, the reader can consider them as interchangeable. However, for the sake of consistency, the term "behavior modification" will be used throughout this chapter.

Theoretical Foundations

Behavior modification refers to the application of learning principles to effect changes in human behavior (Franks, 1969). Most of the behavioral procedures that have been employed with the mentally retarded are based upon the principles of operant conditioning as postulated by Skinner (1938), who distinguished between two types of behavior, called "respondents" and "operants." Respondents are behaviors that are elicited by specific stimuli and that appear whenever the particular triggering stimulus is present. Constriction of the pupils when exposed to bright lights and the characteristic knee jerk when the patella is tapped are examples of respondents. These behaviors are controlled by the antecedent stimuli. In contrast, operants are not elicited by specific stimuli, but are emitted from time to time and appear to be voluntary. Although operants certainly do occur in the presence of various stimuli, these antecedent events do not control whether or not the operant is emitted. Rather, operants are controlled by the consequences that follow them.

Skinner (1938) assumed that when an operant is emitted, it operates or acts upon the environment to generate consequences that influence the future probability of the response. The relationship between operant behavior and its consequences as posited by Skinner was similar to the Law of Effect proposed by Thorndike (1911). This law specified that responses followed by rewards are likely to recur, whereas those followed by aversive consequences are not likely to be repeated. Most of the behavioral research conducted with the mentally retarded has evolved from the operant paradigm, and the techniques that have been developed focus on the systematic manipulation of response consequences.

Basic Principles of Operant Conditioning

The principles of operant conditioning specify the lawful relationships that are presumed to exist between behavior and the particular environment in which it occurs. Although the role of antecedent events is important in the control of behavior, operant conditioning research has focused on the effects of consequences. Thus, the major emphasis in this section will be on both the various events that contingently follow behaviors and their effects on future behavior. The basic operant principles will only be described briefly in this chapter. However, additional information can be found in Reynolds (1968), Bandura (1969), and Honig and Staddon (1977).

Reinforcement

Perhaps the most significant concept in operant theory is reinforcement. As with other concepts, reinforcement is functionally defined in terms of its effects on behavior. More specifically, reinforcement refers to the process in which a stimulus which follows a response increases the frequency or probability of that response occurring again under similar circumstances. The specific stimuli that affect the operant response are called reinforcers. Although events such as requests can serve to increase the future probability of a response, they would not be considered reinforcers since they do not follow the response. Thus, a reinforcer must both follow a response and increase its probability.

There actually are two types of reinforcement procedures, positive and negative reinforcement. Positive reinforcement is the most common and it involves the presentation of a stimulus after a response. For example, taking a child out for an ice cream cone after he has helped rake the lawn increases the likelihood that the child will help with the yard work again. The ice cream cone is a positive reinforcer for raking. In a contrasting situation, the removal of a stimulus after a response can also increase its probability, and this would be defined as negative reinforcement. A good example of negative reinforcement can be seen when a person has a headache. If the person takes an aspirin and the headache goes away, then that individual is more likely to take an aspirin the next time he gets a headache. In this example, the response of taking an aspirin is negatively reinforced by the cessation of pain, and it is the aversive stimulus (e.g., pain) that is the negative reinforcer.

Some stimuli such as food or water satisfy basic biological needs and function as reinforcers without a person having to learn their value. These reinforcers are referred to as primary reinforcers. While the value of primary reinforcers does not have to be learned, it should be noted that these stimuli do not always function as reinforcers. For example, food would not be reinforcing to someone who has just finished eating a large meal. In fact, in this case, food might be aversive.

Many stimuli do not satisfy basic needs, yet they still function as reinforcers. Money, a pat on the back, or even a smile all can increase the future probability of behavior. These stimuli which are called secondary or conditioned reinforcers are not inherently reinforcing. Rather, they acquire reinforcing value through the repeated association with other stimuli that already are reinforcing. A $20.00 bill is really nothing more than a green piece of paper. But, because it can be used to buy things, it is more valuable than most other pieces of green paper. Conditioned reinforcers acquire their reinforcement property through learning. Although all of the examples of primary and conditioned reinforcers provided thus far would be classified as positive reinforcers, negative reinforcers also fit into these same categories. A continuous shock could be a primary negative reinforcer, while verbal reprimands or a frown could function as conditioned negative reinforcers if they have been repeatedly paired with other aversive events.

There are a number of factors that influence the success of reinforcement to alter behavior. One important consideration is the identification of potent reinforcers. There really is no such thing as a universally effective reinforcer. Strong individual preferences exist such that what is a powerful reinforcer for one person may be highly aversive to someone else (e.g., anchovy pizza, opera). Even known reinforcers for a person may not always be effective (e.g., ice cream cone in August versus December), illustrating how important it is to evaluate the potency of a particular stimulus before assuming that it will be reinforcing. In addition to the selection of an effective reinforcer, that reinforcer must be applied correctly. The stimulus must be contingently delivered. That is, the reinforcer should be administered every time the desired behavior occurs but not at other times. If a reinforcer is delivered noncontingently, some alternative to the target response might be strengthened. Finally, to maximize increases in response probability, reinforcers should also be delivered on a continuous schedule, i.e., every time the specific target behavior is emitted. Although it is usually possible to maintain behavior on an intermittent schedule once consistent responding is occurring (Ferster & Skinner, 1957), continuous reinforcement should be used when trying to establish behavior.

Shaping and Prompting

Although reinforcement can increase the future probability of a behavior, some desired behaviors never occur and therefore cannot be reinforced. In such cases, it may be necessary to use prompting, shaping, and fading procedures to establish new behaviors which then can be reinforced.

Some individuals may have the desired behavior in their response repertoire, but need to be prompted before they will initiate the response. These prompts could be verbal instructions, gestural as in the case of pointing and modeling, or physical where the person is actually guided through the behavior by a trainer. In all of these instances, the prompts increase the probability of responding, but they would not be classified as reinforcers since they precede rather than follow the target behavior. Although prompts do assist in the establishment of behavior, the goal of training should be to fade out prompts gradually, so that the target behavior is emitted without them. If prompts are not faded, a person may become dependent upon their presence and never engage in the specific desired behavior unless the prompts are present.

Another strategy for establishing and developing behaviors which are not part of a person's repertoire is shaping. This procedure involves the reinforcement of responses that already exist in the repertoire, but reinforcing slight changes in the behavior that more closely resemble the desired response on subsequent trials. Thus, successive approximations of the target behavior are reinforced during shaping. Initially, reinforcement is contingent upon rough approximations of the desired behavior, but gradually only more precise or exact approximations are reinforced until the target response is emitted. Shaping is most often used in the development of relatively complex behaviors, which can then be strengthened through reinforcement.

Punishment

Punishment refers to the process where an event that follows a response decreases the future probability of that response. People have often equated punishment with the presentation of an aversive or painful stimulus. Although this may be an example of punishment, the key is that the probability of behavior occurring again must be reduced. Thus, if what most people consider an aversive or painful stimulus does not decrease the future probability of a behavior, then punishment did not occur.

As with reinforcement, there are two different ways in which punishment can occur. In the first type, an unpleasant stimulus is presented after a response, which reduces the likelihood that the response will occur in the future. For example, a slap on the hand for raiding the cookie jar could be an effective punisher. In the second form of punishment, a stimulus is removed after a response. Generally, the stimulus that is withdrawn is something the person finds to be pleasant and desirable. To illustrate, a child who throws a tantrum may lose access to his favorite toy for the rest of the day. If this reduces the likelihood

Table 22.1. Comparison of Reinforcement
and Punishment

EFFECT ON	CONTINGENT STIMULUS	
BEHAVIOR	APPLIED	WITHDRAWN
Increase	Positive reinforcement	Negative reinforcement
Decrease	Punishment	Punishment

of future tantrums, then the contingent loss of the toy was punishing.

Because they both involve aversive events, punishment and negative reinforcement are often confused. The differences between these concepts are quite clear, and are illustrated in Table 22.1. The major distinction is that negative reinforcement by definition leads to an increase in behavior. On the other hand, punishment procedures result in a decrease in behavior. A second difference involves the specific way in which the aversive stimulus is employed. In punishment, an aversive stimulus is applied, while the aversive stimulus is removed when negative reinforcement occurs.

Extinction

It was noted above that reinforced behaviors increase in frequency. Extinction refers to a procedure in which responses which were previously reinforced no longer receive reinforcement. As a result, the nonreinforcement of a behavior gradually leads to a reduction of the behavior and sometimes even its elimination. Since extinction involves the nonreinforcement of behavior, it is important that all sources of reinforcement be identified and withheld. If this cannot be done, the behavior will continue to be reinforced at least on an intermittent schedule and it will persist. Because extinction leads to a reduction in behavior, it is sometimes confused with punishment, but they really are two different operations. In extinction, the consequence following a response is simply withheld and there is nothing the person can do to influence this. However, in punishment, an aversive stimulus is presented or some pleasant event is removed contingent upon the person's behavior.

The principles outlined above have provided the foundation for most of the operant-based treatment approaches for dealing with the problematic behaviors of the mentally retarded. These principles illustrate the relationships that exist between operant behavior and the contingent consequences that follow these responses. In the following sections, attention will be given to the specific techniques which have evolved from these principles.

Operant-Based Treatment Procedures

Although a large body of literature exists demonstrating the efficacy of operant-based procedures with the mentally retarded, it must be reiterated that this is a relatively young area of research. The basic behavioral principles of reinforcement, punishment, and extinction studied in the animal literature were first applied to retarded and normal children in the late 1950's (Bijou, 1958). These laboratory studies confirmed that the mentally retarded can learn and provide the foundation for the technology of behavior modification and the applied research to be discussed in the remainder of this chapter.

The current status of the operant literature with the mentally retarded will be reviewed by examining the specific procedures commonly used with this population. Each subsection will focus on a particular intervention technique and discuss some illustrative studies which used this treatment strategy. It should be noted, however, that researchers generally do not rely on a single procedure to deal with the behavior problems of the retarded, but often use several different techniques in a treatment package. In their review, Whitman and Scibak (1981) found that approximately 75% of their sample of 280 studies with severely and profoundly mentally retarded subjects used a combination of two or more procedures. Thus, the reader should not assume that each of the techniques to be described must be applied in a vacuum. In many cases, they are systematically introduced in a complex package in order to bring about more effective and more efficient changes in behavior.

Differential Reinforcement

Differential reinforcement involves the reinforcement of one or more behaviors and the nonreinforcement of other behaviors that might also occur. Actually, there are several procedural variations that could appropriately be labeled differential reinforcement. In all these instances, some behavior or class of behaviors is positively reinforced, while another behavior or class of behaviors is placed on extinction.

Probably the most common differential reinforcement procedure appearing in the literature is referred to as differential reinforcement of other behavior or a DRO procedure. The DRO procedure involves the reinforcement of any behavior other than the specific target response. Because the client receives reinforcement whenever s/he omits the target behavior, some researchers have also used the term "omission training" to describe this procedure (Weiher & Harmon, 1975). Repp, Deitz, and Deitz (1976) used a DRO procedure to reduce a variety of inappropriate behaviors including self-injurious behavior in six mentally retarded children. Initially, the reinforcement interval corresponded to the average amount of time between responses seen during baseline. For one subject, this meant that reinforcement was delivered for every second that he refrained from biting, but this was gradually lengthened. Repp et al. found that in all six cases, the DRO procedure substantially reduced the frequency and variability of inappropriate behavior relative to baseline.

In the second type of differential reinforcement procedure, the reinforcer is dependent upon the emission of a particular response form. To illustrate, Favell (1973) relied on this strategy and reinforced three severely retarded children for appropriate toy play as a means of reducing stereotypy. The data revealed that this approach was successful, as stereotypy declined and appropriate play increased. Similarly, Mulick, Hoyt, Rojahn and Schroeder (1978) used a prompting procedure in which subjects were told to get a toy and were reinforced for toy play. As in the Favell study, Mulick et al. noted that stereotypy decreased and appropriate toy contact was higher.

Researchers choosing to reinforce specific alternative responses generally have a wide variety of potential behaviors from which to choose. Some of these are incompatible with the target response, so that one or the other can occur but not simultaneously. It is also possible to reinforce specific behaviors whose appearance does not necessarily preclude the occurrence of the target behavior. However, Tarpley and Schroeder (1979) found that the differential reinforcement of incompatible behavior (DRI) resulted in more rapid and greater suppression of self-injury than the differential reinforcement of other behavior in three profoundly mentally retarded subjects.

In the final differential reinforcement procedure to be discussed, the target behavior may be occurring at a very high rate during baseline conditions and the researcher determines that the response rate needs to be reduced but not necessarily eliminated. It is possible to provide differential reinforcement of low rates of behavior (DRL) in these situations. For example, Dietz and Repp (1973) used this procedure with 10 moderately mentally retarded children who would frequently talk out in class. After baseline had revealed a rate of 32.7 talk-outs per 50-minute period, a contingency was introduced where candy was distributed at the end of the day whenever there were five or fewer talk-outs during the 50-minute period. This strategy was successful in reducing disruptive classroom behavior in this study, but the DRL procedure has not been used very often with the mentally retarded.

Differential reinforcement procedures have been used to control several diverse categories of problem behavior in the mentally retarded, including self-stimulation (Mulhern & Baumeister, 1965; Repp, Deitz, & Deitz, 1976), self-injurious behavior (Weiher & Harmon, 1975; Ragain & Anson, 1976), aggression (Repp, Deitz, & Deitz, 1976), ruminative vomiting (O'Neil, White, King, & Carik, 1979), and stripping (Lutzker, 1974). One reason for the frequent use of this treatment strategy is the mandate that clinicians employ the least restrictive treatment alternative available (*Wyatt v. Stickney*, 1972). Differential reinforcement affords clients the opportunity to earn reinforcement and is considered less intrusive or restrictive than other options such as punishment procedures.

The specific stimuli which have been effective reinforcers with the mentally retarded have also been diverse, ranging from food items (Hopkins, 1968), social praise (Kazdin, 1973), nonverbal attention (Kazdin & Klock, 1973), free time (Deitz & Repp, 1973), vibration (Bailey & Meyerson, 1969), and tokens which could be exchanges for candy, toys, balloons, and trinkets (Zimmerman, Zimmerman, & Russell, 1969). Even stimuli such as physical restraint (Favell, McGimsey, & Jones, 1978) and isolated time-out (Solnick, Rincover, & Peterson, 1977) have functioned as reinforcers for some clients.

For the clinician interested in using differential reinforcement procedures, several issues require careful consideration. First, potent reinforcers must be identified and introduced. As indicated earlier, distinct individual preferences exist and effective reinforcers should be empirically determined. Second, since differential reinforcement procedures provide reinforcement for the absence of a target behavior during a given interval, the specific interval must be selected carefully. If the response requirements are too difficult, reinforcers will not be earned and no changes in the target behavior will occur. Third, the success of differential reinforcement is dependent upon consistent nonreinforcement of the behavior to be decreased. Unless the clinician can identify and control the stimuli that serve to reinforce the target behavior, differential reinforcement should not be utilized as a treatment strategy.

Removal of Positive Reinforcement

In the DRO procedures, reinforcement is not provided whenever the target behavior occurs, but a reinforcer is delivered for the absence of the target response or the occurrence of a specific alternative. In this section, attention will be directed toward procedures that remove positive reinforcers after an inappropriate response.

EXTINCTION

As discussed earlier, extinction refers to the process of withholding reinforcement from a previously reinforced response. Since reinforcement increases the future probability of behavior, extinction should lead to a reduction in responding. Consequently, clinicians and researchers have often relied on extinction procedures to suppress problematic behaviors. In many cases, extinction has involved the removal of social attention for inappropriate behavior with the response being ignored (cf. Laws, Brown, Epstein, & Hocking, 1971). Although ignoring problem behavior may constitute an extinction procedure, the key is whether attention functions as a reinforcing stimulus for such behavior. As Repp and Brulle (1981) noted, ignoring an inappropriate response when the behavior is not being reinforced by attention would probably be ineffective and may constitute a no-treatment, baseline condition.

For clients whose behavior is maintained by the social consequences of attention, extinction can be an effective strategy. Hall, Fox, Willard, Goldsmith, Emerson, Owen, Davis, and Porcia (1971) controlled arguing in a 15-year-old mentally retarded boy through extinction. Whenever the boy began arguing or disputing with his teacher, the teacher stopped all further interaction by turning away and walking off. The behavior was dramatically reduced within a few days and a six-week follow-up revealed that arguing was no longer a problem. In another application, Martin and Foxx (1973) assumed that the response of a victim could reinforce aggression. The treatment procedure in this study involved the withdrawal of social reinforcement by the victim who was trained to try to ignore all instances of aggression. The results indicated that extinction eliminated all acts of aggression, thus confirming the role of attention by the victim.

Although much of the extinction research has focused on the removal or withholding of social attention, the strategy can be utilized with any stimuli that function as reinforcers. For example, Rincover (1978) hypothesized that inappropriate behaviors are sometimes maintained by the sensory consequences that result. It was also assumed that the removal of these sensory consequences would eliminate intrinsic reinforcers and lead to reductions in the inappropriate responses. In a series of studies, Rincover and his colleagues demonstrated the effectiveness of procedures based on this principle of "sensory extinction." Rincover (1978) found that an autistic client who would repetitively spin objects on a table stopped engaging in the behavior when the auditory consequences of this behavior were eliminated by carpeting the table top. Similarly, Rincover and Devany (1982) introduced sensory extinction procedures to remove the tactile stimulation from head banging and face scratching in three developmentally disabled children. All three subjects showed an immediate and substantial decrease in the rate of self-injury. Moreover, their teachers reported that the procedures could be implemented in the classroom without disrupting other students.

The functional significance of sensory extinction was demonstrated by Rincover, Cook, Peoples and Packard (1979) who found that appropriate toy play could also be developed by introducing toys that produced the same form of sensory reinforcement as the inappropriate response which was placed on extinction. Although the available literature is relatively small, it appears that sensory extinction represents an efficient and relatively convenient application of the principles of extinction to control problematic behavior in the mentally retarded.

There are two potential problems that could affect the selection of extinction as an intervention technique. First, as with differential reinforcement, the success of an extinction procedure is dependent upon the specification and control of all stimuli that are reinforcing the target response. Since behaviors may be maintained and reinforced by multiple stimuli, extinction may prove to be difficult to implement. Additionally, clinicians must be wary of accidental reinforcement of the target behavior particularly by naïve caregivers or visitors since behavior could return to original baseline levels from only one or two "accidental" reinforcements. A second concern is that extinction generally is a slow process with gradual reductions in behavior occurring. Lovaas and Simmons (1969) noted that 9,000 responses occurred before one of their clients' self-injurious behaviors ceased. Thus, if a clinician is seeking rapid suppression or if the occurrence of the target behavior could result in physical harm, the use of extinction would probably be inappropriate.

TIME-OUT

Probably the most common procedure involving the removal of reinforcement is time-out. This strategy involves a client losing the opportunity for earning or having access to reinforcers for a specific period of time. Time-out usually consists of physical removal from others. For example, Wolf, Risley, and Mees (1964) sent a severely disturbed boy to his room whenever he threw his glasses or exhibited a temper tantrum. Because the physical isolation precludes interaction with others, time-out has been a popular procedure in dealing with aggressive behavior (e.g., Hamilton, Stephens, & Allen, 1967; White, Nielsen & Johnson, 1972; Clark, Rowbury, Baer, & Baer, 1973).

Although time-out generally involves isolation, clients do not have to be physically removed from the environment if the clinician is able to control the sources of reinforcement (e.g., attention) that are functional. Foxx and Shapiro (1978) utilized a non-exclusionary form of time-out, whereby clients who were eligible for reinforcement wore ribbons. When a child misbehaved, the ribbon was removed and s/he did not receive teacher attention and could not participate in activities for three minutes. Similarly, Foxx, Jones, Foxx and Kiely (1980) imposed 24 hours of social isolation when their clients were aggressive. The offending individuals wore hospital gowns during the isolation period, which served as a cue for others that the person should be ignored. Thus, although aggression led to social isolation, the client was not removed from the living environment. In both the Foxx and Shapiro (1978) and Foxx et al. (1980) studies, aggression was significantly reduced.

Since the key to the success of time-out is based upon a loss of access to reinforcers, the specific environment in which the client normally functions is a relevant parameter. If the environment is not very reinforcing, such as some institutional wards, then removal of the client from such a setting will probably have little impact.

Punishment

The research described thus far has illustrated how reinforcement and extinction procedures can be employed successfully in the reduction of inappropriate behaviors. These techniques have not always proven effective, however, particularly when the reinforcing events maintaining the problematic behaviors cannot be easily identified or controlled. In such situations, punishment procedures have frequently been used. Punishment is also commonly employed when the inappropriate behavior can cause physical harm to the client or others. Since punishment strategies generally result in rapid suppression, they would be preferable to extinction or reinforcement techniques in such cases, since the latter procedures are less efficient in achieving their effects.

Although a review of the research illustrates the success of punishment procedures with the mentally retarded, the reader must recognize that there is always a risk that staff will misuse and abuse these techniques. Careful monitoring and documentation must be conducted by clinicians whenever aversive techniques are being used. Furthermore, the specific intervention strategy selected must be the least restrictive or intrusive one available and should always include a reinforcement component that establishes or maintains an alternative, more appropriate behavior. Forehand and

Baumeister (1976) noted that the goal of reducing inappropriate behavior is not to produce a passive individual but to create an opportunity for the development of prosocial behavior.

INTRODUCTION OF AVERSIVE STIMULI

It was noted earlier that punishment can either involve the presentation of an aversive, unpleasant event or the withdrawal of some positive stimulus. This section will focus on punishment through the application of some aversive stimulus which has also been referred to as positive punishment (Mikulas, 1978).

Kazdin (1978) noted that the presentation of aversive events is used less frequently than the withdrawal of pleasant events, attributing this to the fact that the use of unpleasant aversive events may be ethically unacceptable. Despite this characterization, a review of the research in this area indicates that various aversive stimuli have been widely used in the suppression of inappropriate behavior in the mentally retarded.

Many early studies relied on the delivery of a contingent electric shock to control undesirable behavior. In these investigations, the delivery of a brief shock led to dramatic reductions in self-injury (Lovaas & Simmons, 1969), aggression (Birnbrauer, 1968), disruptive screaming (Hamilton & Standahl, 1969), inappropriate climbing (Risley, 1968), and vomiting (Kohlenberg, 1970). Recently, however, clinical and ethical concerns have led to a reexamination of the viability of shock as a treatment strategy. More specifically, the suppressive effects of shock appear to be situation specific (Birnbrauer, 1968), although the systematic introduction of the punishment contingency across settings and therapists can result in complete suppression (Risley, 1968). A second issue centers around the use of such an intrusive, noxious procedure in any situation that does not directly threaten the physical well-being of an individual. The courts have ruled that shock shall only be used in extraordinary circumstances to prevent permanent physical damage and only after less restrictive alternatives have failed (*Wyatt v. Stickney*, 1972).

The constraints placed upon the use of shock have led researchers to investigate the efficacy of alternative, less intrusive stimuli which could be introduced contingent upon the emission of inappropriate behavior. These have included lemon juice (Sajwaj, Libet, & Agras, 1974), inhalation of aromatic ammonia (Tanner & Zeiler, 1975), aversive tickling (Greene & Hoats, 1971), physical restraint (Saposnek & Watson, 1974), and verbal reprimands (Doleys, Wells, Hobbs, Roberts & Cartelli, 1976). Although the research literature indicates that these specific stimuli have been utilized in punishment studies with the mentally retarded, individual differences do exist with respect to the effectiveness of these stimuli. As with reinforcers, a clinician cannot assume that a particular stimulus will necessarily be an effective punisher just because it appears to be aversive to the clinician.

Procedures such as aromatic ammonia and lemon juice may cause temporary and mild discomfort to clients, but they are less painful than the administration of shock. Also, because they do not evoke the adverse reactions from guardians and caregivers, these stimuli have become more commonly used in controlling inappropriate behavior as opposed to shock.

OVERCORRECTION

Overcorrection refers to a complex set of procedures, first developed by Foxx and Azrin (1972) to reduce and control various inappropriate behaviors. This intervention strategy requires that a client correct the environmental consequences, if any, of an inappropriate behavior (restitutional overcorrection) and/or repeatedly practice acceptable or overly correct forms of the inappropriate behavior (positive practice). For example, Azrin and Wesolowski (1974) relied on a combination of positive practice and restitutional overcorrection to control vomiting in one profoundly mentally retarded man. Positive practice consisted of 15 trials of "correct" vomiting where the client knelt over the toilet and flushed the toilet, while restitution involved having the client clean up his mess and change his clothing and/or the bed sheets when necessary. As Epstein, Doke, Sajwaj, Sorrell, and Rimmer (1974) noted, overcorrection often incorporates all of the following procedures into one comprehensive package: negative feedback, verbal instructions, response interruption, time out from reinforcement, negative reinforcement, and physical guidance. Although several of these components are not punitive in nature (e.g., verbal instructions, negative reinforcement), overcorrection has been generally considered a punishment procedure.

During the 1970s, overcorrection became the most common punishment technique used to reduce inappropriate behavior in mentally retarded populations. It was applied to a wide variety of behaviors, including stereotyped movements (Foxx & Azrin, 1973; Matson & Stephens, 1981), self-injurious behavior (Azrin, Gottlieb, Hughart, Wesolowski & Rahn, 1975; Matson, Stephens & Smith, 1978), stereotyped verbalizations (Higgs, Burns, & Meunier, 1980), vomiting (Azrin & Wesolowski, 1974), aggression (Foxx & Azrin, 1972; Ollendick & Matson, 1976), pica (Foxx & Martin, 1975), inappropriate vocalizations (Martin & Matson, 1978), and poor attendance at grooming and special education classes (Foxx, 1976).

The effectiveness of overcorrection as a treatment strategy was impressive in the studies listed above. Like shock, overcorrection led to rapid reduction of problematic behavior, usually to a zero level. In addition, the inclusion of positive practice afforded clients the opportunity to learn more appropriate forms of behavior, giving the procedure a positive educative focus. Thus, overcorrection represented a reasonable alternative for clinicians, particularly in light of the concern over the use of more restrictive treatment procedures.

As research progressed, however, data began to appear that indicated that there were limitations to the effectiveness of overcorrection. For example, Rollings, Baumeister, and Baumeister (1977) found that overcorrection was not always effective in reducing stereotypy. For one client, the target response (i.e., head nodding) was unaffected by the introduction of overcorrection, although other inappropriate behaviors including head banging appeared after treatment was introduced. Although overcorrection did reduce rocking with a second subject in the Rollings et al. investigation, the effects were specific to a training room, with no generalized reductions seen on the ward. In addition, the occurrence of negative side effects and situational specificity may necessitate greater staff availability when using overcorrection, particularly if programming is to occur in multiple settings. Thus, clinicians considering the use of overcorrection must carefully weigh these factors, since they could influence whether the specific procedures are implemented correctly and/or consistently. Of course, these issues may simply reflect the relative novelty of overcorrection as a treatment procedure and highlight the need for additional research. More specifically, the critical parameters affecting the efficacy of overcorrection need to be carefully examined. In addition, component analyses may assist in improving the technology by identifying unnecessary components in treatment packages such as overcorrection, ultimately leading to more efficient intervention techniques.

Clinical Applications

The evolution and refinement of the technology of behavior modification has had considerable impact on treatment practices with the mentally retarded. Initially, research attention primarily focused on the control and elimination of self-stimulatory, stereotypic responses (i.e., body rocking, head weaving, hand staring) as well as self-injurious behavior (e.g., head banging). As Whitman and Scibak (1981) noted in a systematic review of the literature, the range of target behaviors has expanded in recent years to include vomiting and rumination (Mulick, Schroeder, & Rojahn, 1980), pica (Ausman, Ball & Alexander, 1974), aggression (Carr, Newsom, & Binkoff, 1980), stripping (Lutzker, 1974), hyperventilation (Singh, Dawson, & Gregory, 1980), echolalic responding (Ausman & Gaddy, 1974), stealing (Azrin & Wesolowski, 1974), and public masturbation (Cook, Altman, Shaw, & Blaylock, 1978).

There are several reasons why behavior modification research has begun to address such a wide range of behavior problems. First, behavior modification techniques have proven successful with various forms of self-stimulatory and self-injurious behavior (see reviews by Baumeister, 1978; Baumeister & Forehand, 1973; Baumeister & Rollings, 1976; O'Brien, 1981; Schroeder, Schroeder, Rojahn & Mulick, 1981). On the basis of these data, clinicians have applied the same procedures to other problem areas. Second, changing patterns in service delivery with the mentally retarded have resulted in clients gaining greater exposure to new environmental stimuli often without needed prerequisite training. For example, the implementation of the normalization principle (Nirje, 1969) meant that barren dayrooms were replaced by small, homelike, furnished living areas with objects and materials available to provide sensory stimulation. In addition, clients were provided with stylish clothing and active attempts made to keep them dressed. Unfortunately, these changes were often introduced without considering the need for training clients how to use and interact with these stimuli appropriately. Consequently, behaviors such as pica, stripping, and property destruction emerged and became problematic with the mentally retarded. Although these behaviors are inappropriate in and of themselves, their occurrence is problematic because they can interfere with active programming. Clients who do not attend to programming efforts being directed toward them simply fail to demonstrate improvements in adaptive functioning.

Finally, many of the inappropriate behaviors exhibited by the mentally retarded can have serious negative implications for the individuals emitting them. For example, staff may be reluctant to work with clients who exhibit high frequencies of vomiting, rumination, or aggressive behavior, either because of their appearance or the risk of physical harm. Consequently, these individuals may not receive the same amount of attention or programming time as their peers and may be social isolates. Unfortunately, this can result in a never-ending circle, where the clients exhibit more inappropriate behavior as means of gaining attention from staff, resulting in negative interactions or even greater avoidance by staff.

Conclusions

The purpose of this chapter has been to review basic operant principles, to provide a brief introduction to the procedures derived from these principles, and to present specific applications which have been conducted with mentally retarded individuals.

As noted in the introduction, over 400 studies have been published which illustrate the successful application of behavior modification techniques with the retarded. Obviously, a comprehensive review of this literature is beyond the scope of this chapter. However, the reader who is interested in exploring this area of research in greater detail should consult specific books (e.g. Matson & McCartney, 1981; Neisworth & Smith, 1973; Thompson & Grabowski, 1972; Whitman, Scibak, & Reid, 1982; Yule & Carr, 1980) and chapters (e.g., Birnbrauer, 1976; Forehand & Baumeister, 1976; Kazdin, 1978; Schroeder, Mulick, & Schroeder, 1979; Whitman & Scibak, 1979) which review the use of behavior modification in the mentally retarded. In addition, relevant articles regularly appear in the following journals: *American Journal of Mental Deficiency, Analysis and Intervention in Developmental Disabilities, Applied Research in Mental Retardation, Behavior Modification, Behavior Research and Therapy, Behavior Research of Severe Developmental Disabilities, Behavior Therapy, Behavioral Analysis and Modification, Journal of Applied Behavior Analysis, Journal of the Association of the Severely Handicapped, Journal of Behavior Therapy and Experimental Psychiatry,* and *Mental Retardation.*

A review of some of the resources listed above will indicate how the technology of behavior modification is evolving. Numerous techniques are available for suppressing most inappropriate responses encountered in clinical settings although many of these techniques have not yet been sufficiently or systematically validated. Since the majority of the studies use single-subject research designs (cf. Hersen & Barlow, 1976), it is imperative that care be taken to control for confounding variables so that the functional relationship between treatment procedures and behavior change can be demonstrated. In addition, there is a need for replications of the findings reported in the literature to determine whether long-term, clinically significant changes occur. Obviously, when dealing with inappropriate behaviors, the primary emphasis is on producing immediate, positive changes in the treatment setting. However, the ultimate goal is to achieve similar changes across settings and over time. Through continued emphasis on the improvement and refinement of the techniques reviewed in this chapter, the technology will advance, as will the clients who are being served.

References

Ausman, J., Ball, T. S., & Alexander, D. Behavior therapy of pica with a profoundly retarded adolescent. *Mental Retardation*, 1974, 12, 16–18.

Ausman, J., & Gaddy, M. R. Reinforcement training for echolalia: Developing a repertoire of appropriate verbal responses in an echolalic girl. *Mental Retardation*, 1974, 12, 20–21.

Azrin, N. H., Gottlieb, L. H., Hughart, L., Wesolowski, M. D., & Rahn, T. Eliminating self-injurious behavior by educative procedures. *Behavior Research and Therapy*, 1975, 13, 101–111.

Azrin, N. H., & Wesolowski, M. D. Theft reversal: An overcorrection procedure for eliminating stealing by retarded persons. *Journal of Applied Behavior Analysis*, 1974, 7, 577–581.

Bailey, J., & Meyerson, L. Vibration as a reinforcer with a profoundly retarded child. *Journal of Applied Behavior Analysis*, 1969, 2, 135–138.

Bandura, A. *Principles of behavior modification*. New York: Holt, Rinehart & Winston, 1969.

Baumeister, A. A. Origins and control of stereotyped movements. In C. E. Meyers (Ed.), *Quality of life in severely and profoundly retarded persons: Research foundations for improvement*. Washington: American Association on Mental Deficiency, 1978.

Baumeister, A. A., & Forehand, R. Stereotyped acts. In N. R. Ellis (Ed.), *International review of research in mental retardation*. Vol. 6. New York: Academic Press, 1973.

Baumeister, A. A., & Rollings, J. P. Self-injurious behavior. In N. R. Ellis (Ed.), *International review of research in mental retardation*. Vol. 9. New York: Academic Press, 1976.

Bijou, S. W. Theory and research in mental (developmental) retardation. *Psychological Record*, 1963, 13, 95–110.

Bijou, S. W. A functional analysis of retarded development. In N. R. Ellis (Ed.), *International review of research in mental retardation*. Vol. 1. New York: Academic Press, 1966.

Bijou, S. W. Operant extinction after fixed-interval schedules with young children. *Journal of the Experimental Analysis of Behavior*, 1958, 1, 25–29.

Birnbrauer, J. S. Generalization of punishment effects: A case study. *Journal of Applied Behavior Analysis*, 1968, 1, 201–211.

Birnbrauer, J. S. Mental retardation. In H. Leitenberg (Ed.), *Handbook of behavior modification and behavior therapy*. Englewood Cliffs, N.J.: Prentice-Hall, 1976.

Carr, E. G., Newsom, C. D., & Binkoff, J. A. Escape as a factor in the aggressive behavior of two retarded children. *Journal of Applied Behavior Analysis*, 1980, 13, 101–118.

Clark, H. B., Rowbury, T., Baer, A. M., & Baer, D. M. Time-out as punishing stimulus in continuous and intermittent schedules. *Journal of Applied Behavior Analysis*, 1973, 6, 443–455.

Clausen, J. A. Mental deficiency: Development of a concept. *American Journal of Mental Deficiency*, 1967, 71, 727–745.

Cook, J. W., Altman, K., Shaw, J., & Blaylock, M. Use of contingent lemon juice to eliminate public masturbation by a severely retarded boy. *Behavior Research and Therapy*, 1978, 16, 131–134.

Dietz, S. M., & Repp, A. C. Decreasing classroom mis-behavior through the use of DRL schedules of reinforcement. *Journal of Applied Behavior Analysis*, 1973, 6, 457–464.

Doleys, D. M., Wells, K. C., Hobbs, S. A., Roberts, M. W., & Cartelli, L. M. The effects of social punishment on noncompliance: A comparison with timeout and positive practice. *Journal of Applied Behavior Analysis*, 1976, 9, 471–482.

Epstein, H., Doke, L., Sajwaj, T., Sorrell, S., & Rimmer, B. Generality and side effects of overcorrection. *Journal of Applied Behavior Analysis*, 1974, 7, 385–390.

Favell, J. E. Reduction of stereotypies by reinforcement of toy play. *Mental Retardation*, 1973, 11, 21–23.

Favell, J., McGimsey, J., & Jones, M. The use of physical restraint in the treatment of self-injury and as positive reinforcement. *Journal of Applied Behavior Analysis*, 1978, 11, 225–241.

Ferster, C. S., & Skinner, B. F. *Schedules of reinforcement*. New York: Appleton-Century-Crofts, 1957.

Forehand, R., & Baumeister, A. A. Deceleration of aberrant behavior among retarded individuals. In M. Hersen, R. M. Eisler, & P. M. Miller (Eds.), *Progress in behavior modification*. Vol. 2. New York: Academic Press, 1976.

Foxx, C. L., Jones, J. R., Foxx, R. M., & Kiely, D. Twenty-four hour social isolation: A program for reducing the aggressive behavior of a psychotic-like retarded adult. *Behavior Modification*, 1980, 4, 130–146.

Foxx, R. M. Increasing a mildly retarded woman's attendance at self-help classes by overcorrection and instruction. *Behavior Therapy*, 1976, 7, 390–396.

Foxx, R. M., & Azrin, N. H. Restitution: A method of eliminating aggressive-disruptive behavior of retarded and brain damaged patients. *Behavior Research and Therapy*, 1972, 10, 15–27.

Foxx, R. M., & Azrin, N. H. The elimination of autistic self-stimulatory behavior by overcorrection. *Journal of Applied Behavior Analysis*, 1973, 6, 1–14.

Foxx, R. M., & Martin, E. D. Treatment of scavenging behavior (coprophagy and pica) by overcorrection. *Behavior Research and Therapy*, 1975, 13, 153–162.

Foxx, R. M., & Shapiro, S. T. The time-out ribbon: A non-exclusionary time-out procedure. *Journal of Applied Behavior Analysis*, 1978, 11, 125–136.

Franks, C. M. (Ed.) *Behavior therapy: Appraisal and status*. New York: McGraw-Hill, 1969.

Greene, R., & Hoats, D. Aversive tickling: A simple conditioning technique. *Behavior Therapy*, 1971, 2, 389–393.

Grossman, H. J. (Ed.) *Manual on terminology and classification in mental retardation*. Washington, D.C.: American Association on Mental Deficiency, 1973.

Hall, R. V., Fox, R., Willard, D., Goldsmith, L., Emerson, M., Owen, M., Davis, F., & Porcia, E. The teacher as observer and experimenter in the modification of disputing and talking-out behaviors. *Journal of Applied Behavior Analysis*, 1971, 4, 141–150.

Hamilton, H., Stephens, L., & Allen, P. Controlling aggressive and destructive behavior in severely retarded institutionalized residents. *American Journal of Mental Deficiency*, 1967, 71, 852–856.

Hamilton, J., & Standahl, J. Suppression of stereotyped screaming behavior in a profoundly retarded institutionalized female. *Journal of Experimental Child Psychology*, 1969, 7, 114–121.

Hersen, M., & Barlow, D. *Single case research designs*. New York: Pergamon Press, 1976.

Higgs, R., Burns, G., & Meunier, G. Eliminating self-stimulatory vocalizations of a profoundly retarded girl through overcorrection. *Journal of the Association for the Severely Handicapped*, 1980, **5**, 264–269.

Honig, W. K., & Staddon, J. E. R. (Eds.) *Handbook of operant behavior*. Englewood Cliffs, N.J.: Prentice-Hall, 1977.

Hopkins, B. L. Effects of candy and social reinforcement, instructions, and reinforcement schedule learning on the modification and maintenance of smiling. *Journal of Applied Behavior Analysis*, 1968, **1**, 121–130.

Jervis, G. A. Medical aspects of mental deficiency. *American Journal of Mental Deficiency*, 1952, **57**, 175–188.

Kazdin, A. E. The effect of vicarious reinforcement on attentive behavior in the classroom. *Journal of Applied Behavior Analysis*, 1973, **6**, 71–78.

Kazdin, A. E. Behavior modification in retardation. In J. T. Neisworth & R. M. Smith (Eds.), *Retardation: Issues, assessment and intervention*. New York: McGraw-Hill, 1978.

Kazdin, A. E., & Klock, J. The effect of nonverbal teacher approval on student attentive behavior. *Journal of Applied Behavior Analysis*, 1973, **6**, 643–654.

Kohlenberg, R. The punishment of persistent vomiting: A case study. *Journal of Applied Behavior Analysis*, 1970, **3**, 241–245.

Laws, D. R., Brown, R. A., Epstein, J., & Hocking, N. Reduction of inappropriate social behavior in disturbed children by an untrained paraprofessional therapist. *Behavior Therapist*, 1971, **2**, 519–533.

Lindsley, O. R. Direct measurement and prosthesis of retarded behavior. *Journal of Education*, 1964, **147**, 62–81.

Lovaas, O. I., & Simmons, J. O. Manipulation of self-destruction in three retarded children. *Journal of Applied Behavior Analysis*, 1969, **2**, 143–157.

Lutzker, J. R. Social reinforcement control of exhibitionism in a profoundly retarded adult. *Mental Retardation*, 1974, **12**, 46–47.

MacMillan, D. L. *Mental retardation in school and society*. Boston; Little Brown & Co., 1977.

Martin, P. L., & Foxx, R. M. Victim control of the aggression of an institutionalized retardate. *Journal of Behavior Therapy and Experimental Psychiatry*, 1973, **4**, 161–165.

Martin, J., & Matson, J. L. Eliminating the inappropriate vocalizations of a retarded adult by overcorrection. *Scandinavian Journal of Behavior Therapy*, 1978, **7**, 203–209.

Matson, J. L., & McCartney J. R. (Eds.) *Handbook of behavior modification with the mentally retarded*. New York: Plenum, 1981.

Matson, J. L., & Stephens, R. M. Overcorrection treatment of stereotyped behaviors. *Behavior Modification*, 1981, **5**, 491–502.

Matson, J. L., Stephens, R. M., & Smith, C. Treatment of self-injurious behavior with overcorrection. *Journal of Mental Deficiency Research*, 1978, **22**, 175–178.

Mikulas, W. L. *Behavior modification*. New York: Harper & Row, 1978.

Mulhern, T., & Baumeister, A. A. An experimental attempt to reduce stereotypy by reinforcement procedures. *American Journal of Mental Deficiency*, 1965, **74**, 69–74.

Mulick, J., Hoyt, R., Rojahn, J., & Schroeder, S. Reduction of a "nervous habit" in a profoundly retarded youth by increasing toy play: A case study. *Journal of Behavior Therapy and Experimental Psychiatry*, 1978, **9**, 381–385.

Mulick, J. A., Schroeder, S. R., & Rojahn, J. Chronic ruminative vomiting: A comparison of four treatment procedures. *Journal of Autism and Developmental Disorders*, 1980, **10**, 203–213.

Neisworth, J. T., & Smith, R. M. *Modifying retarded behavior*. Boston: Houghton Mifflin, 1973.

Nirje, B. The normalization principle and its human management implications. In R. Kugel & W. Wolfensberger (Eds.), *Changing patterns of residential services for the mentally retarded*. Washington, D.C.: President's Committee on Mental Retardation, 1969.

O'Brien, F. Treating self-stimulatory behavior. In J. L. Matson & J. R. McCartney (Eds.), *Handbook of behavior modification with the mentally retarded*. New York: Plenum, 1981.

Ollendick, T. H., & Matson, J. L. An initial investigation into the parameters of overcorrection, *Psychological Reports*, 1976, **39**, 1139–1142.

O'Neil, P. M., White, J. L., King, C. R., & Carik, D. J. Controlling childhood rumination through differential reinforcement of other behavior. *Behavior Modification*, 1979, **3**, 355–372.

Penrose, L. S. *The biology of mental defect*. New York: Grune & Stratton, 1949.

Ragain, R., & Anson, J. The control of self-mutilating behavior with positive reinforcement. *Mental Retardation*, 1976, **14**, 22–25.

Repp, A. C., & Brulle, A. R. Reducing aggressive behavior of mentally retarded persons. In J. L. Matson and J. R. McCartney (Eds.), *Handbook of behavior modification with the mentally retarded*. New York: Plenum, 1981.

Repp, A. C., Deitz, S. M., & Deitz, D. E. D. Reducing inappropriate classroom and prescriptive behaviors through DRO schedules of reinforcement. *Mental Retardation*, 1976, **14**, 11–15.

Reynolds, G. S. *A primer of operant conditioning*. Glenview, Illinois: Scott, Foresman, 1968.

Rincover, A. Sensory extinction: A procedure for eliminating self-stimulatory behavior in psychotic children. *Journal of Abnormal Child Psychology*, 1978, **6**, 299–310.

Rincover, A., Cook, R., Peoples, A., & Packard, D. Sensory extinction and sensory reinforcement principles for programming multiple adaptive behavior change. *Journal of Applied Behavior Analysis*, 1979, **12**, 221–223.

Rincover, A., & Devany, J. The application of sensory extinction procedures to self-injury. *Analysis and Intervention in Developmental Disabilities*, 1982, **2**, 67–81.

Risley, T., The effects and side effects of punishing the autistic behaviors of a deviant child. *Journal of Applied Behavior Analysis*, 1968, **1**, 21–34.

Rollings, J. P., Baumeister, A., & Baumeister, A. The use of overcorrection procedures to eliminate stereotyped behaviors in retarded individuals. *Behavior Modification*, 1977, **1**, 29–46.

Sajwaj, T., Libet, J., & Agras, S. Lemon juice therapy: The control of life-threatening rumination in a six-month-old infant. *Journal of Applied Behavior Analysis*, 1974, **7**, 557–566.

Saposnek, D. T., & Watson, L. S. The elimination of the self-destructive behavior of a psychotic child: A case study. *Behavior Therapy*, 1974, **5**, 79–89.

Schroeder, S., Mulick, J., & Schroeder, C. Management of severe behavior problems of the retarded. In N. R.

Ellis (Ed.), *Handbook of mental deficiency.* (2nd ed.) Hillsdale, N.J.: Erlbaum, 1979.

Schroeder, S. R., Schroeder, C. S., Rojahn, J., & Mulick, J. A. Self-injurious behavior: An analysis of behavior management techniques. In J. L. Matson & J. R. McCartney (Eds.), *Handbook of behavior modification with the mentally retarded.* New York: Plenum, 1981.

Singh, N. N., Dawson, M. J., & Gregory, P. R. Suppression of chronic hyperventilation using response-contingent aromatic ammonia. *Behavior Therapy,* 1980, **11,** 561–566.

Skinner, B. F. *The behavior of organisms: An experimental analysis.* New York: Appleton-Century, 1938.

Solnick, J. V., Rincover, A., & Peterson, C. R. Some determinants of the reinforcing and punishing effects of time-out. *Journal of Applied Behavior Analysis,* 1977, **10,** 415–424.

Tanner, B. A., & Zeiler, M. D. Punishment of self-injurious behavior using aromatic ammonia as the aversive stimulus. *Journal of Applied Behavior Analysis,* 1975, **8,** 53–57.

Tarpley, H., & Schroeder, S. A comparison of DRO and DRI procedures in the treatment of self-injurious behavior. *American Journal of Mental Deficiency,* 1979, **84,** 188–194.

Thompson, T., & Grabowski, J. (Eds.) *Behavior modification of the mentally retarded.* New York: Oxford University Press, 1972.

Thorndike, E. L. *Animal intelligence: Experimental studies.* New York: Macmillan, 1911.

Wecksler, D. *The measurement and appraisal of adult intelligence.* Baltimore: Williams & Wilkins, 1958.

Weiher, R. & Harmon, R. The use of omission training to reduce self-injurious behavior in a retarded child. *Behavior Therapy,* 1975, **6,** 261–268.

White, G., Nielsen, G., & Johnson, S. Time-out duration and the suppression of deviant behavior in children. *Journal of Applied Behavior Analysis,* 1972, **5,** 111–120.

Whitman, T. L., & Scibak, J. W. Behavior modification research with the severely and profoundly retarded. In N. R. Ellis (Ed.), *Handbook of mental deficiency: Psychological theory and research.* (2nd ed.) Hillsdale, N.J.: Erlbaum, 1979.

Whitman, T. L., & Scibak, J. W. Behavior modification research with the mentally retarded: Treatment and research perspectives. In J. L. Matson & J. R. McCartney (Eds.), *Handbook of behavior modification with the mentally retarded.* New York: Plenum, 1981.

Whitman, T. L., Scibak, J. W., & Reid, D. H. *Behavior modification with the severely and profoundly retarded*: Research and applications. New York: Academic Press, 1982.

Wolf, M., Risley, T., & Mees, P. Application of operant conditioning procedures to the behavior problems of an autistic child. *Behavior Research and Therapy,* 1964, **1,** 305–312.

Wyatt v. Stickney, 344 F. Supp, 373, 344 F. Supp, 387 (M.D. Ala., 1972) affirmed sub nom *Wyatt v. Aderholt,* 503 F2d. 1305 (5th Cir. 1974).

Yates, A. J. *Theory and practice in behavior therapy.* New York: Wiley-Interscience, 1971.

Yule, W., & Carr, J. *Behavior modification for the mentally handicapped.* Baltimore: University Park Press, 1980.

Zimmerman, E. H., Zimmerman, J., & Russell, C. D. Differential effects of token reinforcement on instruction-following behavior in retarded students instructed as a group. *Journal of Applied Behavior Analysis,* 1969, **2,** 101–112.

23 PSYCHOTHERAPY

Edward J. Nuffield

Psychotherapy for the mentally retarded should be described in terms of its scope and limitations. This is necessary in order for the presentation to avoid being vague and diffuse, on the one hand, or spilling over into the purview of other methods of psychological assistance to this population on the other. Some authors have spread their nets widely. Thus, Bialer (1967) includes in his discussion such "helping techniques" as casework, social group work, pastoral counseling, art, music, occupational, and recreational therapies as well as remotivation. Kaplan (1963) has tried to delineate the differences between "social work therapy" and "psychiatric psychotherapy." The conclusion is that there is a great deal of overlap between the two in operational terms. The two forms of therapy cannot be distinguished on the basis of such factors as depth of operation or the attainment of insight by the subject; the main difference is that the psychiatrist uses some biological concepts which he has at his disposal, whereas the social worker does not. The disciplinary membership of the therapists is different. In this chapter, I shall focus on what is being done, rather than on the disciplinary affiliation of the person or persons doing it.

A distinction needs to be made between psychotherapy and training. Training or habilitation is a procedure wherein the patient is viewed as a growing and developing organism whose progress has been delayed by various reasons. The mentally retarded individual without any psychiatric complications fits this description. The causes or factors pertinent to this delay are not addressed, but the trainer views his task as one of producing some acceleration in the rate of growth of the individual and attempts to facilitate the acquisition of new skills. On the other hand, therapy views the patient as hampered in his progress by adverse forces, which become the target of the therapist's endeavors. Some of these factors are not psychological but biochemical, genetic, or chromosomal, and even if they are psychological not all of them are capable of being changed. In as much as they are, the mentally retarded person is a suitable subject for psychotherapy.

The currently popular classificatory schema, DSM III, holds to a primarily descriptive principle (pp. 6–8); nevertheless, it fully recognizes the relevance of adverse psychological factors such as inconstant early nurturance and intermittent maternal neglect. These can lead to a variety of nosological entities such as oppositional disorders, pica, or even a pervasive developmental disorder. Such factors can also have an adverse effect on overall developmental progress. The coexistence of mental retardation and a diagnosable psychiatric disorder can have a mutually aggravating effect. Hence it is not surprising that prevalence statistics reflect this interconnection. Investigators have ascertained that some 30 to 40% of mentally retarded individuals have a diagnosable psychiatric disorder (Menolascino, 1965; Rutter, Tizard & Whitmore, 1970). The high prevalence of psychiatric disorder in the mentally retarded population makes a discussion of psychotherapy for this group relevant.

Definitions of Psychotherapy

Writers who approach this issue from the perspective of mental retardation (Bialer, 1967; Cowen, 1955; Cowen & Trippe, 1963) have utilized definitions pertaining to psychotherapy generally which they consider most pertinent to their particular work. A commonly accepted definition (Hinsie & Campbell, 1970) states that:

> Psychotherapy is any form of treatment for mental illnesses, behavioral maladaptations and/or other problems that are assumed to be of an emotional nature in which a trained person deliberately establishes a professional relationship with a patient for the purpose of removing, modifying, or retarding, existing symptoms, of attenuating or reversing disturbed patterns of behavior and of promoting positive personality growth and development.

This broad definition is qualified by the authors, who use the term "definitive forms of psychotherapy." This qualification excludes procedures such as environmental manipulation and general medical treatment, including physical examination, but it does not allow for any of the forms of group psychotherapy. Similarly, Close (1966) and Shoben (1953) confine themselves to defining individual psychotherapy only. Shoben states that psychotherapy is:

> a certain kind of social relationship between two persons who hold periodic conversations in pursuit of certain goals; namely, the lessening of emotional discomfort and the alleviation of various other aspects of client behavior.

This definition does not make any allowance for non-verbal forms of communication between therapist and patient and excludes all forms of activity therapy. Snyder (1947) makes a similar exclusion:

> Psychotherapeutic counseling is a face-to-face relationship in which a psychologically trained individual is consciously attempting by verbal means to assist another person to modify

emotional attitudes that are socially maladjustive and in which the subject is relatively aware of the personality organization through which he is going.

Bertine (1940) defines psychotherapy as "a method of diagnosis and treatment of such illness and malladaptation as cannot, after medical examination, be ascribed to a physical condition but must be understood in terms of the psyche." He is more concerned with etiology than process. English and English (1958) have the broadest definition of psychotherapy possible. They define it as "the use of any psychological technique in the treatment of mental disorder or maladjustment." Grinker, McGregor, Selan, Klein, and Kohrman (1961) define psychological intervention to be "a form of drugless therapy not subject to restrictions of medical licensure."

Cowen (1955) has managed to extract some common factors from a number of definitions. These are as follows:

1. The starting point of therapy is an individual seeking help. (This, of course, is not true in the case of large groups of people such as children and many of the seriously mentally ill and severely retarded. It also does not apply to many nonretarded adolescents who may also be suitable for psychotherapy.)
2. A relationship between the therapist and the client. "The essence of therapy is not the response of the client to therapeutic techniques; it is his response to another person."

Cowen considers that the therapist's personality is crucial. He needs warmth, sensitivity, understanding, spontaneity, and empathy. Another essential ingredient in psychotherapy is the provision of an opportunity for the client or patient to release emotional tension, i.e., an opportunity for catharsis. Cowen recognizes the importance of nonverbal as well as verbal activity on the part of the therapist, but stresses the need for a formally consistent body of therapeutic techniques that can be applied flexibly.

Bialer (1967) is also quite aware that nonverbal techniques are an important inclusion in the practice of psychotherapy. He also negates the necessity for insight on the part of the patient in order for psychotherapy to be successful. His definition of psychotherapy is:

> a systematic utilization of psychological techniques, the chief of which is a close interpersonal relationship by a professionally

trained therapist in order to help individuals who seek or need assistance in the amelioration of emotional or behavioral problems.

In an attempt to differentiate between psychotherapy, counseling psychotherapy, and psychoanalysis, Taraschow (1962) draws the distinction as follows: "Real events are treated as reality in psychotherapy, but in analysis these are treated as products of the patient's fantasies and determined by the requirements of his unconscious conflicts."

Szymanski (1980) follows the realistic approach and defines psychotherapy as:

a treatment procedure performed by a trained mental health professional through application of psychologically based verbal and non-verbal means within the context of a relationship with the patient or client, and with definite goals of improving the patient's coping abilities and/or ameliorating psychopathological symptoms.

In focusing on symptomatic improvement and increased coping abilities on the part of the patient, Szymanski steers away from any idea of fundamental reconstruction of the personality of the mentally retarded patient.

In an attempt to draw together the various concepts of a number of workers in the field of psychotherapy with the mentally retarded, the author proposes the following definition:

Psychotherapy is the formalized exchange between one or more therapists and one or more patients or clients for the purpose of attaining a defined clinical goal. It is an event that can be described in terms of structure, process and content.

This statement does not exclude group methods, but does exclude certain types of chance encounter or casual contacts between therapist and patient. The formality of the procedure implies that institutional sanction is necessary. In practice this occurs in the setting of a clinic or hospital or an institution and introduces an administrative component. The participants in the psychotherapeutic act are parties to a therapeutic contract which may be explicit or implicit. The existence of a defined goal indicates that there is a basic plan to the endeavor. By calling it a clinical goal, it is made clear that the exercise is carried out with the benefit of the patient in view. The descriptive analysis of psychotherapeutic events contains the elements of structure, process, and content. The term structure indicates that there is an agreed upon framework of place and time where and when psychotherapy occurs. The term process indicates that the psychotherapeutic events take on a certain shape, which can be described sequentially. Content is defined as the issues which are being dealt with in the course of psychotherapy.

Varieties of Psychotherapy

There are any number of parameters along which existing forms of psychotherapy can be arranged. The four chosen are those of aim, time frame, numbers, and method. The different aims of psychotherapy will be determined in a practical and realistic way by an answer to the question of what the patient is ultimately capable of. Can he attain sufficient insight into his condition so that he is able to make the necessary readjustments or will he need a crutch for an indefinite time in order to get along in society? There is a wide spectrum of end states between the extreme of total independence on the one hand and ongoing and substantial dependency on the other. Insight therapy operating according to psychodynamic principles will aim at substantial independence. Supportive therapy is appropriate if the patient cannot realistically be brought to a state of even partial independence. In relationship therapy, the aim is somewhat intermediate in that the patient utilizes the dynamics of the interaction between himself and the therapist and through this grows to some measure of independence and maturity.

The second parameter is that of time. It is customary to think of brief therapy as a specific entity but this is quite arbitrary. In a strict sense, every course of therapy should be limited, even if the time span planned is quite extended. The duration of therapy is determined not only by the innate capacity of the patient, but also by certain contingencies in the patient's life situation. The stress that the mentally retarded person is operating under may be of a chronic nature and this will require therapy to be prolonged. Under conditions of acute stress, crisis intervention is as appropriate in mentally retarded individuals as in any other group.

In terms of number, psychotherapies are usually divided into individual and group. Family therapy is a subvariant of group therapy as far as the numbers are concerned, though the members have special relationships. In group psychotherapy, it is customary to have one or two therapists and six to eight patients. In mentally retarded populations, the group may need to be smaller. Sadock (1980, p. 2183) classifies group therapies on the basis of underlying theory or ideology, i.e., Gestalt group therapy, transactional analysis in groups, psychoanalysis of groups, etc. Another variant of group therapy is psychodrama or sociodrama (Morino, 1971). The special features of this form lead to a consideration of the fourth parameter, that of method.

The various methods can be classified as verbal and nonverbal (or activity) methods. Verbal methods range from free association and dream analysis as part of the psychoanalytic method to some didactic approaches. Activities are even more varied and include modalities such as art therapy, music therapy, and dance and movement therapy. The choice of method hinges chiefly on whether the patient is capable of one mode of expression better than another. Thus, one individual may be particularly inhibited in terms of motoric expression but able to communicate relatively freely through verbal means. More often, however, mentally retarded individuals have more difficulty with verbal modes than with the various forms of motor activity. In the overall picture of psychotherapy with the mentally retarded, different forms of activity such as play therapy play a considerable role.

It is necessary to distinguish between methods and strategies on the one hand and techniques on the other. Methods are planned and ongoing activities on the part of the therapist and will be evident throughout its whole course. Thus, in psychoanalysis, free association and dream analysis pervade the course of treatment. Techniques, on the other hand, are employed at certain focal points in therapy and may also occur spontaneously. Confrontation, interpretation, and silence are examples of specific techniques. Sternlicht (1964) has described such techniques as organizing balloon games with a group or engaging a specific member in Indian arm wrestling. It is possible to see how such specific measures have emerged during the course of practicing psychotherapy with the mentally retarded.

History and Evolution of Psychotherapy for the Mentally Retarded

There are early accounts of the care of the feeble-minded (Kanner, 1964) that indicate that psychological methods were used to help these individuals. The treatment of the "Wild Boy of Aveyron" by Itard received a great deal of publicity and Seguin made a similar effort. To some extent, these endeavors were examples of training and habilitation rather than therapy. The focus of early residential centers such as the Abendberg was primarily an educational one, even though these centers were described as healing institutes. The psychoanalytic movement, the mental health movement, and the child guidance movement gave impetus to the practice of formal psychotherapy. Chess (1962) has pointed out that the early child-

guidance clinics did deal with large numbes of mentally retarded children whom they did not turn away, unlike their successors. Psychotherapeutic methods began to be employed at the Vineland Training School from 1908 onwards. As state institutions usually called state schools became larger, the atmosphere became less and less favorable for the development of psychotherapeutic programs. The positive endeavors in these institutions concerned themselves largely with training and habilitation of the inmates. By the second third of the twentieth century, however, accounts of individual psychotherapy being practiced in institutional settings began to appear (Freeman, 1936; Maisner, 1950; Mundy, 1957; Sarbin, 1945; Thorne, 1948). Accounts of group psychotherapy in state schools appeared about the same time or a little later (Astrachan, 1955; Cotzin, 1948; Fisher & Wolfson, 1953; Leland, Walker, & Taboada, 1959; Snyder & Sechrest, 1959; Vail, 1955; Yonge & O'Connor, 1954). Reports of psychotherapeutic activities against a background of psychoanalytic and psychodynamic principles appeared from the Southard School of the Menninger Clinic (Ackerman & Menninger, 1936; Chidester, 1934; Chidester & Menninger, 1936). Outpatient clinics also tended to operate on the basis of psychoanalytic or psychodynamic principles and they presented a few reports of therapy with mentally retarded children (Cooley, 1945; Glassman, 1943; Wegman, 1944). After World War II, special education for the handicapped including the mentally retarded began to be established and a report of psychotherapy against this background was provided by Lavalli and Levine (1954). With the advent of the 1960's, the vast movement of deinstitutionalization emerged and the process of so-called normalization of the mentally retarded began. This has produced a shift of mentally retarded individuals from institutional settings into the community. However, many of the mentally retarded in the community live in settings that are intermediate in terms of restrictions imposed and amount of supervision and support provided. The influence of the context of psychotherapy will be described later.

Principles of Psychotherapy

The necessity for defining principles or guidelines within which psychotherapeutic activities can operate soon became obvious. Thorne (1948) postulated the following principles for treatment:

1. The mentally retarded person had to be accepted by the therapist.
2. He had to be allowed to express his emotions and to ventilate his feelings.
3. He had to be taught to exert emotional control.

(This was most difficult in the case of these individuals.) The situation causing frustration should be analyzed and the retarded person should walk away from it rather than act out.

4. An emphasis on crude suggestion, advice, and persuasion is necessary to establish standards of conduct.
5. Reassurance of the patient in order to build up his confidence is necessary.
6. Steering the child or the individual to use further counseling, i.e., to build up some motivation for seeking help is important.

Abel (1953) postulated the following guidelines:

1. A need for the therapist to have a genuine liking for the subject, that the latter is worthwhile as a human being;
2. Setting up modest goals; and
3. Employing flexible techniques.

Abel (1953) opened up the use of a variety of therapies, including occupational therapy, through his guidelines. Yepson (1952) organized his ideas along the following principles:

1. The counselor must have sufficient information about the client; i.e., there is a certain requirement of diagnostic knowledge before the process of therapy can begin.
2. The counselor should be eclectic in his outlook and should have a broad knowledge about such things as job requirements, community resources etc.
3. The counselor must be supportive.
4. The counselor must give sound advice.
5. He must use constructive emotional appeal.
6. Suggestion and fostering motivation are important ingredients of therapy.
7. Small steps need to be taken at one time and nothing should be taken for granted with the mentally retarded. The use of simple language is advised.
8. The possibility of the mentally retarded gaining insight into his capabilities and limitations should be kept open.

Yepson recognized that the mentally retarded person has special problems with society due to the latter's misunderstanding of retardation.

Sarason (1953), who has been rather influential in this field, had some different principles or preconditions for successful psychotherapy:

1. The therapist should have enough time for psychotherapy.
2. He should have administrative authority.

3. The child should be able to see the therapist whenever he or she wishes.
4. The therapist should not have any punitive or disciplinary role.

Sarason's principles keep an eye on the administrative and institutional context within which psychotherapy takes place. He does open up the possibility of a conflict between the therapist's administrative and clinical functions.

DeMartino (1957) utilized Maslow's (1954) account of the basic ingredients of psychotherapy: (1) release and catharsis, (2) the provision of basic gratification, support, love and respect, (3) protection of the patient and removal of threat, (4) the attainment of insight, (5) the employment of suggestion or authority, and (6) positive self-actualization and growth as a goal. DeMartino emphasized the need for an "eclectic approach" and for flexibility on the part of the therapist.

Cowen (1955) summarized the essential ingredients of successful therapy as follows:

1. a person who seeks psychological help,
2. the presence of a unique client-therapist relationship,
3. an opportunity for release of emotional tension,
4. the presence of a consistent body of therapeutic techniques, and
5. the impact of nonverbal aspects of therapy and the personality of the therapist.

He recognized that the reorganization of the personality and an increase in self-understanding leading to psychological growth is not always possible in the case of the mentally retarded. Regarding his first principle, it must be said that the seeking of help is not always done on the part of the patient but by others close to him. This does not absolutely preclude a successful outcome.

Jakab (1970) recognized this fully and indicated that the contract can be made between the therapist and the society around the patient. She stressed the need for a planned structured approach and the fact that the child has an emotional disturbance as well as the handicap of being mentally retarded.

In summarizing all the foregoing contributions, one can discern a consensus among different authors along the following lines: (1) The therapist needs to have a positive attitude toward at least the possibility that retarded individuals may improve with psychotherapy. (2) The approach needs to be planned and not haphazard. (3) Specific goals are necessary though they can be quite limited. (4) Flexibility in terms of techniques employed is necessary. I would add a fifth principle, namely that *the practice of psychotherapy should be clearly documented and subjected to critical scrutiny by professionals other than the therapist.*

Goals and Objectives

It is possible to describe goals and objectives for the whole population of mentally retarded individuals suitable for psychotherapy or to describe them specifically with one group in mind. As an example of the former, Jakab (1970) considers the goals of psychotherapy to be:

1. the alleviation of painful or uncomfortable symptoms,
2. an improvement or disappearance of socially unaccepted behavior patterns,
3. a realization of intellectual potentials,
4. the accumulation of positive affective experience (love, gratification, and acceptance), and
5. as a consequence of the preceding four) a more integrated interactional development of the total personality toward emotional and intellectual maturity.

The achievement of the first two goals indicates an approach that aims at dealing with the surface phenomena of the disturbance, whereas the last two goals point to a more fundamental change in the individual as being a desirable endpoint. The goal of realization of the individual's intellectual potential is one that is specifically pertinent with regard to mentally retarded patients. The inference, however, is that this goal will be achieved indirectly if the other objectives have been gained.

Leland and Smith (1965), who are concerned primarily with children, describe the following goals: (1) recognition of self, (2) understanding that impulses can be controlled, and (3) living within social boundaries. The third item can be clearly translated into behavioral change, whereas the first two refer to more fundamental aspects of the child's personality. The idea that mentally retarded individuals have a poor self-image or little awareness of self occurs again and again in the literature. Thus, Balthazar and Stevens (1975, p. 91) recognize that when the patient has improved in social adjustment in personality and in adaptive behavior, he will achieve a sense of increased satisfaction and improved worth.

In setting objectives of a more concrete kind, Wilcox and Guthrie (1957) have postulated the following:

1. to reduce the suspicions that patients felt towards outsiders,
2. to release aggression,
3. to encourage feelings of self-confidence and self-worth, and

4. to develop a feeling of responsibility for their actions.

These authors had treated a specific group of institutionalized adolescent girls and young women. Yepson (1952) saw the importance of setting limited goals that have to do with solving problems around certain real-life issues such as friendship, marriage, and recreation.

There has been considerable discussion as to the appropriateness of defining intellectual potential as a goal of psychotherapy and, by corollary, as a measure of its success or failure. Bialer (1967, p. 146) saw a trend away from this emphasis toward stressing the importance of improved emotional adjustment. Beier (1964, p. 480) considered that reports of an increase in intellectual measures as a result of psychotherapy were generally suspect. Robinson and Robinson (1976, p. 395) considered it short-sighted to gauge psychotherapy success by a single dimension such as IQ.

Szymanski (1980) has not concerned himself with any changes in intellectual functioning, but sees the goals of psychotherapy in quite different terms. He stresses improving frustration tolerance, achieving better impulse control, and the learning of social coping skills as significant objectives. He also points to the importance of the patient being able to deal with conflicts around dependency and guilt as well as overcoming a certain egocentricity and being able to express emotions more appropriately.

In summary, it is possible to point to certain recurring themes when considering a priority list of issues for the mentally retarded patient to deal with in psychotherapy: (1) The attainment of a position of greater social acceptability. In order to attain this the mentally retarded individual may need to gain greater emotional maturity. On the other hand, this may involve little more than the removal of a symptom which is socially obnoxious. (2) An appreciation of greater self-worth on the part of the patient. This would appear to be the most fundamental feature of a successful psychotherapeutic outcome. (3) As a result of the latter, the mentally retarded individual would be able to achieve a greater measure of independence with significant others.

As subheadings or subsections of these basic goals, one can point to various coping abilities such as an ability to resist infantilization by parents, a better sexual awareness during adolescence, an ability to make vocational choices, the ability to cope with marriage and the duties of parenting, all being pertinent goals of psychotherapy. Some of these specific issues may be beyond the attainment of the individual mentally retarded person. In these cases, only one or two specifics may be relevant.

Context of Psychotherapy

It is difficult to exaggerate the importance of the context in which psychotherapy takes place, particularly in carrying out the actual work of therapy. Some writers (e.g., Ackerman & Menninger, 1936; Heiser, 1954; Thorne, 1948; Weinstock, 1979) are so preoccupied with the milieu or setting in which psychotherapy occurs that there is little time or space left to describe the therapeutic process. The climate within which different workers have been operating has varied greatly. In general, Wiest (1955) found that the hospital of his day was poorly equipped to deal with emotional disorder in mentally retarded individuals. On the other hand, Albini and Dinitz (1965) and Yonge and O'Connor (1954) gave little description of the climate and the setting in which they worked psychotherapeutically. Fine and Dawson (1965) described a self-contained psychiatric program in a state hospital. In their case, the psychotherapeutic plan was embedded in a total program with a very positive approach. Similarly, Weinstock (1979) described group therapy within the context of a total treatment program, which is sharply demarcated from a residential center with a presumably nontherapeutic atmosphere. The basic and essential feature of a therapeutic milieu consists of the establishment of a therapeutic atmosphere.

In the case of mentally retarded individuals living in the community, the context is very different. In this instance, the psychological environment is much more complicated than in the case of the institutionalized person. Irrespective of whether the patient lives with his family, in a group home, or in some other nonfamilylike residential setting, he is likely to have contact with his family, so that emotional ties will have to be considered as part of his psychological situation. In order to make a therapeutic impact on these factors, it is essential that professional contact with parent or family be established. Szymanski (1980) has pointed out that these contacts may range from intensive psychotherapy with family members to occasional advice on finding resources. It is important to remember that parents and relatives are not by themselves patients. Jakab (1970) recommended that the therapists should have occasional teamlike meetings with all the adults who are part of the patient's environment. This approach would include not only parents but other relatives who were in some significant contact with the patient. Traditionally, a coworker or another professional who is often a social worker will operate in this area. Descriptions of the interplay between individual psychotherapy and formal work with families are given by Pueschel and Yeatman (1977) and Satten and Singer (1979). Walker (1977),

who has a basic family-centered approach, not surprisingly sees involvement of the whole family as an essential part of psychotherapy. Similarly, Chess (1970) made it apparent that she considers the involvement of the family to be essential in order for a treatment plan to be effective.

In the case of the mentally retarded child living with his family of origin, the situation is the same as that of the similarly placed nonretarded child. A more complex configuration occurs where a mentally retarded adult lives in a community setting and is in contact with his family of origin, but does not live with them. In this case, however, family members are best involved on a collaborative basis, i.e., where the psychotherapist enlists the aid of a fellow professional who helps family members independently. In such instances, good team work is essential as it is whenever one is dealing with complex social systems.

Process of Psychotherapy

For the sake of clarity, it will be necessary to separate the process of psychotherapy in children from that in adolescents and adults. Before describing the process and techniques employed with children, it is necessary to address an issue that is basic to child development.

The Role of Play in the Development of the Mentally Retarded Child

It is widely recognized that play has an important role in the development of children. Its effect on cognitive development has been widely documented by many developmental psychologists (Bruner, 1965; Florey, 1976; Piaget, 1951; Pulaski, 1976). The sequential features of this development have been described by Parten (1932) and Piaget (1951) through their description of play hierarchies. Investigators who have compared the play of mentally retarded children with that of nonretarded children have found significant qualitative differences (Weiner, Ottinger, & Tilton, 1969; Weiner & Weiner, 1974; Woodward, 1959). Opposite findings were produced by Hulme and Lunzer (1966). In investigating the social aspects of play, Copabianco and Cole (1960) found mentally retarded children comparing unfavorably with nonretarded children along this parameter. The work of Wing, Gould, Yeates, and Brierley (1977) indicated that the lack of symbolic play was a feature of children with autistic behaviors.

Play Therapy with the Retarded Child

Strictly speaking this should be described as psychotherapy through play methods. Axline (1949) was one of the pioneers of this form of therapy. Her goal was to bring the mentally retarded children to a level of normal intelligence. Maisner (1950) described four phases in the process of play therapy: (1) acceptance and rapport, (2) clarification and desensitization, (3) diagnosis and interpretation, and (4) termination. Mundy (1957) proceeding from a basis of psychoanalytic ideology also used interpretations of a simple kind. She considered that maternal deprivation had played an important part in producing the mental retardation and saw "scientific mothering" as an essential technique. Davidson (1975) aimed to unblock conscious and unconscious feelings in order to bring about more adequate behavior or responses. She used the technique of literal reflections very consistently. Smith, McKinnon, and Kessler (1976) and Schwartz (1979) stressed the content of therapy in their cases. The play technique is considered a move which will lead to regression which may not be a useful strategy. Schwartz also describes the necessity for setting limits. Leland and Smith (1962, 1965) have done the most to describe in detail psychotherapy with mentally retarded children. They consider psychotherapy to be essentially a learning experience for the child. Their main contribution has been to divide the play therapies into unstructured vs. structured, both as far as method and materials are concerned. Thus, they can describe separately the unstructured approach with unstructured materials (U-U therapy), unstructured materials with a structured approach (U-S therapy), structured materials with an unstructured approach (S-U therapy), and structured materials with a structured approach (S-S therapy). It is the third of these, i.e., the structured materials with an unstructured approach, that represents the most commonly employed type of play therapy, whereas the S-S approach, utilizing structured materials with a structured approach, focuses on the end product of the therapy. This type is essentially identical with educational therapy, as the authors admit. Gair, Hersch, and Wiesenfeld (1980) describe a case which falls into the category of the S-U approach. Dolls were used as structured material which helped the patient to act out his fantasies and these were responded to by the therapist through doll stories.

Group Therapy with Mentally Retarded Children

Activity group therapy as prescribed by Slavson and Schiffer (1975) was used by a number of early workers (Cotzin, 1948; Fisher and Wolfson, 1953; Sarbin, 1945). The common experience was a transition from group techniques that were permissive to ones that became more directive as described by Leland, Walker,

and Taboada (1949). Newcomer and Morrison (1974) described and investigated the difference between directive and nondirective techniques. In directive techniques, specific activities are planned in advance. When a nondirective approach is used, the therapist lays out different groups of toys and materials, which children can utilize as they see fit.

A variant of group therapy is a technique called peer play therapy as described by Nuffield and co-workers (Note 1). This form of structured therapy aims at facilitating social interaction between children in a dyadic configuration. There are structured materials that do not vary from session to session, and the therapist promotes interaction through modeling and verbal and physical prompting. While social praise is used when successful interactions occur, no other contingency management is involved.

Other Psychotherapies with Retarded Children

ART THERAPY

Freeman (1936) described methods of therapy using drawing as an aid to communication when dealing with children who lack verbal expression. Kadis (Note 2) used figure painting for similar reasons. Roth and Barrett (1980) described a case where both art therapy and play therapy were utilized. Those two types of therapy had a synergistic effect. Combinations of art, dance, and music therapy were illustrated by Cantalapiedra, DeWeerdt, and Frederick (1977) and Fino (1979) combined art and movement therapy in children.

MUSIC THERAPY

A considerable volume of literature on music therapy with mentally retarded children exists (Heimlich, 1960; Joseph & Heimlich, 1959; Nordoff & Robbins, 1965; Weigl, 1959). The goal of these therapies is not so much to turn the child into a musician but to produce positive behavioral changes. Grant (1977) also claimed that the child's socialization skills and gross and fine motor development were enhanced through this form of therapy. Social relations may also be improved (Perlman & Patterson, 1977).

Counseling of Mentally Retarded Children

Although somewhat uncommonly employed, Deblassie and Lebsock (1979) have described specific techniques for assisting handicapped children in a school setting. Group counseling with the purpose of enhancing the self-image of children has been described by Blohm (1978) and Eldridge, Witmer, Barcikowski, and Bauer (1977).

The Process of Psychotherapy in Mentally Retarded Adolescents and Adults

Individual Psychotherapy and Counseling

Individual methods have received less attention than group techniques. One of the first contributions in the former area was that of Thorne and Dolan (1953). These authors paid much attention to the contextual aspects of the therapy and to the need for constant supervision, but they also utilized nondirective techniques.

The process of individual psychotherapy is often divided into three segments: an initial phase; a middle main working phase; and a termination phase. Both Szymanski (1980) and Jakab (1970) follow this schema. Lack of motivation in the mentally retarded adult has been pointed out again and again. This may apply even more strongly to the mentally retarded adolescent. It has to be stressed that individual psychotherapy may only be one part of the total treatment package. The importance of making a therapeutic contract with a mentally retarded individual, however, should not be forgotten and this should be established at the outset. While recognizing the importance of family dynamics in the case of adults and adolescents living at home, both Walker (1977) and Selan (1979) made a strong plea for individual psychotherapy.

Miscellaneous Therapies for Adults and Adolescents

As in the case of children, the adjunctive therapies, i.e., art, music, dance, and movement therapy can have two separate purposes: (1) the achievement of specific clinical or psychological goals, such as the attainment of self-confidence, the facilitation of communication with others, or the removal of symptoms; and (2) the acquisition of certain technical skills. It is the former goals, however, which make these techniques basically therapeutic. In the case of art therapy, this has been pointed out by several authors (Kunkle-Miller, 1978; Espenak, 1981). Espenak (1981) described conjoint art therapy of a child and her mother, which leads into the commonly used practice of family art sessions. These are useful in understanding family dynamics and reshaping family relationships. Males and Males (1979) and Wilson (1977) have also described art therapy programs. Cassity (1977) has adapted a specific guitar technique for the use of mentally

retarded individuals whose fine motor control may be deficient. A sense of mastery and competence that is obtained through this method and a subsequent enhancement of self-esteem is the common factor to music therapy, as well as in a program of horticulture therapy described in a U.S. Department of Health, Education, and Welfare pamphlet (1977). Shuman-Carpenter (1977) has combined both movement therapy and art therapy in mentally retarded patients and again these modalities can be seen as being complementary. Dance therapy as described by Ohwaki (1976) is intended to enhance the body image which may be evident by the change in human figure drawings. This hypothesis was investigated and the results were in a positive direction. Rogers (1977), using dance therapy, employed a technique that emphasized intervention without interpretation. She considered that both cognitive and emotional functioning could be enhanced through dance therapy.

The common factor underlying all the adjunctive therapies is that they bypass the need for verbal expression. They are therefore particularly useful in those individuals who are deficient in language. These modalities have considerable use in the mentally retarded since lack of verbal facility is one of their prominent features. The individual use of these methods is particularly indicated when an intensification of the therapist-patient relationship is desirable. Art or graphic expression lends itself to extensive employment in the intimate atmosphere of a one-to-one therapeutic situation, whereas dance movement and music therapy would seem to fit in better with group situations.

Group Therapy and Counseling

The grouping together of a number of individuals who have common problems is an attractive proposition for the clinical therapist. The two factors of retardation and institutionalization have given mentally retarded individuals a great deal in common. Group methods are also appealing on economic grounds. Cotzin (1948) gave the first description of this method with mentally retarded residents, although previous work by Slavson, Wiener, and Scheidlinger had been carried out. Cotzin (1948) used some psychodramatic techniques with mildly retarded adolescent boys. Very early in the history of this endeavor, the need for some structure and direction was recognized. Michal-Smith, Gottsegen, and Gottsegen (1955) treated a group of moderately retarded adults who were living with their families. They used a mixture of verbal and activity methods. They were chiefly interested in psychodynamic features such as transference and interpersonal relationships. Fisher and Wolfson (1953) depended heavily on Slavson's work in their treatment of early adolescent girls. They described six phases: (1) testing the limits, (2) a regressive period, (3) a transitional period from ego centeredness to group centeredness, (4) positive sibling transference, (5) an awakening of interest in the outside community, and (6) an interest in acceptance and desire for conformity. Most later authors tend to collapse some of these phases into three or four sections. Thus Szymanski and Rosefsky (1980) described four stages. During the first of these the group members produced seemingly trivial issues and tested out their peers and their leader. The second stage was considered a transitional one, where there was more aggression but still some testing of the limits. The third stage is the main working phase and during this time progress is made in terms of group cohesion and group consolidation. The last stage as described by Szymanski and Rosefsky is a period of regression, which precedes the termination of the group with its incumbent separation problems. Sarbin (1945) aimed at training subjects in spontaneity and used essentially psychodramatic techniques. Similarly, role playing was the important technique used by Lavalli and Levine (1954). Ringelheim and Polatsek (1957) divided the process of group therapy into three phases. During the first or organizational phase, an individual member attempted to usurp the group leadership, which caused the other six members to become negative. During the second phase, there was a reorganization taking place around the new leader. The final phase was called integrative and consisted of problem solving of common difficulties encountered in the everyday existence within the institution. The authors described the role of the therapists as being codiscussants rather than leaders. Evidently this group ran down through the members losing interest. Astrachan (1955) described her experiences with a number of groups in some detail. There were eight patients to one therapist. The therapist excluded nonverbal activities such as taking walks and eating during the group or any planned activity; the methods were purely verbal. There appeared to be an absence of structure. Interpersonal interactions between group members were few at first but gradually increased. Fine and Dawson (1965) treated several groups of adolescent girls and young women in a special section of a state hospital. Each group consisted of two therapists and eight patients. The issues dealt with were the common problems of everyday living and the goal and objective was to get as many patients discharged from the institution as possible. This was also the aim of the group run by Empey (1977). Ultimate adjustment in the community

including obtaining employment and living independently were the issues dealt with. There was little description of the emergence of dynamic themes although the therapist at all times paid attention to group process. Dealing also with process, J. A. Lee (1977) described her group in terms of beginnings, working and doing together, working and meaningful talk, and, finally, termination. Discussion was interspersed with craftwork, music, and dancing. This group also used food as part of the process and had trips and outings. Welch and Sigman (1980) pointed to some of the difficulties in selecting appropriate subjects for group therapy in the mentally retarded population. They stressed the importance of reasonable matching of subjects for mental age. However, they do recognize that the variety of problems that individual members have can be advantageous to group process. Positive feedback to individual patients by therapists and by group members was considered very important. Davis and Shapiro (1979) were led to group therapy by the prevalence of social isolation among mentally retarded adults living in the community. They treated a somewhat older group of females who had been engaged in individual treatment before. The range of mental retardation in their population was quite wide ranging from borderline to severe. Little activity took place in the groups since they were essentially discussion groups. The author mentioned that it took about three months for the group to become a cohesive unit, by which time a spirit of camaraderie became manifest. Both therapists and patients felt termination to have been a painful process. Another essentially verbal group using existential techniques as proposed by Rollo May was described by Deal (1977). The therapist used an unusual method of structuring the group by pairing each member with a member of the opposite sex. Contingency measures such as rewarding subjects with edible treats were used. The focus was on concrete experiences and concrete relationships. Norman (1977) in treating moderately mentally retarded adolescents in a school setting described her program as a group guidance one. The students met weekly to listen to stories about children and their problems, with discussion ensuing. The therapist found that modeling of conversational behavior was necessary to get the group going. Hynes and Young (1976) treated a school population of similar age with three specific goals for their subjects: to develop an increased awareness of physical maturation; to gain a better sense of identity; and to be able to make choices about future vocation and living arrangements. The methods employed were a mixture of activities, such as food preparation, shopping excursions, and group discussions. The authors preferred such methods as role playing, drawing, using audiovisual equipment, pantomime, and music. Role playing and modeling were also stressed in a paper by D. Y. Lee (1977), who treated moderately mentally retarded adults of both sexes in an institutional setting. Techniques were verbal instructions, discrimination training, role playing and discussion with social praise given; no primary reinforcers were used. The goal was improved social adjustment.

The issue of nondirective vs. directive techniques has preoccupied workers in this area for a number of decades. After nondirective techniques ran into difficulties (Ringelheim & Polatsek, 1955; Vail, 1955), Snyder and Sechrest (1959) used more directive methods. They described the therapist as a guiding, manipulative leader who organized the group when necessary. He also prodded members by asking pertinent questions. On the other hand, Yonge and O'Connor (1954) used a nondirective technique exclusively. Sternlicht (1964, 1965, 1966) has paid more attention to techniques than any other writer. His emphasis is on the need to overcome the communication barrier between therapist and patient. He has described the "silence insult" technique as one useful in establishing initial therapeutic movement (1966). Other techniques were engaging a volunteering patient in Indian arm wrestling in order to establish the therapist's position of superiority (1964), the use of mirrors and balloons, and pantomime dramatizations.

Wilcox and Guthrie (1957), using more conventional methods of a verbal nature treated a group of adolescent girls and young women in an institution. They used techniques of reassurance, clarification of feelings, and interpretations. Parson (1980) once again stressed the importance of feedback from either therapists or other group members. Weinstock (1979) used a very tight structure, which included a token economy, time-out procedures, systematic feedback, and behavioral goals. This author treated delinquent, moderately mentally retarded adolescent boys and found the use of discussion alone to be quite ineffective. Crenshaw (1976) employed techniques such as role-playing scenes, role training, and structured group exercises. His rationale for these methods was a strong reality orientation, and a focusing on present rather than future problems.

In summary, then, it is evident that group therapists who are in the mainstream and who treat mentally retarded adolescents and mentally retarded adults tend to employ structure, to set concrete goals, to limit the number of sessions, and to use discussion and

verbal communication sparingly. Behavioral tactics such as reinforcement, feedback and contingency management are occurring in the practice of group therapy in varying degrees.

Outcome and Effectiveness of Psychotherapy Studies: A Critical Analysis of Results

Methodological Problems

Complaints about the absence of good research in this area have been made by a number of writers (Bialer, 1967; Crowley, 1965; Li, 1981). A plea has been made for process research, which is a close study of what is actually being done, as well as for the more obvious outcome research, i.e., the efficacy of the various psychotherapies. Process research is hypothesis generating, as described by Trent and Brodie (1980). Gunzberg (1974) pointed to methodological shortcomings, such as fuzzy and poor description of the process of psychotherapy, inadequate description of context, and, most of all, a failure to pay heed to intercurrent events. The last item means that so-called controlled studies are not in fact controlled. A further difficulty lies in the fact that there is no adequate measuring instrument applicable to the process of change. Cowen and Trippe (1963) had a similar list of complaints: (1) the presence of inadequate sampling methods, (2) poor design, including a lack of patient follow-up, (3) the lack of proper controls, and (4) the absence of criteria of success or failure. Gunzberg has also mentioned a lack of follow-up in most reports. As stated by Cowen and Trippe, the difficulties of sampling are great indeed and it is particularly hard to find a comparison group of subjects in the community. Jakab (1970) has addressed the problem of measuring change. She recommended a combination of psychological testing, including a behavioral rating scale carried out by teachers and a series of social evaluations. For example, the Devereux Behavior Rating Scale should be done by parents and teachers. Narrative descriptions by therapist, social worker, and the testing psychologist supplement the test results. Objective observational rating scales on the process of verbal and nonverbal interaction are furthermore recommended. Murstein (1975) recommended splitting a projective test, half to be given before therapy and the other half after therapy. The validity of projective tests in this case, however, is very much in doubt. Adjustment ratings to be used before and after therapy as described by Mehlman (1953) may be more appropriate. The study of Craft (1965) used the Stott

Social Adjustment Guide as well as the MMPI and the Porteus Maze test. Unfortunately, the variable of psychotherapy was not isolated in this study. Johnson (1953) used various tests, including the Raven's Progressive Matrices, the Binet, and the Klopfer Prognostic Scale on The Rorschach for purposes of predicting success in play therapy.

Description of the Results

Many of the earliest reports relied on IQ measurements to document change. Thus, in the case described by Chidester and Menninger (1936), the IQ rose from 62 to 90, which is remarkable. Axline (1949) also used the IQ as a dependent measure. Her treated group gained 15 to 26 points, whereas an untreated group showed no change. Other early workers were less precise in their reports. Thorne (1948) gave results in terms of improved (45), unchanged (15), and worse (7). Neham (1951) quoted Bernadine Schmidt (1948), who affirmed that mental retardation could be cured by psychotherapy. Her methods were criticized by Hill (1948) and Kirk (1948). Cooley (1945) used a different method in counting the number of treatments needed as the outcome dependent variable when comparing 25 dull children with 25 bright ones. Allegedly the outcome was equally successful in both groups and both groups of children had the same amount of treatment. Cotzin (1948) described the outcome in his cases as good, fair, or poor. He included some follow-up data but had no controls. Fisher and Wolfson (1953) reported 8 of 12 subjects improved substantially, but no change in IQ was reported. Ringelheim and Polatsek (1957) had a small group of seven individuals, of whom two were discharged with excellent adjustment, three were unchanged, and two "acted out." On follow-up, there was little in change of personality dynamics or mental level. It is not clear why these authors were inclined to be optimistic on the basis of such meager results.

Vail (1955), in a burst of honesty, described the process of his group in a paper entitled "An unsuccessful experiment." Astrachan (1955) enumerated her results. Of 31 patients, nine dropped out. Of the other 22, 14 improved successfully to be discharged although two of these relapsed. Of the remaining eight, four improved but were not discharged, and four were unimproved. Albini and Dinitz (1965) set out to establish whether group psychotherapy was really as effective as other authors had indicated. They used an experimental treated group of 37 patients and an untreated group of 36 patients. On various dependent measures the results of both were the same, but the groups were not well matched, since the control sub-

jects were less disturbed. No conclusions can be drawn from that study, as Gunzberg (1974) also pointed out. Subotnik and Callahan (1959) also obtained negative results, although they used a control period rather than a control group for comparison. The control period consisted of eight weeks without treatment, followed by eight weeks of treatment; follow-up was carried out eight weeks after treatment had been concluded. Snyder and Sechrest (1959) had three groups of delinquent, defective boys. The treated group were given a good deal of encouragement and positive feedback. There was a placebo group who sat in some sort of nondirective group therapy. There was also a group who had no treatment whatever. There was a significant improvement in the treated group in terms of the frequency of conduct violations as compared with the placebo and no-treatment groups. Yonge and O'Connor (1954) also used a control group with positive results. Dependent measures were an attitude checklist and workshop behavior ratings. No follow-up was done on their cases. Chess (1962) used a series of psychotherapeutic sessions to reclassify the children into her five groups of mentally retarded children with behavior problems. In terms of results, these were described only in the broadest terms of improvement vs. no improvement. Humes, Adamczyk, and Myco (1969) used a control group and obtained somewhat mixed results. The instruments measuring change were a behavior rating scale, the California Test of Personality, and a variety of instruments measuring self-concept, as well as two sociometric measures. There were positive differences on the behavior rating scale and the personality test, but none on the self-concept measures. There were some differences on one of the sociometric tests. Hayes (1977) carried out a detailed and extensive retrospective study matching 20 mentally retarded adolescents with 20 adolescents of average intelligence. They were treated at different outpatient clinics in New York City. The incidence of behavioral problems was similar in the two groups and the length of treatment was comparable as was socioeconomic status. The frequency of collateral treatments was the same also. The dependent measure was the outcome as rated by the individual therapist on a five-point scale. There was actually a slight difference in favor of the mentally retarded group, which was replicated on the Anna Freud developmental profile. The experimental subjects were familially retarded and almost certainly in the mild category. This study is interesting because the matching procedure was done carefully. Gorlow, Butler, Einig, and Smith (1963) compared group therapy in 38 patients with no therapy in 31 subjects. Their dependent variable was a series of estimations of self-attitudes and the results were negative. Unfortunately the subject selection was somewhat skewed in that the authors omitted the most suitable subjects, who happened to be on a summer vacation at the time. Schachter, Meyer, and Loomis (1962) compared mentally retarded children with schizophrenic children in terms of their response to prolonged psychotherapy lasting over two years. The dependent measures were IQ tests, the Gesell Developmental Scale, and standardized play observations which yielded a number of separate scores. Six mentally retarded children were compared with 12 schizophrenic children, who were in turn divided into six who received psychotherapy and six who received Benadryl. Unfortunately, the type of psychotherapy was not well matched since all the schizophrenics had group therapy, whereas three of the mentally retarded had individual therapy and three had group therapy. The result was that the retarded group gained more than the schizophrenic groups and the children on drugs actually got worse. Wilcox and Guthrie (1951) compared 97 girls in therapy groups with 17 girls in a control group. Thirty-six of the girls dropped out. Measurements were carried out through a hospital adjustment rating scale and incidence reports. Of the treated girls, 52 improved, 38 got worse, and 7 showed no change. Of the untreated, 4 improved and 13 got worse. Although statistically significant, the results are so complex that it is difficult to come to a positive conclusion about group therapy from them.

Mundy (1957) compared 15 treated with 10 untreated children matched for age, neurologic involvement, and IQ. She carried out individual psychotherapy over a period of 9 to 12 months and had a follow-up after one and a half years following the conclusion of therapy. Improvement in social adjustment in the treated group was more impressive than the gain of nine IQ points. Mundy then employed another design using an untreated period of 12 months prior to a treatment period. Change in IQ was the only dependent variable and the results were striking. The number of children was only eight, however. During the untreated period the mean IQ rose from 56 to 58; after treatment it rose to 80. At follow-up after treatment, the mean IQ was 78. Leland, Walker, and Taboada (1959) simply compared results before and after treatment. Their subjects were eight boys aged four to eight who had 90 therapy hours. Measurements used were the WISC and the Vineland Social Maturity Scale. The gains on those measures were insignificant except in one case. There was some difference between the four withdrawn subjects and the four aggressive ones; the former did considerably better than the latter. Newcomer and Morrison (1974) compared the effects of individual play therapy with those of group therapy. They also had a control group of children having no therapy. Both the individually and the group treated children improved significantly over the controls, who showed no change. In a follow-up study, Morrison and Newcomer (1975) compared five children who received group therapy with directive methods with five children receiving nondirective group therapy, and four children receiving no therapy. The results were largely negative, but the groups were poorly matched since the group receiving directive treatment was particularly low in the area of fine motor skills at the beginning of treatment. Furthermore, the treatment series was too short (only 11 sessions) and the therapists were largely inexperienced.

Strain (1975) attempted to assess the effect of sociodramatic play activities on the social play of severely mentally retarded four-year-old children. He used an observational technique which measured social play in children such as sharing, building together, holding hands, etc. The results showed clearly that therapeutic intervention has a positive effect on social play activities. Their incidence returned to baseline when intervention was suspended, increasing again during a second intervention period. Knapczyk and Yoppi (1975) used a technique of teaching children to play nicely together with house parents acting as therapists. Positive reinforcement was given contingent on cooperative play. Their assessment used a series of categories of onlook or solitary, parallel, cooperative, and competitive play. They used an ABAB design and found that cooperative play increased during the first treatment phase and competitive play became more paramount during the second treatment phase. This is not surprising, since competitive play occurs developmentally later than cooperative play.

Results by many authors tend to be largely qualitative and impressionistic. Those with a psychoanalytic background are included in this group (Schwartz, 1979; Smith, McKinnon & Kessler, 1976). Others are Roth and Barrett (1980), Kunkle-Miller (1978), J. A. Lee (1977), and Walker (1977). Welch and Sigman (1980) stated very honestly that "we have not formally assessed outcome for our groups and would find it difficult to separate the effects of our groups from the effects of the milieu or from individual treatment and various other therapeutic experiences offered." Deal (1977) reported very favorable results in a group of 10 mentally retarded adults but had no controls. On the other hand, Zapf (1976), in using Glasser's Reality Therapy, found that the subjects showed no significant change as a whole. Blohm (1978) compared counseling with no counseling for not only mentally retarded students but also learning disabled students. Personality factors and self-concept measures showed virtually no difference. In this case there seemed to have been some side-effects from the treatment, in that the teachers found the children more distractible after a period of group counseling. On the other hand, Parsons (1980), using a technique of therapists modeling feedback delivery so that mildy mentally retarded students could signal back their positive impressions to group members, found a relationship between the quality of feedback and the change in self-concept. This is one of the few studies which shows positive results in this particular area.

Impressionistic results are presented again by Pueschel and Yeatman (1977) and Satten and Singer (1979). Weinstock (1979) pointed to the ineffectiveness of a discussion type of group as compared to the improvement that occurred once games were introduced and controls were imposed.

Ohwaki (1976) used human figure drawings as a means to measure the effect of dance therapy in 19 mentally retarded adults. He showed significant increase in the Goodenough score of these drawings but used no controls. Schweisheimer and Walberg (1976) assessed the effectiveness of peer counseling in mildly mentally retarded students. They did use a control group and found that in the experimental group attendance and decisiveness improved most significantly. Some of the most strikingly positive results were produced by D. Y. Lee (1977), who split a group of mentally retarded adults in an institutional setting into an experimental and a control group. Using the AAMD adaptive behavior scale and the Peabody Picture Vocabulary Test as measures of change, his experimental group did much better than the control group. The sociometric tests were even more significantly different, but were probably exaggerated by the fact that the staff knew which subjects were treated and which were not.

Comment

It can be seen from the foregoing that the quality of outcome research with the mentally retarded has not been high. The problem of controlling for intervening variables seems formidable, perhaps even insurmountable. As this population becomes more and more assimilated into the community, obtaining proper comparison groups and matched controls may well become impossible. On the other hand, the elaboration and refinement of instruments of assessment has progressed and has good prospects for the future. The methodological problems are roughly the same as those of psychotherapy with nonretarded populations, and it may well be that the traditional design comparing a treated with an untreated group of subjects is becoming out of date and sterile. In this field there is a great need for generating new hypotheses rather than testing the old ones.

Prevailing Attitudes towards Psychotherapy and Conclusion

It is evident that the prevailing climate has changed over the past 30 or 40 years and that the question is no longer whether one is for or against psychotherapy for the mentally retarded. Early authors were usually strongly antagonistic, some of them blaming psychoanalytic doctrine for the neglect of the mentally retarded (Abel, 1953). Already in 1957, DeMartino thought that this question was closed and that there was no longer any doubt that psychotherapy with the mentally retarded could yield fruitful results. He asked a number of questions that had to do with selection of subjects, the influence of contextual factors such as the setting in which psychotherapy takes place, the relationship of psychotherapy to drug treatment and to family counseling, the qualities required of the successful therapist and a number of questions regarding technique. All these questions lead one in the direction of what Bialer (1967) has described as process research. In spite of an improvement in climate some recent authors (e.g. Walker, 1980) still find that developmentally disabled individuals are consistently denied intensive counseling services. Empey (1977) makes a special plea for services for the multiply handicapped and Weinstock (1979) considers the combination of delinquency or characterological deficit with mental retardation to be underserved.

In conclusion, it can be stated that the proper application of psychotherapeutic methods in the mentally retarded will hinge on a proper understanding of the relationship between mental retardation and emotional disorder. It should be clear that mental retardation and emotional disorder can coexist and run parallel, being sometimes due to common causes, but also at times due to separate ones. On the other hand, it is a rare mentally retarded person who finds the path through the various phases of life as smooth as the nonretarded individual. More mentally retarded persons may need some sort of assistance during times of developmental crises, i.e., school entry, adolescence, the middle-life crisis. In order for them to require formal psychotherapy, however, there should be a well defined and diagnosable emotional illness. It may well be that the fact of developmental disability or retardation alone constitutes a significant factor in the evolution of such an emotional illness. On the other hand, the unfolding of severe emotional illness during the earliest developmental periods, especially in the case of psychosis of early onset, will almost invariably lead to some degree of mental retardation. This does not mean that psychotherapy is the cornerstone of the treatment approach to such an individual, especially since there is evidence that psychosis may be based on what are essentially biological, i.e., genetic and biochemical malfunctions. Nevertheless, psychotherapy will be indicated in a considerable number of mentally retarded individuals of all ages as part of an overall treatment plan.

Reference Notes

1. Nuffield, E. J., McGonigle, J. J., and Russell, R. *Increasing peer interaction through peer play therapy.* Paper presented at the 105th Annual Meeting of the American Academy of Mental Deficiency, Detroit, May 1981.
2. Kadis, A. L. *The use of fingerpainting in psychotherapy with mentally retarded children.* Paper presented at the 75th Annual Meeting of the American Association on Mental Deficiency, Detroit, May 1951.

References

Abel, T. M. Resistances and difficulties in psychotherapy of mental retardates. *Journal of Clinical Psychology*, 1953, 9, 107–109.

Ackerman, N. W., & Menninger, C. F. Treatment techniques for mental retardation in a school for personality disorders in children. *American Journal of Orthopsychiatry*, 1936, 6, 294–312.

Albini, J. L., & Dinitz, S. Psychotherapy with disturbed and defective children. An evaluation of changes in behavior and attitudes. *American Journal of Mental Deficiency*, 1965, 69, 560.

American Psychiatric Association. *Diagnostic and statistical manual mental disorders* (DSM III). (3rd ed.) Washington, D.C.: American Psychiatric Association, 1980.

Astrachan, M. Group psychotherapy with mentally retarded female adolescents and adults. *American Journal of Mental Deficiency*, 1955, 60, 152–156.

Axline, V. M. Mental deficiency: Symptom or disease? *Journal of Consulting Psychology*, 1949, 13, 313–327.

Balthazar, E. E., & Stevens, H. A. *The emotionally disturbed, mentally retarded: A historical and contemporary perspective.* Englewood Cliffs, N.J.: Prentice Hall, Inc., 1975.

Beier, D. C. Behavioral disturbances in the mentally retarded. In H. A. Stevens & R. Heber (Eds.), *Mental retardation: A review of research.* Chicago: University of Chicago Press, 1964.

Bertine, E. Areas of agreement in psychotherapy. *American Journal of Orthopsychiatry*, 1940, 10, 699.

Bialer, I. Psychotherapy and other adjustment techniques with the mentally retarded. In A. A. Baumeister (Ed.), *Mental retardation, appraisal, education and rehabilitation.* Chicago: Aldine Publishing Co., 1967.

Blohm, A. L. A. Group counseling with moderately mentally retarded and hearing disabled elementary school children. *Dissertation Abstracts International*, 1978, 39(6A), 3362.

Bruner, J. L. Man: a course of study. *Educational Services, Inc. Quarterly Report*, 1965, 3, 85–95.

Cantalapiedra, M. A., Deweerdt, C., & Frederick, F. Le rôle psychothérapique de l'éducateur dans un externat pour jeunes enfants. *Revue de Neuropsychiatrie Infantile*, 1977, 25, 787–811.

Cassity, M. D. Nontraditional guitar techniques for the educable and trainable mentally retarded residents in music therapy activities. *Journal of Music Therapy*, 1977, 14, 39–42.

Chess, S. Psychiatric treatment of the mentally retarded child with behavior problems. *American Journal of Orthopsychiatry*, 1962, 32, 863.

Chess, S. Treatment of the emotional problems of the retarded child and of the family. In F. J. Menolascino (Ed.), *Psychiatric approaches to the diagnosis and treatment of the mentally retarded.* New York: Basic Books, 1970.

Chidester, L. Therapeutic results with mentally retarded children. *American Journal of Orthopsychiatry*, 1934, 4, 464–472.

Chidester, L., & Menninger, K. A. The application of psychoanalytic methods to the study of mental retardation. *American Journal of Orthopsychiatry*, 1936, 6, 616–625.

Close, H. T. Psychotherapy. *Voices*, 1966, 2, 124.

Cooley, J. M. The relative amenability of dull and bright children to child guidance. *Smith College Studies in Social Work*, 1945, 16, 26–43.

Copabianco, R. J., and Cole, D. A. Social behavior of mentally retarded children. *American Journal of Mental Deficiency*, 1960, 64, 638–651.

Cotzin, M. Group therapy with mentally defective problem boys. *American Journal of Mental Deficiency*, 1948, 53, 268–283.

Cowen, E. L. Psychotherapy and play techniques with the exceptional child. In W. H. Cruikshank (Ed.), *Psychology of exceptional children and youth.* (1st ed.) Englewood Cliffs, N.J.: Prentice-Hall, Inc., 1955.

Cowen, E. L., & Trippe, M. J. Psychotherapy and play techniques with the exceptional child. In W. M. Cruikshank (Ed.), *Psychology of exceptional children and youth.* (2nd ed.) Englewood Cliffs, N.J.: Prentice-Hall, 1963.

Craft, M. *Ten studies into psychopathic personality.* Bristol: John Wright and Lews, 1965.

Crenshaw, D. A. Teaching adaptive interpersonal behavior: Group techniques in residential treatment. *Child Care Quarterly*, 1976, 5, 211–220.

Crowley, F. J. Psychotherapy for the mentally retarded: A survey and projective consideration. *Training School Bulletin (Vineland)*, 1965, 62, 5–11.

Davidson, C. D. Psychotherapy with mentally handicapped children in a day school. *Psychotherapy: Theory, research and practice*, 1975, 12, 13–21.

Davis, K. R., Shapiro, L. J. Exploring group process as a means of reaching the mentally retarded. *Social Casework*, 1979, 60, 330–337.

Deal, G. A. Existential group therapy with mentally retarded adults. *Dissertation Abstracts International*, 1977, 37(7A), 4128–4129.

Deblassie, R. R., & Lebsock, M. S. Counseling with handicapped children. *Elementary School Guidance and Counseling*, 1979, 13, 199–206.

DeMartino, M. F. Some observations concerning psychotherapeutic techniques with the mentally retarded. In C. L. Stacey & M. F. DeMartino (Eds.), *Counseling and psychotherapy with the mentally retarded.* Glencoe, Ill.: Free Press, 1957.

Eldridge, M. S., Witmer, J. M., Barcikowski, R. & Bauer, L. The effects of a group counseling program on the self-concepts of EMR children. *Measurement and Evaluation in Guidance*, 1977, **9**, 184–191.

Empey, L. J. Clinical group work with multi-handicapped adolescents. *Social Caseworker*, 1977, **58**, 593–599.

English, H. B., & English, A. C. *A comprehensive dictionary of psychological psychoanalytic terms*. New York: Longman, Green and Co., 1958.

Espenak, L. *Dance therapy, theory and application*. Springfield, Ill.: Charles C. Thomas, 1981.

Fine, R. H., & Dawson, J. C. A therapy program for the mildly retarded adolescent. *American Journal of Mental Deficiency*, 1965, **69**, 23–30.

Fino, J. K. Guided imagery and movement as a means to help disturbed children draw together. *American Journal of Art Therapy*, 1979, **18**, 61–62.

Fisher, L. A. & Wolfson, I. N. Group therapy of mental defectives. *American Journal of Mental Deficiency*, 1953, **57**, 463–476.

Florey, L. Development through play. In C. E. Schaefer (Ed.), *Therapeutic use of child's play*. New York: Jason Aronson, 1976.

Freeman, M. Drawing as a psychotherapeutic intermedium. *American Journal of Mental Deficiency*, 1936, **41**, 182–187.

Gair, D. S., Hersch, C., & Wiesenfeld, S. Successful psychotherapy of severe emotional disturbance in a young, retarded boy. *Journal of American Academy of Child Psychiatry*, 1980, **19**, 257–269.

Glassman, L. A. Is dull normal intelligence a contraindication for psychotherapy? *Smith College Studies in Social Work*, 1943, **13**, 275–298.

Gorlow, L., Butler, A., Eining, K. G. & Smith, J. A. An appraisal of self-attitudes and behavior following group psychotherapy with retarded young adults. *American Journal of Mental Deficiency*, 1963, **67**, 893–898.

Grant, R. E. A developmental music therapy curriculum for the mildly mentally retarded, ages six through twelve. (Dissertation, University of Michigan, 1977). *Dissertation Abstracts International*, 1977 (Microfilms No. 77-29760.)

Grinker, R. R., McGregor, H., Selan, K., Klein, A., & Kohrman, J. *Psychiatric social work: a transactional casebook*. New York: Basic Books, 1981.

Gunzberg, H. C. Psychotherapy. In A. M. Clarke & A. D. B. Clarke (Eds.), *Mental deficiency: The changing outlook*. New York: The Free Press, 1974.

Hayes, M. The responsiveness of mentally retarded children to psychotherapy. *Smith College Studies in Social Work*, 1977, **47**, 112–153.

Heimlich, E. P. Music as therapy with emotionally disturbed children. *Child Welfare*, 1960, **39**, 3–7.

Heiser, K. F. Psychotherapy in a residential school for mentally retarded children. *The Training School Bulletin*, 1954, **50**, 211–218.

Hill, A. S. Does special education result in improved intelligence for slow-learning children? *Journal of Exceptional Children*, 1948, **14**, 208–213, 224.

Hinsie, L. E., & Campbell, R. J. *Psychiatric dictionary*. New York, London & Toronto: Oxford University Press, 1970.

Hulme, I. & Lunzer, E. A. Play language and reasoning in subnormal children. *Journal of Child Psychology and Psychiatry*, 1966, **7**, 107–116.

Humes, C. W., Adamczyk, J. S., & Myco, R. W. A school study of group counseling with educable retarded adolescents. *American Journal of Mental Deficiency*, 1969, **74**, 191–195.

Hynes, J., & Young, J. Adolescent group for mentally retarded persons. *Education and Training for the Mentally Retarded*, 1976, **11**, 226–231.

Jakab, I. Psychotherapy of the mentally retarded child. In N. Bernstein (Ed.), *Diminished people*. London: Little, Brown & Co., 1970.

Johnson, E. Z. The clinical use of Raven's progressive matrices to appraise potential for progress in play therapy: a study of institutionalized mentally and educationally retarded children. *American Journal of Orthopsychiatry*, 1953, **23**, 391–398.

Johnson, E. Z. Klopfer's prognostic scale used with Raven's progressive matrices in play therapy prognosis. *Journal of Projective Techniques*, 1953, **17**, 320–326.

Joseph, H., & Heimlich, E. P. The therapeutic use of music with "treatment resistant" children. *American Journal of Mental Deficiency*, 1959, **64**, 41–49.

Kanner, L. *A history of the care and study of the feebleminded*. Springfield, Ill.: Charles C. Thomas, 1964.

Kaplan, A. H. Social work therapy and psychiatric psychotherapy. *Archives of General Psychiatry*, 1963, **9**, 497–503.

Katz, G. H. Re-educational therapy. *The Nervous Child*, 1942, **2**, 37–43.

Kirk, S. An evaluation of the study of Bernadine G. Schmidt. *Journal of Exceptional Children*, 1948, **15**, 34–40, 54.

Knapczyk, D. R., & Yoppi, J. O. Development of cooperative and competitive play responses in developmentally disabled children. *American Journal of Mental Deficiency*, 1975, **80**, 245–255.

Kunkle-Miller, C. Art therapy with mentally retarded adults. *Art Psychotherapy*, 1978, **5**, 123–133.

Lavalli, A., & Levine, M. Social and guidance needs of mentally handicapped adolescents as revealed through sociodrama. *American Journal of Mental Deficiency*, 1954, **58**, 544–552.

Lee, D. Y. Evaluation of a group counseling program designed to enhance social adjustment of mentally retarded adults. *Journal of Counseling Psychology*, 1977, **24**, 318–323.

Lee, J. A. Group work with mentally retarded foster adolescents. *Social Casework*, 1977, **58**, 164–173.

Leland, H., & Smith, D. *Play therapy with mentally subnormal children*. New York: Grune & Stratton, 1965.

Leland, H., & Smith, D. Unstructured material in play therapy for emotionally disturbed, brain damaged mentally retarded children. *American Journal of Mental Deficiency*, 1962, **66**, 621–627.

Leland, H., Walker, J., & Taboada, A. N. Group play therapy with a group of post-nursery male retardates. *American Journal of Mental Deficiency*, 1959, **63**, 848–851.

Li, A. Play and the mentally retarded child. *Mental Retardation*, 1981, **19**, 121–126.

Maisner, E. A. Contributions of play therapy techniques to total rehabilitative design in an institution for high-grade mentally deficient and borderline children. *American Journal of Mental Deficiency*, 1950, **55**, 235–250.

Males, J., & Males, B. Art therapy: A creative approach to the care of mentally handicapped people. *Australian Journal of Mental Retardation*, 1979, **5**, 275–277.

Maslow, A. H. *Motivation and personality*. New York: Harper & Bros., 1954.

Mehlman, B. Group play therapy with mentally retarded children. *Journal of Abnormal and Social Psychology*, 1953, **48**, 53–60.

Menolascino, F. J. Emotional disturbance and mental retardation. *American Journal of Mental Deficiency*, 1965, 70, 248–256.

Michal-Smith, H., Gottsegen, M. G., & Gottsegen, G. B. A group therapy technique for mental retardates. *International Journal of Group Psychotherapy*, 1955, 5, 84–90.

Morino, J. L. Psychodrama. In H. I. Kaplan & B. J. Sadock (Eds.) *Comprehensive group therapy*. (2nd ed.) Baltimore: Williams & Wilkens, 1971.

Morrison, T. L., & Newcomer, B. L. Effects of directive vs. nondirective play therapy with institutionalized mentally retarded children. *American Journal of Mental Deficiency*, 1975, 79, 666–669.

Mundy, L. Therapy with physically and mentally handicapped children in a mental deficiency hospital. *Journal of Clinical Psychology*, 1957, 13, 3–9.

Murstein, B. I. *Handbook of projective techniques*. New York: Basic Books, 1975.

Neham, S. Psychotherapy in relation to mental deficiency. *American Journal of Mental Deficiency*, 1951, 55, 557–572.

Newcomer, B. L., & Morrison, T. L. Play therapy with institutionalized mentally retarded children. *American Journal of Mental Deficiency*, 1974, 78, 727–733.

Nordoff, P., & Robbins, C. *Music therapy for handicapped children: Investigations and experiences*. Blauvelt, N.Y.: Rudolph Steiner Publications, 1965.

Norman, M. I. A counseling program for TMR students. *School Counselor*, 1977, 24, 274–277.

Ohwaki, S. An assessment of dance therapy to improve retarded adults' body image. *Perceptual and Motor Skills*, 1976, 43, 1122.

Parson, J. A. Effects of therapist modeling of feedback delivery on member feedback and self concept in group therapy with EMR students. *Dissertation Abstracts International*, 1980, 41(3B), 1122.

Parten, M. B. Social participation among preschool children. *Journal of Abnormal and Social Psychology*, 1932, 27, 243–269.

Perlman, E., & Patterson, M. Group singing provided unexpected means for rousing T.M.R. responses. *Journal of Special Educators of the Mentally Retarded*, 1977, 13, 101–102.

Piaget, J. *Play, dreams and imitation in childhood*. London: Kleinemann, 1951.

Pueschel, S. M., & Yeatman, S. An educational and counseling program for phenylketonuric adolescents and their parents. *Social Work in Health Care*, 1977, 3, 29–36.

Pulaski, M. A. Play symbolism in cognitive development. In C. E. Schaefer (Ed.), *Therapeutic uses of child's play*. New York: Jason Aronson, Inc., 1976.

Ringelheim, D., & Polatsek, I. Group therapy with a male defective group (A preliminary study). *American Journal of Mental Deficiency*, 1957, 62, 157–162.

Robinson, N. M., & Robinson, H. B. *The mentally retarded child: A psychological approach*. (2nd ed.) New York: McGraw-Hill Co., 1976.

Rogers, S. B. Contributions of dance therapy in a treatment program for retarded adolescents and adults. *Art Psychotherapy*, 1977, 4, 195–197.

Roth, E. A., & Barrett, R. P. Parallels in art and play therapy with a disturbed retarded boy. *The Arts in Psychotherapy*, 1980, 7, 19–26.

Rutter, M., Tizard, J., & Whitmore, K. *Education, Health, & Behavior*. London: Longman, 1970.

Sadock, B. J. Group psychotherapy, combined individual and group psychotherapy, and psychodrama. In H. I. Kaplan, A. M. Freedman, and B. J. Sadock (Eds.), *Comprehensive textbook of psychiatry*. (3rd ed.) Baltimore/London: Williams and Wilkins, 1980.

Sarason, S. B. *Psychological problems in mental deficiency*. New York: Harper & Bros., 1953.

Sarason, S. B. Individual psychotherapy with mentally defective individuals. *American Journal of Mental Deficiency*, 1952, 56, 803–805.

Sarbin, T. R. Spontaneity training of the feebleminded. *Sociometry*, 1945, 8, 389–393.

Satten, N. R., & Singer, M. Successful treatment in a woman with Down's Syndrome. *Psychiatric Opinion*, 1979, 16, 36–40.

Schacter, F. F., Meyer, L. R., & Loomis, E. A. Childhood schizophrenia and mental retardation: Differential diagnosis after one year of psychotherapy. *American Journal of Orthopsychiatry*, 1962, 32, 584–594.

Schmidt, B. G. Changes in personal, social and intellectual behavior of children originally classified as feebleminded. *Psychological Monograph*, 1948, 60, No. 5. American Psychological Association, Washington.

Schwartz, C. The application of psychoanalytic theory to the treatment of the mentally retarded child. *Psychoanalytic Review*, 1979, 66, 133–141.

Schweisheimer, W., & Walberg, H. J. A peer counselling experiment: High school students as small-group leaders. *Journal of Counseling Psychology*, 1976, 23, 398–401.

Scott, W. C. M. Psychotherapy of mental defectives. *Canadian Psychiatric Association Journal*, 1964, 8, 293.

Selan, B. H. Psychotherapy with the mentally retarded. *Social Work*, 1979, 24, 263.

Shoben, E. J. Some observations on psychotherapy and the learning process. In O. H. Mowrer (Ed.), *Psychotherapy: Theory and research*. New York: Ronald Press, 1953.

Shuman-Carpenter, B. S. The effects of two methods of therapy on the body image of emotionally disturbed, retarded female adolescents. (Dissertation, University of Michigan, 1977.) *Dissertation Abstracts International*, 1977 (Microfilms No. 77-13526.).

Slavson, S. R., & Schiffer, M. *Group therapies for children: A textbook*. New York: International Universities Press, Inc., 1975.

Smith, E., McKinnon, R., & Kessler, J. W. Psychotherapy with mentally retarded children. *Psychoanalytic Study of Childhood*, 1976, 31, 493–514.

Snyder, R., & Sechrest, L. An experimental study of directive group therapy with defective delinquents. *American Journal of Mental Deficiency*, 1959, 64, 117–123.

Snyder, W. V. The present status of psychotherapeutic counseling. *Psychological Bulletin*, 1947, 44, 297–386.

Sternlicht, M. Establishing an initial relationship in group psychotherapy with delinquent retarded male adolescents. *American Journal of Mental Deficiency*, 1964, 69, 39–41.

Sternlicht, M. Psychotherapeutic techniques useful with the mentally retarded: A review and critique. *Psychiatric Quarterly*, 1965, 39, 84–90.

Sternlicht, M. Treatment approaches to delinquent retardates. *International Journal of Group Psychotherapy*, 1966, 16, 91–93.

Strain, P. Increasing social play of severely retarded preschoolers with socio-dramatic activities. *Mental Retardation*, 1975, 13, 7–9.

Subotnik, L., & Callahan, R. J. A pilot study in short-term play therapy with institutionalized educable mentally retarded boys. *American Journal of Mental Deficiency*, 1959, **63**, 730–735.

Szymanski, L. S. Individual psychotherapy with retarded persons. In L. S. Szymanski & P. E. Tanguay (Eds.), *Emotional disorders of mentally retarded persons*. Baltimore: University Park Press, 1980.

Szymanski, L. S. & Rosefsky, Q. B. Group psychotherapy with retarded persons. In L. S. Szymanski & P. E. Tanguay (Eds.), *Emotional disorders of mentally retarded persons*. Baltimore: University Park Press, 1980.

Taraschow, S. Interpretation and reality in psychotherapy. *International Journal of Psychoanalysis*, 1962, **43**, 377–387.

Thorne, F. C. Counseling and psychotherapy with mental defectives. *American Journal of Mental Deficiency*, 1948, **52**, 263–271.

Thorne, F. C., & Dolan, K. M. The role of counseling in a placement program for mentally retarded females. *Journal of Clinical Psychology*, 1953, **9**, 110–113.

Trent, P. J., & Brodie, K. H. Psychiatric research: A process view. In H. I. Kaplan, A. M. Freedman, & B. J. Sadock (Eds.), *Comprehensive treatment of psychiatry*. Baltimore: Williams & Wilkins Co., 1980.

U.S. Department of Health, Education and Welfare. Horticulture therapy for mental retardates. *Journal of the Special Educators of the Retarded*, 1977, **13**, 99–100.

Vail, D. J. An unsuccessful experiment in group therapy. *American Journal of Mental Deficiency*, 1955, **60**, 144–151.

Walker, P. W. Premarital counseling for the developmentally disabled. *Social Casework*, 1977, **58**, 475–479.

Wegman, B. S. Intelligence as a factor in the treatment of problem children. *Smith College Studies in Social Work*, 1944, **14**, 244–245.

Weigl, V. Functional music, a therapeutic tool in working with the mentally retarded. *American Journal of Mental Deficiency*, 1959, **63**, 672–678.

Weiner, B. J., Ottinger, D. R., & Tilton, J. F. Comparison of the toy-play behavior of autistic, retarded, and normal children: A reanalysis. *Psychological Reports*, 1969, **25**, 223–227.

Weiner, E. A. & Weiner, B. J. Differentiation of retarded and normal children through toy-play analysis. *Multivariate Behavioral Research*, 1974, **9**, 245–252.

Weinstock, A. Group treatment of characterologically damaged developmentally disabled adolescents in a residential treatment center. *International Journal of Group Psychotherapy*, 1979, **29**, 369–381.

Welch, V. O., & Sigman, M. Group psychotherapy with mildly retarded, emotionally disturbed adolescents. *Journal of Clinical Child Psychology*, 1980, **9**, 209–212.

Wiest, G. Psychotherapy with the mentally retarded. *American Journal of Mental Deficiency*, 1955, **59**, 640–644.

Wilcox, G. T., & Guthrie, G. M. Changes in adjustment of institutionalized female defectives following group psychotherapy. *Journal of Clinical Psychology*, 1957, **13**, 9–13.

Wilson, L. Theory and practice of art therapy with the mentally retarded. *American Journal of Art Therapy*, 1977, **16**, 87–97.

Wing, L., Gould, J., Yeates, S. P., & Brierley, L. M. Symbolic play in severely mentally retarded and in autistic children. *Journal of Child Psychology and Psychiatry*, 1977, **18**, 167–178.

Woodward, W. M. The behavior of idiots interpreted by Piaget's theory of sensori-motor development. *British Journal of Educational Psychology*, 1959, **29**, 60–71.

Yepson, L. N. Counseling the mentally retarded. *Journal of Mental Deficiency*, 1952, **57**, 205–213.

Yonge, K. A., & O'Connor, N. Measurable effects of group psychotherapy with defective delinquents. *Journal of Mental Science*, 1954, **100**, 944–952.

Zapf, R. F. Group therapy with retarded adults: A reality therapy approach. *Dissertation Abstracts International*, 1976, **37**(3A), 1418.

24 INTERVENTIONS WITH PARENTS OF THE MENTALLY RETARDED*

Alexander J. Tymchuk

There have been numerous changes in the ways that society, primarily through its professionals, has been involved with parents and families of the mentally retarded. Although it is difficult to document, before this century and during the early part of it, there appears to have been a virtual disregard for parents coupled with the well documented limited interest in the mentally retarded. There were individuals and groups scattered throughout the country who attended to the needs of parents, but these were few in number. Beginning in the 1940's, largely in response to the voices of the parents themselves, greater attention was paid to their needs so that today society works in many ways with parents of the mentally retarded. The understanding of this transition, from a lack of interest in parents to today's greater sensitivity to their needs, is of great importance, because there are aspects from the past that still influence how we view parents today, which in turn influences how we work with parents. These aspects of the past may or may not be beneficial and should be considered critically in light of present day knowledge (Powell, 1981).

The purpose of this chapter is to describe the historical and present treatment of parents of the mentally retarded, the evidence on which those treat-

ments are based, and to offer some suggestions for future efforts.

Some Considerations

Before beginning the chapter, a few statements must be made regarding some of the problems in writing such a chapter. Since there has been a great deal written about parents of the mentally retarded from varying perspectives, both historically and more recently, writing such a chapter must take into account the full range of perspectives that have been offered.

DEFINITIONS OF TREATMENT

Since so many different words are used to describe similar behaviors, the author has chosen the word interventions to describe those behaviors that are generally considered to be part of psychological treatment, therapy, education, counseling or training of parents. The word intervention is selected too, as one which is least likely to imply pathology or deviance, for it is the author's contention that pathology or deviance cannot be assumed in parents of the mentally retarded and, therefore, unless verified with empirical data, such "loaded" terms should not be used.

[1] To appear in Matson, J. & Mulick, J. *Handbook on Mental Retardation*, to be published by Pergamon Press.

Of critical importance in understanding interventions with parents of the mentally retarded is the definition of the population upon which these interventions are based. In the past, just what constituted mental retardation and who were those considered to be mentally retarded varied according to the definition used, how knowledgeable the people were who applied a given definition, and how consistently the definition was applied. Thus, before the advent of tests of intelligence the phrase mental retardation and related terms were applied in a general way to include people with emotional disturbances and organic disorders, including epilepsy and cerebral palsy. With the advent of intelligence tests, scores on those tests were used as sole determiners of the societal construct of mental retardation for a period of time. In 1963, the American Association on Mental Deficiency (AAMD) adopted a tripartite definition of mental retardation to include social adaptation and lowered the IQ cutoff to 70. However, the American Psychiatric Association's definition maintained the IQ cutoff at 80 until 1980, when the Diagnostic and Statistical Manual (DSM II) was published. Thus, to be a parent of a mentally retarded person today is vastly different from being a parent before 1905, between then and 1963, and between 1963 and the present.

A further complication is the fact that much of what is known about parents of the mentally retarded historically has been derived from the study of parents of children who were recognized at birth as being physiologically different and thus, having a high probability of slow or limited development and being considered to be mentally retarded. Since children born with an organic basis for their behavioral deficits, including those with biochemical, chromosomal, or neurologic etiologies, constitute only about 25 to 30% of the population considered to be mentally retarded, data about parents of these children cannot be generalized to parents whose children constitute the other 75% (Tarjan & Keeran, 1974). In general, very little is known about the parents whose children come to be considered mentally retarded later in their development. These children generally are physiologically normal at birth and may be seen as being at risk for the development of problems later, but they are not seen to be at the same degree of risk that children with obvious handicaps are. As these children participate in socialization activities and particularly the educational system, they fall behind their peers developmentally and may be labeled mentally retarded.

Intervention with the parents then begins. However, particularly after the school years, these children may or may not be seen as being mentally retarded and may become assimilated into the general population. This is vastly different from the lifelong needs of the other group and thus, again influences how we intervene with the parents.

Finally, much has been written about interventions with parents of children with other disorders including autism and behavior and/or learning problems but with normal intelligence. Whether data gathered on parents of children in other diagnostic categories can be generalized to parents of the mentally retarded needs to be established empirically.

An Historical Perspective

Although much has been written about how the mentally retarded person has been viewed and treated historically, it is important for the purpose of this chapter to mention some of those views and treatments, particularly as they relate to the family. The predominant view of the mentally retarded has been one of worthlessness (President's Committee on Mental Retardation, 1976). The mentally retarded individual was seen as being less than a person, since the construct of intelligence was considered to be an attribute of personhood and, because of some of the physical changes associated with mental retardation, they were seen again as being different and again less than a person, despite the huge variations in what constitutes normal appearance. This view was predominant even though the majority of those considered to be mentally retarded by whatever definition did not look physically different from anyone else, although some dressed differently and/or exhibited unusual behavior.

Another view of the mentally retarded was based upon economics. They were seen as being unable to care for themselves (despite the fact that organized care was custodial rather than habilitative) or to work and contribute to society economically (despite the fact that they were denied opportunities to work). In addition, the mentally retarded were bereft of rights. They were not allowed to speak for themselves by virtue of being institutionalized, but, again, the view that predominated was that the mentally retarded were incapable of making knowledgeable decisions or speaking for themselves.

The general view of the mentally retarded then was overwhelmingly pejorative and negative. Parents, siblings, the mentally retarded themselves and professionals could not help but be influenced by those views.

TREATMENT OF THE MENTALLY RETARDED

Either as a result of these views mentioned above or coincident with them, the treatment of the mentally retarded was generally custodial and not habilitative. For parents, there were few options. One possibility was to maintain their child in the home without public services, which meant that often one parent was forced to remain at home full time virtually forever in a society that generally devalued anyone not fitting the norm, however defined. A second option was to institutionalize their offspring, either at a young age or later, after attempting the first option. Both possibilities usually meant a total and often final separation, since institutions were usually some distance away from population bases and there usually was rapid deterioration of abilities in the person institutionalized. To maintain contact in these circumstances, parents would repeatedly have to question and rationalize their earlier decision. Many parents, in the face of these practical and emotional issues, did not maintain contact with their offspring (Fliederbaum, 1951).

VIEW OF THE PARENT OF A MENTALLY RETARDED PERSON

Much less has been written historically about parents and families of the mentally retarded than has been about the mentally retarded themselves. The views that can be gleaned from the literature include: that parents of the mentally retarded are themselves somehow different from other parents because of having a mentally retarded offspring (Farber, 1959, 1960); that it is axiomatic that to have a mentally retarded offspring is to feel that disaster has struck (e.g., Schell, 1981); and that the best that a parent of a mentally retarded person could do was to institutionalize that person (Anonymous, 1973).

VIEW THAT PARENTS OF THE MENTALLY RETARDED ARE DIFFERENT THAN OTHER PARENTS

Whether intentional or not, the early literature on parents of the mentally retarded presented the view that being such a parent somehow made them different from other parents (Birenbaum, 1979; Redner, 1980). This early literature, influenced as it was by the psychoanalytic view that children were extensions of the parents, implied that if something was different about the child then something was different about the parents (Benedek, 1959; Solnit & Stark, 1961; Waterman, 1948). And since intelligence was highly valued, a child considered less intelligent was devalued and hence, by extension, so were the parents. Although

there was no explicit doctrine indicating that these parents were different from other parents, this attitude also has been adopted by some parents themselves as attested to by their own statements of worthlessness (e.g., Waisbren, 1980). However, it is important to emphasize that these attitudes, either explicit or implicit in the way parents of the mentally retarded were treated and in how the parents viewed themselves, were derived from a single theoretical view espoused during a particularly pessimistic period of treatment of the mentally retarded. Contrary to these attitudes, there is no evidence at all that parents of the mentally retarded are different from any other parents solely by virtue of the fact that the former are parents of the mentally retarded. No one has studied people before they became parents of mentally retarded children; and Mahoney (1958) suggests that these people are a heterogeneous group beforehand and afterwards. Waisbren (1980) studied parents of normal children and those of children with Down syndrome and found them more alike than different during the first year and a half after the birth of their child. In general, the parents of the Down syndrome children did report in later life that they were affected more negatively.

VIEW THAT IT MUST BE A TRAUMA TO HAVE A MENTALLY RETARDED OFFSPRING

Another commonly held attitude is that it is axiomatic that having a mentally retarded offspring is traumatic. When people become parents, they have expectations regarding what the child will be like. At the birth of a physically normal child, these expectations are met. Later in development, if there is difficulty, these expectations may change and it is at this time that such labels as developmentally delayed, slow learner, and mentally retarded may be used with the parents. Parents are ill prepared for such words and for their implications regarding psychological, educational or medical services. When a child's delay is confirmed, parents have to enter systems that are at variance from those to which they have been accustomed and that are usually segregated from services used by other parents whose children do not carry such labels. The reason for this divergence is the belief that special or different services are required for children bearing these labels and, to be sure, this belief is sometimes appropriate, but not to the extent of indicating total segregation. For the parent, however, segregation raises the psychological specter of differentness or low self-esteem— a specter that they may or may not resist, depending upon the perspectives of the professionals involved who may perpetuate the view of the parent as traumatized (Anderson & Garner, 1973). Parents may resist the view of trauma by virtue of their own psychological capabilities or previous experience or support systems, they may accept professional help but not the implications of that help, of they may not accept the help, having received better help already. On the other hand, those parents without support systems or strong psychological capabilities might come to believe in their own differentness or the justification for low self-esteem.

Although the birth of a mentally retarded child usually requires some adjustment on the parts of the parents, the reactions attributed to parents may be exaggerated and are still not well understood. The commonly held attitude that it is axiomatic that having a mentally retarded offspring is traumatic, derives from the psychoanalytic view mentioned above that the child is an extension of the parent. To give birth to a physiologically different child reflects upon the parents who, by virtue of the fact of this birth, must react negatively, since being different has often been equated with unworthiness. Much has been written about the negative reactions of parents to the birth of a physiologically different child, but there are a number of very serious difficulties with these writings. First and foremost, recognition must be given to the state of the psychological art when only one theoretical viewpoint predominated. Without other theories to draw from, early workers used psychoanalytic theory to characterize parent reactions. Even at that time, however, the data upon which these characterizations were made were limited. Early studies of parents of physiologically different children were descriptive in nature, based upon single cases, and influenced by the tenets of a single theory. Grebler (1952), as one example of these early studies, reviewed the patients, whose IQ's were 75 or below, that had been referred to a clinic in a 10-month period from 1949 to 1950 and where there were interviews with parents. Based on 11 cases, Grebler concluded that three mothers were rejecting, six were ambivalent, one was accepting, and a judgement could not be made on the last. Although there were no data presented on the fathers, Grebler generalized to all parents of the mentally retarded.

Several things stand out regarding this study. First, conclusions were drawn from a small number of cases without any method to ascertain the representative nature of the population; second, one person reviewed interview data and categorized them without consideration of any personal biases; and third, there was no measure of paternal attitudes other than one person's review.

The conclusions by Grebler (1952) were uncritically ratified and accepted by numerous other early writers. A review of the references of many of these articles shows the inbred nature of the data. Numerous references are made even today to the articles by Zuk (1959), Fabrega and Haka (1967), Olshansky (1963), and Solnit and Stark (1961), although the articles are little more than personal experiences and observations. Based as they were on limited data, deriving from a single theoretical framework, at a time when there were few trained professionals in mental retardation (Potter, 1965) and when there were few treatment alternatives for the mentally retarded, the conclusions from these studies should no longer influence professional thinking.

A second difficulty with much of what has been written about parents has been mentioned, but needs to be emphasized here. A great deal of the work on parental reactions was done with parents of children with obvious biomedical pathologies in addition to their mental retardation (a subpopulation consisting of only 25% of the mentally retarded population) and the results generalized to other parents. A third difficulty has been that much early work was done primarily with mothers, so that when one speaks of parental reactions it is inappropriate to include the fathers until relevant data are gathered. A fourth difficulty has been that parents have been treated as a homogeneous group without consideration of what they were like before the birth of their mentally retarded child.

The third view that can be gleaned from the early literature is the view that institutionalization was the best alternative for parents of the mentally retarded. This view was influenced by the lack of services in the community for anyone who was handicapped. The only other alternative was to maintain the child in the home and to have the child participate in one of the few special education programs available (Doll, 1967). Although institutionalization was considered appropriate by some for the more severely mentally retarded, many individuals, who also could have benefitted from less restricted alternatives, were also institutionalized (Tarjan, Wright, Eyman, & Keeran, 1973).

Historically, interventions with parents/families of the mentally retarded have been limited in terms of extent, availability, and type. Few available alternatives for treatment influenced, in part, how parents were treated.

Furthermore, since work with the mentally retarded was generally viewed as being of low priority *endeavor* and even distasteful, there were very few university or other training programs to prepare professionals. There was, consequently, a lack of trained professionals (Ainsworth, in Hormuth, 1970). Counselling, for the most part, was related to helping parents separate from their child in the course of institutionalizing the child.

This counselling often was done at the birth of a child with biomedical pathologies who presumably would become mentally retarded later, by the physician or other medical personnel. These personnel often had little or no training in working with parents around these issues. Cummings and Stock (1962), for example, began groups for parents (because one author had had experience with hospitalized veterans) stating "We did not know what to expect (p. 741)." Since there were few public services, parents with children who did not have obvious physical handicaps at birth, but who had delays in learning and/or behavioral difficulties later, obtained counselling, if they could afford it, from private professionals who also were ill prepared (Menolascino, 1970). Many of these professionals, trained in a dynamic and primarily a psychoanalytic modality in work with adults who had emotional problems, presumed to generalize that training to work with parents of the mentally retarded and the mentally retarded themselves. It is not surprising that they often said the mentally retarded could not be helped. Schools by and large maintained the traditional separation of school and home.

The Recent Past

Beginning in the 1950s, several things occurred that coincided with or influenced society's views of the mentally retarded and with a consequent change in how families of the mentally retarded were treated.

Parent Movement

Although it is difficult to pinpoint the sequence of events, for convenience the parent movement will be presented first. It also is hard to present accurately the climate of the times, which was heavily reliant upon the available professional literature, because there probably were many dissatisfied people questioning the treatment of the mentally retarded and their families before the 1950's. It was, however, at this time that the National Association of Retarded Citizens, as it is now called, began. The mission of this organization was precisely to achieve optimal growth for the mentally retarded and their families.

Theoretical Changes

Simultaneously, there were several important philosophical and theoretical changes. First, intelligence was no longer seen as being totally derived from heredity and the influence of environment was acknowledged (Hunt, 1972). Head Start began on this premise, with a focus on providing children at risk for developmental delay with an enriched environment. Initially, parents were not provided with much service or involvement, thus perpetuating separation of school from home (Winton & Turnbull, 1981).

Data from early intervention projects influenced the concept of mental retardation at this time, so that the definition adopted by the AAMD changed from an upper limit of IQ 85 to IQ 70, along with poor social adaptation and occurrence during the developmental period. Parents of children who had been labeled mentally retarded under the old definition with whatever resultant effect, now had to reevaluate their situations. Adding to the confusion was the fact that the American Psychiatric Association's definition of mental retardation remained the same as the earlier AAMD definition for another 10 years. The result was that parents were treated differently, depending upon whom they saw for service.

It was at this time that the view of the mentally retarded person's abilities was drastically changed, in large part as a result of the use of behavioral techniques. In 1961, behavioral techniques could not be used with patients traditionally seen by analytically or dynamically oriented mental-health professionals (see Ball, 1968, for a discussion), but they were applied to institutionalized adult and child populations. Mentally retarded and other institutionalized populations who were previously viewed as limited in their abilities suddenly learned. Other researchers applied behavioral techniques to populations outside the institution, including the school and home. Not all people viewed the use of behavioral techniques positively; to the present day, parents are faced with conflicting messages regarding the use of behavioral techniques. However, where traditional educational or psychotherapeutic practices had limited efficacy leading to the view that the mentally retarded had limited abilities, the application of behavioral techniques coupled with educational curricula demonstrated that the mentally retarded could in fact do a great deal.

These developments, coupled with the rights movement, culminated in a push for deinstitutionalization with an emphasis upon obtaining the optimal environment for the individual. Alternative living arrangements were sought and developed for mentally retarded adults. Yet sterilization laws still remained on the books and marriage of the mentally retarded was implicitly discouraged by perpetuating segregation of the sexes in these living arrangements. In 1975, Public Law 94-142, the Education of All Handicapped Children Act, was passed. Now, parents theoretically had many more options available to them. Schools incorporated mental health techniques after much trepidation, since personnel soon recognized that placement in a school for several hours and returning home without parent involvement did little to maintain growth in the children. Head Start now was mandated to integrate 10% handicapped children, but again with limited parental involvement. Only recently has Head Start and Project Outreach funded by BEH recognized the importance of not only child, but also of parental services and training (Tymchuk, Dahlman, & Asher, 1981).

A final influencing factor has been the rapid development of technology, including media, devices, and medication. The former has allowed for dissemination of varying views and data about many things including how different parents view and grow with their mentally retarded offspring. The development of specialized devices has allowed for greater freedom for mentally retarded persons. Similarly, the portrayal of people using these devices in the media may have influenced the public's perception and parents' use of these devices in a positive way.

The Legacy of the Past

This section summarized the historical treatment of parents and families of the mentally retarded. It is critical to understand this past treatment and the influence it has upon our present view and treatment of parents of the mentally retarded. We must evaluate what is currently done to determine whether what we now do is new or merely a continuation of past practices.

The remainder of this chapter will discuss some of the methodological issues that need to be considered when describing any method of intervening with parents and will describe the current models of intervention.

Issues in Evaluating Methods of Interventions with Parents of the Mentally Retarded

There are great variations in the quality of the literature about interventions with parents of the mentally retarded, and because there are such variations, it is difficult to establish the validity of the data reported. There are a number of reasons for such variability, including the historical reason that this literature was reliant upon descriptions of personal experience by professionals not formally trained in the field of mental retardation. There is also the fact that the mentally retarded are served by an array of disciplines each of whom have their own concepts of the adequacy of research.

Populations Studied

It has been mentioned earlier that historically, studies written about parents of the mentally retarded were largely about parents of children diagnosed at birth or shortly thereafter, including those with identifiable phenotypes like those associated with Down syndrome, but for whom the etiologies still were unknown. Additionally, these parents were often white, middle-class people who could afford psychological services, and as such were not representative of most parents of mentally retarded people.

This situation continued to exist until the late 1960s and early 1970s, when the use of behavioral techniques in the training of parents emerged and educational and early intervention programs began focusing on parent-child relationships. There continues to be an emphasis upon maternal factors in all of the literature, regardless of the author's discipline or theoretical orientation. There also continues to be a focus upon parents of children identifiable at birth, although more is being written about fathers and parents of mentally retarded children without physical handicaps.

Because of these variations, it is difficult to make generalizations regarding parents, or mothers and fathers, of the mentally retarded. A further problem stems from the fact that parents have been studied when children are young. Consequently, there is virtually nothing written about parents of young adult, adult, or aged mentally retarded people.

Research Design

A further difficulty in evaluating the validity of the information on parents reported in the literature is the sophistication of the research design. Virtually all of the literature published on parents of the mentally retarded before the 1960's failed to attend to rudimentary aspects of research design. The same criticism can be made about much of the clinical research antedating that time. This criticism does not mean that the data presented are not useful, but it does mean that a great deal of care must be taken in interpreting these data.

The primary research shortcomings include inadequate sampling and the excessive use of case studies. Often, little attention was paid to observer bias. The instruments used for assessment purposes were primarily investigator-made, without evidence of meeting adequate test construction requirements. It is often unclear how or by whom these instruments were administered. There is often no evidence of efforts to control for expectancy effects. None of the earlier studies utilized contrast groups.

Some of these shortcomings have been overcome in the more recent literature, but their presence in the earlier literature raises serious questions about validity of the data. Still lacking are appropriate outcome measures and their consistent use, including measures of absenteeism and follow-through.

Intervention Issues

There is a paucity of published materials on interventions with parents of the mentally retarded. In those studies published however, there are a number of issues other than those mentioned earlier regarding populations studied and adequacy of research design that make generalizations and comparisons difficult. Content of intervention is often difficult to ascertain. The content may include discussions of whatever issues parents raise at that moment and may be viewed from the particular theoretical orientation of the author. Or the content may include step-by-step activities and exercises for the parents designed in response to assessment of their perceived needs. Tymchuk (1979), for example, after assessing parental attitudes towards child rearing, parental self-concept, marital adjustment, knowledge of child development, knowledge of resources and of their child's disorders, as well as observing at least the mother in interaction with the child, designed a time-limited group or individual intervention that addressed the parental profile. Other intervention issues include the use of media, the length, frequency and duration of the intervention, the age of the child when the intervention occurs, the discipline, experience, and training of the intervenor, the site of the intervention, whether there was individual or group intervention and thus considerations of group size and composition, whether payment by the parents or by the investigators as an incentive and demographics of the parents including marital status, experience, age, race, ethnicity, religion, socioeconomic status, experience with counselling, family size, support systems, and most importantly their psychological capabilities.

Current Models of Interventions with Parents of the Mentally Retarded

There are several models currently in use in intervening with parents of the mentally retarded.

Dynamic Model

A dynamic model for counselling parents of the mentally retarded is one which has as a basic premise that internal factors or dynamics of the parents relate directly to how parents will behave. Treatment is directed toward the parent to explore these dynamics. Resolution of negative feelings then will translate into better acceptance of the child.

Treatment can occur immediately following the birth of a physiologically different child, while the mother is still hospitalized. Few hospitals are equipped to provide such intervention, but greater attention is being paid to the content of such intervention as well as timing and the training of providers (Barnard & Erickson, 1976). Lipton and Svarstad (1977), for example, found that professional communication style was directly related to parental acceptance of the diagnosis of mental retardation and that professional experience was related to that style. The development of alternative models is another issue that needs to be addressed. Schroeder (1974), for example, in a text for nurses admits that she has had only a few opportunities to see how nurses work with people with "defective babies," and yet states that "when a baby is born with a defect the family immediately enters into a process of grieving not unlike the grieving process seen in families who have experienced the death of a loved one" (p. 159). Such uncritical acceptance and generalization of a global concept borrowed from work with the dying only perpetuates the view that such a birth is tragic. Such a presumption that grief is omnipresent also does not allow for consideration of no grief, but happiness at the birth of a child, nor does it allow for degrees of responses in relation to parental psychological capabilities, support services, previous experiences or preparation or in relation to type and degree of child disorder or what is known about it or in relation to preparation of personnel in work with parents. Parents are often depressed after birth of normal as well as handicapped children.

Treatment can be given at other points in time when difficulties in the marital relationship, intra-personally, financially, or with the child are at issue. The focus of dynamically based interventions usually is with the parents either individually or conjointly addressing feelings or attitudes toward one another, toward the child, or toward any of the myriad of issues facing them. The style of treatment is usually face-to-face verbal discussion an hour weekly for several months. Parent groups have been used and play therapy with the children has been used with interpretations made to the child or the parents.

More recently, the use of the concept of attachment has provided impetus for observing and influencing the interactions of parents (usually the mother) with their mentally retarded offspring. The suggestion has been that mothers will be more accepting of their children, depending upon the strength of the bond or attachment. This concept has a great deal of merit, for it provides a focus upon mother-child interaction while also addressing the psychodynamic needs. Bromwich (1981) has adopted what she terms an interactional approach whereby the parent, usually only the mother, is shown how to interact with her preterm infant more effectively. The mother also learns activities in which to engage her infant. Bromwich's approach has merit, since it deals with specific observable behaviors between mother and child. More attention is now needed to determine which mothers, fathers, and significant others do well in interaction with the child.

Interventions with parents of the mentally retarded based upon a dynamic model in general seem to have utility both in conceptualizing parental behavior and in intervening with parents. However, little more can be said regarding the efficacy of such treatment or the identification of which parents benefit from such interventions (see Wolfensberger, 1967). Although there are numerous examples of case studies in the literature, there has been little effort to identify parents who would benefit from dynamically based interventions. The presumption seems to be that all parents would benefit, but this should be empirically established. In addition, comparisons between proponents of the different models as to the criteria for success as well as the criteria for research are needed. Tavormina (1975) addressed this comparative issue with groups of mothers of mentally retarded children with unknown characteristics who were assigned to behavioral, reflective counselling or control (no treatment) procedures. Mothers responded to a letter sent to 300 mothers from two facilities for the mentally retarded. Although there were no maternal differences between groups before involvement, there were no reasons given why only 51% of 300 mothers participated. The generalizability of the results then is limited. Since the control group did not receive Placebo treatment, reported differences could be accounted for in part by session attendance. No report is made of how many mothers missed sessions, but only three dropped out of the two reflective groups. There were a total of 21 measures including parent attitudinal, child problematic and direct behavioral observation of mother-child interaction during free play and command periods. Of six parent attitudinal measures, on only one did the behavioral groups and the reflective

groups improve differently from the control group and from themselves, with the behavioral groups doing better. Of seven child behavior rating scores, there were no significant changes on three of them, while on three both treatment groups differed from the control and not between themselves and only on one was behavioral treatment superior to the reflective, which was superior to no treatment. There were no differences or change on free play for any of the groups, but there were for the command periods in favor of behavioral treatment. In general, mothers in the behavioral groups showed more satisfaction than did those in the reflective groups. Tavormina concluded from this that the behavioral method was superior to the reflective method and that the former was more cost efficient. However, this conclusion must be tempered a great deal by virtue of the fact that there were so few significant differences. Bernal, Klinnert, and Schultz (1980) made a similar comparison between behavioral parent training, client-centered parent counselling and no treatment (waiting list) for parents of children with conduct problems and found equivocal results similar to those reported by Tavormina (1975). Although none of the parents in the Bernal et al. study had children who were mentally retarded, both studies demonstrate the need for further efforts that identify and manipulate fewer variables.

Behavioral Models of Parent Intervention

More recently, behavior modification or operant learning techniques have been utilized with parents of the mentally retarded. These techniques have varied from training parents to ignore excessive crying in a child (Williams, 1959) to training in the systematic collection of data on both adaptive and maladaptive behavior. Programs have been developed both in the clinic and home (Baker, Heifetz & Murphy, 1980). Other variations have included doing the training in groups (Sadler, Seyden, Howe, & Kaminsky, 1976) rather than individually (Brehony, Benson, Solomon & Luscumb, 1980), providing training by one parent for another (Adubato, Adams & Budd, 1981), and utilizing booklets—for general (Patterson & Gullion, 1968; Tymchuk, 1974), as well as for specific knowledge (Heifetz, 1977)—and other media, including videotape (Tymchuk, 1975) and filmstrips with devices that enhance learning, such as a walkie-talkie (Tymchuk, 1973) or a bug-in-the-ear.

Several formats for training have been developed, including what has become a standard eight-session program to cover key aspects of behavioral technology, including observation and measurement, reinforcement principles, program planning, application of reinforcement techniques, program implementation and punishment techniques. Assessments have included pretesting for knowledge about behavioral principles and less frequently on direct observation of parents relative to treatment effectiveness.

There are a number of reviews available that discuss behavioral models of parent intervention in detail (e.g., Berkowitz & Graziano, 1972; Johnson & Katz, 1973). The majority of the studies available, however, have focused upon families of children with behavior problems and few have worked with families of the mentally retarded.

Whereas behavioral interventions with families in general have become very sophisticated methodologically, there are still some difficulties with the lack of data regarding participation of parents. Weinrott, Bauske, and Patterson (1979) reported a 34% dropout rate, which is similar to that which the author has calculated from data provided by Heifetz (1977) and Bernal et al. (1980). Furthermore, relatively few parents are involved in any one project and those who participate are not necessarily representative of parents who come to clinics independently. It is unclear, therefore, for whom behavioral training works. What is required is an assessment of those people who do not participate. In addition, behavioral training has been used primarily with mothers and has largely focused upon eliminating problem behaviors. Child rearing is a family affair and even more so with a mentally retarded child, so that paternal involvement in any intervention is virtually mandated for successful outcome. In addition, since mentally retarded children require a great deal of training for many behaviors during their development, behavioral parent training may be only effective in certain situations or at certain times or in combination with other dynamic or educational approaches. Further efforts are needed to delimit the conditions under which behavioral training is appropriate.

Lobitz and Johnson (1975) have suggested the need for a broader intervention with families, since approximately a third of their families dropped out of their behavioral training program. Heifetz (1977) studied the use of the manuals in comparison with several other conditions with parents of the mentally retarded and found that parents with manuals alone did as well as did those with more intensive involvement. This study is instructive for this finding, but care must be taken in considering the results, since the parents were self-selected by responding to an advertisement. After an initial group of 222 were selected, only 165 came to the first sessions, 160 then continued, with 111 finishing. This fact is important,

since a unitary approach, whether behavioral or dynamic, may not be optimal, depending upon the criteria used for success. Studies using behavioral methods with parents have some methodological shortcomings which are similar to those mentioned about studies using dynamically based methods, including sampling and follow-up issues. Interestingly, it appears that those parents treated by the dynamists are very different from those treated by the behaviorists, since the former never refer to parent training and the latter never refer to interfering dynamic variables. This points out a major difficulty in comparing studies from different theoretical orientations, since orientation influences what the focus is and what to use to evaluate outcome.

Family Therapy

Another method of intervening with parents of the mentally retarded has been family therapy. Family therapy actually describes several approaches including the traditional approach, where family members meet as a group to discuss feelings about each other. Behavioral family therapy describes a hybrid approach, where, in addition to the discussion of feelings, there is a learning of new styles of interaction. Although originally developed with families of the mentally ill adult, family therapy has been adapted for use with families of children who are considered to be mentally ill, behaviorally disordered, or otherwise disordered, including the mentally retarded. Family therapy, like behavioral training, is used a great deal with families of the mentally retarded, but, although several reports have described effectiveness with families of other populations, little has been written about the efficacy of such an approach, either by itself or in comparison to other approaches, with families of the retarded (e.g., Christensen, Johnson, Phillips & Glasgow, 1980); and little has been written regarding suitability of clients for family therapy (DeWitt, 1978).

Early Intervention/Educational Approaches

Although historically there was a separation of school from hospital or clinic, soon after the advent of educational programs for children with special needs, it became evident that having children in school for several hours and then returning them home for the remainder of the day or for weekends and holidays did not provide enough of an effort either for training or in maintenance without providing a parent component. Similarly, where first efforts at early intervention were focused primarily upon the child at risk in Head Start and later in the integration of handicapped children including the retarded into Head Start, later efforts included parents, primarily mothers, with a variety of support services (Tymchuk, Dahlman, & Asher, 1981). Tymchuk (1979) adapted his model of parent therapy developed in a medical school setting for use with families with handicapped children in Head Start and in a special class setting and found that parents, who were virtually all mothers, had similar needs to those seen in clinics, but who functioned within their communities. Participation in parent groups increased the parent's knowledge of child development, resources and techniques and positively changed their attitudes towards parenting. Since there was no measure of mother-child interaction, whether improved attitudes translated into improved interaction could not be determined. There is an obvious difference between families who go to clinics versus those who do not related to the severity of difficulties that the parents may have either as a family or as individuals. Still, in this case, services were provided in a community and in an educational setting where interventions with mothers could be tied to their child's training in naturalistic settings.

Obviously, although more information is required in comparing interventions with families at different sites, expanding the roles of educational programs to include parental and familial interventions may have merit.

Combined Models of Intervention

Parents in general have many needs in order to fulfill their multiplicity of roles. Parents with mentally retarded offspring too have many needs. Although the multiplicity of needs of parents of the retarded is recognized, responses to those needs generally focus upon or emanate from single dimensions, either as a result of theoretical orientation, discipline level and extent of training of persons approached to respond to those needs, or as a result of agency policies and/or funding availability.

In the dynamic literature, for example, the focus has primarily been upon resolution of parental feelings without addressing the parent's needs for help in raising their child or for information regarding services and how to access them among other needs. In the behavioral literature the focus has been upon helping the parents deal with problem behavior in their child with some attempt to learn how to participate in the education of their child in acquiring adaptive behaviors while ignoring any informational needs or any feelings the parents may have regarding themselves, their offspring, or their situation. The early intervention literature more recently has provided a focus upon the child's deficits with some intervention upon mother-

child interaction, while not addressing other needs (Mash & Terdal, 1973). Although some professionals would contend that they do all of the above, the evidence in the literature is lacking.

It is interesting to conjecture what the dynamists say to a parent whose son has just bitten her, what the behaviorists do when a mother states that she does not want to be trained but wants to talk about her role, what the early intervenors say when a child no longer meets their age requirements, or what the educator says when the parents break down crying during a parent-teacher conference. These issues are all real and each one should be addressed. Unfortunately, little has been written regarding the use of several approaches, either concomitantly or in some sequence at different stages in a family's life cycle. Data are needed to determine which approach is optimal with which families at which time in a child's or family's development.

That there are many almost nonoverlapping approaches to intervening with parents of the mentally retarded, each with different concepts and content as well as techniques, is evidence that parents have many needs. Tymchuk (1979) has suggested that parents have a number of needs to varying degrees, including help in addressing any feelings that they may have regarding having a retarded child, about themselves or about professionals, about child development and how this may change when the child is delayed, about resources and how to access them, about mental retardation, and about techniques to enhance their child's development. These factors may vary over time as a child develops and may vary for both mothers and fathers (Gumz and Gubruim, 1972).

Summary and Conclusions

Currently, there are numerous ways in which professionals intervene with parents of the mentally retarded. This is vastly different from a time only a few decades ago when little was done for parents. Since then, there have been rapid changes beginning with the use of psychoanalytically based concepts to interpret the feelings of parents and then to counsel them regarding those feelings. More recently, behavioral, family, and educational approaches have been implemented. Although the initial parent intervention efforts were primarily with parents of children who were physiologically different at birth, interventions have expanded to include both parents and families with children at different levels of ability and/or of etiology and at different developmental periods. As the interventions evolved, so too did the sophistication of the research related to these interventions and the training of the personnel who participated. Where the early literature was largely descriptive, methodologically unsophisticated and based on small, unrepresentative samples, this has changed somewhat and where previously virtually no one, regardless of discipline, had formal training in the field of mental retardation, currently this has changed.

It is important to recognize the impact that these changes are having upon both how we view parents of mentally retarded and how we work with them. Since early efforts at intervening with parents were done during a period of time when treatment alternatives for the retarded themselves were limited and when psychoanalytically based concepts were being applied to these parents, it is little wonder that pessimism prevailed and such concepts as grief, guilt, and denial were applied, since one's theoretical orientation influences how one will view parents. Currently, there are numerous intervention alternatives both for parents and their offspring that allow for alternative perspectives on the parent and hence how we intervene with parents. Because of these changes, it is difficult to make firm conclusions regarding any intervention with parents or between interventions. Although the conclusions that can be drawn must be general ones, recommendations for future efforts can be very specific.

How a parent is viewed by a professional is determined by the theoretical construct used. The certainty with which one can base conclusions regarding those constructs is determined by the sophistication of the instruments to measure those constructs as well as the sophistication of the research design. One future direction is the development of suitable instruments to measure the efficacy of intervention. Another is the dissemination of suitable research designs that will allow us to make statements regarding intervention efficacy with some level of confidence. It is even difficult to make the observation that interventions work, since the criteria for success vary so greatly from orientation to orientation. What can be said is that interventions are done; whether they work individually or in some combination with others, is still to be determined. Other research needs include the development of predictive criteria for inclusion of parents or families into various interventions and the follow-up of those parents. Finally, there remains a critical need to determine whether the provision of periodic, ongoing, and longitudinal interventions would help prepare to anticipate needs as their child develops.

References

Adubato, S., Adams, M. & Budd, K. Teaching a parent to train a spouse in child management techniques. *Journal of Applied Behavioral Analysis*, 1981, **14**, 193–205.

Anderson, K., & Garner, A. Mothers of retarded children: Satisfaction with visits to professional people. *Mental Retardation*, 1973, August, 36–39.

Anonymous. Having a congenitally deformed baby. *Lancet*, 1973, **1**, 1499–1501.

Baker, B., Heifetz, L., & Murphy, D. Behavioral training for parents of mentally retarded children: One-year follow-up. *American Journal of Mental Deficiency*, 1980, **85**, 31–38.

Ball, T. The re-establishment of social behavior. *Hospital and Community Psychiatry*, 1968, **19**, 230–232.

Barnard, K., & Erickson, M. *Teaching children with developmental problems*. St. Louis: Mosby, 1976.

Benedek, T. Parenthood as a developmental phase. *Journal of the American Psychoanalytic Association*, 1959, **7**, 389–417.

Berkowitz, B., & Graziano, A. Training parents as behavior therapists. *Behavior Research and Therapy*, 1972, **10**, 297–317.

Bernal, M., Klinnert, M., & Schultz, L. Outcome evaluation of behavioral parent training and client-centered parent counselling for children with conduct problems. *Journal of Applied Behavioral Analysis*, 1980, **13**, 677–691.

Birenbaum, A. On managing a courtesy stigma. *Journal of Health and Social Behavior*, 1979, **11**, 196–206.

Brehoney, K., Benson, B., Solomon, L., & Luscomb, R. Parents as behavior modifiers: Intervention for three problem behaviors in a severely retarded child. *Journal of Clinical Child Psychology*, 1980, Fall, 213–216.

Bromwich, R. *Working with infants and parents*. Baltimore: University Park Press, 1981.

Christensen, A., Johnson, S., Phillips, S., & Glasgow, R. Cost effectiveness in behavioral family therapy. *Behavior Therapy*, 1980, **11**, 108–226.

Cummings, S., & Stock, D. Brief group therapy of mothers of retarded children outside of the speciality clinic setting. *American Journal of Mental Deficiency*, 1962, **66**, 739–748.

DeWitt, K. The effectiveness of family therapy. *Archives of General Psychiatry*, 1978, **35**, 549–561.

Doll, E. Trends and problems in the education of the mentally retarded: 1800–1940. *American Journal of Mental Deficiency*, 1967, **72**, 175–183.

Fabrega, A., Jr., & Haka, K. Parents of mentally handicapped children. *Archives of General Psychiatry*, 1967, **16**, 202–209.

Farber, B. Effects of a severely mentally retarded child on family integration. *Monographs of the Society for Research in Child Development*, 1959, **24**, 1–108.

Farber, B. Family organization and crisis: maintenance of integration in families with a severely mentally retarded child. *Monographs of the Society for Research in Child Development*, 1960, **25**, 1–93.

Fliederbaum, S. Effect of parent group participation in state schools. *American Journal of Mental Deficiency*, 1951, **56**, 180–184.

Grebler, A. Parental attitudes toward mentally retarded children. *American Journal of Mental Deficiency*, 1952, **56**, 475–483.

Gumz, E., & Gubruim, J. Comparative parental perceptions of mentally retarded children. *American Journal of Mental Deficiency*, 1972, **77**, 175–180.

Heifetz, L. Behavioral training for parents of retarded children: Alternative formats based on instructional manuals.

American Journal of Mental Deficiency, 1977, 82, 194–203.

Hormuth, R. Social work. In J. Wortis (Ed.), Mental retardation. Vol. II. New York: Grune & Stratton, 1970.

Hunt, J. (Ed.) Human intelligence. New Brunswick: Transaction Books, 1972.

Johnson, C., & Katz, R. Using parents as change agents for their children: A review. Journal of Child Psychology and Psychiatry, 1973, 14, 181–200.

Kelman, H. The effect of a brain-damaged child on his family. In H. Birch (Ed.), Brain damage in children. Baltimore: Williams & Wilkins, 1964.

Lipton, H., & Svarstad, B. Sources of variations in clinicians' communication to parents about mental retardation. American Journal of Mental Deficiency, 1977, 82, 155–161.

Lobitz, G., & Johnson, S. Normal versus deviant children: A multimethod comparison. Journal of Abnormal Child Psychology, 1975, 3, 353–374.

Mahoney, S. Observations concerning counselling with parents of mentally retarded children. American Journal of Mental Deficiency, 1958, 63, 81–86.

Mash, E., & Terdal, L. Modification of mother-child interactions: Playing with children. Mental Retardation, October 1973, 44–49.

Menolascino, F. Psychiatry's past, current and future role in mental retardation. In F. Menolascino (Ed.), Psychiatric approaches to mental retardation. New York: Basic Books, 1970.

Olshansky, S. Chronic sorrow: A response to having a mentally defective child. Social Casework, 1963, 43, 190–193.

Patterson, G., & Gullion, M. Living with children. Champaign: Research Press, 1968.

Potter, H. Mental retardation: The Cinderella of psychiatry. Psychiatric Quarterly, 1965, 39, 537–549.

Powell, M. Assessment and management of developmental changes and problems in children. St. Louis: Mosby, 1981.

President's Committee on Mental Retardation. Mental Retardation: Century of Decision. Washington, 1976.

Redner, R. Others' perceptions of mothers of handicapped children. American Journal of Mental Deficiency, 1980, 85, 176–183.

Sadler, O., Seyden, T., Howe, B., & Kaminsky, T. An evaluation of "groups for parents": A standardized format encompassing both behavior modification and humanistic methods. Journal of Community Psychology, 1976, 4, 157–163.

Schell, G. The young handicapped child: A family perspective. Topics in Early Childhood Special Education, 1981, 1, 21–27.

Schroeder, E. The birth of a defective child: A course for

grieving. In J. Hale & B. Weaver (Eds.), Nursing of families in crises. Philadelphia: Lippincott, 1974.

Solnit, A., & Stark, M. Mourning and the birth of a defective child. Psychoanalytic Studies of the Child, 1961, 16, 523–537.

Tarjan, G., & Keeran, C. An overview of mental retardation. Psychiatric Annuals, 1974, 4, 5–11.

Tarjan, G., Wright, S., Eyman, R., & Keeran, C. Natural history of mental retardation: Some aspects of epidemiology. American Journal of Mental Deficiency, 1973, 77, 360–379.

Tavormina, J. Relative effectiveness of behavioral and reflective group counseling with parents of mentally retarded children. Journal of Consulting and Clinical Psychology, 1975, 43, 22–31.

Tymchuk, A. A mobile communication device for use in training behavior modifiers. Behavior Therapy, 1973, 4, 481.

Tymchuk, A. Behavior modification with children. Springfield: Thomas, 1974.

Tymchuk, A. Training parent therapists. Mental Retardation, 1975, October, 19–22.

Tymchuk, A. Parent and family therapy. Jamaica, N.Y.: Spectrum, 1979.

Tymchuk, A., Dahlman, A., & Asher, K. Extending the benefits of a demonstration program for handicapped preschool children to community based programs. Exceptional Children, 1981, 48, 70–72.

Waidell, W. Case work with parents of mentally deficient children. American Journal of Mental Deficiency, 1951, 56, 180–187.

Waisbren, S. Parents' reactions after the birth of a developmentally disabled child. American Journal of Mental Deficiency, 1980, 84, 345–351.

Waterman, J. Psychogenic factors in parental acceptance of feebleminded children. Diseases of the Nervous System, 1948, 9, 184–187.

Weinrott, M., Bauske, B., & Patterson, G. Systematic replication of a social learning approach to parent training. In P. Sjoden & S. Bates (Eds.), Trends in behavior therapy. New York: Academic Press, 1979.

Williams, C. The elimination of tantrum behavior by extinction procedures. Journal of Abnormal Psychology, 1959, 58, 269.

Winton, P., & Turnbull, A. Parent involvement as viewed by parents of preschool handicapped children. Topics in Early Childhood Special Education, 1981, 1, 11–19.

Wolfensberger, W. Counselling the parents of the retarded. In A. Baumeister (Ed.), Mental Retardation. Chicago: Aldine, 1967.

Zuk, G. The religious factor and the role of guilt in the parental acceptance of the retarded child. American Journal of Mental Deficiency, 1959, 64, 139–147.

25 CONSULTATION AND TECHNICAL ASSISTANCE

James F. Budde and
Jean Ann Summers

The mental retardation/developmental disabilities field is a rapidly changing and interdisciplinary specialty. Philosophical, legal, technological and economic changes reverberate across the disciplinary and service spectrum and demand responses from providers and administrators at all levels. One tool that can be used to ease the process of change is consultation or technical assistance.

Consultation and technical assistance, in some form, have been used throughout history to solve one person's problems with another person's expertise. While the basic purpose—to solve problems—has not changed over time, consultation or technical assistance today involves a bewildering array of sophisticated technologies and procedures. Without a clear understanding of the process involved, consultation can create more problems than it solves, both for the giver and the receiver of the service. This chapter is designed to provide that understanding. We hope to do so by tracing the steps involved in consultation from beginning to end—from entry and needs assessment through intervention and evaluation—and in the process to highlight some of the major elements of a successful consulting relationship.

First, however, it is important to understand precisely what we mean by consultation or technical assistance. As there is a great deal of confusion surrounding the meaning of these two terms, this is not an easy task. In fact, many writers proceed without defining the terms at all, leaving their readers to infer meanings as best they can.

Technical assistance is a term originating in military jargon. It relates to the loan (or gift or sale) of skilled people and accompanying high-technology equipment from a developed country to a less developed one, with the expressed aim of improving the recipient's capabilities in one area or another (Domergue, 1968). As this term spread from international politics to the domestic scene, it has come to be applied to many kinds of helping relationships, but is still generally confined to the public sector, and still generally connotes the transference of some new technology, be it "hard" or "soft." Thus, Tracy (1977) defines technical assistance as "the marketing of planned change" (p. 5). Though never an explicit part of the definition, the term "technical assistance" is usually applied when a federal or state agency contracts with an organization of professionals competent in some area, to provide assistance to a group of service agencies (usually funded by the same sponsoring agency).

Consultation, on the other hand, has been defined as "a helping process whereby an expert or specialist (consultant) attempts to assist a consultee (person, group, system) with some problem usually related to the consultee's work situation" (Marino, 1969, p. 4). Bell and Nadler (1979) define consultation as "the provision of information or help by a professional helper (consultant) to a help-needing person or system (client) in the context of a voluntary, temporary relationship which is mutually advantageous" (p. 2). Under these definitions, anyone can be a consultant who undertakes the task of helping anyone else. In the developmental disabilities field, a consultant might be a psychologist called in by a group home director to evaluate a client with a behavior disorder and prescribe a treatment plan. Or a consultant might be a large technical assistance organization employed by a state developmental disabilities council to design an evaluation system. Budde (1979) defines three levels of clients (or consumers) of technical assistance: primary (developmentally disabled people themselves), secondary (parents, service providers, advocates), and tertiary (state councils, state and federal agencies, and professional organizations). Consultation or technical assistance can be provided at any of these three levels, but the kinds of help required by each group will be different.

The actual process of technical assistance is really not different from consultation, except for the fact that in technical assistance there is usually a third party—the funding agency—involved in the relationship. Although the presence of a third party is not insignificant and raises special issues which will be discussed later, we will consider these two terms synonymous in all other respects. Therefore, because technical assistance is a more recent term and still has the somewhat disreputable aura of jargon, we shall most often use the term consultation for our discussion.

Through all the definitions of both consultation and technical assistance, there are three common themes that emerge to distinguish these activities from any other. First, there is a problem situation, a need for change perceived by somebody. This need for change may be seen as urgent, as for example, in the case of a community agency facing imminent loss of federal funds and needing to develop new funding strategies; or it may be evolutionary, as in the case of an agency wishing to develop staff awareness of Section 504 compliance requirements. Second, the help provided is systematic in nature. Consultants and technical assistants follow a variety of procedures and espouse a range of philosophical orientations. The conceptual framework may be defined in varying levels of detail, and may change as the consultant adapts to the client's problem situation. But whether general or detailed, flexible or rigid, the approach is systematic. It is the systematic approach to problem solving that sets the professional consultant apart from

gratuitous advisors. Third, consultation services are temporary and come from outside the situation where the perceived need for change resides. This does not mean that a consultant may not be a permanent employee of the organization (though it often does). For example, a school district's reading specialist may give consultation services to a classroom teacher. But the distinguishing characteristic remains: the consultant comes from outside the problem situation, provides help, and then leaves.

The emphasis on change as the primary objective of consultation leads many authorities to characterize the consultant as a "change agent" (e.g., Neufeld, 1977). This situation in turn leads to such discussions as the client's "resistance to change" and strategies for overcoming that resistance (e.g., Harrison, 1970). But if change is the primary objective, the temporary nature of consultation places limits on the ways in which that change may be achieved. Thompson (1981) points out that perception of a consultant as a change agent is in fact one of the biggest obstructions to effective consultation. The real change agents in a problem situation are the actors in that situation who will remain after the consultant leaves and who will— if the consultation is successful—be acting differently. Thus, a much more useful characterization of the consultant is that he or she serves as a catalyst for change. Such a characterization underscores the importance of the consultant's ability to use personal relationships to achieve the desired results. Furr (1979) draws a rather nice analogy by comparing the consultant to a judo expert, "in that the consultant should employ the energy and momentum of the client" (p. 125) to achieve the desired change.

At any rate, if change is the desired result, but the consultant is not the change agent, then the proper focus of any step-by-step guide to successful consulting should not be on the consultant alone, but on the client-consultant relationship. This notion leads us to define successful consultation as the achievement of desired change through mutual participation of a client (person, group, or system) and a consultant in a systematic process of analysis and intervention.

Regardless of the consultant's theoretical orientation and the actual substance of the problem being addressed, the process of consultation is inevitably dictated by a combination of its systematic and temporary nature. Numerous models of the consultation or technical assistance process are in existence, but in general most authorities agree there are four basic steps:

1. The entry, or bonding process—in which the client discovers a need for change and a need for help in effecting that change; selects an appropriate con-

sultant; and in which client and consultant establish the parameters of their relationship.

2. The needs assessment, or diagnosis—in which client and consultant explore the problem and define it more systematically.

3. The intervention, or service delivery—in which the consultant and client develop a solution to the problem and implement it.

4. Evaluation, or feedback—in which the client judges the effectiveness of the consultant's work and assesses the value of the intervention in meeting perceived needs.

A successful consultation requires that both client and consultant understand their roles and responsibilities at each step. With this as our conceptual framework, then, we will next analyze the interactive roles at each of the four major stages in the consulting process, and then explore the ethical issues surrounding consultation. We will conclude with a few speculations about the future for consultation and technical assistance.

The Bonding Process

The fact that a consultant is a temporary participant in a problem situation creates both advantages and drawbacks to his or her involvement. On the positive side, the consultant brings the fresh perspective of an outsider who is not (presumably) affected by the proverbial forest-and-trees syndrome. Furthermore, the problem may be similar to one (or many) the consultant has experienced and resolved in the past. And finally, the consultant is hired for the express purpose of dealing with the problem, and is thus free to concentrate on it without being bogged down in day-to-day job duties.

All these advantages, however, can be offset by the problems that may easily attach to the introduction of a new face into the milieu. If a consultant is not made totally familiar with the problem in relation to the unique needs of the agency, the recommended solution might be based too much on the consultant's prior experiences and therefore be inapplicable to the problem at hand. Or an imperfect understanding of the resources and energies at the disposal of the agency might lead to unrealistic recommendations (Ford, 1974). And there is always the danger that a consultant or technical assistant called in by management or a sponsoring agency will be sabotaged by a suspicious and resentful staff who see the consultant as a useless intruder or—worse—a spy for the authorities.

If the pitfalls are to be avoided and the advantages maximized, very careful attention must be paid to the way a consultant is introduced to the problem

situation. In fact, it is fair to say that this first stage is the most crucial one in assuring a successful consulting relationship. While descriptions of this stage are labeled "entry" or "selection" by other writers, we prefer to think of it as a bonding process. It is during this stage that consultant and client come together, fashion a relationship, and are bound into a team working toward a common purpose. In general, the bonding process involves three essential steps: (1) a decision to seek outside help, (2) selection of a consultant, and (3) negotiation of the client-consultant roles.

The Decision to Seek Help

A perceived need for change does not automatically imply the necessity of a consultant. But this rather obvious fact does raise a question: When should an agency apply its own resources to a problem, and when should it call in help from outside?

Frankenhuis (1977) notes three basic reasons for seeking the help of a consultant: for savings, for an independent view, and for expertise. Fuchs (1975) lists several reasons for employing a management consultant. Those applicable to social service agencies include: involvement of a consultant in developing long-term strategies, lack of in-house capability to solve an unplanned technical problem requiring specialized skill, and unforeseen conditions with which the staff cannot cope.

Developmental disabilities agencies can effect a great savings through the use of consulting professionals to deal with some of their client's problems. For example, a sheltered workshop might hire a speech therapist on a regular basis to provide services to particular clients. Such an arrangement is in reality a quasi-permanent employment contract, but it retains the flavor of a consultancy by its intermittent nature and by the fact that the permanent staff is often charged with the responsibility of carrying out the treatment regimen prescribed by the "outsider." Whether the agency hires its own specialized staff or develops consulting arrangements depends on the size of the agency and expertise or availability of its staff, and the nature and problems of the developmentally disabled people served.

Beyond this rather specialized use, the decision of whether or not to call in a consultant is less easily resolved. For example, should a residential program director develop a plan for expanding to transition apartments by hiring a consultant or by appointing a task force composed of existing staff? Should an instructional consultant be asked to design and deliver a training program to teach effective IPP (Individualized Program Planning) development techniques to the entire staff—or should one staff member be sent away for the training and asked to bring it back to the others? Again, the question resolves to a consideration of available alternatives and their relative costs.

More important than how the decision is made to use a consultant, is the question of who makes the decision. A need for change may be perceived by the agency's management or board of directors, or even by the government funding agency. But in order to achieve that change, the need for it must be recognized by the people who will actually be doing the changing. The consultant who is "imposed" on a problem situation by decision makers outside that environment can expect stiff resistance and ultimate failure. Tracy (1977) labels this the "problem of forced entry" (p. 9). It is, therefore, not a waste but a saving of time for agency directors to work through the problem with line staff and arrive at a democratic consensus that a consultant would be helpful. Failure to do so has been cited as one of the chief reasons for failure of the consulting process (Ford, 1974; Davey, 1971).

This maxim is especially true in the case of technical assistance projects funded by a third party, sponsoring agency. Neufeld (1977) identifies four alternative styles of funding for technical assistance (TA) projects, including:

1. government resources given directly to the client, enabling the client to request TA and pay for it with government funds;
2. government resources provided directly to a TA system, with the client able to obtain free or partially-free TA;
3. a governmentally established TA system for its clients; and
4. technical assistance sought in the TA marketplace by the client with its own private funds (pp. 23–24).

In Neufeld's opinion, the second and third of these alternatives are the least preferable, because they carry the danger that the technical assistance offered can become directive rather than responsive. We would add that it is more than that: without a conviction that the technical assistance offered is relevant and useful within the client's immediate environment, the technical assistance offered is not likely to be implemented at all.

Selection of a Consultant

Once the decision is made to seek help from a consultant, the next issue to be faced is who to hire. Consultants come in all sizes and shapes. They include specialists and generalists, large organizations and freelance, moonlighting academicians. Large organizations usually have a broad ranging staff of consulting talent, and technical assistance programs frequently expand this base still further by serving as brokers—bringing the appropriate consultant in touch with the appropriate client. Some management support organizations even broker volunteers (e.g., retired business executives or professionals) to nonprofit service agencies (Raebel, 1981).

A specialist is a consultant with a very specific skill or knowledge, such as speech therapy, while a generalist has access to a broad range of information and analysis. In deciding the type of consultant needed, the scope and specificity of the problem should be considered; the broader the scope, the greater the range of skills required by the consultant (or consultant team). Jackson (1980) suggests a rule of thumb for deciding the specialist-generalist question: if the agency knows what the problem is, a specialist is appropriate. For example, a need to train staff in Section 504 regulations is a rather straightforward problem requiring a search for a specialist in that area. If, on the other hand, there is only a conviction that "something is wrong" with the agency's operation, e.g., a bottleneck at the work activity center with very few clients moving on into the sheltered workshop program and a waiting list piling up, then a generalist may be needed to analyze the situation. In short, the agency director should be able to define the problem in terms that point him or her in the general direction of the right consultant.

From the consultant's point of view, marketing one's wares is a major difficulty. Keeps and Jackson (1980) point out that independent consultants who are just entering the field should have from three months to a year's financial reserve in the bank, and should be prepared to spend as much as a third of their time in marketing activities. Often, marketing involves not only "selling" oneself, but also convincing prospective clients that they need and can use consultation services (Tracy, 1977).

From the client's perspective, finding consultants is usually no problem—most of them have already deluged the agency with brochures, folders, and letters of introduction. Failing these, it is possible to get referrals from other nearby agencies, programs, or professional associations. Raebel (1981) lists four directories of management support and technical assistance organizations geared to serve nonprofit social service agencies; these are reproduced in Table 25.1. From these listings, it is possible to select several likely candidates and to request copies of brochures and annual reports.

Selection, however, should not be based on the consultant's advertising material. It is wise to contact

Table 25.1. Directories of Management Support and Technical Assistance

Can Do II—A Technical Assistance Guide
Donors Forum of Chicago
208 S. La Salle St.
Chicago, IL 60604
Individual copies are $5; $6 prepaid by mail. There is a 10% discount on orders of 5 or more copies

The Management Support Organization: Services for Twin Cities Nonprofits
Center for Youth Development and Research
48 McNeal Hall
1985 Buford Ave.
University of Minnesota
St. Paul, MN 55108
Copies are $3 each

On Technical Assistance Programs: A Directory of Resources for New York City Nonprofit Organizations
Public Interest Public Relations
50 W. 57th St., Suite 1200
New York, NY 10029
Copies are $4.95 each

National Directory of Nonprofit Management Support Organizations
The Support Center
1709 New Hampshire Ave. NW
Washington, D.C. 20009
Copies are $8. It should be noted that this directory is intended for other MSOs, but consumers may find it useful.

Source: Raebel, 1981, page 24.

several consultants of consulting organizations, and talk with them personally. Interested consultants should be interviewed as carefully as prospective employees because, after all, that is what they are. Remember that the consultant will be an "outsider" charged with the task of entering an established group and quickly gaining enough acceptance that he or she will be entrusted with an honest view of all the good and bad in the problem situation. As every consultant knows, people in established groups have a natural tendency to "cover up" problems when faced with an outsider. Thus, the consultant must not only be able to have a mastery of his or her field, but must also demonstrate interpersonal skills that inspire trust and open doors.

When the field is narrowed to one or two, the agency should request a written proposal. Raine (1980) provides a checklist for evaluating the proposal, which we have paraphrased and applied to developmental disabilities programs:

1. How well does the consultant understand the developmental disabilities field in general and your agency's problems in particular? Is the consultant's philosophical approach consonant with yours?
2. Are the consultant's objectives and sub-objectives measurable? Do the objectives fit with your perspectives?
3. Is the work plan specified in sequential order? Is it logical?
4. Is there an estimated timeline?

5. Who will actually be doing the job? What are their qualifications?
6. What are the costs? How are they estimated?
7. What is the specific final product (i.e., will the consultant develop recommendations or will he or she help implement them as well)?
8. Does the consultant have the time and resources to do what he or she proposes to do?

Finally, the prospective consultant should provide references, and these should be checked thoroughly.

The Consulting Agreement

If the developmental disabilities program has requested a proposal as outlined above, the actual contract should be relatively simple. At this point, however, we should reemphasize the reciprocal nature of the consulting process. That is, a contract that merely repeats the consultant's proposal and outlines his or her responsibilities, is only half a contract. The agency's responsibilities should likewise be spelled out. Will the consultant have access to the agency's clerical staff? To confidential client files? Other specifics related to the needs assessment, the actual service delivery, and evaluation, should also be specified in the contract. These will be highlighted at appropriate points in the discussion below.

It should also be remembered the terms of the contract can and often do change as the problem situation is clarified and the client and consultant come to have a better understanding of the needs at hand and the interventions required. Thus, most contracts contain an "escape clause," or provision for renegotiation, as the circumstances dictate. The important point is to maintain flexibility and at the same time keep both parties informed and in agreement about what is going on.

Some technical assistance programs are funded by the same governmental agency that also funds the service program to which the technical assistance is to be delivered. In such cases a contract with the actual client is even more imperative. Since the technical assistance recipient usually has little or no choice in the matter of who will provide the assistance, it is crucial that a contract be developed specifying exactly what and how assistance will be rendered. In these cases of "forced entry" (Tracy, 1977), such deference to the unique needs of and respect for the autonomy of the client is vital to the bonding process. Furthermore, the contract should spell out the relationship of both parties to the sponsoring agency. Finally, there should be some assurance of confidentiality, i.e., the technical assistance provider should explicitly agree not to disclose any information about the TA recipient to the sponsoring agency. There should be no doubt among any of the three parties involved that the technical assistant is performing no evaluative function whatsoever. Although this may pose an ethical problem to the TA provider, it is vital to gain and maintain an atmosphere of mutual trust if technical assistance is to be effective.

At this point, we should discuss an additional facet of the technical assistance relationship: the relationship between the technical assistant and the sponsoring agency. Usually a technical assistance project is established through a competitive grant or contract award. The project application in such cases is a peculiar one, as grants go, because it must lack specificity, owing to the fact that the applicant is offering to provide assistance to a service delivery system and not directly to the granting agency. The technical assistant can only offer to provide services, but cannot yet state exactly what those services will be. In addition, the special nature of the client-consultant relationship leaves little room for the third party sponsoring agency. How, then, can the technical assistant be held accountable to the funding agency?

The best way to establish accountability is to demonstrate competence in the consulting process, and to agree with the funding agency that formal evaluation of the consulting process—but not of the program being served—will be made available to the sponsor (we will discuss evaluation methods at length, in a later section). Another assurance of accountability is

found in the frequent agreement between technical assistant and sponsor that training materials (often manuals or films or both) will be developed either in conjunction with the technical assistance or before the technical assistance phase of the contract begins. Finally, most technical assistance projects assure their responsiveness both to the field and to the sponsor by establishing an advisory board consisting of both sponsor and potential client representatives, to guide the technical assistant in the development and delivery of its services.

Needs Assessment

Needs assessment, or diagnosis, is an indispensable part of the consulting process. To some degree this stage overlaps with the bonding process. Many will suppose that the client's definition of the problem as a first step in the selection of a consultant, coupled with the consultant's preliminary data gathering as he or she prepares the proposal, is all the needs assessment required. Indeed, in some cases this may be true; for example, if an already-prepared training program is all that is required the consultant can move directly to delivery. But in more complicated cases, a preliminary definition of the problem is not enough, and a true understanding of the client's needs must be accomplished through more intensive interviews or collection of some hard data.

The temporary nature of the consulting process makes needs assessment one of the consultant's strong points. Many a consultant has been called in with the idea that a formal needs assessment, or "feasibility study" was to be the entire product of his or her labors. For example, a consultant may be hired to survey the need for transportation services for handicapped people in a community. But in this discussion we are speaking more of the needs of the problem situation itself; that is, the objective of the needs assessment is to determine what kind of intervention service the consultant should provide. In this sense perhaps the more traditional term, diagnosis, is more appropriate.

If the ultimate goal of consulting is to empower the client to effect some change, then the diagnosis should be conducted in such a way as to involve the client in the change process from the very beginning. Furr (1979) discusses the purposes of diagnosis and identifies some complex reasons for paying careful attention to this stage.

> We can identify six interrelated aspects of the purpose of diagnosis. The first is to precipitate change itself. Secondly, the diagnosis should provide an assessment of the variables relevant to the change goal. Thirdly, the diagnosis can

create an expanded awareness and growth in the client. Fourth, and very specific to the relationship, it should create in the client a personal value out of the relationship separate from his objective organizational purpose. The fifth aspect is to energize momentum toward the change. The sixth is to focus on the client's attention to the variables necessary to create the change and achieve the goal [p. 120].

A careful reading of Furr's remarks should reveal that empowering the people in the problem situation means more than simply helping them see how to change. It means developing the client's ability and motivation, as well as changing the organizational conditions (Furr, 1979). Thus, diagnosis is a twofold process of (1) providing the consultant with information on behaviors, motivations, and environmental conditions that need to change; and (2) allowing the process of exploring the problem to serve as a key motivating tool for the clients to begin moving in the direction of change. If the consultant moves too fast or gets too far ahead of the client, his or her task of convincing the client that change X is needed will be doubly hard. It is much easier if the client moves hand in hand with the consultant as the problem situation is explored. Discovery is an active process much more likely to leave an impression on the participant than the passive act of listening to or reading a report.

The importance of discovery must be emphasized. It is a part of the needs assessment process, but it is also much, much more: it is an initial step in the process of change and as such can be characterized as an essential intervention tool as well. The good consultant uses discovery throughout the consulting process to stimulate change and move toward resolution of the problem situation.

When the consultant enters a problem situation he or she does so with a preliminary understanding of the purpose of the consultation. The diagnostic phase is in reality a kind of context evaluation (Dunst, 1979) in which the problem is defined and expanded (or narrowed), and obstacles to the problem's solution are identified. Obstacles might include a number of factors both tangible and intangible (which we might term political). For example, suppose a client is assigned to teach ward attendants in an institution to control self-injurious behavior. In the diagnostic phase, the consultant must analyze current procedures with self-injurious clients, assess the staff's level of training and familiarity with behavioral therapy, and survey the reinforcing and punishing contingencies naturally available in the environment, preliminary to developing an intervention program. But the consultant must also gain an understanding of less tangible aspects of the environment. For instance, suppose the procedure at this institution is to transfer self-injurious clients to psychiatric wards if the behavior is not controlled within a given time period. Such a rule might serve as a disincentive to staff's bringing the behavior under control, since failure to control eventually results in a loss of the troublesome client altogether. This information, then, is grist for the diagnostic mill; it should be taken into account as the consultant designs the training program (e.g., staff might be sensitized to overcrowding on the psychiatric ward, etc.), and perhaps also enlarges the consultant's role, as he/she might go beyond staff training and recommend procedural changes to the administration.

Many authorities on consulting discuss "resistance management" as a part of the diagnostic process. Certainly, in cases of forced entry resistance to and even resentment of the consultant is a difficult problem. If great care is taken during the bonding phase to establish trust, this problem should be minimized. Further, the consultant should make certain that the goals of the consultation are in line with the expectations and perceptions of the clients in the problem situation. In short, the best resistance management strategy is for the consultant to play his or her role in such a way that there is little to resist (Bell & Nadler, 1979). Even so, however, there may be cases of clients who find that the results of needs assessment are not what they expected, or whose fear of the unknown leads them to contemplate change in a kind of approach-avoidance posture. It is here that the consultant's interpersonal skills come into play, that he turns counselor and helps the client through the process of discovering and gaining the motivation for change. Once again, a thorough exploration of the problem situation can be an important means of achieving that end.

Intervention

The actual intervention or modification is of course the *raison d'être* of the whole consulting process. It is the motivating force for the bonding phase, the purpose of the needs assessment, and the target of the subsequent evaluation. Yet in many ways this phase is the most difficult to describe. Intervention may range from a simple training workshop lasting a half day, to a complete restructuring of an organization requiring many months. In all cases, however, it should be remembered that the target of intervention is change; and change ultimately means some altered behavior of the agency staff or clients, even though the actual intervention might only manipulate the environment. Thus, once more, we must repeat that for change to occur the consultant must somehow serve as a catalyst who motivates the principal actors to change.

Methods to achieve the motivation for change are nearly as numerous as there are consultants. Terms like simulation gaming, systems analysis, human resources development, organizational development, and management by objectives present a bewildering array of processes and options to a client looking for a consultant. It is important to realize that the method(s) employed by the consultant nearly always shape his or her perspective of the problem situation from beginning to end. Thus, a consultant steeped in management by objectives might see a problem as a need for clarification of roles through establishing measurable objectives. But a human resources development specialist may see the same problem as a dysfunction in interactions among staff and set about designing an intervention that includes team building, intergroup activities, confrontation sessions, and so on. Neither consultant would be incorrect according to his or her own views of the world in general and the problem situation in particular. It is also conceivable that both approaches could solve the problem.

But trouble arises when the approach used does not reflect the prevailing view of the people in the problem situation. For example, an agency staff trained to use behavioral techniques with developmentally disabled clients may not see the value of a transactional analysis approach applied to themselves. In our discussion of the selection process we listed consonance with agency philosophy as an important criterion for selection. As Raebel (1981) pointed out, such consonance is of paramount importance if the intervention is to work. This approach is especially vital in the mental retardation/developmental disabilities field, where controversies abound concerning both philosophy and method. While a certain amount of divergence is healthy and provides fresh input to the problem situation, too much divergence will impair the consultant's ability to enter the group successfully.

One of the factors affecting the group's ability to accept an intervention is the level at which the intervention occurs. Harrison (1978) arranges the many possible intervention methods on a continuum of five levels or depths of intervention. The first, or surface level, is exemplified by operations analysis and is generally concerned with task distribution, lines of authority, etc.—all organizational relationships that may be altered without directly requiring change in any individual's behavior.

The second level essentially involves operations analysis of individuals, and includes performance evaluations, management by objectives, etc. The distinguishing feature at this level is that the consultant is concerned with changing individual behavior, but accomplishes change mainly by focusing on outcome or ends and by manipulating his incentives.

It follows that Harrison's third intervention level shifts the focus from ends to means. Harrison terms these interventions "instrumental process analyses," in which the consultant analyzes a person's style and process of work, and the impact of that style on others. The focus is on changes in work behavior and working relationships. This is to be distinguished from the fourth level, in which interventions are directed at interpersonal relationships and include such methods as T-groups, sensitivity training, etc., designed to make people more comfortable with each other. The fifth and deepest level of intervention is the intrapersonal focus, which basically employs a counseling methodology to explore an individual's feelings, attitudes and conflicts.

Harrison stresses that this taxonomy suggests

> Two criteria for choosing the appropriate depth of intervention: first, *to intervene at a level no deeper than that required to produce enduring solutions to the problem at hand* and second, *to intervene at a level no deeper than that at which the energy and resources of the client can be committed to problem solving and to change* [1978, p. 180, emphasis in original].

Harrison's model places the burden for selection of the intervention on the consultant. It assumes the consultant is a highly versatile individual with a multiple array of methodological approaches at his or her command. We argue, however, that such a multifaceted consultant is rare. It is, therefore, incumbent on both the consultant and the client to understand these dynamics and to make the proposed level of intervention explicit during the negotiation of the consulting agreement.

Of course, not all consultations require such a sophisticated analysis. Certainly, the design of a fund raising campaign for an agency is a straightforward activity requiring no in-depth behavior changes on the part of staff. Likewise, the development of a statewide data management system requires behavioral change of direct care staff only insofar as they must be convinced of the importance of filling out data sheets (accurately!). But if problems emerge in the implementation of these activities, the consultant might be recalled, and might then, after redefining the problem, intervene at a deeper level. Thus, we can conclude that the selection of a successful intervention approach involves several discrete considerations:

1. the theoretical and methodological philosophy of the people in the problem situation;
2. the nature of the problem or change desired; and
3. the depth of intervention both required by the problem and tolerated by the people in the problem situation.

These factors should be considered at three main points during the consultation process: (1) they should be part of the formula for selection of the consultant, (2) they should be part of the contract negotiation between consultant and client, and (3) they should be consciously assessed throughout the diagnostic phase. In short, if the method in intervention is established before the process moves into that phase, then intervention itself is more likely to run smoothly and be successful.

Evaluation

Evaluation, like needs assessment, is sometimes the expected product of a consultation. Consultants may be hired specifically to provide a "friendly" evaluation to a service program as it gears up for JCAH or CARF accreditation or sponsoring agency site visit. Or the consultant may be hired by the sponsoring agency to conduct the evaluation itself (Guba & Lincoln, 1981). It should be clear by now, however, that in this discussion we are interested in evaluating the consultation process *per se*. The methods of evaluating the consultation process are really very similar to the methods of program analysis. Thus, evaluation of the consulting process becomes a matter of applying the vast evaluation literature to this particular activity. This is of course no small feat; but at least, viewed from this light, it is possible.

Some informal evaluation of the consulting process will take place naturally. An informal evaluation is usually a subjective impression of the level of satisfaction, expressed in terms of whether the consultation was "good" or "bad." Its principal value is as an indicator to the consultant or administrator of the general usefulness of the consultation while it is still in midprocess. Informal reactions and attitudes can provide cues about the type or level of intervention required, the need to change direction or slow down, etc. Beyond serving as a diagnostic barometer, however, an informal evaluation can only provide a general gestalt of the success or failure of the consultation. It is our intention, therefore, to provide clients, consultants and third parties with a more objective set of tools designed not only to determine whether the consultation was successful (and in what ways) but also to serve as a basis for future improvement.

Two major factors come into play in the design of an evaluation plan for the consulting process. First, the purpose or purposes of the evaluation must be explicitly identified; and second, the methods by which these purposes will be achieved must be specified. We will deal with each of these considerations in turn.

Purposes of Evaluation

One classic taxonomy of evaluation purposes was outlined by Stufflebeam in 1971 (Dunst, 1979; Guba & Lincoln, 1981). The model postulates four major types of evaluation: context, input, process, and product. Context evaluation is in reality a type of needs assessment, in which the needs in a problem situation are identified and the obstacles to meeting those needs are pinpointed. Input evaluation is the identification, comparison, and evaluation of alternative approaches to meeting those needs; presumably this process results in the selection of one of those alternatives. Process evaluation involves monitoring the implementation of the problem solution. This type of evaluation is not concerned with results but with performance, and assesses the extent to which planned activities are achieved. Finally, product evaluation is concerned with the ultimate results of the total program. It reaches back to the beginning—the needs assessment—and determines the extent to which those needs have been met.

A first impression of this taxonomy is that context and input evaluation might not properly be considered evaluative processes. Indeed, we have included many of these issues in our discussion of the needs assessment and intervention phases of the consultation process. But if evaluation is to be effective it must be grounded in solid data; and to achieve this grounding it must be necessary not only to conduct a needs assessment and an inventory of alternative solutions, but also to document that such a process was carried out. In this sense, context and input evaluation provide the base line for the process and product evaluations.

Another system to classify evaluation purposes is to distinguish between formative and summative evaluation (Tracy, 1977). The purpose of formative evaluation is refinement and improvement, while the goal of summative evaluation is to determine impact or outcomes (Guba & Lincoln, 1981). This implies that formative evaluation occurs throughout the consultation process and in fact provides some form of continuous feedback to allow constant modification of the activities. On the other hand, summative evaluation is a discrete assessment taken at the end of the process (or at the end of each phase) to determine the outcome of the process.

In addition to quality of the product itself, most evaluators include as part of summative evaluation an assessment of any unanticipated effects (Gallagher, 1981). That is, in addition to an assessment of achievement or nonachievement of the stated goals of the consultation, one should look for and take into account any unintended consequences of the process. These might be either good or bad; for example, in the process of designing a new fund-raising campaign, intensive interaction with the consultant might foster greater staff cohesion and "team feeling." Some scholars, in fact, have asserted that the entire summative process be "goal free," i.e., conducted without reference to any stated goals in order to avoid biasing the conclusion of the evaluation (see Guba & Lincoln, 1981, for a review). But in the case of an evaluation of the consulting process, such a position does not seem practicable, since the evaluators are usually also participants in the original design of the goals of the consultation.

These classifications are not mutually exclusive. We might roughly equate formative evaluation with Stufflebeam's context, input, and process evaluative categories; likewise, summative and product evaluation are analogous. The point is that each of these categories reflects a different goal to be achieved through the process of evaluation. Needless to say, the purposes of the evaluation should be an explicit part of the consulting contract at the outset of the relationship.

Methods of Evaluation

Once the purposes of evaluation are known, one can move on to the methods by which those purposes are to be achieved. This involves development of some way to measure effects and processes. Within the issue of measurement lie two basic questions: (1) what is to be measured? and (2) how is it to be measured? Having answered the question of what is to be measured, however, the question of how is a little more complex. There are three basic measurable phenomena associated with the consulting process: (1) cost-benefit comparisons, (2) behavioral change, and (3) reaction criteria (Swartz & Lippitt, 1979).

(1) Cost-benefit comparisons involve the translation of benefits received from the consultation into some unit (usually dollars), and comparison with costs. Costs include not only the consultant's fee, but also the cost of staff time spent in workshops and meetings with the consultant, secretarial services, materials, printing or copying expenses, and so on. Dollar benefits are relatively easy to measure in the private sector; they include increases in profits which can be attributed to the consultation. In nonprofit social services, how-

ever, finding a dollar-based index for comparison to costs is more difficult, but still not impossible. One might include, for example, reductions in program costs or increased earning power of mentally retarded clients as a result of more effective rehabilitation methods attributable to the consultation.

The method for cost-benefit analysis involves collection of data both before and after the consultation, on specified cost measures. Thus, the use of cost-benefit analysis requires that the consultant and client agree at the outset to compute from raw data available in agency records a base-line cost-benefit ratio. If possible, the analysis should be confined to the unit or section with the problem situation to which the consultant is to be assigned. The postmeasure then would simply involve recollection of the same data elements. Such an evaluation should occur after allowing sufficient time for anticipated effects to show up, e.g., six months to a year.

(2) Behavioral change data are more often used than cost-benefit ratios in evaluating consultation with developmental disabilities programs. Behavioral measures involve documentation of observable behaviors exhibited by developmentally disabled people, by staff, or by both. The term "observable" is the distinguishing term here. Behaviors must be overt and definable to the extent that independent observers can agree whether the behavior did or did not occur.

Behavioral measure can range from simple to complex. Measures are usually in quantitative terms, for example, the number of widgets produced on the sheltered workshop floor in a specified time period. Or the evaluator might measure the number of negative versus positive interactions between staff and residents in a group home. Once again, however, there is a need for pre- and postintervention measures.

(3) Reaction criteria are more subjective reports of feelings, attitudes, and points of view as these change over time. For example, the evaluation might attempt to assess agency staff's feelings about the consulting relationship, utilizing participant feedback on a training event. A more complex evaluation might probe attitudes at various points of the consulting process (Swartz & Lippitt, 1979). Measurement of reactions might be quantitative, e.g., use of a Likert-type scale to assess levels of degrees of satisfaction with the consultation. Or it might be more qualitative in nature; e.g., it might use open-ended questionnaires or interviews to get various participants' impressions of the consulting process.

Whichever of these three means of measurement is chosen, three important points should be taken into account. First, the measurement must be related to the original purpose of the evaluation. For example, specific measures might be devised to achieve a process evaluation, while others might be specified for the product assessment. Second, evaluation of the consultation must be distinguished from evaluation of the program in which the consultation is taking place. This is an especially important point in the case of technical assistance projects in which a third party sponsor is involved. In short, evaluation must carry no threat to the recipient of the consultation. Third, evaluation should be distinguished from research. Although measurement instruments and methods used in evaluation may be identical to those used in many social science research designs, the purpose of the evaluation is not to explore the dimensions of some human dynamic, but rather to prove to the satisfaction of client and consultant that the consultation was useful. Therefore, it is not necessary to establish rigorous attributions of cause through correlations between measurement and hypotheses. It is sufficient for client and consultant to agree beforehand that measurement X will be taken as satisfactory evidence of effect Y.

This last point returns us to the most important consideration in developing a plan to evaluate the consulting process: the details should be included in the initial consulting agreement. This does not mean that the evaluation plan cannot be changed in mid-consultation if events warrant it; but if a need for change does emerge, then that too should be negotiated in writing. The evaluation plan specified in the consulting agreement should contain a number of elements, including:

- the purpose(s) of the evaluation;
- what is to be evaluated
- how these elements are to be measured;
- when and how often the measurements will be taken;
- who (client or consultant) will collect the measurement data; and who will pay for it; and
- who will be allowed to see the results of the evaluation.

In the final analysis, specification of an evaluation plan insures more than a sound basis for evaluating the consulting process. Because it clarifies roles and defines outcome measures, it forces the client and consultant to come to terms with the basic purpose of the consulting relationship. If both parties can agree that a specified outcome measure will signify satisfactory achievement of the tasks at hand, we can be reasonably certain that there is no misunderstanding about the goals and approach to the consulting relationship. In short, a good evaluation plan helps everyone to row in the same direction.

Ethical Issues in Consultation

Ethical considerations arise in any professional relationship between two or more parties. Ethical constraints in many respects undergird the whole relationship, defining the boundaries and the "rules" of interaction. The consulting relationship is no different; consultants and clients alike need to know the ground rules for their conduct with respect to one another. The special nature of the consulting relationship—especially the temporary and insider-outsider characteristics—presents several specific ethical issues in which consultant and/or client may be faced with legitimate dilemmas requiring guidelines for behavior. These include (1) representation and promotion of the consultant to the client, (2) contracts and fees issues, (3) conflicts of interest, and (4) ownership of ideas and/or products.

(Mis)representation

The question of how to "drum up" business plagues both public and private sector consultants. Freelancers and firms like to employ a variety of techniques, including brochures, flyers, letters of introduction, and word of mouth. The business of getting grants or contracts from sponsoring agencies involves developing a plan of action, but also building throughout the proposal an "aura of competence" to do the job. The ethical question arises when the consultant crosses that fine line between "selling" credentials and "inflating" those credentials.

The line is crossed more often by silence than by blatant misrepresentation (Pfeiffer & Jones, 1977). By allowing the client to harbor an untrue impression of past activities or credentials, the consultant runs the risk of severe damage to his or her credibility if the truth emerges later. For example, suppose an agency director is giving a prospective consultant a tour of the agency and introduces her to staff as "Dr." Smith, when in actuality, she is a "Ms." This seems innocent enough; for Ms. Smith to correct her host then and there, one might argue, would cause more embarrassment than it is worth. But if she does not, and later during the consulting process the truth emerges that Ms. Smith has a master's degree but no doctorate, her credibility with the staff might be damaged. What else, they might ask, has been misrepresented? In a relationship that is temporary and yet involves changing behaviors—an intrinsically stress-producing situation—the establishment of trust is too crucial to risk even small indiscretions.

Misrepresentation need not be confined to the consultant. Clients, through design or otherwise, can fail to let the consultant know the real reason behind the assignment (e.g., to gather information supporting a "hatchet job" on one staff member). Or a client may fail to let the consultant know the full extent (or lack) of resources available to address the target problem. This could result in the consultant developing a solution beyond the client's capability to implement, with the result that the consultant is frustrated, and the client is left firmly convinced that consultants are useless (Ford, 1974).

Contracts and Fees

Ethical questions usually arise over negotiated contract terms and fees when unforeseen events arise during the consulting process. If the unanticipated circumstance requires more work on the part of the consultant, who pays for it? Schwartz (1980) describes the feelings of both consultant and client in this situation:

> Most consultants claim that their personal integrity prevents them from refusing to perform work that goes beyond their understanding of their obligations. And that's nice. But, the problem arises when having done so, they decide to bill the client for their integrity. The client feels that this is improper. Since it usually happens after the fact, the client is put in a peculiar position. Clients believe they should be party to the decision whether or not to go beyond the contractual understanding. I suspect they have that right. [p. 42]

This issue is especially important in an era of tight budgets in the public sector. The savings to be gained through the use of a consultant might be wiped out by the unpredictability of the final fee. Under no circumstances should the consultant assume there will be enough money in the budget to cover any unanticipated additional activities. Such an assumption might leave the consultant with an ugly surprise, an unpaid bill, and an embarrassed—and unhappy—client.

Conflicts of Interest

Conflicts of interest frequently develop for consultants in the public sector who, having worked for one firm, feel constrained to turn down jobs with industry competitors. This particular issue is fortunately not a problem in mental retardation services, but that does not mean that there are no conflict of interest problems to be addressed. The most difficult questions surround technical assistance projects sponsored by a third-party funding agency. To whom does the technical assistant ultimately respond: the client service program or the sponsoring agency? Should the technical assistant report "damaging" information about the client back to the sponsoring agency? The answer, from our point of view, is that the client-consultant relationship is primary and that consultants should hold the same "privileged information" status vis-à-vis the sponsoring agency that the court appointed lawyer holds with respect to confidences from his or her client. This does not mean that the technical assistant should not inform the client agency when it is out of compliance or engaging in some questionable activity. But there is a big difference between letting the agency know about potential problems and violating the confidential client-consultant relationship by reporting those problems to a third party.

Ownership of Ideas

Ownership of ideas is an issue to which our complex copyright laws are addressed. The law in most cases provides relatively clear guidelines for behavior, but the peculiar relationship between client and consultant throws the picture out of focus. Certainly, training materials and other products developed by a consulting organization *outside* of any specific consultantship are the property of that organization. But what about products developed in the course of a specific consulting job, using the client's money and the consultant's brainpower? Schwartz (1980) points out that, by law, the product is the client's property. But does this mean the consultant cannot use the product with another client? Can the client market the product without sharing the proceeds with the consultant? It would be impossible to prevent the consultant from at least capitalizing on the experience gained from the previous consultancy. One cannot, after all, legislate against human growth. This problem is not as difficult in the nonprofit human services field as it is in the private sector; the issue is uncomplicated by the need to sequester information away from competitors, and by the fact that ideas and products are seldom sold for profit. But what remains is the issue of *credit*. It is our position that products developed in a consultancy may be used, but with acknowledgement of and credit given to both the agency and the consultant who participated in the development of the product.

For that matter, all training products should be scrupulously documented, footnoted, and referenced. Too many training documents are shoddy pieces of scholarship, containing little or no reference to the background materials used to compile them. At a practical level, this reduces the usefulness of the document for those who might want to pursue the topic further. It also gives the impression—probably correctly—that the document was poorly researched and written "off the cuff." But on an ethical level, failure to acknowledge other research and/or writings of professionals whose ideas are synthesized in a training document is nothing short of plagiarism. In the public sector, payment for use of ideas may not be necessary, but acknowledgement always is.

Conclusion: Future Trends in Consultation

In summary, successful consultation or technical assistance is the achievement of some desired change through mutual participation of a client and a consultant through a systematic process of analysis and intervention. The central focus is on the development of a productive relationship in which the consultant serves as the catalyst and the client is the change agent. That relationship passes through four major phases:

1. bonding, in which the consultant enters the client's environment and becomes a part of it;
2. needs assessment or diagnosis, in which client and consultant together explore that environment and discover the underlying elements of a problem situation;
3. intervention, in which client and consultant select and implement a solution to the problem; and
4. evaluation, in which client and consultant measure the processes and products of the consultation to determine its effectiveness.

Within each major phase, there are positive action steps suggested for both client and consultant to help assure that the relationship will be successful. The one element these steps hold in common is that they are all designed to open the channels of communication between the parties. In fact, if we were asked to draw a single maxim from our analysis, it would be this: that the consultation process will be successful to the extent client and consultant are able to achieve total communication in an atmosphere of mutual trust and respect.

Given this maxim, then, what is the future for consultation in the developmental disabilities/mental retardation field? Since human services in general, and mental retardation/developmental disabilities programs in particular, are currently so dependent on public funds (most often, federal funds), this question inevitably leads us to speculate on the effects of the current economic and political climate in Washington.

At this writing it is universal knowledge that the aim of the current administration is to achieve economic recovery through drastic reductions in federal spending. The effects of that policy have already been felt in the technical assistance community. By fiscal year 1981, technical assistance projects funded by federal Regional Office discretionary funds were already a thing of the past. As the supply of federal dollars begins to dwindle (at least, those reserved for human services), one could expect technical assistance programs to be sacrificed in order to keep vital direct services going as long as possible.

This is as it should be. We do not presume to imply that money for technical assistance should take priority over direct services. While one could argue that a well-run technical assistance program can maximize resources and increase cost effectiveness of service programs, such an argument has little merit in the face of human suffering and need.

As Tracy (1977) pointed out, and as we have highlighted throughout this chapter, technical assistance projects sponsored by a third-party funding agency are fraught with the most impediments to the establishment of trust between technical assistant and client. What the budget cuts may do for us, then, is remove the weakest and least efficient consulting arrangement from the array of options available.

Of course, the scarcity of human-service dollars may also mean that individual agencies will have no resources available to bring in outside help. But as human services administrators turn increasingly to the private sector to support activities, there is also the possibility that, along with the money, they will pick up some applicable *modus operandi* from the business world. And among those methods is the judicious use of consultants to maximize efficiency of the operation. Indeed, it is here that consultant programs and technical assistance projects can come into their own. The challenge is to convince service providers and state agency directors that consultants are more than worth their cost—*if* both client and consultant are committed to the solution of a given problem, and *if* that commitment leads to mutual effort in an open and productive client-consultant relationship.

References

Bell, C. R., & Nadler, L. (Eds.) *The client-consultant handbook*. Houston: Gulf Publishing Co., 1979.

Budde, J. F. *Measuring performance in human service system*. New York: AMACOM, 1979.

Davey, N. G. The consultant's role in organizational change. *MSU Business Topics*, Spring 1971, 76–79.

Domergue, M. *Technical assistance*. New York: Praeger Publishers, 1968.

Dunst, C. J. Program evaluation and the Education for All Handicapped Children Act. *Exceptional Children*, Sept. 1979, 24–30.

Ford, C. H. Developing a successful client-consultant relationship. *Human Resource Management*, 1974, **13**, 2–11.

Frankenhuis, J. P. How to get a good consultant. *Harvard Business Review*, November–December, 1977.

Fuchs, J. H. *Making the most of management consulting services*. New York: AMACOM, 1975.

Furr, R. M. Surviving as a messenger: The client-consultant relationship during diagnosis. In C. R. Bell & L. Nadler (Eds.), *The client-consultant handbook*. Houston: Gulf Publishing Co., 1979.

Gallagher, J. J. Models for policy analysis; Child and family policy. In R. Haskins & J. J. Gallagher (Eds.), *Models for social policy analysis: An introduction*. Norwood, N.J.: Ablex Pub. Corp., 1981.

Guba, E. G., & Lincoln, Y. S. *Effective evaluation*. San Francisco: Jossey-Bass Publishers, 1981.

Harrison, R. Choosing the depth of organizational intervention. *The Journal of Applied Behavioral Science*, 1978, **6**, 181–202.

Jackson, S. What do consultants do, anyway? *NSPI Journal*, 1980, **19**, 5–7.

Keeps, E. J., & Jackson, S. F. Starting out as an independent consultant or small consulting firm. *NSPI Journal*, 1980, **19**, 34–39.

Marino, F. *Consultation in mental health and related fields*. Chevy Chase, Md.: National Institute of Mental Health, 1969.

Neufeld, R. Technical assistance systems in human services: An overview. In S. Sturgeon, M. L. Tracy, A. Ziegler, R. Neufeld, & R. Wiegerink (Eds.), *Technical assistance: Facilitating change*. Proceedings of a conference on the provision and use of technical assistance. Bloomington, Ind.: Developmental Training Center, 1977.

Pfeiffer, J. W., & Jones, J. E. Ethical considerations in consulting. In J. E. James & J. W. Pfeiffer (Eds.), *The 1977 Annual Handbook for Group Facilitators*. La Jolla, Ca.: University Associates, 1977.

Raebel, J. Management support organizations. *The Grantsmanship Center News*, 1981, **9**, 16–27.

Raine, R. V. Selecting the consultant. *Personnel Administrator*, Dec. 1980, **25**:12, 41–43.

Schwartz, L. Ethical issues in consulting. *NSPI Journal*, 1980, **19**, 40–43.

Swartz, D., & Lippitt, G. Evaluating the consulting process. In C. R. Bell & L. Nadler (Eds.), *The client-consultant handbook*. Houston: Gulf Publishing Co., 1979.

Thompson, J. T. Helping line managers to be change agents. *Training and Development Journal*, April 1981, **35**:4, 52–56.

Tracy, M. L. Technical assistance: The marketing of change. In S. Sturgeon, M. L. Tracy, A. Ziegler, R. Neufeld, & R. Wiegerink (Eds.), *Technical assistance: Facilitating change*. Proceedings of a Conference on the Provision and Use of Technical Assistance. Bloomington, Ind.: Developmental Training Center, 1977.

PART VII
EDUCATIONAL AND DEVELOPMENTAL APPROACHES

26 LANGUAGE TRAINING

Janis C. Rusch and George R. Karlan

The goal of language intervention, regardless of its theoretical basis, should be to teach appropriate semantic and syntactical rules that enable individuals to convey their needs and intents across the ecological scope of their environment (Schiefelbusch, 1978). Research on methods to achieve this objective has only recently begun. In the past, most research and language training with the mentally retarded has focused upon the acquisition of language skills that may not have had any functional communicative outcome. For example, in Snyder, Lovitt, and Smith's (1975) review of 23 behavior analytic studies, receptive and expressive language skills were taught to mentally retarded persons largely without consideration for the communicative value of those skills. Harris's (1975) review of operant procedures used to teach language skills to nonverbal children suggests that some of these procedures (e.g., imitation of gross motor actions) were implemented without regard for communicative utility. Other more recent reviews also indicate that the majority of language training efforts have focused more upon teaching specific receptive and expressive skills (e.g., receptive discrimination of comparative and superlative forms of adjectives) than upon teaching mentally retarded persons to use those skills to communicate with others (Goetz, Schuler, & Sailor, 1979; Guess, Keough, &

Sailor, 1978). Thus, many mentally retarded persons who were involved in early studies of language training failed to acquire communication skills that could be used to express a variety of functions and ideas with a variety of people in different settings and at different times. Clearly, in order to more closely match the current view of language intervention postulated by Schiefelbusch (1978), the gap between teaching linguistic behaviors and teaching communication skills will have to be narrowed.

The purpose of this chapter will be to review and discuss past language training with the mentally retarded, to discuss emerging trends in language intervention research and to suggest directions future research might take. This chapter will focus, primarily, upon the research data available for the moderately to severely handicapped because of the breadth of work done with this population. Since nonspeech communication in the mentally retarded will be covered below, in chapter 27, this chapter will focus only on verbal skills. Since space limitations preclude an exhaustive review of the literature, the reader will be referred to other relevant reviews on specific topics dealing with language training. This chapter will present past work, emerging areas, and future trends within the framework of the type of program goal suggested by Schiefelbusch (1978). That is, literature on language intervention with the mentally retarded will be reviewed from four perspectives: (a) theoretical constructs and issues in language training, (b) training efforts designed to teach semantic and syntactic rules, (c) strategies used to teach communicative use, and (d) research on generalization strategies or teaching mentally retarded persons to use their language abilities across the ecological scope of their environment.

Theoretical Constructs and Issues in Language Training

The study of language has rapidly gone through many theoretical changes. This situation is most clearly represented in the developmental literature. For example, the current cognitive-pragmatic approach to language training was preceded by the "semantic revolution" and before that the transformational analysis or "structural approach" (Waryas & Stremel-Campbell, 1978). At the same time, behaviorists were advocating the use of a remedial rather than a developmental approach to language training (Guess, Sailor, & Baer, 1977). This argument (developmental vs. remedial) had its roots in the writings of Chomsky (1957, 1965) and Skinner (1957). As a consequence of varying beliefs, models for language training used with the mentally retarded have clearly reflected the theoretical bias of the language teachers. Subsequent changes in these theoretical bases and the ensuing discussions also underscore the complexity of understanding the acquisition of language, as well as the complexity of teaching language skills to mentally retarded persons. The goal of this section is not to resolve all of these issues, but to review the most prominent issue in the field today, that is, the existence and nature of cognitive prerequisites to language intervention.

Those who have advocated sensorimotor-cognitive curriculum approaches for teaching language skills to mentally retarded individuals (e.g., Bricker, Dennison, & Bricker, 1975; Kahn, 1975, 1978, Reichle & Yoder, 1979) have based their approaches primarily upon the developmental theory of Piaget (1962). According to Piaget, there are certain cognitive structures that are necessary, though not sufficient, for the learning of symbolic activities such as language. He has hypothesized (1951, 1963) that meaningful expressive language will not be present until the child has mastered certain cognitive structures and is functioning at Stage 6 in the sensorimotor period. Others (Bloom, 1973; Brown, 1973; Leonard, 1974; Moerk, 1975; Morehead & Morehead, 1974) have also hypothesized that cognitive structures are prerequisites for language development.

The relationship between cognitive development and language acquisition has been studied extensively with nonretarded populations. Even among these studies, however, disparity exists regarding the nature of this relationship. For example, Corrigan (1978), in a longitudinal study of three children, reported only a rough correspondence between beginning language (onset of words) and the period of transition from sensorimotor Stage 5 to Stage 6 of object permanence. Ingram (1977), on the other hand, indicated a correspondence between sensorimotor Stage 6 and the onset of words. Bates, Benigni, Bretherton, Camaioni, and Volterra (1977) reported that only certain subareas within late Stage 5 (Uzgiris & Hunt, 1975) seemed to be indicative of communicative development. They found that nonretarded children's performance on sensorimotor tasks dealing with imitation, means-end, and play with objects were good predictors of their gestural and verbal communicative development, whereas performance on tasks dealing with object permanence and spatial relations were poor predictors. Snyder (1978) also suggested that language-delayed children did not suffer from the inability to acquire a word to refer to an object (Stage 6-object permanence), but rather suffered from the inability to use language as a tool in social interaction (Stage 6-means-end).

The relationship between attainment of a sensorimotor stage and production of two-word combinations has also been studied (Corrigan, 1978; Ingram, 1977; Folger & Leonard, 1978). Although these investigators reported a correspondence between linguistic and cognitive stages, individual differences among children led these investigators to conclude that there was limited evidence that attainment of a particular cognitive stage was a prerequisite to production of two-word combinations. In fact, when age was partialled out, the correlation between children's utterance length and their performance on the means-end scale was eliminated (Folger & Leonard, 1978).

Rubin, Fein, and Vandenberg (in press) have noted that the majority of studies investigating the relationship between language and cognition have focused on language production rather than language comprehension. They asserted that, for Piaget (1962), cognitive development was not so much concerned with the development of speech as it was with the child's understanding that one thing could stand for something else, even when that something was not present. Thus, Rubin et al. postulated that studies of language meaning might have more theoretical significance than studies concerning language production.

Miller, Chapman, Branston, and Reichle (1980) conducted a cross-sectional study of language comprehension in relation to cognitive functioning with 48 normal 10-21-month-old children. Their results showed that although there were significant correlations between comprehension and five sensorimotor subscales, age was the only significant predictor in a multiple regression analysis. They also concluded that Stage 6 functioning was not a necessary prerequisite to the development of one- and two-word comprehension in the semantic roles they assessed. Further, Miller et al. (1980) suggested that their data offered little support for programs that made sensorimotor tasks a prerequisite for work on comprehension tasks and that "directly working on comprehension skills appropriate for the child's cognitive level would constitute more productive use of language programming time" (p. 210).

A number of investigators have directly studied the relationship between cognitive functioning and language development with mentally retarded populations. As with many of the studies with nonretarded populations, the Uzgiris and Hunt (1975) scales are often used to assess cognitive functioning. Kahn (1976) reported that the Uzgiris and Hunt (1975) scales were reliable and ordinal with severely and profoundly mentally retarded children. Karlan (1980a), on the other hand, reported that preference for the object used (i.e., motivation to respond) in the assessment of object permanence or means-end had direct bearing on the reliability of performance. Karlan found that the performance of severely mentally retarded individuals on these two scales was not stable and that ordinality was violated 20% of the time. He suggested that with mentally retarded populations optimal motivation should be established before assessment of cognitive functioning is begun.

Kahn (1975, 1978) supports the notion that cognitive structures exist that are prerequisites for the development of language in mentally retarded children. He further asserts that those mentally retarded children who are not functioning at Stage 6 should not be expected to learn meaningful expressive language and that remediation should concentrate upon raising their cognitive level. In 1975, Kahn investigated the relationship of Stage 6 and the acquisition of meaningful expressive language with eight profoundly mentally retarded children with meaningful language and eight profoundly mentally retarded children without meaningful expressive language. He found that a strong relationship existed between meaningful expressive language and Stage 6 attainment as measured by the Uzgiris and Hunt (1975) ordinal scales of cognitive development.

Two studies (Greenwald & Leonard, 1979; Lobato, Barrera, & Feldman, 1981) have looked at the relationship between prelinguistic communication and cognitive ability with mentally retarded persons. Two kinds of prelinguistic behavior have been studied. One behavior is the imperative performative (Bates, Camainoni, & Volterra, 1975), which represents attempts by the child to enlist adult help in gaining access to an object (e.g., looking, pointing, vocalizing). The other prelinguistic behavior is the declarative performative (Bates et al., 1975), which involves the use of objects to gain the adult's attention (e.g., grasping, showing, vocalizing).

Greenwald and Leonard (1979) investigated imperative and declarative performatives used by nonretarded and Down's syndrome children operating at two stages of sensorimotor intelligence. Generally, their results showed that more advanced forms of performative behavior were associated with the attainment of late Stage 5 behavior for both groups. Their data confirmed the findings of Bates et al. (1977), suggesting that certain levels of sensorimotor development in the domain of means-end, causality, and schemes for relating to objects were associated with different behavior in levels of communication skills.

One interesting finding of the Greenwald and Leonard (1979) work was that the older Down's syndrome children in Stage 5 used more advanced performatives than the younger nonretarded children who were also at Stage 5. One explanation offered for this occurrence was that for some tasks, CA level rather than cognitive level, may dictate particular performance of mentally retarded children (Cromer, 1972). Another explanation offered was that the length of time in Stage 5 (whether due to intervention or natural causes) could account for the higher linguistic abilities since attainment of a stage is progressive rather than abrupt.

Lobato, Barrera, and Feldman (1981) observed similar relationships in the communication behavior of 40 institutionalized severely and profoundly mentally retarded persons. With respect to the question of whether age made a difference in communication development, their results did not suggest that, owing to age, linguistic skills might be more developed than would be expected at the particular cognitive level of the subjects. However, Lobato et al. speculated that differences between these results and those of Greenwald and Leonard (1979) may be due to different populations studied, place of residence (i.e., institution vs. home), or to the nature of measures used (i.e., mean frequencies which masked variability among individuals).

Although most research has been descriptive, two studies successfully demonstrated that object permanence could be taught to mentally retarded individuals. Brassell and Dunst (1976) compared the effects of two training procedures (one conventional and the other systematic instruction) upon the acquisition of object permanence among 21 severely mentally retarded individuals. They found that both training procedures worked equally well in facilitating acquisition but neither resulted in long-term retention.

Kahn (1978) found large improvement in performance on object permanence measures after training a group of severely and profoundly mentally retarded children. After 12 months, there was still a large degree of retention for the experimental subjects; Kahn attributed this retention to the use of a longer training period than was used by Brassell and Dunst (1976).

Summary

At this time, it appears that there is a relationship between cognitive development and language acquisition. This relationship, though, seems to be more direct for some cognitive schemes (e.g., means-end, relating to object, and imitation) than for others (e.g., object permanence). Relationship, however, does not imply causality. Even though Brassell and Dunst (1976) and Kahn (1978) were able to train object permanence with mentally retarded individuals, the more practical and intriguing question is not so much whether these individuals achieved object permanence, but whether attainment of object permanence affected language development. Theoretically, as suggested by Bates et al. (1977), it is not that sensorimotor task performance precedes communication development, but that the two abilities should occur simultaneously. In a study with nonretarded children, Steckol and Leonard (1981) demonstrated that experimental treatment of children's schemes for relating to objects resulted in a developmental increase in these schemes and also resulted in an increase in the children's use of performatives. However, Steckol and Leonard also suggested that future research should now explore the effect of training language performatives upon children's schemes for relating to objects. This research approach is also needed for mentally retarded children, that is, language behaviors should be trained and the influence on cognitive development noted.

Thus, although certain cognitive factors may be necessary, they are not sufficient to totally explain the acquisition of language and cannot be regarded as prerequisites for language training at this time. Certainly, as behaviorists have suggested, the environment directly influences language development. Support for this position comes from behaviorists themselves (Guess, 1980), from studies showing cognitive and communication variability among children,

and from those studies indicating that age was the primary factor in predicting communication development (Folger & Leonard, 1978; Miller et al., 1980). As pointed out by Leonard (1978), even the Piagetian position accepts the importance of the child's environment.

Semantic and Syntactic Rules

Communication is a social process by which one person attempts to influence the thought and hence the behavior of a second person in order to increase his or her own adaptation to the environment and its demands. Because the forms that can function as communicative behaviors are greatly varied and the experiences of one person can be very different from the experiences of another, the process of communicating can be inhibited by these differences; one person's idiosyncratic gestures about a personally unique experience will mean little, if anything, to another person. Thus, the establishment of a communication system requires that the communicating partners:

1. possess a set of referents, values, or experiences in common;
2. share a common set of tokens or symbols with which to identify the referents, values, or experiences; and
3. both be familiar with some relationships or rules for combining the tokens or symbols into larger units of meaning (Sanders, 1976).

Language has evolved to fulfill the second and third requirements of a communication system. "Language is a shared system with rules for correct use in given context, the knowledge of these rules and the ability to apply them are . . . referred to as 'Communicative Competence' " (Rees, 1978, p. 194). To expand Rees's (1978) "shared system" definition of language somewhat, language is a *code* through which ideas about the world are represented via a *conventional system* of *arbitrary* signals for the purposes of communication (Bloom & Lahey, 1978).

The linguistic code may be broken down into three components: a morphemic component, a semantic component, and a syntactic component. The morphemic component is further divided into words and bound or grammatical morphemes. Morphemes are the smallest units of the code that impart meaning. Words are one class of morphemes. Words can be substantive, that is referring to specific objects or classes of objects (e.g., Mother, juice, car, money). Words can also be relational, that is referring to relationships shared by objects, e.g., attribution, location, action, possession, or to relationships such as recurrence of a thing (more), rejection (no), or noting the disappearance of a thing (all gone) (Bloom & Lahey, 1978). Some morphemes are used to modulate the meaning of words; these have been called the grammatical morphemes (Brown, 1973). These grammatical morphemes can be used to indicate number as with the plural morphemes (-s, -es); e.g., glass becomes glasses, boat becomes boats. They can also indicate time as with the tense endings (past, -ed, or present, -s, -ing); e.g., push becomes pushed, run becomes runs or running.

Semantic relations are the basic meaning relationships which pertain in a sequence of words. Brown (1973) has identified a series of two- and three-word semantic relations that can be found in the speech of young children prior to the use of well formed "grammatical" sentences. These relations include:

Agent-action	(Daddy throw)
Action-object	(throw ball)
Agent-object	(Daddy ball)
Action-location	(put those, put in)
Entity-location	(sweater chair)
Possessor-possession	(Mommy briefcase)
Entity-attribute	(big train, soup hat)
Demonstrative-entity	(that hat)

As language develops, such two-term relationships grow to include three terms, e.g., agent-action-object or action-object-location. Early semantic relations also included what Brown (1973) called "operations of reference:"

Recurrence	(more cookie)
Rejection	(no want)
Nonexistence	(all gone, no more)
Cessation of Action	(no push)

As can be concluded from the above examples, semantic relations convey basic meaning, but they are not "well formed" in a grammatical sense.

The syntactic component contains the sequencing rules that govern the production of well formed, or grammatically appropriate, sentences. It is through such rules that a speaker can create an infinite number of sentences, any of which will be understood by a listener who shares knowledge of the rule system with the speaker. In addition, these rules need not be "known" in the sense of stating the rule; an individual who can hear sentences like "the boy hit the ball" and repeatedly restate them as "the ball was hit by the boy" is behaving in a rulelike fashion and need not (and probably cannot) state the rules for transforming active sentences into passive ones.

With respect to research on training in the area of semantics and syntax, the basic issue is whether it can be demonstrated that the mentally retarded individual understands or uses semantic relations or syntactic rules. This implies that the individual is able to comprehend or to produce more than just the particular word sequences trained; it must be shown that novel, untrained sequences representing the relations or rules must be understood or expressed. Within behavioral research, the notion of a generalized response class has often been used as a model for training these generalized semantic or syntactic skills. Baer, Guess, and Sherman (1972) first suggested that certain grammatical classes (representing surface structure failures) can be analyzed as response class phenomena. A generalized response class exists when a manipulation is done in relation to a few members of a supposed class and the effect is shown by all members of the class with no further training (Wheeler & Sulzer, 1970). This analysis has been applied to morphological, inflectional, and syntactical responding.

With the grammatical morphemes, generalized use of the plural morpheme and plural allomorphs has been studied (Guess, 1969; Guess & Baer, 1973; Guess, Sailor, Rutherford, & Baer, 1968; Sailor, 1971). Of the inflectional morphemes, receptive adjectival inflections (Baer & Guess, 1971), productive noun suffixes (Baer & Guess, 1973), and productive verb tense inflections (Clark & Sherman, 1975; Schumaker & Sherman, 1970) have been established as generalized response classes.

Wheeler and Sulzer (1970) conducted a study that involved the establishment of syntactical as well as morphological and inflectional response classes in the appropriate use of sentence structure. Other studies of syntax as a response class phenomenon have investigated smaller structural units within the sentences such as subject-verb agreement with regard to the number feature (singular/plural) of the subject (Garcia, Guess, & Byrnes, 1973; Lutzker & Sherman, 1974). Another group of studies has reported the development of descriptive sentence forms (Bennet & Ling, 1972; Hester & Hendrickson, 1977), simple and compound sentence structures (Stevens-Long & Rasmussen, 1974), and question asking in the presence of unknown stimuli (Twardosz & Baer, 1973).

While there has been relatively less work focusing upon the development of semantic relations, the studies that have been reported have been concerned with generalized responding. Generalized comprehension of locative (prepositional) relations (Frisch & Schumaker, 1974), action-object relations (Striefel, Wetherby, & Karlan, 1976, 1978) and action-attribute-object relations (Striefel, Wetherby, & Karlan, 1978) has been demonstrated. Only two studies have examined the training of expressive use of semantic relations. Sailor and Taman (1972) reported generalized acquisition of locative (prepositional) relations. Generalized expression of action-object relations was taught using a matrix-training strategy (Karlan, Brenn-White, Lentz, Hocher, Egger, & Frankoff, 1982).

Summary

Research has clearly demonstrated that various generalized or rulelike syntactic and semantic skills can be developed with mentally retarded individuals. For the most part, the training strategies have followed a "train sufficient examplars" approach (Stokes and Baer, 1977) to the development of generalized responding. In this approach training merely proceeds across examplars until generalization begins to occur. A few studies have, however, attempted to develop an approach, the matrix strategy, that would more systematically develop generalization (Striefel, Wetherby & Karlan, 1976, 1978; Karlan et al., 1982). These studies have not specifically demonstrated that a nonlanguage user can be trained to produce complete grammatical language. However, taken as a whole, they do indicate that such an outcome is a possibility given enough training.

Pragmatics: The Communicative Use of Language

In the last section, this chapter reviewed language training with retarded persons in the areas of form (syntax and morphology) and content (semantics). Although research studies have shown that mentally retarded individuals can acquire these two aspects of language, little work has been done demonstrating spontaneous uses of these newly acquired structures in natural contexts. The study of language use in context, or pragmatics, is the third perspective on language intervention. In order to be an effective language user, a person not only needs something to say and a way to say it, but also a reason to say it (Miller & Yoder, 1972; Karlan, 1982). As suggested by Rees (1978), language exists in order for information to be communicated between speaker and listener.

Pragmatics examines language in relation to its contextual control; in order for it to be appropriate language use, what is said must be "matched to the context of use in predictable ways" (Hart, 1981, p. 300). For example, the type of verbal behavior that occurs at a party may be very different from the type of verbal behavior that occurs in the lecture hall.

Each type of verbal behavior can be fairly accurately predicted, depending upon the context.

The study of pragmatics regards the "speech act" rather than the sentence as the basic unit of communication. Sentences or utterances are not analyzed according to their internal structure but rather analyzed according to their function in the communicative act (Rees, 1978). As stated by Gallagher and Darnton (1978), the speech act model "considers word selections and combinations to be contextually based uses of language reflecting the intentions and beliefs of speakers and the impact of utterances on listeners" (p. 118).

As with semantics, syntax, and morphology, much of the field of pragmatics has its primary research base in normal child development. Rather than reviewing the research on and the theoretical approach to the study of pragmatics, we refer readers to Bates (1976), Hart (1981), Rees (1978), and McLean and Snyder-Mclean (1978). The goal of this section will be to review that research focused upon mental retardation and those aspects of pragmatics relating to the functional use of language and the analysis of conversation.

Functional Use of Language

Speech acts have been classified according to the manner in which they affect the environment or mediate the behaviors of others. According to Rogers-Warren and Warren (1981), "successful mediation depends on (1) discrimination of the critical stimulus conditions [context], and (2) production of a communication form that is responsive to those conditions" (p. 392). Mentally retarded individuals frequently have difficulties in both of these areas. Not only might they be unable to match their language to the appropriate context, but they may not even realize their language can affect another's behavior and, subsequently, change their environment. Often, creating a need to communicate is a critical first step in working with the more severely mentally retarded. These types of programs have frequently been referred to as "functional language training programs."

Numerous writers have advocated using "functional language training programs" with the mentally retarded to establish initial vocabulary (cf. Goetz et al., 1979; Guess, Sailor, & Baer, 1978a; Karlan, 1980b; Sosne, Handleman, & Harris, 1979; Sailor, Guess, Goetz, Schuler, Utley, & Baldwin, 1980). Guess, Sailor, and Baer (1978a) described functional responses as ones that "(1) produce an immediate consequence for the child; (2) the consequence is potentially reinforcing; (3) the consequence is specific to the response; and (4) the response is natural to the child's interaction with the environment" (p. 114). For example, a functional response would occur when a child is taught to say the work "drink" in the presence of juice at snack time in order to obtain a drink of the juice.

Although research is limited in this area, a number of investigators have shown that the idea of "functionality" is a viable concept for teaching language to the mentally retarded. Janssen and Guess (1978) found that receptive labeling was learned faster when mentally retarded individuals pointed to an object in response to a label and the function of the object was used as a consequence for the correct response. Similarly, Saunders and Sailor (1979) found that two-choice discrimination was facilitated with response-specific reinforcement. Guess, Sailor, and Baer (1977, 1978b) have developed a language curriculum that teaches four basic functions: control, self-extended control, reference, and integration. For a more detailed review of response functionality, that also includes work with autistic children, see Goetz et al. (1979).

Hart (1981) further expands the notion of teaching the functional use of communication by discussing language in relation to context, generalized imitation, and rate. Because differences in context call for differing language responses, mentally retarded persons need to learn to match language responses to these varying context situations. Language trainers can begin to train the contextual use of language by cuing appropriate matching responses in differing contexts and then by training the mentally retarded person to respond appropriately to predictable trainer prompts. Hart suggests the use of two types of prompts: (*a*) very predictable prompts in varying settings, such as "What do you want?" during snack or "Can I help you?" at a restaurant, and (*b*) delay, or pause, prompts where eye-contact is maintained and the language trainer waits for the other person to speak (Halle, Marshall, & Spradlin, 1979). Once appropriate responses are made in the training situation, they are then used and faded into generalized contexts.

Generalized imitation (Baer & Sherman, 1964) is another useful strategy to teach to mentally retarded persons (Hart, 1981). By learning to observe others in varying contexts and learning to match (imitate) verbal behavior observed, generalized language use could occur without direct teaching. Hart (1981) suggested that language be taught as part of interactional scripts or routines (e.g., getting dressed, eating dinner, going to the grocery store) and that once the language in these routines is learned language use in generalized contexts may be facilitated.

Hart and Risley (1980) have suggested that the more a person talks (rate) the more elaborate language becomes. If language is appropriately matched to the context, the more a person talks the more the person is likely to comment on people, objects, events, and relationships within the context, as well as responding to the "subtle ways with [which] every utterance [is] introduced into that context" (p. 309). Thus, language trainers would want to increase the rate of language use by creating interesting (reinforcing) contexts, prompting language, and using incidental teaching methods (i.e., focusing on the topic the person has verbally initiated, repeating it to confirm understanding, and then asking for more language on that topic).

In summary, the idea of functionality of responses seems to be a worthwhile concept to explore for teaching language to mentally retarded persons. That, in combination with emphasizing contextual variables, generalized imitation, and rate should serve as a beginning technology to teach mentally retarded individuals the social use of language.

Conversational Analysis

One of the highest levels of language use is conversation (Karlan, 1980b). Even at this complex level, one of the most important variables is context. The context of the conversation may be physically present or entirely absent, but it is usually established as a function of the conversation. According to Karlan, "the context will be established either specifically in the initial stages of conversation or by the experience held in common by conversations and implied by initial discourse" (p. 135). Grice (1975) has formulated rules for conversation while Sacks, Schegloff, and Jefferson (1974) have developed a descriptive model of turn-taking based on normal adult conversations.

A number of investigators have descriptively analyzed the communicative functions expressed in conversations by mentally retarded adults. Abbeduto and Rosenberg (1980), Bedrosian and Prutting (1978), Owings and McManus (1980), and Sabsay (1975) indicated that mildly to severely mentally retarded adults are active verbal communicators. In a study with institutionalized Down syndrome adults, Sabsay (1975), found essentially normal conversational patterns, especially within retarded-retarded conversations. Bedrosian and Prutting (1978) showed that moderately mentally retarded adults, speaking to a normal adult, utilized similar conversational control but took more of a submissive, rather than dominant, role in conversation. Similarly, Owings and McManus (1980) found that their adult subject was aware of the social conventions necessary for using various communicative functions in different speaking situations. Abbeduto and Rosenberg (1980) analyzed peer conversations and concluded that their sample of mildly mentally retarded adults made few turn-taking errors and recognized illocutionary acts obliging them to respond.

Several studies have successfully taught different conversational skills to mentally retarded adolescents and adults using social skill training packages. Conversational behaviors selected for training have included positive conversational feedback statements (Arnold, Sturgis, & Forehand, 1977; Rychtarik & Bornstein, 1979), self-disclosing statements, complimentary comments (Kelly, Furman, Phillips, Hathorn, & Wilson, 1979; Kelly, Wildman, Urey, & Thurman, 1979) and conversational questions (Rusch, Karlan, Riva, and Rusch, Note 1).

Summary

The most important issue facing language trainers is the issue of generalized use of language. Although generalization is discussed more fully in the next section of this chapter, it is impossible not to mention it with respect to pragmatics as well. The concepts of generalization and pragmatics are intertwined. Both concepts involve language use within the broad notion of "context" or "natural" environments. As suggested by Hart (1981) "in order to arrange for the generalization of language use from the carefully structured contexts of training into 'natural' environments, trainers and teachers need to know how language is 'naturally' used" (p. 299).

Research on the ways mentally retarded persons use language is limited, however. More descriptive and naturalistic observational studies, such as those studies investigating communication functions in conversation (cf. Abbeduto & Rosenberg, 1980), are needed. These studies need to be expanded, however, to include the use of language within a number of differing contextual variables (e.g., setting, people, purpose of communication, etc.). In addition, more normative data on the way both children and adults use language in varying contexts is necessary.

As Hart (1981) noted, an effective technology for teaching communicative use is in its infancy. Clearly, research investigating effective intervention strategies with the mentally retarded is warranted. A beginning point would be to study the effect of context, generalized imitation, and rate on communication. These research suggestions, admittedly, are broad in nature. But as more research on pragmatics and mental retardation is done, more specific questions will evolve.

Generalization and Language Use

Language training research with the mentally retarded has demonstrated successful acquisition of cognitive, syntactic, semantic, and certain aspects of pragmatic skills. What remains to be done, and indeed is the more challenging task, is to demonstrate the generalization of these skills across the ecological scope of an environment. The complexity of this endeavor has been presented by Rogers-Warren and Warren (1981).

> The goal of language training is to teach a repertoire of communication skills that will be used outside training, with persons who are not trainers, to describe objects and events that are usually physically different from, but conceptually similar to, those described in training. The complexity of the communication system requires discrimination and generalization at the phonological level, in labeling, in producing multi-word utterances describable in terms of syntactic or semantic classes, in receptive understanding of all aspects of language, and in adapting language to fit the listener, the occasion, and the speaker's immediate behavioral goals. A generative communication repertoire requires the formation of multiple stimulus and response classes, which are dynamic, responsive to changing contingencies and increasing information about the context and the communication system. [p. 390]

The issue of generalization has been addressed in a number of cogent papers (Cooke, Cooke, & Apollini, 1976; Garcia & Dehaven, 1974; Guess, 1980; Guess, Keogh, & Sailor, 1978; Rogers-Warren & Warren, 1981; Stokes & Baer, 1977; Warren, Rogers-Warren, Baer, & Guess, 1980).

Definitions and Measures

Although the concept of generalization is complex, two general types have been defined: (*a*) stimulus generalization and (*b*) response generalization. Stimulus generalization occurs when language skills are used within varying stimulus conditions (i.e., persons, objects, settings, time) that differ from those conditions used during training. Response generalization occurs when language behaviors are similar in use, but topographically different, from the trained language behaviors. This is the type of generalization discussed with respect to research on syntactic training. In order for language to be used within an ecological framework, stimulus and response generalization need to occur at the same time. The ecological framework can be thought of as the complex interrelationships and interdependencies between organisms, behaviors, and environments that occur in natural contexts (Rusch, Note 2).

Table 26.1. Generalization Studies

		GENERALIZATION	
REFERENCE	DEPENDENT VARIABLE	STIMULUS	RESPONSE
Anderson & Spradlin (1980)	Labeling	X	
Garcia (1974)	Rudimentary conversation skill	X	
Halle, Marshall, & Spradlin (1979)	Meal requests	X	
Rincover & Koegel (1975)	Nonverbal imitation, direction following	X	
Stokes, Baer, & Jackson (1974)	Greetings	X	
Welch & Pear (1980)	Labeling	X	
Baer & Guess (1971)	Comparative and superlative adjectives		X
Baer & Guess (1973)	Noun suffixes		X
Clark & Sherman (1975)	Verb-inflections		X
Garcia, Guess, & Byrnes (1973)	Singular and plural sentences		X
Guess (1969)	Plurals		X
Guess & Baer (1973)	Plurals		X
Guess, Sailor, Rutherford, & Baer (1968)	Plurals		X
Hester & Hendrickson (1977)	Three-element syntactic responses		X
Jeffree, Wheldall, & Mittler (1973)	Two-element syntactic responses		X
Lutzker & Sherman (1974)	Subject-verb agreement		X
Mithaug (1978)	Instruction-following		X
Sailor (1971)	Plurals		X
Schumaker & Sherman (1970)	Past-tense		X
Smeets & Striefel (1976)	Article-noun responses		X
Striefel & Wetherby (1973)	Instruction-following		X
Striefel, Wetherby, & Karlan (1976, 1978)	Instruction-following		X
Twardosz & Baer (1973)	Question-asking		X
Wheeler & Sulzer (1970)	Articles & verbs in sentences		X

Although many language investigations have included generalization measures, few studies have actually sought to train generalization specifically. Table 26.1 lists those language studies that sought to develop generalization and classifies them according to stimulus or response generalization. As can be seen, many more studies have focused upon response generalization than have examined stimulus generalization. Guess, Keogh, and Sailor (1978) concluded "that when certain speech and language behaviors belonging to a response class (i.e., plurals, comparative suffixes, superlative suffixes, and imitation) were trained directly, other members of that response class were also established even though they had not been trained directly" (p. 380). In general, however, research on the acquisition of language behaviors has not proceeded from the concept of a response class (Guess et al., 1978). This is particularly true of cross-modal transfer (i.e., generalization from receptive to productive behaviors and vice versa). Generalization across modalities has been demonstrated in some studies (Bucher & Keller, 1981; Cuvo & Riva, 1980; Mann & Baer, 1971; Ruder, Hermann, & Schiefelbusch, 1977), but not in others (Anderson & Spradlin, 1980; Guess, 1969; Guess & Baer, 1973; Miller, Cuvo, & Borakove, 1977).

All of the studies listed in Table 26.1, with the exception of Hester and Hendrickson (1977) and Jeffree, Wheldall, and Mittler (1973), assessed generalization via structured probes. Structured probes attempt to elicit specific language responses under stimulus and response conditions that differ from the ones used in training (Warren et al., 1980). The other way to measure generalization is to assess the spontaneous use of trained language in the natural environment. Here, trained language is not specifically elicited, but instead, is observed to occur as a function of "real world use" (Warren et al., 1980). Even though natural environment generalization is the most desirable type of generalization to measure, Warren et al.'s (1980) longitudinal study revealed that through the use of structured probes, specifically elicited generalization needed to occur first before spontaneous language was used in the natural settings.

Strategies for Facilitating Generalization

Expanding upon the earlier recommendations of Harris (1975) and Stokes and Baer (1977), the socioecological approach advocated by Guess, Keogh, and Sailor (1978), and the milieu intervention model proposed by Hart and Rogers-Warren (1978), Guess (1980) outlined a number of factors that can facilitate language generalization. Guess divided these factors into two broad categories: (a) training procedures and (b) environmental variables. Training procedures included using multiple trainers, sufficient exemplars, varied settings, appropriate content and sufficient duration, and modifying schedules of reinforcement. Environmental variables that facilitated generalization included person variables (i.e., the availability of persons and the availability of prompts, reinforcers, and models for language) and physical variables (i.e., common stimulus dimensions and arrangements that facilitate verbal and social interactions). Similar analyses have been done by Guess, Keogh, and Sailor (1978), Stokes and Baer (1977), and Warren et al. (1980).

Summary

The ability to generalize acquired language behaviors is critical to achieving communicative competence. That many mentally retarded persons fail to generalize language behaviors without specific intervention underscores the importance of this concern. The research reviewed in this section has demonstrated an initial technology for teaching generalization. This technology must continue to evolve before we can successfully train mentally retarded persons to use language in a functional and appropriate manner. For example, little research exists on assessing generalization in natural environments. Although longitudinal measures of natural language used in context are desirable, they are also expensive and time consuming (Rogers-Warren & Warren, 1980). Rogers-Warren and Warren suggested developing better and more naturalistic generalization probe techniques, which would lend themselves to reliable data collection and replicable procedures. Furthermore, although response class generalization has received the majority of the research attention, these studies have primarily examined syntactic or morphological elements. Research is needed to demonstrate the application of the concept of response class to cross-modal transfer, to semantic and pragmatic development, and to the longitudinal evaluation of prelinguistic behaviors through more complex, multiword utterances.

Many of the strategies for facilitating generalization suggested by Guess (1980) have received limited study. For example, little is known about the type of stimulus control that exists in natural environments for encouraging and reinforcing generalized language. We need to develop "social awareness" (Greenspan, 1979) in the mentally retarded, so that they can assess the environment, make the appropriate linguistic responses, and be judged appropriate. Investigative efforts studying schedules of reinforcement existing in the natural environment and exploring more effective teaching procedures in the natural environment would provide valuable information for the further devel-

opment of specific generalization strategies. Finally, as both Rogers-Warren and Warren (1981) and Warren et al. (1980) have suggested, language generalization research should provide further information toward a comprehensive model of language learning. Thus, the theoretical and applied aspects of generalization point to it as a significant area of research priority with the mentally retarded.

Conclusions

The majority of persons labeled as mentally retarded have significant communication handicaps (Bensberg & Sigelman, 1976). As mentally retarded persons are integrated into community settings, they will require more effective and appropriate linguistic and communicative skills than have been trained. Past language training research has concentrated primarily upon linguistic structures without regard for communicative utility. It has only been recently that the roles of cognition, semantics, pragmatics, and generalization have been stressed as important parts of language training efforts. Although language trainers have debated what to teach and when to teach it, most would agree that applied behavior analysis techniques are the most effective teaching techniques to use with mentally retarded persons.

Schiefelbusch (1981) has recently stated that language training should be viewed as an integral part of all daily activities, within a range of contexts, that are mediated by social constraints, rules, intentions, and contingencies. He thus repeats the statement he made in 1978: that the goal of language intervention programs, regardless of theoretical constructs, should be to teach appropriate semantic and syntactic rules that enable individuals to convey their needs and intents across the ecological scope of their environment.

Reference Notes

1. Rusch, J. C., Karlan, G. R., Riva, M. T., & Rusch, F. R. Teaching mentally retarded adults conversational skills in employment settings. Unpublished manuscript, University of Illinois, Department of Special Education, Champaign, 1981.
2. Rusch, J. C. An ecobehavioral approach to community integration: A review and analysis. Unpublished manuscript, University of Illinois, Special Education Department, 1981.

References

Abbeduto, L., & Rosenberg, S. The communicative competence of mildly retarded adults. *Applied Psycholinguistics*, 1980, 1, 405–426.

Anderson, S. R., & Spradlin, J. E. The generalized effects of productive labeling training involving common object classes. *Journal of Association for Severely Handicapped*, 1980, **5**, 143–157.

Arnold, S., Sturgis, E., & Forehand, R. Training a parent to teach communication skills. *Behavior Modification*, 1977, **1**, 259–276.

Baer, D. M., & Guess, D. Receptive training of adjectival inflections in mental retardates. *Journal of Applied Behavior Analysis*, 1971, **4**, 129–139.

Baer, D., & Guess, D. Teaching productive noun suffixes to severely retarded children. *American Journal of Mental Deficiency*, 1973, **77**, 498–505.

Baer, D. M., Guess, D., & Sherman, J. A. Adventures in simplistic grammar. In R. L. Schiefelbusch (Ed.), *Language of the mentally retarded*. Baltimore: University Park Press, 1972.

Baer, D. M., & Sherman, J. A. Reinforcement control of generalized imitation in young children. *Journal of Experimental Child Psychology*, 1964, **1**, 37–49.

Bates, E. *Language and context*. New York: Academic Press, 1976.

Bates, E., Benigni, L., Bretherton, I., Camaioni, L., & Volterra, V. From gesture to first word: On cognitive and social prerequisites. In M. Lewis & L. Rosenbaum (Eds.), *Interaction, conversation, and the development of language*. New York: John Wiley, 1977.

Bates, E., Camaioni, L., & Volterra, V. The acquisition of performatives prior to speech. *Merrill-Palmer Quarterly*, 1975, **21**, 205–226.

Bedrosian, J. L. & Prutting, C. A. Communicative performance of mentally retarded adults in four conversational settings. *Journal of Speech and Hearing Research*, 1978, **21**, 79–95.

Bennet, C. W., & Ling, D. Teaching a complex verbal response to a hearing-impaired girl. *Journal of Applied Behavior Analysis*. 1972, **5**, 321–328.

Bensberg, G., & Sigelman, C. Definitions and prevalence. In L. L. Lloyd (Ed.), *Communication, assessment and intervention strategies*. Baltimore: University Park Press, 1976.

Bloom, L. *One word at a time*. The Hague: Mouton, 1973.

Bloom, L., & Lahey, M. *Language development and language disorders*. New York: John Wiley, 1978.

Brassell, W. R., & Dunst, C. J. Comparison of two procedures for fostering the development of the object construct. *American Journal of Mental Deficiency*, 1976, **80**, 523–528.

Bricker, D., Dennison, L., & Bricker, W. *Constructive interaction-adaption approach to language training*. MCCD monograph series, No. 1. Miami: Mailman Center for Child Development, University of Miami, 1975.

Brown, R. *A first language: The early stages*. Cambridge: Harvard University Press, 1973.

Bucher, B., & Keller, M. F. Transfer to productive labeling after training in comprehension: Effects of three training variables. *Analysis and Intervention in Developmental Disabilities*, 1981, **1**, 315–331.

Chomsky, N. *Syntactic Structures*. The Hague: Mouton, 1957.

Chomsky, N. *Aspects of the theory of syntax*. Cambridge: M.I.T. Press, 1965.

Clark, H., & Sherman, J. Teaching generative use of sentence answers to three forms of questions. *Journal of Applied Behavior Analysis*, 1975, **8**, 321–330.

Cooke, S., Cooke, T., & Apollini, T. Generalization of language training with the mentally retarded. *Journal of Special Education*, 1976, **10**, 299–304.

Corrigan, R. Language development as related to stage 6 object permanence development. *Journal of Child Language*. 1978, **5**, 173–190.

Cromer, R. Learning of linguistic surface structure cues to deep structure by educationally subnormal children. *American Journal of Mental Deficiency*, 1972, **77**, 346–353.

Cuvo, A. J., & Riva, M. T. Generalization and transfer between comprehension and production: A comparison of retarded and nonretarded persons. *Journal of Applied Behavior Analysis*, 1980, **13**, 315–331.

Folger, M. K., & Leonard, L. B. Language and sensorimotor development during the early period of referential speech. *Journal of Speech and Hearing Research*, 1978, **21**, 519–527.

Frisch, S. A., & Schumaker, J. B. Training generalized receptive prepositions, in retarded children. *Journal of Applied Behavior Analysis*, 1974, **7**, 611–621.

Gallagher, T. M., & Darnton, B. A. Conversational aspects of the speech of language-disordered children: Revision behaviors. *Journal of Speech and Hearing Research*, 1978, **21**, 118–135.

Garcia, E. The training and generalization of a conversational speech form in nonverbal retardates. *Journal of Applied Behavior Analysis*, 1974, **7**, 137–149.

Garcia, E. E., & DeHaven, E. J. Use of operant techniques in the establishment and generalization of language: A review and analysis. *American Journal of Mental Deficiency*, 1974, **79**, 169–178.

Garcia, E., Guess, D., & Byrnes, J. Development of syntax in a retarded girl using procedures of imitation, reinforcement, and modeling. *Journal of Applied Behavior Analysis*, 1973, **6**, 299–310.

Goetz, L., Schuler, A., & Sailor, W. Teaching functional speech to severely handicapped: Current issues. *Journal of Autism and Developmental Disorders*, 1979, **9**, 324–344.

Greenspan, S. Social intelligence in the retarded. In N. R. Ellis (Ed.), *Handbook of mental retardation: Psychological theory and research*. (2nd ed.) Hillsdale, N.J.: Erlbaum, 1979.

Greenwald, C. A., & Leonard, L. B. Communicative and sensorimotor development of Down's syndrome children. *American Journal of Mental Deficiency*, 1979, **84**, 296–303.

Grice, H. P. Logic and conversation. In P. Cole & J. L. Morgan (Eds.), *Syntax and semantics*. Vol. 3. *Speech acts*. New York: Academic Press, 1975.

Guess, D. A functional analysis of receptive language and productive speech: Acquisition of the plural morpheme. *Journal of Applied Behavior Analysis*, 1969, **2**, 55–64.

Guess, D. Methods in communication instruction for severely handicapped persons. In W. Sailor, B. Wilcox, & L. Brown (Eds.), *Methods of instruction for severely handicapped students*. Baltimore: Paul Brookes, 1980.

Guess, D., & Baer, M. An analysis of individual differences in generalization between receptive and productive language in retarded children. *Journal of Applied Behavior Analysis*, 1973, **6**, 311–331.

Guess, D., Keogh, W., Sailor, W. Generalization of speech and language behavior: Measurement and training tactics. In R. L. Schiefelbusch (Ed.), *Bases of language intervention*. Baltimore: University Park Press, 1978.

Guess, D., Sailor, W., & Baer, D. M. A behavioral-remedial approach to language training for the severely handicapped. In E. Sontag (Ed.), *Educational programming for the severely handicapped*. Reston, Va.: A special publication of the Division on Mental Retardation, Council for Exceptional Children, 1977.

Guess, D., Sailor, W., & Baer, D. M. Children with limited language. In R. L. Schiefelbusch (Ed.), *Language intervention strategies*. Baltimore: University Park Press, 1978.(a)

Guess, D., Sailor, W., & Baer, D. *Functional speech and language training for the severely handicapped*. Lawrence, Kansas: H & H Enterprises, 1978.(b)

Guess, D., Sailor, W., Rutherford, G., & Baer, D. An experimental analysis of linguistic development: The productive use of the plural morpheme. *Journal of Applied Behavior Analysis*, 1968, 1, 297-306.

Halle, J. W., Marshall, A. M., & Spradlin, J. E. Time delay: A technique to increase language use and facilitate generalization in retarded children. *Journal of Applied Behavior Analysis*, 1979, 12, 431-441.

Harris, S. L. Teaching language to nonverbal children— with emphasis on problems of generalization. *Psychological Bulletin*, 1975, 82, 563-580.

Hart, B. Pragmatics: How language is used. *Analysis and Intervention in Developmental Disabilities*, 1981, 1, 299-311.

Hart, B., & Risley, T. R. In vivo language intervention: Unanticipated generalized effects. *Journal of Applied Behavior Analysis*, 1980, 13, 407-432.

Hart, B., & Rogers-Warren, A. A milieu approach to teaching language. In R. L. Schiefelbusch (Ed.), *Language intervention strategies*. Baltimore: University Park Press, 1978.

Hester, P., & Hendrikson, J. Training functional expressive language: The acquisition and generalization of five-element syntactic responses. *Journal of Applied Behavior Analysis*, 1977, 10, 316.

Ingram, D. Sensorimotor intelligence and language development. In H. Lock (Ed.), *Action, gesture, and symbol: The emergence of language*. New York: Academic, 1977.

Janssen, C., & Guess, D. Use of function as a consequence in training receptive labeling to severely and profoundly retarded individuals. *AAESPH Review*, 1978, 3, 246-258.

Jeffree, D., Wheldall, K., & Mittler, P. Facilitating two-word utterances in two Down's syndrome boys. *American Journal of Mental Deficiency*, 1973, 78, 117-122.

Kahn, J. V. Relationship of Piaget's sensorimotor period to language acquisition of profoundly retarded children. *American Journal of Mental Deficiency*, 1975, 79, 640-643.

Kahn, J. V. Utility of the Uzgiris and Hunt Scales of sensorimotor development with severely and profoundly retarded children. *American Journal of Mental Deficiency*, 1976, 80, 663-665.

Kahn, J. V. Acceleration of object permanence with severely and profoundly retarded children. *AAESPH Review*, 1978, 3, 15-22.

Karlan, G. R. The effects of preference for objects and repeated measures upon the assessed level of object permanence and means/end ability in severely handicapped students. *Journal of Association for Severely Handicapped*, 1980, 5, 174-193.(a)

Karlan, G. Issues in communication research related to integration of developmentally disabled individuals. In A. R. Novak & L. W. Heal (Eds.), *Integration of developmentally disabled individuals into the community*.

Baltimore, Paul H. Brookes, 1980.(b)

Karlan, G. Issues in communication research related to integration of developmentally disabled individuals. In A. R. Novak & L. W. Heal (Eds.), *Integration of developmentally disabled individuals into the community*. Baltimore, Paul H. Brookes, 1980.(b)

Karlan, G. R., Brenn-White, B., Lentz, A., Hocher, P., Egger, D., & Frankoff, D. Establishing generalized, productive verb-noun phrase usage in a manual language system with moderately handicapped children. *Journal of Speech & Hearing Disorders*, 1982, 47, 101-112.

Kelly, J. A., Furman, W., Phillips, J., & Hathorn, S., & Wilson, T. Teaching conversational skills to retarded adolescents. *Child Behavior Therapy*, 1979, 1, 85-97.

Kelly, J. A., Wildman, B. G., Urey, J., & Thurman, C. Group skills training to increase the conversational repertoire of retarded adolescents. *Child Behavior Therapy*, 1979, 1, 323-336.

Leonard, L. From reflex to remark. *Acta Symbolica*, 1974, 5, 67-99.

Leonard, L. B. Cognitive factors in early linguistic development. In R. L. Schiefelbusch (Ed.), *Bases of language intervention*. Baltimore: University Park Press, 1978.

Lobato, D., Barrera, R. D., & Feldman, R. S. Sensorimotor functioning and prelinguistic communication of severely and profoundly retarded individuals. *American Journal of Mental Deficiency*, 1981, 85, 489-496.

Lutzker, J., & Sherman, J. Producing generative sentence usage by imitative and reinforcement procedures. *Journal of Applied Behavior Analysis*, 1974, 7, 447-460.

Mann, R., & Baer, D. M. The effects of receptive language training on articulation. *Journal of Applied Behavior Analysis*, 1971, 4, 291-298.

McLean, J. E., & Snyder-McLean, L. K. *A transactional approach to early language training*. Columbus, Ohio: Charles E. Merrill, 1978.

Miller, J. F., Chapman, R. S., Branston, M. B., & Reichle, J. Language comprehension in sensorimotor stages V and VI. *Journal of Speech and Hearing Research*, 1980, 23, 284-311.

Miller, J. F., & Yoder, D. E. On developing content for a language teaching program. *Mental Retardation*, 1972, 10, 9-11.

Miller, M. A., Cuvo, A. J., & Borakove, L. S. Teaching naming of coin values: Comprehension before production U.S. production alone. *Journal of Applied Behavior Analysis*, 1977, 10, 735-736.

Mithaug, D. E. Case study in training generalized instruction-following responses to preposition-noun combinations in a severely retarded young adult. *AAESPH Review*, 1978, 3, 94-115.

Moerk, E. L. Piaget's research as applied to the explanation of language development. *Merrill-Palmer Quarterly*, 1975, 21, 151-169.

Morehead, D. M., & Morehead, A. From signal to sign: A Piagetian view of thought and language during the first two years. In R. L. Schiefelbusch & L. L. Lloyd (Eds.), *Language perspectives: Acquisition, retardation, and intervention*. Baltimore: University Park Press, 1974.

Owings, N. O., & McManus, M. D. An analysis of communicative functions in the speech of a deinstitutionalized adult mentally retarded client. *Mental Retardation*, 1980, 18, 309-314.

Piaget, J. *Play, dreams, and imitations in childhood*. New York: W. W. Norton, 1951.

Piaget, J. *The language and thought of the child*. New York:

World Publishing, 1962.

Piaget, J. *The origins of intelligence in children.* New York: W. W. Norton, 1963.

Rees, N. S. Pragmatics of language: Applications to normal and disordered language development. In R. L. Schiefelbusch (Ed.), *Bases of language intervention.* Baltimore: University Park Press, 1978.

Reichle, J. E., & Yoder, D. E. Assessment and early stimulation of communication in the severely and profoundly mentally retarded. In R. L. York & E. Edgar (Eds.), *Teaching the severely handicapped.* Vol. IV. Columbus, Ohio: Special Press, 1979.

Rincover, A., & Koegel, R. L. Setting generality and stimulus control in autistic children. *Journal of Applied Behavior Analysis,* 1975, **8,** 235–246.

Rogers-Warren, A., & Warren, S. F. Form and function in language learning and generalization. *Analysis and Intervention in Developmental Disabilities,* 1981, **1,** 389–404.

Rubin, K., Fein, G., & Vandenberg, B. Play. In P. H. Mussen (Ed.), *Carmichael's Manual on Child Psychology.* (4th ed.) New York: John Wiley. In press.

Ruder, K. F., Hermann, P., & Schiefelbusch, R. L. Effects of verbal imitation and comprehension training on verbal productions. *Journal of Psycholinguistic Research,* 1977, **6,** 59–72.

Rychtarik, R. G., & Bornstein, P. H. Training conversational skills in mentally retarded adults: A multiple baseline analysis. *Mental Retardation,* 1979, **17,** 289–293.

Sabsay, S. L. *Communicative competence in Down's syndrome adults.* Unpublished doctoral dissertation, University of California at Los Angeles, 1979.

Sacks, H., Schegloff, E. A., & Jefferson. A simplest systematics for the organization of turn-taking for conversation. *Language,* 1974, **50,** 696–735.

Sailor, W. Reinforcement and generalization of productive plural allomorphs in two retarded children. *Journal of Applied Behavior Analysis,* 1971, **4,** 305–310.

Sailor, W., Guess, D., Goetz, L., Schuler, A., Utley, B., & Baldwin, M. Language and severely handicapped persons: Deciding what to teach to whom. In W. Sailor, B. Wilcox, & L. Brown (Eds.), *Methods of instruction for severely handicapped students.* Baltimore: Paul Brookes, 1980.

Sailor, W., & Taman, T. Stimulus factors in the training of prepositional usage in three autistic children. *Journal of Applied Behavior Analysis,* 1972, **5,** 183.

Sanders, D. A. A model for communication. In L. L. Lloyd (Ed.), *Communication assessment and intervention strategies.* Baltimore: University Park Press, 1976.

Saunders, R., & Sailor, W. A comparison of three strategies of reinforcement on two-choice learning problems with severely retarded children. *AAESPH Review,* 1974, **4,** 323–333.

Schiefelbusch, R. L. Introduction. In R. L. Schiefelbusch (Ed.), *Bases of language intervention.* Baltimore: University Park Press, 1978.

Schiefelbusch, R. L. A philosophy of intervention. *Analysis and Intervention in Developmental Disabilities,* 1981, **1,** 373–388.

Schumaker, J., & Sherman, J. Training generative verb usage by imitation and reinforcement procedures. *Journal of Applied Behavior Analysis,* 1970, **3,** 273–287.

Skinner, B. F. *Verbal behavior.* New York: Appleton-Century-Crofts, 1957.

Smeets, P. M., & Striefel, S. Training the generative usage of article-noun responses in severely retarded males. *Journal of Mental Deficiency Research,* 1976, **20,** 121–127.

Snyder, L. Communicative and cognitive abilities and disabilities in the sensorimotor period. *Merrill-Palmer Quarterly,* 1978, **24,** 161–180.

Snyder, L. K., Lovitt, T. C., & Smith, J. O. Language training for the severely retarded: Five years of behavior analysis research. *Exceptional Children,* 1975, **42,** 7–15.

Sosne, J. B., Handleman, J. S., & Harris, S. L. Teaching spontaneous-functional speech to autistic-type children. *Mental Retardation,* 1979, **17,** 241–245.

Steckol, K. F., & Leonard, L. Sensorimotor development and the use of prelinguistic performatives. *Journal of Speech and Hearing Research,* 1981, **24,** 262–268.

Stevens-Long, J., & Rasmussen, M. The acquisition of simple and compound sentence structure in an autistic child. *Journal of Applied Behavior Analysis,* 1974, **7,** 473–480.

Stokes, T. F., & Baer, D. M. An implicit technology of generalization. *Journal of Applied Behavior Analysis,* 1977, **10,** 349–367.

Stokes, T. F., Baer, D. M., & Jackson, R. L. Programming the generalization of a greeting response in four retarded children. *Journal of Applied Behavior Analysis,* 1974, **7,** 599–610.

Striefel, S., & Wetherby, B. Instruction-following behavior of a retarded child and its controlling stimuli. *Journal of Applied Behavior Analysis,* 1973, **6,** 123–135.

Striefel, S., Wetherby, B., & Karlan, G. R. Establishing generative verb-noun instruction-following skills in retarded children. *Journal of Experimental Child Psychology,* 1976, **22,** 247–260.

Striefel, S., Wetherby, B., & Karlan, G. R. Developing generalized instruction-following behavior in the severely retarded. In C. E. Meyers (Ed.), *Quality of life in profoundly and severely retarded persons: Research foundations for improvement.* (American Association on Mental Deficiency Monograph Series, No. 3) Washington, D.C.: American Association on Mental Deficiency, 1978.

Twardosz, S., & Baer, D. M. Training two severely retarded adolescents to ask questions. *Journal of Applied Behavior Analysis,* 1973, **6,** 655–661.

Uzgiris, I. C., & Hunt, J. M. *Assessment in infancy.* Urbana: University of Illinois Press, 1975.

Warren, S. F., Rogers-Warren, A., Baer, D. M., Guess, D. Assessment and facilitation of language generalization. In W. Sailor, B. Wilcox, & L. Brown (Eds.), *Methods of instruction for severely handicapped students.* Baltimore: Paul H. Brookes, 1980.

Waryas, C. L., & Stremel-Campbell, K. Grammatical training for the language-delayed child. In R. L. Schiefelbusch (Ed.), *Language intervention strategies.* Baltimore: University Park Press, 1978.

Welch, S. J., & Pear, J. J. Generalization of naming responses to objects in the natural environment as a function of training stimulus modality with retarded children. *Journal of Applied Behavior Analysis,* 1980, **13,** 629–643.

Wheeler, A. J., & Sulzer, B. Operant training and generalization of a verbal response form in a speech-deficient child. *Journal of Applied Behavior Analysis,* 1970, **3,** 139–147.

27 NONSPEECH COMMUNICATION

Brian M. Campbell and
Audrey Shore Schwartz

Disorders of communication represent one of the most pervasive problems among the mentally retarded (Fristoe & Lloyd, 1979a). Difficulties range from minor problems in speech production to more or less total absence of speech and functional communication. Approximately one-fifth of all mentally retarded persons are functionally "speechless"—that is, they use few or no words and experience difficulty expressing even the most basic needs and wants (Miller, 1978, p. 388; Swann & Mittler, 1976).

In the past, the primary focus of intervention with nonvocal mentally retarded persons was to teach them to talk; that is, to develop normal speech, or speech at least adequate for communication purposes. More recently, interest has increasingly shifted to a communication orientation, where the primary goal of intervention is to help individuals develop the ability to communicate by whatever means at a level adequate to meet communication needs (Silverman, 1980). This new orientation has permitted the examination of what was formerly regarded by many as less desirable than having no speech at all, namely, the use of some form of nonvocal or nonspeech method of communication to augment or replace spoken communication that has failed to reach a functional level (Fristoe & Lloyd, 1979a).

In the following chapter, two broad categories of nonspeech communications are examined in relation to the field of mental retardation: manual signing and device-assisted communication systems.

Manual Signing

Although the field is still in its infancy, research on the use of manual signing systems with mentally retarded persons is growing steadily, and preliminary data strongly suggest that signing can represent a viable communication option for many mentally retarded individuals.

After briefly tracing the early history and evolution of the field, we will present and discuss the results of a critical review of 32 articles published within the past decade dealing with the use of signing by mentally retarded/developmentally disabled persons (including the deaf mentally retarded, the hearing mentally retarded, and persons with a primary diagnosis of autism). Our overall objective is to acquaint the reader with what has already taken place in the field and to point out directions for future research needs and priorities.

Historical Perspectives

Within the past decade, there has been a marked increase in the use of signing with mentally retarded persons having severe communication disorders. Tracing the history of its use with this population leads in two separate directions: to the field of deaf education in the United States, and to the laboratories of primate communication research.

Manual signing systems were originally developed in response to the needs of the deaf. Their history in the United States dates to the early 19th century, where deaf education for a long time was virtually synonymous with sign language. However, the uses of signing subsequently declined in the United States, largely because of assumptions adopted by deaf educators concerning the potential negative or harmful effect of signing on oral speech development. That is, it was believed that training in an alternative communication system such as manual signing would in some way inhibit, or otherwise interfere with, the development of oral speech.

A major consequence of this "oral-only" (or at least "oral first and foremost") philosophy was that typically no attempt was made to introduce signing to deaf children until after the child had reached the age of 11 (Moores, 1978)—and only then when it was established beyond a reasonable doubt that he/she was making little progress toward developing oral speech.

This climate of thought prevailed until the early 1960's, when the long-standing bias against manual signing began to lessen. In the wake of this change, it became much more acceptable to teach deaf children the use of manual signing simultaneously with oral speech, rather than simply as a "last resort." Importantly, this shift in orientation paved the way for considering the use of signing systems with deaf (nonvocal) mentally retarded persons (Berger, 1972; Hall & Talkington, 1970; Hoffmeister & Farmer, 1972; Kopchick, Rombach, & Smilovitz, 1975; Smeets & Striefel, 1976) and, more recently, with other nonvocal, but auditorily intact mentally retarded individuals.

Developments within the field of primate communication research also contributed to the history of signing in mental retardation. In 1969, Gardner and Gardner, making use of the chimpanzee's manual dexterity and propensity for imitation, successfully trained a baby chimp named Washoe signs from American Sign Language (ASL). Among Washoe's accomplishments were her ability to spontaneously name objects, generalize the use of a sign from the original object used in training to a wide class of referents, and appropriately use combinations of signs. This pioneer research (1) prepared the way for controlled studies of a number of issues related to the teaching of signs, including identification of the most efficient method and optimal order of teaching signs

(e.g., Fouts, 1973), (2) provided valuable information for planning and designing sign language programs for exceptional human populations, (3) served as a stimulus for renewed thinking about communication deficits experienced by nonverbal persons (Hobson & Duncan, 1979), and (4) gave impetus to the exploration of signing as a possible alternative method of communication for the severely communicatively impaired (Hobson & Duncan, 1979). Taken together, the developments within the field of deaf education and the chimp research combined to set the stage for the consideration of signing as a valid alternative to speech for the mentally retarded.

As the feasibility and potential benefits of signing became familiar to those people involved in educational planning for the mentally retarded, signing programs were initiated in many training settings. However, as the results of the surveys to be described below reveal, these initial efforts were often marked by confusion due to lack of basic knowledge.

Survey Perspectives

By the mid-1970s, it was clear to observers that sign programs (as well as other nonspeech programs) were appearing in increasing numbers in applied clinical settings in the United States. In an effort to assess the situation more closely, a number of national surveys were conducted. The results of the surveys (which produced some surprising findings) provide a picture of the past status of sign programs in applied settings in the United States and give insight into the types of unanswered questions and issues that remain today.

In 1975, Fristoe, in a national survey of speech, hearing, and language services for the mentally retarded, reported that over 10% of 689 respondents had used some type of nonspeech communication system in language training programs. The system most frequently reported was manual signing simultaneously with speech. The respondents wrote that they turned to a nonspeech system only after attempts to teach speech had failed, and that they were often surprised to experience success. Interestingly, most respondents stated that they were unaware that others in the field were using such systems.

Three years later, Fristoe and Lloyd (1978) published the results of a follow-up questionnaire sent to the 86 respondents from the 1975 survey who stated that they were using nonspeech communication systems. The results of the study are of special importance with regard to the status of manual signing systems, for the investigators analyzed in more detail the particular type of manual signing system used, and the reasons for choosing one system over another.

Of those respondents using manual signs, American Sign Language (ASL) was reported as the system most frequently used. (*Note*: ASL is the language used by most deaf adults in the United States today. It has its own morphological rules, and word order is not the same as English.) The pedagogical sign systems (i.e., those that are not a true language but use ASL and other signs in English word order) most frequently reported in use were Signed English and Signing Exact English (SEE-II).[1] However, Fristoe and Lloyd (1978) questioned the reliability of these findings, for they found a discrepancy between what the respondents actually *called* the systems, and their description of how they actually *used* the signs. Apparently, those claiming to have used ASL were actually using some of the signs of ASL in English word order, i.e., one of the pedagogical sign systems. When asked on what basis they had chosen a particular system, most respondents indicated that the choice was based simply on whether or not someone on the staff had any knowledge of a particular system.

Shortly after Fristoe's 1975 survey, the Division of Speech Pathology and Audiology of the American Association on Mental Deficiency was commissioned to survey the use of sign language programs in special education. The survey was designed to gather detailed information on the reasons for choosing signing as the preferred nonspeech system, the types of signing systems used, how and where they were being taught, and how their effectiveness was being assessed. The results of the survey were subsequently reported by Goodman, Wilson, and Bornstein (1978), who evaluated 138 questionnaires returned from a total of 28 states, representing approximately 4,000 clients. Although no distinction was made between primary and multiple diagnosis, it was reported that the largest diagnostic group in which signing was utilized was the severely mentally retarded (79%), followed by moderately mentally retarded (72%), cerebral palsied (56%), profoundly mentally retarded (53%), and autistic (42%). Four out of five programs were less than three years old, and 79% of the programs had fewer than 25 clients. Unfortunately, no breakdown of the types of training settings represented (e.g., residential institution, public school, etc.) was given. A speech pathologist directed most programs, but identification of who was actually teaching the signs was not reported. Although clients of all ages were being taught signs, the respondents of this survey reported that approximately half of the clients were children (most of whom were under five years old).

When asked why signing was selected as the nonspeech system of choice, respondents stated that their decision was based solely on an evaluation of the client's manual dexterity. If the client was physically capable of making signs, signing was preferred over other nonspeech systems because of its convenience (allowing for more spontaneous and frequent communication) and because it is based on an existing natural language. As Fristoe and Lloyd had found earlier, the choice of a particular sign system was based primarily on staff familiarity with a given system. Confusion over which sign system was actually being used was also evident.

Although 70% of the respondents said that the choice of sign lexicon was based on the "needs and interests of the client," available data led the authors to believe it was determined more by which signs were included in the reference books used and/or which materials were available for testing sign comprehension. The survey data on teaching procedures were also confusing. Many of the respondents made no distinction between the formal teaching of signs and the mere use of signs in the presence of the clients, in the hope that they would "pick it up."

Research Perspectives

The results of a critical review of 32 recently published articles dealing with the use of signs by mentally retarded/developmentally disabled persons are summarized and discussed below. The major findings from the analysis are presented in Table 27.1. The articles included in the review are not exhaustive of the field. However, the sample is broadly representative of current research in the area.

OVERVIEW

Fifteen of the articles involved subjects with a primary diagnosis of mental retardation, five dealt with subjects with a combined diagnosis of deafness and mental retardation, and twelve involved subjects with a primary diagnosis of autism (with or without a secondary or combined diagnosis of mental retardation). Approximately half (47%) of the articles were *experimental* (involving procedures that would allow for statistical inferences regarding relationships among variables) and the other half were *outcome oriented* (before-and-after, or AB, designs). Approximately one-fourth (28%) were single-subject studies.

Nearly all of the studies indicated that operant training techniques were used in teaching signs. However, the studies varied greatly in the number of procedural details given, thus often making replication difficult, if not impossible. There were also major differences in the length of the studies (which ranged from under one month [16%] to over six months [22%] and in the length and frequency of training sessions.

SUBJECT SELECTION CRITERIA

Approximately two-thirds of all the articles reviewed made no mention of criteria for inclusion in the sign program or experiment other than lack of speech. The remaining articles (37%) specified various criteria, including (1) ability to imitate signs (Kohl, Karlan, & Heal, 1979; Kotkin, Simpson, & DeSanto, 1978; Stremel-Campbell, Cantrell, & Hall, 1977; Van Biervliet, 1977), (2) ability to imitate words (Kotkin et al., 1978; Van Biervliet, 1977), (3) receptive abilities such as understanding "What's this?" (Kotkin et al., 1977), and (4) ability to discriminate objects visually-verbally (Stremel-Campbell et al., 1977). Other criteria mentioned were specific to the requirements of the particular experiment (Bricker, 1972; Kohl et al., 1979).

The time and energy investment necessary to learn manual signing would undoubtedly be substantial for many handicapped persons, and the question of who would be most likely to benefit from training in such systems deserves careful attention and empirically based answers. Although research has thus far served to demonstrate the feasibility of teaching signing to mentally retarded and other developmentally disabled persons (see below), it has by no means been established that signing is universally applicable within this heterogeneous population, or preferable over nonspeech methods of communication to be discussed later in this chapter.[2]

THE CHOICE OF A SIGN SYSTEM

Over half (56%) of the articles reviewed gave no explanation or description of the sign system used in the training program or experiment. In most instances, it appeared that isolated individual signs (typically ASL) were taught by pairing the sign with a particular spoken word and its referent. The remaining articles claimed to use a signed speech approach. That is, in teaching signs the instructor spoke in English sentences and simultaneously signed the spoken words. However, the specific pedagogical system, e.g., Signed English, or Signing Exact English (SEE-II) was usually not specified. In many instances it was difficult to determine whether a sign was used for every spoken word in the sentence or whether some parts of speech were omitted. This situation was the case regardless of the signs used.[3] The few exceptions included one study which reported using Manual English, a system in which all words are signed or finger spelled with their morphological markers (Grinnell et al., 1976), and another that described the use of the Paget-Gorman Sign System in combination with spoken English (Fenn & Rowe, 1975).

At present, little is known about the relative merits of signed speech systems as compared with other manual signing systems. However, recent research is beginning to yield important data relevant to the consideration of such systems for the mentally retarded. For example, Brady and Smouse (1978), working with an autistic child, found increased instruction following with simultaneous sign and speech as compared with signing alone or speech alone. Similar results have been reported by Barrerra, Lobato-Barrerra, and Sulzer-Azaroff (1980). One recent study attempted a comparison of two signed speech systems (Kohl et al., 1979), and found that complete signing and partial signing of sentences yielded significantly more instruction-following behavior than speech alone.

Two studies dealing with autistic children have used an augmented signed speech approach. Krug et al. (1979) integrated signed speech with the Non-SLIP program, a program in which a system of coded chips is used to teach certain prespeech skills such as matching, sequencing, and associating concrete symbols with abstract concepts. Benaroya et al. (1977) describe their training as a "multisensory-intrusion approach," utilizing various audiovisual instructional devices during training.

THE CHOICE OF A SIGN VOCABULARY

Many of the articles (37%) reviewed gave either no rationale for the choice of particular signs used in training, or no description of the vocabulary other than the number of words or word class (e.g., nouns, verbs, animals, foods). Several studies indicated that signs were chosen because of either their reinforcement value (12%) or the assumed high interest level of the object and/or activity referents (12%). However, only one study (Krug et al., 1979) provided evidence that the referents were, in fact, relevant to the clients.

Other studies (19%) indicated that vocabulary items were chosen because of their meaningfulness and functional relevance to the person's environment, but no evidence was presented to suggest that a functional analysis of the client's environment was actually conducted. Other decisions regarding choice of vocabulary were based on (a) the client's familiarity with the referents (16%), (b) the availability of pictures for training (12%), (c) iconicity (12%), (d) ease of movement in making the sign or motoric complexity (16%), (e) whether motoric elements of the sign were already present in the client's repertoire (3%), (f) the ability of the client to discriminate movements involved in a particular sign (12%), (g) whether signs were "touch signs" (6%), and (h) whether the referent elicited an active response from the listener (3%).

The issue of selecting a sign vocabulary has only recently emerged as an area of special concern within the manual signing literature. However, important

Table 27.1. Manual Signing: A Critique of Recent Literature in Mental Retardation/Developmental Disabilities

	NUMBER OF SUBJECTS			PRIMARY DIAGNOSIS			SUBJECT SELECTION CRITERIA		RESEARCH DESIGN		PROCEDURAL DETAILS		LENGTH OF STUDY			
	1	2	3	4	5	6	7	8	9	10	11	12	13	14	15	16
Booth (1978)	X			X			X		X	X	X		X			
Bricker (1972)			X	X				X			X		X			X
Grinnel et al. (1976)			X	X				X	X	X		X		X		
Hobson & Duncan (1979)			X	X			X			X		X		X		
Kahn (1977)			X	X			X		X		X	X		X	X	
Kohl (1981)				X			X	X	X						X	
Kohl et al. (1979)		X		X				X	X		X		X	X		
Kotkin et al. (1978)		X		X				X	X		X		X	X		
Linville (1977)				X			X			X		X	X		X	
Reich (1978)			X	X			X		X		X		X			
Richardson (1975)			X	X			X			X	X	X		X		
Salisbury et al. (1978)		X		X				X	X	X	X	X		X		X
Stremel-Campbell et al. (1977)	X		X	X			X		X		X	X		X		
Topper (1975)	X		X	X			X		X	X	X	X		X		X
Van Biervliet (1977)			X	X				X	X	X	X					X
Fenn & Rowe (1975)			X		X		X	X	X		X	X		X		
Hall & Talkington (1970)			X		X		X			X		X		X		
Hoffmeister & Farmer (1972)			X		X		X					X		X		
Kopchick et al. (1975)			X		X		X		X		X	X				
Smeets & Striefel (1976)	X				X		X	X	X		X					X
Barrera et al. (1980)	X					X	X	X	X	X	X	X			X	
Benaroya et al. (1977)			X			X	X			X		X				X
Bonvillian & Nelson (1976)	X					X	X			X	X			X		X
Brady & Smouse (1978)	X					X	X		X		X			X		
Carr et al. (1978)		X				X	X		X			X		X		
Casey (1978)		X				X	X		X			X		X	X	
Fulwiler & Fouts (1976)	X					X			X	X	X					
Konstantareas et al. (1979)		X				X		X		X	X				X	
Krug et al. (1979)			X			X		X		X	X				X	
Salvin et al. (1977)	X					X	X			X				X	X	
Schaeffer et al. (1977)		X				X	X			X				X		
Webster et al. (1973)	X					X	X			X		X		X		
Number out of total	9	8	15	15	5	12	20	12	15	17	17	15	5	14	7	6
Percentage of total	28	25	47	47	16	37	63	37	47	53	53	47	16	44	22	19

Table continued on p. 416.

Table 27.1. (continued)

	SIGN VOCABULARY USED			SIGN SYSTEM USED		SIGN SELECTION CRITERIA												BEHAVIORAL IMPACTS				COMMUNICATION IMPACTS		GENERALIZATION	
	17	18	19	20	21	22	23	24	25	26	27	28	29	30	31	32	33	34	35	36	37	38	39	40	41
Booth (1978)	X			X																					
Bricker (1972)		X			X																			X	X
Grinnel et al. (1976)	X			X						X	X											X		X	X
Hobson & Duncan (1979)	X		X		X		X	X											X		X				X
Kahn (1977)	X				X	X						X	X	X	X	X									X
Kohl (1981)	X			X								X	X	X											X
Kohl et al. (1979)	X		X		X							X	X		X										X
Kotkin et al. (1978)	X			X	X							X	X												X
Linville (1977)	X			X	X					X	X											X			X
Reich (1978)			X		X			X											X		X	X			X
Richardson (1975)			X		X												X					X	X		X
Salisbury et al. (1978)			X		X		X															X	X		X
Stremel-Campbell et al. (1977)	X		X	X	X	X	X	X								X			X	X		X	X		X
Topper (1975)		X		X																					X
Van Biervliet (1977)		X		X	X							X													X
Fenn & Rowe (1975)		X	X	X					X	X								X				X		X	
Hall & Talkington (1970)			X		X						X							X				X			X
Hoffmeister & Farmer (1972)	X				X						X									X		X			X
Kopchick et al. (1975)			X	X																		X			X
Smeets & Striefel (1976)			X		X																			X	
Barrera et al. (1980)	X			X	X					X												X			X
Benaroya et al. (1977)			X	X	X					X			X					X			X	X	X		X
Bonvillian & Nelson (1976)	X			X	X										X					X		X			X
Brady & Smouse (1978)			X		X													X	X	X	X	X			
Carr et al. (1978)	X			X	X														X					X	
Casey (1978)	X			X					X									X	X	X				X	
Fulwiler & Fouts (1976)	X			X		X	X											X	X	X	X	X	X	X	X
Konstantareas et al. (1979)		X		X		X	X																		
Krug et al. (1979)			X	X				X														X	X	X	X
Salvin et al. (1977)	X		X		X																	X		X	X
Schaeffer et al. (1977)	X		X																			X	X	X	X
Webster et al. (1973)	X			X	X															X				X	X
Number out of total	17	4	11	15	18	4	5	6	2	5	4	4	5	1	4	2	1	6	7	7	4	16	8	7	25
Percentage of total	53	12	34	47	56	12	16	19	6	16	12	12	16	3	12	6	3	19	22	22	12	50	25	22	78

416

KEY

Number of Subjects
1. One only
2. Two-five
3. Over five

Primary Diagnosis
4. Mentally retarded
5. Deaf mentally retarded
6. Autistic

Subject Selection Criteria
7. No selection criteria other than lack of speech
8. Certain selection criteria specified

Research Design
9. Experimental
10. Outcome oriented

Number of Procedural Details Given
11. Many
12. Few or none

Length of Study
13. Under one month
14. One-six months
15. Over six months
16. Unspecified

Sign 'Vocabulary' Used
17. ASL or ASL derivations
18. Other
19. Unspecified

Sign 'System' Used
20. Signed speech
21. Unspecified

Sign Selection Criteria
22. Reinforcement value
23. S's preference for objects, activities, etc.
24. Meaningfulness & functional relevance
25. Appropriateness to situational demands
26. S's familiarity with referents
27. Availability of pictures for training
28. Iconicity
29. Ease of movement in making sign or motoric complexity
30. Whether motoric elements of sign in client's repertoire
31. Ability to discriminate movements
32. Touch signs?
33. Whether sign elicits active response from listener

Behavioral Impacts
34. Increased self help/independence
35. Increased social interaction/positive effect
36. Decreased disruptive behavior
37. Increased attention

Communication Impacts
38. Spontaneous signing
39. Spontaneous vocalizations

Generalization Planned and Tested For?
40. Yes
41. No

information has already been forthcoming. For example, Fristoe and Lloyd (1980), in an article which gives suggestions and a rationale for planning an initial expressive sign lexicon, have recently addressed the question of which signs should be taught from a developmental perspective. Their insightful and thorough evaluation is an excellent source of information for anyone planning a signing program.

Elsewhere, two experimental studies have shed light on the issues of iconicity and motoric requirements in the acquisition of manual signs. Griffith and Robinson (1980) found that iconic (transparent or guessable) signs increased learning in 36 moderate to severely mentally retarded children. Visual similarity of signs interfered with acquisition. In a similar fashion, Kohl (1981) varied sign dimensions according to iconic vs. abstract, touch vs. nontouch, and symmetrical vs. asymmetrical. She found that touch signs and symmetrical signs were learned faster by eight severely handicapped students.

Another area of recent investigation concerns the order of teaching certain signs. Stremel-Campbell et al. (1977) reported an increase in errors in those training sets in which two signs representing the same conceptual class (e.g., "shirt" and "pants") were taught. Watters, Wheeler, and Watters (1981) varied the order of receptive and expressive training with four autistic children. They found that fewer acquisition trials were needed when expressive skills were taught before receptive skills, which suggests that expressive use facilitated the learning of receptive use. Teaching the receptive use first interfered with the expressive use of signs.

IMPACTS

All studies reviewed reported positive findings, as measured by (a) changes in receptive skills, as indicated by the ability to follow instructions; and/or (b) changes in expressive skills, as demonstrated by the ability to label or describe objects, pictures, or activities; and/or (c) changes in both expressive and receptive skills, as shown by the ability to respond by signing to simple signed questions or commands. Taken as a class, the research articles strongly support a conclusion that signing can be successfully taught to mentally retarded/developmentally disabled persons.

In addition to these impacts, a number of favorable changes were also reported (primarily in anecdotal form). For example, one-fifth (19%) of the studies reported an increase in self-help/independent behaviors, and approximately one-fourth (22%) reported increased social interaction and/or positive affect. In addition, approximately one-fourth (22%) reported a decrease in disruptive and/or bizarre behavior. Many of the studies were represented in more than one category.

Perhaps the most significant impacts noted were those of spontaneous signing (observed in half [50%] of the studies) and spontaneous vocalizations (reported in one-fourth [25%] of the studies). These findings provide a fertile source of hypotheses for future research into sign use as (a) a means of functional communication and (b) serving a facilitating function in speech production. This latter finding has particularly intriguing implications. It is somewhat ironic that the use of signing, most frequently chosen after a history of failure in speech intervention programs, may actually be gaining acceptance because of its possible speech facilitating function. Schaeffer (1980) presents an especially cogent discussion of theories, methods, and directions for future research in teaching signed speech as an intermediate stage between spontaneous sign language and spontaneous speech.

GENERALIZATION

The importance of generalization of learning from training settings to other environments, such as the residential setting, or home, has been widely recognized in the field of mental retardation. However, only a handful (22%) of the studies gave evidence of systematically building this into the intervention program or experimental design. Earlier, we reported that many of the studies considered the importance, meaningfulness, and relevance of sign referents when selecting a lexicon; however, the usefulness of this strategy is questionable if the client is unable to communicate with significant others outside the training setting.

Only about one-third (31%) of the total sample of studies made reference to the participation of parents and/or caretakers as part of the program. Among those that did, participation ranged from merely encouraging the use of signs, to providing signing classes, to structured programs with counseling for parents and/or caretakers (Bonvillian & Nelson, 1976; Casey, 1978; Schaeffer et al., 1977; Konstantareas et al., 1979). Of particular note is the program designed by Schaeffer et al. (1977), which provides for parental observations of therapist-client training sessions, therapist observation and feedback of the parent-child interaction, sign language classes, and counseling sessions. In addition, Casey (1978) has investigated the use of a manual sign language program in daily mother-child laboratory sessions; she found that her parent-child program facilitated generalization of communicative behavior to the child's total environment. In summary, it would appear that parental/caretaker participation is an important factor to consider when designing sign programs for children.

The use of signing with the mentally retarded is a relatively new phenomenon. Nonspeech communication programs are often based on those originally designed for clients with a primary diagnosis other than mental retardation, such as the deaf mentally retarded, autistic, and severely physically handicapped. Actually, it is often the case that a study of reporting group results is composed of a heterogeneous group of "severely dysfunctional" or "severely communicatively impaired" clients. This situation not only makes it difficult to assess the results of a particular study, but also challenges the validity of generalizing the results to any particular population. As the field grows and more information is assimilated into the planning of sign programs, it is hoped that it will be possible to determine an optimal intervention program for a particular individual. Among the client-related variables that should be considered and specifically examined in future research (in addition to diagnostic label) are:

1. cognitive skills,
2. information-processing, perceptual, and physical capabilities,
3. handicapping conditions, and
4. reinforcement history for communication.

Future research on program development should investigate the following variables as they relate to each of the populations which may use signing as a primary means of communication:

1. salience of vocabulary items, including the importance of visual, motoric, tactual, and motivational aspects of the signs;
2. appropriateness of the sign system, including the relative efficacy of initially emphasizing functional communication as opposed to emphasis on the structure of language;
3. frequency and length of training sessions;
4. training procedures, including the best order and grouping of signs to be taught and the optimal order of teaching receptive and expressive skills; and
5. generalization of skills to different settings and people, including analysis of opportunities for communication outside the training setting.

Finally, perhaps the most intriguing area of future research will be the investigation of the phenomenona

of spontaneous signing and spontaneous speech— why they occur, and how they can be facilitated.

Device-Assisted Systems

Mentally retarded persons who are severely physically handicapped and motorically restricted would undoubtedly have a poor prognosis for developing functional communication by means of the manual sign systems discussed in the previous section. In the past, our options for helping such persons were limited. However, recent advances and innovations in the field of nonspeech communication aids and devices for the handicapped (Silverman, 1980; Vanderheiden & Grilley, 1976) are beginning to unlock new potentials for this formerly isolated population. It is becoming increasingly clear that many of the traditional barriers to communication can be overcome.

However, the use of device-assisted systems within the field of mental retardation has thus far been remarkably limited (Fristoe & Lloyd, 1978) and systematic experimental research meagre (Fristoe & Lloyd, 1979a; Mulick, Scott, Gaines & Campbell, 1983). The present section provides basic information about device-assisted systems, reviews pertinent literature, and discusses factors relevant to future developments and applications in relation to the field of mental retardation.

Design Features of Device-Assisted Systems

Communication products differ in physical appearance and range from simple communication (or conversation) boards, to sophisticated electronically controlled systems (Vanderheiden & Harris-Vanderheiden, 1976; Vanderheiden, 1978). But despite their seeming heterogeneity, all such systems are reducible to a limited number of design features, or components (Silverman, 1980).

PHYSICAL RESPONSE

All device-assisted systems are activated by some type of physical response made by the user. This may involve the combined coordinated action of several muscle groups and consist of a fairly sophisticated skill (such as pointing to a word located on a static display), or it may involve the action of more or less isolated muscle groups and less complex motor patterns (such as raising or lowering the index finger). Our technology has advanced to the point where virtually any controlled motor movement can serve as the basis for establishing functional communication. By means of the switching mechanisms described below, physical responses that could serve communication purposes would include those involving: the upper extremities (e.g., moving the shoulder, elbow, wrist, finger, or thumb), the face and neck (e.g., moving the head from side to side, looking to the left or to the right, smiling, blowing, biting, or extending and retracting the tongue), and those involving the trunk and lower extremities (e.g., trunk flexion or rotation, hip rotation, knee flexion, or knee extension). In general, the more intact the individual's motor function, the greater the number of systems and the more efficient the systems which it would be possible for him or her to use (Silverman, 1980).

SWITCHING MECHANISMS

Switching mechanisms interface the user with the communication system. The user pushes, pulls, touches, blows on, or makes any of a variety of movements in association with one or more switching mechanisms. These include: push switches, push plates, position switches, proximity switches, pneumatic switches, or sound-controlled switches.

CONTROL ELECTRONICS

The primary function of control electronics is to interface the switching mechanism with the display (or displays) (see below). This function may be accomplished by something as simple as supplying electrical power to the communication system, or may involve complex operations such as storing, retrieving, or transforming information within the system (based, for example, on the signals introduced by the user via the switching mechanism). In many instances the control electronics of a system consist of a microprocessor (Silverman, 1980). Control electronics, especially in the form of microcomputers (both hardware and software), will undoubtedly play a major role in the future development of systems for the mentally retarded. Many of the restrictions to communication previously imposed by severely limited cognitive skills (such as deficits in short- and long-term memory) may be offset by the memory and retrieval systems available via the computer.

DISPLAYS

Electronic switching mechanisms, in association with appropriate control electronics, can be used to indicate or reproduce messages on several types of readout devices, or displays. These include: noise, light, or vibration generators; rotary scanning displays; rectangular matrix displays; CRT (cathode ray tube) displays; LED (light-emitting diode) displays; electric typewriters; and speech generators (synthesizers). In nonelectronic device-assisted systems, the display generally consists of some type of communication board (containing a predetermined set of communication symbols) or some type of magnetic board, or tray (on which symbols are placed in a specified sequence).

SYMBOL SYSTEMS

The purpose of all device-assisted systems of communication is to help the user gain access to, or develop, systems of symbolic formulation and expression. A basic knowledge of symbols and symbol systems is therefore essential to understanding the range of possible assistive devices.

Briefly, a symbol is a patterned group of stimuli that have come to be associated with a particular object, event, activity, etc. Symbols "stand for" something else, in the sense that they are not the actual objects, events, activities, etc., but rather they are merely associated with these through past learning. Two types of symbols can be distinguished. First, there are symbols that resemble the thing they are intended to represent (e.g., a "stick-figure" of a human male, standing for the concept "man"). Secondly, there are symbols that are more or less arbitrary, in that they bear no relationship to their referents in terms of appearance (e.g., the printed word "dog," standing for the concept "dog"). At times, both classes of symbol are used in combination (e.g., rebuses). Individual symbols usually form part of a symbol system, whose members share a common derivational history, various criterial features for inclusion in the set, and associated rules (syntactic, semantic, and pragmatic) governing permissible combinations and sequences of two or more elements. It is important to point out that most symbols can be encoded in more than one physical medium and spatial dimension, including two-dimensional and three-dimensional solids, light, or sound. Depending on the medium selected they can be made available to one or more sensory modalities—including visual, auditory, or tactile. For example, the letters of the English language can be represented in two-dimensional solid form (e.g., written or printed letters on a piece of paper), three-dimensional solid form (e.g., plastic letters of the alphabet), light (e.g., subtitles of foreign movies), and sound (e.g., saying, or speaking, each letter in a word). Through these various mediums, letter symbols could be made available to sight, touch, and hearing. Symbols and symbol systems are not intrinsic to any particular device-assisted system of communication, although some may lend themselves more to one than to another.

At present, there are no clearly established guidelines for selecting one symbol system over another.

The subject is complex, and will undoubtedly demand a good deal of consideration in the future. Factors that will need to be weighed in relation to each system (a number of which are reviewed in more depth by Silverman [1980]) include (1) the specific medium in which symbols can be conveyed (this might be important, for example, in relation to an individual's sensory deficits or strengths), (2) the type of symbol involved (e.g., symbols that resemble referents may be easier to acquire than arbitrary symbols), (3) the rules for combining or sequencing symbols (e.g., syntactic and semantic rules may differ in terms of complexity, and concomitantly, in terms of ease of learning), (4) the ability of the system to convey information concerning the past, present, or future, as well as concrete or abstract ideas (such factors would be important, for example, in relation to an individual's current and/or anticipated communication needs), (5) the restrictiveness of the system, in terms of acceptability to others (e.g., the least restrictive system would generally be preferable, and (6) whether, or to what degree, the system would be understandable to relatively untrained or unsophisticated observers (this might be especially important, for example, in terms of the amount of reinforcement the other person receives for helping the individual to communicate). With these points in mind, the following are among the symbol systems which have already been used, or which could be potentially used, in association with device-assisted communication systems for the mentally retarded.

Artificial Speech. The English language is available in spoken form by means of machine-generated (recorded or synthesized) speech. Words, phrases, or sentences can be generated, or reproduced, which are more or less structurally equivalent to spoken English.

Blissymbolics (or Semantography). This is a pictographic, idiographic, and arbitrary symbol system developed by Charles K. Bliss (Bliss, 1965). The system consists of about 100 basic elements, which can be used without modification, or combined in various ways to form a vocabulary of almost infinite size. While most Blissymbols are semantically based (i.e., they encode meaning), a few encode strictly grammatical information. The English word equivalent (or other language equivalent) is always printed under each Blissymbol. Vocabulary items can be used singly, or concatenated in a fashion similar to the linguistic structure of English (or some other language).

Braille. This alternative method of encoding and decoding spelled English was developed by Louis Braille in 1824 for use by the visually impaired or totally blind. There are 63 characters in the system, which are made from raised dot patterns. The characters represent letters of the alphabet, numbers, and frequently used letter combinations. Braille can be used to encode any word or sentence in the English language. Characters can be "written" by a device called a slate, or by a Braille typewriter. The system is usually decoded (read) by passing the fingers lightly over the characters.

English Language (Spelled). This symbol system is highly flexible and needs little explanation. It consists of 26 conventional elements (the letters of the alphabet), which are combined to form words, which in turn are concatenated, according to syntactic and semantic rules of combination, to form meaningful phrases, or complete sentences.

Picture Systems. Two-dimensional photographs or drawings, used singly or in combination, can form the basis of a nearly limitless variety of symbol systems. Such systems appear to be especially useful for communicating basic needs and wants.

Premack's Plastic Symbol Language. This symbol system was developed by David Premack (Premack, 1971; Premack & Premack, 1972) to investigate the ability of the chimpanzee to acquire human language. As originally described, the system consists of pieces of plastic, each representing a specific word, that are backed with metal so that they will adhere to a magnetized slate. Sentences are formed by arranging symbols vertically on a magnetized writing board. Rules for sequencing symbols were derived from an analysis of the English language. Individual symbols are abstract in configuration and do not resemble the word or concept they are intended to represent.

Rebuses. Rebuses are used in a predominantly pictographic symbol system which uses a single line drawing, several drawings, or a combination of letters of the alphabet and drawings, to represent standard English words. They can be used singly, or combined in the same manner as English words, to form meaningful phrases or sentences. A dictionary-like compilation of rebus symbols has been prepared by Clarke, Davies, and Woodcock (1974), which contains rebuses for more than 2,000 words.

Yerkish Language. Developed by von Glasersfeld (1977) for the LANA Project at Yerkes Regional Research Center (Rumbaugh, 1977), this system was also developed to study language acquisition of the chimpanzee. Yerkish consists of nine abstract design elements, readily discernible from each other, which can be used singly, or in combinations of two, three, or four (by superimposing one upon the other), to yield 225 different lexigrams. Each lexigram is reproduced on one of seven background colors, which categorize lexigrams on the basis of meaning (e.g., a blue background signifies lexigrams that can encode activities). Lexigrams generally correspond to a single English word, and can be combined, in a manner roughly corresponding to English syntactic and semantic structure to form longer messages. Yerkish symbols are arbitrary; their meaning is assigned through training.

Major Categories of Device-Assisted Systems

Three major categories of device-assisted systems may be distinguished: (a) *manipulable symbol systems*, where the user communicates by picking up a type of manipulable language symbol (such as a plastic letter of the alphabet) and placing it on some form of display (such as a wooden tray, magnetic board, table top, or other surface), (b) *communication (conversation) boards*, where the user communicates by indicating directly (e.g., with a head-stick pointer or patterned movements of the eyes) or indirectly (e.g., by means of electronic control systems) the particular symbol desired from a limited array available on some type of surface, and (c) *electronic communication systems*, where the user encodes and transmits symbols by means of electrically activated switching mechanisms and one or more electrically activated displays. Research relevant to each of these systems is discussed below.

MANIPULABLE SYMBOL SYSTEMS

As was the case with manual sign systems, our knowledge and understanding of device-assisted systems has profited greatly from research efforts aimed at teaching language to nonhuman primates. In particular, the pioneer work of D. Premack and his associates represents a signal contribution to the field of communication prosthetics.

Initially, Premack and an associate (Premack & Schwartz, 1966) embarked on a project to produce a mechanical device capable of producing complex auditory stimuli for communication purposes. The device (which may be thought of as a forerunner to modern-day speech synthesis devices) was activated by a joy stick and the sound produced was similar to that of an electric organ. Although the system was eventually abandoned (most likely because of inadequate technology), there remained good reason to use the chim-

panzee as a "drawing board for delineating strategies and tactics relevant to communication problems" (Hollis & Carrier, 1975, p. 407). Several years later, Premack (1971) developed a much more successful prosthetic communication system.

Premack devised a communication system based on manipulable plastic symbols. Each piece of plastic (consisting of meaningless geometric shapes) corresponded to a word in the English language. The chimp was taught to communicate by placing the appropriate piece of plastic (backed with metal) on a magnetized slate. Premack was highly successful at teaching his subject to "read" and to "write" by means of manipulable symbols, so that his chimp eventually acquired a functional vocabulary of over 130 words. The training included a functional analysis of language behavior, step-by-step training procedures, and errorless training methods (where only one unknown was introduced at a time).

Premack's work demonstrated that the ability to produce spoken language is not a *sine qua non* for effective communication. That is, the functions of language are not limited to the auditory-vocal modality. He was able to show the fundamental equivalence of plastic symbol "words" with spoken language, and that linguistic communication, per se, "can exist independent of many of the characteristics traditionally considered basic to its existence" (Carrier, 1976, p. 527). Importantly, he also demonstrated the applicability of learning theory to the analysis of device-assisted communication systems, and the successful use of applied behavioral analysis procedures and operant training techniques.

Following in Premack's footsteps, Carrier and his associates (Parsons & Carrier, 1971; Schmidt, Carrier, & Parsons, 1971; see Carrier, 1976) successfully replicated the same basic procedures used by Premack with three severely mentally retarded children (aged 8, 12, and 14) and with seven 2–3-year-old Down's syndrome children. Apart from the obvious importance of demonstrating the feasibility of utilizing such systems with human subjects, the study contained an important, and somewhat surprising, result. It was found that the use of the plastic symbol system generalized to the child's natural language, spoken English. That is, it appeared that the device-assisted system facilitated the development of oral speech. Premack (Premack & Premack, 1974) himself later added additional supportive evidence regarding the facilitative effect of his symbol system in a study involving an 8-year-old autistic child who was totally lacking in speech. Like Carrier, Premack found that training in the plastic symbol system generalized to the child's spoken language. He hypothesized that the acquisition of the artificial symbol system might prove to be a useful "crutch," which could be discarded later, for helping language deficient persons acquire natural language.

McLean and McLean (1974) subsequently reported another successful utilization of the Premack-type symbol system with nonverbal autistic children. Importantly, the authors extended the scope of previous research methodology and the strength of previous findings by demonstrating interexperimenter and intersetting generalizations, as well as maintenance of trained responses.

Carrier (1974) later attempted a broaded based and more impressive demonstration of the use of Premack-type symbols with the mentally retarded. For this study, six severely and profoundly mentally retarded institutionalized children served as subjects. Of the 60 subjects who learned the prerequisite motor behavior (i.e., picking up a symbol and placing it on a tray) for utilizing the system, all subjects successfully learned the use of 10 nouns, and subjects showed generalization to post-test (magazine) pictures. Error rates for all subjects were low, and the approximate time necessary to complete the training was a very modest two hours.

The pilot work of Carrier and his associates finally culminated in the development of a comprehensive set of training programs (based on similar behavioral methodology) referred to as the Non-Speech Language Initiation Program (Non-SLIP). As the title suggests, this program (which is commercially available, Carrier and Peak, 1975) was not intended as a total language training program; rather; its aim was to utilize Premack-type symbols in an effort to introduce the fundamental cognitive operations involved in learning and using symbol systems, or languages (Carrier, 1976). The basic assumption underlying the program was established several years earlier, namely, that learning to use the symbols will facilitate other ways of communicating.

Despite some promising beginnings, many questions and issues remain regarding the use of Premack-type symbols with the mentally retarded. The standard Premack-type symbol system does not readily provide the user with a functional communication system for use in the natural environment. This is because such symbols are unintelligible to untrained observers unless they are accompanied by English words attached to them. Another disadvantage of the Premack-type communication system is that the user is limited by physical space requirements as to the number of symbols that would be practical to have freely available. Another issue that needs to be clarified is that of selection criteria for those who would be most likely to benefit from training with the Premack-type symbols. The rule of thumb in the past seems to have been

to use the systems with persons who are severely or profoundly mentally retarded, are more or less totally lacking in functional speech, have consistently failed to respond to traditional speech therapy, and possess sufficient motor function to make the prerequisite motor responses.

Several advantages of Premack-type symbols should also be noted. The cost of components is minimal. The motor movements involved in the system do not appear to require the same degree of elaborate differentiation as would be involved in oral speech. The symbols can be both seen and felt, which might be of particular advantage for persons with visual acuity problems. Finally, because symbols are on permanent display during the process of encoding messages, they place minimal demands on factors involving short-term memory and sustained attention.

Finally, other systems based on a manipulable symbol format could also be developed and various combinations of systems could be constructed. For example, English word equivalents could be written under Yerkish symbols, and reproduced on a small piece of plastic. Some such systems could potentially offer distinct advantages over the Premack-type manipulable symbol system in terms of their intelligibility to the dominant linguistic community.

COMMUNICATION BOARDS

Communication boards can vary along several parameters including size, shape, protability, construction materials, the number of symbols involved, the arrangement of symbols on a display, the type of symbol system utilized, and the methods of which the user indicates the symbol (or symbol sequence) to be communicated. General information regarding the design and clinical application of communication boards is available in several sources (e.g., McDonald, 1976; McDonald & Schultz, 1973; Silverman, 1980; Vanderheiden & Grilley, 1976; Vanderheiden & Harris-Vanderheiden, 1976).

The use of communication boards with the mentally retarded is a relatively recent development, which appears to have been stimulated largely by reports of the successful use of such systems with cerebral palsied children (e.g., McDonald & Schultz, 1973; Sayre, 1963), and the emergence of Blissymbolics as an alternative symbol system for the nonverbal mentally retarded (Fristoe & Lloyd, 1978; Harris-Vanderheiden, 1976a; Harris-Vanderheiden, Brown, Mackenzie, Reinen, & Schiebel, 1975; McNaughton, 1976; Olson, 1976). Today, communication board systems are used widely throughout the field of mental retardation, but formal experimental research on such systems is limited (but see Reid & Hurlbut, 1977).

Blissymbolics is currently the symbol system favored for utilization in conjunction with communication boards for the mentally retarded. However, as indicated by Archer (1977), there are many questions that need to be asked and studied in relation to this symbol system. For example, although it has been suggested that Bliss symbols are easier to learn than traditional English orthography (e.g., Harris-Vanderheiden et al., 1975), this has not been clearly established through formal research. Also, current instructional programs are largely based on intuition and have not been formally evaluated (e.g., Harris-Vanderheiden et al., 1976; McNaughton, 1976; Vanderheiden & Harris-Vanderheiden, 1976).

ELECTRONIC COMMUNICATION SYSTEMS

In the past several years, a variety of sophisticated communication devices have been developed to meet the needs of the nonverbal communicatively impaired (Vanderheiden & Harris-Vanderheiden, 1976; Vanderheiden, 1978). But although inventions and innovations are taking place at a rapid rate, scarcely any attempts have been made to evaluate formally the more sophisticated of the currently available electronic systems specifically with the mentally retarded (but see Hagen, Porter, & Brink, 1973). The vast majority of published reports consist of clinical demonstrations rather than controlled research, and most studies involving developmentally disabled persons have focused on cerebral palsied (or other physically handicapped) children of normal or near normal intelligence (e.g., Bullock, Dalrymple, & Danca, 1975; Harris-Vanderheiden, 1976b; Hill, Campagna, Long, Munch, & Naecker, 1968; Law, Lewis, & Parks, 1980; Morasso, Sandini, Suetta, Tagliasco, Vernazza, & Zaccario, 1978; Park, Roy, Warrick, & Côtè, 1979; Workman, 1979).

There is clearly a great need for future research aimed at exploring the use of sophisticated electronic communication systems for the mentally retarded. It is likely that such studies have not already been undertaken because of factors such as the relatively high cost of components, lack of public awareness of the availability of such systems, the desire of most researchers to have quick and positive results, and assumptions regarding the basic limitations of mentally retarded persons in the area of communication.

One of the most exciting developments that is currently taking place in connection with electronic communication systems is the recent interest in artificial (machine-generated) speech (Freidman, Cheung, Entine, & Bartell, 1979; Vanderheiden, 1976; Warrick, Nelson, Cossalter, Côtè, McGillis, & Charbonneau, 1977). As Warrick et al. (1977)

note, there are many advantages in speech output systems, especially as compared with visual outputs. Audible speech helps facilitate communication from a distance, such as from one side of the room to another, or outdoors. It also facilitates the user's ability to address more than one listener at a time. Perhaps most importantly, synthetic speech would have a high degree of acceptability and intelligibility to persons within the user's natural environment. Portable speech synthesis devices are already commercially available, and their use within the field of mental retardation will probably be commonplace in the near future.

Summary and Discussion

Until recently, many professionals have tended to equate communication with speech, and speech with man. Without consciously intending to, we have placed a priority on spoken communication and have regarded other methods of expression as less than perfect creations. Professionals have insisted on teaching people to speak, even when there was little hope of success, and we have "stacked the deck" of our intelligence tests by loading them with questions that require verbal responses or verbal understanding. But all this is beginning to change. We have learned much about the nature of communication in recent years, and a variety of *nonspeech* alternatives to spoken communication are now being recognized.

In this chapter, we have looked at developments within the fields of manual signing and device-assisted communication systems. We have at times been critical of the literature, but our intent has been benign and our hope was to present a favorable impression of what has already taken place in these fields, and of what the future holds in store.

With current trends towards deinstitutionalization and mainstreaming, it is likely than an increased number of mentally retarded individuals will be seeking entrance into our speech dominant society. The process of "normalization" will be greatly enhanced if we provide them with an effective means of communicating, and if our society is tolerant of the fact that the systems that they use may be slightly different relative to those traditionally accepted.

At one point, professionals feared that providing someone with a nonspeech mode of communication might be doing mentally retarded persons more harm than service. This assumption was based on the high regard placed on speech, and the belief that other "less preferred" forms of communication would in some way block its development. But as noted in this chapter, we no longer need fear the potentially harmful effects of learning a nonspeech mode of communication. For evidence is accumulating that far from being a hindrance or impediment to speech, nonspeech communication may in fact promote and facilitate spoken communication. Although we do not yet know exactly *why* this happens, it is almost assuredly related to the fact that we have reawakened in some persons, or helped establish for the first time in some, the pleasure that comes with being able to control social aspects of one's environment—and thus to cause things to happen and to enjoy the benefits and rewards of one's actions.

It would be difficult to underestimate the importance of being able to communicate effectively with others. Failure to communicate often leads to anger, frustration, or withdrawal. Undoubtedly, the absence of an effective means of communication has contributed greatly to many of the disruptive, bizarre, or unusual behaviors that we frequently observe among the mentally retarded. Support for this contention has recently emerged from the nonspeech literature. For it has been found that when you provide mentally retarded persons with an effective means of communicating, many of these behaviors decrease. This impact would seem to be especially important as we proceed in our efforts of normalization.

The fact that nonspeech systems have thus far been extremely successful in helping unlock the communication potentials of many mentally retarded persons is a sobering thought. For one immediately thinks of those persons who might have benefited from such systems had they been available in the past. Communication is a basic human right that should be secured, as far as possible, for all retarded people. It is encouraging that meaningful dialogue is beginning to take place, and that through the help of nonspeech communication systems, we are beginning to learn to understand one another and to talk together—often for the first time.

Notes

1. See Moores (1974; 1978; 1981) and Wilbur (1976) for more detailed information concerning the formal characteristics and historical origins of sign systems.
2. The issue of alternate nonspeech systems was recently addressed by Stremel-Campbell et al. (1977). Elsewhere Carr et al. 91978), Oxman et al. (1978), Bonvillian, Nelson, and Rhyne (1981), provide a rationale for the use of manual communication based on theories of perception and information processing in severely dysfunctional (autistic) nonverbal children.
3. Ontario Sign Language was used by Konstantareas et al., 1979.

References

Archer, L. A. Blissymbolics: A nonverbal communication system. *Journal of Speech and Hearing Disorders*, 1977,

42, 568–579.

Barrerra, R. D., Lobato-Barrerra, D., & Sulzer-Azaroff, B. A simultaneous treatment comparison of three expressive language training programs with a mute autistic child. *Journal of Autism and Developmental Disorders*, 1980, 10, 21–37.

Benaroya, S., Wesley, S., Ogilvie, H., Klein, L. S., & Meaney, M. Sign language and multisensory input training of children with communication and related developmental disorders. *Journal of Autism and Childhood Schizophrenia*, 1977, 7, 23–31.

Berger, S. A clinical program for developing multimodal responses with atypical deaf children. In J. McLean, D. Yoder, & R. Schiefelbusch (Eds.), *Language intervention with the retarded*. Baltimore: University Park Press, 1972.

Bliss, C. K. *Sematography (blissymbolics)*. (2nd ed.) Coogee, Sydney, Australia: Author, 1965.

Bonvillian, J. D., & Nelson, K. E. Sign language acquisition in a mute autistic boy. *Journal of Speech and Hearing Disorders*, 1976, 4, 339–347.

Booth, T. Early receptive training for the severely and profoundly retarded. *Language, Speech and Hearing Services in Schools*, 1978, 9, 151–154.

Brady, D. O., & Smouse, A. D. A simultaneous comparison of three methods for language training with an autistic child: An experimental single case analysis. *Journal of Autism and Childhood Schizophrenia*, 1978, 8, 271–279.

Bricker, D. D. Imitative sign training as a facilitator of word-object association with low-functioning children. *American Journal of Mental Deficiency*, 1972, 76, 509–516.

Bullock, A., Dalrymple, G. F., & Danca, J. M. Communication and the nonverbal multihandicapped child. *The American Journal of Occupational Therapy*, 1975, 29, 150–152.

Carr, E. G., Binkoff, J. A., Kologinsky, E., & Eddy, M. Acquisition of sign language by autistic children. I. Expressive labelling. *Journal of Behavior Analysis*, 1978, 11, 489–501.

Carrier, J. K., Jr. Nonspeech noun usage training with severely and profoundly retarded children. *Journal of Speech and Hearing Research*, 1974, 17, 510–517.

Carrier, J. K., Jr. Application of a nonspeech language system with the severely language handicapped. In L. L. Lloyd (Ed.), *Communication assessment and intervention strategies*. Baltimore: University Park Press, 1976.

Carrier, J. K., Jr., & Peak, T. *Program manual for non-SLIP (non-speech language initiation program)*. Lawrence, Kansas: H. & H. Enterprises, Inc., 1975.

Casey, L. O. Development of communicative behavior in autistic children: A parent program using manual signs. *Journal of Autism and Childhood Schizophrenia*, 1978, 8, 45–59.

Chapman, R. S., & Miller, J. F. Analyzing language and communication in the child. In R. L. Schiefelbusch (Ed.), *Nonspeech language and communication: Analysis and intervention*. Baltimore: University Park Press, 1980.

Clarke, C. R., Davies, C. O., & Woodcock, R. W. *Standard rebus glossary*. Minneapolis: American Guidance Service, 1974.

Fenn, G., & Rowe, J. A. An experiment in manual communication. *British Journal of Disorders of Communication*, 1975 10, 3–16.

Fouts, R. Acquisition and testing of gestural signs in four young chimpanzees. *Science*, 1973, 180, 978–980.

Freidman, R. B., Cheung, S., Entine, S., & Bartell, T. Verbal communication aid for nonvocal patients. *Medical and Biological Engineering and Computing*, 1979, **17**, 103–106.

Fristoe, M. *Language intervention systems for the retarded.* Decatur, Alabama: L.B. Wallace Developmental Center, 1975.

Fristoe, M., & Lloyd, L. L. A survey of the use of non-speech systems with the severely communication impaired. *Mental Retardation*, 1978, **16**, 99–103.

Fristoe, M., & Lloyd, L. L. Nonspeech communication. In N. R. Ellis (Ed.), *Handbook of mental deficiency, psychological theory and research.* (2nd ed.) Hillsdale, N.J.: Lawrence Erlbaum Associates, 1979.(a)

Fristoe, M., & Lloyd, L. L. Signs used in manual communication training with persons having severe communication impairment. *American Association for the Education of the Severely-Profoundly Handicapped Review*, 1979, **4**, 364–373.(b)

Fristoe, M., & Lloyd, L. L. Planning an initial expressive sign lexicon for persons with severe communication impairment. *Journal of Speech and Hearing Disorders*, 1980, **45**, 170–180.

Fulwiler, R. L., & Fouts, R. S. Acquisition of American Sign Language by a non-communicating autistic child. *Journal of Autism and Childhood Schizophrenia*, 1976, **6**, 43–51.

Gardner, R. A., & Gardner, B. T. Teaching sign language to a chimpanzee. *Science*, 1969, **165**, 664–672.

Goodman, L., Wilson, P. S., & Bornstein, H. Results of a national survey of sign language programs in special education. *Mental Retardation*, 1978, **16**, 104–106.

Griffith, P. L., & Robinson, J. H. Influence of iconicity and phonological similarity on sign learning by mentally retarded children. *American Journal of Mental Deficiency*, 1980, **85**, 291–298.

Grinnell, M. F., Detamore, K. L., & Lippke, B. A. Sign it successful: Manual English encourages expressive communication. *Teaching Exceptional Children*, 1976, **8**, 123–124.

Hagen, C., Porter, W., & Brink, J. Nonverbal communication: An alternative mode of communication for the child with cerebral palsy. *Journal of Speech and Hearing Disorders*, 1973, **38**, 448–455.

Hall, S. M., & Talkington, L. W. Evaluation of a manual approach to programming for deaf retarded. *American Journal of Mental Deficiency*, 1970, **75**, 378–380.

Harris-Vanderheiden, D. Blissymbols and the mentally retarded. In G. C. Vanderheiden and K. Grilley (Eds.), *Non-vocal communication techniques and aids for the severely physically handicapped.* Baltimore: University Park Press, 1976.(a)

Harris-Vanderheiden, D. Field evaluation of the autocom. In G. C. Vanderheiden and K. Grilley (Eds.), *Non-vocal communication techniques and aids for the handicapped.* Baltimore: University Park Press, 1976.(b)

Harris-Vanderheiden, D., Brown, W. P., Mackenzie, P., Reinen, S., & Schiebel, C. Symbol communication for the mentally handicapped: An application of blissymbols as an alternate communication mode for non-verbal mentally retarded children with motoric impairment. *Mental Retardation*, 1975, **13**, 34–37.

Hill, S. D., Campagna, J., Long, D., Munch, J., & Naecker, S. An exploratory study of the use of two response keyboards as a communication for the severely handicapped child. *Perceptual and Motor Skills*, 1968, **26**, 699–704.

Hobson, P. A., & Duncan, P. Sign learning and profoundly retarded people. *Mental Retardation*, 1979, **17**, 33–37.

Hoffmeister, R. J., & Farmer, A. The development of manual sign language in mentally retarded deaf individuals. *Journal of the Rehabilitation of the Deaf*, 1972, **6**, 19–26.

Hollis, J. H., & Carrier, J. K. Research implications for communication deficiencies. *Exceptional Children*, 1975, **41**, 405–412.

Kahn, J. V. A comparison of manual and oral language training with mute retarded children. *Mental Retardation*, 1977, **15**, 21–23.

Kellog, W. N., & Kellogg, L. A. The ape and the child. New York: McGraw-Hill, 1933.

Kohl, F. L. Effects of motoric requirements on the acquisition of manual sign responses by severely handicapped students. *American Journal of Mental Deficiency*, 1981, **85**, 396–403.

Kohl, F. L., Karlan, G. R., & Heal, L. W. Effects of pairing manual signs with verbal signs with verbal cues upon the acquisition of instruction-following behaviors and the generalization to expressive language with severely handicapped students. *American Association for the Education of the Severely-Profoundly Handicapped Review*, 1979, **4**, 291–300.

Konstantareas, M. M., Webster, C. D., & Oxman, J. Manual language acquisition and its influence on other areas of functioning in four autistic and autistic-like children. *Journal of Child Psychology and Psychiatry and Allied Disciplines*, 1979, **20**, 337–350.

Kopchick, G. A., Jr., Rombach, D. W., & Smilovitz, R. A total communication environment in an institution. *Mental Retardation*, 1975, **13**, 22–23.

Kotkin, R. A., Simpson, S. B., & DeSanto, D. The effect of sign language on picture naming in two retarded girls possessing normal hearing. *Journal of Mental Deficiency Research*, 1978, **22**, 19–25.

Krug, D., Arick, J., Scanlon, C., Almond, P., Rosenblum, J., & Border, M. Evaluation of a program of systematic instructional procedures for preverbal autistic children. *Improving Human Performance Quarterly*, 1979, **8**, 29–41.

Law, J., Lewis, J., & Parks, A. L. Using the verbalizer with a nonverbal cerebral palsied child: A case history. *Behavioral Engineering*, 1980, **6**, 19–24.

Linville, S. E. Signed English: A language teaching technique with totally nonverbal, severely mentally retarded adolescents. *Language, Speech, and Hearing Services in Schools*, 1977, **8**, 170–175.

McDonald, E. T., & Schultz, A. R. Communication boards for cerebral palsied children. *Journal of Speech and Hearing Disorders*, 1973, **38**, 73–88.

McDonald, E. T. Design and application of communication boards. In G. C. Vanderheiden & K. Grilley (Eds.), *Non-vocal communication techniques and aids for the severely physically handicapped.* Baltimore: University Park Press, 1976.

McLean, L. P., & McLean, J. E. A language training program for nonverbal autistic children. *Journal of Speech and Hearing Disorders*, 1974, **39**, 186–193.

McNaughton, S. Bliss symbols: An alternative symbol system for the non-vocal pre-reading child. In G. C. Vanderheiden & K. Grilley (Eds.), *Non-vocal communication techniques and aids for the severely physically handicapped.* Baltimore: University Park Press, 1976.

Miller, J. F. On specifying what to teach: The movement

from structure, to structure and meaning, to structure and meaning and knowing. In E. Sontag (Ed.), *Educational programming for the severely and profoundly handicapped*. Reston, Va.: The Council for Exceptional Children, 1978.

Moores, D. F. Nonvocal systems of verbal behavior. In R. L. Schiefelbusch & L. L. Lloyd (Eds.), *Language perspectives: Acquisition, retardation, and intervention*. Baltimore: University Park Press, 1974.

Moores, D. F. *Educating the deaf: Psychology, principles, and practices*. Boston: Houghton Mifflin Co., 1978.

Morasso, P., Sandini, G., Suetta, G., Tagliasco, V., Vernazza, T., & Zaccario, R. Logos: A microprocessor-based device as a writing aid for the motor handicapped. *Medical and Biological Engineering and Computing*, 1978, **16**, 309–315.

Mulick, J. A., Scott, F. D., Gaines, R. F., & Campbell, B. M. Devices and instrumentation for skill development and behavior change. In J. L. Matson & F. Andrasik (Eds.), *Treatment issues and innovations in mental retardation*. New York: Plenum Press, 1983.

Olson, T. Return of the nonverbal. *Asha*, 1976, **18**, 823.

Oxman, J., Webster, C. D., & Konstantareas, M. M. The perception and processing of information by severely dysfunctional nonverbal children: A rationale for the use of manual communication. *Sign Language Studies*, 1978, **21**, 289–316.

Park, G. C., Roy, O. Z., Warrick, A., & Côtè, C. Mechanical pointer for use with handicapped children. *Medical and Biological Engineering and Computing*, 1979, **17**, 246–248.

Parsons, S., & Carrier, J. K., Jr. *A proposed language program based on David Premack's program for Sarah, a chimpanzee*. Paper presented at the meeting of the Oklahoma Speech and Hearing Association, Oklahoma City, April, 1971.

Premack, A. J., & Premack, D. Teaching language to an ape. *Scientific American*, 1972, **222**, 92–99.

Premack, D. Language in chimpanzees. *Science*, 1971, **172**, 808–822.

Premack, D. A functional analysis of language. *Journal of Experimental Analysis of Behavior*, 1978, **59**, 440–442.

Premack, D., & Premack, A. J. Teaching visual language to apes and language-deficient persons. In R. L. Schiefelbusch & L. L. Lloyd (Eds.), *Language perspectives: Acquisition, retardation, and intervention*. Baltimore: University Park Press, 1974.

Premack, D., & Schwartz, A. Preparations for discussing behaviorism with Chimpanzee. In F. Smith & G. A. Miller (Eds.), *The genesis of language*. Cambridge: Massachusetts Institute of Technology Press, 1966.

Reich, R. Gestural facilitation of expressive language in moderate/severely retarded preschoolers. *Mental Retardation*, 1978, **16**, 113–117.

Reid, D. H., & Hurlbut, B. Teaching nonvocal communication skills to multihandicapped retarded adults. *Journal of Applied Behavior Analysis*, 1977, **10**, 591–603.

Richardson, T. Sign language for the SMR and PMR. *Mental Retardation*, 1975, **13**, 17.

Rumbaugh, D. M. *Language learning by a chimpanzee: The LANA project*. New York: Academic Press, 1977.

Salisbury, C., Wambold, C., & Watter, G. Manual communication for the severely handicapped: An assessment and instructional strategy. *Education and Training of the Mentally Retarded*, 1978, **13**, 393–396.

Salvin, A., Routh, O. K., Foster, R. E., Jr., & Lovejoy, K. M. Acquisition of modified American Sign Language by a mute autistic child. *Journal of Autism and Childhood Schizophrenia*, 1977, **7**, 359–371.

Sayre, J. M. Communication for the non-verbal cerebral palsied. *CP Review*, 1963, **24**, 3–8.

Schaeffer, B. Teaching spontaneous sign language to nonverbal children: Theory and method. *Sign Language Studies*, 1978, **21**, 317–352.

Schaeffer, B. Teaching signed speech to nonverbal children: Theory and method. *Sign Language Studies*, 1980, **26**, 29–63.

Schaeffer, B., Kollinzas, G., Musil, A., & McDowell, P. Spontaneous verbal language for autistic children through signed speech. *Sign Language Studies*, 1977, **17**, 287–328.

Schmidt, M. J., Carrier, J. K., Jr., & Parsons, S. *Use of a non-speech mode for teaching language*. Paper presented at the American Speech and Hearing Association Convention, Chicago, 1971.

Shane, H. C. Approaches to assessing the communication of non-oral persons. In R. L. Schiefelbusch (Ed.), *Nonspeech language and communication: Analysis and intervention*. Baltimore: University Park Press, 1980.

Shane, H. C., & Bashir, A. S. Election criteria for the adoption of an augmentative communication system: Preliminary considerations. *Journal of Speech and Hearing Disorders*, 1980, **45**, 408–415.

Silverman, F. H. Communication for the speechless. Englewood Cliffs, N.J.: Prentice-Hall, Inc., 1980.

Smeets, P. M., & Striefel, S. Acquisition and cross modal generalization of receptive and expressive signing skills in a retarded deaf girl. *Journal of Mental Deficiency Research*, 1976, **20**, 251–260.

Stremel-Campbell, K., Cantrell, D., & Halle, J. Manual signing as a language system and as a speech initiator for the non-verbal severely handicapped student. In E. Sontag (Ed.), *Educational programming for the severely and profoundly handicapped*. Reston, Va.: Division on Mental Retardation, Council for Exceptional Children, 1977.

Swann, W., & Mittler, P. A survey of language abilities in ESNS children. *Special Education: Forward Trends*, 1976, **3**, 24–27.

Topper, S. Gesture language for the nonverbal severely retarded. *Journal of Autism and Developmental Disorders*, 1975, **13**, 30–31.

Van Biervliet, A. Establishing words and objects as functionally equivalent through manual signing. *American Journal of Mental Deficiency*, 1977, **82**, 178–186.

Vanderheiden, G. C. Introduction and framework. In G. C. Vanderheiden and K. Grilley (Eds.), *Non-vocal communication techniques and aids for the severely physically handicapped*. Baltimore: University Park Press, 1976.

Vanderheiden, G. C. (Ed.) *Non-vocal communication resource book*. Baltimore: University Park Press, 1978.

Vanderheiden, G. C., Brown, W. P., & Fothergill, J. Master chart of communication aids. In C. Vanderheiden (Ed.), *Non-vocal communication resource book*. Baltimore: University Park Press, 1978.

Vanderheiden, G. C., & Grilley, K. (Eds.). *Non-vocal communication techniques and aids for the severely physically handicapped*. Baltimore: University Park Press, 1976.

Vanderheiden, G. C., & Harris-Vanderheiden, D. H. Communication techniques and aids for the nonvocal severely handicapped. In L. L. Lloyd (Ed.)., *Communication assessment and intervention strategies.* Baltimore: University Park Press, 1976.

von Glasersfeld, E. The yerkish language and its automatic parser. In D. M. Rumbaugh (Ed.), *Language learning by a chimpanzee: The LANA project.* New York: Academic Press, 1977.

Warrick, A., Nelson, P. J., Cossalter, J. C., Côtè, C., McGillis, J., & Charbonneau, J. R. Synthesized speech as an aid to communicating language for the non-verbal. *Proceedings of the Workshop on Communication for the Non-Verbal Physically Handicapped.* Ottawa, Canada, June 1977.

Watters, R. G., Wheeler, L. J., & Watters, W. E. The relative efficiency of two orders for training autistic children in the expressive and receptive use of manual signs. *Journal of Communication Disorders,* 1981, **14**, 273–385.

Webster, C. D., McPherson, H., Sloman, L., Evans, M. A., & Kuchar, E. Communicating with an autistic boy by gestures. *Journal of Autism and Childhood Schizophrenia,* 1973, **3**, 337–346.

Wilbur, R. B. The linguistics of manual systems and manual sign languages. In L. L. Lloyd (Ed.), *Communication assessment and intervention strategies.* Baltimore: University Park Press, 1976.

Workman, A. A. Communication system for the nonverbal severely disabled. *American Journal of Occupational Therapy,* 1979, **33**, 194–195.

28 TEACHING SELF-HELP SKILLS

Dennis H. Reid,
Philip G. Wilson, and
Gerald D. Faw

One of the most prevalent areas of concern among caregivers and researchers working with the mentally retarded has been the teaching of self-help skills. This concern has been due, at least in part, to the recognition that acquisition of self-help skills by mentally retarded persons is a crucial step in the overall developmental process (Reid, 1982; Van Etten, Arkell, & Van Etten, 1980; Whitman & Scibak, 1979). Moreover, from the point of view of caregivers, a considerable amount of time and effort is reduced if mentally retarded individuals provide for their basic care as opposed to relying on the caregivers. An additional and equally important reason for the concern over teaching self-help skills is the widespread deficits in self-help skill functioning among mentally retarded populations (e.g., Lovaas, 1981; Van Etten et al., 1980).

Because of the recognized importance of self-help skills and the pervasive skill deficiencies among the mentally retarded, a considerable amount of research has been conducted to develop and evaluate methods of teaching these skills. A milestone in this line of research occurred in the early 1960s, when the first applications of behavior modification procedures to train self-help skills were reported. The early successes of behavior modification procedures provided the impetus for more than 75 investigations which refined

and improved basic behavioral methods of training self-help skills. In fact, the development and subsequent efficacy of behavior modification procedures for assisting the development of independent self-help functioning has been cited as one of the most influential factors in improving the care and training of the mentally retarded in the last 15 to 20 years (Whitman, Scibak, & Reid, in press).

The purpose of this chapter is to discuss the behavior modification research on teaching self-help skills to the mentally retarded. More specifically, this chapter will briefly review the research on the development of behavioral training procedures in the self-help area, summarize the current status of the training technology to date, and note areas in need of investigation. Initially, a brief overview of the early history of behavior modification research in the general self-help area will be provided. Next, a discussion of the behavior modification work in specific self-help skill areas will be presented. However, owing to the availability of a number of detailed reviews of various aspects of the self-help skill literature (Osarchuck, 1973; Reid, 1982; Snell, 1978; Watson & Uzzell, 1980; Whitman & Scibak, 1979; Whitman et al., in press), as well as to space limitations here, an in-depth review of all investigations within each self-help area will not be provided. Rather, key studies and developments will be noted and the interested reader is encouraged to consult previous reviews to follow up particular areas of concern.

History of Early Behavior Modification Research in the General Self-Help Area

The initial behavior modification research in the general self-help skill area was typically concerned with demonstrating that behavioral procedures, based primarily on principles of operant conditioning, could be used to teach self-help skills to the mentally retarded. Generally, the investigations were quite comprehensive in terms of including participants with all levels of retardation and attempting to train a number of self-help skills simultaneously (see Table 28.1 for summary characteristics of the early investigations).

Summaries of the early behavioral programs have been provided in a number of reports, including those of Whitman and Scibak (1979), Whitman et al. (in press) and Reid (1982). As reported by Whitman et al., the usual format in the early studies involved a group of caregivers (e.g., institutional attendants) receiving in-service training in behavior modification procedures and then being expected to conduct training programs intermittently during the day with groups of clients. Typically, the programs were not conducted with a very rigorous research format (Reid, in press; Whitman et al., in press), frequently lacking in experimental controls, such as no control group measures (Colwell, Richards, McCarver, & Ellis, 1973; Girardeau, & Spradlin, 1964) and/or no reliability on measures of client progress (Cuvo, 1973). Additionally, procedural descriptions were often too global to allow for experimental replication of the programs (Gray & Kasteler, 1969; Murphy & Zahm, 1975) and lack of data on individual client progress prohibited a thorough evaluation of the results (e.g., Girardeau & Spradlin, 1964; Gray & Kasteler, 1969; Murphy & Zahm, 1975).

Despite methodological problems in much of the early research, the reports did suggest the efficacy of behavior modification procedures in training self-help skills in the mentally retarded. Regardless of the degree of retardation of the participants in the various programs, as well as differences in the type of assessment procedures used (see Table 28.1), at least some progress was reflected in essentially all of the reports. Moreover, these early investigations provided the impetus for additional and more methodologically rigorous research in the mid to late 1970's and early 1980's. However, the more recent research frequently focused on individual self-help skills in separate investigations, as opposed to targeting several self-help skills simultaneously as in the earlier reports. Typically, the skills

addressed were within one of four main self-help areas; toileting, feeding, dressing, and personal hygiene.

Behavior Modification Research in Specific Self-Help Areas

Teaching Independent Toileting

For a number of reasons, toileting skills have received a large amount of attention from behavioral investigators. Perhaps foremost, the unpleasantness and amount of time and effort required of caregivers to clean clients and the physical environment following toileting accidents have evoked research on training toileting skills (Whitman & Scibak, 1979). Additional reasons for the special concern with this self-help skill include the health hazards resulting from incontinence (Osarchuk, 1973), the degrading impact of incontinence on the mentally retarded (Azrin, Bugle, & O'Brien, 1971), and the fact that the lack of independent toileting frequently prohibits participation of the mentally retarded in other therapeutic activities (Smith, Britton, Johnson, & Thomas, 1975). As the forthcoming discussion will suggest, results of the research offer strong support for the efficacy of behavior modification procedures in teaching independent toileting to the mentally retarded, although a number of research questions still remain.

SUMMARY OF DEVELOPMENT OF
BEHAVIORAL PROCEDURES FOR TEACHING
INDEPENDENT TOILETING

A significant milestone in the development of toilet training procedures for the mentally retarded was a report by Ellis (1963) in which he proposed a training approach from a molar behavior theory viewpoint. Ellis's report is generally given credit for providing the impetus for the development and professional dissemination of behavioral toilet training programs (Whitman et al., in press). Initially, applications of Ellis's recommendations, or modifications thereof, were represented in case reports that were published in the mid-1960s (e.g., Baumeister & Klosowski, 1965; Dayan, 1964). Although these initial programs typically were not evaluated experimentally (see Osarchuk, 1973, for a review of the early behavioral literature on toilet training regimes), they did reflect the potential efficacy of behavioral procedures for toilet training and provided support for the earlier optimism of Ellis (1963).

Following the initial case reports, more experimentally oriented reports of behavioral toilet training procedures appeared in the literature (e.g., Giles & Wolf, 1966; Hundziak, Maurer, & Watson, 1965). Generally, these investigations reflected successively

Table 28.1. Types of Skills Targeted, Range of Retardation Levels of Participants, and Assessment Device Used in Early Behavior Modification Research on Self-Help Skills

SKILLS TARGETED[a]	NUMBER AND RETARDATION LEVEL OF PARTICIPANTS	ASSESSMENT DEVICE[b]	REFERENCE
Dressing, undressing, tooth brushing, hand washing, toileting	7 severely retarded males	Modified Vineland Social Maturity Scale	Bensberg, Colwell, & Cassel, 1965
Dressing, toileting, feeding, bathing	70 moderately to profoundly retarded males and females	Vineland Social Maturity Scale	Gray & Kasteler, 1969
Toileting, feeding, grooming, dressing	20 severely and profoundly retarded males and females	Modified Vineland Social Maturity Scale	Roos & Oliver, 1969
Toileting, feeding, dressing, and undressing	47 moderately to profoundly retarded males and females	Behavior Checklist	Colwell, Richards, McCarver, & Ellis, 1973
Tooth brushing, showering, dressing, shoe tying, bed-making, feeding	48 severely retarded males	Fairview Self-Help Scale; Situation Specific Test	Brody, Esslinger, Casselman, McGlinchey, & Mitala, 1975
Dressing, feeding, grooming, toileting	24 severely and profoundly retarded males	Fairview Self-Help Scale	Murphy & Zahm, 1975

[a] Skills listed do not necessarily include all behaviors targeted in each investigation.
[b] Assessment devices listed do not necessarily include all measurement procedures used.

increasing rigor in the evaluation of the programs as well as increasing behavioral sophistication in the design and implementation of the procedures. Additionally, four other directions or trends were reflected in the toilet training research during this time; a focus on *training a more complete and naturally sequential set of toileting behaviors,* the use of *automated training devices, training night-time toileting skills* to eliminate bed wetting, and the use of *rapid and intensive toilet training programs.*

The first trend just noted is best represented in the work at Arizona State University in the late 1960s and early 1970s (Mahoney, Van Wagenen, & Meyerson, 1971; Van Wagenen, Meyerson, Kerr, & Mahoney, 1969). Prior to that time, the basic format for toilet training was a "potting procedure" (Van Wagenen et al., 1969), in which a client was placed on a toilet (pot) and the caregiver waited for a voiding response in order to provide reinforcement. The rationale for the potting procedure was that by catching the client voiding in the toilet and reinforcing that behavior while not reinforcing (or punishing) voiding in other situations, the client would learn to discriminate where to void and where not to void. Van Wagenen et al. (1969) and Mahoney et al. (1971) argued that a more effective approach would be to teach a more comprehensive set of behaviors in the sequence in which they occur during normal toileting. That is, instead of a caregiver placing a client on the toilet at various caregiver-determined intervals and waiting for the client to void, the client should first be taught to go to the toilet after the presentation of stimuli associated with a full bladder, and then sequentially be taught to lower his/her pants, to assume the appropriate voiding position and to void in the toilet. Finally, the client should be taught to pull his/her pants up after voiding. Empirical support for this "forward moving" procedure was provided in two investigations involving children with retardation levels ranging from profound to moderate (Mahoney et al., 1971; Van Wagenen et al., 1969).

One aspect of the forward training approach just described essentially resulted in the second trend in the toileting research: *the use of automated devices.* More specifically, in order for a caregiver to teach a client to go to the toilet in response to relevant body cues, the caregiver must first be able to immediately detect the initiation of voiding by the client. Because such detection is almost impossible for caregivers under typical living conditions, portable devices were developed for automatically signalling the occurrence of a client wetting his/her pants (Azrin et al., 1971; Azrin & Foxx, 1971; Mahoney et al., 1971; Van Wagenen et al., 1969). Basically, such devices involve

the closing of an electrical circuit in the specially designed pants due to moisture from the voiding, which in turn activates a small battery-operated auditory alarm worn by the client. Similarly, a second type of automated toilet-training device was designed for use in the actual toilet to signal voiding (Azrin et al., 1971; Azrin & Foxx, 1971; Herreshoff, 1973; Passman, 1975). The latter apparatus facilitates the quick delivery of a reinforcer by a caregiver following the clients' appropriate voiding.

A third type of automated device used in behavioral toilet training programs was designed for *remediating inappropriate night-time incontinence or bed-time wetting* (enuresis). Basically, the devices are the same in principle to the pants-alarm and potty-alarm apparatus just described, in that an auditory signal is activated when urination in the bed causes an electrical circuit to be completed (see Foxx & Azrin, 1974 for a more complete description). The use of such devices simply to cause an individual to be awakened contingent on wetting the bed (and perhaps then requiring the individual to go to the toilet) has been reported to be somewhat successful in reducing bed-wetting with some institutionalized mentally retarded persons (Kennedy & Sloop, 1968; Sloop & Kennedy, 1973), although results have been inconsistent (Azrin, Sneed, & Foxx, 1973). When the bed-wetting alarm has been used as part of a comprehensive behavioral program, more significant results have been obtained (Azrin et al., 1973). For instance, Azrin et al. developed a rapid training program for remediating enuresis that included a variety of behavioral components and was effective in significantly reducing the bed wetting of 12 profoundly mentally retarded, institutionalized adults within one week of training.

The format of the Azrin et al. program for eliminating enuresis is representative of the fourth direction in the behavioral research on toilet training: *the use of intensive training procedures.* Such procedures were developed and disseminated by Azrin and Foxx (Azrin & Foxx, 1971; Foxx & Azrin, 1974) and represented a major habilitative advancement with mentally retarded populations. The Azrin and Foxx approach involved numerous procedures in order to provide a rapid and comprehensive program for toilet training. Specific procedural components included reinforcement for appropriate toileting, inhibitory training (punishment) for inappropriate toileting, automatic urine detection devices including the pants-alarm and potty-alarm, increased operant level of toileting by increasing the consumption of liquids, training in toilet-related skills such as dressing and undressing, and initially requiring the clients to be near and frequently on the toilet (i.e., at least every hour) to increase the probability of a correct voiding response (Azrin & Foxx, 1971). Azrin and Foxx demonstrated the effectiveness of the intensive approach with nine institutionalized mentally retarded persons with IQ's ranging from 7 to 45. Training required eight hours per day for an average of six days across all nine participants and was accompanied by reductions from an average of two toileting accidents per eight-hour day per client to approximately one accident every four days.

CURRENT STATUS OF BEHAVIORAL PROCEDURES FOR TEACHING INDEPENDENT TOILETING

The current status of behavioral procedures for toilet training the mentally retarded is best represented by the intensive approach developed by Azrin and Foxx as just noted. The Azrin and Foxx program presents a well-described approach that can be effective in an extremely short period of time (i.e., only a few days) relative to previous procedures that typically required at least several months. Since the initial research with the Azrin and Foxx program, other investigations have provided support for the intensive training format with a variety of mentally retarded populations, such as persons with retardation levels ranging from trainable (Raborn, 1978) to profound (Sadler & Merkert, 1977), adults (Smith et al., 1975) and children (Doleys & Arnold, 1975), and individuals with multiple handicaps including blindness (Song, Song, & Grant, 1976) and deaf/blindness (Lancioni, 1980). Additionally, the Azrin and Foxx program, or a modification thereof, has been used with mentally retarded persons in numerous settings such as institutions (Smith et al., 1975), classrooms (Raborn, 1978; Song et al., 1976), day training centers (Sadler & Merkert, 1977), and normal homes (Doleys & Arnold, 1975).

AREAS FOR FUTURE RESEARCH

Despite the noted success of the Azrin and Foxx toileting approach, significant problems still remain in toilet training programs with the mentally retarded. This section attempts to delineate specific problems and subsequent areas in need of research. However, before discussing specific research areas, it should be noted that there is a general need for more experimental sophistication in research on the efficacy of behavioral toilet training procedures. With minimal exceptions (e.g., Lancioni, 1980), most investigations of toilet training procedures have not been conducted with very much experimental rigor (see Whitman et al., in press, for a more critical review).

One area that is especially in need of research is the evaluation of caregiver acceptance (Kazdin, 1980) of intensive toilet training programs. Our experience, as well as that of others (Sadler & Merkert, 1977), has indicated that a concern with the intensive approach is that staff members dislike it, apparently because of the perceived amount and intensity of the behaviors required of staff. Such a lack of acceptability might reduce the probability of widespread utilization of the program. Similarly, lack of staff adherence to designed training regimes also has been a problem with intensive training formats (Smith et al., 1975). Hence, methods of obtaining staff compliance with the designated procedures warrant investigation. One potential method might be to determine ways of enhancing the acceptability of the training programs for staff.

A second area warranting research is component analyses of the intensive training programs. For instance, although several components of the Azrin and Foxx program have been investigated in previous research, it is not clear what impact each of the numerous procedures has on the overall success of the program when the components are used in combination with each other. An example of such a component is the method of reducing the dependency of the client on the trainer and the highly structured environment in order to develop complete self-initiation of toileting by the client. Although varying methods of reducing client dependency have been described (e.g., Azrin & Foxx, 1971; Lancioni, 1980), a detailed evaluation of this component has been lacking and we have found it to be a frequent source of difficulty in training endeavors.

A third research area is the development of effective and practical training procedures for use with non-ambulatory mentally retarded persons. This population includes individuals who can use a wheelchair for locomotion and transfer from the wheelchair to a toilet and vice versa. Also included are individuals whose physical disabilities prohibit effective mobility such that use of a portable device (e.g., bedpan) would be a necessary part of training.

A fourth area warranting research is the teaching of independent toileting as part of community survival skills for those mentally retarded persons preparing to live in noninstitutional environments (see Whitman et al., in press, for a discussion of the retarded and community survival skills). In many respects, toileting skills needed by mentally retarded persons in community settings are very different from the skills needed in institutions. Examples of skills that would represent useful target behaviors for such research include locating public restroom facilities in community settings, using urinals as opposed to toilets, using pay toilets, and recognizing public signs distinguishing male and female facilities. Methods of teaching these types of skills that allow for a generalized use of the skills across a variety of community situations would be particularly useful.

A final area in need of research is enuresis. Only a small number of studies have evaluated methods of reducing bedwetting by the mentally retarded, with inconsistent results. It has been our experience that bedwetting, especially in institutional settings, is a serious and prevalent problem. Hence, research to develop and refine practical methods of reducing enuresis would be valuable, for both mentally retarded persons and their caregivers.

Teaching Self-Feeding

Behavioral research on teaching feeding skills to the mentally retarded has been at least as frequent as the research on teaching independent toileting. One reason for the attention given to self-feeding is that it is considered the first self-help skill to be acquired in the normal developmental sequence (Whitman & Scibak, 1979) and hence is a necessary set of behaviors to develop before other independent living skills are targeted in training programs. Moreover, the feeding process is very amenable to a behavioral training strategy because of the inherent reinforcer (food) involved (Watson, 1967). Results of the investigations on self-feeding indicate that a behavioral approach is generally an effective training strategy.

SUMMARY OF DEVELOPMENT OF
BEHAVIORAL PROCEDURES FOR TEACHING
SELF-FEEDING

The development of programs for teaching self-feeding followed a different course than the development of toilet training procedures. Specifically, whereas the toilet training research is characterized by key investigations that stimulated noticeably different research directions, the feeding research consists of studies that only gradually refined previous work without any apparent radical differences in the basic training format. However, the sophistication in implementing the basic procedures and the comprehensiveness regarding types of feeding skills targeted have increased considerably from the early to more recent research (Reid, in press). Additionally, the degree of experimental rigor in evaluating the training programs has improved significantly over the last 15 years (Whitman et al., in press).

The similarity in the approaches to teaching feeding skills just noted is due in large part to the reliance on three basic training procedures. First, the process of self-feeding is viewed as a sequence of behaviors

and is task analyzed into specific behavioral components. Second, chaining strategies are used in which successively larger combinations of separate behaviors are systematically reinforced in order to form more complex skills (Sulzer-Azaroff & Mayer, 1977). Chaining can be in a forward format by sequentially training each behavior in the order that it normally occurs or in a backward format by training the behaviors in a reverse order. Generally, backward chaining has been the more common approach used with self-feeding. The third basic procedure involves contingent reinforcement (food consumption and/or social praise) after correct feeding responses.

In addition to the three basic strategies just noted, other behavioral techniques have been employed commonly in feeding training regimes. For instance, physical guidance has been used frequently (Berkowitz, Sherry, & Davis, 1971; Song & Gandhi, 1974). Physical guidance involves a trainer manually guiding a client's hand through the feeding process and then reducing the amount of guidance as the client demonstrates progress (O'Brien, Bugle, & Azrin, 1972). In addition, various prompting sequences have been used to evoke appropriate feeding behaviors by a client such that reinforcement can be delivered following the desired behavior. Often, the sequence begins with a minimally intensive prompt such as a general instruction and then continues with successively more intensive prompts (e.g., a specific instruction, modeling, and then physical guidance) if the client does not respond appropriately (Johnson & Cuvo, 1981; Marholin, O'Toole, Touchette, Berger, & Doyle, 1979; O'Brien & Azrin, 1972). However, the reverse sequence in which successive prompts become less intensive has also been used, with apparently little difference in the relative effectiveness of the two prompting formats (Walls, Crist, Sienicki, & Grant, 1981). A more detailed description of these basic training procedures for self-feeding, as well as for other self-help areas, is provided by Watson and Uzzell (1980) and Whitman et al. (in press).

Essentially all of the procedures just noted have been combined in an attempt to provide a maximally efficient and effective training program (Azrin & Armstrong, 1973). Basically, the Azrin and Armstrong program is similar in concept to the intensive toilet training format noted earlier (Azrin & Foxx, 1971; Foxx & Azrin, 1974). However, the impact of the intensive feeding approach on subsequent research has been significantly less than the impact of the Azrin and Foxx toileting reports. That is, with few exceptions (e.g., Stimbert, Minor, & McCoy, 1977) investigators have not attempted to use and/or evaluate intensive approaches for teaching feeding skills.

In addition to the investigations of programs for *training feeding skills* to the mentally retarded, studies have focused on methods of *reducing inappropriate feeding/mealtime behaviors* of this population. Generally, the inappropriate behaviors involve activities that are socially unacceptable such as stealing food (Barton, Guess, Garcia, & Baer, 1970), or involve potential health hazards such as eating extremely quickly (Favell, McGimsey, & Jones, 1980). In order to reduce such behaviors, a variety of deceleration procedures have been investigated. However, the basic behavior change strategy has been similar throughout most of the reports in that the undesirable activities are behaviorally defined and punishment is provided contingent on their occurrence. Frequently, the punishment involves some type of time-out procedure whereby the mealtime process is interrupted or terminated via removal of the food from the client (Christian, Hollomon, & Lanier, 1973; Groves & Carroccio, 1971; O'Brien & Azrin, 1972) or escorting the client away from the dining area (Albin, 1977; Hamilton & Allen, 1967; Martin, McDonald, & Omichinski, 1971). Time-out generally has been effective in reducing inappropriate mealtime behaviors, although some inconsistencies in the results have been reported (Plummer, Baer, & LeBlanc, 1977). In addition to time-out strategies, punishment routines have involved the use of brief, contingent restraint (Favell et al., 1980; Henriksen & Doughty, 1967; Song & Gandhi, 1974) and verbal reprimands (O'Brien & Azrin, 1972). Additionally, differential reinforcement of more appropriate mealtime behaviors (Cipani, 1981; Favell et al., 1980; Martin et al., 1971) has been used to reduce undesirable mealtime activities.

CURRENT STATUS OF BEHAVIORAL PROCEDURES FOR TEACHING SELF-FEEDING

A summary of the current status of behavioral procedures for training self-feeding to the mentally retarded includes a large degree of optimism. Using basic training strategies as discussed briefly in this section, numerous investigations have reported success in assisting mentally retarded persons in acquiring appropriate feeding skills. Such success has occurred with clients at all levels of mental retardation and with a variety of mealtime behaviors including elementary spoon-feeding (Zeiler & Jervey, 1968), multiple utensil usage (Nelson, Cone, & Hanson, 1975), cafeteria-line skills (Stolz & Wolf, 1969), table manners (Matson, Ollendick, & Adkins, 1980), dining in public restaurants (Marholin et al., 1979; van den Pol, Iwata, Ivancic, Page, Neef, & Whitley, 1981), and cooking (Johnson & Cuvo, 1981; Robinson-Wilson, 1977). However, despite the significant impact that behavioral procedures have had on the development of feeding skills, caution has been expressed against forming the conclusion that all serious mealtime problems of the mentally retarded have been resolved (Reid, 1982). As the next section indicates, considerably more research is needed in a number of areas in order to overcome the comprehensive problems mentally retarded persons encounter in learning to eat with total independence.

AREAS FOR FUTURE RESEARCH

There are four general areas related to developing feeding skills in the mentally retarded that are in particular need of research. First, the development and/or refinement of pretraining assessment procedures would be useful in order to better match new and existing training technologies with specific skill deficiencies of clients. Second, continued research on intensive training programs and other methods of accelerating the acquisition of feeding skills would be helpful. Third, investigations are needed on procedures for promoting generalization of newly acquired feeding skills across settings and time. Research on generalization of skills is especially warranted with the severely and profoundly mentally retarded, as opposed to the less seriously retarded. Finally, new deceleration procedures for reducing inappropriate mealtime activities that are not primarily punitive in nature would be a useful line of research. Such research is particularly needed in state institutions for the mentally retarded. In these settings, mealtime is often an enriched period for clients because of increased contact with staff and the reinforcing power of food and drink. Hence, mealtimes in institutions are well suited for training a variety of social skills in addition to the usual feeding skills (Halle, Marshall, & Spradlin, 1979; Schepis, Reid, Fitzgerald, Faw, van den Pol, & Welty, 1982; Van Biervliet, Spangler, & Marshall, 1981). However, an over-reliance on punishing techniques during the mealtime process may have a generalized suppressive effect and interfere with the potential multiple-skill development that can occur during mealtimes.

Additional feeding related areas that warrant the attention of investigators have been discussed elsewhere (e.g., Reid, in press). One such area that is in particular need of research is the development and evaluation of procedures for teaching more advanced (e.g., teaching nutritional eating practices) and normal (e.g., teaching family-style dining to profoundly retarded individuals) mealtime skills. Similarly, research has been called for on procedures to assist mentally retarded persons in overcoming physical disabilities that interfere with self-feeding (see also Korabek, Reid, & Ivancic, 1981).

Teaching Independent Dressing

The acquisition of independent dressing and undressing skills is important to the mentally retarded for a variety of reasons (Whitman et al., in press). Perhaps foremost, self-sufficient dressing skills allow mentally retarded individuals more control over their lives than if they had to rely on caregivers to dress them. Such skills also relieve caregivers of the time-consuming task of dressing clients. Additionally, self-dressing is important in a social context. For instance, by affecting appearance, dressing skills affect the social interactions mentally retarded persons have with nonretarded individuals (Reid, 1982).

Despite the well recognized importance of independent dressing, there has been considerably less behavioral research on training dressing skills than on training skills in the toileting and feeding areas. The research that is available provides support for the efficacy of behavioral procedures in improving self-dressing among mentally retarded populations, although the overall success of the behavioral programs has been less than the success with those self-help skills previously discussed.

SUMMARY OF DEVELOPMENT OF
BEHAVIORAL PROCEDURES FOR TEACHING
INDEPENDENT DRESSING

The development of behavioral procedures for teaching dressing skills was similar to the development of training programs in the self-feeding area in three general respects. First, as in the research on self-feeding, recent investigations (mid 1970's to early 1980's) on self-dressing were generally conducted with more experimental rigor than the early studies (1960's). Second, whereas the early research in both self-help areas typically focused on relatively simple skills (e.g., putting on a baggy pair of pants), recent research (see Reid, 1982) focused on more complex behaviors (e.g., selecting clothing garments according to popular color standards). Third, the same basic behavioral strategy that was used to teach feeding skills has been used throughout the investigations on self-dressing (Watson & Uzzell, 1980), with a trend over time to gradually refine the training approach. However, as with the research on self-feeding, different investigations focused more heavily on specific components of the behavioral teaching strategy.

One set of training components that has warranted special concern in dressing programs involves the generalization of newly acquired dressing skills across different settings and time. The concern for such generalization is crucial because of where and when self-dressing typically occurs. Normally, dressing skills are used in the privacy of an individual's bedroom or bathroom at specified times such as early morning and late evening. However, owing primarily to practical reasons such as availability of trainers, research on training self-dressing frequently has been conducted at other times of the day (e.g., Martin, Kehoe, Bird, Jensen, & Darbyshire, 1971; Minge & Ball, 1967) and in other settings (e.g., Nutter & Reid, 1978). When training is conducted under these latter conditions, measures are needed to ensure the skills acquired in the formal program generalize to the situation and time in which they are required on a day-to-day basis. Traditionally, such measures have been lacking in the available research, although informal indications of generalization have been reported (Karen & Maxwell, 1967). More recent investigations (e.g., Cronin & Cuvo, 1979; Nutter & Reid, 1978) have directed more attention to the generalization issue by including specific procedures to promote generalization of skills (Stokes & Baer, 1977) and/or presenting data to document that generalization did occur.

Similar to the concern for generalization across settings and time in dressing training research, special attention is needed on the issue of generalization of new skills across the presence of different trainers. That is, when caregivers of mentally retarded persons are not the ones responsible for carrying out training programs, specific procedures are needed to ensure that the dressing skills demonstrated for the trainers are also displayed for the caregivers in the normal living situation. In studies where the caregivers were not the trainers (e.g., Brody et al., 1975; Fenrick & McDonnell, 1980; Gray & Kasteler, 1969; King & Turner, 1975; Nutter & Reid, 1978), such procedures typically have been lacking and/or no measures of generalization were reported.

An additional set of training components related to dressing programs that warrants extra attention is maintenance of newly acquired skills over extended time periods. This is of particular concern with dressing skills relative to other self-help skills such as feeding and toileting. More specifically, with self-dressing, there typically are not immediate and normally occurring consequences to maintain independent behaviors (except possibly the warmth provided by clothes during cold weather) as there are with self-feeding and toileting (Reid, in press). As noted previously, feeding processes have an inherent reinforcer via food consumption that can maintain eating skills once acquired. With toileting, the avoidance of the aversiveness of wet or soiled clothing can function to maintain independent skills. In contrast, the usual consequence for self-dressing is not directly related to the behaviors per se, but more indirect and social (i.e., the social approval people provide to individuals who dress attractively). Hence, specific maintenance components, such as frequent but intermittent caregiver or peer approval (Matson, DiLorenzo & Esveldt-Dawson, 1981), need to be incorporated into dressing-training programs. Typically, investigations in the dressing area have not specifically programmed long-term maintenance. However, several researchers have evaluated maintenance by including follow-up measures, with inconsistent results reported as to the durability of newly acquired dressing skills (Ball, Seric, & Payne, 1971; Cronin & Cuvo, 1979; Cuvo, Jacobi, & Sipko, 1981; King & Turner, 1975; Lawrence & Kartye, 1971; Nutter & Reid, 1978).

Throughout most of the behavioral research on dressing skills, the emphasis has been on demonstrating methods of teaching the mentally retarded to dress and undress themselves more independently. A related line of investigation has been the evaluation of methods to reduce inappropriate dressing-related behaviors. For instance, several investigators have attempted to reduce the public disrobing of mentally retarded persons, often involving institutionalized, severely or profoundly retarded individuals. Frequently, differential reinforcement of other behavior (DRO) either by itself or with other procedures (e.g., time-out and response cost) has been used to reduce public disrobing (Paul & Miller, 1971; Schaeffer & Martin, 1969; Thompson & Grabowski, 1972). However, some inconsistency with DRO has also been reported (Durana & Cuvo, 1980). Additional deceleration strategies have included overcorrection (Foxx, 1976) and time out with physical restraint (Hamilton, Stephens, & Allen, 1967).

CURRENT STATUS OF BEHAVIORAL PROCEDURES FOR TEACHING INDEPENDENT DRESSING

A summary of the current status of behavioral procedures for teaching dressing skills to the mentally retarded does not include the degree of optimism that was presented earlier in the corresponding summary on feeding procedures. While there is little doubt that behavioral techniques can effectively teach mentally retarded individuals certain dressing skills, there are few experimental data to demonstrate that the procedures effectively teach the mentally retarded to dress themselves at a level commensurate with non-retarded persons. The next section summarizes some

areas in which future research could help advance the training technology in this respect.

AREAS FOR FUTURE RESEARCH

A recent review of areas related to dressing skills of the mentally retarded that are in need of research has been provided by Reid (in press), who discusses four general areas that particularly warrant attention by investigators. First, investigations are needed on methods of teaching the mentally retarded advanced dressing skills, such as determining the appropriate fit of clothing and coordinating clothes according to societal functions during which the clothes are worn. Second, research would be useful on developing effective methods of training mentally retarded persons with physical handicaps to dress themselves, possibly with the assistance of prosthetic equipment. Third, behavioral procedures for managing the performance of caregivers (e.g., institutional attendants) in proficiently carrying out training strategies in dressing-related areas over extended periods of time warrant additional research. Finally, the addition of social validity components (Kazdin, 1977) to dressing training regimes would be useful. For example, social validity procedures would be helpful in determining what to teach to mentally retarded individuals in terms of normal clothing fashion (Nutter & Reid, 1978).

In addition to the research areas just noted, investigations are needed to better articulate specific components involved in intensive training programs for self-dressing and to more systematically demonstrate the effectiveness and efficiency of the intensive approaches. Such programs could be particularly useful for training dressing skills because of the large amount of time typically required of current dressing programs (Adelson-Bernstein, & Sandow, 1978). To date, however, intensive training procedures have not been used in the dressing area as frequently as in the toileting and feeding areas, despite some initial results that are quite promising (Azrin, Schaeffer, & Wesolowski, 1976).

Teaching Personal Hygiene Skills

Personal hygiene skills, or grooming, are typically considered to encompass all self-care activities except toileting, feeding, and dressing. Hence, a wide variety of self-help tasks are included within the personal hygiene area, including, for example, bathing, teeth brushing, shaving, and hair care. Mastery of such skills by the mentally retarded is an integral step toward independent or semi-independent living. However, despite the importance of mentally retarded persons' acquiring personal hygiene skills, relatively little research has occurred on the development and evaluation of behavioral training methods in this area. Where research has occurred, it typically has been conducted with less experimental rigor than research with other self-help skills (Whitman & Scibak, 1979).

The first reports of the use of behavior modification procedures to train personal hygiene skills to the mentally retarded targeted such skills along with other self-help activities in comprehensive training programs (e.g., Bensberg et al., 1965; Cassell & Colwell, 1965; Cuvo, 1973; Girardeau & Spradlin, 1964). Several recent investigations also have focused on personal hygiene tasks in conjunction with other self-help skills in multi-component behavior change projects (Brody et al., 1975; Murphy & Zahm, 1975, 1978). As noted previously, procedures used in the comprehensive programs were often poorly articulated and experimental controls necessary for thorough analyses of the results were frequently lacking.

Outside of the focus on multiple-skill programs, there have been no readily apparent, systematic trends in behavioral research on teaching personal hygiene skills to the mentally retarded. Most of the literature that addresses these skills consists of descriptions of general training programs (e.g., Crnic & Pym, 1979; Wambold & Salisbury, 1978) and/or curriculum materials (see Van Etten et al., 1980 for a review of different curricula), with minimal data to document that the suggested teaching methods are effective. As noted earlier, the small number of investigations that do present experimental data generally were plagued with methodological problems. However, one exception is a report by Horner and Keilitz (1975). Horner and Keilitz convincingly demonstrated the effectiveness of basic behavioral procedures such as verbal instructions, modeling, physical guidance, and contingent reinforcement in teaching tooth brushing skills to moderately and mildly mentally retarded persons. Other studies also have focused on teeth-brushing skills, but have generally been too briefly reported (Wehman, 1974), lacking in experimental controls (Abramson & Wunderlich, 1972), and/or did not directly evaluate effects of the program on tooth brushing per se (Fowler, Johnson, Whitman, & Zukotynski, 1978) such that sound conclusions on the efficacy of the procedures are prohibited.

In addition to the relatively few investigations that evaluated methods of assisting the mentally retarded in acquiring personal hygiene skills, a small number of investigators have evaluated procedures for reinstating and/or maintaining use of previously acquired skills. Doleys, Stacy, and Knowles (1981) used a token system (Kazdin & Bootzin, 1972) to increase the frequency with which mentally retarded persons in group homes used their previously developed skills in such areas as bathing, teeth brushing, hair washing, and shaving. Similarly, Thinesen and Bryan (1981) used picture cues of desired activities to reinstate grooming behaviors (e.g., face washing, cleaning glasses, shaving, teeth brushing) of mildly and moderately mentally retarded persons in a group home. These investigations suggest that personal hygiene skills are similar to dressing skills (see previous section), in that long-term maintenance is not an automatic process and training programs need to include specific maintenance components.

The current status of behavioral procedures for teaching personal hygiene skills is probably best represented in the recent work of Matson and colleagues (e.g., Matson et al., 1981; Matson, Marchetti, & Adkins, 1980). Matson et al. (1980, 1981) expanded the typical behavioral acquisition strategy (see earlier description of the Horner & Keilitz 1975 program) to include methods for training mentally retarded persons to evaluate their own progress in personal hygiene tasks (e.g., showering) and to give each other feedback during training programs. The packaged approach, labeled independence training, has appeared more effective than the usual behavioral training strategy (Matson et al., 1980) and currently appears to be the most effective format in the personal hygiene area. However, independence training is still too recent to have received widespread attention from investigators. Consequently, research is warranted to more thoroughly evaluate the approach, as is research in other areas related to personal hygiene.

The main area warranting additional research in the personal hygiene category is the development (or application) and evaluation of training procedures for a larger variety of skills than targeted to date. Procedures with documented effectiveness and cost efficiency are needed for skills ranging from independent feminine hygiene behaviors to socially appropriate hair care. Such research would be useful for clients at all levels of mental retardation. However, studies with severely and profoundly mentally retarded populations would

Table 28.2. Examples of Areas Reported in Need of Research Regarding the Training of Personal Hygiene Skills to the Mentally Retarded

RESEARCH AREA	REFERENCE
Development and evaluation of training strategies for a wider variety of personal hygiene skills	Whitman, Scibak, & Reid, 1981, Chapter 5
More rigorous analysis of effectiveness of training strategies	Horner & Keilitz, 1975
Use of self-control procedures by clients receiving training	Matson, Marchetti, & Adkins, 1980
Training personal hygiene skills to clients in noninstitutional settings	Doleys, Stacy, & Knowles, 1981
Evaluation of staff acceptability of client training procedures	Whitman, Scibak, & Reid, 1981, Chapter 5
Comparison of training procedures for effects on long-term maintenance of initial behavior changes	Matson, DiLorenzo, & Esvedt-Dawson, 1981

be especially useful since previous evaluations of personal hygiene programs have involved primarily the mildly and/or moderately retarded.

Besides expanding the types of personal hygiene skills targeted, a number of other research questions exist. Table 28.2 summarizes examples of areas that other investigators have noted as being in need of research. In addition to the areas noted in Table 28.2, research attention would be particularly useful on the evaluation of the social validity of behavior changes that accompany training programs in personal hygiene skills (see also Matson et al., 1981). Research on social validity is needed because of the difficulty in determining successful achievement in many personal hygiene tasks (e.g., hair combing, use of makeup, and hand washing) since such skills do not easily lend themselves to objective measurement. Hence, methods of incorporating cost efficient measures of the social validity of client progress into personal hygiene training programs need to be developed.

General Summary

This chapter has attempted to review the developments in research on behavior modification procedures for teaching self-help skills to the mentally retarded. Clearly, behavioral approaches are effective in teaching these types of skills and very considerable progress has occurred in the refinement and widespread application of the procedures. However, this chapter also has attempted to indicate gaps in the research and subsequent areas for future investigation. Each self-help skill area presents particular problems that warrant the attention of investigators. Additionally, there are several areas in need of research that are common across all the self-help domains. In the latter respect, perhaps the most pressing need is for research on methods of training self-help skills in noninstitutional settings such as normal homes and group homes. Although several of the investigations cited in this chapter occurred in homes (e.g., Doleys &

Arnold, 1975; King & Turner, 1975; Fowler et al., 1978), group homes (e.g., Doleys et al., 1981; Thinesen & Bryan, 1981), and short-term residential settings (e.g., Stimbert et al., 1977), the vast majority of the studies involved institutions. Whether or not the effectiveness of behavioral procedures for training self-help skills as noted in the investigations conducted in institutions will be similar in noninstitutional settings is currently unclear.

A foundation for self-help training programs and research in noninstitutional environments rests with the relatively large body of literature on programs and research on training behavioral skills to parents of mentally retarded children (Baker, 1976; Baker, Heifetz, & Murphy, 1980; Baker & Heifetz, 1976; Heifetz, 1977; Jenkins, Stephens, & Sternberg, 1980; Rose, 1974; Tymchuk, 1975; Watson & Bassinger, 1974). Since parents or group-home parents are the caregivers in most noninstitutional settings, they are in an advantageous position to conduct behavioral self-help training procedures. However, reviews and/or summaries of the parent training research have indicated that experimental rigor has been lacking in many of the investigations (Baker, 1976; Whitman et al., 1981). Subsequently, definitive conclusions regarding the effectiveness of various parent training programs on the skill acquisition of mentally retarded children are often prohibited. Hence, a goal for future research in this area would be to improve the experimental sophistication of investigations in order to more conclusively demonstrate the utility of various training methods. Such research is needed, as well as research in other areas noted earlier in this chapter, if the field of behavior modification is to continue to significantly enhance the care and training of the mentally retarded as it has in the last 15 years.

References

Abramson, E. E., & Wunderlich, R. A. Dental hygiene training for retardates: An application of behavioral techniques. *Mental Retardation*, 1972, 10, 6–8.

Adelson-Bernstein, N., & Sandow, L. Teaching buttoning to severely/profoundly retarded multihandicapped children. *Education and Training of the Mentally Retarded*, 1978, **13**, 178–183.

Albin, J. B. Some variables influencing the maintenance of acquired self-feeding behavior in profoundly retarded children. *Mental Retardation*, 1977, **15**, 49–52.

Azrin, N. H., & Armstrong, P. M. The "mini-meal." A method for teaching eating skills to the profoundly retarded. *Mental Retardation*, 1973, **11**, 9–13.

Azrin, N. H., Bugle, C., & O'Brien, F. Behavioral engineering: Two apparatuses for toilet training retarded children. *Journal of Applied Behavior Analysis*, 1971, **4**, 249–253.

Azrin, N. H., & Foxx, R. M. A rapid method of toilet training the institutionalized retarded. *Journal of Applied Behavior Analysis*, 1971, **4**, 89–99.

Azrin, N. H., Schaeffer, R. M., & Wesolowski, M. D. A rapid method of teaching profoundly retarded persons to dress by a reinforcement-guidance method. *Mental Retardation*, 1976, **14**, 29–33.

Azrin, N. H., Sneed, T. J., & Foxx, R. M. Dry bed: A rapid method of eliminating bedwetting (enuresis) of the retarded. *Behaviour Research and Therapy*, 1973, **11**, 427–434.

Baker, B. L. Parent involvement in programming for developmentally disabled children. In L. L. Lloyd (Ed.), *Communication assessment and intervention strategies*. Baltimore: University Park Press, 1976.

Baker, B. L., & Heifetz, L. J. The READ Project: Teaching manuals for parents of retarded children. In T. D. Tjossen (Ed.), *Intervention strategies for high risk infants and young children*. Baltimore: University Park Press, 1976.

Baker, B. L., Heifetz, L. J., & Murphy, D. M. Behavioral training for parents of mentally retarded children: One-year follow-up. *American Journal of Mental Deficiency*, 1980, **85**, 31–38.

Ball, T. S., Seric, K., & Payne, L. E. Long-term retention of self-help skill training in the profoundly retarded. *American Journal of Mental Deficiency*, 1971, **76**, 378–382.

Barton, E. S., Guess, D., Garcia, E., & Baer, D. M. Improvement of retardates' mealtime behaviors by timeout procedures using multiple baseline techniques. *Journal of Applied Behavior Analysis*, 1970, **3**, 77–84.

Baumeister, A., & Klosowski, R. An attempt to group toilet train severely retarded patients. *Mental Retardation*, 1965, **3**, 24–26.

Bensberg, G. J., Colwell, C. N., & Cassel, R. H. Teaching the profoundly retarded self-help activities by behavior shaping techniques. *American Journal of Mental Deficiency*, 1965, **69**, 674–679.

Berkowitz, S., Sherry, P. J., & Davis, B. A. Teaching self-feeding skills to profound retardates using reinforcement and fading procedures. *Behavior Therapy*, 1971, **2**, 62–67.

Brody, J. F., Esslinger, S., Casselman, G., McGlinchey, M., & Mitala, R. The itinerant training team: Variations on a familiar concept. *Mental Retardation*, 1975, **13**, 38–42.

Cassell, R. H., & Colwell, C. N. Teaching the profoundly retarded self-help activities by behavior shaping techniques. In G. J. Bensberg (Ed.), *Teaching the mentally retarded: A handbook for ward personnel*. Atlanta, Georgia: Southern Regional Education Board, 1965.

Christian, W. P., Hollomon, S. W., & Lanier, C. L. An attendant operated feeding program for severely and profoundly retarded females. *Mental Retardation*, 1973, **11**, 35–37.

Cipani, E. Achieving clinical significance, durability and consumer satisfaction in modifying food spillage behavior in an institutionalized retarded client. *Journal of Behavior Therapy & Experimental Psychiatry*, 1981, **12**, 261–266.

Colwell, C. N., Richards, E., McCarver, R. B., & Ellis, N. R. Evaluation of self-help habit training of the profoundly retarded. *Mental Retardation*, 1973, **11**, 14–18.

Crnic, K. A., & Pym, H. A. Training mentally retarded adults in independent living skills. *Mental Retardation*, 1979, **17**, 13–16.

Cronin, K. A., & Cuvo, A. J. Teaching mending skills to mentally retarded adolescents. *Journal of Applied Behavior Analysis*, 1979, **12**, 401–406.

Cuvo, A. J. Child care workers as trainers of mentally retarded children. *Child Care Quarterly*, 1973, **2**, 25–37.

Cuvo, A. J., Jacobi, L., & Spiko, R. Teaching laundry skills to mentally retarded students. *Education and Training of the Mentally Retarded*, 1981, **16**, 54–64.

Dayan, M. Toilet training retarded children in a state residential institution. *Mental Retardation*, 1964, **2**, 116–117.

Doleys, D. M., & Arnold, S. Treatment of childhood encopresis: Full cleanliness training. *Mental Retardation*, 1975, **13**, 14–16.

Doleys, D. M., Stacy, D., & Knowles, S. Modification of grooming behavior in adult retarded. *Behavior Modification*, 1981, **5**, 119–128.

Durana, I. L., & Cuvo, A. J. A comparison of procedures for decreasing public disrobing of an institutionalized profoundly mentally retarded woman. *Mental Retardation*, 1980, **18**, 185–188.

Ellis, N. R. Toilet training the severely defective patient: An S-R reinforcement analysis. *American Journal of Mental Deficiency*, 1963, **68**, 98–103.

Favell, J. E., McGimsey, J. F., & Jones, M. L. Rapid eating in the retarded: Reduction by nonaversive procedures. *Behavior Modification*, 1980, **4**, 481–492.

Fenrick, N. J., & McDonnell, J. J. Junior high school students as teachers of the severely retarded. Training and generalization. *Education and Training of the Mentally Retarded*, 1980, **15**, 187–194.

Fowler, S. A., Johnson, M. R., Whitman, T. L., & Zukotynski, G. Teaching a parent in the home to train self-help skills and increase compliance in her profoundly retarded adult daughter. *AAESPH Review*, 1978, **3**, 151–161.

Foxx, R. M. The use of overcorrection to eliminate the public disrobing (stripping) of retarded women. *Behaviour Research and Therapy*, 1976, **14**, 53–61.

Foxx, R. M., & Azrin, N. H. *Toilet training the retarded: A rapid program for day and nighttime independent toileting*. Champaign, Illinois: Research Press, 1974.

Giles, D. K., & Wolf, M. M. Toilet training institutionalized, severe retardates: An application of operant behavior modification techniques. *American Journal of Mental Deficiency*, 1966, **70**, 766–780.

Girardeau, F. L., & Spradlin, J. E. Token rewards in a cottage program. *Mental Retardation*, 1964, **2**, 345–351.

Gray, R. M., & Kasteler, J. M. The effects of social reinforcement and training on institutionalized mentally retarded children. *American Journal of Mental Deficiency,* 1969, **74,** 50–56.

Groves, I. D., & Carroccio, D. F. A self-feeding program for the severely and profoundly retarded. *Mental Retardation,* 1971, **9,** 10–12.

Halle, J. W., Marshall, A. M., & Spradlin, J. E. Time delay: A technique to increase language use and facilitate generalization in retarded children. *Journal of Applied Behavior Analysis,* 1979, **12,** 431–439.

Hamilton, J., & Allen, P. Ward programming for severely retarded institutionalized residents. *Mental Retardation,* 1967, **5,** 22–24.

Hamilton, J., Stephens, L., & Allen. P. Controlling aggressive and destructive behavior in severely retarded institutionalized residents. *American Journal of Mental Deficiency,* 1967, **71,** 852–856.

Heifetz, L. J. Behavioral training for parents of retarded children: Alternative formats based on instructional manuals. *American Journal of Mental Deficiency,* 1977, **82,** 194–203.

Henriksen, K., & Doughty, R. Decelerating undesired mealtime behavior in a group of profoundly retarded boys. *American Journal of Mental Deficiency,* 1967, **72,** 40–44.

Herreshoff, J. K. Two electronic devices for toilet training. *Mental Retardation,* 1973, **11,** 54–55.

Horner, R. D., & Keilitz, I. Training mentally retarded adolescents to brush their teeth. *Journal of Applied Behavior Analysis,* 1975, **8,** 301–309.

Hundziak, M., Maurer, R. A., & Watson, L. S. Operant conditioning in toilet training of severely mentally retarded boys. *American Journal of Mental Deficiency,* 1965, **70,** 120–124.

Jenkins, S., Stephens, B., & Sternberg, L. The use of parents as parent trainers of handicapped children. *Education and Training of the Mentally Retarded,* 1980, **15,** 256–263.

Johnson, B. F., & Cuvo, A. J. Teaching mentally retarded adults to cook. *Behavior Modification,* 1981, **5,** 187–202.

Karen, R. L., & Maxwell, S. J. Strengthening self-help behavior in the retardate. *American Journal of Mental Deficiency,* 1967, **71,** 546–550.

Kazdin, A. E. Assessing the clinical or applied importance of behavior change through social validation. *Behavior Modification,* 1977, **1,** 427–452.

Kazdin, A. E. Acceptability of alternative treatments for deviant child behavior. *Journal of Applied Behavior Analysis,* 1980, **13,** 259–273.

Kazdin, A. E., & Bootzin, R. R. The token economy, an evaluative review. *Journal of Applied Behavior Analysis,* 1972, **5,** 343–372.

Kennedy, W. A., & Sloop, E. W. Methedrine as an adjunct to conditioning treatment and nocturnal enuresis in normal and institutionalized retarded subjects. *Psychological Reports,* 1968, **22,** 997–1000.

King, L. W., & Turner, R. D. Teaching a profoundly retarded adult at home by non-professionals. *Journal of Behavior Therapy and Experimental Psychiatry,* 1975, **6,** 117–121.

Korabek, C. A., Reid, D. H., & Ivancic, M. T. Improving needed food intake of profoundly handicapped children through effective supervision of institutional staff. *Applied Research in Mental Retardation,* 1981, **2,** 69–88.

Lancioni, G. E. Teaching independent toileting to profoundly retarded deaf-blind children. *Behavior Therapy,* 1980,
11, 234–244.

Lawrence, W., & Kartye, J. Extinction of social competency skills in severely and profoundly retarded females. *American Journal of Mental Deficiency,* 1971, **75,** 630–634.

Lovaas, O. I. (Ed.) *Teaching developmentally disabled children: The ME book.* Baltimore: University Park Press, 1981.

Mahoney, K., Van Wagenen, R. K., & Meyerson, L. Toilet training of normal and retarded children. *Journal of Applied Behavior Analysis,* 1971, **4,** 173–181.

Marholin, D., O'Toole, K. M., Touchette, P. E., Berger, P. L., & Doyle, D. A. "I'll have a Big Mac, large fries, large Coke, and apple pie," . . . or teaching adaptive community skills. *Behavior Therapy,* 1979, **10,** 236–248.

Martin, G. L., Kehoe, B., Bird, E., Jensen, V., & Darbyshire, M. Operant conditioning in dressing behavior of severely retarded girls. *Mental Retardation,* 1971, **9,** 27–31.

Martin, G. L., McDonald, S., & Omichinski, M. An operant analysis of response interactions during meals with severely retarded girls. *American Journal of Mental Deficiency,* 1971, **76,** 68–75.

Matson, J. L., DiLorenzo, T. M., & Esveldt-Dawson, K. Independence training as a method of enhancing self-help skills acquisition of the mentally retarded. *Behaviour Research and Therapy,* 1981, **19,** 399–405.

Matson, J. L., Marchetti, A., & Adkins, J. A. Comparison of operant- and independence-training procedures for mentally retarded adults. *American Journal of Mental Deficiency,* 1980, **84,** 487–494.

Matson, J. L., Ollendick, T. H., & Adkins, J. A comprehensive dining program for mentally retarded adults. *Behaviour Research and Therapy,* 1980, **18,** 107–112.

Minge, M. R., & Ball, T. S. Teaching of self-help skills to profoundly retarded patients. *American Journal of Mental Deficiency,* 1967, **71,** 864–868.

Murphy, M. J., & Zahm, D. Effects of improved ward conditions and behavioral treatment on self-help skills. *Mental Retardation,* 1975, **13,** 24–27.

Murphy, M. J., & Zahm, D. Effect of improved physical and social environment on self-help and problem behaviors of institutionalized retarded males. *Behavior Modification,* 1978, **2,** 193–210.

Nelson, G. L., Cone, J. D., & Hanson, C. R. Training correct utensil use in retarded children: Modeling vs. physical guidance. *American Journal of Mental Deficiency,* 1975, **80,** 114–122.

Nutter, D., & Reid, D. H. Teaching retarded women a clothing selection skill using community norms. *Journal of Applied Behavior Analysis,* 1978, **11,** 475–487.

O'Brien, F., & Azrin, N. H. Developing proper mealtime behaviors of the institutionalized retarded. *Journal of Applied Behavior Analysis,* 1972, **5,** 389–399.

O'Brien, F., Bugle, C., & Azrin, N. H. Training and maintaining a retarded child's proper eating. *Journal of Applied Behavior Analysis,* 1972, **5,** 67–72.

Osarchuk, M. Operant methods of toilet-behavior training of the severely and profoundly retarded: A review. *Journal of Special Education,* 1973, **7,** 423–437.

Passman, R. H. An automatic device for toilet training. *Behaviour Research and Therapy,* 1975, **13,** 215–220.

Paul, H. A., & Miller, J. R. Reduction of extreme deviant behaviors in a severely retarded girl. *Training School Bulletin,* 1971, **67,** 193–197.

Plummer, S., Baer, D. M., & LeBlanc, J. M. Functional

considerations in the use of procedural timeout and an effective alternative. *Journal of Applied Behavior Analysis*, 1977, **10**, 689–705.

Raborn, J. D. Classroom applications of the Foxx-Azrin toileting program. *Mental Retardation*, 1978, **16**, 173–174.

Reid, D. H. Trends and issues in behavioral research on training feeding and dressing skills. In J. L. Matson, & F. Andrasik (Eds.), *Treatment issues and innovations in mental retardation*. New York: Plenum, 1982.

Robinson-Wilson, M. A. Picture recipe cards as an approach to teaching severely and profoundly retarded adults to cook. *Education and Training of the Mentally Retarded*, 1977, **13**, 69–73.

Roos, P., & Oliver, M. Evaluation of operant conditioning with institutionalized retarded children. *American Journal of Mental Deficiency*, 1969, **74**, 325–330.

Rose, S. D. Training parents in groups as behavior modifiers of their mentally retarded children. *Journal of Behavior Therapy and Experimental Psychiatry*, 1974, **5**, 135–140.

Sadler, O. W., & Merkert, F. Evaluating the Foxx and Azrin toilet training procedure for retarded children in a day training center. *Behavior Therapy*, 1977, **8**, 499–500.

Schaeffer, H. H., & Martin, P. L. *Behavioral therapy*. New York: McGraw-Hill, 1969.

Schepis, M. M., Reid, D. H., Fitzgerald, J. R., Faw, G. D., van den Pol, R. A., & Welty, P. A. A program for increasing manual signing by autistic and profoundly retarded youth within the daily environment. *Journal of Applied Behavior Analysis*, 1982, **15**, 363–380.

Sloop, E. W., & Kennedy, W. A. Institutionalized retarded nocturnal enuretics treated by a conditioning technique. *American Journal of Mental Deficiency*, 1973, **77**, 717–721.

Smith, P. S., Britton, P. G., Johnson, M., & Thomas, D. A. Problems involved in toilet-training profoundly mentally handicapped adults. *Behaviour Research and Therapy*, 1975, **13**, 301–307.

Snell, M. E. (Ed.) *Systematic instruction of the moderately and severely handicapped*. Columbus, Ohio: Charles E. Merrill Publishing Co., 1978.

Song, A. Y., & Gandhi, R. An analysis of behavior during the acquisition and maintenance phases of self-spoon feeding skills of profound retardates. *Mental Retardation*, 1974, **12**, 25–28.

Song, A. Y., Song, R. H., & Grant, P. A. Toilet training in the school and its transfer in the living unit. *Journal of Behavior Therapy & Experimental Psychiatry*, 1976, **7**, 281–284.

Stimbert, V. E., Minor, J. W., & McCoy, J. F. Intensive feeding training with retarded children. *Behavior Modification*, 1977, **1**, 517–529.

Stokes, T. F., & Baer, D. M. An implicit technology of generalization. *Journal of Applied Behavior Analysis*, 1977, **10**, 349–367.

Stolz, S. B., & Wolf, M. M. Visually discriminated behavior in a "blind" adolescent retardate. *Journal of Applied Behavior Analysis*, 1969, **2**, 65–77.

Sulzer-Azaroff, B., & Mayer, R. G. *Applying behavior analysis procedures with children and youth*. New York: Holt, Rinehart, and Winston, 1977.

Thinesen, P. J., & Bryan, A. J. The use of sequential pictorial cues in the initiation and maintenance of grooming behaviors with mentally retarded adults. *Mental Retardation*, 1981, **19**, 247–250.

Thompson, T., & Grabowski, J. *Behavior modification of the mentally retarded*. New York: Oxford University Press, 1972.

Tymchuk, A. J. Training parent therapists. *Mental Retardation*, 1975, **13**, 19–22.

Van Biervliet, A., Spangler, P. F., & Marshall, A. M. An ecobehavioral examination of a simple strategy for increasing mealtime language in residential facilities. *Journal of Applied Behavior Analysis*, 1981, **14**, 295–305.

van den Pol, R. A., Iwata, B. A., Ivancic, M. T., Page, T. J., Neef, N. A., & Whitley, F. P. Teaching the handicapped to eat in public places: Acquisition, generalization, and maintenance of restaurant skills. *Journal of Applied Behavior Analysis*, 1981, **14**, 61–69.

Van Etten, G., Arkell, C., & Van Etten, C. *The severely and profoundly handicapped: Programs, methods, and materials*. St. Louis: C. V. Mosby Company, 1980.

Van Wagenen, R. K., Meyerson, L., Kerr, N. J., & Mahoney, K. Field trials of a new procedure for toilet training. *Journal of Experimental Child Psychology*, 1969, **8**, 147–159.

Walls, R. T., Crist, K., Sienicki, D. A., & Grant, L. Prompting sequences in teaching independent living skills. *Mental Retardation*, 1981, **19**, 243–246.

Wambold, C., & Salisbury, C. H. The development and implementation of self-care programs with severely and profoundly handicapped children. *AAESPH Review*, 1978, **3**, 178–184.

Watson, L. S. Application of operant conditioning techniques to institutionalized severely and profoundly retarded children. *Mental Retardation Abstracts*, 1967, **4**, 1–18.

Watson, L. S., & Bassinger, J. F. Parent training technology: A potential service delivery system. *Mental Retardation*, 1974, **12**, 3–10.

Watson, L. S., & Uzzell, R. Teaching self-help skills, grooming skills, and utensil feeding skills to the mentally retarded. In J. L. Matson & J. R. McCartney (Eds.), *Handbook of behavior modification with the mentally retarded*. New York: Plenum Press, 1980.

Wehman, P. Maintaining oral hygiene skills in geriatric retarded women. *Mental Retardation*, 1974, **12**, 20.

Whitman, T. L., & Scibak, J. W. Behavior modification research with the severely and profoundly retarded. In N. R. Ellis (Ed.), *Handbook of mental deficiency, psychological theory of research*. Hillsdale, New Jersey: Erlbaum, 1979.

Whitman, T. L., Scibak, J. W., & Reid, D. H. *Behavior modification with the severely and profoundly retarded: Research and application*. New York: Academic Press, In press.

Zeiler, M. D., & Jervey, S. S. Development of behavior: Self-feeding. *Journal of Consulting and Clinical Psychology*, 1968, **32**, 164–168.

29 PROGRAMMED INSTRUCTION

Nancy H. Huguenin, Leslie E. Weidenman, and James A. Mulick

Programmed instruction from a behavioral standpoint consists of the application of operant-conditioning principles to the development of new skills. It involves the arrangement of specific environmental events, both antecedents and consequences, that permit behavior to be acquired. Without the arrangement of these contingencies, it is unlikely that the behavior would occur (Skinner, 1965). The basic elements of programmed instruction include the materials or stimuli, the students' responses, and the consequences (Popovich, 1981). Educational material is arranged so that desired responses occur in the presence of appropriate environmental stimuli. When this takes place, reinforcement is provided to strengthen and maintain the target behavior (Silverman, 1978). Programmed materials are designed to minimize errors, as they represent a loss of instructional control. Should errors occur, the educational program is altered to reduce the chance of errors and to insure that a high density of positive reinforcement continues throughout instruction.

Many mentally retarded students failed to acquire basic skills when traditional teaching procedures were utilized. Programmed instruction, however, has had amazing success with even the most seriously impaired individuals. Investigators comparing different teaching procedures consistently have demonstrated the su-periority of programmed instruction for mentally retarded individuals (Frederiksen & Frederiksen, 1977; Haring & Krug, 1975; Walls, Zane & Thvedt, 1980). The highly individualized nature of this form of instruction plays a crucial role in its utility with the heterogeneous mentally retarded population. The present chapter will discuss specific instructional techniques that have been used successfully with mentally retarded students. A variety of goals can be achieved using the methodology of programmed instruction. Three major areas in which programming has been used effectively will be considered: (1) establishing new behaviors, (2) bringing target behaviors under stimulus control, and (3) programming for generalization. A review of some of the relevant literature in these areas will be provided as well as a discussion of future research needs.

Establishing New Forms of Behavior

There are many ways by which children acquire new skills. For example, they may discover a principle or concept through interaction with the environment or they may learn by imitating the behavior of others. In a more structured setting, such as the classroom, new skills often are transmitted in a more directed, formal way through specific performance feedback.

Teachers, other students, or even the instructional materials themselves can provide the student with feedback on his or her performance. Feedback can be delivered in a variety of ways, thus accounting for the numerous teaching procedures outlined in traditional teacher-training programs and methods courses. One of the more successful methods, generally referred to as a behavioral approach, describes a systematic way of arranging the environment, outlining objectives, creating opportunities for the student to respond, and providing corrective feedback on the performance. A well designed behavioral program may teach skills more efficiently and with better retention than a less structured method (e.g., Becker & Englemann, 1973; Englemann & Sterns, 1972). When teaching children with learning problems or mentally retarded students, efficiency and effectiveness of the procedures becomes even more important. Research has demonstrated that, given the proper learning environment, severely and profoundly retarded students can acquire new skills. These students have been taught a variety of self-help and preacademic skills such as dressing, toileting, color and picture matching, as well as speech and object identification, and many others.

Shaping

One feature commonly used in behavioral training to establish new behaviors is shaping. Shaping refers to a systematic method of reinforcement by which new behaviors are developed from already existing skills or actions. It consists of reinforcing successive approximations of the desired behavior (also called terminal or target behavior) as they occur until the acceptable form of the behavior has been achieved. The term successive approximations refers to an ordered series of behaviors each one slightly different from the preceding one in the direction of the desired behavioral outcome. Thus, each small change brings the behavior closer in topography to the target behavior. The shaping process begins with a behavior present in the child's repertoire. Of the series, this behavior is the least similar or roughest approximation to the final behavior. At first, reinforcement is provided for these dissimilar forms. When this behavior has been strengthened, the teacher changes the behavioral criteria and provides reinforcement only when a closer approximation occurs. Through this process of differential reinforcement, the child's behavior gradually takes the desired form. After the behavior is shaped, maintenance procedures can be instituted. Numerous factors will determine the success or failure of a particular shaping program. One of the most important factors is how well the program corresponds to the students' abilities and needs. Problems can arise, for example, if the approximations are too finely graded or are too far apart. In the former case, the student may become disinterested, or the program may be too time consuming. The latter situation, on the other hand, might cause frustration or distress. Difficulties can also occur if any one step in the series receives too much reinforcement. The student may get "stuck" at that level and not emit the next approximation. When planning a shaping program (or any behavioral program), careful selection of reinforcers is crucial. Reinforcers, like the steps in the series, must be tailored for the individual student to maximize effectiveness.

Shaping has proven to be an effective technique in teaching many useful skills to severely handicapped people. Both preacademic and nonacademic skills have been trained. For example, institutionalized retarded children were toilet trained (Azrin & Foxx, 1971), and a retarded child with spina bifida was taught to use crutches (Horner, 1971). Other self-help skills such as eating and dressing have been trained successfully using shaping (O'Brien, Bugle, & Azrin, 1972). Recent studies demonstrated that severely multihandicapped children could be taught to put on their own hearing aids (Tucker & Berry, 1980), and asthma patients could learn to use inhalation therapy equipment (Renne, 1976). In more academic areas, speech training, voice loudness, and following directions have all been trained using shaping procedures (Jackson & Wallace, 1974; McReynolds, 1969). It has succeeded when other approaches have failed partly because the response requirements at any one time are within the learner's ability, and it begins with behaviors already in the repertoire. Other factors, such as the use of immediate feedback, positive consequences, and active responding also contribute to its effectiveness. As most readers are aware, behaviors are strengthened or diminished by their consequences. Careful structuring of the consequences in a systematic, ordered fashion is the basis on which shaping occurs. One obvious disadvantage of shaping is that the trainer or teacher utilizing the procedure must wait for the behavior (or its component) to occur before reinforcement can be provided and the behavior strengthened. This disadvantage can be overcome easily, however, by using prompting procedures in conjunction with shaping. These techniques are considered later in the chapter.

Task Analysis

To plan a shaping or other behavioral-instruction program, one needs to examine carefully both the behavior to be taught and the capabilities of the students for whom the program is intended. It is important that the components of the behavior and the skills required to perform it be determined and arranged in a logical order. This type of analysis will enable the teacher to tailor a program for individual students. An analysis leading to the sequence of steps involved in the performance of the behavior often is referred to as a task analysis. The definition of task analysis offered by Sulzer-Azaroff & Mayer (1977) is: "breaking down a complex skill or behavioral chain into its component behaviors, sub-skills, or sub-tasks. Each component is stated in the order of occurrence and sets the occasion for the occurrence of the next behavior" (p. 524).

To conduct a task analysis, most program planners begin by observing the behavior, listing the components in the order of occurrence, and listing the subskills required for its performance. For example, if the behavior analyzed is toothbrushing, the following components might be listed:

- unscrewing cap of toothpaste
- holding toothbrush
- squeezing proper amount of toothpaste on brush
- brushing teeth (front, side, back, etc.)
- rinsing brush
- spitting out toothpaste
- rinsing mouth

the necessary sub-skills might include:

- fine motor control to unscrew cap and hold brush
- ability to turn on water faucet

This initial attempt, based on common sense and logic, is considered only a first step and not a finished task analysis. As Bijou (1981) points out, "an instructional program based on common sense task analysis rarely coincides with the way a particular child actually learns. Some of the steps may be too easy, some may be too short, and some may produce boredom or distractible behavior; other steps may be too difficult or too long and some may result in frustration, escape or avoidance behaviors" (p. 101). Obviously, the sequence needs to be validated empirically by trying it with the appropriate population and revising it as needed. Once the program has been completed, it still will require tailoring for each individual student. It is at this point that the student's abilities or entering skills are considered. For example, if handwriting was the behavior for which a task analysis was devised, modifications would be needed for a physically impaired child who did not have adequate motor control to hold a pencil. In this case, adaptive equipment could be utilized or perhaps the performance criteria could be altered to accommodate the student's abilities.

The process of conducting a task analysis is very useful for educators. It focuses attention on the relation between the individual's skills and the abilities required to perform a specific behavior. The sequence of component behaviors enables teachers, parents, and the children themselves to observe progress towards the behavioral goal, even if progress occurs slowly. Task analysis is an instructional tool that is meant to be used flexibly. For example, if the teacher finds the child is gaining skills rapidly, it may be possible to skip steps and advance the child at a faster pace. On the other hand, if a particular step is too difficult, the teacher may need to break it down further, creating smaller steps the child can accomplish.

It is not always necessary to develop task analyses on each behavior to be taught. Task analyses on numerous behaviors in many different skill areas have been published in both the educational and behavioral literature. Several sources have entire curriculums developed for handicapped children. For example, Fredericks et al. (1976) and Wheeler and his colleagues (1977) provide programs for self-help, preacademic, and prevocational skills, to name a few. Other materials focus on specific areas of functioning such as Wehman's (1977) text. In it, leisure activities such as roller skating, painting, and playing checkers are outlined.

Chaining

Once task analysis is completed, any necessary modifications for the individual's skills can be made, and appropriate reinforcers can be selected in preparation for instruction. The teaching process involves establishing the behavior, one component at a time. The components or subskills outlined sequentially in the task analysis often are referred to as a behavioral chain. Each component represents a link in the chain, and each link is necessary for the performance of the behavior. The training procedure by which the skills are acquired is called chaining. Chaining is a "procedure in which simple responses already in the repertoire of the individual are reinforced in a sequence to form more complex behaviors" (Sulzer-Azaroff & Mayer, 1977, p. 513). The success of chaining as a teaching procedure can be partly accounted for by the notion of conditioned reinforcement. The behavioral components or links in the chain may develop reinforcing properties over time through frequent pairings with a strong reinforcer. That is, they may become conditioned reinforcers. At the same time, the frequent pairings of component events leading to reinforcement may result in the components taking on discriminative properties. After a period of time, the behavior preceding the reinforced event will come to "signal" or occasion the behavior that follows.

Thus, each link in the chain can be thought of as developing two stimulus functions: serving as a conditioned reinforcer for the preceding link (component in the chain), and acting as a discriminative stimulus or signal to occasion the following link in the chain.

Bringing Behavior Under Stimulus Control

A major goal of programmed instruction is to bring the student's behavior under the control of antecedent stimuli. A stimulus is said to control a response if the response's probability of occurrence is higher in the presence of the stimulus than in its absence (Reynolds, 1968). For example, if a child remained seated only when his teacher was in the classroom, the teacher would be an antecedent stimulus which exerted control over the student's sitting. One method of establishing stimulus control is differential reinforcement. With this technique, the target response is reinforced only in the presence of a particular stimulus. When other stimuli are present, no reinforcement is provided; that is, the response is under extinction. A discrimination between the antecedent stimuli is formed if they determine response probability.

Differential reinforcement has been found to be an inefficient technique for bringing about stimulus control with mentally retarded individuals. When mentally retarded and normal children are compared on discrimination-learning tasks, mentally retarded children typically required significantly more trials to reach criterion (Ullman & Routh, 1971). Other investigators have discovered that mentally retarded children exhibit many more errors than nonretarded children when a series of successive compound-discrimination tasks are administered (Kaufman & Peterson, 1958; Stevenson & Swartz, 1958; Wischner & O'Donnell, 1962). Finally, in experiments where only one stimulus dimension reliably was associated with reinforcement and extinction, stimulus control was achieved more slowly for mentally retarded children because of their greater number of errors (Brown, 1970).

Errors are thought to represent behavior under the control of irrelevant features of instructional materials (Touchette, 1968). Responding to irrelevant properties can continue indefinitely if reinforced intermittently and also can prevent the student from attending to the relevant dimensions of the task. Zeaman and House (1963) propose that mentally retarded students are likely to respond persistently to irrelevant stimuli since they attend to fewer (and possibly different) aspects of their environment than normal students. Therefore, stimulus-control procedures which reduce

the possibility of errors, or responding to irrelevant features, are especially crucial for mentally retarded individuals.

Stimulus Fading

Stimulus fading is a teaching procedure used to bring target behaviors gradually under the control of environmental stimuli (Fig. 29.1). It is designed so that stimulus control develops with few or no errors. This feature makes stimulus fading a particularly useful technique to use with mentally retarded students. The important components of stimulus fading, sometimes called extrastimulus prompting (Schreibman, 1975; Wolfe & Cuvo, 1978), consist of presenting two stimuli simultaneously. One stimulus already produces the desired response reliably. The second stimulus is the training stimulus which does not yet exert control over the response. During teaching, the training stimulus remains unaltered while the added stimulus prompt is progressively decreased in magnitude until it finally is eliminated. Stimulus control is transferred from the prompting cue to the training stimulus by reinforcing and maintaining the target response as the stimulus prompt is faded. Stimulus

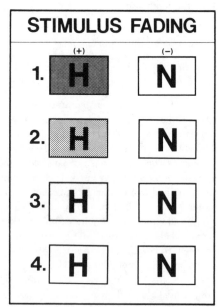

Fig. 29.1. Diagram of a stimulus-fading procedure for teaching a letter discrimination. In this example, a red background (represented by varying shades of gray) is used to prompt the correct (+) response choice. The color prompt is reduced by decreasing its intensity during the fading sequence. In the final step, only the training stimuli (letters H and N) remain.

fading has been effective for mentally retarded students in many different instructional programs that include teaching visual discriminations (Sidman & Stoddard, 1967; Touchette, 1968), enhancing language skills (Carr, Binkoff, Kologinsky, & Eddy, 1978; Reid & Hurlbut, 1977), and teaching compliance with verbal instructions (Striefel & Wetherby, 1973).

Carr and his associates (1978) provided a clear illustration of stimulus fading when they employed this stimulus-control technique to teach sign language to nonverbal autistic children. Their procedure involved training the correct sign for five common foods which prior to the instructional program the children did not know. In the first step, the teacher presented the object and named it. A physical prompt was provided simultaneously, and it entailed molding the child's hand into the appropriate sign configuration. Following execution of the sign, immediate reinforcement was provided. These steps were repeated over successive trials as the physical prompt was faded. Fading was accomplished by gradually decreasing the amount of manual guidance in forming the sign. The fading sequence resulted in a transfer of stimulus control from the physical prompt to the training cues, and eventually each of the students produced the correct sign unaided when the corresponding object was displayed.

Different types of prompts have been used in stimulus-fading programs. They include verbal instruction, gestural prompts, arranging the environment so the target response is likely to occur, physical guidance, and modeling (Favell, 1977). Past research has shown that not all prompts are equally effective with mentally retarded students. Nelson, Cone, and Hanson (1975), for instance, demonstrated that physical guidance was more successful than modeling in teaching mealtime skills. Which kind of prompt is selected then, must depend on which one consistently evokes the target response with the particular student.

Verbal instruction is one type of prompt where the teacher simply tells the student to perform the target response. Social behaviors (Gibson, Lawrence, & Nelson, 1977; Petersen, Austin, & Lang, 1979) and language skills (Twardosz & Baer, 1973) have been enhanced by this technique. A verbal prompt is faded by either speaking in a progressively softer voice or gradually reducing the number of words in the verbal instruction (Popovich, 1981).

Gestural prompts also have been utilized to increase the frequency of target behaviors for mentally retarded individuals. A teacher could prompt a student to brush his/her teeth by simply pointing to the toothbrush. The gestural prompt is faded subsequently by gradually reducing the size of the gesture (Popovich, 1981) and

its topographical completeness (Favell, 1977). This kind of prompt was attenuated in one study (Wolfe & Cuvo, 1978) by the teacher slowly increasing the distance between his pointed finger and the correct choice in a discrimination-learning task.

Arranging the physical environment to insure the likelihood of specified behaviors is a third prompting technique that has been used to teach retarded students simple discriminations (Touchette, 1968), self-help skills (Thinesen & Bryan, 1981), and reading comprehension (Dorry, 1976). The average environment is supplemented with additional stimulus cues that either physically promote the occurrence of the target response (e.g., Stoddard & Gerovac, 1981) or make the correct answer more distinctive than incorrect choices (Favell, 1977). The added features are then gradually removed. Dorry (1976) taught retarded students to identify printed words of familiar objects using this technique. Initially, appropriate labeling was induced by simultaneously presenting a picture of each object with the word. Next, the picture prompts were faded by reducing their visibility over trials until only the printed words remained.

Physical prompts also are incorporated in many stimulus-fading procedures (Carr, Binkoff, Kologinsky, & Eddy, 1978; Reid & Hurlbut, 1977; Striefel & Wetherby, 1973; Walls, Crist, Sienicki, & Grant, 1981). They involve physical contact since the teacher either manually guides the student through the target behavior or prompts the response with a touch or a tap. Walls and his associates (1981) employed physical prompts to teach retarded adults shirt folding, table setting, and how to use a cassette-tape recorder. The teacher began the instructional program providing full physical assistance until each response was completed. Partial physical prompts during fading involved moving the student's hand to the appropriate materials and finally a nudge on the student's arm without guidance.

Modeling is a fifth prompting procedure that could evoke target behaviors for mentally retarded students possessing imitative skills. Correct responses performed by the teacher in front of the student have increased social behaviors (Gibson, Lawrence, & Nelson, 1977), expressive speech (Garcia, Guess, & Byrnes, 1973; Martin, 1975), and dressing skills (Nutter & Reid, 1978). A modeling prompt is attenuated by showing only partial components of the target behavior and systematically reducing the extent of the demonstration (Favell, 1977).

Doran and Holland's (1979) investigation succeeded in unraveling some of the necessary ingredients for predicting whether stimulus fading will be an errorless mode of instruction. They used a brightness fading procedure to train size discriminations. Choosing the larger of two circles was reinforced, and initially the target response was prompted by increasing the luminance level of the larger circle. The luminance cues were then faded until the circles were of equal brightness. At that point, only the relevant size cues remained. Throughout the 50-trial fading sequence, test trials were administered to detect any transfer in stimulus control from the prompting (brightness) stimuli to the training (size) cues. One test stimulus had the same luminance as the positive stimulus but was of smaller size. The second test stimulus equalled the size of the positive stimulus but had a lower luminance. These test trials were presented to resolve the specific stimulus features each student was attending to in the early, intermediate, and final stages of fading.

With this testing technique, Doran and Holland discovered that prior to learning the size discrimination most children attended simultaneously to the luminance and size components of the positive stimulus. If stimulus control was not displayed concurrently for both the prompting and training cues in early or intermediate phases of the fading sequence, children usually failed to acquire the size discrimination after the prompting stimuli were completely removed. Although in either situation, the students responded errorlessly until the final stages of fading, test trials revealed substantial differences and accurately predicted their terminal performance.

Stimulus Shaping

Another technique that frequently has brought the behavior of mentally retarded individuals under control of instructional cues with relatively few errors is stimulus shaping. This technique is also referred to as within-stimulus prompting (Schreibman, 1975; Wolfe & Cuvo, 1978). It consists of initially emphasizing distinctive features of training stimuli so that the student consistently responds in an appropriate fashion (Fig. 29.2). Errorless performance is maintained by gradually reducing exaggertion of distinctive features until the criterion level of the training stimuli is finally reached. Stimulus shaping differs from stimulus fading in that it does not employ an added stimulus cue to prompt correct responses. In addition, it brings the student under control of the relevant instructional stimuli at the beginning of the teaching sequence.

One of the earliest demonstrations of stimulus shaping was a laboratory investigation conducted by Stoddard and Sidman (1967). Both mentally retarded and normal children participated in the program. During training, children sat facing a display panel containing nine response keys arranged in a 3-by-3

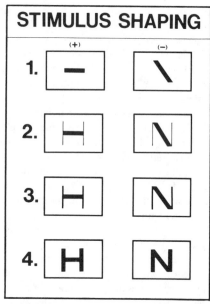

Fig. 29.2. Diagram of a stimulus-shaping procedure for teaching a letter discrimination. In this example, the distinctive features of the training stimuli (letters H and N) are presented alone to prompt the correct (+) response choice. The distinctive features are next maintained while the redundant features of the training stimuli are gradually introduced.

matrix. Stimuli were projected on the keys, and a correct choice resulted in the automatic delivery of tokens and candy. A stimulus-shaping procedure was used to teach a difficult circle-ellipse discrimination. It was achieved by first training each child to select the key with a circle projected on it from keys that contained relatively flat ellipses. As training progressed, the vertical height of the ellipses was gradually increased while the circle remained constant. Their procedure, which progressively increased similarity of the circle and ellipses, successfully taught each child to discriminate very small differences with virtually errorless performance.

More recently Stoddard and Gerovac (1981) demonstrated that stimulus-shaping methods could also be used for teaching severely and profoundly mentally retarded individuals a complex motor response. The methods differed from the use of stimulus shaping in discrimination learning where the response remains invariant. Instead, progressive changes in stimuli were used to produce changes in the spatial topography of the response. Briefly, the subjects learned to insert a token into the proper slot of an automatic device to produce food deliveries through a series of graded steps. First, touching a token which projected only slightly from the illuminated slot led to reinforcement. On subsequent trials, the token projected more and more, was then dangled by a string from the slot at increasing distances, and finally ended up in the underlying tray where they would drop if delivered by the automatic dispenser mechanism. Thus, progressive alteration of spatial stimulus properties that already controlled responding led to gradual alterations in the movements required until the terminal performance was achieved.

Stimulus shaping has also been employed in more applied instructional programs as well. Wolfe and Cuvo (1978), for example, utilized stimulus shaping to teach letter-recognition skills to 24 severely retarded young adults. The instructor placed three cards, containing the selected target letter and two distractors, before the student. In the full prompt condition, the distinctive feature of the target letter was emphasized by increasing both its height and width. The prompting conditions that followed gradually reduced the size of the target letter's distinctive feature to criterion level. Throughout the prompting sequence, correct choices were reinforced. The mentally retarded students learned with a high level of accuracy to pick target letters upon verbal request. They were not observed to exhibit this skill before the stimulus-shaping program was introduced.

Numerous investigators have compared the relative effectiveness of stimulus shaping vs. stimulus fading as teaching methods for developmentally delayed individuals. Schreibman (1975) discovered that, when the two prompting procedures were employed to teach visual discriminations to autistic children, more children learned the tasks with stimulus shaping. Stimulus fading involved presenting a gestural prompt (pointed finger) simultaneously with the correct visual cue and then gradually removing the pointing prompt. Stimulus shaping, in contrast, consisted of expanding in size the critical components of the visual cues, followed by a gradual size reduction, and then progressively introducing the redundant features of the training stimuli. Each time the stimulus-fading procedure was applied, it failed. In the majority of cases, however, stimulus shaping successfully taught difficult visual discriminations to the autistic students. Wolfe and Cuvo (1978) compared the effects of similar prompting procedures to train severely retarded individuals to identify target letters. They also demonstrated that stimulus shaping was a more successful form of instruction than stimulus fading.

The superiority of stimulus shaping for severely retarded and autistic students may possibly be explained by past research indicating that these client populations

exhibit extreme selective attention compared to non-disabled individuals (Koegel & Wilhelm, 1973; Lovaas & Schreibman, 1971; Lovaas, Schreibman, Koegel, & Rehm, 1971; Wilhelm & Lovaas, 1976). They have difficulty in attending simultaneously to more than one feature of instructional stimuli. A disadvantage of stimulus fading is that it requires simultaneous attention to both the added stimulus prompt and the training stimulus in order for a transfer of stimulus control to occur (Doran & Holland, 1979). This may partially explain why stimulus fading programs are not always successful with mentally retarded students. Since stimulus shaping brings the student's behavior under the control of relevant training cues by emphasizing their distinctive features and without necessarily introducing a prompt from a differing stimulus dimension, it has greater utility with overselective populations.

Although stimulus shaping may be preferred for mentally retarded individuals, Irvin and Bellamy's (1977) findings suggest that a combination of stimulus shaping and stimulus fading may be a more powerful instructional tool than either prompting procedure used in isolation. They compared three conditions for teaching vocational skills to retarded adults. Stimulus fading in this investigation was adding a color prompt to the training stimulus (raised face of an axle nut) and then fading the color cue. Stimulus shaping involved increasing the dissimilarity of the axle nuts on the relevant shape dimension and then progressively reducing their dissimilarity to the normal level. In the combined condition, the shape of the face of the axle nut was exaggerated, and it was also colored red. Next, both prompts were attenuated. The combined fading and shaping condition permitted the mentally retarded students to learn the assembly task with the fewest errors.

Delayed Cue

Stimulus fading is an errorless instructional procedure that involves presenting the prompt in spatial and temporal contiguity with the training stimulus during initial introduction and gradual removal. The magnitude of the stimulus prompt is reduced while it continues to occur concurrently with the training stimulus (Fig. 29.3). The delayed-cue technique, however, is an errorless stimulus-control method where the intensity of the stimulus prompt is constant throughout but its temporal relationship with the training stimulus is manipulated (Touchette, 1971). In the initial trials, the stimulus prompt is delivered at the same time as the training stimulus. As trials continue, the onset of the stimulus prompt is delayed

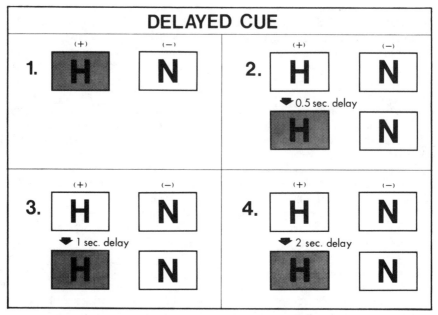

Fig. 29.3. Diagram of a delayed-cue procedure for teaching a letter discrimination. In this example, a red background (represented by dark gray) is used to prompt the correct (+) response choice. The color prompt is removed by progressively delaying its onset following the presentation of the training stimuli (letters H and N).

progressively. At first, the prompt and training stimulus occur together, but if the target response is consistently observed, the amount of time separating the introduction of the training stimulus and subsequent appearance of the prompt is gradually increased.

Delayed-cue prompting taught severely retarded adolescents to form discriminations without errors (Touchette, 1971). A color prompt was chosen in this study, because each student had already learned to press a red key consistently when a white response key was simultaneously available. The first trial, therefore, involved superimposing two different forms on the red and white keys. If the student picked the form on a red background, the color prompt was delayed 0.5 seconds after the forms were presented on the following trial. Each correct response in the teaching session delayed the prompt on succeeding trials an extra 0.5 seconds. Choosing the positive form either before or after the addition of the red cue ended the trial and immediately was reinforced. In relatively few trials, each student began to respond to the positive form before the color prompt was supplied and without making any response to the negative form. A delayed prompt for these students transferred stimulus control errorlessly from one set of stimuli to another.

The delayed-cue technique in another investigation brought the motor behavior of profoundly-retarded students under the control of verbal cues when a modeling prompt was progressively withheld (Striefel, Bryan, & Aikins, 1974). Initially, a verbal instruction to perform a specific motor response was given while the teacher simultaneously modeled the behavior. After the student imitated the teacher, reinforcement was provided. On following trials, a delay was inserted between the verbal instruction and the modeling prompt. Each occurrence of the target response gradually increased the time separation. Within a few trials, students began to comply with the verbal instructions before the teacher modeled the behavior. The delayed-cue prompting method trained these profoundly-retarded individuals to follow verbal directions with a low level of errors and efficiently transferred instructional control from a visual to an auditory modality.

Delaying a stimulus prompt can successfully transfer stimulus control to training stimuli without errors. This technique, however, has not been employed as widely as stimulus fading and stimulus shaping, and its limitations have not yet been determined. Future investigations need to directly compare the delayed-cue procedure with other errorless stimulus-control procedures to specify any advantages and disadvantages it might have.

Programming Generalization

A third aim of programmed instruction is to promote generalization of the newly acquired behavior. Generalization is observed when target behaviors occur in nontraining conditions where the full treatment program has never been applied (See Stokes & Baer, 1977). Discovering techniques that actively produce generalization is particularly important for mentally retarded students, as they frequently fail to transfer recently acquired behaviors to environments outside of the treatment setting (Handleman, 1979; Koegel & Rincover, 1974; Murdock, Garcia, & Hardman, 1977; Rincover & Koegel, 1975). Murdock and her colleagues (1977) illustrated this when they taught mentally retarded students to articulate four words correctly when appropriate pictures were displayed. Although the students learned to verbally identify stimulus cards in the classroom, they did not articulate target words in most cases when other teachers presented pictures in different settings. Similarly, Rincover and Koegel's (1975) findings revealed that mentally retarded children did not generalize responses across environments because of incidental aspects of the training setting gaining stimulus control. If these incidental features were not available in other areas, students did not exhibit newly taught behaviors.

Common Stimuli

One technique for encouraging generalization is to insure that target behaviors come under the control of specific antecedent stimuli which are common to other environments (Stokes & Baer, 1977). Some investigators have accomplished this objective by developing a high level of stimulus control for designated stimuli in the original setting and then introducing identical cues in additional environments where previously they never have been observed. Target behaviors are frequently produced in settings where the contrived stimuli are provided (Halle, Marshall, & Spradlin, 1979; Huguenin & Mulick, 1981). An alternative approach has been to duplicate in the classroom stimuli that appear normally in other settings. When the reproduced stimuli exhibit appropriate control, the same or similar stimuli in the natural environment also increase the probability of the target behavior's occurrence (Nutter & Reid, 1978; Page, Iwata, & Neef, 1976; Welch & Pear, 1980).

Varied Instruction

Enhancing the diversity of the teaching procedure during original training is another technique for facilitating generalization (Stokes & Baer, 1977). When either more than one teacher provides instruction (Garcia, 1974; Stokes, Baer, & Jackson, 1974) or the training program is conducted in at least two settings (Murdock, Garcia, & Hardman, 1977), greater transfer of newly acquired behaviors to untrained conditions is obtained. Varied instruction may cause this result, because it reduces the possibility of incidental training features acquiring stimulus control which would then reduce generalization effects (Rincover & Koegel, 1975).

Summary and Conclusions

Programmed instruction, which is a successful educational approach for a wide variety of student populations, has proven to be especially important for the education and training of mentally retarded individuals. Shaping and task analysis are two basic programmed instruction procedures which have taught many essential living skills to students with differing degrees of mental retardation who failed to profit from a more traditional format. Stimulus fading, stimulus shaping, and delayed-cue prompting are techniques that have efficiently trained retarded students to exhibit acquired behaviors in appropriate environmental contexts. Finally, programming for generalization by bringing target behaviors under the control of antecedent stimuli common to other environments or increasing the diversity of original training has promoted the occurrence of learned skills in nontraining settings. Unfortunately, although programmed instruction has been demonstrated to have by far the greatest utility for developmentally-disabled students, greater application of this educational methodology is still needed.

Future aims of programmed instruction should include additional research directed at comparisons of existing educational procedures to determine which techniques are the most powerful for mentally retarded individuals. Although some studies have already shown that similar procedures can vary greatly in their teaching success with this population, more experiments must be performed. We also need to pinpoint specific student characteristics which dictate how programmed instruction should be administered. Studies which include nonretarded children as controls can permit us to identify behavior patterns peculiar to mentally retarded students that must be considered when choosing a specific educational format. Applying new technology is perhaps one of the more exciting future prospects for programmed instruction (Mulick, Scott, Gaines, & Campbell, 1983). Increasing the range and complexity of target behaviors and administering precise and complex behavioral contingencies without direct teacher supervision are some of the many benefits that computer-mediated instruction may have in future classrooms for the mentally retarded.

References

Azrin, N. H., & Foxx, R. M. A rapid method of toilet training the institutionalized retarded. *Journal of Applied Behavior Analysis*, 1971, **4**, 89–99.

Becker, W. C., & Englemann, S. *Summary analyses of five-year data on achievement and teaching progress with 14,000 in 20 projects, Technical Report 73-2.* Eugene, Oregon: University of Oregon Follow Through Project, Dec. 1973.

Bijou, S. W. Behavioral teaching of young handicapped children: Problems of application and implementation. In S. W. Bijou & R. Ruiz (Eds.), *Behavior modification: Contributions to education.* Hillsdale, N.J.: Lawrence Erlbaum, 1981.

Brown, A. L. Subject and experimental variables in the oddity learning of normal and retarded children. *American Journal of Mental Deficiency*, 1970, **75**, 142–151.

Carr, E. G., Binkoff, J. A., Kologinsky, E., & Eddy, M. Acquisition of sign language by autistic children. 1. Expressive labelling. *Journal of Applied Behavior Analysis*, 1978, **11**, 489–501.

Doran, J., and Holland, J. G. Control by stimulus features during fading. *Journal of the Experimental Analysis of Behavior*, 1979, **31**, 177–187.

Dorry, G. W. Attentional model for the effectiveness of fading in training reading-vocabulary with retarded persons. *American Journal of Mental Deficiency*, 1976, **81**, 271–279.

Englemann, S., & Sterns, S. *Distar reading level III: Reading to learn.* Chicago: Science Research Associates, 1972.

Favell, J. E. *The power of positive reinforcement.* Springfield: Charles C. Thomas, 1977.

Fredericks, H. D., Grove, D. N., Baldwin, V. L., Moore, W. G., Riggs, C., Furey, V., Hanson, Jordan, E., McDonnell, J. J., & Wadlow, U. *The teaching research curriculum for the moderately and severely handicapped.* Springfield: Charles C. Thomas, 1976.

Frederiksen, L. W., & Frederiksen, C. B. Experimental evaluation of classroom environments: Scheduling planned activities. *American Journal of Mental Deficiency*, 1977, **81**, 421–427.

Garcia, E. The training and generalization of a conversational speech form in nonverbal retardates. *Journal of Applied Behavior Analysis*, 1974, 7, 137–149.

Garcia, E., Guess, D., & Byrnes, J. Development of syntax in a retarded girl using procedures of imitation, reinforcement, and modelling. *Journal of Applied Behavior Analysis*, 1973, **6**, 299–310.

Gibson, F. W., Lawrence, P. S., & Nelson, R. O. Comparison of three training procedures for teaching social responses to developmentally disabled adults. *American Journal of Mental Deficiency*, 1977, **81**, 379–387.

Halle, J. W., Marshall, A. M., & Spradlin, J. E. Time delay: A technique to increase language use and facilitate generalization in retarded children. *Journal of Applied Behavior Analysis*, 1979, **12**, 431–439.

Handleman, J. S. Generalization by autistic-type children of verbal responses across settings. *Journal of Applied Behavior Analysis*, 1979, **12**, 273–282.

Haring, N. G., & Krug, D. A. Evaluation of a program of systematic instructional procedures for extremely poor retarded children. *American Journal of Mental Deficiency*, 1975, **79**, 627–631.

Horner, R. D. Establishing the use of crutches by a mentally retarded spina bifida child. *Journal of Applied Behavior Analysis*, 1971, **4**, 183–189.

Huguenin, N. H., & Mulick, J. A. Nonexclusionary timeout: Maintenance of appropriate behavior across settings. *Applied Research in Mental Retardation*, 1981, **2**, 55–67.

Irvin, L. K., & Bellamy, G. T. Manipulation of stimulus features in vocational-skill training of severely retarded individuals. *American Journal of Mental Deficiency*, 1977, **81**, 486–491.

Jackson, D. A., & Wallace, R. F. The modification and generalization of voice loudness in a fifteen-year-old retarded girl. *Journal of Applied Behavior Analysis*, 1974, **7**, 461–471.

Kaufman, M. E., & Peterson, W. M. Acquisition of a learning set by normal and mentally retarded children. *Journal of Comparative and Physiological Psychology*, 1958, **51**, 619–621.

Koegel, R. L., & Rincover, A. Treatment of psychotic children in a classroom environment. 1. Learning in a large group. *Journal of Applied Behavior Analysis*, 1974, **7**, 45–59.

Koegel, R. L., & Wilhelm, H. Selective responding to the components of multiple visual cues by autistic children. *Journal of Experimental Child Psychology*, 1973, **15**, 442–453.

Lovaas, O. I., & Schreibman, L. Stimulus overselectivity of autistic children in a two stimulus situation. *Behavior Research and Therapy*, 1971, **9**, 305–310.

Lovaas, O. I., Schreibman, L., Koegel, R. L., & Rehm, R. Selective responding by autistic children to multiple sensory input. *Journal of Abnormal Psychology*, 1971, **77**, 211–222.

Martin, J. A. Generalizing the use of descriptive adjectives through modelling. *Journal of Applied Behavior Analysis*, 1975, **8**, 203–209.

McReynolds, L. V. Application of timeout from positive reinforcement for increasing the efficiency of speech training. *Journal of Applied Behavior Analysis*, 1969, **2**, 199–205.

Mulick, J. A., Scott, F. D., Gaines, R. F., & Campbell, B. M. Devices and instrumentation for skill development and behavior change. In J. L. Matson & F. Andrasik (Eds.), *Treatment issues and innovations in mental retardation.* New York: Plenum Press, 1983.

Murdock, J. Y., Garcia, E. E., & Hardman, M. L. Generalizing articulation training with trainable mentally retarded subjects. *Journal of Applied Behavior Analysis*, 1977, **10**, 717–733.

Nelson, G. L., Cone, J. D., & Hanson, C. R. Training correct utensil use in retarded children: Modeling vs. physical guidance. *American Journal of Mental Deficiency*, 1975, **80**, 114–122.

Nutter, D., & Reid, D. H. Teaching retarded women a

clothing selection skill using community norms. *Journal of Applied Behavior Analysis*, 1978, **11**, 475–487.

O'Brien, F., Bugle, C., & Azrin, N. H. Training and maintaining a retarded child's proper eating. *Journal of Applied Behavior Analysis*, 1972, **5**, 67–72.

Page, T. J., Iwata, B. A., & Neef, N. A. Teaching pedestrian skills to retarded persons: Generalization from the classroom to the natural environment. *Journal of Applied Behavior Analysis*, 1976, **9**, 433–444.

Petersen, G. A., Austin, G. J., & Lang, R. P. Use of teacher prompts to increase social behavior: Generalization effects with severely and profoundly retarded adolescents. *American Journal of Mental Deficiency*, 1979, **84**, 82–86.

Popovich, D. *Effective educational and behavioral programming for severely and profoundly handicapped students*. Baltimore: Paul H. Brookes, 1981.

Reid, D. H., & Hurlbut, B. Teaching nonvocal communication skills to multihandicapped retarded adults. *Journal of Applied Behavior Analysis*, 1977, **10**, 591–603.

Renne, C. M., & Creer, T. L. Training children with asthma to use inhalation therapy equipment. *Journal of Applied Behavior Analysis*, 1976, **9**, 1–11.

Reynolds, G. S. *A primer in operant conditioning*. Glenview: Scott, Foresman and Company, 1968.

Rincover, A., & Koegel, R. L. Setting generality and stimulus control in autistic children. *Journal of Applied Behavior Analysis*, 1975, **8**, 235–246.

Schreibman, L. Effects of within-stimulus and extra-stimulus prompting on discrimination learning in autistic children. *Journal of Applied Behavior Analysis*, 1975, **8**, 91–112.

Sidman, M., & Stoddard, L. T. The effectiveness of fading in programming a simultaneous form discrimination for retarded children. *Journal of the Experimental Analysis of Behavior*, 1967, **10**, 3–15.

Silverman, R. E. Programmed instruction. In A. C. Catania & T. A. Brigham (Eds.), *Handbook of applied behavior analysis: Social and instructional processes*. New York: Irvington Publishers, 1978.

Skinner, B. F. The technology of teaching. *Proceedings of the Royal Society*, 1965, **162**, 427–443.

Stevenson, H. W., & Swartz, J. D. Learning set in children as a function of intellectual level. *Journal of Comparative and Physiological Psychology*, 1958, **51**, 755–757.

Stoddard, L. T., & Gerovac, B. J. A stimulus shaping method for teaching complex motor performance to severely and profoundly retarded individuals. *Applied Research in Mental Retardation*, 1981, **2**, 281–295.

Stoddard, L. T., & Sidman, M. The effects of errors on children's performance on a circle-ellipse discrimination. *Journal of the Experimental Analysis of Behavior*, 1967, **10**, 261–270.

Stokes, T. F., & Baer, D. M. An implicit technology of generalization. *Journal of Applied Behavior Analysis*, 1977, **10**, 349–367.

Stokes, T. F., Baer, D. M., & Jackson, R. L. Programming the generalization of a greeting response in four retarded children. *Journal of Applied Behavior Analysis*, 1974, **7**, 599–610.

Striefel, S., Bryan, K. S., & Aikins, D. A. Transfer of stimulus control from motor to verbal stimuli. *Journal of Applied Behavior Analysis*, 1974, **7**, 123–135.

Striefel, S., & Wetherby, B. Instruction-following behavior of a retarded child and its controlling stimuli. *Journal of Applied Behavior Analysis*, 1973, **6**, 663–670.

Sulzer-Azaroff, B., & Mayer, G. R. *Applying behavior analysis procedures with children and youth*. New York: Holt, Rinehart, and Winston, 1977.

Thinesen, P. J., & Bryan, A. J. The use of sequential pictorial cues in the initiation and maintenance of grooming behaviors with mentally retarded adults. *Mental Retardation*, 1981, **19**, 247–250.

Touchette, P. E. The effects of graduated stimulus change on the acquisition of a simple discrimination in severely retarded boys. *Journal of the Experimental Analysis of Behavior*, 1968, **11**, 39–48.

Touchette, P. E. Transfer of stimulus control: Measuring the moment of transfer. *Journal of the Experimental Analysis of Behavior*, 1971, **15**, 347–354.

Tucker, D. J., & Berry, G. W. Teaching severely multihandicapped students to put on their own hearing aids. *Journal of Applied Behavior Analysis*, 1980, **13**, 65–75.

Twardosz, S., & Baer, D. M. Training two severely retarded adolescents to ask questions. *Journal of Applied Behavior Analysis*, 1973, **6**, 655–661.

Ullman, D. G., & Routh, D. K. Discrimination learning in mentally retarded and nonretarded children as a function of the number of relevant dimensions. *American Journal of Mental Deficiency*, 1971, **76**, 176–180.

Walls, R. T., Crist, K., Sienicki, D. A., & Grant, L. Prompting sequences in teaching independent living skills. *Mental Retardation*, 1981, **19**, 242–245.

Walls, R. T., Zane, T., & Thvedt, J. E. Trainers' personal methods compared to two structured training strategies. *American Journal of Mental Deficiency*, 1980, **84**, 495–507.

Wehman, P. *Helping the mentally retarded acquire play skills: A behavioral approach*. Springfield: Charles C. Thomas, 1977.

Welch, S. J., & Pear, J. J. Generalization of naming responses to objects in the natural environment as a function of training stimulus modality with retarded children. *Journal of Applied Behavior Analysis*, 1980, **13**, 629–643.

Wheeler, A. J., Miller, R. A., Duke, J., Salisbury, E. A., Merritt, V., & Horton, B. *Murdoch center C & Y program library: A collection of step-by-step programs for the developmentally disabled*. Butner, N.C.: Murdoch Center, 1977.

Wilhelm, H., & Lovaas, O. I. Stimulus overselectivity: A common feature in autism and mental retardation. *American Journal of Mental Deficiency*, 1976, **81**, 26–31.

Wischner, G. J., & O'Donnell, J. P. Concurrent learning-set formation in normal and retarded children. *Journal of Comparative and Physiological Psychology*, 1962, **55**, 524–527.

Wolfe, V. F., & Cuvo, A. J. Effects of within-stimulus and extra-stimulus prompting on letter discrimination by mentally retarded persons. *American Journal of Mental Deficiency*, 1978, **83**, 297–303.

Zeaman, D., & House, B. J. The role of attention in retardate discrimination learning. In N. R. Ellis (Ed.), *Handbook of mental deficiency*. New York: McGraw-Hill, 1963.

30 VOCATIONAL TRAINING AND PLACEMENT*

Frank R. Rusch,
Richard P. Schutz, and Laird W. Heal

dvances in the field of vocational (re)habilitation have resulted in a new optimism regarding the best practices to employ mentally retarded persons. These advances are particularly noteworthy with regard to training severely mentally retarded persons. Severely mentally retarded persons, once believed incapable of performing valued work behavior, have been taught to assemble complex, multistep tasks that vary along several dimensions, including size, color, and form (Rusch & Schutz, 1981). Most impressive has been new data reported by Horner and his colleagues in their investigation of generalization (Colvin & Horner, 1982; Horner & McDonald, 1982; see also Walls, Sienicki, & Crist, 1981). Certainly, if advances in this area can be made, there is a much greater likelihood that the level of work produced by mentally retarded adults will be high enough and the cost of training low enough that both public and private employers will consider employing this group.

This chapter reviews research over the past 25 years. Following this overview is a review of an ecological perspective (Brooks & Baumeister, 1977a,b) that should continue to influence diverse areas of mental retardation research and, in particular, work behavior research. This chapter also introduces a more recent overview of the research that has been conducted in sheltered workshop settings and in competitive em-

ployment settings. Finally, a discussion of current and future trends in the area of response maintenance and generalization is offered.

Overview of Vocational Rehabilitation Research

Over the past 25 years, research into the vocational rehabilitation of mentally retarded persons has focused primarily upon three lines of inquiry. Initially, investigators attempted to isolate specific factors affecting the employability of the mentally retarded adult (Cobb, 1972; Kolstoe, 1961; Shafter, 1957; Windle, 1962). This was followed closely by efforts focused on vocational evaluation and prediction of employment potential (Ferguson, 1958; Fry, 1956; Patterson, 1964; Tobias & Gorelick, 1960). The third, and most recent area of research, has concentrated primarily on skill acquisition (Evans & Spradlin, 1966; Zimmerman, Stuckey, Garlick, & Miller, 1969) and modification (Huddle, 1967; Schoeder, 1972) in sheltered workshops and work activity centers.

Factors Affecting Employability

Those studies reporting specific factors that influence the employability of the mentally retarded adult include

* Special thanks are extended to Sister Diane Owens for her editorial services. This chapter was completed during the first author's appointment to the Bureau of Educational Research, College of Education, University of Illinois.

positive relationships' between employability and intelligence (Abel, 1940; Collman & Newlyn, 1956; Conley, 1973; Reynolds & Stunkard, 1960), chronological age (Hartzler, 1951), academic attainment (Erickson, 1966), influence of family (Greene, 1945), and personality (Neff, 1959). Researchers have also discounted the influence of intelligence (Bobroff, 1956; Cowan & Goldman, 1959), chronological age (Shafter, 1957), and academic attainment (Greene, 1945). Most investigations have noted the salutary effects of the family on employment success of the mentally retarded adult (Abel, 1940; Greene, 1945; Jackson & Butler, 1963; Neff, 1959). Personality correlates of employability have included emotional stability (Bronner, 1933), gregariousness (Whitcomb, 1961), ambition and self-respect (Abel, 1940), and attitude and motivation (Thomas, 1965).

Vocational Evaluation and Prediction

The literature on vocational evaluation and prediction has indicated that intelligence test scores and manual dexterity test scores correlate with each other (Tobias & Gorelick, 1960) and with employment potential (Distefano, Ellis, & Sloan, 1958). For example, the Stanford-Binet intelligence Test was found to be significantly correlated with the O'Connor Tweezer Dexterity Test and the Minnesota Rate of Manipulation Placing Test (Wagner & Hawver, 1965). Appel, Williams, and Fischell (1962) found that competitively employed mentally retarded adults scored higher than those in sheltered employment on the performance sections of the Wechsler Adult Intelligence Scale and the Wechsler-Bellevue Intelligence Scale.

Skill Acquisition and Modification in Sheltered Settings

Training the mentally retarded adult to acquire work-related behaviors in sheltered settings has been a growing area of inquiry in the field of vocational rehabilitation. This literature indicates two primary areas of concentration—vocational skill training and production training. Much of the research on vocational skill training has been aimed at demonstrating that mentally retarded individuals can acquire complex assembly skills. Recent studies by Bellamy, Peterson, and Close (1975), Crosson (1969), Friedenberg and Martin (1977), Gold (1972, 1976), Irvin (1976), and Martin and Flexer (1975) have amply demonstrated that mentally retarded individuals can acquire complex vocational tasks requiring multiple discriminations of form, color, color-form compounds, size, judgment, and the use of tools.

Production-oriented training has ranged from identifying more efficient job methods and designing work stations (Martin & Flexer, 1975), and adopting task analysis procedures (Bellamy, Peterson, & Close, 1975; Gold, 1972, 1976) to strengthening reinforcing contingencies to increase production rates (Brown, Van Deventer, Perlmutter, Jones, & Sontag, 1972; Crosson, 1969; Huddle, 1967; Trybys & Lacks, 1972; Zimmerman, et al., 1969). The use of behavior graphs (Jens & Shores, 1969) and videotaped feedback of performance (DeRoo & Haralson, 1971) have also been applied to the training of work performance. Recent vocational rehabilitation training research in combination with that completed over the last two decades provides compelling evidence that mentally retarded individuals who are provided appropriate learning experiences can acquire and perform complex tasks reliably. Bellamy (1976) has prepared an extended review of this research.

Although it is not the intent of this chapter to present a historical overview of the research efforts in the field of vocational rehabilitation, it is important to understand that there exists little consensus among researchers concerning correlates of rehabilitation success (Butler & Browning, 1974) and that the extensive literature on evaluation and prediction generally lacks practical significance (Gold, 1973a). While response consequences and general characteristics of work settings can be arranged to increase production rates, and antecedent events can have transitory facilitation, the differences between accumulated research results and actual practices have long been apparent (Rogers, 1970).

An Ecological Perspective

A number of professionals have raised concerns regarding past and future research in the area of mental retardation (Brooks & Baumeister, 1977a, 1977b; Gaylord-Ross, 1979; House, 1977). Although House (1977) lauds the contributions of basic research, suggesting that a better understanding has resulted from such practices, Brooks and Baumeister (1977b) and Gaylord-Ross (1979) have argued persuasively for a different type of research focus. In their plea for ecological validity, Brooks and Baumeister (1977a) raise the point that laboratory research devoted to the study of analog behavior has not increased our understanding of mental retardation.

The meaning of *ecological validity* (Brooks & Baumeister, 1977a,b) still appears to be evolving, and the reported state of its evolution varies with the reporter's purpose and perspective. As a construct in research methodology, it is a subset of the larger construct, external validity; defined as the extent to which a particular observed phenomenon or relationship represents a general class of phenomena or relationships that occur reliably under a variety of conditions (Bracht & Glass, 1968). Special concern is for generalizability to the conditions that arise in "everyday life," as opposed to those of carefully controlled experimental settings. There are four conceptually distinct variations of external validity: population, social, referent, and ecological. Population generality is achieved when one is confident that an observed phenomenon is replicable in some defined population of subjects (Bracht & Glass, 1968; Campbell & Stanley, 1963). Social validation is a variation of population validity in which one seeks to establish that a phenomenon targeted for one population (usually one that is perceived to be deviant) is typical of that manifested in another (Kazdin, 1977; Kazdin & Matson, 1981; Wolf, 1978). Referent generality, sometimes called response generalization, refers to a system of intrapersonal behaviors (Baer, 1977; Holman, 1977; Snow, 1974; Willems, 1974). The subject is viewed as demonstrating a complex set of interrelated behaviors, and changes in one behavior may result in generalization to other behaviors. Finally, the ecological perspective focuses on the subject within the physical and contingency milieu. Ecological validity is achieved when one is confident that an observed phenomenon or relationship is replicable in a variety of settings, especially "everyday" settings.

While the intrapersonal and ecological views of external validity are somewhat divergent, they share a common base, as both are person-centered analyses of behavior. The approach represented by these views has been labeled as "ecobehavioral," because it encompasses the tenets and goals of both behavior analysis and ecological validity. This perspective, then, represents a union of the outcome-oriented treatment approach with the ecological premise that the environment is reactive to all changes, whether systematically or unsystematically imposed (Warren, 1977). This ecobehavioral perspective has led Warren (1977) to recommend that research procedures focus on various response dimensions (e.g., rate, durability, diversity). Warren (1977) recommended the collection of more measures: measuring more behaviors, measuring for generalization across settings, measuring over time for durability, and measuring consumer satisfaction to detect side effects and treatment usability.

Ecobehavioral procedures proposed by Rogers-Warren (1977) go beyond Warren's (1977) by suggesting the success of treatment may depend on a more thorough assessment of the setting prior to intervention. A suggested advantage of such assessments is that they may indicate modification in nonsocial (environmental) variables, such as organization of activities or physical design, thereby reducing or eliminating the need to manipulate social antecedents or consequences of the response. Rogers-Warren's proposed strategy for conducting ecobehaviorally valid research includes identifying target behaviors, evaluating the physical setting, evaluating the contingency environment, and determining setting-imposed limits and facilities for desired behaviors. It is the thesis of the present chapter that while vocational rehabilitation research has fallen short of the ecobehavioral standard, ecobehaviorally valid research is feasible and examples of its occurrence can be cited.

Sheltered Workshops Research: A Problem in Scope?

The ability of mentally retarded individuals to acquire a variety of difficult and potentially remunerative vocational skills has been amply documented by Bellamy (1976) and Gold (1973b). That this literature cumulatively supports the importance of systematic applications of learning principles and behavioral interventions cannot be disputed. However, from a generalizability perspective, the vocational habilitation literature manifests a severe limitation in scope.

For example, with the exception of Crosson's (1969) work, most production studies have involved subjects who were either already involved in vocational research programs or specifically selected for those programs. It is difficult to evaluate whether this selection systematically eliminated some individuals whom community sheltered workshops are expected to serve, thereby reducing population validity. Furthermore, a specific issue in applicability across individuals is the possibility that many interventions documented to be effective with a small number of research subjects may have less influence on the behavior of other workers or when attempts are made to manipulate these interventions by those not involved in university-related research programs.

The existing literature on vocational habilitation in sheltered settings has focused almost exclusively on vocational skill acquisition and production problems. Unquestionably, completing one's job and producing at an acceptable rate are essential for successful vocational rehabilitation. However, there are certainly other behaviors that affect maintaining one's job, i.e., that have greater social validity (Rusch, 1979b). For example, Mithaug and Hagmeier (1978), in a survey of sheltered workshops' entry requirements, found that the ability to communicate basic needs, move safely about the workshop, and to participate vocationally were listed as the three behaviors most agreed upon by workshop supervisors to ensure vocational survival. The ability to learn new tasks was tied in rank (7th) with maintaining proper grooming. These data suggest that vocational rehabilitation researchers have not necessarily addressed the same problems as those identified by the most likely consumers of their research efforts—those individuals admitting the mentally retarded adult into sheltered settings.

A general ecological problem relates to the fact that much of this research has been conducted in laboratories and experimental vocational settings as opposed to ecologically representative settings. Consequently, the practitioner has limited confidence in using this research to develop strategies for generalization and maintenance, identify optimal methods of staff training when experimenters are not present, and design studies and environments for simultaneous change in a variety of behaviors.

Maintenance and Generalization of Training

The failure of workshops to utilize research findings may in part reflect the practical realities of staff ratios, staff expertise, and equipment budgets. However, specific to the literature, most of the research has evaluated the relationship between supervision procedures and work performance during constricted time periods. Whether performance during the first few weeks in a training setting is representative of performance several months or years later, or in another vocational setting, can be questioned. Changes in work rates over time are found in several studies. However, in many of these studies, gradual improvement over time appeared to reflect the effects of practice or exposure (Brown et al., 1972; Crosson, 1969; Gold, 1973b; Kahn & Burdett, 1967). Evidence is also available that the effectiveness of various contingency arrangements may decrease considerably over time (Loos & Tizard, 1955). Ecobehaviorally valid research must necessarily concern itself with the generality of a training intervention over time as well as across settings.

Multiple-Treatment Interference

Confidence in the generalizability of research findings is also threatened by the possibility of multiple-treatment interference. Several studies have demonstrated that the effects of both antecedents and consequences on work behavior are different depending on other treatments that may have preceded them (Gordon, O'Connor, & Tizard, 1954; Noonan & Barry, 1967; Siegel, Williams, & Forman, 1967). These data suggest that multiple-treatment interference

can reduce the generality of findings. Reactive effects of experimental arrangements may also confound generalizability of findings. In vocational research, these include the presence of observers in the work setting, the use of simple tasks, and the use of shortened work days during experiments. Because of the reliance on short repetitive tasks, it is also unclear whether relations between various stimulus events and productivity will hold given the variety and complexity of sheltered workshop contracts. Similarly, generality of findings from brief experimental periods (Brown et al., 1972; Gold, 1972, 1976) to full work days has not been ascertained.

Conclusion

While the vocational rehabilitation literature collectively indicates that the mentally retarded adult can acquire vocational skills, it suffers from several ecologically oriented weaknesses. We do not know the exact conditions under which many of the reported training effects can be expected. Nor is it clear what combination of setting characteristics will produce maximum productivity. Specific details of antecedent and consequent arrangements are similarly unknown. In addition, the research to date has not concerned itself with the four facets of external validity defined above, and consequently there is a gap between existing experimental results and current practices in rehabilitation. Thus, extensive as the research is, it does not provide an ecologically valid basis for vocational training.

Nonsheltered Workshop Research: A New Frontier?

A very recent trend in the vocational habilitation research literature has been the investigation of vocational behavior in nonsheltered settings (Cuvo, Leaf, & Borakove, 1978; Rusch, 1979a; Rusch, Connis, & Sowers, 1979; Schutz, Rusch, & Lamson, 1979; Sowers, Rusch, Connis, & Cummings, 1980; Wehman, Hill, & Koehler, 1979). Similar to sheltered workshop studies these efforts have attended to skill acquisition and performance problems. Different from sheltered vocational rehabilitation studies has been the focus upon maintenance and generalization of acquired vocational behaviors and the reliance upon potential consumers, i.e., employers, to validate the relevancy of the goals set, procedures tried, and results ultimately attained. This focus on the consumer lends social validation to all aspects of the rehabilitative effort, and reflects, in part, a concern for ecological validity (Gaylord-Ross, 1979).

The research just cited has focused on tasks found in various service industry occupations, e.g., janitorial and kitchen laborer positions. For example, Cuvo et al. (1978) taught six mentally retarded adolescents to clean a restroom using a task analysis that featured 181 separate response components. Each of the participants in this investigation acquired the necessary responses when provided varying levels of instructional feedback. In a restaurant setting, Rusch et al. (1979) trained a single individual to work continuously throughout a six-hour work day. Rusch et al. found that combining praise and feedback (points) for continuous work and response cost (loss of points) for discontinuing work resulted in maximum work effort as compared to praise or praise and feedback without response cost.

Additional studies by Sowers et al. (1980) and Rusch (1979a) have also investigated the acquisition and performance of nonsheltered vocational behavior. Sowers et al., trained three mentally retarded persons to manage their time behaviors during lunches and breaks. Baseline data suggested that all three persons in this study required considerable, if not total, feedback to go to and return from their respective lunches and breaks. Introduction of a time-management card, pre-instruction on the use of the card, and feedback on correctness of use, resulted in the subjects' self-monitoring their departure and arrival times by matching the hands on their time-management cards to the hands of clocks displayed in each of their respective work stations and their lunch/break rooms.

Rusch (1979a) addressed the relationship between attending to task and speed to task completion. Six mentally retarded adults were trained to clean 15 tables prior to their involvement in this investigation. Subsequent to this training each was assigned, randomly, to two experimental groups. Group 1 received reinforcement for speed of task completion; group 2 received reinforcement for time spent attending to the task. The findings of this study suggested that directly reinforcing speed of task completion resulted in speedier task completion. Further, token reinforcement of either attending or producing appeared to result in considerable improvements in the nonreinforced measures. This finding supports Warren's (1977) suggestion that ecobehavioral validity is best established by a variety of outcome measures—what Wahler (1969) has called response clusters.

Maintenance and Generalization

A unique feature of each of the vocational rehabilitation research efforts described in this section, with the exception of Rusch (1979a), has been the investigator's interest in preserving acquired behaviors and, in the case of Cuvo et al., (1978), generalizing these gains to nontreatment settings. This focus is rare in the vocational literature, although maintaining and generalizing vocational behaviors is an essential and necessary link in the overall rehabilitative efforts of vocational researchers, regardless of setting (Rusch & Mithaug, 1980).

Typically, generalization research suggests inconsistent and often contradictory findings. Schutz, Jostes, Rusch, and Lamson (1980) and Cuvo et al. (1978) indicated that acquired skills generalized to a second, untrained setting. Cuvo et al. (1978), however, also reported these same skills did not generalize across subtasks. Although authors have questioned the generality of trained behaviors (see Sowers et al., 1980), such efforts are not included in the majority of the studies conducted in various work settings.

Social Validation in Vocational Training Research

Kazdin (1977) and Kazdin and Matson (1981) have proposed that behavioral changes be considered important only if performance is brought within the range of socially acceptable levels, as evidenced by peer group performance. In a recent article entitled "Toward the validation of social/vocational survival skills," Rusch (1979b) suggested that researchers and trainers alike be responsive to targeted job placement settings and, specifically, to the key factors that in all likelihood account for successes or failures in these settings. This concern was expressed by Rogers-Warren (1977) in her suggestion to evaluate physical settings and behavior-setting interactions prior to designing interventions.

In recent years, social validation methodology has been applied to the identification of entry skills thought to be necessary for admittance into a variety of work settings. For example, Mithaug and his colleagues (Mithaug & Hagmeier, 1978) employed descriptive validation assessment (e.g., questionnaires) to identify the skills supervisors believed were necessary for entrance into sheltered workshops. The skills identified by this research, and the corresponding standards for skill performance, were then found to discriminate successful workers in sheltered workshops from clients with lower competency levels enrolled in work activity centers (Mithaug, Mar, Stewart, & McCalmon, 1980). More recently, attention has been directed toward the identification of job requisites employers state would lead to employment in the competitive work force. Specifically, employers representing service (Rusch, Schutz, & Agram, in press) and light industrial occupations (Schutz & Rusch, unpublished ms.) have been surveyed to identify specific requisite skills and the minimum proficiency of skill performance necessary for mentally retarded persons to obtain entry-level, competitive employment positions. In addition to these efforts, social validation methodology has been used to assess employers' acceptance of alternative training procedures that are typically used to prepare handicapped persons for competitive employment (Menchetti, Rusch, & Lamson; 1981).

Social validation procedures have also been applied to obtaining input from potential employees, i.e., handicapped individuals. For example, Mithaug and Mar (1980) assessed the prevocational work preferences of two severely mentally retarded persons. The results of this study demonstrated the reinforcing and punishing effects of working on different tasks. The effects of working a punishing task were demonstrated by decreases in work performed; the effects of working a reinforcing task were demonstrated by increases in work performed. This relationship, between the task selected and the work performed, suggests that the selection response is a valid indicator of employee preference for different types of work: a relationship initially suggested in an earlier study conducted by Mithaug and Hanawalt (1978).

Social validation methodology has also been used to guide individual training/research efforts. To date, measures of social acceptability have included corroboration by employers of the relevance of training goals (Rusch, Weithers, Menchetti, & Schutz, 1980), procedures employed (Schutz, Rusch, & Lamson, 1979), and the results of instruction (Schutz, Jostes, Rusch, & Lamson, 1980). For example, Schutz et al. (1980) asked supervisors to state whether they believed kitchen floors were adequately swept and mopped by two mentally retarded persons training for kitchen laborer positions. Supervisory ratings of performance collected during baseline, training, and maintenance phases were found to favorably compare with direct observation measures collected by trainers across the same phases. Schutz et al. (1979) sought to determine the effectiveness of two employer-selected supervisory procedures applied to the verbally abusive behavior of three moderately mentally retarded adults. A warning and a one-day suspension were identified as the procedures a potential employer used when employees were verbally abusive or generally socially inappropriate. After the use of warnings alone, these investigators applied one-day suspensions in combination with warnings. The use of a one-day suspension had an immediate impact on the inappropriate behavior of each of the three potential employees. This study exemplifies Rogers-Warren's (1977) suggestion to de-termine the contingencies to be found in the eventual placement setting for individuals.

Both descriptive and comparative validation were utilized by Rusch, Weithers, Menchetti, and Schutz (1980). Supervisors and nonhandicapped employees complained that topics repeated by a moderately mentally retarded employee during lunches and dinners were excessive and annoying. Following baseline measurement, coworkers were provided preinstruction in how to give feedback when a topic was repeated. Results indicated that coworkers were effective in reducing topic repetition only when they were prompted to provide feedback themselves by trained follow-up personnel. Data collected on the number of coworker topical repeats (comparative validation measure) revealed that the mentally retarded employee and his nonhandicapped peers repeated themselves equally often. Of particular interest, however, was the finding that ratings by the coworkers (descriptive validation assessment) indicated that they believed the mentally retarded employee had not reduced his repeats, a finding contrary to the direct, comparison measure. The investigators offered at least two reasons why the observed and rated measures did not correspond. First, it was suggested that the comparative measure used by coworkers may have been more broadly defined than that used by the trained observers. Second, the coworkers may have let topic repetitions during other periods of the day influence their ratings during two separate meal times.

Summary and Limitations

Recent rehabilitation research conducted in non-sheltered settings appears to reflect a focus on individual functioning in an environmental context. Moreover, these research efforts have tended to concentrate on skills that, when acquired and maintained, would prove functional to persons wishing access to non-sheltered employment settings. This focus has led to expanded efforts to examine factors affecting long-term behavior change as demonstrated, in part, by the inclusion of the programming for maintenance and generalization of behavior change as components of overall vocational training packages (Schutz et al., 1980). This research also demonstrates a greater responsiveness to the work environment through the adoption of ecobehavioral and social validation criteria to assist in the evaluation of obtained results. The use of social validation measures to direct behavioral programs is not new (e.g., Patterson, 1974; Patterson, Cobb, & Ray, 1972; Walker & Hops, 1976); however, the use of such a measure in vocational rehabilitation has not been applied previously. The studies reviewed suggest that if vocational (re)habilitation researchers included potential consumers in their research design, considerable attention would be redirected toward those behaviors, apart from completing one's job, that comprise a larger class of social/vocational survival skills (Rusch, 1979b).

Generally, nonsheltered rehabilitation research has addressed applied issues (i.e., behaviors exhibited in natural settings), which in turn, has facilitated the potential for the attainment of results with immediate implications for the delivery of services to mentally retarded persons outside laboratory settings. While this research represents a shift toward a more ecologically valid approach in (re)habilitation research, information voids still exist. For example, while some of these "applied," separate research efforts have incorporated social validation to help guide their overall direction, very little is known about these settings beforehand. In addition, as pointed out by Rusch (in press) problems exist if verbal reports, alone, are used to validate objective measures. For example, in the Rusch et al. (1980) investigation, little attention was paid to what topics were being discussed by coworkers as opposed to those by the new employee. This investigation sought to reduce topics repeated, not topics discussed. It could be that had topic change been reinforced, not repetition per se, the ratings by coworkers would have changed. In short, the vocational (re)habilitation research efforts in nonsheltered settings appear to suffer from a lack of data relevant to direct behavioral programming and, therefore, fall short of changing the quality of life of the persons treated individually.

Maintenance and Generalization: A Future Trend?

The areas of maintenance and generalization, until recently, have received little attention in the vocational (re)habilitation literature. At this time, studies that have incorporated maintenance as part of the overall evaluation effort can be divided into two major subtypes: those utilizing externally-produced and monitored cues and those utilizing externally-produced cues that are monitored by the subject (Rusch & Schutz, 1981).

Externally-produced and Monitored Cues

The majority of the vocational (re)habilitation research reported, to date, has used procedures implemented and monitored by an external change agent (e.g., a trainer). Only a handful have focused upon the issue of response maintenance—that is, the degree to which

behaviors are performed at an acceptable level, once training is eliminated. Illustrative of these research efforts are investigations by Matson and Martin (1979), Schutz et al. (1980), Rusch et al. (1980), and Rusch, Connis, and Sowers (1979). Matson and Martin (1979) demonstrated the utility of a social learning-based training package to increase work efficiency and decrease unwanted social behaviors (e.g., chin wiping) of three severely mentally retarded subjects. The training package combined the strategies of instruction, feedback, and role playing. Follow-up, conducted four weeks after training, indicated behavioral gains had been maintained. However, the Matson and Martin (1979) study could have been improved upon in two critical respects. First, since the study was conducted in a sheltered workshop setting, it is unknown whether these gains would have generalized to an extratraining setting; it is also unknown if the strategies employed would have been as effective in a nonresidential context. Second, follow-up was conducted four weeks after the termination of training and consisted of only a three-day observation period. Although this approach to acquisition and maintenance exemplifies studies in the vocational rehabilitation literature, studies of genuine relevance to the issue of maintenance must incorporate follow-up observations for a protracted period, such as a month or a year.

In another study, Schutz et al. (1980) reported the utility of contingent preinstruction in the acquisition training of two work skills (mopping and sweeping skills) to two mentally handicapped workers employed in a restaurant setting. A three-month follow-up indicated that these acquired skills were maintained as contingent preinstruction was systematically faded. However, the Schutz et al. (1980) study must be regarded as an exploratory training effort. An in-depth investigation of contingent preinstruction that incorporates a larger number of subjects and a greater variety of vocational tasks is warranted.

Rusch et al. (1980) successfully utilized coworker feedback in order to reduce topic repetition of a single mentally handicapped worker competitively employed in a nonsheltered setting. The training program was developed in response to the indications of three coworkers and a supervisor that topical repetition was a troublesome feature of the handicapped person's social/work behavior. The results of this study indicated that topical repeats by the worker could be significantly reduced via coworker feedback. Of particular interest was the finding that, although coworkers were willing to attempt to modify the behavior of the handicapped person, they did not do so without a prompt from the experimenter/observer involved. However, this investigation was important, because it suggested that peers in a vocational setting can deliberately and effectively apply procedures to decrease undesirable behavior. Future research which employs coworkers as change agents would be a valuable addition to the vocational (re)habilitation literature. What could be established is a reciprocal reinforcing environment capable of promoting the maintenance of worker behavior and hence his/her long-term employment.

Finally, Rusch, Connis, and Sowers (1979) utilized the combined effects of praise, tokens, and response cost to increase a single subject's time-spent working in a restaurant setting. The experiment incorporated a sequential-withdrawal design (Rusch & Kazdin, 1981) in an effort to assess which component of this training package was most influential in promoting maintenance. A sequential withdrawal of single components was initiated after experimental control by the combined treatment components has been established. One finding reported was that a five-phase withdrawal sequence of the token component indicated no loss in acquired behavior. Clearly, this design constitutes a potentially powerful maintenance tool. In this case, the design allowed for the specification of the training component critical to the maintenance of behavior, and thus targeted where additional procedures were needed to promote maintenance.

Externally-produced and Self-monitored Cues (Self-control)

Self-control refers to behaviors intentionally performed by an individual to achieve desired outcomes (Kazdin, 1980). Until recently, mentally retarded individuals were regarded as unable to achieve self-control without external supervision. Such a deficit has been regarded as a primary obstacle to successful competitive employment (Wehman, 1975). However, Kurtz and Neisworth (1976) concluded, in an extensive review of the self-control research literature, that the strategies of self-monitoring, self-reinforcement, and antecedent cue regulation could be especially useful with mentally retarded individuals.

Fortunately, a small body of research has recently appeared that has examined the use of self-control in facilitating the maintenance of vocational behavior. The ability of mentally retarded individuals to self-administer and self-determine reinforcement was examined in three studies by Wehman, Schutz, Bates, Renzaglia, and Karan (1978). Two of these investigations compared the effect of external, self-administered and self-determined reinforcement on production rates in a sheltered setting. In the first study a severely mentally retarded adult was sequentially introduced to external, then self-administered, and finally self-determined reinforcement. Work production rates increased with the introduction of each new reinforcement phase; the self-determined reinforcement phase produced the highest level of production. In the second study, a mildly mentally retarded adult was exposed to similar reinforcement conditions. Replicating the results of the first study, each reinforcement phase produced higher production rates— the self-administered and self-determined phases were more effective than external reinforcement, with self-determined reinforcement being the most effective. The third case example compared the effects of noncontingent, externally administered, and self-administered reinforcement upon a profoundly mentally retarded individual's production of floor pulleys. Unlike the other two studies, external reinforcement was the most effective, followed by self-administered and non-contingent reinforcement.

Helland, Paluck, and Klein (1976) compared the effect of self-reinforcement on workshop task production to external reinforcement. Twelve mildly and moderately mentally retarded young adults were divided into two groups. Subjects in the self-reinforcement group were trained to give self-compliments and select a reinforcer upon completing a paper-collating task. The individuals in the external reinforcement group were praised following completion of the same paper-collating task. Analysis of the results indicated that both reinforcement conditions significantly improved performance, as well as no significant difference between the results of the two reinforcement methods. That is, self-reinforcement was as effective as external reinforcement. The self-reinforcement subjects were free of external supervision during their production trials.

Connis (1979) examined the effects of sequential pictorial cues, self-recording, and praise on job task sequencing. Four moderately mentally retarded adults were introduced to the use of picture schedules and self-recording following a baseline period. Each subject's photographed schedule represented his or her daily assigned tasks. The photograph, combined with self-recording, enabled the subjects to successfully sequence their job tasks. Withdrawal of picture-cue training resulted in continued high levels of independent task change, indicating that self-directed use of sequenced photographs enabled successful maintenance of the acquired behaviors.

Finally, Sowers, Rusch, Connis, and Cummings (1980) trained time-management in a vocational setting utilizing self-control strategies. Three mildly to moderately mentally retarded adults were trained in a competitive employment setting to go and return from lunch and breaks on time. After a stable baseline had been established, preinstruction in time management, instructional feedback, and the use of a pictorial time card were introduced. This self-control training package quickly enabled the individuals to learn to manage their own time. When preinstruction and then instructional feedback were sequentially withdrawn (Rusch & Kazdin, 1981), the time-management skills were maintained at high levels.

Obviously, the rehabilitation literature has examined only a few of the many areas pertinent to self-control training with the mentally retarded individual. Much more research is needed that would investigate the utility of self-control strategies in the maintenance of valued social and vocational survival skills.

The objective of vocational rehabilitation must involve more than training isolated skills and maintenance strategies. If mentally retarded adults are to function in diverse work situations, skills will need to be reliably performed across a number of situations and settings. Although there is not an instructional technology that has produced reliable generalized skills, generalization as a process has received some recent attention (Drabman, Hammer, & Rosenbaum, 1979; Stokes & Baer, 1977). In the vocational (re)habilitation research literature, generalization has been evaluated with respect to the extent that operations transfer across several new tasks to be learned.

Operations Training (Generalization)

An operation is a set of response characteristics that form a particular response class. If an operation has been trained, "all members of the response class are performed in the presence of the appropriate stimulus, and responses wholly or partly outside that class are not performed" (Walls et al., 1981, p. 357). The goal of operations training is transfer of learned responses to several new tasks with stimulus dimensions similar to those which existed during training. Bellamy, Wilson, Adler, and Clarke (1980) proposed four advantages of operations training in vocational rehabilitation, including the ability of an adult to (a) adapt to changes of tasks and jobs to be performed in the work setting, (b) learn marketable and valued vocational skills, (c) adjust to changes in job station design, and (d) develop flexible, marketable learning strategies competencies.

The results of a limited number of studies in this area suggest significant time and error savings in task training when potential employees are trained, via operations, following the guidelines proposed by Becker, Engelmann, and Thomas (1975). For example, Walls et al. (1981) taught 15 mentally retarded adults generic vocational operations (e.g., bolt or nut

loosening with a ratchet and socket) prior to training of specific tasks, resulting in less time spent learning new tasks. Horner and McDonald (1982) suggested "general case" or operations training was superior to single instance training in tht all four subjects made fewer errors and performed new tasks more quickly when provided the former. Similarly, Colvin and Horner (1982) reported results that suggest teaching the operations of one particular tool (screwdriver) across several dimensions (i.e., hex, square, phillips, slot) and levels (e.g., 3 in., 4 in.) resulted in improved performance on nontrained tasks. Furthermore, as subjects progressed through a curriculum package and were trained on a wider range of screwdriver tasks, their performance on nontrained probe tasks improved. These findings are consistent with the suggestion that to the extent that operations generalize across new tasks, training of the basic operations should facilitate mastery of new tasks (Horner & Bellamy, 1978).

Conclusion

This chapter overviewed past and current practices in the area of vocational (re)habilitation. An overview of ecological validity as it relates to both sheltered and competitive employment research efforts was also provided. With attention focused upon the ecological validity of past research in mental retardation (Brooks & Baumeister, 1977; Haywood, 1977) it would appear that vocational (re)habilitation researchers have a challenging task ahead, i.e., conducting research that has both societal and scientific value. Although not without its many problems, current research in the areas of maintenance and generalization training is suggesting some new and potentially fruitful areas of inquiry.

References

Abel, T. M. A study of a group of subnormal girls successfully adjusted in industry and the community. *American Journal of Mental Deficiency*, 1940, **45**, 66–72.

Appel, M. R., Williams, C. M., & Fischell, K. N. Significant factors in placing mental retardates from a workshop situation. *Personnel and Guidance Journal*, 1962, **41**, 260–265.

Baer, D. M. Some comments on the interaction of ecology and applied behavior analysis. In A. Rogers-Warren and S. F. Warren (Eds.), *Ecological perspectives in behavior analysis*. Baltimore: University-Park Press, 1977.

Becker, W. C., Englemann, S., & Thomas, D. *Teaching: A course in applied psychology*. Chicago: Science Research Associates, 1975.

Becker, R., Widener, Q., & Soforenko, A. Career education for trainable mentally retarded youth. *Education and Training of the Mentally Retarded*, 1979, **14**, 101–105.

Bellamy, G. T. Habilitation of the severely and profoundly

retarded: A review of research on work productivity. In G. T. Bellamy (Ed.), *Habilitation of severely and profoundly retarded adults.* Eugene: Center on Human Development, Specialized Training Center, University of Oregon, 1976.

Bellamy, G. T., Peterson, L., & Close, D. Habilitation of the severely and profoundly retarded: Illustrations of competence. *Education and Training of the Mentally Retarded.* 1975, **10**, 174–187.

Bellamy, G. T., Wilson, D. J., Adler, E., & Clarke, J. Y. A strategy for programming vocational skills for severely handicapped youth. *Exceptional Education Quarterly,* 1980, **1**, 85–97.

Bobroff, A. Economic adjustment of 121 adults formerly students in classes for mental retardates. *American Journal of Mental Deficiency,* 1956, **60**, 525–535.

Bracht, G. H., & Glass, G. V. The external validity of experiments. *American Educational Research Journal.* 1968, **5**, 437–474.

Bronner, A. F. Follow-up studies of mental defectives, procedures, and address. *American Journal of Mental Deficiency,* 1933, **38**, 258–267.

Brooks, P. H., & Baumeister, A. A. A plea for consideration of ecological validity in the experimental psychology of mental retardation: A guest editorial. *American Journal on Mental Retardation,* 1977, **81**, 407–416.(a)

Brooks, P. H., & Baumeister, A. A. Are we making a science of missing the point? *American Journal of Mental Deficiency,* 1977, **81**, 543–546.(b)

Brown, L., Van Deventer, P., Perlmutter, L., Jones, S., & Sontag, E. Effects of consequences on production rates of trainable retarded and severely emotionally disturbed students in a public school workshop. *Education and Training of the Mentally Retarded,* 1972, **7**, 74–81.

Butler, A. J., & Browning, P. L. Predictive studies on rehabilitation outcome with retarded: A methodological critique. In P. L. Browning (Ed.), *Mental retardation: Rehabilitation and counseling.* Springfield, Illinois: Charles C. Thomas, 1974.

Campbell, D. T., & Stanley, J. C. *Experimental and quasi-experimental designs for research.* New York: Rand McNally and Company, 1963.

Cobb, H. V. *The forecast of fulfillment.* New York: Teachers College Press, 1972.

Collman, R. D., & Newlyn, D. Employment success of educationally subnormal ex-pupils in England. *American Journal of Mental Deficiency,* 1956, **60**, 733–743.

Colvin, G. T., & Horner, R. H. Experimental analysis of generalization: An evaluation of a general case program for teaching motor skills to severely handicapped learners. Eugene: Specialized Training Program, Center on Human Development, University of Oregon, 1982.

Conley, R. W. *The Economics of Mental Retardation.* Baltimore: Johns Hopkins Press, 1973.

Connis, R. T. The effects of sequential cues, self-recording, and praise on the job task sequencing of retarded adults. *Journal of Applied Behavior Analysis,* 1979, **12**, 355–361.

Cowan, L., & Goldman, M. Selection of the mentally deficient for vocational training and the effect of this training on vocational success. *Journal of Consulting Psychology,* 1959, **23**, 78–84.

Crosson, J. E. A technique for programming sheltered workshop environments for training severely retarded workers.

American Journal of Mental Deficiency, 1969, **73**, 814–818.

Cuvo, A. J., Leaf, R. B., & Borakove, L. S. Teaching janitorial skills to the mentally retarded: Acquisition, generalization, and maintenances. *Journal of Applied Behavior Analysis,* 1978, **11**, 345–355.

DeRoo, W. M., & Haralson, H. L. Increasing workshop production through seslf-visualization on videotape. *Mental Retardation,* 1971, **9**, 22–25.

Distefano, M. K., Ellis, N. R., & Sloan, W. Motor proficiency in mental defectives. *Perceptual and Motor Skills,* 1958, **8**, 231–234.

Drabman, R. S., Hammer, D., & Rosenbaum, M. S. Assessing generalization in behavior modification with children: The generalization map. *Behavioral Assessment,* 1979, **1**, 203–219.

Erickson, R. C. Part II, The relationship between selected variables and success of the retarded in the cooperative work-study program: An analysis of predictive power. Final Report of Project NIMH 1159. Washington, D.C.: National Institute of Mental Health, 1966.

Evans, G., & Spradlin, J. Incentives and instructions as controlling variables in productivity. *American Journal of Mental Deficiency,* 1966, **71**, 129–132.

Ferguson, R. G. Evaluating vocational aptitudes and characteristics of mentally retarded young adults in an industrial agricultural workshop. *American Journal of Mental Deficiency,* 1958, **62**, 787–791.

Friedenberg, W. P., & Martin, A. S. Prevocational training of the severely retarded using task analysis. *Mental Retardation,* 1977, **15**, 16–20.

Fry, L. M. A predictive measure of work success for high grade mental defectives. *American Journal of Mental Deficiency,* 1956, **61**, 401–408.

Gaylord-Ross, R. J. Mental retardation research, ecological validity, and the delivery of longitudinal education programs. *Journal of Special Education,* 1979, **12**, 6980.

Gold, M. Stimulus factors in skill training of the retarded on a complex assembly task: Acquisition, transfer, and retention. *American Journal of Mental Deficiency,* 1972, **76**, 517–526.

Gold, M. Research on the vocational rehabilitation of the retarded: The present, the future. In N. R. Ellis (Ed.), *International review of research in mental retardation.* Vol. VI. New York: Academic Press, 1973.(a)

Gold, M. Factors affecting production by the retarded: Base rates. *Mental Retardation,* 1973, **11**, 41–45.(b)

Gold, M. Task analysis of a complex assembly task by the retarded blind. *Exceptional Children,* 1976, **43**, 78–84.

Gordon, S., O'Connor, N., and Tizard, J. Some effects of incentives on the performance of imbecils. *British Journal of Psychology* 1954, **45**, 277–289.

Greene, C. L. A study of personal adjustment in mentally retarded girls. *American Journal of Mental Deficiency,* 1945, **49**, 472–476.

Hartzler, E. A follow-up study of girls discharged from the laurelton school. *American Journal of Mental Deficiency,* 1951, **55**, 612–618.

Haywood, H. C. The ethics of doing research and not doing it. *American Journal of Mental Deficiency,* 1977, **81**, 311–317.

Helland, C. D., Paluck, R. J., & Klein, M. A comparison of self- and external reinforcement with the trainable mentally retarded. *Mental Retardation,* **14**, 22–23.

Hill, M., & Wehman, P. Employer and nonhandicapped

co-worker perceptions of moderately and severely retarded workers. *Journal of Contemporary Business*, 1979, **8**, 107–112.

Holman, J. The moral risk and high cost of ecological concern in applied behavior analysis. In A. Rogers-Warren and S. F. Warren (Eds.), *Ecological perspectives in behavior analysis*. Baltimore: University Park Press, 1977.

Horner, R. H., & Bellamy, G. T. A conceptual analysis of vocational training with the severely retarded. In M. Snell (Ed.), *Systematic instruction of the moderately and severely handicapped*. Columbus, Ohio: Charles E. Merrill, 1978.

Horner, R. H., & McDonald, R. S. A comparison of single instance and general case instruction in teaching a generalized vocational skill. Eugene: Specialized Training Program, Center on Human Development, University of Oregon, 1982.

House, B. I. Scientific explanation and ecological validity: A reply to Brooks and Baumeister. *American Journal of Mental Deficiency*, 1977, **81**, 534–542.

Huddle, D. Work performance of trainable adults as influenced by competition, cooperation, and monetary reward. *American Journal of Mental Deficiency*, 1967, **72**, 198–211.

Irvin, L. K. General utility of easy to hard discrimination training procedures with the severely retarded. *Education and Training of the Mentally Retarded*, 1976, **4**, 21–26.

Jackson, S. K., & Butler, A. J. Prediction of successful community placement of institutionalized retarded. *American Journal of Mental Deficiency*, 1963, **68**, 211–17.

Jens, K., & Shores, R. Behavioral graphs as reinforcers for work behavior of mentally retarded adolescents. *Education and Training of the Mentally Retarded*, 1969, **4**, 21–26.

Kahn, R. L., & Burdett, A. D. Interaction of practice and rewards on motor performance of adolescent mental retardates. *American Journal of Mental Deficiency*, 1967, **72**, 422–427.

Kazdin, A. E. Assessing the clinical or applied importance of behavior change through social validation. *Behavior Modification*, 1977, **1**, 427–451.

Kazdin, A. E. *Behavior modification in applied settings*. Homewood, Ill.: The Dorsey Press, 1980.

Kazdin, A. E., & Matson, J. L. Social validation in mental retardation. *Applied Research in Mental Retardation*, 1981, **2**, 39–54.

Kolstoe, O. P. An examination of some characteristics which discriminate between employed and non-employed mentally retarded males. *American Journal of Mental Deficiency*, 1961, **66**, 472–482.

Kurtz, P. D., & Neisworth, J. T. Self-control possibilities for exceptional children. *Exceptional Children*, 1976, **42**, 212–217.

Loos, F., and Tizard, J. The employment of adult imbeciles in a hospital workshop. *American Journal of Mental Deficiency*, 1955, **59**, 394–403.

Martin, A. S., & Flexer, R. W. *Three studies on training work skills and work adjustment with the severely retarded*. Research and Training Center in Mental Retardation, Texas Tech. University, 1975.

Matson, J., & Martin, J. A social learning approach to vocational training of the severely retarded. *Journal of Mental Deficiency Research*, 1979, **23**, 9–17.

Menchetti, B. M., Rusch, F. R. & Lamson, D. S. Employers' perceptions of acceptable training procedures for use in competitive employment settings. *Journal of the Association for the Severely Handicapped*, 1981, **6**, 6–16.

Mithaug, D. E., & Hagmeier, L. D. The development of procedures to assess prevocational competencies of severely handicapped young adults. *ASESPH Review*, 1978, **3**, 94–115.

Mithaug, D. E., & Hanawalt, D. A. The validation of procedures to assess prevocational task preferences in retarded adults. *Journal of Applied Behavior Analysis*, 1978, **11**, 153–162.

Mithaug, D. E., & Mar, D. K. The relation between choosing and working prevocational tasks in two severely retarded young adults. *Journal of Applied Behavior Analysis*, 1980, **13**, 177–182.

Mithaug, D., Mar, D., Stewart, J., & McCalmon, D. Assessing prevocational competencies of profoundly, severely, and moderately retarded persons. *Journal of the Association for the Severely Handicapped*, 1980, **5**, 270–284.

Neff, W. S. *The success of a rehabilitation program: A follow-up study of clients of the vocational adjustment center*. Monograph #3. Chicago: The Jewish Vocational Service, 1959.

Noonan, J., & Barry, J. Differential effects of incentives among the retarded. *The Journal of Educational Research*, 1967, **61**, 108–111.

Patterson, C. Y. Methods of assessing the vocational adjustment potential of the mentally handicapped. *The Training School Bulletin*, 1964, **61**, 129–152.

Patterson, G. R. Interventions for boys with conduct problems: Multiple settings, treatments, and criteria. *Journal of Consulting and Clinical Psychology*, 1974, **42**, 471–481.

Patterson, G. R., Cobb, J. A., & Ray, R. S. Direct intervention in the classroom: A set of procedures for the aggressive child. In F. W. Clark, D. R., Evans, and L. A. Hamerlynck (Eds.), *Implementing behavior programs for schools and clinics*. Proceedings of the Third International Conference on Behavior Modification. Champaign, Illinois: Research Press, 1972.

Reynolds, M. C., & Stunkard, C. L. A comparative study of day class vs. institutionalized educable retardates. Project 192. Minneapolis: College of Education, University of Minnesota, 1960.

Rogers, E. Research utilization in rehabilitation. In N. Neff (Ed.), *Rehabilitation psychology*. Washington, D.C.: American Psychological Association, 1970.

Rogers-Warren, A. Planned change: Ecobehaviorally based interventions. In A. Rogers-Warren and S. R. Warren (Eds.), *Ecological perspectives in behavior analysis*. Baltimore: University Park Press, 1977.

Rusch, F. R. A functional analysis of the relationship between attending to task and producing in an applied restaurant setting. *The Journal of Special Education*, 1979, **13**, 399–411.(a)

Rusch, F. R. Toward the validation of social/vocational survival skills. *Mental Retardation*, 1979, **17**, 143–145.(b)

Rusch, F. R. Competitive employment. In M. Snell (Ed.), *Systematic instruction of the moderately and severely handicapped*. (2nd ed.) Columbus, Ohio: Charles E. Merrill Publishing Co., in press.

Rusch, F. R., Connis, R. T., and Sowers, J. The modification and maintenance of time spent attending to task using social reinforcement, token reinforcement and response cost in an applied restaurant setting. *Journal of Special Education Technology,* 1979, **2,** 18–28.

Rusch, F. R., & Kazdin, A. E. Toward a methodology of withdrawal designs for the assessment of response maintenance. *Journal of Applied Behavior Analysis,* 1981, **14,** 131–140.

Rusch, F. R., & Mithaug, D. E. *Vocational training for mentally retarded adults: A behavior analytic approach.* Champaign, Illinois: Research Press, 1980.

Rusch, F. R., & Schutz, R. P. Vocational and social work behavior: An evaluative review. In J. L. Matson and J. R. McCartney (Eds.), *Handbook of behavior modification with the mentally retarded,* New York: Plenum Press, 1981.

Rusch, F. R., Schutz, R. P., & Agram, M. Validating entry-level survival skills for service occupations: Implications for curriculum development. In press.

Rusch, F. R., Weithers, J. A., Menchetti, B. M., & Schutz, R. P. Social validation of a program to reduce topic repetition in a nonsheltered setting. *Education and Training of the Mentally Retarded,* 1980, **15,** 208–215.

Schroeder, S. Parametric effects of reinforcement frequency, amount of reinforcement, and required response force on sheltered workshop behavior. *Journal of Applied Behavior Analysis,* 1972, **5,** 431–441.

Schutz, R., Jostes, K., Rusch, F. R., & Lamson, D. The use of contingent preinstruction and social validation in the acquisition, generalization, and maintenance of sweeping and mopping responses. *Education and Training of the Mentally Retarded,* 1980, **15,** 306–311.

Schutz, R. P., & Rusch, F. R. Assessing light and service industry employers' expectations for competitive employment: A comparative analysis. Manuscript submitted for publication.

Schutz, R. P., Rusch, F. R., & Lamson, D. S. Evaluation of an employer's procedure to eliminate unacceptable behavior on the job. *Community Services Forum,* 1979, **1,** 4–5.

Shafter, A. J. Criteria for selecting institutionalized mental defectives for vocational placement. *American Journal of Mental Deficiency,* 1957, **61,** 599–616.

Siegel, P., Williams, J., & Foreman, C. Instrument behavior in the retardate in relation to qualitative variation in the incentive. *American Journal of Mental Deficiency,* 1967, **72,** 450–454.

Snow, R. E. Representative and quasi-representative designs for research on teaching. *American Educational Research Journal,* 1974, **44,** 265–291.

Sowers, J., Rusch, F. R., Connis, R. T., & Cummings, L. E. Teaching mentally retarded adults to time manage in a vocational setting. *Journal of Applied Behavior Analysis,* 1980, **13,** 119–128.

Stokes, T. F., & Baer, D. M. An implicit technology of generalization. *Journal of Applied Behavior Analysis,* 1977, **10,** 349–367.

Thomas V. Curricular implications of work experience. Unpublished paper, Council for Exceptional Children Convention, Portland, Oregon, April, 1965.

Tobias, J., & Gorelick, J. The utility of the Goodenough Scale in the appraisal of retarded adults. *American Journal of Mental Deficiency,* 1960, **65,** 64–68.

Trybys, R. J., & Lacks, P. B. Modification of vocational behavior in a community agency for mentally retarded adolescents. *Rehabilitation Literature,* 1972, **33,** 258–266.

Wagner, E. E., & Hawver, D. A. Correlations between psychological tests and sheltered workshop performance for severely retarded adults. *American Journal of Mental Deficiency,* 1965, **69,** 685–691.

Wahler, R. G. Setting generality: Some specific and general effects of child behavior therapy. *Journal of Applied Behavior Analysis,* 1969, **2,** 239–246.

Walker, H. M., & Hops, H. Increasing academic achievement by reinforcing direct academic performance and/or facilitative nonacademic responses. *Journal of Educational Psychology,* 1976, **68,** 218–225.

Walls, R. T., Sienicki, D. A., & Crist, K. Operations training in vocational skills. *American Journal of Mental Deficiency,* 1981, **85,** 357–367.

Warren, S. F. A useful ecobehavioral perspective for applied behavior analysis. In A. Rogers-Warren and S. F. Warren (Eds.), *Ecological perspectives in behavioral analysis.* Baltimore: University Park Press, 1977.

Wehman, P. Behavioral self-control with the mentally retarded. *Journal of Applied Rehabilitation Counseling,* 1975, **6,** 27–34.

Wehman, P., Hill, J. W., & Koehler, F. Helping severely handicapped persons enter competitive employment. *AAESPH Review,* 1979, **4,** 274–290.

Wehman, P., Schutz, R., Bates, P., Renzaglia, A., & Karan, O. Self-management programs with mentally retarded workers: Implications for developing independent vocational behavior. *British Journal of Social and Clinical Psychology,* 1978, **17,** 57–64.

Whitcomb, M. A. A comparison of social and intellectual levels of 100 high-grade adult mental defectives. *American Journal of Mental Deficiency,* 1961, **66,** 213.

Willems, E. P. Behavioral technology and behavioral ecology. *Journal of Applied Behavior Analysis,* 1974, **7,** 151–165.

Windle, C. D. Prognosis of mental subnormals. Monograph Supplement, *American Journal of Mental Deficiency,* 1962, **66,** 1–180.

Wolf, M. M. Social validity: The case for subjective measurement of how applied behavior analysis is finding its heart. *Journal of Applied Behavior Analysis,* 1978, **11,** 203–214.

Zimmerman, J., Stuckey, T., Garlick, B., & Miller, M. Effects of token reinforcement on productivity in multiply handicapped clients in a sheltered workshop. *Rehabilitation Literature,* 1969, **30,** 34–41.

31 EARLY INTERVENTION*

Craig T. Ramey and
Donna M. Bryant

Current definitions of mental retardation include both significantly subaverage general intellectual functioning and deficits in adaptive behavior (American Psychiatric Association's Diagnostic and Statistical Manual of Mental Retardation, 1980; Grossman, 1977). Because intelligence and adaptive behavior are regarded as modifiable by environmental contingencies, many intervention programs have been established to prevent or ameliorate mental retardation. This chapter will review those efforts for both severe and mild retardation. Emphasis will be placed on reviewing those programs that have used adequate experimental procedures to assess effectiveness and which have conducted effectiveness assessments over a significant developmental period. The chapter will conclude with a discussion of some general principles that help us to understand the effectiveness of programs in both the severe and mild areas of retardation.

* This research was supported by grants from the National Institute of Child Health and Human Development (No. HD09130), the Office of Special Education and Rehabilitation Services, U.S. Department of Education (No. OSERS 1106), and the Administration for Children, Youth, and Families (No. 90-CW-602).

Distinction Between Types of Retardation

Although recent definitions of mental retardation include a deficit in adaptive behavior, in practice the diagnosis of mental retardation is still most often made on the basis of IQ scores. Individuals with the Stanford Binet IQ scores of 52–67 are usually designated as mildly retarded. IQ's of 36–51 indicate moderate retardation; 20–35, severe retardation; and below 20, profound mental retardation. Although not an absolute distinction, most of the people in the last three categories are mentally retarded because of biological factors such as genetic or infectious diseases or toxic environmental conditions. These three groups make up about 0.3–0.6% of the general population (Kushlick & Blunden, 1974) and about 20–25% of the mentally retarded. For the purposes of simplicity we shall refer to these groups collectively in the rest of this chapter as the severely retarded.

Individuals with mild mental retardation comprise about 1–3% of the population and about 75–80% of all cases of mental retardation. Researchers who take the "two groups approach" (severe vs. mild) (Penrose, 1963; Zigler, 1967) typically consider the mildly retarded to be the lower tail of a normal Gaussian distribution of human intelligence (Moser, Ramey, & Leonard, in press). Individuals in this group often have no known biological pathology or dysfunction to account for their disorder.

Establishing one of these subtype diagnoses involves some error of measurement. Thus, the various IQ cut points should be regarded more as administrative guidelines than as definitive diagnostic criteria. However, early intervention and prevention efforts are generally quite different for the mildly mentally retarded compared with the more severely mentally retarded. Therefore, this chapter will be divided into separate sections for severely and mildly retarded persons.

Distinction Between Prevention and Remediation

For most types of severe mental retardation, preventive efforts must be effective before a child's birth and, in some cases, even before conception. Most efforts after that are remedial in nature.

We have chosen to use the age of two as the time marker distinguishing prevention and remediation programs for the mildly mentally retarded. This age was chosen because several studies (e.g., Golden, Birns, Bridger, & Moss, 1971; Knoblock & Pasamanick, 1953; Ramey & Cambell, 1979) have demonstrated that it is during the second year of life that differences in cognitive abilities of children from different socioeconomic strata become apparent, differences that almost always favor children of more economically advantaged families. Prior to 12 months of age, measurable cognitive deficits have not been reliably detected in lower class children who are disproportionately represented among the mildly mentally retarded. Whether the failure to identify significant differences before 12 months is a function of the sensitivity of our measuring instruments is, at present, not established.

Severe Mental Retardation

There are many different kinds of programs for the moderately to severely mentally retarded, ranging from training and rehabilitation programs to programs that simply provide custodial care. Some training programs have been effective at promoting learning of cognitive and social skills. Advances have also been made in research on genetic and environmental causes of severe mental retardation. As a result, prevention of some severe mental retardation is becoming possible through genetic counseling, environmental change, and other methods. Much of the material relevant to the causes

and prevention of biomedical problems associated with mental retardation is covered elsewhere in this book in chapters on chromosomal disorders, genetic disorders, genetic counseling, brain damage, and nutrition. These chapters should be consulted by the interested reader for more detailed information on prevention of severe mental retardation, a topic which will be mentioned only briefly in this chapter.

Preventive Intervention for Severe Retardation

Recent genetic findings have helped put to rest some of the assumptions on which "eugenic mythologies" were based (Berg, 1976) as well as provide the basis for a preventive approach to severe mental retardation. Research about the environmental contributors to moderate and severe retardation has also led to preventive strategies.

GENETIC ABNORMALITIES

There are two types of genetic causes of mental deficiency, chromosomal abnormalities and genetic diseases. Over 100 different types of chromosomal abnormalities have been documented, some common and some rare. In Down syndrome, for example, an extra chromosome is found on the 21st pair of chromosomes. The degree of risk for a given couple desiring children can be estimated with a fair degree of accuracy using this information. Through genetic counseling about these risks, a couple can make informed decisions about childbearing.

The second type of genetically caused retardation is due to specific gene defects. In these conditions, specific genes, carried on normal chromosomes, result in mental retardation. An example of such a genetic disease is unresponsive Vitamin B_{12} methylmalonic acidemia. A couple might be able to prevent recurrence of this kind of genetically caused retardation through effective contraception. Amniocentesis can also detect these kinds of genetic disorders once pregnancy has occurred, providing information that the parents can use in deciding to continue or end the pregnancy through abortion.

Although genetic counseling, amniocentesis, abortion, and other procedures are possible ways to prevent severe mental retardation, they are procedures which raise many difficult ethical questions. There is no question, though, that genetic information and intervention procedures, if more widely available and properly used, have the power to substantially reduce the incidence of severe mental retardation.

ENVIRONMENTAL ABNORMALITIES

Environment, broadly defined, includes both the internal and external forces that alter behavior. Nutrition, drugs, alcohol, toxic chemicals, and viruses are all aspects of the environment that can affect intellectual functioning.

Brain development can be affected by diet deficiencies and, in fact, malnutrition may be the largest cause of lack of normal brain development in the world (Isaacson & Van Hartesveldt, 1978). Malnourished infants have both behavioral and intellectual problems, and are usually smaller in body and brain size than babies whose mothers had good diets during pregnancy (Dobbing, 1971). However, babies who were malnourished in utero are usually also from poor families, thus making it difficult to separate the effects of fetal nutrition from other factors associated with socioeconomic status.

Drugs and alcohol are aspects of the environment that can cause mental retardation to varying degrees. Mothers who drink heavily during pregnancy can produce infants with fetal alcohol syndrome (Jones & Smith, 1975). These infants can have congenital malformations of the brain and body, poor coordination, retardation, and character disorders. Eliminating, or at least reducing, a pregnant woman's intake of harmful chemicals would decrease the chances of mental retardation in the infant.

The way in which the rubella virus has been brought under control is an example of a good effort at prevention of one type of severe mental retardation. If a woman contracts rubella, or German measles, during the first three months of pregnancy, the chances are much higher that her child may be affected. The problems most commonly seen are deafness, glaucoma, heart defects, and microcephaly with severe mental retardation (Menolascino & Egger, 1978). Irregular epidemics are believed to occur at 5- to 12-year intervals, but the last large epidemic occurred in the U.S. in 1963–64. The results of that epidemic were about 50,000 stillbirths and abortions and more than 20,000 defective babies. Now, however, such drastic effects of rubella are rare. Public health officials in the United States have successfully mounted a campaign to immunize all school children with a rubella vaccine, thus limiting its spread to pregnant women. Young women who were part of the first vaccination efforts are now of childbearing age themselves and are immune to rubella. As a result, prevention of rubella has essentially prevented rubella-caused retardation.

The reduction of pollution and industrial wastes, such as methylmercury, could also prevent some mental retardation. As with the rubella vaccine, this would involve a national commitment and years of time and effort—high costs but potentially high benefits, considering the savings in human suffering and in effort involved in caring for a retarded person for life.

Treatment of Severe Retardation

The range of problems usually accompanying severe mental retardation—physical and emotional handicaps in addition to severe developmental delays and adaptive behavior problems—makes it obvious that no best single type of treatment for the condition has been found. A treatment program for the severely mentally retarded often means doing those things that prevent the condition from getting worse, rather than providing hope for future improved behavior. Remedial programs for the severely mentally retarded may make home care more possible for those who would otherwise, without treatment, have to be institutionalized. Training programs in adaptive behavior may allow for higher levels of social participation than would otherwise be possible, for example, going to movies, eating at a restaurant, or spending part of one's school day in a nonhandicapped classroom.

Severe mental retardation usually involves neurobiological factors in addition to retarded mental development and possible behavior problems. Pharmacological treatment is often used in addition to various types of environmental treatments, such as behavior management and deinstitutionalization.

PHARMACOLOGICAL TREATMENT

Many severely retarded people suffer to some extent from epilepsy, although their seizures may not be *grand mal* seizures. Many also have behavior problems such as head banging, ruminating, and aggressive outbursts. Major tranquilizers such as chlorpromazine and minor tranquilizers such as diazepam (Valium) and barbiturates may be used to control such behaviors (Craft, 1979). Amphetamines and methylphenidate have been used to decrease hyperactivity (Freeman, 1970). Usually, these drugs are prescribed to help control behaviors that are collateral to the actual intellectual deficit of the retarded. They are the same drugs that would be used for such behaviors in a nonretarded individual and may cause similar side effects. The reader is referred to Sprague and Baxley's (1978) review for an extensive discussion of drugs used with the mentally retarded, including a section on the legal implications of drug use, particularly for those in institutions.

DIET AND VITAMIN TREATMENTS

The reason that drugs are effective in changing behaviors is that they can affect neurotransmission in the brain. More controversial approaches to changing behavior involve modifying brain chemistry through dietary control or megavitamin therapy. High doses of vitamin B6 have been used to treat autistic children (Rimland, Callaway, & Dreyfus, 1978). Harrell, Capp, Davis, Peerless, and Ravitz (1981) reported obtaining marked benefits from providing nutritional supplements to school-age retarded children. The supplement contained minerals and large amounts of 11 vitamins. There are no additional scientific data available to support these claims.

PKU is one of the conditions where dietary control is specifically warranted. An infant with PKU cannot adequately metabolize phenylalanine, a substance that occurs in many foods. If a special synthetic food diet is started within weeks of birth, a PKU infant may grow up normally. Even when dietary treatment begins later, there are modest improvements in behavior and appearance, although generally not in intelligence (Menolascino & Egger, 1978).

BEHAVIORAL TREATMENT

Early intervention studies with severely handicapped infants and young children have taken many different forms that could be considered environmental or experiential in nature. These forms include the use of physical, occupational, and speech therapy and various combinations of therapies. Simeonsson (1978) recently reviewed several treatment procedures for training social competence in the severely handicapped. He concluded that modeling and operant learning strategies, instructional approaches, and group interaction and counseling have each had success in promoting socialization skills and behaviors.

Remediation programs for the severely handicapped are often not based on a formal developmental theory or an overall treatment approach to severe mental retardation. This lack of a formal, comprehensive approach may be due in part to the multiple and sometimes idiosyncratic problems of severely mentally retarded children. Therefore, treatment research often takes the form of single-subject experiments targeting one particular behavior, such as self-injurious behavior or rumination, for modification. Behavior management techniques are most often used to deal with such behaviors. Schroeder, Mulick, and Schroeder (1979) reviewed techniques such as positive reinforcement, time out, punishment, avoidance conditioning, and overcorrection, and provided examples of their use with the severely mentally retarded.

The question of overall effectiveness of these early intervention procedures was raised in both the Simeonsson (1978) and Schroeder et al. (1979) reviews, as well as in other places. Researchers and clinicians do not agree on the most effective treatments, and well designed experimental comparisons of comprehensive treatment programs are not often conducted, because of logistical and ethical constraints. For example, samples of severely mentally retarded individuals are often heterogeneous, with respect to etiology and severity, therapeutic procedures frequently differ from one experiment to another, and determining the appropriate summary measures of effectiveness is a difficult task. In addition, the skills learned in a treatment program may not generalize to other settings unless specific procedures are used to train generalization (Stokes & Baer, 1977).

A minimal requirement for determining effectiveness of a program is the assessment of a child's abilities on two or more occasions to see if changes have occurred. Simeonsson, Cooper, and Scheiner (in press) found only 25 studies since 1975 that met this requirement. Of those studies, 40% reported statistical support for effectiveness. Only five of the 25 studies used random assignment to treatment or control groups.

In another review of 34 studies, Dunst and Rheingrover (in press) evaluated each available study's resistance to internal validity threats as discussed by Campbell and Stanley (1966). Only three of those studies used random assignment, although other studies showed creative use of multiple-baseline design, or a good single subject methodology. Even so, the authors conclude that most studies yield results that are fundamentally uninterpretable because they have failed to use sound design and evaluation techniques. Their review, and that of Simeonsson and colleagues should make researchers aware of the need for better experimental designs when studying treatments for moderate and severely handicapped children. Unfortunately, the efficacy of intervention efforts can be scientifically determined only when sound designs and adequate evaluations are used.

Mild Mental Retardation

Mild mental retardation is a term similar to the educational category "educable." Stanford-Binet IQs of the mildly retarded range from 52 to 67 and they make up about 80% of the mentally retarded population. Prevalence of mild mental retardation seems to be highest between ages 6 and 19, the school years. During preschool, mildly retarded individuals probably develop communication and social skills. After school-age, they can sometimes adjust to community life and function independently, generally at the lower level of socioeconomic status (Tizard, 1974). It appears that many mildly mentally retarded persons are better able to meet the adaptive behavior criteria of adult life than the academic criteria required during the school-age years.

Whereas mental retardation due to known biological factors is spread throughout the entire socioeconomic spectrum, there are proportionately more children from the lower socioeconomic class who are diagnosed as mildly mentally retarded. This is often attributed to being reared in impoverished environments, but it is also true that many other potential causes of developmental retardation are associated with low socioeconomic status. Medical complications of pregnancy are more prevalent among the poor. Lack of education or financial resources to provide for basic necessities such as food, clothing, and shelter is also associated with poverty.

The distinction between prevention and treatment is less clear with mild mental retardation than with moderate to severe mental retardation. The age of diagnosis is usually much later for mild mental retardation than for more severe types. The severely retarded are usually diagnosed within the first 18 months of life, and show a variety of symptoms suggesting the causes of the delay. The moderately mentally retarded are usually diagnosed before the age of three or four, and also show a range of physical signs and symptoms. However, the mildy mentally retarded are rarely evaluated before school entry, and show few signs suggesting the cause of the delay. There may be some abnormalities of brain structure or function associated with mild mental retardation, but current techniques are unable to demonstrate such abnormalities.

The mildly mentally retarded are usually referred for treatment when they begin having school problems with language and number concepts. Thus, the point at which a treatment program for mild mental retardation changes from prevention to remediation depends on how early the signs of developmental delay can be diagnosed.

The Concept of Risk

Prevention of mild mental retardation depends on identifying susceptible people who are likely to develop the condition, but identifying them before they actually do develop the condition. Treatment is then directed toward those at risk. Recent educational intervention programs have been based on the assumption that intervention is most effective when it begins early and

is prevention-oriented (Ramey, Collier, Sparling, Loda, Campbell, Ingram, & Finkelstein, 1976).

As mentioned earlier, we have chosen the age of two as the time marker distinguishing prevention programs from remediation programs for the mildly mentally retarded. If early intervention is to prevent this kind of developmental retardation, the earlier that identification can occur, the better. Several recent studies have identified prenatal or early infancy indicators of later psychosocial retardation.

Ramey, Stedman, Borders-Patterson and Mengel (1978) reported that information available on birth certificates, including the education and marital status of the mother, race and birth order of the child, can be used to discriminate between school-age children who are one or more standard deviations below the mean on intelligence, achievement, and adaptive behavior measures, and children who are at or above the mean on those measures. Finkelstein and Ramey (1980), also using birth certificate information, were able to generate a classification equation correctly predicting 80% of low scoring children on measures of intelligence, achievement, and adaptive behavior, but the equation also resulted in a high false positive rate which undermines its practical value. Most recently, Ramey and Brownlee (1981) have used information about mothers' attitudes, children's early development, and children's early caregiving arrangements to predict IQ scores of above or below 85 at age two. Their procedures demonstrated 75% correct identification, with a miss rate of 20% and a false positive rate of 30%, which is a substantial improvement over their earlier efforts. Although more empirical research is needed to develop more accurate early identification procedures, these results from relatively easily obtained data are encouraging in their implications for preventive intervention.

Prevention of Mild Retardation

From the mid-1960s to the 1980s, programs for prevention of mild mental retardation have varied in the target of intervention, the form of program delivery, and the content of the curriculum. Eighteen exemplary prevention-oriented programs have been reviewed recently by Ramey, Sparling, Bryant, and Wasik (1982). The programs all began during the first two years of life and focused on infants at risk for mild mental retardation.

The targets for intervention have typically been the infant and the mother. The major program delivery forms have included educational home visitation (e.g., Gordon & Guinagh, 1978; Gutelius, Kirsch, MacDonald, Brooks, & McErlean, 1976; Schaefer & Aaronson, 1977), group educational day care (e.g.,

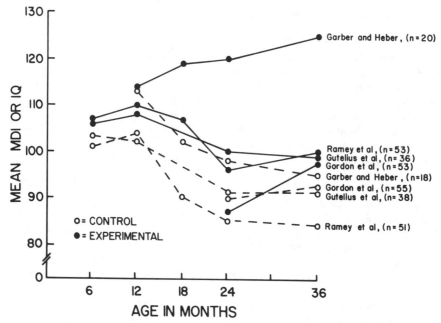

Fig. 31.1. Summary of intellectual results for experimental and control children who were enrolled continuously from birth to 36 months in early intervention programs that had randomly constituted groups.

Caldwell & Richmond, 1968; Robinson & Robinson, 1971), home visit-day care combinations (e.g., Ramey & Haskins, 1981), and parent group sessions (e.g., Badger, 1981). In addition, some programs have included job training for parents (e.g., Garber & Heber, 1977), and medical care for children (e.g., Ramey & Haskins, 1981). Curriculum content of these programs is difficult to divide into distinct categories, because it has varied across a wide spectrum within programs and included content as diverse as sensorimotor infant exercises (e.g., Painter, 1971), parent teaching styles (e.g., Gordon & Guinagh, 1978), and problem solving skills (e.g., Ramey, Sparling, & Wasik, 1981).

Most of these projects had small sample sizes which may limit the generality of the results. Further, few studies have been replicated. Depending on the manner in which subjects were selected, some studies had a problem of self-selection initially or of attrition at a later point. The majority of the prevention-oriented studies included a test-only comparison group, either randomly assigned or selected from another sample and matched with the subjects receiving treatment. Of course, randomization to treatment and control groups is the most powerful experimental procedure to assure initial equivalence of groups, but very few programs have used this critical design feature.

Fig. 31.1 contains what we think are the primary intellectual results from experimentally adequate re-

search programs concerned with the prevention of mild mental retardation. To construct this figure we invoked the following criteria to select projects: (1) the project had to enroll high-risk infants prior to six months of age, (2) infants had to be enrolled continuously in the project until at least 36 months of age, (3) periodic assessments of infants' development using standardized tests had to be accomplished, and (4) assignment to treatment or control groups had to be at random. These criteria resulted in identifying four completed projects (i.e. all children having reached or exceeded three years of age) and one that is in progress (Ramey, Sparling, & Wasik, 1981). We will briefly characterize the four completed projects.

The Milwaukee Project (Garber & Heber, 1977) provided experimental group children with educational group daycare, beginning at four months of age, on a five-day-a-week basis. In addition, families were involved in a parental education component. Mothers also received vocational education, plus on-the-job training. The Milwaukee Project control group participated only in periodic assessments.

In the *Carolina Abecedarian Project* (Ramey & Campbell, 1979), the experimental group received daily education in a group daycare setting, beginning prior to three months of age. Like the Milwaukee Project, this program operated five days a week, 50 weeks a year. In addition, the children received medical care and adequate nutrition, and the families received social work services. The control group in the Abecedarian Project received nutritional supplements, social work services, and medical care.

In the program directed by *Gutelius* (Gutelius et al., 1977), the experimental group children received well-baby care at a clinic and their parents participated in bimonthly parent educational meetings, as well as receiving educational home visits from a public health nurse and phone consultations. The children in that program also received nutritional supplements. Gutelius' control group children were referred to local health departments for routine services and were assessed with the same assessment schedule as the experimental group.

In the *Gordon* Project (Gordon & Guinagh, 1978), the most intensively treated experimental group received weekly home visits for the first two years. During the third year of life, the experimental group children also participated in small play groups for about two hours per day, two days each week. The control group received only periodic assessments.

Each of the four completed programs has reported statistically significant differences between experimental and control groups by 36 months of age. Therefore, each program has provided evidence for its effectiveness. Further, all four treated groups were superior to all four control groups. As can be noted in Fig. 31.1, there was no overlap in the distributions of mean performance of treated and control groups, even though the children came from different projects. It is also important to note that the form of the difference between experimental and control groups within projects is due primarily to a decline in performance of the control groups over time, which confirms that the control groups were at risk for retarded development. Another important point is that these levels of performance for the control groups at 36 months are not likely to be their final or lowest levels. Because these children were still early in their development when assessed, it remains to be seen at what age point these developmental declines will stabilize. It is also important to note that these four projects represent a variety of educational treatment approaches including home visitation (Gordon), home visitation plus parent meetings (Gutelius), developmental daycare (Ramey et al.) and developmental daycare plus parent education (Garber & Heber).

Another interesting finding emerges when the four completed projects are rank-ordered on intensity of treatment in the experimental groups. If intensity is defined as the typical amount of time that the projects had direct involvement or contact with the children and/or families, plus the variety of services offered, then the following order of intensity is likely: Garber and Heber > Ramey et al. > Gutelius et al. >

Gordon et al. It is interesting to note that this ordering also corresponds to the rank ordering of the mean intellectual performance of the four treated groups at 36 months of age.

Further, from descriptions by the projects of the services offered to the control groups, it is also possible to rank the relative discrepancy of treatment intensity between experimental and control groups within projects (Ramey & Bryant, 1982). The discrepancy rankings indicate maximal discrepancy between treated and control groups in the Garber and Heber project followed by Ramey et al., Gutelius et al., and Gordon et al., in that order. At 36 months the discrepancy in experimental and control group IQ scores in these four projects is proportional to the discrepancy in differential treatment. Thus, both the absolute level of IQ performance for treated children, and their relative discrepancy from the performance of their control group, seems to depend upon differences in intensity of treatment. However, at present this conclusion must be regarded as an inference derived from comparing results across projects, and there exist no experimentally adequate data directly relevant to this point.

SUMMARY OF PREVENTION STUDIES CONCERNING MILD RETARDATION

From the studies that have been reviewed, several major conclusions seem likely. First, a variety of educational formats can be successfully implemented with socially defined high-risk families that can prevent developmental retardation at least through the age of three. Second, in the absence of educational intervention such high-risk children are likely to show declines in intellectual performance over time, relative to normative samples. Third, intensity of educational treatment is plausibly related to levels of intellectual functioning in such high-risk populations. However, intensity of treatment has not been systematically manipulated in previous studies, so that this interpretation must be regarded as an hypothesis rather than as an empirically demonstrated finding. Fourth, most of the evaluation data from early intervention programs have been restricted to global measures of intellectual functioning and little information exists concerning the psychological and social mechanisms through which such interventions have had their effects. Fifth, almost no information exists on differential response to treatment either within or between various kinds of intervention programs.

Treatment of Mild Mental Retardation

For reasons previously discussed, we have chosen the age of two as the age to distinguish between prevention and remediation of mild mental retardation. Projects that begin to work with children from low-income families after the age of two are usually dealing with already manifest developmental delays. Several major experimental preschool programs for disadvantaged children were conducted in the 1960's and 1970's, and the federal government made a national commitment to such programs by initiating Project Head Start in 1965.

The most important evidence for the effectiveness of these remedial preschool programs comes from the recent work of the Consortium for Longitudinal Studies (Darlington, Royce, Murray, Snipper, & Lazar, 1980; Lazar & Darlington, 1982). The research was conducted by pooling the original data of 12 principal investigators who had independently designed and conducted experimental preschool programs for children from low-income families. A common follow-up of the original participants (both experimental and control children) was conducted in 1976–77. Of approximately 2,700 subjects and controls in the original 12 projects, 1,599 children who were between the ages of 9 and 19 were located. Follow-up data included an IQ test, school record information, scores on school-administered achievement tests, and interviews with participants and parents.

The 12 original preschool programs have each been described individually in the Consortium's *Society for Research in Child Development Monograph* (Lazar & Darlington, 1982), as well as elsewhere. The subjects in the programs were typically black children (94%) from low-income families in which the mother had completed an average 10.3 years of school and in which the average head of household was a semiskilled or unskilled worker. The median preprogram IQ of the children was 92.1. With the exception of Ira Gordon's Florida project, all of the children were two years old or older at the time of entry into the programs. (We included Gordon's project in our earlier discussion of preventive programs.)

The 12 projects differed in important ways, although all were explicitly concerned with the attainment of basic cognitive concepts and many of the programs placed special emphasis on language development. Six programs used preschool centers, two used a home-visit format, and three used a combination of center and home contacts. Curricula in the centers were based on Piagetian theory, on Montessori's methods, on the Bereiter-Engelmann method, and others.

The projects also differed in how subjects were assigned to groups. Only four projects closely approximated a truly randomized design: Gordon's, Gray's Early Training Project (Gray & Klaus, 1970), Palmer's Harlem Training Project (Palmer & Siegel, 1977),

and Weikart's Perry Preschool Project (Weikart, Bond, & McNeil, 1978).

A description of Gordon's home visit program was included in the earlier section on prevention because subjects entered his project at three months of age. Gray's Early Training Project was both center-based and home-based. Beginning at age four or five, children attended a center-based preschool for three summers and received weekly home visits during the school year. The home visitor served as a liaison between the school and home.

Palmer's project tested two types of curricula—a structured, concept training program and a less structured "discovery" program. Children were tutored in one-to-one situations for 45 minutes two times per week for eight months. Children participated for eight months between the ages of two and three, three and four, or for both years, between two and four.

Weikart's Perry Preschool Project included both half-day, center-based preschool for eight months a year and weekly home visits. The preschool curriculum was based on Piaget's theories and placed heavy emphasis on cognitive objectives. Children entered at the age of three and continued for two years.

The overall findings of the Consortium show that early education has lasting effects in some areas. Participation in an early remedial education program significantly reduced the likelihood that a child would be assigned to a special education class later in school, with 29% of the control group and only 14% of the treatment group being assigned to remedial classes. Early education significantly reduced the number of children retained in grade, with 31% in the control group and 25% in the treatment group being held back a year or more in school. These median percentages are from eight of the 11 projects that collected special education and grade retention data. However, if we restrict discussion to the four programs that used random assignment to treatment or control groups, the combined results are even stronger, particularly for retention in grade. In these studies, 25% of the treatment group and 37% of the control group were held back a year in school. This difference is highly significant statistically. These results are also true after controlling for the effects of children's initial IQ scores, sex, ethnic background, and home background. This is true for all the studies combined with even stronger results when only the experimentally designed studies are included in the analyses.

The Consortium also combined the grade retention and special education variables into a single measure of failure to meet school requirements (Darlington et al., 1980). The median failure percentage for the four experimental design projects was 32% for the treatment group and 53% for the control group, a highly statistically significant difference (Pooled $p <$ 0.001). However, among the individual studies, the differences were significant only for the Palmer and Weikart studies. Weikart's Perry Preschool Project was the most comprehensive, so that result might have been expected. The Gordon project was probably the least intensive, and seemed to have modest effects in the desired direction, although not statistically significant. This result might also have been expected, given that Gordon's project was less intense than the other three. Gray's program was a three-month daycare plus home visit program and Palmer's was a one-to-one tutor program twice weekly. Gray had many more hours of child contact, although not all of it one-to-one, as was Palmer's study. In the area of failure to meet school requirements, Palmer's results were significant but Gray's were not. One cannot conclude, however, that tutoring is more effective than daycare plus home visits because subjects were not randomly assigned to these treatment groups. Also, data were collected when the children were at various points in their school careers. Therefore, as in the prevention studies, intensity of the remediation program is plausibly related to the child's outcome, but experimentally adequate studies directly relevant to this point do not exist.

OTHER RESULTS FROM THE CONSORTIUM STUDIES

The Consortium failed to find any lasting effects in IQ attributable to program participation. There were large effects of IQ tests taken soon after the programs ended, but these gradually tapered off to nonsignificant differences. Without continued differential treatment into public schools it is reasonable to expect more congruence in performance on standardized tests over time as the specific content of the early education program becomes progressively less relevant to test performance and the content of the public school curriculum becomes more relevant. Perhaps the treatment children received an early cognitive head start, which better prepared them to try harder to adapt to the demands of the public schools. Indeed, these children were more likely than controls to give achievement-type answers to the follow-up questionnaires administered by the Consortium. In addition, their mothers had even higher vocational aspirations for them than the children had for themselves, a difference not found in control group mothers and children.

There was, however, some evidence for improved school achievement test scores for treatment group children. They scored significantly higher on the fourth grade mathematics achievement tests than did control children, and somewhat higher on reading achievement tests.

SUMMARY OF REMEDIATION STUDIES

It must be noted that the results from these remediation projects indicate only what *can* be some consequences of preschool education for disadvantaged children but not necessarily what those consequences *will* be. The discrepancy between *can* and *will* is the domain of public policy. That these 12 experiments in preschool education achieved a measure of success in no way guarantees that this is the best that preschool education can achieve or even that similar high-quality educational programs will be available in the future. Nor do the results indicate that poorly planned and implemented copies of these programs will enjoy a similar measure of success. What they do indicate is that remedial intervention programs can be developed and researched with greater confidence in their long-range importance and impact.

Common Principles Underlying Early Intervention

Having reviewed the effects of early intervention in this chapter and in other articles (e.g. Ramey, Sparling, Bryant, & Wasik, 1982; Ramey & Bryant, 1982; Ramey & Baker-Ward, 1982), it is apparent that this is an area characterized by diverse theoretical orientations and diverse intervention practices. However, there are several principles or unifying constructs that we feel could well serve as guideposts to generate additional systematic inquiry for both preventive and remedial educational programs.

We believe that it is useful to construe the developing child as a dynamic part of an evolving family system which has the potential to accelerate or retard development. From this systems-theory perspective, discussed in detail by Ramey, MacPhee, and Yeates (1982), the child and his development become an output of a complex network of genetic, social, and cultural factors, which interact to codetermine developmental status. Therefore, it is possible, to the extent that the child is indeed part of a system, to influence his development by systematically altering various elements which are thought to be causally implicated in developmental change.

From this systems perspective, several derivative principles can be generated as working hypotheses. These include: (a) *Intensity of programming*. Given that truly causal elements affecting development have been isolated, the more intensely the program is applied the greater will be the resulting developmental yield. (b) *Breadth of programming.* Educational programs that effectively manipulate more, rather than fewer elements in the causal network, will result in greater developmental gains. For example, a program that works directly with the parents as well as with the child will have greater benefits than a program that focuses only on the children or the parents. (c) *Structure of educational programming.* Development is not construed as a haphazard process, but rather as a delicate interlacing of many forces that codetermine a given outcome; therefore, for intervention to be optimally effective, it should be embedded within a structured conceptual system that provides a coherent philosophy of development and therefore intervention. To the extent that programs are more structured, rather than less structured, they are likely to be more successful. (d) *Timing of intervention.* Because development is a process begun at conception and is the result at any given point in time of the dynamic interplay between biological, social, and cultural factors, interventionists are best advised to begin their efforts as early in the life span as practical. To advocate intervention that begins early does not imply that one must adopt a critical period hypothesis, one which suggests that if intervention is not begun by a particular time it will be ineffective (see Ramey & Baker-Ward, 1982, for a fuller description of this issue). Rather, to begin early simply recognizes that adaptation to a given set of circumstances is a fundamental characteristic of living organisms, and that the longer a system has adapted to a given set of circumstances the more difficult change is likely to be. Therefore, the advocacy for early intervention derives more from an appreciation of the tendency of systems to approach adaptation to their environment, rather than the acceptance of a particular theoretical perspective on critical periods.

In addition to these parametric implications of general systems theory for early educational intervention, recent research breakthroughs in the study of development hold several theoretical implications which should be considered in designing the next generation of intervention studies. These include the following: (a) *Context generality.* The acquisition of a skill, whether it is a cognitive or motor or social skill, is initially learned in a particular context or location. Frequently these skills do not generalize to other contexts or locations. For example, social skills mastered in a resource room do not necessarily become displayed in a different classroom setting. Without explicit attention to the mechanisms of generalization, the effect of a given training program may be unduly limited. Therefore, it is recommended that particular attention be given to mechanisms which will facilitate generalization across settings. (b) *Developmental generality.* Early intervention researchers have frequently been disappointed when the gains that were obtained from a given educational intervention were no longer detectable in older children after the intervention program had ceased. Yet in almost all instances, the cognitive and social functions that were assessed at a later time, for example cognitive functions tested by an IQ test given at school age, are really different functions from those that were initially taught in the intervention program administered during the preschool period. This phenomenon has frequently been labeled, erroneously we believe, as a *fade-out* effect. However, it has not been established in the literature that early skills that were taught, for example, pre-reading skills, were in fact lost from the child's repertoire at a later point in time. Rather, later developmental skills frequently have not been mastered at the level that early interventionists have desired. In Piagetian terms, there has been limited success at accelerating *vertical decollages.* At present, there is only limited theory and even more limited empirical research on this important topic.

Finally, there are three broad areas of research endeavor that, in our opinion, the next generation of early intervention projects could pay better attention to. The first of these is the area of *epidemiology.* As Hayden & Beck (1982) have pointed out, we have limited knowledge of the epidemiology of pathologies that express themselves after the neonatal period. This is particularly true for conditions that are characterized by mild, rather than severe, intellectual retardation. Therefore, for early intervention programs to target their limited resources most effectively toward those individuals who are most likely to need additional services, we need a better understanding of which specific children are most in danger of nonoptimal development.

Second, in the past, early intervention programs have been evaluated almost exclusively with respect to improvements in cognitive or intellectual development, as opposed to social aspects of personality. This history of concentration on cognition is likely due to the existence of better assessment and evaluation techniques for the intellectual domain of functioning than for social functioning. Nevertheless, it is obvious that social characteristics play a major role in the effectiveness with which a child negotiates his environment. Therefore, greater effort needs to be expended on program development for *social aspects of early human development*, with an accompanying emphasis on instrument development and validation.

Third, and finally, it should be noted that there is at present a paucity of *formal theory* about early human development which can inform and guide new and innovative intervention attempts. Great effort needs to be expended in this area, and these efforts need not be independent from early educational interventions. In fact, as Gray and Wandersman (1980) and others have argued, experimental studies of early intervention are one way to perform basic experiments on the process of human development. Therefore, within the context of early intervention research, there can be the simultaneous and reciprocal advancement of educational techniques and formal theory.

References

American Psychiatric Association. *Diagnostic and statistical manual of mental disorders.* (3rd ed.) Washington, D.C.: American Psychiatric Association, 1980.

Badger, E. Effects of parent education on teenage mothers and their offspring. In K. G. Scott, T. Field, & E. Robertson (Eds.), *Teenage parents and their offspring.* New York: Grune & Stratton, 1981.

Berg, J. M. Genetics and genetic counseling. In J. Wortis (Ed.), *Mental retardation and developmental disabilities.* Vol. VIII. New York: Brunner/Mazel Publishers, 1976.

Caldwell, B. M., & Richmond, J. B. The Children's Center in Syracuse, New York. In L. L. Dittmann (Ed.), *Early child care: The new perspectives.* New York: Atherton Press, 1968.

Campbell, D. T., & Stanley, J. *Experimental and quasi-experimental designs in research.* Chicago: Rand McNally, 1966.

Craft, M. Medication. In M. Craft (Ed.), *Tredgold's mental retardation.* (12th ed.) London: Bailliere Tindall, 1979.

Darlington, R. B., Royce, J. M., Snipper, A. S., Murray, H. W., & Lazar, I. Preschool programs and later school competence of children from low-income families. *Science,* 1980, *208,* 202–204.

Dobbing, J. Undernutrition and the developing brain: The use of animal models to elucidate the human problem. *Psychiatria, Neurologia, Neurochirurgia,* 1971, *74,* 433–442.

Dunst, C. J., & Rheingrover, R. M. An analysis of the efficacy of infant intervention programs with organically handicapped children. *Evaluation and Program Planning,* 1981, *4.* In press.

Finkelstein, N. W., & Ramey, C. T. Information from birth certificate data as a risk index for school failure. *American Journal of Mental Deficiency,* 1980, *84,* 546–552.

Freeman, R. D. Psychopharmacology and the retarded child. In F. J. Menolascino (Ed.), *Psychiatric approaches in mental retardation.* New York: Basic Books, 1970.

Garber, H., & Heber, F. R. The Milwaukee Project: Indications of the effectiveness of early intervention in preventing mental retardation. In P. Mittler (Ed.), *Research to practice in mental retardation.* Vol. 1. Baltimore: University Park Press, 1977.

Golden, M., Birns, B., Bridger, W., & Moss, A. Social class differentiation in cognitive development among black preschool children. *Child Development,* 1971, *42,* 37–45.

Gordon, I. J., & Guinagh, B. J. A home learning center approach to early stimulation. *JSAS Catalog of Selected Documents in Psychology,* 1978, *8,* 6. (Ms. No. 1634)

Gray, S. W., & Klaus, R. A. The early training project: A seventh year report. *Child Development,* 1970, *41,* 909–924.

Gray, S. W., & Wandersman, L. P. The methodology of home-based intervention studies: Problems and promising strategies. *Child Development,* 1980, *51,* 993–1009.

Grossman, H. J. (Ed.), *Manual on terminology and classification in mental retardation,* 1977 revision. American Association on Mental Deficiency. Special Publication Series No. 2., 1977.

Gutelius, M. F., Kirsch, A. D., MacDonald, S., Brooks, M. R., & McErlean, T. Controlled study of child health supervision: Behavioral results. *Pediatrics,* 1976, *60,* 294–304.

Harrell, R. F., Capp, R. H., Davis, D. R., Peerless, J., & Ravitz, L. R. Can nutritional supplements help mentally retarded children? An exploratory study. *Proceedings of the National Academy of Science,* 1981, *78,* 574–578.

Hayden, A. H., & Beck, G. R. The epidemiology of high-risk and handicapped infants. In C. T. Ramey & P. L. Trohanis (Eds.), *Finding and educating high-risk and handicapped infants.* Baltimore: University Park Press, 1982.

Isaacson, R. L., & Van Hartesveldt, C. The biological basis of an ethic for mental retardation. In N. R. Ellis (Ed.), *International Review of Research in Mental Retardation.* Vol. 9. New York: Academic Press, 1978.

Jones, K. L., & Smith, D. W. The fetal alcohol syndrome. *Teratology,* 1975, *12,* 1–10.

Knoblock, H., & Pasamanick, B. Further observation on the behavioral development of Negro children. *Journal of Genetic Psychology,* 1953, *83,* 137–157.

Kushlick, A., & Blunden, R. The epidemiology of mental subnormality. In A. M. Clarke & A. D. B. Clarke (Eds.), *Mental deficiency: The changing outlook.* New York: The Free Press, 1974.

Lazar, I., & Darlington, R. B. Lasting effects of early education: A report from the Consortium for longitudinal studies. *Monographs of the Society for Research in Child Development,* 1982, *47,* 2–3, Serial No. 195.

Menolascino, F. J., & Egger, M. L. *Medical dimensions of mental retardation.* Lincoln: University of Nebraska Press, 1978.

Moser, H. W., Ramey, C. T., & Leonard, C. O. Mental retardation. In A. E. H. Emery & D. L. Rimoin (Eds.), *The principles and practices of medical genetics.* New York: Churchill Livingstone Inc. In press.

Painter, G. *Teach your baby.* New York: Simon and Schuster, 1971.

Palmer, F. H., & Seigel, R. J. *Harlem Study follow up: Cognitive and social characteristics of the sample at ages 13 to 15.* Final Report, Grant no. 90-C1274(01) from the Administration for Children, Youth and Families (OHDS, DHEW), October, 1978.

Penrose, L. S. *The biology of mental defect.* (2nd ed.) New York: Grune & Stratton, 1963.

Ramey, C. T., & Baker-Ward, L. Psychosocial retardation and the early experience paradigm. In D. Bricker (Ed.), *Intervention with at-risk infants.* Baltimore: University Park Press, 1982, 269–289.

Ramey, C. T., & Brownlee, J. R. Improving the identification of high-risk infants. *American Journal of Mental Deficiency,* 1981, *85,* 504–511.

Ramey, C. T., & Bryant, D. M. Evidence of primary prevention of developmental retardation during infancy. *Journal of the Division for Early Childhood,* 1982, *5,* 73–78.

Ramey, C. T., & Campbell, F. A. Early childhood education

for disadvantaged children: The effects on psychological processes. *American Journal of Mental Deficiency*, 1979, **83**, 645–648.

Ramey, C. T., Collier, A. M., Sparling, J. J., Loda, F. A., Campbell, F. A., Ingram, D. L., & Finkelstein, N. W. The Carolina Abecedarian Project: A longitudinal and multidisciplinary approach to the prevention of developmental retardation. In T. Tjossem (Ed.), *Intervention strategies for high-risk infants and young children*. Baltimore: University Park Press, 1976. Pp. 629–665.

Ramey, C. T., & Haskins, R. Causes and treatment of school failure: Insights from the Carolina Abecedarian Project. In M. J. Begab, H. Garber, & H. C. Haywood (Eds.), *Prevention of retarded development in psychosocially disadvantaged children*. Baltimore: University Park Press, 1981.

Ramey, C. T., MacPhee, D., & Yeates, K. O. Preventing developmental retardation: A general systems model. In L. Bond & J. Joffee (Eds.), *Facilitating infant and early childhood development*. Hanover, N.H.: University Press of New England, 1982, 343–401.

Ramey, C. T., Sparling, J. J., Bryant, D. M., & Wasik, B. H. Primary prevention of developmental retardation during infancy. *Prevention in Human Services*, 1982, **1**, 61–83.

Ramey, C. T., Sparling, J., & Wasik, B. H. Creating social environments to facilitate language development. In R. Schiefelbusch & D. Bricker (Eds.), *Early language intervention*. Baltimore: University Park Press, 1981.

Ramey, C. T., Stedman, D. J., Borders-Patterson, A., & Mengel, W. Predicting school failure from information available at birth. *American Journal of Mental Deficiency*, 1978, **82**, 525–534.

Rimland, B., Callaway, E., & Dreyfus, P. The effect of high doses of vitamin B6 on autistic children: A double-blind crossover study. *American Journal of Psychiatry*, 1978, **135**, 472–475.

Robinson, H., & Robinson, N. Longitudinal development of very young children in a comprehensive day-care program: The first two years. *Child Development*, 1971, **42**, 1673–1683.

Schaefer, E. S., & Aaronson, M. Infant Education Research Project: Implementation and implications of the home tutoring program. In M. E. Day & R. K. Parker (Eds.), *The preschool in action*. (2nd ed.) Boston: Allyn and Bacon, 1977.

Schroeder, S. R., Mulick, J. A., & Schroeder, C. S. Management of severe behavior problems of the retarded. In N. R. Ellis (Ed.), *Handbook of mental deficiency, psychological theory and research*. (2nd ed.) Hillsdale, N.J.: Lawrence Erlbaum Associates, 1979.

Simeonsson, R. J. Social competence. In J. Wortis (Ed.), *Mental retardation and developmental disabilities*. New York: Brunner/Mazel, 1978.

Simeonsson, R. J., Cooper, D. H., & Scheiner, A. P. A review and analysis of the effectiveness of early intervention programs. *Pediatrics*. In press.

Sprague, R. L., & Baxley, G. B. Drugs for behavior management, with comment on some legal aspects. In J. Wortis (Ed.), *Mental retardation and developmental disabilities*. New York: Brunnel/Mazel, 1978.

Stokes, T. F., & Baer, D. M. An implicit technology of generalization. *Journal of Applied Behavior Analysis*, 1977, **10**, 349–367.

Tizard, J. Longitudinal studies: Problems and findings. In A. M. Clarke and A. D. B. Clarke (Eds.), *Mental deficiency: The changing outlook*. New York: The Free Press, 1974.

Weikart, D. P., Bond, J. T., & McNeil, J. T. The Ypsilanti Perry Preschool Project: Preschool years and longitudinal results through fourth grade. *Monographs of the High/Scope Educational Research Foundation*, No. 3, 1978.

Zigler, E. Familial mental retardation: A continuing dilemma. *Science*, 1967, **155**, 292–298.

32 ATTENTION, MEMORY, AND COGNITION*

John G. Borkowski, Virginia A. Peck, and Patrick R. Damberg

A straightforward question about the nature of mental retardation was frequently asked a decade ago: "Why don't mentally retarded children learn and remember as well as normal children?" The typical response of many psychologists reflected a strong conviction on the matter: "The mentally retarded have deficient *attentional* and *rehearsal* processes. This is a major problem for the retarded since these two activities are necessary for good encoding and efficient processing of information in short- and long-term memory."

If the same question is asked today, a more complex response is required if it is to square with contemporary research on memory and cognition in the mentally retarded. This chapter attempts to draw upon recent literature and to identify structures, processes, and environmental contingencies that influence learning, remembering, and thinking in the mentally retarded.

The framework used to direct our review is illustrated in the multistage model presented in Fig. 32.1. This model represents the flow of information in the mind and is a composite sketch of the theories of memory and information processing provided by Atkinson and Shiffrin (1968), Butterfield and Belmont

* The writing of this paper was supported in part by NIE Grant #G-80-0134. The second author was supported by an NIH Training Grant (HD-071844).

(1977), Detterman (1979; 1982), Ellis (1970), Estes (1981), and Zeaman and House (1963). Most of the ideas and data sets presented in this chapter can be located within the confines of the schematic representation.

Although we use the model in Fig. 32.1 principally as a heuristic to guide our search for memory and cognitive deficits in the mentally retarded, structures, stages, and processes in the model have been chosen to reflect postulates that mirror current thinking in cognitive psychology. We will discuss the function of each component of the model in the various sections of this chapter. Before proceeding to this analysis, however, we will briefly contrast the current view of how learning in mentally retarded and normal people differs with the dominant position of a decade ago.

In the 1960s, Zeaman and House (1963) and Ellis (1970) pinpointed attentional processes and rehearsal activity as two key components distinguishing normal and retarded performance. We can now add to or amplify these critical components with several new or revised processes that are contained in the composite model in Fig. 32.1: (1) *Very short-term memory* (e.g., the sensory representation of a stimulus, such as in iconic memory; this state has very rapid decay characteristics. (2) *Primary, secondary,* and *long-term memory* (these stages of memory were described by

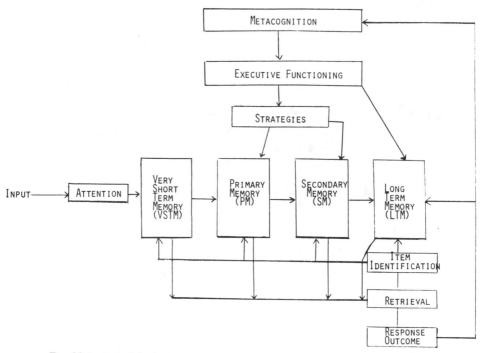

Fig. 32.1. A model of cognitive functioning (after Ellis, Detterman, and others).

Ellis in 1970; there is now some evidence to suggest that primary memory is also a source of memory difficulties in the mentally retarded). (3) *Item identification* is the component that draws upon knowledge in long-term memory to give specificity and identity to a stimulus. (4) *Strategies* augment the flow of information through the system. This can be accomplished by holding information in a memory store (e.g., the role of maintenance rehearsal in secondary memory) or by moving information into long-term memory (e.g., using clustering with categorized items or elaborative imagery with unrelated words). In the latter case, the role of a strategy is to transform the stimulus in order to make it easier to learn or remember (cf. Taylor & Turnure, 1979). (5) *Metacognition* and *executive functioning* are two components that guide the implementation, operation, and revision of lower-level strategies and skills. Metacognition refers to the knowledge an individual has about how the memory and cognitive systems work in meeting the challenges of problem solving in multiple contexts. Executive functioning refers to coordinating processes such as strategy selection, monitoring, and revision. (6) *Retrieval* is the decoding aspect of memory, wherein information in one of the memory stages is selected for output. (7) Most responses we make have an effect on the environment around us or upon ourselves.

Either a problem is solved, partially solved, or an error results. *Response outcomes* become part of both long-term memory (in terms of strengthening specific factual memories) and metacognitive knowledge (i.e., judgments are made about the relative effectiveness of a particular strategy in leading to successful problem solution or to knowledge acquisition). We now proceed to search for processes, structures, and stages within the context of our composite model, as well as from other theoretical perspectives, that will help us understand learning, memory and cognition in mentally retarded people.

Attentional and Perceptual Processes

Attention theories in the past decade have become more general in scope, encompassing cognitive processing as well as structural components of performance deficits in the mentally retarded. Several major theories will be outlined below, followed by a review of the most recent research on retardation that flows from these models of attention. The section will conclude with a summary of the literature on the modification of attentional processes in the mentally retarded.

Theories of Attention

Zeaman and House (1963) developed a theory of attention to explain performance deficits of mentally retarded persons on simple discrimination tasks. They sought to relate constants in discrimination learning equations to intellectual functioning. The theory was based on a chained discrimination learning paradigm that consisted of (1) attending to the relevant dimension (color and/or shape) and (2) approaching the correct cue for that dimension (e.g., red or blue). Individual differences in intelligence were found to be related to the initial direction of attention, but stable aspects of this parameter were not included in the model. Initial cue preferences and the number of competing dimensions were not found to vary with intelligence. Similarly, learning rate parameters were found to be relatively constant across levels of intelligence.

In 1973, Fisher and Zeaman proposed an attention-retention theory of discrimination learning which combined the original Zeaman and House (1963) attention theory with the memory model of Atkinson and Shiffrin (1968), Luce's (1959) decision rule, a feedback mechanism from control theory, and the multiple-look hypothesis from the earlier House and Zeaman (1963) model. This theory described discrimination learning performance as consisting of the processes of learning and retention. The former included attention both in terms of dimension selection as well as cue selection on the preferred dimension; these components were influenced by reward outcomes. The new aspect of the 1973 model was the important role assigned to retention. Changes in the focus of attention resulting from changes in the contents of memory were described as processes of retention (Fisher & Zeaman, 1973).

In a recent update of the 1973 model, Zeaman and House (1979) report that several components of their theory were related to intelligence. In the original Zeaman and House (1963) attention theory, the initial probability of attending to the relevant dimension was not considered to be a structural or fixed component related to intelligence. This statement, however, is incompatible with the finding that the initial probability of attending to the relevant dimension distinguished mentally retarded subjects of lower and higher intelligence on initial performance. Zeaman and House (1979) were led to include direction of attention as a fixed component in their model.

House and Zeaman (1963) concluded that the learning and extinction rate parameters of attention (or thetas) were not related to intelligence. Recently, Okada (1978) found that the experimental designs used in discrimination learning were more sensitive to individual differences in the direction of attention than learning rate parameters. Data reported in Zeaman and House (1979), using Okada's theta sensitive designs,

have shown reliable differences in theta parameters for two groups of mentally retarded subjects varying in MA. Finally, Zeaman and House (1979) reported evidence to suggest that the size of the rehearsal buffer (the capacity of the STM system), as well as the ability to attend to more than one dimension, are related to intelligence.

Whereas Zeaman and House (1979) focused on the structural, unmodifiable, components of the processing system, other theories have focused more on functional features believed to control processing within the structural system. Shiffrin and Schneider (1977) incorporated attentional parameters into a theory of information processing in which a distinction is drawn between automatic and controlled processing. Automatic processing is described as an activation of a learned sequence of elements in long-term memory (LTM) that does not necessarily demand attention. Controlled processing is involved in the temporary activation of sequences of elements not yet learned. This process requires attentional capacity and is therefore initiated by the subject. Craik and Lockhart (1972) similarly emphasize functional features as the limiting aspect of information processing. They proposed degrees of processing flexibility in terms of the depth to which stimuli are analyzed. The more attention given to the semantic processing of a stimulus the greater the amount of retention.

Mosley (unpublished ms.) has posited a theory of selective attention in mild mentally retarded individuals which expands upon the Zeaman and House theory. The theory is a combination of the Atkinson and Shiffrin (1968) structure and control process model and the Craik and Lockhart (1972) depth of processing model. Selective attention is hypothesized to be a control process, similar to rehearsal and coding in the memory system. According to Mosley, the process of selective attention consists of three components: (1) Information is initially registered in pre-attentive sensory receptors that are essential for narrowing the visual field. (2) Stimuli are then attended to through the use of an orienting component and an internal cue selection component that operate simultaneously. The orienting component indicates awareness or readiness to respond and consists, in part, of reflex actions such as pupil dilation or changes in heart rate. (3) The internal cue selection component relates the present input to stored information.

Recently, Nettelbeck and Brewer (1981) concluded that the inferior performance of mentally retarded individuals on a variety of reaction time tasks is due to a general attentional deficit affecting all aspects of the information processing system. They propose that attention is a flexible executive component involved in such activities as preparedness, perceptual encoding, stimulus translation, and response processes.

Carr (in press) described attention as an executive process working within a limited capacity system. Attentional processes are involved in goal selection and planning sequences of operations to reach that goal. They have executive control properties that monitor the execution of plans. In addition, attentional processes are involved in filtering irrelevant and storing relevant perceptual information. Finally, attention is involved with active processing of relevant information in short-term memory. Carr contends that the mentally retarded have a limited capacity system that is drained by each attentional component. Compensation in terms of speed-accuracy tradeoffs, work-storage trade-offs, and task-task tradeoffs result in deficits in performance for mentally retarded individuals. It seems clear that we will hear more about the role of attention in explaining speed/accuracy tradeoff functions in the mentally retarded in the decade ahead.

Information Processing and Attention

Recent research in information processing has shifted focus from a preoccupation with strategies and memory to a concern for perceptual processing. The emphasis is on short-term sensory processing, perceptual encoding, central processing capacity, and preparedness of mentally retarded and nonretarded persons on tasks in which higher level strategic processing is not likely to occur. The duration of the sensory store has been investigated by means of the partial report paradigm and various visual persistence tasks. Visual masking procedures have been used to measure perceptual encoding, while memory scanning, stimulus probability tasks, and redundancy tasks have been used to measure central processing capacity.

SENSORY AND PERCEPTUAL PROCESSING

In partial report procedures, subjects are cued at various intervals after a stimulus offset (the interstimulus interval) to report only a portion of a stimulus array. Mentally retarded persons have been shown to perform more slowly at all interstimulus intervals on partial report tasks (Friedrich, Libkuman, Craig, & Winn, 1977; Libkuman & Friedrich, 1972; Mosley, 1978b; Pennington & Luszcz, 1975, experiment 4). In addition, mentally retarded individuals do more poorly than nonretarded subjects on a variety of visual persistence tasks.

Ross and Ross (1971) and Ross (1972) compared trace and delay classical eyelid conditioning in mentally retarded subjects. In the trace procedure, the con-

ditioned stimulus (CS) is terminated at varying durations before the onset of the unconditioned stimulus (UCS). For the delay procedure, the CS continues at least until the onset of the UCS. Poorer trace conditioning reflects the inability of the subject to maintain a CS trace of sufficient duration to establish a CS-UCS association. Results indicated that when the time between the CS onset and the UCS onset (interstimulus interval) was longer than 500 msec. delay conditioning was superior to trace conditioning, suggesting an inability to maintain the CS trace (Ross, 1972). Ross and Ross (1975) found evidence supporting an alternative explanation. They suggested that trace-delay conditioning differences in the mentally retarded were due to the trace interval (time between CS offset and duration).

On visual persistence tasks using tachistoscopically presented stimuli, mentally retarded subjects required longer stimulus durations in order to recognize the material (Clausen, 1966; Deich, 1968, 1971; Griffith, 1960). Also they have more difficulty reporting briefly presented multiple stimulus arrays (Clausen, 1966; Hoats, 1971; Mosley, 1978b), and reporting dark intervals between successive flashes of light (Thor, 1973).

As evinced by this review of sensory processing efficiency, mentally retarded individuals generally perform more poorly than nonretarded individuals on a variety of tasks measuring short-term sensory, perceptual, and central processing. It is unclear whether these deficits are a function of developmental level, intellectual level, or both. Stanovich (1978) reports evidence to suggest that the processing deficits of mentally retarded individuals are more likely related to MA than IQ. The support comes from the absence of intelligence level-x performance interactions in studies of sensory store processing (Pennington & Luszcz, 1975; Berkson, 1960), perceptual encoding (Thor, 1970; Spitz & Thor, 1968) and central processing (Spitz & Borland, 1971). The failure to find intelligence level-x performance interactions on specific processing tasks has spurred theorizing about the existence of more general deficits in information processing performance related to intellectual functioning. Several theories have emerged pointing to the conclusion that intellectual functioning is related to executive parameters of attention.

In a series of discrimination and choice reaction time studies, Nettelbeck, Brewer and their colleagues found mentally retarded subjects to be slower at processing information and less efficient at organizational responses than nonretarded subjects (cf. Nettelbeck & Brewer, 1981). The conclusion reached was that the mentally retarded lacked general attentional skills involved in three aspects of information processing.

They proposed that mentally retarded individuals were less efficient at accumulating perceptual information (Lally & Nettelbeck, 1977, experiment 1; Nettelbeck & Lally, 1976, 1979), detecting appropriate stimuli, and translating it into an appropriate response (Brewer, 1978; Lally & Nettelbeck, 1977, experiment 2; Lally & Nettelbeck, 1980).

Nettelbeck and Lally (1976) analyzed the discrimination performance of mentally retarded and non-retarded people on a task hypothesized to produce a measure of encoding efficiency for sensory information, as well as its translation into short-term memory. Subjects were required to report which of two tachistoscopically presented lines was shorter. The lines viewed without restrictions were easily distinguishable. However, when a visual mask was presented at varying intervals after the stimulus offset, sensory registration was also restricted. Inspection time served as a measure of the stimulus exposure duration at which an individual was correct nearly all of the time. Since stimulus exposure duration was controlled by the experimenter and reaction time controlled by the subject, independent measures could be obtained for each. Nettelbeck and Lally (1976) analyzed the inspection time and latency data of 10 individuals with WAIS Full Scale IQ scores ranging from 119 to 47. Overall latency was found to be unrelated to IQ scores, which was surprising in view of the slow performance usually attributed to the mentally retarded. Inspection time scores, however, correlated negatively with IQ.

Lally and Nettelbeck (1977, experiment 1) replicated these findings with a population of subjects ranging in IQ from 57 to 130. Using the same discrimination procedure, inspection time again correlated negatively with intelligence. The reaction times of nonretarded subjects increased as the stimulus exposure durations decreased, while the reaction time for the mentally retarded subjects remained relatively constant across exposure durations. The inspection data suggest that mentally retarded individuals need more time than nonretarded individuals to accumulate sufficient sensory information to make a correct discrimination. However, despite this deficit, the stable reaction time performance of the mentally retarded indicated that they were willing to respond with less information than normals.

Nettelbeck, Kirby, Haymes, and Bills (1980) tested the hypothesis that the inspection time performance of the mentally retarded was the result of a speed-accuracy tradeoff. Mentally retarded and normal subjects were encouraged to slow down before making a response. Retarded persons had reaction times that were constant across various exposure durations. In addition, reaction times for errors were similar to reaction times for correct responses in the mentally retarded population, while reaction times for errors in the nonretarded populations were slower than for correct responses. Again, mentally retarded subjects tended to respond on the basis of much less information, regardless of instructions to slow down. It should be noted that Nettelbeck and Lally (1979) have suggested that normal-retarded inspection time differences are not simply a function of MA. For instance, inspection time measures of subjects ranging in age from seven years to adulthood were similar, whereas estimates of mildly retarded adults were about twice as long as for normal adults. Comparisons of speed/accuracy tradeoff functions hold promise of telling us more about central processing limitations associated with mental retardation.

In another series of studies by Lally and Nettelbeck (1977, 1980) and Brewer (1978), stimulus-response translational parameters were analyzed using data obtained from mentally retarded and nonretarded subjects on choice reaction time (CRT) tasks. Deficits in performance of the mentally retarded were associated with deficits in attentional skills resulting from the increase in central processing demands required in these tasks. Lally and Nettelbeck (1977, experiment 2) analyzed the CRT of a sample of 10 mentally retarded and 10 nonretarded subjects who had participated in an initial experiment. Two measures were taken—a decision measure reflecting the time taken to detect and identify a simple stimulus and a movement measure representing the gross movement time required to press the response key. Results indicated that decision times for both groups became slower as the number of stimulus alternatives increased, but the decrease was more prominent in the mentally retarded group. Movement times also slowed in both groups as stimulus choice increased. Mentally retarded individuals were much slower overall but the differences between the groups were consistent across the number of choices. Lally and Nettelbeck (1977, experiment 2) concluded that differences in CRT performance between mentally retarded and nonretarded people are influenced more by central perceptual factors involved in response selection.

Lally and Nettelbeck (1980) tested the hypothesis that the longer inspection time scores obtained for the mentally retarded might have been due to organizational difficulties in responding and not to slower perceptual speed. Under the assumption that increasing response complexity requires longer organizational time, mentally retarded and normal subjects were required to respond using both index fingers (keys 30 cm apart) or using the index and middle fingers on the same hand (keys 1 cm apart). Retarded subjects responded with some deliberation on both tasks, resulting in more errors on the complex task that required more response organization. Retarded subjects traded accuracy for speed, leading to a decision based on insufficient information. In a study by Brewer (1978), the CRT performance of mentally retarded subjects was also attributed to central processing capacity limitations rather than to peripheral motor responses. The task involved an eight-choice reaction time decision in which the correct finger for a response was stimulated, thereby reducing central processing requirements. In this instance, CRT latencies for mentally retarded subjects were not significantly different than for nonretarded subjects.

Carr (in press) has taken an approach similar to Nettelbeck and Brewer (1981) with regard to the information processing abilities of the mentally retarded. Carr has focused on the intellectual and developmental functions of attention involved in data regulation and manipulation, citing research with the mentally retarded on the attention-demanding functions of dual task performance, selective attention, and memory maintenance. For instance, research with mentally retarded individuals using the Psychological Refractory Period Paradigm has revealed complex findings. As the interstimulus interval between two stimuli decreases, the response to the second stimulus is generally slower and less accurate than response to the first stimulus. When simple choice reaction time tasks are employed, intelligence does not correlate with the length of the interstimulus interval. However, when two choice reaction time tasks are used, intelligence correlates with the magnitude of the interstimulus interval (cf. Stanovich, 1980). Carr (in press) attributes this correlation to individual differences in attentional capacity available for data management.

Selective attention skills of the mentally retarded have also been shown to be related to intelligence. As reported earlier, Zeaman and House (1979) suggest that the ability to focus on more than one dimension on a discrimination learning task, termed breadth of attention, is related to intelligence. Incidental learning, another selective attention task, has also been found to be related to intelligence. Hagen and Huntsman (1971) found that mentally retarded subjects were less able than nonretarded subjects to select relevant information on tasks of this kind. Carr (in press) interprets this as an indication that the mentally retarded do not effectively allocate their limited attentional capacities.

Another function of attention suggested by Carr (in press) is the process of memory maintenance. Research from different areas suggests that the attention parameter is related to intelligence. For example, Bachhelder and Denny (1977a,b) proposed that

memory span is related to intelligence. Along the same line, Zeaman and House (1979) suggested that the size of the rehearsal buffer is related to intelligence. The ability to keep more than one code active simultaneously in primary memory (Cohen & Nealon, 1979), and the ability to keep relevant codes and disregard irrelevant codes (Bray, Justice, & Simon, 1978) also seem to be related to intelligence. Apparently, the mentally retarded are less able than normal individuals to selectively attend to and maintain pertinent information in the memory system.

Based on a group of studies on tachistoscopic task performance of the retarded, Mosley (1978a,b) concluded, as did Nettelbeck and Brewer (1981) and Carr (in press), that deficits in performance of the mentally retarded are due to components relevant to attention. Mosley's theory of selective attention (unpublished ms.) contains three components: a preattentive sensory component, an orienting component, and an internal cue selection component. By varying the number of tachistoscopically presented stimuli and the response requirements, Mosley has assessed the relationship of each component to the perceptual performance of retarded and nonretarded subjects. Mosley (1978a) varied the distance between two tachistoscopically presented letters to analyze differences in retarded and normal performance on the preattentive sensory component of selective attention. Decrements in performance were similar for both groups at all interletter distances, leading Mosley (1978a) to conclude that perceptual differences were not localized at the receptor level.

Mosley (1978b), using a cued partial report procedure with a multistimulus display, tested the hypothesis that the difference in retarded tachistoscopic performance was due to the orienting response component. Recall for mentally retarded adults was significantly poorer than nonretarded CA matched adults, but above chance level. Error analyses revealed that the response patterns for mentally retarded and nonretarded groups were similar. The most frequently made errors for both groups were reporting the letter next to the cued letter. This error was an indication that the orienting response for both groups was inefficient. Mosley (1978b) also found that mentally retarded subjects reported letters that had not been on the original display (intrusion errors) significantly more often than nonretarded subjects. Mosley concluded that the match between stimulus items and already stored information (internal cue selection) was less efficient for mentally retarded than nonretarded subjects.

A whole report procedure with a multistimulus display was used to analyze the difference between mentally retarded and nonretarded persons in internal cue selection performance (Mosley, 1978b). In theory, the more letters in the display the more time should be required to perform internal cue selection, matching each stimulus with its appropriate long-term memory cue. This time requirement works to the detriment of the orienting response in that the stimulus materials decay rapidly. It is possible that the stimulus material will be lost before the internal cue selection process is completed. In the Mosley (1978b) study, mentally retarded adults and CA matched nonretarded adults were shown a tachistoscopically presented array of ten letters and asked to report as many letters as possible. Subjects reported the correct letter in its appropriate position in order to gain a correct response. Nonretarded adults recalled significantly more letters than the mentally retarded adults. In addition, nonretarded subjects made a relatively high percentage of position errors and relatively low percentage of nonspecific errors, whereas the reverse was true for mentally retarded adults. Normal subjects spent more time retrieving information from long-term memory, resulting in a loss of letter orientation information. Mentally retarded subjects, on the other hand, were much slower in internal cue selection, resulting in a correct spatial assignment but incorrect long-term memory match.

Mosley (1980) varied stimulus familiarity (letters vs. Chinese characters) and stimulus onset asynchrony (i.e., the interval between target stimulus offset and mask onset) with a group of mentally retarded adolescents, a CA matched group, and an MA matched group of nonretarded adolescents and children. When the stimulus load was minimal (single letters), the internal cue selection processes were similar for the two groups. In other words, as stimulus onset asynchrony (SOA) increased errors decreased. Response patterns changed, however, when the unfamiliar Chinese characters were presented. At the longer SOA, older normal adults performed better than mentally retarded adolescents and MA matched children. When the SOA became shorter, adults performed more poorly than both groups. These results suggest that while internal cue selection will be rapid for familiar stimuli, internal cue selection of unfamiliar stimuli takes much more time, resulting in decreased performance. As in the Mosley (1978b) study, "time drain" effects recall of briefly presented stimuli in an adverse way for mentally retarded subjects.

OFF-TASK GLANCING

It has been well documented that mentally retarded populations respond more slowly than nonretarded populations on a variety of simple reaction time tasks (Baumeister & Kellas, 1968). In addition, mentally retarded individuals show greater between-subject and within-subject variability in reaction time performance (Baumeister & Kellas, 1968; Krupski, 1976; Liebert & Baumeister, 1973). These performance deficits have been attributed, in part, to the finding that mentally retarded individuals are less likely to maintain adequate attentional levels during reaction time tasks (Baumeister & Kellas, 1968; Denny, 1964; Krupski, 1975, 1976). Turnure (1970, study 1) reported more off-task glancing by mentally retarded children than CA-matched nonretarded children while working on oddity problems. Similarly, Turnure and Zigler, (1964, study 2; Turnure, 1970) found more off-task glancing by mentally retarded subjects on object assembly tasks. Krupski (1977) reported slower reaction times and more off-task glancing by mentally retarded adolescents during a preparatory interval between a warning signal and a reaction time signal. All of these findings suggest difficulty in maintaining attentional direction on the part of the mentally retarded.

PREPAREDNESS AND EXPECTANCY

Nettelbeck and Brewer (1981) proposed that response preparedness and stimulus expectancy are attentional components differentiating the mentally retarded from normal individuals. Studies on preparatory intervals, serial reaction time, and heart rate can be cited in support of this contention. For instance, Baumeister and Kellas (1968) examined the relationship between reaction time and the length of the preparatory interval (PI) between a warning signal and a reaction stimulus. In one instance, the PI was consistent within a block of trials and varied between blocks (regular procedure). In a second instance, PI was variable across trials (irregular procedure). For the regular procedure, the reaction times of mentally retarded subjects were slower with increasing PI, but with the irregular procedure faster reaction times followed the longer PI. Retarded subjects had slower reactions than nonretarded subjects in all conditions, but the differences were less in the irregular procedure when the PIs were less. Baumeister and Kellas (1968) concluded that it was more difficult for the mentally retarded subjects to focus attention for extended periods of time required by long PI. Joubert and Baumeister (1970) found reaction times to a second stimulus that followed at varied intervals a response to an initial stimulus to be slower than for mentally retarded subjects. An attentional deficiency related to preparatory sets was used to account for the normal-retarded differences. What may be occurring is that the limited processing capacity of mentally retarded subjects may make it difficult to process two stimuli in close succession (cf. Carr, in press; Stanovich, 1980). Whenever the task is freed of this condition,

RT differences between normal and retarded individuals may be less extreme (cf. Friedrich, Libkuman, & Hawkins, 1974).

Modification of Attention

A limited number of studies have focused on increasing attention in the mentally retarded. Burgio, Whitman, and Johnson (1980) assessed the feasibility of increasing attending behaviors in EMR children through a self-instruction technique developed by Meichenbaum (1977). The children were taught to verbalize a series of steps to guide the learning process, including instructions on how to cope with errors and distractions. Burgio et al. (1980) were successful in teaching self-instructions, showing that the complex strategy transferred to the classroom. Results also indicated a reduction in off-task, attentive behavior. A consistent improvement in classroom performance across other domains, however, was not found. Self-instructional (Guralnick, 1976), operant (Maier & Hogg, 1974), and differential reinforcement (Jackson, 1979) procedures have been successful in enhancing general, on-task attention in the mentally retarded. However, research is needed on the development of methods for producing generalization of attention across time and tasks.

Components of Memory

Memory research with the mentally retarded has been based almost exclusively on a model developed by Ellis (1970), a variant of the multistore or stage approach to memory (Atkinson & Shiffrin, 1968; Waugh & Norman, 1965). The Ellis model consists of four independent stores: (1) very short-term memory (VSTM), (2) primary memory (PM), (3) secondary memory (SM), and (4) tertiary memory (TM), with the last added by Ellis to account for overlearned information in long-term storage. Each structure is differentiated by the nature of the retention interval, storage capacity, and cause of forgetting. Additionally, Ellis included two processes in the model to account for movement between stores—attentional/perceptual mechanisms utilized to transfer information from VSTM to PM, and rehearsal activity to recirculate an item through PM to maintain the stimulus and prevent decay or to move an item from PM to SM.

Research within this paradigm has focused on the detection of deficits within stores or processes that might account for differences on memory task performance between normal and retarded groups. Most individual studies have studied only one portion of the system, and yet have often claimed deficits

throughout the system. Detterman (1979), following a stage-by-stage, process-by-process review of the literature, suggested that in light of the frequency of findings citing deficits in memory for retarded individuals that every memory process is to some degree deficient. Ellis (1978) reached a similar conclusion in suggesting that a deficit occurs "from stimulus onset and persisting." Nevertheless, on the basis of the methodological shortcomings common to many studies claiming deficits, and the general disagreement in the literature as to what specific deficits are present in the mentally retarded, a brief review of selected studies within each of the stages and processes is necessary.

Very Short-term Memory (VSTM)

Very short-term memory (Ellis, 1970) is basically a sensory-specific representation of stimulus events. It has been labeled iconic memory, owing to the fact that much of the research concerns visual stimulation. The structure of VSTM has been operationally defined by Sperling (1960), and Averbach and Coriell (1961) as being of relatively limitless capacity and of extremely brief duration (250–2,000 msec). Information is lost from VSTM through either decay or masking (covering of prior stimulus by a new stimulus). There is obviously considerable overlap between VSTM and attentional mechanisms discussed in the previous section. This is to be expected, given the interdependence of attention and prememory processing.

Researchers have studied VSTM structures of mentally retarded individuals in comparison with normal MA- or CA-matched individuals, in hopes of defining the structural similarities or differences between groups. Several studies have found the mentally retarded to be deficient in VSTM (Headrick & Ellis, 1964; Libkuman & Friedrich, 1972; Pennington & Luszcz, 1975). All of these investigators have relied on a partial-report technique, citing main effects as evidence for deficient performance by the mentally retarded. Ross and Ward (1978) concluded that partial-report data might be more susceptible to confounding factors such as strategy use, or prior learning, accounting for differential effects between groups. This suggestion is supported by the findings of Sheingold (1973). However, from the partial-report data we have tentative evidence to suggest that qualitative deficits may exist in visual VSTM for mentally retarded individuals (Pennington & Luszcz, 1975).

An alternative method for studying VSTM, one claimed to be relatively free of confounds, is the masking techniques (Sperling, 1963). Several studies have used this method (Galbraith & Gliddon, 1972;

Spitz & Thor, 1968; Welsandt & Meyer, 1974), reporting that the mentally retarded are deficient in the efficiency of processing information as reflected in reduced VSTM capacity. Welsandt and Meyer (1974) reported significant interstimulus interval (delay of onset of masking stimuli) X intelligence interactions between retarded, CA-, and MA-matched groups.

Hornstein and Mosley (1979) found that a combined partial-report and visual masking procedure, using unfamiliar stimuli (Chinese characters), resulted in comparable performance at the sensory level between mentally retarded, MA-, and CA-matched children. These authors concluded that differences found in performance between groups in previous studies must have been due to processes other than VSTM. In a similar vein, Stanovich (1978) concluded that the lack of intelligence X experimental factor interactions in a number of studies precluded a conclusion about differential factors or structures influencing VSTM or perceptual encoding in the mentally retarded. They may have the structural integrity necessary for VSTM (in terms of capacity and duration of the icon), but lack the development of attentional/perceptual processing skills involved in extracting information from the stimulus event (Pennington & Luszcz, 1975). The assumption of a structural deficit in VSTM associated with mental retardation does not appear justifiable according to Stanovich (1978).

Primary Memory (PM)

Primary memory (Waugh & Norman, 1965; Ellis, 1970) is often equated with the short-term store (Atkinson & Shiffrin, 1968). It is limited in capacity and of longer duration than VSTM. Perhaps, the simplest operational definition of PM is that it is represented by the recency effect, or superior recall of the last items in a serial list. If groups of subjects performed equally well on the last few positions, it can be concluded that the groups were functionally similar in PM (cf. Ellis, 1970). This method of defining PM provided the impetus for the conclusion that there were no differences in PM between mentally retarded and normal subjects (Ellis, 1970; Belmont & Butterfield, 1969). Since the groups performed equally well on the recall of the last items, differences in overall memory performance were thought to be the result of the lack of active strategy use (Ellis, 1970). That is, the deficit occurred in the strategies involved in holding and transferring the information to secondary memory (SM) rather than in PM.

The rehearsal deficit position is one of the most significant findings in memory research with the mentally retarded. The conclusion that passive mem-

ory, or the structure of PM, is essentially of equal integrity in both retarded and nonretarded populations has held wide acceptance in the literature. However, several recent studies claim that passive memory deficits characterize the performance of mentally retarded individuals.

Scott and Scott (1968) suggest that on tasks of short-term retention the mentally retarded are deficient in PM. Similarly, Dugas and Kellas (1974) found that the mentally retarded were deficient in performance on the Sternberg (1966) scanning task and concluded that the deficit was due to a PM deficiency, consistent with Scott and Scott (1968). However, studies designed to detect passive memory deficits in the retarded have sometimes faced methodological problems, such as failure to control for strategic involvement, measurement differences, or failure to equate for initial acquisition level (cf. Ferretti, in press). Strong conclusions about PM deficits cannot be drawn in light of these problems. Nevertheless, some studies have reported the presence of passive memory deficits in the retarded even after procedures were employed that attempted to control for methodological difficulties in separating PM effects from other memory components (Clark & Detterman, 1981; Ross & Ross, 1976; Cohen & Sandberg, 1977).

In one of the more carefully designed studies to date, Ferretti (in press) tested two competing predictions concerning differences between nonrehearsing (passive) normal and retarded persons. The predictions tested were the following: (1) all retention differences can be attributed to differences in cognitive strategy usage, so that no differences should occur in retention of nonrehearsing subjects (supported by Ellis, 1970; Belmont & Butterfield, 1969); and (2) in the absence of cognitive strategies, retention differences should be found between normal and retarded subjects (supported by Ross & Ross, 1976). Results showed equal forgetting for mentally retarded and nonretarded subjects when the demands of acquisition were equated and rehearsal was negated, suggesting that passive memory (PM) is indeed similar for mentally retarded and nonretarded individuals (Ferretti, in press).

Rehearsal Strategies and Secondary Memory (SM)

Secondary memory (SM) is a limited storage system but of greater capacity and duration than PM. Transfer to and from SM occurs after various rehearsal strategies (e.g., chunking, grouping, imaging) are applied to the materials to be learned. Rehearsal, a process by which information is transferred from one memory state to another, can be accomplished through simple repetition of stimulus items (maintenance rehearsal) or it can involve planning, organization, and transformation (elaborative rehearsal). The effectiveness of rehearsal, that is, how efficiently transfer from PM to SM occurs, depends upon a complex array of situational and subject variables, not least of which is the ability to activate the rehearsal processes appropriately.

Rehearsal processes in the mentally retarded may well be the most researched topic in the memory area (cf. Detterman, 1979). Much of the interest in rehearsal in the mentally retarded was spurred by the theory and data of Ellis (1970), who concluded that the differential performances on memory tasks between mentally retarded and nonretarded individuals was due to the former's failure to use active rehearsal processes. It appeared that the retarded were suffering from a rehearsal deficit. Ellis (1970) found that on a variety of serial learning tasks, mentally retarded individuals performed as well as nonretarded subjects on the last few positions on the list (PM), but recalled significantly fewer items than normals from the early positions of the lists (the primacy effect, reflective of SM). Increased exposure time did not noticeably enhance SM for mentally retarded individuals.

Several researchers have claimed that the mentally retarded do not lack the strategic processes necessary for accurate performance, but lack spontaneous access to these processes and the coordination among them. In other words, the mentally retarded have been found to be production-deficient. Brown (1974) concluded that the mentally retarded could be expected to be deficient to some extent on tasks requiring active strategy use (e.g., rehearsal, clustering). On tasks requiring no strategy usage, however, they would be expected to show minimal deficits. The mentally retarded seemed to lack the ability to adopt strategies spontaneously, although they could be successfully instructed to do so through systematic training.

Another research approach supporting the production deficiency hypothesis is the paradigm developed by Belmont and Butterfield (Belmont & Butterfield, 1969, 1971; Butterfield & Belmont, 1977; Butterfield, Walbold, & Belmont, 1973). These investigators developed a self-paced memory task in which a complex strategy is applied following training to an experimental task. By observing the "executive functioning" of nonretarded individuals over a variety of tasks, Butterfield et al. (1973) developed a method for inducing a complex strategy package, featuring the coordinating of input and output processing, in mildly mentally retarded adolescents.

Production deficiency may be remediated through a variety of training procedures designed to increase learning and retention of information by mentally retarded individuals. Instructional research appears to be moderately effective in training the retarded to use strategies and thereby increasing performance on memory tasks. However, many of the benefits attributed to training are often short-lived in that the mentally retarded fail to maintain the instructed strategy in their rehearsal repertoire (cf. Borkowski & Cavanaugh, 1979). Additionally, Detterman (1979) points out that training studies often involve the manipulation of several variables, any or all of which might have had an effect on memory performance. It is difficult to identify a single variable as being responsible for the performance increase demonstrated by the retarded following most training studies.

Training studies can be classified into two general, procedural paradigms: (1) active strategy-inducing procedures in which subjects are taught strategies and encouraged to use them on experimental tasks, and (2) passive strategy-inducing methods, where a mnemonic is demonstrated by the experimenter, but the subject does not actively manipulate the strategy on the experimental task (cf. Glidden, 1979). The results of a number of studies suggest that retention and transfer of passive strategies are generally poor for mentally retarded individuals (e.g., Mar & Glidden, 1977), whereas a growing number of studies have reported long-term retention of active strategies (e.g., Wanschura & Borkowski, 1975). Butterfield et al. (1973) remediated large individual differences in memory performance between mentally retarded and CA-matched adolescents. Utilizing a procedure in which extensive systematic instructions on both rehearsal and retrieval strategies were given to mentally retarded subjects, the investigators demonstrated that pretraining deficits were alleviated through training. In fact, the trained mentally retarded subjects actually performed better than their untrained CA-matched counterparts on a self-paced, six-item single-exposure recall task. Butterfield et al. (1973) suggested that not only do the mentally retarded suffer from a rehearsal deficit, but additionally they fail to properly sequence rehearsal and nonrehearsal learning techniques. They neither coordinate multiple retrieval strategies, nor coordinate retrieval strategies with acquisition strategies. Therefore, training must focus on executive processes so that the selecting, sequencing, and coordinating of rehearsal and retrieval strategies are synchronized, thereby improving retention.

Wanschura and Borkowski (1975) compared different groups of moderately retarded children on a paired-associate task, in which the children received prepositional mediators (*is, on,* or *under*) on some, all, or none of the pairs in a list. The results demonstrated unusually large individual differences among mentally retarded children, especially on an unstructured transfer task designed to assess the maintenance of the acquired mediational strategy. Those trained to use the mediational strategy showed either perfect strategy maintenance or zero maintenance on the nonprompted, paired-associate transfer task. The authors conclude that individual differences must be carefully monitored when training the mentally retarded, as the results showed that learning a strategy may not be sufficient for applying that strategy on a transfer task.

A study by Reichhart, Cody, and Borkowski (1975) showed the importance of carefully monitoring individual differences when training subjects to use strategies. In one of the few studies to train a variety of strategies, Reichhart et al. (1975) compared the effects of clustering-instruction, cumulative rehearsal, and a combined cumulative clustering strategy on nine-item categorized lists of pictures. Subjects were assigned to one of the experimental groups (cumulative rehearsal or cumulative clustering) or to the clustering-instructed control group, with the groups balanced for higher functioning (mean IQ = 55) and lower functioning (mean IQ = 40) mentally retarded adolescents. Use of the instructed strategy failed to improve recall for the cumulative-clustering group on an immediate transfer task, and failed for both rehearsal groups after two weeks. Further analysis revealed that lower functioning individuals did not transfer strategy training in either rehearsal group, even immediately after training. These findings suggest once again that individual differences between mentally retarded subjects must be understood if we are to explain the variability in strategy transfer, demonstrated by Reichhart et al. (1975), Wanschura and Borkowski (1975), Butterfield et al. (1973), and Belmont, Ferretti, and Mitchell (in press).

Turnure, Buium, and Thurlow (1976) posited that a production deficiency is not a viable explanation of learning differences, especially if the deficient children can easily be taught to use more appropriate strategies. The investigators presented mentally retarded individuals with an interrogative (questioning) strategy to aid paired-associate learning. Interrogative cues provided the opportunity for greater semantic analysis by the child, and consequently improved recall. Kendall, Borkowski, and Cavanaugh (1980) found that transfer of the interrogative strategy to a nonprompted maintenance task occurred for EMR children. This finding questions the conceptual usefulness of "production deficiency." That is, if adequate instruction can raise memory performance and maintain that performance on a transfer test at some later point,

the effect seems due more to a failure in instruction than a cognitive deficit in the child.

Burger, Blackman, Holmes, and Zetlin (1978) showed that mentally retarded children given explicit training on a sorting strategy for lists of pictures, performed comparably to nonretarded children averaging one year (MA) above the retarded group. Additionally, Burger et al. (1978) found that good retention of the sorting strategy occurred on a transfer task three weeks following training. Once again, it appears that explicit training resulted in improved performance by retarded individuals, a result consistent with findings by Turnure et al. (1976) and Kendall et al. (1980).

Brown, Campione, and Barclay (1979) taught mentally retarded children to make recall-readiness estimations of their own memory capacities, a self-monitoring process. Brown et al. were successful in producing strategy generalization with EMR children. One year following original training, older EMR children (MA8) not only maintained the recall-readiness strategy, but also showed evidence for generalization in that they used the strategy to aid list recall of prose passages. Brown et al. (1979) demonstrated that a general process could be taught that will induce mentally retarded children to actively implement a strategy that will generalize across time and transfer task.

Borys, Spitz, and Dorans (1982) tested mentally retarded young adults (institutionalized) and average, nonretarded six, seven, eight, and 10 year olds on the Tower of Hanoi task. The investigators were interested in assessing problem-solving differences between subject groups as a function of the number of moves required for solution of the Tower of Hanoi problem. Borys et al. (1982) found that all subjects had difficulty in solving the standard seven-move tower problem, but showed a dramatic improvement on a six-move problem. The authors attributed this result to the fact that a seven-move problem required a three-level depth-of-search, whereas a six-move problem required a one-level depth-of-search. Overall, Borys et al. found that the mentally retarded group suffered from a limited search capacity responsible for a maturational lag of about 1½ years for the educable group. Specifically, the maturational lag was most pronounced on the seven-move problem, and then dissipated, probably because of ceiling effects, on the five-move problem for the educable and borderline groups, and on the three-move problem for the trainable group. Additionally, Borys et al. (1982) found that children spontaneously solved problems in a hard-to-easy progression (e.g., first solving an experimenter-guided six-move problem, and then applying the move to the seven-move problem). Borys et al. (1982) suggested that the use of superior strategies by the more mature groups is related to an increasing depth-of-search capacity, and that the mentally retarded groups' limited search capacity is largely responsible for the pronounced maturational lag. The extent to which strategy instructions can be successfully applied to this deficit in problem solving is unknown.

Along the lines of the Borys et al. study (1982), McCauley, Kellas, Dugas, and Devillis (1976), and Clark and Detterman (1981) suggested that deficits in processes other than rehearsal might be responsible for lower STM performance by mentally retarded individuals. For instance, Clark and Detterman (1981) postulate that architectural differences in capacity might account for deficits demonstrated when rehearsal is controlled in a memory task. Such factors are probably not easy to remediate.

In conclusion, it appears that mentally retarded individuals typically exhibit a deficit in rehearsal and in SM. However, the growing number of successful training studies in which attention is paid to both rehearsal (or acquisition) strategies and retrieval techniques, and, more importantly, to explicit methods for generalizing these strategies to transfer tasks suggests that deficits in SM may be reduced by providing the mentally retarded with adequate cognitive instructions. The extent of improvement, however, seems limited.

Tertiary Memory (TM)

Ellis (1970) described TM as the durable, long-term store of overlearned information. It is relatively limitless in capacity and duration, although information may be lost through interference or may be inaccessible due to retrieval difficulties. Detterman (1979) reports that a majority of studies done on the TM structures of mentally retarded individuals are hampered by methodological problems, for example, level of initial learning has often not been equated across groups (cf. Underwood, 1964). Belmont (1966), in perhaps the most complete review of the TM capabilities of the mentally retarded to date, found that in the literature on long-term memory methodological problems precluded conclusions about TM integrity in the mentally retarded. He suggested that researchers should consider standardizing experimental procedures, use procedures that are relatively simple to apply, and then study such variables as difficulty and meaningfulness, degree of learning, frequency and intensity of presentation, and length of retention interval, for an assessment and explanation of TM in mentally retarded subjects.

Belmont (1966) found only one study (Klausmeier, Feldhusen, & Check, 1959) in which methodological

difficulties did not preclude acceptance of conclusions about TM deficits. Klausmeier et al. (1959) found that high IQ children (over 120) learned rapidly and forgot rapidly whereas low IQ children (55–80) learned slowly and forgot slowly. Also, retention was equal for high, average, and low IQ subjects when the original learning task was graded to the learners' achievement level. Additionally, retention was reported to decrease over time for all groups on a variety of tasks. In contrast to this conclusion, Prehm and Mayfield (1970) reported that mentally retarded subjects demonstrate deficient long-term retention when compared with nonretarded individuals.

Too few sound studies can be found in the literature to support or refute a TM deficit in mentally retarded individuals. Present conclusions must be speculative, especially in light of the variability in findings. Since deficits have been claimed in VSTM, attentional/perceptual processes, PM, rehearsal strategies, and SM, we must wonder whether TM can ever be unequivocally measured in view of these initial differences in the memory chain.

Retrieval Processes

Since deficits have been posited to exist throughout the memory systems of mentally retarded individuals, we might look to retrieval processes to provide explanations for some of the deficits. To retrieve an item successfully from SM or TM, the individual must first encode the item, rehearse it, transfer it from PM to SM (or TM), and then catalog the item within the vast capacity of the TM structure. The individual must access the correct location in SM or TM to retrieve an item successfully, and this process must often occur rapidly amid a bombardment of alternative selection routes. Research on retrieval processes has suggested that the mentally retarded are unable to store information so that it can be efficiently retrieved (e.g., R. M. Brown, 1974; Harris, 1972; Spitz, 1973). Other investigators have suggested that the mentally retarded fail to use this information to their advantage (Sperber, Ragain, & McCauley, 1976).

The availability of category information should help individuals store items in such a way to allow for efficient retrieval to occur. Several researchers have suggested that the mentally retarded are deficient in the knowledge of category information in memory or its availability (e.g., Blount, 1968; Glidden & Mar, 1978; Haywood & Switzky, 1974; Stephens, 1964, 1966). Davies, Sperber, and McCauley (1981) have suggested that the poor performance of mentally retarded individuals on tests of category usage may not result from a deficiency in category knowledge, but may instead be attributable to a failure to retrieve information that is available. The results of the Davies et al. (1981) study support the hypothesis of "differential accessibility." Retarded and nonretarded subjects did not differ in the degree to which stored information about subordinate/superordinate category relationships automatically influenced picture processing in a semantic processing task, but when subjects were required to make simple decisions that involved active retrieval of superordinate information, the mentally retarded took consistently longer than the nonretarded group.

Winters and Burger (1980) also suggested that the speed with which information is retrieved from semantic memory might indicate the processing, structure, and organization of that information. These investigators compared an age-of-acquisition measure and ratings on seven semantic dimensions for words presented to nonretarded adults, and the codability and retrieval speed of those items by mentally retarded individuals. Winters and Burger (1980) found that the retrieval mechanisms of retarded and nonretarded individuals are similar for semantic variables that represent intragroup performance (the codability variable) or intergroup ratings (e.g., meaningfulness, imagery, or age of acquisition). These results support earlier studies (e.g., Winters & Cundari, 1979; Winters, Winter, & Burger, 1978) on retarded deficits in speed of retrieval.

Winters (in press) has studied the effects of proactive interference (PI) on retrieval in a series of studies designed to test the cue-overload principle (Watkins & Watkins, 1975, 1976). Mentally retarded subjects were tested on a modified Brown-Peterson task (1958, 1959). Winters hypothesized that the cue-overload principle might explain the process of PI build-up (the interference of previously learned items on the recall of recently presented items) and PI release. The principle states that the efficiency of a retrieval cue in recalling an item decreases as the number of items it subsumes under the same cue increases (Watkins & Watkins, 1975, 1976). PI build-up occurs when a category cue overloads. Perhaps mentally retarded and normal individuals suffer from an inability to match encoding cues (or features extracted in the acquisition of material) with retrieval cues. This would account for PI build-up due to cue-overload and to PI release when a new cue is presented.

Winters (in press) concluded that the PI paradigm lends itself to the study of the organization and encoding of information in the PM of the mentally retarded, and how that processing may affect later retrieval. Winters found, in a series of studies on PI release, that mentally retarded subjects perform very much like nonretarded individuals. Results support the

findings of Cody and Borkowski (1977), who concluded that overall performance at recall was poorer for the mentally retarded, and that it was probably due more to their lack of use of category knowledge than to their lack of category knowledge itself. In the Winters study, the mentally retarded had a tendency to encode specific items instead of category-matching during PI build-up, causing greater interference. In other words, they fail to use efficient encoding skills (lack of category information extraction) and fail therefore to match the information they possess with retrieval cues that might aid them in recall. In conclusion, the area of retrieval offers a new and promising research focus for the analysis of memory processes. It might be a basis for detecting links between deficient encoding processes and poor overall performance by the mentally retarded. Further research should aim to clarify the availability/accessibility dichotomy as it influences retrieval performance in this population.

Executive Processes

There are two major approaches to the study of executive processes in the mentally retarded. The first emphasizes the role of executive functioning—such as strategy invention, monitoring, and revision (cf. Butterfield & Belmont, 1977). The second approach is called metacognition. It reflects the importance of prior knowledge about cognitive-memory processes as precursors of strategic behavior (cf. Borkowski, Reid, & Kurtz, in press). Both approaches focus on the failure of mentally retarded children to generalize strategies over time and settings.

Executive Functioning

Butterfield and Belmont (1977) state that "when the subject spontaneously changes a control process or sequence of control processes as a reasonable response to an objective change in an information task (p. 284)," executive functioning has occurred. In other words, if strategy A is used with task X, and then strategy B replaces A when a new task (Y) is introduced, conditions have satisfied the operational definition of executive functioning.

Recent research has been directed at understanding how executive functioning operates in the mentally retarded. Belmont, Butterfield, and Borkowski (1978) measured executive functioning in terms of the transfer of trained study strategies to near and far generalization tests. They hypothesized that generalization might best be taught by guiding children through at least two highly similar training procedures and calling attention to their similarities and differences. Results showed that mentally retarded children learned to transfer study strategies to both near and far generalization tasks. The extent of the generalization was highly dependent on multiple training sessions, each focusing on slightly different study strategies and the reason for their effectiveness. It is interesting to note that generalization was more apparent on later than on earlier trials in the final phases of this experiment. The reinstatement or revision of an acquired strategy apparently took time to accomplish in the face of changing task demands. These findings begin to provide insights as to how strategy monitoring operates in the problem-solving routines of the mentally retarded. More extensive research is needed on how to train children to monitor output requirements and then select reasonable study strategies. Perhaps we should turn our attention to the direct training of matching, monitoring, and revising input-output strategies as tasks change.

Belmont, Ferretti, and Mitchell (in press) found that mentally retarded adolescents who recalled accurately on late trials, but who did poorly on early trials, invented study strategies over trials. These new strategies, in turn, were responsible for the successful recall. In this study, 40 untrained mentally retarded and 32 untrained nonretarded adolescents were given eight trials of practice on a self-paced memory problem with lists of letters or words. Each trial was a new list, requiring ordered recall of terminal list items followed by ordered recall of initial items. Subgroups of solvers and nonsolvers were identified for each group in terms of recall accuracy. Direct measures of mnemonic activity showed that over trials, normal and mentally retarded "solvers" (those who recalled well on late trials) tended to fit a theoretically ideal memorization method. Nonsolvers failed to show similar strategy inventions. Furthermore, on early trials, for both IQ levels, fit to the ideal strategy was uncorrelated with recall accuracy. On late trials, fit and recall were highly correlated at both IQ levels. These results support a theory of executive functioning in children's memory performance. Some mentally retarded children are capable of sizing up task demands and inventing strategies that lead to good performance. We need to understand why large individual differences in strategy invention exist among the mentally retarded. What factors in learning history or process capabilities are responsible for strategy invention? Also, research is needed to determine whether mentally retarded children who invent strategies on one task will also invent other strategies on dissimilar tasks. Is strategy invention a relatively consistent aspect of general intelligence?

Metacognition

Once a child knows when, where, and how to employ a strategy, specific metacognitive information about that strategy can be assessed and put to use (cf. Flavell, 1978). Metacognitive knowledge can be operationally defined as one aspect of general knowledge—information about one's own cognitive processes. One component of metacognition is called metamemory or knowledge about memory processes and operations. Metamemory is indexed by means of an interview technique in which we question children about their memories. We try to tap existing knowledge structures that contain information about the nature of memory processes and events (cf. Borkowski, Reid, & Kurtz, in press).

Recently, we have assessed the validity of metacognition by examining metamemory-strategy use-recall accuracy connections with EMR children in strategy transfer contexts (Kendall, Borkowski, & Cavanaugh, 1980). Our hypothesis was that metamemorial knowledge is important to the retarded insofar as it predicts learning. In this study we analyzed the role of metamemory in relation to the maintenance and generalization of an acquired interrogative strategy with paired-associate (PA) tasks. Children learned pairs of unrelated items by posing questions about them, then answering these inquiries with semantic elaborations associating the main attributes of each item together. For example, if the pair to be learned was nurse-toaster, the child might say: "Why is the *nurse* holding the *toaster?*" Then a relationship was formed: "The *nurse* is holding the *toaster* so that she can make toast for the sick people." Two groups of EMR children ($\overline{MA}$ = 6 and 8) participated in pre- and posttest metamemory assessments (the Story-List, Study Plan, and Preparation-Object subtests from the Kreutzer, Leonard, and Flavell, 1975, questionnaire), four training sessions in which a four-part self-instructional study strategy was taught, a long-term test for retention of the pairs learned during the final training session, a strategy maintenance test with a new PA task (and new experimenter), and a strategy generalization test to lists of word triads. An index of strategy use based on probe tests at maintenance and generalization assessed the extent of elaboration for each pair immediately after the recall trial. The most important results were the significant correlations relating quality of elaborations at strategy transfer to metamemory pretest ($r = 0.50$) and to metamemory posttest ($r = 0.46$). Individual differences in memory knowledge among a group of EMR children predicted differences in strategy transfer. One of the more interesting questions concerning metamemory theory and retardation arises out of these correlation data: Is metamemory a prerequisite for strategy transfer in the mentally retarded, or more generally, is metacognition a prerequisite for cognition and comprehension?

From a theoretical perspective, we might expect quite different dynamic properties in the relationship of metacognition to cognition for EMR and TMR children. For instance, Catino (1976) found that higher functioning mentally retarded children exhibited metamemory skills similar to matched MA normal children. In contrast, mentally retarded children with MA of five years or less showed delays and distortions on several metamemory tasks. These findings square with the results of Campione, Brown, and their colleagues who have reported a number of projects with the mentally retarded in which interactions between MA levels and long-term effects of strategy training were found (cf. A. L. Brown, 1978).

Response Outcome

A major aspect of executive functioning in the mentally retarded is the ability to realize the environmental impact produced by a response. Has a momentary response solved the problem at hand, put the learner on the path to a more complex solution, or proven totally inadequate in reaching a successful solution? While successful learners often derive information about response outcomes without explicit aid from others, the mentally retarded often need to be led into a pattern of correct responding based on prearranged sequences of reinforcement. An example here is the work of Konarski, Crowell, Johnson, and Whitman (1982) on the response deprivation hypothesis. More research is needed on the ability of mentally retarded children to abstract information from performance about the role of specific processes in improving problem solving and memory.

Conclusions and Future Perspectives

Throughout our review of research on memory and cognition in the mentally retarded, recurring themes that have been with us for several decades were much in evidence. At a general level, these interrelated themes are the defect versus developmental perspectives and structural versus process deficits (cf. Winters, 1977). More specifically, we see these positions reflected in the research orientation on attention and VSTM versus SM and executive functioning. Those holding to the developmental perspective are likely to do instructional research on lower- or higher-level processes (strategies or metacognition) in an attempt to show that aspects of mental retardation can be, in

part, remediated. In contrast, those adhering to a deficit perspective are likely to search for the loci of deficiencies in attention, perception, or sensory-based memory that clarify limitations in information processing capabilities. These perspectives will probably remain with us, influencing the theoretical emphases and research directions in attempts to understand learning, memory, and cognition in the mentally retarded. The last decade has given us revised theoretical perspectives and new methodologies that will continue to guide the search for more precise knowledge about the nature of mental retardation.

Research in the next decade will continue to study the processes and structures in the memory systems of the mentally retarded. As methodological procedures become more elegant, training studies will be designed to assess pretraining performance and to match individuals to specific training methods, to provide instructions on a wide variety of acquisition and retrieval strategies, and to induce generalization across useful transfer tasks. However, we must first gain detailed knowledge about existing deficits and then work to remediate those deficits, if possible.

Recently, a good deal of interest has been expressed in the dynamic approach to intellectual performance. This approach has been developed by Campione and Brown (1978) in line with the Soviet notion of the zone of proximal or potential development (Vygotsky, 1978). The zone is a measure of the child's potential to benefit from the mediational interactions with adults or older peers. With continued refinements in measurement, the zone approach holds promise of becoming a more sensitive measure of differences in intellectual functioning and for detecting individual deficits, as the child progresses through a series of highly defined tasks. Feuerstein (1969, 1979) has developed the Learning Potential Assessment Device (LPAD) and the Instrumental Enrichment (IE) program to diagnose and remediate learning problems in mentally retarded individuals, borrowing heavily from the dynamic approach. Budoff (1974) has employed a similar program to aid learning. The zone of potential development will likely continue to be a useful research paradigm for studying mental retardation because of its sensitivity to individual differences and its fundamental, dialectic nature (cf. Borkowski, Reid, & Kurtz, in press). The dialectic orientation has the advantage of returning motivation to its legitimate place in the study of cognition and is especially germane to the problem of generalization (cf. Borkowski et al., in press).

Levine, Zetlin, and Langness (1980) studied memory tasks that retarded children encounter in everyday classroom environments. This study was essentially observational in nature, with memory tasks classified along five major dimensions: (1) the agent who presented the task, (2) the kind of memory requirement, (3) the frequency of occurrence, (4) the variability in response requirement, and (5) the type of feedback. Levine et al. (1980) concluded that poor classroom performance of the educable mentally retarded might be attributable to their exposure to highly routine tasks for which more emphasis is placed on appropriateness of a response than on its correctness. The potential of observational procedures, such as the paradigm implemented by Levine et al. (1980), provides us with an ecologically valid indication of what the mentally retarded may lack in memory performance on everyday tasks. Naturalistic observation will likely become more common as a research strategy for studying memory, cognition, and intelligence in the retarded.

Perhaps the most promising approach to studying the mentally retarded will be an eclectic method, including information processing assessments, attentional and efficiency concepts, the zone of potential development as a prognostic measure of capability, and the observational perspective. The combination of information processing and naturalistic methods will not be easy to implement; yet the integration holds promise of yielding new insights into the nature of memory and cognition in the mentally retarded.

References

Atkinson, R. C., & Shiffrin, R. M. Human memory: A proposed system and its control processes. In K. W. Spence & J. T. Spence (Eds.), *The psychology of learning and motivation*. Vol. 2. New York: Academic Press, 1968.

Averbach, E. & Coriell, A. S. Short-term memory in vision. *Bell System Technical Journal*, 1961, **40**, 309–328.

Bachhelder, B. L., & Denny, M. R. A theory of intelligence. I. Span and the complexity of stimulus control. *Intelligence*, 1977, **1**, 127–150.(a)

Bachhelder, B. L., & Denny, M. R. A theory of intelligence. II. The role of span in a variety of intellectual tasks. *Intelligence*, 1977, **1**, 237–256.(b)

Baumeister, A. A., & Kellas, G. Reaction time and mental retardation. In N. R. Ellis (Ed.), *International review of research in mental retardation*. Vol. 3. New York: Academic Press, 1968.

Belmont, J. M. Long-term memory in mental retardation. In N. R. Ellis (Ed.), *International Review of Research in Mental Retardation*. Vol. 1. New York: Academic Press, 1966.

Belmont, J. M., & Butterfield, E. C. The relations of short-term memory to development and intelligence. In L. P. Lipsitt & H. W. Reese (Eds.), *Advances in Child Development and Behavior*. Vol. 4. New York: Academic Press, 1969.

Belmont, J. M., & Butterfield, E. C. Learning strategies as determinants of memory deficiencies. *Cognitive Psychology*, 1971, **2**, 411–420.

Belmont, J. M., Butterfield, E. C., & Borkowski, J. G. Training retarded people to generalize memorization methods across memory tasks. In M. M. Gruneberg, P. E. Morris, & R. N. Sykes (Eds.), *Practical Aspects of Memory*. London: Academic Press, 1978.

Belmont, J. M., Ferretti, R. P., & Mitchell, D. W. Memorizing: A test of untrained retarded children's problem solving. *American Journal of Mental Deficiency*. In press.

Berkson, G. An analysis of reaction time in normal and mentally deficient young men. I. Duration threshold experiment. *Journal of Mental Deficiency Research*, 1960, **4**, 59–67.

Blount, W. R. Concept usage research with the mentally retarded. *Psychological Bulletin*, 1968, **69**, 281–294.

Borkowski, J. G., & Cavanaugh, J. C. Maintenance and generalization of skills and strategies by the retarded. In N. R. Ellis (Ed.), *Handbook of mental deficiency, psychological theory and research*. (2nd ed.) Hillsdale, N.J.: Erlbaum, 1979.

Borkowski, J. G., Reid, M. K., & Kurtz, B. Metacognition and retardation: Paradigmatic, theoretical, and applied perspectives. In R. Sperber, C. McCauley, & P. Brooks (Eds.), *Learning and cognition in the mentally retarded*. Baltimore: University Park Press. In press.

Borys, S. V., Spitz, H. H., & Dorans, B. A. Tower of Hanoi performance of retarded young adults and nonretarded children as a function of solution length and goal state. *Journal of Experimental Child Psychology*, 1982, **33**, 87–110.

Bray, N. W., Justice, E. M., & Simon, D. L. The sufficient conditions for directed forgetting in normal and educable mentally retarded adolescents. *Intelligence*, 1978, **2**, 153–168.

Brewer, N. Motor components in the choice reaction time of mildly retarded adults. *American Journal of Mental Deficiency*, 1978, **82**, 565–572.

Brown, A. L. The role of strategic behavior in retardate memory. In N. R. Ellis (Ed.), *International review of research in mental retardation*. Vol. 7. New York: Academic Press, 1974.

Brown, A. L. Knowing when, where, and how to remember: A problem of metacognition. In R. Glaser (Ed.), *Advances in instructional psychology*. Hillsdale, N.J.: Erlbaum, 1978.

Brown, A. L., Campione, J. C., & Barclay, C. R. Training self-checking routines for estimating test readiness: Generalization from list learning to prose recall. *Child Development*, 1979, **50**, 501–512.

Brown, J. Some tests of the decay theory of immediate memory. *Quarterly Journal of Experimental Psychology*, 1958, **10**, 12–21.

Brown, R. M. Effects of recall order, cue placement, and retention interval on short-term memory of normal and retarded children. *Perceptual and Motor Skills*, 1974, **39**, 167–178.

Budoff, M. *Learning potential and educability among the educable mentally retarded*. Final report project no. 312312 OEG-0-8-080506-4597. Washington, D.C.: Department of Health, Education, and Welfare, December, 1974.

Burger, A. L., Blackman, L. S., Holmes, M., & Zetlin, A. Use of active sorting and retrieval strategies as a facilitator of recall, clustering, and sorting by EMR and nonretarded children. *American Journal of Mental Deficiency*, 1978, **83**, 253–261.

Burgio, L. D., Whitman, T. L., & Johnson, M. J. A self-instructional package for increasing attending behavior in educably mentally retarded children. *Journal of Applied Behavior Analysis*, 1980, **13**, 443–460.

Butterfield, E. C., & Belmont, J. M. Assessing and improving the cognitive functions of mentally retarded people. In I. Bialer & M. Sternlicht (Eds.), *The psychology of mental retardation: Issues and approaches*. New York: Psychological Dimensions, 1977.

Butterfield, E. C., Wambold, C., & Belmont, J. M. On the theory and practice of improving short-term memory. *American Journal of Mental Deficiency*, 1973, 77, 654–669.

Campione, J. C., & Brown, A. L. Toward a theory of intelligence: Contributions from research with retarded children. *Intelligence*, 1978, **2**, 279–304.

Carr, T. H. Attention, skill, and intelligence: Some speculations on extreme individual differences in human performance. In R. Sperber, C. McCauley, & P. Brooks (Eds.), *Learning and Cognition in the Mentally Retarded*. Baltimore: University Park Press. In press.

Catino, C. *Metamemorial processes in normal and retarded children*. Unpublished doctoral dissertation, University of Notre Dame, 1976.

Clark, P. A., & Detterman, D. K. Performance of mentally retarded and nonretarded persons on a lifted-weight task with strategies reduced or eliminated. *American Journal of Mental Deficiency*, 1981, **85**, 530–538.

Clausen, J. *Ability structure and subgroups in mental retardation*. Washington, D.C.: Spartan Books, 1966.

Cody, W. J., & Borkowski, J. G. Proactive interference and its release in short-term memory of mildly retarded adolescents. *American Journal of Mental Deficiency*, 1977, **82**, 305–308.

Cohen, R. L., & Nealon, J. An analysis of short-term memory differences between retardates and nonretardates. *Intelligence*, 1979, **3**, 65–72.

Cohen, R. L., & Sandberg, T. Relation between intelligence and short-term memory. *Cognitive Psychology*, 1977, **9**, 534–554.

Craik, F. I. M., & Lockhart, R. S. Levels of processing: A framework for memory research. *Journal of Verbal Learning and Verbal Behavior*, 1972, **11**, 671–684.

Davies, D., Sperber, R. D., & McCauley, C. Intelligence-related differences in semantic processing speed. *Journal of Experimental Child Psychology*, 1981, **31**, 387–402.

Deich, R. F. Reproduction and recognition as indices of perceptual impairment. *American Journal of Mental Deficiency*, 1968, 73, 9–12.

Deich, R. F. Tachistoscopic perception of disoriented shapes by nonretarded and retarded children. *American Journal of Mental Deficiency*, 1971, **75**, 525–526.

Denny, M. R. Research in learning and performance. In H. Stevens & R. Heber (Eds.), *Mental Retardation*. Chicago: University of Chicago Press, 1964.

Detterman, D. K. Does *g* exist? *Intelligence*. 1982, **6**, 99–108.

Detterman, D. K. Memory in the mentally retarded. In N. R. Ellis (Ed.), *Handbook of mental deficiency, psychological theory and research*. (2nd Ed.) Hillsdale, N.J.: Erlbaum, 1979.

Dugas, J. L., & Kellas, G. Encoding and retrieval processes in normal children and retarded adolescents. *Journal of Experimental Child Psychology*, 1974, **17**, 177–185.

Ellis, N. R. Memory processes in retardates and normals. In N. R. Ellis (Ed.), *International review of research in mental retardation*. Vol. 4. New York: Academic Press, 1970.

Ellis, N. R. Do the mentally retarded have poor memory? *Intelligence*, 1978, **2**, 41–54.

Estes, W. K. Intelligence and learning. In M. P. Friedman, J. P. Das, & N. O'Connor (Eds.), *Intelligence and learning*. New York: Plenum, 1981.

Ferretti, R. P. An analysis of passive memory in normal and mentally retarded persons. *Intelligence*. In press.

Feuerstein, R. *The instrumental enrichment method: An outline of theory and technique*. Unpublished paper. Hadassah-Wiza-Canada Research Institute, 1969.

Feuerstein, R. *The dynamic assessment of retarded performers: The learning potential assessment device, theory, instruments, and techniques*. Baltimore: University Park Press, 1979.

Fisher, M. A., & Zeaman, D. An attention-retention theory of retardate discrimination learning. In N. R. Ellis (Ed.), *International review of research in mental retardation*. Vol. 6. New York: Academic Press, 1973.

Flavell, J. H. Metacognitive development. In J. M. Scandura & C. J. Brainerd (Eds.), *Structural/process theories of complex human behavior*. Alphen a.d. Rijn, The Netherlands: Sijthoff & Noordhoff, 1978.

Friedrich, D., Libkuman, T., Craig, E., & Winn, F. Read-out times from iconic memory in normal and retarded adolescents. *Perceptual and Motor Skills*, 1977, **44**, 467–473.

Friedrich, D., Libkuman, T., & Hawkins, W. F. Response-stimulus interval performance of nonretarded and institutionalized retarded subjects. *American Journal of Mental Deficiency*, 1974, 79, 64–69.

Galbraith, G. C., & Gliddon, J. B. Backward visual masking with homogeneous and patterned stimuli: Comparison of retarded and nonretarded subjects. *Perceptual and Motor Skills*, 1972, **34**, 903–908.

Glidden, L. M. Training of learning and memory in retarded persons: Strategies, techniques, and teaching tools. In N. R. Ellis (Ed.), *Handbook of mental deficiency, psychological theory and research*. (2nd ed.) Hillsdale, N.J.: Erlbaum, 1979.

Glidden, L. M., & Mar, H. H. Availability and accessibility of information in the semantic memory of retarded and nonretarded adolescents. *Journal of Experimental Child Psychology*, 1978, **25**, 33–40.

Griffith, A. H. The effects of retention interval, exposure interval, and IQ on recognition in a mentally retarded group. *American Journal of Mental Deficiency*, 1960, **64**, 1000–1003.

Guralnick, M. J. Solving complex perceptual discrimination problems: Techniques for the development of problem-solving strategies. *American Journal of Mental Deficiency*, 1976, **81**, 118–125.

Hagen, J. W., & Huntsman, N. Selective attention in mental retardates. *Developmental Psychology*, 1971, **5**, 151–160.

Harris, G. J. Input and output organization in short-term serial recall by retarded and nonretarded children. *American Journal of Mental Deficiency*, 1972, 76, 423–426.

Haywood, H. C., & Switzky, H. N. Children's verbal abstracting: Effects of enriched input, age, and IQ. *American Journal of Mental Deficiency*, 1974, 78, 556–565.

Headrick, M. W., & Ellis, N. R. Short-term visual memory in normals and retardates. *Journal of Experimental Child Psychology*, 1964, **1**, 339–347.

Hoats, D. L. Numerosity discrimination of homogeneous and subgrouped dot patterns by EMR adolescents and normals. *American Journal of Mental Deficiency*, 1971, **76**, 220–224.

Hornstein, H. A., & Mosley, J. L. Iconic memory processing of unfamiliar stimuli by retarded and nonretarded individuals. *American Journal of Mental Deficiency*, 1979, **84**, 40–48.

House, B. J., & Zeaman, D. Miniature experiments in the discrimination learning of retardates. In L. P. Lipsitt & C. C. Spiker (Eds.), *Advances in child development and behavior*. Vol. 1. New York: Academic Press, 1963.

Jackson, G. M. The use of visual orientation feedback to facilitate attention and task performance. *Mental Retardation*, 1979, **17**, 280–284.

Joubert, C. E., & Baumeister, A. A. Effects of varying the length and frequency of response-stimulus interval on the reaction times of normals and mentally deficient subjects. *Journal of Comparative and Physiological Psychology*, 1970, **73**, 105–110.

Kendall, C. R., Borkowski, J. G., & Cavanaugh, J. C. Maintenance and generalization of an interrogative strategy by EMR children. *Intelligence*, 1980, **4**, 255–270.

Klausmeier, H. J., Feldhusen, J., & Check, J. *An analysis of learning efficiency in arithmetic of mentally retarded children in comparison with children of average and high intelligence*. Madison: University of Wisconsin Press, 1959.

Konarski, E. A., Jr., Crowell, C. R., Johnson, M. R., & Whitman, T. L. Response deprivation, reinforcement, and instrumental academic performance in an EMR classroom. *Behavior Therapy*, 1982, **13**, 94–102.

Kreutzer, M. A., Leonard, C., & Flavell, J. H. An interview study of children's knowledge about memory. *Monographs of the Society for Research in Child Development*, 1975, **40** (Serial No. 159).

Krupski, A. Heart rate changes during a fixed reaction-time task in normal and retarded adult males. *Psychophysiology*, 1975, **12**, 262–267.

Krupski, A. Heart rate changes during reaction time: An approach for understanding deficient attention in retarded individuals. In R. Karrer (Ed.), *Developmental Psychophysiology of Mental Retardation*. Springfield, Ill.: Charles C. Thomas, 1976.

Krupski, A. The role of attention in the reaction time performance of mentally retarded adolescents. *American Journal of Mental Deficiency*, 1977, **82**, 79–83.

Lally, M., & Nettelbeck, T. Intelligence, reaction time, and inspection time. *American Journal of Mental Deficiency*, 1977, **82**, 273–281.

Lally, M., & Nettelbeck, T. Inspection time, intelligence, and response strategy. *American Journal of Mental Deficiency*, 1980, **84**, 553–560.

Levine, H. G., Zetlin, A. G., & Langness, L. L. Everyday memory tasks in classrooms for TMR learners. *The Quarterly Newsletter of the Laboratory of Comparative Human Cognition*, 1980, **2**, 1–6.

Liebert, A. M., & Baumeister, A. A. Behavioral variability among retardates, children and college students. *The Journal of Psychology*, 1973, **83**, 57–65.

Likbuman, T., & Friedrich, D. Threshold measures of sensory register storage (perceptual memory) on normals and retardates. *Psychonomic Science*, 1972, **27**, 357–358.

Luce, R. D. *Individual choice behavior: A theoretical analysis*. New York: Wiley, 1959.

Maier, I., & Hogg, J. Operant conditioning of sustained visual fixation in hyperactive severely retarded children.

American Journal of Mental Deficiency, 1974, **79**, 297–304.

Mar, H. H., & Glidden, L. M. Semantic and acoustic processing in free and cued recall by educable mentally retarded adolescents. *Intelligence*, 1977, **1**, 298–309.

McCauley, C., Kellas, G., Dugas, J., & Devillis, R. F. Effects of serial rehearsal training on memory search. *Journal of Educational Psychology*, 1976, **68**, 474–481.

Meichenbaum, D. *Cognitive-behavior modification: An integrative approach*. New York: Plenum, 1977.

Mosley, J. L. Retinal locus and the identification of tachistoscopically presented letters by retarded and nonretarded individuals. *American Journal of Mental Deficiency*, 1978, **82**, 380–385.(a)

Mosley, J. L. The tachistoscopic recognition of letters under whole and partial report procedures as related to intelligence. *British Journal of Psychology*, 1978, **69**, 101–110.(b)

Mosley, J. L. Selective attention of mildly mentally retarded and nonretarded individuals. *American Journal of Mental Deficiency*, 1980, **84**, 568–576.

Mosley, J. L. Selective attention as a contributor to strategic inadequacies in mild mental retardation. Unpublished manuscript. University of Calgary, Calgary, Alberta, Canada.

Nettelbeck, T., & Brewer, N. Studies of mild mental retardation and timed performance. In N. R. Ellis (Ed.), *International Review of Research in Mental Retardation*. Vol. 10. New York: Academic Press, 1981.

Nettelbeck, T., Kirby, N. H., Haymes, G., & Bills, A. Influence of procedural variables on estimates of inspection time for mildly mentally retarded adults. *American Journal of Mental Deficiency*, 1980, **85**, 274–280.

Nettelbeck, T., & Lally, M. Inspection time and measured intelligence. *British Journal of Psychology*, 1976, **67**, 17–22.

Nettelbeck, T., & Lally, M. Age, intelligence, and inspection time. *American Journal of Mental Deficiency*, 1979, **83**, 398–401.

Okada, Y. C. A critical analysis of the attention hypothesis of Zeaman and House: Problems of parameter interaction in multiparameter models. *Journal of Experimental Child Psychology*, 1978, **25**, 173–182.

Pennington, F. M., & Luszcz, M. A. Some functional properties of iconic storage in retarded and nonretarded subjects. *Memory and Cognition*, 1975, **3**, 295–301.

Peterson, L. R., & Peterson, M. J. Short-term retention of individual verbal items. *Journal of Experimental Psychology*, 1959, **58**, 193–198.

Prehm, M. J., & Mayfield, S. Paired-associated learning and retention in retarded and nonretarded children. *American Journal of Mental Deficiency*, 1970, **74**, 622–625.

Reichhart, G. J., Cody, W. J., & Borkowski, J. G. Training and transfer of clustering and cumulative rehearsal strategies in retarded individuals. *American Journal of Mental Deficiency*, 1975, **79**, 648–658.

Ross, L. E., & Ward, T. B. The processing of information from short-term visual store: Developmental and intellectual level differences. In N. R. Ellis (Ed.), *International review of research in mental retardation*. Vol. 9. New York: Academic Press, 1978.

Ross, S. M. Trace and delay classical eyelid conditioning in severely and profoundly retarded subjects as a function of interstimulus interval. *American Journal of Mental Deficiency*, 1972, **77**, 39–45.

Ross, S. M., & Ross, L. E. Comparison of trace and delay

classical eyelid conditioning as a function of interstimulus interval. *Journal of Experimental Psychology*, 1971, **91**, 165–167.

Ross, S. M., & Ross, L. E. Stimulus input recruitment and stimulus trace decay factors in the trace conditioning deficit of the severely retarded. *American Journal of Mental Deficiency*, 1975, **80**, 109–113.

Ross, S. M., & Ross, L. E. The conditioning of skeletal and autonomic responses: Normal-retardate stimulus trace differences. In N. R. Ellis (Ed.), *International review of research in mental retardation*. Vol. 8. New York: Academic Press, 1976.

Scott, K. G., & Scott, M. S. Research and theory in short-term memory. In N. R. Ellis (Ed.), *International review of research in mental retardation*. Vol. 3. New York: Academic Press, 1968.

Sheingold, K. Developmental differences in intake and storage of visual information. *Journal of Experimental Child Psychology*, 1973, **16**, 1–11.

Shiffrin, R. M., & Schneider, W. Controlled and automatic human information processing: II. Perceptual learning, automatic attending, and a general theory. *Psychological Review*, 1977, **84**, 127–190.

Sperber, R. D., Ragain, R. D., & McCauley, C. Reassessment of category knowledge in retarded individuals. *American Journal of Mental Deficiency*, 1976, **81**, 227–234.

Sperling, G. The information available in brief visual presentations. *Psychological Monographs*, 1960, **74**(11, whole No. 498).

Sperling, G. A model for visual memory tasks. *Human Factors*, 1963, **5**, 19–31.

Spitz, H. H. Consolidating facts into the schematized learning and memory system of educable retardates. In N. R. Ellis (Ed.), *International review of research in mental retardation*. Vol. 6. New York: Academic Press, 1973.

Spitz, H. H., & Borland, M. D. Effects of stimulus complexity on visual search performance of normals and educable retardates. *American Journal of Mental Deficiency*, 1971, **75**, 724–728.

Spitz, H. H., & Thor, D. H. Visual backward masking in retardates and normals. *Perception and Psychophysics*, 1968, **4**, 245–246.

Stanovich, K. E. Information processing in mentally retarded individuals. In N. R. Ellis (Ed.), *International review of research in mental retardation*. Vol. 9. New York: Academic Press, 1978.

Stanovich, K. E. Toward an interactive-compensatory model of individual differences in the development of reading fluency. *Reading Research Quarterly*, 1980, **16**, 32–71.

Stephens, W. E. A comparison of performance of normal and subnormal boys on structured categorization tasks. *Exceptional Children*, 1964, **30**, 311–315.

Stephens, W. E. Category usage by normal and mentally retarded boys. *Child Development*, 1966, **37**, 355–361.

Sternberg, S. High-speed scanning in human memory. *Science*, 1966, **153**, 652–654.

Taylor, A. M., & Turnure, J. E. Imagery and verbal elaboration with retarded children: Effects on learning and memory. In N. R. Ellis (Ed.), *Handbook of mental deficiency, psychological theory and research*. (2nd Ed.) Hillsdale, N.J.: Erlbaum, 1979.

Thor, D. H. Discrimination of succession in visual masking by retarded and normal children. *Journal of Experimental Psychology*, 1970, **83**, 380–384.

Thor, D. H. Counting and tracking of sequential visual

stimuli by EMR and intellectually average children. *American Journal of Mental Deficiency*, 1973, **78**, 41–46.

Turnure, J. E. Reactions to physical and social distractors by moderately retarded institutionalized children. *The Journal of Special Education*, 1970, **4**, 283–294.

Turnure, J. E., Buium, N., & Thurlow, M. L. The effectiveness of interrogatives for promoting verbal elaboration productivity in young children. *Child Development*, 1976, **47**, 851–855.

Turnure, J., & Zigler, E. Outer-directedness in the problem solving of normal and retarded children. *Journal of Abnormal and Social Psychology*, 1964, **69**, 427–436.

Underwood, B. J. Degree of learning and the measurement of forgetting. *Journal of Verbal Learning and Verbal Behavior*, 1964, **3**, 112–129.

Vygotsky, L. S. *Mind in society: The development of higher psychological processes*. M. Cole, V. John-Steiner, S. Scribner, & E. Souberman (Eds.). Cambridge, Mass.: Harvard University Press, 1978.

Wanschura, P. B., & Borkowski, J. G. Long-term transfer of a mediational strategy by moderately retarded children. *American Journal of Mental Deficiency*, 1975, 80, 323–333.

Watkins, M. J., & Watkins, O. C. Cue-overload theory and the method of interpolated attributes. *Bulletin of the Psychonomic Society*, 1976, 7, 289–291.

Watkins, O. C., & Watkins, M. J. Buildup of proactive inhibition as a cue-overload effect. *Journal of Experimental Psychology: Human Learning and Memory*, 1975, **104**, 442–452.

Waugh, N. C., & Norman, D. A. Primary memory. *Psychological Review*, 1965, **72**, 89–104.

Welsandt, R. F., & Meyer, P. A. Visual masking, mental age, and retardation. *Journal of Experimental Child Psychology*, 1974, **18**, 512–519.

Winters, J. J., Jr. Methodological issues in psychological research with retarded persons. In I. Bialer & M. Sternlicht (Eds.), *The psychology of mental retardation: Issues and approaches*. New York: Psychological Dimensions, 1977.

Winters, J. J., Jr. Proactive inhibition in retarded persons: Factors influencing accumulation and release. In K. D. Gadow & I. Bialer (Eds.), *Advances in learning and behavioral disabilities: An annual compilation of theory and research*. Vol. 1. Greenwich, Conn.: JAI Press. In press.

Winters, J. J., Jr., & Burger, A. L. Retrieval speed, age-of-acquisition estimates, uncertainty, and semantic-dimension comparisons with mentally retarded persons. *American Journal of Mental Deficiency*, 1980, **85**, 90–93.

Winters, J. J., Jr., & Cundari, L. Speed of retrieving information from the lexicon of mentally retarded adolescents. *American Journal of Mental Deficiency*, 1979, **83**, 566–570.

Winters, J. J., Jr., Winter, L., & Burger, A. L. Confidence in age-of-acquisition estimates and its relationship to children's labeling performance. *Bulletin of the Psychonomic Society*, 1978, **12**, 361–364.

Zeaman, D., & House, B. The role of attention in retardate discrimination learning. In N. R. Ellis (Ed.), *Handbook of mental deficiency*. New York: McGraw-Hill, 1963.

Zeaman, D., & House, B. A review of attention theory. In N. R. Ellis (Ed.), *Handbook of mental deficiency, psychological theory and research*. (2nd ed.) Hillsdale, N.J.: Erlbaum, 1979.

33 NEUROPSYCHOLOGY

Ralph E. Tarter and Gregg Slomka

europsychology is the study of brain-behavior relationships. Within the realm of clinical application, it is concerned with describing behavioral capacity and style as they relate to known or implicated disturbances of brain functioning.

Three fundamental principles guide efforts to delineate the relationships between brain functioning and psychological processes. First, psychological impairment can be manifest as a result of a disorder at any level of neurological organization. Hence, morphological, chemical, or physiological disturbances can have psychological sequelae. Second, psychological deficits can result from either acquired brain pathology or, alternatively, reflect genetic endowment and/or defective embryogenesis. Thus, both intrinsic and extrinsic neurological events can result in a psychological deficit. And third, psychological impairments consequential to a disruption of the developing brain are quite different from damage incurred by an already mature organism.

Thus, there are multiple pathways to a psychological deficit. With respect to the group of disorders that are collectively labeled "mental retardation," numerous biological, as well as environmental, factors have been shown to result in the manifest intellectual impairments. The natures of the intellectual deficits are comprehensively reviewed in Ellis (1979), Bialer and

Sternlich (1977), and Clarke and Clarke (1973), and thus will not be discussed here. Rather, this chapter will address the research and theory which have been concerned with relating the psychological deficit to cerebral dysfunction. Although the body of research is small, it will be seen that a neuropsychological analysis can contribute to the development of a systematic framework for understanding the deficits in mental retardation, and clarify some of the existing confusion regarding the classification and mechanisms of impairment, as well as have direct clinical application for diagnosis and habilitation.

Research Issues in Neuropsychology

Classification

During the past four decades, the definition and concept of mental retardation has undergone significant changes. Essentially, there has been a shift from a biological or medical model to a behavioral multidimensional model (American Association on Mental Deficiency Manual on Terminology and Classification in Mental Retardation, Grossman, 1977). Currently, mental retardation is defined as a developmental disorder in which there is significantly subaverage intellectual functioning that is accompanied by deficits in adaptive behavior and onset prior to 18 years of age.

Three important characteristics distinguish the medical and behavioral orientations. First, the biomedical approach is concerned primarily with explaining the structural basis or mechanisms underlying the intellectual deficit, while the behavioral perspective emphasizes the descriptive aspects of the disability. Second, adherents of the biomedical orientation aim to *explain* psychological impairment on the basis of disturbed brain functioning. The behavioral orientation, on the other hand, recognizes the organic substrate for many conditions and, in addition, maintains that not all disorders are, or ever will be, found to be due to measurable neurological pathology. Furthermore, the behavioral approach stresses the importance of diverse environmental factors such as economic and social deprivation, neglect and familial discord, as well as deficient parental rearing style, all of which can produce developmental retardation. Third, the tradition of the biomedical perspective is to attempt to classify individuals into mutually exclusive categories, although clear-cut psychiatric and neurological syndromes have not, to date, been revealed by empirical research. In contrast, the behavioral approach, by recognizing individual differences, is concerned with describing psychological processes (e.g., language, memory, motor coordination, etc.) within a dimensional framework, thereby eliminating the need to "shoehorn" individuals into somewhat artificial and poorly validated categories.

Neuropsychology can make a number of contributions in bridging the biomedical and behavioral orientations. By employing the techniques of multivariate behavioral assessment, neuropsychological measurement can improve our understanding of the various patterns of behavioral sequelae that arise from different types of neurological disturbances (Hecaen & Albert, 1978; Reitan & Davison, 1974). In addition, neuropsychological techniques afford the opportunity to determine how psychological processes are functionally organized in the brain (Luria, 1966). Moreover, where etiology is unknown, neuropsychological procedures can help determine whether subaverage level intellectual functioning is the consequence of focal or diffuse brain pathology (Lezak, 1976; Walsh, 1978). Consequently, neuropsychological procedures can assist in differential diagnosis where the presence, pattern and severity of central nervous system dysfunction needs to be clarified. Thus, neuropsychological measures, being sensitive to detecting impaired cerebral integrity, are compatible with both the biomedical and behavioral orientations.

Because neuropsychological techniques interrelate brain functioning and behavior, the information accrued has both descriptive and explanatory power. As such, it is feasible to generate heuristic etiological hypotheses that could form a basis for the development of a comprehensive classification system incorporating both neurological and psychological information. In addition, since the brain is the organ most responsible for mediating communication with the organism's other biological systems, as well as with the external environment, it is the ultimate determinant of adaptive capacity. Through extensive *functional* assessment of behavioral processes (e.g., language, memory, spatial orientation, etc.), which are known to be subserved by specific cerebral regions and systems, it is possible to determine both the level and style of transaction with the social environment. To this extent, neuropsychological techniques have a contribution to make in delineating the current status and potential adaptive success of mentally retarded individuals who have one form or another of disturbed brain functioning.

Research Strategies

Two basic approaches, the *clinical inferential* and the *statistical inferential*, are used to investigate neuropsychological impairment. In the first strategy, individuals who meet certain selection criteria (for example, Down's syndrome) are assessed for neuropsychological style and capacity. The selection criteria utilized in research of this type are somewhat arbitrary, and usually involve such variables as etiological factors, IQ, or neurological status. The clinical inferential strategy, therefore, entails the testing of hypotheses in well defined samples. There is, however, a major limitation in this approach. Because of inherent exclusionary criteria in defining a sample, it is not possible to determine whether certain variables, which are omitted, contribute to the obtained results. The process of selection is, therefore, itself potentially responsible for yielding results that could be spurious, or at the very least, produce findings of limited generalizability.

The statistical inferential approach is generally identified with the multivariate orientation. Subtypes are statistically derived that feature commonalities between individuals on neuropsychological performance. A population is identified (e.g., all 10 year olds in a school district) and regardless of medical status, family history, IQ, or any other factor, all individuals are admitted into the investigations. The homogeneous groupings describe subjects who have similar neuropsychological characteristics. Once the subtypes are established, it can be determined how they differ from each other in ways beyond their pattern of neuro-psychological performance. For example, it can be ascertained if a certain neuropsychological profile is related to a particular etiology, socioeconomic status, perinatal injury, premature birth, or specific MR disorder. Hence, the statistical inferential strategy is superior to the clinical inferential approach, in that it enables the empirical derivation of neuropsychological types that are atheoretical and, thus, are not encumbered by *a priori* assumptions or selection criteria.

Methodological Limitations

While neuropsychological methods can make a substantial contribution in furthering an understanding of brain-behavior relationships, it should be pointed out that these techniques also have several drawbacks. First, because mental retardation is a summary designation based on an IQ score, the population of individuals encompassed by this label is very heterogeneous in terms of both etiology and manifest characteristics. It is, therefore, highly improbable that specific neuropsychological characteristics can be found to describe all individuals. Depending on the type and severity of brain dysfunction, different patterns and severity of deficits are likely to be manifest. For example, even within a particular disorder of known etiology there is a substantial influence exerted by environmental factors on neuropsychological development (Milner, 1967).

Second, most of what is known about brain-behavior relationships is based on studies of adults where the brain is already developed. In contrast, mental retardation, as a developmental disorder, first becomes manifest at a relatively early age. Consequently, the neuropathological process prevents optimal acquisition of psychological functions. While neuropsychological procedures are very useful in detecting localized brain damage in adults (Walsh, 1978), the validity of extrapolating the same procedures and findings to the developmental disorders raises complex issues which, if not considered, could lead to dubious interpretations (Isaacson, 1975; Kinsbourne, 1974). It should be emphasized that findings from research on adults can provide a useful model for the developmental disorders, even though the specific findings may not be readily generalizable across age. However, even if the mechanisms underlying the particular qualitative aspects of a disorder differ between children and adults, it is noteworthy that the same categories

of deficits (e.g., reading, verbal expression, arithmetic, etc.) are found as sequelae to brain pathology.

Third, neuropsychological performance is influenced by the social environment. These factors can attenuate, as well as exacerbate, the effects of a brain lesion (Baumeister & MacLean, 1979).

Fourth, because MR individuals most probably have experienced many adverse events from the time of conception to the time of testing, it is difficult, if at all possible, retrospectively to ascertain the relative contribution of these events and their mode of interaction that eventuated in the observed neuropsychological impairments (Clarke & Clarke, 1975). The fact that neuropsychological development continues into midadolescence, illustrates how long a time span there is for adverse events to exert limiting effects on the realization of one's cognitive potential (Haywood, 1970; Montagu, 1971).

And fifth, since etiological factors are so diverse, vary in severity, and affect the individual in idiosyncratic ways, it is unlikely that there is a one-to-one correspondence between the presence of brain pathology and pattern of neuropsychological performance. Although there may be numerous causes for a brain disorder, there can be only a limited number of effects produced in the brain that are measured and differentiated from each other by neuropsychological techniques.

Developmental Parameters

The time in life the central nervous system is disrupted determines to a large extent the neuropsychological outcome. Moreover, the vulnerability to certain adverse events varies according to the stage of development. For instance, because the immune system is not fully functional at birth, the neonate is exceptionally susceptible to infections like encephalitis and meningitis. In addition, because skull formation is incomplete during early postnatal life, the child is vulnerable to the effects of even modest head trauma. Thus, the potential influence of any factor is, to a major extent, a function of the child's age.

The various developmental stages where a neuropsychological disruption can occur which has lasting effects are briefly described below.

Genetics

Intellectual potential (Clarke & Clarke, 1975) and neuropsychological processes (DeFries, Vanderberg, & McClearn, 1976) are to some extent inherited. Genetic disturbances can be expressed in three ways:

(a) Mendelian or single gene transmission, (b) through polygenic or multifactorial transmission and, (c) by chromosomal abnormalities. The genetic disorders discussed elsewhere in this volume have a well defined etiology and a more or less predictable outcome insofar as intelligence is concerned. As yet, little systematic research aimed at elucidating differentiating neuro-psychological features among the genetic disorders has been conducted. While numerous deficits have been identified in the genetic disorders, there is a dearth of information about the neuropsychological features that may distinguish one condition from another.

Intrauterine Events

Numerous intrauterine factors can increase the risk for mental retardation in the developing embryo and fetus. Infection (e.g., syphilis and rubella), metabolic (e.g., RH incompatability), and toxic (e.g., alcohol, drugs) factors are commonly recognized risk factors. Medical illnesses that cause vaginal bleeding, nutritional deficiency, and hydramnios, as well as a myriad of other influences are commonly known to augment the risk for mental retardation in the offspring of persons who have such illnesses. While a general relationship between the above factors and heightened risk for an unfavorable outcome has been established, there is little known about the relationship between specific prenatal events and their neuropsychological correlates.

Prenatal Development

Complications during labor and delivery significantly increase the risk for a developmental disability. The severity of the outcome has been described along a continuum of "reproductive casualty" that ranges from relatively benign conditions like tics, to more debilitating disorders such as learning disability, infantile autism, and mental retardation (Pasamanick & Knob-lock, 1966). The term "reproductive wastage" (Graves, Freeman & Thomson, 1970) has also been invoked to encompass the factors that limit the organism's fulfillment of its biological potential.

Many birth related variables have been identified which augment the risk for mental retardation. The most common ones include an occiput posterior presentation (Rosenbaum, 1970) and small pelvic size of the mother (Willerman, 1970). These as well as other factors such as a breech presentation, prolonged labor, and low forceps delivery have been known for quite some time to increase the risk for various developmental disturbances, including mental retar-

dation. Anoxia, trauma, infection, and poor nutrition are also commonly recognized risk factors.

The number of postnatal factors that can impact on subsequent development are too numerous to review here, but are discussed elsewhere in this volume. It is nonetheless apparent that mental retardation can result from a variety of causes occurring at different stages of development, beginning at conception and continuing through the period of neurobehavioral maturation. It is important to note that these causal factors are also associated with conditions other than mental retardation, suggesting that they probably exert a nonspecific effect (Tarter & Hegedus, in press). Why some children become mentally retarded while most do not, despite experiencing the same events, is unknown. Perhaps there is a specific vulnerability to the various disorders in some individuals. Alternatively, it is possible that a general vulnerability is exacerbated by other biological factors and/or environmental influences to culminate in mental retardation in some people. The association between the plethora of known risk factors and neuropsychological outcome is poorly understood, although there is some evidence that a stimulating home environment can militate against, or even ameliorate, the effects of a perinatal injury (Werner, Simonian, Bierman, & French, 1967).

Developmental versus Deficit Theories

In the area of research on cognition and the developmental disabilities, there has existed a long running debate and theoretical speculation over two models that attempt to describe the nature of the cognitive deficits seen in mental retardation. One model views mental retardation within the context of a cognitive lag, while the other view holds that a disruption of the underlying structure of the CNS is responsible for the manifest cognitive deficits. The former position has been labeled the *developmental or similar-sequence model* and the latter the *deficit or difference model*. A cardinal assumption of the *sequence or developmental theory* is that the acquisition of cognitive skills, usually defined according to Piagetian criteria (Weisz & Zigler, 1979; Zigler, 1967, 1969, 1973), proceeds through an invariant path. The retarded and normal child are hypothesized to differ in regard to the rate of cognitive development and the ultimate plateau that is attained. Thus, a retardate matched for mental age with a normal chronologically younger child would be expected to demonstrate the same level of cognitive functioning.

Support for this theory comes from a number of sources. Iano (1971) found that retarded persons, matched with normals for chronological age, were inferior in learning ability. No differences were found, however, when the two groups were matched on mental age and then compared. Similar findings have been reported in studies of hypothesis-testing capacity (Weisz, 1977). Lackner (1968) also found that sentence length, along with language transformations and initiations, were at a level consistent with the mental age of the child. Retarded children were qualitatively the same as normals in language capacity, and when the groups were matched for mental age, were quantitatively indistinguishable. These latter results confirm the earlier findings by Karlin and Strazzula (1952) who studied three samples of subjects; those with IQ's between 15 and 25, 26 and 50, and 51 and 70. They observed that mentally retarded and normal children proceeded through the same developmental sequence of language development, but that the former group progressed at a slower rate.

Proponents of the deficit or difference theory advance the view that all retarded persons have some form of disturbed brain functioning. Cognitive processes in the mentally handicapped are hypothesized to be structurally different from normals, even when mental age is accounted for (Das, 1972; Greenspan, 1979). Stephens and McLaughlin (1973) tested mentally retarded and normal subjects on a variety of Piagetian tasks and found that the two groups differed in ways that could not be attributed to either chronological or mental age. Milgram (1971) argues that primitive cognitive strategies continue to persist during development and that there is also a tendency for retarded persons to regress to earlier developmental stages. Das, Kirby, and Jarman (1975) concluded that the mentally handicapped have impaired integrative skills for simultaneous information processing relative to sequential processing capacity. Other investigators, measuring language development (Semmel, Barritt, & Bennett, 1970) also obtained results that could not be explained on the basis of only a developmental slowing.

Much of the confusion and controversy surrounding the sequence and deficit theories stems from sampling characteristics. As pointed out previously, the population of mentally retarded children is very heterogeneous in terms of etiology and overt characteristics. Weisz and Yeates (1981) reviewed 20 studies and concluded that when mentally retarded children who did not exhibit obvious neurological disorder were studied, the results supported the developmental sequencing theory. If neurologically impaired children were included, the findings tended to confirm the deficit theory. Thus, it appears that each of these theories is confirmed when tested in specifically selected samples.

The dichotomy of retarded persons into neurological and nonneurological types, each having particular associated cognitive characteristics, has several ramifications for neuropsychology. First, clinical neuropsychological assessment, as a technique for revealing brain dysfunction, may be very useful for detecting the nature of the particular mental retardation syndrome, as well as the concomitant pattern of impairment. As such, a neuropsychological evaluation may have prognostic value for habilitation and educational planning (Feuerstein, 1980). Moreover, neuropsychological techniques offer a finer degree of analysis and precision in the measurement of cognitive level than is revealed by psychometric indices such as mental age. Second, neuropsychological procedures may detect evidence of cerebral dysfunction that is not otherwise observed by routine neurological, neuroradiological, or EEG examination. Thus, the developmental lag, proposed by Weisz and Yeates (1981), to describe retarded persons who do not have a CNS disorder may, upon close examination, be the result of such a disorder. Third, a neuropsychological analysis could elucidate the mechanisms underlying a cognitive deficit. For example, it is possible to determine whether there is a focal cortical disorder. Circumscribed processes such as visual scanning, auditory reception, and spatial orientation may be disturbances that are militating against optimal cognitive development. Hence, many of the issues addressed by the various theorists could be somewhat clarified through neuropsychological procedures (Balla & Zigler, 1971; Humphreys & Parsons, 1979).

A few neuropsychological studies have been conducted in which mentally retarded subjects have been dichotomized and compared to each other according to the presence or absence of neurological disorder. Garfield, Benton, and MacQueen (1966) reported that 50% of brain-damaged mentally retarded subjects exhibited motor impersistence, while only 9% of "cultural-familial" subjects had this impairment. Mathews (1963) evaluated a sample of mentally retarded subjects who were grouped into cultural-familial, brain-damaged, undifferentiated and undifferentiated plus psychosis or personality disorder categories. He administered two types of tests—those that required problem-solving capacity that was supposedly unrelated to past experience and those in which performance was presumed to be influenced by past history. It was found that the cultural-familial group performed better than the three other groups on tests that required problem solving, but were more impaired on tests that were contingent on past history. These findings indicate that neuropsychological techniques can differentiate the various types of mental retardation disorders and, as such, may have value in elucidating the validity and generalizability of the deficit and sequencing models.

Models of Brain Organization

How are psychological capacities organized in the brain? This question has intrigued scholars since the time of Hippocrates, but it is only within the last hundred years that researchers and clinicians have made strides in furthering our understanding of this complex problem. These advances have been directly tied to the refinement of neurosurgical techniques in tandem with the development of standardized psychological procedures that are both reliable and valid.

Insofar as the type of research methods employed and problems addressed are influenced by the model that the investigator adheres to, it is important to discuss how the different models can enhance our understanding of mental retardation. As will be seen below, each of the four models discussed is capable of systematizing and accommodating a portion of the neuropsychological findings.

Connectionist Model

The school of associationist philosophers was represented by John Locke, George Berkeley, David Hume, James Mill, and John Stuart Mill, all of whom are generally identified with the British empiricism school of thought. A cardinal assumption held by each was that all knowledge was the product of experience. This position contrasted with rationalist philosophers like Emmanuel Kant, who argued for the notion of innate ideas or knowledge. The empiricists believed that by associating stimuli that are spatially and temporally contiguous, new ideas are codified in the brain. At birth, the child has a clean slate, or *tabula rasa*, upon which sensory experiences are imprinted and connected to each other to produce more complex ideas or knowledge.

Classical neurology subsequently embraced the associationist position. However, instead of sensory units, it was hypothesized that there are specialized cell groups in the cerebral cortex that are functionally integrated by discrete fiber connections. The particular psychological sequelae of a lesion depended on which cell groupings or connections were disrupted. Because of the presumed specificity of the brain-behavior relationships, it was maintained that a systematic psychological analysis could enable the localization of a lesion. Given the manifold and complex pattern of neuronal interconnections, the number of possible neuropsychological syndromes was, therefore, believed

to be almost unlimited. Thus, the connectionists theorized that psychological functions were localized to specific brain regions. If for whatever reason, a lesion occurred at a particular site, then circumscribed psychological deficits resulted.

The connectionist model dominated neurological thinking until the second decade of the twentieth century. Based on numerous clinical case studies, as well as more formal research efforts, major strides were made in our understanding of brain-behavior relationships. Among the most salient contributions was the elucidation of the cortical representation of language processes by such neurologists as Wernicke, Liepmann, and Broca. Because of space limitations, it is not possible to present a more detailed discussion of the connectionist model, but a comprehensive review and synthesis can be found in Geschwind (1965a, 1965b).

Given the implied specificity of brain-behavior relationships, it is apparent that the model is best applied to situations where the objective is to detect the nature of a psychological deficit in relation to focal cortical pathology. For example, Benton (1964) reported that it was possible to identify specific psychological impairments in individuals exhibiting general mental subnormality. Unfortunately, this study is unique, inasmuch as systematic neuropsychological investigations have not been conducted that are directed to lesion localization in mental retardation. This is largely due to the limited number of instruments available that are also sensitive to detecting focal cortical pathology, and can be administered to persons of low intellectual capacity.

Stratified Model

Evolutionary concepts and geological research in the latter part of the nineteenth century exerted a major influence on psychological and neurological theory. Herbert Spencer advanced a teleological theory that emphasized the adaptational qualities of behavior. A model of brain organization proposed by Hughlings Jackson (see Taylor, 1958) conceptualized the nervous system as being hierarchically arranged, with each ascending level replicating and elaborating the functions of the lower levels. The basic sensory-motor unit is innervated in the spinal cord. Similar, but more complex, sensory-motor units are replicated in the midbrain, diencephalon, and telencephalon. At the highest level, the cortex, numerous connections form sensory-sensory and sensory-motor associative networks. In agreement with the connectionist model, Jackson believed that the higher order cognitive processes could be reduced to simpler sensory and motor elements.

In addition to the replicating and progressively greater elaboration of sensory-motor circuits, Jackson theorized that each successively higher level also possessed inhibitory control over lower levels of the nervous system. These inhibitory mechanisms play a critical role in mediating cognitive and behavioral processes. For example, the ability to inhibit extraneous stimuli is necessary for vigilance or attention. In addition, the capacity to inhibit responding to repetitive stimuli involves inhibitory mechanisms. Inhibitory regulation is also integral for the planning, patterning, and sequencing of behavior, thereby enabling cognitive regulatory processes such as foresight, decision making, and discriminative responding.

The stratified model has some applicability for understanding the mechanisms underlying certain of the deficits in mental retardation. For instance, Mednick and Wild (1961) observed impaired inhibitory processes as inferred from generalization gradients to a conditioned stimulus. However, there is also contrary evidence which indicates that retarded persons are not differentially impaired in attentional tasks or are more susceptible to distraction (Baumeister & Ellis, 1963; Girardeau & Ellis, 1964; Tizard, 1968). On the other hand, discrimination learning (House & Zeaman, 1959, 1962; House, 1964) and response sequencing and coding (Das, Kirby, & Jarmon, 1979) also require inhibitory control and sensory-motor integration and have been found to be impaired in retarded persons. Thus, while the stratified model has some degree of explanatory power and can account for some of the findings, not all of the deficits can be predicted from the assumption of an inhibitory impairment.

Equipotential Model

The belief that there are circumscribed cerebral loci connected by discrete fiber systems subserving specific psychological processes was commonly accepted until the second decade of the twentieth century. Partly as a result of the influence of the phenomenological movement in Europe and partly as a reaction against stimulus-response reflex theories of behavior as espoused by Watson and Pavlov, a conceptualization of brain organization was advanced, based on the assumption that the whole brain was integrally and equally involved in subserving all psychological processes. The concept of specialization of function by different cerebral regions was thus rejected.

The most prominent neurologist identified with this movement was Kurt Goldstein (1939), whose thinking was complemented by the Gestalt movement in psychology (Kohler, 1947). The subjective and qualitative aspects of experience were the primary interests of Gestalt theorists. Complex mentalistic processes such as "insight" and "perceptual closure" and phenomena such as illusions constituted the research focus.

Given the phenomenological emphasis, it is not surprising that the notion of localization of psychological function was rejected. Research into the neurological correlates of animal learning confirmed the belief in a holistic representation of psychological processes, rather than specialization of function in the cortex. Based on the observation that the severity of a behavioral deficit was related to the amount and not the location in the cerebrum from which cortical tissue was ablated, Lashley (1938) advanced the principles of *equipotentiality* and *mass action*. Though subsequent research has refuted the above two "principles," even with animals, they nonetheless confirmed at the time the assumptions of the Gestalt theory regarding the indivisibility of brain functioning. Studies, however, of humans who have undergone various neurosurgical procedures, such as focal ablation (Walsh, 1978), lobotomy (Benton, 1968), and electrical brain stimulation (Penfield & Roberts, 1959) have provided unequivocal evidence for cortical localization of psychological function.

Equipotential theory of brain functioning, though not corroborated by recent investigations, has had a persisting influence in neuropsychology. Piagetian theory of cognitive development is the successor of the phenomological movement. The theory has been applied to research in mental retardation, particularly in attempts to resolve the developmental-deficit controversy. However, because the constructs utilized by cognitively oriented researchers are not correlated with specific cortical regions or systems, Gestalt and Piagetian approaches are of limited relevance for neuropsychological investigations aimed at lateralizing or localizing a brain lesion or for determining the psychological sequela of a lesion. For example, the loss of the "abstract attitude" is often a sequela of brain damage (Goldstein, 1942), but is generally not the consequence of a focal lesion. By reducing this construct to simpler elements of cognition (e.g., attention, hypothesis testing, visuospatial organization, response persistence, perseveration, etc.) it is conceivable that neuropsychological analyses could help delineate the nature of the disordered brain-behavior relationships involving the "abstract attitude" in mental retardation. Hence, while a concrete mode of thinking may accurately describe reduced level of brain development, a condition originally labeled by Tredgold (1952) as "simple primary amentia," it is not sufficiently specific to be of explanatory value in a neuropsychological analysis. Similarly, while Piaget's contribution to our understanding of the psychology of cognitive development has been very substantial, the concepts and measures as presently utilized are not amenable to a neuropsychological analysis.

Regional Equipotentiality Model

Luria (1966) proposed a model of brain functional organization that offers a compromise between the connectionist and equipotential models. Primary analyzers in the cortex for the sensory and motor modalities are concentrically surrounded by, and connected to, secondary and tertiary association fibers. The different analyzer systems are also reciprocally connected to each other by cortical neurons from the secondary and tertiary areas. The tertiary association areas, consisting of the richest, most elaborate and finely arrayed neuronal interconnections, compose the substrate for the higher cognitive functions. Thus, while the physical properties of a stimulus are processed by the primary analyzer, the interpretative and symbolic aspects are analyzed in the secondary and tertiary associative areas. In addition, because the tertiary association areas are ontologically the last to achieve functional maturity, their development is influenced by environmental factors. Hence, postnatal environmental deprivation would be predicted to have a deleterious effect on the acquisition of the higher order cognitive capacities. Conversely, an enriching environment would be expected to have a beneficial effect on cognitive development. Tentative evidence has been obtained to suggest that neuropsychological development is indeed modifiable by the environment. Eisenberg (1967) reported that educational interventions provided through Head Start resulted in increments in performance that subsequently declined when the interventions were discontinued. Heber and Garber (1972) found that three- and four-year-old children of mothers with IQ's less than 70 had a 33 IQ point improvement after tutoring and academic help. These latter studies underscore the importance of the environment, particularly for cultural-familial retardation, on cognitive and intellectual development. In addition, they illustrate the reciprocal interaction between neuropsychological development and environmental influences.

The interaction between neuropsychological development and environmental influences is a cornerstone of Luria's model (Luria, 1961). For instance, it is argued that the acquisition of language skills is greatly determined by the reinforcing effects of adult speech. Initially, words have a directive function from parent to child. By five years of age, the directive functions are internalized so that covert language, or

"thinking," is the process by which behavior is guided or mediated. Internal language mediation is required for such functions as memory, problem solving, complex perceptions, and logical analysis. Behavioral activation and inhibition is also internally regulated by language mediated processes.

From the perspective of Luria's model, mentally retarded children can be viewed as suffering from a dysfunction of incompletely developed tertiary association networks. The observation that these children more readily form phonic than semantic generalizations to words indicates that there is greater responsiveness to the physical properties of the stimulus than to its symbolic meaning (Luria & Vinogradova, 1959). These latter authors interpreted their findings by hypothesizing that there is a dissociation between the speech and motor signaling systems due to an inertia of the underlying cortical mechanisms.

While Luria espouses a defect model of impaired language capacity, Leneberg, Nichols, and Rosenberg (1964) argue their position from a developmental standpoint, claiming that language acquisition is simply slowed down. However, apart from their theoretical differences, there is some convergence of empirical findings. For example, Leneberg et al. (1964) found that chronological age and motor capacity predicted language development in a sample of 61 Down's syndrome subjects who ranged in age between 3 and 22 years, indicating that the development of language is linked to prior acquisition of other neuropsychological processes. Thus, a lesion in the region of the motor analyzer would be expected to adversely affect language development. In a broader sense, optimal language development would thus be contingent on the integrity of all the sensory and motor analyzer systems. To illustrate the point, Kamhi (1981) reported that mentally retarded as well as nonretarded children performed better than a language impaired group of normal intelligence on several Piagetian tasks. Though the three groups were matched for mental age on the Leiter International Performance Scale (a nonverbal intelligence scale) it is intriguing to note that it was the latter group who performed poorest on haptic recognition, classification, number conservation, and water level estimation from different orientations. These findings strikingly illustrate the interrelationship between language processes and other aspects of cognitive and perceptual development.

Until recently, Luria's theories have not been subjected to neuropsychological research outside of the Soviet Union. This has, in large part, been due to unfamiliarity with Luria's instruments and his individualized process of assessment. With the recent development and standardization of the Luria-Nebraska

Neuropsychological Battery (Golden, Hemmeke, & Purish, 1980), it is now possible to conduct a quantified neuropsychological analysis aimed at lesion localization that is consistent with Luria's conceptual framework of functional brain organization. As yet, no systematic research, however, has been conducted on mentally retarded individuals.

Neuropsychological Disorders

A variety of neuropsychological sequelae of focal brain lesions have been described. The disorders discussed below, though not by any means a complete inventory, constitute the majority of conditions encountered by the clinical neuropsychologist. As will be readily seen, these disorders have the appearance of comprising syndromes, but it should be emphasized that in reality they are not generally observed as mutually exclusive categories of impairment. However, for the benefit of clarity, and to familiarize the reader with the clinical approach to brain-behavior relationships, the various disorders are presented as if they are discrete clinical entities. For more extensive discussions of these disorders, the reader is referred to Walsh (1978), Hecaen and Albert (1978), and Lezak (1976).

Acalculia

Acalculia refers to an impairment in performing arithmetic calculations. The cardinal features of this deficit, in its pure form, are an inability to recognize the value of a number in terms of its numerical category (tens, hundreds, etc.), an inability to carry out arithmetic operations (addition, subtraction, etc.), and an inability to develop appropriate schemas for the resolution of problems. Acalculia can also be found in conjunction with other neuropsychological disorders. These include:

ACALCULIA SECONDARY TO ALEXIA AND AGRAPHIA FOR NUMBERS

This condition is usually associated with extensive left hemisphere dysfunction, found in conjunction with aphasia, and is manifest as an impairment in the *written* expression and/or comprehension of number concepts.

ACALCULIA ASSOCIATED WITH SPATIAL DISORGANIZATION OF NUMBERS

This disorder is characterized by inversion and reversal errors, misalignment of digits, visual neglect, and inability to maintain decimal points. The presence of a fundamental spatial deficit implies a right hemisphere dysfunction.

ANARITHMETRICA

This deficit corresponds most closely to primary acalculia. It is defined by an impairment in calculation ability. Focal lesions in the temporal or occipital regions of the dominant hemisphere often produce this disturbance.

Agraphia

Agraphia refers to a group of disorders of written language. These disturbances can arise from a motor, perceptual, or linguistic dysfunction. Not surprisingly, therefore, the study of agraphic disorders has been closely linked to studies of aphasia.

Writing disorders typically coexist with oral language disorders. However, it is possible to distinguish agraphic defects that are interactively associated with aphasia from agraphia where no other language deficit exists. However, because of the intimate association between orally and graphically expressed language, it is usually found that a cerebral lesion leads to diminution in both functions to a greater or lesser degree. Agraphia may also emerge because of an incapacity to execute the gestures necessary for writing or as a result of a lesion in the right hemisphere due to a disruption of spatial organization.

Apraxia

Apraxia pertains to an impairment in the skilled performance of purposeful movements that is not due to paralysis, weakness, motor skills, or sensory loss. The apraxias have been described in four major forms. In *ideomotor apraxia*, the person is unable to carry out a single purposeful act upon request or to perform a specific gesture (e.g., wave goodbye). In *ideational apraxia*, the incapacity is evident when the patient must execute a series of responses to achieve a certain end product. The apractic individual may stop after the first step is achieved, omit steps, or confound the sequence of the steps.

The third type, *constructional apraxia*, consists of an inability to construct or manually reproduce a geometric pattern by drawing or copying an arrangement of objects. In this disorder, the person cannot integrate behavior so as to reproduce a stimulus figure. Finally, *dress apraxia*, has been considered one of the major types of disorders, and refers to the inability to orient articles of clothing to the respective limb while engaging in the sequence of dressing. Again, it is important to reiterate that the deficit in apraxia is not a perceptual one, but rather reflects a disturbance in translating perceptions into complex motor acts.

Alexia

Alexia is generally defined as an inability to comprehend written language. Two forms of alexia have been traditionally accepted. *Developmental alexia* (or dyslexia) denotes the condition in which reading abilities never developed. On the other hand, *acquired alexia* corresponds to the loss of reading comprehension in an individual who had already developed normal reading skills. A common practice has been to further subclassify alexia into four types.

LITERAL ALEXIA

is an inability to recognize letters while maintaining the capacity to read words.

VERBAL ALEXIA

is an inability to read words even though letter recognition is intact.

GLOBAL ALEXIA

is defined by an incapacity to read letters, as well as words, while reading numbers is intact.

SENTINAL ALEXIA

is defined by an inability to read sentences with intact capacity to read letters and words.

By differentiating alexic, aphasic, and agraphic symptoms, a neuropsychological assessment can often precisely localize a cortical lesion. For example, alexia concomitant to receptive aphasia is often found in individuals with a lesion in the mid to posterior temporal lobe of the left hemisphere. Alexia with agraphia is likely found where the lesion is more posterior, such as in the angular gyrus of the left hemisphere. Hence, a clinical analysis of the manifest disturbances in reading, language, and writing has direct implications for lesion localization.

Agnosia

Agnosia is an impairment in the ability to recognize the form and nature of objects.

A lesion in the cortical association area adjacent to a respective sensory area can result in a recognitive deficit despite normal sensory functioning. For example, a disorder of visual recognition, *visual agnosia*, is characterized by an inability to respond appropriately to visually presented material. Although the perceptual apparatus for seeing and describing an object is intact, this modality alone is insufficient to enable object recognition. If, however, the person is permitted to touch, manipulate, or hear the object in use, the

additional and separate sensory input results in correct recognition.

A specific, and rather dramatic form of visual agnosia is *prosopagnosia*. The term is applied when the person cannot recognize familiar faces. Although affected individuals can discriminate between different faces, they are incapable of identifying an individual by only facial features. It is not uncommon for a recognition failure to be manifest in situations where the face is very familiar to the individual. In the most severe form, it has been reported that the person may not be able to even recognize his own face in a mirror.

In *auditory agnosia*, despite normal findings on audiometric screening, the individual is incapable of recognizing the nature of sounds. While in Wernicke's aphasia, the individual is cognizant of the fact that language is being spoken, although he is incapable of comprehending it, the agnosic patient, in contrast, is not capable of distinguishing language from non-language. The third major type, *tactile agnosia*, is an inability to recognize or name objects upon manipulation. Thus, the agnosias are frequently manifestations of lesions in the cortical association areas.

Aphasia

Aphasia can be broadly defined as an impairment in language that is due to brain damage. It is important to differentiate between disorders of speech, such as dysarthria (articulation deficit) or dysphonia (difficulty in vocalization) from aphasia. The former are disorders of vocal production, while aphasia comprises a group of disorders pertaining to symbolic communication. There are several different forms of aphasia:

BROCA'S APHASIA

This condition is characterized by nonfluent verbal output, sparse effortful speech production, overly simplified grammar and, on occasion, telegraphic speech. Comprehension is essentially normal, although it is not uncommon for some mild impairment to be present. Specific difficulties in repetition are noteworthy. Reading is generally mildly impaired, while writing is typically more substantially disrupted. Lesions that are anterior to the Sylvian and Rolandic fissures in the left hemisphere (an area referred to as Broca's region) compose the anatomical substrate of this type of aphasia.

WERNICKE'S APHASIA

This condition is dramatically different from Broca's aphasia in that the primary deficit is in comprehension and not language production. Although verbal production is fluent, it is contaminated by paraphasia, usually in the form of semantic substitutions. Naming and word finding deficits, along with difficulties in repetition, reading and writing are usually noted as well. Pathology in this form of aphasia is generally in the dominant temporal lobe in the posterior portion of the superior temporal gyrus.

CONDUCTION APHASIA

A severe disability in repetition characterizes this disorder. Additional deficits include paraphasias, impairments in reading aloud, spelling, and writing. Other language characteristics are essentially normal with comprehension of written and spoken language being intact. Conduction aphasia can be a sequelae of lesions either above or below the Sylvian fissure.

ANOMIC APHASIA

A severe and selective loss of lexical items (word-finding difficulty) characterizes this disorder. These difficulties are manifest in conversational speech in the form of "empty speech," that is, verbosity that lacks specificity because of the inability to select appropriate words or substitutes. Lesion locus is variable, but is most frequently in the temporoparietal region.

TRANSCORTICAL MOTOR APHASIA

This condition is characterized by intact repetition capacity in an individual who has lost the ability for spontaneous output. Verbal expression is nonfluent except for the ability to echo. Reading comprehension is generally preserved, but writing is severely impaired. A lesion producing this type of aphasia is most often localized to the region anterior or superior to Broca's area.

TRANSCORTICAL SENSORY APHASIA

This is a less common variety of aphasia. It is characterized by well preserved repetition, but limited comprehension and paraphasic speech patterns. Reading and writing are severely impaired. Exact anatomical referents are not well defined, although it is often associated with lesions in the border zones between the parietal and temporal lobes while sparing Wernicke's area.

GLOBAL APHASIA

This condition, sometimes referred to as total aphasia, is featured by an inability to both express and comprehend language. It is usually found in conjunction with lesions in the perisylvian region and is typically accompanied by a right hemiplegia, as well as marked sensory loss.

Summary

From the above, it can be seen that a neuropsychological evaluation can elucidate the nature of a functional disorder and relate it to the neuroanatomical substrate. Psychological processes (e.g., language) are broken into their elements (e.g., comprehension, repetition, naming, etc.) which, in conjunction with a consideration of the particular modality (e.g., auditory, tactile, etc.) enable a precise description and explanation of the manifest impairment. In addition, once a lateralization and localization inference is derived from the neuropsychological assessment, it is possible to predict other associated aspects of the deficit that are not directly tested, but which would be expected on the basis of knowledge of the CNS dysfunction. The next section addresses the issues and techniques of conducting such an assessment.

Measurement Issues

Quantitative versus Qualitative Analysis

For over five decades there has been an intensive debate between the Gestalt theorists and behaviorists concerning the type of information needed and the best technique for gathering information in a clinical assessment. The Gestaltists emphasize the subjective and qualitative aspects, whereas the behaviorists stress the objective and quantitative features of behavior.

There still persists much controversy as to which of these two strategies is more clinically useful in the evaluation of cerebral dysfunction or damage (Goldstein, 1941). Those who adhere to the quantitative approach argue that the focus must be on measurable aspects of behavior, while those who maintain a qualitative orientation insist that the stylistic aspects of performance and self-report provide important information as well. As can be readily seen, the quantitative perspective derives from the psychometric tradition of test validation, while the qualitative approach stresses observation and subjective clinical judgment.

The Halstead-Reitan Battery (Reitan, 1955) exemplifies the quantitative orientation to neuropsychological assessment. The patient is administered a battery of cognitive, motor, and perceptual tests, from which is derived an impairment index. Each of the tests has proven validity and reliability in detecting cerebral damage, thereby enabling the interpretation of scores without the need to exercise subjective observations in making a clinical judgment. Indeed, the battery can be utilized as an actuarial instrument, so that the diagnosis of brain damage and localization of a lesion can be made at a very high level of accuracy without the clinician having to even interview the patient (Russell, Neuringer, & Goldstein, 1970).

In contrast, the qualitative approach places much more weight on observation of the client's behavior and on information about the style of performance, in making a clinical judgment. For example, how the person draws the designs, and not just accuracy, on the Bender Gestalt Test is considered valuable information. The qualitative approach also aims for categorical classifications (e.g., concrete vs. abstract thinking), rather than describing performance dimensionally or along a continuum. Moreover, unlike quantitatively oriented neuropsychologists, the clinician who adheres to a qualitative approach cannot rely on an examination conducted by a technician since astute observation and subjective judgments are essential for valid interpretation of test findings. Thus, the qualitative perspective is concerned with *how* and not only *how well* the client or patient performs. Typical among qualitative tests that distinguish normals from brain damaged are the Bender-Gestalt (1938), the Goldstein-Scheerer (1941) Object Sorting Test and the Rod and Frame Test (Witkin, Lewis, Hertzman, Machover, Meissner, & Wapner, 1954). These instruments were developed by researchers who were aligned with the Gestalt school to evaluate integration and organization processes in perception and cognition.

The issue of the relative merit of the qualitative versus quantitative approach in the assessment of mental retardation is of major importance in neuropsychology. By definition, mental retardation is diagnosed quantitatively on the basis of performance on standardized intelligence tests. Within the context of low level of intelligence, circumscribed neuropsychological deficits have been observed (Benton, 1968). In this latter study, a dyspraxic syndrome was revealed, suggesting a disorder in the parietal region of the right hemisphere. *Of particular significance was the finding that the deficits were observed in persons who did not otherwise evidence positive neurological findings*, indicating that the manifest deficits were the result of a disturbance in functional cortical organization, rather than due to the effects of an acquired lesion. In another study, Mathews, Falk, and Zerfas (1966) found lateralized finger agnosia in mentally retarded subjects. The above investigations, by identifying specific syndromes in persons of low intellectual capacity, illustrate the value of obtaining both qualitative and quantitative information. Thus, while the debate between the qualitatively and quantitatively oriented clinicians continues to generate intense heat, it is apparent that the two approaches are not necessarily mutually exclusive, and can indeed even complement each other.

Differential Diagnosis

As previously noted, there are many pathways to the mental retardation conditions or syndromes. Consequently, mentally retarded individuals compose a very heterogeneous population in terms of etiology and overt characteristics. It is, therefore, not surprising that other concurrent neuropsychological conditions such as learning disability, autism, hyperactivity, cerebral palsy, and epilepsy are manifested by mentally retarded individuals.

Faced with the problem of heterogeneous and overlapping disorders, the neuropsychological examination aims to elucidate specific aspects of dysfunction in the context of general intellectual impairment. Such an assessment is difficult, because intellectual tests measure a limited range of functions. Hence, mental retardation may be implicated when, in fact, the impairment is due to noncognitive factors. For example, a child suffering from cerebral palsy, by virtue of the neuromotor disability, will perform very poorly on timed tests that require motor dexterity, such as the Wechsler Performance Scales. Though cognitive capacities may be intact, or even superior, classification of the child on the basis of an IQ score alone would be invalid. Similarly, a child of normal intelligence suffering from an attention deficit disorder will perform poorly on tests that require sustained concentration. The ensuing low summary IQ score could thus result in a misdiagnosis.

One way to offset the risk of neuropsychological misdiagnosis is to utilize a comprehensive assessment protocol that taps a broad range of functions. From such an approach, the extent to which a low IQ is due to a specific impairment in attentional, perceptual, memory, language, or motor skills can be determined.

Clinical Neuropsychological Assessment

In a comprehensive evaluation, neuropsychological capacity is assessed in the context of psychometric intelligence, educational achievement, psychopathological status and learning aptitude. In conducting such an integrated evaluation, two aspects of neuropsychological performance must be considered: *severity of deficit* and *rate of change*. Inasmuch as a single evaluation yields only information about the individual's status at one particular time, the results are limited in both scope and validity. Serial assessments, on the other hand, permit an appraisal of the level of functioning across the developmental span, so that the rate of change, if any, can be determined.

To fulfill these objectives, it is recommended that full scale IQ testing be first conducted, using either the child or adult form of the Weschler scales. Where intellectual capacity is severely limited, the Binet scales are suggested, inasmuch as they can yield information that is pertinent to a neuropsychological interpretation. However, it is important to note that intellectual capacity is only modestly correlated with performance on neuropsychological tests (Mathews, 1974). Nonetheless, the process of intelligence testing affords the opportunity to observe performance style (e.g., perseveration, response segmentation, concreteness), and inspect profile patterns (e.g., discrepancy between verbal and performance IQ), which could facilitate the formulation of neuropsychological hypotheses for subsequent in-depth exploration utilizing specialized instruments. For example, response perseveration would suggest extensive testing of frontal lobe dysfunction. Substantially inferior verbal IQ compared with performance IQ suggests the need for additional testing for left hemisphere disturbance. Thus, intellectual testing at the outset of the evaluation process, in addition to providing an index of severity of intellectual impairment, also affords the opportunity to formulate neuropsychological hypotheses.

Depending on the specific information requirements, the neuropsychological evaluation can be conducted as an in-depth assessment of an extensive range of processes, or if preliminary information is first desired, via a brief screening procedure. The Luria-Nebraska and Halstead-Reitan are two commonly used comprehensive neuropsychological batteries. Recently, a screening device was developed by Tarter, Goldstein, and Shelly (1982) that yields about 35 age-corrected scaled scores and permits the direct comparison of capacity across a broad range of psychological functions, so that a hierarchical ranking of abilities and limitations can be described along a standard scale. Thus, for example, memory and visuospatial processes can be directly compared with each other, as well as with intellectual capacity. Moreover, this latter screening battery has the added advantage of rapid scoring, inasmuch as a computer program converts the data into standard scores and plots a profile. Thus, an eyeball inspection of the profile permits a quick determination of areas of competency and deficiency.

When there are educational ramifications, particularly if mainstreaming is contemplated, it is important to evaluate the degree to which achievement and learning aptitude deficiencies can be explained by neuropsychological disturbances. Achievement level measured in relation to intellectual capacity and neuropsychological deficit can assist in predicting the individual's potential in an educational environment, where specific skill acquisition is required. For instance, a child presenting a pattern of left hemisphere dys-

function will do poorly in subjects requiring language skills such as reading, spelling and communication, but may perform well on visuospatial tasks. Thus, measures of learning aptitude involving attention, memory, orientation, and ability to follow directions need also to be evaluated insofar as they may point to areas of cerebral dysfunction which, combined with neuropsychological tests, can assist in formulating an educational and vocational habilitation program.

Finally, since emotional disturbance disrupts cognitive, motor, and perceptual processes, it is important to delineate the contribution of psychopathology to the manifest deficits. A number of rating scales, observational techniques, and self-report tests are available, which together with an interview, enables the clinician to assess for psychopathology and to gauge its effects on the intellectual, neuropsychological, and educational measures. In addition, certain psychopathological disorders, such as aggression, and depression may stem from cerebral dysfunction, particularly in the seizure disorders. Hence, the possibility of an "organic" substrate for the behavioral or affective disorder needs to be examined. Furthermore, since certain psychopathological conditions are associated with distinctive neuropsychological deficits (Gruzelier & Flor-Henry, 1979), it is essential to determine whether the impairments are reflective of an acute psychopathological disorder or, alternatively, are the result of a cerebral lesion.

Summary

The specialized clinical and research techniques in neuropsychology, though having certain limitations, can potentially make a substantial contribution to our understanding of brain-behavior relationships in mental retardation. Moreover, these procedures may help resolve some of the difficulties involved in classification, as well as provide a new perspective on the developmental-deficit controversy.

Neuropsychological sequelae can occur from pathology at any level of biological organization and from insult at any time from the beginnings of embryonic development to maturation in adulthood. Little is known, however, of the factors that determine the specific features of neuropsychological impairment. Nor have systematic neuropsychological studies been conducted comparing the different forms of mental retardation conditions. The fact that there are several models of neuropsychological organization indicates that there is a heuristic basis and conceptual framework to pursue research aimed at delineating the brain-behavior relationships in the mental retardation disorders. Neuropsychology can also assist in assessment and suggest habilitation strategies. Such information, considered in the context of general intellectual capacity and incorporated in other assessment approaches could then be utilized for comprehensive educational intervention as well as for vocational planning.

References

Balla, D., & Zigler, E. Luria's verbal deficiency theory of mental retardation and performance on sameness, symmetry and opposition tasks: A critique. *American Journal of Mental Deficiency*, 1971, **75**, 400–413.

Baumeister, A., & Ellis, N. Delayed response performance of retardates. *American Journal of Mental Deficiency*, 1963, **67**, 714–722.

Baumeister, A., & MacLean, W. Brain damage and mental retardation. In N. Ellis (Ed.), *Handbook of mental deficiency: Psychological theory and research*, Hillsdale, N.J.: Lawrence Erlbaum, 1979.

Bender, L. *A visual motor gestalt test and its clinical use.* New York: American Orthopsychiatric Association Research Monographs, 1938.

Benton, A. Differential behavioral effects of frontal lobe disease. *Neuropsychologia*, 1968, **6**, 53–60.

Bialer, J. & Sternlich, M. *The psychology of mental retardation: Issues and approaches.* New York: Psychological Dimensions, 1977.

Clarke, A., & Clarke, A. Mental subnormality. In H. Eysenck (Ed.), *Handbook of abnormal psychology*. (2nd ed.) San Diego: Robert R. Knapp, 1973.

Clarke, A. & Clarke, A. Genetic-environmental interactions in cognitive development. In A. Clarke & A. Clarke (Eds.), *Mental deficiency: The changing outlook*, New York: The Free Press, 1975.

Das, J. Patterns of cognitive ability in nonretarded and retarded children. *American Journal of Mental Deficiency*, 1972, **77**, 6–12.

Das, J., Kirby, J., & Jarman, R. Simultaneous and successive synthesis: An alternative model for cognitive abilities. *Psychological Bulletin*, 1975, **82**, 87–103.

Das, J., Kirby, J., & Jarman, R. *Simultaneous and successive cognitive processes.* New York: Academic Press, 1979.

DeFries, J., Vandenberg, S. & McClearn, G. Genetics of specific cognitive abilities. *Annual Review of Genetics*, 1976, **10**, 179–207.

Eisenberg, L. Clinical considerations in the psychiatric evaluation of intelligence. In J. Zubin & G. Jervis (Eds.), *Psychopathology of mental development*, New York: Grune and Stratton, 1967.

Ellis, N. (Ed.) *Handbook on mental deficiency: Psychological theory and research.* Hillsdale, N.J.: Lawrence Erlbaum, 1979.

Feuerstein, R. *Instrumental enrichment: An intervention program for cognitive modifiability.* Baltimore: University Park Press, 1980.

Garfield, J., Benton, A., & MacQueen, J. Motor impersistence in brain damaged and cultural familial defectives. *Journal of Nervous & Mental Disease*, 1966, **142**, 434–440.

Geschwind, N. Disconexion syndromes in animals and man (Part I). *Brain*, 1965, **88**, 237–294.(a)

Geschwind, N. Disconexion syndromes in animals and man (Part II). *Brain*, 1965, **88**, 585–644.(b)

Girardeau, F., & Ellis, N. Rote verbal learning by normal and mentally retarded children. *American Journal of Mental Deficiency*, 1964, **68**, 525–532.

Golden, C., Hemmeke, T.,.& Purish, A. *The Luria-Nebraska Neuropsychological Battery.* Los Angeles: Western Psychological Services, 1980.

Goldstein, G. Some recent developments in clinical neuropsychology. *Clinical Psychological Review*, 1981, **1**, 245–268.

Goldstein, K. *The organism.* New York: American Book, 1939.

Goldstein, K. *After effects of brain injuries in war.* New York: Grune and Stratton, 1942.

Goldstein, K., & Scheerer, M. Abstract and concrete behavior: An experimental study with special tests. *Psychological Monographs*, 1941, **53**, 239.

Graves, W., Freeman, M., & Thompson, J. Culturally related reproduction factors in mental retardation. In C. Haywood (Ed.), *Sociocultural aspects of mental retardation.* New York: Appleton-Century-Crofts, 1970.

Greenspan, S. Social intelligence in the retarded. In N. Ellis (Ed.), *Handbook of mental deficiency: Psychological theory and research.* (2nd ed.) Hillsdale, N.J.: Lawrence Erlbaum, 1979.

Grossman, H. (Ed.) *Manual on terminology and classification in mental retardation.* Washington, D.C.: American Association on Mental Deficiency, 1977.

Gruzelier, J., & Flor-Henry, P. (Ed.) *Hemisphere asymmetries of function in psychopathology.* New York: Elsevier/North Holland Biomedical Press, 1979.

Haywood, H. *Socio-cultural aspects of mental retardation.* New York: Appleton-Century-Crofts, 1970.

Heber, R., & Garber, H. An experiment in prevention of cultural-familial mental retardation. In D. Primrose (Ed.), *Proceedings of the second congress of the International Association for the Scientific Study of Mental Deficiency.* Amsterdam: Swets & Zeitlinger, 1972.

Hecaen, H. & Albert, M. *Human neuropsychology.* New York: John Wiley & Sons, 1978.

House, B. The effect of distinctive responses on discrimination reversals in retardates. *American Journal of Mental Deficiency*, 1964, **69**, 79–85.

House, B., & Zeaman, D. Position descrimination and reversals in low-grade retardates. *Journal of Comparative & Physiological Psychology*, 1959, **52**, 564–565.

House, B., & Zeaman, D. Reversal and nonreversal shifts in discrimination learning in retardates. *Journal of Experimental Psychology*, 1962, **63**, 444–451.

Humphreys, L., & Parsons, C. Piagetan tasks measure intelligence and intelligence tests assess cognitive development: A reanalysis. *Intelligence*, 1979, **3**, 369–382.

Iano, R. Learning deficiency vs. developmental conceptions of mental retardation. *Exceptional Children*, 1971, **38**, 301–311.f

Isaacson, R. The myth of recovery from early brain damage. In N. R. Ellis (Ed.) *Aberant development in infancy: Human and animal studies.* N.Y.: Halstad Press, 1975.

Kamhi, A. Developmental versus difference theories of mental retardation: A new look. *American Journal of Mental Deficiency*, 1981, **86**, 1–7.

Karlin, J., & Strazzula, M. Speech and language problems of mentally deficient children. *Journal of Speech & Hearing Disorders*, 1952, **17**, 286–294.

Kinsbourne, M. Mechanisms of hemispheric interaction in man. In M. Kinsbourne & W. Smith (Eds.) *Hemispheric disconnection and cerebral function.* Springfield, IL.: Charles C. Thomas, 1974.

Kohler, W. *Gestalt psychology.* New York: Liveright Publishing Corp., 1947.

Lackner, J. A developmental study of language behavior in retarded children. *Neuropsychologia,* 1968, **6,** 301–320.

Lashley, K. Factors limiting recovery after central nervous lesions. *Journal of Nervous & Mental Disease,* 1938, **88,** 733–755.

Leneberg, E., Nichols, I., & Rosenberg, E. Primitive stages of language development in mongolism. In D. McRioch & E. Weinstein (Eds.), *Disorders of communication.* Baltimore: Williams and Wilkins, 1964.

Lezak, M. *Neuropsychological assessment.* New York: Oxford University Press, 1976.

Luria, A. *The role of speech in the regulation of normal and abnormal behavior.* New York: Pergamon Press, 1961.

Luria, A. *Higher cortical functions in man.* New York: Basic Books, 1966.

Luria, A. & Vinogradova, O. An objective investigation of the dynamics of semantic systems. *British Journal of Psychology,* 1959, **50,** 89–105.

Mathews, C. Problem-solving and experimental background determinants of test performance in mentally retarded subjects. *Psychological Review,* 1963, **13,** 391–401.

Mathews, C. Applications of neuropsychological test methods in mentally retarded subjects. In R. Reitan & L. Davison (Eds.), *Clinical neuropsychology: Current status and applications,* New York: John Wiley & Sons, 1974.

Mathews, C., Falk, E., & Zerfas, P. Lateralized finger localization deficits and differential Wechsler-Bellevue results in retardation. *American Journal of Mental Deficiency,* 1966, **70,** 695–702.

Mednick, S., & Wild, C. Stimulus generalization in brain damaged children. *Journal of Consulting Psychology,* 1961, **25,** 525–527.

Milgram, N. Cognition and language in mental retardation: A reply to Balla and Zigler. *American Journal of Mental Deficiency,* 1971, **76,** 33–41.

Milner, E. *Human neural and behavioral development.* Springfield, Ill.: C. C. Thomas, 1967.

Montagu, A. Sociogenetic brain damage. *Developmental Medicine & Child Neurology,* 1971, **13,** 597–605.

Pasamanick, B., & Knoblock, H. Retrospective studies on the epidemiology of reproductive casualty: Old and new. *Merrill-Palmer Quarterly,* 1966, **12,** 1–26.

Penfield, W., & Roberts, L. *Speech and brain mechanisms.* Princeton, N.J.: Princeton University Press, 1959.

Reitan, R. An investigation of the validity of Halstead's measures of biological intelligence. *Archives of Neurology & Psychiatry,* 1955, **73,** 28–35.

Reitan, R., & Davison, L. *Clinical neuropsychology: Current status and applications.* Washington, D.C.: V. H. Winston, 1974.

Rosenbaum, A. Neuropsychological outcome of children born via the occiput posterior position. In C. Angle & A. Bering (Eds.), *Physical trauma as an etiological agent in mental retardation,* Bethesda, Maryland: U.S. Dept. of Health, Education and Welfare, 1970.

Russell, E., Neuringer, C., & Goldstein, G. *Assessment of brain damage: A neuropsychological key approach.* New York: Wiley-Interscience, 1970.

Semmel, M., Barritt, L., & Bennett, S. Performance of EMR and non-retarded children on a modified cloze task. *American Journal of Mental Deficiency,* 1970, **74,** 681–688.

Stephens, B., & McLaughlin, J. Two year gains in reasoning by retarded and nonretarded persons. *American Journal of Mental Deficiency,* 1973, **77,** 311–313.

Tarter, R., Goldstein, G., & Shelly, C. *Computer assisted neuropsychological evaluation.* Pittsburgh: International Neuropsychology Society, 1982.

Tarter, R., & Hegedus, A. Developmental disorders. In R. Tarter (Ed.), *The child at psychiatric risk.* New York: Oxford University Press. In press.

Taylor, J. (Ed.) *Selected writings of John Hughlings Jackson.* New York: Basic Books, 1958.

Tizard, B. Habituation of EEG and skin potential changes in normal and severely subnormal children. *American Journal of Mental Deficiency,* 1968, **73,** 209–213.

Tredgold, A. *A textbook of mental deficiency.* (8th ed.) Baltimore: Williams and Wilkins, 1952.

Walsh, K. *Neuropsychology: A clinical approach.* New York: Churchill Livingstone, 1978.

Weisz, J. R. A follow-up developmental study of hypothesis behavior among mentally retarded and nonretarded children. *Journal of Experimental Child Psychology,* 1977, **24,** 108–122.

Weisz, J. & Yeates, K. Cognitive development in retarded and nonretarded persons. Piagetian test of the similar structure hypothesis. *Psychological Bulletin,* 1981, **90,** 153–178.

Weisz, J., & Zigler, E. Cognitive development in retarded and nonretarded persons: Piagetian tests of the similar sequence hypothesis. *Psychological Bulletin,* 1979, **86,** 831–851.

Werner, E., Simonian, K., Bierman, J., & French, F. Cumulative effects of perinatal complications and deprived environment on physical, intellectual and social development of preschool. *Pediatrics,* 1967, **39,** 490–505.

Willerman, L. Maternal pelvic size and neuropsychological outcome. In C. Angle & A. Bering (Eds.), *Physical trauma as an etiological agent in mental retardation.* Bethesda, Maryland: U.S. Dept. of Health, Education and Welfare, 1970.

Witkin, H., Lewis, H., Hertzman, M., Machover, K., Meissner, P., & Wapner, S. *Personality through perception: An experimental and clinical study.* New York: Harper, 1954.

Zigler, E. Familial mental retardation: A continuing dilemma. *Science,* 1967, **157,** 578–579.

Zigler, E. Developmental versus difference theories of mental retardation and the problem of maturation. *American Journal of Mental Deficiency,* 1969, **73,** 536–556.

Zigler, E. The retarded child as a whole person. In D. K. Routh (Ed.), *The experimental psychology of mental retardation,* Chicago, Ill.: Aldine, 1973.

34 DEVELOPMENTAL PROCESSES

Rune J. Simeonsson

An overview of research and theory suggests a dichotomy of perspectives in the study of cognition and mental retardation. This dichotomy is reflected by a quantitative perspective on the one hand, focusing on differences between mentally retarded and nonretarded persons on such cognitive tasks as memory (Detterman, 1979) and attention (Zeaman & House, 1979). On the other hand, and to a lesser degree, a qualitative perspective has focused on commonalities of cognitive stages and structures (Woodward, 1979). The extent to which either of these perspectives is adopted as an approach to the study of mental retardation determines the kind of questions explored, the kind of assessment strategies devised and the nature of intervention efforts implemented.

Heal (1970) has proposed four major goals for research in mental retardation: (a) defining retardation/delay, (b) defining defect/impairment, (c) studying developmental processes, and (d) studying exceptionality for its own sake. In the context of Heal's proposed goals, defining defect/impairment and studying developmental processes have often involved comparisons of CA-matched, or MA-matched groups of mentally retarded and nonretarded persons on quantitatively measured cognitive tasks. Representative contributions from the extensive literature of the quantitative per-spective are made elsewhere in this volume (see chapters by Barkowski et al. and Tarter et al.). The study of cognition from a qualitative perspective seems more compatible with Heal's proposed goals of defining retardation/delay and the study of exceptionality for its own sake. This chapter will focus on this latter approach to the study of cognition and mental retardation exemplified by the constructivist theory developed by Piaget (1970). While the contributions of other theorists such as Vygotsky and Luria (Schiefelbusch, Copeland, & Smith, 1967) and Montessori (Jordan, 1976) also may be seen as qualitative in nature, theoretical and empirical extensions to mentally retarded populations have been less comprehensive than that of Piaget's theory (Inhelder, 1966; Piaget & Inhelder, 1947; Reiss, 1970; Simeonsson, 1978; Woodward, 1963).

The purpose of this chapter is to identify current and emerging issues of significance to a cognitive-developmental approach to mental retardation. This will be done by drawing on representative theoretical and empirical contributions, meeting criteria for significance as issues. One criterion to be met was that the issue should be inclusive of normal as well as pathological development. Secondly, to be significant, an issue should also be comprehensive, rather than limited, in scope. With these qualifications in mind, a review of selected literature yielded two major issues advancing the study of mental retardation by examining (a) the structure of cognition and (b) the content of cognition. Research bearing on these issues will be reviewed and summarized and implications for research and practice identified.

Prior to reviewing research findings, several assumptions of cognitive-developmental theory will be identified, as they provide the basis for the study of mental retardation. One important assumption is that the child is an interactive-generative transformer of knowledge (Cowan, 1978). Cognition is therefore not a passive act of copying information but rather the active structuring and restructuring of reality by the child. A second assumption is that such structuring of cognition is qualitative in nature, and that cognitive development is thus reflected by transitions that are invariant in their order of appearance.

A derivation of the above assumptions for research in mental retardation is that variation may be found in the rate, but not the sequence, of cognitive development. In a systematic consideration of the implications of cognitive developmental theory, Inhelder (1966) has proposed that the cognition of mentally retarded persons will be characterized by delays and fixations in development. Structural development is seen as limited, resulting in incomplete (false equilibrium) cognitive structures at maturity. Mental retardation is thus defined as the failure to achieve the stage of formal operations at maturity with severity levels of mental retardation corresponding to fixations at one of the three lower stages of cognitive development. These characteristics of delays and fixations of cognitive-development have been the focus for substantial research with mentally retarded populations and have expanded the knowledge base regarding the structure and content of their cognition.

Structure of Cognition

In reviewing research findings dealing with the structure of cognition in mentally retarded persons, it may be productive to use the qualitative stages of development as a framework. Research addressing sensorimotor, preoperational and concrete-operational functioning will thus be reviewed in sequence.

The relevance of systematically investigating sensorimotor elements of cognition in the severely and profoundly mentally retarded individual has been recognized for some time. Whereas earlier efforts were directed at adults and older children (Woodward, 1963), more recent efforts have investigated this level of functioning in mentally retarded infants and young children. Two representative studies have focused on

the issues of parallelism (Rogers, 1977) and ordinality of emergence of sensorimotor substages (Wohlheuter & Sindberg, 1975). In an investigation of 40 profoundly mentally retarded children between 8 and 14 years of age (IQ range 7–17), Rogers (1977) hypothesized that sensorimotor development would be invariant and parallel stage acquisitions would be found across domains. The results revealed significant indices of scaleability for four of five sensorimotor scales providing support for the invariance of development in the profound mentally retarded child. Parallelism of stages was not observed, indicating horizontal decalage in cognitive development. Moderate associations were found between mental age measures and sensorimotor task achievement. Adopting a somewhat different approach, Wohlheuter and Sindberg (1975) investigated the acquisition of object permanence in a longitudinal study of 67 one- to six-year-old children ranging in severity from moderate to profound levels of mental retardation. Twenty of the subjects achieved the criterion of object permanence development. Of those children who did not reach the criterion, three different patterns were observed. One of the patterns was defined as variable, one as plateau, and one as an upward pattern. While all but one of the subjects characterized by a plateau pattern were profoundly mentally retarded, subjects in the other two groups included profoundly mentally retarded children, indicating that object concept development does not correspond in a one-to-one fashion with severity of mental retardation.

A major qualitative characteristic of the preoperational stage is the emergence of representational competence, that is, the ability to distinguish between a symbol and the object it signifies. This representational competence gives the child freedom to deal with symbols in the absence of the objects they represent. Preoperational functioning, however, is limited by precausal and prelogical thinking characterized by artificialistic, animistic, syncretistic, and transductive thought. These limitations of thought have been demonstrated in mentally retarded subjects in representative studies involving conservation and causal inference problems. Several studies, for example, have served to confirm the fact that children diagnosed as mentally retarded progress through qualitative stages but do so at later ages than their CA peers. McManis (1969) compared the MA levels at which conservation of mass, weight, and volume were attained by 90 institutionalized mentally retarded children and young adults (CA range 7–21) with those of 90 elementary school students (CA range 5–10) of similar mental ages. The mental age placements for mass and weight conservation among the mentally retarded subjects were comparable to the CA placements for their nonretarded peers. The overall sequence of conservation attainment of mass to weight to volume was generally confirmed among the mentally retarded subjects. It was interesting to note that conservation of volume, defined as a formal operation skill, was documented only with mentally retarded subjects whose IQ exceeded 70 and who had MA's above 11 years. In a subsequent study comparing mentally retarded and nonretarded subjects matched for MA's between 5–0 and 11–11, McManis (1970) found a significant deficit in seriation performance among the mentally retarded having MA's between five and seven years. McManis interpreted these and earlier findings as supportive of interrelated deficits in the sequence of operations from conservation to seriation to transitivity in mentally retarded subjects.

In an elaborate study analyzing the association of MA, CA, and IQ with conservation skills, Brown (1973) compared the performance of normal, mentally retarded, and bright children matched for a mental age of six years. Two groups of nonretarded children were also matched on CA with the bright children (CA = 4) and with the mentally retarded children (CA = 8). Results indicated that the conservation performance of mentally retarded children was comparable to that of nonretarded MA peers, but lower than that of CA peers. The children did not perform as well as their mentally retarded or nonretarded MA peers. Brown interpreted these results to support the position that acquisition of conservation skills involved both experiential and intellectual factors. This finding qualifies the more general association assumed to hold between MA and conservation performance (Boland, 1973).

The intuitive, perceptually dominated characteristic of preoperational thought has been investigated with mentally retarded children. Smith (1977) compared the perceptual decentering skills of nonretarded eight-year olds with MA and CA matched mentally retarded children. The responses of the CA matched mentally retarded children were significantly different from those of the other two groups, showing greater perceptual centering in figures requiring the integration of parts and wholes. The relationship between perceptual decentering and conservation of substance was evident in the fact that only 27% of CA matched mentally retarded children gave conserving responses, whereas the values for nonretarded and retarded MA-matched peers were 83 and 70%, respectively.

The perceptual correlates of conservation skills have also been examined in the context of concrete operational functioning in mentally retarded children. Wilton and Boersma (1974) compared the visual scanning activities of MA matched (MA = 7) mentally retarded and nonretarded children grouped on the bases of being conservers and nonconservers. For both mentally retarded and nonretarded conservers, greater visual scanning activities were observed. Eye movements that differentiated conservers from nonconservers were those reflective of greater overall perceptual activity and less centration. Wilton and Boersma (1974) interpreted these findings of a decrease in perceptual centration accompanying acquisition of conservation as supportive of Piaget's notion of perceptual correlates of operational thought. Another study by Cardozo and Allen (1975) provides additional clarification of the role of visual perception in operational thinking. Conservation performance of 30 retarded children was compared with that of CA-matched (CA = 12) and MA-matched (MA = 7) nonretarded children relative to visual-perceptual competence. The conservation performance of retarded children was significantly lower than that of MA matched nonretarded children in spite of comparable visual-perceptual skills as measured by Frostig tasks. The findings indicated that the variables of MA, CA and visual perception could not account for differences in conservation between retarded and nonretarded children. These variables may thus be necessary but insufficient to account for the acquisition of conservation skills.

A substantial number of studies additional to those reviewed above have examined conservation and related skills such as classification in mentally retarded populations (Klein & Safford, 1977). In general, these applications of Piaget's theory to the study of mental retardation suggest several conclusions regarding the development of cognitive structures. Findings have provided support for the fact that the sequence of qualitative transitions is invariant among mentally retarded subjects as it is in nonretarded subjects. The rate of movement through stages however is characterized by substantial delays, relative to the severity of mental retardation. Measures of intellectual ability such as MA are associated with, but not equivalent to, the development of cognitive structures. Visual perceptual skills, while also found to be correlated with concrete operations, may be necessary but not sufficient to account for operational thought. These conclusions provide documentation for the nature of thought among the mentally retarded in terms of common developmental sequences, as well as specificity of structural characteristics. Furthermore, the conclusions demonstrate that a qualitative approach contributes a unique perspective on cognition and mental retardation, not redundant with traditional indices such as IQ and other quantitative variables.

Content of Cognition

Complementing contributions to the study of the

structure of cognition, the second major issue considered in this chapter is research dealing with the content of cognition. While substantial research has been carried out on the former in the context of Piaget's cognitive-developmental theory, applications to cognitive content, such as understanding of personal and social phenomena, are an area of limited and relatively recent interest. Given the fact that mental retardation is defined jointly by intellectual and social competence deficits, the study of social understanding would constitute a very relevant domain of investigation. Prior approaches to the study of social competence in mentally retarded populations has often focused on self-help skills, vocational/occupational adjustment, adaptive/maladaptive behavior and instrumental competence (Simeonsson, 1978). Such approaches emphasize behaviors or skills with limited attention to the underlying developmental dimensions of social awareness and insight. A model of interpersonal competence has been proposed by Kleck (1975) for the mentally retarded, which is compatible with a developmental orientation and which encompasses the nature of social understanding. Kleck's model draws on the sociological approach of purposiveness in interpersonal relationships (Weinstein, 1973) and specifies three components: (a) the ability to take the role of others, (b) the possession of varied repertoires of lines of action, and (c) the possession of interpersonal resources allowing the application of effective tactics in varied situations.

Research on the child's emerging understanding of personal and social phenomena has been quite extensive in the field of child development since the late 1960s and early 1970s. Shantz (1975) defined social cognition as "the child's intuitive or logical representation of others, that is, how he characterizes others and makes inferences about their covert inner psychological experiences" (p. 258). In a more generic sense, social understanding can be defined as an understanding that mediates social behavior. Factors such as intelligence, personality, and motivation may also influence social behavior, but are not equivalent to social understanding. This unique nature of social understanding has been emphasized by Damon (1979), who maintained that "social cognition cannot be derived from, or be reduced to, the study of physical cognition" (p. 209). Piaget's early work (1929) on the child's construction of social reality contributed to assumptions that qualitative transitions in understanding the physical environment would be paralleled by similar transitions in knowledge of the social environment. Central to these transitions are sequential changes in self-other differentiation from an egocentric, self-referenced standpoint toward more decentered,

reciprocal perspectives in social exchanges. The nature of social understanding thus involves the progressive ability to differentiate self from personal phenomena, from the world of others, and effectively to apply such understanding in purposive social behavior. Differentiation of one's phenomenological world has been approached through the study of causality concepts. Investigation of social understanding has considered the domains of social communication, role-taking, and moral judgment. Social inference and social comprehension have also been proposed as elements of a comprehensive model of social intelligence (Greenspan, 1979).

Recent research contributions have extended the study of cognition to the area of content to include intrapersonal and interpersonal domains. One aspect of the intrapersonal domain is that of causality conceptions of such phenomena as life and dreams (Laurendau & Pinard, 1962). Drawing on Piaget's (1929) original work, Laurendau and Pinard identified four stages in the responses of children to questions on the concept of life, reflecting changes from animism to the restriction of life to plants and animals. Smeets (1974) has compared the attribution of life and life traits to objects in 11-year-old mentally retarded children and their chronological and mental age peers. A 70-item questionnaire was used to assess the child's attribution of life and life traits to animate and inanimate objects. The results revealed significant differences between older and younger nonretarded children and the attribution of life to animate objects and of life traits to inanimate objects. Responses of the mentally retarded children, however, were not significantly different from either CA or MA peers, leading Smeets to conclude that attribution of life and life traits are dependent upon the interaction of CA and MA. Analyses of responses indicated that the mentally retarded children and their CA peers tended to make their attribution on the basis of perceptual characteristics, whereas older nonretarded children considered biological and/or logical dimensions in their attributions. These findings are of value in documenting an aspect of thought not often assessed psychometrically, and may reflect the role of experience in cognitive development. Further research on other aspects of intrapersonal thought such as dream conceptions may be valuable not only in broadening the knowledge base on cognition and mental retardation, but may also provide an index of reality orientation as it has in emotionally disturbed children (Evans, 1973). Such information could have practical diagnostic and treatment implications.

Advances in the study of cognition have also come through research on the nature of interpersonal understanding in mentally retarded populations. The typical area of social cognition, focusing on the child's understanding of others' perspectives, motives, attributes, and informational needs has been investigated in role-taking, moral judgment, person perception and referential communication tasks, respectively.

Assessment of role-taking skills typically draws on a situation in which the subject, given a present perspective, is required to assume the perspective of another. One type of perspective taking task involves three-dimensional displays in which the task is to correctly assume a spatial perspective different from one's own. Using this type of task, Houssiades and Brown (1967) found the performance of eight- to 15-year-old mentally retarded children to be delayed but to follow the same sequence as nonretarded peers, while Rubin and Orr (1974) found the performance of mentally retarded children to be comparable to that of MA (mean ca. eight years) but not CA-equated (mean ca. 12 years) peers. Other tasks involving cognitive perspective taking have attempted to assess the child's ability to infer what others are thinking. Feffer (1970) and Affleck (1975a,b, 1976) have utilized a projective instrument (Make A Picture Story) to investigate the role-taking skills of mentally retarded children and young adults. While their findings have revealed a limited relationship between role-taking ability and MA, higher role-taking skills were associated with more effective interpersonal tactics. Utilizing a somewhat different task, Simeonsson and his colleagues (Blacher-Dixon & Simeonsson, 1978, Monson, Greenspan, & Simeonsson, 1979) assessed the ability of mentally retarded children and adolescents to suppress privileged information while assuming another's limited perspective. Findings from these studies have revealed variability of role-taking skills in mentally retarded children and associations of such skills with social competence measures (Monson et al., 1979). Experimental manipulation of privileged information was differentially effective in task performance as a function of initial role-taking ability in spite of similar MA and IQ characteristics of the children (Blacher-Dixon & Simeonsson, 1978). A one-year follow-up study provided evidence for the stability of role-taking skills in the subjects (Blacher-Dixon & Simeonsson, 1979). In a recent comparative study, Perry and Krebs (1980) found no differences in role-taking performance between mildly mentally retarded adolescents and MA-matched children. Thus, while the above research shows that mentally retarded children and adults are characterized by greater egocentricity than that of nonretarded peers, acquisition of role-taking skills is not determined solely by intelligence level. Findings of positive relationships between role-taking ability

and interpersonal competence and the differential effectiveness of experimental manipulations of shared perspectives holds promise for the systematic provision of social experiences to promote interpersonal competence.

Assessment of person perception has focused on the manner in which the mentally retarded person makes inferences about the characteristics and attributes of others. In studies of nonhandicapped populations, Secord and Peevers (1973) have found descriptions of others to become less self referenced and more differentiated with development. Research on this aspect of social cognition has been limited among the mentally retarded and not carried out with common theoretical or methodological aspects. Gardner and Barnard (1969) found differences between mentally retarded, nonretarded, and gifted children of similar mean mental ages of 12 years in representation of different affect. The authors concluded that level of intelligence does determine person perception in the mentally retarded. In a comparison of CA-matched mentally retarded and nonretarded adolescents, Wooster (1970) found mentally retarded boys to rate others on a simpler and less differentiated basis. In a descriptive study using Secord and Peevers' (1973) methods with 20 moderately mentally retarded adults, Monson, Greenspan, and Simeonsson (1979) found descriptions similar to those of preschoolers for dimensions of descriptiveness and personal involvement and with seventh graders for the depth dimension. On a tentative basis, it can be concluded that mentally retarded persons are likely to perceive others in relatively immature egocentric and nondifferentiated ways, characteristics that are likely to influence successful interaction with others.

Research on moral judgment has sought to determine developmental changes in the evaluation of the ethical or moral nature of specified behavior. In the context of cognitive-developmental theory, research has generally taken one of two forms. Studies based on Piaget's (1929) original work have sought to document the transition from consequence-based to moral judgments which counter intentionality reflective of morality of constraint and morality of cooperation, respectively. Conversly, studies drawing on Kohlberg's (1969) six-stage model of moral development have focused on the structural analysis of responses to moral dilemmas to determine stage assignment. Compared with other areas of social cognitive research, studies of moral judgment in the mentally retarded have had a longer and more comprehensive history. Representative research extensions of Piaget's approach were initiated more than four decades ago (Abel, 1941) and are continuing to be applied in a variety of ways

(Foye & Simeonsson, 1979). A review of studies using Piagetian type tasks within this period indicated that the moral judgment performance of mentally retarded persons is inferior to that of CA peers, but generally comparable to that of MA peers (Simeonsson, Monson & Blacher, 1982). Support has also been found for the developmental sequence of consequence based on judgments recognizing the interaction of intent and consequence. Research based on Kohlberg's paradigm has provided evidence for the comparability of moral judgments of mentally retarded children with those of MA-matched peers qualified on the basis of an organic versus a cultural-familial etiology (Simeonsson et al., 1982). The value of further research on this topic is supported by findings linking reasoning, moral conduct and behavior with moral judgment in mentally retarded persons.

An area of fairly recent investigation among mentally retarded subjects is that of referential communication as an aspect of social cognitive research. While specific tasks have varied somewhat, most involve the assessment of speaker-listener effectiveness. Findings with nonhandicapped children have demonstrated that communication becomes less self-referenced and more accurate from preschool through early school years. There is also evidence linking family interaction style and referential communication skills of children (Bearison & Cassel, 1975). Studies of referential communication skills with mentally retarded subjects have typically involved older children and adolescents although at least one study has focused on preschoolers (Blacher, 1982). Utilizing variations of two-person communication tasks, findings have revealed that the referential communication skills of mentally retarded speakers, while relatively deficient, are not simply a function of intelligence level or vocabulary skills (Longhurst, 1974).

Research on the content of cognition, as represented by these selected studies provides documentation on the manner in which mentally retarded individuals understand their personal and social worlds. Further work in this relatively new area is needed to isolate and identify the dimensions of social understanding which contribute to effective interpersonal behavior.

Emerging Directions

The application of cognitive-developmental theory to the study of mental retardation has, at present, demonstrated the general relevance and utility of a qualitative, structural examination of cognition among mentally retarded persons. From an analysis of structure as well as content, research evidence supports Inhelder's (1966) formulation that mental retardation is defined

as the failure to achieve formal operations at maturity, with fixations at lower cognitive stages representative of greater severity of mental retardation. Findings from cognitive-developmental research have thus not only expanded our knowledge of cognition, but have also identified alternate methods and strategies to assess cognitive functioning in the mentally retarded. Structural assessment, for example, can have as a primary objective, the differentiation of sensorimotor substage functioning among profoundly mentally retarded adults not readily differentiated on the basis of psychometric criteria. In such an instance the difference between measured IQ's of 10 and 15 may have little conceptual meaning, whereas the difference between primary and secondary circular reactions conveys meaning with conceptual as well as practical implications. Assessment of personal and social understanding may, for example, have practical utility by documenting levels of self-other differentiation in the process of planning community placement.

Recent findings from child development research and from studies with mentally retarded subjects suggest at least two emerging directions for future investigations of cognitive-developmental processes. One of these emerging research directions is that of more precise and systematic delineation of variables contributing to cognitive development. A second, and related, emerging research direction is that of investigations of the modifiability of cognition in mentally retarded individuals.

Unraveling the complexity of factors influencing performance of handicapped populations has been an important objective in efforts to delineate variables in cognitive growth. Representative of this effort is a study by Ilmer et al. (1981), which assessed object permanence in severely/profoundly handicapped children differentiated on the basis of motor ability level (low vs. high) and instructional prompt (verbal vs. combined verbal and physical guidance). The authors found evidence for the differential effectiveness of the combined prompt for the higher motor ability level group. Also focusing on object permanence characteristics of severely/profoundly mentally retarded children was a study by Silverstein et al. (1981). Three successive administrations of sensorimotor scales, six months apart, yielded test-retest correlation coefficients ranging from 0.67 to 0.87. These coefficients and minimal point change on the scales were seen as indicative of stability of these measures in this population. The above findings yield evidence regarding the stability and complexity of sensorimotor functioning in the severely mentally retarded. In this context, ordinal assessment of primary communication skills and responsiveness to physical and social objects may have particular value with children and adults functioning at very basic sensorimotor levels and can contribute to more comprehensive multivariate documentation strategies (Simeonsson et al., 1980).

The second emerging direction in research from a cognitive-developmental perspective is represented by investigations seeking to promote qualitative/structural change in retarded subjects. Sensorimotor gains have been found for mentally retarded infants by Brassell and Dunst (1978) following several months of intervention designed to foster object construct growth. Promoting transition to concrete operations thought has been the focus of several studies. Boersma and Wilton (1976) provided perceptual attention training to one of two randomly assigned groups of non-conserving EMR children. Not only was the training effective in promoting conservation performance, but differences in eye movements were observed to accompany conservation skills (i.e., more visual exploration, less perceptual centration). In another study Field (1974) found that a verbal rule approach was differentially effective over a learning set approach in training conservation of nonconserving EMR children. The modifiability of cognitive processes however appears to be a function of subject as well as task characteristics. Klein and Safford (1976), for example, found that a six-week intervention program focusing on classification skills did result in improved classification of representational materials such as toys, whereas transfer of such skills to nonrepresentational, abstract materials was limited. In another study involving TMR children Litrownik et al. (1978) compared the effectiveness of training, using a model demonstrating identity-equivalence conservation. While there was some evidence that training did contribute to performance gains, conservation skills were minimal and were not maintained after a three-week period. Finally, in a study seeking to train formal operations thought, Kahn (1974) compared the outcomes of EMR adolescents from middle and low SES background. Differential effects were found, in that none of the middle SES EMR subjects demonstrated formal thought, whereas successful performance was demonstrated by a number of the EMR adolescents from low SES background. These findings of differential modifiability of cognitive processes as a function of subject characteristics are consistent with Inhelder's (1966) proposed classification of mental retardation by severity levels and suggest alternative ways of matching individuals to programs.

Intervention efforts focusing on social understanding have been limited compared to research on non-social phenomena. A few studies, however, have experimentally manipulated social experiences to enhance social understanding of mentally retarded subjects. Perry and Cerreto (1977) investigated the effectiveness of social skills training through role playing of relevant behaviors. Borderline to severely mentally retarded young adults were randomly assigned to an experimental group, a contrast group (discussion) or a nontreatment control group. Predicted changes were found favoring subjects given training but differences between groups were of marginal significance. In the area of moral judgment, Rackman (1973) assigned 57 EMR adolescents to one of three groups to investigate the effectiveness of training in resolution of moral dilemmas. Although significant improvements were found for the training group initially, gains were not maintained at follow-up three months later.

Research based on cognitive-developmental theory has demonstrated the applicability of a qualitative approach to cognitive processes in mentally retarded persons. This approach assumes that development is reflected by successive transitions from sensorimotor to symbolic representations of reality and from centered to decentered thought. Given that a primary focus of education and habilitation programs for mentally retarded persons is to promote transitions from dependent toward independent functioning (Simeonsson et al., 1976), cognitive-developmental theory provides a useful framework for assessment and training efforts. As such, it can represent a mentally retarded person's understanding of physical, intrapersonal and interpersonal phenomena along common developmental gradients. In addition to the goal of charting the delays in development, it can also document the unique cognitive characteristics essential for individual program planning.

References

Abel, T. M. Moral judgments among subnormals. *Journal of Abnormal and Social Psychology*, 1941, **36**, 478.

Affleck, G. Role-taking ability and interpersonal conflict resolution among retarded young adults. *American Journal of Mental Deficiency*, 1975, **80**, 233–236. (a)

Affleck, G. Role-taking ability and the interpersonal competencies of retarded children. *American Journal of Mental Deficiency*, 1975, **80**, 312–316. (b)

Affleck, G. Role-taking ability and the interpersonal tactics of retarded children. *American Journal of Mental Deficiency*, 1976, **80**, 667–670.

Bearison, D. J., & Cassel. Cognitive decentration and social codes: Communicative effectiveness in young children from differing family contexts. *Developmental Psychology*, 1975, **11**, 29–31.

Blacher, J. Assessing social cognition in young retarded and non-retarded children. *American Journal of Mental Deficiency*, 1982, **86**, 473–484.

Blacher-Dixon, J., & Simeonsson, R. J. The effect of shared experience on role-taking performance in retarded children. *American Journal of Mental Deficiency*, 1978, **83**,

21–28.

Blacher-Dixon, J., & Simeonsson, R. J. Perspective-taking in retarded children: A one year followup. *American Journal of Mental Deficiency*, 1981. In press.

Boersma, F. J. & K. M. Wilton. Eye movements and conservation acceleration in mildly retarded children. *American Journal on Mental Deficiency*, 1976, **80**, 636–643.

Boland, S. K. Conservation tasks with retarded and non-retarded children. *Exceptional Children*, 1973, **40**, 209–211.

Brassell, W. R. & Dunst, C. J. Comparison of two procedures for fostering the development of the object construct. *American Journal of Mental Deficiency*, 1976, **80**, 523–528.

Brown, A. L. Conservation of quantity in normal, bright, and retarded children. *Child Development*, 1973, **44**, 376–379.

Cardozo, C. W., & Allen, R. M. Contribution of visual perceptual maturation to the ability to conserve. *American Journal of Mental Deficiency*, 1975, **79**, 701–704.

Cowan, P. A. *Piaget with feeling*. New York: Holt, Rinehart and Winston, 1978.

Damon, W. Why study social-cognitive development? *Human Development*, 1979, **22**, 206–211.

Detterman, D. K. Memory in the mentally retarded. In N. R. Ellis (Ed.), *Handbook of mental deficiency: Psychological theory and research*. (2nd ed.) Hillsdale, N.J.: Lawrence Erlbaum Associates, Pub., 1979.

Evans, R. C. Dream conception and reality testing in children. *Journal of the American Academy of Child Psychiatry*, 1973, **12**, 73–92.

Feffer, M. H. *Role-taking behavior in the mentally retarded*. (Final Report No. 42-2029). New York: Yeshiva University, 1970.

Field, D. Long-term effects of conservation training with educationally subnormal children. *Journal of Special Education*, 1974, **8**, 237–245.

Foye, H., & Simeonsson, R. J. Quantitative and qualitative analyses of moral reasoning in children, adolescents, and adults of similar mental age. *Journal of Pediatric Psychology*, 1979, **4**, 197–209.

Gardner, T. D., & Barnard, J. W. Intelligence and the factorial structure of person perception. *American Journal of Mental Deficiency*, 1969, **74**, 212–217.

Greenspan, S. Social intelligence in the retarded. In N. R. Ellis (Ed.), *Handbook of mental deficiency: Psychological theory and research*. (2nd ed.) Hillsdale, N.J.: Erlbaum, 1979.

Heal, L. Research strategies and research goals in the scientific study of the mentally subnormal. *American Journal of Mental Deficiency*, 1970, **75**, 10–19.

Houssiades, L. & Brown, L. B. The co-ordination of perspectives by mentally defective children. *Journal of Genetic Psychology*, 1967, **110**, 211–215.

Ilmer, S., Rynders, J., Sinclair, S. & Helfrich, D. Assessment of object permanence in severely handicapped students as a function of motor and prompting variables. *Journal of the Association for the Severely Handicapped*, 1981, **6**, 30–39.

Inhelder, B. Cognitive-developmental contributions to the diagnosis of some phenomena of mental deficiency. *Merrill-Palmer Quarterly*, 1966, **12**, 299–319.

Jordan, T. E. *The mentally retarded*. Columbus, Ohio: Charles E. Merrill Publishing Co., 1976.

Kahn, J. V. Training MER and intellectually average adolescents of low and middle SES for formal thought. *American Journal of Mental Deficiency*, 1974, **79**, 397–403.

Kleck, R. E. Issues in social effectiveness: The case of the mentally retarded. In M. Begab, & S. Richardson (Eds.), *The mentally retarded and society: A social science perspective*. Baltimore: University Park Press, 1975.

Klein, N. K., & Safford, P. L. Effects of representation level of materials on transfer of classification skills in TMR children. *Journal of Special Education*, 1976, **10**, 47–52.

Klein, N. K., & Safford, P. L. Application of Piaget's theory to the study of thinking of the mentally retarded: A review of research. *Journal of Special Education*, 1977, **11**, 201–216.

Kohlberg, L. Sage and sequence: The cognitive-developmental approach to socialization. In D. H. Goslin (Ed.) *Handbook of socialization theory and research*. Chicago: Rand McNally, 1969.

Laurendau, M., & Pinard, A. *Causal thinking in the child*. New York: International Universities Press Inc., 1962.

Litrownik, A. J., Franzini, L. R., Livingston, M. K., & Harvey, S. Developmental priority of identity conservation: Acceleration of identity and equivalence in normal and moderately retarded children. *Child Development*, 1978, **49**, 201–208.

Longhurst, T. M. Communication in retarded adolescents: Sex and intelligence level. *American Journal of Mental Deficiency*, 1974, **78**, 607–618.

McManis, D. L. Conservation of mass, weight, and volume by normal and retarded children. *American Journal of Mental Deficiency*, 1969, **73**, 762–767.

McManis, D. L. Conservation, seriation and transitivity performance by retarded and average individuals. *American Journal of Mental Deficiency*, 1970, **74**, 784–791.

Monson, L. B., Greenspan, S., & Simeonsson, R. J. Correlates of social competence in retarded children. *American Journal of Mental Deficiency*, 1979, **83**, 627–630.

Perry, J. E., & Krebs, D. Role-taking, moral development and mental retardation. *Journal of Genetic Psychology*, 1980, **136**, 95–108.

Perry, M. A., & Cerreto, M. C. Structured learning training of social skills for the retarded. *Mental Retardation*, 1977, **15**, 31–34.

Piaget, J. (1929) *The child's conception of the world*. Totowa, N.J.: Littlefield, Adams & Co., 1975.

Piaget, J. Piaget's theory. In P. H. Mussen (Ed.), *Carmichael's manual of child psychology*. (3rd ed.) Vol. 1. New York: Wiley, 1970.

Piaget, J., & Inhelder, B. Diagnosis of mental operations and theory of intelligence. *American Journal of Mental Deficiency*, 1947, **51**, 401–406.

Rackman, B. M. Improving moral judgments made by educable mentally retarded adolescents. New York: Teachers College, Columbia University. Dissertation, 1973.

Reiss, P. Implications of Piaget's developmental psychology for mental retardation. *American Journal of Mental Deficiency*, 1967, **72**, 361–369.

Rogers, S. Characteristics of the cognitive development of profoundly retarded children. *Child Development*, 1977, **48**, 837–843.

Rubin, K. J., & Orr, R. R. Spatial egocentrism in nonretarded and retarded children. *American Journal of Mental Deficiency*, 1974, **79**, 95–97.

Rueda, R., & Chan, K. S. Referential communication skill levels of moderately mentally retarded adolescents.

American Journal of Mental Deficiency, 1980, **85**, 45–52.

Schiefelbusch, R. L., Copeland, R. H., & Smith, J. O. (Eds.) *Language and mental retardation*. New York: Holt, Rinehart & Winston, Inc., 1967.

Secord, B. H., & Peevers, P. F. Developmental changes in attributions of descriptive concepts to persons. *Journal of Personality and Social Psychology*, 1973, **27**, 120–128.

Shantz, C. V. The development of social cognition. In E. M. Hetherington (Ed.), *Review of child development research*. Vol. 5. Chicago: University of Chicago Press, 1975.

Silverstein, A. B. Mental growth from six to sixty in an institutionalized mentally retarded sample. *Psychological Reports*, 1979, **45**, 643–646.

Simeonsson, R. J. Social competence. In J. Wortis (Ed.), *Mental retardation and developmental disabilities: An annual review*. X. New York: Brunner/Mazel, Inc., 1978. Pp. 130–171.

Simeonsson, R. J., Grunewald, K., & Scheiner, A. P. Piaget and normalization: Developmental humanism. *Research Exchange and Practice*, 1976, **2**, 299.

Simeonsson, R. J., Huntington, G. S., Parse, S. A. Expanding the developmental assessment of young handicapped children. *New Directions for Exceptional Children*, 1980, **3**, 51–74.

Simeonsson, R. J., Monson, L., & Blacher, J. Social understanding and mental retardation. In P. Brooks et al. (Eds.) *Learning cognition and mental retardation*. Baltimore: University Park Press, 1982.

Smeets, P. M. The influence of MA and CA on the attribution of life and life traits to animate and inanimate objects. *Journal of Genetic Psychology*, 1974, **124**, 17–27.

Smith, J. D. Perceptual decentering in EMR and nonretarded children. *American Journal of Mental Deficiency*, 1977, **81**, 499–501.

Weinstein, E. A. The development of interpersonal competence. In D. A. Goslin (Ed.), *Handbook of socialization theory and research*. Chicago: Rand McNally College Publishing Co., 1973.

Wilton, K. M., & Boersma, F. J. Conservation research with the mentally retarded. In N. R. Ellis (Ed.), *International review of research in mental retardation*. Vol. III. New York: Academic Press, 1974.

Wohlheuter, M. J., & Sindberg, R. M. Longitudinal development of object permanence in mentally retarded children: An exploring study. *American Journal of Mental Deficiency*, 1975, **79**, 513–518.

Woodward, M. The application of Piaget's theory to research in mental deficiency. In N. R. Ellis (Ed.), *Handbook of mental deficiency: Psychological theory and research*. New York: McGraw-Hill Book Co., 1963.

Woodward, M. Piaget's theory and the study of mental retardation. In N. R. Ellis (Ed.), *Handbook of mental deficiency: Psychological theory and research*. (2nd ed.) Hillsdale, N.J.: Lawrence Erlbaum Associates, Publishers, 1979.

Wooster, A. D. Formation of stable and discrete concepts of personality by normal and mentally retarded boys. *Journal of Mental Subnormality*, 1970, **16**, 24–28.

Zeaman, D., & House, B. J. A review of attention theory. In N. R. Ellis (Ed.), *Handbook of mental deficiency: Psychological theory and research*. (2nd ed.) Hillsdale, N.J.: Lawrence Erlbaum Associates, 1979.

PART VIII
METHODOLOGY

35 SOME TRENDS IN RESEARCH DESIGN*

Douglas K. Detterman

The purpose of this chapter is to examine trends in past mental retardation research and, if possible, to extrapolate those trends to make some prediction of future research directions in the area. This will be accomplished in two ways, as is the case for most historical analyses. First, artifacts reflecting historical development will be considered empirically. Primary artifacts in research are published research reports. General characteristics of these reports will be analyzed to determine whether there have been major changes in the way in which research is carried out.

The second method of historical investigation is far more subjective. It requires the analysis of historical artifacts in an effort to determine the motivations of those who produced them. What questions were mental retardation researchers attempting to answer? This form of analysis is obviously much more prone to bias, because it depends, to a large extent, on the views of the interpreter. Despite these problems, this form of analysis is the major source of historical insight.

The major focus of this chapter is on basic research. However, it is inevitable that some consideration be

given to applied issues, since there is not a clear dividing line between the two types of research. The discussion of applied research is confined to the first half of the chapter. When applied research is discussed, the purpose of the discussion is generally to differentiate it from basic research. The last half of this chapter is devoted to a detailed consideration of the questions asked and the methodology used in basic research.

A Comparison of Past Trends

Three periods were selected in order to investigate what researchers in mental retardation have actually done. These periods are 1951, 1976, and 1980. The last two periods were selected close together so that it might be possible to detect any recent changes in research trends if these are present. Estimating that it takes a minimum of two years for research to be published, reports appearing in 1976 would have been begun in 1974 or before and, likewise, those in 1980 would have been started in 1978. These time periods are particularly significant because they are the times when Federal court cases had large effects on access to subject populations.

In addition to problems with the availability of subjects, another trend that occurred during this period was an increased perception that mental retardation

* Preparation of this manuscript was partially supported by Grants HD-07176 and HD-15518 from the National Institute of Child Health and Human Development. I would like to thank David Caruso, Peter Legree, and John Mayer for suggestions for improving this chapter.

Table 35.1. Selected Characteristics of Mental Retardation Research
Reported in the American Journal of Mental Deficiency
for Three Periods

CHARACTERISTIC	PERIOD		
	1951	1976	1980
Report			
Number of reports surveyed	14	25	25
Proportion reporting basic research	1.00	.79	.67
Number of experiments reported	14	28	30
Mean number of citations per report	7.64	16.60	18.37
Mean number of tables per report	3.21	1.92	1.93
Mean number of figures per report	.29	1.56	.48
Subjects			
Proportion of experiments reporting			
N for MR subjects	.93	1.00	.86
Mean age for MR subjects	.71	.86	.83
Mean IQ for MR subjects	.79	.61	.70
N for normal subjects	.21	.36	.60
Mean age for normal subjects	.14	.36	.40
Mean IQ for normal subjects	.14	.11	.13
Reporting experiments demographics			
N of MR subjects (except N > 500)	74.00	43.73	49.27
Mean age of MR subjects (years)	14.93	15.70	17.95
Mean IQ of MR subjects	65.18	58.70	57.34
N of normal subjects (except N > 500)	25.00	62.90	41.71
Mean age of normal subjects (years)	10.09	13.14	12.57
Mean IQ of normal subjects	99.75	100.70	101.32
Variables reported			
Mean number independent variables	3.50	3.70	3.63
Mean number dependent variables	1.21	2.17	2.03
Descriptive statistics reported			
Means	.71	.71	.80
Standard deviations	.43	.25	.47
Correlations	.29	.11	.23
Inferential statistics reported			
Analysis of variance	.21	.68	.70
t-tests	.29	.07	.10
Correlations	.29	.07	.07
Factor analysis	.00	.07	.07
Multiple regression	.00	.07	.10
Additional analyses	.57	.39	.53

research was closely related to individual differences research in cognitive psychology. That is, there was a growing awareness that research conducted with the mentally retarded was generally relevant to experimental psychologists and not solely relevant to mental retardation. From about 1960 onward, basic researchers had been attempting to achieve such a confluence, but those efforts did not reach fruition until the mid- to late-1970s. Until that time, research in mental retardation had been an isolated, and, in my opinion, undervalued endeavor.

A 25- rather than 50-year period was selected, because research in mental retardation was reasonably constant in number of published reports during the first half of this century (Detterman, 1977). Changes

began to occur sometime after World War II. Thus, 1951 is approximately in the middle of a transitional period in mental retardation research from a period of level production to one of substantial growth, at least in psychological research. The year 1951 seems most appropriate as a benchmark against which to gauge the effects of this growth.

In order to have some objective data concerning a sample of what research in mental retardation consists of, up to 25 reports were randomly selected from the *American Journal of Mental Deficiency*, which is one of the most prominent journals in the field, for each of the three periods under consideration. (For 1951, only 14 studies met the criteria for inclusion.) Review articles were excluded, so that comparisons across time periods reflect research actually being done. That is, these comparisons do not reflect differences in the amount of research being conducted. Rather, they are an attempt to see whether the reported research during these time periods differs in any important way.

Table 35.1 shows the main results of the survey. Results are grouped by the major sections of research reports. The first portion of the table presents general characteristics of the reports. The following sections report either the proportion of studies reporting a particular characteristic or the mean value reported by study. Note that these statistics are by study and not report. When a report included more than one study, each was considered separately. Mean values include only those studies that reported the characteristic as indicated by proportion reporting.

The focus of this table is on general characteristics that could be tabulated for each experiment reported. A more detailed analysis of experimental characteristics would certainly be possible, but, given the small sample size, it would probably not be very instructive. Therefore, in the following discussion, no attention will be given to statistical significance of obtained differences. Instead, an attempt will be made to find consistent trends.

Early Trends: 1951

Inspection of Table 35.1 indicates that there are far more similarities than differences between research reported in 1951 and the later two years. It should, however, be remembered that data for 1951 include all of the 14 reports that could be considered psychological research. There was obviously a much lower rate of production during this period.

The most obvious differences between 1951 and the later periods relate to what could be called sophistication. Studies reported in later periods tended to have a larger number of dependent variables, use more complex statistics more frequently, and contain a larger number of citations. Reports during the later two periods also showed a slight tendency to include more than one study. Although 1951 reports contain more tables than later periods, descriptive statistics do not seem to be any more fully reported. In summary, it seems reasonable to conclude that even superficial characteristics of reported research reflect an increasing sophistication in mental retardation research.

Recent Trends

Comparisons of the years 1976 and 1980 show far more similarities than differences. Indeed, at first glance the factors postulated earlier to affect research during these periods seem to have had little effect on these data. There are, however, some trends worth examining. The first obvious difference in the table is the proportion of basic research reported in the two years. In 1976, 79% of research reported was considered basic, but by 1980 only 67% was basic. Basic research was defined as any research which did not answer a question of immediate, practical concern. Classification of research as applied or basic was done by an advanced undergraduate, so that it would be as free as possible from my own biases.

The high proportion of basic research reported for both years is partly a function of the criterion adopted by the rater. To be an applied study, an immediate application had to be apparent. For example, one study on the effects of physician counseling of Down syndrome parents was classified as basic because it was designed to assess the effect of current practices rather than the modification of those practices.

To determine whether the criterion used to classify basic and applied research affected differences in amount of basic research for the two years, I reclassified studies according to a more lenient criterion. A study was considered to be applied if it had immediate, practical applications or suggested such applications. According to this criterion, 68% of the experiments in 1976 reported basic research, but only 40% in 1980. When research intermediate between basic and applied research is counted as applied research, the decline in basic research becomes even more pronounced.

There are several possible reasons for this decline in basic research. One is that basic researchers were attempting to promote the applied implications of their research, no matter how distant those applications, although the experiments surveyed do not seem to support this argument. Another possibility is that availability of subjects has more severely affected basic researchers than applied researchers. The characteristics of subjects reported for these two years have not markedly changed. In fact, a larger mean number of mentally retarded subjects was used in experiments reported in 1980 than in those reported in 1976.

Of course, this difference in sample size is confounded with changes in types of research; it could still be possible that subjects are less available for certain kinds of research. To test this possibility, the sample sizes for basic experiments (using the author's definition of basic) for the two periods were tabulated. For experiments reported in 1976, mean sample size was 50.11, but for those reported in 1980 it was 27.92.

Is the decline in the amount of basic research simply an artifact? It may well be, but probably not.

Researchers in mental retardation to whom I have spoken are not surprised by this finding. It agrees with their subjective impressions that theoretically motivated studies are declining. What does surprise them is the magnitude of the decline and the ease with which it can be documented.

Other findings for the years 1976 and 1980 are consistent with the conclusion that basic research is declining. The fact that fewer experiments report sample sizes for mentally retarded subjects (100 vs. 86%) does not reflect an increase in poor reporting. Rather, it reflects the fact that some of the studies used populations that were not primarily identified as mentally retarded. In 1980, it was more common to find the population defined in terms of the continuum of intellectual functioning than on the basis of the mental retardation-normal dichotomy. This trend is also reflected in the increased reporting of characteristics of normal subject samples.

Movement away from dichotomous subject samples to those reflecting the normal distribution may be a result of difficulty in obtaining subjects from traditional sources. The trend probably not only reflects political difficulties in obtaining subjects but also the *changes in residence* of some mentally retarded subjects. (Only a small percentage of MR people were ever institutionalized. Deinstitutionalization has only broken up large concentrations of MR people at various functional levels. The large institutions are a bit smaller today and have lower functioning populations.) I believe the conceptualization of mental retardation as a point on a continuum of intellectual functioning is a positive development and should be encouraged, although it will undoubtedly make research more expensive. However, a psychology based on the institutionalized mentally retarded is even less representative than one based on the college sophomore. Considering the full range of intellectual development rather than just the retarded-nonretarded dichotomy is certainly a potentially more fruitful approach.

A finding that is probably not explained by the decline in basic research is the increased reporting of descriptive statistics and the trend toward more complete and elaborate use of inferential statistics. While these effects are small ones, they reflect changes over a four-year period, and it is to be hoped that they will continue.

In summary, a consideration of research reported in 1951, 1976, and 1980 suggests several trends in mental retardation research. First, research between 1951 and the later two periods has shown a substantial increase in sophistication, even when fairly superficial characteristics of that research are considered. Second, when recent short-term trends are considered by com-

paring research reported in 1976 and 1980, a disturbing decline in the amount of basic research reported is discovered. One reason for this decline may be difficulty in obtaining mentally retarded participants but it is doubtful that this entirely accounts for the finding.

What Are the Questions Being Asked?

In this section, a more subjective approach will be taken to attempt to determine what questions mental retardation researchers have been trying to answer with their research. First, an attempt will be made to determine whether there is a small set of questions that generally characterize research in the area. Next, finer gradations of these major questions will be considered. In the following section, the methods used to answer these questions will be discussed.

To attempt to characterize research in mental retardation in terms of a few questions that researchers in the area could endorse as typifying the goal of their research is not an easy thing to do. There are many questions that any particular piece of research poses simultaneously. The attempt here will be to find as few superordinate categories as possible which are capable of subsuming all of these questions.

Though the major focus of this chapter is on basic research, initial consideration will be given to applied research. The questions asked by applied research must be considered to understand how they are different from the questions asked by basic research. Following the discussion of applied research, basic research questions will be considered.

Applied Research

One question that provides an obvious motivation for a good portion of the research done in mental retardation, and for nearly all applied research, is, "How can we make life better for the mentally retarded?" This is quite a simple question on the surface, but as anyone who has spent time doing research in mental retardation knows, it turns out to be very complex. Indeed, more effort has been devoted to debates on this issue than any other, even though only about half of the research in the area is done on this question. When published articles which are not primary reports of research are taken into account, the space devoted to this question certainly dwarfs the amount used to present research results.

What makes this question so difficult is that it is really two questions in one. The first question is a moral one: What constitutes a better life? The second question is a technological one: Given the definition of a "better life," what is the most efficient way to accomplish it? The emphasis of this second question, as for most technological questions, is on obtaining a currently useful answer. To complicate matters further, these questions are not independent but interact, especially when resource and knowledge limitations are taken into account.

The portion of this two part question that is the most difficult to resolve is the moral aspect. At about the turn of this century, there was no doubt in anyone's mind that institutional living was the way to provide a better life for the mentally retarded. An institution would provide the specialized services required by this special segment of the population. Now the prevailing attitude is that the mentally retarded should be provided with as close to a "normal" environment as possible. Each of these positions can, and have, been argued from a utopian perspective quite independent of what is being done or what it is technologically possible to do. That is, utopian arguments can be advanced independently of research findings.

Proponents of the Institutional Movement defined a better life for the mentally retarded as access to required services in an emotionally supportive environment physically tailored to their special needs. A "better" life, according to this argument, was to have access to all of the concentrated technology that could be made available for self-improvement and, failing restoration to normality, to live comfortably among peers in an environment whose complexity was suitable to the individual's ability level. Thus, a better life for the non-MR population was one of the primary early motivators of institutions in this century.

On the other hand, proponents of normalization argue that it is essential for the mentally retarded to remain in the community among family and friends. For them, the "better" life is defined by a sense of being an integral part of the larger society. Every person has an inalienable right to be an important part of the social fabric and if he cannot take his place in society alone, society must provide the support for him to do so.

It is well to remember that these are moral positions, as are any positions that state that something is "better" or "best." It is not possible now, nor will it ever be possible, to answer these questions using research. The issue raised by these two alternatives is whether it is better to live in a world tailored to your needs or to live in the same world as everyone else. In even more basic terms, the argument is whether an individual acquires value by individual accomplishment or by his contribution to society. Normalization places the greatest emphasis on an individual's relationship to society, while the Institutional Movement emphasized the structuring of society to provide individual

self-fulfillment. The moral question of the relationship between an individual and society is a very old one. It is unlikely that the general question will be resolved any time in the near future and even more unlikely that the special case involving the mentally retarded will be resolved any sooner.

It is sometimes difficult for technologists to appreciate the moral implications of the questions they ask. The reason for this is that research results often have important implications for the practical implementation of these ideal positions. Whether someone can be taught basic social skills is bound to be an important variable in determining how easily he will assume his rightful place in society. While the philosopher may always argue about the "best of all possible worlds," the technologist may only consider the practicality of all possible worlds. It is often disconcerting to the technologist that consideration of the practicality of alternative positions plays little or no role in deciding on the positions' relative merits. This is particularly true in the social sciences.

While technologists will never be able to provide definitive answers to moral questions through research, they can decide on the current practical implications of these questions. It is possible to determine, through research, whether institutionalization or community placement lead to greater educational achievement, more social development, or greater contentment. They may also determine the cost of each of the alternatives and develop new technologies to make each more effective. However, research will never decide which position is "best" in an ultimate sense.

Despite recent controversy, I believe that there is one moral question that dominates all others. That is the degree to which society feels an obligation to provide assistance to the mentally retarded person. In my opinion, the answer to this question has been ambiguous and cyclical. Until there is endorsement of the principle that the less able are deserving of the unwavering support of society, fair tests of technological solutions from any moral perspective will be difficult to obtain.

Basic Research

The second major question addressed by mental retardation research has no immediate practical implications. That question is, "Why are some people smarter than others?" This question has been at the heart of nearly all basic research in mental retardation in one form or another since the beginning of such research. The basic goal of this research has been to find a satisfactory explanation for the observed differences between mentally retarded and normal subjects. As the next section shows, the approach to answering this question has changed dramatically as has the criterion for what would constitute a satisfactory explanation, but the question has not changed.

The larger question of why some people are smarter than others has manifested itself in a number of more specific questions that generally focus on a particular aspect of the real problem. These more specific questions have been so frequently debated that there is a tendency to dismiss them as pseudo-issues. However, their persistent ability to trouble researchers suggests that they are far more than that. Perhaps the tendency to classify them as pseudo-issues is simply a reaction to the difficulty of finding adequate answers.

The following sections will consider a number of specific questions that have been almost continually debated. These are: difference vs. developmental approaches, number of causes of differences in intelligence, biological vs. environmental influences, the degree of modifiability of intellectual functioning, and the level of analysis required to understand intelligence. The current status of each of these specific questions will be summarized and an attempt will be made to suggest directions research on these questions might take in the future. During the discussion of these specific issues it should be kept in mind that each is simply a facet of the larger question of why some people are smarter than others.

Difference vs. Developmental Approaches

The difference vs. development controversy is a most familiar one in mental retardation. The developmental position (Zigler, 1969) proposes that mental retardation represents retarded development. Subjects matched for mental age, according to this position, should show very nearly equivalent performances of cognitive tasks. On the other hand, resulting differences in performance in cognitive tasks are explained by the effects slow development has on other processes. Thus, any differences between mentally retarded and normal individuals at the same MA might be explained by motivational or personality differences resulting from slowed development and its sequela.

This position has been referred to by its critics as the "Little Man" theory of mental retardation because it suggests that mentally retarded persons are not qualitatively different than normal persons. This position characterizes differences in mental ability much as the effects of differences in height might be characterized from a psychological perspective. What is important is not that people vary in height but the effects this difference has on psychological functioning.

The difference position (Ellis, 1969), on the other hand, states that there is one or more differences between mentally retarded and normal persons which cause their differences in ability. A difference theorist would argue that the appropriate comparison is between chronologically matched mentally retarded and normal persons because that is what defines mental retardation and it is this difference that research should account for. The goal of research, then, is to provide a catalog of more basic "differences" which are predictive of differences in intellectual ability.

The major difficulty with the developmental position is that there must be some cause or causes for every effect. This position would seem to ignore those causes and, instead, focus on the effects of the resulting differences on other spheres of psychological functioning. The developmental position, as I understand it, regards differences in intellectual ability as an independent variable whose effects should be understood. The difference position, on the other hand, regards differences in intellectual ability as a dependent variable for which the cause must be specified (Detterman, 1974). Certainly, regarding differences in intellectual ability as either an independent or dependent variable both result in legitimate, researchable questions. I simply believe that the Difference position's regard for intellectual differences as an independent variable results in questions that are more fundamental to understanding why some people are smarter than others.

A further objection to the developmental position is that mental age matches are inappropriate because they match subjects on the variable of chief interest, intellectual ability, and thereby eliminate the possibility of finding the differences which may exist.

Developmental theorists, on the other hand, raise a number of objections to the difference position. They suggest that regarding people as mentally retarded in development rather than defective produces far more positive social attitudes. This is no small matter, because the major difficulties faced by retarded persons concern social adjustment.

Furthermore, they would argue that, even though difference theorists have been looking for the defects which produce mental retardation, they have not been particularly successful. Indeed, as will be discussed later, a major finding resulting from research conducted within this theoretical framework is that chronologically matched mentally retarded subjects show deficits in nearly everything when compared to normals (Detterman, 1979). In response to these criticisms, difference theorists would point out that social attitudes do not determine the correctness of scientific endeavors and that just because something has not yet been accomplished does not mean that it cannot be.

Number of Causes

Another major issue has been common in mental retardation as well as all other branches of psychology that study individual differences. This controversy concerns whether differences in intelligence are produced by a single cause or by a set of different causes. The debate has been most persistent in the psychometric and factor analytic literature.

When Spearman (1904) first set about to analyze a set of mental tests, he noted that there were positive correlations between all of the tests. He suggested that these moderate correlations among different tests represented a general factor (cause) measured by all of the tests which he referred to as *g*, or general intellectual ability. The opposite position is represented by the work of Thurstone (1938), who attempted to find a set of independent, uncorrelated factors, each represented by separate tests.

The same traditions are represented today, in slightly elaborated form, by the work of Guilford (1967) and Cattell (1971), respectively. More recently this argument has taken another form. Jensen (1979) has suggested that choice reaction time is a good representative of *g*. He has shown that measures of choice reaction time are moderately to highly correlated with the general intellectual factor derived from factor analysis. He suggests that choice reaction time is a measure of mental speed or efficiency and that this factor may be the chief cause in differences in intellectual ability. The independent factors approach has also been employed with basic experimental tasks by Carroll (1980). He has presented evidence for the operation of 10 independent factors represented by different experimental tasks traditionally considered to be tests of perception, memory, and learning.

The same issue arises in the study of mental retardation. For a number of years, researchers have been searching for one or more deficits that could account for mental retardation. Most researchers have parsimoniously sought a single deficit. A recent example is the work of Belmont and Butterfield (e.g., Belmont, Butterfield, & Ferretti, in press). They suggest that differences in intellectual ability can be accounted for by differences in executive processing, that part of the information processing system which selects and controls strategy use. However, when all of the work of individual investigators is put together, it

would appear that they have been highly successful in isolating deficits. Mentally retarded persons show deficits in nearly every aspect of intellectual functioning. Accounting for all of these observed deficits in terms of a single variable may seem to be parsimonious but may not be practical. There will certainly be greater attention paid to this issue in mental retardation in the future.

Biological versus Environmental Influences

Perhaps one of the most sharply debated issues in all of psychological research is the degree to which biological factors determine intellectual capability. The point has received particular attention since Jensen (1969) suggested that the high heritability of intelligence might account for the ineffectiveness of compensatory education programs. Researchers in mental retardation have not been particularly active participants in this debate, perhaps because they have never taken extreme positions on the issue.

There is a good reason for this moderate position. The mentally retarded are composed of a significant number, though not a majority, of cases whose intellectual impairment can be directly traced to a biological cause. Furthermore, even in those cases where no specific biological cause can be identified, familial factors are frequently potential contributors. To balance this trend, researchers in mental retardation have actively pursued environmental influences on intelligence in a more systematic fashion than any other discipline. Unfortunately, this research has not resulted in many systematic statements concerning the role of environmental influences on intellectual development. In fact, the only theory I know of which presents a systematic, quantitative description of environmental influences is the confluence model (Zajonc & Markus, 1975).

What has resulted from the extensive research on environmental effects is a large set of potential variables, each accounting for only a few percent of total variance. Even the confluence model, which makes quite precise predictions on large data sets, accounts for only a few percentage points of total variance. It would seem that if systematic environmental models are developed, it will be in terms of numerous small effects.

While there are well worked out theories about the heritability of intelligence, we know next to nothing about the biological mechanisms that might account for these differences. Theories about the way brain functioning might account for mental retardation or even about what parts of the brain might be involved in intellectual functioning are nearly nonexistent. Recent efforts by John (1977) have focused on using electrophysiological indicators of brain functioning as diagnostic tools, and such efforts may become more common in the future. However, well developed biological theories may have to await more specific definitions of intellectual functioning.

Degree of Modifiability

An issue quite separate from, but often confused with, the biological vs. environmental contributions to intelligence is the degree to which intelligence can be modified. It is often thought that if a characteristic has a strong biological basis, it cannot be modified. Actually, all evidence would seem to indicate that biological characteristics are the most easily modified. I know of a few cases in which planned changes in environments have produced unambiguously positive changes. On the other hand, examples of positive biological interventions are too numerous to mention. Indeed, the success of modern medical technology is dependent almost entirely on biological interventions.

The issue of modifiability has been most debated within mental retardation with respect to the effects of early educational intervention (e.g., Caruso & Detterman, 1981; Garber & Heber, 1982; Ramey, McPhee, & Yeates, 1982). The main issue is not whether, but how much, intelligence can be increased through environmental intervention. This is an important issue because a good theory of intelligence must not only describe what intelligence is but also predict how and how much it can be changed. The only theoretical position I am familiar with that actually makes such quantitative predictions is the genetic model (Jensen, 1973).

It is unlikely that the degree to which intelligence can be modified will be decided any time in the near future. However, as society becomes increasingly complex, this issue will certainly become more important. Certainly there is some threshold of social complexity beyond which a civilization of a given mean intelligence cannot pass. We are probably not yet near that threshold, but as we approach it researchers outside of mental retardation will become more concerned with this issue. Since our only choices are to modify the individuals composing society or the social environment and each of these alternatives will probably have different social and economic costs, a large number of ethical questions will be raised by the alternatives developed for the modifiability of intelligence.

Level of Analysis

Another question of significance which has motivated researchers in mental retardation is the selection of the appropriate level of analysis for best understanding differences in intelligence. While this question has been a persistent philosophical one, it has not had many practical implications, because behavioral analyses have been the chief instrument for understanding human intelligence. Research conducted from a biological perspective has been more concerned with finding conditions associated with an impairment in intellectual functioning than with attempting to explain why such conditions impair intellectual functioning. Indeed, the literature is strangely silent on why it is a particular syndrome, for example Down syndrome, should lead to a reduction in intellectual performance. Certainly there is no systematic theory to suggest how all of the various identified syndromes which lead to mental retardation have their effect.

It must be expected that such theories will be developed. There are two potential sequences for the development of these theories. First, it is possible that biological theories will require well developed behavioral theories. That is, behavioral parameters of intellectual functioning will have to be well specified before they can be identified at the biological level. A second possibility is that more molecular theories will be developed independently of behavioral theories. In this case, the two levels of explanation may conflict. I suspect that the first possibility is the more likely since it would seem difficult to identify the biological basis of a behavior which is not well defined.

Methodologies in Basic Research

The focus of this chapter is on basic research. The topic to be considered in this section is how researchers have gone about answering the questions they have posed (as discussed in the previous section). As will be shown, specification of what would provide a satisfactory answer to the question, "Why are some people smarter than others?" has changed significantly. Those changes have been reflected in changes in methodology.

In fact, the basic question has been answered several times in various forms. Each time it has been answered, it has been reformulated to reflect increasing sophistication. Thus, while the ultimate question of researchers in mental retardation has remained the same, the concensus concerning the adequate answer to that question has changed drastically.

Early Research

The goal of early researchers in mental retardation was simply to find a measure that would represent degrees of intelligence. It was the belief of these researchers that once such a measure was found, the question of why some people were smarter than others would be adequately answered. This assumption is well represented in the work of Binet, though the work of others, such as Galton or Cattell, could as easily be used as an illustration.

Before developing the intelligence test, Binet had been what we would today call a developmental cognitive psychologist. He had done research in the areas of perception, memory, and language (Matarazzo, 1972). He had conducted substantial amounts of this research with his own children and with children in public schools and he had founded a journal devoted to this type of research. The theoretical foundations for the test of intelligence he later developed were clearly presented in terms of cognitive abilities he thought should be represented by such a test (Brody & Brody, 1972). These abilities are not very different from the sorts of abilities current researchers suggest be involved in intellectual functioning (e.g., Carroll, 1980).

The history of the development of the Binet test of intelligence is well known and need not be repeated here. However, that Binet thought his test would provide an explanation of differences in intellectual ability has generally not been acknowledged. This is clear, though, from at least two aspects of the test's development. First, the test was theoretically grounded. Therefore, successful development of the test could be regarded as support for Binet's theory of intelligence. Second, it is clear that Binet intended to put his test to immediate practical applications suggesting that he felt successful development of such a test would support its theoretical underpinnings.

The society of which Binet was a founder and member was shocked by the treatment given the mentally retarded in France and felt that France was losing its international position of leadership in the area. To remedy this, they drafted a resolution to the French Ministry of Public Instruction. One part of that resolution proposed the development of an intelligence test for the express purpose of differentiating children who would require additional educational help from those who were fully capable of taking advantage of the educational system as it existed. A second part of this resolution proposed the establishment of a special education demonstration project that would provide help to children identified by the intelligence test as needing it. Both parts of the resolution were adopted

by the French Ministry of Public Instruction and The Society was given responsibility for putting them into effect. Thus, it is clear that Binet fully expected that his test would not only be diagnostic but also prescriptive.

It is clear from our perspective that Binet was remarkably successful at developing a diagnostic instrument that would differentiate between the mentally retarded and nonretarded. It is also clear that the test was not, unfortunately, prescriptive. Simply being able to predict the degree to which a person would succeed in school did not provide the means for altering that prognosis.

Cataloging Capabilities

The development of the intelligence test was greeted with enthusiasm in this country, at least in some circles. Goddard, at the Vineland Institute, put it to immediate use as a classification device (Kanner, 1964). Once researchers had convinced themselves that the Binet test could make more accurate classifications than subjective impressions, the next very natural question to ask was what characteristics were associated with differences in test scores. This question produced a substantial body of research that made simple comparisons on a number of characteristics between individuals who scored high and low on the test. Such characteristics as the degree of family resemblance, type of environment, and presence of physical pathology were thoroughly investigated.

The cataloging of differences resulted in the establishment of functional relationships between intelligence and a number of other variables. For example, it was shown that the mentally retarded could learn and remember material in experimental situations but that they did so with more difficulty than subjects of normal intelligence. These findings seem naive to us now but were quite important at the time and often contradicted popular notions about the mentally retarded. Such findings were an important first step toward understanding intellectual functioning. The problem was that showing a single difference between groups did not indicate that the particular variable under consideration affected the mentally retarded any differently than normals. It only showed that the two groups were different. These differences could as easily be explained on the basis of differences in past experience or differences in psychological processes. For any demonstrated difference between groups, there was a large number of potential explanations.

The cataloging of differences did answer the question of why some people are smarter than others at one level of explanation. It demonstrated which areas of functioning were good candidates for further investigation. It did not, however, provide a sufficiently detailed account of those differences to be explanatory in any scientifically satisfactory sense.

The Academic Pursuit of Individual Differences

The cataloging of differences took place largely outside of academic institutions. At about the same time that the intelligence test was brought to the United States, academic psychologists were busy pursuing the relationships among "mental tests" derived from a different tradition. Galton (1883) had been the founder of this second tradition and his mental tests consisted of very basic tests of psychological functioning and measures of physical characteristics. The mental tests consisted of measures of reaction time, simple perceptual tasks, and basic measures of memory. This tradition of attempting to relate basic processes to intellectual functioning was brought to the United States by James McKeen Cattell (1890).

Tuddenham (1963) has described the unfortunate history of this movement in the United States. There is no doubt that there was substantial interest in the development of mental tests of basic psychological processes. Whipple (1910) published a volume of these tests and by 1915 his manual had grown to two volumes. This interest was short. The main reason for the sudden decline seems to have been two studies reporting negative results.

Sharp was a student of Titchner with an interest in mental tests. She tested seven graduate students on a number of tests designed to measure memory, attention, and discrimination among other basic processes. Her results (Sharp, 1898) showed no relationship between the tests and academic performance. Critics failed to realize that little else could be expected from her small, highly selected sample of subjects.

The second negative study was reported by Wissler (1901). He was a student of Cattell at Columbia. Cattell had collected data on a group of entering freshmen with the plan of relating their test performance to their subsequent academic performance at graduation. While he was waiting for students to graduate, Cattell described this study to groups of teachers and administrators from around the country who came to the Mecca of modern education as the study which would be the model for modern scientific educational practice. It was, therefore, somewhat embarrassing for Cattell to find, when the data were finally analyzed, that the correlations between mental tests and grades were in the low to moderate range. The data were given to Wissler to report alone without the coauthorship of Cattell.

Wissler's conclusions were not entirely negative: "This general negative statement is likely to impress the reader in such a way that he will feel disposed to declare that psychological tests are of no value, and that the time spent in making them is mere waste. The writer can not share in such a feeling" (Wissler, 1901, p. 55). Despite Wissler's conclusions, such positive expectations had been developed about the study that the results were regarded as completely negative.

The effect of these two studies combined was to suppress the study of intellectual functioning in academic environments, except in a very limited way, until sometime after the middle of this century. The study of intelligence was not considered a potentially fruitful endeavor.

Interactions

About 1960, interest in the study of mental retardation and intellectual functioning began to grow once again. The methodological difficulties inherent in a simple cataloging of differences quickly became apparent to this new wave of researchers trained in the rigorous Hullian tradition. They suggested that understanding mental retardation would require showing that some variables had different effects on mentally retarded persons than on normal persons. Furthermore, at some level of the variable, the two groups would have to perform identically to show that the demonstrated differences were not due to differences in past experience or other potentially confounded variables. Thus, the minimum requirement for finding differences between mentally retarded and normal groups was the demonstration of an interaction with the two groups performing equally at one level of the independent variable and differently at another (Baumeister, 1967; Cronbach, 1957; Ellis, 1963).

A good illustration of the application of this methodology is Ellis' (1963) Stimulus Trace Deficit Theory or the Zeaman and House (1963) Attention Theory. In the Ellis theory, retarded subjects are viewed as deficient in integrity of the central nervous system, which produces reduced stimulus trace persistence. This results in more rapid forgetting of stimulus material by retarded than by normal subjects. Thus, an interaction between intellectual status and retention interval is predicted. Retarded and normal subjects should be equivalent when tested for immediate retention, but because retarded persons lose material from memory more quickly than normal persons, they should show increasingly poorer performance as the retention interval grows longer.

There were numerous tests of the Stimulus Trace Theory. The results were generally mixed but the major problem with these tests was methodological. The way in which the theory was tested allowed numerous alternative explanations of the obtained results. Clearly, a more elaborate theoretical framework was required.

Box Psychology

As tests of theories predicting simple interactions proliferated, it became clear that a single variable was not sufficient to capture the complexity of all of the new findings. Information processing models of memory and learning were coming into fashion and were replacing the earlier S-R models that had dominated the field for several decades. These information processing models represented the flow of information through the mind as a series of boxes, each box representing a separate stage or process. Researchers in mental retardation quickly adopted and modified the existing models, seeing in them the potential for representing the complexity they had been discovering.

Perhaps one of the best examples of a box model is that proposed by Ellis (1970). According to this model, information flowed from a very short-term memory to primary memory to secondary memory and finally to tertiary memory. Each memory store was represented by a box and each box could be operationally defined. The stores were differentiated by their capacity, mechanism of forgetting, and other characteristics. The processes for moving information from store to store were also specified. Tests of this model suggested that it was rehearsal, the mechanism for moving information from primary to secondary memory and for maintaining it in primary memory, that was deficient in mentally retarded subjects. This was supported chiefly by the demonstration of an interaction between intellectual level and portions of the serial position curve which operationally defined primary and secondary memory. Those parts representing primary memory showed little difference between mentally retarded and normal groups, while portions representing secondary memory showed large differences.

Although box psychology offered a method for developing more elaborated models of mental functioning, these models were still tested with the interaction approach. Numerous tests of the Ellis model and others like it led to the conclusion that everything in the information processing system of the mentally retarded was deficient (Detterman, 1979). This finding was most disconcerting because it produced no greater understanding of why some people were smarter than others than had the cataloging of simple differences.

One approach to resolving this problem was to postulate higher-order processes whose deficiencies

were expressed in every part of the system. An example of such a model is the one proposed by Belmont and Butterfield (see, for example Belmont, Butterfield, & Ferretti, 1982). They suggested that the rehearsal deficit demonstrated by Ellis was simply a special case of a more general deficit. They localized this deficit to a box called Executive Processing, which was responsible for the development and selection of information processing strategies, rehearsal being one example of such a strategy. But since Executive Processing supervised the flow of information throughout the entire system, the deficit would be observed in every part of the system.

System Psychology

Chapman and Chapman (1973, 1974) have suggested an alternate interpretation for the finding of such a large number of deficits using the interaction approach with box models. They suggest that many of the findings are artifactual. The reason for this is that when absolute level of performance changes so does sensitivity to differences between groups. This change in sensitivity is quite independent of floor and ceiling effects which mental retardation researchers had been well aware of for some time (Baumeister, 1967).

As an example, suppose we gave a vocabulary test to groups of retarded and normal subjects. All subjects are required to give a synonym to the test word and their response is graded either right or wrong. After administration, data for both groups are combined and each item is scored according to the number of subjects passing it. Now we examine the items which half of the combined group of subjects pass. It is these items of moderate difficulty for which we will find the largest difference between groups. The absolute difference between number of normal and retarded subjects passing will be larger than for either easier or harder items. The reason for this is that test items of moderate difficulty are more reliable and, therefore, more discriminating between groups.

The relationship between difficulty and reliability or discriminating power has serious implications for the interaction approach. Suppose that we compare mentally retarded and normal groups on items which, for both groups combined, were found to be either very difficult or moderately difficult. We would find larger differences between them for the moderately difficult items because they are more reliable than the very difficult items. Since items of moderate difficulty show a larger difference between groups than very difficult items, we would conclude that as items become easier, mentally retarded subjects show an increasing deficit.

However, if we compared the two groups on items

of moderate difficulty with easy items, we would come to the opposite conclusion. As with difficult items, items of moderate difficulty are more reliable, hence more discriminating, than easy items. Finally, if we compared groups of normal and mentally retarded subjects on items which are either easy or difficult for both groups combined, we could well find no difference between groups if the easy and difficult items are equal in reliability and so discriminate equally between groups.

Because reliability changes with task difficulty, the interaction approach is highly subject to artifactual results. Chapman and Chapman suggest a resolution to this problem. Their suggestion is simple in principle, but difficult to carry out. They suggest that two independent variables be equated at two separate points for groups of normal subjects on reliability and difficulty. Next groups of retarded subjects are tested on the four resulting tasks representing the two points for the two variables. Because the easy and hard points for each of the variables for normal subjects are matched, performance of retarded subjects should not be expected to differ at the easy or hard levels for each of the variables. If, however, it should be found that retarded subjects perform more poorly on one of the variables than the other, it is possible to conclude that they show a deficit on that variable *relative to the other*.

The important point, though Chapman and Chapman do not explicitly say so, is that deficits can only be expressed relative to other parts of the system. They cannot be expressed in any absolute sense. What this suggests is that an understanding of why some people are smarter than others will depend on a clear definition of the entire system regulating intellectual functioning and a comparison of the *relative* strength of its parts. This will be a most challenging undertaking but seems far more desirable than attempting to explain the findings in terms of higher-order deficits (Detterman, 1980b).

Future Directions

In summary, this short exposition of the important questions that researchers have consistently asked and the history of the methods they have used to answer them has shown that the major question of why some people are smarter than others has actually been answered several times. Each time, however, the answer has been found wanting and a new approach to the problem has been developed. Each new approach has added sophistication to the old approach. In a very short time, research in mental retardation has gone from asking the same question in a very simple way to asking it in a most sophisticated way. This increase in sophistication has moved mental retardation research from second-class citizenship to a position of leadership in individual differences research. The basic research now being conducted in mental retardation is more sophisticated and better conceived than the individual differences research in any other area of psychology that I know of.

What of the future? I have discussed what I would like the future to be elsewhere (Detterman, 1980b, 1982). I am sure, however, that no matter what direction research in mental retardation takes, it will continue to become more sophisticated. We will have a firmer grasp on the important questions and better methods with which to answer them.

It would probably be unproductive to attempt to make specific predictions about what research in mental retardation will accomplish in the future. As is frequently the case, I believe the future will exceed the present's expectations. There is much more reason for optimism than there has ever been before. Although there may not be a satisfactory answer to why some people are smarter than others in my lifetime, the progress that has been made should be gratifying to those who have contributed to it. They have established a strong foundation for future accomplishment.

References

Baumeister, A. A., Jr. Problems in comparative studies of mental retardates and normals. *American Journal of Mental Deficiency*, 1967, **71**, 869–875.

Belmont, J. M., Butterfield, E. C., & Ferretti, R. P. To secure transfer of training, instruct self-management skills. In D. K. Detterman and R. J. Sternberg (Eds.), *How and how much can intelligence be increased?* Norwood, N.J.: Ablex Publishing Corp., 1982.

Brody, E. B., & Brody, N. *Intelligence: Nature, determinants, and consequences*. New York: Academic Press, 1976.

Carroll, J. B. *Individual difference relations in psychometric and experimental cognitive tasks*. Technical Report #163, L. L. Thurstone Psychometric Laboratory, University of North Carolina, Chapel Hill, N.C., 1980.

Caruso, D. R., & Detterman, D. K. Intelligence research and intelligent policy. *Phi Delta Kappa*, 1981, **63**, 183–186.

Cattell, J. McK. Mental tests and measurements. *Mind*, 1890, **15**, 373–381.

Cattell, R. B. *Abilities: Their structure, growth, and action*. New York: Houghton Mifflin, 1971.

Chapman, L. J., & Chapman, J. P. Problems in the measurement of cognitive deficits. *Psychological Bulletin*, 1973, **79**, 380–385.

Chapman, L. J., & Chapman, J. P. Alternatives to manipulating a variable to compare retarded and nonretarded subjects. *American Journal of Mental Deficiency*, 1974, **79**, 404–411.

Cronbach, L. S. Two disciplines of scientific psychology. *American Psychologist*, 1957, **12**, 671–684.

Detterman, D. K. M.R. is M.R. is M.R.: Mental retardation and the philosophy of science. *Mental Retardation*, 1974, **12**, 26–28.

Detterman, D. K. Is *Intelligence* necessary. *Intelligence*, 1977, **1**, 1–4.

Detterman, D. K. Memory in the mentally retarded. In N. R. Ellis (Ed.), *Handbook of mental deficiency* (2nd ed.) Norwood, N.J.: Lawrence Erlbaum Assoc., 1979.

Detterman, D. K. A job half done: The road to intelligence testing in the year 2000. In R. J. Sternberg & D. K. Detterman (Eds.), *Human intelligence: Perspectives on its theory and measurement.* Norwood, N.J.: Ablex Publishing Corp., 1980.(a)

Detterman, D. K. Understand cognitive components before postulating metacomponents. *Brain and Behavioral Science*, 1980, **3**, 589.(b)

Detterman, D. K. Questions I would like answered. In D. K. Detterman & R. J. Sternberg (Eds.), *How and how much can intelligence be increased?* Norwood, N.J.: Ablex Publishing Corp., 1982.

Ellis, N. R. A research strategy for mental retardation. In N. R. Ellis (Ed.), *Handbook of mental deficiency.* New York: McGraw-Hill, 1963.

Ellis, N. R. The stimulus trace deficit hypothesis. In N. R. Ellis (Ed.), *Handbook of mental deficiency.* New York: McGraw-Hill, 1963.

Ellis, N. R. A behavioral research strategy in mental retardation: Defense and critique. *American Journal of Mental Deficiency*, 1969, **73**, 557–566.

Ellis, N. R. Memory processes in retardates and normals. In N. R. Ellis (Ed.), *International review of research in mental retardation.* Vol. 4. New York: Academic Press, 1970.

Galton, F. *Inquiries into human faculty and its development.* London: Macmillan, 1883.

Garber, R., & Heber, R. Modification of predicted cognitive development in high-risk children through early intervention. In D. K. Detterman & R. J. Sternberg (Eds.), *How and how much can intelligence be increased?* Norwood, N.J.: Ablex Publishing Corp., 1982.

Guilford, J. P. *The nature of human intelligence.* New York: McGraw-Hill, 1967.

Humphreys, L. G. A factor analytic model for research on intelligence and problem solving. In L. B. Resnick (Ed.), *The nature of intelligence.* Hillsdale, N.J.: Lawrence Erlbaum Assoc., 1976.

Jensen, A. R. How much can we boost IQ and scholastic achievement? *Harvard Educational Review*, 1969, **39**, 1–114.

Jensen, A. R. Let's understand Skodak and Skeels, finally. *Educational Psychologist*, 1973, **10**, 30–35.

Jensen, A. R. g: Outmoded theory or unconquered frontier? *Creative Science and Technology*, 1979, **11**(3), 16–29.

Jensen, A. R. *Bias in Mental Testing.* New York: Free Press, 1980.

John, E. R. Neurometrics. *Science*, 1977, **196**, 1393–1410.

Kanner, L. *The history of the care and study of the mentally retarded.* Springfield, Ill.: Charles C. Thomas, 1964.

Matarazzo, J. D. *Wechsler's measurement and appraisal of adult intelligence.* (5th ed.) Baltimore: Williams and Wilkins, 1972.

Ramey, C. T., MacPhee, D., & Yeates, K. O. Preventing developmental retardation: A general systems model. In D. Detterman & R. S. Sternberg (Eds.), *How and how much can intelligence be increased?* Norwood, N.J.: Ablex Publishing Corp., 1982.

Sharp, S. E. Individual psychology: A study in psychological method. *American Journal of Psychology*, 1898, **10**, 329–391.

Spearman, C. E. General intelligence objectively defined. *American Journal of Psychology*, 1904, **15**, 206–221.

Thurstone, L. L. *Primary mental abilities.* Chicago: Chicago University Press, 1938.

Tuddenham, R. D. The nature and measurement of intelligence. In L. Postman (Ed.), *Psychology in the making.* New York: Knopf, 1963.

Whipple, G. M. *Manual of mental and physical tests.* Baltimore: Warwick & York, 1910.

Wissler, C. The correlation of mental and physical tests. *Psychological Review Monograph Supplement*, 1901, **3**, No. 6.

Zajonc, R. B., & Markus, G. B. Birth order and intellectual development. *Psychological Review*, 1975, **82**, 74–88.

Zeaman, D., & House, B. J. The role of attention in retardate discrimination learning. In N. R. Ellis (Ed.), *Handbook of mental deficiency.* New York: McGraw-Hill, 1963.

Zigler, E. Developmental versus difference theories of mental retardation and the problem of motivation. *American Journal of Mental Deficiency*, 1969, **73**, 536–556.

36 EPIDEMIOLOGICAL METHODS*

Michele Kiely and
Robert A. Lubin

The present chapter is designed to provide an introduction to the methodology of epidemiological research as a tool in the study of the causes, distribution, and prevention of mental retardation. We will also discuss the contribution of epidemiological research to the design and evaluation of public health screening and prevention programs. Additionally, sufficient references will be provided to allow the interested reader to pursue methodological or content areas further. The present chapter is not designed to be a review of the literature of the epidemiology of mental retardation. For this purpose, the reader is referred to Abramowicz and Richardson (1975), Clarke and Clarke (1975), Hansen, Belmont and Stein (1980), Heber (1970), and Stein and Susser (1971, 1980).

Epidemiology is both derived from and historically associated with the word epidemic, which is most commonly associated with communicable diseases. This association is now inappropriate, as the study of epidemiology is much broader than the study of epidemics. Epidemic actually means an increased frequency of disease, clearly in excess of the normal expectancy (Beneson, 1975). Contemporary epidemiology is used to study chronic as well as infectious conditions, and may be broadly defined as the study of diseases and disorders in populations. As with most medical disciplines, epidemiology is interested in the determinants of disease. However, epidemiology is unique in that it studies the determinants of disease based on the frequency and distribution of disease in populations (Fox, Hall, & Elveback, 1970; MacMahon & Pugh, 1977).

The methodology used to study mental retardation is also based upon traditional epidemiological concerns with the distribution and determinants of disorders in the population and the factors that influence the distribution. However, the study of the epidemiology of mental retardation has a unique problem. While epidemiological studies of cancer or heart disease can relate environmental or personal factors to physiological conditions, mental retardation is not as readily described. Mental retardation is not a unique syndrome, but a label for a multitude of observable or hidden disabilities. The concept of mental retardation generally refers to persons with impaired intellectual and behavioral functioning (AAMD, 1977). In order to define mental retardation better or to consider issues of etiology, treatment, and prevention, it is necessary to have additional descriptive or diagnostic information (Begab,

* We would like to acknowledge the many valuable comments of John L. Kiely. We also wish to thank Carole Griffo for typing the manuscript. The preparation of this manuscript was supported, in part, by the New York State Advisory Council on Mental Retardation and Developmental Disabilities (Grant No. 914-6000A).

1980; Thoene, Higgins, Krieger, Schmickel, & Weiss, 1981; Van Den Berghe, Fryus, Parloir, Deroover, & Keulemans, 1980).

Uses of Epidemiology

Epidemiology may be utilized for a variety of research purposes in the study of mental retardation. In particular, it has been used:

- To describe the underlying causal mechanisms for specific disorders associated with mental retardation.
- To describe incidence, prevalence, and mortality patterns of disorders and to identify associated risk factors.
- To describe the natural course of specific forms of mental retardation.
- To utilize new and existing sources of information for studying specific disorders and designing public health prevention programs.

The primary use of epidemiology is the elucidation of causal mechanisms of health disorders. In the study of mental retardation, epidemiological research is concerned with the etiological contribution of genetic, infectious, or environmental factors. Additionally, epidemiological methods have been used to study the causal factors that (1) influence physiological processes (e.g., growth and fertility) and (2) lead to subsequent developmental disabilities.

Epidemiology has also been used to describe and explain patterns of disorders (i.e., how the number of persons in the population with the disorder varies over time or by geographical area). For example, research is conducted to determine whether the likelihood of mental retardation is associated with certain characteristics or exposures. The characteristics may be group attributes, a history of exposure to toxic agents, or environmental factors uniquely associated with the geographical region. If there is a basis for hypothesizing specific associations between the occurrence of the disorder and the characteristics of persons or groups having (or not having) the disorder, then various methodological strategies can be used to measure the presence or extent of any causal link. Epidemiology can be used to describe the course or "natural history" of disorders associated with mental retardation, and age-dependent mortality or morbidity patterns associated with the disorder.

One of the long-range goals of epidemiological research is the establishment of effective primary or secondary prevention programs. Prevention programs may take the form of public health education or screening. Public-health education programs are usually designed to provide information concerning strategies to reduce or eliminate the risks of exposure or disease. Recent programs, for example, have focused on discouraging pregnant women from drinking alcohol and smoking tobacco, as each of these exposures has been related to adverse pregnancy outcomes.

Screening programs are designed to identify persons who have a disorder from an apparently healthy population. To be efficient and cost effective, it is generally best to screen among groups considered to have a high prevalence of the disorder (Mausner & Bahn, 1974; Vecchio, 1966). Screening tests are only feasible if there are appropriate testing and treatment programs for identifying persons presumed to be at increased risk (Cochrane & Holland, 1971). The screening procedures are usually structured to provide further diagnostic testing for persons with positive screening test results. Therapeutic intervention may be provided for all cases identified within the screening program. For example, the identification of the genetic and metabolic mechanisms underlying phenylketonuria (PKU) led to the establishment of effective postnatal prevention programs. Newborns diagnosed through postnatal screening programs as having this relatively rare metabolic disorder can be placed on a prophylactic low phenylalanine diet (Berry, Sutherland, Umbarger, & O'Grady, 1976; Kennedy, Wertelecki, Gates, Sperry, & Cass, 1967; Sutherland, Umbarger, & Berry, 1966). In most cases, the restricted diet serves to prevent the neurological damage associated with severe mental retardation. In a similar manner, the observed association between maternal exposure to Rubella virus (i.e., German measles) during the first trimester of pregnancy and subsequent birth defects led to the development of prophylactic immunization programs (Siegal, Fuerst, & Guinee, 1971; Ueda, Nishida, Oshima, & Shepard, 1979).

The four-fold table set out in Table 36.1 illustrates the manner in which a screening procedure is evaluated. The entries in the four-fold table allow for an assessment of the sensitivity (TP/(TP + FN)) and specificity (TN/(TN + FP)) of the screening program. The sensitivity measures the likelihood that a positive screening result will be found among persons having the disorder. The specificity measures the likelihood that a negative screening result will be found among persons not having the disorder. The purpose of the

Table 36.1. Results of Screening Test

SCREENING TEST RESULTS	DISEASE STATE	
	DISEASE	NO DISEASE
Positive	True positive (TP)	False positive (FP)
Negative	False negative (FN)	True negative (TN)

epidemiological assessments is to evaluate the efficacy of the screening test and the need for varying the screening standards. The severity of the disorder in conjunction with the establishment of sensitivity and specificity standards guides public health officials in deciding whether it is more serious to have missed cases or to have falsely identified healthy individuals as cases. Such decisions are complex, and the reader is referred elsewhere for a fuller explanation of the procedures for establishing screening standards (Bay, Flathman, & Nestman, 1976).

Causality

A primary aim of epidemiological research is to describe the causal pathways or associations from a set of independent variables to a dependent variable (i.e., a disorder or a disease). An association between two variables occurs when the presence of one variable changes the probability of observing another variable (Fleiss, 1981). For example, a woman with a history of Rubella during pregnancy has an increased probability of having a child with mental retardation (Siegal et al., 1971; Ueda et al., 1979).

In many situations, statistical analyses will reveal that an association between an independent variable and a dependent variable is not due to chance. Yet, a statistically significant association between two variables does not imply that they are *causally* associated. If the independent variable is found to be statistically related to the dependent variable, the two variables may be noncausally associated by their common link to another variable. Events which are associated, but are noncausal, are usually due to an association with a third factor. In other words, when variable A increases at the same time that variable B increases, it should not be assumed that variable A is causing a change in variable B. It is also possible that the change in both variables is caused by a change in another variable, C. In such a case, the apparent association between A and B is only due to their individual association with C.

$$
\begin{array}{c}
A \\
C \qquad ? \\
B
\end{array}
$$

In the diagram above, C is the real causal variable, B is the dependent variable (i.e., the disorder), and A is the hypothetical causal variable. A researcher studying children of low birthweight (hypothesized causal variable, or A), for example, is interested in intellectual functioning and mental retardation (the dependent variable, or B). Since low birthweight and

mild mental retardation are associated, examining these two variables alone could lead to the conclusion that low birthweight causes mild mental retardation. In actuality there is a third variable (i.e., low social class) which is the real causal variable (or C) and is associated with both low birthweight and mild mental retardation (Kiely & Paneth, 1981). These factors are pictorially represented below.

$$
\begin{array}{c}
\text{Low birthweight} \\
\text{Low social class} \\
\text{Mild mental retardation}
\end{array}
$$

Much of epidemiological research is concerned with establishing the presence and direction of causal relationships among variables. Susser (1973) has described criteria that can be used to determine whether an association is causal (i.e., consistency, strength of association, time, specificity, and coherence).

Consistency

This criterion requires that similar findings are obtained when studies are performed under varying conditions (e.g., different populations or study designs). For example, two studies investigated alcohol consumption and spontaneous abortion and found consistent results. One addressed the problem prospectively (Harlap & Shiono, 1980), the other retrospectively (Kline, Stein, Shrout, Susser & Warburton, 1980). Both these studies are consistent in that they found excessive drinking increased the risk of spontaneous abortion.

It should be noted that if methodological errors are repeated between studies, the results may be consistent but spurious.

Strength of Association

The degree to which variables occur together is a measure of their strength of association. The stronger the association, the more probable that the association

Table 36.2. Cerebral Palsy Rates by Birthweight

BIRTH-WEIGHT IN GRAMS	CEREBRAL PALSY RATE PER 1000	RELATIVE RISK (COMPARED WITH THE GROUP WITH BIRTHWEIGHTS ≥ 2501 GRAMS)
≥ 2501	3.70	1.00
1501–2500	13.91	3.76
≤ 1500	90.43	24.43

From the Collaborative Perinatal Project of the National Institute of Neurological and Communicative Disorders and Stroke (data from Ellenberg & Nelson, 1979).

is causal. The relative risk (i.e., the rate of a disorder among persons exposed to a factor relative to the rate of the disorder among persons not exposed to the factor) serves as an index of the strength of association in epidemiological research. For example, Ellenberg and Nelson (1979) reported rates of cerebral palsy by birthweight. The rate of cerebral palsy increased with decreasing birthweight (Table 36.2). The strength of the association between low birthweight and cerebral palsy is demonstrated by the rise in the relative risk as the birthweight decreases.

Time

In order for a factor to be considered causally related to a disorder, the exposure to the factor must precede the manifestation of the disorder. The time sequence between prenatal exposure to infectious diseases and postnatal outcome is relatively simple to describe. However, with chronic diseases having an insidious onset (e.g., multiple sclerosis), the time order between an hypothesized exposure and outcome is often difficult to establish.

Specificity

This criterion of judgment refers to the extent to which the occurrence of one variable predicts the occurrence of another variable. The highest level of specificity is when a certain event always predicts the occurrence of a disorder and the disorder occurs only after that event. An example of complete specificity is an extra 21st chromosome and the constellation of characteristics associated with Down's syndrome (e.g., mental retardation, epicanthal folds, simian creases, etc.). A person who has trisomy 21 always has Down's syndrome and a person who manifests Down's syndrome always has an extra 21st chromosome. (More accurately, 4% of persons with Down's syndrome have the extra chromosomal material as a translocation rather than as a separate chromosome.) A high level of specificity is one indication that the variable being studied is causally associated with the observed effect. However, it is important to remember that even though high specificity increases the likelihood that a relationship is causal, it does not prove the causal association.

Coherence

The criterion of coherence considers the credibility of the association of two variables. An association between two variables is considered coherent if the relationship is plausible in terms of current scientific knowledge.

Rates

The field of epidemiology has adopted standard terms to address simultaneously the issue of case identification, population size, and time period. Specifically, the number of persons with a certain characteristic or disorder are described in terms of a unit population size and a unit time period. The relationship between the number of persons with a condition and the size of the population is expressed as a rate. In epidemiological studies of mental retardation, the numerator of the rate could be the number of persons in a given time period diagnosed to have Down's syndrome, Tay-Sachs disease, etc. The denominator of the rate would be the overall number of persons in the same population and over the same time period from which the cases were identified.

A rate is derived by comparing a count of all individuals diagnosed as having a disorder with the number of persons in a population in a given area. For example, a study in northern Israel found 735 cases of epilepsy in an area that had a population of 316,017 (Wajsbort, Haral, & Alfandary, 1967). The rate of epilepsy would be *calculated* as:

$$\frac{735 \text{ cases of epilepsy in northern Israel}}{316,017 \text{ people in northern Israel}} = 0.00232.$$

Rates are expressed in terms of standard bases such as 100, 1,000 or 100,000. In practice, the size of the numerator usually determines the size of the denominator. In the present example, the rate of epilepsy is expressed as a function of 1,000 persons.

$$0.00232 \times 1,000 = \frac{2.32 \text{ cases of epilepsy}}{1,000 \text{ persons}}$$

There are a number of different rates used in studies of the epidemiology of mental retardation. The most frequently used rates are incidence, prevalence, and mortality.

Incidence is the number of new cases which are manifest during a specified period of time. Incidence rates are the number of new cases of a disorder occurring in a population during a specified period of time relative to the number of persons at risk for the disorder in the same time period. One study, for example, found that there were 65 new cases of epilepsy in Rochester, Minnesota, between the three years 1965 and 1967 (Hauser & Kurland, 1975). The population of Rochester was derived for this study to be 46,698. The incidence rate of epilepsy was calculated as 46.4 cases per 100,000 population per year. Specifically,

65 new cases of epilepsy

$$\frac{\text{from 1965 to 1967}}{46,698 \text{ persons}} \times 100,000 \div 3 \text{ years} =$$

$$\frac{\begin{array}{c} 46.4 \text{ cases of epilepsy} \\ \text{per year} \end{array}}{100,000 \text{ population}}$$

Prevalence refers to the number of cases of a condition (whether old or new cases) that are present in a population at a designated time point. Prevalence rates are the number of cases relative to the total population from which the cases were ascertained. The total population, or denominator, includes all cases (i.e., the numerator) as well as all persons unaffected by the disorder.

Mortality rates express the number of deaths among the total number of persons in the same group over a specific time period. The numerator of a mortality rate is the number of deaths during a specified period and the denominator is the total population in which the deaths occurred. Rates may also be used to calculate the number of deaths among persons with a specific syndrome relative to all persons with the disorder. This factor is referred to as the *case fatality rate*. Such a rate serves as an indication of the relative severity of a disorder.

Mortality rates are also used to reflect issues associated with life expectancy. A relatively high mortality rate among specific groups would indicate that there are factors contributing to a low life expectancy among those groups. Conversely, if the mortality rate among groups of persons with a given disorder does not exceed the mortality rate of the population at large, then there is no basis for assuming any association of the disorder with a lower life expectancy. Mortality rates are useful in describing factors that are associated with changes in life expectancy. Studies of the age-specific mortality rates among mentally retarded persons relative to the population-at-large have shown that these persons

have a lower life expectancy (Forssman & Akesson, 1965; Richards, 1975). However, these studies have also shown an historical decline in mortality rates among mentally retarded persons (Fabia & Drolette, 1970; Gallagher & Lowry, 1975; McCurley, Mackay & Scally, 1972; Oster, Mikkelson, & Nielsen, 1975). While the changes in the mortality rates vary widely across specific syndromes and the age groups being studied, the general increase has been linked to such factors as improved health and social services. In a similar manner, the decline in mortality rates among newborns has been associated with improved perinatal services (Kiely, Paneth, Stein, & Susser, 1981).

In calculating rates, it is necessary to apply the same restrictions to the denominator as apply to the numerator. If the numerator considers only persons of a specific age, sex, or ethnicity, the persons in the denominator must be similarly restricted. Such restrictions can increase the usefulness of the rate. For example, a survey of infants born with Down's syndrome in Victoria, Australia found a rate of 1.45 cases/1,000 livebirths. When the rate was restricted to infants born to women 40 years of age or older, it increased to 10.9 infants with Down's syndrome per 1,000 livebirths (Collman & Stoller, 1962). The increased risk of older women for bearing a child with Down's syndrome becomes readily apparent when the rates are presented as a function of maternal age.

Incidence, prevalence, and duration are interrelated. Prevalence rates vary as a function of incidence and duration. In the hypothetical situation in which incidence and duration do not change, the prevalence will equal the incidence times the duration, i.e., $P = I \times D$ (MacMahon & Pugh, 1977). The interrelationships among incidence, prevalence, and duration are demonstrated in Table 36.3. For example, the incidence rate of Tay-Sachs disease, a genetically determined metabolic disorder among Jews of Ashkenazi descent, is approximately 27.7 cases per 100,000 births per year (Thompson & Thompson, 1973). Since

Table 36.3. Prevalence Varies as the Product of Incidence and Duration

DISEASE	INCIDENCE	PROBABLE CAUSE	DURATION	PROBABLE CAUSE	PREVALENCE
Down's syndrome	Decreasing	Decrease in maternal age	Increasing	Medical care[a]	Increasing
Spina bifida	Probably decreasing	?	Varying over time	Surgical intervention policies[b]	Varies
Prenatally determined cerebral palsy?	Stable?		Increasing?	Neonatal intensive care	Increasing?

[a] Stein, 1975.
[b] Adelstein, 1975.

the life expectancy of infants with Tay-Sachs is only two to four years, the prevalence rate of Tay-Sachs could be estimated to be between 55.4 and 110.8 affected children/100,000 children born to Ashkenazi Jews.

Person, Place, and Time

As with any disorder of known or unknown etiology, mental retardation is associated with a multitude of factors. In order to describe the association between factors of interest and a given disorder, the epidemiologist often uses descriptive variables that characterize person, place, and time. The predominant "person" factors are age, gender, ethnic group or race, and socioeconomic status. All of these factors have been shown to be associated with the distribution of mental retardation (Drillien, Jameson, & Wilkinson, 1966; Heber, 1970).

Age should always be considered in epidemiological studies. There is usually more variation in the frequency of a disorder due to age than to any other variable. In other circumstances, age may have little to do with the disorder, but can affect diagnosis. For example, it is quite difficult to diagnose accurately cerebral palsy before two years of age.

The association between gender and a disease may be demonstrated by a difference in disease rates for each sex. For example, the inheritance pattern of certain types of mental retardation (e.g., Fragile X syndrome) where only males are affected, leads to the conclusion that the disorder is due to an X-linked recessive gene (Herbst, Dunn, Dill, Kalousek, & Krywaniuk, 1981; Howard-Peebles & Stoddard, 1980; Turner, Daniel, & Frost, 1980).

The observations of incidence, prevalence, or mortality rates differing as a function of descriptive variables does not always indicate causal relationships. Such trends may serve as the basis for further investigation. For example, epidemiological studies have demonstrated the strong association between maternal age and incidence rates of Down's syndrome. It appears that older women are at significantly greater risk for bearing an infant with Down's syndrome than are younger women (Ferguson-Smith, 1978; Hook & Cross, 1981; Stein, Goldsmith, Kline, Margolis, Sadow, & Zybert, 1975). This finding does not imply that advanced maternal age causes Down's syndrome. Rather, the strong association between maternal age and the incidence of Down's syndrome suggests the need for further studies on the physiological and genetic mechanisms associated with development which may be dependent upon maternal age.

Rates of specific forms of mental retardation have also been shown to vary as a function of race or ethnic background. For example, the incidence rate of Tay-Sachs is approximately 27.7/100,000 among Jews of Ashkenazi descent, but about 0.27/100,000 in other populations (Thompson & Thompson, 1973). Early studies of this condition showed the strong association between Tay-Sachs disease and ethnic background, and suggested a probable genetic cause.

Findings from epidemiological studies which look at descriptive variables may also be useful in designing prevention programs. For example, the finding that there is a strong association between maternal age and the incidence of Down's syndrome led to the use of age as a screening factor in determining whether women should consider prenatal testing (i.e., amniocentesis and chromosomal analysis of fetal cells). For conditions of relatively low incidence, it is more efficient to establish prevention programs which target services to persons at highest risk for the disorder. Since Tay-Sachs disease has a genetic etiology, it is only worthwhile to conduct genetic screening if both prospective parents are of Ashkenazi descent (Beck, Blaichman, Scriver, & Clow, 1974; Childs, Gordis, Kaback, & Kazazian, 1976).

Cohort Studies

Cohort studies are designed to compare rates of disorders in groups of people who differ in certain personal characteristics or exposures. The groups of people, or cohorts, are observed over time to determine the rates of disorders within each group. Such studies are conducted to determine whether certain characteristics or exposures are causally related to the outcome of interest.

There are two types of cohort studies: prospective and retrospective. In a prospective cohort study, the characteristics or exposure may or may not have taken place, but the disorder will not have occurred. Rather, the study must follow individuals over time to determine whether, and what rate, the disorder occurs. In a retrospective cohort study, both the exposure and the disorder will have already occurred when the study begins. The advantage of a retrospective study is that the cohorts can be identified from available information and the waiting period between exposure and outcome is eliminated. Retrospective cohort studies can only be conducted if sufficient information on exposure and subsequent disability is available.

Selection of Study Cohorts

Several factors influence the selection of participants in cohort studies. Individuals who have undergone an unusual occupational or environmental exposure are prime sources of cohorts, and may be selected in order to investigate the effects of those exposures. For example, groups of pregnant women with a common history of radiation exposure (Blot & Miller, 1973; Blot, Shimizu, Kato, & Miller, 1975; Miller & Blot, 1972) or of nutritional deprivation (Stein, Susser, Saenger, & Marolla, 1975) have been studied to examine the long-term effects upon their offspring. Information on the exposure serves as the basis for identifying the cohorts. The extent of any adverse outcome on the offspring serves as the basis for identifying the risk due to exposure.

In both retrospective and prospective cohort studies, there is no critical period of follow-up of the cohorts. The cohorts may be identified during an exposure and then followed to determine outcome. Alternatively, the cohorts may be identified shortly after or well after the exposure has occurred. It is only necessary that sufficient information on exposure and outcome is available and that this information is uniformly accessible for all cohorts.

In some situations, the cohorts are assembled to study the effects of a known exposure. In other situations, cohorts are assembled without knowledge of exposure history. For example, persons in prepaid group health plans are particularly useful for participation in cohort studies because (1) their records will be uniform across the cohorts and of relatively high quality, (2) loss to follow-up is minimized as use of prepaid health plans centralizes the provision of services, and (3) longitudinal information is available through periodic follow-up of all groups. Other groups which provide unique resources for cohort studies include occupational groups, obstetrical populations, insured persons, hospital patients, and volunteer groups. However, cohort studies which utilize volunteer groups should be conducted with caution. While information from volunteers is often readily available, there is a risk of biased results. Volunteer groups are, by definition, self-selected and may not be representative of the population.

Data on Exposure

When the exposed and nonexposed cohorts are to be established without prior knowledge of exposure history (e.g., members of a prepaid group health plan), researchers must obtain information to determine exposure status. Such information on exposure can be gathered from a variety of sources. Information from records allows for the cohorts to be designated as exposed or not exposed, and provides pertinent demographic and clinical information. Other types of information, such as the medical characteristics of

cohort members can only be obtained through diagnostic examinations. In some instances, exposure status can be determined directly through an evaluation of environmental attributes (e.g., air or water pollution). Information from personal interviews can be obtained from visits or telephone calls, or from mailed questionnaires. When information is collected from cohort members or their families, it is possible that the proportion responding will not be the same for the exposed and unexposed cohorts. The researcher must then evaluate the response patterns. The relationship between exposure and outcome will be misrepresented if there is bias with respect to exposure and outcome categories. If nonresponse is biased with respect to the exposure (e.g., persons with heavy exposure fail to respond to the questionnaire), the direction of the relationship between exposure and outcome in the study cohort will be accurate. However, it will not be possible to measure the rate of exposure in the population. If nonresponse is biased with respect to outcome (e.g., persons in poor health fail to respond), then the rates of disease in the study cohort will be spuriously lower than the actual rate of disease in the population, but the ratio of high exposure to low exposure will accurately reflect the ratio in the population. If response patterns are not biased by exposure or outcome, then the influence of the missing information may safely be ignored (MacMahon & Pugh, 1977).

It is often difficult to ascertain whether response patterns are biased. The presence and extent of any bias can be evaluated in part by (1) obtaining exposure and outcome information on a subsample of nonrespondents to determine whether they are comparable to respondents, (2) contrasting demographic information for respondents and nonrespondents to determine the comparability of groups, and (3) using alternative sources of information to determine the rate of exposure of outcome among nonrespondents.

Selection of Comparison Groups

There are three main strategies of establishing comparison groups in cohort studies: within group, between group, and population comparisons. A within-group comparison is actually a single large cohort within which all individuals are classified as either exposed or not exposed. This single large cohort can mitigate the need for an outside comparison group. A between group comparison involves the establishment of a nonexposed cohort which is demographically similar to the exposed cohort. The third strategy for establishing a comparison group is the use of the population at large as the nonexposed cohort. The rate of the disorder in the exposed cohort is compared with the rate of

Relative Risk. The ratio of the rate of disease among those exposed to the rate among those not exposed.

ETIOLOGIC CHARACTERISTIC	DISEASED	NONDISEASED	TOTAL
Exposed	a	b	a + b
Not exposed	c	d	c + d
Total	a + c	b + d	a + b + c + d = N

I_e, Incidence among exposed $\quad = \dfrac{a}{a + b}$

I_o, Incidence among not exposed $\; = \dfrac{c}{c + d}$

$$\text{Relative risk} \; = \; \frac{\dfrac{a}{a + b}}{\dfrac{c}{c + d}} \; = \; \frac{I_e}{I_o}$$

Example: Very Low Birthweight and Cerebral Palsy: (Data from the Collaborative Perinatal Project).

BIRTHWEIGHT	CP	NOT AFFECTED	TOTAL
< 1501 grams	17	170	183
> 2501 grams	124	33,142	33,266

Incidence in very-low-birthweight group $\quad = \dfrac{17}{183} \; = \; 92.9 \text{ per } 1,000$

Incidence in normal and high weight group $\; = \dfrac{124}{33266} \; = \; 3.7 \text{ per } 1,000$

$$\text{Relative Risk} \; = \; \frac{92.9}{3.7} \; = \; 25.1$$

Fig. 36.1. Calculation of the relative risk. (Data from Ellenberg & Nelson, 1979.)

the disorder in the population. This last strategy is limited to those circumstances in which (1) the rate of the disorder is known for the population and (2) the characteristics (e.g., demographic and geographical) of the study cohort and the population are comparable.

Longitudinal Follow-up

Cohort studies include a follow-up component in order to determine outcome among cohort members. During the follow-up, the researcher will determine whether there are any differences between the exposed and unexposed cohorts in morbidity or mortality rates. Several factors should be considered in the follow-

up of cohorts. Ascertainment should be comparable across all exposure categories. Persons responsible for follow-up should be blind to exposure category, as judgment of outcome may be biased by a knowledge of exposure. Finally, attention should be given to completing data collection on as many nonrespondents as possible. In long-term studies that are concerned with morbidity and mortality, the number of cohort members examined over time decreases and becomes increasingly selected.

Analysis

The analysis of a cohort study is basically a comparison of the rates of the outcome of interest (i.e., morbidity and mortality) between persons exposed and persons not exposed. The numerator in the rates is the number of persons with the outcome. The denominator is expressed as a function of both cohort size and time (i.e., person-years). The denominator is calculated by multiplying the number of persons in each group by the total number of years each person was in the study. Person-years are used because longitudinal studies not only lose subjects over time, but also must account for the varying time periods in which different subjects enter and remain in the study.

There are three risk estimates which are commonly used as a measure of association between exposure and outcome: "relative risk" refers to the ratio of the rate of disorder among the non-exposed group to the rate of disorder among the exposed group (see Fig. 36.1). The relative risk provides a direct measure of the risk due to an exposure.

"Attributable risk" refers to the rate of disease in exposed individuals than can be attributed to the exposure. It is calculated by subtracting the rate of disorder among the non-exposed group from the rate among the exposed group (see Fig. 36.2). "Population attributable risk fraction" refers to the proportion of all cases in a defined population which can be directly attributed to an exposure or characteristic. This measure provides an estimate of the impact that a specific exposure or characteristic may have on the outcome in the population (see Fig. 36.3). The population attributable risk fraction also allows for an estimation of the relative benefit to the population of reducing or eliminating the exposure.

Advantages and Disadvantages of Cohort Studies

The main advantage of cohort studies is that they provide a direct estimate of the risk of developing a disorder due to a specific exposure or characteristic. When information is collected prospectively, and the disorder has not yet occurred, the exposure data are not biased by knowledge of outcome. Cohort studies also enable the researcher to monitor changes over time in the exposure of the cohort, and how these changes in exposure may be related to outcome. In addition to the disorder under study, the relationship of the characteristic or exposure to other outcomes may be investigated. Finally, in most circumstances the results of cohort studies are not biased by subject loss attributable to the characteristic or exposure being studied, as information on all members of the cohort is gathered prior to the onset of the disorder. While the advantages of cohort studies are numerous, there are also several disadvantages. Specifically, cohort studies are difficult and expensive to conduct, require long periods of observation, and necessitate large study populations (Lilienfeld, 1976).

Cohort studies are inefficient for studying rare disorders (Lilienfeld, 1976). For example, the Collaborative Perinatal Project was designed to study cerebral palsy prospectively. For eight years the study collected information on approximately 54,000 pregnancies. Among the 38,500 children with a known outcome at age seven years, only 202 cases of cerebral palsy were found.

Attributable Risk: Rate of the disease in exposed individuals that can be attributed to exposure.

$$\text{A.R.} = \frac{a}{a+b} - \frac{c}{c+d} = I_e - I_o$$

Example: The Effect of Maternal Smoking on the Subsequent Health of the Child.

Diseases of the Respiratory System, Blood and Blood-forming Organs, Nervous System and Sense Organs During First 5 Years of Life

SMOKED DURING PREGNANCY?	AFFECTED	DENOMINATOR (SURVIVED FIRST 28 DAYS)	RATE
Smokers	527	1,776	297 per 1,000
Nonsmokers	294	1,793	164 per 1,000

Attributable risk = 297 − 164 = 133 per 1,000

Fig. 36.2. Calculation of the attributable risk. The amount of morbidity among children born to smoking mothers attributable to maternal smoking is approximately 133 per 1,00. (Data from Rantakallio, 1978.)

Proportion of all cases in a total defined population which can be ascribed to a factor.

$$\text{Population attributable risk fraction} = \frac{I_t - I_o}{I_t},$$

where

$$I_o = \text{Incidence rate among those not exposed to factor,}$$

$$I_t = \text{Incidence rate in total population.}$$

Example: Low birthweight

NEONATAL MORTALITY RATE[1]	
< 2501 grams	87.2 per 1,000
≥ 2501 grams	2.9 per 1,000
Total	12.6 per 1,000

* Data from New York City Department of Health, 1977.

$$\text{Population attributable risk fraction} = \frac{12.6 - 2.9}{12.6} = 77\%$$

CEREBRAL PALSY RATE[2]	
< 2501 grams	18.3 per 1,000
≥ 2501 grams	3.7 per 1,000
Total	5.1 per 1,000

$$\text{Population attributable risk fraction} = \frac{5.1 - 3.7}{5.1} = 27\%$$

Fig. 36.3. Calculation of the population attributable risk fraction. 77% of neonatal deaths and 27% of cerebral palsy could be avoided if low birthweight were eliminated. (Data from [1]New York City Department of Health, 1977 and [2]Ellenberg and Nelson, 1979.)

Case Control Studies

Case-control studies are designed to contrast the rate of characteristics or exposures among persons who either manifest or do not manifest a given disorder. Individuals considered to have the disorder are defined as cases, and individuals who are considered not to have the disorder are defined as controls. Cases and controls are compared to determine characteristics or exposures which are more common to one group and are relevant to the hypothesized etiology of the disorder. Case control studies are most useful in testing hypotheses about etiological factors associated with a specific disorder.

Selection of Cases

As the purpose of case-control studies is to identify characteristics or exposures associated with a disorder, precise diagnostic criteria are crucial. Ideally, there should be no ambiguity about the diagnosis of cases or controls. The erroneous identification of cases or controls could mask valid group differences.

Cases are generally recruited for case-control studies from specific target populations (i.e., cases in treatment) or from the population at large. Selecting cases from existing registries or treatment programs is the most efficient strategy. However, such selection procedures may result in a nonrepresentative group of cases. The cases may be unrepresentative in terms of the severity of their disorder or their personal characteristics (i.e., age, gender, race). Selecting cases from the population will increase the difficulty and expense of case-finding. Such efforts will enable researchers to estimate the rates and severity of the disorder in the population.

Selection of Controls

The purpose of controls is to determine whether the frequency of the exposure or characteristic differs between cases and a comparable group without the disorder (i.e., controls). If the frequency of the characteristic or exposure differs between cases and controls, one can assess the contribution of the hypothesized etiologic factor to the manifestation of the disorder. On the other hand, if the frequency of the characteristic or exposure does not vary between cases and controls, it is unlikely that those factors are causally associated with the disorder.

There are several considerations to be made in defining a control group. Specifically, one must be careful to obtain all information on personal characteristics or exposures in a similar manner for cases and controls. Biases in collecting such information could potentially mask or lead to spurious group differences. The researcher must be careful of the validity and reliability of respondent's recall. For example the recall patterns concerning prenatal events may differ between parents of mentally retarded children and parents of nonretarded children.

Cases and controls should be drawn from the same or similar populations. In selecting a control group it is often important to consider the associated economic and logistic costs. At a minimum, controls should be representative of the population from which they are drawn, or the manner in which they are not representative should be known. There are several sources of controls for case-control studies. Subjects from the same medical facility as the cases may be a source for controls. This source is often the most practical since access to a data base has already been established and the quality of the information will likely be comparable for both cases and controls. However, this source of controls may be unrepresentative of the population-at-large, making it difficult to extrapolate from any study findings. When control groups are selected from a clinical facility, it is important that they are drawn from a range of diagnostic categories, rather than from a single category. If a single diagnostic group is chosen for the control group and group differences are found, it will be difficult to determine

whether it is the cases or controls who differ from the general population.

Family members (e.g., spouse or siblings) may also be used as a source of controls. The advantage of family members as controls is that they will likely have the same ethnic and social background as the cases. However, family controls are inappropriate when the factor being studied is common to both the cases and their family members (e.g., environmental exposures). Another source for controls may be associates of cases (e.g., neighbors, classmates or fellow employees). It can be time consuming to recruit associates of cases and collect the necessary information.

In some studies, it may be possible to use population controls by defining them as all noncases within an administrative area (e.g., health area or census tracts). Population controls are appropriate only when most or all of the cases were selected from the same population. There are two problems with the use of population controls. First, the response rate from population controls tends to be lower than the response rate when controls are selected from a circumscribed population such as a medical or other clinical program. Second, the selection and interviewing of population controls is more time consuming and expensive than with other sources of controls. It is also feasible to use all noncases as controls if the necessary information is routinely collected on an entire population (e.g., birth or death certificates). In most instances, the necessary detailed information is not available for the entire population. In such instances, it is necessary to select a sample of controls from a more circumscribed population.

In addition to selecting an appropriate control group, the researcher must also decide on the number of persons within the control group(s). When the cost of obtaining data is high and there are a potentially unlimited number of cases, the best choice is to have equal numbers of cases and controls. If the number of cases is limited or if the cost of obtaining data is low, then the best choice is to have multiple controls. By selecting more controls than cases, the statistical power of the study can be increased. However, minimal power is gained if there are more than four controls for each case (Gail, Williams, Byar, & Brown, 1976).

The sampling of controls for a case-control study can either be systematic or random. A systematic sample is one in which the entire list of potential controls is ordered in terms of one or more characteristics and the controls are then systematically selected (i.e., every nth control). When systematic sampling is used, the order of the list of potential controls should not be arranged so that it varies with the factors of interest. Systematic sampling is done to ensure a representative distribution in the control group. Another strategy for selecting controls involves the pairwise matching of controls to individual cases. The goal of matching procedures is to ensure that cases and controls are similar on variables which may have an effect on the dependent variable and also vary with the independent variable (Susser, 1973). The most common matching characteristics are age, gender, and ethnicity (Mausner & Bahn, 1974). Failure to match cases and controls on the necessary characteristics may lead to spurious results. However, it may become difficult to assemble a control group, if too many matching criteria are chosen, as an insufficient number of controls will meet all matching criteria.

Analysis of Case-Control Studies

The analysis of case-control studies is a comparison of the frequency of the suspected etiological factors among cases with the frequency of the same factor among controls. The comparison of cases and controls is the odds ratio. The odds ratio is derived from the four-fold table shown in Fig. 36.4. The odds ratio is calculated as equal to $(A \times D)/(B \times C)$, and provides an estimate of the "true" relative risk. The chi square test can be used to evaluate the probability that the group differences are statistically significant (Fleiss, 1981).

The likelihood of demonstrating actual differences between cases and controls is increased if subjects are classified across multiple categories. For example, the relationship between alcohol consumption and fetal alcohol syndrome (Olegard, Sabel, Aronsson, Sandin, Johansson, Carlsson, Kyllerman, Iverson, & Hrbek, 1979; Russell, 1977) can be assessed by contrasting infants born to mothers who consumed alcohol during gestation with infants born to mothers who abstained from alcohol. The hypothesized relationship would be easier to demonstrate if the drinking mothers were classified as a function of their quantity or frequency of drinking. If a dose-response pattern is demonstrated as a function of alcohol consumption, more strength could be given to the hypothesis that prenatal alcohol consumption leads to fetal alcohol syndrome.

Advantages and Disadvantages of Case-Control Studies

Lilienfeld (1976) has described the advantages and disadvantages of case-control studies. Specifically, (1) case-control studies are relatively inexpensive to conduct in comparison with cohort studies, (2) relatively few subjects are needed to demonstrate the existence of group differences, (3) results can be obtained relatively quickly, as there is no need for longitudinal follow-up, and (4) case-control studies are the only practical approach for studying the etiology of rare disorders. The disadvantages of case-control studies are (1) risk estimates can only be obtained indirectly, (2) the history of exposure to the conditions being studied is often totally dependent upon the individual's

CHARACTERISTIC OR EXPOSURE OF INTEREST	DISEASED	NOT DISEASED	
Present	a	b	a + b
Absent	c	d	c + d

$$\text{Odds ratio} = \frac{ad}{cb}$$

Example: Clinical illness with or exposure to mumps virus during maternal gestation or during first 18 months of life, Massachusetts Autism Study, June 1975–January 1977.

	AUTISM CASES	SIBLING CONTROLS
Illness or exposure to mumps	21	18
Not exposed	142	333
Total	163	355

$$\text{Odds ratio} = \frac{21 \times 333}{142 \times 18} = 2.74$$

Fig. 36.4. Calculation of the odds ratio. (Data from Deykin & MacMahon, 1979.)

memory of past events or on the availability of records. This dependence upon memory or records is a particular problem, as the level of recall or the quality of health records may not be equivalent for cases and controls, (3) case-control studies are necessarily limited to individuals who have survived sufficiently long after the exposure to participate in the study. If the characteristics or exposure of interest are related to an increased mortality risk, only survivors can participate in the study. Since people who have died prior to the study cannot be included, the odds ratio obtained may be spuriously low, and (4) it may be particularly difficult to otain a control group which differs from cases only in terms of the exposure or characteristics under study.

Prevalence Studies

Prevalence studies, per se, are not usually included in a discussion of epidemiological methodology. However, the concept of prevalence is important in the study of epidemiology of mental retardation. Knowledge about the prevalence of various forms of mental retardation is crucial to the planning, administration, and evaluation of specialized programs and services. The concept of prevalence is often more meaningful than the concept of incidence in the study of the epidemiology of mental retardation. Since it is often difficult to establish when the disorder began, it may be impossible to determine incidence rates. Accordingly, prevalence rates are the only reliable index of the relative frequency of a given disorder.

There is no set methodology which is most appropriate to the study of the prevalence of mental retardation. A variety of methodologies have been used to determine prevalence rates of mental retardation. Studies which demonstrate a variety of approaches in estimating the prevalence of mental retardation are described. In addition to the studies described in this section, the reader is referred to reviews of community-based prevalence studies for further illustrations of survey methodologies (Abramowicz & Richardson, 1975; Kushlick & Blunden, 1974; LaPouse & Weitzner, 1970; Stein & Susser, 1974). Studies which demonstrate a variety of approaches for estimating prevalence are described.

Birch, Richardson, Baird, Horobin, and Illsley (1970) conducted a clinical and epidemiological study of "mental subnormality" in Aberdeen, Scotland. The study was designed to estimate the number of persons in the population, as well as which groups were at increased risk of being mentally retarded. Aberdeen was selected as the site for the study for several reasons. First, health and school authorities were especially

cooperative and interested in the project. In addition, the city had a relatively stable population with little in- or out-migration. Finally, uniform longitudinal records on social, familial, and health characteristics were available for most mothers on the course and complications of their pregnancies and deliveries.

The study population included all children between 8 and 10 years of age residing in Aberdeen. Prevalence estimates were derived by using the health and education records of children in special classes, group test results, and individual psychological assessments for all children identified by local authorities as "subnormal." Their best estimate of the overall prevalence rate of "mental subnormality" among children 8 to 10 years of age was 27.4/1,000 children. The estimated prevalence rate for children with an IQ below 50 was 3.7/1,000 children age 8–10.

Riverside, California was the site of a large study to determine the prevalence of mental retardation (Mercer, 1973). Individuals were identified as being mentally retarded under either of two approaches: (1) social system epidemiology where individuals were considered mentally retarded by the various social systems in the community, and (2) clinical epidemiology where the researchers identified and studied prospective cases on the basis of clinical attributes.

The social system epidemiology approach was conducted by requesting all private and public organizations in the community to identify all mentally retarded persons known to their organization. The concept of mental retardation was undefined by the project and each organization was instructed to apply their own definition(s).

In the clinical epidemiology approach, an adult from each of 3,192 randomly selected households was interviewed about the sociocultural background, intelligence, adaptive behavior, and extent of any physical disability for every family member. Interview information was gathered on a total of 6,998 persons. This information was used to design and standardize two new measures: an adaptive behavior scale and a physical disability scale. An IQ test was administered to a stratified subsample, including persons of all ages. On the basis of the IQ test only, the weighted prevalence of mental retardation (defined as IQ < 70) was estimated to be 21.4/1,000 total population. When the diagnosis of mental retardation included adaptive behavior as well as IQ, the estimated prevalence rate declined to 9.7/1,000.

Stein, Susser, and Saenger (1976a,b) estimated the prevalence of mental retardation in the Netherlands on the basis of a survey of 19-year-old men born between 1944 and 1947. The prevalence estimates were based upon a larger study designed to determine sequelae to in utero exposure to famine (Stein et al., 1975). The strength of this study comes from the completeness of the data and the large size of the data base (i.e., approximately 400,000 men).

During their 19th year, all Dutch male citizens participated in a limited but highly systematic induction examination to determine their suitability for military training. A clinical record completed by an individual's physician was substituted for the induction examination for some individuals, including a group considered to be severely mentally retarded. On the basis of this information, the overall prevalence of severe mental retardation was estimated to be 3.7/1,000 adult males age 19. Most men who were mildly retarded underwent the medical examination for military induction. On the basis of the wide range of information collected during the examinations, the researchers were also able to estimate prevalence rates of mild mental retardation. Specifically, three criteria were considered: attendance at a special school, failure to perform or score a class 6 on the Raven Progressive Matrices Test, and clinical diagnosis using 1948 International Classification of Diseases (ICD) codes. The prevalence rates of mild mental retardation per 1,000 19-year-old males were estimated as 30.5 based upon schooling, 57.5 based upon scores on the Raven test, and 61.4 based upon the ICD code.

Another method of estimating prevalence utilizes multiple sources of information and is called the multinomial capture-recapture method, or Bernoulli census (Hook, Albright & Cross, 1980; Wittes, 1974; Wittes, Colton, & Sidel, 1974; Wittes & Sidel, 1968). The method estimates prevalence based upon the extent of overlap between data sources. For example, Hook et al. (1980) used three sources of data (i.e., birth certificates, death certificates, and records of individuals receiving services from the medical rehabilitation program) to estimate the prevalence of spina bifida in New York.

It should be possible to conduct studies of the prevalence of developmental disabilities using the multinomial capture-recapture method with the existent service registries. However, the derived prevalence rates may vary or give biased estimates of true prevalence rates. Given three sources of data, it is possible to derive seven estimates of prevalence: one estimate that considers all three sources jointly, three estimates obtained by pooling any two sources of data, and three individual estimates obtained by ignoring one data source (Hook et al., 1980; Neugebauer & Golden, 1981). The derived prevalence rates may be biased if the sources of data are not independent. The prevalence will be underestimated if two sources of data are positively dependent, that is being listed by

one source increases the likelihood of being listed by another source (e.g., agencies share lists). The prevalence will be overestimated if the sources of data are negatively dependent, that is being listed by one source decreases the likelihood of being listed by the other sources (e.g., agencies are assigned unique lists by an umbrella organization). Nevertheless, this problem of bias may be avoided by pooling dependent data sources.

Conclusion

The researcher has the responsibility for selecting an appropriate study design. In order to make the proper selection, the researcher should consider a number of questions: What is the purpose of the study? What are the disorders, exposures, or characteristics of persons under investigation? What are the implications of a given research design and how quickly can the study be accomplished? Is the study feasible, given the available resources? The answers to these questions will help direct the selection of a research design and the choice of a study population.

References

Abramowicz, H. K., & Richardson, S. A. Epidemiology of severe mental retardation in children: Community studies. *American Journal of Mental Deficiency*, 1975, **80**, 18–39.

Adelstein, A. M., National statistics. *Postgraduate Medicine*, 1975, **51**(Suppl. 2), 57–67.

American Association on Mental Deficiency. *Manual on terminology and classification in mental retardation.* Washington, D.C., 1977.

Bay, K. S., Flathman, D., & Nestman, L. The worth of a screening program: An application of a statistical decision model for the benefit evaluation of screening projects. *American Journal of Public Health*, 1976, **66**, 145–150.

Beck, E., Blaichman, S., Scriver, C. R., & Clow, C. L. Advocacy and compliance in genetic screening: Behavior of physicians and clients in a voluntary program of testing for the Tay-Sachs gene. *New England Journal of Medicine*, 1974, **291**, 1160–1170.

Begab, M. Presidential address: Frontiers of knowledge in mental retardation. In P. Mittler (Ed.), *Frontiers of knowledge in mental retardation.* Vol. II. *Biomedical Aspects.* Baltimore: University Park Press, 1980.

Beneson, A. S. (Ed.) *Control of communicable diseases in man.* (12th ed.) Washington, D.C.: American Public Health Association, 1975.

Berry, H. K., Sutherland, B. S., Umbarger, B., & O'Grady, D. Treatment of phenylketonuria. *American Journal of Diseases of Children*, 1976, **113**, 2–5.

Birch, H., Richardson, S. A., Baird, D. Horobin, G., & Illsley, R. *Mental subnormality in the community.* Baltimore: Williams & Wilkins, 1970.

Blot, W. J., & Miller, R. W. Mental retardation following in utero exposure to the atomic bombs of Hiroshima and Nagasaki. *Radiology*, 1973, **106**, 617–619.

Blot, W. J., Shimizu, Y., Kato, H., & Miller, R. W. Frequency of marriage and live birth among survivors prenatally exposed to the atomic bomb. *American Journal of Epidemiology*, 1975, **102**, 128–136.

Childs, B., Gordis, L., Kaback, M., & Kazazian, H. Tay-Sachs screening: Motives for participating and knowledge of genetics and probability. *American Journal of Human Genetics*, 1976, **28**, 537–549.

Clarke, A. M., & Clarke, A. D. B. (Eds.). *Mental deficiency: The changing outlook*. New York: The Free Press, 1975.

Cochrane, A. L., & Holland, W. W. Validation of screening procedures. *British Medical Bulletin*, 1971, **27**, 3–8.

Collman, R. D., & Stoller, A. A survey of mongoloid births in Victoria, Australia 1942–1957. *American Journal of Public Health*, 1962, **52**, 813–829.

Deykin, E. Y., & MacMahon, B. Viral exposure and autism. *American Journal of Epidemiology*, 1979, **109**, 628–638.

Drillien, C. M., Jameson, S., & Wilkinson, E. M. Studies in mental handicap: I. Prevalence and distribution by clinical type and severity of defect. *Archives of Disease in Childhood*, 1966, **41**, 528–538.

Ellenberg, J. H., & Nelson, K. B. Birth weight and gestational age in children with cerebral palsy or seizure disorders. *American Journal of Diseases of Children*, 1979, **133**, 1044–1048.

Fabia, J., & Drolette, M. Life tables up to age 10 for mongols with and without congenital heart defect. *Journal of Mental Deficiency Research*, 1970, **14**, 235–242.

Ferguson-Smith, M. A. Maternal age and Down's syndrome. *Lancet*, 1978, **2**, 213.

Fleiss, J. L. *Statistical methods for rates and proportions*. (2nd ed.) New York: John Wiley & Sons, 1981.

Forssman, H., and Akesson, H. O. Mortality in patients with Down's syndrome. *Journal of Mental Deficiency Research*, 1965, **9**, 146–149.

Fox, J. P., Hall, C. E., & Elveback, L. R. *Epidemiology: Man and disease*. New York: Macmillan Company, 1970.

Gail, M., Williams, R., Byar, D. P., & Brown, C. How many controls? *Journal of Chronic Diseases*, 1976, **29**, 723–731.

Gallagher, R. P., & Lowry, R. B. Longevity in Down's syndrome in British Columbia. *Journal of Mental Deficiency Research*, 1975, **19**, 157–163.

Hansen, H., Belmont, L., & Stein, Z. A. Epidemiology. In J. Wortis (Ed.), *Mental retardation and developmental disabilities*. Vol. XI. New York: Brunner/Mazel, 1980.

Harlap, S., & Shiono, P. H. Alcohol, smoking, and incidence of spontaneous abortions in the first and second trimester. *Lancet*, 1980, **2**, 173–176.

Hauser, W. A., & Kurland, L. T. The epidemiology of epilepsy in Rochester, Minnesota, 1935–1967. *Epilepsia*, 1975, **16**, 1–66.

Heber, R. F. *Epidemiology of mental retardation*. Springfield, Ill.: Charles C. Thomas, 1970.

Herbst, D. S., Dunn, H. G., Dill, F. J., Kalousek, D. K., & Krywaniuk, L. W. Further delineation of X-linked mental retardation. *Human Genetics*, 1981, **58**, 366–372.

Hook, E. B., Albright, S. G., & Cross, P. K. Use of Bernoulli census and log-linear methods for estimating the prevalence of spina bifida in livebirths and the completeness of vital record reports in New York State. *American Journal of Epidemiology*, 1980, **112**, 750–758.

Hook, E. B., & Cross, P. K. Temporal increase in the rate of Down syndrome livebirths to older mothers in New York State. *Journal of Medical Genetics*, 1981, **18**, 29–30.

Howard-Peebles, P. N., & Stoddard, G. R. Familial X-linked mental retardation with a marker X chromosome and its relationship to macro-orchidism. *Clinical Genetics*, 1980, **17**, 125–128.

Kennedy, J. L., Wertelecki, W., Gates, L., Sperry, B. P., & Cass, V. M. The early treatment of phenylketonuria. *American Journal of Diseases of Children*, 1967, **113**, 16–21.

Kiely, J. L., & Paneth, N. Follow-up studies of low-birthweight infants: Suggestions for design, analysis and reporting. *Developmental Medicine and Child Neurology*, 1981, **23**, 96–100.

Kiely, J. L., Paneth, N., Stein, Z. A., & Susser, M. W. Cerebral palsy and newborn care. II: Mortality and neurological impairment in low-birthweight infants. *Developmental Medicine and Child Neurology*, 1981, **23**, 650–659.

Kline, J. K., Stein, Z. A., Shrout, P., Susser, M. W., & Warburton, D. Drinking during pregnancy and spontaneous abortion, *Lancet*, 1980, **2**, 176–180.

Kushlick, A., & Blunden, R. The epidemiology of mental subnormality. In A. M. Clarke and A. D. B. Clarke (Eds.), *Mental deficiency*. New York: The Free Press, 1974. Pp. 31–81.

LaPouse, R., & Weitzner, M. Epidemiology. In J. Wortis (Ed.), *Mental retardation: An annual review*. Vol. I. New York: Grune & Stratton, 1970. Pp. 197–223.

Lilienfeld, A. M. *Foundations of epidemiology*. New York: Oxford University Press, 1976.

MacMahon, B., & Pugh, T. F. *Epidemiology: Principles and methods*. Boston: Little, Brown and Company, 1977.

Mausner, J. S., & Bahn, A. K. *Epidemiology: An introductory text*. Philadelphia: W.B. Saunders Co., 1974.

McCurley, R., Mackay, D. N., & Scally, B. G. The life expectation of the mentally subnormal under community and hospital care. *Journal of Mental Deficiency Research*, 1972, **16**, 57–66.

Mercer, J. R. *Labelling the mentally retarded*. Berkeley: University of California Press, 1973.

Miller, R. W., & Blot, W. J. Small head size after in-utero exposure to atomic radiation. *Lancet*, 1972, **2**, 784–787.

Neugebauer, R., & Golden, R. Application of a capture-recapture method (the Bernoulli census) in historical epidemiology. Presented at the Society for Epidemiological Research XIVth annual meeting, Snowbird, Utah, June, 1981.

New York City Department of Health. *Summary of Vital Statistics*. 1977.

Olegard, R., Sabel, D. G., Aronsson, M., Sandin, B., Johansson, P. R., Carlsson, C., Kyllerman, M., Iverson, K., & Hrbek, A. Effects on the child of alcohol abuse during pregnancy, *Acta Paediatrica Scandinavica*, Suppl. **275**, 1979, 112–121.

Oster, J., Mikkelsen, M., & Nielsen, A. Mortality and life-table in Down's syndrome. *Acta Paediatrica Scandinavica*, 1975, **64**, 322–326.

Rantakallio, P. The effect of maternal smoking on birthweight and subsequent health of the child. *Early Human Development*, 1978, **2**, 371–382.

Richards, B. W. Mental retardation. In J. G. Howells (Ed.), *Modern perspectives in the psychiatry of old age*. New York: Brunner/Mazel, 1975.

Russell, M. Intra-uterine growth in infants born to women

with alcohol-related psychiatric disorders. *Alcoholism: Clinical and Experimental Research*, 1977, **1**, 225–231.

Siegal, M., Fuerst, H. T., & Guinee, V. F. Rubella epidemicity and embryopathy: Results of a long-term prospective study. *American Journal of Diseases of Children*, 1971, **121**, 469–473.

Stein, Z. A. Strategies for the prevention of mental retardation. *Bulletin of the New York Academy of Medicine*, 1975, **51**, 130–142.

Stein, Z. A., Goldsmith, R., Kline, J., Margolis, S., Sadow, M., & Zybert, P. Public health aspects of Down's syndrome (Mongolism). *Public Health Reviews*, 1975, **4**, 229–253.

Stein, Z. A., & Susser, M. W. Changes over time in the incidence and prevalence of mental retardation. In J. Hellmuth (Ed.), *Exceptional infant*. Vol. 2. *Studies in abnormalities*. New York: Brunner/Mazel, 1971, 305–340.

Stein, Z. A., & Susser, M. W. The epidemiology of mental retardation. In S. Arietti (Ed.), *American handbook of psychiatry*. (2nd ed.) New York: Basic Books, Inc., 1974.

Stein, Z. A., & Susser, M. W. Mental retardation. In J. M. Last (Ed.), *Maxcy-Rosenau public health and preventive medicine*. (11th ed.) New York: Appleton-Century-Crofts, 1980.

Stein, Z. A., Susser, M. W., & Saenger, G. Mental retardation in national population of young men in the Netherlands. I. Prevalence of severe mental retardation. *American Journal of Epidemiology*, 1976, **103**, 477–485. (a)

Stein, Z. A., Susser, M. W., & Saenger, G. Mental retardation in a national population of young men in the Netherlands. II. Prevalence of mild mental retardation. *American Journal of Epidemiology*, 1976, **104**, 159–169. (b)

Stein, Z. A., Susser, M. W., Saenger, G., & Marolla, F. *Famine and human development: The Dutch hunger winter of 1944/45*. New York: Oxford University Press, 1975.

Susser, M. W. *Causal thinking in the health sciences: Concepts and strategies in epidemiology*. New York: Oxford University Press, 1973.

Sutherland, B. S., Umbarger, B., & Berry, H. K. The treatment of phenylketonuria: A decade of results. *American Journal of Diseases of Children*, 1966, **111**, 505–523.

Thoene, J., Higgins, J., Krieger, I., Schmickel, R., & Weiss, L. Genetic screening for mental retardation in Michigan. *American Journal of Mental Deficiency*, 1981, **85**, 335–340.

Thompson, J. S., & Thompson, M. W. *Genetics in medicine*. (2nd ed.) Philadelphia: W.B. Saunders Co., 1973.

Turner, G., Daniel, A., & Frost, M. X-linked mental retardation, macro-orchidism, and the Xq27 fragile site. *Journal of Pediatrics*, 1980, **96**, 837–841.

Ueda, K., Nishida, Y., Oshima, K., & Shepard, T. H. Congenital rubella syndrome: Correlation of gestational age at time of maternal rubella with type of defect. *Journal of Pediatrics*, 1979, **94**, 763–765.

Van Den Berghe, H., Fryus, J., Parloir, C., Deroover, J., & Keulemans, M. Genetic causes of severe mental handicap: Preliminary data from a University of Leuven study. In P. Mittler (Ed.), *Frontiers of knowledge in mental retardation*. Vol. II. *Biomedical aspects*. Baltimore: University Park Press, 1980.

Vecchio, J. J. Predictive value of a single diagnostic test in unselected populations. *New England Journal of Medicine*, 1966, **274**, 1171–1173.

Wajsbort, J., Haral, N., & Alfandary, I. A study of the epidemiology of chronic epilepsy in northern Israel. *Epilepsia*, 1967, **8**, 105–116.

Wittes, J. T. Applications of a multinomial capture-recapture model to epidemiological data. *Journal of the American Statistical Association*, 1974, **69**, 93–97.

Wittes, J. T., Colton, T., & Sidel, V. W. Capture-recapture methods for assessing the completeness of case ascertainment when using multiple information sources. *Journal of Chronic Diseases*, 1974, **227**, 25–36.

Wittes, J. T., & Sidel, V. W. A generalization of the simple capture-recapture model with applications to epidemiological research. *Journal of Chronic Diseases*, 1968, **21**, 287–301.

37 NONEXPERIMENTAL FIELD RESEARCH METHODS

Marsha Mailick Seltzer

N onexperimental field research methods encompass a series of research designs and statistical analytical models that are intended
to be used in conduct of research in natural or field
settings when classical experimental designs that involve
randomization procedures cannot feasibly be employed. Thus, nonexperimental field research methods
have two key characteristics: (1) these studies are generally located in field settings, not in laboratories and
(2) these studies do not employ randomization procedures. In this chapter, examples of nonexperimental
field research will be presented along with a discussion
of appropriate research designs.

Studies employing nonexperimental field research
methods tend to be action oriented and applied. That
is, the focus of these studies is generally on producing
descriptive and evaluative data about services that are
provided to mentally retarded persons, about their
families, and about their interactions with members
of the broader community. Basic research about the
physiological causes of mental retardation and epidemiological research about the distinctive features
of the mentally retarded population are beyond the
purview of this methodology. Examples of issues frequently raised in nonexperimental field research include: evaluation of the effects of deinstitutionalization,
mainstreaming, and early intervention; assessment of
the extent to which community integration efforts

have been successful; examination of the phenomenon
of labeling and its correlates; and investigation of
relationships among mentally retarded persons, between mentally retarded persons and their families,
and between mentally retarded persons and the staff
who have responsibility for them.

Empirical evidence about these issues is spotty at
best, both because of the limited amount of research
conducted in this area, and because the results of
those studies that have been conducted often do not
confirm one another (Gottlieb, 1981; Landesman-
Dwyer, 1981). This lack of evidence remains a serious
problem. Haywood (1981), in his Presidential Address
to the American Association on Mental Deficiency,
remarked that

> ignorance is still our most plentiful commodity
> in this field. We are called to do things that we
> simply do not know how to do. We have
> embarked on whole national social movements
> without the knowledge necessary to chart the
> course of such movements, and without the
> highly trained personnel necessary to carry out
> and evaluate new programs. [p. 193]

For example, as of the early 1970s evidence regarding
the relative benefits of placement of educable mentally
retarded children in separate special classrooms vs.

mainstreamed classrooms was not available and, as Meyers, MacMillan, and Yoshida (1980) noted, this "empirical ambiguity permitted other forces, both political and philosophical, to push the change [to mainstreaming]" (p. 197).

The optimal research methodology to use when investigating "real-life" problems faced by mentally retarded persons—especially about the effects of services on them—is the randomized experiment. When this methodology is used, conclusions about the effects of an intervention on its recipients can be made with a considerable degree of confidence. However, there are many times when political and practical constraints make the conduct of randomized experiments in natural settings very difficult or impossible. For example, in the investigation of the relative benefits of group homes vs. institutional wards on the performance of mentally retarded persons, it is generally not possible to release a randomly selected group of clients from the institution to group homes and to retain the others in the institution as a control group. It is in situations such as this one that nonexperimental field research methods can make an important contribution.

Nonexperimental field research methods are also useful when randomization is logically impossible, such as when the independent variable is not manipulable. For example, if a researcher is interested in comparing elderly mentally retarded persons with nonelderly mentally retarded adults with respect to their functional skills, it is obviously impossible to manipulate the independent variable, i.e., to assign persons randomly to the elderly group and to the nonelderly group. Instead, such comparisons can be made when members of the two groups are matched on key characteristics in order to make the two groups as comparable as possible. Matching is one of several nonexperimental field research methods that can be used in this situation. There are also times when manipulation of the independent variable would cause suffering to the subjects (e.g., taking medications that have serious side effects), and in such instances nonexperimental field research methods can be used as well.

Brooks and Baumeister (1977) have challenged experimental researchers in the field of mental retardation to "leave the security of their laboratories, tolerate greater ambiguity, and go where people actually live in order to analyze adaptive behavior" (p. 415). This chapter is intended to present one body of research methods for use in field situations such as those discussed by Brooks and Baumeister. In the sections that follow, three major considerations in the design of nonexperimental field research will be discussed, including (*a*) the analytic objective of a study (description

vs. causation), (*b*) the type of research design (three types of nonexperimental field research designs for use in situations when randomization is not feasible, not possible, or not desirable), and (*c*) the method of data collection to be employed.

Analytic Objective

In nonexperimental field research, there are two possible analytic objectives that a study may attempt to achieve. One analytic objective involves the *description* of services, clients, situations, families, and so on, while the other analytic objective entails drawing a *causal link* between two sets of phenomena, such as deinstitutionalization and community adjustment, or increased contact between mentally retarded and nonretarded children and reduced stigmatization of mentally retarded children by others. In general, much more descriptive research than causal research is conducted and published on topics such as deinstitutionalization, community adjustment, vocational adjustment, mainstreaming, social interaction among mentally retarded persons, labeling, etc. However, causal research provides much more useful evaluative information than does descriptive research. The characteristics of each and the differences between the two will be briefly described below.

Descriptive Research

Descriptive studies may be either cross-sectional or longitudinal in design. For example, if the objective is to study different types of sheltered workshops and compare their graduates' rates of placement into and adjustment to competitive jobs, there are two possible research designs. One approach is to survey a sample of sheltered workshops, collect data about the number of clients served by each workshop in the course of a year, the number of graduates who have obtained competitive jobs, etc. The sample of sheltered workshops could be divided into a series of subgroups on the basis of some key dimension or dimensions (e.g., size) and the placement rates of the different subgroups, or types, could be calculated and compared. All graduates, or a random sample, who are placed in competitive jobs could then be visited and interviewed, and on the basis of their responses to questions posed to them, their adjustment could be assessed. This is the cross-sectional approach to the problem.

An alternative methodology would be to use a longitudinal (or prospective) design in which a sample of sheltered workshops would be studied over a period of time (e.g., two years). Workshops could be divided into types, as above, and placement rates could be calculated at the end of each year. However, an advantage of the longitudinal design is that it allows for more than one assessment of the outcome of interest, which, in this case, is adjustment to a competitive job. Thus, *change* in adjustment over time could be detected. If, hypothetically, adjustment shortly after placement is poor but improves over time, a longitudinal design with two or more assessments would detect this change, whereas a cross-sectional design would have a great deal more difficulty in doing so. Also, with longitudinal descriptive studies, all subjects can be assessed at the same point in time relative to their date of release (e.g., two months after release), whereas in cross-sectional research, since client assessment is conducted only once, it is likely that at the time of assessment, clients would have been in their jobs for varying lengths of time. Although it is possible to analyze for the relationship between length of time on the job and adjustment using data collected from a cross-sectional study, this issue can be more directly addressed in longitudinal research. Thus, longitudinal descriptive studies can provide substantially more useful information than cross-sectional descriptive studies.

However, both types of descriptive studies differ from causal studies in that in descriptive studies it is more difficult to draw valid causal connections. Thus, in the example used above, if larger workshops were found to have higher competitive placement rates than smaller workshops, it would be unwarranted to assume that the size of the workshop was the cause of the differential placement rate, unless the two types of workshops were alike in all other respects besides size, or unless special statistical procedures are used to "control for" the effects of characteristics of the workshops other than size on the placement rates. It may be that the services provided to clients in larger workshops differed systematically from the services provided in smaller workshops and that it was the difference in services not the difference in size that accounted for the different placement rates.

It is also possible that different placement rates might be the result of different types of clients; that is, it is possible that the more capable clients were accepted by the larger workshops, and thus differences in placement rates might be more a function of the different levels of skills possessed by the clients before they entered their respective workshops than of any effect that the workshops actually had on them. If the objective of the study is purely descriptive, then such preplacement differences in the two groups of workshops are not problematic. However, if the goal is to try to determine whether differences in workshops cause differences in placement rates, then additional controls must be introduced into the research design or the statistical analysis to maximize the extent to which the two groups are comparable. Differences in outcome cannot be assumed to be caused by differences in the workshops unless there is reason to believe that clients who attended the different types of workshops were comparable to begin with.

Causal Studies

Unlike descriptive studies, causal studies are intended to assess the impact of an intervention on the service recipients. For example, it is possible to investigate the impact of deinstitutionalization on the community adjustment of mentally retarded persons. In this example, the impact of deinstitutionalization can be defined as being the difference between how the deinstitutionalized clients fared in the community and how they would have fared at that same point in time had they remained in the institution. In order to draw conclusions about this impact, one must first have a basis to say that the deinstitutionalized clients' level of adjustment would not have been achieved without the particular intervention (in this case, movement from an institution to a community living arrangement).

Changed behavior in clients alone is not evidence of the impact of an intervention such as deinstitutionalization. Before it is possible to say that deinstitutionalization has had an impact, it must be demonstrated that the change in behavior would not have occurred without the change in environment. Some change in behavior will occur naturally over time as individuals develop and mature; thus, change should not be confused with impact. In fact, no change may be shown to be a positive impact of deinstitutionalization. For example, it is possible for deinstitutionalization to enable persons to sustain skills already learned that would have deteriorated had they remained in the institutional setting. If it were established that this behavioral regression is associated with remaining in an institution and that such a regression did not take place or was arrested or slowed down by a community placement, there would be reason to conclude that deinstitutionalization had an impact on the clients even though no improvements occurred in their behavior.

To summarize, descriptive studies provide useful data about phenomena of interest (e.g., mainstreamed classrooms, community residences, friendship patterns), either through one-shot (cross-sectional) or over-time (longitudinal) methods. Changed client behavior as detected by longitudinal descriptive studies cannot alone be taken as evidence of the impact of a service intervention on the clients. In order to infer impact (or cause and effect), research designs must be employed that provide estimates of how the clients would have fared had they not received the intervention; quasi-experimental designs are available for use when randomization cannot be conducted but when causal inferences are still desired.

Research Design

The previous section presented two alternative analytic objectives that may be characteristic of a study that utilizes nonexperimental field research methods, namely (1) description and (2) inferring a cause-and-effect relationship. In this section, three quasi-experimental research designs are discussed for use when the analytic objective is inferring causation. According to Cook and Campbell (1979), quasi-experiments are studies that have "treatments (i.e., interventions), outcome measures, and experimental units, but do not use random assignment to create comparisons from which treatment-caused change is inferred" (p. 6).

The central methodological issue in quasi-experiments is estimating what the behavior of the clients would have been had they not received the intervention; this estimation must be made using methods other than a randomized control group. In quasi-experimental research designs, an attempt is made to rule out "threats to internal validity." Threats to internal validity are defects in the research design that allow for alternative explanations (other than the key hypothesis) to account for the obtained findings. Unless the research design is successful in ruling out most of these alternative explanations, there can be little confidence that the findings of a study actually provide evidence to support the research hypothesis. For example, in comparing two groups of mentally retarded school aged children, one group may be placed in a self-contained classroom while the other group is mainstreamed. Unless the research design insures that the two groups of children are equivalent before the school year begins, any differences in the extent to which the children in the two groups interact with the other children at the end of the year might be due to a host of causes other than the effect of mainstreaming. The children in the self-contained classroom, for instance, might have had more behavior problems at the beginning of the year than the mainstreamed children and it is possible that the poor behavior manifested by these children—and not the fact that they were in a self-contained classroom— was the reason that they interacted less often with the nonretarded children in the school. This is the threat

to internal validity of "selection"; the children were differentially selected into two groups. If the research design cannot insure equivalence of groups prior to the beginning of the intervention, certain data analytic techniques must be used to attempt to rule out the threats to internal validity that otherwise would reduce the usefulness of the study.

In the discussion that follows, three research designs/ data analytic techniques are presented which are commonly used in nonexperimental field studies. Each approach attempts to rule out threats to internal validity so that a causal inference can be made with more or less confidence about the effect of the independent variable on the dependent variable. Each research design has been accepted with more or less controversy by methodologists, but in general, the attempt to infer impact (or causation) using quasi-experimental methods remains somewhat controversial in social science research. Examples of studies employing each of the three designs from the mental retardation literature are also provided.

Nonrandomized Control Group Design

The nonrandomized control group design involves a comparison between a group of individuals who receive an intervention (e.g., a service) and another group of individuals who do not. In this design, the individuals are assigned to the groups by some method other than randomization. The comparison between the groups is made so that the individuals who did not receive the service can provide an estimate of how those who did receive the service would have functioned had they not received the service. This design is also used when two (or more) alternative interventions are compared with each other, either in the absence of a no-treatment control group or in conjunction with a no-treatment control group. A comparison between the alternative interventions provides an estimate of how those who received one intervention would have functioned had they received the other intervention. If significant differences are found between the groups at posttest, an inference may be made about the effect of the service on the recipients. The validity of this inference is largely a function of the comparability of the groups prior to the beginning of the research and the similarity of intervening experiences other than the service; that is, if the groups are similar at pretest, any differences between the groups at posttest may be due to the effect of the service. However, since randomization is not an available strategy for use in creating the groups and making them equivalent, it is likely that the groups will not be perfectly comparable at pretest. The reader of a study in which the nonrandomized control group design is used must thus be on the alert for systematic differences between the groups that may account for posttest differences on the key dependent variable. Several threats to internal validity that are frequently encountered in nonrandomized control group studies will be briefly discussed below.

As noted above, the most serious threat to the internal validity of the nonrandomized control group design is selection—systematic differences between the groups at pre-test. For example, in comparing small group home settings with large group home settings, if the clients who are placed in the smaller residences have higher IQ's and fewer years of institutionalization than those in the larger settings, it is impossible to interpret any posttest differences between the groups in community adjustment as being due to the differential effects of residences of different sizes. Since the two groups differed to begin with, the posttest differences may be partly or entirely a function of characteristics possessed by the clients before their placement rather than a function of the effect of facility size on clients. In order to make a valid inference about the effect of residence size on community adjustment, there should be reason to believe that the clients who live in the two types of settings were comparable on key characteristics prior to their placement in the residences.

Pretest comparability is one important prerequisite for determining whether an intervention had an effect on the clients. However, there are other design requirements that must be met in order to make a valid inference about the effect of the independent variable on the dependent variable. During the course of the study, if one group experienced different external events than the other group, the effect of the key intervention may be confounded. This is the threat to internal validity of "history." To illustrate this point the example presented above regarding residence size will be used. If the smaller residences were located in city A and the larger residences were located in city B, and furthermore if in city A a new community integration program was begun during the period of time that the research project was ongoing, any posttest advantages in community adjustment on the part of residents of the smaller facilities might in fact be due to the effect of the community integration program rather than the differences in facility size. Thus, even when the two groups are comparable at pretest, the effects of different external events can confound size effects.

Another issue to keep in mind when designing or reading about a study employing a nonrandomized control group design concerns the problem of differential rates of maturation between the two groups. Thus, for example, if the larger facilities include residents who are younger in age than the residents of the smaller facilities, any posttest differences in community adjustment may be a function of the faster development occurring among the younger residents rather than the effect of differential residential size. In this case, both the threats of selection and maturation are operative.

To summarize, when a study contains an experimental and control group that were not created by means of randomization, it is necessary for caution to be exercised prior to inferring that the intervention had an impact on the clients. Threats to internal validity, such as differential external events, differential rates of maturation, or pre-intervention differences between the members of the two groups must be ruled out.[1] Threats to internal validity may result in differences between the groups that are not a function of the impact of the intervention. If there is reason to believe that these threats to internal validity did not occur with respect to a particular study and if posttest between-group differences were found, it is possible to conclude that the intervention probably had an impact on the clients.

The nonrandomized control group design is commonly used in nonexperimental field research, primarily because fewer political constraints are encountered with this design than when attempting to create equivalent groups through randomization procedures. It also enables the comparison of groups of individuals who already are placed in different settings or who already receive different types of interventions. An attempt is made to match pairs (or triplets, quadruplets, etc.) of clients on relevant characteristics. For example, Berkson (1981) compared three groups of clients—those who lived in sheltered care, those who lived with their families, and those who lived independently—with respect to various measures of social behavior and work performance. He matched the "triplets" on four variables: AAMD level of retardation, age, sex, and specific workshop placement. The design assumption was that if the groups were comparable on these four variables, any differences among the groups in the dependent variables would be the result of the differential effects of the three living environments. However, no dependent variable differences were found.

It should be noted that although Berkson matched his subjects on four variables, the hope was that they would also be comparable with respect to many other variables that were correlated with the four matching variables. He reported that no significant differences were found among the groups on three other variables (length of time in the workshop, number of observations made, and physical attractiveness), suggesting general comparability of subjects across groups. However, the extent to which subjects were actually comparable on still other key variables remains unknown and may in fact account for the lack of dependent variable differences. Although this may be unlikely, the possibility nevertheless remains with the nonrandomized control group design. Sherwood, Morris, and Sherwood (1975) present a multivariate matching procedure which minimizes this problem considerably.

Interrupted Time Series Design

The interrupted time series design involves multiple observations of a phenomenon over time, with an intervention occurring at some point during the course of the observation period. For example, the variable being observed (the dependent variable) could be the number of staff in a sheltered workshop who resign each month. In an effort to reduce the amount of staff turnover, a staff training intervention is planned. Using the interrupted time series design, the number of resignations per month for the five months prior to the beginning of the two week training program and for the five months after are plotted (see Fig. 37.1).

The logic of the interrupted time series design is that with a sufficient number of measurements prior to the intervention, a stable trend line can be drawn which reflects the preintervention base-line level of the dependent variable—in this case, number of staff resignations per month. If a break or interruption in this line occurs coterminous with the introduction of the intervention, an inference can be made that it was the staff training intervention that was responsible for the change in the number of staff resignations per month.

It is much better to use this design than to compare one measure of the dependent variable to the intervention with one measure of the dependent variable following the intervention. Pre-post change often is incorrectly assumed to be caused by an intervention

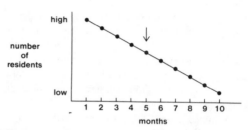

Fig. 37.2. Number of residents in an institution per month.

when in fact it simply may be the result of an ongoing trend, as shown in Fig. 37.2.

In the example presented in Fig. 37.2, in an effort to speed up deinstitutionalization, the superintendent of an institution introduced a new set of procedures and forms at the fifth month. Although a simple look at the number of residents who lived in the institution during months 4, 5, and 6 would suggest that new procedures and forms had their desired effect, in actuality all that is occurring is an ongoing trend of increasing deinstitutionalization each month, with no apparent additional effect of the new forms and procedures. Thus, with the interrupted time series design, the probability of incorrectly inferring an effect is much lower than with a simple pre-post change design. It is therefore necessary to include as many preintervention assessments of the dependent variable as possible in order to maximize the validity of cause-and-effect inferences.

The interrupted time series design has a number of strengths. First, when introducing an innovation in a setting such as a sheltered workshop, a community residence, or institution, there are times when it is very difficult to set up a control group that does not receive the innovation or that receives an alternative service. When such feasibility problems arise, the interrupted time series design can be conducted so that a reasonably valid inference of impact can be made even though all persons are exposed to the intervention. Additionally, it is a very useful design to use when examining data in records in order to determine the impact of an intervention that occurred in the past, since it is obviously impossible to set up a control group situation after the fact. The interrupted time series design is also used in clinical situations when an intervention is attempted with only one client.

However, there are a number of problems with the interrupted time series design. First, it is vulnerable to the threat to internal validity of history—the possibility that an external event other than the intervention occurred coterminous with the intervention and ac-

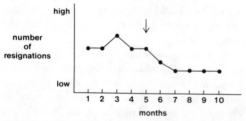

Fig. 37.1. Number of staff resignations per month.

tually caused the change observed in the dependent variable. Second, it is very difficult to detect the impact of interventions that have delayed effects or gradual effects. Third, since it is necessary to take repeated measurements of the dependent variable prior to the intervention, it is possible that those who are eager to begin the intervention would be reluctant to wait until a sufficient number of preintervention measurements are made. Furthermore, the measurement process can often be extremely intrusive if the subjects are aware that they are being assessed. However, when measurement is accomplished by observation of subjects rather than by interviewing, intrusiveness may be somewhat less of a problem, and when data are culled from records, intrusiveness is obviously not a problem at all.

A variation on the basic interrupted time series design entails the following steps: (1) preintervention observations, (2) the introduction of the intervention, (3) postintervention observations, (4) removal of the intervention, (5) observation after the intervention is removed, (6) reintroduction of the intervention, and (7) observation. This design is known as the interrupted time series with multiple replications or the ABAB design. According to Cook and Campbell (1979), "a treatment effect would be suggested if the dependent variable responded in a similar fashion each time the treatment was introduced and in a similar fashion each time it was removed. However, the direction of the responses must be different in the case of introduction when compared to removals" (p. 222). This design is often used in behavioral research such as the study conducted by Mayhew, Enyart, and Anderson (1978), which sought to determine whether severely and profoundly mentally retarded persons could increase their rate of social responses when socially reinforced for this behavior. Using an ABAB design, a five-session period of base-line observation was followed by a five-session period of social reinforcement; next, the social reinforcement was removed for five sessions, and finally, reinforcement was reintroduced for the final five sessions. As hypothesized, the rate of social responses increased during the two reinforcement periods and decreased during the nonreinforced period.

The primary advantage of the ABAB design over the usual interrupted time series design concerns the ability to rule out the threat to internal validity of history. The probability that an outside event would coincidentally occur and stop and reoccur at precisely those times that the intervention is introduced and removed and reintroduced is very low. Thus, the inference of causation can be made more confidently when the threat of history is ruled out. However,

ethical concerns have been raised about the removal of beneficial treatments, and such concerns often limit the use of this design.

The Statistical Control Design

In nonexperimental field research, it is common to encounter highly complex naturally occurring experiments that are amenable to neither the nonrandomized control group design nor to the interrupted time series design. For example, in some naturally occurring experiments, the researcher does not have control over the experimental situation, making the conduct of many repeated measures impossible and thus ruling out the use of the interrupted time series design. Moreover, it may be that the construction of comparable nonrandomized groups through matching procedures cannot easily be accomplished because of the large number of categories of the independent variable. For example, if the independent variable is "type of residence", the categories could include the following five types: group home, foster home, independent apartment, semi-independent apartment, institution. In such instances, rather than attempt to match quintuplets, it is possible to use statistical controls to conduct a quasi-experimental analysis of the effects of an intervention such as type of residence.

An example of such a complex naturally-occurring experiment is described by Berkson and Romer (1980). Over 300 mentally retarded adults in five settings (four sheltered workshops and one residence) were studied and in one analysis (Romer & Berkson, 1980), an attempt was made to examine the relative importance of personal variables and setting variables in predicting the affiliative behavior of the subjects. Matching apparently was not attempted because of the probable difficulty in identifying sets of five individuals, one from each of the five settings, who were comparable with respect to the matching or "control" variables (sex, IQ, age, and diagnosis). Instead, a multiple regression analysis[2] was conducted in which the relationship between these personal variables and the dependent variable of affiliation was calculated and the extent to which setting characteristics were successful in accounting for additional variability in affiliation was determined. Since the types of individuals who were included in the five types of settings were somewhat different, it was necessary to statistically adjust for such differences before analyzing the effect of setting characteristics on affiliative behavior.

In another example of the statistical control design, Seltzer, Seltzer, and Sherwood (in press) used multiple regression analysis to examine the extent to which clients who were placed in different types of residential settings actually differed in their performance of community living skills. In this analysis, the independent variable (the intervention) was type of residential setting and the dependent variable was level of performance. The methodological challenge posed by this naturally occurring experiment was to determine whether the observed performance differences were actually the result of the effects of different environments, or, alternatively, the result of the characteristics possessed by the clients before they were placed in these environments. The issue raised in that analysis is that differences in client outcome in different types of settings may exist because settings differentially selected clients. That is, it is possible that settings which possessed "better" characteristics (e.g., high degree of autonomy) selected for admission those clients who possessed "better" characteristics (e.g., higher intelligence); the fact that later on in time these clients still possessed the favorable characteristics and functioned at a higher level does not necessarily say anything about the effect of the residential environment on the client. In order to make an inference about the effect of the residential environment, it is necessary first to statistically control for the relationship between type of client (as measured by background demographic characteristics) and performance level, by entering the control variables first into a regression equation.[3] Then, any additional variance in the dependent variable that can be accounted for by the intervention provides an estimate of the extent to which the intervention is having an effect. As Cook and Campbell (1979) summarize, in the statistical control design, "a treatment effect is inferred if there is a statistically significant regression coefficient relating the dummy variable (the intervention) to the dependent variable after adjusting for the effect of the covariates (the control variables) introduced to try to correct for selection" (p. 298).

In the statistical control design, the objective of entering the control variables into the multiple regression equation first is comparable to the objective of matching subjects across groups in the nonrandomized control group design. In both of these designs, an attempt is made to correct for the threat to internal validity of selection, so that the true effect of an intervention can better be estimated.

Methods of Data Collection

Earlier in this chapter, a distinction was drawn between research in which the analytic objective is description and research in which the analytic objective is inferring causation. If a study attempts to draw causal inferences, it is necessary to employ a research design that maximizes the validity of such cause-and-effect conclusions. In contrast, when the analytic objective is description, the study should be designed in such a way as to maximize the extent to which the data collection procedures provide the desired descriptive information.[4]

In the discussion that follows, four methods of data collection are presented. Although, as noted above, the selection of the appropriate methods of data collection is a particularly important consideration in descriptive research, the discussion presented below is also applicable to quasi-experimental (i.e., causal) studies, and also for that matter to true experiments.

The method of data collection is a particularly important issue for the field of mental retardation, because it is difficult for some mentally retarded persons to provide reliable and valid information about their performance of skills, their lifestyles, and the services they receive. In such cases, the researcher must either collect the data from significant others (such as parents or supervising staff), from direct observations of mentally retarded persons, or from test results obtained from formalized and standardized testing procedures. Each of these approaches has advantages and disadvantages in reliability, validity, and focus. These issues will be discussed below. A discussion of the data collection problems encountered when collecting information about settings follows the more detailed discussion of methods of collecting data about mentally retarded persons on the individual level.

The Collection of Data about Individuals

INTERVIEWING THE MENTALLY RETARDED PERSON

A number of reports are available in the literature in which the retarded person was interviewed directly to gather data regarding some aspect of his or her community adaptation (Gollay, Friedman, Wyngaarten, & Kurtz, 1978; Seltzer & Seltzer, 1978; Seltzer, 1981). In general, such interviews are intended to generate data about the extent to which mentally retarded persons are satisfied with various aspects of their lifestyles, including their residential situations, work settings, friendships, relationships with family, etc. To the extent to which a research study includes a focus on client satisfaction, this method is central to adequate data collection.

In one study, for example, the job satisfaction of 65 deinstitutionalized mildly and moderately mentally retarded persons was assessed by means of interviews held directly with these individuals (Seltzer, 1981). The findings of this study suggested that the responses given by the mentally retarded persons were generally quite adequate. Alpha reliability (measuring the internal consistency of a set of items) of the five subscales that were included in the interview averaged 0.77, indicating relatively high internal reliability in the responses provided by the interviewees. Regarding the validity of their responses, favorable results were reported as well. Sample members who had experienced downward vocational mobility were significantly less satisfied than those who had either maintained or improved the level of their jobs, indicating a certain degree of criterion validity of the measurement.

Sigelman and her colleagues have conducted a number of very important studies on the process of interviewing retarded children and adults (Sigelman, Schoenrock, Spanhel, Hromas, Winer, Budd & Martin, 1980; Sigelman, Budd, Spanhel, & Schoenrock, 1981; Sigelman, Schoenrock, Winer, Spanhel, Hromas, Martin, Budd, & Bensberg, 1981). They found that there was a significant relationship between IQ and the likelihood of answering a question appropriately, with over 80% of the mildly mentally retarded children and adults in one sample able to answer appropriately and no profoundly mentally retarded person in the sample able to do so. These authors also studied the relative benefits of using various types of questions, and found that although a high percentage of mentally retarded persons could respond to "yes-no" questions, acquiescence (i.e., saying "yes" irrespective of one's real feeling) was a problem with this type of question, particularly with moderately and severely mentally retarded persons. The authors recommended the use of "either-or" questions. However, the results of their research raise serious questions about the validity of data collected by interviewing all but mildly and some moderately mentally retarded persons. Alternatives to this method are discussed below.

INTERVIEWING AN INFORMANT

By far the most frequently utilized approach in gathering data about mentally retarded persons is obtaining information from a parent or staff person, either through an interview or by having the informant complete a self-administered rating scale. This is the approach utilized with the Adaptive Behavior Scale (Nihira, Foster, Shellhaas, & Leland, 1975), the Minnesota Development Programming System (Bock & Weatherman, 1975), the Personal Competency Scale (Reynolds, 1981), and the Progress Adjustment Chart (Gunzberg, 1969).

A major advantage of this approach is that it is not very expensive. The informant can draw upon months and often years of experience with the mentally

retarded person across many situations, and can thus conceptualize maximum and minimum levels of performance as well as "typical" levels. Although interviewing an informant has the advantages of both low cost and drawing upon a broad base of familiarity with the mentally retarded person's behavior, there are also disadvantages. Although a number of researchers report successful use of this approach with respect to the issues of reliability (e.g., Heifetz, 1977), others have found limited reliability and validity of the reports or judgments made by informants (e.g., Isett & Spreat, 1979; Seltzer & Seltzer, in press). Problems of poor memory, unintentional (or intentional) distortion, and overall inflation or deflation of ratings present serious measurement limitations. In addition, the possibility that the ratings given by the informant do not reflect the single "true score" performance of the subject but rather capture the performance of the subject *as he or she interacts with the informant* must be considered.

In one study, for example, Millham, Chilcutt, and Atkinson (1978) compared the results obtained when a sample of mentally retarded persons was assessed, using the data provided by an informant (using the Adaptive Behavior Scale) and through direct observation of behavior using the same items. When the data gathered by the two methods were compared, differences were found in over 50% of the items. Although this study did not determine which method was correct, it raised questions about the validity of informant recall as a data-gathering approach in research on skill assessment.

OBSERVING THE MENTALLY RETARDED PERSON

The use of direct observation of the mentally retarded person presents an alternative to interviewing an informant in order to collect data about the behavior of mentally retarded persons. Two general approaches to this method have been used, namely participant observation and systematic observation. *Participant observation* has been used by Edgerton and his colleagues (Bercovici, 1981; Edgerton, 1967; Edgerton & Bercovici, 1976) in providing detailed descriptions of the everyday lives of mentally retarded persons. By studying the same person over time in multiple settings, an in-depth understanding of the individual within the context of the environment is said to be achieved. Of course, participant observation involves informal interviews with mentally retarded persons, and thus shares the advantages and disadvantages of interviewing mentally retarded persons that were discussed earlier in this chapter. Participant observation also has been criticized for its expense, subjectivity, and reliance on small samples. However, an advantage of this method is that it does not rely on brief, "snapshot" views of the mentally retarded person. The researcher has an extended period of time with which to gather data and note fluctuations in behavior.

Systematic observation is increasingly used as a method of collecting data about mentally retarded persons. In one study utilizing this approach (Landesman-Dwyer, Stein, & Sackett, 1978), more than 400 mentally retarded persons in 23 group homes were studied. Over 16,000 hours of behavior were sampled and data were gathered using over 50 coded categories. An advantage of systematic observation is that with high degrees of interrater reliability and with detailed codes, a great deal of valuable information can be collected about the mentally retarded individual and systematic analyses of the observed behavior can be made. Systematic observation is not dependent upon the memory of an informant or the impressions of a participant observer, and it generates data that can be easily analyzed. However, the data are completely limited to what a subject *does*, not what he or she *can* do; that is, skills that the subject actually can perform but fails to perform during the observation period are scored as "does not perform." Of course, with extended periods of observation, this disadvantage is likely to diminish, but then the costs of observation may become prohibitive. Finally, there is some evidence that the data that are collected through systematic observation are a function not only of the behavior of the person being observed but also of the environmental context in which the person is observed, suggesting that observations are best conducted in the setting in which behavior naturally occurs.

TESTING THE MENTALLY RETARDED PERSON

A fourth method of data collection involves testing the mentally retarded person. The utilization of standardized tests has a long and well documented history in the field of mental retardation. The most commonly used standardized tests are IQ tests. Other tests are intended to gather data about the subject's present level of performance on functional activities. The Bayley Scales of Infant Development (Bayley, 1969) is a test characteristic of the category of tests of performance. Others include the Social and Prevocational Information Battery (Halpern, Raffeld, Irwin & Link, 1975), the Uzgiris and Hunt Scales of Sensorimotor Development (Uzgiris and Hunt, 1975), and various academic achievement tests.

This approach to data gathering has both advantages and disadvantages. Its apparent advantages include objective observations of behavior (as opposed to subjective recall of performance by an informant), relatively rapid administration (as compared with the time needed to make observations in natural settings), the provision of information regarding behaviors that would otherwise be difficult to observe (e.g., the inclusion in the test protocol of infrequently occurring behaviors), and often the availability of normative standards with which to compare an individual's level of performance. Its primary disadvantage is that discrepancies are likely to occur between behavior observed in an artificial testing situation and in a naturally occurring situation, reducing the utility and generalizability of the findings.

RELATIVE ADVANTAGES AND DISADVANTAGES

After reviewing the four methods of collecting data about the behavior of mentally retarded persons, it may be useful to consider the method or combination of methods that is most desirable or advantageous. Although each method has strengths and weaknesses, direct observation of behavior is probably the most reliable and valid approach to the assessment of the performance of mentally retarded persons. Conducting observations in a natural setting as opposed to constructing an artificial testing situation is more appealing; the generalizability of findings and avoiding reliance on the reporting of possibly biased informants is also an advantage. Systematic observation is more likely to yield reliable data than participant observation. Thus, when reviewing reports of nonexperimental field research, the reader should probably be more confident in the quality of data collected by systematic observation than by the other methods reviewed above. However, since the expense of conducting observations is high and since practical difficulties are often encountered when conducting observations, there are significant obstacles to the use of this method of data collection in nonexperimental field research.

In contrast, the use of an informant's reports does not pose serious cost or implementation problems. A parent, teacher, houseparent, or other individual who knows the mentally retarded person well can be interviewed. Because of the ease of administration, there is widespread reliance on the Adaptive Behavior Scale and on other similar interview-based scales. However, the reliability and validity of data collected from an informant are potentially low. This discussion is not intended to suggest that data generated in this manner are not valuable. Rather, readers of studies that employ data collected by informant recall should perhaps be somewhat more cautious in accepting the results than when systematic observational methods are employed.

The utilization of several different methods of data collection is perhaps the strongest approach. In addition to conducting systematic observations or interviewing an informant to determine the level at which a mentally retarded person functions, it is also often desirable to interview the individual, if this is possible, in order to gain an understanding of his or her feelings, preferences, and aspirations. Similarly, when collecting descriptive information about clients in settings, it may be useful to augment quantifiable data collected by either systematic observation or interviewing an informant with data generated by participant observation in order to more fully describe the qualitative aspects of personal behavior and client experience. Methodologically, a strong case has been made by Campbell and Fiske (1959) that the validity of data can be more confidently established if two or more methods of collecting data about a single dimension (such as performance) are found to produce comparable results.

The Collection of Data About Settings

Many of the points raised above about the collection of data about individuals are also applicable to the collection of data about settings. Observation of events that occur in settings is generally superior to relying exclusively upon the reports made by staff, although when interested in learning about historical events (such as the extent of community resistance encountered when a community residence first opened), staff reporting is often the only reasonable approach. Similarly, the utilization of multiple methods of data collection is an advantage in research on settings.

There are a number of additional points to be made, however, regarding the collection of data about settings or environments. First, although the collection of data through mailed surveys is not restricted to the collection of data about settings, this approach is more likely to be used when the setting is the unit of analysis. For example, a number of mailed surveys of community residences have been conducted (Baker, Seltzer, & Seltzer, 1977; Bruininks, Hauber, & Kudla, 1979; Bruininks, Hill, & Thorsheim, 1980; O'Connor, 1976). A problem often encountered when conducting mailed surveys is poor response rate. If the objective of a study is to describe the total universe of settings of a particular type at a given time, then concern about nonresponses is in order, because one does not know whether the settings that did not respond are systematically different from the ones that did respond, and potentially misleading inferences about the proportion of settings that fall into a particular type may

be made. However, if the purpose of a study is to identify types of settings, without emphasizing the distribution of settings across types, the response rate may not be as serious a consideration, although the research of course runs the risk of failing to describe types of settings from which responses were not obtained.

Regardless of the manner in which the data about settings are collected—through mailed surveys, interviews, or observations—a key issue pertaining to the collection of data about settings is the conceptual definition of "the setting." Settings can be conceptualized narrowly—the physical environment—or more broadly—the physical environment, the staff, the other retarded persons who are found in the setting, the program of services, the characteristics of the community in which the setting is found, the extent of autonomy given to the retarded persons in the setting, the philosophical or ideological orientation of the staff, and so on. When investigating the effects of the community residential environment, for example, on the performance level of retarded persons, it is necessary first to identify the conceptual and operational boundaries of the concept of environment before selecting the data collection strategy to use.

An additional problem relevant to the conceptualization of the environment concerns the issue of the extent to which an environment is the same for all persons who experience it. Most measures of settings (e.g., PASS-3, Wolfensberger & Glenn, 1975) assume that the environment is constant for all clients. Another perspective hypothesizes that an environmental element may be favorable for one type of person, unfavorable for a second, and neutral for a third. For example, being provided with a key to the front door of the residence may be a positive environmental feature for clients who are learning or have learned to come and go from the residence independently, but for clients who have a history of running away, the key would possibly be a negative environmental feature. There also might be a type of client for whom a front door key might be irrelevant, such as a very young or very severely disabled person. The collection of data about each client's environment is certainly a more expensive and time-consuming effort than the collection of a single set of data about the environment for all subjects. However, the validity of such individual-specific data may be superior.

Summary and Conclusions

Three designs were presented in this chapter that are useful in different field research situations. The *nonrandomized control group design* is used when no-treatment control groups or alternative treatment comparison groups can be set up in the field research situation and subjects in the various groups are matched to increase comparability of groups. The *interrupted time series design* is used when all subjects are exposed to a single intervention—and thus there are no possible control or comparison groups—and when multiple pre- and postmeasures of the dependent variable can be taken. The *statistical control design* is used when for whatever reason matching is not employed as a method of insuring comparability between groups and when multiple dependent variable pre- and post-measures are not available but when between-group differences must be controlled for in order to examine the unique dependent variable variance that can be accounted for by the intervention.

In each of these designs, an attempt is made to obtain an estimate of what the behavior of the subjects would have been had they not been exposed to the intervention. If there are differences between the pre- and postintervention behavior levels, there may be reasons to believe that these differences are due to the effect of the intervention. The estimate of what the behavior of the subjects would have been had they not been exposed to the intervention is provided by the control group in the nonrandomized control group design and by the preintervention base line in the interrupted time series design. In the statistical control design, the unique dependent variable variance accounted for by the intervention when it is entered last into the regression equation provides an estimate of the effect of the intervention.

When designing or evaluating nonexperimental field research, it is crucial to determine whether threats to internal validity are operative that seriously jeopardize the study. Different threats are particularly problematic for each of the three designs. With the nonrandomized control group design and the statistical control design, the most serious threat to internal validity is selection, defined as systematic preintervention differences between groups. If posttest differences between groups are found, it may be difficult to determine whether these differences are due to the effect of the intervention or, alternatively, to selection. The remedy is to attempt to insure that the groups are as comparable as possible prior to the introduction of the intervention and to adjust for preintervention differences through matching or statistical control. With the interrupted time series design, the most serious threat to internal validity is history, defined as the effect of an event external to the study on the subjects. If the external event and the intervention occur at the same time, it is probably impossible to determine whether any dependent variable difference was due to the intervention or to the external event.

If these and other threats to internal validity are believed not to be operative in a given quasi-experimental situation, then it may be possible to make an inference about the effect of the intervention on the subjects. However, even when threats to internal validity do not jeopardize a study, data collection problems may be encountered that may limit the utility of the findings. As was discussed earlier, different findings may be obtained when different data collection methods are used and it is thus important that nonexperimental field research studies be critically evaluated with respect to the appropriateness of the data collection method used.

Obviously, many research design and data collection problems may be encountered when conducting nonexperimental field research. However if efforts are made to maximize the extent to which the research design controls for threats to internal validity and to utilize the most appropriate data collection techniques, then nonexperimental field research methods can play an important role in evaluating the effects of interventions and building the knowledge base of the field of mental retardation. In an era of scarce and shrinking resources, data about the effects of interventions can be very valuable in advocating for continued funding, should the research findings support the effectiveness of these interventions. Regarding many evaluation issues in the field of mental retardation, methodologists who argue from a purist perspective that anything other than experimental research cannot provide any valid evidence regarding the effects of an intervention are likely to find little evidence available to them because of the difficulty in conducting true experiments in field situations. On the other extreme, those who conduct descriptive research with no attempt to make causal inferences about the effects of intervention produce knowledge that may be useful in building programs but that offers little evaluative data. As Sherwood and Morris (1975) point out,

All service programs may be considered experiments in the sense that an effort is being made to intervene in a system of process with the aim of making events turn out to be different than they would have been without intervention efforts; but they are seldom carefully controlled experiments. The problem, then, is to find ways of designing and implementing intervention programs in such a way that it is possible to make sound empirically based inferences as to whether they make a difference, and, if they do, why they make a difference. [p. 641]

Nonexperimental field research methods can provide valuable strategies for use when there is a need for data about the effectiveness of interventions and when randomization cannot be accomplished. The potential of nonexperimental field research methods to make an important contribution in the field of mental retardation exists, but the extent to which this potential will be realized is dependent upon both designers and consumers of studies employing this methodology. It becomes the responsibility of those who conduct nonexperimental field research to be rigorous in their designs. At the same time, it is the responsibility of those who read nonexperimental field research to be critical consumers and to search for confirmation of findings across studies.

Notes

1. For a full discussion of the problem of these and other threats to internal validity, see Campbell and Stanley (1963) and Cook and Campbell (1979).
2. In this section, the statistical procedure of multiple regression is discussed for illustrative purposes. It should be noted that other similar statistical techniques are also often used in the statistical control design, such as analysis of covariance and path analysis.
3. In the statistical control design, the order in which the independent variables are entered into the regression equation is determined by the hypothesis to be tested. Stepwise multiple regression techniques therefore cannot be used in the statistical control design.
4. Another key consideration in the design of descriptive research is sampling procedures, which due to space limitations are not included in this chapter. For a discussion of sampling procedures, see Blalock (1979).

References

Baker, B. L., Seltzer, G. B., & Seltzer, M. M. *As close as possible: Community residences for retarded persons.* Boston: Little, Brown, 1977.

Bayley, N. *Manual for the Bayley Scales of Infant Development.* New York: The Psychological Corporation, 1969.

Bercovici, S. Qualitative methods and cultural perspectives in the study of deinstitutionalization. In R. H. Bruininks, C. E. Meyers, B. B. Sigford, & K. C. Lakin (Eds.), *Deinstitutionalization and Community Adjustment of Mentally Retarded People.* Monograph No. 4. Washington, D.C.: American Association on Mental Deficiency, 1981.

Berkson, G. Social ecology of supervised communal facilities for mentally disabled adults: V. Residence as a predictor of social and work adjustment. *American Journal of Mental Deficiency*, 1981, 86, 39–42.

Berkson, G., & Romer, D. Social ecology of supervised communal facilities for mentally disabled adults: I. Introduction. *American Journal of Mental Deficiency*, 1980, 85, 219–228.

Blalock, H. M. *Social Statistics.* (2nd ed.) New York: McGraw-Hill, 1979.

Bock, W., & Weatherman, R. *Minnesota developmental*

programming system. St. Paul: University of Minnesota, 1975.

Brooks, P. H., & Baumeister, A. A. A plea for consideration of ecological validity in the experimental psychology of mental retardation: a guest editorial. *American Journal of Mental Deficiency*, 1977, 81, 407–416.

Bruininks, R. H., Hauber, F., & Kudla, M. *National survey of community residential facilities: A profile of facilities and residents in 1977.* Minneapolis: Department of Psychoeducational Studies, University of Minnesota, 1979.

Bruininks, R. H., Hill, B. K., & Thorsheim, M. J. *A profile of foster home services for mentally retarded persons in 1977.* Minneapolis: Department of Psychoeducational Studies, University of Minnesota, 1980.

Campbell, D., & Fiske, D. Convergent and discriminant validation by the multitrait-multimethod matrix. *Psychological Bulletin*, 1959, 56, 81–105.

Campbell, D. T. & Stanley, J.C. *Experimental and quasi-experimental designs for research.* Chicago: Rand McNally College Publishing Co., 1963.

Cook, D., & Campbell, D. T. *Quasi-experimentation: Design and analysis issues for field settings.* Chicago: Rand McNally, 1979.

Edgerton, R. B. *The cloak of competence: Stigma in the lives of the mentally retarded.* Berkeley: University of California Press, 1967.

Edgerton, R. B., & Bercovici, S. M. The cloak of competence: Years later. *American Journal of Mental Deficiency*, 1976, 80, 485–497.

Gollay, E., Friedman, R., Wyngaarten, M., & Kurtz, N. *Coming Back.* Cambridge, Mass.: Abt Books, 1978.

Gottlieb, J. Mainstreaming: Fulfilling the promise? *American Journal of Mental Deficiency*, 1981, 86, 115–126.

Gunzberg, H. C. *The P-A-C Manual.* London: National Association for Mental Health, 1969.

Halpern, A. S., Raffeld, P., Irwin, L., & Link, R. *Social and prevocational information battery.* Monterrey: CTB/ McGraw Hill, 1975.

Haywood, H. C. Reducing social vulnerability is the challenge of the eighties. *Mental Retardation*, August 1981, 190–195.

Heifetz, L. J. Behavioral training for parents of retarded children: alternative formats based on instructional manuals. *American Journal of Mental Deficiency*, 1977, 82, 194–203.

Isett, R. D., & Spreat, S. Test-retest and interrater reliability of the AAMD Adaptive Behavior Scale. *American Journal of Mental Deficiency*, 1979, 84, 93–95.

Landesman-Dwyer, S. Living in the community. *American Journal of Mental Deficiency*, 1981, 86, 223–234.

Landesman-Dwyer, S., Stein, J. G., & Sackett, G. P. A behavioral and ecological study of group homes. In G. P. Sackett (Ed.), *Observing behavior.* Vol. 1. *Theory and applications in mental retardation.* Baltimore: University Park Press, 1978.

Mayhew, G. L., Enyart, P., & Anderson, J. Social reinforcement and naturally-occurring social responses of severely and profoundly retarded adolescents. *American Journal of Mental Deficiency*, 1978, 83, 164–170.

Meyers, C. E., MacMillan, D. L., & Yoshida, R. K. Regular class education of EMR students, from efficacy to mainstreaming: a review of issues and research. In J. Gottlieb (Ed.), *Educating mentally retarded persons in the mainstream.* Baltimore: University Park Press, 1980.

Millham, J., Chilcutt, J., & Atkinson, B. L. Comparability of naturalistic and controlled observation assessment of adaptive behavior. *American Journal of Adaptive Behavior*,

1978, **83**, 52–59.

Nihira, K., Foster, R., Shellhaas, M., & Leland, H.: *AAMD-Adaptive Behavior Scale*. Washington, D.C.: American Association on Mental Deficiency, 1975.

O'Conner, G. *Home is a good place: A national perspective of community residential facilities for developmentally disabled persons*. Washington, D.C.: American Association on Mental Deficiency, 1976.

Reynolds, W. M. Measurement of personal competence of mentally retarded individuals. *American Journal of Mental Deficiency*, 1981, **85**, 368–376.

Romer, D., & Berkson, G. Social ecology of supervised communal facilities for mentally disabled adults: II. Predictors of affiliation. *American Journal of Mental Deficiency*, 1980, **85**, 229–242.

Seltzer, M. M. Deinstitutionalization and vocational adjustment, in P. Mittler (Ed.), *Frontiers of Knowledge in Mental Retardation*. Vol. 1. Baltimore: University Park Press, 1981.

Seltzer, M. M., & Seltzer, G. B. *Context for competence: A study of retarded adults living and working in the community*. Cambridge, Mass.: Educational Projects, Inc., 1978.

Seltzer, M. M., & Seltzer, G. B. Functional assessment of persons with mental retardation. In C. V. Granger & G. E. Gresham (Eds.), *Functional assessment in rehabilitation medicine*. Boston: Williams & Wilkins. In press.

Seltzer, M. M., Seltzer, G. B., & Sherwood, C. C. The residential environment and its relationship to client behavior. In K. T. Kernan, M. J. Begab, and R. B. Edgerton (Eds.), *Impact of specific settings on development and behavior of retarded persons*. Baltimore: University Park Press. In press.

Sherwood, C. C., & Morris, J. N. Strategies for research and innovation. In S. Sherwood (Ed.), *Long-term care: A handbook for researchers, planners, and providers*. New York: Spectrum Publications, 1975.

Sherwood, C. C., Morris, J. N., & Sherwood, S. A multivariate, non-randomized technique for studying the impact of social interventions. In E. L. Struening, and M. Guttentag, *Handbook of evaluation research*. Vol. 1. Beverly Hills: Sage Publications, 1975.

Sigelman, C. K., Budd, E. C., Spanhel, C. L., & Schoenrock, C. J. When in doubt, say yes: Acquiescence in interviews with mentally retarded persons. *Mental Retardation*, April 1981, 53–58.

Sigelman, C. K., Schoenrock, C. J., Spanhel, C. L., Hromas, S. G., Winer, J. L., Budd, E. C., & Martin, P. W. Surveying mentally retarded persons: Responsiveness and response validity in three samples. *American Journal of Mental Deficiency*, 1980, **84**, 479–486.

Sigelman, C. K., Schoenrock, C. J., Winer, J. L., Spanhel, C. L., Hromas, S. G., Martin, P. W., Budd, E. C., & Bensberg, G. J. Issues in interviewing: Mentally retarded persons. In R. H. Bruininks, C. E. Meyers, B. B. Sigford, & K. C. Lakin (Eds.), *Deinstitutionalization and community adjustment of mentally retarded people*. Washington, D.C.: American Journal of Mental Deficiency, 1981.

Uzgiris, I. C., & Hunt, J. McV. *Assessment in infancy: Ordinal scales of psychological development*. Urbana: University of Illinois Press, 1975.

Wolfensberger, W., & Glenn, L. *PASS 3-Program Analysis of Service Systems: A Method for the Quantitive Evaluation of Human Services*. Toronto: National Institute on Mental Retardation, 1975.

AUTHOR INDEX

SUBJECT INDEX

ABOUT THE EDITORS AND CONTRIBUTORS

The Editors

Johnny L. Matson received his Ph.D. in Psychology in 1976 from Indiana State University, and he completed an internship in clinical psychology which was approved by the American Psychological Association. He has been employed as a program director at Partlow State School and Hospital (for the mentally retarded). He has also been employed as an Assistant Professor in Child Psychiatry at the University of Pittsburgh School of Medicine and in Clinical Psychology at the University of Pittsburgh. Currently, he is Associate Professor of Learning and Development at Northern Illinois University. Dr. Matson has published or is currently completing 14 books. He is the founder and editor of *Applied Research in Mental Retardation*, a journal published by Pergamon Press. He is on the editorial board of four journals and serves as an occasional reviewer for 22 journals in psychology and psychiatry. He has published over 90 papers in scientific and professional journals and has made numerous paper presentations. Dr. Matson has been involved in the training of doctoral students from the University of Pittsburgh, Northern Illinois University and two universities in India, the University of Calcutta and Delhi University. Recent honors include an early career research award from the Spencer Foundation.

James A. Mulick received his A.B. degree in psychology from Rutgers College. He completed graduate studies in psychology at the University of Vermont, where he received both the M.A. and Ph.D. degrees. He completed a postdoctoral fellowship in clinical child psychology at the Child Development Institute, Division for Disorders of Development and Learning at the University of North Carolina at Chapel Hill. He has held the position of program director in the self-injurious behavior program at Murdoch Center in Butner, North Carolina, chief psychologist in the Community Evaluation and Rehabilitation Center of the Eunice Kennedy Shriver Center for Mental Retardation, Inc. in Waltham, Massachusetts, and Visiting Assistant Professor of Psychology at Northeastern University. He is currently Director of Psychology and Training Coordinator at the University Affiliated Program at the Child Development Center of Rhode Island Hospital, Clinical Assistant Professor of Pediatrics in the Brown University Program in Medicine, and Adjunct Associate Professor of Psychology at the University of Rhode Island. He is licensed or certified to practice psychology in three states. Dr. Mulick has published numerous papers in the areas of learning, developmental psychobiology, and mental retardation. He has edited a number of books on mental retardation and serves as a reviewer for several journals in this area. He has held advisory positions to state government and to various mental retardation facilities. Dr. Mulick has been Psychology Division Chairperson and Chairman of the Northeast Region X American Association on Mental Deficiency. Current research interests include experimental and applied behavior analysis, instructional technology, severe childhood psychopathology, and public policy analysis relating to children and the handicapped.

The Contributors

Dianne Abuelo, M.D., is a board certified geneticist and serves as medical director for the Rhode Island Statewide Genetics Program as well as Director of the Rhode Island Hospital Genetic Counseling Center. She serves as a Clinical Assistant Professor of Pediatrics in the Brown University Program in Medicine and at Tufts University, and holds staff appointments at the Rhode Island Hospital, The Women and Infants Hospital in Providence, Rhode Island and the Tufts-New England Medical Center.

Mark Alter, Ph.D. received his doctorate in special education from Yeshiva University in New York City. He is currently Assistant Professor of Special Education at New York University.

Michael G. Aman, Ph.D. is an MRC Senior Research Fellow with the Department of Psychiatry at the University of Auckland in New Zealand. He is interested in the psychoactive effects of drugs, particularly in mental retardation, childhood epilepsy, and hyperactivity.

Henry A. Beyer, J.D. is presently Interim Director of the Center for Law and Health Sciences at the Boston University School of Law. For the past seven years, Mr. Beyer has directed projects providing technical assistance to New England advocates for people with developmental disabilities. He currently serves on the Human Rights Committee of the Massachusetts Development Disabilities Council, the Board of Trustees of the Walter E. Fernald State School, and the Board of Directors of Delta Projects, Inc., Cambridge, Massachusetts.

John G. Borkowski, Ph.D. received his doctorate from the University of Iowa. He has held the position of instructor at Oberlin College and is currently Professor of Psychology at the University of Notre Dame and Director of the Graduate Program in Mental Retardation.

Donna M. Bryant, Ph.D. received her doctorate in experimental psychology at the University of North Carolina at Chapel Hill. She is presently an investigator at the Frank Porter Graham Child Development Center, University of North Carolina at Chapel Hill. She organizes and conducts the longitudinal research with children and families in Project CARE, a study comparing daycare and home visit interventions for disadvantaged children at risk for mental retardation. She also conducts observational studies of social interactions among daycare children.

James F. Budde, Ed.D. is Director of the Research and Training Center on Independent Living at the University of Kansas, and has managed a number of technical assistance projects through the Kansas University Affiliated Facility. His major area of interest is using research and technical assistance to improve human service systems. He has recently served as President of the American Association of University Affiliated Programs (AAUAP) in Mental Retardation and Developmental Disabilities.

Brian Matthew Campbell, Ph.D. received his doctorate in psychology at the University of St. Andrews in Scotland, U.K. He is presently Assistant Professor of Psychology in the Ph.D. clinical psychology program at Nova University in Ft. Lauderdale, Florida. He serves as a behavioral consultant for several state funded programs for the mentally retarded and developmentally disabled and is also in private practice. His research interests include psycholinguistics and computer-assisted instruction.

Paul J. Castellani, Ph.D. is a political scientist with the Program Research Unit of the New York State Office of Mental Retardation and Developmental Disabilities. He has recently directed research projects on community support services for the developmentally disabled, case management, and protection of human subjects.

Patrick R. Damburg is currently a graduate student in the Mental Retardation Program at the University of Notre Dame and expects to receive his MA degree in 1983.

Douglas K. Detterman, Ph.D. is presently Chair of the Department of Psychology at Case Western Reserve University in Cleveland, Ohio. He is also Editor of *Intelligence: A Multidisciplinary Journal* and his current research concerns the relationship of cognitive abilities and intelligence in mentally retarded and nonretarded persons.

Gerald D. Faw is currently enrolled in the behavior modification graduate program at Southern Illinois University and is involved in clinical and research activities in mental retardation and developmental disabilities.

Steven R. Forness, Ed.D. is presently Professor of Psychiatry and Biobehavioral Sciences at UCLA and Director of Special Education at the UCLA Neuropsychiatric Institute.

Sterling D. Garrard, M.D. is currently a Professor of Family and Community Medicine and Pediatrics and is Vice-Chairman of the Department of Family and Community Medicine at the University of Massachusetts Medical School in Worcester, Massachusetts. He is also the Director of the University of Massachusetts Medical Center's Contract Medical Programs in State Residential Facilities. He has formerly held the position of Director of the University Affiliated Training Program at the Indiana University Medical Center and Co-Director of the Eunice Kennedy Shriver Center UAF Training Program. He has served as President of the American Academy on Mental Retardation. His current research interests include the epidemiology of hepatitis and intestinal parasitosis in mentally retarded populations and the comparative health status of groups in institutional and community residential settings.

Amy Goldstein, M.S. is currently a Genetic Counselor with the Statewide Rhode Island Genetic Counseling Program. She recently became a Diplomate of the Board of Medical Genetics.

Barbara W. Gottlieb, Ed.D. received her doctorate in special education from Northern Illinois University. She is presently Assistant Professor in the Department of Specialized Services and Education and Director of the Developmental Learning Center at Herbert Lehman College of the City University of New York.

Jay Gottlieb, Ph.D. received his doctorate from Yeshiva University in New York City. He is currently Associate Professor of Educational Psychology and Director of the Program in Special Education at New York University.

Laird W. Heal, Ph.D. is currently Professor of Special Education at the University of Illinois. Professor Heal is interested in policy research related to deinstitutionalization.

Agnes M. Huber, Ph.D., R.D. is currently Associate Professor of Nutrition at Sargent College of Boston University. She is also Director of Nutrition at the Eunice Kennedy Shriver Center for Mental Retardation in Waltham, Massachusetts. Her research interests are in the area of trace mineral nutrition.

Nancy H. Huguenin, Ph.D. is currently Director of the Programmed-Instruction Laboratory in the School of Graduate Studies and Research and Adjunct Assistant Professor of Psychology at the University of Massachusetts in Amherst. Her research interests include behavioral analysis in mental retardation and stimulus control during discrimination learning.

John W. Jacobson, M.S. is a planner and research analyst with the New York State Office of Mental Retardation and Developmental Disabilities, and was project manager for the New York Developmental Disabilities Information System from 1978 to 1981. He is a co-investigator in the Living Alternatives Research Project. His current responsibilities include management and consultation activities in policy, program, and research development.

Matthew P. Janicki, Ph.D. is currently Director of Program Research and Planning at the New York State Office of Mental Retardation and Developmental Disabilities. He has been involved with developing and implementing developmental disabilities program needs assessments, standards, and planning methodologies for the state of New York. He is currently actively involved in research on group home systems and on problems facing elderly developmentally disabled persons.

George R. Karlan, Ph.D. is currently an Associate Professor of Special Education at Purdue University. His research interests include language development and non-speech communication.

Michele Kiely, M.P.H. is a Research Scientist in the Department of Epidemiology at the New York State Institute for Basic Research in Developmental Disabilities and a doctoral candidate at the Columbia University School of Public Health. Her main research interests are in the etiology of cerebral palsy and other developmental disabilities.

Henry Leland, Ph.D. is currently Professor of Psychology and Director of Psychology at the Nisonger Center for Mental Retardation and Developmental Disability at Ohio State University. His major research and publication has been in the areas of adaptive behavior, play therapy, and psychological training of MR/DD specialists.

Ira T. Lott, M.D. is presently the Director of Pediatric Neurology and Associate Professor of Pediatrics and Neurology at the University of California Medical School, Irvine. He has held the positions of Assistant Professor of Neurology at the Harvard Medical School, and Clinical Director at the Eunice Kennedy Shriver Center in Waltham, Massachusetts.

Robert A. Lubin, Ph.D., M.P.H. is currently the Head of the Department of Epidemiology at the New York State Institute for Basic Research in Developmental Disabilities. He is also affiliated with the Columbia University School of Public Health and teaches at the New School for Social Research.

Murry Morgenstern, Ph.D. is currently the Director of Psychology at the University Affiliated Facility Mental Retardation Institute at the Westchester County Medical Center in Valhalla, New York. He is also a consultant with the Association for Children with Retarded Mental Development in New York City and serves on the Professional Advisory Board for the Willowbrook Consent Decree for the State of New York. He is actively involved in developing policies on sexuality in public and private mental retardation facilities.

Robert G. Norris is currently First Deputy Commissioner of the New York State Office of Mental Retardation and Developmental Disabilities. During the past several years, he has been instrumental in shifting New York State's developmental services structure toward a community-oriented system through both regulatory and legislative activities.

Edward J. Nuffield, M.D. is currently an Assistant Professor of Child Psychiatry and Pediatrics at the University of Pittsburgh School of Medicine. He also serves as Acting Medical Director of the John Merck Program for Multiply Disabled Children.

Virginia A. Peck, Ph.D. received her doctorate in psychology from the University of Notre Dame. She presently holds a research position in Cognitive Studies at the University of Washington.

Siegfried M. Pueschel, M.D., M.P.H. received his doctorate from the Medical Academy in Dusseldorf, Germany. Following his pediatric residency and fellowship training, Dr. Pueschel attended the Harvard School of Public Health where he earned a Master of Public Health degree. Subsequently, he was employed at the Developmental Evaluation Clinic of Boston Children's Hospital Medical Center and the Harvard School of Medicine. Dr. Pueschel is currently Director of the Child Development Center at Rhode Island Hospital in Providence, Rhode Island. He is certified by the American Board of Pediatrics and recently became a Diplomate of the American Board of Medical Genetics. His current academic appointments include Lecturer in Pediatrics at the Harvard Medical School and Associate Professor in Pediatrics at the Brown University Program in Medicine. He has published widely in the areas of Down Syndrome and amino acid disorders.

Craig T. Ramey, Ph.D. is currently Director of Research at the Frank Porter Graham Child Development Center and holds the rank of Professor in the Department of Psychology at the University of North Carolina at Chapel Hill. Since 1972, he has directed two longitudinal studies concerning intervention strategies for disadvantaged children at risk for mental retardation. He is currently planning an evaluation program for a national study of intervention procedures with low birthweight infants.

Dennis H. Reid, Ph.D. is a Senior Psychologist at Western Carolina Center in Morganton, North Carolina and is involved in clinical, administrative, and research activities in mental retardation and developmental disabilities.

Johannes Rojahn, Ph.D. received his doctorate from the University of Vienna, Austria. He is currently on the Faculty of Psychology at the University of Marburg, West Germany. He has published extensively in both the United States and Europe on behavioral assessment issues in handicapped populations.

Philip Roos, Ph.D. has served for many years as National Executive Director of the Association for Retarded Citizens of the United States. He is currently President of P. S. Roos and Associates, Inc., a firm in the practice of clinical psychology and training for business and industry.

Frank R. Rusch, Ph.D. is an Associate Professor of Special Education at the University of Illinois. He is primarily interested in community-integration and employment education for moderately and severely mentally retarded adults.

Janis C. Rusch is a Letitia Walsh Scholar and doctoral candidate in special education at the University of Illinois. Her research interests include language intervention, psychotropic medication, and ecobehavioral research methodology with mentally retarded persons.

Edward A. Sassaman, M.D. received his doctorate from the Harvard Medical School and completed a fellowship in developmental pediatrics at the Developmental Evaluation Clinic and University Affiliated Program at Boston Children's Hospital Medical Center. He is currently Associate Director of the University Affiliated Program at the Child Development Center of Rhode Island Hospital and is an Assistant Professor of Pediatrics at the Brown University Program in Medicine. Dr. Sassaman's current research interests include the treatment of children with spina bifida and Duchenne muscular dystrophy.

Stephen R. Schroeder, Ph.D. received his doctorate from the University of Pittsburgh. He is currently a Research Scientist at the Biological Sciences Research Center and on the Faculties of Psychiatry and Psychology at the University of North Carolina at Chapel Hill. He has conducted research in a broad variety of areas related to mental retardation, habilitative programming, self-injurious behavior, and the behavioral consequences of lead exposure in children.

Richard P. Schutz is an Assistant Professor of Special Education at the Center for Developmental Disabilities of the University of Vermont. Mr. Schutz is primarily interested in model program development in the area of competitive employment.

Allen A. Schwartz, Ph.D. is a licensed psychologist in New York State, and is presently Director of Planning and Special Projects with the New York City County Service Group of the New York State Office of Mental Retardation and Developmental Disabilities. A co-investigator in the Living Alternatives Research Project, his research interests and publications are in the area of deinstitutionalization, changes in adaptive skills, staff attitudes, and the administration of MR/DD services.

Audrey Schore Schwartz is an Instructor in Psychology at Broward Community College in Florida and a Ph.D. candidate in Applied Developmental Psychology at Nova University. She is currently conducting research on social interaction in hearing impaired children and on prosthetic communication devices.

John W. Scibak, Ph.D. received his doctorate in psychology at the University of Notre Dame. He has held the position of Assistant Professor of Special Education and Coordinator of Field Based Training for Teachers of the moderately, severely, and profoundly retarded at Indiana University. He is currently Director of Psychological Services at Belchertown State School in Massachusetts and Adjunct Assistant Professor of Psychology at the University of Massachusetts, Amherst. His research interests include applied behavior analysis in mental retardation, cognitive behavior modification, and the legal rights of mentally retarded persons.

Gary B. Seltzer, Ph.D. received his doctorate in Clinical Psychology from Harvard University. He is currently an Assistant Professor in the Brown University Program in Medicine with appointments in the Departments of Family Medicine and Community Health. He is also Project Director of a training grant in rehabilitation and family medicine and serves as the Director of Rehabilitation Psychology at Pawtucket Memorial Hospital in Rhode Island. He is co-author of the book *As Close As Possible: Community Residences for Retarded Adults* as well as many articles and chapters in the areas of deinstitutionalization, long-term care, and rehabilitation. His present research involves the affects of various experimental clinical interventions on the physical and psychosocial functioning of elderly persons.

Marsha Mailick Seltzer, Ph.D. received her doctorate from Brandeis University. She is currently an Assistant Professor in the Research Department at the Boston University School of Social Work, where she teaches research methods and statistics. She has conducted research in the area of deinstitutionalization and the provision of community-based services for mentally retarded persons. She co-authored the book *As Close As Possible: Community Residences for Retarded Adults* and has authored numerous articles and chapters in the field of mental retardation. Her current research interests include community attitudes about community residences for mentally retarded persons, and the affect of family involvement on the maintenance of frail elderly persons in the community. She has been a consultant to community-based programs for mentally retarded persons and to national research studies on deinstitutionalization.

Rune J. Simeonsson, Ph.D. received his doctorate from George Peabody College. He has held the position of Assistant Professor of Pediatrics, Psychiatry, and Psychology at the University of Rochester School of Medicine. He is currently Professor of Education in the Departments of Special Education and School

Psychology as well as a Research Professor at the Frank Porter Graham Child Development Center at the University of North Carolina at Chapel Hill. His research interests include social cognitive development and developmental disabilities.

Esther Sinclair, Ph.D. is currently Assistant Professor of Psychiatry and Biobehavioral Sciences and is on the staff of the Neuropsychiatric Institute at the University of California at Los Angeles.

Nirbhay N. Singh is currently with the Department of Psychology at the University of Canterbury, Christchurch, New Zealand. His research interests are in childhood psychopathology and psychopharmacology.

Gregory Slomka, M.Ed. is a Speciality Counselor with the Mental Retardation Unit at the Western Psychiatric Institute and Clinic in the Department of Psychiatry at the University of Pittsburgh School of Medicine.

Jean Ann Summers is Acting Director of the Lawrence campus of the Kansas University Affiliated Facility and is active in the Kansas Developmental Disabilities Planning Council. Her areas of interest include administration and policy analysis of human service programs.

Ralph E. Tarter, Ph.D. is currently Associate Professor of Psychiatry and Neurology at the Western Psychiatric Institute and Clinic of the University of Pittsburgh School of Medicine.

Horace C. Thuline, M.D. is currently Supervisor of the Genetic Program in the Department of Social and Health Services in Seattle, Washington. He is also Clinical Associate Professor in Pediatrics at the University of Washington. Dr. Thuline has worked in the field of medical genetics and has contributed significantly in the field of chromosomal disorders.

H. Rutherford Turnbull, III is a graduate of Johns Hopkins University, the University of Maryland Law School, and Harvard Law School. He is currently Chairman and Professor of Special Education and Courtesy Professor of Law at the University of Kansas.

He is a senior officer in the Association for Retarded Citizens of the United States and of the American Association on Mental Deficiency. He is the author of numerous books, chapters, and articles concerning law and mental retardation. He is the father of a handicapped child.

Alexander J. Tymchuk, Ph.D. attended the University of Victoria and the University of Western Ontario in Canada and received his doctorate at George Peabody College. He is currently an Associate Professor of Medical Psychology and Director of the Mental Retardation/Developmental Disabilities Program in the Department of Psychiatry of the School of Medicine at the University of California at Los Angeles. He has published numerous articles and chapters in the field of mental retardation. His books include *Behavior Modification with Children, The Mental Retardation Dictionary,* and *Parent and Family Therapy.* His research interests include the prediction of which parents of developmentally disabled children are most likely to profit from various types of professional intervention, assessment of parent/child interaction in mental retardation, and ethical decision making.

Leslie E. Weidenman, Ph.D. received her doctorate in Educational Psychology at the University of Massachusetts, Amherst. She is now at the University Affiliated Program at the Child Development Center at Rhode Island Hospital. She works as a psychologist with the Early Intervention Program.

Mary J. Wheat is a graduate of Baylor University and of the University of Kansas Law School. She served as a staff expert in the area of disabilities law for Senator Robert Dole (R., Kansas) for several years in Washington, D.C. She has co-authored an article on Least Restrictive Educational Placement of Handicapped Children with Mr. Turnbull.

Philip G. Wilson is currently in the behavior modification graduate program at Southern Illinois University. He is currently involved in clinical and research activities in mental retardation and developmental disabilities.

Pergamon General Psychology Series

Editors: Arnold P. Goldstein, Syracuse University
Leonard Krasner, SUNY at Stony Brook

DATE			
APR 14 1985	NOV 1 5 1995		
DEC 0 5 1985	NOV 2 9 1995		
	MAY 2 6 2000		
APR 0 7 1986	MAY 2 6 2000		
JAN 3 1 1988			
APR 0 3 1989			
NOV 2 5 1989			
DEC 1 6 1990			
MAR 1 6 1994			